Lecture Notes in Computer Science　10706

Commenced Publication in 1973
Founding and Former Series Editors:
Gerhard Goos, Juris Hartmanis, and Jan van Leeuwen

Advanced Research in Computing and Software Science
Subline of Lecture Notes in Computer Science

A Min Tjoa · Ladjel Bellatreche
Stefan Biffl · Jan van Leeuwen
Jiří Wiedermann (Eds.)

SOFSEM 2018: Theory and Practice of Computer Science

44th International Conference on Current Trends
in Theory and Practice of Computer Science
Krems, Austria, January 29 – February 2, 2018
Proceedings

 Springer

Editors
A Min Tjoa
Vienna University of Technology
Vienna
Austria

Ladjel Bellatreche
ISAE-ENSMA
Chasseneuil-du-Poitou
France

Stefan Biffl
Vienna University of Technology
Vienna
Austria

Jan van Leeuwen
Utrecht University
Utrecht
The Netherlands

Jiří Wiedermann
Academy of Sciences
Prague
Czech Republic

ISSN 0302-9743   ISSN 1611-3349 (electronic)
Lecture Notes in Computer Science
ISBN 978-3-319-73116-2   ISBN 978-3-319-73117-9 (eBook)
https://doi.org/10.1007/978-3-319-73117-9

Library of Congress Control Number: 2017962878

LNCS Sublibrary: SL1 – Theoretical Computer Science and General Issues

Printed on acid-free paper

This Edizioni della Normale imprint is published by Springer Nature
The registered company is Springer International Publishing AG
The registered company address is: Gewerbestrasse 11, 6330 Cham, Switzerland

Preface

This volume contains the invited and contributed papers selected for presentation at SOFSEM 2018, the 44th International Conference on Current Trends in Theory and Practice of Computer Science, which was held at Danube University Krems from January 29 to February 2, 2018. For the first time, Austria was the host country of the prestigious SOFSEM conference series.

SOFSEM (originally SOFtware SEMinar) is devoted to leading research and fosters the cooperation among researchers and professionals from academia and industry in all areas of computer science. As a well-established and fully international conference, SOFSEM has kept the best of its original Winter School aspects, such as a substantial number of invited talks (seven for the year 2018) and an in-depth coverage of novel research results in selected areas of computer science. SOFSEM 2018 was organized around the following three tracks:

- Foundations of Computer Science
  (chaired by Jan van Leeuwen and Jiří Wiedermann),
- Software Engineering: Advanced Methods, Applications, and Tools – SEMAT
  (chaired by Stefan Biffl),
- Data, Information, and Knowledge Engineering
  (chaired by Ladjel Bellatreche).

With these three tracks, SOFSEM 2018 covered the latest advances in both theoretical and applied research in leading areas of computer science. The SOFSEM 2018 Program Committee consisted of 89 international experts from 33 different countries, representing the track areas with outstanding expertise.

An integral part of SOFSEM 2018 was the traditional SOFSEM Student Research Forum (chaired by Roman Špánek) organized with the aim of presenting student projects on both the theory and practice of computer science, and to give the students feedback on the originality of their results. The papers presented at the Student Research Forum are published in separate local proceedings.

In response to the call for papers, SOFSEM 2018 received 108 submissions by 246 authors from 32 different countries. The submissions were distributed in the conference tracks as follows: 60 in Foundations of Computer Science, 25 in Software Engineering: Advanced Methods, Applications, and Tools, and 23 in Data, Information, and Knowledge Engineering. From these, 25 submissions fell in the student category.

After a detailed reviewing process, with approximately three reviews per paper in every track, a careful selection procedure was carried out using the EasyChair Conference System for an electronic discussion. Following strict criteria of quality and originality, 41 papers were selected for presentation, namely: 26 in Foundations of Computer Science, 7 in Software Engineering: Advanced Methods, Applications, and Tools, and 8 in Data, Information, and Knowledge Engineering. From these, 10 were student papers.

Based on the recommendation of the chair of the Student Research Forum and with the approval of the track chairs and Program Committee members, seven more student papers were chosen for the SOFSEM 2018 Student Research Forum.

We are greatly indebted to the many colleagues who contributed to the scientific program of the conference, especially the invited speakers and all authors of the submitted papers. We also thank the authors of the accepted papers for their prompt responses to our editorial requests.

SOFSEM 2018 was the result of a concerted effort by many people. We would like to express our special thanks to the members of the SOFSEM 2018 Program Committee and all external reviewers for their precise and detailed reviewing of the submissions, Roman Špánek for his handling of the Student Research Forum, Fajar J. Ekaputra for his efforts on the proceedings, Springer's LNCS team for its great support, and the local Organizing Committee for the support and preparation of the conference.

Finally we want to thank the Danube University Krems and the Austrian Computer Society (especially Christine Haas) for their invaluable support, which made it possible to host SOFSEM in Austria for the first time.

January 2018

A Min Tjoa
Ladjel Bellatreche
Stefan Biffl
Jan van Leeuwen
Jiří Wiedermann

Organization

Steering Committee

Barbara Catania	University of Genoa, Italy
Miroslaw Kutylowski	Wroclaw University of Technology, Poland
Tiziana Margaria-Steffen	University of Limerick, Ireland
Branislav Rovan	Comenius University, Bratislava, Slovakia
Petr Šaloun	Technical University of Ostrava, Czech Republic
Július Štuller (Chair)	Academy of Sciences, Prague, Czech Republic
Jan van Leeuwen	Utrecht University, The Netherlands

Program Committee

Program Chair

A Min Tjoa	Vienna University of Technology, Austria

Track Chairs

Ladjel Bellatreche	ISAE-ENSMA, France
Stefan Biffl	Vienna University of Technology, Austria
Jan van Leeuwen	Utrecht University, The Netherlands
Jiří Wiedermann	Academy of Sciences, Prague, Czech Republic

Student Research Forum Chair

Roman Špánek	Technical University of Liberec, Czech Republic

Program Committee

Parosh Aziz Abdulla	Uppsala University, Sweden
Andris Ambainis	University of Latvia, Latvia
Ioannis Anagnostopoulos	University of Thessaly, Greece
Claudia P. Ayala	Technical University of Catalunya, Spain
Christel Baier	Technical University of Dresden, Germany
Ladjel Bellatreche	ISAE-ENSMA, France
Salima Benbernou	Université Paris Descartes, France
Djamal Benslimane	University of Lyon 1, France
Fadila Bentayeb	ERIC Lab, University of Lyon 2, France
Jorge Bernardino	ISEC - Polytechnic Institute of Coimbra, Portugal
Mária Bieliková	Slovak University of Technology in Bratislava, Slovakia
Stefan Biffl	Vienna University of Technology, Austria
Premek Brada	University of West Bohemia, Czech Republic

Barbara Catania	DIBRIS-University of Genoa, Italy
Gabriel Ciobanu	Romanian Academy - Iasi, Romania
Alain Crolotte	Teradata Corporation, USA
Alfredo Cuzzocrea	ICAR-CNR and University of Calabria, Italy
Josep Diaz	Technical University of Catalunya, Spain
Anton Dignös	Free University of Bozen-Bolzano, Italy
Johann Eder	Alpen Adria Universität Klagenfurt, Austria
Thomas Erlebach	University of Leicester, UK
Javier Esparza	Technical University of Munich, Germany
Michael Felderer	University of Innsbruck, Austria
Bernd Fischer	Stellenbosch University, South Africa
Martin Fürer	The Pennsylvania State University, USA
Johann Gamper	Free University of Bozen-Bolzano, Italy
Leszek Gąsieniec	University of Liverpool, UK
Cyril Gavoille	Université Bordeaux-1, France
Tibor Gyimóthy	University of Szeged, Hungary
Allel Hadjali	ISAE-ENSMA, France
Brahim Hamid	IRIT, University of Toulouse, France
Theo Härder	Technische Universität Kaiserslautern, Germany
Pinar Heggernes	University of Bergen, Norway
Juraj Hromkovič	ETH Zurich, Switzerland
Anna Ingolfsdottir	Reykjavik University, Iceland
Mirjana Ivanovic	University of Novi Sad, Serbia
Kazuo Iwama	Kyoto University, Japan
Marcos Kalinowski	Pontifical Catholic University of Rio de Janeiro, Brazil
Jarkko Kari	University of Turku, Finland
Zoubida Kedad	University of Versailles, France
Selma Khouri	Ecole nationale Supérieure d'Informatique, France
Rastislav Královič	Comenius University, Slovakia
Evangelos Kranakis	Carleton University, Canada
Milos Kravcik	DFKI GmbH, Germany
Stefano Leonardi	Sapienza University of Rome, Italy
Sebastian Link	The University of Auckland, New Zealand
Óscar Pastor Lopez	Universitat Politècnica de València, Spain
Martin Lopez-Nores	University of Vigo, Spain
Leszek Maciaszek	Wrocław University of Economics, Poland
Yannis Manolopoulos	Aristotle University of Thessaloniki, Greece
Pierre-Etienne Moreau	Inria-LORIA Nancy, France
Rim Moussa	ENICarthage, Tunisia
Iveta Mrázová	Charles University, Prague, Czech Republic
Rolf Niedermeier	Technical University Berlin, Germany
Boris Novikov	St. Petersburg University, Russia
Mirosław Ochodek	Poznan University of Technology, Poland
Alexander Okhotin	St. Petersburg State University, Russia
Pekka Orponen	Aalto University, Finland
Claus Pahl	Dublin City University, Ireland

Catuscia Palamidessi	Inria, France
George Papadopoulos	University of Cyprus, Cyprus
Alfonso Pierantonio	University of L'Aquila, Italy
Jaroslav Porubän	Technical University of Košice, Slovakia
Franck Ravat	IRIT, University of Toulouse, France
Karel Richta	Czech Technical University in Prague, Czech Republic
Gunter Saake	University of Magdeburg, Germany
Sherif Sakr	The University of New South Wales, Australia
Petr Šaloun	VSB-TU Ostrava, Czech Republic
Eike Schallehn	University of Magdeburg, Germany
Markus Schordan	Lawrence Livermore National Laboratory, USA
Lukáš Sekanina	Technical University Brno, Czech Republic
Miroslaw Staron	University of Gothenburg, Sweden
Krzysztof Stencel	University of Warsaw, Poland
A Min Tjoa	Vienna University of Technology, Austria
Farouk Toumani	Blaise Pascal University, France
Mark van den Brand	Eindhoven University of Technology, The Netherlands
Peter van Emde Boas	University of Amsterdam, The Netherlands
Jan van Leeuwen	Utrecht University, The Netherlands
Panos Vassiliadis	University of Ioannina, Greece
Valentino Vranić	Slovak University of Technology in Bratislava, Slovakia
Marina Waldén	Åbo Akademi University, Finland
Igor Walukiewicz	Université Bordeaux-1, France
Jiří Wiedermann	Academy of Sciences, Prague, Czech Republic
Dietmar Winkler	Vienna University of Technology, Austria
Damien Woods	Inria, France
Shmuel Zaks	Technion, Haifa, Israel
Apostolos Zarras	University of Ioannina, Greece
Jaroslav Zendulka	Brno University of Technology, Czech Republic
Wolf Zimmermann	Martin Luther University Halle-Wittenberg, Germany

Additional Reviewers

Luca Aceto	Valérie Berthé	Paul Dorbec
Achilleas Achilleos	Michael Blondin	Jeremias Epperlein
Mario S. Alvim	Hans-Joachim	Till Fluschnik
Bogdan Aman	Böckenhauer	Vincent Froese
Kazuyuki Amano	Guillaume Bonfante	Anastasios Gounaris
Pradeesha Ashok	Broňa Brejová	Peter Hegedus
Önder Babur	Leizhen Cai	Mika Hirvensalo
Dénes Bán	Yu-Fang Chen	Ludovico Iovino
Kfir Barhum	Van Cyr	Szabolcs Iván
Ion Barosan	Bui Phi Diep	Sanjay Jain
Matthias Bentert	Stefan Dobrev	Tomasz Kociumaka

Yang Li	Martin Nehez	Grzegorz Stachowiak
Richard Lipka	André Nichterlein	Nimrod Talmon
Allan Lo	Reino Niskanen	Zoltan Toth
Zvi Lotker	Marta Olszewska	Richard Trefler
Michael Luttenberger	Dana Pardubska	Mirco Tribastone
David Manlove	Boaz Patt-Shamir	Charlotte Truchet
Jieming Mao	Daniel Paulusma	Ming-Hsien Tsai
Russell Martin	Krišjānis Prūsis	Theodoros Tzouramanis
George Mertzios	Karol Rástočný	David Wehner
Christos Mettouris	Othmane Rezine	Prudence Wong
Othon Michail	Matthias Rungger	Alexandros Yeratziotis
František Mráz	Eike Schallehn	

Organizing Committee

Proceedings Chair

Fajar J. Ekaputra   Vienna University of Technology, Austria

Local Committee

Wilfried Baumann	Austrian Computer Society, Austria
Ronald Bieber (Chair)	Austrian Computer Society, Austria
Gerlinde Ecker	Austrian Computer Society, Austria
Christine Haas	Austrian Computer Society, Austria
Karin Hiebler	Austrian Computer Society, Austria
Sandra Pillis	Austrian Computer Society, Austria
Wolfgang Resch	Austrian Computer Society, Austria
Johann Stockinger	Austrian Computer Society, Austria
Christine Wahlmüller-Schiller	Austrian Computer Society, Austria

Contents

Invited Talks

Keynote Talk

Swift Logic for Big Data and Knowledge Graphs:
Overview of Requirements, Language, and System   3
   Luigi Bellomarini, Georg Gottlob, Andreas Pieris,
   and Emanuel Sallinger

Foundations of Computer Science

On Architecture Specification   19
   Manfred Broy

The State of the Art in Dynamic Graph Algorithms   40
   Monika Henzinger

Software Engineering: Advanced Methods, Applications, and Tools

Diversity in UML Modeling Explained: Observations, Classifications
and Theorizations   47
   Michel R. V. Chaudron, Ana Fernandes-Saez, Regina Hebig,
   Truong Ho-Quang, and Rodi Jolak

Self-managing Internet of Things   67
   Danny Weyns, Gowri Sankar Ramachandran, and Ritesh Kumar Singh

Data, Information and Knowledge Engineering

LARS: A Logic-Based Framework for Analytic Reasoning over Streams
(Extended Abstract).   87
   Harald Beck, Minh Dao-Tran, and Thomas Eiter

Network Analysis of the Science of Science: A Case Study in SOFSEM
Conference.   94
   Antonia Gogoglou, Theodora Tsikrika, and Yannis Manolopoulos

Regular Papers

Network Science and Parameterized Complexity

The Parameterized Complexity of Centrality Improvement in Networks   111
  Clemens Hoffmann, Hendrik Molter, and Manuel Sorge

Local Structure Theorems for Erdős–Rényi Graphs and Their Algorithmic
Applications   125
  Jan Dreier, Philipp Kuinke, Ba Le Xuan, and Peter Rossmanith

Target Set Selection Parameterized by Clique-Width
and Maximum Threshold   137
  Tim A. Hartmann

Model-Based Software Engineering

Combining Versioning and Metamodel Evolution in the ChronoSphere
Model Repository   153
  Martin Haeusler, Thomas Trojer, Johannes Kessler, Matthias Farwick,
  Emmanuel Nowakowski, and Ruth Breu

Automated Change Propagation from Source Code to Sequence Diagrams . . .   168
  Karol Rástočný and Andrej Mlynčár

Multi-paradigm Architecture Constraint Specification and Configuration
Based on Graphs and Feature Models   180
  Sahar Kallel, Chouki Tibermacine, Ahmed Hadj Kacem,
  and Christophe Dony

Computational Models and Complexity

Lower Bounds and Hierarchies for Quantum Memoryless Communication
Protocols and Quantum Ordered Binary Decision Diagrams
with Repeated Test   197
  Farid Ablayev, Andris Ambainis, Kamil Khadiev, and Aliya Khadieva

Computational Complexity of Atomic Chemical Reaction Networks   212
  David Doty and Shaopeng Zhu

Conjugacy of One-Dimensional One-Sided Cellular Automata
is Undecidable   227
  Joonatan Jalonen and Jarkko Kari

Software Quality Assurance and Transformation

Formal Verification and Safety Assessment of a Hemodialysis Machine.   241
  Shahid Khan, Osman Hasan, and Atif Mashkoor

Automatic Decomposition of Java Open Source Pull Requests:
A Replication Study   255
  Victor da C. Luna Freire, João Brunet, and Jorge C. A. de Figueiredo

Transformation of OWL2 Property Axioms to Groovy.   269
  Bogumiła Hnatkowska and Paweł Woroniecki

Graph Structure and Computation

Simple Paths and Cycles Avoiding Forbidden Paths   285
  Benjamin Momège

External Memory Algorithms for Finding Disjoint Paths
in Undirected Graphs.   295
  Maxim Babenko and Ignat Kolesnichenko

On Range and Edge Capacity in the Congested Clique   305
  Tomasz Jurdziński and Krzysztof Nowicki

Business Processes, Protocols, and Mobile Networks

Global vs. Local Semantics of BPMN 2.0 OR-Join   321
  Flavio Corradini, Chiara Muzi, Barbara Re, Lorenzo Rossi,
  and Francesco Tiezzi

AODVv2: Performance vs. Loop Freedom   337
  Mojgan Kamali, Massimo Merro, and Alice Dal Corso

Multivendor Deployment Integration for Future Mobile Networks   351
  Manuel Perez Martinez, Tímea László, Norbert Pataki,
  Csaba Rotter, and Csaba Szalai

Mobile Robots and Server Systems

Patrolling a Path Connecting a Set of Points with Unbalanced
Frequencies of Visits.   367
  Huda Chuangpishit, Jurek Czyzowicz, Leszek Gąsieniec,
  Konstantinos Georgiou, Tomasz Jurdziński, and Evangelos Kranakis

Exploring Graphs with Time Constraints by Unreliable Collections
of Mobile Robots   381
   Jurek Czyzowicz, Maxime Godon, Evangelos Kranakis,
   Arnaud Labourel, and Euripides Markou

The *k*-Server Problem with Advice in *d* Dimensions and on the Sphere   396
   Elisabet Burjons, Dennis Komm, and Marcel Schöngens

Automata, Complexity, Completeness

Deciding Universality of ptNFAs is PSpace-Complete   413
   Tomáš Masopust and Markus Krötzsch

Theoretical Aspects of Symbolic Automata   428
   Hellis Tamm and Margus Veanes

Complete Algorithms for Algebraic Strongest Postconditions and Weakest
Preconditions in Polynomial ODE'S   442
   Michele Boreale

Recognition and Generation

Influence of Body Postures on Touch-Based Biometric
User Authentication   459
   Kamil Burda and Daniela Chuda

Michiko: Poem Models used in Automated Haiku Poetry Generation   469
   Miroslava Hrešková and Kristína Machová

Optimization, Probabilistic Analysis, and Sorting

House Allocation Problems with Existing Tenants and Priorities
for Teacher Recruitment   479
   Ana Paula Tomás

Runtime Distributions and Criteria for Restarts   493
   Jan-Hendrik Lorenz

Inversions from Sorting with Distance-Based Errors   508
   Barbara Geissmann and Paolo Penna

Filters, Configurations, and Picture Encoding

An Optimization Problem Related to Bloom Filters with Bit Patterns   525
   Peter Damaschke and Alexander Schliep

Nivat's Conjecture Holds for Sums of Two Periodic Configurations   539
  Michal Szabados

Encoding Pictures with Maximal Codes of Pictures   552
  Marcella Anselmo, Dora Giammarresi, and Maria Madonia

Machine Learning

ARCID: A New Approach to Deal with Imbalanced
Datasets Classification   569
  *Safa Abdellatif, Mohamed Ali Ben Hassine, Sadok Ben Yahia,
  and Amel Bouzeghoub*

Fake Review Detection via Exploitation of Spam Indicators and Reviewer
Behavior Characteristics.   581
  Ioannis Dematis, Eirini Karapistoli, and Athena Vakali

Mining Spatial Gradual Patterns: Application to Measurement
of Potentially Avoidable Hospitalizations   596
  *Tu Ngo, Vera Georgescu, Anne Laurent, Thérèse Libourel,
  and Grégoire Mercier*

Text Searching Algorithms

New Variants of Pattern Matching with Constants and Variables.   611
  Yuki Igarashi, Diptarama, Ryo Yoshinaka, and Ayumi Shinohara

Duel and Sweep Algorithm for Order-Preserving Pattern Matching   624
  *Davaajav Jargalsaikhan, Diptarama, Yohei Ueki, Ryo Yoshinaka,
  and Ayumi Shinohara*

Longest Common Prefixes with k-Mismatches and Applications   636
  *Hayam Alamro, Lorraine A. K. Ayad, Panagiotis Charalampopoulos,
  Costas S. Iliopoulos, and Solon P. Pissis*

Data and Model Engineering

Managing Reduction in Multidimensional Databases   653
  Franck Ravat, Jiefu Song, and Olivier Teste

UML2PROV: Automating Provenance Capture in Software Engineering   667
  Carlos Sáenz-Adán, Beatriz Pérez, Trung Dong Huynh, and Luc Moreau

Validating Data from Semantic Web Providers   682
  *Jacques Chabin, Mirian Halfeld-Ferrari, Béatrice Markhoff,
  and Thanh Binh Nguyen*

Author Index   697

Keynote Talk

Swift Logic for Big Data and Knowledge Graphs
Overview of Requirements, Language, and System

Luigi Bellomarini[1], Georg Gottlob[1,2(✉)], Andreas Pieris[3],
and Emanuel Sallinger[1]

[1] Department of Computer Science, University of Oxford, Oxford, UK
georg.gottlob@gmail.com
[2] Institute of Information Systems, TU Wien, Vienna, Austria
[3] School of Informatics, University of Edinburgh, Edinburgh, UK

Abstract. Many modern companies wish to maintain knowledge in the form of a corporate knowledge graph and to use and manage this knowledge via a knowledge graph management system (KGMS). We formulate various requirements for a fully-fledged KGMS. In particular, such a system must be capable of performing complex reasoning tasks but, at the same time, achieve efficient and scalable reasoning over Big Data with an acceptable computational complexity. Moreover, a KGMS needs interfaces to corporate databases, the web, and machine-learning and analytics packages. We present KRR formalisms and a system achieving these goals. To this aim, we use specific suitable fragments from the Datalog$^\pm$ family of languages, and we introduce the VADALOG system, which puts these swift logics into action. This system exploits the theoretical underpinning of relevant Datalog$^\pm$ languages and combines it with existing and novel techniques from database and AI practice.

1   Introduction

The so-called *knowledge economy*, characteristic for the current Information Age, is rapidly gaining ground. According to [1], as cited in [29], "The knowledge economy is the use of knowledge [...] to generate tangible and intangible values. Technology, and, in particular, knowledge technology, help to transform a part of human knowledge to machines. This knowledge can be used by decision support systems in various fields and generate economic value." The importance of knowledge as an essential economic driving force has been evident to most corporate decision makers since the late 1970s, and the idea of storing knowledge and processing it to derive valuable new knowledge existed in the context of *expert systems*. Alas, it seems that the technology of those 'early' times was not sufficiently mature: the available hardware was too slow and main memory too tight for more complex reasoning tasks; database management systems were too slow and too rigid; there was no web where an expert system could acquire data; machine learning, and, in particular, neural networks were ridiculed as

This paper is a significantly abbreviated and slightly updated version of [4].

© Springer International Publishing AG 2018
A. M. Tjoa et al. (Eds.): SOFSEM 2018, LNCS 10706, pp. 3–16, 2018.
https://doi.org/10.1007/978-3-319-73117-9_1

largely unsuccessful; ontological reasoning was in its infancy and the available formalisms were much too complex for Big Data applications. Meanwhile, there has been huge technological progress, and also much research progress that has led to a better understanding of many aspects of knowledge processing and reasoning with large amounts of data. Hardware has evolved, database technology has significantly improved, there is a (semantic) web with linked open data, companies can participate in social networks, machine learning has made a dramatic breakthrough, and there is a better understanding of scalable reasoning mechanisms.

Because of this, and of some eye-opening showcase projects such as IBM Watson [18], thousands of large and medium-sized companies suddenly wish to manage their own *knowledge graphs*, and are looking for adequate *knowledge graph management systems (KGMS)*.

The term *knowledge graph* originally only referred to Google's Knowledge Graph, namely, "a knowledge base used by Google to enhance its search engine's search results with semantic-search information gathered from a wide variety of sources" [30]. Meanwhile, further Internet giants (e.g. Facebook, Amazon) as well as some other very large companies have constructed their own knowledge graphs, and many more companies would like to maintain a private corporate knowledge graph incorporating large amounts of data in form of facts, both from corporate and public sources, as well as rule-based knowledge. Such a corporate knowledge graph is expected to contain relevant business knowledge, for example, knowledge about customers, products, prices, and competitors rather than mainly world knowledge from Wikipedia and similar sources. It should be managed by a KGMS, i.e., a knowledge base management system (KBMS), which performs complex rule-based reasoning tasks over very large amounts of data and, in addition, provides methods and tools for data analytics and machine learning, whence the equation:

$$\boxed{\text{KGMS} \;=\; \text{KBMS} + \text{Big Data} + \text{Analytics}}$$

The word 'graph' in this context is often misunderstood to the extent that some IT managers think that acquiring a graph database system and feeding it with data is sufficient to achieve a corporate knowledge graph. Others erroneously think that knowledge graphs necessarily use RDF triple stores instead of plain relational data. Yet others think that knowledge graphs are limited to storing and analyzing social network data only. While knowledge graphs should indeed be able to manipulate graph data and reason over RDF and social networks, they should not be restricted to this. For example, restricting a knowledge graph to contain RDF data only would exclude the direct inclusion of standard relational data and the direct interaction with corporate databases.

Not much has been described in the literature about the architecture of a KGMS and the functions it should ideally fulfil. In Sect. 2 we briefly list what we believe are the main requirements for a fully fledged KGMS. As indicated in Fig. 1, which depicts our reference architecture, the central component of a KGMS is its core reasoning engine, which has access to a rule repository. Grouped around it are various modules that provide relevant data access and analytics

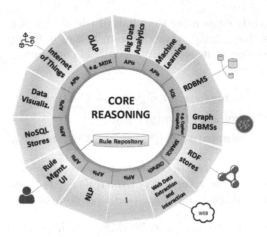

Fig. 1. KGMS reference architecture.

functionalities (see [4] for details). We expect a KGMS to fulfil many of these functions.

The reasoning core of a KGMS needs to provide a language for knowledge representation and reasoning (KRR). The data format for factual data should, as said, match the standard relational formalism so as to smoothly integrate corporate databases and data warehouses, and at the same time be suited for RDF and graph data. The rule language and reasoning mechanism should achieve a careful balance between expressive power and complexity. In Sect. 3 we present VADALOG, a Datalog-based language that matches this requirement. VADALOG belongs to the Datalog$^\pm$ family of languages that extend Datalog by existential quantifiers in rule heads, as well as by other features, and restricts at the same time its syntax so as to achieve decidability and data tractability; see, e.g., [5–8]. The logical core of the VADALOG language corresponds to *Warded Datalog$^\pm$* [2,16], which captures plain Datalog as well as SPARQL queries using set semantics [22] under the entailment regime for OWL 2 QL [15], and is able to perform ontological reasoning tasks. Reasoning with the logical core of VADALOG is computationally efficient.

While the logical core of VADALOG has a number of beneficial properties, several features that have been added to it for achieving more powerful reasoning and data manipulation capabilities [4]. To give just one example here, the language is augmented by monotonic aggregations [26], which permits the use of aggregation (via summation, product, max, min, count) even in the presence of recursion. This enables us to swiftly solve problems such as the *company control* problem (studied e.g. in [10]) as explained in the following example.

Example 1 (**Example**). Assume the ownership relationship among a large number of companies is stored via facts (i.e., tuples of a database relation) of the following form Own($comp_1, comp_2, w$) meaning that company $comp_1$ directly owns a fraction w of company $comp_2$, with $0 \leq w \leq 1$. A company x controls a company y if x directly owns more than half of the shares of y or if x controls a set S of companies that jointly own more than half of y. Computing a predicate Control(x, y) expressing that company x controls company y, is then achieved in VADALOG by two rules:

$$\mathrm{Own}(x, y, w), w > 0.5 \rightarrow \mathrm{Control}(x, y)$$
$$\mathrm{Control}(x, y), \mathrm{Own}(y, z, w),$$
$$v = \mathtt{msum}(w, \langle y \rangle), v > 0.5 \rightarrow \mathrm{Control}(x, z).$$

Here, for fixed x, the aggregate construct $\mathtt{msum}(w, \langle y \rangle)$ forms the sum over all values w such that for some company y, Control(x, y) is true, and Own(y, z, w) holds, i.e., company y directly owns fraction w of company z.   ■

In [4] we introduce the VADALOG KGMS, which builds on the VADALOG language and combines it with existing and novel techniques from database and AI practice such as stream query processing, dynamic in-memory indexing and aggressive recursion control. The VADALOG system is Oxford's contribution to the VADA (*Value Added Data Systems*) research project [14, 20, 28], which is a joint effort of the universities of Edinburgh, Manchester, and Oxford.

2   Desiderata for a KGMS

In this section we briefly summarize what we think are the most important desiderata for a fully-fledged KGMS. We will list these requirements according to three categories, keeping in mind, however, that these categories are interrelated.

Language and System for Reasoning

There should be a logical formalism for expressing facts and rules, and a reasoning engine that uses this language, which should provide the following features.

Simple and Modular Syntax: It should be easy to add and delete facts and to add new rules. As in logic programming, facts should conceptually coincide with database tuples.

High Expressive Power: Datalog [10, 19] is a good yardstick for the expressive power of rule languages. Over ordered structures (which we may assume here), Datalog with very mild negation captures PTIME; see, e.g., [11]. A rule language should thus ideally be at least as expressive as plain recursive Datalog, possibly with mild negation.

Numeric Computation and Aggregations: The basic logical formalism and inference engine should be enriched by features for dealing with numeric values, including appropriate aggregate functions.

Probabilistic Reasoning: The language should be suited for incorporating appropriate methods of probabilistic reasoning, and the system should propagate probabilities or certainty values along the reasoning process, that is, compute probabilities or certainty values for derived facts, and make adjustments wherever necessary. Probabilistic models may range from simple triangular norm operators (T-norm – cf [17]) over probabilistic database models [27] to Markov logic networks [23].

Ontological Reasoning: Ontological reasoning and query answering should be provided. We have two yardsticks here. First, ontological reasoning to the extent of tractable description logics such as DL-Lite$_R$ should be possible. Recall that DL-Lite$_R$ forms the logical underpinning of the OWL 2 QL profile of the Web Ontology Language as standardized by the W3C. Second, it should be expressive enough to cover all SPARQL queries under set semantics [22] over RDF datasets under the entailment regime for OWL 2 QL [15].

Low Complexity: Reasoning should be tractable in data complexity (i.e. when the rules are assumed to be fixed and the fact base is considered the input). Whenever possible, the system should recognize and take profit of rule sets that can be processed within low space complexity classes such as NLOGSPACE (e.g. for SPARQL) or even AC$_0$ (e.g. for traditional conjunctive database queries).

Rule Repository, Rule Management, and Ontology Editor: A library for storing recurring rules and definitions should be provided, as well as a user interface for rule management in the spirit of the ontology editor protégé [21].

Dynamic Orchestration: For larger applications, there must be a master module to allow the orchestration of complex data flows. For simple systems, the process must be easily specifiable. For complex systems, the process must be dynamically controllable through intelligent reasoning techniques or external control facilities and tools (e.g. BPM).

Accessing and Handling Big Data

Big Data Access: The system must be able to provide efficient access to Big Data sources and systems and fast reasoning algorithms over Big Data. In particular, the possibility of out-of-memory reasoning must be given in case the relevant data does not fit into main memory. Integration of Big Data processing techniques should be possible where the volume of data makes it necessary (see e.g. [25]).

Database and Data Warehouse Access: Seamless access to relational, graph databases, data warehouses, RDF stores, and major NoSQL stores should be granted. Data in such repositories should be directly usable as factual data for reasoning.

Ontology-Based Data Access (OBDA): OBDA [9] allows a system to compile a query that has been formulated on top of an ontology into one directly on the database. OBDA should be possible whenever appropriate.

Multi-query Support: Where possible and appropriate, partial results from repeated (sub-)queries should be evaluated once [24] and optimized in this regard.

Data Cleaning, Exchange and Integration: Integrating, exchanging and cleaning data should be supported both directly (through an appropriate KRR formalism that is made available through various applications in the knowledge repository), and by allowing integration of third-party software.

Web Data Extraction, Interaction, and IoT: A KGMS should be able to interact with the web by (i) extracting relevant web data (e.g. prices advertised by competitors) and integrating these data into the local fact base, and (ii) exchanging data with web forms and servers that are available through a web interface. One way to achieve this is given in [4]. Similar methods can be used for interacting with the IoT through appropriate network accessible APIs.

Embedding Procedural and Third-Party Code

Procedural Code: The system should have encapsulation methods for embedding procedural code (proprietary and third party) written in a variety of programming languages and offer a logical interface to it.

Third-Party Packages for Machine Learning, Text Mining, NLP, Data Analytics, and Data Visualization: The system should be equipped with direct access to powerful existing software packages for machine learning, text mining, data analytics, and data visualization. Given that excellent third-party software for these purposes exists, we believe that a KGMS should be able to use a multitude of such packages via appropriate logical interfaces.

3   Overview of the VADALOG Language and System

We here only give a brief overview of the VADALOG language and system. A more extensive overview of both language and system is given in [4] and the system is presented in detail in a forthcoming paper.

As said before, VADALOG is a KR language that achieves a careful balance between expressive power and complexity, and it can be used as the reasoning core of a KGMS. In Sect. 3.1 we discuss the logical core of VADALOG and some interesting fragments of it, while in Sect. 3.2 we discuss how this language can be extended with additional features that are much needed in real-world applications.

3.1 Core Language

The logical core of VADALOG is a member of the Datalog$^\pm$ family of knowledge representation languages, which we call Warded Datalog$^\pm$. The main goal of Datalog$^\pm$ languages is to extend the well-known language Datalog with useful modeling features such as existential quantifiers in rule heads (the '+' in the symbol '$\pm$'), and at the same time restrict the rule syntax in such a way that the decidability and data tractability of reasoning is guaranteed (the '$-$' in the symbol '$\pm$').

The core of Datalog$^\pm$ languages consists of rules known as *existential rules* or *tuple-generating dependencies*, which essentially generalize Datalog rules with existential quantifiers in rule heads; henceforth, we adopt the term existential rule. An example of such an existential rule is

$$\text{Person}(x) \;\rightarrow\; \exists y \, \text{HasFather}(x, y), \text{Person}(y)$$

which encodes that every person has a father who is also a person. In general, an existential rule is a first-order sentence

$$\forall \bar{x} \forall \bar{y} (\varphi(\bar{x}, \bar{y}) \;\rightarrow\; \exists \bar{z} \, \psi(\bar{x}, \bar{z}))$$

where φ (the *body*) and ψ (the *head*) are conjunctions of atoms with constants and variables.

The semantics of a set of existential rules Σ over a database D, denoted $\Sigma(D)$, is defined via the well-known chase procedure. Roughly, the chase adds new atoms to D (possibly involving null values used for satisfying the existentially quantified variables) until the final result $\Sigma(D)$ satisfies all the existential rules of Σ. Notice that, in general, $\Sigma(D)$ is infinite. Here is a simple example of the chase procedure.

Example 2. Consider the database $D = \{\text{Person}(Bob)\}$, and the existential rule

$$\text{Person}(x) \;\rightarrow\; \exists y \, \text{HasFather}(x, y), \text{Person}(y).$$

The database atom triggers the above existential rule, and the chase adds in D the atoms

$$\text{HasFather}(Bob, \nu_1) \quad \text{and} \quad \text{Person}(\nu_1)$$

in order to satisfy it, where ν_1 is a (labeled) null representing some unknown value. The new atom $\text{Person}(\nu_1)$ triggers again the existential rule, and the chase adds the atoms

$$\text{HasFather}(\nu_1, \nu_2) \quad \text{and} \quad \text{Person}(\nu_2),$$

where ν_2 is a new null. The result of the chase is the instance

$$\{\text{Person}(Bob), \text{HasFather}(Bob, \nu_1)\} \;\cup$$
$$\bigcup_{i>0} \{\text{Person}(\nu_i), \text{HasFather}(\nu_i, \nu_{i+1})\},$$

where $\nu_1, \nu_2, \dots$ are (labeled) nulls. ∎

Given a pair $Q = (\Sigma, \text{Ans})$, where Σ is a set of existential rules and Ans an n-ary predicate, the evaluation of Q over a database D, denoted $Q(D)$, is defined as the set of tuples over the set C_D of constant values occurring in the database D that are entailed by D and Σ, i.e., the set

$$\{\langle t_1, \ldots, t_n \rangle \mid \text{Ans}(t_1, \ldots, t_n) \in \Sigma(D) \text{ and each } t_i \in C_D\}.$$

The main reasoning task that we are interested in is *tuple inference*: given a database D, a pair $Q = (\Sigma, \text{Ans})$, and a tuple of constants $\bar{t}$, decide whether $\bar{t} \in Q(D)$. This problem is very hard; in fact, it is undecidable, even when Q is fixed and only D is given as input [5]. This has led to a flurry of activity for identifying restrictions on existential rules that make the above problem decidable. Each such restriction gives rise to a new Datalog$^\pm$ language.

Warded Datalog$^\pm$: The Logical Core of VADALOG. The logical core of VADALOG relies on the notion of wardedness, which gives rise to Warded Datalog$^\pm$ [16]. In other words, VADALOG is obtained by extending Warded Datalog$^\pm$ with additional features of practical utility that are discussed in the next section.

Wardedness applies a restriction on how the "dangerous" variables of a set of existential rules are used. Intuitively, a "dangerous" variable is a body-variable that can be unified with a labeled null value when the chase algorithm is applied, and it is also propagated to the head of the rule. For example, given the set Σ consisting of the existential rules

$$P(x) \rightarrow \exists z\, R(x, z) \quad \text{and} \quad R(x, y) \rightarrow P(y),$$

the variable y in the body of the second rule is "dangerous" (w.r.t. Σ) since starting, e.g., from the database $D = \{P(a)\}$, the chase will apply the first rule and generate $R(a, \nu)$, where ν is a null that acts as a witness for the existentially quantified variable z, and then the second rule will be applied with the variable y being unified with ν that is propagated to the obtained atom $P(\nu)$. The goal of wardedness is to tame the way null values are propagated during the construction of the chase instance by posing the following conditions:

1. all the "dangerous" variables should coexist in a single body-atom α, called the ward, and
2. the ward can share only "harmless" variables with the rest of the body, i.e., variables that are unified only with database constants during the construction of the chase.

Warded Datalog$^\pm$ consists of all the (finite) sets of warded existential rules. The rule in Example 2 is clearly warded. Another example of a warded set of existential rules follows:

Example 3. Consider the following rules encoding part of the OWL 2 direct semantics entailment regime for OWL 2 QL (see [2, 16]):

$$\underline{\text{Type}(x, y)}, \text{Restriction}(y, z) \rightarrow \exists w \, \text{Triple}(x, z, w)$$
$$\underline{\text{Type}(x, y)}, \text{SubClass}(y, z) \rightarrow \text{Type}(x, z)$$
$$\underline{\text{Triple}(x, y, z)}, \text{Inverse}(y, w) \rightarrow \text{Triple}(z, w, x)$$
$$\underline{\text{Triple}(x, y, z)}, \text{Restriction}(w, y) \rightarrow \text{Type}(x, w).$$

It is easy to verify that the above set is warded, where the underlined atoms are the wards. Indeed, a variable that occurs in an atom of the form $\text{Restriction}(\cdot, \cdot)$, or the form $\text{SubClass}(\cdot, \cdot)$, or $\text{Inverse}(\cdot, \cdot)$, is trivially harmless. However, variables that appear in the first position of Type, or in the first/third position of Triple can be dangerous. Thus, the underlined atoms are indeed acting as the wards.

Let us now intuitively explain the meaning of the above set of existential rules: The first rule states that if a is of type b, encoded via the atom $\text{Type}(a, b)$, while b represents the class that corresponds to the first attribute of some binary relation c, encoded via the atom $\text{Restriction}(b, c)$, then there exists some value d such that the tuple (a, d) occurs in the binary relation c, encoded as the atom $\text{Triple}(a, c, d)$. Analogously, the other rules encode the usual meaning of subclasses, inverses and the effect of restrictions on types. ∎

Let us clarify that Warded Datalog$^{\pm}$ is a refinement of the language of *Weakly-Frontier-Guarded Datalog$^{\pm}$*, which is defined in the same way but without the condition (2) given above [3]. Weakly-Frontier-Guarded Datalog$^{\pm}$ is highly intractable in data complexity; in fact, it is EXPTIME-complete. This justifies Warded Datalog$^{\pm}$, which is a (nearly) maximal tractable fragment of Weakly-Frontier-Guarded Datalog$^{\pm}$.

Warded Datalog$^{\pm}$ enjoys several favourable properties that make it a robust core towards more practical languages:

- Tuple inference under Warded Datalog$^{\pm}$ is data tractable; in fact, it is PTIME-complete when the set of rules is fixed.
- Warded Datalog$^{\pm}$ contains full Datalog as sub-language without increasing the complexity. Indeed, a set Σ of Datalog rules is trivially warded since there are no dangerous variables (w.r.t. Σ).
- Warded Datalog$^{\pm}$ generalizes central ontology languages such as the OWL 2 QL profile of OWL, which in turn relies on the prominent description logic DL-Lite$_R$.
- Warded Datalog$^{\pm}$ is suitable for querying RDF graphs. Actually, by adding stratified and grounded negation to Warded Datalog$^{\pm}$, we obtain a language, called TriQ-Lite 1.0 [16], that can express every SPARQL query using set semantics [22] under the entailment regime for OWL 2 QL.

3.2 Extensions

In order to be effective for real-world applications, we extend the logical core of VADALOG described above with a set of additional features of practical utility.

Although the theoretical properties of the language are no longer guaranteed, our preliminary evaluation has shown that the practical overhead for many of these features remains reasonable in our streaming implementation. In the future, we plan to perform a more thorough complexity analysis and isolate sets of features for which beneficial complexity upper bounds are met and runtime guarantees are given.

Data Types: Variables and constants are typed. The language supports the most common simple data types: integer, float, string, Boolean, date. There is also support for composite data types, such as sets.

Expressions: Variables and constants can be combined into expressions, which are recursively defined as variables, constants or combinations thereof, for which we support many different operations for the various data types: algebraic sum, multiplication, division for integers and floats; containment, addition, deletion of set elements; string operations (contains, starts-with, ends-with, index-of, substring, etc.); Boolean operations (and, or, not, etc.). Expressions can be used in rule bodies (1) as the left-hand side (LHS) of a *condition*, i.e., the comparison ($>, <, >=, <=, <>$) of a body variable with the expression itself; (2) as the LHS of an *assignment*, i.e., the definition of a specifically calculated value, potentially used as an existentially quantified head variable. In our running example, variable v is calculated with the expression $\mathtt{msum}(w, \langle y \rangle)$ and used in the condition $v > 0.5$.

Skolem Functions: Labeled null values can be suitably calculated with functions defined on-the-fly. They are assumed to be deterministic (returning unique labeled nulls for unique input bindings), and to have disjoint ranges.

Monotonic Aggregations: VADALOG supports aggregation (*min, max, sum, prod, count*), by means of an extension to the notion of monotonic aggregations [26], which allows adopting aggregation even in the presence of recursion while preserving monotonicity w.r.t. set containment. The company control example shows the use of $\mathtt{msum}$, which calculates variable v, as the monotonically increasing sum of the quota w of company z owned by y, in turn controlled by x. The sum is accumulated so that above the threshold 0.5, we have that x controls z. Recent applications of VADALOG in challenging industrial use cases showed that such aggregations are very efficient in many real-world Big Data settings.

Data Binding Primitives: Data sources and targets can be declared by adopting *input/output annotations*, a.k.a. *binding patterns*. Annotations are special facts augmenting sets of existential rules with specific behaviours. The unnamed perspective used in VADALOG can be harmonized with the named perspective of many external systems by means of *bind* and *mapping* annotations, which also support *projection*. A special *query bind* annotation also supports binding predicates to queries against inputs/outputs (in the external language, e.g., SQL-queries for a data source or target that supports SQL). In our example, the extension of the Own predicate is our input, which we denote with an @input("Own") annotation. The actual facts then may be derived, e.g., from a relational or graph database, which we would respectively access with the two following annotations (the latter one using neo4j's cypher graph query language):

```
@bind("Own", "rdbms", "companies.ownerships").
    @qbind("Own", "graphDB",
        "MATCH (a)-[o:Owns]->(b)
        RETURN a,b,o.weight").
```

A similar approach is also used for bridging external machine learning and data extraction platforms into the system. This uses binding patterns as a form of *behaviour injection*: the atoms in rules are decorated with binding annotations, so that a step in the reasoning process triggers the external component. We give a simple example using the OXPath [13] large-scale web data extraction framework (developed as part of the DIADEM project [12]) – an extension of XPath that interacts with web applications to extract information obtained during web navigation. In our running example, assume that our local company ownership information is only partial, while more complete information can be retrieved from the web. In particular, assume that a company register acts as a web search engine, taking as input a company name and returning, as separate pages, the owned companies. This information can be obtained as follows:[1]

```
@qbind("Own", "oxpath",
    "doc('http://company_register.com/ownerships')
    /descendant::field()[1]/{$1}
    /following::a[.#='Search']/{click/}
        /(//a[.#='Next']/ {click/})*
            //div[@class='c']:<comp>
            [./span[1]:<name=string(.)>]
            [./span[3]:<percent=string(.)>]").
```

The above examples show a basic bridging between the technologies. Interesting interactions can be seen in more sophisticated scenarios, where the reasoning process and external component processing is more heavily interleaved.

Probabilistic Reasoning: VADALOG offers support for the basic cases in which scalable computation can be guaranteed. Facts are assumed to be probabilistically independent and a minimalistic form of probabilistic inference is offered as a side product of query answering. Facts can be adorned with probability measures according to the well-known possible world semantics [27]. Then, if the set of existential rules respects specific syntactic properties that guarantee probabilistic tractability (namely, a generalization of the notion of *hierarchical queries* [27]), the facts resulting from query answering are enriched with their marginal probability, safely calculated in a scalable way. In the following extension to our running example, we use probabilistic reasoning to account for uncertain ownerships (e.g., due to unreliable sources), prefixing the facts

---

[1] Concretely, the first position of the Own predicate is bound to the $1 placeholder in the OXPath expression.

with their likelihood, so as to derive non-trivial conclusions on company control relationships:

0.8 :: Own("ACME", "COIN", 0.7)
0.3 :: Own("COIN", "SAVERS", 0.3)
0.4 :: Own("ACME", "GYM", 0.55)
0.6 :: Own("GYM", "SAVERS", 0.4).

In total, the language allows bridging logic-based reasoning and machine learning in three ways. First, the language supports scalable probabilistic inference in basic cases as seen above. Second, the extensions to the core language provide all the necessary features to abstract and embed advanced inference algorithms (e.g. belief propagation) so that they can be executed directly by the VADALOG system, and hence leverage its optimization strategies. Third, for the more sophisticated machine learning applications, data binding primitives allow a simple interaction with specialized libraries and systems as described before.

Post-processing Annotations: Since specific computations are often needed after the result has been produced, VADALOG supports many of them by means of annotations for the following features: *ordering* of the resulting values, as set semantics is assumed on the output, and yet a particular ordering of the facts may be desired by the consumer: for example, @orderby("Control", 1) sorts the obtained control facts by the controlling company; *deduplication*, in specific conditions (e.g. in presence of calculated values), the output may physically contain undesired duplicates; *non-monotonic aggregations* on the final result, without the limitations induced by recursion; and *certain answers*.

4   Conclusion

In this paper, we have formulated a number of requirements for a KGMS, which led us to postulate our reference architecture (see Fig. 1). Based on these requirements, we introduced the VADALOG language whose core corresponds to Warded Datalog$^\pm$. The basic VADALOG language is extended by features for numeric computations, monotonic aggregation, probabilistic reasoning, and, moreover, by data binding primitives used for interacting with the corporate and external environment. These binding primitives allow the reasoning engine to access and manipulate external data through the lens of a logical predicate. The external data may stem from a corporate database, may be extracted from web pages, or may be the output of a machine-learning program that has been evaluated over previously computed data relations. The VADALOG system, which is being implemented at the University of Oxford, puts these swift logics into action. This system exploits the theoretical underpinning of Warded Datalog$^\pm$ and combines it with existing and novel techniques from database and AI practice.

Many core features of the VADALOG system [4] are already integrated and show good performance. Our plan is to complete the system in the near future. A detailed report on the key technical features of the VADALOG reasoning system and on their implementation is already available on request from the authors. We believe that the VADALOG system is a well-suited platform for applications that integrate machine learning (ML) and data analytics with logical reasoning. We are currently implementing applications of this type and will report about them soon.

Acknowledgments. This work has been supported by the EPSRC Programme Grant EP/M025268/1 "VADA – Value Added Data Systems". The VADALOG system as presented here is the intellectual property of the University of Oxford.

References

1. Amidon, D.M., Formica, P., Mercier-Laurent, E.: Knowledge Economics: Emerging Principles. Tartu University Press Tartu, Pactices and Policies (2005)
2. Arenas, M., Gottlob, G., Pieris, A.: Expressive languages for querying the semantic web. In: PODS, pp. 14–26 (2014)
3. Baget, J.F., Leclère, M., Mugnier, M.L., Salvat, E.: On rules with existential variables: walking the decidability line. Artif. Intell. **175**(9–10), 1620–1654 (2011)
4. Bellomarini, L., Gottlob, G., Pieris, A., Sallinger, E.: Swift logic for big data and knowledge graphs. In: Sierra, C. (ed.) Proceedings of the Twenty-Sixth International Joint Conference on Artificial Intelligence, IJCAI 2017, Melbourne, Australia, 19–25 August 2017, pp. 2–10. ijcai.org (2017). https://doi.org/10.24963/ijcai.2017/1
5. Calì, A., Gottlob, G., Kifer, M.: Taming the infinite chase: query answering under expressive relational constraints. J. Artif. Intell. Res. **48**, 115–174 (2013)
6. Calì, A., Gottlob, G., Lukasiewicz, T.: A general datalog-based framework for tractable query answering over ontologies. J. Web Sem. **14**, 57–83 (2012)
7. Calì, A., Gottlob, G., Lukasiewicz, T., Marnette, B., Pieris, A.: Datalog+/−: a family of logical knowledge representation and query languages for new applications. In: LICS, pp. 228–242 (2010)
8. Calì, A., Gottlob, G., Pieris, A.: Towards more expressive ontology languages: the query answering problem. Artif. Intell. **193**, 87–128 (2012)
9. Calvanese, D., De Giacomo, G., Lembo, D., Lenzerini, M., Poggi, A., Rodriguez-Muro, M., Rosati, R., Ruzzi, M., Savo, D.F.: The mastro system for ontology-based data access. Semant. Web **2**(1), 43–53 (2011)
10. Ceri, S., Gottlob, G., Tanca, L.: Logic Programming and Databases. Springer, Heidelberg (2012). https://doi.org/10.1007/978-3-642-83952-8
11. Dantsin, E., Eiter, T., Gottlob, G., Voronkov, A.: Complexity and expressive power of logic programming. ACM Comput. Surv. **33**(3), 374–425 (2001)
12. Furche, T., Gottlob, G., Grasso, G., Guo, X., Orsi, G., Schallhart, C., Wang, C.: DIADEM: thousands of websites to a single database. PVLDB **7**(14), 1845–1856 (2014). http://www.vldb.org/pvldb/vol7/p1845-furche.pdf
13. Furche, T., Gottlob, G., Grasso, G., Schallhart, C., Sellers, A.J.: Oxpath: a language for scalable data extraction, automation, and crawling on the deep web. VLDB J. **22**(1), 47–72 (2013)
14. Furche, T., Gottlob, G., Neumayr, B., Sallinger, E.: Data wrangling for big data: towards a lingua franca for data wrangling. In: AMW (2016)
15. Glimm, B., Ogbuji, C., Hawke, S., Herman, I., Parsia, B., Polleres, A., Seaborne, A.: SPARQL 1.1 entailment regimes, 2013. W3C Recommendation, 21 March 2013

16. Gottlob, G., Pieris, A.: Beyond SPARQL under OWL 2 QL entailment regime: rules to the rescue. In: IJCAI, pp. 2999–3007 (2015)
17. Hájek, P.: Metamathematics of Fuzzy Logic. Springer, Heidelberg (1998). https://doi.org/10.1007/978-94-011-5300-3
18. High, R.: The era of cognitive systems: an inside look at IBM Watson and how it works. IBM, Redbooks (2012)
19. Huang, S.S., Green, T.J., Loo, B.T.: Datalog and emerging applications: an interactive tutorial. In: SIGMOD, pp. 1213–1216. ACM (2011)
20. Konstantinou, N., Koehler, M., Abel, E., Civili, C., Neumayr, B., Sallinger, E., Fernandes, A.A.A., Gottlob, G., Keane, J.A., Libkin, L., Paton, N.W.: The VADA architecture for cost-effective data wrangling. In: SIGMOD, pp. 1599–1602 (2017)
21. Noy, N.F., Sintek, M., Decker, S., Crubézy, M., Fergerson, R.W., Musen, M.A.: Creating semantic web contents with protege-2000. IEEE IS **16**(2), 60–71 (2001)
22. Pérez, J., Arenas, M., Gutierrez, C.: Semantics and complexity of SPARQL. ACM Trans. Database Syst. **34**(3), 16:1–16:45 (2009). https://doi.org/10.1145/1567274.1567278
23. Richardson, M., Domingos, P.M.: Markov logic networks. Mach. Learn. **62**(1–2), 107–136 (2006)
24. Roy, P., Seshadri, S., Sudarshan, S., Bhobe, S.: Efficient and extensible algorithms for multi query optimization. In: SIGMOD, pp. 249–260 (2000)
25. Shkapsky, A., Yang, M., Interlandi, M., Chiu, H., Condie, T., Zaniolo, C.: Big data analytics with datalog queries on spark. In: SIGMOD, pp. 1135–1149 (2016). http://doi.acm.org/10.1145/2882903.2915229
26. Shkapsky, A., Yang, M., Zaniolo, C.: Optimizing recursive queries with monotonic aggregates in deals. In: ICDE, pp. 867–878 (2015)
27. Suciu, D., Olteanu, D., Ré, C., Koch, C.: Probabilistic Databases. Morgan & Claypool, San Rafael (2011)
28. VADA: Project Website (2016). http://vada.org.uk/. Accessed 19 May 2017
29. Wikipedia: Knowledge economy (2017). https://en.wikipedia.org/wiki/Knowledge_economy. Accessed 19 May 2017
30. Wikipedia: Knowledge graph (2017). https://en.wikipedia.org/wiki/Knowledge_graph. Accessed 19 May 2017

Foundations of Computer Science

Foundation of Computer Science

On Architecture Specification

Manfred Broy[⊠]

Institut für Informatik, Technische Universität München,
80290 Munich, Germany
broy@in.tum.de
http://www.broy.informatik.tu-muenchen.de

Abstract. The design, specification, and correct implementation of an architectural design are after the task of requirements specification the perhaps most important design decisions, when building large software or software based systems. Architectures are responsible for software quality, for a number of quality attributes such as maintainability, portability, changeability, reusability but also reliability, security, and safety. Therefore, the design of architectures is a key issue in system and software development. For highly distributed, networked systems and for cyber-physical systems we need a design concept which supports composition, parallelism, and concurrency and finally real time but keeps all of the general advantages of object-oriented programming. We describe an approach to specify and implement systems along the lines of some of the established concepts of object-orientation – such as inheritance and class instantiation. This leads to an approach that nevertheless provides an execution model which is parallel and concurrent in nature and supports real time and modular composition. This way, it lays the foundation of a software and systems engineering style where classical object-orientation can be extended to cyber-physical systems in straightforward way.

Keywords: Specification · Design · Contracts · Assumptions · Commitments
System specification · Interface · Architecture

1 Introduction

Object-oriented programming is currently the perhaps most widely used programming style in software development. It combines a number of useful concepts in programming in a way that, in particular, the development of large software systems is supported by it. Nevertheless, object-oriented programming shows a number of deficiencies when dealing with distributed cyber-physical systems. First of all, in classical object-oriented programming the execution model is inherently sequential. All attempts to extend or generalize it to parallel execution models without significant changes in the underlying execution model make the understanding and design of object-oriented programs utterly complicated. Secondly, the composition of object-oriented programs shows some weaknesses and open issues. This is related to the recognized lack of a clear notion of component, a lack of parallel composition, and the lack of a parallel execution model as needed usually for the development of

© Springer International Publishing AG 2018
A M. Tjoa et al. (Eds.): SOFSEM 2018, LNCS 10706, pp. 19–39, 2018.
https://doi.org/10.1007/978-3-319-73117-9_2

cyber-physical systems as we see them nearly everywhere nowadays. A further issue is time and probability which are first class citizens in cyber-physical applications.

When looking at software families and product lines, architecture becomes even more significant, because it determines the possibilities and options of variability and reusability (see [8]). With this in mind, it is a key issue to have an appropriate methodology with a calculus for the design of architectures. This includes a number of ingredients.

- A key concept for *subsystems*, also called components, as building blocks of architectures: this means that we have to determine what the concept of a subsystem is and, in particular, what the concept of an *interface* and *interface behavior* is. Interfaces are the most significant concept for architectures. Subsystems are composed and connected via their interfaces.
- The second ingredient is *composition*. We have to be able to compose systems by composition via their interfaces. Composition has to reflect parallel execution.
- This requires that interfaces of subsystems can be structured into a *family* of sub-interfaces, which are then the basis for the composition of subsystems, more precisely the composition of sub-interfaces of subsystems with other sub-interfaces of subsystems. For this we need a syntactic notion and a notion of behavior interface.
- In addition, we are interested in options to specify properties of interface behaviors in detail.
- Moreover, we have to be able to deal with interface types and subsystem types. These concepts allow us to introduce a notion of subsystems and their types, called system classes as in object-oriented programs, and these can also be used to introduce types of interfaces, properties of assumptions of the interfaces of subsystems which we compose.
- As a result, we also talk about the concept of refinement of systems and their interfaces as a basis of inheritance.

A key is the ability to specify properties of subsystems in terms of their interfaces and to compose interface specifications in a modular way.

In the following, we introduce a logical calculus to deal with interfaces and show how we can use it to define subsystems via properties of their interface assumptions also be able to deal with architectural patterns such as layered architectures.

2   A Formal Model of Interfaces

The key to software and system design is interface specifications where we do not only describe syntactic interfaces but also specify interface behavior.

2.1   Data Models

Systems exchange messages. Messages are exchanged between systems and their operational context and also between subsystems. Systems have states. States are composed of attributes. In principle, we can therefore work out the data model for a service-oriented architecture which consists, just as an object-orientation, of all the attributes which are part of the local states of the subsystems which consists of the description of the data which are communicated over the interfaces between the subsystems.

2.2   Syntactic Interfaces and Interface Behavior

We choose a very general notion of interface where the key is the concept of a channel. A channel is a directed typed communication line on which data of the specified type are transmitted. As part of an interface, a channel is a possibility to provide input or output to a system. Therefore, we speak about input channels and output channels.

Syntactic Interfaces
An interface defines the way a system interacts with its context. Syntactically an interface is specified by a set C of channels where each channel has a data type assigned that defines the set of messages, events, or signals that are transmitted over that channel.

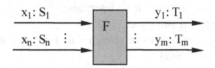

Fig. 1. Graphical representation of a system F as a data flow node with its syntactic interface consisting of the input channels $x_1, ..., x_n$ of types $S_1, ..., S_n$ and the output channels $y_1, ..., y_m$ of types $T_1, ..., T_m$, resp.

In this section, we briefly introduce syntactic and semantic notions of discrete models of *systems* and their *interfaces*. This theoretical framework is in line with [1] called the Focus approach. Systems own input and output channels over which streams of messages are exchanged. In the following we denote the universe of all messages by IM.

Let I be a syntactic interface of typed input channels and O be a syntactic interface of typed output channels that characterize the syntactic interface of a system. (I▶O) denotes this *syntactic interface*. Figure 1 shows system F with its syntactic interface in a graphical representation as a data flow node.

System Interaction: Timed Data Streams
Let IN denote the natural numbers (including 0) and IN^+ denote the strictly positive natural numbers.

The system model is based on the concept of a global clock. The system model can be described as time synchronous and message asynchronous. In the following, we work with streams that include discrete timing information. Such streams represent histories of communications of data messages transmitted within a time frame. By this model of discrete time, time is structured into an infinite sequence of finite time intervals of equal length. We use the natural numbers IN^+ to number the time intervals.

Definition. Timed Streams

Given a message set $M \subseteq IM$ of data elements of type T we represent a *timed stream* s of type T by a function

$$s : \mathbb{N}^+ \to M^*$$

In a timed stream s a sequence of messages s(t) is given for each time interval $t \in \mathbb{N}^+$; $s(t) = \varepsilon$ indicates that in time interval t no message is communicated. By $(M^*)^\infty$ we denote the set of timed streams. ❑

Throughout this paper, we work with a couple of basic operators and notations for streams over the message set that are shortly summarized as follows:

$\langle \rangle$ empty sequence or empty finite stream,

$\langle m \rangle$ one-element sequence containing m as its only element,

a^s   concatenation of the finite sequence with the finite or infinite sequence s,

s(t)   element in the t-th time interval of the stream s,

s↓t   prefix of length $t \in \mathbb{N}$ of the stream s (which corresponds to a sequence of message in t time intervals),

s↑t   the stream s without its first t time intervals,

#s   number of messages in stream s,

M#s   number of copies of messages of stream s that are in a given set $M \subseteq IM$ (for $\{m\}\#x$ we also write m#x),

$\bar{x}$ denotes the result $x(1)^\wedge x(2)^\wedge \ldots$ of concatenating the sequences x(1), x(2), x(3), … resulting in a finite stream in M^* or an infinite stream in $(\mathbb{N}^+ \to M)$.

A channel history for a set C of typed channels (which is a set of typed identifiers) assigns to each channel $c \in C$ a timed stream of messages communicated over that channel.

Let C be a set of typed channels; a (total) *channel history* x is a mapping

$$x : C \to (\mathbb{N}^+ \to M^*)$$

such that x(c) is a timed stream of type Type(c) for each channel $c \in C$. We denote the set of all channel histories for the channel set C by $\vec{C}$. A finite (partial) channel history is a mapping

$$x : C \to (\{1, \ldots, t\} \to M^*)$$

with some number $t \in \mathbb{N}$ such that x(c) respects the channel type of c. ❑

As for streams, for every history $z \in \vec{C}$ and every time $t \in \mathbb{N}$ the expression z↓t denotes the partial history (the communication on the channels in the first t time intervals) of z until time t. z↓t yields a finite history for each of the channels in C represented by a mapping of the type $C \to (\{1, \ldots, t\} \to IM^*)$. z↓0 denotes the history with the empty sequence associated with all its channels.

Interface Behavior

For a given syntactic interface (I▶O) a relation that relates the input histories in $\overrightarrow{I}$ with output histories in $\overrightarrow{O}$ defines its behavior. It is called *system interface behavior* (see [10]). We represent the relation by a set-valued function. In the following we write $\wp$ (M) for the power set over M.

Definition. Interface Behavior and Causal Interface Behavior

A function

$$F: \overrightarrow{I} \to \wp(\overrightarrow{O})$$

is called an I/O-behavior; F is called *causal in input x* if (for all times $t \in \mathbb{N}$ and input histories x, $z \in \overrightarrow{I}$):

$$x{\downarrow}t = z{\downarrow}t \Rightarrow \{y{\downarrow}t: y \in F(x)\} = \{y{\downarrow}t: y \in F(z)\}$$

F is called *strongly causal* if (for all times $t \in \mathbb{N}$ and input histories x, $z \in \overrightarrow{I}$):

$$x{\downarrow}t = z{\downarrow}t \Rightarrow \{y{\downarrow}t + 1: y \in F(x)\} = \{y{\downarrow}t + 1: y \in F(z)\} \qquad \square$$

Causality indicates consistent time flow between input and output histories (for an extended discussion of causality see [1]).

Notation: Extension of predicates on infinite histories to finite ones. Throughout the paper, we use the following notation: Given a predicate

$$p: \overrightarrow{C} \to \mathbb{B}$$

on infinite histories, we extend it also to finite histories x of length t by the definition:

$$p(x) \equiv \exists x' \in \overrightarrow{C}, t \in \mathbb{N} : x = x'{\downarrow}t \land p(x') \qquad \square$$

In other words, assertion p(x) holds for a finite history x if there exists some infinite history x' for which predicate p holds and which is identical to x till time t. This notation is easily extended to n-ary predicates on histories.

Interface Assertions

The interface behavior of systems can be specified in a descriptive logical style using interface assertions.

Definition. Interface Assertion

Given a syntactic interface (I▶O) with a set I of typed input channels and a set O of typed output channels, an *interface assertion* is a formula in predicate logic with channel identifiers from I and O as free logical variables which denote streams of the respective types. $\qquad \square$

We specify the behavior F_S for a system with name S with syntactic interface $(I \blacktriangleright O)$ and an *interface assertion* Q by a scheme:

spec S
in I
out O
Q

Q is an assertion containing the input and the output channels as free variables for channels. We also write q(x, y) with $x \in \overrightarrow{I}$ and $y \in \overrightarrow{O}$ for interface assertions. This is only another way to represent interface assertions which is equivalent to the formula $Q[x(x_1)/x_1, \ldots x(x_n)/x_n), y(y_1)/y_1, \ldots y(y_m)/y_m]$.

Definition. Meaning of Specifications and Interface Assertions

An interface behavior F fulfills the specification S with interface assertion q(x, y) if

$$\forall x \in \overrightarrow{I}, y \in \overrightarrow{O} : y \in F(x) \Rightarrow q(x, y)$$

S and q(x, y) are called *(strongly) realizable* if there exists a "realization" which is a strongly causal function f: $\overrightarrow{I} \to \overrightarrow{O}$ that fulfills S.   ❑

The purpose of a specification and an interface assertion is to specify systems.

Composing Interfaces

Finally, we describe how to compose systems from subsystems described by their interface behavior. Syntactic interfaces $(I_k \blacktriangleright O_k)$ with k = 1, 2 are called *composable*, if their channel types are consistent and $O_1 \cap O_2 = \emptyset, I_1 \cap O_1 = \emptyset, I_2 \cap O_2 = \emptyset$.

Definition. Composition of Systems – Glass Box View

Given for k = 1, 2 composable interface behaviors F_k : $(I_k \blacktriangleright O_k)$ with composable syntactic interfaces; let I = $I_1 \backslash O_2 \cup I_2 \backslash O_1$, O = $O_1 \cup O_2$ and C = $I_1 \cup I_2 \cup O_1 \cup O_2$; we define the composition $(F_1 \times F_2)$: $(I \blacktriangleright O)$ by

$$(F_1 \times F_2)(x) = \{y \in \overrightarrow{O} : \exists z \in \overrightarrow{C} : x = z|I \wedge y = z|O \wedge z|O_1 \in F_1(z|I_1) \wedge z|O_2$$
$$\in F_2(z|I_2)\}$$

where | denotes the usual restriction operator for mappings.   ✣

In the glass box view the internal channels and their valuations are visible. In the black box view the internal channels are hidden. From the glass box view we can derive the black box view of composition.

Definition. Composition of Systems – Black Box View – Hiding internal channels

Given two composable interface behaviors F_k : $(I_k \blacktriangleright O_k)$ with k = 1, 2; let I = $I_1 \backslash O_2$ $\cup$ $I_2 \backslash O_1$ and O = $O_1 \backslash I_2 \cup O_2 \backslash I_1$ and C = $I_1 \cup I_2 \cup O_1 \cup O_2$

$$(F_1 \otimes F_2)(x) = \{y \in \overrightarrow{O} : \exists z \in \overrightarrow{C} : y = z|O \wedge z \in (F_1 \times F_2)(x)\}$$

Shared channels in $(I_1 \cap O_2) \cup (I_2 \cap O_1)$ are hidden by this composition.   ✤

Black box composition is commutative and associative as long as we compose only systems with disjoint sets of input channels.

A specification approach is called *modular* if specifications of composed systems can be constructed from the specification of their components. The property of modularity of composition of two causal interface specifications F_k, $k = 1, 2$, where at least one is strongly causal is as follows. Given system specifications by specifying assertions P_k:

spec F_1
in I_1 **out** O_1
P_1

spec F_2
in I_2 **out** O_2
P_2

We obtain the specification of the composed system $F_1 \otimes F_2$ as a result of the composition of the interface specification F_1 and F_2 as illustrated in Fig. 3: $L_1 \cup L_2$ denotes the set of shared channels.

spec $F_1 \otimes F_2$
in $I_1 \backslash L_2 \cup I_2 \backslash L_1$ **out** $O_1 \backslash L_1 \cup O_2 \backslash L_2$
$\exists L_1, L_2: P_1 \wedge P_2$

The specifying assertion of $F_1 \otimes F_2$ is composed in a modular way from the specifying assertions of its components by logical conjunction and existential quantification over streams denoting internal channels (Fig. 2).

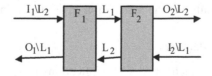

Fig. 2. Composition $F_1 \otimes F_2$

In a composed system, the internal channels are used for internal communication.

The composition of strongly causal behaviors yields strongly causal behaviors. The set of systems together with the introduced composition operators form an algebra. For properties of the resulting algebra, we refer to [1, 4]. Since the black box view hides internal communication over shared channels, the black box view provides an abstraction of the glass box composition.

Note that this form of composition works also for instances. Then, however, often it is helpful to use not channels identified by instance identifiers but to connect the channels of classes and to use the instance identifiers to address instances.

3 Specifying Contracts

Contracts are used in architectures (see [7, 9, 11–16]). In the following we show how to specify contracts.

3.1 Interface Assertions for Assumption/Commitment Contracts

Specifications in terms of assumptions and commitments for a system S with syntactic interface (I▶O) and with input histories $x \in \vec{I}$ and output histories $y \in \vec{O}$ are syntactically expressed by interface assertions asu(x, y) and cmt(x, y). We write A/C-contracts by the following specification pattern:

$$\textbf{assume :} \qquad \text{asu}(x, y)$$
$$\textbf{commit :} \qquad \text{cmt}(x, y)$$

with interface assertions asu(x, y) and cmt(x, y). In the following section we explain why, in general, in the assumption not only the input history occurs but also the output history y. We interpret this specification pattern as follows:

- Contracts as Context Constraints: the assumption asu(x, y) is a specifying assertion for the context with syntactic interface (I▶O)

Understanding the A/C-contract pattern as context constraints leads to the following meaning: if the input x to the system generated by the context on its input y, which is the system output, fulfills the interface assertion given by the assumption asu(x, y) then the system fulfills the promised assertion cmt(x, y). This leads to the specification:

$$\text{asu}(x, y) \Rightarrow \text{cmt}(x, y)$$

Assertion asu(x, y) is a specification indicating which inputs x are permitted to be generated by context E fulfilling the assumption given the output history y.

3.2 Contracts in Architectures

In this section, we discuss methodological applications of the A/C-pattern in system development with emphasis on system architecture design. We study contracts for

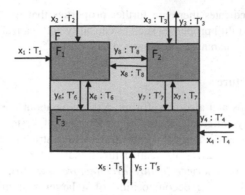

Fig. 3. Architecture of a system with interface behavior $F = F_1 \otimes F_2 \otimes F_3$

subsystems and their role in designing and reasoning about architectures and their relationship to the A/C-contract of the composite system. This provides a basis for a method for supporting steps in architecture design.

Architectures are blue prints to build and structure systems. Architectures contain descriptions of subsystems and specify how to compose the subsystems. In other words, architectures are described by the sets of subsystems where the subsystems are described by their syntactic interfaces and their interface behavior. Shared channels describe internal communication between the subsystems.

In the following we assume that each system used in an architecture as a component has a unique identifier k.

4 On Systems, Their Interfaces and Properties

In the following, we use the term system in a specific way. We address discrete systems, more precisely discrete real-time system models with input and output. For us, a system is an entity that shows some specific behavior by interacting with its operational context. A system has a boundary, which determines what is inside and what is outside the system. Inside the system there is an encapsulated internal structure. The set of actions and events that may occur in the interaction of the system with its operational context at its border determines the syntactic ("static") interface of the system. At its interface, a system shows some *interface behavior*.

From the behavioral point of view, we distinguish between

- the *syntactic interface* of a system that describes which actions may be executed at the interface and which kind of information is exchanged by these actions across the system border,
- the *semantic interface* (also called *interface behavior*) which describes the behavior evolving over the system border in terms of the specific information exchanged in the process of interaction by actions according to the syntactic interface.

For specifying predicates there are further properties that we expect. We require that system behaviors fulfill properties such as causality and realizability. However, not all interface assertions guarantee these properties (see [3, 5]).

4.1 About Architecture

Architecture of systems and also of software systems is about the structuring of systems. There are many different aspects of structuring of systems and therefore of architecture. Examples are functional architectures which structure systems in terms of their offered services (see [2]) – also called functional features. We speak of a *functional architecture* or of a *service feature architecture* (see [6]). Another very basic concept of architecture is the decomposition of a larger system into a number of subsystems that are composed and provide this way the behavior of the overall system. We speak of a *sub-system architecture*.

This shows that architecture is the structuring of a system into smaller elements, a description how these elements are connected and behave in relationship to each other. A key concept of architecture is the notion of element and interface. An interface shows at the border of a system how the system interacts with its operational context.

4.2 On the Essence of Architecture: Architecture Design is Architecture Specification

Architecture is not what is represented and finally implemented in code but a description of architectural structures and rules which are required by the design for implementations leading to code that is correct w.r.t. the specified architecture. The rules, structure, and therefore the principles of architecture usually cannot be reengineered from the code but provide an additional design frame that is documented in the architecture specification. An architecture design is the specification of the system's structures, rules, and principles.

Implemented systems realize architectures, more precisely architecture designs described by specifications. Architectures define the overall structure of systems. Consequently, architectures have to be specified. Designs of sub-system architectures are specifications of the sets of subsystems, relevant properties of their interfaces including their interface behavior, and the way the interfaces are connected. This defines the way the subsystems are composed following the design of an architecture in terms of their interfaces that follow the rules and principles of the architectural design.

4.3 Logical Sub-system Architectures

Logical sub-system architectures including service-oriented architectures are execution platform independent. They consist of the following ingredients

- A set of elements called sub-systems, each equipped with a set of interfaces
- A structure connecting these interfaces

This shows that a key issue in architectural design is the specification of interfaces including their interface behavior and the description of the architectural structure.

5 Interfaces and Their Composition

An interface is structured into a syntactic part, which describes the set of available activities on the system border, separated in activities of the context (which are input to the system) and activities of the system (which are output of the system). The syntactic part is the basis for the behavior part which describes the logic of behavior.

A system has a syntactic interface and an interface behavior. The interface can be formalized as we shown by sets of input and output channels and the relationship of their valuations. The interface of a system can be structured into a set of sub-interfaces that may serve as connectors to other sub-systems.

Two interfaces that fit syntactically together can be connected by a composition of the two systems over their interfaces, if their syntactic interfaces fit together (formally, what is an input channel of one of the interfaces is an output channel of the other system and vice versa).

A system has an interface the behavior of which is specified by an interface assertion L. If we want to use the system in context with a number of other systems we partition the syntactic interface into a number of sub-interfaces. Each sub-interface can be specified by an assertion L' for which we require

$$L \Rightarrow L'$$

In the following, we show how to deal with export, import and assumption/ commitment interfaces.

5.1 Export Interfaces

We consider the following example illustrated by Fig. 4. We specify subsystem K1 as follows: y1, z2: {req}, x1, z1: D

$$L1 \equiv [\#z1 = \min(\#x1, \#z2) \wedge \forall d \in D : d\#z1 \leq d\#x1 \wedge y1 = z2]$$

We specify K2 in analogy as follows: z2, x2: {req}, z1, y2 : D

$$L2 \equiv [\#y2 = \min(\#z1, \#x2) \wedge \forall d \in D : d\#y2 \leq d\#z1 \wedge z2 = x2]$$

Composing the two components results into the following interface assertions

$$\#z1 = \min(\#x1, \#z2) \wedge \forall d \in D : d\#z1 \leq d\#x2$$
$$\wedge \#y2 = \min(\#z1, \#x2) \wedge \forall d \in D : d\#y2 \leq d\#z1 \wedge y1 = z2 \wedge z2 = x2$$

Hiding z1 and z2 by existential quantification we get

$$\#y2 = \min(\#x1, \#x2) \wedge \forall d : d\#y2 \leq d\#x2 \wedge y1 = x2$$

In this special case, the composed system fulfills the same assertion as the two sub-systems.

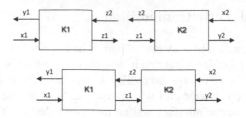

Fig. 4. Example of two sub-systems and their composition

For the hidden channels, we get the assertions

$$z2 = y1 \wedge z2 = x2$$

and

$$\#y2 = \min(\#z1, \#x2) \wedge \forall d : d\#y2 \leq d\#x1 \leq d\#x1 \wedge \#z1 = \min(\#x1, \#z2)$$

This assertion characterizes the properties of the internal channels of this little architecture.

However, we may also specify an assertion for the internal channels:

$$\exists x1, y1, x2, y2 : \#z1 = \min(\#x1, \#z2) \wedge \forall d \in D : d\#z1 \leq d\#x2$$
$$\wedge \#y2 = \min(\#z1, \#x2) \wedge \forall d \in D : d\#y2 \leq d\#z1 \wedge y1 = z2 \wedge z2 = x2$$

which can be simplified to

$$\exists x1, y2 : \#z1 = \min(\#x1, \#z2) \wedge \forall d \in D : d\#z1 \leq d\#z2$$
$$\wedge \#y2 = \min(\#z1, \#z2) \wedge \forall d \in D : d\#y2 \leq d\#z1$$

This condition is an assertion for the internal channels $z1$ and $z2$.

We call interfaces that describe the service offered of a system *export* interfaces. They describe the export a service without any assumptions about properties of their context.

5.2   Import Interfaces

If a component requires a certain interface to be able to fulfill its task this is expressed by an import interface. An import interface is a specification of a requested interface. Given a system with interface assertion G and the input assumption A we compose it with a system with interface B if the composition condition holds

$$B \Rightarrow A$$

A is called *assumption*. We get the interface specification of the composed component

$$(A \Rightarrow G) \wedge B$$

which is equivalent to

$$G \wedge B$$

Example: Consider the component K1 in Fig. 4 with the specification as before and the additional assumption

$$Asu_1 \equiv \forall t : \#z2{\downarrow}t \leq (\#z1{\downarrow}t) + 1$$

For the second component, we add the assertion Asu_1 to the specifying assertion of sub-system K2 leading to interface assertion

$$L2' = (L2 \wedge Asu_1)$$

We get obviously

$$L2' \Rightarrow Asu_1$$

Only if component K2 with specification $L2'$ fulfills the assumption Asu_1 we may compose the components and get the assertion

$$(L1 \wedge L2') \equiv (L1 \wedge L2 \wedge Asu_1)$$

We get assumptions as additional condition for the internal channels. To fulfill these assumptions, we have to add the following assumption to K2 – note $z2 = y1 \wedge z2 = x2$

$$\forall t : \#x2{\downarrow}t \leq (\#z1{\downarrow}t) + 1$$

This demonstrates how assumptions are part of specifications and how they have to be distributed.

5.3   Assumption/Commitment Specifications

We may also work with interfaces that provide assumptions and commitments at the same time. Consider interface specifications with interface assertions L_1 and L_2 where

$$L_1 \Rightarrow (A_1 \Rightarrow C_1) \qquad L_2 \Rightarrow (A_2 \Rightarrow C_2)$$

and interface specifications with an assumption A_1 and a commitment C_1 and with assumption A_2 and commitment C_2 such that

$$(A_1 \Rightarrow C_1) \Rightarrow A_2$$
$$(A_2 \Rightarrow C_2) \Rightarrow A_1$$

In other words, the specifications fulfil mutually the resp. assumptions. Then the interface assertion

$$L_1 \wedge L_2$$

implies assumption A_1 as well as assumption A_2.

Example: We introduce an additional assumption Asu_2 and commitment Com_2 for the second component

$$Asu_2 \equiv \forall t : \#(z_1 {\downarrow} t) \leq \#(z_2 {\downarrow} t)$$
$$Com_2 \equiv \forall t : \#(z_1 {\downarrow} t) \leq \#(z_2 {\downarrow} t) + 1$$

and a commitment for the first component

$$Com_1 \equiv \forall t : \#z_1 {\downarrow} t \leq \#z_2 {\downarrow} t$$

and add Asu_2 to L1 and Asu_1 to L2:

$$L1' \equiv Asu_2 \wedge L1 \qquad\qquad L2' \equiv Asu_1 \wedge L2$$

We get obviously

$$L1' \Rightarrow Asu_2 \qquad\qquad L2' \Rightarrow Asu_1$$

and by composition a component that fulfills the specification

$$L1' \wedge L2'$$

This demonstrates how we compose systems specified by assumptions and commitments.   □

We get a logical calculus of interface assertions for the composition of systems.

5.4   Using Different Types of Interfaces Side by Side

We distinguish the following three types of interfaces:

- *export interfaces*: they describe services offered by the system to its outside world
- *import interfaces*: they describe services required by the system from its outside world
- *assumption/commitment interfaces*: they describe assumptions about the behavior of the outside world and the commitment of the system under the condition that the assumption holds.

We consider the following cases:

- Connecting export and import interfaces: Given an export interface described by interface assertion P and an import interface described by interface assertion Q which fit together syntactically we speak of a sound connection if

$$P \Rightarrow Q$$

- Connecting two export interfaces: Given two export interfaces with interface assertions A_1 and A_2 that fit together syntactically then we speak of a sound connection annotated by (see Fig. 6)

$$A_1 \wedge A_2$$

- Connecting two assumption/commitment interfaces: Given two assumption/ commitment interfaces with assumptions A_1 and A_2 and commitment P_1 and P_2 that fit together syntactically and where if

$$(A_2 \Rightarrow P_2) \Rightarrow A_1$$
$$(A_1 \Rightarrow P_1) \Rightarrow A_2$$

We speak of a sound connection; the connection is annotated by $P_1 \wedge P_2$.

The case of connecting an export interface with an assumption/commitment interface is considered as a special case of connecting two assumption/commitment interfaces where one assumption is true.

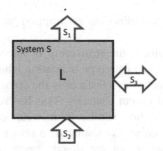

Fig. 5. System S with 3 sub-interfaces of different types

Similarly, the composition of an export interface with an input interface can be understood as a special case where one assumption is true (for the export interface) and one commitment is true (for import interface). This shows that the general case is the assumption of two assumption/commitment interfaces that cover all other cases as special cases.

A system has an interface that can be structured into a family of sub-interfaces each of which is determined by an interface specification. Now we show how these sub-interfaces can be combined into a comprehensive interface. Let us consider a simple example of a system with three sub-interfaces S_1, S_2, and S_3 as described in Fig. 5.

The interface specification of a sub-system defines the contract for the subsystem between its implementer and the architect that uses the subsystem. Each implemented subsystem may fulfill many contracts. The sub-interfaces shown in Fig. 4 describe

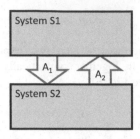

Fig. 6. Connecting subsystem S1 with subsystem S2 via their interfaces

three different types of interfaces. S_1 is the assertion specifying a service, offered by the system (called provided service). S_3 is a service that is structured into an assumption A_3 and a commitment C_3. S_2 is an interface assertion that specifies a service which is assumed to be provided called required service.

The three sub-services are put together into the over-service specified by the following interface specification in terms of interface assertions. This finally leads to a complete overall interface specification for the system S.

$$(S_2 \wedge A_3) \Rightarrow (C_3 \wedge S_1)$$

Here the assertion $S_2 \wedge A_3$ defines an assumption while the assertion defines a commitment $C_3 \wedge S_1$.

Channels allow us, in addition, the structuring of interfaces. Interfaces consist of channels where each channel has a data type indicating which data are communicated.

An important aspect in structuring interfaces is the separation of the set of channels of the interface into input and output channels. This has semantic consequences. We require causality which is a notion similar to monotonicity in a domain theoretic approach. Causality for an interface consisting of a set of input channels and output channels where the input and output are timed streams indicating the asymmetry between input and output. Causality basically says that the output produced till time t does only depend on input received before time t. The reverse does not hold. Input generated at time t can be arbitrary and does not have to depend on the output produced till time t.

6   Composition: Interfaces in Architectures

Given specifications of S1 and S2 by interface assertions A_1 and A_2 we define the interaction assertion

$$A_1 \wedge A_2$$

which specifies the interaction between the subsystems that are connected via their interfaces.

Another specification may give only the interaction assertion Q which describes the result $A_1 \wedge A_2$.

We may introduce a layering between subsystems, if we specify only one interface, by assertion P and do only specify the behavior of the other one by assertion A. For instance, for a layer in a layered architecture the interface looks as shown in Fig. 7.

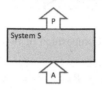

Fig. 7. Interface between two layers

6.1 Interaction Assertions

Given a set of systems with interface assertions we may compose them into an architecture, provided the semantic interfaces fit together. We call the architecture *well-formed*, if all assumptions are implied by the interface assertions the interfaces they are composed with.

For each pair of connected interfaces, we speak of a *connector*, we derive an *interaction assertion* which describes the properties of the data streams that are communicated over this connector. An example of an interaction assertion is given at the end of Sect. 5.1 specifying the properties of the internal channels z1 and z2 of the composition shown in Fig. 4.

6.2 Layered Architectures

Layered architectures have many advantages. In many applications, therefore layered architectures are applied. In a layered architecture as shown in Fig. 8 the key idea is that system S2 offers some service that does not include any assumptions about the way it is used. Therefore, we describe the service by some interface assertion A_2. The interface P of system S1 can be arbitrary. However, the specification of the interface Q of S1 reads as follows

$$Q = [A_1 \Rightarrow P]$$

and P is an interface specification for the reverse interface, then the interface can only be used in a meaningful way if the assumption is fulfilled by system S1. Note that S2 does not rely in any way on the behavior of S1 – it is supposed only to offer export interface A.

Figure 8 shows the composition of layer S2 providing service A_1 with system S1 requiring this service. We get

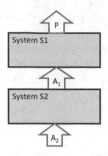

Fig. 8. Composition of two layers

$$(A_1 \Rightarrow P) \wedge (A_2 \Rightarrow A_1)$$

which hiding interface A_1 results in

$$A_2 \Rightarrow P$$

If we replace the component S2 with the interface assertion A_2 by the component S′ with interface assertion $A_2 \Rightarrow B$ where

$$B \Rightarrow A_1$$

then the arguments work as well. S2′ is a refinement of S2 and we get for the composition

$$(A_2 \Rightarrow B) \wedge (B \Rightarrow A_1)$$

which results the hiding interface B again into

$$A_2 \Rightarrow P$$

The sub-systems of a layered architecture are partitioned in layers. The set of layers is in a linear order and sub-systems of layer k are only connected to layer k − 1 or k + 1.

However, this definition is not sufficient. The key idea of a layered architecture is that layer k offers services to layer k + 1 but does not assume anything about layer k + 1. Layer k may use services offered by layer k − 1 but has to know nothing more about layer k − 1. In other terms, a layer imports a number of services (from layer k − 1) and exports a number of services (for layer k + 1). The only relationship between the layers is by the services that are exported to the next layer.

The idea of layered architecture thus is therefore not captured by data flow (by the idea that data may only flow from lower to higher layers or vice versa) nor by control flow (by the idea that calls may only be issued by higher to lower layers) but by the "design flow". Lower layers can be designed without any knowledge of the higher layers – only knowing the services that are requested at the higher layer.

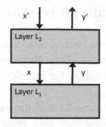

Fig. 9. Composition of the two layers L_1 and L_2

Example: Layered Architecture of a Question Answering System

We describe a simple layered architecture of two layers L_1 and L_2 as shown in Fig. 9. We start by defining two types of messages

Qst   the set of questions
Asw   the set of answers

Let the predicate

$$asw : Qst \times Asw \rightarrow B$$

specify by asw(q, a) that a is an answer for question q. We define for $x \in (Qst^*)^\infty$ and $y \in (Asw^*)^\infty$ the two assertions

$$P = \forall k \in \mathbb{N} : k \leq \#\bar{x} \Rightarrow asw(\bar{x}(k), \bar{y}(k))$$
$$A = \forall t \in \mathbb{N} : \#x{\downarrow}t \leq 1 + \#y{\downarrow}t$$

P expresses that all questions are answered and A expresses that no further question is asked before all previous questions are answered. We specify the layer L_1 with input channel x and output channel y by

$$A \Rightarrow P$$

We can add a layer L_2 with input channel x' and y and output channel x and y' which controls x and satisfies this way the assumption. Let x' be an infinite sequence of questions. A solution for the layer is given by the specification p(x, y, x', y') which holds if

$$y' = y$$

and (for all t)

$$x(t) = \begin{cases} \varepsilon & \text{otherwise} \\ x'(k) & \text{if } \#(y{\downarrow}(t-1)) = k \wedge \#(x'{\downarrow}(t-1)) = k \end{cases}$$

The layer makes sure that the system gets only one question at a time. ❑
The example shows a classical assumption/commitment specification.

7   Concluding Remarks and Future Work

The purpose of this paper is to show that architecture can be specified by assertions similar to assertion logic in programs. This includes also on assertion calculus for architecture. The key here is a denotation for interaction in our case in terms of timed streams.

An interesting question is the logical flow of the assertions through an architecture. An example are assumptions and how they propagate through the architecture.

Acknowledgement. It is a pleasure to thank my colleagues for stimulating discussions.

References

1. Broy, M., Stølen, K.: Specification and Development of Interactive Systems: Focus on Streams, Interfaces, and Refinement. Monographs in Computer Science. Springer, New York (2001). https://doi.org/10.1007/978-1-4613-0091-5
2. Broy, M., Krüger, I., Meisinger, M.: A formal model of services. TOSEM - ACM Trans. Softw. Eng. Methodol. **16**, 5 (2007)
3. Broy, M.: Interaction and realizability. In: van Leeuwen, J., Italiano, G.F., van der Hoek, W., Meinel, C., Sack, H., Plášil, F. (eds.) SOFSEM 2007. LNCS, vol. 4362, pp. 29–50. Springer, Heidelberg (2007). https://doi.org/10.1007/978-3-540-69507-3_3
4. Broy, M.: A logical basis for component-oriented software and systems engineering. Comput. J. **53**(10), 1758–1782 (2010)
5. Broy, M.: Computability and realizability for interactive computations. Inf. Comput. **241**, 277–301 (2015)
6. Broy, M.: Multifunctional software systems: structured modeling and specification of functional requirements. Sci. Comput. Program. **75**, 1193–1214 (2010)
7. Broy, M.: Theory and Methodology of assumption/commitment based system interface specification and architectural contracts, to appear
8. Clements, P., Bachmann, F., Bass, L., Garlan, D., Ivers, J., Little, R., Merson, P., Nord, R., Stafford, J.: Documenting Software Architectures: Views and Beyond, 2nd edn. Addison-Wesley, Boston (2010)
9. Derler, P., Lee, E.A., Tripakis, S., Törngren, M.: Cyber-physical system design contracts. In: Proceedings of the ACM/IEEE 4th International Conference on Cyber-Physical Systems (ICCPS 2013), pp. 109–118. ACM, New York, (2013)
10. Henzinger, Th.A., Qadeer, S., Rajamani, S.K.: Decomposing refinement proofs using assume-guarantee reasoning. In: Proceedings of the International Conference on Computer-Aided Design (ICCAD), pp. 245–252. IEEE Computer Society Press (2000)
11. Meyer, B.: Applying "Design by Contract". Computer **25**(10), 40–51 (1992). IEEE
12. Sangiovanni-Vincentelli, A., Damm, W., Passerone, R.: Taming Dr. Frankenstein contract-based design for cyber-physical systems. Europ. J. Control **18**(3), 217–238 (2012)
13. Soderberg, A., Vedder, B.: Composable safety-critical systems based on pre-certified software components. In: 2012 IEEE 23rd International Symposium on Software Reliability Engineering Workshops (ISSREW), pp. 343–348, November 2012

14. Toerngren, M., Tripakis, S., Derler, P., Lee, E.A.: Design contracts for cyber-physical systems: making timing assumptions explicit. Technical report UCB/EECS-2012–191, EECS Department. University of California, Berkeley, August 2012
15. Tripakis, S., Lickly, B., Henzinger, Th.A., Lee, E.A.: A theory of synchronous relational interfaces. ACM Trans. Program. Lang. Syst. **33**(4), 14:1–14:41 (2011)
16. Westmann, J.: Specifying safety-critical heterogeneous systems using contracts theory. KTH, Industrial Engineering and Management. Doctoral thesis Stockholm, Sweden (2016)

The State of the Art in Dynamic Graph Algorithms

Monika Henzinger[(✉)]

Fakultät für Informatik, University of Vienna, Vienna, Austria
monika.henzinger@univie.ac.at

A dynamic graph algorithm is a data structure that supports operations on dynamically changing graphs. Typically there are two type of operations:

Graph update operations, which insert and delete edges or nodes;
Query operations, that either output a desired graph property (such as a minimum cost spanning tree) or the *value* of the desired graph property (such as the cost of the minimum cost spanning tree).

In the following we assume that n is the number of nodes in the graph and m is the number of edges. Frequently one assumes that the set of nodes in the graph remains unchanged (or that only degree-0 nodes are inserted or deleted) and that only the set of edges that changes and all the work cited below refers to this setting.

There has been a lot of progress in dynamic graph algorithms in the last decade. One fundamental contribution was the development of (conditional) lower bounds (initiated by [2] and extended by [1,17,24,32]) for a large set of dynamic problems and variants thereof. These lower bounds are based on popular conjectures such as the subexponential time hypothesis and assume that only polynomial (and sometimes even only $O(n^2)$) preprocessing time is allowed. They are interesting as they are frequently linear in $n^{1-\epsilon}$ or $m^{1-\epsilon}$ for an arbitrarily small $\epsilon > 0$, while prior lower bounds for dynamic graph algorithms in the cell probe model were only *polylogarithmic* in n [28,33,35].

There is a small set of problems (among them the connected, 2-edge connected, and 2-vertex connected components [27,29] and the minimum spanning tree [29]) that can by maintained in polylogarithmic time per operation[1]. The recent conditional lower bounds give an explanation why not more progress has been made for many dynamic graph problems: Given a sublinear-time algorithm for one of them would contradict popular conjectures. For example, even (i) maintaining whether a graph is strongly connected, (ii) maintaining the length of the shortest path between two fixed nodes s and t in an undirected, unweighted graph, or (iii) maintaining a perfect matching in an unweighted graph cannot be done in time polylogarithmic time for both query and update (assuming the popular conjectures hold): There exists a graph with $m = \Theta(n^2)$ edges such

---

[1] There are still some openresearch question regarding the *amortized* versus the *worst-case* time per operation, but we will not discuss them here.

© Springer International Publishing AG 2018
A M. Tjoa et al. (Eds.): SOFSEM 2018, LNCS 10706, pp. 40–44, 2018.
https://doi.org/10.1007/978-3-319-73117-9_3

that it is not possible to perfom updates in time $O(m^{1/2-\epsilon})$ *and* queries in time $O(m^{1-\epsilon})$ if only polynomial preprocessing time is allowed[2].

As a result research in dynamic graph algorithms is now mainly concentrating on (a) approximate solutions, (b) special classes of graphs, and (c) restricted types of update operations such as deletions-only or insertions-only settings. In these cases very efficient solutions are possible, as shown by the following examples.

(1) *Approximate matching algorithms.* As mentioned above the exact maximum cardinality matching cannot be maintained efficiently under edge insertions and deletions (see [38] for the best known non-trivial upper bound). However, a $(1+\epsilon)$-approximate matching can be maintained in time $O(\sqrt{m}\epsilon^{-2})$ per operation [22,37], already beating the conditional lower bound for the exact setting. Furthermore, there has been a sequence of work on maintaining a (usually small) constant approximate matching [5,7,9,10,12–14,34] which finally resulted in a constant expected time randomized algorithm for a 2-approximate matching [39] and a constant deterministic time algorithm for a $O(1)$-approximate maximum matching [11].

(2) *Restricted graph classes.* There is a sequence of work on dynamic graph algorithms for planar graphs that achieve sublinear-time update times [19,21, 30,31,40] such as for shortest-paths and single-source reachability. However, there exist also conditional lower bounds for dynamic graph algorithms in planar graphs [1], for example for the maximum weight bipartite matching in planar weighted graphs. More recently, further improvements have been achieved on even more restricted graph classes such as graphs with low highway dimension [3].

(3) *Restricted types of update sequences.* Insertions-only (aka *incremental*) settings and deletions-only (aka *decremental*) setttings can sometimes be solved more efficiently. For example, maintaining single-source reachability from a source node s (in a directed graph) under a sequence of edge insertions can be done with an "incremental" breadth-first (or depth-first) search: Mark every node that can be reached from s. Ignore every newly inserted edge into a marked node and store every newly inserted edge between two unmarked nodes. Whenever, however, a newly inserted edge goes from a marked node to an unmarked node u, then mark u and start a breadth-first search from u in the current graph that only calls itself recursively on unmarked nodes. In this way the total work for all insertions is $O(m)$, i.e., the amortized time per insertion is only constant. Another example is maintenance of single-source shortest paths to all nodes in an undirected, unweighted graph under a sequence of edge deletions. It is possible to maintain a $(1+\epsilon)$-approximation in amortized time $O(m^{O(\sqrt{\log\log n/\log n})}) = O(m^{o(1)})$ per deletion [23]. However, there are also conditional lower bounds known for the incremental and decremental setting [17], for example for maintaining the s-t maximum flow and for maximum cardinaltiy bipartite matching.

---

[2] Note, however, that this does not exclude an algorithm that takes time $O(m^{1/2})$ for both updates and queries.

We briefly sketched in this abstract the main trends in the standard dynamic graph algorithms model. However, we want to point out that there are also other dynamic graph models such as the *kinetic algorithms model* [4,6], the *subgraph model* [15,20,26], and the sensitivity model [8,16,18,25,36].

References

1. Abboud, A., Dahlgaard, S.: Popular conjectures as a barrier for dynamic planar graph algorithms. In: FOCS (2016)
2. Abboud, A., Williams, V.V.: Popular conjectures imply strong lower bounds for dynamic problems. In: FOCS (2014)
3. Abraham, I., Fiat, A., Goldberg, A.V., Werneck, R.F.: Highway dimension, shortest paths, and provably efficient algorithms. In: Proceedings of the Twenty-First Annual ACM-SIAM Symposium on Discrete Algorithms, pp. 782–793. Society for Industrial and Applied Mathematics (2010)
4. Agarwal, P.K., Eppstein, D., Guibas, L.J., Henzinger, M.R.: Parametric and kinetic minimum spanning trees. In: Proceedings of the 39th Annual Symposium on Foundations of Computer Science, 1998, pp. 596–605. IEEE (1998)
5. Anand, A., Baswana, S., Gupta, M., Sen, S.: Maintaining approximate maximum weighted matching in fully dynamic graphs. In: D'Souza, D., Kavitha, T., Radhakrishnan, J. (eds.) FSTTCS. LIPIcs, vol. 18, pp. 257–266. Schloss Dagstuhl - Leibniz-Zentrum fuer Informatik (2012)
6. Basch, J., Guibas, L.J., Hershberger, J.: Data structures for mobile data. J. Algorithms **31**(1), 1–28 (1999)
7. Baswana, S., Gupta, M., Sen, S.: Fully dynamic maximal matching in $\mathcal{O}(\log n)$ update time. In: FOCS (2011). http://dx.doi.org/10.1137/130914140
8. Bernstein, A., Karger, D.: A nearly optimal oracle for avoiding failed vertices and edges. In: Proceedings of the Forty-First Annual ACM Symposium on Theory of Computing, pp. 101–110. ACM (2009)
9. Bernstein, A., Stein, C.: Fully dynamic matching in bipartite graphs. In: Halldórsson, M.M., Iwama, K., Kobayashi, N., Speckmann, B. (eds.) ICALP 2015. LNCS, vol. 9134, pp. 167–179. Springer, Heidelberg (2015). https://doi.org/10.1007/978-3-662-47672-7_14
10. Bernstein, A., Stein, C.: Faster fully dynamic matchings with small approximation ratios. In: Proceedings of the Twenty-Seventh Annual ACM-SIAM Symposium on Discrete Algorithms, pp. 692–711. Society for Industrial and Applied Mathematics (2016)
11. Bhattacharya, S., Chakrabarty, D., Henzinger, M.: Deterministic fully dynamic approximate vertex cover and fractional matching in $O(1)$ amortized update time. In: Eisenbrand, F., Koenemann, J. (eds.) IPCO 2017. LNCS, vol. 10328, pp. 86–98. Springer, Cham (2017). https://doi.org/10.1007/978-3-319-59250-3_8
12. Bhattacharya, S., Henzinger, M., Italiano, G.F.: Deterministic fully dynamic data structures for vertex cover and matching. In: SODA (2015)
13. Bhattacharya, S., Henzinger, M., Nanongkai, D.: New deterministic approximation algorithms for fully dynamic matching. In: STOC 2016
14. Bhattacharya, S., Henzinger, M., Nanongkai, D.: Fully dynamic approximate maximum matching and minimum vertex cover in o(log3 n) worst case update time. In: Proceedings of the Twenty-Eighth Annual ACM-SIAM Symposium on Discrete Algorithms. pp. 470–489. SIAM (2017)

15. Chan, T.M.: Dynamic subgraph connectivity with geometric applications. SIAM J. Comput. **36**(3), 681–694 (2006)
16. Chechik, S., Langberg, M., Peleg, D., Roditty, L.: F-sensitivity distance oracles and routing schemes. Algorithmica **63**(4), 861–882 (2012)
17. Dahlgaard, S.: On the hardness of partially dynamic graph problems and connections to diameter. In: ICALP, pp. 48:1–48:14 (2016)
18. Duan, R., Pettie, S.: Connectivity oracles for failure prone graphs. In: Proceedings of the Forty-Second ACM Symposium on Theory of Computing, pp. 465–474. ACM (2010)
19. Eppstein, D., Galil, Z., Italiano, G.F., Spencer, T.H.: Separator based sparsification for dynamic planar graph algorithms. In: Proceedings of the Twenty-Fifth Annual ACM Symposium on Theory of Computing, pp. 208–217. ACM (1993)
20. Frigioni, D., Italiano, G.F.: Dynamically switching vertices in planar graphs. Algorithmica **28**(1), 76–103 (2000)
21. Frigioni, D., Marchetti-Spaccamela, A., Nanni, U.: Fully dynamic algorithms for maintaining shortest paths trees. J. Algorithms **34**(2), 251–281 (2000)
22. Gupta, M., Peng, R.: Fully dynamic $(1 + \epsilon)$-approximate matchings. In: FOCS (2013)
23. Henzinger, M., Krinninger, S., Nanongkai, D.: Decremental single-source shortest paths on undirected graphs in near-linear total update time. In: 2014 IEEE 55th Annual Symposium on Foundations of Computer Science (FOCS), pp. 146–155. IEEE (2014)
24. Henzinger, M., Krinninger, S., Nanongkai, D., Saranurak, T.: Unifying and strengthening hardness for dynamic problems via the online matrix-vector multiplication conjecture. In: STOC (2015)
25. Henzinger, M., Lincoln, A., Neumann, S., Williams, V.V.: Conditional hardness for sensitivity problems. In: ITCS (2017)
26. Henzinger, M., Neumann, S.: Incremental and fully dynamic subgraph connectivity for emergency planning. In: ESA (2016)
27. Henzinger, M.R., King, V.: Randomized fully dynamic graph algorithms with poly-logarithmic time per operation. J. ACM (JACM) **46**(4), 502–516 (1999)
28. Henzinger, M.R., Fredman, M.L.: Lower bounds for fully dynamic connectivity problems in graphs. Algorithmica **22**(3), 351–362 (1998)
29. Holm, J., De Lichtenberg, K., Thorup, M.: Poly-logarithmic deterministic fully-dynamic algorithms for connectivity, minimum spanning tree, 2-edge, and biconnectivity. J. ACM (JACM) **48**(4), 723–760 (2001)
30. Italiano, G.F., La Poutré, J.A., Rauch, M.H.: Fully dynamic planarity testing in planar embedded graphs. In: Lengauer, T. (ed.) ESA 1993. LNCS, vol. 726, pp. 212–223. Springer, Heidelberg (1993). https://doi.org/10.1007/3-540-57273-2_57
31. Klein, P.N., Subramanian, S.: A fully dynamic approximation scheme for shortest paths in planar graphs. Algorithmica **22**(3), 235–249 (1998)
32. Kopelowitz, T., Pettie, S., Porat, E.: Higher lower bounds from the 3 sum conjecture. In: SODA, pp. 1272–1287 (2016)
33. Larsen, K.G., Weinstein, O., Yu, H.: Crossing the logarithmic barrier for dynamic boolean data structure lower bounds. arXiv preprint arXiv:1703.03575 (2017)
34. Neiman, O., Solomon, S.: Simple deterministic algorithms for fully dynamic maximal matching. In: STOC (2013)
35. Patrascu, M., Demaine, E.D.: Logarithmic lower bounds in the cell-probe model. SIAM J. Comput. **35**(4), 932–963 (2006)

36. Patrascu, M., Thorup, M.: Planning for fast connectivity updates. In: 48th Annual IEEE Symposium on Foundations of Computer Science, 2007, FOCS 2007, pp. 263–271. IEEE (2007)
37. Peleg, D., Solomon, S.: Dynamic $(1+\epsilon)$-approximate matchings: a density-sensitive approach. In: SODA (2016)
38. Sankowski, P.: Faster dynamic matchings and vertex connectivity. In: SODA (2007)
39. Solomon, S.: Fully dynamic maximal matching in constant update time. In: 2016 IEEE 57th Annual Symposium on Foundations of Computer Science (FOCS), pp. 325–334. IEEE (2016)
40. Subramanian, S.: A fully dynamic data structure for reachability in planar digraphs. In: Lengauer, T. (ed.) ESA 1993. LNCS, vol. 726, pp. 372–383. Springer, Heidelberg (1993). https://doi.org/10.1007/3-540-57273-2_72

Software Engineering: Advanced Methods, Applications, and Tools

Diversity in UML Modeling Explained: Observations, Classifications and Theorizations

Michel R. V. Chaudron[1]([✉]), Ana Fernandes-Saez[2], Regina Hebig[1],
Truong Ho-Quang[1], and Rodi Jolak[1]

[1] Chalmers | Gothenburg University, Gothenburg, Sweden
michel.chaudron@cs.gu.se, {regina.hebig,rodi.jolak}@cse.gu.se,
truongh@chalmers.se
[2] University Castilla La-Mancha, Ciudad Real, Spain
AnaMaria.Fernandez@uclm.es

Abstract. Modeling is a common part of modern day software engineering practice. Little evidence exists about how models are used in software development and how they help in producing better software. In this talk we introduce a classification-matrix and a theoretical framework that helps explain the large variety of models and modeling styles found in industrial practice. As part of this explanation, we will explore empirical findings on the uses of UML modeling in practice. We intersperse this paper with some insights about modeling in software development that may be common to some, but certainly not generally accepted throughout the software engineering community.

1 Introduction

There exists a large variety of modeling languages in the field of software engineering. These range from languages for modeling user interfaces, business processes, data-exchange formats, and software designs. In this paper we focus on the use of UML in the modeling of the design of software systems. The UML language has emerged in the mid-1990's after a phase in which many software design notations existed. Often each of these design notations was proposed in conjunction with a software design method. The naissance of UML was no different: it came together with an object-oriented design method. However, nowadays, UML is considered mostly a notation. Ever since its introduction, the use of UML in software development has been subject to (almost religious) debate. In this paper we aim to contribute to clarifying the field of modeling by explaining different type of approaches to modeling.

The structure of this paper is as follows: First, we describe models as they can be found in current software development. In order to understand the differences found across such models, we present two classifications based on different distinguishing characteristics. Next, we discuss different purposes of models in software development, and explain that the different ways of modeling can be understood by recognizing different goals and contexts of different projects. Then, we reflect

© Springer International Publishing AG 2018
A M. Tjoa et al. (Eds.): SOFSEM 2018, LNCS 10706, pp. 47–66, 2018.
https://doi.org/10.1007/978-3-319-73117-9_4

on some insights and findings from empirical studies into modeling. Finally we discuss selected future directions.

We intersperse this paper with some propositions that highlight insights about modeling in software development that may be familiar to some, but are certainly not commonly accepted throughout the software engineering community.

2   Classifications of Software Models and Their Uses

Nowadays, we have come to realize that software modeling (using UML) is done in a large variety of ways. Indeed various terms are used to suggest different ways of using models in software development: model-driven sw development, model-based sw development, model-based engineering, model-centric development. Unfortunately, there is no common agreement on the meaning or characteristics of these terms. This has o.a. led to the running (and publishing) of survey studies that lump together every respondent that says that they do 'model-* development'. Yet, in order to properly perform and interpret scientific studies on modeling in software development, we need a way to precisely define the object of study. Based on the empirical studies from the last decades, we next propose multiple classifications for characterizing UML modeling and their uses in software development.

2.1   A Classification of Models by Abstraction Level

In this section we illustrate how modeling can be classified by looking at the abstraction level of the system that they aim to capture. We recognize the following levels of abstraction:

- A-type: Architecture modeling
- D-type: Design modeling
- I-type: Implementation modeling.

We give a brief characterization of each of these approaches:

Architecture modeling targets a high level of abstraction of the system. Following [1], architecture targets the overall structure and behaviour of a system as defined by the components, their relations and their interactions. Also, as part of the architecting activity, a model is used to assess whether the design meets the extra-functional[1] requirements of the system. An architecture is typically defined in terms of the main system components and layers. Rarely do architecture designs include actual mention of classes, methods or attributes. At the abstraction level that they target, architectures aim to be complete in the sense that all important components are included in the model. For completeness sake, one could distinguish two different levels of architecture: (i) software/ system-architecture, and (ii) enterprise architecture - which can be seen as

---

[1] Also known as non-functional.

systems-of-systems abstraction. UML can be used for the enterprise architecture level, but we will not make this distinction in this paper.

In Design modeling, there is a medium abstraction of the implementation of the system. The design level model of a system is typically represented in terms of classes (or components or packages) and the relations between them. For some classes, details such as methods and attributes are defined. Models at the design-level of abstraction typically focus on important parts of the system. Importance is relative to the producers and consumers of the model, but generally is driven by importance and risk (see [18]).

For implementation modeling, there is a close correspondence between the system model and the implementation: In principle, every class in the model can be mapped onto one of more classes (or other artifacts) in the implementation. Hence, because the model mirrors the implementation, the model must be complete.

Some projects use modeling at all three levels of abstraction. Modeling at more than one level of abstraction introduces the challenge of keeping the models at different levels consistent with each other.

An insightful diagram (Fig. 1 about the spectrum of approaches to the use of modeling in software development was presented by Brown [2]. His spectrum is organized around different types of key uses of models in a project. The top row in the original paper only stated 'Model' in all boxes. The use of the same term 'Model' across all boxes is actually a bit misleading. Based on our studies of the use of models, we have come to understand that the models for the types of use suggested in the diagram are quite different. Hence, we have added letters 'A' (Architecture), 'D' (Design), and 'I' (Implementation) to indicate that the models in the types of use suggest are typically of various levels of abstraction.

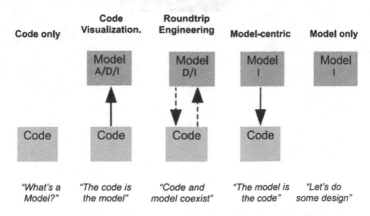

Fig. 1. Spectrum of modeling approaches by Brown [2] - Annotated

2.2   A Classification of Models by Stage of Development

In this section, we explain a complementary classification of models in software development from the perspective of the stage of development for which they are used. The scientific field of Design recognizes several stages of a design in the process of developing a product [4]. In the context of software development, we state these stages and their use of models as follows. We illustrate these stages in Fig. 2[2]:

- Ideation/Conceptualization: The main objective of this step is to create a concept of the system to be created. This is one of the most creative and synthetic steps in the design: it requires the exploration, formation and combination of ideas.
- Externalization: The main objective of this step is to construct an external/ explicit (as opposed to internal (to the mind of the designer)/tacit) representation of the system to be built. This representation serves as a vehicle for achieving shared understanding in a team/organization, and as persistent reference for a complicated abstraction that cannot be maintained in the memory of the engineers.
- Production/Implementation: In this stage, the system is actually being constructed. The model of the system is used to produce specifications of the parts that need to be constructed, as well as recipes on how to assemble the parts. In software engineering, models can indeed be used to generate (parts of) the implementation.

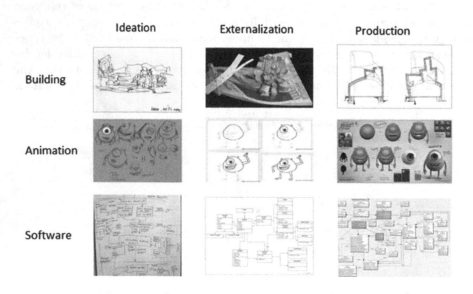

Fig. 2. Models in different stages of development

Ideation or conceptualization in software development is commonly done by sketching on a whiteboard or on a piece of paper. At this stage, the syntax of

---

[2] Images of Bilbao Guggenheim Museum (c) by Gehry, and Mike from Monsters Inc. (c) by Pixar.

the actual representation is not considered critical. Presumably, this is because the people involved in the ideation share the same room, hence can clarify issues by talking to each other. Ideation sessions tend to range on a timescale of tens of minutes to a few hours. This ideation effort is independent of the size of the system.

Externalization can be done in different ways. The quick and dirty way is to take a picture of the drawing on the whiteboard using a smartphone and then store the image in the project repository. The next step up in rigour is to create a design using a generic drawing tool, such as Powerpoint, or Visio. The advantage of generic Office tools is that the resulting diagrams can be easily integrated into overall 'Software Architecture Design' (SAD) documents that typically are a mix of text and diagrams. The most rigorous representations are made using a UML-CASE tool. Such representation supports basic forms of version management, but are considered a bit more complicated to integrate with word-processors for creating SAD documents. Using a CASE tool to create a UML model for a modest system can take a few hours, while creating a detailed UML model for a complex system can be a matter of days.

For using models in the production of software, the models need to be complete in the sense that they cover all of the implementation functionality and also in strict conformance to the syntax of the modeling language so that a compiler/code generator can produce implementation code. Creating such models requires dedicated CASE tools and (as they represent the main implementation activity) can take a large part of the effort of the overall project (say 30–40%).

A key difference between on the one hand the ideation and externalization stage and on the other hand the production stage, is that in the ideation and externalization stage, the main consumer/audience of the models are people, whereas for the production stage computers are an essential consumer of the models - see Fig. 3. Aiming for a computer as consumer requires that models are specified following a rigorous syntax and semantics. The fact that humans are the audience of models can be used to tailor the approach to modeling

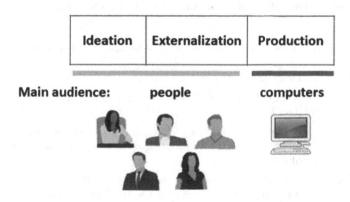

Fig. 3. Main audience of models in different stages of design

to the audience's needs: One best practice observed in industry is to test a 'design model/document': before committing a document as 'stable', the document should be reviewed/tested by the consuming party/parties.

Proposition 1. *When created wisely, design models (and by generalization: documentation) are consulted much more often than that they are created/modified. For the 'consumption' of models to work well, producers and consumers of models should agree (from early on in a project) on representation (detail, conventions for naming and layout), organization (layering), and conventions for navigation in- and searching for models.*

2.3   Syntactic Characterization of Software Design Models

The previous sections have introduced two key dimensions for classifying models. In this section, we will introduce some characteristics by which models differ from each other. We see these characteristics as mostly syntactical, and also more as a resultant of the dimensions 'abstraction' and 'development stage' than as additional angles by which to classify models. Table 1 shows an overview of these characteristics. Detail of a models can be seen by the amount of aspects of elements that are represented in the model. For example a class can be represented only by a rectangle with a class name (which would be low detail). Alternatively, a class can additionally be represented by attributes and methods. The latter can have public/private attributes, signature with typing. Using all these aspects represents a class in a high level of detail. Nugroho et al. introduced a metric for level of detail for UML models in [19]. Using this metric, this paper shows that a higher level of detail in sequence diagrams correlates with a lower defect density in the implementation of the corresponding classes.

Rigour refers to the degree to which a representation conforms to a formal syntax. A low conformance to formal syntax is common in the ideation stage. However, also in industrial SAD documents we frequently find that the design diagrams are enhanced by 'free format' shapes and icons which are not part of the UML syntax. We call a low adherence to a formal syntax 'sketchy'.

Table 1. Syntactic dimensions of software design models

Dimension	Description of range
Detail	A model can be represented in low detail or very high detail
Rigour	A model can precisely follow the syntax of the language or largely ignore the syntax (e.g. sketchy) (even mixed levels of rigour are common)
Completeness	A model can focus on representing key parts only or can be a complete mirror-image of the implementation
Consistency	A model can be consistent or contain many inconsistencies

Completeness refers to the degree to which all parts of the system are represented by the model. From the work of Osman [20] we know that UML models (made as part of forward design) contain only between 50% and 10% of the classes of the corresponding implementation (See Fig. 4. Moreover, we know from [17] that designers focus on parts of the system that is complex and critical, hence follow a risk-driven approach to choosing which information to include and leave out of a design.

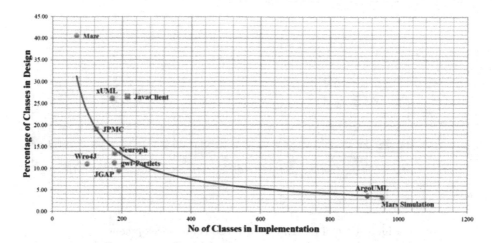

Fig. 4. Ratio of #Classes in UML design vs #Classes in implementation (from [20])

Consistency refers to the degree of intrinsic consistency in the model. The issue of consistency arises mostly from the fact that UML supports multiple types of diagrams that are logically linked to each other through reference to the same classes (and states). The problem of inconsistency has been identified in the early 2000's. A recent mapping study aimed to establish a definitive collection of consistency rules [22]. As part of an overall research program that aimed at assessing quality of UML models, Lange et al. [13] describe an empirical study in which they show that the amount of inconsistencies that exists in UML models of a few industrial case studies is very high. Partially this is due to the fact that incompleteness of a model can often also be interpreted as an inconsistency, and we know from our aforementioned empirical study on completeness of UML models [17] that designers leave out many parts of the implementation. In a follow-up experiment [14] we found that inconsistencies in UML models increase the divergence of interpretations of the models and thus increase the risk of various mistakes.

2.4   A Classification of the Uses of Software Design Models

At first the huge diversity of types of models found across industry puzzled us. Was there not one right way or best way to do modeling in software projects? In the previous section we have already explained that there are different project settings that drive modeling practices. In addition to those, we explain in this section that design models are used in support of many different activities. Figure 5 shows an overview of different activities that have been reported in various industrial case studies to use UML models (see e.g. [6] as a starting point).

| | Generic | | Management | | | | | | | Analysis & Design | | | Implementation | | V & V | | ... |
	Overview	Understanding	Planning	Progress Monitoring	Cost Estimation	Risk Management	Compliance / Certification	Coordination - Standardization	Communication - Knowledge Sharing	Ideation	Analysis - Domain	Analysis - XFP	Prototyping	Code-generation	Traceability	Testing	
Architecture Modeling	X	X	X	X	X	X	X	X	X	X	X	X			R->D		
Design Modeling	X	X	X	X		X	X	X	X	X	X				R/A->I		
Implementation Modeling				X			X		X				X	X	D->I	X	

Fig. 5. Uses of design models in software development

We have classified the uses into several global categories: Generic: 'create overview' and 'understanding': these apply to all types of models. There is a surprisingly large number of project management type of activities that are supported by design models:

– *Planning:* a design model allows to split the work in parts and delegate these to different teams/developers.
– *Progress monitoring:* a design model can be uses to track progress by providing an overview of the progress of individual components, or - at a higher abstraction level - by showing which components have been completed.
– *Cost estimation:* similarly to planning, the fact that a design model provides a breakdown of the system into components, allows the estimation of costs for parts which can then be used to estimate cost (and schedule) for the entire system.
– *Risk management:* a design model makes explicit, and helps discover, which components are needed in a system, this in turn triggers discussion about possible risks that may arise in the construction and composition of components into the overall system.
– *Compliance:* One typical use of design models is to use them to verify that the implementation indeed conforms to the design. When no design model exist, there is a higher risk of 'drift' in the implementation. Additionally, models can be used to verify that particular policies are integrated in the system

(such policies exist in the banking-domain); alternatively, some domains (e.g. medical, automotive) ask that certain models are constructed and used for analysis of critical properties of the system.

- *Coordination/standardization:* For teams that work across multiple locations, it is important that a common standard on how to handle the design and implementation is available. Design models play such a role.
- *Knowledge sharing:* modeling a system is a way of capturing knowledge about a system. Through its representation this knowledge can be shared in a development team.
- *Ideation:* Ideation is the formation, exploration and combinations of ideas. In the case of software, these apply to the design (and analysis) of a system. Having an explicit model serves as an aid in inventing ideas and exploring new directions.
- *Analysis (XFP):* a design model can be used for various types of analysis of the system: ranging from more qualitative 'what if' scenarios (e.g. about maintainability) to quantitative analysis of extra-functional properties such as performance, reliability, safety and others.
- *Prototyping:* design models may be (partially) executable and can hence by used to demonstrate and try out how the system will work.
- *Code-generation:* models of the system are essential for code-generation. The main objective of this, is to increase the overall development speed of the project.
- *Traceability:* design models provide an intermediate abstraction esp. between requirements and the implementation. As such design models can act as a pivot point and aid in establishing traceability between requirements and the implementation.
- *Testing:* models can be the basis for specifying and prioritizing tests.

Figure 5 shows that that are many uses of design models and that these uses serve different stakeholders in software engineering projects. Indeed, some of these uses are secondary or by-catch of other more important uses of design models. So, the use of design models should not be seen as exclusive to one purpose. Moreover, the main purposes of a model change during the execution of a project. We will elaborate this theme in Sect. 4. We summarize the findings on the multiple uses of models through the following propositions:

Proposition 2. *Models of software designs serve a multitude of purposes in software development projects.*

Proposition 3. *In software development projects, the purposes of models of software designs change focus over time.*

Proposition 4. *The value of models in achieving the goals changes over time.*

Proposition 4 applies to various goals, but we will explain it using one example that is illustrated by Fig. 6. Figure 6 depicts the utility of documentation (as a generalization of models) as a function of the experience of developers. For developers that are new to a system, the documentation is of much value/utility because it helps them understand the system which they need in order to do their work effectively. However, as developers work for longer time on the same system, they build up in their working memory an understanding of the system. Hence, the value of the documentation becomes less to them (while the documentation itself has not changed - only the context has changed!).

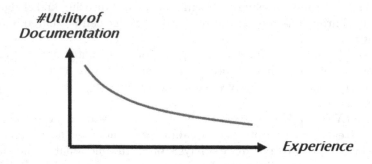

Fig. 6. Utility of documentation over time

Thus the purpose of models is a moving target. Clearly, this complicates finding empirical evidence for effectiveness of modeling because this has to be assessed relative to the purpose.

Interestingly, when going over the list of uses of models, there are only few uses for which models are indispensable. For most other uses, alternative approaches can be used. Clearly this is unlike the inevitability of producing implementation-code of systems. Indeed, in general models are a means to an end - the end being: the efficient development of (quality) software. This 'weakens' the commitment to modeling. And if alternatives work better than modeling, then projects are indeed better served with such alternatives. Possibly a good metaphor for the use of models is that they function as lubricant: they make many task run more smoothly.

Proposition 5. *There are many uses of models that do not directly follow from the main goals for using modeling.*

Various surveys have explored the main goals of using modeling approaches in software development projects. The commonly mentioned goals are: reduce development time/increase productivity/agility/velocity, improve quality (of code and of design), improve efficiency/reduce cost. When looking at the uses of models in Fig. 5, then there is not a very direct contribution of the uses of models to the aforementioned goals. Again through its diversity of uses, modeling has contributions to many goals in many ways. Empirical evidence regarding the 'effect-size' of modeling is still elusive. We point to two attempt at collecting evidence on the effectiveness of modeling: In [3] Chaudron et al. propose a theory that offers a causal explanation of the impact of UML modeling on quality and productivity. Some steps in this chain are supported by evidence from research papers, for other causal steps no empirical evidence is mentioned. For a more general perspective, Garousi et al. provide studies into the factors that affect the use and usefulness of documentation [7]. Their study culminates in the formulation of costs and benefits of technical documentation and a theory (meta-model) for the quality of software documentation [24]. However, their study does not look at the process of the use of documentation over a development project. In the next section we propose a theory that explains the different types of modeling found.

3 A Theory for Explaining the Plethora of Approaches to Modeling

In this section, we propose a theoretical framework that captures the insights from the previous sections that modeling practices are linked to project goals. Our theoretical framework is shown in Fig. 7. In this diagram 'SE' stands for Software Engineering. The interpretation of the framework is as follows: Projects happen in a context, have stakeholders and·can be in a particular stage of development. Context may include may facets (See e.g. [5]). For example, one can think of: risk-propensity of the organization, available time/money, organizational culture (e.g. [11]), but also size and geographic distribution. In practice many more factors of the context may play significant roles. Stakeholders have goals, such as increase development speed, a particular quality-level of the final product and so on. The goals may change across the stages of execution of a project. These goals of the stakeholders drive the development process used and the practices used in the overall approach to SE. A process denotes the collection of (formalized) steps of tasks that the project follows to engineer software. The processes and practices in turn drive the choice and use of tools. The next aspects of the diagram we explain are the nested rounded rectangles: The outermost rounded rectangle denotes the overall approach to software engineering including all its processes, practices and tools. Part of the overall approach to SE are the approach to documentation (AtD) and the approach to implementation (AtI). AtD and AtI refer to a combination of processes, practices and tools for documentation and implementation respectively. Together these AtD and AdI drive the approach to modeling (AtM). The approach to modeling itself again consists of a modeling process, a set of modeling practices and a collection of modeling tools. To summarize, this theoretical framework enables explaining which modeling approach is followed in a project by tracing it to the goals of the stakeholders and the project context.

For explanation purposes we have used 'drives' arrows between process, practice and tools in one direction. In reality, there may as well be arrows in the opposite direction where tools make a practice (im)possible or constrain possible processes. The same applies for the arrows between concepts specific to modeling and concepts general for SE: a modeling approach may enable or constrain the general SE approach.

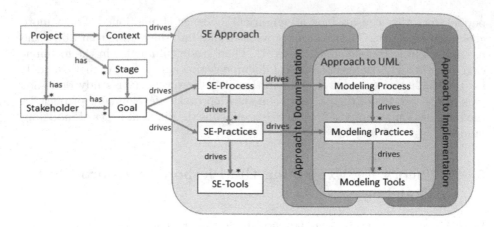

Fig. 7. Theoretical framework for modeling practices

4 Modeling Pathways

Earlier we observed that models of software designs serve multiple purposes to different stakeholders of software development projects. In this section we will zoom into how the types of models used in a project change as a project progresses. We explain this by means of Fig. 8. This diagram combines the main dimensions for classifying models that were introduced in Sect. 2. In the horizontal direction this diagram shows stages of modeling: moving from ideation into production. The vertical direction shows the abstraction levels: architecture, design and implementation. A project's modeling practices can occupy zero or more cells in this matrix. In this matrix, we have drawn a pathway that illustrates the evolution of the focal role of design models over time. Together with a change of their focal role, design models also change their abstraction level, their rigour as well as other dimensions mentioned in Table 1.

The first phase of the pathway is denoted 'I' and deals with ideation. Typically ideation addresses the architecture and/or design levels of abstraction. It is not common for models to be used for ideation of the implementation of a whole system, but ideation is not uncommon for designing parts of an implementation - such as e.g. use of patterns. A typical next use of design models (denoted 'II') is for externalization (communication, standardization, persistence). This can happen for the architecture and for the design. Also externalization is not common for the whole implementation - because the source code is a good source of information for the implementation. The third stage (denoted 'III') is production. Here the model is used to guide or produce the implementation. For this stage, the model must contain all the details necessary for a developer or compiler to generate the implementation. Its level of abstraction is therefore generally medium to low ('implementation level'). Please note that such pathways focus on the process of creating and refining a design. As development of the system progresses and also in the maintenance of the system, all of the design models created along a pathway will have to be updated when significant changes are made.

Indeed, a key problem for most modeling-pathways is that of updating more abstract design models to reflect (the significant parts of) increments of models at a lower level of abstraction. In theory, this 'continuous synchronization' of models at different levels of abstraction seems technically possible when both levels are described in a rigorous/formal manner and there exist clear traceability between two representations. Osman has demonstrated a prototype for synchronizing models across different levels of abstraction [21], yet much more work is needed in this direction.

A company may have a design-flow that supports the creation of a next system model on the basis of a set of systematic transformations of a model from a preceding stage. In this case there is high traceability between successive models. Alternatively, subsequent design models may be created largely independently from previous models. This happens for example when the models are used mostly for supporting the own understanding of the designers (at that stage). In the latter case there is poor traceability between successive models.

	Ideation	Externalization	Production
Architecture	I		
Design		II	
Implementation			III

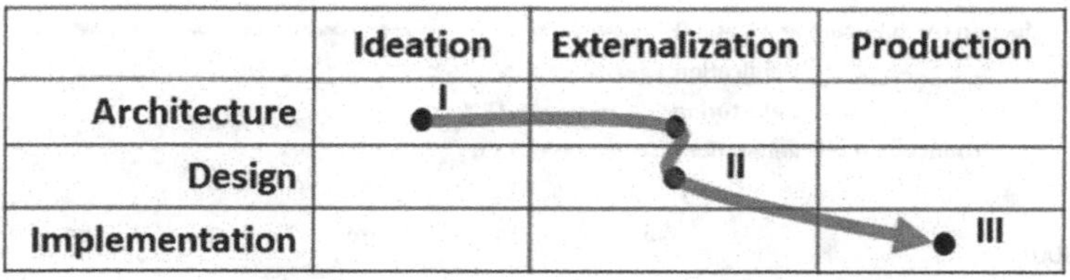

Fig. 8. Pathway of models in software development

In the future, we aim to show how these pathways can be used to illustrate the different approaches to modeling found across different projects.

5 Observations on Modeling in Open Source Projects

We set out to look into open source projects for empirical evidence on the use of modeling.

To answer these question, we mined GitHub for open source projects that use UML. We identified more than 20,000 projects that use UML [9]. Then, we ran a survey to collect information from more than 400 open source developers who work on these projects [10]. In this section, we report a brief selection of our findings.

Stage of Development: In our set of open source projects models are introduced at all phases on the life-cycles. Yet we found a concentration of first appearance of models around the start of projects [9]. Furthermore, for 26% of the projects we found that models were updated as projects progressed over time. The questionnaire confirmed that models are used for all three stages of development: ideation, externalization, and production. For ideation we found a large number of photos of sketches of UML diagrams. As documentation (i.e. externalization), models most commonly targeted the design-level of abstraction. Also, reverse engineered diagrams are also frequently used to serve as documentation. However, code generation based on implementation-level models, was only reported for few of the OSS projects [10]. Possibly because this requires an advanced level of training on methods and tools, and advanced coordination amongst the contributors.

Use of Models: Our survey asked after the use of models through a multiple choice questions to which multiple responses were possible. The responses are shown in Fig. 9[3]. By far the most common uses are for documentation (an externalization use) and for ideation and production of designs at the architecture- and design-level.

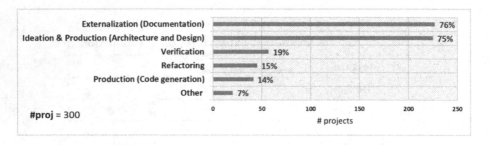

Fig. 9. Uses of models in open source software development

The responses to the survey confirm the non-negligible use of models for less obvious uses: 19% of the respondents uses models for verification tasks and 15% of the respondents uses models as part of doing refactoring. Another observation from our survey is that novices often use existing UML models as one of the most important sources for gaining an understanding of a system. Interestingly, the developers who create these models often seem unaware that other project members use their models in this way.

Models for coordinating distribution of work (planning): To investigate one other use of UML models, we explored whether models are used to coordinate work. The first interesting observation was that the design model was implemented by only a single person (no coordination) in only 33% of our set of open source projects. In 41% of the projects 3 or more persons participated in the implementation of a design. This suggests that models indeed are frequently used

---

[3] The categories have been renamed to be consistent with the naming used in this paper.

to coordinate implementation tasks. When asked for the involvement of these developers in the modeling process, it turned out that 88% of the persons implementing a modeled design also participated in the creating of that model. Thus, it seems that many open source projects adopt a *team modeling* approach, where developers create models together. This may be a particular trait of open source projects as the open source community values 'equality' and 'transparency'.

For more findings on these studies we refer to [9,10].

6   Future Directions

In this section we discuss selected ideas on future directions for improving the effective use of modeling in software development.

6.1   Aligning the Tools with the Tasks and the Process

Tooling continues to be mentioned as a problematic area in model-based development. In this section we use our classification matrix together with design pathways to understand why tooling continues to be problematic.

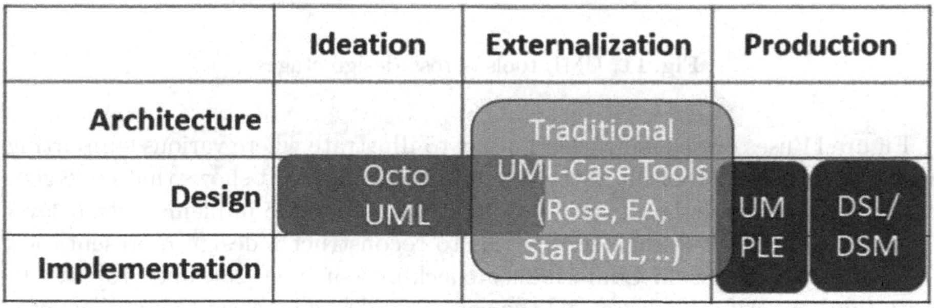

	Ideation	Externalization	Production	
Architecture		Traditional		
Design	Octo UML	UML-Case Tools (Rose, EA,	UM PLE	DSL/ DSM
Implementation		StarUML, ..)		

Fig. 10. UML tools across design stages

There are several major challenges related to modeling-tooling: One challenge is the large diversity in modeling styles. It is very difficult for any one tool to be a good match in supporting so many different uses. Integrating all possible uses of modeling in a tool would lead to a 'universal Swiss army knife': it becomes too complicated to use. Hence, this diversity of uses also explains the continued existence of a large variety of UML-based software modeling and design tools.

Figure 10 uses our classification matrix to explain that different tools focus on supporting different stages of development: Traditional UML CASE tools focus on creating UML models that strictly follow the UML syntax. One can consider them 'UML editors'. They can cover parts of the implementation- and production-stage (through code generation), but generally ignore informal notations and sketching that is typical for the ideation stage. Tools that aim to support MDA with code-generation force developers to model at the implementation level of abstraction. One example of such a tool is UMPLE [8]. Moreover, while there are certainly benefits of these types of tools, their use is mostly limited to the production stage. Other tools aim to bridge the gap between ideation and externalization by offering both informal sketchy modeling and transformations of these into rigorous/geometric UML shapes. One example of such a tool is for example OctoUML [12]. In summary, in practice models are developed along pathways that cross different stages of development and change in abstraction level. None of the modeling tools that is currently around efficiently supports a complete pathway.

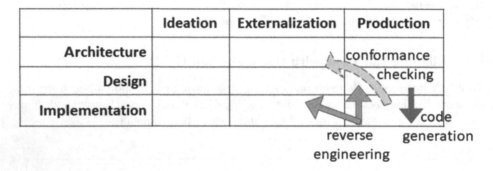

Fig. 11. UML tools across design stages

Figure 11 uses our classification matrix to illustrate where various supporting features of modeling tools fit in the development process. It shows that code generation transforms design level representations into code implementation level representation. Reverse engineering tries to reconstruct a design representation from an implementation. Conformance checking (such as [23], and [16]) try to verify (and quantify the degree of) the correspondence between the implementation and design. To this end, conformance checking techniques need to find ways to represent the abstractions that are made between design and implementation.

Future Direction 1. *Future software design tooling should support the mixing of text, sketches, formal diagrams, and source code in a flexible manner.*

Motivation: (i) different developers have a need for different combinations of text, sketches, diagrams and code. (ii) some artifacts evolve from one form (sketch) into another form (formal diagram). If this is a common use of models, then tools should support this.

Future Direction 2. *We need to move away from documentation as a static source of information about a system. Instead, we should move to dynamic 'information/knowledge' management about a design: multiple sources of data about a system should be combined dynamically and smart selections and abstractions of these data should be presented in an interactive way is both user-centric and task-centric.*

The aforementioned issues are related to two key aspects of modeling tools: (i) usability, and (ii) efficient chaining of tools in tool-chains.

6.2   A Promising Future: Domain Specific Architecture- and Modeling

There are interesting model-based approaches in practice that counter the aforementioned usability and tool-chaining issues: One notable example are so-called 'low-code' platforms as offered by e.g. Mendix and OutSystems. Their approaches capitalize on the fact that the most common architecture is a 3-layered architecture that consists of a data-layer, a business logic layer and a user-interaction layer. The 'low-code' approach offers 3 separate modeling languages (each of which can be considered a domain-specific modeling language): one modeling language for specifying data-models, one modeling language for defining business processes, and one for specifying user-interaction (user interface, possibly with user-processes). This approach is illustrated in Fig. 12.

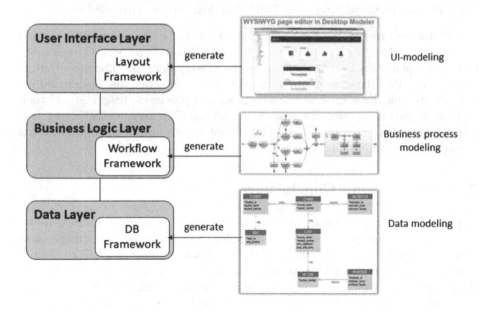

Fig. 12. Low-code approach to modeling for 3-layered architectures

These approaches are called 'low-code' because an entire running system can be generated out of a triplet of three types of models - hence no (textual) code is involved. Through specializing for particular types of software architecture, and separating the concerns in different modeling languages, the modeling of an application becomes fairly simple. Indeed these companies have shown factors of 3×–10× of speed-up in application development. One other key aspect of these new approaches is that the development pipeline is highly automated and even includes automated deployment (e.g. in the cloud) and automated production of app's for mobile platforms. In our view, this is one example of how modeling can be used in a very effective way by specializing the modeling language and linking it to a common architecture and architectural style in a particular domain.

One complementary study evaluated the impact of migrating of an existing (legacy) 3-layered architecture that was programmed 'manually' from scratch into a format that was generated out of a (3-layered) domain specific model (DSM) [15]. The results show that after introducing the DSM-approach the defect density lowered, defects were found earlier, but resolving defects took longer. Other observed benefits are that the number of developers and the number of person-hours needed for maintaining the system decreased, and the portability to new platforms increased.

When seen together, the use of the combination of a domain specific architecture and domain specific modeling languages promise to offer higher levels of abstraction while still being able to generate the implementation.

6.3   Practical Guidelines for Tailoring Modeling Approaches

Our theoretical framework Fig. 7 argues that project goals and project context are the drivers for the approach to modeling that is used in project. Currently the theory is explanatory in character: we can use it to explain the differences that we observe. Possibly the same framework could be made actionable if we could use it to create guidelines on *how to* chose modeling processes, practices and tools to best fit particular projects goals and context. This requires collecting best practices in modeling approaches and systematic ways for documenting contexts as part of case studies [5].

7   Summary and Conclusions

The term 'modeling' is a general term and it is used in a large variety of meanings. Possibly some people even want 'modeling' to mean certain things. However, as a result many scientific studies in software engineering fail to provide sufficiently precise characterizations of the modeling-practices that are used in the projects that they study. This lack of precise characterization leads to confusion and contradictions about the findings of modeling in software development. In this paper, we introduce several classification to more precisely describe the types of modeling encountered in software development. The main dimensions of these classification are: (i) the different levels of abstraction, and (ii) different stages of development. We introduced a classification matrix that combines these dimensions. This matrix can be used to characterize models as well as illustrate pathways that characterize how the focus of models evolve as projects progress.

Additionally, we proposed a theoretical framework that explains how the use of different modeling practices can be explained by looking at how they are driven by different context and different project goals. Further, we showed that

UML models are used for many more activities than only the guiding of the implementation.

All these extra uses of models impose additional requirements on the tools and processes used for the creation and maintenance of UML models throughout software projects. UML tools have to cater for interoperability with other processes and tools used in software development in order to support software engineers in moving tasks through differ stages of development. Only by recognizing and embracing the diversity of uses of models throughout software projects can we improve the tools needed to support their effective use. Currently, usability of modeling tools is one of the main challenges in modeling. In order for modeling to be more effective and achieve higher adoption, tools should become a better fit with the tasks of developers and better support various uses of models throughout the entire software development process.

References

1. Bass, L., Clements, P., Kazman, R.: Software Architecture in Practice, 3rd edn. Addison-Wesley Professional, Boston (2012)
2. Brown, A.W.: Model driven architecture: principles and practice. Softw. Syst. Model. **3**(4), 314–327 (2004)
3. Chaudron, M.R.V., Heijstek, W., Nugroho, A.: How effective is UML modeling? Softw. Syst. Model. **11**(4), 571–580 (2012)
4. Cross, N.: Design Thinking: Understanding How Designers Think and Work. Berg, Oxford (2011)
5. Dybå, T.: Contextualizing empirical evidence. IEEE Softw. **30**(1), 81–83 (2013)
6. Fernández-Sáez, A.M., Chaudron, M.R.V., Genero, M.: Exploring costs and benefits of using UML on maintenance: preliminary findings of a case study in a large it department. In: EESSMOD@ MoDELS, pp. 33–42 (2013)
7. Garousi, G., et al.: Usage and usefulness of technical software documentation: an industrial case study. Inf. Softw. Technol. **57**, 664–682 (2015)
8. Garzón, M.A., Aljamaan, H., Lethbridge, T.C.: Umple: a framework for model driven development of object-oriented systems. In: 2015 IEEE 22nd International Conference on Software Analysis, Evolution and Reengineering (SANER), pp. 494–498. IEEE (2015)
9. Hebig, R., Quang, T.H., Chaudron, M.R.V., Robles, G., Fernandez, M.A.: The quest for open source projects that use UML: mining GitHub. In: Proceedings of the ACM/IEEE 19th International MODELS Conference, pp. 173–183. ACM (2016)
10. Ho-Quang, T., Hebig, R., Robles, G., Chaudron, M.R.V., Fernandez, M.A.: Practices and perceptions of UML use in open source projects. In: Proceedings of the 39th International Conference on Software Engineering: Software Engineering in Practice Track, pp. 203–212. IEEE Press (2017)
11. Hofstede, G., Hofstede, G.J., Minkov, M.: Cultures and Organizations - Software of the Mind: Intercultural Cooperation and its Importance for Survival, 3rd edn. McGraw-Hill, New York (2010)
12. Jolak, R., Vesin, B., Chaudron, M.R.V.: OctoUML: an environment for exploratory and collaborative software design. In: ICSE 2017, vol. 17 (2017)

13. Lange, C., Chaudron, M.R.V., Muskens, J., Somers, L.J., Dortmans, H.M.: An empirical investigation in quantifying inconsistency and incompleteness of UML designs. In: Workshop Consistency Problems in UML-Based Software Development II, pp. 26–34 (2003)
14. Lange, C.F.J., Chaudron, M.R.V.: Effects of defects in UML models: an experimental investigation. In: Proceedings of the 28th International Conference on Software Engineering, pp. 401–411. ACM (2006)
15. Mellegård, N., Ferwerda, A., Lind, K., Heldal, R., Chaudron, M.R.V.: Impact of introducing domain-specific modelling in software maintenance: an industrial case study. IEEE Trans. Softw. Eng. **42**(3), 245–260 (2016)
16. Muskens, J., Bril, R.J., Chaudron, M.R.V.: Generalizing consistency checking between software views. In: Fifth Working IEEE/IFIP Conference on Software Architecture (WICSA 2005), 6–10 November 2005, USA, pp. 169–180. IEEE Computer Society (2005)
17. Nugroho, A., Chaudron, M.R.V.: A survey of the practice of design-code correspondence amongst professional software engineers. In: ESEM 2007, September 2007, Spain, pp. 467–469. ACM/IEEE Computer Society (2007)
18. Nugroho, A., Chaudron, M.R.V.: A survey into the rigor of UML use and its perceived impact on quality and productivity. In: Proceedings of the 2nd International Symposium on Empirical Software Engineering and Measurement, ESEM 2008, 9–10 October 2008, Germany, pp. 90–99. ACM (2008)
19. Nugroho, A., Flaton, B., Chaudron, M.R.V.: Empirical analysis of the relation between level of detail in UML models and defect density. In: Czarnecki, K., Ober, I., Bruel, J.-M., Uhl, A., Völter, M. (eds.) MODELS 2008. LNCS, vol. 5301, pp. 600–614. Springer, Heidelberg (2008). https://doi.org/10.1007/978-3-540-87875-9_42
20. Osman, M.H., Chaudron, M.R.V.: UML usage in open source software development: a field study. In: Proceedings of the 3rd International Workshop on Experiences and Empirical Studies in Software Modeling Co-located MODELS 2013, USA, vol. 1078, pp. 23–32. CEUR-WS.org (2013)
21. Osman, M.H., Chaudron, M.R.V., van der Putten, P.: Interactive scalable abstraction of reverse engineered UML class diagrams. In: APSEC 2014, South Korea, December 2014, pp. 159–166. IEEE (2014)
22. Torre, D., Labiche, Y., Genero, M.: UML consistency rules: a systematic mapping study. In: EASE 2014, UK, 13–14 May 2014. ACM (2014)
23. van Opzeeland, D.J.A., Lange, C.F.J., Chaudron, M.R.V.: Quantitative techniques for the assessment of correspondence between UML designs and implementations. In: 9th ECOOP Workshop on Quantitative Approaches in Object-Oriented Software Engineering (2005)
24. Zhi, J., et al.: Cost, benefits and quality of software development documentation: a systematic mapping. J. Syst. Softw. **99**, 175–198 (2015)

Self-managing Internet of Things

Danny Weyns[1]([✉]), Gowri Sankar Ramachandran[2], and Ritesh Kumar Singh[1]

[1] Department of Computer Science, KU Leuven, Leuven, Belgium
danny.weyns@kuleuven.be
[2] University of Southern California, Los Angeles, USA

Abstract. Internet of Things (IoT) are in full expansion. Applications range from factory floors to smart city environments. IoT applications consist of battery powered small computing devices (motes) that communicate wirelessly and interact with the environment through sensors and actuators. A key challenge that IoT engineers face is how to manage such systems that are subject to inherent uncertainties in their operation contexts, such as interferences and dynamic traffic in the network. Often these uncertainties are difficult to predict at development time. In practice, IoT applications are therefore typically over-provisioned at deployment; however, this leads to inefficiency. In this paper, we make a case for IoT applications that manage themselves at runtime to deal with uncertainties. We contribute: (1) a set of concerns that motivate the need for self-management for IoT systems, (2) three initial approaches that illustrate the potential of realising self-managing IoT systems, and (3) a set of open challenges for future research on self-adaptation in IoT.

Keywords: Internet-of-Things · IoT · Uncertainties
Self-adaptation · Self-management

1 Introduction

Internet of Things (IoT) consist of tiny embedded and battery powered computing device (motes) that are equipped with a low-power wireless radio, sensors and actuators. These motes form networks that are capable of monitoring and controlling the physical world and thereby connecting digital processes to our physical environment. IoT applications are widely deployed in the context of industries and smart cities, see for example [5,18,21]. Typically, IoT applications require resources for computation, sensing, actuation and communication. Continuous management and maintenance of these resources is critical for accomplishing the desired stakeholder goals. This problem is particularly challenging due to the large scale nature of IoT deployments and the conditions under which they may need to operate that are often difficult to predict [17].

Consider an application example in the context of factory floor monitoring: an IoT application is deployed on the factory floor to monitor the operational conditions of the machines and production lines. In order to maintain the productivity and the efficiency of the factory floor, machines have to be operational

© Springer International Publishing AG 2018
A. M. Tjoa et al. (Eds.): SOFSEM 2018, LNCS 10706, pp. 67–84, 2018.
https://doi.org/10.1007/978-3-319-73117-9_5

24/7. To ensure this requirement, the machines are equipped with sensors that continuously monitor the temperature and the vibration profile of the machines. Whenever an abnormality is detected, the application is reconfigured to sense additional parameters of the machine. This allows fine-grained tracking of the factory environment and alarming operators in case an intervention is required. In such an application scenario, the IoT application must have capabilities to manage the resources for sensing, computation and communication. In addition, this application scenario highlights the dynamic nature of IoT applications.

Resource demands of IoT applications fluctuate during run-time due their event-driven nature [29]. Consider another application in the context of a smart building that monitors the comfort level of employees and actuates the heating when the temperature is too low, or alternatively the air condition when the temperature is too warm, and regulates the light when the light condition change. However, in the event of a fire detected in the building, the application has to be reconfigured to actuate an alarm, and stream a video to assist the fire personnel to rescue people. While monitoring the comfort level, the application requires low bandwidth, since the transmission of temperature and light reading requires few bytes of data. However, in the event of fire, the application requires high bandwidth, since the streaming of video requires at least kilo bytes of data. The ability of an IoT application to manage such dynamics autonomously and correctly is highly critical in such application scenarios.

A key underlying problem that IoT engineers face are uncertainties in the operation contexts of the applications, internal dynamics, and even changes in the requirements during operation. Often these uncertainties are difficult to predict at development time and can only be resolved during operation. To tackle these run-time uncertainties, IoT applications are typically over-provisioned at deployment. Although such an approach fulfil some of the desired application goals, e.g. the reliability, it comes at a cost of high energy consumption. Since IoT applications are battery powered, it is important to minimise its battery consumption to maximise their lifetime. With over-provisioning, IoT applications tend to be configured for worst case demands, which result in high radio use for wireless communication. According to literature, radio dominates the energy consumption in IoT application [22]. Minimising the radio usage is a major requirement for achieving a longer lifetime. Self-management frameworks that track the system and its context at runtime to resolve uncertainties during operation is essential for resource and energy constrained IoT applications.

The contributions of this paper are: (1) a set of concerns that motivate why we need self-management for IoT systems, (2) an overview of three initial approaches towards tackling some of the challenges in realising self-managing IoT systems, and (3) a set of open problems for future research on self-adaptation in the IoT domain.

The remainder of this paper is structured as follows. In Sect. 2, we provide a brief introduction to self-adaptation. Section 3 elaborates on the need for self-management in IoT and its specific challenges. Section 4 highlights a number of our initial efforts that aim to contribute towards tackling some of the challenges. Finally, Sect. 5 presents a set of open problems for future research in this area that we identified from our experiences.

2 Background on Self-adaptation

Dealing with uncertainties is an increasingly important challenge for software engineers. Here our focus is on the ability of software systems to deal with uncertainties that needs to be resolved at runtime [7,16,20]. A prominent approach to deal with uncertainties at runtime is so called self-adaptation [8,12,13,19,33]. Self-adaptation equips a software system with a feedback loop that collects data of the system and its environment that was difficult or impossible to determine before deployment. The feedback loop uses the collected data to reason about itself and to adapt itself to changes in order to provide the required quality goals, or gracefully degrade if needed. A typical example is a self-managing Web-based client-server system that continuously tracks and analyzes changes in work load and available bandwidth and dynamically adapts the server configuration to provide the required quality of service to its users, while minimising costs [8].

Self-adaptation can be considered from two perspectives [30]: (1) the ability of a system to adjust its behaviour in response to the perception of the environment and the system itself [3,15]; the *self* prefix indicates that the system decides and adapts autonomously (i.e., without or with minimal interference of humans) [2], and (2) the mechanisms that are used to realises self-adaptation, typically by means of a closed feedback loop [1,8,32], i.e. there is an explicit separation between a part of the system that deals with the domain concerns (goals for which the system is built) and a part that deals the adaptation concerns (the way the system realises its goals under changing conditions). Figure 1 shows the basic building blocks of a self-adaptive system, taken from [30].

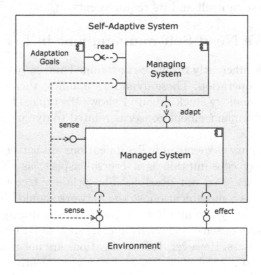

Fig. 1. Basic building blocks of a self-adaptive system [30]

The environment refers to the part of the external world with which the self-adaptive system interacts and in which the effects of the system can be observed [10]. The managed system comprises the application code that realizes the systems domain functionality. The managing system manages the managed system; that is, the managing system collects runtime data, reasons about this data and adapts the managed system to deal with one or more adaption goals. The adaptation goals are concerns of the managing system over the managed system; they usually relate to the software qualities of the managed system. Adaptation goals themselves can be subject of change (which is not shown in Fig. 1). A typical approach to structure the software of the managing system is by means of a so-called Monitor-Analyser-Planner-Executer + Knowledge feedback loop [4,12,26] (MAPE-K loop in short). The Monitor collects runtime data from the managed system and the environment and uses this to update the content of the Knowledge. Based on the current knowledge, the Analyser determines whether there is a need for adaptation of the managed system using the adaptation goals. If adaptation is required, the Planner puts together a plan that consists of a set of adaptation actions that are then enacted by the Executor that adapts the managed system as needed.

In the past few years, research in this area has particularly been focussing on how to provide assurances for the adaptation goals of self-adaptive systems that operate under uncertain operating conditions [14,31]. This is particularly important for systems with strict quality goals. Such systems require the provision of evidence that the system requirements are satisfied during its entire lifetime, from inception to and throughout operation. It is important to highlight that this evidence must be produced despite the uncertainty in the environment, the behaviour of the system itself and its requirements.

3 Why Do We Need Self-management in IoT?

IoT applications are inherently resource-constrained and subject to various types of dynamics during operation. These dynamics manifest themselves at different layers of the IoT technology stack. Figure 1 shows the typical layers of IoT applications. We highlight management concerns related to dynamics and uncertainties at different layers.

Things. The primary elements of IoT applications are battery powered motes. Consequently, energy consumption is a crucial aspect, as changing batteries is costly, or sometimes even not possible. The primary factor that determines energy consumption is communication, so the network should be configured carefully to avoid unnecessary communication. Motes of monitoring applications are equipped with sensors to sense the environment, such as RFID sensors, infrared and temperature sensors. However, IoT applications are not restricted to merely sensing and may also control elements in the environment, such as lightbulbs, heating devices, valves etc. Sensors and actuators are subject to all kind of uncertainties, ranging from inaccurate sampling or actuating up to failure.

Communication. IoT deployments primarily rely on wireless communication to relay sensor data to a central server. Wireless communication is subject to

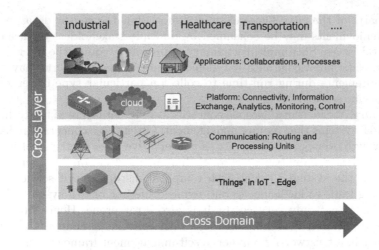

Fig. 2. Typical layers of IoT applications

runtime uncertainties, such as interferences, noise, and multi-path fading effects. Different communication technologies with dedicated protocols are applied to support different settings. For example, bluetooth enables establishing on the fly local networks between mobile entities, while a LoRa mesh network can support efficient very long range communication. Mobility may introduce particular challenges to reliable communication. Run-time uncertainties in communication result in packet loss. In such cases, it is important to reconfigure the wireless communication network to minimise packet loss (e.g. route messages differently in a multi-hop network setting).

Platform. Platforms provide the glue between user applications and the underlying IoT resources. An IoT platform offers a variety of services to applications and application developers, including a runtime environment, programming APIs etc. Platform services may range from the provision of basic resources to storage facilities up to advanced analytics and control management of underlying IoT resources. Crucial aspects in a distributed context are information exchange, monitoring and control services. Platforms can be deployed on various infrastructures, ranging from dedicated machines to a public cloud. IoT platforms and the infrastructure on which they are deployed can be subject of various sources of dynamics, typical examples are changes in the availability of resources, and dynamics in load (e.g. in a multi-tenant setting).

Applications. Application themselves can be subject of change, which in turn may affect the configuration of underlying layers. In the data-driven society, IoT deployments are acting as a catalyst to meet the demands of stakeholders in various disciplines. In the context of a smart city for example, garbage management units can support collection schedules for different parts of the city by knowing the status of individual garbage cans. Similarly, traffic regulators can dynamically alter the traffic routes in a city by knowing the traffic flows in various parts of the city. These examples show that the sensor data produced by IoT deployments may be consumed by multiple stakeholders to tackle various societal issues. Such multidisciplinary approaches require the integration of domain specific knowledge into IoT deployments. Domain experts may modify their requirements during run-time to collect a particular type of sensor data with a specific setting.

Summary. We identified various concerns at different layers of the technology stack of IoT systems that require management. Often these concerns are handled either through over-provisioning (e.g. a conservative power settings of motes to ensure sufficient reliability), or through human intervention (e.g. an operator reconfigures the system to deal with temporal disruptions of service). Over-provisioning leads to inefficiencies and reduced lifetime of IoT systems. Manual intervention is not only very costly, it is also error prone. Hence, in order to fulfil the application demands and deal with continuous change and runtime uncertainty in a trustworthy manner, a self-management framework is essential.

4   Initial Contributions to Self-management in IoT

We highlight three initial contributions from our work that illustrate how self-adaptation techniques enable IoT systems to manage themselves autonomously. We start with Dawn that supports autonomous bandwidth allocation for IoT systems. Then we show how Hitch Hiker enables self-adaptation for concerns that cross multiple layers of IoT systems. Finally, we demonstrate how simulation and statistical techniques can be exploited at runtime to provide guarantees for a set of adaptation goals of an IoT application.

4.1   Autonomous Bandwidth Allocation Using Dawn

Dawn [24] is a self-management middleware for automatically configuring and reconfiguring 6TiSCH [28] networks based upon the requirements of their resident software. 6TiSCH [28] is a de-facto standard in high-reliability, low-power networking for the IoT. 6TiSCH networks are time synchronised and follow a communication schedule that repeats over time. The atomic unit of the communication schedule is a *time slot*. Time slots have a fixed, predefined duration, long enough for a single radio transmission and acknowledgment. Each platform is allocated a number of time slots in the schedule, that it then uses for communication. Platforms save energy by sleeping during inactive time slots. Each allocated time slot adds a quantum of communication bandwidth to the platform. The more time slots are allocated in the schedule for a given platform, the more data the platform can transmit per unit of time (higher bandwidth) and has more frequent transmission opportunities (lower latency), at the cost of higher energy consumption.

The schedule is typically created and maintained by an entity called the network manager. For periodic application traffic with static requirements, this process is straightforward. However, application dynamism, traffic periodicity and traffic heterogeneity render approaches based on static bandwidth provisioning suboptimal. On one hand, over-provisioning bandwidth to account for the worst case increases energy consumption. On the other hand, under-provisioning bandwidth results in packet loss for non-deterministic traffic patterns due to insufficient bandwidth and thus lower reliability. The challenge is therefore to handle these non-deterministic traffic patterns while meeting requirements on low latency or high bandwidth, as well as the application dynamism that arises due to software and hardware reconfiguration. Practically, this means that each individual node should be provisioned with the optimum amount of bandwidth, and that this should be adjusted to meet the demands of runtime reconfiguration.

Dawn builds on top of LooCI binding model [9]. LooCI is a component based middleware for developing and managing IoT applications. In LooCI, application software is realized in the form of 'compositions' of reusable components. Figure 3 shows an example LooCI composition, where a temperature and light sensor component deployed on *Node A* communicate with an aggregator component on *Node B* via a TEMP and LIGHT type binding, respectively. A LooCI binding connects a component's provided interface (shown as -o) to another component's required interface (shown as)-), and it is depicted as -o)- in Fig. 3.

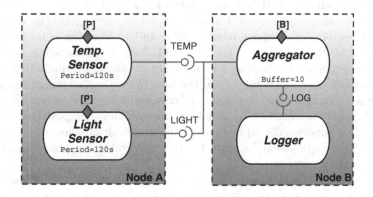

Fig. 3. Example composition of a component-based IoT application.

In the composition shown in Fig. 3, the temperature and light sensor components are sources, while the aggregator component is a sink. All *source* components are required to carry the standard Dawn property, *period* [P], which provides the transmission frequency of the source component in seconds. In this example, the temperature and light reading is transmitted once every 120 s. In cases where a *source* component transmits sporadically, such as the triggering of a PIR sensor, P provides the *maximum* rate at which the component may transmit. As with all LooCI properties, the *period* property may be inspected by external software or users. A component may also choose to allow runtime modification of this property in cases where transmission frequencies are determined by the application composition.

Intermediate components are located between a source and sink in the composition graph. These components may expose either the *period* property or the *buffer* property [B], which determines how many inputs the component will store from its dependent before forwarding a message. In the example composition shown in Fig. 3, the aggregator component buffers 10 sensor readings from the light and temperature interfaces before transmitting the aggregated results to the logger component. For each component in the composition with a *buffer* property [B], the bandwidth requirement of the component is the aggregate bandwidth requirement of its dependents. The property naming conventions such as *period* [P] and *buffer* property [B] are standardised in Dawn, and it enables Dawn to allocate optimal bandwidth for the compositions.

As can be seen from Fig. 3, the bandwidth requirement of a component depends on its *period* and *buffer* properties as well as the properties of all of its dependents in the component graph. The total bandwidth requirement of a node is therefore the aggregate of the transmission frequencies of all components with a *remote binding*. For the composition shown in Fig. 3, Node A has a bandwidth requirement of 8 bytes every 120 s, since the payload sizes of TEMP and LIGHT bindings are 5 and 3 bytes, respectively. However, Node B does not have any bandwidth requirement, as bandwidth assignments are based only on outgoing traffic and Node B has no remote bindings, thus there is no outgoing traffic. All the outgoing traffic on the node, which are determined by the remote bindings of components, require bandwidth resources from the network in order to reliably transmit the data to the intended destination. Existing bandwidth allocation approaches are static, which makes them suboptimal. In addition, such approaches offer less flexibility in the face of runtime reconfiguration.

Runtime reconfiguration of a software composition can significantly impact bandwidth requirements. Let us consider the software composition shown in Fig. 4, which is functionally equivalent to the composition shown in Fig. 3, but with a modified deployment location for the aggregator component and different *period* property settings.

While both compositions are functionally equivalent, the bandwidth allocation required to support the composition in Fig. 4 is 40 bytes every 50 min is 50 times less than the configuration shown in Fig. 3, since the buffer becomes full after receiving five sensor readings from both temperature and light sensor components. From these example compositions, it can be seen that the bandwidth requirement of the composition depends on the components and their properties. An automatic composition analysis approach is therefore required to extract bandwidth requirements from software compositions.

Dawn uses a composition analysis algorithm to derive the bandwidth requirements of application compositions, and then it invokes the bandwidth allocation algorithm to allocate the desired bandwidth for the IoT platform.

Dawn handles runtime reconfiguration by listening for reconfiguration actions at the middleware level. When reconfiguration is detected, the composition analysis and bandwidth allocation algorithms are executed. The process is fully automated and therefore imposes no burden on developers.

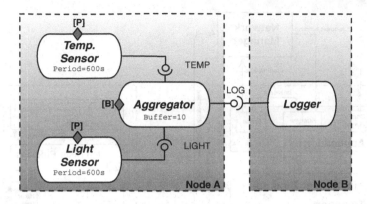

Fig. 4. Reconfigured composition of a component-based IoT application shown in Fig. 3.

Dawn elegantly automates the bandwidth reservation process, which enables the application developer to build extremely flexible and dependable IoT applications. Evaluation results on a 50-node testbed show that Dawn provides 100% reliability and manages to increase the lifetime by *three-fold* with minimal memory and performance overhead. For more information, we refer the interested reader to [24].

4.2 Self-adaptation Across Layers with Hitch Hiker

Internet-of-Things (IoT) devices must operate for long periods on limited power supplies. As discussed earlier, wireless communication is the primary source of energy consumption for IoT devices [22]. The lifetime of IoT applications can therefore be increased by minimising radio communication. Data aggregation has been widely applied to tackle this problem [11,23,27]. Data aggregation is a technique in which multiple messages are combined in to a single datagram, thus reducing radio transmissions and hence, the energy consumption of IoT devices. Furthermore, less frequent transmissions result in fewer collisions and therefore retransmissions. This can significantly improve the performance of IoT devices.

Hitch Hiker is a middleware that uses application knowledge to perform data aggregation based on the priority of the application data. Hitch Hiker allows the application developers to classify its application traffic as high-priority and low-priority based on its criticality. Hitch Hiker creates a data aggregation overlay using the high-priority transmissions, and the low-priority data is aggregated with high- priority transmissions. Hitch Hiker reduces the energy consumption, while offering a flexible data aggregation scheme for application developers.

Figure 5 shows the building blocks of Hitch Hiker distributed across the different layers of network stack. Hitch Hiker supports two types of management: centralized and decentralized. With the centralized scheme, the configuration and maintenance of low priority Hitch Hiker bindings is done by a centralized network manager. In this case, the central manager collects the information

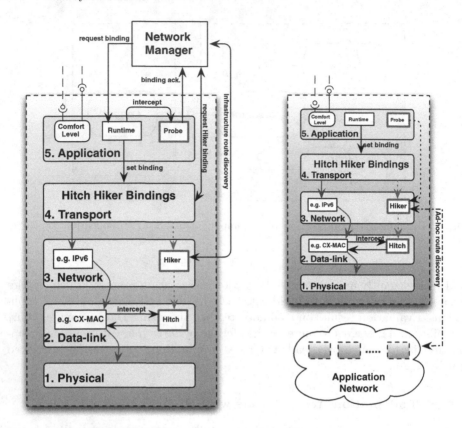

Fig. 5. High level overview of Hitch Hiker [25].

about high priority bindings, and it sets up the network for low priority data aggregation by configuring Hitch and Hiker protocols. In case of the decentralised scheme, the network configuration process is delegated to all the nodes in the network. Nodes self-configure themselves by coordinating and collaborating with each other.

Hitch Hiker autonomously add and remove data aggregation support for IoT applications using the existing high and low priority application bindings. Whenever the application gets reconfigured, Hitch Hiker recompute the route to retain the data aggregation functionality. If data aggregation route cannot be establised using the existing application compositions, Hitch Hiker notifies the application managers to take appropriate action.

Evaluation of the prototype implementation shows that Hitch Hiker consumes minimal memory, introduces limited overhead and that transmitting messages with Hitch Hiker consumes a small fraction of the energy that is required for a standard radio transmission. The interested reader finds more information about Hitch Hiker in [25].

4.3 Area Security Surveillance

In a joint R&D effort between imec-DistriNet and VersaSense[1] we studied self-adaptation for an area security surveillance application. The particular aim of this work was to evaluate whether simulation combined with statistical techniques can be used to provide guarantees for adaptation goals of an IoT system during operation. Figure 6 shows an overview of the deployment that a science campus of KU Leuven that we used in this study.

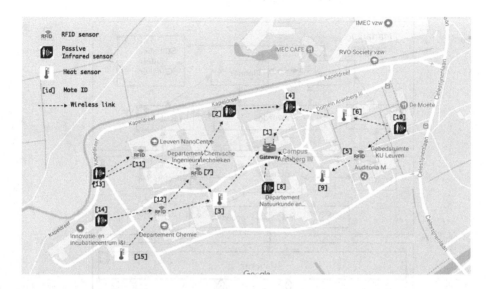

Fig. 6. Configuration area security surveillance application

The network is set up as a mesh network that comprises 15 motes equipped with different types of sensors that communicate over a time synchronised LoRa network. Motes are strategically placed to provide access control to labs (via RFID sensor), to monitor the movements and occupancy status (via Passive infrared sensor) and to sense the temperature (via heat sensor). The sensor data from all the motes are relayed to the IoT gateway, which is deployed at a central monitoring facility. The communication in the network is organised in cycles, each cycle comprising a fixed number of communication slots. Each slot defines a sender and receiver mote that can communicate with one another.

The domain concern for the IoT network is to relay surveillance data to the gateway. The stakeholders defined the adaptation goals as follows: (1) the average packet loss over 24 h should not exceed 10%, (2) the average latency of messages should be less than 5% of the cycle time, (3) the energy consumption of the motes should be minimised to optimise the life time of the network. Achieving these adaptation goals is challenging due to two primary types of

---

[1] www.versasense.com.

uncertainty: (1) network interference and noise caused by external factors such as weather conditions and the presence of other WiFi signals in the neighbourhood of communication links; interference affects the quality of the communication which may lead to packet loss; (2) fluctuating traffic load which may be difficult to predict (e.g., messages produced by a passive infrared sensor are based on the detection of motion of humans).

To solve the problem of the IoT network we applied a self-adaptation approach shown in Fig. 7.

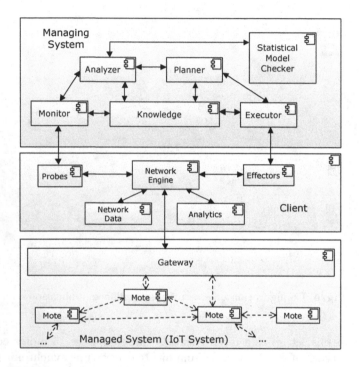

Fig. 7. Self-adaptation approach for the area security surveillance application

The bottom layer consists of the managed system with the network of motes and the gateway. The middle layer comprises a client that runs on a dedicated machine. This client offers an interface to the network using probes and effectors. Probes can be used to monitor the status of motes and links, statistical data about the packet loss, energy consumption, and latency of the network. The effectors allow adapting the mote settings, including power settings of the motes, distribution of messages to parents. The network engine collects the network data in a repository and performs analyses on the data to serve operators or adaptation logic using the analytics component. In manual mode, an operator can access the IoT network via the client to track its status and perform reconfigurations manually. These reconfigurations include changing the power settings per communication link and changing the distribution of packets sent to parents (in case there are multiple parents). In the self-adaptive solution, the top layer is added to the system that automatically adapts the configuration such that the adaptation goals of the IoT network are met.

Self-adaptation is realised using a MAPE-K feedback loop. The Monitor uses the probe to track the recent traffic load and network interferences as well as the statistics for each quality property of interest. This data is used to update a set of models in the knowledge repository, including a model of the IoT system and its environment, a representation of the adaptation goals in the form of a set of rules, and a set of quality models, one for each adaptation goal.

The Analyzer uses a statistical model checker to predict the quality properties for each possible configuration of the IoT application. A configuration is characterised by: (i) a power setting for each communication link (a value between 0 and 15) and (ii) a distribution of packets sent along to links of motes with more than one parent (discretised in steps of 20%). The statistical model checker performs a series of simulations and uses statistical techniques to predict the qualities. Compared to exhaustive model checking, statistical model checking is very efficient in terms of verification time and required resources. The tradeoff is that the results are not exact, but subject to a level of confidence. The engineer can set this level, but higher confidence requires more time and resources. If the currently deployed configuration does not realise the adaptation goals, the planner is triggered to plan an adaptation. The results of analysis is a predicted value for each quality property of interest (average packet loss, average latency, energy consumption) for each possible configuration.

The Planner starts with selecting the best adaptation option based on the quality properties determined by the analyser. If valid configuration is found, a failsafe strategy is applied (i.e., the network is reconfigured to a default setting). Otherwise, the planner creates a plan to adapt the IoT network from its current configuration to the best adaptation option that was found. A plan consists of steps, where each step either adapts the power setting of a mote for a link, or it adapts the distribution of packets sent to a parent of a mote. As soon as the plan is ready, the Executer is triggered that will enact the adaptation steps via the effectors.

We compared the self-adaptation approach with an approach commonly used in practice that uses over-provisioning to deal with uncertainties (power settings are set to maximum and packets are duplicated in case of multiple parents).

We evaluated the packet loss, latency, and energy consumption of the IoT network for both approaches for a period of 24 h. The cycle time was set to 9.5 min, corresponding to 153 cycles in 24 h. During the first 8 min of the cycle the motes can communicate packets downstream to the gateway; during the remaining 1.5 min the gateway can communicate adaptation messages upstream to the motes. For the self-adaptation approach we configured the verification queries with a confidence of 90% and simulations queries with a relative standard error of the mean of 0.5%. Figure 8 shows the main results.

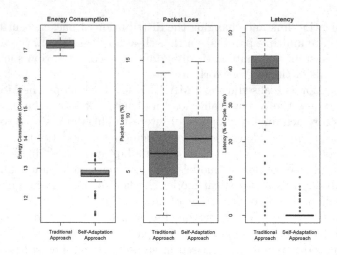

Fig. 8. Test results for the area security surveillance application

The graphs show that the average energy consumption of the self-adaptation solution is significantly better compared to the traditional approach (p-value < 0.000). Similarly, the self-adaptation approach outperforms the traditional approach for latency (p-value < 0.000). For the packet loss, both approaches have similar results (mean of paired differences is 1.4%). We measured also the time required for adaptation. With a mean of 45.7 s, the adaptation time was perfectly fine for a setting with a cycle time of around 9.5 min with 1.5 min to make an adaptation decision.

The area security surveillance application demonstrates how self-adaption techniques can be applied to enable an IoT application to deal with uncertainties at runtime and provide guarantees with sufficient confidence for a set of required quality properties in an automatic manner. For more information, we refer the reader to the DeltaIoT website[2].

5   Open Problems for Self-management in IoT

We conclude this paper with a number of open challenges for future research on self-adaptation of IoT systems that we identified based on the state of the art and our experiences with engineering concrete IoT applications.

Local adaptation. The examples of autonomous bandwidth allocation using Dawn (Sect. 4.1) and area security surveillance (Sect. 4.3) are examples of self-adaptation that is applied locally. Existing solutions such as these have primarily focussed on the benefits and tradeoffs in terms of qualities that can be achieved by self-adaptation. However, in the context of IoT, an important factor is the cost associated with applying the adaptation actions. For example, in a mesh

---

[2] https://people.cs.kuleuven.be/danny.weyns/software/DeltaIoT/.

network, to adjust the network settings of motes, adaptation messages needs to be routed from the gateway upstream to the motes. Communicating these messages requires energy. The cost of this energy may invalidate the expected benefits of the adaptation. Another example of cost may be the time that is required to enact the adaptation actions. Hence, an important challenge for future research is to develop solutions that consider both the benefits and the costs of self-adaptation.

Cross-layer adaption. Hitch Hiker is an approach that supports cross-layer adaptation (Sect. 4.2). In the context of smart cities, IoT applications typically consist of hundreds of motes equipped with various types of sensors and actuators. Continuous adaptation based on context changes of such motes has shown to be useful for understanding sensor data [23]. On the other hand, reconfigurations of applications may also alter the underlying communication demands [24,25]. As a consequence, reconfiguration at one layer of the technology stack may call for reconfigurations at another layer. While traditional layering schemas leads to separation of concerns, it may be less suitable for dynamic IoT applications where concerns inevitably crosscut the layers. An important challenge is to investigate how to deal with dominant crosscutting concerns such as energy efficiency and security in IoT, which may require a new view on layering of the IoT technology stack.

Cross-application adaption. Besides adaptation concerns that span different layers of the IoT technology stack, concerns can also cross domains as shown in Fig. 2. Although generally considered as crucial for the future of IoT, little research has been devoted to interactions and collaborations between different IoT applications. Such collaborations have the potential to generate dramatic synergies [6]. However, at the same time they create dependencies that in a dynamic context may be extremely difficult to handle. Hence, an important challenge for future research is how to investigate the interplay between IoT applications in an ecosystem. This will require solutions for technical alignment and stability, but also suitable business models and methods for establishing trust.

Providing guarantees. One of the crucial aspects of many IoT applications is trustworthiness. Trustworthiness refers to stakeholders' confidence, dependability, and reliability in the applications. As we have highlighted in Sect. 3, given that IoT applications are subject to a zoo of uncertainties, this raises an important challenge: how to obtain trustworthiness in IoT systems that are subject of ongoing uncertainties? Tacking this challenge is hard, in particular in an ecosystem context. It does not only require novel technical solutions to guarantee the concerns of stakeholders throughout the lifetime of IoT systems, it also requires novel legal frameworks that can handle continuous change.

Acknowledgments. We are grateful to the technical staff of VersaSense (https://www.versasense.com/) for the fruitful collaborations.

References

1. Andersson, J., de Lemos, R., Malek, S., Weyns, D.: Modeling dimensions of self-adaptive software systems. In: Cheng, B.H.C., de Lemos, R., Giese, H., Inverardi, P., Magee, J. (eds.) Software Engineering for Self-adaptive Systems. LNCS, vol. 5525, pp. 27–47. Springer, Heidelberg (2009). https://doi.org/10.1007/978-3-642-02161-9_2
2. Brun, Y., et al.: Engineering self-adaptive systems through feedback loops. In: Cheng, B.H.C., de Lemos, R., Giese, H., Inverardi, P., Magee, J. (eds.) Software Engineering for Self-adaptive Systems. LNCS, vol. 5525, pp. 48–70. Springer, Heidelberg (2009). https://doi.org/10.1007/978-3-642-02161-9_3
3. Cheng, B.H.C., et al.: Software engineering for self-adaptive systems: a research roadmap. In: Cheng, B.H.C., de Lemos, R., Giese, H., Inverardi, P., Magee, J. (eds.) Software Engineering for Self-adaptive Systems. LNCS, vol. 5525, pp. 1–26. Springer, Heidelberg (2009). https://doi.org/10.1007/978-3-642-02161-9_1
4. Dobson, S., Denazis, S., Fernández, A., Gaïti, D., Gelenbe, E., Massacci, F., Nixon, P., Saffre, F., Schmidt, N., Zambonelli, F.: A survey of autonomic communications. ACM Trans. Auton. Adapt. Syst. 1(2), 223–259 (2006). http://doi.acm.org/10.1145/1186778.1186782
5. Dohler, M., Barthel, D., Watteyne, T., Winter, T.: RFC5548: routing requirements for urban low-power and lossy networks (2009)
6. Dustdar, S., Nastic, S., Scekic, O.: A novel vision of cyber-human smart city. In: 2016 Fourth IEEE Workshop on Hot Topics in Web Systems and Technologies (HotWeb), pp. 42–47, October 2016
7. Esfahani, N., Malek, S.: Uncertainty in self-adaptive software systems. In: de Lemos, R., Giese, H., Müller, H.A., Shaw, M. (eds.) Software Engineering for Self-adaptive Systems II. LNCS, vol. 7475, pp. 214–238. Springer, Heidelberg (2013). https://doi.org/10.1007/978-3-642-35813-5_9
8. Garlan, D., Cheng, S., Huang, A., Schmerl, B., Steenkiste, P.: Rainbow: architecture-based self-adaptation with reusable infrastructure. Computer 37(10), 46–54 (2004)
9. Hughes, D., Thoelen, K., Maerien, J., Matthys, N., Del Cid, J., Horre, W., Huygens, C., Michiels, S., Joosen, W.: LooCI: the loosely-coupled component infrastructure. In: Proceeding of the 11th IEEE International Symposium on Network Computing and Applications, pp. 236–243 (2012)
10. Jackson, M.: The meaning of requirements. Ann. Softw. Eng. 3, 5–21 (1997). http://dl.acm.org/citation.cfm?id=590564.590577
11. Kalpakis, K., Dasgupta, K., Namjoshi, P.: Maximum lifetime data gathering and aggregation in wireless sensor networks. Proc. IEEE Netw. 2, 685–696 (2002)
12. Kephart, J., Chess, D.: The vision of autonomic computing. Computer 36(1), 41–50 (2003)
13. Kramer, J., Magee, J.: Self-managed systems: an architectural challenge. In: Future of Software Engineering, FOSE 2007. IEEE Computer Society (2007)
14. de Lemos, R., et al.: Software engineering for self-adaptive systems: research challenges in the provision of assurances. In: de Lemos, R., Garlan, D., Ghezzi, C., Giese, H. (eds.) Software Engineering for Self-adaptive Systems III. LNCS, vol. 9640. Springer, Heidelberg (2018, forthcoming). https://people.cs.kuleuven.be/danny.weyns/papers/2018SEfSAS.pdf

15. de Lemos, R., et al.: Software engineering for self-adaptive systems: a second research roadmap. In: de Lemos, R., Giese, H., Müller, H.A., Shaw, M. (eds.) Software Engineering for Self-adaptive Systems II. LNCS, vol. 7475, pp. 1–32. Springer, Heidelberg (2013). https://doi.org/10.1007/978-3-642-35813-5_1

16. Mahdavi-Hezavehi, S., Avgeriou, P., Weyns, D.: A classification of current architecture-based approaches tackling uncertainty in self-adaptive systems with multiple requirements. In: Managing Trade-offs in Adaptable Software Architectures. Elsevier (2016)

17. Mainwaring, A., Culler, D., Polastre, J., Szewczyk, R., Anderson, J.: Wireless sensor networks for habitat monitoring. In: Proceedings of the 1st ACM International Workshop on Wireless Sensor Networks and Applications, WSNA 2002, pp. 88–97. ACM, New York (2002). http://doi.acm.org/10.1145/570738.570751

18. Martocci, J., Mil, P., Riou, N., Vermeylen, W.: Building automation routing requirements in low-power and lossy networks (5867) (2010)

19. Oreizy, P., Medvidovic, N., Taylor, R.: Architecture-based runtime software evolution. In: International Conference on Software Engineering, ICSE 1998. IEEE Computer Society (1998). http://dl.acm.org/citation.cfm?id=302163.302181

20. Perez-Palacin, D., Mirandola, R.: Uncertainties in the modelling of self-adaptive systems: a taxonomy and an example of availability evaluation. In: International Conference on Performance Engineering, ICPE 2014 (2014)

21. Pister, K., Thubert, P., Dwars, S., Phinney, T.: Industrial routing requirements in low-power and lossy networks. Technical report (2009)

22. Raghunathan, V., Schurgers, C., Park, S., Srivastava, M.: Energy-aware wireless microsensor networks. IEEE Sig. Process. Mag. 19(2), 40–50 (2002)

23. Rajagopalan, R., Varshney, P.: Data-aggregation techniques in sensor networks: a survey. IEEE Commun. Surv. Tutor. 8(4), 48–63 (2006)

24. Ramachandran, G.S., Matthys, N., Daniels, W., Joosen, W., Hughes, D.: Building dynamic and dependable component-based internet-of-things applications with dawn. In: 2016 19th International ACM SIGSOFT Symposium on Component-Based Software Engineering (CBSE), pp. 97–106, April 2016

25. Ramachandran, G.S., Proenca, J., Daniels, W., Pickavet, M., Staessens, D., Huygens, C., Joosen, W., Hughes, D.: Hitch hiker 2.0: a binding model with flexible data aggregation for the internet-of-things. J. Internet Serv. Appl. 7(1), 4 (2016). http://dx.doi.org/10.1186/s13174-016-0047-7

26. Salehie, M., Tahvildari, L.: Self-adaptive software: landscape and research challenges. Trans. Auton. Adapt. Syst. 4, 14:1–14:42 (2009)

27. Tan, H.O., Körpeoğlu, I.: Power efficient data gathering and aggregation in wireless sensor networks. SIGMOD Rec. 32(4), 66–71 (2003). http://doi.acm.org/10.1145/959060.959072

28. Watteyne, T., Palattella, M., Grieco, L.: Using IEEE 802.15.4e time-slotted channel hopping (TSCH) in the Internet of Things (IoT): problem statement. RFC 7554, RFC Editor, May 2015

29. Watteyne, T., Weiss, J., Doherty, L., Simon, J.: Industrial IEEE802.15.4e networks: performance and trade-offs. In: 2015 IEEE International Conference on Communications (ICC), pp. 604–609, June 2015

30. Weyns, D.: Software engineering of self-adaptive systems: an organised tour and future challenges. In: Dick Taylor, R., Kang, K., Cha, S. (eds.) Handbook of Software Engineering. Springer, Heidelberg (2018, forthcoming). https://people.cs.kuleuven.be/danny.weyns/papers/2017HSE.pdf

31. Weyns, D., et al.: Perpetual assurances in self-adaptive systems. In: de Lemos, R., Garlan, D., Ghezzi, C., Giese, H. (eds.) Software Engineering for Self-adaptive Systems III. LNCS, vol. 9640. Springer, Heidelberg (2018, forthcoming). https://people.cs.kuleuven.be/danny.weyns/papers/2016SEfSAS.pdf
32. Weyns, D., Iftikhar, U., Söderlund, J.: Do external feedback loops improve the design of self-adaptive systems? A controlled experiment. In: International Symposium on Software Engineering of Self-managing and Adaptive Systems, SEAMS 2013 (2013)
33. Weyns, D., Malek, S., Andersson, J.: FORMS: unifying reference model for formal specification of distributed self-adaptive systems. ACM Trans. Auton. Adapt. Syst. 7(1), 8:1–8:61 (2012)

Data, Information and Knowledge Engineering

LARS: A Logic-Based Framework for Analytic Reasoning over Streams
(Extended Abstract)

Harald Beck, Minh Dao-Tran, and Thomas Eiter[(✉)]

Institute of Information Systems, Vienna University of Technology,
Favoritenstraße 9-11, A-1040 Vienna, Austria
{beck,dao,eiter}@kr.tuwien.ac.at

Abstract. Stream reasoning considers continuously deriving conclusions on streaming data. While traditional stream processing approaches focus on throughput and are often based on operational grounds, reasoning approaches aim at high expressiveness based on declarative semantics; yet according theoretical underpinning in the streaming area has been lacking. To fill this gap, we provide LARS, a Logic-based Framework for Analytic Reasoning over Streams. It provides generic window operators to limit reasoning to recent snapshots of data, and modalities to control the temporal information of data. Building on resulting formulas, a rule-based language is presented which can be seen as extension of Answer Set Programming (ASP) for streams. We study semantic properties and the computational complexity of LARS, its relation to other formalisms and mention various work that builds on it.

Keywords: Answer Set Programming · Stream reasoning
Dynamic data

1 Introduction

Stream Reasoning [15,28] is an emerging field of computation with broad interest[1] in which streams of data are considered. These streams may origin in different ways and at different velocities, ranging from low frequency updates in the realm of minutes, days, or even months, to high frequency changes such as sensor data produced in real-time environment (e.g., in transport and traffic scenarios), to very high speed changes such as of bonds at the stock market. Typically, a large amount of data is produced, and processing these large data streams requires special methods and techniques.

This work has been supported by the Austrian Science Fund (FWF) projects P26471, P27730, and W1255-N23.

[1] Several workshops on this subject have been held in the recent years, e.g. in Vienna 2015 and in Berlin 2016 apart from further workshops at major conferences.

© Springer International Publishing AG 2018
A M. Tjoa et al. (Eds.): SOFSEM 2018, LNCS 10706, pp. 87–93, 2018.
https://doi.org/10.1007/978-3-319-73117-9_6

Many works in databases and data processing follow the approach of the continuous query language (CQL) [4], where only a recent snapshot of the data, a *window*, is kept and other data is dropped. If data arrives in buffers, then the size of the buffer may regulate the contents that can be handled, and only the latest data is kept (tuple-based windows); alternatively, data within a certain time of arrival are kept (time-based window). Furthermore, the way in which windows are changed over time (continuously, periodically, etc.) is another aspect of low-level data management.

2   The LARS Framework

As many stream processing systems have an operational semantics, LARS [10][2] was proposed as a logic-based framework that provides a means to express semantics of stream processing formally, and in a declarative way. Furthermore, LARS has been conceived to model more expressive reasoning than plain filtering, joining and aggregation of data.

Stream and Windows. The LARS framework evaluates streams at time points. We view a *stream* S as a pair (T, v), where the *timeline* $T \subseteq \mathbb{N}$ is a closed interval of natural numbers, and the *evaluation function* $v : T \to 2^{\mathcal{A}}$ maps each time point $t \in T$ to a (possibly empty) set of atoms. A *window function* is any computable function w that takes a stream S and a time point t and returns a substream $S' \subseteq S$, called a *window*.

Formulas. LARS adds to Boolean connectives the following syntactic elements. A unary *window operator* $\boxplus^w$ restricts the evaluation of the subsequent formula to window obtained by w. Dually, the *reset operator* $\triangleright$ re-accesses the original stream. Furthermore, temporal modalities $\Diamond$, $\Box$, and $@_{t'}$ serve to express that the subsequent formula holds at *some* time, *all* the time, and *at* the exact time t' in the current stream, respectively.

The semantics relies on *structures*, i.e., tuples $M = \langle S^\star, W, B \rangle$, where $S^\star$ is a stream, W a set of window functions, and background knowledge $B \subseteq \mathcal{A}$ are atoms. Given a substream $S = (T, v)$ of $S^\star$ and a time point $t \in \mathbb{N}$, *entailment* $M, S, t \Vdash \varphi$ of formulas φ is inductively defined as follows:

$$a \in \mathcal{A} \text{ iff } a \in v(t) \text{ or } a \in B, \qquad \Diamond\phi \text{ iff } M, S, t' \Vdash \phi \text{ for some } t' \in T,$$
$$\neg\phi \text{ iff } M, S, t \not\Vdash \phi, \qquad \Box\phi \text{ iff } M, S, t' \Vdash \phi \text{ for all } t' \in T,$$
$$\phi \wedge \psi \text{ iff } M, S, t \Vdash \phi \text{ and } M, S, t \Vdash \psi, \qquad @_{t'}\phi \text{ iff } M, S, t' \Vdash \phi \text{ and } t' \in T,$$
$$\phi \vee \psi \text{ iff } M, S, t \Vdash \phi \text{ or } M, S, t \Vdash \psi, \qquad \boxplus^w\phi \text{ iff } M, S', t \Vdash \phi, \text{where } S' = w(S, t),$$
$$\phi \to \psi \text{ iff } M, S, t \not\Vdash \phi \text{ or } M, S, t \Vdash \psi, \qquad \triangleright\phi \text{ iff } M, S^\star, t \Vdash \phi.$$

If $M, S, t \Vdash \varphi$ holds, we say that (M, S, t) *entails* φ. Moreover, we say that M *satisfies* φ at time t, if $(M, S^\star, t)$ entails φ. In this case we write $M, t \models \varphi$ and call M a *model* of φ at time t.

---

[2] An extended version with details, examples, and further results is online available [9].

Programs. Based on this, we define a LARS *program* as a set of rules of form

$$\alpha \leftarrow \beta_1, \ldots, \beta_n$$

where head α and each body element β_i $(1 \le i \le n)$ is a LARS formula. In contrast to the monotone semantics of LARS formulas, LARS programs have a stable model (answer set) semantics based on the formulation in [19]. Given an interpretation $I \supseteq D$ for a data stream $D = (T, v)$, define a *model* $M = \langle I, W, B \rangle$ program P for D at time t, denoted by $M, t \models P$, if $M, t \Vdash \beta(r) \rightarrow \alpha$ for every rule $r \in P$ of the above form, where $\beta(r) = \beta_1 \wedge \cdots \wedge \beta_n$. An *answer stream* then is a $\subseteq$-minimal model (w.r.t. I) of the *(FLP) reduct* $P^{M,t} = \{r \in P \mid M, t \models \beta(r)\}$ at time t.

Properties and complexity. LARS extends Answer Set Programming (ASP) [13,23] and inherits properties like minimality and supportedness of models; expressive features like nonmonotonic negation, recursion, or default reasoning carry over as well. The multiple model semantics is amenable to see alternative solutions by model enumeration.

Regarding computational complexity, both satisfiability and model checking are PSpace-complete for propositional (ground) LARS formulas and for LARS programs in general, but have lower complexity if either the nesting depth of window operators is bounded by a constant, or only common window operators as those mentioned above are used. In particular, reasoning in LARS is then not harder than in ASP. Notably, this includes the most practical programs which employ no window nesting. For non-ground LARS formulas and programs (i.e., the Datalog case), the complexity increases up to NExpTime^{NP} for satisfiability, but not much for model checking (for LARS formulas, it remains unchanged). Regarding expressiveness, LARS formulas express only (and in general all) polynomial time recognizable languages, while propositional LARS programs with sliding time-based windows capture the class of regular languages, i.e., all and only regular languages. As non-ground LARS programs subsume disjunctive Datalog and are not harder to evaluate, these programs capture the class of Σ_2^p recognizable languages, and are thus a rather expressive formalism.

3   Relation to Other Formalisms

Stream reasoning is naturally related to temporal logics, where usually infinite state sequences are considered, but typically no window operators. LARS formulas with sliding time-based windows can be translated into linear time temporal logic (LTL). Expressing other window functions like tuple-based windows is more involved and not possible in general for windows evaluable in polynomial time. The more expressive Metric Temporal Logic (MTL) [26] allows for time-based sliding windows with subsequent some resp. all temporal modality, but has no general window operators like LARS. It has a timed state-sequence semantics with arbitrary time increase between successive states, while LARS has a fixed (unit) time tick. In addition, MTL has as LARS formulas a monotone semantics, while the answer set semantics of LARS programs has no counterpart.

The core semantics of CQL [4], which extends SQL for streams, can be captured by LARS. Given a window function w in CQL, the stream-to-relation operator drops the timestamps of the selected tuples to obtain a relation. This amounts in LARS to a formula of form $\boxplus^w \Diamond s$, where the streaming tuple s is directly accessed. The SQL-part (on relations obtained) is then reflected by well-known Datalog translations [20]. LARS also allows us to describe the difference arising from pull-based and push-based querying in model theoretic-terms, as exemplified on the syntactically similar SPARQL extensions C-SPARQL [5] and CQELS [30] for streaming RDF data, respectively.

The explicit access to time points and generic window operators enables us to express intervals as in Allen's interval algebra [2]. Such intervals are used, e.g., in the rule-based language ETALIS [3], which aims at describing complex events (over intervals) based on events (at time points). ETALIS has a canonical model semantics and can express overlapping intervals. Streamlog [33] is another rule-based language, which extends Datalog with temporal rules. Syntactic restrictions on negation ensure unique models; mechanisms to drop data, however, are lacking. Time-decaying logic programs [21] incorporate a limited form of window mechanisms where program parts expire after a fixed number of steps. This lead to the multi-shot solving capabilities of the ASP solver Clingo [22], targeting the control of the grounding and solving processes. LARS programs, on the other hand, explicitly lift the ASP semantics for streams and provide novel language constructs than can be flexibly composed. Related are also the Linked Sensor Middleware [31] and StreamRule [27] which present system architectures.

4   Theoretical Aspects and Applications

Towards optimizations of LARS programs, different notions of equivalence in ASP and their model-theoretic characterizations [32] were lifted to LARS [8]; notably, the computational complexity of equivalence checking does not increase compared to ASP in general. Besides a tailored approach with so-called Bi-LARS models, which capture a large fragment of LARS, a variant for *monotone* windows (e.g. time-based windows) extends the logic of Here-and-There [25] and thus links LARS to Equilibrium logic [29].

Of special interest in stream reasoning, in particular for nonmonotonic languages like LARS, is incremental reasoning. Due to a partial correspondence of ASP and Doyle's [16] justification-based truth maintenance system (JTMS) [18]o, we extended the latter [24] for *plain LARS* programs, which replaces in the definition of logic programs a body atom a by an *extended atom*, given by the grammar $a \mid @_t a \mid \boxplus @_t a \mid \boxplus \Diamond a \mid \boxplus \Box a$; in the head only a or $@_t a$ is allowed. JTMS considers model update when a new rule is added; our extended data structures incorporate intervals in which formulas hold. Introducing a new concept of *stream-stratified* programs, which split the program in layers due to generic window operators, in analogy to stratified negation, we show how the acyclic flow of information can be exploited for efficient update of an answer stream.

Furthermore, incremental reasoning has been considered in [11] which elaborates how a static ASP encoding of a plain LARS program can be updated incrementally. Using JTMS as specific update technique (for the resulting model), where also removal of rules is provided, a performance benefit over repeated one-shot solving with Clingo is shown. The resulting prototype engine Ticker works for sliding time-based and sliding-tuple based windows. A slight variant of plain LARS, where negation is occurs only in front of atoms, has been employed as formal underpinning in another prototype engine called Laser [6], which extends evaluation techniques from Datalog [1]. Targeting the same windows as Ticker, it focuses on highly efficient update of the model, which is unique due to the restriction to programs with stratified negation.[3]

Further work has employed LARS as formal tool. In Content-Centric Networking (CCN) research [7] for future internet architectures, where routers can store popular content (like video chunks) for faster delivery to end users, we built a simulation architecture for switching caching strategies based on the popularity distribution of chunks. The decision control was specified in LARS and implemented using the dlvhex solver [17]. Furthermore, in [14], bridge rules of nonmonotonic multi context systems (MCS) [12] that interlink knowledge bases (contexts) were extended to streaming utilizing a fragment of LARS for processing data streams that are dynamically generated by contexts. Moreover, the semantic key concept of equilibrium was lifted in a nontrivial way to an asynchronous execution model.

5 Conclusion

LARS offers a theoretical underpinning for stream processing and reasoning approaches, based on which the declarative semantics of stream languages can be expressed, analyzed and compared. LARS programs extend ASP with explicit means to handle streams, i.e., generic window operators and temporal modalities. We highlighted some properties of the framework, its relation to other formalisms, and recent work building on LARS. The potential for future work is manifold, ranging from comparative studies, e.g., with variants of MTL, to algorithmic issues like fully incremental grounding. In particular, incremental model update, especially in the nonmonotonic setting, remains a challenging yet intriguing issue due to the trade-off between throughput and expressiveness.

References

1. Abiteboul, S., Hull, R., Vianu, V.: Foundations of Databases. Addison-Wesley, Reading (1995)
2. Allen, J.F.: Maintaining knowledge about temporal intervals. Commun. ACM **26**(11), 832–843 (1983)

---

[3] Source code: https://github.com/hbeck/ticker, https://github.com/karmaresearch/laser.

3. Anicic, D., Fodor, P., Rudolph, S., Stühmer, R., Stojanovic, N., Studer, R.: A rule-based language for complex event processing and reasoning. In: Hitzler, P., Lukasiewicz, T. (eds.) RR 2010. LNCS, vol. 6333, pp. 42–57. Springer, Heidelberg (2010). https://doi.org/10.1007/978-3-642-15918-3_5

4. Arasu, A., Babu, S., Widom, J.: The CQL continuous query language: semantic foundations and query execution. VLDB J. **15**(2), 121–142 (2006)

5. Barbieri, D.F., Braga, D., Ceri, S., Della Valle, E., Grossniklaus, M.: C-SPARQL: a continuous query language for RDF data streams. Int. J. Semant. Comput. **4**(1), 3–25 (2010)

6. Bazoobandi, H.R., Beck, H., Urbani, J.: Expressive stream reasoning with laser. In: Proceeding of ISWC (2017) (to appear). http://arxiv.org/abs/1707.08876

7. Beck, H., Bierbaumer, B., Dao-Tran, M., Eiter, T., Hellwagner, H., Schekotihin, K.: Stream reasoning-based control of caching strategies in CCN routers. In: Mao, S., Marina, M.K., Senouci, S.M. (eds.) IEEE ICC 2017 Next Generation Networking and Internet Symposium (2017).https://arxiv.org/abs/1610.04005

8. Beck, H., Dao-Tran, M., Eiter, T.: Equivalent stream reasoning programs. In: Kambhampati, S., Brewka, G. (eds.) Proceeding of 25th International Joint Conference on Artificial Intelligence, IJCAI 2016, pp. 929–935. AAAI Press/IJCAI (2016)

9. Beck, H., Dao-Tran, M., Eiter, T.: LARS: A Logic-Based Framework for Analytic Reasoning over Streams. Technical report INFSYS RR-1843-17-03, Institute of Information Systems, TU Wien, October 2017. http://www.kr.tuwien.ac.at/research/reports/rr1703.pdf

10. Beck, H., Dao-Tran, M., Eiter, T., Fink, M.: LARS: a logic-based framework for analyzing reasoning over streams. In: Bonet, B., Koenig, S. (eds.) Proceeding of 28th Conference on Artificial Intelligence, AAAI 2015, pp. 1431–1438. AAAI Press (2015)

11. Beck, H., Eiter, T., Folie, C.: Ticker: a system for incremental ASP-based stream reasoning. Theory and Practice of Logic Programming (2017) (to appear). special issue on ICLP 2017

12. Brewka, G., Eiter, T.: Equilibria in heterogeneous nonmonotonic multi-context systems. In: Proceeding of 22nd Conference on Artificial Intelligence, AAAI 2007, pp. 385–390. AAAI Press (2007)

13. Brewka, G., Eiter, T., Truszczyński, M. (eds.): AI Magazine: special issue on Answer Set Programming, vol. 37, no. 3. AAAI Press (2016) (Fall issue)

14. Dao-Tran, M., Eiter, T.: Streaming multi-context systems. In: Sierra, C., Bacchus, F. (eds.) Proceeding of 26th International Joint Conference on Artificial Intelligence, IJCAI 2017, pp. 1000–1007. IJCAI (2017)

15. Della Valle, E., Ceri, S., van Harmelen, F., Fensel, D.: It's a streaming world! reasoning upon rapidly changing information. IEEE Intell. Syst. **24**, 83–89 (2009)

16. Doyle, J.: A truth maintenance system. Artif. Intell. **12**(3), 231–272 (1979)

17. Eiter, T., Ianni, G., Fink, M., Krennwallner, T., Redl, C., Schüller, P.: A model building framework for ASP with external computations. Theory Pract. Logic Program. **16**(4), 418–464 (2016)

18. Elkan, C.: A rational reconstruction of nonmonotonic truth maintenance systems. Artif. Intell. **43**(2), 219–234 (1990)

19. Faber, W., Pfeifer, G., Leone, N.: Semantics and complexity of recursive aggregates in answer set programming. Artif. Intell. **175**(1), 278–298 (2011)

20. Garcia-Molina, H., Ullman, J.D., Widom, J.: Database Systems - The Complete Book, 2nd edn. Pearson Education, London (2009)

21. Gebser, M., Grote, T., Kaminski, R., Obermeier, P., Sabuncu, O., Schaub, T.: Stream reasoning with answer set programming. Preliminary report. In: KR, pp. 613–617 (2012)

22. Gebser, M., Kaminski, R., Kaufmann, B., Schaub, T.: Multi-shot ASP solving with clingo. CoRR abs/1705.09811 (2017). http://arxiv.org/abs/1705.09811

23. Gelfond, M., Lifschitz, V.: Classical negation in logic programs and disjunctive databases. New Gener. Comput. **9**, 365–385 (1991)

24. Beck, H., Dao-Tran, M., Eiter, T.: Answer update for rule-based stream reasoning. In: Yang, Q., Wooldridge, M. (eds.) Proceeding of 24th International Joint Conference on Artificial Intelligence, IJCAI 2015, pp. 2741–2747. AAAI Press/IJCAI (2015)

25. Heyting, A.: Die formalen Regeln der intuitionistischen Logik. In: Sitzungsberichte der Preußischen Akademie der Wissenschaften, phys.-math. Klasse, pp. 42–65, 57–71, 158–169 (1930)

26. Koymans, R.: Specifying real-time properties with metric temporal logic. Real-Time Syst. **2**(4), 255–299 (1990)

27. Mileo, A., Abdelrahman, A., Policarpio, S., Hauswirth, M.: StreamRule: a non-monotonic stream reasoning system for the semantic web. In: Faber, W., Lembo, D. (eds.) RR 2013. LNCS, vol. 7994, pp. 247–252. Springer, Heidelberg (2013). https://doi.org/10.1007/978-3-642-39666-3_23

28. Mileo, A., Dao-Tran, M., Eiter, T., Fink, M.: Stream reasoning. In: Liu, L., Özsu, M.T. (eds.) Encyclopedia of Database Systems, 2nd edn. Springer, New York (2017). https://doi.org/10.1007/978-1-4899-7993-3_80715-1

29. Pearce, D.: Equilibrium logic. Annals Math. Artif. Intell. **47**(1–2), 3–41 (2006)

30. Le-Phuoc, D., Dao-Tran, M., Xavier Parreira, J., Hauswirth, M.: A native and adaptive approach for unified processing of linked streams and linked data. In: Aroyo, L., Welty, C., Alani, H., Taylor, J., Bernstein, A., Kagal, L., Noy, N., Blomqvist, E. (eds.) ISWC 2011. LNCS, vol. 7031, pp. 370–388. Springer, Heidelberg (2011). https://doi.org/10.1007/978-3-642-25073-6_24

31. Phuoc, D.L., Nguyen-Mau, H.Q., Parreira, J.X., Hauswirth, M.: A middleware framework for scalable management of linked streams. J. Web Sem. **16**, 42–51 (2012)

32. Woltran, S.: Characterizations for relativized notions of equivalence in answer set programming. In: Alferes, J.J., Leite, J. (eds.) JELIA 2004. LNCS (LNAI), vol. 3229, pp. 161–173. Springer, Heidelberg (2004). https://doi.org/10.1007/978-3-540-30227-8_16

33. Zaniolo, C.: Logical foundations of continuous query languages for data streams. In: Barceló, P., Pichler, R. (eds.) Datalog 2.0 2012. LNCS, vol. 7494, pp. 177–189. Springer, Heidelberg (2012). https://doi.org/10.1007/978-3-642-32925-8_18

Network Analysis of the Science of Science: A Case Study in SOFSEM Conference

Antonia Gogoglou[1](✉), Theodora Tsikrika[2], and Yannis Manolopoulos[1]

[1] Department of Informatics, Aristotle University, 54124 Thessaloniki, Greece
{agogoglou,manolopo}@csd.auth.gr
[2] Centre for Research and Technology Hellas, 57001 Thessaloniki, Greece
theodora.tsikrika@iti.gr

Abstract. A rising issue in the scientific community entails the identification of temporal patterns in the evolution of the scientific enterprise and the emergence of trends that influence scholarly impact. In this direction, this paper investigates the mechanism with which citation accumulation occurs over time and how this affects the overall impact of scientific output. Utilizing data regarding the SOFSEM Conference (International Conference on Current Trends in Theory and Practice of Computer Science), we study a corpus of 1006 publications with their associated authors and affiliations to uncover the effects of collaboration network on the conference output. We proceed to group publications into clusters based on the trajectories they follow in their citation acquisition. Representative patterns are identified to characterize dominant trends of the conference, while exploring phenomena of early and late recognition by the scientific community and their correlation with impact.

Keywords: Scientometrics · Bibliographic data
Time series clustering · Trends

1 Introduction

With the extensive recording of scientific endeavors in large scale online databases and a rising interest in assessing scientific impact, the "science of science" [1] has attracted significant attention. However, the age old question in the quantification and evaluation of scientific impact still remains: Does a pattern for success exist and what can cause a publication or scholar to stand out? First, it is necessary to quantify success effectively and then investigate the process that leads to high performance levels. Since the seminal work of Eugene Garfield [10], the acknowledgment received by peers in the form of citations serves as the most straightforward measure for representing visibility and recognition by one's cohorts; therefore it is the most widely used metric for popularity. Even though many different approaches exist for measuring citations and correlating them with impact [20], the timing of each received citation is also of high importance. How do citations accumulate? Is the process unique for each individual or are

© Springer International Publishing AG 2018
A M. Tjoa et al. (Eds.): SOFSEM 2018, LNCS 10706, pp. 94–108, 2018.
https://doi.org/10.1007/978-3-319-73117-9_7

there identifiable trends and, if so, how do they relate to impact? What is the role of collaboration in citation acquisition?

Across different scientific disciplines, countries and performance levels, the process of accumulating citation varies widely. Efforts have focused on profiling scholars and their publications to compartmentalize their growth and identify similarities amongst seemingly unrelated scientific entities (e.g. publications from different authors or time periods). In [4] an extensive study of Computer Science publications revealed six dominant categories based on their citation attraction process and associated this categorization with year of publication, publishing venue and topological features of the citation network. At author level, in [11], five scholarly profiles were distinguished for Computer Scientists in terms of temporal evolution and their overall impact was correlated with frequency of publications ("publish or perish effect" [8]). Grouping of scientific entities in profiles proves to be of assistance to the estimation of future impact evolution [3,7], since past behavior may not only determine current but also future status. Given the diversity of observed profiles, building a specialized prediction model for each profile can produce more accurate predictions.

Modeling citation trajectories as spatio-temporal objects can shed light into the process that leads to success. More specifically, the citation time series of a paper reveals whether the number of citations increases steadily, or it saturates after some time, or whether the paper seems to receive a belated citation explosion. Citation time series have been utilized for identifying scientific breakthroughs [17,21], while entire citation networks have been studied accounting for temporal degeneracy [5]. Focusing specifically on the timing of citation shifts [9], citation cascades have been associated with paradigm shifting in scientific discoveries [15]. These cascading events were also found to reveal unique patterns, such as the "sleeping beauty" effect [13] where a publication exhibits a long hibernation period before receiving recognition or early discoveries, where a citation boost occurs soon after publication [6]. It turns out that these distinguishing citation patterns do not constitute an isolated scarce phenomenon, but occur often in science highly affecting careers, future visibility and even award giving or fund allocation.

The real challenge in these efforts is to determine a trend given the diversity of publishing behaviors that arise in science. Essentially, fair comparisons need to be computed amongst publishing and citing patterns of scientists of different age and background in different time periods. In this work, we attempt to tackle this challenge and contemplate the following research questions:

– What is the dominant trend in the temporal evolution of publications in e.g. a particular conference? Are they steady, rising or decaying over time?
– When does the peak of citations occur for most publications and does increased output mean deviation from trends?
– And finally, is there a correlation between these temporal patterns and the total output or other academic features (e.g. affiliations)?

To address the aforementioned questions, we contemplate the temporal popularity dynamics of the citation curves for individual publications associated with the SOFSEM conference[1]. We conduct a bibliometric analysis of the conference records and identify prominent participants, frequent contributors and associated communities. Next, we extract citation curves from the historical data of the conference; a *citation curve* is defined as the set of points that represent citations acquired at given time steps (e.g. yearly). We attempt to fit these curves into representative profiles, while characterizing the members in each profile according to their collective output, set of authors, and associated affiliations. Indeed, our goal is not to perfectly model the popularity evolution of all possible trajectories, but rather capture the most prevalent tendencies based on shape similarity, regardless of differences in amplitude and phase. We build upon similar efforts that address online content growth as a time series pattern mining problem studying how different pieces of user generated content compete for attention in mircoblogs (e.g. Twitter) [22]. Apart from the shape of the total curve, we additionally micro-analyze the timing of shifts in the time series of citations to comprehend the mechanism causing citation boosts and how it relates to the total impact.

The rest of the paper is organized as follows: Sect. 2 describes the process for collecting the data, while Sect. 3 provides an overview of our bibliometric analysis for the SOFSEM conference. Section 4 focuses on the temporal evaluation of publications and Sect. 5 concludes the article.

2   Data Acquisition

SOFSEM (SOFtware SEMinar) was first held in 1974 as a local Czechoslovakian event to bring together theorists and practitioners of computing. Since 1995 it has been steadily evolving into a fully-fledged annual multidisciplinary international conference on Current Trends in Theory and Practice of Informatics with participants from multiple European countries including UK, France, Germany, and Spain. For the next 21 years, the conference location has alternated between Czech Republic and Slovakia, while in 2017 it was first held in a different location (Limerick, Ireland). Since 1995, the conference proceedings have featured in the Lecture Notes in Computer Science (LNCS) series by Springer.

To obtain the SOFSEM 1995–2017 publication data, the DBLP XML dump [14] (as downloaded on June 23, 2017) was processed using appropriate XQuery queries that featured the "conf/sofsem" keyword. This led to the collection of 1027 publication titles in the *main* SOFSEM proceedings (i.e., excluding papers/posters published in the SOFSEM Student Research Forum proceedings) over 22 years[2], resulting in an average of 47 publications per year. The next step was to gather metadata and citation records on these publications.

Regarding the citation data, many online data sources are available, either proprietary, such as the Web of Science[3] by Clarivate Analytics and Scopus[4]

---

[1] https://link.springer.com/conference/sofsem.

[2] The SOFSEM 2003 proceedings are not listed in DBLP and thus omitted from this study.

[3] https://apps.webofknowledge.com/.

[4] https://www.scopus.com/.

by Elsevier, or open source ones, such as Google Scholar[5] and Microsoft Academic[6]. Each follows a different data collection policy that affects both the publications covered and the number of citations found, while differences in their coverage may affect the assessment of scholarly impact metrics [12]. For the purposes of our analysis, we focused on freely available databases that do not require subscriptions and we opted for the newly introduced Beta 2.0 version of Microsoft Academic. Even though Google Scholar also offers wide coverage of citation records, Microsoft includes a more structured collection of scientific entities (conferences, journals, author and institutional profiles). Therefore, we queried its database for the publication titles collected from DBLP adding the keyword SOFSEM, since publications with the same title are often published later on in other venues (e.g. journals) as well. Additionally, Microsoft Academic offers author profiles which alleviates author name disambiguation issues that often arise in other citation databases. Out of the original publication set, 1006 publication titles (98%) were identified in Microsoft Academic and their publication year, authors with related affiliations, as well as yearly citation records were obtained.

3   Bibliometric Analysis

First, we conduct a bibliometric analysis of the records collected to identify the most prominent participants in the conference over the years, the diversity of participants and their institutions and explore the dynamics of collaboration amongst them. Table 1 illustrates the highest ranking publication based on various citation rates (total, average and peak), while Tables 2 and 3 illustrate, respectively, authors and institutions with the highest participation rates in the conference and the biggest impact, as measured by the total citations acquired by their publications in SOFSEM. An interesting observation in the selected publication titles is that the ones with the highest total citation count are not necessarily the ones that received the biggest boost in citations or the ones with a steady average citation rate over the years. This leads us to the realization that different citation patterns can lead to increased overall impact. Another intriguing finding regarding authors and their affiliated institutions is that high productivity, meaning a high participation rate, does not guarantee a higher impact level. Therefore the question rises, what makes an author stand out in this conference?

To explore the presence of each author amongst their collaborators and the effects of it on their impact, we created the co-authorship network that is represented as an undirected graph where nodes correspond to authors and edges correspond to a co-authored publication. The resulting graph is depicted in Fig. 1 filtered by size and color based on two centrality metrics: *degree* and *betweeness* centrality. *Degree centrality* is computed by counting the neighbors of each node, whereas *betweeness centrality* is equal to the number of shortest paths from all

---

[5] https://scholar.google.com.
[6] http://academic.research.microsoft.com/.

Table 1. Top rated publications in the SOFSEM proceedings.

# Total citations		
Chevaleyre et al.: A short introduction to computational social choice	2007	155
Appelt: WWW based collaboration with the BSCW system	1999	143
Rahman & Iliopoulos: Indexing factors with gaps	2007	136
Allauzen et al.: factor oracle: a new structure for pattern matching	1999	115
Bodlaender: Discovering treewidth	2005	115
# Average citations		
Chevaleyre et al.: A short introduction to computational social choice	2007	14
Lee et al.: Efficient group key agreement for dynamic TETRA networks	2007	13
Rahman & Iliopoulos: Indexing factors with gaps	2007	12
Navigli: A quick tour of word sense disambiguation	2012	11
Dolog: Designing adaptive web applications	2008	8
# Citations peak		
Lee et al.: Efficient group key agreement for dynamic TETRA networks	2007	34
Chevaleyre et al.: A short introduction to computational social choice	2007	28
Rahman & Iliopoulos: Indexing factors with gaps	2007	22
Appelt: WWW based collaboration with the BSCW system	1999	20
Navigli: A quick tour of word sense disambiguation	2012	16

Table 2. Most prolific and cited authors

# Publications		# Citations	
Mária Bieliková	11	Yann Chevaleyre	155
Costas S. Iliopoulos	7	Ulle Endriss	155
Shunsuke Inenaga	7	Nicolas Maudet	155
Friedrich Otto	7	M. Sohel Rahman	152
Henning Fernau	6	Costas S. Iliopoulos	146

Table 3. Most prolific and cited institutions

# Publications		# Citations	
Charles University in Prague	64	ETH Zurich	662
Slovak Univ. of Technology in Bratislava	50	King's College London	449
University of Latvia	49	University of Amsterdam	392
Masaryk University	47	University of Latvia	318
ETH Zurich	40	Lamsade (Univ. Paris-Dauphine)	316

Fig. 1. Visualization of the SOFSEM co-authorship network, with darker colored nodes representing high number of authored publications and bigger sized nodes representing higher betweeness centrality values.

nodes to all others that pass through that specific node (i.e. author). *Closeness centrality* was also calculated for the participating authors, which is the mean distance from a node to others. For our co-authorship graph, as it contained a number of disconnected nodes, we utilized the harmonic mean to calculate representative values for the closeness centrality [18]. Essentially a high degree centrality indicates a scientist with a large number of co-authors, while betweeness centrality gives highest values to individuals through whom information is more likely to pass, i.e. they bridge different groups of collaborators. Closeness centrality, in turn, highlights the actors who will be able to contact easily all other members of the network, meaning they share many common collaborators with other participants. As seen in Fig. 1, a large number of small author communities appear that are seemingly disconnected from the rest of the network. We observe though some densely connected groups formed around nodes with high betweeness centrality further indicating these nodes' level of influence.

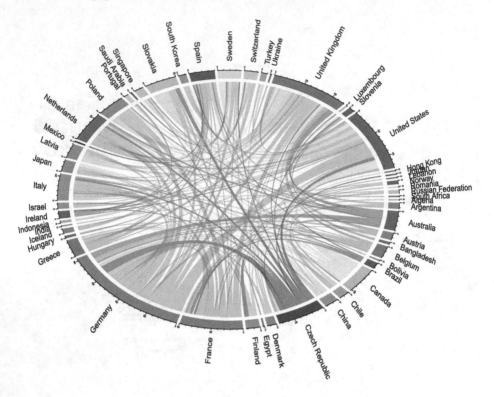

Fig. 2. Co-authorship network based on the countries of the authors' affiliations.

We also performed a similar analysis on a higher level of granularity by considering the co-authorship network where the nodes correspond to the countries of the authors' affiliations and edges to the co-authored publications. The analyzed SOFSEM publications were collaboratively produced by authors affiliated with institutions in 55 countries. Figure 2 shows the collaborations between the different countries in the SOFSEM community and depicts 51 countries and 158 edges. The most prolific country in terms of publications (Germany) is also the most extrovert with the most collaborations. On the other hand, the second most prolific country in terms of publications authored (Czech Republic) is fifth in terms of collaborations, indicating a more conservative approach.

Apart from collaboration relationships, we identify the set of authors that have consistently participated in SOFSEM and received high recognition to distinguish the patterns that led to their increased status. The citation time series of the selected authors are included in Table 4 along with their closeness and betweeness centrality values. The selected scientists are ranked in descending order of publication number (size of citation vector) in SOFSEM conference. As we observe, they appear to follow very different citation patterns, with some achieving high boosts in citations (e.g. Keith G. Jeffrey) while others displaying a moderate but steady rate (e.g. Michal Barla). However, the majority of the selected prominent scientists share high values in betweeness centrality indicating that obtaining strategic collaborations with scientists from diverse coauthorship groups and bridging them together is the most effective pattern for overall increased visibility and popularity. On the other hand, establishing multiple co-authorship relationships (higher closeness centrality) appears to have little effect on impact.

Table 4. Citation records, closeness and betweeness centrality values for authors with more than 2 SOFSEM publications and more than 10 citations overall.

Author name	Citation vector	Closeness centrality	Betweeness centrality
Costas S. Iliopoulos	[136, 1, 11, 1, 0, 0, 16]	1.25	22
Keith G. Jeffrey	[143, 1, 0, 2, 0]	1.00	12
Hans L. Bodlaender	[115, 1, 0, 0, 4]	1.00	17
Juraj Hromkovi	[0, 11, 56, 0, 5]	1.25	45
Petr Jancar	[12, 0, 13, 30]	1.30	3
Michal Barla	[6, 7, 13, 20]	2.00	74.3
Hans-Joachim Bckenhauer	[1, 11, 56, 1]	1.00	12.5
Nieves R. Brisaboa	[0, 17, 39]	1.80	9
Oscar Pedreira	[0, 17, 39]	1.00	22
Michal Tvaroek	[6, 13, 20]	2.60	6
Maxime Crochemore	[115, 11, 1]	1.00	9
Wojciech Rytter	[0, 11, 27]	1.42	1
Johannes Uhlmann	[17, 5, 12]	1.40	1
Ngoc Thanh Nguyen	[27, 5, 1]	1.00	3

Next, we will explore the patterns that lead to high impact at publication level and how they correspond to author impact.

4   Temporal Dynamics of Scholarly Impact

Time-series sequences, such as citation curves, advance with respect to two axis, time and scale (or magnitude). We propose two different approaches to study a set of such sequences and identify temporal patterns: one is macroscopic focusing on the *shape* of the resulting curves regardless of citation scale or timing of shifts, while the other one is microscopic contemplating the *relationship* between magnitude of citations and the timing of occurrence. The result of the first approach is a set of profiles of publications going through similar stages of impact.

The second approach provides a different categorization of publications with respect to the timing of their recognition and their aging process.

4.1 Publication Profiles

The need for clustering time series with scale- and shift-invariant methods has emerged in multiple fields, such as business, social media, medicine, biology, etc. [11,16], with the goal to identify and summarize interesting patterns and correlations in the underlying data. In this work, we employ a recently proposed time series clustering algorithm called K-spectral clustering (KSC) [22] that has been utilized to discover common trends in the spread of online content. The KSC algorithm groups times series based on the shape of the curve and thus respects invariants of scale in the popularity axis and shifts in the time axis. That is, two entities that have their popularity evolving according to similar processes (e.g. linear growth) will be assigned to the same cluster by KSC, regardless of the popularity values. KSC requires that all time series are comprised of the same number of points.

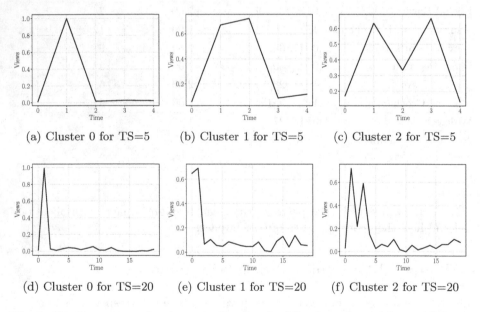

(a) Cluster 0 for TS=5   (b) Cluster 1 for TS=5   (c) Cluster 2 for TS=5

(d) Cluster 0 for TS=20   (e) Cluster 1 for TS=20   (f) Cluster 2 for TS=20

Fig. 3. Citation patterns for the centroids of each of the three clusters for two different time spans: short-term $TS = 5$ (top) and long-term $TS = 20$ (bottom).

Regarding the citation vectors, we represent each publication with a series of t points each corresponding to the citations this particular publication acquired in one particular year, starting from its publication year. Because publication

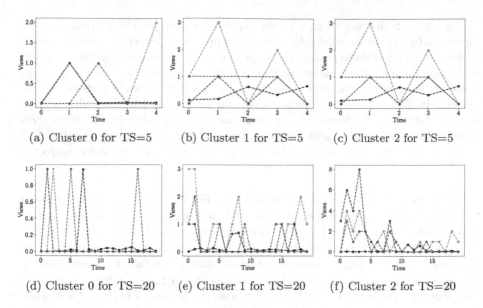

(a) Cluster 0 for TS=5   (b) Cluster 1 for TS=5   (c) Cluster 2 for TS=5

(d) Cluster 0 for TS=20   (e) Cluster 1 for TS=20   (f) Cluster 2 for TS=20

Fig. 4. Four examples of members from each of the three clusters for two different time spans: short-term $TS = 5$ (top) and long-term $TS = 20$ (bottom).

ages vary from 1 to 22 for our given time period (1995–2017), we define four time spans ($t = TS$) that correspond to the minimum age of the publications included in each span and consider only the first t years of a publication's life. We consider $TS = 5, 10, 15$ *and* 20 years so that patterns for both long- and short-term impact can be studied. A predefined number of clusters k also needs to be determined and in our case we opted for $k = 3$ based on optimal inter- and intra-cluster distance amongst publications.

The implementation of KSC we adopted[7] closely resembles the classic k-means but with a different definition for the distance metric. The similarity between two vectors x and y (in our case of citations) is calculated as follows:

$$d(x,y) = \min_{a,q} \frac{||x - \alpha y_{(q)}||}{||x||} \tag{1}$$

where $y_{(q)}$ represents the shift of vector y by q units and $||.||$ the l^2-norm [2]. In the above dual minimization problem there is no straightforward way to compute q; therefore, we follow a heuristic proposed in the original paper [22] that includes searching for the optimal value of q in the range of all integers $(-t, t)$, where t is the size of the time series, as mentioned above. Given a fixed q, the exact solution for α can be obtained by computing the minimum distance d from Eq. 1.

---

[7] http://github.com/flaviovdf/pyksc

By shifting citation vectors to find optimal values for the distance metric, we were able to match publications to three prevalent patterns. The interesting finding here is that these patterns, as represented by the cluster centroids, appear to be similar over time, meaning that analogous patterns are identified when contemplating either the first 5 or 20 years of a publication's history. As can be seen in Fig. 3, the three patterns can be summarized as one with a steep peak (referred to as cluster 0), another one with a peak followed by a more smooth decay (cluster 1) and, finally, a curve with two prominent peaks and a relatively steady acquisition rate (cluster 2). Figure 4 displays four examples of citation trajectories from each cluster for two selected time spans ($TS = 5$ and 20 years).

How do these patterns relate to impact? Fig. 5 depicts the distribution of total citation count for each cluster over all time spans. A clear pattern here is that cluster 2 is associated with higher citation counts, whereas cluster 0 that includes single peak publications leads to lower overall impact. Therefore, one can assume that a single boost of citations does not relate to actual impact, whereas a pattern of multiple peaks amongst a steady rate of citations indicates an influential publication over time. But does the timing of the peak/s matter?

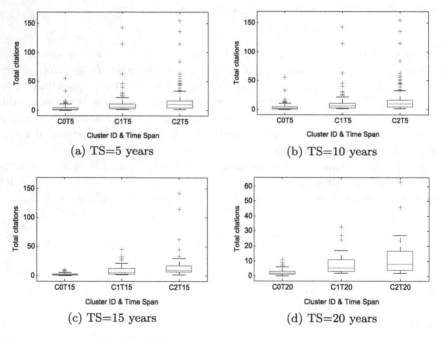

Fig. 5. Boxplots of total citation counts for all three clusters for each of the four time spans; e.g. C0T5 represents cluster 0 at time span equal to 5 years.

4.2   Publication Recognition: Timing and Aging

In this subsection, we explore the timing of citation shifts and the aging process of publications. Studies examining citation patterns have identified different behaviors of early recognition or long hibernation periods for publications. As introduced in [19], a metric to calculate the obsolescence of publications, without examining each citation curve individually to identify shifts, is defined as:

$$G_s = 1 - \frac{2 \times [n \times C_1 + (n-1) \times C_2 + ... + C_n] - C}{C \times n} \tag{2}$$

where n is the age of a publication, C is the total number of citations, and C_i corresponds to the citations until the ith year. We refer to G_s as the *aging coefficient* and dependent on its calculated values, we can assign publications to groups related to the timing of their recognition.

For the purposes of our study and given the citation rates observed in our dataset, we employ the following thresholds to define three distinct *timing* categories for publications with "extra-ordinary" citation trajectories:

- $0.1 < G_s < 1$ and $C > 10$ indicates a *sleeping beauty*, meaning a publication that received recognition after a long period of time;
- $G_s < 0$ and $C > 10$ indicates a *flash in a pan*, meaning a publication that received a citation boost soon after its release; and
- $0 < G_s < 0.05$ and $C > 10$ indicates an *aging gracefully* publication, meaning it maintains a steady citation rate for longer periods.

Table 5 contains information on publications categorized in one of the above groups based on their aging coefficient. We observe highly prestigious institutions and authors in all three categories indicating that the timing of impact does not directly relate to the size of impact. Moreover, one of the most seminal publications of the conference, "A Short Introduction to Computational Social Choice", managed to acquire citations steadily leading to a graceful aging period, while another highly popular publication, "Automatic Testing of Object-Oriented Software", appears to have acquired 59 citations in total with the majority of them occurring soon after publication. On the other hand, a comprehensive survey by A. Goldberg, "Point-to-Point Shortest Path Algorithms with Preprocessing", did not rise in popularity until several years after publication. Looking into the citation ranges and the categories that mostly populate them in Fig. 6, we further realize that publications from all categories can obtain high citation counts, with a slight competitive edge attributed to the flashes in a pan category.

Table 5. Examples of publications belonging to each timing category based on the timing of their recognition including title, authors and affiliations.

Category	Titles and # of citations	Authors
Flashes in a pan	Automatic testing of object-oriented software (59)	Bertrand Meyer Ilinca Ciupa Andreas Leitner Lisa Ling Liu (ETH Zurich)
	Sample method for minimization of OBDDs (27)	Anna Slobodova (Comenius University in Bratislava), Christoph Meinel (Università Potsdam)
	Improving watermark resistance against removal attacks using orthogonal wavelet adaptation (40)	Jan Stolarek (University of Edinburh), Piotr Lipiski (University of Edinburh)
	Explicit connectors in component based software engineering for distributed embedded systems (16)	Dietmar Schreiner (Vienna University of Technology), Karl M. Gschka (Vienna University of Technology)
Sleeping beauties	On the NP-completeness of some graph cluster measures (50)	Jiri Sima (Academy of Sciences Czech Republic), Satu Elisa Schaeffer (Helsinki University of Technology)
	Domain engineering: a software engineering discipline in need of research (11)	Dines Bjrner (Technical University of Denmark)
	Fuzzy set theory and medical expert systems: survey and model (14)	Nguyen Hoang Phuong (Academy of Sciences Czech Republic)
	Point-to-point shortest path algorithms with preprocessing (25)	Andrew V. Goldberg (Microsoft)
Aging gracefully	A short introduction to computational social choice (155)	Yann Chevaleyre (Lamsade), Ulle Endriss (University of Amsterdam), Jrme Lang (Centre national de la recherche scientifique), Nicolas Maudet (Lamsade)
	Complexity of model checking for modal dependence logic (21)	Johannes Ebbing (Leibniz University of Hanover), Peter Lohmann (Leibniz University of Hanover)
	Spatial selection of sparse pivots for similarity search in metric spaces (39)	Oscar Pedreira (University of A Corua), Nieves R. Brisaboa (University of A Corua)
	Recent challenges and ideas in temporal synthesis (13)	Orna Kupferman (Hebrew University of Jerusalem)

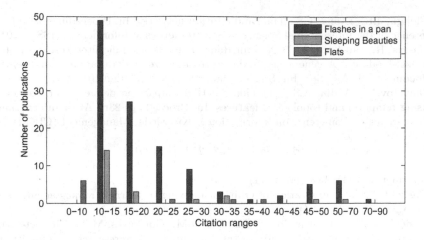

Fig. 6. Number of publications from each timing category that belong to various citation ranges.

5 Conclusions

In this work, we conducted a bibliometric analysis of publication and citation records of the SOFSEM conference to determine the mechanism that leads to high impact scientific output. Exploring the effects of affiliations and co-authorship we realized that scientists bridging together different communities through collaboration are more likely to produce popular publications. We then focused on identifying citation patterns over the years and an interesting finding was that there exist three distinct trajectory patterns in citation acquisition for both long- and short-term impact irrespective of timing and magnitude of popularity. Going one step further, we revealed publications with different timing in receiving recognition and concluded that the timing of citation boosts does not correlate to impact in the same degree as the overall shape of the citation time series. Therefore, increased popularity is mostly achieved by publications that obtain multiple citation sprees and manage to age gracefully over time.

References

1. Börner, K., Dall'Asta, L., Ke, W., Vespignani, A.: Studying the emerging global brain: analyzing and visualizing the impact of co-authorship teams. Complexity **10**(4), 57–67 (2005)
2. Bourbaki, N., Eggleston, H., Madan, S.: Topological Vector Spaces. Éléments de mathématique. Springer, Heidelberg (1987)
3. Chakraborty, T., Kumar, S., Goyal, P., Ganguly, N., Mukherjee, A.: Towards a stratified learning approach to predict future citation counts. In: Proceedings 14th ACM/IEEE-CS Joint Conference on Digital Libraries (JCDL), pp. 351–360 (2014)
4. Chakraborty, T., Kumar, S., Goyal, P., Ganguly, N., Mukherjee, A.: On the categorization of scientific citation profiles in computer science. Communi. ACM **58**(9), 82–90 (2015)

5. Clough, J.R., Evans, T.S.: Time and citation networks. In: Proceedings 16th Conference of the International Society of Scientometrics & Informetrics (ISSI) (2015)
6. Costas, R., van Leeuwen, T.N., van Raan, A.F.: Is scientific literature subject to a 'sell-by-date'? A general methodology to analyze the "durability" of scientific documents. J. Am. Soc. Inf. Sci. Technol. **61**(2), 329–339 (2010)
7. Davletov, F., Aydin, A.S., Cakmak, A.: High impact academic paper prediction using temporal and topological features. In: Proceedings 23rd ACM International Conference on Conference on Information & Knowledge Management (CIKM), pp. 491–498 (2014)
8. Publish or perish: Editorial. Nature **467**, 252–252 (2010)
9. Egghe, L., Bornmann, L., Guns, R.: A proposal for a first-citation-speed-index. J. Informetrics **5**(1), 181–186 (2011)
10. Garfield, E.: The application of citation indexing to journals management. Curr. Contents **33**, 3–5 (1994)
11. Gonçalves, G.D., Figueiredo, F., Almeida, J.M., Gonçalves, M.A.: Characterizing scholar popularity: a case study in the computer science research community. In: Proceedings IEEE/ACM Joint Conference on Digital Libraries (JCDL), pp. 57–66 (2014)
12. Harzing, A., Alakangas, S.: Google scholar, scopus and the web of science: a longitudinal and cross-disciplinary comparison. Scientometrics **106**(2), 787–804 (2016)
13. Ke, Q., Ferrara, E., Radicchi, F., Flammini, A.: Defining and identifying sleeping beauties in science. Proc. Natl. Acad. Sci. **112**(24), 7426–7431 (2015)
14. Ley, M.: DBLP: some lessons learned. Proc. VLDB Endowment **2**(2), 1493–1500 (2009)
15. Mazloumian, A., Eom, Y., Helbing, D., Lozano, S., Fortunato, S.: How citation boosts promote scientific paradigm shifts and nobel prizes. PLoS ONE **6**(5), 1–6 (2011)
16. Paparrizos, J., Gravano, L.: k-shape: efficient and accurate clustering of time series. In: Proceedings ACM International Conference on Management of Data (SIGMOD), pp. 1855–1870 (2015)
17. Revesz, P.Z.: A method for predicting citations to the scientific publications of individual researchers. In: Proceedings 18th International Database Engineering & Applications Symposium (IDEAS), pp. 9–18 (2014)
18. Rochat, Y.: Closeness centrality extended to unconnected graphs: the harmonic centrality index. In: ASNA, No. EPFL-CONF-200525 (2009)
19. Sun, J., Min, C., Li, J.: A vector for measuring obsolescence of scientific articles. Scientometrics **107**(2), 745–757 (2016)
20. Wildgaard, L., Schneider, J.W., Larsen, B.: A review of the characteristics of 108 author-level bibliometric indicators. Scientometrics **101**(1), 125–158 (2014)
21. Wolcott, H.N., Fouch, M.J., Hsu, E.R., DiJoseph, L.G., Bernaciak, C.A., Corrigan, J.G., Williams, D.E.: Modeling time-dependent and-independent indicators to facilitate identification of breakthrough research papers. Scientometrics **107**(2), 807–817 (2016)
22. Yang, J., Leskovec, J.: Patterns of temporal variation in online media. In: Proceedings 4th ACM International Conference on Web Search and Data Mining (WSDM), pp. 177–186 (2011)

Network Science and Parameterized Complexity

The Parameterized Complexity of Centrality Improvement in Networks

Clemens Hoffmann[1], Hendrik Molter[1], and Manuel Sorge[1,2]([✉])

[1] Institut für Softwaretechnik und Theoretische Informatik,
TU Berlin, Berlin, Germany
h.molter@tu-berlin.de
[2] Department of Industrial Engineering and Management,
Ben-Gurion University of the Negev, Beer Sheva, Israel
sorge@post.bgu.ac.il

Abstract. The centrality of a vertex v in a network intuitively captures how important v is for communication in the network. The task of improving the centrality of a vertex has many applications, as a higher centrality often implies a larger impact on the network or less transportation or administration cost. In this work we study the parameterized complexity of the NP-complete problems CLOSENESS IMPROVEMENT and BETWEENNESS IMPROVEMENT in which we ask to improve a given vertex' closeness or betweenness centrality by a given amount through adding a given number of edges to the network. Herein, the closeness of a vertex v sums the multiplicative inverses of distances of other vertices to v and the betweenness sums for each pair of vertices the fraction of shortest paths going through v. Unfortunately, for the natural parameter "number of edges to add" we obtain hardness results, even in rather restricted cases. On the positive side, we also give an island of tractability for the parameter measuring the vertex deletion distance to cluster graphs.

1 Introduction

Measuring the centrality of a given vertex in a network has attracted the interest of researchers since the second half of the 20th century [11], see Newman's book [16] for an overview. There are various interpretations of what makes a vertex more central than another vertex in a network. Two popular measures for the centrality of a vertex z are *closeness centrality* c_z and *betweenness centrality* b_z [11]. They are based on the distances of the given vertex z to the remaining vertices and on the number of shortest paths going through z, respectively.

MS supported by the People Programme (Marie Curie Actions) of the European Union's Seventh Framework Programme (FP7/2007–2013) under REA grant agreement number 631163.11 and the Israel Science Foundation (grant no. 551145/14).

A. M. Tjoa et al. (Eds.): SOFSEM 2018, LNCS 10706, pp. 111–124, 2018.
https://doi.org/10.1007/978-3-319-73117-9_8

$$c_z = \sum_{\substack{u \in V \\ d(u,z) < \infty \\ u \neq z}} \frac{1}{d(z,u)} \qquad\qquad b_z = \sum_{\substack{s,t \in V \\ s \neq t; s,t \neq z \\ \sigma_{st} \neq 0}} \frac{\sigma_{stz}}{\sigma_{st}}$$

Herein, $d(s,t)$ is the distance between two vertices s and t, that is, the number of edges on a shortest s-t path, σ_{st} is the number of shortest s-t paths, and σ_{stz} is the number of shortest s-t paths that contain z. Intuitively, if z has many close-by vertices, then its closeness centrality is large, and if z is on shortest paths between many vertices, then its betweenness centrality is large. The closeness centrality as defined above is also known as the *harmonic centrality*.[1]

Analyzing vertex centrality in networks has been studied intensively (e.g. [4,11,16–18]) and comprises a diverse set of applications in, e.g., biological [21], economic [19], and social networks [11].

Some examples: A transport company might be interested in placing its depots centrally such that the transportation costs are rather low. The value of an airport might be influenced by its centrality in the flight-connection network between airports. The most central nodes in a computer network may be useful for determining the locations of data centers where the routes are short and peering costs are low. In social networks, economically important influencers are presumably more central than other users.

Since it is so desirable to find vertices with large centrality in a graph, vertices have incentive to improve their own centrality. E.g., a social network member might want to increase her impact on other users by increasing her own centrality, or an airport operator wants to increase the appeal of her airport for investors (as measured by the centrality). In both cases, natural operations are to introduce new links into the network, i.e., to make new acquaintances or incentivise airlines to offer certain routes. In this work, we hence study the complexity of improving the centrality of a given vertex by introducing new links into the network. Formally, the computational problems that we study are defined as follows.

CLOSENESS (BETWEENNESS) IMPROVEMENT

Input: An undirected, unweighted graph $G = (V, E)$, a vertex $z \in V$, an integer k and a rational number r.
Question: Is there an edge set S, $S \cap E = \emptyset$, of size at most k such that $c_z \geq r$ ($b_z \geq r$) in $G + S := (V, E \cup S)$?

We also say that an edge set S as above is a *solution*.

The above two problems were introduced by Crescenzi et al. [5] and D'Angelo et al. [8], respectively, who gave approximation algorithms and showed that their empirical approximation ratios are close to one on random graphs with up to 100 vertices and up to 1000 vertices, respectively. In a corresponding presentation Crescenzi et al. [5] noted that finding the optimal solution for comparison was

---

[1] There are several definitions for closeness centrality in the literature. We use the present one because it is natural [16] and it was used in closely related work [5].

very time consuming. Here, we study the parameterized complexity of CLOSE-NESS IMPROVEMENT and BETWEENNESS IMPROVEMENT with the ultimate goal to design efficient exact algorithms. That is, we aim to find *fixed-parameter (FPT) algorithms* with running time $f(k) \cdot n^{O(1)}$, where n is the input length and k is some secondary measure, called *parameter*, or we show W[1] or W[2]-hardness, meaning that there are presumably no FPT algorithms.

Our Results. Our results for CLOSENESS IMPROVEMENT are as follows. From two reductions from DOMINATING SET it follows that CLOSENESS IMPROVEMENT is NP-hard on (disconnected) planar graphs with maximum degree 3 and W[2]-hard with respect to k, the number of added edges, on disconnected split graphs, for example (Corollary 2). Split graphs are a simple model of core-periphery structure, which occurs in social and biological networks [6]. In particular, we can derive that a straightforward $n^{O(k)}$-time algorithm for CLOSENESS IMPROVE-MENT is asymptotically optimal. Motivated by the fact that social networks often have small diameter in conjunction with small H-index [9], we show that CLOSENESS IMPROVEMENT remains NP-hard on (connected) graphs of diameter at most 6 and H-index 4 (Theorem 2). On the positive side, we show that CLOSENESS IMPROVEMENT allows a fixed-parameter algorithm with respect to the parameter *distance to cluster graph*, that is, the smallest number of vertices to delete in order to obtain a cluster graph. DIRECTED CLOSENESS IMPROVE-MENT is NP-hard and W[2]-hard with respect to k even if the input graph is acyclic (Theorem 4) or has diameter 4 (Theorem 5).

For BETWEENNESS IMPROVEMENT the picture is similar. It is W[2]-hard with respect to k (Theorem 6) also in the directed case (Theorem 8), NP-hard for graphs of H-index 4 (Corollary 5), and BETWEENNESS IMPROVEMENT is f ixed-parameter tractable with respect to k and the distance to cluster graph combined. Due to space constraints, results marked by $*$ are deferred to a full version.

Preliminaries and Notation. We use standard notation from graph theory [20]. Throughout, we refer to the number of vertices as n and to the number of edges (arcs) as m. For two vertices u, v we denote by $d(u, v)$ the *distance* between u and v, i.e. the number of edges on a shortest path from u to v. If u and v are not connected by a path, then $d(u, v) = \infty$. A *split graph* allows for a partition of the vertex set into a clique and an independent set. In a *cluster graph* each connected component is a clique. The *diameter* of a graph is ∞ if it is disconnected and the maximum distance of any two vertices otherwise. The *H-index* of a graph is the largest integer h such that there h vertices of degree at least h.

We also use standard notation from parameterized complexity [7]. Importantly, a *parameterized reduction* from a parameterized problem $L \subseteq \Sigma^* \times \mathbb{N}$ with parameter k to a problem $L' \subseteq \Sigma^* \times \mathbb{N}$ with parameter k' is a $g(k) \cdot |I|^{O(1)}$-time computable function $f : \Sigma^* \times \mathbb{N} \to \Sigma^* \times \mathbb{N} : (I, k) \to (I', k')$ such that $k' \leq h(k)$ for some computable function h and $(I, k) \in L \Leftrightarrow (I', k') \in L'$.

The *Exponential Time Hypothesis* roughly states that satisfiability of a Boolean formula in conjunctive normal form with clauses of size 3 cannot be decided in $2^{o(n)}$ time, see Impagliazzo and Paturi [13], Impagliazzo et al. [14].

2   Closeness Centrality

In this section, we present algorithmic and hardness results for CLOSENESS IMPROVEMENT. First, we make an important observation that will help us in our proofs. Intuitively, we show that to improve the closeness of a vertex by adding edges, it always makes sense to add only edges adjacent to that vertex. From this observation we get an XP algorithm with respect to k.

Lemma 1 ($*$). *Let $I = (G = (V, E), z, k, r)$ be a CLOSENESS IMPROVEMENT instance. If I is a YES-instance, then c_z can be increased to r by adding at most k edges, all of which contain z.*

Corollary 1. CLOSENESS IMPROVEMENT *is solvable in $O(n^k \cdot (n + m))$ time where k is the number of edge additions, and thus is in XP with respect to k.*

Hardness Results. Next, we present several hardness results for CLOSENESS IMPROVEMENT which are based on two reductions from DOMINATING SET. From results on DOMINATING SET we can then infer corresponding results for CLOSENESS IMPROVEMENT. In particular, we show that the $n^{O(k)}$-time algorithm from Corollary 1 is essentially optimal unless the Exponential Time Hypothesis is false.

Theorem 1 ($*$). CLOSENESS IMPROVEMENT *is NP-hard and W[2]-hard with respect to the number k of edge additions (on disconnected graphs). Moreover, unless the Exponential Time Hypothesis fails, CLOSENESS IMPROVEMENT does not allow an algorithm with running time $f(k) \cdot n^{o(k)}$.*

Corollary 2 ($*$). CLOSENESS IMPROVEMENT *is*

1. *NP-hard even on disconnected planar graphs with maximum degree 3,*
2. *NP-hard and W[2]-hard on disconnected split graphs, and*
3. *NP-hard and W[2]-hard on disconnected graphs in which each connected component has diameter two.*

Applications in social networks, which have both small diameter and small H-index[2] [9], motivate the following more special hardness result where both these values are small constants. It also shows that CLOSENESS IMPROVEMENT remains hard on connected graphs, which was left open by Theorem 1.

Theorem 2. CLOSENESS IMPROVEMENT *is NP-hard and W[2]-hard with respect to the parameter number k of edge additions even on connected graphs with diameter 4. Moreover, CLOSENESS IMPROVEMENT is NP-hard even on graphs which simultaneously have diameter 6 and H-index 4.*

---

[2] Recall that the H-index of a graph is the largest integer h such that there are h vertices of degree at least h.

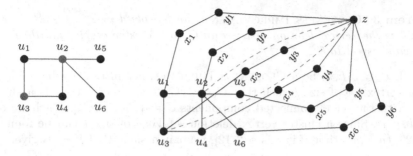

Fig. 1. Parameterized reduction from DOMINATING SET to CLOSENESS IMPROVEMENT on graphs with diameter 4. Left: A DOMINATING SET instance $I = (G, k = 2)$. The red colored vertices u_2 and u_3 form a solution for I. Right: The constructed CLOSENESS IMPROVEMENT instance $(I' = G', z, k' = 2, 2n + \frac{k}{2})$. The red, dashed edges form a solution for I'. (Color figure online)

Proof. The proof is by a parameterized reduction from two variants of DOMI-NATING SET, detailed below. Let $I = (G = (V, E), k \in \mathbb{N})$ be a DOMINATING SET instance where $V = \{u_1, \ldots, u_n\}$. We construct a CLOSENESS IMPROVE-MENT instance $I' = (G' = (V', E'), z, k, 2n + \frac{k}{2})$ as follows (see Fig. 1): Given the input graph G, we add $2n$ vertices $x_1, \ldots, x_n, y_1, \ldots, y_n$ such that each vertex x_i is adjacent to u_i and y_i. Furthermore, we add z and add edges between z and each $y_1, \ldots, y_n$. Formally, $V' = V \cup \{x_i, y_i \mid 1 \leq i \leq n\} \cup \{z\}$ and $E' = E \cup \{\{u_i, x_i\}, \{x_i, y_i\}, \{z, y_i\} \mid 1 \leq i \leq n\}$. We partition V' into the subsets $Y' := \{y_1, \ldots, y_n\}, X' := \{x_1, \ldots, x_n\}$, and $U' := \{u_1, \ldots, u_n\}$. Note that the vertices in Y' have distance 1 to z, the vertices in X' have distance 2 to z and the vertices in U' all have distance 3 to z. This completes the construction which can clearly be carried out in polynomial time.

Suppose the reduction is correct. To get NP-hardness and W[2]-hardness with respect to k on diameter 4 graphs, we reduce from DOMINATING SET on graphs of diameter two, which is NP-hard [1] and W[2]-hard with respect to k [15]. It is not hard to see that the resulting graph G' indeed has diameter 4. To get NP-hardness on graphs with simultaneously diameter 6 and H-index 4, reduce instead from DOMINATING SET on graphs G with maximum degree 4. By the connections via x_i, y_i, and z, any two vertices of G are connected in G' by a path of length at most 6. Graph G' has H-index 4, because it has maximum degree 4 apart from z. The correctness of the reduction is deferred to a full version.   □

We note that it is not hard to show that CLOSENESS IMPROVEMENT is polynomial-time solvable on graphs of diameter 2. The case of diameter 3 remains open.

Algorithmic Result. Now we present an algorithm for CLOSENESS IMPROVE-MENT, which shows that the problem is fixed-parameter tractable when param-eterized by the distance of the input graph to a cluster graph.

Theorem 3. CLOSENESS IMPROVEMENT *can be solved in* $2^{2^{2^{O(\ell)}}} \cdot n^{O(1)}$ *time, where ℓ is the vertex deletion distance of G to a cluster graph, and thus is in FPT with respect to ℓ.*

Proof. Let (G, z, k, r) be a CLOSENESS IMPROVEMENT instance, where $V_{\mathsf{VDS}} \subset V$ is a vertex set of size ℓ such that $G_C = (V_C, E_C) := G - V_{\mathsf{VDS}}$ is a cluster graph with the set of connected components $\mathcal{C} = \{C_1, \ldots, C_s\}$ which we also call *clusters*. Since a cluster vertex deletion set V_{VDS} of size ℓ can be found in $O(1.92^\ell \cdot (n + m))$ time if it exists [2, 12], we may assume that V_{VDS} is given. By Lemma 1 we may assume that the edges in an optimal solution E^* to (G, z, k, r) all have endpoint z. Hence, in the following we denote by a solution V' the endpoints different from z of the corresponding edge set. Any solution can thus be divided into vertices in V_{VDS} and those in $V \setminus V_{\mathsf{VDS}}$. Let V^*_{VDS} be the intersection of an optimal solution V^* with V_{VDS}. The first step in our algorithm is to find V^*_{VDS}, by trying all 2^ℓ possibilities. It remains to determine $V^* \setminus V_{\mathsf{VDS}}$. Intuitively, if there are vertices which have the same neighborhood in V_{VDS} and are in clusters that also have the same neighborhood in V_{VDS}, then each such vertex after the first one does not help to shorten distances to z for any vertex except itself. Hence, if we know that the optimal solution contains vertices in clusters both with some specified neighborhood in V_{VDS}, then we can assume that these vertices are distributed among the largest clusters with that neighborhood. In the algorithm we thus first determine for which neighborhoods in V_{VDS} there are clusters and vertices in these clusters in the optimal solution. Then we distribute the vertices in the solution optimally among the chosen neighborhoods. The proof that this yields an optimal solution is unfortunately technical and we need the following notation.

We say that the *signature* $\mathsf{sig}(C_i)$ *of a cluster* C_i, $i = 1, \ldots, s$, is the set of neighbors in $V_{\mathsf{VDS}} \cup \{z\}$ of vertices in C_i, that is, the signature is $\{v \in V_{\mathsf{VDS}} \cup \{z\} \mid \exists u \in C_i : \{u, v\} \in E\}$. Similarly, the *signature* $\mathsf{sig}(v)$ *of a vertex* $w \in V \setminus V_{\mathsf{VDS}}$ is $N(v) \cap (V_{\mathsf{VDS}} \cup \{z\})$. For some subset $V_i \subseteq C_i$ of some cluster $C_i \in \mathcal{C}$ denote by the *signature* $\mathsf{sig}(V_i)$ of V_i the tuple $(\mathsf{sig}(C_i), \{\mathsf{sig}(v) \mid v \in V_i\})$. Say also that C_i is V_i's *cluster*. Now the *signature* $\mathsf{sig}(\hat{V})$ *of a solution* $\hat{V}$ is the set $\{\mathsf{sig}(V_i) \mid C_i \in \mathcal{C} \wedge C_i \cap \hat{V} = V_i \neq \emptyset\}$. That is, the signature of $\hat{V}$ encodes the signatures of the clusters touched by $\hat{V}$ along with, for each touched cluster, the signatures of all vertices touched by $\hat{V}$ in that cluster. Say that a vertex subset V_j of some cluster C_j is *eligible* for some signature $\mathsf{sig}(V_i)$ of a vertex subset V_i of a cluster C_i if $\mathsf{sig}(V_j) = \mathsf{sig}(V_i)$. Accordingly, for some solution $\hat{V}$ with signature $\mathsf{sig}(\hat{V})$, say that a vertex subset $V_i \subseteq C_i$ of some cluster C_i is *eligible* for $\mathsf{sig}(\hat{V})$ if $\mathsf{sig}(V_i) \in \mathsf{sig}(\hat{V})$. Finally, the *reduct* of a solution $\hat{V}$ is a subset $V' \subseteq \hat{V}$ such that, for each cluster $C_i \in \mathcal{C}$ with $\hat{V} \cap C_i \neq \emptyset$ and each vertex signature $S \in \{\mathsf{sig}(v) \mid v \in \hat{V} \cap C_i\}$, there is exactly one vertex $u \in V' \cap C_i$ with signature S. Observe that, if V' is the reduct of $\hat{V}$ and $V'' \supseteq V'$ is any superset of V' with $|V''| = |\hat{V}|$, then $\mathsf{sig}(\hat{V}) = \mathsf{sig}(V') \subseteq \mathsf{sig}(V'')$ and the closeness centrality of z achieved by V'' is at least the one achieved by $\hat{V}$.

Let S be the signature of some vertex subset of some cluster. Call a vertex subset $V_i \subseteq C_i$ of some cluster $C_i \in \mathcal{C}$ *most potent* for S if it is eligible for S

and among all vertex subsets of some cluster in $\mathcal{C}$ that are eligible for S we have that V_i's cluster is the largest. If the signature S is clear from the context, we say that V_i is most potent.

Let V^* be the reduct of an optimal solution. We claim that there is an optimal solution with reduct V_2^* with signature $\mathsf{sig}(V_2^*) = \mathsf{sig}(V^*)$ such that, for each $S \in \mathsf{sig}(V_2^*)$, there is a vertex subset V_j of some cluster contained in V^* that is most potent among vertex subsets eligible for S. Assume the claim does not hold. Then there exists the reduct V_3^* of some optimal solution such that V_3^* contains the largest number of most potent vertex sets and at least one signature $S \in \mathsf{sig}(V_3^*)$ such that no vertex subset of some cluster which is most potent for S is contained in V_3^*. Observe however, that some vertex subset $V_i \subseteq C_i$ with $\mathsf{sig}(V_i) = S$ is contained in V_3^*. Let V_j be most potent among vertex sets with signature $\mathsf{sig}(V_i)$ and let $V_4^* = (V_3^* \setminus V_i) \cup V_j$. Note that, $\mathsf{sig}(V_4^*) = \mathsf{sig}(V_3^*)$ and, because of that, each vertex in $V \setminus (C_i \cup C_j)$ has the same distance to z according to V_3^* and to V_4^*. However, since $|C_i| < |C_j|$, $\mathsf{sig}(V_i) = \mathsf{sig}(V_j)$, and since, for each vertex signature in $\mathsf{sig}(V_i)$ there is at most one vertex in each of V_4^* and V_3^* with that signature, more vertices have distance 2 to z according to V_4^* than to V_3^*. This is a contradiction to V_3^* being the reduct of an optimal solution. Hence, the claim holds. Thus, once we know the signature of an optimal solution, we know it is optimal to take the most potent (according to that signature) vertex sets into our solution.

Let V^* again be the reduct of an optimal solution. The *remainder* of V^* is the subset of V^* resulting from removing for each $S \in \mathsf{sig}(V^*)$ a most potent vertex set V_j with signature $\mathsf{sig}(V_j) = S$ from V^* (note that the V_j's are present without loss of generality by the previous claim).

We claim that there is some optimal solution with reduct V_2^* with signature $\mathsf{sig}(V_2^*) = \mathsf{sig}(V^*)$ such that the remainder of V_2^* contains among all vertex subsets of some cluster with a signature in $\mathsf{sig}(V_2^*)$ those vertex subsets in the largest clusters. Assume otherwise. Then there exists the reduct V_3^* of some optimal solution such that the remainder $V_3^{*,R}$ of V_3^* contains some $V_i \subseteq C_i$ such that $V_3^{*,R} \cap C_i = V_i$, and there is a cluster C_j and a vertex subset $V_j \subseteq C_j$ such that $V_3^{*,R} \cap V_j = \emptyset$, $\mathsf{sig}(V_j), \mathsf{sig}(V_i) \in \mathsf{sig}(V_3^*)$, and $|C_j| > |C_i|$. Let $V_4^* = (V_3^* \setminus V_i) \cup V_j$. Note that $\mathsf{sig}(V_3^*) = \mathsf{sig}(V_4^*)$ and, because of that, each vertex in $V \setminus (C_i \cup C_j)$ has the same distance to z according to V_3^* and to V_4^*. By the same argument as in the previous claim, we obtain a contradiction to V_3^* being the reduct of an optimal solution. Hence, also this claim holds. Thus, once we know the signature S of an optimal solution, we know it is optimal to take into the remainder of the optimal solution those vertex subsets with a signature in S that are contained in the largest clusters.

The algorithm to compute an optimal solution V^* is now as follows. Try all possibilities for the intersection $V^* \cap V_{\mathsf{VDS}}$. Next, try all possibilities for the signature S of V^*. Put into V^*, for each $S' \in S$, a vertex subset of some cluster which is most potent for S'. Then, find the smallest vertex subsets of the clusters which have some signature in S and add them to V^* in decreasing order of the size of their cluster as long as $|V^*| \leq k$. Finally, add to V^* arbitrary vertices until $|V^*| = k$. This algorithm finds an optimal solution because at least one of the possibilities checked above corresponds to an optimal solution and by the claims above.

It remains to show the running time: There are at most 2^ℓ possibilities for $V^* \cap V_{\text{VDS}}$. For each signature of a cluster C_i, of which there are at most 2^ℓ, there are at most 2^{2^ℓ} possibilities for the set of vertex signatures of a subset of C_i. Hence, the signature of V^* is the subset of a set of size $2^\ell \cdot 2^{2^\ell}$, meaning that there are at most $2^{2^{2^{O(\ell)}}}$ possibilities for the signature of V^*. Hence, the algorithm checks at most $2^{2^{2^{O(\ell)}}}$ possibilities. To see that the cluster vertex subsets added to V^* for each possibility can be computed in polynomial time, observe that the it suffices to iterate over each cluster, find its signature and the signature of its vertices and accumulate the largest ones into a dictionary data structure indexed by the size of the clusters.   □

Directed Closeness Improvement. We now investigate the problem DIRECTED CLOSENESS IMPROVEMENT of improving the closeness centrality of a vertex z on directed, unweighted graphs. Herein, the closeness centrality is measured by sum of the multiplicative inverse distances *from z the other vertices*[3]. We show that the problem remains W[2]-hard with respect to the number k of added arcs, even on directed acyclic graphs and even if the diameter of the graph is 4. Analogously to the undirected variant, we show that we can maximize the closeness centrality of a vertex z in a directed graph by adding arcs adjacent to z. Again, this directly implies that DIRECTED CLOSENESS IMPROVEMENT is in XP with respect to the number of arc additions:

Lemma 2 (∗). *Let $I = (G = (V, E), z, k, r)$ be a DIRECTED CLOSENESS IMPROVEMENT instance. If I is a YES-instance, then there is a solution S for I where for each arc $a \in S$, the source vertex is z.*

Corollary 3. DIRECTED CLOSENESS IMPROVEMENT *can be solved in $O(n^k \cdot (n + m))$ time, where k is the number of arc additions and thus is in XP with respect to k.*

With two similar reductions from SET COVER we get the following two hardness results for DIRECTED CLOSENESS IMPROVEMENT.

Theorem 4 (∗). DIRECTED CLOSENESS IMPROVEMENT *is NP-hard and W[2]-hard with respect to the number k of edge additions on directed acyclic graphs.*

Theorem 5 (∗). DIRECTED CLOSENESS IMPROVEMENT *is NP-hard and W[2]-hard with respect to the number k of edge additions on directed graphs with diameter 4.*

---

[3] It is easy to check that all our results also hold if the closeness centrality is measured by sum of the multiplicative inverse distances *from the other vertices to z.*

3 Betweenness Centrality

We now investigate the problem of increasing the betweenness centrality of a vertex in a graph by inserting a certain number of edges into the graph. We remark that the betweenness centrality of a vertex in an undirected graph can be computed in $O(n \cdot m)$ time [3]. We show that, similar to CLOSENESS IMPROVEMENT, BETWEENNESS IMPROVEMENT is W[2]-hard with respect to the parameter number of edge additions and we also present algorithmic results.

First, we make an important observation that will help us in our proofs. Analogous to Lemma 1, we show that to improve the betweenness of a vertex by adding edges, it always makes sense to add only edges adjacent to that vertex.

Lemma 3 (*). *Let* $I = (G, z, k, r)$ *be a* BETWEENNESS IMPROVEMENT *instance. If* I *is a* YES-*instance, then there is an optimal solution that only contains edges where one endpoint is* z.

Hence, if we compute a solution for some BETWEENNESS IMPROVEMENT instance, we need to find a subset of the graph's vertices of size k such that adding an edge between z and these vertices maximally increases the betweenness centrality of z. This directly implies the following corollary:

Corollary 4. BETWEENNESS IMPROVEMENT *is solvable in* $O(n^k \cdot (n+m))$ *time where* k *is the number of edge additions and thus is in XP with respect to* k.

Hardness Results. We show that BETWEENNESS IMPROVEMENT is W[2]-hard with respect to the parameter number of edge additions by a parameterized reduction from DOMINATING SET on graphs with diameter 3. Furthermore, we show that the problem is NP-hard on graphs with diameter 3 and H-index 4.

Theorem 6. BETWEENNESS IMPROVEMENT *is NP-hard and W[2]-hard with respect to the parameter number* k *of edge additions on graphs with diameter 3. Moreover, unless the Exponential Time Hypothesis fails,* BETWEENNESS IMPROVEMENT *does not allow an algorithm with running time* $f(k) \cdot n^{o(k)}$.

Proof. We give a parameterized reduction from DOMINATING SET, which also directly implies the running time lower bound when assuming ETH [7]. Let $I = (G = (U, E), k)$ be a DOMINATING SET instance, where $U = \{u_1, \ldots, u_n\}$. We construct a BETWEENNESS IMPROVEMENT instance

$$I' = \left(G' = (V, E'), z_1, k, r = \alpha k + \frac{2}{3}\alpha(n - k) + \frac{1}{2}\left(k + \alpha + \binom{\alpha}{2} \right) \right),$$

where $\alpha > \frac{3k(k-1)}{2}$. The graph G' is constructed as follows. For each $u_i \in U$, we add a vertex u_i' to G'. Also, for each edge $\{u_i, u_j\} \in E$, we add an edge $\{u_i', u_j'\}$ to E'. We set $U' := \{u_1', \ldots, u_n'\}$. Next, we add the vertices $\{z_1, z_3, z_4\}$ and $Z_2 = \{z_{2_1}, \ldots, z_{2_\alpha}\}$ to G'. For each $z_{2_i} \in Z_2$, we add two edges $\{z_1, z_{2_i}\}$ and $\{z_{2_i}, z_3\}$ to G'. Furthermore, we add the edges $\{z_1, z_3\}, \{z_1, z_4\}$ and $\{z_3, z_4\}$. Finally, for

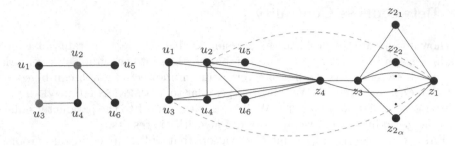

Fig. 2. Parameterized reduction from DOMINATING SET to BETWEENNESS IMPROVE-MENT. Left: A DOMINATING SET instance $(I = (G, k = 2))$. The red colored vertices u_2, u_3 form a solution. Right: The constructed BETWEENNESS IMPROVEMENT instance $I' = (G, z_1, k, r)$. The red, dashed edges form a solution. (Color figure online)

each vertex $u_i' \in U'$, we add an edge $\{z_4, u_i'\}$. Figure 2 illustrates the construction. It is easy to check that G' has diameter 3.

As z_1 is adjacent to all vertices except the ones in U', a solution S for I' contains only edges where one endpoint is z_1 and each other one is in U' (Lemma 3). The correctness of the reduction is deferred to a full version.   □

By closer inspection of the reduction, we can also show that BETWEENNESS IMPROVEMENT remains hard on graphs with diameter 3 and H-index 4.

Corollary 5 (∗). BETWEENNESS IMPROVEMENT *is NP-hard on graphs with diameter 3 and H-index 4.*

Algorithmic Result. We also derive a positive result for BETWEENNESS IMPROVEMENT. We show that the problem is fixed-parameter tractable with respect to the combined parameter distance to cluster and number of edge additions.

Theorem 7. BETWEENNESS IMPROVEMENT *is solvable in time* $2^{O(2^{2^\ell} \cdot k \log k)} \cdot n^{O(1)}$, *where ℓ is the distance of G to a cluster graph, and thus is in FPT with respect to the combined parameter (k, ℓ).*

Proof. Let (G, z, k, r) be a BETWEENNESS IMPROVEMENT instance, where the set $V_{\text{VDS}} \subset V$ is a cluster vertex deletion set of size ℓ, that is, $G[V \setminus V_{\text{VDS}}]$ is a cluster graph with connected components (*clusters*) $\{C_1, \ldots, C_s\} =: C$. Since a cluster vertex deletion set of size ℓ can be found in $O(1.92^\ell \cdot (n + m))$ time if it exists [2,12], we may assume that V_{VDS} is given. The basic idea is similar to Theorem 3. First, we determine the intersection of an optimal solution with V_{VDS}. To find the vertices in $V \setminus V_{\text{VDS}}$ we assign signatures to clusters and vertices in clusters based on their neighborhood in V_{VDS}. We then find the signatures in an optimal solution and the optimal vertices for each signature. A difference to Theorem 3 is that, once we have determined the signatures of vertices in an optimal solution, it still matters how many vertices we take for each signature.

Let V^* be the set of endpoints different from z of the edges in an optimal solution. By Lemma 3 we may assume that $|V^*| = k$. The first step in the algorithm is to iterate over all 2^ℓ possibilities for putting $V^* \cap V_{\text{VDS}}$ in the output solution. Assume henceforth that we are in the iteration in which we have found $V^* \cap V_{\text{VDS}}$.

Define for each cluster C_i its *cluster signature* as the set of neighbors of C_i in $V_{\text{VDS}} \cup \{z\}$. From V^* we get a subset $\mathcal{S}$ of the set of all 2^ℓ possible cluster signatures by putting into $\mathcal{S}$ all signatures of clusters which have nonempty intersection with V^*. That is, $\mathcal{S} = \{N(C_i) \cap (V_{\text{VDS}} \cup \{z\}) \mid i \in \{1, \ldots, s\}\}$, where $N(C_i) = \bigcup_{v \in C_i} N(v)$. The second step in the algorithm is to iterate over all 2^{2^ℓ} possibilities for $\mathcal{S}$. Assume below that we are in the iteration in which we have found $\mathcal{S}$.

Define for each vertex $v \in V \setminus (V_{\text{VDS}} \cup \{z\})$ its *vertex signature* as the set $N(v) \cap (V_{\text{VDS}} \cup \{z\})$. From V^*, for each cluster signature $S \in \mathcal{S}$, we obtain a family T_S of sets of vertex signatures by, for each cluster C_i with signature S that has nonempty intersection with V^*, putting into T_S the set $\{N(v) \cap V_{\text{VDS}} \mid v \in C_i \cap V_{\text{VDS}}\}$. The third step in the algorithm is to iterate for each $S \in \mathcal{S}$ over all 2^{2^ℓ} possible families T_S. In total, these are at most $2^\ell \cdot 2^{2^{2^\ell}}$ possibilities. Assume henceforth that we are in the iteration in which we have found T_S for each $S \in \mathcal{S}$.

As fourth step in the algorithm we find for each $S \in \mathcal{S}$ and each $S' \in T_S$ the number $n_{S,S'}$ of clusters C_i such that $C_i \cap V^* \neq \emptyset$, C_i has signature S', and the set of vertex signatures of vertices in $C_i \cap V^*$ is exactly S'. We do this by iterating over all at most $(2^\ell \cdot 2^{2^\ell})^k$ possibilities. Assume henceforth that we are in the iteration in which we have found $n_{S,S'}$ for each $S \in \mathcal{S}$ and each $S' \in T_S$.

As a fifth step in the algorithm we find for each of the $n_{S,S'}$ clusters C_i as above, for each vertex signature in $s \in S'$ the number $n_{S,S',s}$ of vertices in $C_i \cap V^*$ with signature s. Again, we iterate over all at most $(2^\ell \cdot 2^{2^\ell} \cdot 2^\ell \cdot k)^k$ possibilities. Assume henceforth that we are in the iteration in which we have found $n_{S,S',s}$.

Say that a cluster C_i is *eligible* for S, S' if it has cluster signature S and for each vertex signature $s \in S'$ there are $n_{S,S',s}$ vertices with signature s in C_i. We now claim that, without loss of generality, among clusters that are eligible for S, S', set V^* contains only vertices from the k largest such clusters. Assume otherwise. Hence, there is a cluster C_i among the k largest clusters eligible for S, S' and a cluster C_j which is eligible for S, S' but not among the k largest such clusters. (Recall that we are in an iteration in which we have found S, S', $n_{S,S'}$, and $n_{S,S',s}$ as defined and hence, C_j exists.) Obtain W^* from V^* by replacing each vertex in $C_j \cap V^*$ with a vertex in C_i with the same signature; call the vertices in $C_i \cap W^*$ the *replacements* of the vertices in V^*. The betweenness centrality of z with respect to W^* is at least the one with respect to V^*. Indeed, each shortest path with respect to V^* that contains z and some vertices in $C_j \cap V^*$ induces a shortest path with respect to W^* containing z and the corresponding replacements in $C_i \cap W^*$. Thus, the claim holds.

The sixth and final step in the algorithm is thus to try all possibilities to mark $n_{S,S'}$ clusters which are eligible for S, S' and to put, for each marked cluster and each $s \in S'$ a set of $n_{S,S',s}$ arbitrary vertices of signature s in the marked cluster into the output solution. There are at most $(2^{\ell} \cdot 2^{2^{\ell}} \cdot k^2)^k$ possibilities. By the claim and since we can replace vertices with the same signatures in the marked clusters in V^*, in one of the tried possibilities, we will find an optimal solution.   □

Directed Betweenness Improvement. We now cover results for the problem of improving the betweenness centrality of a vertex in a directed, unweighted graphs. First, we define betweenness centrality for directed, unweighted graphs, as the definition due to Freeman [10] only measures the centrality over all unordered subsets of vertices of size two. A very natural definition, which is equivalent to the one used in further literature (e.g. by White and Borgatti [22]) is to measure the ratio of shortest paths containing a certain vertex z for both orders of any pair of vertices: $b_z = \sum_{s \in V} \sum \frac{\sigma_{stz}}{\sigma_{st}}$. Herein $s, t \neq z$ and the second sum is taken over all $t \in V$ such that $t \neq s$ and $\sigma_{st} \neq 0$. Using this definition, DIRECTED BETWEENNESS IMPROVEMENT is defined analogously to BETWEENNESS IMPROVEMENT.

Analogously to the undirected problem variant, we show that we can maximize the betweenness centrality of a vertex z by adding arcs incident to z.

Lemma 4 (∗). *If a* DIRECTED BETWEENNESS IMPROVEMENT *instance* $I = (G = (V, A), z, k, r)$ *is a* YES-*instance, then there is a solution S that only contains arcs where either the source or the target is z.*

However, note that a solution S for a YES-instance $I = (G, z, k, r)$ may also contain arcs where z is the source. For instance, $(G = \{z, v_1, v_2\}, A = \{(v_1, z)\}, z, 1, 1)$ is a YES-instance with solution $S = \{(z, v_2)\}$.

Corollary 6. DIRECTED BETWEENNESS IMPROVEMENT *is solvable in* $O((2n)^k \cdot (n + m))$ *time where k is the number of edge additions, and thus is in* XP *with respect to the parameter number of edge additions.*

Substantial improvement of this running time is unlikely, as Theorem 8 shows.

Theorem 8 (∗). DIRECTED BETWEENNESS IMPROVEMENT *is NP-hard and* W[2]-*hard with respect to the parameter number of arc additions k on directed acyclic graphs.*

4   Outlook

Our tractability results yield running times that are impractical and need to be improved. Some further questions that we left open are as follows. First, it is not hard to show that CLOSENESS IMPROVEMENT polynomial-time solvable on graphs of diameter 2. Is this also true for diameter 3? As we showed, for diameter 4 it is NP-hard. Noticeable is also that the problem seems to be harder on disconnected graphs. In particular, our reductions also imply NP-hardness for *disconnected* graphs where every connected component has diameter 2.

There seem to be similarities between DOMINATING SET and CLOSENESS IMPROVEMENT, as indicated by our hardness reductions. DOMINATING SET is fixed-parameter tractable with respect to the combined parameter maximum degree and k. Does the same hold for CLOSENESS IMPROVEMENT? Similar questions extend to BETWEENNESS IMPROVEMENT. For BETWEENNESS IMPROVEMENT it would also be interesting to see, whether in our fixed-parameter algorithm for the combined parameter solution size k and the distance to cluster graph, we can remove the dependency on k.

References

1. Ambalath, A.M., Balasundaram, R., Rao H., C., Koppula, V., Misra, N., Philip, G., Ramanujan, M.S.: On the kernelization complexity of colorful motifs. In: Raman, V., Saurabh, S. (eds.) IPEC 2010. LNCS, vol. 6478, pp. 14–25. Springer, Heidelberg (2010). https://doi.org/10.1007/978-3-642-17493-3_4
2. Boral, A., Cygan, M., Kociumaka, T., Pilipczuk, M.: A fast branching algorithm for cluster vertex deletion. Theor. Comput. Syst. **58**(2), 357–376 (2016)
3. Brandes, U.: A faster algorithm for betweenness centrality. J. Math. Sociol. **25**(2), 163–177 (2001)
4. Brandes, U.: On variants of shortest-path betweenness centrality and their generic computation. Soc. Netw. **30**(2), 136–145 (2008)
5. Crescenzi, P., D'angelo, G., Severini, L., Velaj, Y.: Greedily improving our own closeness centrality in a network. ACM Trans. Knowl. Discov. Data **11**(1), 9 (2016)
6. Csermely, P., London, A., Wu, L.-Y., Uzzi, B.: Structure and dynamics of core/periphery networks. J. Complex Netw. **1**(2), 93–123 (2013)
7. Cygan, M., Fomin, F.V., Kowalik, Ł., Lokshtanov, D., Marx, D., Pilipczuk, M., Pilipczuk, M., Saurabh, S.: Parameterized Algorithms. Springer, Heidelberg (2015). https://doi.org/10.1007/978-3-319-21275-3
8. D'Angelo, G., Severini, L., Velaj, Y.: On the maximum betweenness improvement problem. Electron. Notes Theor. Comput. Sci. **322**, 153–168 (2016)
9. Eppstein, D., Spiro, E.S.: The h-index of a graph and its application to dynamic subgraph statistics. J. Graph Algorithms Appl. **16**(2), 543–567 (2012)
10. Freeman, L.C.: A set of measures of centrality based on betweenness. Sociometry **40**, 35–41 (1977)
11. Freeman, L.C.: Centrality in social networks conceptual clarification. Soc. Netw. **1**(3), 215–239 (1978)
12. Hüffner, F., Komusiewicz, C., Moser, H., Niedermeier, R.: Fixed-parameter algorithms for cluster vertex deletion. Theory Comput. Syst. **47**(1), 196–217 (2010)
13. Impagliazzo, R., Paturi, R.: Complexity of k-SAT. In: Proceeding of the 14th Annual IEEE Conference on Computational Complexity (CCC 1999), pp. 237–240 (1999)
14. Impagliazzo, R., Paturi, R., Zane, F.: Which problems have strongly exponential complexity? In: Proceedings 39th Annual Symposium on Foundations of Computer Science (FOCS 1998), pp. 653–662 (1998)
15. Lokshtanov, D., Misra, N., Philip, G., Ramanujan, M.S., Saurabh, S.: Hardness of r-DOMINATING SET on Graphs of Diameter $(r + 1)$. In: Gutin, G., Szeider, S. (eds.) IPEC 2013. LNCS, vol. 8246, pp. 255–267. Springer, Cham (2013). https://doi.org/10.1007/978-3-319-03898-8_22

16. Newman, M.: Networks: An Introduction. Oxford University Press, Oxford (2010)
17. Newman, M.E.: A measure of betweenness centrality based on random walks. Soc. Netw. **27**(1), 39–54 (2005)
18. Okamoto, K., Chen, W., Li, X.-Y.: Ranking of closeness centrality for large-scale social networks. In: Preparata, F.P., Wu, X., Yin, J. (eds.) FAW 2008. LNCS, vol. 5059, pp. 186–195. Springer, Heidelberg (2008). https://doi.org/10.1007/978-3-540-69311-6_21
19. Opsahl, T., Agneessens, F., Skvoretz, J.: Node centrality in weighted networks: generalizing degree and shortest paths. Soc. Netw. **32**(3), 245–251 (2010)
20. Diestel, R.: Graph Theory. Graduate Texts in Mathematics, vol. 173, 5th edn. Springer, Heidelberg (2016). https://doi.org/10.1007/978-3-662-53622-3
21. Rubinov, M., Sporns, O.: Complex network measures of brain connectivity: uses and interpretations. Neuroimage **52**(3), 1059–1069 (2010)
22. White, D.R., Borgatti, S.P.: Betweenness centrality measures for directed graphs. Soc. Netw. **16**(4), 335–346 (1994)

Local Structure Theorems for Erdős–Rényi Graphs and Their Algorithmic Applications

Jan Dreier[1], Philipp Kuinke[1], Ba Le Xuan[2], and Peter Rossmanith[1(✉)]

[1] Theoretical Computer Science, Department of Computer Science,
RWTH Aachen University, Aachen, Germany
{dreier,kuinke,rossmani}@cs.rwth-aachen.de
[2] The Sirindhorn International Thai-German Graduate School of Engineering,
King Mongkut's University of Technology North Bangkok, Bangkok, Thailand
ba.l-sse2015@tggs-bangkok.org

Abstract. We analyze local properties of sparse Erdős–Rényi graphs, where $d(n)/n$ is the edge probability. In particular we study the behavior of very short paths. For $d(n) = n^{o(1)}$ we show that $G(n, d(n)/n)$ has asymptotically almost surely (a.a.s.) bounded local treewidth and therefore is a.a.s. nowhere dense. We also discover a new and simpler proof that $G(n, d/n)$ has a.a.s. bounded expansion for constant d. The local structure of sparse Erdős–Rényi graphs is very special: The r-neighborhood of a vertex is a tree with some additional edges, where the probability that there are m additional edges decreases with m. This implies efficient algorithms for subgraph isomorphism, in particular for finding subgraphs with small diameter. Finally, experiments suggest that preferential attachment graphs might have similar properties after deleting a small number of vertices.

Keywords: Graph theory · Random graphs · Sparse graphs
Graph algorithms

1 Introduction

One of the earliest and most intensively studied random graph models is the Erdős–Rényi model [1,2]. Graphs from this class are usually depicted as a random variable $G(n, p)$, which is a graph consisting of n vertices where each pair of vertices is connected independently uniformly at random with probability p. The edge probability p may also depend on the size of the graph, e.g., $p = d/n$. Many properties of Erdős–Rényi graphs are well studied including but not limited to, threshold phenomena, the sizes of components, diameter, and lengths of paths [1]. One particular impressive result is the 0-1 law: Let φ be a first-order formula. If we take a random graph $G = G(n, 1/2)$, then the probability of $G \models \varphi$ is either 0 or 1 as $n \to \infty$ [3].

"Instead of the worst case running time, it is also interesting to consider the average case. Here even the most basic questions are wide open." as Grohe

© Springer International Publishing AG 2018
A M. Tjoa et al. (Eds.): SOFSEM 2018, LNCS 10706, pp. 125–136, 2018.
https://doi.org/10.1007/978-3-319-73117-9_9

puts it [4]. One can find an optimal coloring of $G(n, p)$ in expected linear time for $p < 1.01/n$ [5]. The 0-1 law on the other hand has (not yet) an efficient accompanying algorithm that can decide whether $G \models \varphi$ for $G = G(n, 1/2)$ and a fixed formula φ.

One possibility to open up a whole graph class to efficient algorithms are algorithmic meta-theorems. Such meta-theorems were developed for more and more general graph classes: planar, bounded genus, bounded degree, H-minor free, H-topological minor free etc. In all these graph classes we can decide properties that are expressible in first-order logic in linear time for a fixed formula φ [6,7]. Unfortunately, random graph classes do not belong to any of these classes. For example $G(n, 1.1/n)$ has a.a.s. linear treewidth and does contain constant-size cliques of arbitrary size [8]. Recently, however, graph classes of bounded expansion were introduced by Nešetřil and de Mendez [9]. These classes also admit linear time FO-model checking and generalize the older meta-theorems [10]. The most general model checking algorithm runs in time $O(n^{1+\epsilon})$ on nowhere-dense classes [11]. In $G(n, d/n)$, the value d is the expected density of a random graph. For constant d it was shown that $G(n, d/n)$ has a.a.s. bounded expansion [12]. Unfortunately, this does not automatically imply that one can test first-order properties on $G(n, d/n)$ in linear (expected) time, but only that we can test such a property in linear time with a failure probability of $o(1)$ while the expected runtime might be unbounded. This is for example the case if the runtime grows faster than the failure probability converges to zero. One example of an (expected-time) fpt-algorithm is one that finds a k-clique in $G(n, p(n))$ in time $f(k)n^{O(1)}$, for many choices of p [13].

In Sect. 3 we find an easier proof for the fact that $G(n, d/n)$ has a.a.s. bounded expansion for constant d and give concrete probability bounds, which were missing up to now. Then we investigate local properties of Erdős–Rényi graphs. The expected density of $G(n, d(n)/n)$ is $d(n)$ and therefore, if $d(n)$ is not constant, unbounded. This implies that $G(n, d(n)/n)$ does a.a.s. not have bounded expansion. Nevertheless, we show that subgraphs with small diameter are treelike with only a few additional edges. From this it follows that $G(n, n^{o(1)}/n)$ has a.a.s. locally bounded treewidth, which implies that they are a.a.s. nowhere dense. Locally bounded treewidth [14] and more generally, locally excluding a minor [15] are useful concepts for developing first-order model checking algorithms that run in time $O(n^{1+\epsilon})$.

We discussed that a random graph class that is a.a.s. nowhere dense or has a.a.s. bounded expansion may not directly admit efficient algorithms. It is known that one can check first-order properties in $G(n, d(n)/n)$ in time $O(g(|\varphi|)n^{1+o(1)})$ for $d(n) = n^{o(1)}$ and some function g [4,16]. For constant d one can check first-order properties in time $O(g(|\varphi|)n)$. In Sect. 4 we use the locally tree-like structure of Erdős–Rényi graphs to construct an efficient algorithm for subgraph isomorphism. We show that one can find a subgraph H with h vertices and radius r in $G(n, d(n)/n)$ in time $2^{O(h)}(d(n) \log n)^{O(r)} n$, while a naive algorithm may need time $O(d(n)^h n)$. Therefore, our method may be faster for finding large pattern graphs with small radius.

It can be argued that Erdős–Rényi graphs are not a good model for real-world networks and therefore efficient algorithms for Erdős–Rényi graphs admit only limited practical applications. Recently, there were more and more efforts to model real world networks with random graph models. One candidate to meet this goal were the Barabási–Albert graphs, which use a preferential attachment paradigm to produce graphs with a degree distribution that tries to mimic the heavy-tailed distribution observed in many real-world networks [17].

This model is particularly interesting from the point of mathematical analysis because of its simple formulation and interesting characteristics, which is why they have been widely studied in the literature [18–20]. It was also shown that this model does *not* have a.a.s. bounded expansion [21].

In Sect. 5 we discuss experiments to see how similar the local structure of Barabási–Albert graphs is to Erdős–Rényi graphs. Not surprisingly, it seems that they are quite different and the former contain dense subgraphs and are likely to be somewhere dense. If we, however, remove the relatively small dense early part of these graphs, the local structure of the remaining part looks quite similar to Erdős–Rényi graphs and indicators hint that the remaining part is indeed nowhere dense. As the dense part is quite small it gives us hope that hybrid algorithms exist that combine different methods for the dense part and the structurally simple part. To search for a subgraph H, for example, could be done by guessing which vertices of H lie in the dense part and then using methods from Sect. 4 to find the remaining vertices in the simple part.

2 Preliminaries

In this work we will denote probabilities by $\mathbb{P}[\ldots]$ and expectation by $\mathbb{E}[\ldots]$. We use common graph theory notation [22]. For a graph G let $V(G)$ be its vertex set and $E(G)$ its edge set. For $v \in V(G)$ we denote the r-neighborhood of v by $N_r(v)$. The degree of a vertex v in graph G is denoted by $\deg(v)$. We write $G' \subseteq G$ if G' is a subgraph of G. For $X \subseteq V(G)$ we denote by $G[X]$ the subgraph of G that is induced by the vertices in X. The graph $G[V(G) - X]$ obtained from G by deleting the vertices in X and their incident edges, is denoted by $G - X$. The treewidth $\mathrm{tw}(G)$ of a graph G is a measure how tree-like a graph is. We denote Erdős–Rényi graphs by a random variable $G(n, d/n)$ and distinguish between graphs with constant d and graphs $G(n, d(n)/n)$, where we allow d to grow (slowly) with n. We will use various ways to measure the sparsity of a graph or graph class.

Definition 1 (Shallow topological minor [9]). *A graph M is an r-shallow topological minor of G if M is isomorphic to a subgraph G' of G if we allow the edges of M to be paths of length up to $2r + 1$ in G'. We call G' a model of M in G. For simplicity we assume by default that $V(M) \subseteq V(G')$ such that the isomorphism between M and G' is the identity when restricted to $V(M)$. The vertices $V(M)$ are called* nails[1] *and the vertices $V(G')\backslash V(M)$ subdivision*

---

[1] Also known as principal vertices.

vertices. *The set of all r-shallow topological minors of a graph G is denoted by* $G \widetilde{\triangledown} r$.

With that we can define the clique size over all topological minors of G as

$$\omega(G \widetilde{\triangledown} r) = \max_{H \in G \widetilde{\triangledown} r} \omega(H).$$

Definition 2 (Topological grad [23]). *For a graph G and an integer* $r \geq 0$, *the topological grad at depth r is defined as*

$$\widetilde{\triangledown}_r(G) = \max_{H \in G \widetilde{\triangledown} r} \frac{|E(H)|}{|V(H)|}$$

For a graph class $\mathcal{G}$, *define* $\widetilde{\triangledown}_r(\mathcal{G}) = \sup_{G \in \mathcal{G}} \widetilde{\triangledown}_r(G)$.

Definition 3 (Bounded expansion [23]). *A graph class* $\mathcal{G}$ *has bounded expansion if and only if there exists a function f such that* $\widetilde{\triangledown}_r(\mathcal{G}) < f(r)$ *for all* $r \geq 0$.

Definition 4 (Locally bounded treewidth). *A graph class* $\mathcal{G}$ *has locally bounded treewidth if and only if there exists a function f, such that for all* $r \geq 0$ *every subgraph with radius r has treewidth at most* $f(r)$.

Definition 5 (Nowhere dense [23]). *A graph class* $\mathcal{G}$ *is nowhere dense if there exists a function f such that* $\omega(G \widetilde{\triangledown} r) < f(r)$ *for all* $G \in \mathcal{G}$ *and all* $r \geq 0$.

If a graph class has locally bounded treewidth it is also nowhere dense [23].

3   Local Structure and Algorithmic Applications

In this section, we observe the local structure of Erdős–Rényi graphs and how to exploit it algorithmically. It is already known that Erdős–Rényi graphs have a.a.s. bounded expansion if the edge probability is d/n for constant d [12]. We present a simpler proof via a direct method, that also gives concrete probability bounds. The original proof did not give such concrete bounds so we feel that this new proof has applications in the design of efficient algorithms. To make our calculations easier we assume that $d \geq 2$, since Erdős–Rényi graphs are only sparser for smaller d, our techniques will also work in this case.

3.1   Bounded Expansion

The technique we use to bound the probability that certain shallow topological minors exists is to bound the probability that a path of length at most r exists between two arbitrary vertices.

Lemma 1. *Let* p_r *be the probability that there is a path of length at most* r *between two arbitrary but fixed vertices in* $G(n, d/n)$. *It holds that*

$$\frac{d}{n} \leq p_r \leq \frac{2d^r}{n}.$$

Proof. Since all edges are independent, we do not need to identify the start and end vertices of the path. We prove by induction over r that the probability of the existence of a path of length exactly r is bounded by $\frac{d^r}{n}$. For $r = 1$ the statement holds: $p_1 \leq \frac{d}{n}$. The probability of a path of length r is at most that of some path of length $r - 1$ times the probability of a single edge:

$$p_r \leq \sum_{k=0}^{n} p_{r-1} p_1 \leq \sum_{k=0}^{n} \frac{d^{r-1} d}{n^2} \leq \frac{d^r}{n}$$

By using the union bound and assuming that $d \geq 2$, the joint probability is bounded by $\frac{2d^r}{n}$. □

Having this bound in place, we can show that $G(n, d/n)$ has a.a.s. no r-shallow topological minors of large density from which it follows that they are contained in a graph class of bounded expansion a.a.s. The proof of this theorem can be found in the full version.[2]

Theorem 1. $G(n, d/n)$ *is a.a.s. contained in a graph class of bounded expansion. In particular, for $d \geq 16$ the probability that such a random graph contains some r-shallow topological minor of size k and at least $8kd^{2r+1}$ edges is at most* $\max\{n^{-2k}, 2^{-n^{2/3}}\}$. *For $d < 16$ the same result holds for at least $8k16^{2r+1}$ edges.*

3.2 Locally Simple Structure

It is known that even for constant d the treewidth of $G(n, d/n)$ grows with $\Omega(n)$ [8]. Furthermore, $G(n, d(n)/n)$ does a.a.s not have bounded expansion if $d(n)$ is unbounded. We now show that $G(n, n^{o(1)}/n)$ nevertheless has locally bounded treewidth and thus is a.a.s. nowhere dense. We start by counting the expected number of occurrences of a certain subgraph in $G(n, d(n)/n)$.

Lemma 2. *The expected number of induced subgraphs with k vertices and at least $k + m$ edges in $G(n, d(n)/n)$ is at most $k^{2k+2m} d(n)^{k+m}/n^m$.*

Proof. There are $\binom{n}{k} \leq n^k$ induced subgraphs H of size k in G. For each such H there are $\binom{\binom{k}{2}}{k+m} \leq k^{2k+2m}$ ways to choose $k + m$ edges. The probability that these $k + m$ edges are present in H is then exactly $(d(n)/n)^{k+m}$ and the probability that H has $k + m$ edges is at most $k^{2k+2m}(d(n)/n)^{k+m}$. Finally, the expected number of such induced subgraphs is at most $k^{2k+2m} d(n)^{k+m}/n^m$. □

From Lemma 2 we can conclude a well known property of Erdős–Rényi graphs: The expected number of cycles of fixed length r is $O(d(n)^r)$ (which is a constant if d is constant) by setting $k = r$ and $m = 0$. We now use this Lemma to make statements about the density of neighborhoods.

Lemma 3. *The probability that there is an r-neighborhood in $G(n, d(n)/n)$ with m more edges than vertices is at most $f(r, m)d(n)^{2r}(d(n)^{2r+1}/n)^m$ for some function f.*

---

[2] https://arxiv.org/abs/1709.09152

Proof. Consider any r-neighborhood with ℓ vertices. Assume the neighborhood contains at least m more edges than vertices. Let T be a breadth-first search spanning tree of this neighborhood. Since T contains ℓ vertices and $\ell - 1$ edges, there are $m + 1$ edges which are not contained in T. Each extra edge is incident to two vertices. Let U be the set of these vertices. Let H be the graph induced by the union of the $m + 1$ extra edges and the unique paths in T from u to the root of T for each $u \in U$. Since $|U| \leq 2(m + 1)$ and each path to the root in the breadth-first-search tree T has length at most r, the number of vertices of H is bounded by $2r(m + 1)$.

In summary, if there exists an r-neighborhood with at least m more edges than vertices then there exists a subgraph with $k \leq 2r(m + 1)$ vertices and m more edges than vertices. But according to Lemma 2, the expected number of such subgraphs is bounded by

$$\frac{\left(\left(2r(m + 1)\right)^2 d(n)\right)^{2r(m+1)+m}}{n^m} = f(r, m)d(n)^{2r}\left(\frac{d(n)^{2r+1}}{n}\right)^m.$$

This also bounds the probability that such a subgraph exists. $\qquad\square$

Theorem 2. *Let $d(n) = n^{o(1)}$. Then $G(n, d(n)/n)$ has a.a.s. locally bounded treewidth.*

Proof. The show that a graph has locally bounded treewidth we have to show that the treewidth of every r-neighborhood is bounded by a function of r alone.

Since $d(n) = n^{o(1)}$, there exists a monotone decreasing function $g(n)$ with $d(n) \leq n^{g(n)}$ and $\lim_{n \to \infty} g(n) = 0$. Let $h(r)$ be the inverse function of $1/8g(r)$. Since $g(n)$ is monotone decreasing, $h(r)$ exists and is monotone increasing. We show that for all $r \geq 0$ every subgraph with radius r has a.a.s. treewidth at most $h(r)$. We distinguish between two cases. The first case is $r < 1/8g(n)$ and $f(r, 1) < n^{1/4}$.

According to Lemma 3, an r-neighborhood of G has more edges than vertices with probability at most

$$f(r, 1)\frac{d(n)^{4r+1}}{n} \leq f(r, 1)n^{g(n)(4\frac{1}{8g(n)}+1)-1} \leq f(r, 1)n^{-1/2+g(n)} = o(1)$$

We can conclude that every r-neighborhood has a.a.s. treewidth at most 2.

The second case is $r \geq 1/8g(n)$, which means $h(r) \geq n$, so even the treewidth of the whole graph is a.a.s. bounded by $h(r)$ and the third case is given by $f(r, 1) \geq n^{1/4}$ and the (total) treewidth is a.a.s. bounded by $f(r, 1)^4$.

Altogether, the treewidth of an r-neighborhood is a.a.s. bounded by 2, by $h(r)$, or by $f(r, 1)^4$. $\qquad\square$

4   Algorithm for Subgraph Isomorphism

In this section we solve SUBGRAPH ISOMORPHISM, which given a graph G and a graph H asks, whether G contains H as a subgraph. This is equivalent to FO-model checking restricted to only existential quantifiers.

Let H be a connected graph with h vertices and radius r. In this section we discuss how fast it can be decided whether $G(n, d(n)/n)$ contains H as a subgraph. We first discuss the runtime of simple branching algorithms on Erdős–Rényi graphs and how exploiting local structure may lead to better run-times. We discovered that if the radius r of the pattern graph is small, an approach based on local structure is significantly faster.

For low-degree graphs there exists a simple branching algorithm to decide whether a graph G contains H as a subgraph in time $O(\Delta^h n)$, where Δ is the maximal degree in G. Let us first assume that $d(n) = d$ is constant. There is nevertheless a non-vanishing probability that the maximal degree of $G(n, d/n)$ is as large as $\sqrt{\log n}$. Therefore, the maximal degree cannot be bounded by any function of d. This implies that a naive, maximal degree based algorithm may have at least a quasi-linear dependence on n, while we present an algorithm which has only a linear dependence on n.

Let us also assume that $d(n)$ is of order $\log n$ and even that the maximum degree is bounded by $O(d(n))$. A naive branching algorithm may therefore decide whether $G(n, d(n)/n)$ contains H in expected time $O(d(n))^h n$. We improve this result, not making any assumption about the maximal degree, by replacing the factor $O(d(n))^h$ in the runtime with $2^{O(h)} (d(n) \log n)^{O(r)}$, where r is the radius of H. For graphs with small radius, the runtime is no longer dominated by a factor $O(d(n))^h$. The new algorithm may be significantly smaller when $d(n)$ is, for example, of order $\log n$.

So far we only discussed connected subgraphs. Using color-coding techniques, the results in this section can easily be extended to disconnected subgraphs, where the radius of each component is bounded by r. Color-coding may, however, lead to an additional factor of c^h in the runtime: Assume H has c components where the size of H is h. We want to color each vertex of G uniformly at random. Assume G contains H, then the probability that every component of H can be embedded using vertices of a single color is at least $1/c^h$. So if H can be embedded in G we will answer yes after an expected number of c^h runs.

For the following result notice that if $d(n)$ is poly-logarithmic in n the runtime is quasi-linear in n. For $d(n) = n^{o(1)}$ the dependence on n is $n^{1+o(1)}$. The algorithm is given in the proof for Theorem 3.

Lemma 4. *In $G(n, d(n)/n)$ holds with probability of at least $1 - n^{-\frac{1}{4}\log(n)}$ that every r-neighborhood has size at most $\log(n)^{2r} d(n)^r$.*

Proof. The Chernoff Bound states for the degree D of an individual vertex that $\mathbb{P}[D \geq x] \leq e^{-(\frac{1}{3}\frac{x}{d(n)} - 1)d(n)}$ and therefore $\mathbb{P}[D \geq \log(n)^2 d(n)] \leq n^{-\frac{1}{4}\log(n)}$. Let $\hat{D}$ be the maximal degree of the graph. With the union bound we have a similar bound for $\hat{D}$. Every r-neighborhood has size at most $\hat{D}^r$.   □

Theorem 3. *Let H be a connected graph with h vertices and radius r.*

There is a deterministic algorithm that can find out whether H occurs as a subgraph in $G(n, d(n)/n)$ in expected time $2^{O(h)} (d(n) \log n)^{O(r)} n$.

Proof. We sketch the algorithm briefly. The algorithm works on a graph $G = G(n, d(n)/n)$. In the following we assume that every r-neighborhood in G has size at most $d(n)^r \log(n)^{2r}$. By Lemma 4 this assumption holds with a probability of at least $1 - n^{\log(n)/4}$ and we can easily check it within the stated time bounds. Should the assumption be wrong, we can use a brute force algorithm without affecting the average running time.

In a preprocessing step we look at the connected graph H and construct a subgraph H' that is also connected, but consists only of a tree with two additional edges (if possible, otherwise we set $H' = H$).

We enumerate all r-neighborhoods in G and try to find H in every one of them as follows: By using color-coding we enumerate all subgraphs in the r-neighborhood that are isomorphic to H'. This can be done by using the algorithm for finding a graph of bounded treewidth [24] with the enumeration techniques in [25]. The expected time needed is $2^{O(h)}(d(n)\log(n))^{O(r)}$ times the number of subgraphs that are found. However, by Lemma 2 the latter number is bounded by a constant.

After enumerating all subgraphs isomorphic to H' we have to find out whether G contains H as a subgraph. If this turns out to be true, then H can be found only somewhere where H' was found. Hence, it suffices to look at all found H' in G and see whether by adding a subset of the possible $\binom{h}{2}$ edges we can find H. This can be done in time $O(2^{h^2} d(n)^r \log(n)^2)$, which is asymptotically faster than the remaining part. □

5   Experimental Evaluation of Barabási–Albert-Graphs

In the previous section, we showed that Erdős–Rényi graphs have bounded expansion for edge probability $p = d/n$ (with constant d) and are nowhere dense with $p = n^{o(1)}/n$. In this section, we discuss the sparsity of the Barabási–Albert model. It is known that this model has *not* a.a.s. bounded expansion, because it contains an unbounded clique with non-vanishing probability [21]. It is not known, however, if it is (or is not) a.a.s. somewhere-dense. Our experiments seem to imply that on average Barabási–Albert graphs seem to be dense but that this density is limited to early vertices: In the Barabási–Albert model, vertices with high degree tend to be preferred for new connections. This means that edge probabilities are not independent. Moreover, the expected degree $d(i) = \sqrt{n/i}$ for a vertex i is less uniform than it is for Erdős–Rényi graphs, where $d(i) = pn$.

To evaluate the expansion properties of the Barabási–Albert-model, we compute transitive fraternal augmentations and p-centered colorings. These have been introduced by Nešetřil and de Mendez, and are highly related to bounded expansion and a tool for developing new and faster algorithms. A graph class has bounded expansion if and only if the maximum in-degree of transitive fraternal augmentations is bounded, or the graph admits a p-centered coloring with bounded number of colors.

Definition 6 (Transitive fraternal augmentation [9]). *Let $\overrightarrow{G}$ be a directed graph. A 1-transitive fraternal augmentation of $\overrightarrow{G}$ is a directed graph $\overrightarrow{H}$ with* *the same vertex set, including all the arcs of $\overrightarrow{G}$ and such that, for any vertices* x, y, z,

- *if (x, z) and (z, y) are arcs of $\overrightarrow{G}$ then (x, y) is an arc of $\overrightarrow{H}$ (transitivity),*
- *if (x, z) and (y, z) are arcs of $\overrightarrow{G}$ then (x, y) or (y, x) is an arc of $\overrightarrow{H}$ (fraternity).*

A transitive fraternal augmentation of a directed graph $\overrightarrow{G}$ is then the consecutive application of 1-transitive fraternal augmentations.

Definition 7 (p-centered coloring [26]). *For an integer p, a p-centered coloring of G is a coloring of the vertices such that any connected subgraph H induced on the vertices of an arbitrary set of i colors ($i \leq p$), H must have at least one color that appears exactly once.*

Showing that the maximum in-degree of a transitive fraternal augmentation or the number of colors needed for a p-centered coloring does not grow with the size of the graph is a way to prove that a graph has bounded expansion [9]. When designing algorithms, p-centered colorings can be used to solve hard problems efficiently. By using p-centered colorings, we can decompose a graph into small, well-structured subgraphs such that NP-hard problems can be solved easily on each subgraph before combining these small solutions to get a solution for the entire graph. It is important that the number of colors needed for a p-centered coloring for a fixed p is small, as the runtime usually is a function of the number of colors needed. If a graph class does not have bounded expansion; that is, the number of colors grows with n, but very slowly, such as $\log \log n$, using these algorithms might still be practical.

One example problem which can be solved directly using p-centered colorings is Subgraph Isomorphism, where one asks if a graph H is contained in a graph G as a subgraph. In general graphs, this problem is W[1]-hard when parameterizing by the size of H [27]. However, there exist an algorithm, whose runtime is a function of the number of colors needed for a p-centered coloring, where p depends on the size of H [23]. So, regardless of the fact whether Barabási–Albert graphs are theoretically sparse or not, calculating the number of colors of a p-centered coloring for different graph sizes has direct impact on the feasibility of a whole class of algorithms on these graphs.

5.1   Barabási–Albert Graphs are Empirically Dense

First, we analyze the maximum in-degree of transitive fraternal augmentations. We ran the previously described algorithm on random Barabási–Albert graphs with $d = 2$ for different sizes ($500 \leq n \leq 3000$) and calculated the maximum in-degree of up to five transitive fraternal augmentation steps. The results are shown in Fig. 1a. Each data point is an average over ten runs with the same n. For all graphs both the maximum in-degree grows with n, which would not be the case for graphs with bounded expansion.

To evaluate how well the expansion properties of Barabási–Albert graphs can be practically exploited, we analyzed the number of colors needed to construct p-centered colorings. We constructed 3- and 4-centered colorings. With the same graph parameters and sizes than before. The results are shown in Fig. 1b. For the analyzed range, the number of colors needed grows steadily. Furthermore, the number of colors needed to construct 4-centered colorings is substantially higher than the number of colors needed for 3-centered colorings. Computing higher order colorings or colorings for larger graphs was infeasible with the used algorithm. It seems practically impossible to use p-centered colorings algorithmically for Barabási–Albert graphs. We have to note that the used algorithm is only a heuristic and the real values might be much better than what we have computed. But since these heuristics work well for graphs that have low treedepth colorings, it is unlikely that the graphs have bounded coloring number for p-centered colorings. Previously, we showed that the colors needed to construct p-centered colorings of small graphs can be very high. In this section we discover that the early vertices of the random process heavily affect these results. We remove the first 10% of the vertices added in the random process and analyze the maximum in-degree of transitive fraternal augmentations and number of colors needed to construct p-centered colorings. By removing those 10%, we can construct p-centered colorings for much larger graphs ($5000 \leq n \leq 30000$), see Fig. 2a and b. The required number of colors for p-centered colorings and maximum in-degree of transitive fraternal augmentations remain stable and do not seem to depend on the number of vertices. This suggests that these 10% of the early vertices contain almost all of the density of Barabási–Albert graphs. This is of course a linear factor and it remains to see if one can use much smaller functions of n, like for example $\log n$. The sizes of the graphs at hand, however, were not large enough to investigate sub-linear functions of n with a meaningful result.

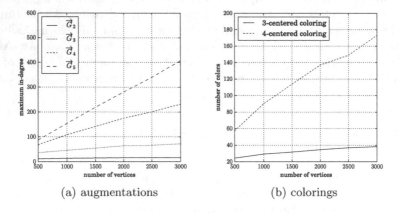

(a) augmentations   (b) colorings

Fig. 1. Results for Barabási–Albert graphs with $d = 2$ for increasing n.

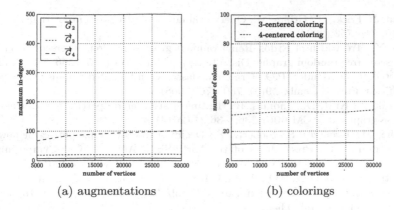

(a) augmentations   (b) colorings

Fig. 2. Results for Barabási–Albert graphs with $d = 2$ for increasing n after deleting the first 10% of vertices.

6 Conclusion

In this work we gave an alternative proof that $G(n, d/n)$ has a.a.s. bounded expansion and have shown that $G(n, d(n)/n)$ with $d(n) = n^{o(1)}$ has a.a.s. locally bounded treewidth. Our results are based on the fact that local neighborhoods of Erdős–Rényi graphs are tree-like with high probability. It is known [4] that for a graph $G = G(n, d(n)/n)$ with $d(n) = n^{o(1)}$ and a first-order formula φ one can decide whether $G \models \varphi$ in expected time $f(|\varphi|)n^{1+o(1)}$ for some functions f and g. This result can also be proven using our techniques. It remains to show whether it is possible to answer this question in linear expected fpt-time (where $d(n)n$ is the expected number of edges), i.e. $O(f(|\varphi|)d(n)n)$. In this paper, we also presented a more efficient algorithm for the subgraph isomorphism problem on Erdős–Rényi graphs if the pattern graph has small radius. It would be interesting to consider other measures for the pattern graph as well, such as treewidth or treedepth. Furthermore, we gathered empirical evidence which suggests that Barabási–Albert graphs are somewhere dense. It would be interesting to prove this conjecture.

References

1. Bollobás, B.: Random Graphs, 2nd edn. Cambridge University Press, Cambridge (2001)
2. Erdős, P., Rényi, A.: On random graphs. Publ. Math. **6**, 290–297 (1959)
3. Fagin, R.: Probabilities on finite models. J. Symb. Log. **41**(1), 50–58 (1976)
4. Grohe, M.: Logic, graphs, and algorithms (2007)
5. Coja-Oghlan, A., Taraz, A.: Colouring random graphs in expected polynomial time. In: Alt, H., Habib, M. (eds.) STACS 2003. LNCS, vol. 2607, pp. 487–498. Springer, Heidelberg (2003). https://doi.org/10.1007/3-540-36494-3_43
6. Dawar, A., Grohe, M., Kreutzer, S.: Locally excluding a minor. In: 22nd Annual IEEE Symposium on Logic in Computer Science (LICS 2007), pp. 270–279, July 2007

7. Flum, J., Frick, M., Grohe, M.: Query evaluation via tree-decompositions. J. ACM **49**(6), 716–752 (2002)
8. Gao, Y.: Treewidth of Erdős–Rényi random graphs, random intersection graphs, and scale-free random graphs. Discrete Appl. Math. **160**(4–5), 566–578 (2012)
9. Nešetřil, J., de Mendez, P.O.: Grad and classes with bounded expansion I. Decompositions. Eur. J. Comb. **29**(3), 760–776 (2008)
10. Dvořák, Z., Kráĺ, D., Thomas, R.: Testing first-order properties for subclasses of sparse graphs. J. ACM **60**(5), 36:1–36:24 (2013)
11. Grohe, M., Kreutzer, S., Siebertz, S.: Deciding first-order properties of nowhere dense graphs. In: Proceedings of the Forty-Sixth Annual ACM Symposium on Theory of Computing, STOC 2014, pp. 89–98. ACM, New York (2014)
12. Nešetřil, J., de Mendez, P.O., Wood, D.R.: Characterisations and examples of graph classes with bounded expansion. Eur. J. Comb. **33**(3), 350–373 (2012). Topological and Geometric Graph Theory
13. Fountoulakis, N., Friedrich, T., Hermelin, D.: On the average-case complexity of parameterized clique. Theoret. Comput. Sci. **576**, 18–29 (2015)
14. Frick, M., Grohe, M.: Deciding first-order properties of locally tree-decomposable structures. J. ACM **48**(6), 1184–1206 (2001)
15. Dawar, A., Grohe, M., Kreutzer, S.: Locally excluding a minor. In: Proceedings of the 22nd IEEE Symposium on Logic in Computer Science (LICS 2007), Wroclaw, Poland, 10–12 July 2007, pp. 270–279. IEEE Computer Society (2007)
16. Grohe, M.: Generalized model-checking problems for first-order logic. In: Ferreira, A., Reichel, H. (eds.) STACS 2001. LNCS, vol. 2010, pp. 12–26. Springer, Heidelberg (2001). https://doi.org/10.1007/3-540-44693-1_2
17. Barabási, A.L., Albert, R.: Emergence of scaling in random networks. Science **286**(5439), 509–512 (1999). American Association for the Advancement of Science
18. Cohen, R., Havlin, S.: Scale-free networks are ultrasmall. Phys. Rev. Lett. **90**, 058701 (2003)
19. Kamrul, M.H., Hassan, M.Z., Pavel, N.I.: Dynamic scaling, data-collapse and self-similarity in Barabási–Albert networks. J. Phys. A: Math. Theoret. **44**(17), 175101 (2011)
20. Klemm, K., Eguíluz, V.M.: Growing scale-free networks with small-world behavior. Phys. Rev. E **65**, 057102 (2002)
21. Demaine, E.D., Reidl, F., Rossmanith, P., Villaamil, F.S., Sikdar, S., Sullivan, B.D.: Structural sparsity of complex networks: random graph models and linear algorithms. CoRR abs/1406.2587 (2014)
22. Diestel, R.: Graph Theory. Springer, Berlin (2010)
23. Nešetřil, J., de Mendez, P.O.: Sparsity: Graphs, Structures, and Algorithms. Springer, Berlin (2014)
24. Alon, N., Yuster, R., Zwick, U.: Color-coding. J. ACM **42**(4), 844–856 (1995)
25. Chen, J., Kanj, I.A., Meng, J., Xia, G., Zhang, F.: On the effective enumerability of NP problems. In: Bodlaender, H.L., Langston, M.A. (eds.) IWPEC 2006. LNCS, vol. 4169, pp. 215–226. Springer, Heidelberg (2006). https://doi.org/10.1007/11847250_20
26. Nešetřil, J., de Mendez, P.O.: Grad and classes with bounded expansion II. Algorithmic aspects. Eur. J. Comb. **29**(3), 777–791 (2008)
27. Downey, R.G., Fellows, M.R.: Parameterized Complexity. Springer, Berlin (2012)

Target Set Selection Parameterized by Clique-Width and Maximum Threshold

Tim A. Hartmann[⊠]

Lehrstuhl für Informatik 1, RWTH Aachen University, Aachen, Germany
`hartmann@algo.rwth-aachen.de`

Abstract. The TARGET SET SELECTION problem takes as an input a graph G and a non-negative integer threshold $\text{thr}(v)$ for every vertex v. A vertex v can get active as soon as at least $\text{thr}(v)$ of its neighbors have been activated. The objective is to select a smallest possible initial set of vertices, the target set, whose activation eventually leads to the activation of all vertices in the graph.

We show that TARGET SET SELECTION is in FPT when parameterized with the combined parameters clique-width of the graph and the maximum threshold value. This generalizes all previous FPT-membership results for the parameterization by maximum threshold, and thereby solves an open question from the literature. We stress that the time complexity of our algorithm is surprisingly well-behaved and grows only single-exponentially in the parameters.

1 Introduction

The TARGET SET SELECTION problem (TSS) suits to model irreversible propagation of all sorts of conditions or information in a network. This may be for example a word-of-mouth-effect, disease spreading or fault influence in distributed systems [15]. The input is an undirected graph G and a non-negative integer threshold $\text{thr}(v)$ for every vertex v. The task is to select a smallest possible set S of initially active vertices, the target set, whose activation eventually leads to the activation of all vertices in the graph. A vertex v can become active as soon as at least $\text{thr}(v)$ of its neighbors have been activated.

Our view on the activation of a vertex is that it is *allowed* to become active if enough neighbors are active before, in contrast to that it is *obligated* to get active as soon as possible. We ask for a smallest possible set S, the target set, and a permutation of the vertices π, which is the ordering in which the vertices get active. Then, for every non-target set vertex v, to assure its activation we require that at least threshold $\text{thr}(v)$ many neighbors of v are ordered before v. In particular, our permutation may order the target set vertices S not at the beginning. This definition is more robust towards re-orderings of the permutation of vertices. We can re-order the permutation and not have to bother that for example the target set no longer consists of the very first vertices of the ordering. In the literature the problem is commonly defined via rounds of activations that

© Springer International Publishing AG 2018
A. M. Tjoa et al. (Eds.): SOFSEM 2018, LNCS 10706, pp. 137–149, 2018.
https://doi.org/10.1007/978-3-319-73117-9_10

define sets of active vertices for each round. Our definition is equivalent while being much more convenient for our techniques.

TARGET SET SELECTION

Input: An undirected graph G, a non-negative threshold for every vertex $\text{thr} : V(G) \to \mathbb{N}$, and $k \in \mathbb{N}$.

Question: Is there a set of vertics $S \subseteq V(G)$ of size at most k and a permutation of the vertices $\pi : V(G) \to [|V(G)|]$ such that for every vertex $v \in V(G) \setminus S$ we have $|\{u \in N_G(v) \mid \pi(u) < \pi(v)\}| \geq \text{thr}(v)$?

The problem was first introduced by Kempe et al. [14]. It proves to be computationally extremely difficult. It is NP-hard even for the restriction to split-graphs of diameter two [15]. Chen showed that minimizing the size of the target set is APX-hard [4]. More recently, Bazgan et al. showed that for every functions f and ρ this problem cannot be approximated within a factor of $\rho(k)$ in $f(k) \cdot n^{\mathcal{O}(1)}$ time [1]. The parameterized complexity studies focus on the original problem and two variants that limit the allowed thresholds. These are *constant thresholds*, where all thresholds are at most a constant $t_{\max}$, and *majority thresholds*, where a vertex can get active as soon as at least the majority of its neighborhood is active before. The general TSS is W[1]-hard for each of the parameterization, "distance to cluster," [5] "distance to forest" and pathwidth [15]. The strongest positive FPT-membership results for constant thresholds are the parameterization by treewidth [2], the parameterization by "distance to cluster" [5], and the parameterization by neighborhood diversity [11]. There are a lot more parameterized complexity results for these three variants of TSS [5,15]. Further, Cicalese et al. study a variant of TSS which asks if a set of vertices A can be activated in a given number of activation rounds [6]. They give a polynomial time algorithm when the number of activation rounds and the clique-width of the input graph are constant. Their exponential dependency on the clique-width is unlikely to be improved, as even TSS for one activation round is W[1]-hard with respect to the treewidth [3]. For a more extend introduction to the history of the problem as well as other algorithmic aspects and similar models see for example [5,15].

Dvořák et al. raised the question of the complexity of the parameterization by the modular-width [11]. The structural graph parameter modular-width was introduced by Gajarský et al. [13]. We give a positive answer by showing FPT-membership for a more general question. We consider the clique-width which is upper bounded by the parameters modular-width and treewidth [7], and by further common structural parameters for which the parametrized complexity of TSS was open. Thereby, we generalize all positive FPT-memberships results for TSS with constant thresholds. Further, our result does not rely on the maximum threshold $t_{\max}$ being a constant, but allows that $t_{\max}$ is a parameter. Moreover, the time complexity of our algorithm behaves surprisingly well and grows only single-exponentially in the parameters clique-width and maximum threshold.

A related result is that TSS is in FPTwhen parameterized by treewidth and maximum threshold, by Ben-Zwi et al. [2]. They use a dynamic program that works along the bags of a computed tree decomposition. They fix the local ordering in which the vertices of the currently observed bag get active. Our approach also uses such an recursive approach, while working on a computed ℓ-expression. Informally, an ℓ-expression is a tree-decomposition in the context of clique-width. Such an ℓ-expression f uses three types of recursive operations that work on labeled vertices using at most ℓ different labels. Analogously to the approach for a tree decomposition, for every subexpression a current state fixes a part of the global ordering of the vertices.

However, the described vertices of a current subexpression is not bounded by our parameters. Our algorithm has to remember an ordering of a limited number of vertices and further has to address these vertices indirectly. Crucial for the activation of a vertex is its threshold and neighborhood. However, we cannot address the neighborhood even for vertices of currently equal label and threshold since they can have very different neighborhoods as subexpression may reveal. Consequently, our approach explores the ℓ-expression top down, and fixes an ordering of the important vertices of the up to now described graph. The up to now encountered operations define a common neighborhood for all vertices of a fixed label. This is because for every outer operations, vertices of the same label behave equally. Thus, our local ordering indirectly references the vertices solely by their label and threshold.

Further, vertices of the same label that occur late enough in a global ordering behave equally. There is only one type of edge operation of ℓ-expression, namely $\eta_{\alpha,\beta}$ adding all edges between vertices of some labels α and β. There, for a vertex v of label α we have to account the contribution to the activation of v due to vertices of label β. Only the first $\mathsf{thr}(v) \leq t_{\max}$ active vertices of label β are important. If the activation of v is between the activation of the first $t_{\max}$ of label β, we fix their relative positioning in our local ordering. Otherwise, the activation of v does not differ from other late vertices of label α.

However, we need to guarantee that a vertex v of label α that is not referenced by our local ordering is indeed ordered late enough. That is, the first $t_{\max}$ vertices of label β occur before vertex v. We denote such a global ordering as nice to the current subexpression $\eta_{\alpha,\beta}f'$. It is possible to modify any valid global ordering to be nice to all subexpressions. We extend our local ordering to also include the $(t_{\max} + 1)$-st vertex of every label. Then, whether the underlying global ordering π is nice, is reflected in our local ordering. Therefore, we can restrict our algorithm to consider nice global orderings only.

The resulting procedure for our algorithm at each operation of the given ℓ-expression then is as follows. For a current edge operation $\eta_{\alpha,\beta}$, for each vertex v we simply have to adjust the number of neighbors contributing to the activation of v according to our fixed local ordering. We remember this contribution as the *activation from outside*. For a current operation that combines two subgraphs, consider the unknown partition of the vertices fixed by the local ordering in either subgraph. In that case, the algorithm tries all possibilities. The approach for the operation that re-labels a label is very similar. For every subexpression, the number of possible states is single-exponentially bounded by our parameters, which yields to an overall FPT-runtime.

Theorem 1. *Let* $t_{max}, \ell \in \mathbb{N}$. *There is an algorithm that, given a graph* G, *a threshold for each vertex* thr : $V(G) \to [0, t_{max}]$ *and an* ℓ-*expression* f *of* G, *computes the minimal size of a target set in time* $\mathcal{O}(\ell^{3\ell t} \cdot t^{\ell(4t+1)} \cdot |f|)$, *where* $t := t_{max} + 1$ *and* $|f|$ *is the length of* f.

An easy upper bound for the length of the ℓ-expression f is $|V(G)|^2$. Further, one can obtain a minimum target set, and not only its size, by tracking such sets throughout our dynamic program.

Oum gave an algorithm that either outputs an $(8^\ell - 1)$-expression of graph G or confirms that the clique-width of G is larger than ℓ, and that runs in time $\mathcal{O}(g(\ell) \cdot |V(G)|^3)$, where $g(\ell)$ only depends on the clique-width ℓ [17]. Combined with the algorithm of Theorem 1 it follows that TSS parameterized by the clique-width and the maximum threshold is in FPT.

Corollary 1. TARGET SET SELECTION *is in FPT with respect to the combined parameters clique-width of the given graph and the maximum threshold.*

Following the preliminaries in Sect. 2, we prove Theorem 1 in Sect. 3. We conclude in Sect. 4. Due to space constraints, we omit some proofs or only give a proof sketch. For the full proof, we refer to an online version at https://arxiv.org/abs/1710.00635.

2 Preliminaries

For integers $i < j$, let $[i] := \{1, 2, \ldots, i\}$ and $[i, j] := \{i, (i+1), \ldots, j\}$. For a list (or vector) A, we describe the i-th element as $A[i]$.

All our graphs are simple, finite and undirected. For a graph G, we denote by $V(G)$ its set of vertices. We use $N_G(v)$ as the neighborhood of vertex $v \in V(G)$. Usually we consider graphs with thresholds for each vertex thr : $V(G) \to [0, t_{max}]$ which are at most a constant t_{max}, and assume that its thresholds thr and t_{max} are given, if needed.

In this work, we consider parameterized complexity. For an introduction see for example [9,10,12,16]. For a graph class, for example clusters (the disjoint union of cliques), the parameter "distance to cluster" is the minimal number of vertices one needs to delete from the input graph in order to obtain a cluster.

The clique-width $\mathsf{cw}(G)$ of a graph G was introduced in [8]. A graph has clique-width at most $\ell \in \mathbb{N}$, if it can be constructed by an ℓ-expression that uses four types of operations and a labeling of the vertices of at most ℓ labels, as we describe in the following. Let $\mathsf{labels}(f)$ be the set of labels used by f. To avoid confusion with thresholds, we use small Greek letters α, β, γ for the labels. An ℓ-expression defines a graph $G(f)$ with labels per vertex $\mathsf{lab}_G : V(G) \to \mathsf{labels}(f)$. The graph $G(f)$ is recursively defined as

- $G(v(\alpha))$, a single vertex v of label $\alpha \in \mathsf{labels}(f)$,
- $G(f_1 \oplus f_2)$, the disjoint union of $G(f_1)$ and $G(f_2)$ for ℓ-expressions f_1, f_2,
- $G(\eta_{\alpha,\beta}f')$, the graph $G(f')$ where there is an edge between every vertex of label α and every vertex of label β, for ℓ-expression f', and
- $G(\rho_{\alpha \to \beta}f')$, the graph $G(f')$ where all vertices of label α are re-labeled to label β, for ℓ-expression f'.

The subexpressions of f are all expressions f_1, f_2, f' used in the recursive definition of f. Especially f is a subexpression of f. We drop the $G(\cdot)$ when using $G(f)$ as a nested term. For example, instead of $V(G(f))$, we simply write $V(f)$. Further, we also refrain from specifying the set of labels $\mathsf{labels}(f)$ if it is clear from the context.

An ℓ-expression is irredundant if for every subexpression $\eta_{\alpha,\beta}f'$ the graph $G(\eta_{\alpha,\beta}f')$ has no edge between vertices of label α and β. We assume that the given ℓ-expression is irredundant, which we can assure by a simple preprocessing step [8].

3 Dynamic Program

A good way to convince someone that a graph G with thresholds has a target set of size at most k is to state a complete ordering in which the vertices get active. We denote this permutation of the vertices as a *global ordering* $\pi : V(G) \to [|V(G)|]$. We say that π is k-activating for graph G if there is a k-vertex set $S \subseteq V(G)$, the target set, such that for every other vertex v the neighbors of v that are ordered before v outnumber the threshold $\mathsf{thr}(v)$.

Definition 1. *A* global ordering *of a graph G is a permutation of the vertices $\pi : V(G) \to [|V(G)|]$. Further, π is* k-activating *(for G) if there is a k-vertex set $S \subseteq V(G)$ such that for every vertex $v \in V(G) \setminus S$ we have*

$$\pi_G^{\leq}(v) := \left|\{u \in \mathsf{N}_G(v) \mid \pi(u) < \pi(v)\}\right| \geq \mathsf{thr}(v).$$

Graph G has a target set of size k if there is a global ordering π such that π is k-activating for G.

Example 1. The following graph G has global ordering $\pi : v_i \mapsto i$, which is 1-activating (for $S = \{v_1\}$). Further, $f = \eta_{\beta,\gamma}f' = \eta_{\beta,\gamma}(v_6(\gamma) \oplus v_8(\gamma) \oplus v_{11}(\gamma) \oplus v_9(\gamma) \oplus v_7(\beta) \oplus \rho_{\gamma \to \alpha}\eta_{\beta,\gamma}(v_{10}(\gamma) \oplus \rho_{\gamma \to \alpha}\eta_{\alpha,\beta}\eta_{\beta,\gamma}(v_2(\gamma) \oplus v_1(\beta) \oplus v_3(\beta) \oplus v_4(\alpha) \oplus v_5(\alpha))))$ is a 3-expression of G. For each vertex, the label among $\{\alpha, \beta, \gamma\}$ and threshold at most $t_{\max} = 2$ is given as a tuple.

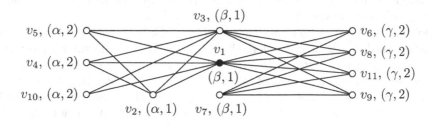

For later examples, let $A := ((\beta, 1), (\alpha, 1), (\beta, 1), (\alpha, 2), (\alpha, 2), (\gamma, 2), (\beta, 1),$ $(\gamma, 2), (\gamma, 2))$, and further $\eta_{\alpha,\beta} f'$, G and π be as defined here.

An ℓ-expression f describes a graph $G(f)$ with three types of recursive operations that rely on ℓ different labels assigned to the vertices. We formulate a dynamic program over the subexpressions of f. At a current subexpression f, a *state* fixes a part of a global ordering π. Whether such a state is a part of a k-activating global ordering, is verified by considering the subexpressions with suitable states.

In order to obtain the desired FPT-runtime, we may only work with states that fix an ordering of a number of vertices bounded by our parameters, which are maximum threshold $t_{\max}$ and clique-width ℓ. However, the number of all vertices described by a current subexpression is not bounded by our parameters. Our algorithm thus can only remember an ordering of a limited number of vertices and further cannot address these vertices directly. We identify the important verices and a suitable way to remember them. Crucial for the activation of a vertex is its threshold and neighborhood. Our local ordering can very well remember the threshold of vertices. However, it cannot address the neighborhood even for vertices of currently equal label and threshold since they can have very different neighborhoods as subexpression may reveal.

Consequently, our approach explores the given ℓ-expression top down, and fixes an ordering of the important vertices of the graph described by the up to now seen part of the ℓ-expression. The up to now seen operations define a common neighborhood for all vertices of a fixed label. This is because for every outer operation, two vertices of equal label behave equally. Thus, our local ordering can indirectly reference the vertices solely by their label and threshold.

Now, let us identify the vertices whose relative ordering is crucial. We can observe that vertices of the same label that occur late enough in a global ordering behave equally. An ℓ-expression has only one type of operation that adds edges, namely $\eta_{\alpha,\beta}$ for some labels α and β, which adds all edges between vertices of labels α and β. There, for a vertex v of label α we have to account for the contribution to the activation of v by the vertices of label β. Only the first $\mathrm{thr}(v) \leq t_{\max}$ vertices of label β of the global ordering π are important. Consequently, if π orders v somewhere between the first $t_{\max}$ vertices of label β, the local ordering fixes the ordering of v relatively to those first vertices of label β as well. If π orders v after the first $t_{\max}$ of label β, we can neglect its exact ordering. This is because the number of neighbors of label β that contribute to its activation do not differ from other such late vertices of label α. Our plan therefore is that the local ordering fixes the relative positioning of these crucial first $t_{\max}$ vertices of every label.

Doing so, we need to guarantee that a vertex v of label α that is not referenced by our local ordering is indeed ordered late enough. That is, the first $t_{\max}$ vertices of label β occur before vertex v. In particular, the first $t_{\max}$ vertices of label β are ordered before the $(t_{\max} + 1)$-st of label α. Then, given that v is not referenced by our local ordering, there are at least $t_{\max}$ of label β ordered before, or if there are not even as many of label β, accordingly less. We denote such an ordering as nice to the current subexpression $\eta_{\alpha,\beta} f'$. It is possible to modify any valid global ordering such that it is nice to every subexpression. Therefore, our algorithm may only consider nice global orderings. We extend our local ordering to also include the $(t_{\max} + 1)$-st vertex of every label. Then, whether the underlying global ordering π is nice to a current expression $\eta_{\alpha,\beta} f'$, is reflected in our local ordering. Our algorithm may then ignore states with such not nice local orderings.

We define the local ordering A for a current ℓ-expression f that fixes the relative ordering of the first $(t_{\max} + 1)$ activate vertices for each label α (or if there are not even as many vertices of label α, accordingly less), which we denote by t^{α}. We indirectly remember a vertex v by fixing the label and threshold of v. For technical reasons, we define a local ordering as possibly incomplete. Our algorithm only considers complete local orderings.

Definition 2. *Let G be a graph with labels* lab $: V(G) \rightarrow$ labels(G). *For label α, let $t^{\alpha}(G) := \min\{t_{\max}(G)+1, |\{v \in V(G) \mid \mathsf{lab}(v) = \alpha\}|\}$. A local ordering A of G is a list of tuples of label and threshold $(\alpha, a) \in \mathsf{labels}(G) \times [0, t_{\max}(G)]$ such that for every label α there are at most t^{α} tuples of label α; and A is complete if, for every label α, there are exactly t^{α} tuples of label α.*

The local ordering A is our limited view on a global ordering π. Let condense(π) be the ordered list of vertices consisting of the first t^{α} vertices of each label α. A global ordering π *extends* A if the tuples of label and threshold of condense(π) are equal to A. As a technical tool, we also define condense(π, A) as the first ordered vertices consisting of each label α, such that the number of vertices labeled α is equal to as there are in A.

Definition 3. *Let graph G have global ordering π. Consider the list of vertices according to the global ordering $\pi^{-1}(1), \ldots, \pi^{-1}(|V(G)|)$. For every label α, remove all vertices of label α but the first t^{α} vertices of label α. Then, the resulting list is* condense(π). *Global ordering π extends a local ordering A (for G) if the list tuples of label and threshold of* condense(π) *is equal to A.*

Let condense(π, A) *be the remaining list, after, for every label α, removing all vertices of label α but the first $|\{i \mid \mathsf{lab}(A[i]) = \alpha\}|$ of label α.*

Example 2. We have $t^{\alpha}, t^{\beta}, t^{\gamma} = 3$ and A is a complete local ordering of G. Further, condense$(\pi) = $ condense$(\pi, A) = (v_1, \ldots, v_9)$, whose list of tuples of label and threshold is equal to A. Thus, A extends π. Let incomplete local ordering A^* contain only one tuple per label. Then, condense(π, A^*) is the list of vertices (v_1, v_2, v_6). The list of tuples of label and threshold is equal to A^*.

For an edge operation $\eta_{\alpha,\beta}$, which adds all edges between vertices of two distinct labels, we simply have to adjust the number of neighbors contributing to an activation of a vertex according to our fixed local ordering. We remember this contribution as the *activation from outside*. The mapping afo maps to a value $[0, t_{\max}]$ for each position of the local ordering A, as well as maps to a value for each label. That way we have a value for every vertex indirectly referenced by

A. Further, there is a value for every vertex v not referenced by A, which we identify via the label of v.

A *state* of a current subgraph $G(f)$ is a tuple consisting of a local ordering A and an activation from outside afo. To reference the activation from outside for a concrete vertex v we define $A^\pi(v)$ such that $\mathsf{afo}(A^\pi(v))$ is the activation from outside for v. Thus, $A^\pi(v)$ maps v to its according position in A if it exists and otherwise to the label of v. A global ordering π is k-activating for a state (A, afo) of G if it is k-activating for G while supported by the activation from outside afo.

Definition 4. *Let f be an ℓ-expression, and graph $G(f)$ have local ordering A. An* activation from outside *for A is a mapping* $\mathsf{afo} : [|A|] \cup \mathsf{labels}(f) \to [0, t_{\max}]$. *Then, the tuple (A, afo) is a* state *of $G(f)$. For a global ordering π of $G(f)$, let* $A^\pi : V(f) \to [|A|] \cup \mathsf{labset} f)$,

$$A^\pi(v) \mapsto \begin{cases} i, & i \in [|A|], \ v = \mathsf{condense}(\pi, A)[i], \\ \mathsf{lab}(v), & else. \end{cases}$$

A global ordering π of $G(f)$ is k-activating for (A, afo) if there is k-vertex set $S \subseteq V(G)$ such that for every vertex $v \in V(G) \setminus S$ we have that

$$\pi^{\leq}_G(v) \geq \mathsf{thr}(v) - \mathsf{afo}(A^\pi(v)).$$

Example 3. Let $\mathsf{afo}(1) = 1$, and for $x \in \{2, \ldots, 6, \alpha, \beta, \gamma\}$, let $\mathsf{afo}(x) = 0$. The activation from outside for vertex v_1 is $\mathsf{afo}(A^\pi(v_1)) = \mathsf{afo}(1) = 1$ and for vertex v_{10} it is $\mathsf{afo}(A^\pi(v_{10})) = \mathsf{afo}(\alpha) = 0$. Further, π is 0-activating for state (A, afo).

We define nice orderings, analogously for global orderings π and local orderings A. As we show in the following, for every k-activating global ordering π there is a slightly modified k-activating global ordering π which is nice to every subexpression of f. Our local ordering A includes the $(t_{\max} + 1)$-st vertex of every label. Thus, whether π is to nice the current expression f is expressed in the ordering of A. Therefore, our algorithm can avoid not nice global orderings by ignoring states where the local ordering A is not nice to f.

Definition 5. *Let G be a graph with global ordering π. Let f be an ℓ-expression describing a subgraph of G. For label α, let $v_\alpha[1], v_\alpha[2], \cdots \in V(f)$ be the vertices of label α of $G(f)$ ordered ascending according to π. For every label α, let $t^\alpha_{\max} := \min\{t_{\max}(G), |\{v \in V(G) \mid \mathsf{lab}(v) = \alpha\}|\}$. Then, π is nice to f if $f = \eta_{\alpha,\beta} f'$ implies that (if those respective positions exist)*

$$\pi(v_\alpha[t_{\max}+1]) > \pi(v_\beta[t^\beta_{\max}]) \quad and \quad \pi(v_\beta[t_{\max}+1]) > \pi(v_\alpha[t^\alpha_{\max}]).$$

Let A be the list of tuples of label and threshold of $\mathsf{condense}(\pi \restriction_{V(f)})$ for graph $G(f)$, where $\pi \restriction_{V(f)}$ is π restricted to vertices $V(f)$. Then, A is nice to f if (and only if) π is nice to f.

Example 4. Global ordering π is not nice to $\eta_{\beta,\gamma}f'$ since $\pi(v_\beta[t_{\max}+1]) = \pi(v_7) = 7 \not> 8 = \pi(v_8) = \pi(v_\gamma[t_{\max}])$. By switching the 7th and 8th position π becomes nice to $\eta_{\beta,\gamma}f'$. Likewise, A is not nice to $\eta_{\beta,\gamma}f'$, but $A' = ((\beta,1), (\alpha,1), (\beta,1), (\alpha,2), (\alpha,2), (\gamma,2), (\boldsymbol{\gamma},\boldsymbol{2}), (\boldsymbol{\beta},\boldsymbol{1}), (\gamma,2))$ is nice to $\eta_{\beta,\gamma}f'$.

Lemma 1. *Let f be an ℓ-expression and π a global ordering that is k-activating for graph $G(f)$. Then, there is a global ordering π' that is k-activating for graph $G(f)$ and nice to every subexpression of f.*

Proof (Sketch). There may be subexpressions $\eta_{\alpha,\beta}f'$ where the $(t_{\max}+1)$st vertex of label α is ordered before the first $t_{\max}$ vertices of label β, formally $\pi(v_\alpha[t_{\max}+1]) =: i < \pi(v_\beta[t^\beta_{\max}])$. We repair such a violation by moving all vertices of $v_\beta[1], \ldots, v_\beta[t^\beta_{\max}]$ that did not occur already between positions $(i-1)$ and i. Since there are $t_{\max}$ vertices of label α ordered before position i, the modified local ordering is still activating. We repair all such violations top-down. Following this order prevents recursive violations for already fixed subexpression $\eta_{\alpha',\beta'}$. For a full proof see online version.

Definition 6. *Graph $G(f)$ is k-activating for a state (A, afo) if there is a global ordering π that extends A, is k-activating for (A, afo), and is nice to every subexpression of f.*

Lemma 2. *Let f be an ℓ-expression. Then, graph $G(f)$ has a target set of size k if and only if there is a complete local ordering A of $G(f)$ such that $G(f)$ is k-activating for state $(A, \boldsymbol{0})$, where $\boldsymbol{0} : [\|A\|] \cup \mathsf{labels}(G) \to \{0\}$.*

Proof (Sketch). Use Lemma 1. For a full proof see online version.

It remains to specify the recursive dependency of our computation. We distinguish the three operations, which are adding edges if $f = \eta_{\alpha,\beta}f'$, taking the disjoint union if $f = f_1 \oplus f_2$, and re-labeling if $f = \rho_{\alpha\to\beta}f'$.

Consider a current ℓ-expression $\eta_{\alpha,\beta}f'$ and a state (A, afo). The operation $\eta_{\alpha,\beta}$ adds the edges between all vertices of label α and β. We adjust the activation from outside such that it replaces the edges between vertices of label α and β. The relative ordering of the first $(t_{\max}+1)$ vertices of label α and label β is already fixed by the local ordering A. We increase the activation from outside of a position y of A of label β for every prior position x of A of label α. For the activation from outside for vertex v of label α that is not referenced by A, every position x of A of label β increases the activation from outside. We denote the result as $\eta_{\alpha,\beta}\mathsf{afo}$.

Definition 7. *Let graph G with labels α and β have local ordering A. For $y \in [\|A\|] \cup \mathsf{labels}(G)$, let*

$$(\eta_{\alpha,\beta}\mathsf{afo})(y) := \min\{t_{\max}, \mathsf{afo}(y) + \mathsf{add}(y)\}, \quad \textit{where}$$

$$\mathsf{add}(y) := |\{x \in [\|A\|] \mid x < y, \{\mathsf{lab}(x), \mathsf{lab}(y)\} = \{\alpha, \beta\}\}|,$$

where $1 < 2 < \cdots < |A| < \gamma$, *for every label* γ; *and where* $\mathsf{lab}(x)$, *for* $x \in [|A|]$, *is defined as* $\mathsf{lab}(A[x])$. *For every vertex* $v \in V(G)$, *let*

$$\mathsf{e}_\pi(v) := |\{u \in V(G) \mid \pi(u) < \pi(v), \ \{\mathsf{lab}(u), \mathsf{lab}(v)\} = \{\alpha, \beta\}\}|.$$

The number of edges that additionally contribute to the activation of a vertex v, denoted by $\mathsf{e}_\pi(v)$, is equal to the increase of the activation from outside $\mathsf{add}(v)$ (while ignoring an overall activation exceeding $t_{\max}$).

Lemma 3. *Let global ordering* π *extend local ordering* A, *which is nice to* $\eta_{\alpha,\beta}f'$. *For every vertex* $v \in V(\eta_{\alpha,\beta}f')$, *we have that*

$$\min\{t_{\max}, \ \mathsf{afo}(A^\pi(v)) + \mathsf{e}_\pi(v)\} = (\eta_{\alpha,\beta}\mathsf{afo})(A^\pi(v)).$$

Proof (Sketch). We need to show for every vertex v that the number of new neighbors ordered before, $\mathsf{e}_\pi(v)$, is equal to how much we increase $\mathsf{afo}(A^\pi(v))$, when capped by $t_{\max}$. Since A is nice to $\eta_{\alpha,\beta}f'$, this number of new neighbors is correctly expressed by comparing v with its neighbors of label β in A, which is how $\mathsf{add}(A^\pi(v))$ is computed. For a full proof see online version.

Lemma 4. *Graph* $G(\eta_{\alpha,\beta}f')$ *is* k-*activating for state* (A, afo) *if and only if* A *is nice to* $\eta_{\alpha,\beta}f'$ *and* $G(f')$ *is* k-*activating for* $(A, \eta_{\alpha,\beta}\mathsf{afo})$.

Proof (Sketch). We assume that the ℓ-expression $\eta_{\alpha,\beta}f'$ is irredundant as mentioned in the preliminaries. Then, every edge between vertices of label α and β is new to $G(f')$ such that $\pi^<_{\eta_{\alpha,\beta}f'}(v) = \pi^<_{f'}(v) + \mathsf{e}_\pi(v)$. For the forward direction, let $G(\eta_{\alpha,\beta}f)$ have global ordering π that extends A, is k-activating for state (A, afo) and nice to every subexpression of $\eta_{\alpha,\beta}f'$. It follows directly that A is nice to $\eta_{\alpha,\beta}A$. We in particular show that the same ordering π is k-activating for the modified state $(A, \eta_{\alpha,\beta}\mathsf{afo})$. That is, every non-target set vertex v has $\pi^<_{f'}(v) \geq \mathsf{thr}(v) - (\eta_{\alpha,\beta}\mathsf{afo})(A^\pi(v))$. We can follow this result from our initial observation and by applying Lemma 3. The backward direction is similar. For a full proof see online version.

In case of a current expression $f = f_1 \oplus f_2$, we have to show how to recursively rely on the subexpressions f_1 and f_2, analogously for $f = \rho_{\alpha \to \beta}f'$, on subexpression f'. For both cases, vertices of label β potentially come from different sets of vertices. In case of a re-labeling form α to β, a vertex of label β possibly had label α before or already had label β. In case of a disjoint union of subgraphs, a vertex of label β (or any other label) can be from either subgraph $G(f_1)$ or $G(f_2)$. For our indirect referenced vertices of our local ordering A, we do not know the true origin. Thus, we have to try all possible partitions of label β into labels α and β, respective all partitions of label β (and every other label) into either subgraph. As the possible local orderings A are bounded by our parameters, also the possible partitions are bounded by our parameters.

Definition 8

(1) *A state* (A, afo) *of graph* $G(f)$ *completes a state* (A^*, afo^*) *if* A *is complete, and removing from* A, *for every label* α, *the last tuples of label* α *from* A *until as many as in* A^* *remain, results in* A^*; *and* $\mathsf{afo} : [\|A\| \cup \mathsf{labels}(f) \rightarrow [0, t_{\max}]$, *maps* x *to* $\mathsf{afo}^*(x)$, *if defined for* x, *and otherwise to* $\mathsf{afo}^*(\mathsf{lab}(A[x]))$.

(2) *Let* $(f_1 \oplus f_2)$ *be an* ℓ-*expression. Then,* $\mathcal{S}[f_1 \oplus f_2, (A, \mathsf{afo})]$ *is the family of every pair of states* $((A_1, \mathsf{afo}_1), (A_2, \mathsf{afo}_2))$ *that complete the possible incomplete states* $(A_1^*, \mathsf{afo}_1^*)$ *and* $(A_2^*, \mathsf{afo}_2^*)$ *that can be constructed as follows. Start with states* $(A_1^*, \mathsf{afo}_1^*)$, $(A_2^*, \mathsf{afo}_2^*)$ *where* $A_1^* = A_2^* = ()$ *and, for every label* α, *we have* $\mathsf{afo}_i^*(\alpha) = \mathsf{afo}(\alpha)$. *For position* j, *beginning from* 1 *to* $|A|$, *add* $A[j]$ *to the end of either list* $A_i^* \in \{A_1^*, A_2^*\}$ *where possible. For position* $j \in [\|A\|]$, *tuple* $A[j]$ *is added to list* A_i^*, *and let* j' *be the position of* $A[j]$ *in* A_i^*. *Then, let* $\mathsf{afo}_i^*(j') := \mathsf{afo}(j)$.

(3) *Let* (A, afo) *be a state of* $G(\rho_{\alpha \rightarrow \beta} f')$. *Then,* $\mathcal{S}[\rho_{\alpha \rightarrow \beta} f', (A, \mathsf{afo})]$ *is the family of every state* (A', afo') *that completes a state* (A^*, afo^*) *that can be constructed as follows. Re-label* $s \in [0, t_{\max}^{\alpha}(f')]$ *many tuples of* A *of label* β *to* α, *while at most* $t_{\max}^{\beta}(f')$ *of label* β *remain, resulting in* A^*. *Let* afo^* *be defined as* afo *but where* $\mathsf{afo}^*(\alpha) = \mathsf{afo}(\beta)$.

Lemma 5. *Graph* $G(f_1 \oplus f_2)$ *is* k-*activating for state* (A, afo) *if and only if there are states* $((A_1, \mathsf{afo}_1), (A_2, \mathsf{afo}_2)) \in \mathcal{S}[f_1 \oplus f_2, (A, \mathsf{afo})]$ *and partition* $k_1 + k_2 = k$ *such that, for* $i \in \{1, 2\}$, *graph* $G(f_i)$ *is* k_i-*activating for* (A_i, afo_i).

Lemma 6. *Graph* $G(\rho_{\alpha \rightarrow \beta} f')$ *is* k-*activating for state* (A, afo) *if and only if there is a state* $(A', \mathsf{afo}') \in \mathcal{S}[\rho_{\alpha \rightarrow \beta} f', (A, \mathsf{afo})]$ *such that* $G(f')$ *is* k-*activating for* (A', afo').

Finally, we can show our main theorem, which was stated in the introduction.

Theorem 2 (Theorem 1 restated). *Let* $t_{\max}, \ell \in \mathbb{N}$. *There is an algorithm that, given a graph* G, *a threshold for each vertex* $\mathsf{thr} : V(G) \rightarrow [0, t_{\max}]$ *and an* ℓ-*expression* f *of* G, *computes the minimal size of a target set in time* $\mathcal{O}(\ell^{3\ell t} \cdot t^{\ell(4t+1)} \cdot |f|)$, *where* $t := t_{\max} + 1$ *and* $|f|$ *is the length of* f.

Proof. The minimal size of a target set is the minimal k of all local orderings A of $G(f)$ such that $G(f)$ is k-activating for $(A, \mathbf{0})$, as seen in Lemma 2.

Our algorithm computes the minimal k for possibly each subexpression f' of f and state (A, afo) of $G(f')$, in the fashion of dynamic programming. The minimum for a subexpression f' and state (A, afo) of $G(f')$ is remembered for future queries. There are at most $(\ell t)^{\ell t}$ possible local orderings A for a subgraph $G(f')$. And there are at most $t^{\ell t + \ell}$ possible activations from outside $\mathsf{afo} : \|A\| \cup \mathsf{labels}(f) \rightarrow [0, t_{\max}]$. Thus, there are at most $(\ell t)^{\ell t} \cdot t^{\ell t + \ell}$ different states for a fixed subexpression. Further, every computation is the minimum of at most $(\ell t)^{2\ell t}$ entries (an upper bound is guessing A_1, A_2 respectively A' from scratch), and the minimum can be found in linear time. Therefore, the algorithm runs in time $\mathcal{O}((\ell t)^{\ell t} \cdot t^{\ell t + \ell} \cdot (\ell t)^{2\ell t}) \cdot |f| = \mathcal{O}(\ell^{3\ell t} \cdot t^{\ell(4t+1)} \cdot |f|)$. If (A, afo) is not a correct state for $G(f')$, set its minimum to ∞.

If f contains only one operation, then $f = v(\alpha)$ and the only possible global ordering is $\pi : \{v\} \to \{1\}$. Graph $G(f)$ is at least 1-activating, and possibly 0-activating if $\mathsf{thr}(v) \geq \mathsf{thr}(v) - \mathsf{afo}(1)$. Answer accordingly in time $\mathcal{O}(1)$.

Otherwise, if f consists of more than one operation, we have either of the recursive cases that f is $\eta_{\alpha,\beta} f'$, $f_1 \oplus f_2$ or $\rho_{\alpha \to \beta} f'$. According to Lemmas 5 and 6 respectively, graph $G(f_1 \oplus f_2)$ is k-activating for state (A, afo) if and only if there is a pair of states $((A_1, \mathsf{afo}_1), (A_2, \mathsf{afo}_2)) \in \mathcal{S}[f_1 \oplus f_2, (A, \mathsf{afo})]$ and partition $k_1 + k_2 = k$ such that, for $i \in \{1, 2\}$, the graph $G(f_i)$ is k_i-activating for (A_i, afo_i);and graph $G(f \rho_{\alpha \to \beta} f')$ is k-activating if and only if there is a state $(A', \mathsf{afo}') \in \mathcal{S}[\rho_{\alpha \to \beta} f', (A, \mathsf{afo})]$ such that $G(f')$ is k-activating for (A', afo'). Therefore, in those two cases we can recursively obtain a minimum size of a target set by querying for the according subgraphs $G(f'), G(f_1), G(f_2)$ and states $((A_1, \mathsf{afo}_1), (A_2, \mathsf{afo}_2)) \in \mathcal{S}[f_1 \oplus f_2, (A, \mathsf{afo})]$ and $(A', \mathsf{afo}') \in \mathcal{S}[\rho_{\alpha \to \beta} f', (A, \mathsf{afo})]$, respectively. In case of $f = f_1 \oplus f_2$ the minimum size of a target set is the minimum of the sum of the minimum sizes for f_1 and f_2. For $f = \rho_{\alpha \to \beta} f$ the minimum size is equal to the minimum for f'.

According to Lemma 4, graph $G(\eta_{\alpha,\beta} f')$ is k-activating for state (A, afo) if and only if A is nice $\eta_{\alpha,\beta} f'$ and graph $G(\eta_{\alpha,\beta} f')$ is k-activating for state $(A, \eta_{\alpha,\beta}\mathsf{afo})$. Thus, in case of that A is not nice to f we can discard the current computation for a minimal size of a target set for the graph $G(\eta_{\alpha,\beta} f')$ and state (A, afo). Otherwise, the minimum size of a target set is equal to the minimum size of subgraph $G(f)$ with state $(A, \eta_{\alpha,\beta}\mathsf{afo})$.

4   Conclusion

In this work, we gave an FPT-algorithm for TSS for the combined parameters clique-width and maximum threshold. This result generalizes all previous FPT-membership results of TSS with constant thresholds. It would be interesting to explore the whole dichotomy of constant TSS for common structural parameters. Is there a different dichotomy when the maximum threshold is a parameter and not a constant?

References

1. Bazgan, C., Chopin, M., Nichterlein, A., Sikora, F.: Parameterized inapproximability of target set selection and generalizations. Computability **3**(2), 135–145 (2014)
2. Ben-Zwi, O., Hermelin, D., Lokshtanov, D., Newman, I.: Treewidth governs the complexity of target set selection. Discret. Optim. **8**(1), 87–96 (2011)
3. Betzler, N., Bredereck, R., Niedermeier, R., Uhlmann, J.: On bounded-degree vertex deletion parameterized by treewidth. Discret. Appl. Math. **160**(1–2), 53–60 (2012)
4. Chen, N.: On the approximability of influence in social networks. SIAM J. Discret. Math. **23**(3), 1400–1415 (2009)
5. Chopin, M., Nichterlein, A., Niedermeier, R., Weller, M.: Constant thresholds can make target set selection tractable. Theory Comput. Syst. **55**(1), 61–83 (2014)

6. Cicalese, F., Cordasco, G., Gargano, L., Milanic, M., Vaccaro, U.: Latency-bounded target set selection in social networks. Theor. Comput. Sci. **535**, 1–15 (2014)
7. Corneil, D.G., Rotics, U.: On the relationship between clique-width and treewidth. SIAM J. Comput. **34**(4), 825–847 (2005)
8. Courcelle, B., Olariu, S.: Upper bounds to the clique width of graphs. Discret. Appl. Math. **101**(1–3), 77–114 (2000)
9. Cygan, M., Fomin, F.V., Kowalik, Ł., Lokshtanov, D., Marx, D., Pilipczuk, M., Pilipczuk, M., Saurabh, S.: Parameterized Algorithms. Springer, Cham (2015). https://doi.org/10.1007/978-3-319-21275-3
10. Downey, R.G., Thilikos, D.M.: Confronting intractability via parameters. CoRR, abs/1106.3161 (2011)
11. Dvořák, P., Knop, D., Toufar, T.: Target set selection in dense graph classes. CoRR, abs/1610.07530 (2016)
12. Flum, J., Grohe, M.: Parameterized Complexity Theory. Texts in Theoretical Computer Science. An EATCS Series. Springer, Heidelberg (2006). https://doi.org/10.1007/3-540-29953-X
13. Gajarský, J., Lampis, M., Ordyniak, S.: Parameterized algorithms for modular-width. In: Gutin, G., Szeider, S. (eds.) IPEC 2013. LNCS, vol. 8246, pp. 163–176. Springer, Cham (2013). https://doi.org/10.1007/978-3-319-03898-8_15
14. Kempe, D., Kleinberg, J.M., Tardos, É.: Maximizing the spread of influence through a social network. In: Proceedings of the Ninth ACM SIGKDD International Conference on Knowledge Discovery and Data Mining, Washington, D.C., USA, 24–27 August 2003, pp. 137–146 (2003)
15. Nichterlein, A., Niedermeier, R., Uhlmann, J., Weller, M.: On tractable cases of target set selection. Soc. Netw. Anal. Min. **3**(2), 233–256 (2013)
16. Niedermeier, R.: Invitation to Fixed-Parameter Algorithms. Oxford University Press, Oxford (2006)
17. Oum, S.: Approximating rank-width and clique-width quickly. ACM Trans. Algorithms **5**(1), 1–20 (2008)

Model-Based Software Engineering

Combining Versioning and Metamodel Evolution in the ChronoSphere Model Repository

Martin Haeusler[1(✉)], Thomas Trojer[2], Johannes Kessler[1], Matthias Farwick[2], Emmanuel Nowakowski[1], and Ruth Breu[1]

[1] University of Innsbruck, 6020 Innsbruck, Austria
{martin.haeusler,johannes.kessler,emmanuel.nowakowski,
ruth.breu}@uibk.ac.at
[2] Txture GmbH, 6020 Innsbruck, Austria
{thomas.trojer,matthias.farwick}@txture.io

Abstract. Model Driven Engineering (MDE) has gained a lot of popularity in recent years and is being applied in a wide variety of domains. As teams, models and applications grow in size, the need for faster and more scalable technology emerges, in particular in the crucial area of model repositories. These software components are responsible for persisting, querying and versioning the model content and act as central hubs for interaction with the model. However, existing repository solutions do not consider metamodel evolution, which is important in long-running projects. In this paper, we present ChronoSphere, a novel model repository, targeted specifically towards developers working with MDE technology in industry, with a focus on models-at-runtime scenarios. By utilizing the latest innovations in graph databases and version control, ChronoSphere provides transparent and efficient versioning as well as metamodel evolution capabilities. This paper focuses on the core concepts of ChronoSphere, in particular data management, versioning and metamodel evolution. Our open-source implementation serves as proof of concept.

1 Introduction

The discipline of Model Driven Engineering (MDE) is employed in a wide variety of domains with different goals and purposes [1]. One of the most pressing concerns in any larger modeling endeavour is collaboration on model data which also entails model persistence, versioning [2] and model querying. Model repositories serve this very purpose and constitute a major part in the tooling landscape of model engineering and model-driven disciplines. Over the years, a considerable number of approaches and tools have been developed [3]. However, most implementations never exceeded the prototypical stage and have therefore never actually been employed in industrial contexts. The most prominent tool that has passed the test of time is called *Connected Data Objects* (CDO[1]). CDO is

---

[1] https://wiki.eclipse.org/CDO.

© Springer International Publishing AG 2018
A M. Tjoa et al. (Eds.): SOFSEM 2018, LNCS 10706, pp. 153–167, 2018.
https://doi.org/10.1007/978-3-319-73117-9_11

a powerful, full-featured repository for EMF Ecore[2]-based models that provides a client-server architecture, database connectivity, transaction handling as well as a graphical user interface. CDO is widely considered to represent the state-of-the-art in model repositories. However, it offers no solution for metamodel evolution. If a new metamodel version is required, the database needs to be dropped and recreated from scratch, deleting all existing model elements in the process. Metamodel evolution is of crucial importance in several areas, especially in MDE [4] and models-at-runtime scenarios [5,6].

Over the course of the past two years, we have dedicated our efforts to solving these issues by designing and implementing a next-generation model repository that is dedicated to the developers of model-driven applications. In particular we considered the requirements for models-at-runtime scenarios. The result of these efforts is the *ChronoSphere* EMF model repository which is an open-source project[3] that is freely available on GitHub[4]. As we are going to discuss in detail in Sect. 3, ChronoSphere is fundamentally different from existing solutions. It implements the entire data management stack, from high-level Ecore model elements to on-disk data structures, in order to maximize the flexibility, scalability and separation of concerns while adhering to a coherent architecture. It addresses the needs of practitioners to adapt the metamodel without deleting existing instance data and scales well even with large models. The individual architectural layers (c.f. Sect. 3) can also be used as standalone components outside the model repository context. These components have also contributed to the state-of-the-art in database systems in the areas of versioned data management [7] and graph databases [8].

The remainder of this paper is structured as follows. In Sect. 2, we present the requirements we considered in the design and construction of ChronoSphere. In Sect. 3 we give an overview of our proposed solution, which we then compare to related work in Sect. 4. Finally, we present an outlook to future work in Sect. 5 before concluding the paper with a summary in Sect. 6.

2   Requirements Overview

This section is dedicated to the requirements that guided the design and development of ChronoSphere. We synthesized those requirements from related work [3] as well as from our own long-standing experiences with model repositories [9–12].

The following list summarizes some of the requirements that we considered in the design and implementation of our ChronoSphere prototype. There are several other aspects that are already implemented in ChronoSphere (such as model-level queries and secondary indices). These requirements are beyond the scope of this paper.

---

[2] https://www.eclipse.org/modeling/emf/.
[3] This work was partially funded by the research project "txtureSA" (FWF-Project P 29022).
[4] http://tinyurl.com/chronosphere-github.

- [**R1**] *Model Persistence*
  - [**R1.1**] *Persisting Model Data*
    The ability to persist model data is the most fundamental capability of any model repository. Given an arbitrary metamodel and instance model, ChronoSphere must be able to store this data in a persistent format on disk, and reconstruct it as needed, in whole or partially.
  - [**R1.2**] *Transactional Safety*
    In order to cope with concurrent access, ChronoSphere must offer transaction concepts that allow for safe model usage in the presence of parallel modifications. This requirement is closely related to the ACID properties in database systems [13].
  - [**R1.3**] *Scalability*
    Instance models can grow to considerable sizes in practice, in particular in scenarios where instances are not created and managed manually but by an automated process. The ability to efficiently manage models with several 100000 elements (e.g. with respect to query response times, CPU and RAM usage. . .) is paramount for ChronoSphere.
- [**R2**] *Model Versioning and Evolution*
  - [**R2.1**] *Versioning*
    Auditing, traceability of changes and legal compliance are just three examples why versioning capabilities are important in practice. The ability to consistently reproduce the same results for a given query and request version, as well as capabilities for analyzing the history of individual elements, are the essence of this requirement.
  - [**R2.2**] *Lightweight Branching*
    The orthogonal requirement to the linear versioning concept is to have several branches in a repository. Branches have several use cases in practice, for example in planning and comparing different scenarios based on a common ancestor model. Branching should be lightweight, i.e. creating a branch should not entail the creation of a full copy of the model on disk.
  - [**R2.3**] *Metamodel Evolution*
    The ability to evolve the metamodel over time, even in the presence of existing instance elements, is crucial in models-at-runtime contexts. ChronoSphere must be able to support this process, ensuring the conformance of instance model elements to their metamodel at all times.
  - [**R2.4**] *Metamodel Versioning*
    Given requirements [**R2.1**] and [**R2.3**], being able to include the metamodel in the version control mechanism is mandatory. Otherwise, older versions of instance model elements might not conform to an evolved metamodel.

3   Proposed Solution

Figure 1 shows the data management concepts of ChronoSphere. The Ecore-based application, depicted on the far left, is working with EObjects and their corresponding EClasses, EPackages and other Ecore elements. The fact that the model and the metamodel are stored and managed *together* will become a critical factor when dealing with metamodel evolution. This combined model needs to be persisted and versioned [**R1.1, R2.1, R2.3, R2.4**]. In the top left, the programmer is working (A) with the APIs provided by ChronoSphere and Ecore, or formulates model-level queries (which are beyond the scope of this paper). The repository then transforms (B) the model-level request into a request in the underlying graph database called *ChronoGraph*[5] [8]. This graph database implements the concept of a versioned property graph [14] and is fully compliant to the *Apache TinkerPop*[6] graph computing standard. To the best of our knowledge, ChronoGraph is the first TinkerPop graph database that provides full versioning support, and we implemented it primarily in order to serve as a backend for our ChronoSphere repository. Property graphs are conceptually very close to Ecore models [**R1.3**]. Our model-to-graph mapping is inspired by Neo4EMF [15] but uses a custom implementation for technical reasons.

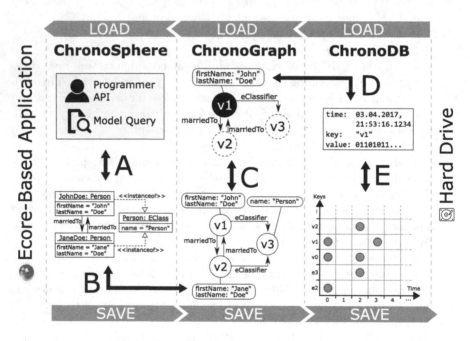

Fig. 1. ChronoSphere data management stack

In order to achieve a serial form for the model data that can be persisted to disk, ChronoGraph disassembles (C) the property graph into individual *Star Graphs*, one for each vertex (i.e. node). A star graph is a sub-graph that is centered around one particular vertex. It contains all properties from this vertex,

---

[5] http://tinyurl.com/chronograph-github.
[6] http://tinkerpop.apache.org/.

as well as all adjacent edges. The star graph also contains the IDs of the neighbour vertices, but has no further information about them. Figure 1 shows the star graph of vertex $v1$ (where $v1$ is depicted as a black circle). Creating star graphs for each vertex is a special kind of *graph partitioning*. This partitioning only affects the data layout, it has no impact on transaction control (i.e. a single transaction can contain multiple star graphs). When linking the star graphs again by replacing IDs by vertices, the original graph can be reconstructed from this partitioning. This reconstruction can occur fully or only partially, which makes this solution particularly suitable for lazy loading techniques [**R1.3**]. For further details on ChronoGraph, we refer the interested reader to our previous work [8].

In the next step (D) we transform the star graph of each vertex into a binary string using the well-known *Kryo*[7] serializer, and pass the result to our underlying versioned Key-Value-Store *ChronoDB*[8] which we describe in detail in our previous work [7]. When the transaction is committed [**R1.2**], the commit timestamp is assigned to each pair of modified keys and corresponding binary values, creating time-key-value triples as shown in Fig. 1 [**R2.1**]. ChronoDB then stores (E) these triples in a *Temporal Data Matrix* [7] which is implemented as a B^+-Tree [16]. Each row in this matrix represents the full history of a single element, each column represents a model revision, and each cell represents the data of one particular element for a given ID at a given timestamp. As history is immutable, unchanged values are reused implicitly in all future versions until they are overridden by another entry, allowing for a very compact representation on disk. Lightweight branching [**R2.2**] is achieved on the ChronoDB layer as well. Each branch has a one-to-one relationship to a temporal data matrix. If an entry is requested in a matrix that is older than the creation timestamp of the matrix, the request will be deferred to the matrix of the origin branch (recursively). As each matrix only stores the changes applied to its own branch, no copying is required, thus achieving *lightweight* branching.

The transformation chain depicted in Fig. 1 is bijective, i.e. it can be applied for saving data as well as loading data. The EObjects which are loaded from the underlying layers by ChronoSphere are fully compliant to the Ecore standard and can therefore be used by any tool in the Ecore ecosystem, such as EMFCompare [17].

The conceptual metamodel of ChronoSphere is shown in Fig. 2. An instance of `ChronoSphere` manages a number of named `Branch`es (with *master* as the predefined one) [**R2.2**], and each Branch refers to its `origin` (recursively). Each Branch contains any number of `Version`s, which in turn contain a (Ecore-based) `Metamodel` and an `InstanceModel`, which is a collection of `EObject`s that adhere to the `EClass`es in the Metamodel. A ChronoSphere instance can then create `Transaction`s on a given Version by starting them on a `transactionTimestamp`, which is usually obtained from a user-provided `java.util.Date`. This is a fairly common setup for versioning- and branching-enabled model repositories. A detail

---

[7] https://github.com/EsotericSoftware/kryo.
[8] http://tinyurl.com/chronodb-github.

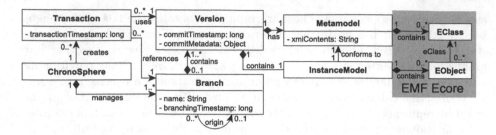

Fig. 2. Conceptual ChronoSphere metamodel (simplified)

deserving special attention is the fact that a Version and a Metamodel are bound to each other in a one-to-one relationship. This is a requirement for metamodel evolution, which we will discuss in the next section.

3.1 Metamodel Evolution

One of the major benefits of employing model repositories is the freedom of defining a custom, domain-specific metamodel for any given use case. In practice, users often cannot take full advantage of this benefit because they are hampered by the lack of proper tool support, in particular in cases where the metamodel evolves over the duration of a project [4]. These cases are very common in industrial contexts with long-running projects. In enterprise scenarios, developers create database scripts that migrate the database schema (and contained data) from one version to the next. There is a wide variety of tools for this purpose (e.g. Flyway[9] and LiquiBase[10]). In a model-based environment, this translates to the concept of *metamodel evolution*, sometimes also referred to as *metamodel adaptation* [18]. The key challenge of metamodel evolution is to keep the instance model consistent with the metamodel, i.e. the instances need to be *co-adapted* such that they conform to the new metamodel [19].

For some evolutionary metamodel changes, no instance co-adaptation is required. For example, when adding a new (optional) `EAttribute` to an existing `EClass`, the existing instances are still valid, they just have no value set for the new attribute. Other basic examples include the addition of new `EClasses` or increasing the multiplicity of an `EAttribute` from multiplicity-one to multiplicity-many. However, far more complex examples exist as well, and in many cases, fully automatic and deterministic instance co-adaptation is not possible. Cicchetti et al. refer to such cases as *unresolvable breaking changes* [19]. For instance, we consider a metamodel that contains an `EClass` A. The next version of the same metamodel does not contain A anymore, but a new `EClass` named B instead. Even though there are algorithms for model differencing [17,20,21], in the absence of unique identifiers (e.g. UUIDs) and change logs we cannot tell if A

---

[9] https://flywaydb.org/.

[10] http://www.liquibase.org/.

was removed and *B* was added, or if *A* was merely renamed to *B*. In the first case, we would have to delete all instances of *A*, in the second case we would need to migrate them to become instances of *B*. This basic example shows that instance co-adaptation requires *semantic information* about the change, which is only available to the *application developer*. For this reason, ChronoSphere provides an API for managing metamodel evolution with instance co-adaptation [**R2.3**]. Rose et al. provide a summary of related approaches [22]. This in-place transformation approach is in line with Wimmer et al. [23] and Meyers et al. [24], with the notable difference that we propose a Java API instead of ATL processes or DSLs [25,26]. The concept is also similar to the Model Change Language [27]. This API offers three different modes of operation:

- **Metamodel Changes without need for instance adaptation**
  This kind of evolution is intended for the most basic changes that do not require any kind of instance co-adaptation, such as adding `EClasses`, adding `EAttributes`, or increasing feature multiplicities from one to many. This category is also known as *non-breaking changes* [19]. The developer only provides the new version of the metamodel and loads it into ChronoSphere, which will create a new version in the history.
- **One-to-one correspondence**
  When instance co-adaptation is required, a common case is that each `EObject` from the old model will still correspond to (at most) one `EObject` in the new model. Examples for changes in this category include the renaming of `EClasses` and `EAttributes`. For such cases, the ChronoSphere metamodel evolution engine provides the developer with a predefined evolution process and a predefined element iteration order. The developer implements an *Incubator* that is responsible for either migrating a given `EObject` to match the new metamodel, or deleting it if it is obsolete. The Incubator is specific to a given source and target metamodel and contains the semantics and domain-specific constraints of the migration, expressed in Java source code.
- **Generic adaptation**
  In more complex cases, a one-to-one correspondence of elements can no longer be established, for example when an `EClass` is refactored and split up into two separate classes. In such cases, ChronoSphere provides a generic *Evolution Controller* interface that is in full control over the instance co-adaptation. It receives the *migration context*, which provides utility methods for querying the old and new model states. The migration process as well as the iteration order of elements are defined by the implementation of the controller. For that reason, implementing an evolution controller is the most powerful and expressive way of defining a migration, but also the most technically challenging one that entails the highest effort for the developer. Just like the incubators from the one-to-one correspondence case, such migration controllers are specific to a given source and target metamodel version.

By offering these features, we implement the metamodel evolution requirement [**R2.3**]. Since we only adapt the latest version of the model to the new metamodel, the old model instances still conform to their corresponding metamodel.

We must not touch these instances, because this would violate the requirements for versioning and traceability of changes [**R2.1**]. Hence we need to put the metamodel under version control as well.

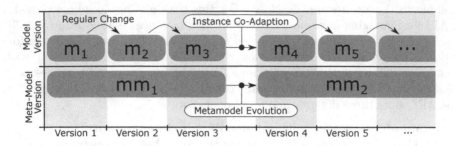

Fig. 3. Metamodel evolution in ChronoSphere

As shown in Fig. 3, every version in every branch of the model can have its own metamodel to which it corresponds [**R2**]. A direct consequence of this approach is that the application developer needs to be aware of those (potentially) multiple metamodels, and create queries dynamically based on that metamodel. While this will entail additional efforts in development, it is the only fully consistent way of managing versioned models with evolving metamodels.

The alternative would be to retroactively adapt every stored version of the model to a single new metamodel. However, since this adaptation process is not guaranteed to conserve all information (e.g. consider a new metamodel where an `EAttribute` has been deleted), we would not be able to guarantee traceability anymore. Consequently, we would introduce a considerable threat to the validity of audits. By storing a new metamodel alongside the co-adapted instance model, we restrict the impact of a metamodel evolution to a single version (e.g. the version that simultaneously introduces m_4 and mm_2 in Fig. 3), and can still guarantee traceability in the remaining sections of our data. As we will discuss in the remainder of this section, in our approach we can guarantee traceability even across metamodel evolutions.

Algorithm 1 shows how metamodel evolution works in ChronoSphere when using an Incubator. In the beginning of the metamodel evolution algorithm, we open *two* transactions on the repository, and we refer to them as *txOld* and *txNew*. We will use *txOld* in order to read the repository state before the evolution has occurred, and *txNew* to perform our modifications. We assume that *txOld* contains a metamodel and a corresponding instance model (otherwise the evolution is a regular insertion). It is crucial at this point that these two transactions are able to work in parallel, and are furthermore completely *isolated* from each other. Our first actual modification is to *override* the previous metamodel in txNew. We can safely do so because the original is still stored in txOld. There is no metamodel differencing taking place in this phase, we perform a plain overwrite. We initially delete all elements in txNew (lines 4 to 5) and start with an

---

Algorithm 1. Metamodel Evolution using an Incubator

Data: Repository; NewMetamodel; Incubator

1   txOld ← Repository.tx();
2   txNew ← Repository.tx();
3   txNew.setMetamodel(NewMetamodel);
4   **foreach** *EObject e in txNew.allInstances* **do**
5   txNew.delete(e)

6   **foreach** *EObject e in txOld.allInstances* **do**
7   newClass ← Incubator.getEClass(NewMetamodel, e);
8   **if** *newClass != NULL* **then**
9   txNew.recreate(e, newClass);

10   **foreach** *EObject e in newTx.allInstances* **do**
11   oldEObject ← oldTx.getEObject(e);
12   Incubator.transferEAttributes(oldEObject, e);

13   **foreach** *EObject e in newTx.allInstances* **do**
14   oldEObject ← oldTx.getEObject(e);
15   Incubator.transferEReferences(oldEObject, e);

16   txNew.commit();
17   txOld.rollback();

---

empty instance model. Afterwards we begin our first instance evolution phase (lines 6 to 9). We iterate over all EObjects stored in the old repository state, and ask our Incubator for a new EClass for this particular EObject. If there is a corresponding EClass in the new metamodel, we *recreate* the EObject with the same ID, preserving the historical traceability link. Otherwise, we discard the EObject. In lines 10 through 12, we iterate over the elements that received a new EClass previously and look for their counterparts in txOld. We ask the Incubator to transfer any desired EAttribute values from the old version to the new one, which may also involve a value transformation step. For the fulfillment of all of its tasks, the Incubator has access to the Ecore API as well as the ChronoSphere API, allowing for very clean and expressive implementations. Finally, we construct the EReference instances by iterating over the EObjects again (lines 13 to 15). Once more, the Incubator is responsible for the actual semantics. In the last phase, we perform the commit that persists our changes to disk (and creates a new entry in the version history), and roll back the historical transaction.

Overall, we have maintained our traceability links (by retaining the IDs of EObjects) and performed a metamodel evolution with instance adaptation that is ACID safe and creates a clean history without partially evolved intermediate states. The evolution process with a full-fledged Evolution Controller works in much the same way. The primary difference is that the lines 6 through 15 are replaced by a call to the controller, allowing for a maximum of flexibility in the controller implementation. This algorithm requires efficient management of RAM in practice, in particular when working with larger models. Since *txNew* needs to manage all changes applied to all model elements, the change set can grow to very large sizes. ChronoSphere provides mechanisms [28] to mitigate this problem while providing the same level of ACID safety and equivalent histories.

3.2 Transaction and Versioning Concepts

Transactional safety [**R1.2**] is the foundation of all collaboration- and evolution-related features in ChronoSphere. Originally coined by the database community, this concept has since been adopted by other domains as well. In the context of modeling and model repositories, transactional safety implies that several clients can work in parallel on a model without interfering with each other.

In ChronoSphere, a *client*[11] requests a transaction, then operates on it by executing queries and applying changes locally in this transaction. Afterwards, the transaction can either be *committed* (local changes will be made available globally [**R1.1**] by creating a new version [**R2.1**]) or *rolled back* (reverting all local changes). The *isolation* property defined in the SQL Standard [13] states that any operation executed within a transaction *must not be affected* by other, concurrent transactions [**R1.2**]. In order to achieve the highest possible isolation level (*serializable* [13], also known as *snapshot isolation*), databases tradition-ally either need to perform excessive pessimistic locking, or allocate considerable amounts of RAM to open transactions in order to retain duplicates of concur-rently modified entries. Thanks to its versioning capabilities, ChronoSphere can provide snapshot isolation with minimal locking, no additional memory overhead and without sacrificing performance. This is a direct consequence of our design: once a model version is committed, it is effectively immutable. Further changes will create new versions. Therefore, as long as a client is working on any given version (i.e. the used transaction timestamp does not change), the model content will not change, thus guaranteeing snapshot isolation.

ChronoSphere is a *full ACID* model repository. A direct consequence of this feature is that Online Transaction Processing (OLTP) and Online Analytics Pro-cessing (OLAP) are supported in parallel. For instance, one client may have a long-running transaction that performs extensive model analysis, while other clients execute short-lived transactions that modify the model content. Due to the snapshot isolation, the long-running analysis transaction will not block the other transactions, and the changes they introduce to the model will not be visible to the analysis transaction. This guarantees that the analysis will be executed without any interference.

4 Related Work

The tool landscape in the area of model repositories is as large as it is varied today, ranging from traditional approaches like CDO and EMFStore [29] to

---

[11] We use the term "client" to refer to application code that operates on top of Chrono-Sphere. This can be a remote method invocation, another thread or simply a method call to the public API.

modern NoSQL-solutions like the Hawk Model Indexer [30] and Neo4EMF [15]. Pierantonio et al. provide a good overview of existing tools in their paper [3]. In this Section, we will compare ChronoSphere to existing tools on a conceptual level. We are also performing comparative benchmarks, but since this process is tightly tied to model queries, which are outside the scope of this paper, these results will be published separately.

Table 1. Feature comparison of model repositories and model indexers

Technology	Storage	F1	F2	F3	F4	F5	F6
CDO	SQL	✓	✓	✓	✓	✗	✓
Hawk	Graph	✗	✗	✓	✓	✗	✗
Neo4EMF	Graph	✗	✗	✓	✓	✗	✗
MORSA	Documents	✓	✗	✓	✗	✗	✗
EMFStore	Diff-Files	✓	✓	✗	✗	✗	✗
ChronoSphere	Graph	✓	✓	✓	✓	✓	✓

Feature	Name
F1	Versioning
F2	Branching
F3	Model Queries
F4	Lazy Loading
F5	Metamodel Evolution
F6	Full ACID Transactions

In ChronoSphere the entire data management stack was implemented from scratch, ranging from data storage and versioning to transaction and model management. To the best of our knowledge, this is an unparalleled effort in the area of model repositories. This approach allows for a complete redesign of the architecture, avoiding the common problems introduced by traditional methods, such as Object-Relational Mapping (e.g. used by CDO) or the storage of model differences for versioning (e.g. EMFStore) while still achieving a comparable feature set in a coherent solution. There are several NoSQL model repositories available, e.g. MORSA [31], but ChronoSphere is the first to fully leverage the potential of graph databases. Approaches like Neo4EMF [15] and Hawk [30] are graph-based and inspired and guided our efforts. However, these tools do not offer the versioning and temporal indexing capabilities provided by ChronoSphere, which are essential for models-at-runtime scenarios. They serve different use cases that only partially overlap with our goals. This also becomes evident when comparing the feature sets of Neo4EMF and Hawk to the requirements we have stated in Sect. 2. Table 1 shows a comparison of features of related technologies.

ChronoSphere is, to the best of our knowledge, the only actively maintained model repository for EMF models that offers metamodel evolution features. These features are enabled by the fact that graph databases, such as ChronoGraph, do not need a fixed schema, whereas most traditional SQL databases require schemas for their tables. Model repositories based on SQL databases, such as CDO, cannot offer metamodel evolution features to the same extent as ChronoSphere, because such a change would require a schema adaptation in SQL. Such an change inevitably affects all rows stored in the modified tables, potentially breaking audit traces in the process. In contrast, a metamodel evolution in ChronoSphere will never affect model elements from previous versions, allowing for highly accurate auditing and version history analysis. Furthermore, by exposing a dedicated Java API to developers, we provide a mechanism for co-adaptation of instances.

The transaction-based nature of this mechanism allows implementations to analyze the pre-evolved as well as the current state of the repository, which greatly reduces the difficulty of the co-adaptation implementation.

5   Outlook and Future Work

In future publications, we will discuss the query framework provided by Chrono-Sphere in detail which is already part of the implementation. It also contains mechanisms for the detection of conflicts that can occur during concurrent transactions. Currently, conflicts are resolved in a "first writer wins" fashion, but more elaborate conflict resolution strategies based on the three-way differencing algorithms [17] employed by version control systems (e.g. GIT) are on our roadmap. This will also allow to merge branches in future versions of Chrono-Sphere. Another major goal for the future is to distribute ChronoGraph across several machines in order to achieve higher scalability and load balancing. Due to the clean layer separation, ChronoSphere will also benefit from these improvements with minimal need for adaptations. This will turn ChronoSphere into a distributed model repository that will be able to work effectively with very large models. We also intend to publish an extensive case study on the industrial application of ChronoSphere in the context of the commercial IT Landscape Management tool Txture[12]. Txture is already using ChronoSphere in production. This software leverages the capabilities of ChronoSphere and its underlying components to bring powerful interactive model-based visualizations to its users. The planned case study will showcase how ChronoSphere supports the critical tasks in such an industrial environment.

6   Summary

In this paper, we presented the model repository ChronoSphere. Incorporating over two years of work and dedication, this open-source project utilizes the latest innovations in graph computing and version control and makes them accessible for the MDE community in the form of a novel, next-generation model repository. We provided a requirements specification for our repository synthesized from related work as well as our own long-standing experience in this area. Based upon these requirements, we showcased the basic principles of ChronoSphere and its unique data management stack. The presented concept for supporting versioning and metamodel evolution in a consistent fashion retains traceability links and allows for effective auditing and history analysis. We concluded the paper with a comparison with related state-of-the-art model repositories. ChronoSphere is an all-new open-source technology that offers unique advantages and possibilities. It is intended to serve as a platform for future projects in research and industry alike.

---

[12] www.txture.io.

References

1. Mohagheghi, P., Gilani, W., Stefanescu, A., Fernandez, M.A., Nordmoen, B., Fritzsche, M.: Where does model-driven engineering help? Experiences from three industrial cases. Softw. Syst. Model. **12**(3), 619–639 (2013)
2. Brosch, P., Kappel, G., Langer, P., Seidl, M., Wieland, K., Wimmer, M.: An introduction to model versioning. In: Bernardo, M., Cortellessa, V., Pierantonio, A. (eds.) SFM 2012. LNCS, vol. 7320, pp. 336–398. Springer, Heidelberg (2012). https://doi.org/10.1007/978-3-642-30982-3_10
3. Di Rocco, J., Di Ruscio, D., Iovino, L., Pierantonio, A.: Collaborative repositories in model-driven engineering. IEEE Softw. **32**(3), 28–34 (2015)
4. Iovino, L., Pierantonio, A., Malavolta, I.: On the impact significance of metamodel evolution in MDE. J. Object Technol. **11**(3), 1–3 (2012)
5. Seybold, D., Domaschka, J., Rossini, A., Hauser, C.B., Griesinger, F., Tsitsipas, A.: Experiences of models@ run-time with EMF and CDO. In: Proceedings of the 2016 ACM SIGPLAN International Conference on Software Language Engineering, pp. 46–56. ACM (2016)
6. Blair, G., Bencomo, N., France, R.B.: Models@ run.time. Computer **42**(10), 22–27 (2009)
7. Haeusler, M.: Scalable versioning for key-value stores. In: Proceedings of 5th International Conference on Data Management Technologies and Applications, Lisbon, Portugal, 24–26 July 2016, DATA 2016, pp. 79–86. http://dx.doi.org/10.5220/0005938700790086
8. Haeusler, M., Nowakowski, E., Farwick, M., Breu, R., Kessler, J., Trojer, T.: ChronoGraph - versioning support for OLTP TinkerPop Graphs. In: Proceedings of the 6th International Conference on Data Science, Technology and Applications, DATA, INSTICC, vol. 1, pp. 87–97. SciTePress (2017)
9. Breu, M., Breu, R., Löw, S.: Living on the move: towards an architecture for a living models infrastructure. In: The Fifth International Conference on Software Engineering Advances, 22–27 August 2010, Nice, France, ICSEA 2010, pp. 290–295. http://dx.doi.org/10.1109/ICSEA.2010.51
10. Breu, R., Agreiter, B., Farwick, M., Felderer, M., Hafner, M., Innerhofer-Oberperfler, F.: Living models - ten principles for change-driven software engineering. Int. J. Softw. Inform. **5**(1–2), 267–290 (2011). http://www.ijsi.org/ch/reader/view_abstract.aspx?file_no=i84
11. Trojer, T., Farwick, M., Häusler, M., Breu, R.: Living modeling of IT architectures: challenges and solutions. In: De Nicola, R., Hennicker, R. (eds.) Software, Services, and Systems. LNCS, vol. 8950, pp. 458–474. Springer, Cham (2015). https://doi.org/10.1007/978-3-319-15545-6_26
12. Trojer, T., Farwick, M., Haeusler, M.: Modeling techniques for enterprise architecture documentation: experiences from practice. In: Multi-level Modelling Workshop Proceedings, MULTI 2014, p. 113 (2014)
13. ISO: SQL Standard 2011 (ISO/IEC 9075:2011) (2011)
14. Rodriguez, M.A., Neubauer, P.: The graph traversal pattern. In: Graph Data Management: Techniques and Applications, pp. 29–46 (2011). http://dx.doi.org/10.4018/978-1-61350-053-8.ch002
15. Benelallam, A., Gómez, A., Sunyé, G., Tisi, M., Launay, D.: Neo4EMF, a scalable persistence layer for EMF models. In: Cabot, J., Rubin, J. (eds.) ECMFA 2014. LNCS, vol. 8569, pp. 230–241. Springer, Cham (2014). https://doi.org/10.1007/978-3-319-09195-2_15

16. Salzberg, B.: File Structures: An Analytic Approach. Prentice-Hall Inc., Upper Saddle River (1988)
17. Toulmé, A., Intalio, Inc.: Presentation of EMF compare utility. In: Eclipse Modeling Symposium, pp. 1–8 (2006)
18. Wachsmuth, G.: Metamodel adaptation and model co-adaptation. In: Ernst, E. (ed.) ECOOP 2007. LNCS, vol. 4609, pp. 600–624. Springer, Heidelberg (2007). https://doi.org/10.1007/978-3-540-73589-2_28
19. Cicchetti, A., Di Ruscio, D., Eramo, R., Pierantonio, A.: Automating co-evolution in model-driven engineering. In: 12th International IEEE Enterprise Distributed Object Computing Conference, EDOC 2008. IEEE, pp. 222–231 (2008)
20. Khelladi, D.E., Hebig, R., Bendraou, R., Robin, J., Gervais, M.-P.: Detecting complex changes during metamodel evolution. In: Zdravkovic, J., Kirikova, M., Johannesson, P. (eds.) CAiSE 2015. LNCS, vol. 9097, pp. 263–278. Springer, Cham (2015). https://doi.org/10.1007/978-3-319-19069-3_17
21. ben Fadhel, A., Kessentini, M., Langer, P., Wimmer, M.: Search-based detection of high-level model changes. In: 2012 28th IEEE International Conference on Software Maintenance (ICSM), pp. 212–221. IEEE (2012)
22. Rose, L.M., Paige, R.F., Kolovos, D.S., Polack, F.A.: An analysis of approaches to model migration. In: Proceedings of the Joint MoDSE-MCCM Workshop, pp. 6–15 (2009)
23. Wimmer, M., Kusel, A., Schönböck, J., Retschitzegger, W., Schwinger, W., Kappel, G.: On using inplace transformations for model co-evolution. In: Proceedings of the 2nd International Workshop Model Transformation with ATL, vol. 711, pp. 65–78 (2010)
24. Meyers, B., Wimmer, M., Cicchetti, A., Sprinkle, J.: A generic in-place transformation-based approach to structured model co-evolution. Electron. Commun. EASST 42 (2012)
25. Rose, L.M., Kolovos, D.S., Paige, R.F., Polack, F.A.C.: Model migration with epsilon flock. In: Tratt, L., Gogolla, M. (eds.) ICMT 2010. LNCS, vol. 6142, pp. 184–198. Springer, Heidelberg (2010). https://doi.org/10.1007/978-3-642-13688-7_13
26. Herrmannsdoerfer, M., Benz, S., Juergens, E.: COPE - automating coupled evolution of metamodels and models. In: Drossopoulou, S. (ed.) ECOOP 2009. LNCS, vol. 5653, pp. 52–76. Springer, Heidelberg (2009). https://doi.org/10.1007/978-3-642-03013-0_4
27. Narayanan, A., Levendovszky, T., Balasubramanian, D., Karsai, G.: Automatic domain model migration to manage metamodel evolution. In: Schürr, A., Selic, B. (eds.) MODELS 2009. LNCS, vol. 5795, pp. 706–711. Springer, Heidelberg (2009). https://doi.org/10.1007/978-3-642-04425-0_57
28. Haeusler, M., Breu, R.: Sustainable management of versioned data. In: Proceedings of the 24th PhD Mini-Symposium. Budapest University of Technology and Economics (2017)
29. Koegel, M., Helming, J.: EMFStore: a model repository for EMF models. In: Kramer, J., Bishop, J., Devanbu, P.T., Uchitel, S. (eds.) ICSE, vol. 2, pp. 307–308. ACM (2010). http://dblp.uni-trier.de/db/conf/icse/icse2010-2.html#KoegelH10

30. Barmpis, K., Kolovos, D.: Hawk: towards a scalable model indexing architecture. In: Proceedings of the Workshop on Scalability in Model Driven Engineering, p. 6. ACM (2013)
31. Espinazo Pagán, J., Sánchez Cuadrado, J., García Molina, J.: Morsa: a scalable approach for persisting and accessing large models. In: Whittle, J., Clark, T., Kühne, T. (eds.) MODELS 2011. LNCS, vol. 6981, pp. 77–92. Springer, Heidelberg (2011). https://doi.org/10.1007/978-3-642-24485-8_7

Automated Change Propagation from Source Code to Sequence Diagrams

Karol Rástočný[(⊠)] and Andrej Mlynčár

Faculty of Informatics and Information Technologies,
Slovak University of Technology in Bratislava,
Ilkovičova 2, 842 16 Bratislava, Slovakia
karol.rastocny@stuba.sk, a.mlyncar@gmail.com

Abstract. Sequence diagrams belong to three most frequently used UML diagrams and they are often an integral part of a software design. Designers utilize sequence diagrams to define and visualize designed software's behavior. But during software development and maintenance, multiple vendor's changes are implemented into a source code. These changes lead to inconsistencies between a software model and the source code, that are omitted due to lack of time. This paper is focused on problems with automated source code changes propagation into UML sequence diagrams. In the paper, we propose the architecture for synchronization of outdated designers' sequence diagrams with current software behavior implemented in a source code. The proposed architecture is focused on updating and not on regenerating sequence diagrams, what helps designers to understand modified behavior and changes provided in it. We evaluated the proposed architecture via implemented extension for Eclipse Papyrus, which analyzes differences between sequence diagrams and source code model, and based on developers' styles, it propagates differences to sequence diagrams.

Keywords: UML · Sequence diagram · Source code · Change propagation

1 Introduction

With the focus on current trends in agile software development, great emphasis is placed on software sustainability. Huge amount of change requests is often required in massive enterprise architectures and long-term projects. Even though change requests and bugs are obviously well documented [1], during applying of these changes, there is regularly a problem that software design documentation is not properly updated and become insufficient [1, 2]. Outdated software design documentation, e.g. in form of a UML model can cause significant obstacles during problem investigation.

To solve this problem, automated tools for change propagation from source code to UML models are required. Tools for automated synchronization of static part of UML models are already developed and integrated in software modelling tools, e.g. Sparx Systems Enterprise Architect[1] or IBM Rational Software Architect Designer[2]. But

---

[1] http://www.sparxsystems.com/.
[2] http://www-03.ibm.com/software/products/en/ratsadesigner.

© Springer International Publishing AG 2018
A M. Tjoa et al. (Eds.): SOFSEM 2018, LNCS 10706, pp. 168–179, 2018.
https://doi.org/10.1007/978-3-319-73117-9_12

software behavior is still uncovered problem. There are already tools (e.g. IBM Rational Rhapsody[3] or Microsoft Visual Studio[4]) and research works [3, 4] that are dealing with generating behavioral UML diagrams from source code. But these tools can only generate new diagrams from source code or a source code execution, but they are not able to update existing diagrams with changes provided in source code. This problem is mainly visible in the third most used UML diagram [5, 6] – sequence diagram, in which designers obviously keep needed abstraction and they do not model all scenarios and interactions. The stable position of sequence diagrams in software models over years is caused by their ability to clarify how software works [5].

To achieve automatic change propagation to UML sequence diagrams, a source code and sequence diagrams synchronization is required. This means that if we want to preserve meaning and level of abstraction of models, every time changes are made in a source code, existing sequence diagrams should be updated. There is also problem with level of abstraction of sequence diagrams, because transforming all source code changes is usually not desired. We propose the solution fully functional synchronization of software source code and sequence diagrams based on change detection and synchronization methods.

2 Related Work

To achieve fully functional synchronization process of UML sequence diagrams and source code, it is required that sequence diagrams' components and source code fragments, that can be transformed into sequence diagrams, need to be represented in identical form suitable for detection of changes. One of promising sequence diagram representation is a hierarchical tree structure [7], where tree node represents sequence diagram lifeline and sequence diagram messages are represented with edge of tree (Fig. 1).

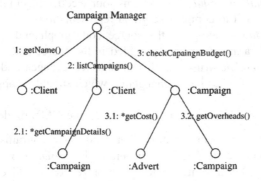

Fig. 1. Example of hierarchical tree representation of a sequence diagram [7]

---

[3] http://www-03.ibm.com/software/products/en/ratirhapfami.

[4] https://www.visualstudio.com/.

Another example of solutions where diagram was transformed into suitable structure for later processing and comparison are Petri nets [9] or control flow graphs [8].

An important part of the synchronization is source code fragments extraction. These fragments are required for comparison and synchronization of source code and a set of sequence diagrams. Source code fragments extraction can be made during source code execution [13] or by manual analysis of program files. Another way to extract information about program structure is static analysis with source code transformation to Abstract Syntax Tree [3] or Knowledge Discovery Metamodel (KDM)[5]. Knowledge Discovery Metamodel is technology independent metamodel developed by OMG, usually used in legacy system to provide intermediate representation of software components and software structure. KDM is separated into 4 layers – Infrastructure layer, Program Elements Layer, Runtime Resource Layer and Abstractions Layer [10]. Program Elements Layer provide us with information about source code structure in XMI format. MoDisco Eclipse Plugin implements KDM standard and it generates KDM XMI structure from Java Standard Edition projects [12].

3 Architecture for Automated Change Propagation

Our proposed solution of automated change propagation from source code to sequence diagrams is designed as modular architecture containing seven modules that expose services (see Fig. 2):

- *KDM Code Analyzer* – analyzes source code described by KDM and transforms it to an object model;
- *UML Analyzer* – analyzes UML model, extracts information about sequence diagrams and transforms them to an object model;
- *Strategy Analyzer* – analyzes design strategies used by designers in sequence diagrams and prepares data for synchronization rules;
- *Graph Transformation module* – transforms source code object model and sequence diagram object model to comparable graph representations;
- *Comparison module* – compares the source code graph and sequence diagrams graphs and builds a list of changes provided in the source code;
- *Synchronization module* – uses the list of detected changes and synchronizations rules to propagate changes into a changelog, which should be applied on sequence diagrams;
- *Interpreter module* – interprets the changelog on the UML model.

The solution can extract information about sequence diagrams from a software UML model and source code fragments generated by MoDisco Eclipse Plugin from source code and use this information to synchronize newly added modifications in source code into existing sequence diagrams.

Each module has defined output and input formats and acts mostly independently of the other modules. This means that even if a core functionality in one of modules has

---

[5] http://www.omg.org/technology/kdm/.

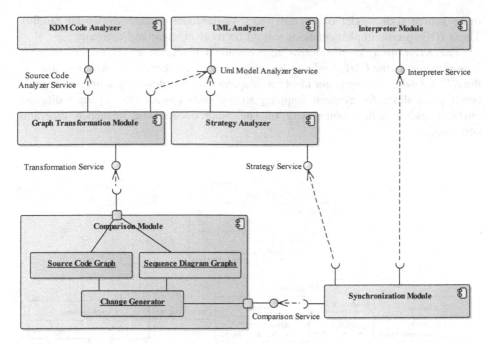

Fig. 2. Modular architecture for automated change propagation from source code to sequence diagrams.

been changed, inputs and outputs of the module remain unchanged so functionality of the rest of modules is sustained. For example, if the *KDM Analyzer* module is replaced with an AST analyzer, it should not affect functionality of other modules. Another example is in comparison module – if another comparison algorithm is used in comparison module, this change does not affect ways of a source code and sequence diagrams synchronization.

3.1 UML Analyzer

The module *UML Analyzer* parses an UML model stored in a XMI file and transforms the model's sequence diagrams to simplified sequence diagram representation (Fig. 3), which contains necessary data for comparing newer source code with outdated sequence diagrams. This simplified representation is efficient for later transformations and it also suitable for representation of algorithms written in the source code.

3.2 KDM Analyzer

The *KDM Analyzer* provides an adapter between the proposed architecture and used tool for static source code analysis. Getting the *KDM Analyzer* apart makes the architecture programming language and technology independent. We can easily implement language specific adapter, and only by implementation of specialized adapter, we can make IDE specific implementation, while the specialized adapter can reuse source code model of an IDE (e.g., CodeModel in case of Visual Studio). These IDE specific implementations should be more efficient and accurate.

The *KDM Analyzer* transforms source code's model in KDM to the common representation as the *UML Analyzer*. Re-usage of the representations adds more logic to the *KDM Analyzer*, what is not ideal for adapters. But nearness to a source code gives better possibilities for efficient mapping source code artifacts to sequence diagram artifacts and it reduce complexity of later source code and sequence diagrams comparison.

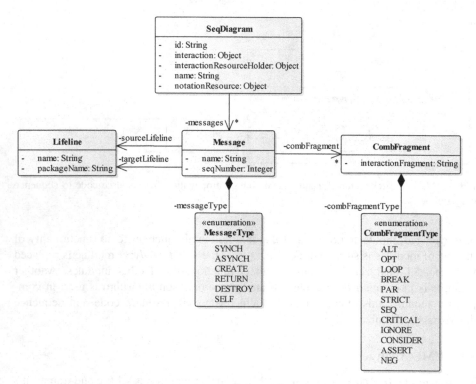

Fig. 3. Simplified sequence diagram representation generated by the *UML analyzer.*

3.3   Graph Transformation Module

The main objective of the *Graph Transformation module* is to transform data created by the *KDM Analyzer* and the *UML Analyzer* to a format which supports efficient change detection between a source code and sequence diagrams. There are several representation solutions mentioned in the Sect. 2. Based on analysis and comparison of these methods we use *Hierarchical tree structure* [7], based on which we proposed our *sequence diagram tree graph structure*. Each tree node (class *Node*) contains lifeline name, execution identifier, list of child nodes, message by which node is created, and list of combined fragments affecting this message.

3.4   Comparison Module

The *Comparison module* detects changes between a source code tree structure and sequence diagram tree structures created by the *Graph Transformation module*. The *Comparison module* process each potentially outdated sequence diagram in three steps:

1. *Find identical subtree* in the source code tree structure – the module tries to match the sequence diagram in the source code. If the sequence diagram is found as identical subtree, the diagram is marked as up-to-date and the next two steps are omitted.
2. *Find the root node of similar subtree* in the source code tree structure – the module tries to identify the root node of the sequence diagram in the source code. To match the root node, the breadth-first search with following conditions is used:
   a. For a root node candidate, a subtree-depth is calculated. If the subtree depth is less than the sequence diagram's tree-depth - 2, the root node candidate is rejected. The difference 2 has been chosen as search algorithm optimization, while it markedly reduces searched space. We defined this heuristic, because the source code is more detailed than sequence diagrams and if the source code's subtree is significantly smaller, than it will been rejected in the following condition with high probability.
   b. If 35% nodes of the root node candidate's subtree are identical with the sequence diagram tree's nodes, the root node candidate is marked as the root node. The ratio of identical nodes has been determined by manual experiments. The value 35% is relatively small, but the source code tree contains precise details like system and external calls at lowest level, that are not modeled in sequence diagrams.
3. *Comparison of the source code's subtree with the sequence diagram tree* – the comparison algorithm is based on [11], which finds an edit script which contains a set of tree modifications to achieve quickest way to reach an isomorphic state between these two trees. In our case, our modified change detection algorithm creates a list of changes detected in compared source code's subtree and the sequence diagram tree. Detected changes are later processed by synchronization module to finalize synchronization process.

The comparison algorithm is proposed to process a source code representable by a tree, i.e. programs with one execution point (e.g. *Main* function). The algorithm can be modified to reflect a source code with multiple execution points, e.g. REST services. In this case, the source code is not a tree, but it is still directed graph with nodes that have not any input edges. These nodes are execution points and they acts as root nodes for their sub-graphs – trees. Therefore, by matching sequence diagrams against all root nodes (execution points), the comparison algorithm became suitable to current software systems that utilize execution frameworks.

3.5   Strategy Analyzer

The *Strategy Analyzer module* analyzes original sequence diagrams and based on this analysis it collects information, that describe a sequence diagrams design style. Current set of analyzed design style information contains:

- Average lifelines count;
- Average messages count;
- Lifelines count in each sequence diagram;
- Messages count in each sequence diagram;
- Frequencies of combined fragment types;
- Usage of get/set messages in each sequence diagram.

3.6   Synchronization Module

The *Synchronization module* is responsible for managing synchronization process. From this module, users can start execution of synchronization process. The module uses lists of changes and sets of design style information for each sequence diagram to build a list of synchronization actions, that should be provided in the UML model.

The list of synchronization actions is built by resolutions, whether a change detected in the *Comparison module* should be interpreted to a software sequence diagram. This feature is fulfilled by set of synchronization rules. Each modification detected in the *Comparison module* is evaluated by following synchronization rules and based on output from rule, it is determined, if the modification is added to the list of synchronization actions:

- Lifeline synchronization rules:
  - if an addition of a lifeline exceeded maximal lifelines count in the sequence diagram, the addition is ignored;
  - if an addition of a lifeline will introduce a package, which has not been used in the sequence diagram, the addition is ignored;
- Messages lifeline synchronization rules:
  - If multiple occurrences of a message should be added to the sequence diagram, but the sequence diagram does not contain any occurrence of the message, all additions of the message are ignored;
  - If the sequence diagram does not contain any get/set messages, all additions of get/set messages are ignored;
- Combined fragments synchronization rules:
  - If multiple combined fragments should be added, but the sequence diagram does not contain any combined fragment, the sequence diagram is evaluated as high level diagram and all additions of combined fragments are ignored;
  - If an opt combined fragment should be deleted and alt combined fragment should be added at the same position, both modifications are ignored and new modify synchronization action, which transforms the opt combined fragment to the alt combined fragment, is added to the list of synchronization actions.

3.7   Interpreter Module

The *Interpreter module* is designed to finalize whole synchronization process. The module interprets actions from the list of synchronizations actions. The *Interpreter module* should be implemented for each UML modelling tool separately. There is also possibility to provide tool independent implementation that modifies XMI files, but each UML modelling tool uses their own XMI extension for sequence diagrams' layout information.

4   Evaluation

To evaluate usability of the proposed architecture we implemented the prototype[6] which synchronizes Java source code analyzed by MoDisco Eclipse Plugin with sequence diagrams modeled in Eclipse Papyrus. In the prototype, we did not implement synchronization of all elements from the sequence diagram metamodel, but we focused on the mainly used elements, via which we can present correctness of change propagation from obviously used source code structures:

- Synchronous messages;
- Reply messages;
- Lifelines;
- Combined fragments: loop, opt.

Modules of the prototype are implemented as OSGi Eclipse Bundles with fully implemented APIs and data structures necessary for supporting whole sequence diagram metamodel. So, this restriction of sequence diagram elements does not affect results of the evaluation and the restriction will be resolved by final implementation of the change detection module and the interpreter module.

We evaluated the proposed architecture via sixteen test cases, that was organized in three test sets based on level of their complexity:

- Evaluation of basic functionalities
    - TC01: Adding a synchronous message
    - TC02: Adding a synchronous message and a lifeline
    - TC03: Removing a synchronous message
    - TC04: Removing a synchronous message and a lifeline
    - TC05: Adding a combined fragment opt
    - TC06: Removing a combined fragment opt
- Evaluation of synchronization rules
    - TC07: Filtration of system calls
    - TC08: Restriction of lifelines count
    - TC09: Filtration of get/set calls
    - TC10: Filtration of external calls
    - TC11: Filtration of combined fragments

---

[6] Replication package: https://github.com/rastocny/SOFSEM_SeqDiag_ChangeProp.

- Evaluation of propagation of complex changes
  - TC12: Replacing two messages with one new message, which contains internally six new calls
  - TC13: Condition change and movement of existing calls to new operation
  - TC14: Part of the functionality has been moved to new operation
  - TC15: Removing a sequence diagram implementation from the source code
  - TC16: Adding a loop over an existing condition and adding a new synchronous call into the condition

For each test case, we defined outdated sequence diagram (Fig. 4), modified source code (List. 1) and expected changelog (List. 2). After execution of all test cases we manually compared expected changelogs with obtained changelogs and evaluated differences. In the next step, we reviewed updated sequence diagrams (Fig. 5) and evaluated their layout and correctness.

During the evaluation of the first test case set, 20 modifications in sequence diagrams were done. The evaluation proved, that the prototype correctly processes the source code and sequence diagrams in *UML Analyzer* and *KDM Analyzer* modules and that the source code and the sequence diagrams are correctly transformed to the *sequence diagram tree graph structure*. This evaluation also showed, that the *Comparison module* can detect modifications on implemented sequence diagram elements and that detected modifications are correctly interpreted by the *Interpreter module*.

The first set of test cases uncover some layout issues in the *Interpreter module*. After deletion of messages, bellow messages are not shifted up. There was also problem with added combined fragment which has not correctly set top and bottom margins.

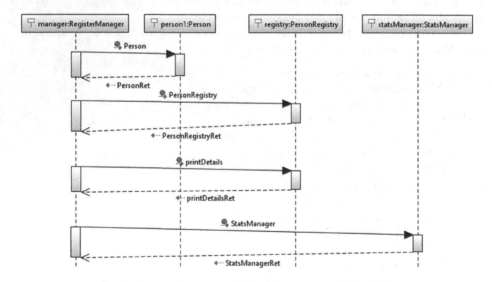

Fig. 4. Outdated sequence diagram for testcases TC01-TC07.

```
public void createRegistry(){
  Person person1 = new Person("Andrej", "Mlyncar", null);
  PersonRegistry registry = new PersonRegistry();
  if(registry != null)
    registry.printDetails();
  StatsManager statsManager = new StatsManager(registry);
}
```

List. 1. Modified source code for TC03.

```
fragment_add = opt:registry!=null; message: printDetails
```

List. 2. Expected change log for TC03.

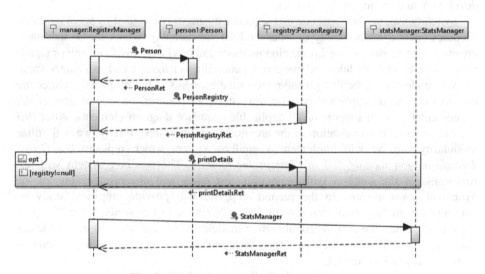

Fig. 5. Updated sequence diagram for TC03.

The second test case set is focused no validation if the proposed architecture is able to detect basics of used design styles. For these test cases, we defined different sequence diagrams and we observed if the *Strategy Analyzer* and the *Synchronization module* correctly detect and interpret used styles. The test cases applied 20 modifications in sequence diagrams and proved that observed design styles are correctly identified independently. We observed only one new issue with calculating horizontal positions of nested execution specifications.

Combinations of multiple design styles and source code modifications were evaluated by the last test case set, which provided 67 modifications. The results showed that proposed architecture can correctly detects complex changes and propagates them to sequence diagrams with respect of a design style. Some issues were observed in layouts of sequence diagrams, where multiple modifications have been done. Some sequence diagram elements did not have correctly calculated heights and x-coordinates, but all elements were semantically and syntactically placed correctly. These problems can be later resolved by reusing Eclipse Papyrus's layouting algorithm in the *Interpreter module*. The layouting algorithm should be also updated to use distances and sizes learned from original sequence diagrams for added and modified elements.

5   Conclusion and Future Work

The work presented in the paper is primarily focused on architectural design of solution which will be able to provide an effective way to automate update of a behavioral documentation of software systems for software architects and developers. The proposed solution can improve process of applying changes to existing software systems by reducing communication about implemented software changes between software developers and architects or analytics.

Synchronization of source code and sequence diagrams is executed by set of modules. Modules operate independently of other modules functionality, which means that interpretation, comparison or synchronization methods can be changed without any or significant effects to other modules and that core functionality is language and tool independent.

We implemented the first prototype to prove concepts of the proposed architecture and to evaluate its applicability. The next steps are focused on completion of the implementation with support of all applicable sequence diagram elements. After that we will provide final evaluation of the architecture in two steps. Firstly, we will utilize modularity and we will implement a sandbox system which replaces the *Graph Transformation module* and the *Interpreter module*. The sandbox system will test robustness of the solution with generating test cases and observing results of the *Synchronization module*. In the second step, we will provide empirical study by applying the implemented prototype in real agile teams. In this study, we will deploy the prototype into the tool for collaborative modelling [14] and we will involve teams from the course Team project and teams from our innovation lab built in cooperation with the project DA-SPACE[7].

Later we will focus also on applying the proposed architecture on other behavioral diagrams. We assume that the architecture is almost directly applicable on communication diagrams, that have equivalent expression power as sequence diagrams. More challenging are activity diagrams, in that same algorithmic concepts (e.g., loops) can be modelled variously.

Acknowledgement. This work was partially supported by the Scientific Grant Agency of the Slovak Republic, grant No. VG 1/0752/14, the Slovak Research and Development Agency under the contract No. APVV-15-0508, and this publication is the partial result of the Research & Development Operational Programme for the project Research of methods for acquisition, analysis and personalized conveying of information and knowledge, ITMS 26240220039, co-funded by the ERDF.

---

[7] http://www.interreg-danube.eu/approved-projects/da-space.

References

1. Voigt, S., von Garrel, J., Müller, J., Wirth, D.: A study of documentation in agile software projects. In: Proceedings of the 10th ACM/IEEE International Symposium on Empirical Software Engineering and Measurement, p. 6. ACM, New York (2016)
2. Rashid, N., Khan, S.: Developing green and sustainable software using agile methods in global software development: risk factors for vendors. In: Proceedings of the 11th International Conference on Evaluation of Novel Software Approaches to Software Engineering, pp. 247–253. SCITEPRESS (2016)
3. Fauzi, E., Hendradjaya, B., Sunindyo, W.D.: Reverse engineering of source code to sequence diagram using abstract syntax tree. In: International Conference on Data and Software Engineering (ICoDSE), p. 6. IEEE (2016)
4. Srinivasan, M., Yang, J., Lee, Y.: Case studies of optimized sequence diagram for program comprehension. In: 24th International Conference on Program Comprehension (ICPC), p. 4. IEEE (2016)
5. Dobing, B., Parsons, J.: How UML is used. Commun. ACM - Two Decades Lang-action Perspect. **49**(5), 109–113 (2006)
6. Reggio, G., Leotta, M., Ricca, F., Clerissi, D.: What are the used UML diagram constructs? A document and tool analysis study covering activity and use case diagrams. In: Hammoudi, S., Pires, L.F., Filipe, J., das Neves, R.C. (eds.) MODELSWARD 2014. CCIS, vol. 506, pp. 66–83. Springer, Cham (2015). https://doi.org/10.1007/978-3-319-25156-1_5
7. Li, X., Liu, Z., Jifeng, H.: A formal semantics of UML sequence diagram. In: Australian Software Engineering Conference 2004, pp. 1–10. IEEE (2004)
8. Rountev, A., Volgin, O., Reddoch. M.: Control flow analysis for reverse engineering of sequence diagrams. Technical report, Ohio State University (2004)
9. Emadi, S., Shams, F.: Transformation of usecase and sequence diagrams to petri nets. In: ISECS International Colloquium on Computing, Communication, Control, and Management 2009, pp. 399–403. IEEE (2009)
10. Pérez-Castillo, R., De Guzman, I.G.R., Piattini, M.: Knowledge discovery metamodel-ISO/IEC 19506: a standard to modernize legacy systems. Comput. Stan. Interfaces **33**(6), 519–532 (2011)
11. Wang, Y., DeWitt, D.J., Cai., J.-Y.: X-Diff: an effective change detection algorithm for XML documents. In: 19th International Conference on Data Engineering, pp. 519–530. IEEE (2003)
12. Bruneliere, H., Cabot, J., Jouault, F., Madiot, F.: MoDisco: a generic and extensible framework for model driven reverse engineering. In: Proceedings of the IEEE/ACM International Conference on Automated Software Engineering, pp. 173–174. ACM, New York (2010)
13. Oechsle, R., Schmitt, T.: JAVAVIS: automatic program visualization with object and sequence diagrams using the Java debug interface (JDI). In: Diehl, S. (ed.) Software Visualization. LNCS, vol. 2269, pp. 176–190. Springer, Heidelberg (2002). https://doi.org/10.1007/3-540-45875-1_14
14. Ferenc, M., Polasek, I., Vincúr, J.: Collaborative modeling and visualisation of software systems using multidimensional UML, In: Proceedings of the Fifth IEEE Working Conference on Software Visualization VISSOFT 2017, p. 5. IEEE, Shanghai (2017)

Multi-paradigm Architecture Constraint Specification and Configuration Based on Graphs and Feature Models

Sahar Kallel[1,2(✉)], Chouki Tibermacine[1], Ahmed Hadj Kacem[2],
and Christophe Dony[1]

[1] LIRMM, CNRS and University of Montpellier, Montpellier, France
{sahar.kallel,tibermacin,dony}@lirmm.fr
[2] ReDCAD, University of Sfax, Sfax, Tunisia
ahmed.hadjkacem@fsegs.rnu.tn

Abstract. Currently, architecture constraints can be specified and checked in different paradigms of software development, the object-oriented, component-based and service-based one. But the current state of the art and practice do not consider their specification at a high level of abstraction, independently from any paradigm vocabulary. We propose in this paper a process combining graphs and feature modeling to specify multi-paradigm architecture constraints. These constraints are expressed with OCL on a particular meta-model of graphs. Then these constraints can be transformed to any chosen paradigm, after their configuration using a feature/variability model. This transformation allows later to handle these constraints in that (chosen) paradigm: to refine them, to generate source code from them, and to check them on models and on source code. A case study is presented in this paper; it concerns architecture constraint specification and configuration under software migration from the object-oriented to the component-based paradigm.

1 Introduction

Documenting software architectures provides a preliminary comprehensive view of the structure and the behavior of the software. This documentation includes the definition of architecture decisions which provide an important element: *Architecture constraints.*

Architecture constraints [11], which are meta-level specifications of invariants on the structure of the entities, constituting a user application (objects for instance), enable to "formalize" the topological/structural conditions imposed by design patterns, architectural styles or any design principle. They are involved throughout the software development life-cycle (from design to implementation stages and in maintenance). Currently, these artifacts can be specified and checked in different programming paradigms: the object-oriented, component-based and service-based one, among others. But constraint specifications in the different paradigms are defined completely separately from each other, while

© Springer International Publishing AG 2018
A. M. Tjoa et al. (Eds.): SOFSEM 2018, LNCS 10706, pp. 180–193, 2018.
https://doi.org/10.1007/978-3-319-73117-9_13

these share a major part of their specification. This part concerns the formalized structural conditions. The variable part between them is the set of architectural entities on which these conditions are checked (objects, object dependencies, components, ports, connectors, services, and so on). For example, in the Façade pattern, the façade entity is an object in an object-oriented application, and what it hides to client entities are the internal methods of the application. In a component-based application, the façade entity is a component which provides a unique port to client entities; it hides the provided services by the other components of the application. The structural conditions here are the same (presence of a unique entity – object or component – which serves client entities).

In our previous works [6, 7], we have studied the use of OCL/UML[1] for architecture constraint specification and their checking at the design and implementation stages in different development paradigms. Our first work presented a process which enables to generate meta-programs that make possible constraint checking on object-oriented applications. The second work proposed another process which enables to generate reusable and executable components deployed in component-based applications, in addition to architecture constraints as services which are reusable, searchable, executable and checkable in service-based applications. We propose in this paper an approach (a language and a process) in which architecture constraints are specified in an abstract way, with a neutral structural constraint vocabulary. They are expressed in ocl and navigate in a meta-model of graphs. Then these constraints can be transformed towards a given paradigm (in our case, the object-oriented, component-based and service-based ones) by configuring a feature model. This feature model expresses the commonality and variability between development paradigms. Once constraints are transformed to a given paradigm, they can be checked on models defined in that paradigm, or be refined and transformed into meta-programs (particular classes or component/service descriptors) to be checked on the code of applications.

The remaining of this paper is organized as follows. In the following section, we present the graph meta-model and the feature model used in our approach. Section 3 explains the process of architecture constraint configuration and transformation. A case study is exposed in Sect. 4. Before concluding, we discuss the related work in Sect. 5.

2   Architecture Constraint Specification and Configuration

We define in the first subsection a meta-model of graphs on which an example of an architecture constraint is specified. In the second subsection, we present the feature model used for the configuration of constraints.

---

[1] OCL/UML means that the constraints are specified with OCL and navigate in the UML meta-model.

2.1   A Meta-model of Graphs

As an underlying software representation we use graphs because they can capture the basic structure in a straightforward and generic way: nodes represent software entities and edges represent relationships between those entities. More precisely, we have used `typed`, `directed` and `labeled` graphs. We have used a `typed` graph to specify that nodes can be nested in other nodes. We have used `directed` graphs, implying that each edge has a source and a target node (directed dependencies between software entities) and `labeled` graphs to attach any number of domain-specific properties to the nodes and edges.

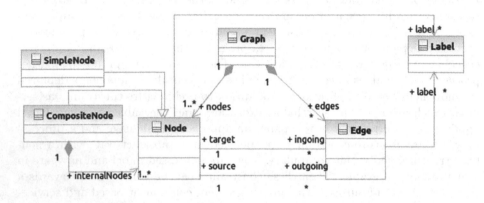

Fig. 1. Meta-model of graphs

Figure 1 shows the meta-model of graphs used in our approach. A graph is composed of edges and nodes. A node has at least one outgoing and ingoing edge. Each edge has exactly one source node and one target node. A node can be composite or simple. The composite node can be composed of simple and also composite nodes. Each node and edge can be labeled in order to refine the graph. According to this meta-model, we can obtain a model (a graph) that contains edges going from inside a composite node to a simple one.

Listing 1.1 presents an architecture constraint characterizing the `Façade` pattern. This constraint is formalized with OCL navigating in the meta-model shown in Fig. 1. It consists of several sub-constraints. We suppose that there exist a set of nodes that represent `clients`, another set represents `systems` and a node represents a `facade`.

```
1  context Graph inv :
2  --Clients have only outgoing edges
3  clients ->forAll(n:Node|n.ingoing->isEmpty())
4  and
5  --Systems have only ingoing edges
6  systems->forAll(n:Node|n.outgoing->isEmpty())
7  and
8  --No edges between clients and systems
9  clients ->forAll(n:Node|n.outgoing->forAll(e:Edge|
10   systems->excludes(e.target)))
11 and
12 --All the edges whose sources are the clients should go to the facade
13 clients ->forAll(n:Node|n.outgoing->forAll(e:Edge|e.target=facade))
14 and
15 --The facade should be linked to at least one system
16 facade.outgoing->exists(e:Edge|systems->includes(e.target))
```

Listing 1.1. Facade constraint specification in the graph meta-model

These node labeled *Client, System, Facade* may give a hint about constraint semantic but it is not clear that these nodes represent objects, components or classes. At this level, we can say that the constraint is formalized in an abstract way, *i.e.* independently from any paradigm. To translate the constraints into a specific paradigm, we have to configure a feature model which is presented in the following section.

2.2 Feature Models

Feature models [8] are simple and hierarchical models that capture the commonality and variability of a set of products in a software product line. In our approach, a feature model is used to express the variability between software development paradigms.

A feature diagram is a representation of a feature model. We have used the notation of Czarnecki *et al.* [5] in the feature diagram developed for our approach because it is a practical way to integrate labels for the nodes and the edges. It is a useful way to configure the constraint which navigates, among others, in **Label**, **Node** and **Edge** meta-classes of the graph meta-model. Moreover, an architecture constraint is generally composed of sub-constraints assembled by the logic operator "and" (see Listing 1.1). In each sub-constraint, we find several (0-n) nodes and/or edges. Each node or edge can be translated to the appropriate element in the chosen paradigm (class, method, connector, port, object, etc.). For doing so, we added a cardinality to the feature diagram in order to be able to do all the required transformation for each sub-constraint and configure each node and each edge.

Since this work is a continuation of our previous works (introduced in the previous section), we have chosen to translate ocl architecture constraints from a graph meta-model to UML[2] meta-model based on feature models. Therefore,

---

[2] UML http://www.omg.org/spec/UML/2.4.1 is an OMG standard and covers both class/object and component modeling.

the features (without considering the leaves) represent, among others, the meta-classes (Ex: Graph, Node, Edge) and the meta-roles (ex: source and target) of the meta-model of graphs, while the leaves of the feature diagram are elements of the UML meta-model (Fig. 2[3]).

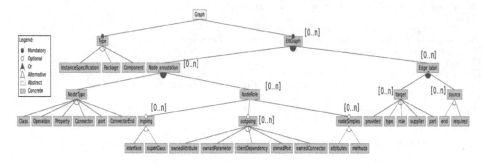

Fig. 2. An excerpt of the feature diagram for constraint transformation from graphs

The root feature of the diagram is the graph representing the architecture on which the constraint is formalized. The feature *Node* is a sub-feature of *EltGraph* (i.e., *Node* is a child of *EltGraph* in the feature tree) and has an attribute for specifying its label, if any. Every feature is qualified by a feature cardinality. It specifies how often the entire sub-tree rooted in the solitary feature can be copied (with the roots of the replicated sub-trees becoming siblings). For example, the features *Node* and Edge have the feature cardinality [0..n]. This means that an *EltGraph* can be formed by 0 or n *Node*s and *Edge*s.

3   Multi-paradigm Architecture Constraints

In this section, we present the different steps of the constraint transformation. We use the `Façade` architecture constraint shown in Listing 1.1 as a running example.

3.1   Constraint Configuration

Constraint configuration consists in selecting, in the feature diagram, the suitable features to build a new constraint in the chosen paradigm. This step is started by configuring first the context of the constraint, then configuring the OCL definitions[4] and OCL let expressions, if any, and finally the sub-constraints by respecting their appearance order in the constraint. A step called *feature model specialization* [5] is performed before the configuration. It consists in choosing the precise values of cardinalities presented in the feature diagram. This facilitates

---

[3] For space limitation, the constraints accompanying the feature diagram are not showed.

[4] OCL queries characterized by the keyword `def:`. They allow to declare and define attribute values (like let expression) and/or to return internal OCL operation values.

the configuration of the constraint by reserving the exact number of features in the configuration interface.

Each sub-constraint, including the OCL let expression, is represented by *EltGraph*. In our constraint, we have 8 *EltGraphs*. We can configure all these *EltGraphs* thanks to the cardinality of this feature. We follow the order of the sub-constraints to configure them. Figure 3 presents a possible configuration of the sub-constraint 5 (in Listing 1.1 without considering the let expressions) in the object-oriented development paradigm.

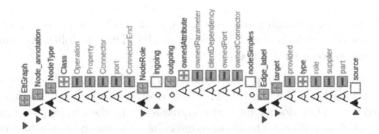

Fig. 3. A possible configuration of Facade constraint in OO paradigm

The constraint configuration is performed using the feature IDE plugin. It shows an interface to configure a feature diagram. We can see all the possible configurations and it produces exceptions if the configuration does not respect the requirements of the feature diagram.

3.2   Constraint Transformation

The implementation of the constraint transformation is performed using the editor of the feature model. The first step is a direct transformation of the constraint. It uses the configured feature model. The second step is based on the abstract syntax tree (AST) generated from the obtained constraint and the XMI document representing the UML meta-model. It has as a goal to make the constraint valid. The tool-set used for configuring the feature diagram provides a document that includes the inputs and the outputs of the configuration (names of features). Our process uses this document and automatically applies the mapping to the constraint. An abstract syntax tree is generated from the constraint (which is specified in the graph meta-model). The AST node names and their types (the meta-class names) are then modified by their corresponding features and are regenerated in order to obtain an architecture constraint written in the UML meta-model.

Listing 1.2 presents the **façade** constraint after the direct transformation. The meta-role *outgoing* in Line 9 in Listing 1.1 is replaced by *clientDependency* and in Line 16 by *ownedAttribute* as the configuration is defined (see Fig. 3).

```
1  context Package inv :
2  ---
3  clients ->forAll (n : Class | n.->isEmpty () )    and
4  systems->forAll (n : Class | n.->isEmpty () )    and
5  clients ->forAll (n : Class | n.clientDependency->forAll (e : Edge |
6    systems->excludes (e.supplier ) ) ) and  .... and
7  facade.ownedAttribute->exists (e : Edge | systems
8    ->includes (e.type ))
```

Listing 1.2. An excerpt from a Facade constraint after a direct transformation

In Listing 1.2, the constraint is specified in UML meta-model, but this transformation does not necessarily produce a valid OCL constraint. OCL exceptions are provided when compiling the constraint in an OCL compiler. For example *Edge* in Line 5 is undefined in UML meta-model. The two following sub-steps are implemented to solve these errors.

1. *Removing unnecessary sub-constraints*: This is the case of the subconstraints 1 and 2 in Listing 1.2. The user does not completely configure the sub-constraints. They do not have any equivalence in the target paradigm: the object-oriented paradigm. These sub-constraints are safely removed from the constraint.

2. *Adding OCL expressions*: There are two cases where we should add OCL expressions. The process here examines the constraint in each case and try to add OCL expressions to make it valid and accurate.

The process in the first case consists first in replacing all the roles and metaclasses that are still written in the graph meta-model by their corresponding modeling elements in the UML meta-model. This transformation is complementary to the direct one. It is based on the AST generated from the constraint. The AST parser, taking into consideration the UML meta-model, indicates the AST nodes which whose types do not belong to the UML meta-model. We take the example presented in Line 5, in Listing 1.2 in which the meta-class **Edge** is not translated yet. According to the UML meta-model, *clientDependency* is a navigation that produces **Set(Dependency)**. So, **Edge** will be replaced by **Dependency**. The same processing is performed for the error located in Line 8 in the same Listing: **Edge** is replaced by **Property**.

The process in the second case consists in adding navigation patterns[5] in the constraint. Indeed, after the direct transformation, we can obtain in a subconstraint an ocl inequality exception. Suppose that we take an example of a constraint that has, in its specification in the graph meta-model, a navigation towards the *Node* meta-class via *target*, to get the target node (one node [1..1]) (see Listing 1.3). The user configures *target* by *end* in the componentbased development paradigm. *end* is a meta-role in the UML meta-model. It provides a set [0..*] of component connectors. So, we face an OCL exception (**Set(Connectors)= a component**). Here, the process adds, among others, an

---

[5] A navigation pattern is a set of navigations. It includes more roles and ocl operations/quantifiers.

appropriate quantifier that takes only one of the sets to complete the constraint transformation. More details are given in the following Listings.

In the first line of Listing 1.3, X and Y are nodes composing the graph of the model. The constraint imposes that the node X should have at least one outgoing edge towards the node Y. To transform this constraint in the component paradigm, the user configured *outgoing* by *ownedPort* and *target* by *end*. The process checks if the constraint has again errors of the first case. The second line represents the constraint specification under the transformation. We observe that the specification of this constraint is wrong. It is violated when evaluating it in the UML meta-model. To solve this problem, we integrate first some meta-roles such as `ownedConnector` and `role` (an application of the first case) and then pattern navigations as presented in Listing 1.4. This Listing shows a possible result.

```
1 X.outgoing->exists(e:Edge|e.target=Y)
2 X.ownedPort->exists(e:Port|e.end  =Y)
```

Listing 1.3. OCL AC before and after direst transformation

```
1 X.ownedPort->exists(e:Port|e. ownedConnector .end->
2    exists(ee:ConnectorEnd | ee.role -> includes(Y.role)) )
```

Listing 1.4. OCL AC specified in the UML meta-model

As we noticed above, the implementation of the process that consists in making the architecture constraint independent to any paradigm uses an Eclipse tool-set. This tool-set generates the abstract syntax tree (AST) and analyzes the UML meta-model. Each output (sub-constraint) provided by this process should be validated by the user.

4 Case Study

We have applied the proposed approach on a particular engineering activity: the automatic software migration from the object-oriented paradigm to the component-based one. In this kind of activities, it is too difficult to directly specify the architecture constraint in the transformed application (component-based application) because many constraints imposed by the initial application (like, inheritance and instantiation) may generate other constraints (new architectural patterns are added under the migration, which are not known by the user, especially if the migration is automatic) and new architectural elements (connectors and ports) which can impose new architecture constraints.

We take the example of an object-oriented application which is designed with UML and implemented with java, and which represents an *information screen* [2]. This application simulates the behavior of an information screen, a software system which displays in a public transportation's embedded screen, the names of stations, the expected time at each station, etc. The *ContentProvider* class implements methods which send text messages (instances of the *Message* class), and time information obtained through *Clock* instances based on the data returned by *TimeZone* instances. The *DisplayManager* is responsible for viewing the provided information through a *Screen*. The design of this application imposed a set of architecture constraints that should be valid on the code. Some of these constraints are presented in the following list.

- *ContentProvider* class should be a singleton class.
- *Clock* and *Message* classes should be kept in relation with the *Content* abstract class (which is an inheritance relation in the OO application).
- The Observer pattern is instantiated in this application. We focus in this case study on a part of this pattern, in which *DisplayManager* class should be in association with *ContentProvider* to invoke methods returning the content.

When migrating an application, major changes of the architecture and then the source code are performed. Some elements are removed, others are added, *e.g.* dependencies between some elements are changed, etc. In fact, each paradigm imposes its own architecture design principles. For example, in the component-based paradigm, each component must hide its internal structure. It should provide its services without exposing the classes that implement them. These conditions should be taken into consideration. In addition, the works cited previously proposed an automatic migration of the applications, which generally produces additional intermediate classes, methods and components in addition to dependencies between them, which are seamless to developers. In this case, rewriting the constraints in the target paradigm is difficult because architectural elements constituting the target application can be unknown.

Our intuition is that our approach can allow to simplify the migration of the architecture constraints of information screen object-oriented application in component-based paradigm. To apply our approach, we have used software migration works that are composed of two steps: architecture recovery then code transformation. These works generate automatically a graph describing the architecture of the target application. This graph contains labeled nodes that may represent the classes, the methods, the attributes and the components representing clusters of cohesive classes, in addition to edges that link between nodes (method invocations, connectors between required/provided interfaces, etc.). Besides, to make component interfaces operational, the graph is extended by other nodes and edges that represent new classes, interfaces and attributes that are generated to transform inheritance into the component-based paradigm [2]. Figure 4 shows an excerpt of this graph.

Based on this graph which contains architecture elements of the source application and also new elements added by the migration, we have rewritten the architecture constraints of the application. It is specified in the meta-model of graphs shown in Fig. 1. For reasons of space limitation, Listing 1.5 presents only an excerpt of this constraint.

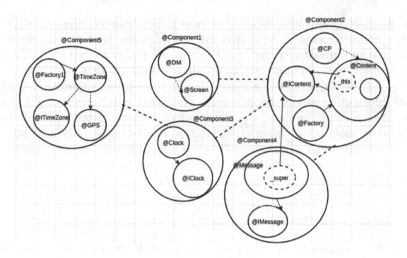

Fig. 4. An excerpt of a graph representing the architecture recovered from the Information Screen application

```
1  context Graph inv :
2  let compo1:Set(CompositeNode)=self.nodes->select(n:Node|n.labels
3     ->exists(a:Label|a.name='Component1')) in
4  -- the same for compo2, compo3, compo4 and compo5
5  let content:Node= compo2.simpleNodes->select(n:Node|n.labels
6     ->exists(a:Label|a.name='Content'))->asOrderedSet()->first() in
7  -- other let expressions ...
8  in
9  compo1.outgoing->one(e:Edge|e.target=compo2)  and
10 compo2.ingoing->forAll(e1,e2|e1.source=compo3 and e2.source=compo4)
11 and ... and
12 content.outgoing->exists(e:Edge|e.target=iContent) and
13 factory.ingoing->one(e:Edge|e.source=content) and
14 content.simpleNodes->select(n|n.outgoing->exists(e|e.target=iContent))
15 and ... and
16 message.simpleNodes->select(n:Node|n.outgoing
17     ->exists(e:Edge|e.target=iContent))
```

Listing 1.5. An excerpt of AC specification in graph meta-model

In this constraint, the let expressions search for the elements composing the application, and which can be classes or components. `compo1` is an example of a variable which references the node named `Component1`. This component was identified in the architecture recovery step; it is considered in this constraint as a graph's node.

4.1   Configuring the Constraint by the Feature Model

There are nodes that represent classes (annotated by CP, Factory, Content and TimeZone), attributes (dashed nodes in Fig. 4), components (annotated by Componenti, i = [1..5]), etc. There are edges that represent connectors (thick dashed edges), others represent inheritance (between classes inside components). There are other nodes which are generated due to solutions kept to transform the instantiation and inheritance. Some of these nodes are annotated with *IContent*, *Factory*, *_this*, *_super*, *ITimeZone*. There are also edges which link them. These elements did not exist in the architecture of the source application (object-oriented information screen application). They imposed a new condition that consists in respecting the factory pattern (which is instantiated in the architecture when transforming an inheritance relation in the chosen migration solution in this case study). The constraint will be configured in our feature model starting by the first sub-constraint and so on as described in Sect. 3. We indicate for each element its equivalent in the new architecture.

4.2   Transforming the Constraint

Following the process explained in Sect. 3 by using the configured feature model of our constraint and after making the constraint well specified in the UML meta-model, we obtain as an excerpt of a result the following Listing.

```
 1  context Component inv :
 2  let internalCompo : Set(Component) ... in
 3  let compo1: Component=internalCompo->select(n:Component|
 4    c.name='Component1')->asOrderedSet()->first()    in
 5  -- the other let expressions ... in
 6  compo1.ownedPort->one(e:Port|e.ownedConnector.end
 7       ->forAll(ee:ConnectorEnd|ee.role->includes(compo2.role))) and
 8  compo2.ownedPort.ownedConnector->forAll(e1,e2|
 9    compo3.role->includes(e1.end.role) and compo4.role
10       ->includes(e2.end.role))    and
11  content.interface->exists(e:Interface|e.name=iContent) and
12  factory.ownedAttribute->one(e:Property|e.type=content)
```

Listing 1.6. An excerpt of AC specification in UML meta-model (Component modeling)

This constraint declares first the internal component which composes the target application. This implies modifications in the let expressions like in Line 3. According to the configured feature diagram, the sub-constraints 1 and 2 (Lines 6 to 10) handle the relations between the generated components, and the remaining of the constraint deals with classes. Indeed, the migration solution used in this case study produces a component-based application in which components are clusters of classes (a hybrid object/component target model). This is the reason why the end of the architecture constraint in the Listing still treats classes. This makes this example a multi-paradigm architecture constraint.

Discussion: The migration of the object-oriented information screen application has produced new architecture elements and new architecture relations. This is observable (in Fig. 4) by the production of 5 components, 6 classes and several attributes. Therefore, a direct transformation of the application's constraints is obviously very complex because they do not treat the newly created architectural elements. After specifying the constraints of the target application in the graph meta-model, based on the generated graph from the architecture recovery step, which should be done only once, the user can transform the constraints after a simple configuration of the feature model. To migrate the application to another paradigm, such as the service-oriented one, with the proposed approach the developer can just configure again the feature model to transform her/his constraints.

In addition, the usage of the graph meta-modeling and the feature model facilitate constraint specification at an abstract level. In the long term, we imagine the development of a catalog of architecture constraints written in the graph meta-model. This catalog can be used in different scenarios. Suppose that we use another software migration solution, like [1], which transforms inheritance and instantiation from object-oriented to component-based paradigm by using the *Adapter* and *Facade* patterns, in contrast to the one used in this case study that is based on the *Factory* pattern. The architecture constraints formalizing these two patterns (*Adapter* and *Facade*) can be checked out from the catalog, then configured (by adding the necessary labels) and at last integrated in the architecture constraint specification of the application.

5   Related Work

Vranic *et al.* proposed a method of multi-paradigm software development called multi-paradigm design with feature modeling (MPDFM) [13]. Feature modeling is used to model both an application and the solution domain. Solution domain concepts (paradigms) are represented as features. These later (called paradigms) are being selected in the feature model in order to obtain code skeleton. This method is evaluated on the AspectJ paradigm as a solution domain. Like our approach, this method uses feature modeling to express variabilities between paradigm instances. But the term paradigm denotes a solution domain concept, which corresponds to a programming language mechanism/extension. In our approach, we used the common definition of a paradigm – a way of development. This covers a larger spectrum.

Balarin *et al.* proposed a formalism for constraint specification at higher levels of abstraction [3]. This formalism use mathematical theorems to remove any ambiguity in its interpretation, and yet it allows quite simple and natural specification of many typical constraints. In our work, we have proposed an abstract specification level of constraints based on graphs. With graphs, we can benefit from a visualization that simplifies the comprehensibility of any kind of constraints. Constraint specification with graphs allows later transformation, refinement and code generation which is very complex when using a pure mathematical formalism.

ACL [12] is a family of languages which allows the specification of constraints associated to architecture decisions, at any stage of the component-based software development process. Independently to any component-based model, architecture constraints can be specified with this language. The authors proposed a generic meta-model that includes the common concepts found in existing component models. This meta-model can be used to specify these constraints, which are independent from component models. Then, through XML transformations, constraints can be checked on a precise component model, like Corba. In contrast to our work, this work deals with the component-based software development paradigm only, and not the other paradigms. Their generic meta-model includes common concepts in component-models and not variable concepts. In our work, thanks to feature modeling, we specified common and variable concepts in development paradigms and used this in constraint transformation.

Many works [4,9,10] handle the specification of constraints with graphs. These works share the same context as our approach but their goal is different from ours. They focus on, among authors, formalizing semantics in UML models and transformations using ocl, verifying them on models. But no one considers ocl **architecture** constraint specification. To the best of our knowledge, there is no work that enables to make architecture constraints specified independently to the paradigm used in the application development.

6   Conclusion

We presented in this paper an approach that enables the specification of multi-paradigm architecture constraints. These constraints are written in an abstract way independently from any paradigm. The key idea is to combine the usage of OCL with a graph metamodel, and a feature model to implement our method. The meta-model of graphs is used to specify the constraints and the feature model is exploited to express paradigm variabilities. The constraints can be translated to any specific paradigm, simply through the configuration of the feature model.

As a future work, we plan to provide a way to express architecture constraints at (yet) a more abstract level, with a natural language syntax, and then combine it with this work and our previous approaches to provide a complete process. A transformation method should be developed to transform the architecture constraint specification from natural language into graph-based specification and then into UML-based one, until source code generation according to a specific paradigm. This will make the architecture constraint specification simpler, yet keep it operational (checkable on source code and at runtime).

References

1. Allier, S., et al.: From object-oriented applications to component-oriented applications via component-oriented architecture. In: WICSA, pp. 214–223. IEEE (2011)
2. Alshara, Z., et al.: Migrating large object-oriented applications into component-based ones. In: ACM SIGPLAN Notices, no. 3, pp. 55–64. ACM (2015)
3. Balarin, F., et al.: Constraints specification at higher levels of abstraction. In: HLDVT Workshop, pp. 129–133. IEEE (2001)
4. Bauer, E.: Enhancing the dynamic meta modeling formalism and its eclipse-based tool support with attributes. Bachelor thesis. University of Paderborn (2008)

5. Czarnecki, K., Helsen, S., Eisenecker, U.: Staged configuration through specialization and multilevel configuration of feature models. Softw. Process: Improv. Pract. **10**(2), 143–169 (2005)
6. Kallel, S., Tibermacine, C., Tramoni, B., Dony, C., Kacem, A.H.: Automatic translation of OCL meta-level constraints into Java meta-programs. In: Lee, R. (ed.) Software Engineering, Artificial Intelligence, Networking and Parallel/Distributed Computing 2015. SCI, vol. 612, pp. 213–226. Springer, Cham (2016). https://doi.org/10.1007/978-3-319-23509-7_15
7. Kallel, S., et al.: Generating reusable, searchable and executable "architecture constraints as services". J. Syst. Softw. **127**, 91–108 (2017)
8. Pohl, K., et al.: Software Product Line Engineering: Foundations, Principles and Techniques. Springer Science & Business Media, Heidelberg (2005). https://doi.org/10.1007/3-540-28901-1
9. Radke, H., Arendt, T., Becker, J.S., Habel, A., Taentzer, G.: Translating essential OCL invariants to nested graph constraints focusing on set operations. In: Parisi-Presicce, F., Westfechtel, B. (eds.) ICGT 2015. LNCS, vol. 9151, pp. 155–170. Springer, Cham (2015). https://doi.org/10.1007/978-3-319-21145-9_10
10. Rutle, A., et al.: A formal approach to the specification and transformation of constraints in MDE. J. Logic Algebraic Program. **81**(4), 422–457 (2012)
11. Tibermacine, C.: Architecture constraints. Softw. Archit. **2**, 37–90 (2014)
12. Tibermacine, C., et al.: A family of languages for architecture constraint specification. J. Syst. Softw. **83**(5), 815–831 (2010)
13. Vranić, V.: Multi-paradigm design with feature modeling. Comput. Sci. Inf. Syst. **2**(1), 79–102 (2005)

Computational Models and Complexity

Lower Bounds and Hierarchies for Quantum Memoryless Communication Protocols and Quantum Ordered Binary Decision Diagrams with Repeated Test

Farid Ablayev[2], Andris Ambainis[1], Kamil Khadiev[1,2](✉), and Aliya Khadieva[2]

[1] Faculty of Computing, Center for Quantum Computer Science,
University of Latvia, Rīga, Latvia
andris.ambainis@lu.lv, kamilhadi@gmail.com
[2] Kazan Federal University, Kazan, Russia
fablayev@gmail.com, aliyakhadi@gmail.com

Abstract. We explore multi-round quantum memoryless communication protocols. These are restricted version of multi-round quantum communication protocols. The "memoryless" term means that players forget history from previous rounds, and their behavior is obtained only by input and message from the opposite player. The model is interesting because this allows us to get lower bounds for models like automata, Ordered Binary Decision Diagrams and streaming algorithms. At the same time, we can prove stronger results with this restriction. We present a lower bound for quantum memoryless protocols. Additionally, we show a lower bound for Disjointness function for this model. As an application of communication complexity results, we consider Quantum Ordered Read-k-times Branching Programs (k-QOBDD). Our communication complexity result allows us to get lower bound for k-QOBDD and to prove hierarchies for sublinear width bounded error k-QOBDDs, where $k = o(\sqrt{n})$. Furthermore, we prove a hierarchy for polynomial size bounded error k-QOBDDs for constant k. This result differs from the situation with an unbounded error where it is known that an increase of k does not give any advantage.

Keywords: Quantum computation · Communication complexity
Branching programs · Binary decision diagrams · OBDD
Quantum models · Hierarchy · Computational complexity

1 Introduction

The quantum communication protocol is a well-known model. That was explored in papers [21, 22, 26, 31]. We consider communication "game" of two players: Alice and Bob. They together want to compute Boolean function. In the paper we consider the "memoryless" model. It means that players do not remember anything

© Springer International Publishing AG 2018
A M. Tjoa et al. (Eds.): SOFSEM 2018, LNCS 10706, pp. 197–211, 2018.
https://doi.org/10.1007/978-3-319-73117-9_14

from previous rounds. So, on each round a player knows only his own part of the input and the message from an opposite player. This type of communication models was explored, for example in [13,18,37]. On the one hand, this model is powerful enough for emulating computational models that store all information in states: automata, OBDDs, streaming algorithms, etc. On the other hand, memoryless protocol requires fewer resources and can be implemented in practice easier. Such model is useful, for example, in web applications for *REST* architecture.

Researchers are often interested in exploring lower bounds for computational models. We can see different lower bounds for quantum communication models and selected functions in following papers: [9,23,24,26,27]. We suggest a lower bound that demonstrates the relation between complexity characteristics of Boolean function (number of subfunctions) and complexity characteristics of the model: $N^\pi(f) \le 2^{l \cdot (Ct2^l)^2}$, where t is a number of rounds, l is a maximal length of a message for all rounds, π is a partition of input variables, $N(f)$ is a number of subfunctions for a Boolean function f and C is some constant. Note, that a number of subfunctions is exactly one-way deterministic communication complexity of a function. We prove this lower bound, using a technique, which was described in [7,18] for classical models. That based on the representation of the computational process in a linear form.

We apply the proven lower bound to Branching programs. The model is one of well-known models of computation. That has been shown useful in a variety of domains such as hardware verification, model checking, and other applications [35]. It is known that the class of Boolean functions computed by polynomial size branching programs coincided with the class of functions computed by non-uniform log-space Turing machines. One of the important restrictive branching programs are oblivious read-once branching programs or Ordered Binary Decision Diagrams (OBDD) [35]. The OBDD model can be considered as a nonuniform automata (see, for example, [3]). In the last decades quantum model of OBDD was considered [4,29,32,33]. Researchers are interested in read-k-times quantum model of OBDD (k-QOBDD), for example [16]. k-QOBDD can be explored from automata point of view. And in that situation, we can find good algorithms for two way quantum classical automata and related models [10,36].

If we apply the lower bound for memoryless protocols to k-OBDD, then we get the relation between the characteristic of a function f (a number of subfunctions, $N(f)$) and characteristics of the model: a width (w) and a number of layers (k). $N(f) \le w^{C \cdot (kw)^2}$, for some $C = const$. Note, that a number of subfunctions is a minimal width of a deterministic OBDD for a function [35]. A relation with another classical k-OBDDs was presented in paper [18]. A relation between deterministic OBDD and probabilistic, quantum OBDDs was presented in [5]. Furthermore, different relations between models were discussed, for example, in [1,6,8,14,15,19,20]. Additionally, we apply this lower bound to *Matrix XOR Pointer Jumping* function and present k-QOBDD for this function. Using this result, we prove a hierarchy of complexity classes for bounded error k-QOBDDs of a sublinear width with a natural order of input variables and up to non-constant k. k-OBDD model of small width is also interesting, because, for example, the class of functions computed by constant width $poly(n)$-OBDD equals to the well-known complexity class NC_1 for logarithmic depth circuits [11,34]. For constant k, we apply a lower bound from communication complexity theory [25,26] to *XOR Reordered Pointer Jumping* function and get a hierarchy for polynomial size k-QOBDD. Recall that if we consider unbounded error k-OBDDs, then we have another situation. Let us consider two classes of Boolean functions: function computed by polynomial size unbounded error k-QOBDDs and 1-QOBDDs. Homeister and Waack [16] have shown equality of these two classes. Note that due to the definition, k-OBDD is polynomial width iff it is polynomial size. Similar hierarchies are known for classical cases [7,12,18,20]. But for k-QOBDD it is a new result.

The paper has the following structure. Section 2 contains definitions of a communication model. In Sect. 3, we prove a lower bound for a bounded error quantum memoryless communication protocol and apply it to the $MXPJ_{k,p}$ function. We apply the lower bound to OBDD in Sect. 4. And use these lower bounds to prove hierarchies of complexity classes for k-QOBDDs.

2   Communication Model

(π, t, l) memoryless communication quantum protocol R is quantum t-round protocol with a partition of input variables π and a maximal length of a message l. On each round, a player does not remember anything about previous rounds and sends a message that depends only on an input of the player and a received message from the opposite player. Both players can measure states on any rounds, after that, they should return 1-answer and stop computation process or continue. On the last round Player B measures qubits and answers 0 or 1, if someone did not do it before. Let us define the model in a formal way:

Definition 1. *Let π be a partition of a set X of variables. We define (π, t, l) memoryless communication quantum protocol R as follows: R is a two party t-round communication protocol. Protocol R uses a partition π of variables X among two quantum players Alice (A) and Bob (B). Let $\nu = (\sigma, \gamma)$ be a partition of the input ν according to π. Alice always starts the computation. All messages contain l qubits.*

Round 1. *A generates the first quantum message $|m^1\rangle$ $(|m^1\rangle = |m^1\rangle(\sigma))$ and sends it to B.*

Round 2. *B generates quantum message $|m^2\rangle$ $(|m^2\rangle = |m^2\rangle(|m^1\rangle, \gamma))$, and sends it to A.*

Round 3. *A generates $|m^3\rangle$ $(|m^3\rangle = |m^3\rangle(|m^2\rangle, \sigma))$, and sends it to B.*

Round 4. *B generates quantum message $|m^4\rangle$ $(|m^4\rangle = |m^4\rangle(|m^3\rangle, \gamma))$, and sends it to A.*

...

Round t. *B receives $|m^t\rangle$ and produces a result of computation 0 or 1, if players do not produce an answer on previous rounds.*

Both players can measure states on any rounds, after that they should return 1-answer and stop computation process or continue. The result $R(\nu)$ of computation R on $\nu \in \{0,1\}^n$ is 1 if the probability of 1-result greats $1/2 + \varepsilon$ and $R(\nu) = 0$ if the probability of 1-result less than $1/2 - \varepsilon$ for some constant $\varepsilon > 0$. If $Pr\{R$ returns $z\} > 1/2 + \varepsilon$, then $R_\varepsilon(\nu) = z$, for $z \in \{0,1\}$. A Boolean function $f(X)$ is computed by protocol R (presented by R) with bounded error if $f(\nu) = R_\varepsilon(\nu)$ for some $0 < \varepsilon < 0.5$ and for all $\nu \in \{0,1\}^n$. We say that protocol R uses $l \cdot t$ bits communication on all rounds.

3   Lower Bounds for Communication Model

Let us start from the necessary definitions and notation.

Let $\pi = (X_A, X_B)$ be a partition of the set X into two sets X_A and $X_B = X \backslash X_A$. Below we will use equivalent notations $f(X)$ and $f(X_A, X_B)$. Let $f|_\rho(X_B)$ be a subfunction of f, where ρ is mapping $\rho : X_A \rightarrow \{0,1\}^{|X_A|}$ such that $\rho = \{x_{i_1} = \sigma_1, \ldots, x_{i_{|X_A|}} = \sigma_{|X_A|}\}$, for $\{x_{i_1}, \ldots, x_{i_{|X_A|}}\} = X_A\}$. Function $f|_\rho(X_B)$ is obtained from f by fixing values of variables from X_A using values from ρ. Let us consider all possible subfunctions with respect to partition π: $SF^\pi(f) = \{f|_\rho$, such that $\rho : X_A \rightarrow \sigma$, for $\sigma \in \{0,1\}^{|X_B|}\}$. Let $N^\pi(f) = |SF^\pi(f)|$ be the number of different subfunctions with respect to the partition π. Let the partition $half = (\{1, \ldots, n/2\}, \{n/2 + 1, \ldots, n\})$.

Theorem 1. *Suppose Boolean function $f(X)$ be computed by (π, t, l) memoryless quantum communication protocol R with bounded error; then we have:*
$$N^\pi(f) \leq 2^{(1.5t + 0.5 + (t-1)\log_2(2^l + 2)) \cdot (0.5t - 0.5)(2^{l+1} + 4)^2}$$

Let us describe the same result in a short way.

Corollary 1. *Suppose Boolean function $f(X)$ be computed by (π, t, l) memoryless quantum communication protocol R with bounded error; then we have:*
$$N^\pi(f) \leq 2^{Cl \cdot \left(t2^l\right)^2}, \textit{ for some } C = const$$

We present proof in the next section.

3.1   Proof of Theorem 1

The proof of Theorem 1 is based on a representation of a protocol's computation process in a matrix form. Then we estimate a number of special matrices, which are used for this representation.

Now we define a sequence of matrices $\mathcal{M}_R(\sigma, \gamma)$ that represents a computation procedure of protocol R on input $\nu = (\sigma, \gamma)$ with respect to partition π. Let $t = 2k - 1$, then the sequence is following:
$$\mathcal{M}_R(\sigma, \gamma) = \left(M_R^{(1)}(\gamma), M_R^{(1)}(\sigma), M_R^{(2)}(\gamma), M_R^{(2)}(\sigma), \ldots, M_R^{(k-2)}(\sigma), M_R^{(k-1)}(\gamma),\right.$$
$$\left. M_R^{(k-1)}(\sigma), M_R^{(k)}(\gamma)\right).$$ The sequence describes a computation on rounds from 2 to t.

The $(2^l+2) \times (2^l+2)$-matrix $M_R^{(i)}(\sigma)$ describes a computation of round $2i+1$. And the $(2^l+2) \times (2^l+2)$-matrix $M_R^{(i)}(\gamma)$ describes a computation of the round $2i$.

Let $\mathcal{M}_R(\sigma) = \left(M_R^{(1)}(\sigma), M_R^{(2)}(\sigma), \ldots, M_R^{(k-2)}(\sigma), M_R^{(k-1)}(\sigma) \right)$ be a part of sequence, which depends on σ, and $\mathcal{M}_R(\gamma) = \left(M_R^{(1)}(\gamma), M_R^{(2)}(\gamma), \ldots, M_R^{(k-1)}(\gamma), M_R^{(k)}(\gamma) \right)$ be a part of the sequence, which depends on γ.

Matrix $M_R^{(i)}(\gamma)$ is a complex-value matrix. It represents transformation that was made by B on the round $2i$:

- Let $s = (s_1, \ldots, s_{2^l+2})$ be the r-th row of $M_R^{(i)}(\gamma)$, for $1 \leq r \leq 2^l$. Elements $(s_1, \ldots, s_{2^l})$ is amplitudes for states of l qubits of a message that B sends on round $2i$, if he receives a message with pure state r. And last two elements of the row $s_{2^l+1} = s_{2^l+2} = 0$.
- Let $s = (0, \ldots, 0, 1, pr)$ be the $(2^l + 1)$-st row of matrix $M_R^{(i)}(\gamma)$. The row represents a measurement event on the round $2i$. pr is probability of getting 1 on the round $2i$.
- Let $s = (0, \ldots, 0, 0, 1)$ be the $(2^l + 1)$-st row of matrix $M_R^{(i)}(\gamma)$. The row represents probability of measurement on previous rounds.

Matrices $M_R^{(i)}(\sigma)$ describe a computation of the round $2i$ and have the similar structure.

Additionally, we define vectors $p_R^0(\sigma)$ and q_R, which describe the first round and accepting states after the last round, respectively. The row vector $p_R^0(\sigma) = (p_1, \ldots p_{2^l+2})$ defines the message, which was formed on the first round of R. Each element of vector corresponds to one of $M_R^{(1)}(\gamma)$ matrix's row. $p_{2^l+1} = 1$ and p_{2^l+1} is the probability of 1-result if we have measurement on the first round.

The column vector $q_R = (q_1, \ldots, q_{2^l}, 0, 1)$. Each element of vector corresponds to one of $M_R^k(\gamma)$ matrix's row. $q_r = 1$ iff r is accepting state, $q_r \in \{0, 1\}$, for $1 \leq r \leq 2^l$.

Let us define sqr operator that describes measurement after the last round. Let operator $sqr : \mathbf{C}^{2^l+2} \to \mathbf{R}^{2^l+2}$ be given by $sqr(z_1 \ldots, z_{2^l+2}) = (s_1 \ldots, s_{2^l+2})$, where $s_i = |z_i|^2$, for $1 \leq i \leq 2^l$ and $s_i = |z_i|$ for $2^l + 1 \leq i \leq 2^l + 2$, $\mathbf{C}$ is a set of complex numbers and $\mathbf{R}$ is a set of real numbers.

Lemma 1. *For any input $\nu \in \{0,1\}^n$, $\nu = (\sigma, \gamma)$ we have:*

$$Pr\{R \text{ reaches } 1 \text{ on } \nu\} = sqr \left(p_R^0(\sigma) \left(\prod_{i=1}^{k-1} M_R^{(i)}(\gamma) M_R^{(i)}(\sigma) \right) M_R^{(k)}(\gamma) \right) \cdot q_R.$$

$$(1)$$

Proof. Let the vector $p^j = (p_1^j, \ldots p_{2^l+2}^j)$ be a vector that describes the computation of R after j rounds on input $\nu = (\sigma, \gamma)$. Then p_r^j for $1 \leq r \leq 2^l$ describes amplitudes for state r, $p_{2^l+1}^j = 1$ and $p_{2^l+2}^j$ is the probability of 1-result if we have measurements on previous rounds and should answer 1.

Vector p^j is computed as follows: $p^j = p_R^0(\sigma) \left(\prod_{i=1}^{\lfloor j/2 \rfloor} M_R^{(i)}(\gamma) M_R^{(i)}(\sigma) \right)$ for even j, and $p^j = p_R^0(\sigma) \left(\prod_{i=1}^{\lfloor j/2 \rfloor} M_R^{(i)}(\gamma) M_R^{(i)}(\sigma) \right) M_R^{(k)}(\gamma)$ for odd j.

By the definition of vector q_R we have the following fact: $sqr\left(p^{2k-1}\right) \cdot q_R$ is the probability of reaching 1 on input $\nu = (\sigma, \gamma)$. Hence (1) is right. $\qquad\square$

Let us discuss the following question: "How similar should be sequences $\mathcal{M}_R(\sigma, \gamma)$ and $\mathcal{M}_R(\sigma', \gamma)$ for equivalence of computation results for inputs (σ, γ) and (σ', γ)?". For simplifying an answer to the question, we convert complex-value matrices and vectors to real-value matrices. We use the trick from the paper [28]. It is well known that complex numbers $c = a + bi$ can be represented by 2×2 real matrix $\mathbf{c} = \begin{pmatrix} a & b \\ -b & a \end{pmatrix}$ The reader can check that multiplication is faithfully reproduced and that $\mathbf{c}^T \mathbf{c} = |\mathbf{c}| \mathbf{1}$. In the same way, a $r \times r$ complex-value matrix can be simulated by a $2r \times 2r$ real-valued matrix. Moreover, this matrix is unitary if the original matrix is. Consequently, we will consider $(2^{l+1} + 4) \times (2^{l+1} + 4)$ real-value matrices $M_R^{(i)}(\sigma)$ and $M_R^{(i)}(\gamma)$, $(2^{l+1} + 4) \times 2$ real-number matrix $p_R^0(\sigma)$ and $2 \times (2^{l+1} + 4)$ real-number matrix q_R. Let us pay attention to matrix $q_R = \begin{pmatrix} q_1, & 0 \\ \cdots & \cdots \\ q_{2^{l+1}+4}, & 0 \end{pmatrix}$. Element $q_r = 1$ iff $\lceil (r+1)/2 \rceil$ is accepting state, $q_r \in \{0, 1\}$, for $1 \leq r \leq 2^l$. $q_{2^{l+1}+1} = q_{2^{l+1}+2} = 0$ and for probability of 1-result on previous rounds we have $q_{2^{l+1}+3} = q_{2^{l+1}+4} = 1$.

Before introduction closeness of matrices, let us consider δ-close metric of number equivalence. Let $\delta \geq 0$. Two real numbers p and p' are called δ-close if both: $-1 \leq p, p' \leq 1$ and $|p - p'| < \delta$. Let $\beta \geq 0$. Two $q \times r$ matrices $M = [s_{ij}]$ and $M' = [s'_{ij}]$ are δ-close iff s_{ij} and s'_{ij} are δ-close, for any $i \in \{1, \ldots, q\}$ and $j \in \{1, \ldots, r\}$. We have the similar definition for vectors.

Now we can discuss an equivalence of inputs according to similarity of answer probability in the following lemma.

Lemma 2. *Suppose inputs (σ, γ) and (σ', γ) such that corresponding matrices in sequences $\mathcal{M}_R(\sigma, \gamma)$ and $\mathcal{M}_R(\sigma', \gamma)$ are δ-close, $p_R^0(\sigma)$ and $p_R^0(\sigma')$ are δ-close; then we have: $|Pr\{R \text{ returns } 1 \text{ on } input(\sigma, \gamma)\} - Pr\{R \text{ returns } 1 \text{ on } input(\sigma', \gamma)\}| < 2^{3k-1}(2^l + 2)^{2k}\delta$, for $t = 2k - 1$ (See arXiv version [2]).*

According to above lemma, we can introduce the δ-equivalence for inputs with respect to the protocol R. Two inputs σ and σ', $(\sigma, \sigma' \in \{0, 1\}^{|X_A|})$ are δ-equivalent if corresponding matrices in sequences $\mathcal{M}_R(\sigma)$ and $\mathcal{M}_R(\sigma')$ are δ-close and $p_R^0(\sigma)$ and $p_R^0(\sigma')$ are δ-close.

Let us obtain possible biggest δ such that it does not affect 1-result probability too much.

Lemma 3. *Suppose inputs $\sigma, \sigma' \in \{0, 1\}^{|X_A|}$ are δ-equivalent and $\delta = \varepsilon 2^{-3k}(2^l + 2)^{-2k}$, then for any $\gamma \in \{0, 1\}^{|X_B|}$ we have: $R_\varepsilon(\sigma, \gamma) = R_{\varepsilon/2}(\sigma', \gamma)$.*

Proof. Let $p = Pr\{R \text{ reaches } 1 \text{ on } (\sigma, \gamma)\}$ and $p' = Pr\{R \text{ reaches } 1 \text{ on } (\sigma', \gamma)\}$.

Probabilities p and p' are $2^{3k-1}(2^l + 2)^{2k}\delta$-close due to Lemma 2. Therefore, p and p' are $\varepsilon/2$-close. Hence, we have: $|p - p'| < \varepsilon/2$. Thus, if $p > 0.5 + \varepsilon$ then $p' > 0.5 + \varepsilon/2$; if $p < 0.5 - \varepsilon$ then $p' < 0.5 - \varepsilon/2$. And the claim of the lemma is right. □

Let protocol R computes Boolean function $f(X)$ with bounded error ε. Let us prove that the number of subfunctions $N^\pi(f)$ is less than or equal to the number of non δ-equivalent inputs σ's with respect to the protocol R and error $\varepsilon/2$, for $\delta = \varepsilon 2^{-3k}(2^l + 2)^{-2k}$. Assume that $N^\pi(f)$ greats the number of non δ-equivalent σ's. Then due to Pigeonhole principle there are two inputs σ and σ' and corresponding mappings ρ and ρ' such that $f|_\rho(X_B) \neq f|'_\rho(X_B)$, but σ and σ' are δ-equivalent inputs. Therefore, there is $\gamma \in \{0,1\}^{|X_A|}$ such that $f|_\rho(\gamma) \neq f|'_\rho(\gamma)$, but $R_{\varepsilon/2}(\sigma, \gamma) = R_{\varepsilon/2}(\sigma', \gamma)$. This is contradiction.

If we compute the number of different non δ-equivalent σ's, we will get a claim of the lemma. Let us compute the number of different non δ-equivalent σ's. It is equal to the number of non δ-close matrices from sequence $\mathcal{M}_R(\sigma)$ multiply the number of non δ-close matrices $p_R^0(\sigma)$. The number of non δ-close matrices in sequence $\mathcal{M}_R(\sigma)$ is at most

$$\left(\frac{2}{\delta}\right)^{(k-1)(2^{l+1}+4)^2} \leq \left(\frac{2^{3k+1}(2^l+2)^{2k}}{\varepsilon}\right)^{(k-1)(2^{l+1}+4)^2}$$
$$= 2^{(3k+1-\log\varepsilon+2k\log_2(2^l+2))\cdot(k-1)(2^{l+1}+4)^2}$$
$$\leq 2^{(3k+1+2k\log_2(2^l+2))\cdot(k-1)(2^{l+1}+4)^2}.$$

Additionally, we have the following bound for the number of non δ-close vectors $p^0(\sigma)$: $2^{(3k+1+2k\log_2(2^l+2))\cdot(2^{l+1}+4)^2}$. Therefore,

$$N^\pi(f) \leq 2^{(3k+1+2k\log_2(2^l+2))\cdot k(2^{l+1}+4)^2} = 2^{(1.5t+0.5+(t-1)\log_2(2^l+2))\cdot(0.5t-0.5)(2^{l+1}+4)^2}. \quad □$$

A Lower Bound for Boolean Function $MXPJ_{k,d}$. Let us consider Boolean function $MXPJ_{k,d}(X)$. It is a modification of Shuffled Address Function from [17] which based on definition of Pointer Jumping (PJ) function from [12,30].

Let us present a definition of PJ function for integers. Let V_A, V_B be two disjoint sets (of vertexes) with $|V_A| = |V_B| = d$ and $V = V_A \cup V_B$. Let $F_A = \{f_A : V_A \to V_B\}$, $F_B = \{f_B : V_B \to V_A\}$ and $f = (f_A, f_B) : V \to V$ defined by $f(v) = f_A(v)$, if $v \in V_A$ and $f = f_B(v)$, $v \in V_B$. For each $j \geq 0$ define $f^{(j)}(v)$ by $f^{(0)}(v) = v$, $f^{(j+1)}(v) = f(f^{(j)}(v))$. Let $v_0 \in V_A$. We want to compute $g_{k,d} : F_A \times F_B \to V$ function. This is defined by $g_{k,d}(f_A, f_B) = f^{(k)}(v_0)$.

The *Matrix XOR Pointer Jumping function*$(MXPJ_{2k,d})$ is modification of PJ. Firstly, we introduce the definition of $MatrixPJ_{2k,d}$ function. Let us consider functions $f_{A,1}, \cdots f_{A,k} \in F_A$ and $f_{B,1}, \cdots f_{B,k} \in F_B$. On iteration $j+1$ function $f^{(j+1)}(v) = f_{j+1}(f^{(j)}(v))$, where $f_i(v) = f_{A,\lceil\frac{i}{2}\rceil}(v)$ if i is odd, and $f_i(v) = f_{B,\lceil\frac{i}{2}\rceil}(v)$ otherwise. $MatrixPJ_{2k,d}(f_{A,1}, \cdots f_{A,k}, f_{B,1}, \cdots f_{B,k}) = f^{(k)}(v_0)$. $MXPJ_{2k,d}$ is modification of $MatrixPJ_{2k,d}$. Here we take $f^{(j+1)}(v) = f_{j+1}(f^{(j)}(v)) \oplus f^{(j-1)}(v)$, for $j \geq 0$.

Finally, we consider a boolean version of these functions. The Boolean function $PJ_{t,n} : \{0,1\}^n \to \{0,1\}$ is $g_{k,d}$, where we encode f_A in a binary string using $d \log d$ bits and do it with f_B as well. The result of the function is a parity of bits from the binary representation of the result vertex's number. For encoding functions in an input of $MXPJ_{2k,d}$, we use following order: $f_{A,1}, \ldots, f_{A,k}, f_{B,1}, \ldots, f_{B,k}$. Let us describe the process of computation on Fig. 1. Function $f_{A,i}$ is encoded by $a_{i,1}, \cdots a_{i,d}$, and $f_{B,i}$ is encoded by $b_{i,1}, \cdots b_{i,d}$, for $i \in \{1 \cdots k\}$. We assume that $v_0 = 0$.

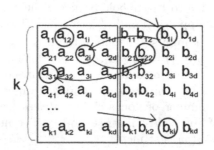

Fig. 1. Boolean function $MXPJ_{k,d}$

Let us discuss a number of subfunctions for $MXPJ_{2k,d}$ in Lemma 4 and apply our lower bound to the function in Lemma 5.

Lemma 4. *For $kd \log d = o(n)$ we have:* $N^{id}(MXPJ_{2k,d}) \geq d^{\lfloor d/3-1 \rfloor (k-3)}$.

Proof. The idea is similar to the proof from [17]. See arXiv version [2].   □

Lemma 5. *$MXPJ_{2k,\lfloor\sqrt{d}\rfloor}$ cannot be computed by any (k/r,half, l) quantum memoryless communication protocol, for $C_1\sqrt{d} \log d - (C2^{2l}kl)/r^2 > 0$ and $C, C_1 = const$ (See arXiv version [2]).*

4   Application to Ordered Binary Decision Diagrams

Let us start with definitions. Ordered Read k-times Branching Programs (k-OBDD) are a well-known model for computation of Boolean functions. For more details see [35].

k-OBDD is a restricted version of a branching program (BP). BP over a set X of n Boolean variables is a directed acyclic graph with two distinguished nodes s (a source node) and t (a sink node). We denote it $P_{s,t}$ or just P. Each inner node v of P is associated with a variable $x \in X$. A *deterministic* P has exactly two outgoing edges labeled $x = 0$ and $x = 1$ respectively for that node v. The program P computes Boolean function $f(X)$ ($f : \{0,1\}^n \to \{0,1\}$) as follows: for each $\sigma \in \{0,1\}^n$ we let $f(\sigma) = 1$ iff there exists at least one $s-t$ path (called *accepting* path for σ) such that all edges along this path are consistent with σ. A *size* of branching program P is a number of nodes. Ordered Binary Decision Diagram (OBDD) is a BP with following restrictions: (i) Nodes can be partitioned into levels $V_1, \ldots, V_{\ell+1}$ such that s belongs to the first level V_1 and sink node t belongs to the last level $V_{\ell+1}$. Nodes from level V_j have outgoing edges only to nodes of level V_{j+1}, for $j \leq \ell$. (ii) All inner nodes of one level are labeled by the same variable. (iii) Each variable is tested on each path only once.

A *width* $w(P)$ of a program P is $w(P) = \max_{1 \leq j \leq \ell} |V_j|$. OBDD P reads variables in its individual order $\theta(P) = (j_1, \ldots, j_n)$. Let $tr_P : \{1, \ldots, n\} \times \{1, \ldots, w(P)\} \times \{0, 1\} \to \{1, \ldots, w(P)\}$ be transition function of OBDD P on the level i. OBDD P is called *commutative* iff for any permutation θ' OBDD P' can be constructed by reordering transition functions and P' still computes the same function. Formally, $tr_{P'}(i, s, x_{\theta'(i)}) = tr_P(\theta^{-1}(\theta'(i)), s, x_{\theta'(i)})$, for θ is the order of P. A BP P is called k-OBDD if it consists of k layers. The i-th ($1 \leq i \leq k$) layer P^i of P is an OBDD. We call order $\theta(P) = \theta$ the order of P, where $\theta(P^1) = \cdots = \theta(P^k) = \theta$. k-OBDD P is commutative iff each layer is commutative OBDD.

Let us define a quantum k-OBDD (k-QOBDD). That is given in different terms, but you can see that they are equivalent, see [4] for more details. For a given $n > 0$, a quantum OBDD P of width w defined on $\{0, 1\}^n$, is a 4-tuple $P = (T, |\psi\rangle_0, Accept, \pi)$, where $T = \{T_j : 1 \leq j \leq n$ and $T_j = (G_j^0, G_j^1)\}$ are ordered pairs of (left) unitary matrices representing the transitions. Here G_j^0 or G_j^1 is applied on the j-th step. And a choice is determined by the input bit. $|\psi\rangle_0$ is a initial vector from w-dimensional Hilbert space over the field of complex numbers. $|\psi\rangle_0 = |q_0\rangle$ where q_0 corresponds to the initial node. $Accept \subset \{1, \ldots, w\}$ is a set of accepting nodes. π is a permutation of $\{1, \ldots, n\}$ defines the order of input bits.

For any given input $\nu \in \{0, 1\}^n$, the computation of P on ν can be traced by a w-dimensional vector from Hilbert space over the field of complex numbers. The initial one is $|\psi\rangle_0$. In each step j, $1 \leq j \leq n$, the input bit $x_{\theta(j)}$ is tested and then the corresponding unitary operator is applied: $|\psi\rangle_j = G_j^{x_{\theta(j)}}(|\psi\rangle_{j-1})$, where $|\psi\rangle_j$ represents the state of the system after the j-th step, for $1 \leq j \leq n$. We can measure one of qubits. Let the program was in state $|\psi\rangle = (v_1, \ldots, v_w)$ before measurement and let us measure the i-th qubit. And let states with numbers $j_1^0, \ldots, j_{w/2}^0$ correspond to 0 value of the i-th qubit, and states with numbers $j_1^1, \ldots, j_{w/2}^1$ correspond to 1 value of the i-th qubit. The result of measurement of i-th qubit is 1 with probability $pr_1 = \sum_{u=1}^{w/2} |v_{j_u^1}|^2$ and 0 with probability $pr_0 = 1 - pr_1$. In the end of computation program P measures all qubits. The accepting (return 1) probability $Pr_{accept}(\sigma)$ of P_n on input σ is $Pr_{accept}(\nu) = \sum_{i \in Accept} v_i^2$, for $|\psi\rangle_n = (v_1, \ldots, v_w)$.

Let $P_\varepsilon(\nu) = 1$ if P accepts input $\nu \in \{0, 1\}^n$ with probability at least $0.5 + \varepsilon$, and $P_\varepsilon(\nu) = 0$ if P accepts input $\nu \in \{0, 1\}^n$ with probability at most $0.5 - \varepsilon$, for $\varepsilon \in (0, 0.5]$. We say that a function f is computed by P with bounded error if there exists an $\varepsilon \in (0, 0.5]$ such that $P_\varepsilon(\nu) = f(\nu)$ for any $\nu \in \{0, 1\}^n$. We can say that P computes f with bounded error $0.5 - \varepsilon$.

Quantum k-OBDD (k-QOBDD) is Quantum Branching program with k layers. Each layer is QOBDD, and each layer has the same order θ. We allow measurement for k-QOBDD during the computation, but after that, it should stop and accept an input or continue the computation. k-id-QOBDD is k-QOBDD with the natural order of input bits $id = (1, \dots, n)$.

Let k-$\mathbf{QOBDD}_{\mathcal{W}}$ be a set of Boolean functions that can be computed by bounded error k-QOBDDs of width w, for $w \in \mathcal{W}$. k-id-$\mathbf{QOBDD}_{\mathcal{W}}$ is the same for bounded error k-id-QOBDDs. As $\mathcal{W}$ we will consider only "good" sets $G_{k,r}$, for integer $k = k(n)$, $r = r(n)$. The set $\mathcal{W}$ belongs to $G_{k,r}$ if this is ths set of integers with following properties: (i) if $w \in \mathcal{W}$, then $\lfloor \sqrt{w} \rfloor, \lfloor \sqrt{w} \rfloor^2 \in \mathcal{W}$; (ii) $k^2 w^2 \log w = o(n)$, for any $w \in \mathcal{W}$; (ii) $C_1 \sqrt{w} \log w - (Cv^2 k \log v)/r^2 > 0$ for any $w, v \in \mathcal{W}$ and $C, C_1 = const$. Let $\mathrm{BQP}_{\varepsilon}$-$k$QOBDD be a set of Boolean functions that can be computed by polynomial size k-QOBDDs with probability of a right answer at most $1 - \varepsilon$ or an error at least ε. We can consider similar classes for deterministic model (P-kOBDD) and bounded error probabilistic model ($\mathrm{BP}_{\varepsilon}$-$k$OBDD).

Lower Bound for Ordered Binary Decision Diagrams. Let us start from necessary definitions and notation. Let $\Theta(n)$ be the set of all permutations of $\{1, \dots, n\}$. Let the partition $\pi(\theta, u) = (X_A, X_B) = (\{x_{j_1}, \dots, x_{j_u}\}, \{x_{j_{u+1}}, \dots, x_{j_n}\})$, for the permutation $\theta = (j_1, \dots, j_n) \in \Theta(n), 1 < u < n$. We denote $\Pi(\theta) = \{\pi(\theta, u) : 1 < u < n\}$. Let $N^{\theta}(f) = \max_{\pi \in \Pi(\theta)} N^{\pi}(f), N(f) = \min_{\theta \in \Theta(n)} N^{\theta}(f)$.

We can emulate k-QOBDD P of width w and order θ with (π, t, l) memoryless communication quantum protocol R, such that $\pi \in \Pi(\theta)$, $t = 2k - 1$ and $2^l = w$. Such emulation is described, for example, in [18]. Therefore, the lower bound for k-QOBDD follows from Theorem 1.

Theorem 2. *Suppose function $f(X)$ is computed by bounded error k-QOBDD P of width w; then $N(f) \leq 2^d$, for $d = \left(3k + 1 + 2k \log_2(w + 2)\right) \cdot k(2w + 4)^2$.*

Corollary 2. *Suppose function $f(X)$ is computed by bounded error k-QOBDD P of width w; then $N(f) \leq w^{C \cdot (kw)^2}$, for some $C = const$.*

Note that this lower bound gives us relation with deterministic OBDD complexity of function, because $N(f)$ is the width of better deterministic OBDD for function [35]. Let us apply this lower bound to $MXPJ_{k,d}(X)$ function.

Lemma 6. *Let $\mathcal{W} \in G_{k,r}$, for integers $k = k(n), r = r(n)$. Then $MXPJ_{2k, \lfloor \sqrt{d} \rfloor} \notin \lfloor k/r \rfloor$-$id$-$\mathbf{QOBDD}_{\mathcal{W}}$ (See arXiv version [2]).*

5   Hierarchy Results

Hierarchy for Sublinear Width. Firstly, let us discuss upper bound for $MXPJ_{k,d}$ function. The Proof is in arXiv version [2].

Lemma 7. *There is exact k-id-QOBDD P of width d^2 which computes $MXPJ_{2k,d}$.*

Using above lemma and lower bound from Lemma 6, we get hierarchy results.

Theorem 3. *Suppose* $W \in G_{k,r}$, *for integers* $k = k(n), r = r(n)$, *then:* $\lfloor k/r \rfloor$-*id*-**QOBDD**$_W \subsetneq k$-*id*-**QOBDD**$_W$ *(See arXiv version [2]).*

Partial cases are hierarchies for the following classes: k-id-**QOBDD**$_{CONST}$, k-id-**QOBDD**$_{PLOG}$ and k-id-**QOBDD**$_{SUBLIN(\alpha)}$. Here $CONST = \{w : w = const\}$, $PLOG = \{w : w = (\log n)^{O(1)}\}$, $SUBLIN(\alpha) = \{w : w = O(n^\alpha)$, for $0 < \alpha < 1\}$.

Corollary 3. *Claim 1.* $\lfloor \sqrt{k}/r \rfloor$-*id*-**QOBDD**$_{CONST} \subsetneq k$-*id*-**QOBDD**$_{CONST}$, *for* $k = o(\sqrt{n})$, $\sqrt{k} > r$, $1 = o(r)$.
Claim 2. $\lfloor \sqrt{k}/n^r \rfloor$-*id*-**QOBDD**$_{PLOG} \subsetneq k$-*id*-**QOBDD**$_{PLOG}$, *for* $k = o(n^{0.5-\delta})$, $\sqrt{k} > n^r$, $r > 0, \delta > 0$.
Claim 3. $\lfloor \sqrt{k}/n^{\alpha+r} \rfloor$-*id*-**QOBDD**$_{SUBLIN(\alpha)} \subsetneq k$-*id*-**QOBDD**$_{SUBLIN(\alpha)}$, *for* $k = o(n^{0.5-\alpha-\delta})$, $\sqrt{k} > n^{\alpha+r}$, $r > 0, \delta > 0$ *and* $0 > \alpha > 1/6 - \delta/3 - 2r/3$.

Proof. Let us consider Claim 1. We get conditions 1 and 2 of $G_{k,r}$, because $W = CONST, k = o(\sqrt{n})$. Let us consider condition 3 and $r' = \sqrt{k}r$. Then $C_1 w \log w - (Cv^2 k \log v)/r'^2 = C' - C''/r^2 > 0$ for $C', C'' = const$, because $1 = o(r)$. Therefore, due to Theorem 3, we have:
$\lfloor k/r' \rfloor$-id-**QOBDD**$_{CONST} \subsetneq k$-id-**QOBDD**$_{CONST}$ and we get Claim 1.

Let us consider Claim 2. We get conditions 1 and 2 of $G_{k,r}$, because $W = PLOG, k = o(n^{0.5-\delta})$. Let us consider condition 3 and $r' = \sqrt{k}n^r$. Then $C_1 w \log w - (Cv^2 k \log v)/r'^2 > C' - C''O(n^r)/n^{2r} = C' - C''/n^r > 0$ for $C', C'' = const$. Therefore, due to Theorem 3, we have:
$\lfloor k/r' \rfloor$-id-**QOBDD**$_{PLOG} \subsetneq k$-id-**QOBDD**$_{PLOG}$ and we get Claim 2.

Let us consider Claim 3. We get conditions 1 and 2 of $G_{k,r}$, because $W = SUBLIN(\alpha), k = o(n^{0.5-\alpha-\delta})$, $\sqrt{k} > n^{\alpha+r}$, $r > 0, \delta > 0$ and $0 > \alpha > 1/6 - \delta/3 - 2r/3$. Let us consider condition 3 and $r' = \sqrt{k}n^{\alpha+r}$. Then $C_1 w \log w - (Cv^2 k \log v)/r'^2 > C' - C''O(n^{2\alpha+r})/n^{2\alpha+2r} = C' - C''/n^r > 0$ for $C', C'' = const$. Therefore, due to Theorem 3, we have:
$\lfloor k/r' \rfloor$-id-**QOBDD**$_{SUBLIN(\alpha)} \subsetneq k$-id-**QOBDD**$_{SUBLIN(\alpha)}$ and we get Claim 3. $\square$

Hierarchy for Polynomial Size. Let us consider a Boolean function $XRPJ_{k,n}$, it is a modification of boolean version of $PJ_{k,n}$ function using reordering method from [20]. We add address for each bit of input and compute with respect to the address in original input. If we meet bits with the same address, then we consider their XOR. $XRPJ_{k,n}$ is a total version of xor-reordered $PJ_{k,n}$, details in [20]. Let us define this formally.

Let us split the input $X = (x_1, \ldots, x_n)$ to b blocks with n/b elements, such that $b\lceil \log_2 b + 1 \rceil = n$, therefore, $b = O(n/\log n)$. And let $Adr(X, i)$ be an integer such that its binary representation is first $\lceil \log_2 b \rceil$ bits of the i-th block. Let $Val(X, i)$ be a value of the bit number $\lceil \log_2 b + 1 \rceil$ from the block i, for $i \in \{0, \ldots, b-1\}$. Let $2d\lceil \log d \rceil = b$ and $V_A = \{0, \ldots, d-1\}$, $V_B = \{d, \ldots, 2d-1\}$.

Hence, $d = O(n/\log^2 n)$. Let function $BV : \{0,1\}^n \times \{0,\ldots,2d-1\} \to \{0,\ldots,d-1\}$ be the following:

$$BV(X,v) = \sum_{j=(v-1)\log b+1}^{v \log b} 2^{j-(v-1)\log b-1} \cdot \bigoplus_{i:Adr(X,i)=j} Val(X,i)$$

Then $f_A(v) = BV(X,v) + d$, $f_B(v) = BV(X,v)$. Let $r = g_{t,a}(f_A, f_B)$, then

$$XRPJ_{t,n}(X) = \bigoplus_{i:(r-1)\log b < Adr(X,i) \leq r \log b} Val(X,i).$$

Let us prove lower and upper bounds for $XRPJ_{k,n}$:

Lemma 8. *Claim 1. Suppose k-QOBDD P of width w computes $XRPJ_{2k-1,n}(X)$ with bounded error at least $1/8$; then $w \geq 2^r$, for $r = n/(k2^{O(k)}) - k \log n$.*

Claim 2. There is exact $2k$-QOBDD P of width $O(n^{2k+1})$ computing $XRPJ_{2k-1,n}(X)$.

Proof. The proof of the first claim is based on lower bound for quantum communication complexity from [25,26]. We apply the bound in the similar way as in [20].

Assume that $XRPJ_{2k-1,n}$ is computed by k-QOBDD P of width $w = 2^{o(r)}$. k-QOBDD P can be simulated by $2k-1$-round quantum communication protocol R, which sends at most $\lceil\log_2 w\rceil(2k-1)$ bits. For prove this fact look, for example, at [18]. Let us consider only inputs from the set $\Sigma \subset \{0,1\}^n$ such that for $\sigma \in \Sigma$ we have $Adr(\sigma,i) = i + b$, for $0 \leq i \leq b-1$ and $Adr(\sigma,i) = i - b$, for $b \leq i \leq 2b-1$, $b \log b = n$. For these inputs, our protocol will just compute $PJ_{2k-1,b}$, but in a communication game B starts the computation. Therefore, from the protocol R we can get the protocol R' such that B starts computation. The protocol R' computes $PJ_{2k-1,b}$ and sends at most $\lceil\log_2 w\rceil(2k-1)$ bits. It means $Q_{1/8}^{B,2k-1}(PJ_{2k-1,b}) = o(r)$. This contradicts with results from quantum communication complexity [25,26].

For the proof of the second claim, we construct $2k$-id-QOBDD for the function. The main idea is to store a pointer for current steps and use new qubits for a new step. And we apply reordering method from [20]. See arXiv version [2] for the full proof. $\square$

Using this lemma, we can prove the following hierarchy result:

Theorem 4. $BQP_{1/8}\text{-}kOBDD \subsetneq BQP_{1/8}\text{-}(2k)QOBDD$, for $k > 0, k = const$ (See arXiv version [2]).

Both hierarchies from Corollary 3 and Theorem 4 are interesting, because we cannot apply lower bound from Theorem 2 to polynomial width, at the same time, we cannot use results from Lemma 8 to sublinear width.

Acknowledgements. The work is partially supported by ERC Advanced Grant MQC. The work is performed according to the Russian Government Program of Competitive Growth of Kazan Federal University.

References

1. Ablayev, F., Gainutdinova, A., Khadiev, K., Yakaryılmaz, A.: Very narrow quantum OBDDs and width hierarchies for classical OBDDs. Lobachevskii J. Math. **37**(6), 670–682 (2016)
2. Ablayev, F., Ambainis, A., Khadiev, K., Khadieva, A.: Lower bounds and hierarchies for quantum memoryless communication protocols and quantum ordered binary decision diagrams with repeated test. arXiv preprint arXiv:1703.05015 (2017)
3. Ablayev, F., Gainutdinova, A.: Complexity of quantum uniform and nonuniform automata. In: De Felice, C., Restivo, A. (eds.) DLT 2005. LNCS, vol. 3572, pp. 78–87. Springer, Heidelberg (2005). https://doi.org/10.1007/11505877_7
4. Ablayev, F., Gainutdinova, A., Karpinski, M.: On computational power of quantum branching programs. In: Freivalds, R. (ed.) FCT 2001. LNCS, vol. 2138, pp. 59–70. Springer, Heidelberg (2001). https://doi.org/10.1007/3-540-44669-9_8
5. Ablayev, F., Gainutdinova, A., Karpinski, M., Moore, C., Pollett, C.: On the computational power of probabilistic and quantum branching program. Inf. Comput. **203**(2), 145–162 (2005)
6. Ablayev, F., Gainutdinova, A., Khadiev, K., Yakaryılmaz, A.: Very narrow quantum OBDDs and width hierarchies for classical OBDDs. In: Jürgensen, H., Karhumäki, J., Okhotin, A. (eds.) DCFS 2014. LNCS, vol. 8614, pp. 53–64. Springer, Cham (2014). https://doi.org/10.1007/978-3-319-09704-6_6
7. Ablayev, F., Khadiev, K.: Extension of the hierarchy for k-OBDDs of small width. Russ. Math. **53**(3), 46–50 (2013)
8. Ablayev, F., Khasianov, A., Vasiliev, A.: On complexity of quantum branching programs computing equality-like boolean functions. In: ECCC (2008, to appear in 2010)
9. Ambainis, A.: A new protocol and lower bounds for quantum coin flipping. In: Proceedings of the Thirty-Third Annual ACM Symposium on Theory of Computing, pp. 134–142. ACM (2001)
10. Ambainis, A., Watrous, J.: Two-way finite automata with quantum and classical states. Theoret. Comput. Sci. **287**(1), 299–311 (2002)
11. Barrington, D.A.M.: Bounded-width polynomial-size branching programs recognize exactly those languages in NC^1. J. Comput. Syst. Sci. **38**(1), 150–164 (1989)
12. Bollig, B., Sauerhoff, M., Sieling, D., Wegener, I.: Hierarchy theorems for kOBDDs and kIBDDs. Theoret. Comput. Sci. **205**(1), 45–60 (1998)
13. Chailloux, A., Kerenidis, I., Laurière, M.: The information cost of quantum memoryless protocols. arXiv preprint arXiv:1703.01061 (2017)
14. Gainutdinova, A.F.: Comparative complexity of quantum and classical OBDDs for total and partial functions. Russ. Math. **59**(11), 26–35 (2015)
15. Gainutdinova, A., Yakaryılmaz, A.: Nondeterministic unitary OBDDs. In: Weil, P. (ed.) CSR 2017. LNCS, vol. 10304, pp. 126–140. Springer, Cham (2017). https://doi.org/10.1007/978-3-319-58747-9_13. arXiv:1612.07015
16. Homeister, M., Waack, S.: Quantum ordered binary decision diagrams with repeated tests. arXiv preprint arXiv:quant-ph/0507258 (2005)

17. Khadiev, K.: Width hierarchy for k-OBDD of small width. Lobachevskii J. Math. **36**(2), 178–183 (2015)
18. Khadiev, K.: On the hierarchies for deterministic, nondeterministic and probabilistic ordered read-k-times branching programs. Lobachevskii J. Math. **37**(6), 682–703 (2016)
19. Khadiev, K., Ibrahimov, R.: Width hierarchies for quantum and classical ordered binary decision diagrams with repeated test. In: Proceedings of the Fourth Russian Finnish Symposium on Discrete Mathematics. TUCS Lecture Notes, no. 26. Turku Centre for Computer Science (2017)
20. Khadiev, K., Khadieva, A.: Reordering method and hierarchies for quantum and classical ordered binary decision diagrams. In: Weil, P. (ed.) CSR 2017. LNCS, vol. 10304, pp. 162–175. Springer, Cham (2017). https://doi.org/10.1007/978-3-319-58747-9_16
21. Klauck, H.: On quantum and probabilistic communication: Las Vegas and one-way protocols. In: STOC 2000: Proceedings of the Thirty-Second Annual ACM Symposium on Theory of Computing, pp. 644–651 (2000)
22. Klauck, H.: Quantum communication complexity. arXiv preprint arXiv:quant-ph/0005032 (2000)
23. Klauck, H.: Lower bounds for quantum communication complexity. In: Proceedings of the 42nd IEEE Symposium on Foundations of Computer Science, pp. 288–297. IEEE (2001)
24. Klauck, H.: Lower bounds for quantum communication complexity. SIAM J. Comput. **37**(1), 20–46 (2007)
25. Klauck, H., Nayak, A., Ta-Shma, A., Zuckerman, D.: Interaction in quantum communication and the complexity of set disjointness. In: Proceedings of the Thirty-Third Annual ACM Symposium on Theory of Computing, pp. 124–133. ACM (2001)
26. Klauck, H., Nayak, A., Ta-Shma, A., Zuckerman, D.: Interaction in quantum communication. IEEE Trans. Inf. Theory **53**(6), 1970–1982 (2007)
27. Linial, N., Shraibman, A.: Lower bounds in communication complexity based on factorization norms. Random Struct. Algorithms **34**(3), 368–394 (2009)
28. Moore, C., Crutchfield, J.P.: Quantum automata and quantum grammars. Theoret. Comput. Sci. **237**(1–2), 275–306 (2000)
29. Nakanishi, M., Hamaguchi, K., Kashiwabara, T.: Ordered quantum branching programs are more powerful than ordered probabilistic branching programs under a bounded-width restriction. In: Du, D.-Z.-Z., Eades, P., Estivill-Castro, V., Lin, X., Sharma, A. (eds.) COCOON 2000. LNCS, vol. 1858, pp. 467–476. Springer, Heidelberg (2000). https://doi.org/10.1007/3-540-44968-X_46
30. Nisan, N., Widgerson, A.: Rounds in communication complexity revisited. In: Proceedings of the Twenty-Third Annual ACM Symposium on Theory of Computing, pp. 419–429. ACM (1991)
31. Raz, R.: Exponential separation of quantum and classical communication complexity. In: Proceedings of the Thirty-First Annual ACM Symposium on Theory of Computing, pp. 358–367. ACM (1999)
32. Sauerhoff, M.: Quantum vs. classical read-once branching programs. In: Complexity of Boolean Functions. Dagstuhl Seminar Proceedings, no. 06111. Internationales Begegnungs- und Forschungszentrum für Informatik (2006)
33. Sauerhoff, M., Sieling, D.: Quantum branching programs and space-bounded nonuniform quantum complexity. Theoret. Comput. Sci. **334**(1–3), 177–225 (2005)

34. Vasiliev, A.V.: Functions computable by boolean circuits of logarithmic depth and branching programs of a special type. J. Appl. Ind. Math. **2**(4), 585–590 (2008). https://doi.org/10.1134/S1990478908040145

35. Wegener, I.: Branching Programs and Binary Decision Diagrams: Theory and Applications. SIAM, Philadelphia (2000)

36. Yakaryılmaz, A., Say, A.C.C.: Succinctness of two-way probabilistic and quantum finite automata. Discret. Math. Theoret. Comput. Sci. **12**(2), 19–40 (2010)

37. Zheng, S., Gruska, J.: Time-space tradeoffs for two-way finite automata. arXiv preprint arXiv:1507.01346 (2015)

Computational Complexity of Atomic Chemical Reaction Networks

David Doty[1(✉)] and Shaopeng Zhu[2]

[1] Computer Science Department, University of California, Davis, Davis, USA
doty@ucdavis.edu
[2] Computer Science Department, University of Maryland, College Park, USA
szhu@terpmail.umd.edu

Abstract. Informally, a chemical reaction network is "atomic" if each reaction may be interpreted as the rearrangement of indivisible units of matter. There are several reasonable definitions formalizing this idea. We investigate the computational complexity of deciding whether a given network is atomic according to each of these definitions.

Primitive atomic, which requires each reaction to preserve the total number of atoms, is shown to be equivalent to mass conservation. Since it is known that it can be decided in polynomial time whether a given chemical reaction network is mass-conserving [28], the equivalence we show gives an efficient algorithm to decide primitive atomicity.

Subset atomic further requires all atoms be species. We show that deciding if a network is subset atomic is in NP, and "whether a network is subset atomic with respect to a given atom set" is strongly NP-complete.

Reachably atomic, studied by Adleman, Gopalkrishnan *et al.* [1,22], further requires that each species has a sequence of reactions splitting it into its constituent atoms. Using a combinatorial argument, we show that there is a polynomial-time algorithm to decide whether a given network is reachably atomic, improving upon the result of Adleman *et al.* that the problem is decidable. We show that the reachability problem for reachably atomic networks is PSPACE-complete.

Finally, we demonstrate equivalence relationships between our definitions and some cases of an existing definition of atomicity due to Gnacadja [21].

1 Introduction

A *chemical reaction network* is a set of reactions such as $A + B \rightleftharpoons C$ and $X \rightarrow 2Y$, intended to model molecular species that interact, possibly combining or splitting in the process. For 150 years [23], the model has been a popular language for describing natural chemicals that react in a well-mixed solution. It is known that in theory *any* set of reactions can be implemented by synthetic DNA complexes [43]. Syntactically equivalent to Petri nets [3,5,18], chemical reaction networks are now equally appropriate as a *programming* language that can be compiled into real chemicals. With advances in synthetic biology heralding a new era

This work was supported by NSF grant 1619343.

A M. Tjoa et al. (Eds.): SOFSEM 2018, LNCS 10706, pp. 212–226, 2018.
https://doi.org/10.1007/978-3-319-73117-9_15

of sophisticated biomolecular engineering [10,29,32,34,35,40,44], chemical reaction networks are expected to gain prominence as a natural high-level language for designing molecular control circuitry.

There has been a flurry of recent progress in understanding the ability of chemical reaction networks to carry out computation: computing functions [2,5,7–9,13,15,16,18,36,38,42], as well as other computational tasks such as space- and energy-efficient search [45], signal processing [25,37], linear I/O systems [31], machine learning [30], and even identifying function computation in existing biological chemical reaction networks [6]. These studies generally assume that any set of reactions is permissible, but not all are physically realistic. Consider, for example, the reaction $X \rightarrow 2X$, which appears to violate the law of conservation of mass. Typically such a reaction is a shorthand for a more realistic reaction such as $F + X \rightarrow 2X$, where F is an anonymous and plentiful source of "fuel" providing the necessary matter for the reaction to occur. The behavior of the two is approximately equal only when the number of executions of $X \rightarrow 2X$ is far below the supplied amount of F, and if F runs out then the two reactions behave completely differently. Thus, although $X \rightarrow 2X$ may be implemented approximately, to truly understand the long-term behavior of the system requires studying its more realistic implementation $F + X \rightarrow 2X$. A straightforward generalization of this "realism" constraint is that each chemical species S may be assigned a *mass* $m(S) \in \mathbb{R}^+$, where in each reaction the total mass of the reactants equals that of the products. Indeed, *conservative* Petri nets formalize this very idea [27,28], and it is straightforward to decide algorithmically if a given network is conservative by reducing to a question of linear algebra.

The focus of this paper is a more stringent condition: that the network should be *atomic*, i.e., each reaction rearranges discrete, indivisible units (atoms), which may be of different noninterchangeable types.[1] (In contrast, mass conservation requires each reaction to rearrange a conserved quantity of continuous, generic "mass".) We emphasize that this is not intended as a study of the atoms appearing in the periodic table of the elements. Instead, we aim to model chemical systems whose reactions rearrange certain units, but never split, create, or destroy those units. For example, DNA strand displacement systems [43,46] have individual DNA strands as indivisible components, and each reaction merely rearranges the secondary structure among the strands (i.e., which bases on the strands are hybridized to others).

Contrary to the idea of mass conservation, there is no "obviously correct" definition of what it means for a chemical reaction network to be atomic, as we will discuss. Furthermore, at least two inequivalent definitions exist in the literature [1,21]. It is not the goal of this paper to identify a single correct definition. Instead, our goal is to evaluate the choices that must be made in formalizing a definition, to place existing and new definitions in this context to

---

[1] This usage of the term "atomic" is different from its usage in traditional areas like operating system or syntactic analysis, where an "atomic" execution is an uninterruptable unit of operation [41].

see how they relate to each other, and to study the computational complexity of deciding whether a given network is atomic. This is a step towards a more broad study of the computational abilities of "physically realistic" chemical reaction networks.

1.1 Summary of Results and Connection with Existing Work

The most directly related previous work is that of Adleman et al. [1] and of Gnacadja [21], which we now discuss in conjunction with our results.

We identify two fundamental questions to be made in formalizing a definition of an "atomic" chemical reaction network:

1. Are atoms also species? (For example, if the only reaction is $2H_2 + O_2 \rightleftharpoons 2H_2O$; then H and O are atoms but not species that appear in a reaction.)
2. Is each species separable into its constituent atoms via reactions?

A negative answer to (1) implies a negative answer to (2). (If some atom is not a species, then it cannot be the product of a reaction.) Thus there are three non-degenerate answers to the above two questions: no/no, yes/no, and yes/yes. We respectively call these *primitive atomic*, *subset atomic*, and *reachably atomic*, defined formally in Sect. 3. Intuitively, a network is *primitive atomic* if each species may be interpreted as composed of one or more atoms, which themselves are not considered species (a species can be composed of just a single atom, but they will have different "names"). More formally, if Λ is the set of species, there is a set Δ of atoms, such that each species $S \in \Lambda$ has an *atomic decomposition* $\mathbf{d}_S \in \mathbb{N}^\Delta \setminus \{\mathbf{0}\}$ describing the atoms that constitute S, such that each reaction preserves the atoms. A network is *subset atomic* if it is primitive atomic and the atoms are themselves considered species; i.e., if $\Delta \subseteq \Lambda$. A network is *reachably atomic* if it is subset atomic, and furthermore, for each species $S \in \Lambda$, there is a sequence of reactions, starting with a single copy of S, resulting in a configuration consisting only of atoms. (If each reaction conserves the atomic count, then this configuration must be unique and equal to the atomic decomposition of S.)

A long-standing open problem in the theory of chemical reaction networks is the global attractor conjecture [12,24], of which even the following special case remains open: is every network satisfying detailed balance *persistence*, i.e., if started with all positive concentrations, do concentrations stay bounded away from 0? Adleman *et al.* [1] defined reachably atomic chemical reaction networks and proved the global attractor conjecture holds for such networks. Gnacadja [21], attacking similar goals, defined a notion of atomicity called "species decomposition" and showed a similar result. We establish links between our definitions and those of both [1,21] in Sect. C. We discuss related complexity issues in Sects. 6 and C. In particular, Adleman *et al.* [1] showed that it is decidable whether a given network is reachably atomic. This is not obvious since the condition of a species being separable into its constituent atoms via reactions appears to require an unbounded search. We improve this result, showing it is decidable in polynomial time.

Mayr and Weihmann [28] proved that configuration reachability graphs for mass conserving chemical reaction networks (i.e., conservative Petri nets) are at most exponentially large in the size of the binary representation of the network, implying via Savitch's theorem [39] a polynomial-space algorithm for deciding reachability in mass-conserving networks. We use these results in analyzing the complexity of reachability problems in reachably atomic chemical reaction networks in Sect. 6.

It is clear that any reasonable definition of atomicity should imply mass conservation: simply assign all atoms to have mass 1, noting that any reaction preserving the atoms necessarily preserves their total count. Perhaps surprisingly, the conditions of primitive atomic and mass-conserving are in fact equivalent, so it is decidable in polynomial time whether a network is primitive atomic and what is an atomic decomposition for each species. A key technical tool is Chubanov's algorithm [11] for finding exact rational solutions to systems of linear equations with a strict positivity constraint.

In their work on autocatalysis of reaction networks [14], Abhishek and Manoj showed that a consistent reaction network is self-replicable if and only if it is critical. Since weak-reversibility implies consistency and our definition of reversibility implies weak-reversibility , we obtain the following equivalence: let a chemical reaction network $\mathcal{C}$ be reversible. Then $\mathcal{C}$ is mass conserving if and only if there does not exist $c_1 < c_2 \in \mathbb{N}^\Lambda$ such that $c_1 \Rightarrow^* c_2$.

Lastly, we note that there have been other models addressing different aspects of atomicity (not necessarily using the term "atomic"). They focus on features of chemical reaction networks not modeled in this paper. For discussions on these works, please see Sect. A of the Appendix in [17].

2 Preliminaries

Let $\mathbb{Z}, \mathbb{N}, \mathbb{R}$ respectively denote the set of integers, nonnegative integers, and reals. Let Λ be a finite set. We write $\mathbb{N}^\Lambda$ to denote $\{f : \Lambda \to \mathbb{N}\}$. Equivalently, by assuming a "canonical" ordering on Λ, an element $c \in \mathbb{N}^\Lambda$ can also be viewed as a $|\Lambda|$-dimensional vector of natural numbers, with each coordinate labeled by $S \in \Lambda$ interpreted as the count of S. $c \in \mathbb{N}^\Lambda$ interpreted this way is called a *configuration*. We sometimes use multiset notation, e.g., $\{3A, 2B\}$ to denote the configuration with 3 copies of A, 2 of B, and 0 of all other species. $\mathbb{Z}^\Lambda, \mathbb{R}^\Lambda, \mathbb{N}^{\Lambda \times \Delta}, \mathbb{N}^\Delta$ (where Δ is also a finite set) are defined analogously.

We write $c \leq c'$ to denote that $(\forall X \in \Lambda) \, c(X) \leq c'(X)$, and $c < c'$ if $c \leq c'$ and $c \neq c'$. We say c and c' are *incomparable* if $c \not\leq c'$ and $c \not\geq c'$.

Definition 2.1. *Given a finite set of chemical species Λ, a reaction over Λ is a pair $\alpha = (r, p) \in \mathbb{N}^\Lambda \times \mathbb{N}^\Lambda$, specifying the stoichiometry of the reactants and products respectively.*[2]

A chemical reaction network is a pair $\mathcal{C} = (\Lambda, R)$, where Λ is a finite set of chemical species, and R is a finite set of reactions over Λ.

---

[2] There is typically a positive real-valued *rate constant* associated to each reaction, but we ignore reaction rates in this paper and consequently simplify the definition.

A chemical reaction network is *reversible* if $(\forall (\mathbf{r}, \mathbf{p}) \in R)\, (\mathbf{p}, \mathbf{r}) \in R$.

For configurations $\mathbf{c}_1, \mathbf{c}_2 \in \mathbb{N}^\Lambda$, we write $\mathbf{c}_1 \Rightarrow_{\mathcal{C}}^* \mathbf{c}_2$ (read "$\mathcal{C}$ reaches $\mathbf{c}_2$ from $\mathbf{c}_1$") if there exists a finite reaction sequence (including the empty sequence) that starts with $\mathbf{c}_1$ and ends with $\mathbf{c}_2$. For simplicity, write $\mathbf{c}_1 \Rightarrow^* \mathbf{c}_2$ (read "$\mathbf{c}_2$ is reachable from $\mathbf{c}_1$") when $\mathcal{C}$ is clear.

Definition 2.2. *Given* $\mathbf{c} \in \mathbb{N}^\Lambda$ *(or* $\mathbb{Z}^\Lambda, \mathbb{R}^\Lambda$ *etc. analogously), the* support *of* $\mathbf{c}$*, written as* $[\mathbf{c}]$*, is the set* $\{S \in \Lambda \mid \mathbf{c}(S) \neq 0\}$.

A few more notational conventions are listed here: write $\mathbf{e}_A \in \mathbb{N}^\Lambda$ as the unit vector that has count 1 on $A \in \Lambda$ and 0 on everything else. Given a vector $\mathbf{x} \in \mathbb{N}^\Lambda$, write $\|\mathbf{x}\| = \|\mathbf{x}\|_1 = \sum_{S \in \Lambda} \mathbf{x}(S)$. When $\cdot$ is any data, write $\langle \cdot \rangle$ for its binary representation as a string, so $|\langle \cdot \rangle|$ is the length of the binary representation of $\cdot$. Given $f : A \to B$ and $C \subseteq A$, $f \upharpoonright C$ is the function $C \to B$, $c \mapsto f(c)$ $(\forall c \in C)$. Lastly, when $\mathbf{M}$ is a matrix, write $\mathbf{M}^T$ as its transposition.

3   Definitions of "Atomic"

This section addresses definitions of several classes of networks, some computational complexity result of which will be exhibited later.

Intuitively, $\mathcal{C} = (\Lambda, R)$ is primitive atomic if all species can be decomposed into combinations of some atoms. Atoms are not required to be species. Each reaction conserves the total count of each type of atom in the species involved (i.e., the reaction can only rearrange atoms but not create or destroy them).

Note that the purpose of studying the primitive-atomic model (as well as all other types of atomic later) is not to analyze "real-world" atoms. Instead, we are trying to study how molecules can be interpreted as decomposable into *exchangeable parts*. In particular, if we know only the reactions but not those exchangeable parts, we are interested in whether the reactions can tell us how the molecules are composed from parts. Proposition 4.2 below, for example, shows that this information can be retrieved by finding a mass distribution vector.

Definition 3.1 (Primitive Atomic). *Let* Δ *be a nonempty finite set and* $\mathcal{C} = (\Lambda, R)$ *a chemical reaction network.* $\mathcal{C}$ *is* primitive atomic with respect to Δ *if for all* $S \in \Lambda$*, there is* $\mathbf{d}_S \in \mathbb{N}^\Delta \setminus \{\mathbf{0}\}$ *such that*

1. $(\forall (\mathbf{r}, \mathbf{p}) \in R)(\forall A \in \Delta) \sum_{S \in \Lambda} \mathbf{r}(S) \cdot \mathbf{d}_S(A) = \sum_{S \in \Lambda} \mathbf{p}(S) \cdot \mathbf{d}_S(A)$ *(reactions preserve atoms), and*
2. $(\forall A \in \Delta)(\exists S \in \Lambda)\ \mathbf{d}_S(A) \neq 0$. *(each atom appears in the decomposition of some species).*

For $S \in \Lambda$*, call* $\mathbf{d}_S$ *in Condition (1) the (atomic)* decomposition *of* S*. We say* $\mathcal{C}$ *is* primitive atomic *if there is a nonempty finite set* Δ *such that* $\mathcal{C}$ *is primitive atomic with respect to* Δ*. In the cases above,* Δ *is called the* set of atoms.

Condition (1) embodies the intuition above. Condition (2) prescribes that each atom appears in the decomposition of at least one species. (See Remark D.1 [17] for comment on Condition 2.) Consider the network $\mathcal{C} = (\{X, Y, W, Z\}, \{((2, 1, 0, 1)^T, (0, 0, 2, 1)^T), ((1, 2, 1, 1)^T, (0, 1, 1, 2)^T)\})$. One may write $\mathcal{C}$ as:

$$\{2X + Y + Z \rightarrow 2W + Z, \ X + 2Y + W + Z \rightarrow Y + W + 2Z.\}$$

$\mathcal{C}$ is primitive-atomic with respect to, say, $\Delta = \{H, O\}$, via the decomposition vector $\mathbf{d}_X = (2, 0)^T, \mathbf{d}_Y = (0, 2)^T, \mathbf{d}_W = (2, 1)^T, \mathbf{d}_Z = (2, 2)^T$. Here $\mathbf{d}_X = (2, 0)^T$ means the species X is composed of 2 units of atom H and 0 unit of atom O, and $\mathbf{d}_Y, \mathbf{d}_W, \mathbf{d}_Z$ can be interpreted likewise. Observe that each of the two reactions in $\mathcal{C}$ preserves the total count of each type of atom on both sides of reactions.

Next, we introduce the definitions of stoichiometric matrix and decomposition matrix. In particular, $\mathbf{A}$ encodes the net change of species caused by execution of one reaction, and $\mathbf{D}$ compiles all decomposition vectors into one data structure.

Definition 3.2 (Stoichiometric Matrix). *The stoichiometric matrix $\mathbf{A}$ for a chemical reaction network $\mathcal{C} = (R, \Lambda)$ is the $|R| \times |\Lambda|$ matrix where the entry $\mathbf{A}_{(\mathbf{r}, \mathbf{p}), S} = \mathbf{p}(S) - \mathbf{r}(S)$ for each $(\mathbf{r}, \mathbf{p}) \in R$ and $S \in \Lambda$.*

Notation-wise, $\mathbf{A}_{(\mathbf{r}, \mathbf{p}), S}$ is the entry whose row is labeled by the reaction $(\mathbf{r}, \mathbf{p})$ and column by the species S. Each row of the stoichiometric matrix represents the change of count of each species via execution of 1 unit of $(\mathbf{r}, \mathbf{p})$. For more illustration, see Example D.1 [17].

Definition 3.3 (Decomposition Matrix). *Let $\mathcal{C} = (\Lambda, R)$ be primitive atomic with respect to Δ. The decomposition matrix, denoted as $\mathbf{D}_\Delta$ for $\mathcal{C}$ with respect to Δ is the $|\Lambda| \times |\Delta|$ matrix whose row vectors are $(\mathbf{d}_S)^T$ ($S \in \Lambda$).*

Note that the set of decomposition vectors $\{\mathbf{d}_S\}_{S \in \Lambda}$ is in general not unique for primitive atomic chemical reaction networks – for example, $A + B \rightarrow C$ is primitive atomic with respect to $\Delta = \{D\}$ via $(k, k, 2k)(\forall k \in \mathbb{N}_{>0})$. Correspondingly, $\mathbf{D}_\Delta$'s are defined with respect to each set $\{\mathbf{d}_S\}_{S \in \Lambda}$. See Example D.2 and Remark D.2 [17] for more discussion on decomposition matrices.

The next definition requires all atoms to be species.

Definition 3.4 (Subset Atomic). *Let $\mathcal{C} = (\Lambda, R)$ be a chemical reaction network and let $\Delta \subseteq \Lambda$ be nonempty. We say that $\mathcal{C}$ is subset-Δ-atomic if $\mathcal{C}$ is primitive atomic with respect to Δ and, for each $S \in \Lambda$:*

1. *$S \in \Lambda \cap \Delta = \Delta \implies \mathbf{d}_S = \{S\}$, and*
2. *$S \in \Lambda \setminus \Delta \implies \|\mathbf{d}_S\| \geq 2$.*

We say $\mathcal{C}$ is subset atomic if $\exists \emptyset \neq \Delta \subseteq \Lambda$ such that $\mathcal{C}$ is subset-Δ-atomic.

By Definition 3.4, no two *atoms* can have the same atomic decomposition, but it is allowed that two distinct *molecular* (i.e. non-atom) species to have the same decomposition. In this case we say the two species are *isomers* (reminiscent of isomers in nature that are composed of the same atoms in different geometrical arrangements). As for the requirement that each non-atom species decompose to a vector of size at least 2, that is to incorporate the idea that generally a molecule should be composed of at least 2 atoms.

For example, the network $C = \{2X + Y + Z \rightarrow 2W + Z, X + 2Y + W + Z \rightarrow Y + W + 2Z\}$ mentioned above is subset-atomic: just redefine $\Delta = \{X\}$ and $\mathbf{d}_X = (1), \mathbf{d}_Y = (2), \mathbf{d}_Z = (3), \mathbf{d}_W = (2)$. One may verify that in the first reaction, each side has 7 atoms X, while in the second each side has 10.

The next definition further requires that decomposition of each molecular species S_i can be "*realized*" via a sequence of reactions, given $\{1S_i\}$ as initial state. As discussed in Subsect. 1.1, this definition was originally developed in [1] to help their approach to the Global Attractor Conjecture in the field of mass action kinetics. Considering the convention for most networks, we relax their requirement of reversibility for each reaction.

Definition 3.5 (Reachably Atomic). *A chemical reaction network $C = (\Lambda, R)$ is reachably atomic if*

1. *C is subset atomic with respect to some $\Delta \subseteq \Lambda$, and*
2. *for each $S \in \Lambda \setminus \Delta$, $\{1S\} \Rightarrow^* \mathbf{d}_S$.*

Here and wherever necessary, with slight abuse of notation, $\mathbf{d}_S$, which represents the atomic decomposition of S, simultaneously represents a configuration in $\mathbb{N}^\Delta$ reachable from $\{1S\}$. Observe that $C = \{2X + Y + Z \rightarrow 2W + Z, X + 2Y + W + Z \rightarrow Y + W + 2Z\}$ is not reachably-atomic unless we add the following reactions: $Y \rightarrow 2X, Z \rightarrow 3X, W \rightarrow 2X$.

Condition 2 is a strong restriction ensuring some nice properties. For example, the atom set of a reachably atomic network is unique:

Lemma 3.6. *If $C = (\Lambda, R)$ is reachably atomic, then the choice of Δ with respect to which C is reachably atomic is unique. Moreover, for each $S \in \Lambda$, $\mathbf{d}_S$ is unique, i.e., if $\{1S\} \Rightarrow^* \mathbf{c} \in \mathbb{N}^\Delta$, then $\mathbf{c} = \mathbf{d}_S$.*

Proof. The intuition is to show that should there exist $\Delta_1 \neq \Delta_2$ and without loss of generality, assume $\exists A \in \Delta_1 \setminus \Delta_2$, then the decomposition of A with respect to Δ_1 violates the preservation of atoms in Δ_2. For details, see Sect. B [17]. $\square$

Conservation laws in "-atomic" networks reminds us of a more familiar type of conservation law, which is mass conservation. The next section exhibits some observations on the relationship between these two types of conservation laws.

4   Mass-Conservation and Primitive Atomicity

This section shows that "primitive atomic" and "mass conserving" are equivalent concepts. We first formalize what it means for a network to conserve mass:

Definition 4.1 (Mass Conserving). *A chemical reaction network* $\mathcal{C} = (\Lambda, R)$ *is* mass conserving *if*

$$(\exists \mathbf{m} \in \mathbb{R}_{>0}^{\Lambda})(\forall (\mathbf{r}, \mathbf{p}) \in R) \sum_{S \in \Lambda} \mathbf{r}(S) \cdot \mathbf{m}(S) = \sum_{S \in \Lambda} \mathbf{p}(S) \cdot \mathbf{m}(S)$$

Equivalently, if $\mathbf{A}$ *is the stoichiometric matrix in Definition 3.2, then* $\mathcal{C}$ *is mass conserving if* $(\exists \mathbf{m} \in \mathbb{R}_{>0}^{\Lambda})$ $\mathbf{A} \cdot \mathbf{m} = \mathbf{0}$. *We call* $\mathbf{m}$ *a mass distribution vector.*

Using our familiar example, $\mathcal{C} = \{2X + Y + Z \rightarrow 2W + Z, X + 2Y + W + Z \rightarrow Y + W + 2Z\}$ is mass conserving with respect to $\mathbf{m} = (0.5, 1, 1.5, 1)^T$. "Mass Conserving" captures the feature that for every reaction in C, the total mass of reactants are equal to the total mass of products. Difference between the definitions of Mass Conserving and Primitive Atomic (as well as all "-atomic" definitions descended therefrom) become clear if we compare the matrix form of their respective conservation laws: mass conservation requires a single conservation relation ($\mathbf{A} \cdot \mathbf{m} = 0^{|R|}$), while primitive atomicity requires $|\Delta|$ of them ($\mathbf{A} \cdot \mathbf{D} = \mathbf{0}$ where $\mathbf{D}$ is a $|\Lambda| \times |\Delta|$) matrix.

However, apparently these two conservation laws are closely related. In fact, the freedom of defining Δ independent of Λ provides us a choice for making Δ a singleton, which enables us to prove the following equivalence:

Proposition 4.2. *For any network* $\mathcal{C}$, $\mathcal{C}$ *is primitive atomic* $\Leftrightarrow \mathcal{C}$ *is mass conserving. Further, there exists an* $O(|\langle \mathbf{A} \rangle|^5)$ *algorithm to decide if* $\mathcal{C}$ *is primitive atomic, with* $\mathbf{A}$ *the stoichiometric matrix of* $\mathcal{C}$.

Proof. Intuitively, the " $\implies$ " direction is shown by assigning mass 1 to each atom, as "homogenizing" the atoms preserves the original conservation law; for the " $\impliedby$ " direction, one may essentially create a Δ of cardinality 1 with respect to which the network is primitive atomic. The proof also reflects the difference in number of conservation relations addressed two paragraphs above. See Sect. B [17] for details and more remarks.

Recall that subset atomicity imposes the restriction that $\Delta \subseteq \Lambda$. As we'll show in the following section, this single restriction increases the computational complexity of the decision problem "is a network '(*prefix*)-atomic'".

5 Complexity of Subset Atomic

We shall determine in this chapter the computational complexity for deciding the subset atomicity of networks. First, we define the relevant languages:

Definition 5.1. *We define the following languages:*

SUBSET-ATOMIC $= \{\langle \Lambda, R \rangle \mid (\exists \Delta \subseteq \Lambda)(\Lambda, R) \text{ is subset atomic with respect to } \Delta\}$
SUBSET-FIXED-ATOMIC $= \{\langle \Lambda, R, \Delta \rangle \mid (\Lambda, R) \text{ is subset atomic with respect to } \Delta\}$

By definition, SUBSET-ATOMIC is the language whose elements are the encoding of a *subset atomic* chemical reaction network. SUBSET-FIXED-ATOMIC, on the other hand, is the language consisting of the encoding of a (network, atom set) pair where the network is *subset atomic* with respect to the given atom set. In this section we determine the complexity classes of these languages.

5.1   Subset-Fixed-Atomic and Subset-Atomic are in NP

It is not immediately obvious that there exists a short witness for either language (which if true would imply that both languages are in NP immediately), so we reduce SUBSET-FIXED-ATOMIC to INTEGER-PROGRAMMING, which is in NP [33].

Proposition 5.2. SUBSET-FIXED-ATOMIC $\leq_m^p$ INTEGER-PROGRAMMING *(here inafter, "IP").*

Proof. The proof is done by exhibiting a polynomial time algorithm to transition the conditions in Definition 3.4 into a linear system. Note that the atom set Δ is given as input. For details, see Sect. B [17]. ∎

Corollary 5.3. SUBSET-FIXED-ATOMIC, SUBSET-ATOMIC $\in$ NP.

Proof. It is proved (e.g., in [33]) that IP $\in$ NP, hence so is SUBSET-FIXED-ATOMIC.

The proof that SUBSET-ATOMIC $\in$ NP is given by an polynomial time verification algorithm using the polynomial-time verifier of SUBSET-FIXED-ATOMIC as an oracle and taking as witness both the atom set and decomposition matrix. For details, see Sect. B [17]. ∎

5.2   Subset-Fixed-Atomic is NP-hard

Our proof shall be based on reduction from MONOTONE-1-IN-3-SAT. Recall that a monotone 3-CNF C is a conjunctive normal form with no negations, and a 1-in-3 satisfying assignment for C is an assignment of Boolean values to all variables such that for each clause in C, exactly one variable is assigned true.

As a well-established result, the following language is NP-complete [19].

MONOTONE-1-IN-3-SAT $= \{\langle V, C \rangle \mid C$ is a monotone 3-CNF over $V = \{v_i\}_{i=1}^n$,

and there exists a 1-in-3 satisfying assignment for C$\}$

Proposition 5.4. MONOTONE-1-IN-3-SAT $\leq_m^p$ SUBSET-FIXED-ATOMIC.

Proof. Given an instance $\langle V, C \rangle$, we design a chemical reaction network $\mathcal{C}$ where

1. Each molecular species consists of 2 atoms T and F (representing "True" and "False" respectively), and
2. reactions guarantees the equivalence: $\mathcal{C}$ is subset-Δ-atomic if and only if the $\langle V, C \rangle \in$ MONOTONE-1-IN-3-SAT.

For details, see Sect. B [17]. ∎

The full proof of Proposition 5.4 uses only coefficients of size $O(1)$ with respect to $|\langle V, C \rangle|$, which combined with Corollary 5.3 establishes the following:

Corollary 5.5. SUBSET-FIXED-ATOMIC *is strongly* NP-*hard (and hence strongly* NP-*complete).*

Remark 5.6. SUBSET-FIXED-ATOMIC *remains* NP-*complete even restricted to instances where R contains only unimolecular and bimolecular reactions. To see details on this, see Sect. B* [17].

The lower bound of the complexity of SUBSET-ATOMIC therefore remains open, but we conjecture that SUBSET-ATOMIC is NP-hard (hence NP-complete).

6   Complexity of Reachably Atomic

Without repeating the intuition of the definition of reachably atomic which has been explained in Subsect. 1.1 and Sect. 3, we proceed with the corresponding definition of languages for deciding reachable atomicity and the reachability problem in reachably atomic networks.

Definition 6.1. *We define the following languages (to save space I use "w.r.t." as shorthand for "with respect to"):*

REACHABLY-ATOMIC $= \{\langle \Lambda, R \rangle \mid (\exists \Delta \subseteq \Lambda)(\Lambda, R)$ *is reachably atomic w.r.t.* $\Delta\}$
REACHABLY-FIXED-ATOMIC $= \{\langle \Lambda, R, \Delta \rangle \mid (\Lambda, R)$ *is reachably atomic w.r.t.* $\Delta\}$

Distinction between REACHABLY-FIXED-ATOMIC and REACHABLY-ATOMIC is analogous to "SUBSET-FIXED-ATOMIC vs. SUBSET-ATOMIC". However, by Lemma 3.6 there is no semantic reason to distinguish between "RREACHABLY-FIXEDATOMIC" and REACHABLY-ATOMIC. So we shall only consider REACHABLY-ATOMIC.

6.1   Reachably-Atomic is in P

As mentioned before, the requirement that $\{1S\} \Rightarrow^* \mathbf{d}_S$ $(\forall S \in \Lambda)$ ensures some interesting results. The complexity results in this subsection confirm this.

Lemma 6.2. *If a network* $\mathcal{C} = (\Lambda, R)$ *is reachably atomic with respect to* Δ *via decompositin matrix* $\mathbf{D}$ *(or equivalently, via the set of decomposition vectors* $\{\mathbf{d}_S\}_{S \in \Lambda}$), *then* $\exists S \in \Lambda \setminus \Delta$ *and* $(\mathbf{r}, \mathbf{p}) \in R$ *s.t.* $\mathbf{r} = \{1S\}$ *and* $\mathbf{p} = \mathbf{d}_S$.

Proof. The claim is saying that if a network is reachably atomic, then there exists a molecular species that can be decomposed into its atomic decomposition in *one* single reaction. Proof is done by assuming otherwise and chasing the decomposition sequence to find an infinite descending chain of species ordered by the size of their decomposition vectors, contradicting the finiteness of species set. For details, see Sect. B [17].

Theorem 6.3. REACHABLY-ATOMIC $\in$ P.

Proof. We need to exhibit a polynomial time algorithm that decides whether there exists a separation of Λ into two non-empty, disjoint sets M (molecules) and Δ (atoms), with elements in M decomposable via sequences of reactions into combination of elements in Δ.

To achieve this goal, we set $M = \{S \in \Lambda \mid (\exists(\mathbf{r}, \mathbf{p}) \in R)\mathbf{r} = \{1S\}\}$, the subset of species which are the single reactant of some reaction; apparently M is non-empty for reachably-atomic networks, by Lemma 6.2. Then recursively, we check if there exist elements in M that can be decomposed into combination of atoms via a reaction sequence of length $i = 1, 2, \cdots$, and reject if we succeed to do so at $i = k$ but fails at $i = k + 1$ while not all elements in M have been examined. When this process terminates (note that M is finite) finding (candidate) atomic decomposition for all molecules, we verify if the necessary conservation laws hold. Details of the proof are included in Sect. B of [17].

6.2 Reachable-Reach is PSPACE-complete

We shall first introduce the definition of configuration reachability graphs, followed by a result proved in [28] (see also Subsect. 1.1), based on which we prove REACHABLE-REACH (see Definition 6.7), a problem motivated by restricting relevant problems such as "exact reachability" [26], is PSPACE-complete.

Definition 6.4 (Configuration Reachability Graph). *An i-initiated Configuration Reachability Graph $G_{\mathcal{C},\mathbf{i}}$ of the chemical reaction network $\mathcal{C} = (\Lambda, R)$ is a directed graph (V, E), where:*

1. *each $v_{\mathbf{c}} \in V$ ($\mathbf{c} \in \mathbb{N}^{\Lambda}$) is labeled by a reachable configuration $\mathbf{c}$ of $\mathcal{C}$;*
2. *$v_{\mathbf{i}} \in V (\mathbf{i} \in \mathbb{N}^{\Lambda})$ is the vertex labeled by the initializing configuration $\mathbf{i}$;*
3. *the ordered pair $(v_{\mathbf{c}_1}, v_{\mathbf{c}_2}) \in E$ if and only if $\mathbf{c}_1 \Rightarrow^1 \mathbf{c}_2$.*

Remark 6.5. For the sake of simplicity, we use $G_{\mathcal{C},\mathbf{i}}$ as shorthand for $G_{\mathcal{C},v_{\mathbf{i}}}$.

For the same $\mathcal{C}$, Configuration Reachability Graphs can be far from isomorphic due to parameterization by different initialization vectors. We have included an example (Example D.3) in [17].

We will soon prove the conclusion on the complexity of the reachability problem for reachably atomic networks. But first, we point out that the following is a straightforward translation of a finding in [28], giving the complexity class of reachability problems for mass-conserving chemical reaction networks.

Observation 6.6 (A result proved in [28]). *For all mass conserving chemical reaction networks $\mathcal{C}$ and initial configuration $\mathbf{i}$ of $\mathcal{C}$, $|\langle G_{\mathcal{C},\mathbf{i}}\rangle| \in O(2^{poly(|\langle \mathcal{C},\mathbf{i}\rangle|)})$. That is, the binary size of the encoding of the configuration reachability graph $G_{\mathcal{C},\mathbf{i}}$ is at most exponential to the binary size of the encoding of the pair $(\mathcal{C}, \mathbf{i})$.*

Furthermore, reachability problem for mass conserving networks is PSPACE-complete. That is, it is PSPACE-complete to decide if an instance is in the following language:

$$\{\langle \Lambda, R, \mathbf{c}_1, \mathbf{c}_2 \mid (\Lambda, R) \text{ is mass conserving}; \ \mathbf{c}_1, \mathbf{c}_2 \in \mathbb{N}^{\Lambda}; \mathbf{c}_1 \Rightarrow^* \mathbf{c}_2\rangle\}$$

Built on Observation 6.6, we now exhibit the proof that the decision problem "Given a Reachably Atomic network, is $\mathbf{c}_2$ reachable from $\mathbf{c}_1$" is PSPACE-Complete.

Definition 6.7 (Reachable-Reach). *We define the language*

$$\text{REACHABLE-REACH} = \{(\Lambda, R, c_1, c_2) \mid (\Lambda, R) \text{ } \underline{\text{is reachably atomic}}; \text{ } c_1, c_2 \in \mathbb{N}^\Lambda;$$
$$c_1 \Rightarrow^* c_2\}$$

Proposition 6.8. REACHABLE-REACH *is* PSPACE-complete.

Proof. REACHABLE-REACH $\in$ PSPACE is a direct application of Observation 6.6 – note that all reachably-atomic chemical reaction networks are primitive atomic, and hence mass conserving (Proposition 4.2). Hardness is shown by simulating polynomial space Turing Machines via reactions. Details in Sect. B [17].

Remark 6.9. The fact that the coefficients of all reactions involved in the proof of Proposition 6.8 are constant also implies that REACHABLE-REACH is PSPACE-hard (and hence complete) in the strong sense. Another remark on the irreversibility of reactions may be found in Sect. D [17].

We also found connections between our definitions of "-atomic" and the concept of "core composition", addressed by Gnacadja [21] and detailed in Sect. C [17]. Some interesting results are:

1. **Lemma C.12** states that a network is subset atomic if and only if it admits a "near-core composition" with certain restrictions;
2. **Lemma C.20** in the same section says reachable-atomicity implies admitting a core composition;
3. **Theorem C.15** gives the equivalence between "reversibly-reachable atomic" and "explicitly-reversibly constructive with no isomeric elementary species".

7 Open Problems

Conjecture 7.1. SUBSET-ATOMIC $\in$ NP-complete.

One may note that there are two sources of indeterminancy in the problem SUBSET-ATOMIC: the choice of Δ and $\mathbf{D}$. For example, the network constructed in the proof of NP-hardness of SUBSET-FIXED-ATOMIC would remain subset atomic if we define $\Delta = \{T, F\}$, and let $\mathbf{d}_P = \mathbf{d}_Q = \{kT, sF\}$ for any $k, s \geq 2$.

There is a formal sense in which chemical reaction networks have been shown to be able to compute functions $f : \mathbb{N}^k \to \mathbb{N}$ [8] and predicates $\mathbb{N}^k \to \{0, 1\}$ [4]. A function/predicate can be computed "deterministically" (i.e., regardless of the order in which reactions occur) $\Longleftrightarrow$ it is semilinear (see [20] for a definition).

Problem 7.2. *What semilinear functions/predicates can atomic chemical reaction networks compute* deterministically, *and how efficiently? What general functions/predicates can atomic chemical reaction networks compute with high probability, and how efficiently?*

Remark 7.3. A partial answer for Problem 7.2 based on results in [8] says that primitive atomic networks and subset atomic networks can stably compute any seminilear functions (For the proof of this, see Sect. [17]), but it is not obvious how to modify the subset-atomic network into reachably-atomic with the stably-computation property maintained, or whether it is even possible to do so.

Acknowledgements. The authors are thankful to Manoj Gopalkrishnan, Gilles Gnacadja, Javier Esparza, Sergei Chubanov, Matthew Cook, and anonymous reviewers for their insights and useful discussion.

References

1. Adleman, L., Gopalkrishnan, M., Huang, M.-D., Moisset, P., Reishus, D.: On the mathematics of the law of mass action. In: Kulkarni, V.V., Stan, G.-B., Raman, K. (eds.) A Systems Theoretic Approach to Systems and Synthetic Biology I: Models and System Characterizations, pp. 3–46. Springer, Dordrecht (2014). https://doi.org/10.1007/978-94-017-9041-3_1
2. Alistarh, D., Aspnes, J., Eisenstat, D., Gelashvili, R., Rivest, R.: Time-space trade-offs in molecular computation. In: Proceedings of the Twenty-Eighth Annual ACM-SIAM Symposium on Discrete Algorithms, pp. 2560–2579 (2017)
3. Angeli, D., De Leenheer, P., Sontag, E.D.: A Petri net approach to the study of persistence in chemical reaction networks. Math. Biosci. **210**, 598–618 (2007)
4. Angluin, D., Aspnes, J., Diamadi, Z., Fischer, M., Peralta, R.: Computation in networks of passively mobile finite-state sensors. Distrib. Comput. **18**, 235–253 (2006). https://doi.org/10.1007/s00446-005-0138-3. Preliminary version appeared in PODC 2004
5. Brijder, R., Doty, D., Soloveichik, D.: Robustness of expressivity in chemical reaction networks. In: Rondelez, Y., Woods, D. (eds.) DNA 2016. LNCS, vol. 9818, pp. 52–66. Springer, Cham (2016). https://doi.org/10.1007/978-3-319-43994-5_4
6. Cardelli, L., Csikász-Nagy, A.: The cell cycle switch computes approximate majority. Sci. Rep. **2** (2012)
7. Chen, H., Cummings, R., Doty, D., Soloveichik, D.: Speed faults in computation by chemical reaction networks. Distributed Computing (2015, to appear). Special issue of invited papers from DISC 2014
8. Chen, H.L., Doty, D., Soloveichik, D.: Deterministic function computation with chemical reaction networks. Nat. Comput. **13**(4), 517–534 (2013). Special issue of invited papers from DNA 2012
9. Chen, H.L., Doty, D., Soloveichik, D.: Rate-independent computation in continuous chemical reaction networks. In: ITCS 2014: Proceedings of the 5th Conference on Innovations in Theoretical Computer Science, pp. 313–326 (2014)
10. Chen, Y.J., Dalchau, N., Srinivas, N., Phillips, A., Cardelli, L., Soloveichik, D., Seelig, G.: Programmable chemical controllers made from DNA. Nat. Nanotechnol. **8**(10), 755–762 (2013)
11. Chubanov, S.: A polynomial projection algorithm for linear feasibility problems. Math. Program. **153**(2), 687–713 (2015)
12. Craciun, G., Dickenstein, A., Shiu, A., Sturmfels, B.: Toric dynamical systems. J. Symb. Computat. **44**(11), 1551–1565 (2009)

13. Cummings, R., Doty, D., Soloveichik, D.: Probability 1 computation with chemical reaction networks. Nat. Comput. 1–17 (2015). https://doi.org/10.1007/s11047-015-9501-x. Special issue of invited papers from DNA 2014
14. Deshpande, A., Gopalkrishnan, M.: Autocatalysis in reaction networks. arXiv preprint arXiv:1309.3957 (2013)
15. Doty, D.: Timing in chemical reaction networks. In: SODA 2014: Proceedings of the 25th Annual ACM-SIAM Symposium on Discrete Algorithms, pp. 772–784, January 2014
16. Doty, D., Hajiaghayi, M.: Leaderless deterministic chemical reaction networks. Nat. Comput. 14(2), 213–223 (2015). Preliminary version appeared in DNA
17. Doty, D., Zhu, S.: Computational complexity of atomic chemical reaction networks. arXiv preprint arXiv:1702.05704 (2017)
18. Esparza, J., Ganty, P., Leroux, J., Majumdar, R.: Verification of population protocols. Acta Inform. 54, 1–25 (2016)
19. Garey, M.R., Johnson, D.S.: Computers and Intractability. W. H. Freeman, New York (1979)
20. Ginsburg, S., Spanier, E.H.: Semigroups, Presburger formulas, and languages. Pac. J. Math. 16(2), 285–296 (1966). http://projecteuclid.org/euclid.pjm/1102994974
21. Gnacadja, G.: Reachability, persistence, and constructive chemical reaction networks (part II): a formalism for species composition in chemical reaction network theory and application to persistence. J. Math. Chem. 49(10), 2137 (2011)
22. Gopalkrishnan, M.: Private communication. Email (2016)
23. Guldberg, C.M., Waage, P.: Studies concerning affinity. In: Forhandlinger: Videnskabs-Selskabet i Christinia, p. 35. Norwegian Academy of Science and Letters (1864)
24. Horn, F.J.M.: The dynamics of open reaction systems. In: SIAM-AMS Proceedings VIII, pp. 125–137 (1974)
25. Jiang, H., Salehi, S.A., Riedel, M.D., Parhi, K.K.: Discrete-time signal processing with DNA. ACS Synth. Bafiology 2(5), 245–254 (2013)
26. Leroux, J.: Vector addition system reachability problem: a short self-contained proof. In: Dediu, A.-H., Inenaga, S., Martín-Vide, C. (eds.) LATA 2011. LNCS, vol. 6638, pp. 41–64. Springer, Heidelberg (2011). https://doi.org/10.1007/978-3-642-21254-3_3
27. Lien, Y.E.: A note on transition systems. Inf. Sci. 10(2), 347–362 (1976)
28. Mayr, E.W., Weihmann, J.: A framework for classical Petri net problems: conservative Petri nets as an application. In: Ciardo, G., Kindler, E. (eds.) PETRI NETS 2014. LNCS, vol. 8489, pp. 314–333. Springer, Cham (2014). https://doi.org/10.1007/978-3-319-07734-5_17
29. Montagne, K., Plasson, R., Sakai, Y., Fujii, T., Rondelez, Y.: Programming an in vitro DNA oscillator using a molecular networking strategy. Mol. Syst. Biol. 7(1) (2011)
30. Napp, N.E., Adams, R.P.: Message passing inference with chemical reaction networks. In: Advances in Neural Information Processing Systems, pp. 2247–2255 (2013)
31. Oishi, K., Klavins, E.: Biomolecular implementation of linear I/O systems. IET Syst. Biol. 5(4), 252–260 (2011)
32. Padirac, A., Fujii, T., Rondelez, Y.: Nucleic acids for the rational design of reaction circuits. Curr. Opin. Biotechnol. 24(4), 575–580 (2013)
33. Papadimitriou, C.H.: On the complexity of integer programming. J. ACM (JACM) 28(4), 765–768 (1981)

34. Qian, L., Winfree, E., Bruck, J.: Neural network computation with dna strand displacement cascades. Nature **475**(7356), 368–372 (2011)
35. Qian, L., Winfree, E.: Scaling up digital circuit computation with DNA strand displacement cascades. Science **332**(6034), 1196 (2011)
36. Salehi, S.A., Parhi, K.K., Riedel, M.D.: Chemical reaction networks for computing polynomials. ACS Synth. Biol. **6**, 76–83 (2016)
37. Salehi, S.A., Riedel, M.D., Parhi, K.K.: Asynchronous discrete-time signal processing with molecular reactions. In: 2014 48th Asilomar Conference on Signals, Systems and Computers, pp. 1767–1772. IEEE (2014)
38. Salehi, S.A., Riedel, M.D., Parhi, K.K.: Markov chain computations using molecular reactions. In: 2015 IEEE International Conference on Digital Signal Processing (DSP), pp. 689–693. IEEE (2015)
39. Savitch, W.J.: Relationships between nondeterministic and deterministic tape complexities. J. Comput. Syst. Sci. **4**(2), 177–192 (1970)
40. Seelig, G., Soloveichik, D., Zhang, D.Y., Winfree, E.: Enzyme-free nucleic acid logic circuits. Science **314**(5805), 1585–1588 (2006). http://www.sciencemag.org/cgi/doi/10.1126/science.1132493
41. Silberschatz, A., Galvin, P.B., Gagne, G., Silberschatz, A.: Operating System Concepts. Addison-Wesley, Reading (2013)
42. Soloveichik, D., Cook, M., Winfree, E., Bruck, J.: Computation with finite stochastic chemical reaction networks. Nat. Comput. **7**(4), 615–633 (2008). https://doi.org/10.1007/s11047-008-9067-y
43. Soloveichik, D., Seelig, G., Winfree, E.: DNA as a universal substrate for chemical kinetics. Proc. Nat. Acad. Sci. **107**(12), 5393 (2010). Preliminary version appeared in DNA 2008
44. Srinivas, N.: Programming chemical kinetics: engineering dynamic reaction networks with DNA strand displacement. Ph.D. thesis, California Institute of Technology (2015)
45. Thachuk, C., Condon, A.: Space and energy efficient computation with DNA strand displacement systems. In: DNA 2012: Proceedings of the 18th International Meeting on DNA Computing and Molecular Programming, pp. 135–149 (2012)
46. Yurke, B., Turberfield, A., Mills Jr., A., Simmel, F., Neumann, J.: A DNA-fuelled molecular machine made of DNA. Nature **406**(6796), 605–608 (2000)

Conjugacy of One-Dimensional One-Sided Cellular Automata is Undecidable

Joonatan Jalonen$^{(\boxtimes)}$ and Jarkko Kari

University of Turku, Turku, Finland
jsjalo@utu.fi

Abstract. Two cellular automata are strongly conjugate if there exists a shift-commuting conjugacy between them. We prove that the following two sets of pairs (F, G) of one-dimensional one-sided cellular automata over a full shift are recursively inseparable:
(i) pairs where F has strictly larger topological entropy than G, and
(ii) pairs that are strongly conjugate and have zero topological entropy.
Because there is no factor map from a lower entropy system to a higher entropy one, and there is no embedding of a higher entropy system into a lower entropy system, we also get as corollaries that the following decision problems are undecidable: Given two one-dimensional one-sided cellular automata F and G over a full shift: Are F and G conjugate? Is F a factor of G? Is F a subsystem of G? All of these are undecidable in both strong and weak variants (whether the homomorphism is required to commute with the shift or not, respectively). It also immediately follows that these results hold for one-dimensional two-sided cellular automata.

1 Introduction

The original setting for cellular automata theory was the theory of computation and computability, as cellular automata were created as a mathematical model of natural computational devices. Thus algorithmic questions have always been a significant part of the study of cellular automata. It is known, for example, that surjectivity and injectivity (and so also reversibility) are decidable for one-dimensional cellular automata [1] and undecidable in higher dimensions [10], and that nilpotency and periodicity are undecidable for one- and higher-dimensional cellular automata [9,13,16]. It is also known that the topological entropy of one- and higher-dimensional cellular automata is uncomputable [8].

The Curtis-Lyndon-Hedlund Theorem, which says that the classical definition of cellular automata is equivalent to saying that cellular automata are shift commuting endomorphisms of the full shift, prompted the fruitful study of cellular automata as topological dynamical systems. One natural question then is to determine if two cellular automata are conjugate dynamical systems.

Combining both views, one ends up asking if conjugacy of cellular automata is decidable. In [6,7] it was conjectured that topological conjugacy of one-dimensional cellular automata is undecidable. We prove that this holds for strong

Research supported by the Academy of Finland Grant 296018.

J. Jalonen—Research supported by the Finnish Cultural Foundation.

A. M. Tjoa et al. (Eds.): SOFSEM 2018, LNCS 10706, pp. 227–238, 2018.
https://doi.org/10.1007/978-3-319-73117-9_16

and weak conjugacy (whether the conjugacy is required to be shift commuting or not, respectively). In fact we prove a stronger result: Consider sets of pairs (F, G) of one-dimensional one-sided cellular automata over a full shift such that

(i) F has strictly larger topological entropy than G,
(ii) F and G are strongly conjugate and both have zero topological entropy.

We prove that these sets of pairs are recursively inseparable. The same result then also holds for one-dimensional two-sided cellular automata, too. As an immediate corollary we get that (strong) conjugacy, being a (strong) factor, and being a (strong) subsystem are undecidable properties for one-dimensional one- and two-sided cellular automata.

2   Preliminaries

2.1   Symbolic Dynamics

Zero is considered a natural number, i.e., $0 \in \mathbb{N}$. For two integers $i, j \in \mathbb{Z}$ such that $i < j$ the interval from i to j is denoted $[i, j] = \{i, i+1, \ldots, j\}$. We also denote $[i, j) = \{i, i+1, \ldots j-1\}$ and $(i, j] = \{i+1, \ldots, j\}$. Notation $\mathbb{M}$ is used when it does not matter whether we use $\mathbb{N}$ or $\mathbb{Z}$. Composition of functions $f : X \to Y$ and $g : Y \to Z$ is written as gf, and defined by $(gf)(x) = g(f(x))$ for all $x \in X$.

The set of infinite sequences over an *alphabet* A indexed by $\mathbb{M}$ is $A^{\mathbb{M}}$. An element $c \in A^{\mathbb{M}}$ is a *configuration*. A configuration is a function $\mathbb{M} \to A$ and we denote $c(i) = c_i$ for $i \in \mathbb{M}$. For any $D \subset \mathbb{M}$ we denote by c_D the restriction of c to the domain D and by A^D the set of all functions $D \to A$. The set of *finite words* is denoted by $A^+ = \bigcup_{n \in \mathbb{N}} A^{[0,n]}$. Let D be finite and $u \in A^D$, then we denote $[u] = \{c \in A^{\mathbb{M}} \mid c_D = u\}$ and call such sets *cylinders*. Let A have the discrete topology and $A^{\mathbb{M}}$ the product topology. Cylinders form a countable clopen (open and closed) base of this topology. We consider $A^{\mathbb{M}}$ to be a metric space with the metric

$$d(c, e) = \begin{cases} 2^{-\min(\{|i| \mid c_i \neq e_i\})}, & \text{if } c \neq e \\ 0, & \text{if } c = e \end{cases},$$

for all $c, e \in A^{\mathbb{M}}$. It is well-known that this metric induces the product topology, and that this space is compact.

A *(topological) dynamical system* is a pair (X, f) where X is a compact metric space and f a continuous map $X \to X$. Let (X, f) and (Y, g) be two dynamical systems. A continuous map $\phi : X \to Y$ is a *homomorphism* if $\phi f = g \phi$. If ϕ is surjective, it is a *factor map*, and (Y, g) is a *factor* of (X, f). If ϕ is injective, it is an *embedding*, and (X, f) is a *subsystem* of (Y, g). And lastly, if ϕ is a bijection, it is a *conjugacy*, and (X, f) and (Y, g) are *conjugate*, denoted by $(X, f) \cong (Y, g)$. Let $\mathcal{U}$ be a finite open cover of X, and denote $h(\mathcal{U})$ the smallest number of elements of $\mathcal{U}$ that cover X. Let $\mathcal{V}$ be another finite open cover of X and denote

$\mathcal{U} \vee \mathcal{V} = \{U \cap V \mid U \in \mathcal{U}, V \in \mathcal{V}\} \setminus \{\varnothing\}$. Then the *entropy of (X, f) with respect to $\mathcal{U}$* is

$$h(X, f, \mathcal{U}) = \lim_{n \to \infty} \frac{1}{n} \log_2 h(\mathcal{U} \vee f^{-1}(\mathcal{U}) \vee f^{-2}(\mathcal{U}) \vee \cdots \vee f^{-n+1}(\mathcal{U})).$$

The *entropy* of (X, f) is

$$h(X, f) = \sup\{h(X, f, \mathcal{U}) \mid \mathcal{U} \text{ is an open cover of } X\}.$$

We need the following:

Proposition 1 [14, Proposition 2.88]. *If (Y, g) is a subsystem or a factor of (X, f), then $h(Y, g) \leq h(X, f)$. It follows that if (X, f) and (Y, g) are conjugate, then $h(X, f) = h(Y, g)$.*

The *direct product* of dynamical systems (X, f) and (Y, g) is $(X \times Y, f \times g)$, where $f \times g : X \times Y \to X \times Y$, $(f \times g)(x, y) = (f(x), g(y))$. It is known that $h(X \times Y, f \times g) = h(X, f) + h(Y, g)$ [14, Proposition 2.89].

The *shift map* $\sigma : A^{\mathbb{M}} \to A^{\mathbb{M}}$, defined by $\sigma(c)_i = c_{i+1}$ for all $i \in \mathbb{M}$, is easily seen to be continuous. The dynamical system $(A^{\mathbb{M}}, \sigma)$ is the *full (A-)shift*. A dynamical system (X, σ), where $X \subset A^{\mathbb{M}}$ is topologically closed and $\sigma^m(X) \subset X$ for all $m \in \mathbb{M}$, is a *subshift*. When it does not cause confusion, we will simply talk about a subshift X. A configuration $c \in A^{\mathbb{M}}$ *avoids* $u \in A^{[0,n)}$ if $\sigma^i(c)_{[0,n)} \neq u$ for all $i \in \mathbb{M}$. Let $S \subseteq A^+$, and let X_S be the set of configurations that avoid S, i.e., $X_S = \{c \in A^{\mathbb{M}} \mid \forall u \in S : c \text{ avoids } u\}$. It is well-known that the given topological definition of subshifts is equivalent to saying that there exists a set of forbidden words S such that $X = X_S$. If there exists a finite set S such that $X = X_S$, then X is a *subshift of finite type (SFT)*. If Y is a factor of an SFT then it is a *sofic shift*. An equivalent characterization of sofic shifts is that the set of forbidden words is a regular language.

The *subword complexity (of length n)* of a subshift X is $p_n(X) = |\{u \in A^+ \mid \exists c \in X : c_{[0,n)} = u\}|$. The entropy of (X, σ) can be calculated using the subword complexity

$$h(X, \sigma) = \lim_{n \to \infty} \frac{1}{n} \log_2(p_n(X)).$$

2.2   Cellular Automata

A *cellular automaton (CA)* is a dynamical system (X, F) where $X \subset A^{\mathbb{M}}$ is a subshift and F commutes with the shift map, i.e., $F\sigma = \sigma F$. In this paper we will only consider CA's over a full shift, i.e., $X = A^{\mathbb{M}}$. When $\mathbb{M} = \mathbb{N}$, the CA is called *one-sided* and, when $\mathbb{M} = \mathbb{Z}$, the CA is called *two-sided*. We will often refer to a CA by the function alone, i.e., talk about the CA F, and in a similar fashion we often omit the phase space from notations. For example, we write $h(F) = h(A^{\mathbb{M}}, F)$ for the entropy. Let $D = [i, j] \subset \mathbb{M}$ and let $G_l : A^D \to A$. Define $G : A^{\mathbb{M}} \to A^{\mathbb{M}}$ by $G(c)_i = G_l((\sigma^i(c))_D)$. It is easy to see that G is continuous and commutes with σ, and so it is a cellular automaton. The set D is the *local neighborhood* of G and the function G_l is the *local rule* of G. According to the Curtis-Hedlund-Lyndon Theorem every CA is defined by a local rule. We will denote the local and global rules with the same G. This will not cause confusion as it will be clear from the context which function G stands for. Let $r \in \mathbb{N}$ be the smallest number such that $D \subseteq [-r, r]$. The number r is the *radius* of G.

Let (A^{M}, F) and (B^{M}, G) be two CA's. If $H : A^{\mathrm{M}} \to B^{\mathrm{M}}$ is a homomorphism from (A^{M}, F) to (B^{M}, G), and also a homomorphism from (A^{M}, σ) to (B^{M}, σ) then it is a *strong homomorphism*. Naturally we define *strong factor, strong subsystem,* and *strongly conjugate,* when the corresponding homomorphism is a strong homomorphism. If F and G are strongly conjugate, we denote $F \cong_s G$. Notice that if ϕ is a strong conjugacy from (A^{M}, F) to (B^{M}, G), then automatically ϕ^{-1} is also strong, i.e., commutes with σ (see, e.g., [11]).

For every $n \in \mathbb{N}$, CA (A^{M}, F) defines the nth *trace subshift*

$$\tau_n(F) = \left\{ e \in \left(A^n \right)^{\mathbb{N}} \mid \exists c \in A^{\mathrm{M}} : \forall i \in \mathbb{N} : e_i = \left(F^i(c) \right)_{[0,n)} \right\}.$$

The entropy of F can be calculated as the limit of the entropies of its trace subshifts

$$h(F) = \lim_{n \to \infty} h(\tau_n(F), \sigma).$$

For a one-sided cellular automaton F with radius r we have that $p_n(\tau_{r+1}(F)) = |A| \cdot p_n(\tau_r(F))$, so we get the following:

Proposition 2. *Let* $F : A^{\mathbb{N}} \to A^{\mathbb{N}}$ *be a CA with radius* r. *Then* $h(F) = h(\tau_r(F), \sigma)$.

Let $F : A^{\mathrm{M}} \to A^{\mathrm{M}}$ and $G : B^{\mathrm{M}} \to B^{\mathrm{M}}$ be two CA's. There are two natural ways to interpret the direct product of F and G. First we can consider $F \times G$ to be a CA that has two separate *tracks* A^{M} and B^{M}, and $F \times G$ operates on the A-track via F and on the B-track via G. On the other hand we can also consider $F \times G$ as a CA on $(A \times B)^{\mathrm{M}}$, where the states have two *layers*. For any $F \times G$ we use which ever interpretation seems more natural. We can, of course, define a CA over $(A \times B)^{\mathrm{M}}$ that is not a direct product of two CA's. For such a CA we will also talk about tracks and layers.

Let F be a CA. If there exist $n, p > 0$ such that $F^{n+p} = F^n$, then F is *eventually periodic,* and if there exists $p > 0$ such that $F^p = \mathrm{id}$, then F is *periodic.* For a state $a \in A$ we denote ${}^\omega a^\omega \in A^{\mathrm{M}}$ the configuration such that ${}^\omega a^\omega(i) = a$ for all $i \in \mathrm{M}$. A state $q \in A$ is *quiescent* if $F({}^\omega q^\omega) = {}^\omega q^\omega$. A cellular automaton is *nilpotent* if there exists a quiescent state q such that for every $c \in A^{\mathrm{M}}$ there exists $n \in \mathbb{N}$ such that $F^n(c) = {}^\omega q^\omega$. A state $s \in A$ is *spreading* if the local rule maps every neighborhood containing s to s. Clearly a spreading state is quiescent. It is known that for cellular automata nilpotency implies uniform nilpotency:

Proposition 3 [3]. *Let* $F : A^{\mathrm{M}} \to A^{\mathrm{M}}$ *be a nilpotent CA. Then there exists* $n \in \mathbb{N}$ *such that for all* $c \in A^{\mathrm{M}}$ *it holds that* $F^n(c) = {}^\omega q^\omega$.

We also need the following, which is a result of a simple compactness argument.

Proposition 4. *Let $F : A^{\mathbb{M}} \to A^{\mathbb{M}}$ be a CA that is not nilpotent, and let $s \in A$ be a spreading state. Then there exists $c \in A^{\mathbb{M}}$ such that $F^n(c)_j \neq s$ for all $n \in \mathbb{N}$ and $j \in \mathbb{M}$.*

Consider a one-sided reversible cellular automaton $F : A^{\mathbb{N}} \to A^{\mathbb{N}}$ such that both F and its inverse F^{-1} have radius 1. In many cases this restriction for radius is not a serious one as every reversible CA is conjugate (though maybe not *strongly* conjugate) to such a CA through suitable grouping of cells. It is easy to see that for every fixed $a \in A$ the map $F(\_a) : A \to A, x \mapsto F(xa)$ has to be a permutation. We will denote this permutation with ρ_a. Notice however that not every set of permutations $\{\rho_a\}_{a \in A}$ define a reversible CA. We refer the reader to [4] for a detailed combinatorial considerations of such reversible one-sided CA's. For our purposes the following simple example will be enough.

Example 1. Define a one-sided CA $F : A^{\mathbb{N}} \to A^{\mathbb{N}}$ where $A = \{0, 1, 2\}$ using the following permutations:

$$
\rho_0 = \rho_2 : \begin{matrix} 0 \mapsto 0 \\ 1 \mapsto 2 \\ 2 \mapsto 1 \end{matrix} \qquad \rho_1 : \begin{matrix} 0 \mapsto 1 \\ 1 \mapsto 2 \\ 2 \mapsto 0 \end{matrix}.
$$

This is reversible, and its inverse also has radius one. Namely the permutations $\pi_0 = \pi_1 = (0)(12), \pi_2 = (021)$ can be verified to define the inverse of F. This example was already considered in [4]. We will compute its entropy.

According to Proposition 2 the entropy is just the entropy of the subshift $\tau_1(F)$. From the local rule we see that 0 maps to 0 or 1, 1 always maps to 2, and 2 maps to 0 or 1. So $\tau_1(F) \subseteq \{0, 12\}^{\mathbb{Z}}$ (which is here considered a subshift of $\{0, 1, 2\}^{\mathbb{Z}}$). Suppose 20^n1 is a factor of some element in $\tau_1(F)$. Notice that the only word of length $n - 2$ that can appear next to 20^n1 in the space-time-diagram of F is $20^{n-2}1$ (consider this with the help of Fig. 1). Inductively this implies that if 20^n1 is a factor of some element in $\tau_1(F)$ then n is even. So we have that $\tau_1(F) \subseteq \{00, 12\}^{\mathbb{Z}}$. But for any $t \in \{00, 12\}^{\mathbb{Z}}$ we can construct a valid space-time-diagram of F that contains t as follows: Consider 00 to represent zero and 12 to represent one, and let t_1 be xor of t (turn to Fig. 2). We see that when lined up correctly, this gives a configuration that is locally compatible with t, i.e., that they could be successive columns of a space-time-diagram of F. This process can be repeated to obtain a valid space-time-diagram of F.

We have seen that $\tau_1(F) = \{00, 12\}^{\mathbb{Z}}$, and so $h(F) = \frac{1}{2}$. Using the direct product construction we can obtain a one-sided reversible CA that has radius one, and whose inverse also has radius one, and that has arbitrarily high entropy.

For an overview of the topics considered here, we refer the reader to [11] (a survey of cellular automata theory), and [14] (a book on topological and symbolic dynamics).

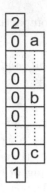

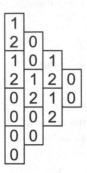

Fig. 1. First notice that c has to be 1, since only ρ_1 maps 0 to 1. The same way a has to be 2, since only π_2 maps 0 to 2. Finally b has to be 0, since b has to satisfy $\rho_b(0) = 0$ and $\pi_b(0) = 0$.

Fig. 2. Fill the leftmost column in an arbitrary way using the blocks 00 and 12. Fill the next column by taking xor (addition modulo 2) interpreting 00 as 0 and 12 as 1. Notice that we get no violations of the local rule of F doing this. Repeat.

3   Main Result

Our proof is based on the undecidability of nilpotency of one-dimensional cellular automata.

Theorem 1 [9,16]. *Nilpotency of one-dimensional one-sided cellular automata with a spreading state and radius 1 is undecidable.*

Now we can prove the main result of this paper.

Theorem 2. *The following two sets of pairs of one-dimensional one-sided cellular automata are recursively inseparable:*

(i) pairs where the first cellular automaton has strictly higher entropy than the second one, and

(ii) pairs that are strongly conjugate and both have zero topological entropy.

Proof. We will reduce the decision problem of Theorem 1 to this problem, which will prove our claim.

Let $H : B^{\mathbb{N}} \rightarrow B^{\mathbb{N}}$ be an arbitrary given one-sided CA with neighborhood radius 1 and a spreading quiescent state $q \in B$. Let $k \in \mathbb{N}$ be such that $k > \log_2(|B|)$, F_{2k} be the $2k$-fold cartesian product of the cellular automaton F of Example 1, and $A = \{0, 1, 2\}^{2k}$ (we are aiming for high enough entropy). Now we are ready to define CA's $\mathcal{F}$ and $\mathcal{G}$ such that

$$H \text{ is not nilpotent} \implies h(\mathcal{F}) > h(\mathcal{G})$$
$$H \text{ is nilpotent} \implies \mathcal{F} \cong_s \mathcal{G} \text{ and } h(\mathcal{F}) = h(\mathcal{G}) = 0.$$

Both of these new CA's work on two tracks $\mathcal{F}, \mathcal{G} : (A \times B)^{\mathbb{N}} \to (A \times B)^{\mathbb{N}}$. The CA $\mathcal{G}$ is simply $\text{id}_A \times H$, i.e.,

$$\mathcal{G}((a_0, b_0)(a_1, b_1)) = (a_0, H(b_0 b_1)),$$

for all $a_0, a_1 \in A$, $b_0, b_1 \in B$. The CA $\mathcal{F}$ acts on the A-track as F_{2n} when the B-track is not going to become q, and as id_A when the B-track is going to become q, i.e.,

$$\mathcal{F}((a_0, b_0)(a_1, b_1)) = \begin{cases} (F_{2n}(a_0 a_1), H(b_0 b_1)), & \text{if } H(b_0 b_1) \neq q \\ (a_0, H(b_0 b_1)), & \text{if } H(b_0 b_1) = q, \end{cases}$$

for all $a_0, a_1 \in A$, $b_0, b_1 \in B$.

(i) Suppose that H is not nilpotent. The entropy of $\mathcal{G}$ is

$$h\big((A \times B)^{\mathbb{N}}, \mathcal{G}\big) = h\left(A^{\mathbb{N}}, \text{id}_A\right) + h\left(B^{\mathbb{N}}, H\right) = h\left(B^{\mathbb{N}}, H\right),$$

since $\mathcal{G} = \text{id}_A \times H$. On the other hand, by Proposition 4, there exists a configuration $e \in B^{\mathbb{Z}}$ such that for all $i, j \in \mathbb{N}$ we have that $H^i(c)_j \neq q$. But then we have that

$$h\big((A \times B)^{\mathbb{N}}, \mathcal{F}\big) \geq h\left(A^{\mathbb{N}}, F_{2k}\right) > \log_2(|B|) \geq h(B^{\mathbb{N}}, H),$$

according to Example 1 and how we chose k. Overall we have that

$$h\big((A \times B)^{\mathbb{N}}, \mathcal{F}\big) > h\big((A \times B)^{\mathbb{N}}, \mathcal{G}\big),$$

as was claimed.

(ii) Suppose that H is nilpotent. Let us first explain informally why we now have that $\mathcal{F} \cong_s \mathcal{G}$. Both $\mathcal{F}$ and $\mathcal{G}$ behave identically on the B-track, so the conjugacy will map this layer simply by identity. Nilpotency of H guarantees that for all configurations the B-track will be $^\omega q^\omega$ after some constant time n. By the definition of $\mathcal{F}$ this means that after n steps $\mathcal{F}$ does nothing on the A-track. Since $\mathcal{G}$ never does anything on the A-track, we can use this fact to define the conjugacy on the A-track simply with $\mathcal{F}^n$. That this is in fact a conjugacy follows since $\mathcal{F}$ is, informally, reversible on the A-layer for a fixed B-layer.

Let us be exact. First we will define a continuous map $\phi : (A \times B)^{\mathbb{N}} \to (A \times B)^{\mathbb{N}}$ such that $\phi \mathcal{F} = \mathcal{G} \phi$. This ϕ will be a CA. Then we show that ϕ is injective, which implies reversibility (see, e.g., [11]), and so $\mathcal{F} \cong_s \mathcal{G}$.

Let $\pi_A : A^{\mathbb{N}} \times B^{\mathbb{N}} \to A^{\mathbb{N}}$ be the projection $\pi_A(c, e) = c$ for all $c \in A^{\mathbb{N}}$ and $e \in B^{\mathbb{N}}$. Define $\pi_B : A^{\mathbb{N}} \times B^{\mathbb{N}} \to B^{\mathbb{N}}$ similarly.

Let $n \in \mathbb{N}$ be a number such that for all $c \in B^{\mathbb{N}}$ we have $H^n(c) = {}^\omega q^\omega$. Such n exists according to Proposition 3, since H is nilpotent. Because $\mathcal{F}$ and $\mathcal{G}$ act identically on the B-track, ϕ will map this layer simply by identity, i.e.,

$$\pi_B \phi(c, e) = e,$$

for all $c \in A^{\mathbb{N}}, e \in B^{\mathbb{N}}$. On the A-layer ϕ is defined using the fact that after n steps $\mathcal{F}$ does nothing on the A-track, i.e., acts the same way $\mathcal{G}$ does. Due to this we define

$$\pi_A \phi = \pi_A \mathcal{F}^n.$$

Now ϕ is a CA, since it is continuous and shift-commuting. Let us show that ϕ is a homomorphism. Of course we have that

$$\phi \mathcal{F} = \mathcal{G} \phi \iff (\pi_A \phi \mathcal{F} = \pi_A \mathcal{G} \phi \text{ and } \pi_B \phi \mathcal{F} = \pi_B \mathcal{G} \phi).$$

It is immediate from the definitions that $\pi_B \phi \mathcal{F} = \pi_B \mathcal{G} \phi$. For the equality on the A-layer notice first that $\pi_A \mathcal{G} = \pi_A$, and then compute:

$$
\begin{aligned}
\pi_A \phi \mathcal{F} &\overset{\text{def.}}{=} (\pi_A \mathcal{F}^n) \mathcal{F} \\
&= \pi_A \mathcal{F} \mathcal{F}^n && \| \text{ after } n \text{ steps } \mathcal{F} \\
&= \pi_A \mathcal{G} \mathcal{F}^n && \text{behaves as } \mathcal{G} \\
&= \pi_A \mathcal{F}^n \\
&\overset{\text{def.}}{=} \pi_A \phi \\
&= \pi_A \mathcal{G} \phi.
\end{aligned}
$$

So we have that $\phi \mathcal{F} = \mathcal{G} \phi$.

To prove that ϕ is a strong *conjugacy* it is enough to show that ϕ is an injection. As the B-layer is mapped by identity, we only need to show that for a fixed $e \in B^{\mathbb{N}}$ we have that for all $c \in A^{\mathbb{N}}$ there exists a unique $c' \in A^{\mathbb{N}}$ such that $\phi(c', e) = (c, e)$. By the definition of ϕ it is clear that this will hold if

$$\pi_A \mathcal{F}^n(\_, e) : A^{\mathbb{N}} \longrightarrow A^{\mathbb{N}}$$

$$c \longmapsto \pi_A \mathcal{F}^n(c, e)$$

is a bijection for every $e \in B^{\mathbb{N}}$. We can consider this step by step. We claim that $(c, e) = (c_0 c_1 c_2 \ldots, e_0 e_1 e_2 \ldots) \in (A \times B)^{\mathbb{N}}$ uniquely defines the A-track of the elements in the set $\mathcal{F}^{-1}(c, e)$. Let $(c', e') = (c'_0 c'_1 c'_2 \ldots, e'_0 e'_1 e'_2 \ldots) \in \mathcal{F}^{-1}(c, e)$. It is enough to show that c'_0 is defined uniquely by (c, e). Suppose first that $e_0 = q$. Then according to the definition $\mathcal{F}$ acted as identity, so we have that $c'_0 = c_0$. Suppose next that $e_0 \neq q$. We have two cases, either $e_1 = q$ or not. Suppose first that $e_1 = q$. Then as before we have that $c'_1 = c_1$. And so $c'_0 = \rho_{c'_1}^{-1}(c_0) = \rho_{c_1}^{-1}(c_0)$. And lastly suppose that $e_1 \neq q$. Then we have that $F_{2n}(c'_0 c'_1 c'_2 \ldots) = (c_0 c_1 \ldots)$ according to the definition of $\mathcal{F}$. But now c'_0 is uniquely determined since F_{2n} is reversible and the inverse also has radius 1: We have that $c'_0 = F_{2n}^{-1}(c_0 c_1)$.

To complete the proof we observe that

$$h(\mathcal{F}) = h(\mathcal{G}) = h(\text{id}_A) + h(H) = 0,$$

since $\mathcal{F} \cong_s \mathcal{G} = \text{id}_A \times H$, and H is nilpotent. $\square$

Since the two-sided variant of Theorem 2 can be reduced to the one-sided case, also the two-sided variant is undecidable. We also get the following corollary.

Corollary 1. *Let* $\mathbb{M} = \mathbb{N}$ *or* $\mathbb{M} = \mathbb{Z}$. *Let* $F, G : A^{\mathbb{M}} \to A^{\mathbb{M}}$ *be two cellular automata. Then the following hold:*

1. *It is undecidable whether* F *and* G *are (strongly) conjugate.*
2. *It is undecidable whether* F *is a (strong) factor of* G.
3. *It is undecidable whether* F *is a (strong) subsystem of* G.

Proof.   *1.* The pairs in the set *(i)* of Theorem 2 can not be (strongly) conjugate, and the pairs in *(ii)* have to be. Thus deciding (strong) conjugacy would separate these sets.

2. The first CA in the pair from the set *(i)* has strictly higher entropy than the second one, and so it can not be a (strong) factor of the other. On the other hand CA's of pairs from the set *(ii)* are (strong) factors of each other. So checking for both CA's of a pair whether it is a (strong) factor of the other one would separate the sets of Theorem 2.

3. In a similar way, since a subsystem can not have higher entropy.   □

4   Other Results

4.1   Decidable Cases

Now that we know conjugacy to be undecidable for one-dimensional cellular automata, we can consider what happens if we restrict to some natural subclass. Recently it was proved that

Theorem 3 [7, Corollary 5.17]. *Conjugacy of periodic cellular automata on one- or two-sided subshifts of finite type is decidable.*

Periodic cellular automata are the least sensitive to changes in the initial configuration. Next we consider the most sensitive cellular automata, i.e., positively expansive ones. A dynamical system (X, f) is called *positively expansive* if

$$\exists \varepsilon > 0 : \forall x, y \in X : \exists n \in \mathbb{N} : x \neq y \implies d(f^n(x), f^n(y)) > \varepsilon.$$

Positively expansive CA's are quite extensively studied which allows us to deduce the following result.

Proposition 5. *Conjugacy of positively expansive cellular automata on one- or two-sided full shifts is decidable.*

Proof. Let $F : A^{\mathbb{M}} \to A^{\mathbb{M}}$ and $G : B^{\mathbb{M}} \to B^{\mathbb{M}}$ be two positively expansive cellular automata. Due to the positive expansivity, F and G are conjugate to $\tau_k(F)$ and $\tau_k(G)$ (resp.) for large enough k. These subshifts are conjugate to subshifts of finite type ([2] for one-sided case, [17] for two-sided case). According to [5, Theorem 36] we can effectively compute these subshifts. The claim follows, as the conjugacy of one-sided subshifts of finite type is decidable [18].   □

Naturally these results raise the question whether strong conjugacy is decidable when restricted to periodic or positively expansive cellular automata. Also the questions whether (strong) conjugacy is decidable for eventually periodic, i.e., equicontinuous, cellular automata [7, Question 8.1], or for expansive cellular automata remain unanswered. It is conjectured that expansive cellular automata are conjugate to two-sided subshifts of finite type (this is known for expansive two-sided cellular automata with one-sided neighborhoods). However the previous proof still wouldn't work, as it is not known whether conjugacy of two-sided subshifts of finite type is decidable.

4.2   Conjugacy of Subshifts

Questions about conjugacy provide perhaps the most well-known open problems in symbolic dynamics. For example it is unknown whether conjugacy of two-sided subshifts of finite type is decidable. It is also unknown whether conjugacy of one- or two-sided sofic shifts is decidable. On the other hand conjugacy of one-sided subshifts of finite type is known to be decidable; we used this fact to show that conjugacy of positively expansive cellular automata is decidable. We can ask if we could work to the opposite direction, i.e., if the classical problems for subshifts could be answered using cellular automata. For example, undecidability of conjugacy for one-sided expansive cellular automata would imply undecidability of conjugacy of two-sided subshifts of finite type, although it seems more likely that conjugacy for one-sided expansive cellular automata is decidable. A more plausible result would be that conjugacy is undecidable for expansive two-sided cellular automata, which together with the conjecture that every expansive cellular automaton is conjugated to a two-sided SFT [15, Conjecture 30], would imply undecidability of conjugacy of two-sided SFT's.

All of the above relied on the connection between cellular automaton and its trace subshift. The problem with this approach is that only expansive cellular automata are conjugate to subshifts. However there could be some more inventive ways to link subshifts and cellular automata to obtain decidability results. We provide the following, somewhat artificial, result.

Proposition 6. *Let $X, Y \subseteq (A \times A)^{\mathrm{M}}$ be two subshifts of finite type. It is undecidable whether X and Y are conjugate via a conjugacy of the form $\phi \times \phi$.*

Proof. The proof is a direct reduction from strong conjugacy of cellular automata. Let $F, G : A^{\mathrm{M}} \to A^{\mathrm{M}}$ be two CA's. Let $X = \{(c, F(c)) \mid c \in A^{\mathrm{M}}\}$ and $Y = \{(c, G(c)) \mid c \in A^{\mathrm{M}}\}$. These subshifts are naturally conjugate to A^{M}. Suppose there exists a conjugacy $\phi \times \phi : X \to Y$. Then ϕ commutes with the shift and for every $c \in A^{\mathrm{M}}$ we have that $(\phi(c), \phi F(c)) = (e, G(e))$, where e has to be $\phi(c)$, and so $\phi F(c) = G\phi(c)$ for all $c \in A^{\mathrm{M}}$. In other words ϕ is a strong conjugacy of (A^{M}, F) and (A^{M}, G).

On the other hand, any strong conjugacy ϕ from (A^{M}, F) to (A^{M}, G) immediately gives a conjugacy $\phi \times \phi$ between X and Y.   □

5   Conclusion

We have proved that the decision problems "are (strongly) conjugate", "is a (strong) subsystem of" and "is a (strong) factor of" are undecidable for one-dimensional one- and two-sided cellular automata. We note that these results provide an example that contradicts the rule of thumb that one time step properties of one-dimensional cellular automata are decidable.

A natural question to ask is whether conjugacy remains undecidable even for reversible cellular automata. Since our proof is based on the undecidability of nilpotency, it is clear that a different approach is needed. We note that though for non-reversible cellular automata one- and two-sided cases differ only little, for reversible cellular automata the one-sided case seems far more distant as there are no known undecidability results for one-sided cellular automata that could be used for the reduction. For two-sided cellular automata periodicity and mortality problems [12,13] are known to be undecidable, and provide a possible replacement for the nilpotency problem in the reversible case. This is of course implicitly assuming that one is expecting the problem to remain undecidable. As a first step one could consider whether topological entropy is computable for one- and two-sided reversible cellular automata.

Lastly it is interesting to consider whether there is way to solve or at least shed new light on the long-standing open problems of symbolic dynamics, namely conjugacy problems of subshifts.

References

1. Amoroso, S., Patt, Y.: Decision procedures for surjectivity and injectivity of parallel maps for tessellation structures. J. Comput. Syst. Sci. **6**, 448–464 (1972)
2. Boyle, M., Kitchens, B.: Periodic points for onto cellular automata. Indag. Math. **10**(4), 483–493 (1999)
3. Culik II, K., Pachl, J., Yu, S.: On the limit sets of cellular automata. SIAM J. Comput. **18**(4), 831–842 (1989)
4. Dartnell, P., Maass, A., Schwartz, F.: Combinatorial constructions associated to the dynamics of one-sided cellular automata. Theoret. Comput. Sci. **304**, 485–497 (2003)
5. Di Lena, P.: Decidable and computational properties of cellular automata. Department of Computer Science, University of Bologna, Ph.D. thesis (2007)
6. Epperlein, J.: Classification of elementary cellular automata up to topological conjugacy. In: Kari, J. (ed.) AUTOMATA 2015. LNCS, vol. 9099, pp. 99–112. Springer, Heidelberg (2015). https://doi.org/10.1007/978-3-662-47221-7_8
7. Epperlein, J.: Topological conjugacies between cellular automata. Fakultät Mathematik und Naturwissenschaften der Technischen Universität Dresden, Ph.D. thesis (2017)
8. Hurd, L.P., Kari, J., Culik, K.: The topological entropy of cellular automata is uncomputable. Ergod. Theory Dyn. Syst. **12**, 255–265 (1992)
9. Kari, J.: The nilpotency problem of one-dimensional cellular automata. SIAM J. Comput. **21**, 571–586 (1992)
10. Kari, J.: Reversibility and surjectivity problems of cellular automata. J. Comput. Syst. Sci. **48**, 149–182 (1994)

11. Kari, J.: Theory of cellular automata: a survey. Theoret. Comput. Sci. **334**, 3–33 (2005)
12. Kari, J., Lukkarila, V.: Some undecidable dynamical properties for one-dimensional reversible cellular automata. In: Condon, A., Harel, D., Kok, J., Salomaa, A., Winfree, E. (eds.) Algorithmic Bioprocesses. NCS, pp. 639–660. Springer, Heidelberg (2009). https://doi.org/10.1007/978-3-540-88869-7_32
13. Kari, J., Ollinger, N.: Periodicity and immortality in reversible computing. In: Ochmański, E., Tyszkiewicz, J. (eds.) MFCS 2008. LNCS, vol. 5162, pp. 419–430. Springer, Heidelberg (2008). https://doi.org/10.1007/978-3-540-85238-4_34
14. Kůrka, P.: Topological and Symbolic Dynamics, vol. 11. Société Mathématique de France (2003)
15. Kůrka, P.: Topological dynamics of cellular automata. In: Meyers, R.A. (ed.) Encyclopedia of Complexity and System Sciences, pp. 9246–9268. Springer, Heidelberg (2009). https://doi.org/10.1007/978-0-387-30440-3_556. Print ISBN 978-0-387-75888-6
16. Aanderaa, S., Lewis, H.: Linear sampling and the $\forall\exists\forall$ case of the decision problem. J. Symb. Logic **39**(3), 519–548 (1974)
17. Nasu, M.: Textile systems for Endomorphisms and Automorphisms of the Shift, vol. 546. Memoirs of the American Mathematical Society (1995)
18. Williams, R.F.: Classification of subshifts of finite type. Ann. Math. **98**, 120–153 (1973)

Software Quality Assurance and Transformation

Formal Verification and Safety Assessment of a Hemodialysis Machine

Shahid Khan[1](✉), Osman Hasan[1], and Atif Mashkoor[2]

[1] School of Electrical Engineering and Computer Science (SEECS),
National University of Sciences and Technology (NUST), Islamabad, Pakistan
{shahid.khan1,osman.hasan}@seecs.nust.edu.pk
[2] Software Competence Center Hagenberg GmbH, Hagenberg, Austria
atif.mashkoor@scch.at

Abstract. Given the safety-critical nature of healthcare systems, their rigorous safety assessment, in terms of studying their behavior in the presence of potential faults and how the malfunctioning components cause system failures, is of paramount importance. Traditionally, the safety assessment of a system is done analytically or using simulation based tools. However, the former is prone to human error and the later does not provide a complete analysis, which makes them inappropriate for the safety assessment of healthcare systems. These limitations can be overcome by using formal methods based safety assessment. This paper presents our experience of applying model based safety assessment and system verification tools on a hemodialysis machine. In particular, we use the nuXmv model checker to formally verify a formal model of the given hemodialysis machine. The formal model of the given system is then extended with various fault modes of the system components and the eXtended Safety Assessment Platform is used to check various undesired behaviors of the system using invariant properties defined as Top Level Events. This way, we can automatically generate the FTA and FMEA to do the safety assessment of the given hemodialysis machine.

1 Introduction

Modern healthcare systems are increasingly incorporating computing and communication technologies to provide a safe and reliable experience to the patients in the most effective manner. Given the integration of many technologies and the safety-critical nature of healthcare systems, where a system failure may even result in the loss of human lives, the healthcare system manufacturers and regulatory bodies are obliged to rigorously analyze and control the production and usage of such machines. On the contrary, due to the complex nature of present-age healthcare systems and stringent constraints on their time-to-market, both

The research presented in this paper is partially supported by the Austrian Ministry for Transport, Innovation and Technology, the Federal Ministry of Science, Research and Economy, and the Province of Upper Austria in the frame of the COMET center SCCH.

© Springer International Publishing AG 2018
A M. Tjoa et al. (Eds.): SOFSEM 2018, LNCS 10706, pp. 241–254, 2018.
https://doi.org/10.1007/978-3-319-73117-9_17

healthcare system manufacturers and regulatory bodies have very limited time and resources to perform a thorough safety analysis [22]. For instance, the Food and Drug Administration (FDA) of the USA has to substantively interact with its clients within 90 calender days of the filing date, which is clearly insufficient to perform a detailed analysis of each incoming equipment. The situation is further complicated as the details about the product, submitted for review, typically consist of several hundred pages [17].

Safety assessment of systems mainly involves a set of methods, such as Failure Mode and Effect Analysis (FMEA) [21] and Fault Tree Analysis (FTA) [5], to study the way the faults are dealt-with by the system. FTA is a widely used top down technique, which provides a graphical model for analyzing the conditions and factors causing an undesired Top Level Event (TLE), i.e., a critical event, which can cause the complete system failure upon its occurrence. FMEA, on the other hand, provides a bottom up approach in which atomic low level events are tabulated to check the way they lead to an undesired event.

Traditionally, both FTA and FMEA are done using human interventions. A safety assessment expert along with domain experts enlist the possible failure events and from these events FTA and FMEA are generated and analyzed using paper-and-pencil based analytical techniques. However, the complex nature of the present-age healthcare systems makes their analysis on paper almost impossible. Moreover, such manual analysis is quite prone to human error as well. Alternatively, the failure assessment of complex systems is conducted using simulation tools, such as ReliaSoft[1]. However, the results obtained through these simulation based tools cannot be fully trusted as well due to the involvement of numerical methods and the sampling based nature of simulation, where the given system is not exhaustively tested for all possible scenarios. This inaccuracy limitation makes the simulation based FTA or FMEA infeasible for the safety-critical healthcare systems, where an undetected system fault may lead to the loss of human life in the worst-case scenario.

Formal methods [15], which are computer based mathematical reasoning techniques, have been successfully used to overcome the above-mentioned limitations of the paper-and-pencil proof methods and simulation. The main idea behind the formal analysis of any given system is to first construct a mathematical model of the given system using a state-machine or an appropriate logic and then use logical reasoning and deduction methods to formally verify that this system exhibits the desired characteristics, which are also specified mathematically using an appropriate logic. Formal methods are mainly categorized into two mainstream techniques: (1) Model checking [3] that is a state-based technique in which system behavior, specified as a state-machine, is analyzed by verifying the temporal properties exhaustively over the entire state-space of the formal model of the given system within a computer, and (2) theorem proving [15] that allows using logical reasoning to verify relationships between a system and its properties as theorems, specified in an appropriate logic, using a computer.

---

[1] ReliaSoft: http://www.reliasoft.com/.

Both model checking and theorem proving have been used for the FT-based failure analysis of many real-world systems such as wheel brake system [10] and satellite solar arrays [1]. To the best of our knowledge, formal safety assessment of healthcare systems has not been reported in the literature so far. We believe that using formal methods for the safety assessment of healthcare systems would not only ensure more accurate results, compared to the traditional simulation and analytical based analysis techniques, but would also allow the manufacturers and regulators to manage the safety assessment of healthcare systems within their resources and time constraints. As a first step towards this direction, we investigate the formal safety assessment of a hemodialysis machine [19], which is used to remove metabolic waste from the blood in case of a kidney failure, making it a very safety-critical machine. The hemodialysis machine is a classical example of cyber-physical system and has been identified as a potential candidate of formal safety analysis of a S# based analysis framework [14]. Another main motivation of choosing a hemodialysis machine as our application is the availability of its detailed description along with the required functional requirements [19] as a case study to promote the usage of formal methods in medical cyber-physical systems. All of the reported work, in response to this case study, focused on the formal specification and/or functional verification of this machine using various formal methods, like Event-B [16,18], Hybrid Event B [4], Algebraic State Transition Diagrams (ASTD) [12] and Abstract State Machines (ASMs) [2]. Thus, in this paper, we extend these recently reported efforts by presenting the formal safety assessment of this hemodialysis machine.

In particular, we chose to build upon the classical ASM based analysis of the hemodialysis machine [2], in which the ASM model of the hemodialysis machine was automatically translated to the corresponding Symbolic Model Verifier (SMV) model for its functional verification by the nuXmv model checker. In this work, we enhance their SMV model with various failure modes for the safety assessment of the given system using the eXtended Safety Assessment Platform (xSAP) tool [9]. The main motivation behind choosing xSAP and the nuXmv model checker for the proposed safety assessment is the ability to conduct a comprehensive analysis using both FTA and FMEA methods since, to the best of our knowledge, the theorem proving based safety analysis does not support FMEA as of now. Moreover, a distinguishing feature of our work is that a formally verified model of the hemodialysis machine is used to integrate the failure modes and analyze the safety aspects.

2 Preliminaries

2.1 Model Checking and nuXmv Model Checker

Model checking [3] is primarily used as a verification technique for reactive systems, i.e., the systems whose behavior is dependent on time and their environment. The inputs to a model checker include a finite-state model of the system that needs to be analyzed along with the intended system properties, which are expressed in *temporal* logic, which is a logic that allows expressing time-dependent behaviors. The model checker automatically and exhaustively verifies if the properties hold for the given system while providing an error trace in case of a failing property. The state-space of a system grows exponentially with the increase in the size of system variables and their possible values. Thus, it becomes computationally impossible to explore the entire state-space with limited resources of time and memory for larger models. This problem, termed as *state-space explosion* [3], is usually resolved by using efficient algorithms and techniques, like symbolic [7] and Bounded Model Checking (BMC) [8]. The main idea behind BMC is to allow the model checker to check the given property for a partial model, based on the user provided depth. The model checker detects the failing property if it fails in this reduced model. Otherwise, the depth of BMC is incrementally increased in search of a failing property.

The nuXmv model checker supports a wide range of systems, including the infinite state systems, by introducing the new data types of *integers* and *reals* and using Satisfiability Modulo Theory (SMT) [6] for verification. The system to be verified is modeled in a modular manner using the SMV language [7], which allows declaring of Variables (VAR), macros (DEFINE), environment variables interacting with system (IVAR), state transition relations (using INIT and NEXT statements) and nondeterminism. The properties [11] to be verified can be specified in nuXmv using the Linear Temporal Logic (LTL) or the Computation Tree Logic (CTL). LTL specifications are written in nuXmv with the help of logical operations like, AND (&), OR (|), Exclusive OR (xor), Exclusive NOR (xnor), Implication (→) Equality (↔), and temporal operators, like Globally (G), Finally (F), neXt (X) and Until (U). Similarly, the CTL specifications can be written by combining logical operations with quantified temporal operators, like Exists Globally (EG), Exists neXt state (EX) and for All Finally (AF). In case a property turns out to be false, a counterexample in the execution trace of the state machine is provided. Although the approaches used by nuXmv are in general incomplete, a Lasso-shaped counter example is always found if it is guaranteed to exist [11].

2.2 eXtended Safety Assessment Platform

xSAP [9] is the safety assessment tool supported by the nuXmv [11] model checker. xSAP requires three inputs, i.e., a nominal model written in the SMV language, Fault Extension Instructions (FEI) written in a dedicated FEI language and fault library to perform the safety assessment of a system. The nominal model is written in the SMV language and consists of a modular architecture of the system under investigation along with some additional variables, called affected symbols. The FEI file provides the fault definitions in a SMV understandable format. xSAP uses its built-in fault library, which is also customizable, to interpret the FEI [9]. The FEI file mainly consists of fault slices, where each fault slice targets an affected symbol of a nominal component, which is a module in nominal model. Upon execution, xSAP forces affected symbols to be stuck at some value to emulate the behavior of fault occurrence in the system. Each fault slice represents a single or a set of basic failure modes targeting single affected symbol. Upon construction of the overall system state space, these failure modes lead to more complex system failures through the mechanism of local and global dynamic models. For the safety assessment of the overall system, TLE are defined as *invariant* properties, which mainly describe the bad behavior of the system. For instance, in the context of the hemodialysis machine, if the system is in the *self test* phase then it is desirable that it eventually successfully completes the self test and goes to the next phase, i.e., *connect concentrate*. The TLE in this case would be !CN.self_test_status. Upon execution, xSAP will identify all fault slices and all basic failure modes that can lead to this undesirable behavior, and these fault slices and failure modes are then used to automatically generate the fault tree for the specific event [9]. The xSAP supports many classical tools for safety analysis, including FTA, FMEA, failure propagation analysis using Timed Failure Propagation Graphs (TFPGs), and Common Cause Analysis (CCA). One of the main strengths of this approach is that it automatically generates these artifacts from a formal model, which has been independently checked for its functional correctness using nuXmv.

3 Proposed Approach

The proposed formal analysis approach for healthcare systems, depicted in Fig. 1, is divided in two phases, i.e., Formal Functional Verification (FFV) phase and Formal Safety Assessment (FSA) phase. The phase of functional verification requires a SMV model of the given healthcare system and the associated *temporal* properties capturing the functional requirements. The nuXmv model checker exhaustively checks the model against the provided *temporal* properties and provides the counterexamples in case of failing properties. These counterexamples can then be investigated to check whether the problem is due to a modeling error or actually a functional bug in the system. The modeling issues can be rectified by iteratively refining the SMV model to remove all issues until all the properties are successfully verified. On the other hand, the system designers can be consulted in case of identifying a design bug. Thus, upon the completion of the FFV phase, we obtain a functionally verified SMV model against all its requirements. We use this model in the FSA phase to introduce the affected symbols and provide the fault extension in the .FEI file. Besides the above-mentioned inputs, we consider the involvement of domain experts in this step very important as they can provide useful insights in the modeling process and greatly facilitate the fault identification due to their past experiences in the domain. Both of these files, i.e., the .SMV file containing the nominal model and the .FEI file containing fault extension instructions, are provided to xSAP for model extension as mentioned in Sect. 2.2. The xSAP extends the provided .SMV model based on the information provided in the .FEI by invoking its fault library, and applies the fault slices written in the .FEI file on the .SMV nominal component affected symbols of the .SMV file. The next step is to provide the TLE along with this extended model to xSAP to perform the safety assessment. The xSAP automatically generates the FTA and the FMEA tables satisfying TLEs. These artifacts

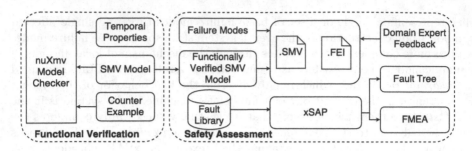

Fig. 1. Proposed Formal Safety Assessment approach

can be subsequently documented and further analyzed for the safety assessment of the given healthcare system.

4   Hemodialysis Machine

Hemodialysis machines are used to remove a controlled amount of metabolic wastes from blood in the case of kidney failures. Their correct operation is the key for the patients wellbeing and thus they can be classified as a safety-critical healthcare system. The machine's internal architecture, as depicted in Fig. 2, can be mainly divided into 8 sub-blocks. Each block further consists of various components having predefined functions. A brief description of each block and its constituent components is given below.

Low Level and High Level Controller. The controller module [19] consist of two sub-modules, i.e., high level and low level controllers. The former mainly interacts between the machine and the operator through a Graphical User Interface (GUI). Moreover, it also connects the machine with the cyberspace to facilitate remote therapy and on-line observation of therapy results. Whereas, the low level controller acts as a coordinator of tasks between the remaining modules of the machine and thus plays an important role for the successful operation of the

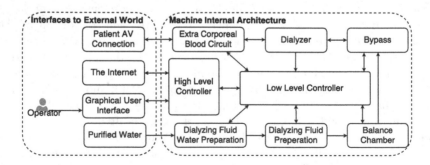

Fig. 2. Hemodialysis machine architecture

overall machine. It receives feedback from different sensors and transmits actuation signals to fulfill the requirements of the machine. For our proposed safety assessment, we have considered the low level controller only. This is because ensuring the cybersecurity is in itself a major challenge and considering it here would divert the focus of this paper to general cybersecurity issues rather than the safety assessment of healthcare systems.

Extracorporeal Blood Circuit (EBC). This module connects the patient to the machine through the Arterial and Vascular (AV) connections. It consists of 2 Venous Peristaltic Pumps (VPP), 1 Arterial Peristaltic Pump (APP), 1 Blood Pump (BP), 1 Heparin Syringe Pump (HSP), a Disposable System (DS) (connectors, drip chambers, tubing), a Safety Air Detector (SAD), 2 Pressure Transducers (1 for Venous (VPT) and other for Arterial (APT) side) and 1 Venous Valve (VV).

Dialyzer. This module mainly performs the dialysis of patient's blood. It consists of a bidirectional diffusive membrane, which filters out a predetermined amount of the metabolic wastes from the blood.

Bypass. It bypasses the dialyzing process when the temperature raises beyond a certain limit or an out-of-proportion concentration of acid and/or bicarbonate is detected in the Dialyzing Fluid (DF). The bypass module mainly consists of two Valves (V1 and V2).

Balance Chamber. The Balance Chamber (BC) keeps a balance between the incoming and outgoing DF. It consist of two chambers with a flexible membrane and two Magnetic Position Sensors (MPS1 and MPS2) to keep track of the flexible membrane position.

Dialyzer Fluid Preparation. This module is mainly responsible for mixing the prepared water with acid and bicarbonate concentrates. It consists of a Conductivity Meter (CM) and a Temperature Sensor (TC) to monitor the parameters of the prepared water.

Dialyzer Fluid Water Preparation (DFWP). The DFWP mainly degasses and heats the refined water and subsequently provides the processed water to the DF preparation module. It comprises of a Degassing Chamber (DC), a Heater (HT) and a Reverse Osmosis (RO) filter.

Failure Modes. Now, we describe the failures of the hemodialysis machine [10,13][2]. These failures are mainly associated with the modules and sub-modules

---

[2] Courtesy: Fresenius Medical Care: url: http://fmcna.com//).

described above. As explained in Sect. 3, these failure modes are first expressed in the FEI file and then integrated with the control logic of the machine to emulate run-time feedback and controlling actuation signal mechanism.

The faults occurring in the *pump* module include permanently being in the off state, not reaching the maximum speed at the maximum voltage, the pump is turning in the wrong direction, the signal of the optical tachometer is going out of range, analog voltage going out of range, rotor turning when it is not supposed to, and pump rate and its setting not being synchronized. The behavior of all pumps, including peristaltic pumps, the heparin pump and blood pump, is captured through the module named *pump*, which is instantiated six times, namely *EBC.APP1*, *EBC.APP2*, *EBC.VPP*, *EBC.HSP* and *BC.UFP* to represent 2 arterial peristaltic pumps, 1 venous peristaltic pump, 1 heparin syringe pump of EBC and 1 ultra filtration pump of the balance chamber, respectively.

The faults occurring in the *disposable tubing system* module include a leak, kinking, clotting and clamping, the fibre clotting of dialyzer, and a closed line. This module is instantiated twice, namely *EBC.DS* and *D.DS*, to represent the disposable system of *EBC* and the disposable assembly of the dialyzer, respectively.

The failure modes of the *valve* module include a failure when the valve is open, failure when it is close, failure at the last commanded position and a failure at an erroneous position. These failure modules are instantiated three times, namely *EBC.VV*, *B.V1*, *B.V2*, to represent the venous valve of the *EBC* and the valve 1 and 2 of the *bypass* module, respectively.

The failure modes of the *chamber* module captures the failing behavior of all chambers, including the balance and degassing chamber, by considering the conditions of low and high fluid levels and low and high pressures. The *chamber* module is instantiated three times, namely *EBC.VC*, *EBC.AC* and *DWP.DC*, to represent the *venous chamber* of the *EBC*, *arterial chamber* of *EBC* and *degassing chamber* of *DWP* stage, respectively.

The conductivity *Meter* module of the DF preparation stage is modeled by undetected erroneous data and no data faults. It is used once, i,e., *DFP.CM*, to represent the *conductivity meter* of DFP module.

The failure modes of sensors associated with temperature, safety air detector and magnetic position are captured by the undetected erroneous data, no data, signal ramping down and signal out of limit events. The *sensor* module is instantiated four times, namely *EBC.SAD*, *BC.MPS1*, *BC.MPS2*, *DFP.TS*, to represent the *air detector* of *EBC* and the magnetic position Sensors 1 and 2 of the balance chamber and the temperature sensor of the DF preparation modules, respectively.

The *Heater* module is required for water heating in the DF water preparation stage. Its failures are captured by the insulation break, burn out of the heating element and malfunctioning or complete failure of heater events. The heater module is instantiated once to represent the heater of dialyzing water preparation stage (*DWP.HT*).

The failure mode of the *Transducer* module is represented by the wet transducer protector (protectors are used to keep interior of pressure transducers from getting wet), obstructed monitor line, erroneous data, no data and data out of limit events. This module is instantiated twice, i.e., *EBC.APT* and *EBC.VPT*, to represent the arterial and the pressure transducers of the EBC module, respectively.

5   Formal Functional Verification and Safety Assessment

The model, described in Sect. 4, is used to conduct the formal functional verification and safety assessment of the hemodialysis machine using the approach outlined in Sect. 3. For verification purposes, we used Version 1.0.0 of nuXmv with an *Intel(R) Core(TM) i5-3320M CPU @ 2.60 GHZ, x64-based processor*. While the safety assessment is carried out using Version 1.1.0 of xSAP. All reported properties are verified using BMC with a depth of 100. However, the TLEs are exhaustively checked for developing of the fault trees and FMEA. Next, we describe four top level events for which we generated the fault trees and FMEA during the safety assessment process[3].

5.1   Self Test Pass

We first verify that there is at least one instance when the self test of the hemodialysis machine, i.e., `CN.prepPhase = SELF_TEST`, during the Preparation Phase succeeds and the system goes to the next Preparation Phase, i.e., Connecting Concentrate [19], `CN.prepPhase = CONNECT_CONCENTRATE`. The CTL property used to check this property is as follows `AG(CN.prepPhase = SELF_TEST -> EF CN.prepPhase = CONNECT_CONCENTRATE)`. It is important to note that the property is not verified for all cases since it obviously fails in the presence of machine faults. To generate the FT and FMEA for the bad conditions, i.e., when the system is stuck at self test, we introduced an undefined state, i.e., `PREP_UNDEF`. Such that, the system goes in this state whenever it is not in any known state of the Preparation Phase. The TLE is `CN.prepPhase = PREP_UNDEF`. The verification of this property allows us to automatically generate the fault tree, which is partially shown in Fig. 3a. It can be clearly seen that a fault occurrence in any component can lead to an overall system failure. The reliability of the overall system can be increased by introducing redundancy in the system components. Thus, we added another venous peristaltic pump *EBC.VPP2* in the system. This change would lead to the addition of an AND gate between both arterial peristaltic pumps, *EBC.VPP1 and EBC.VPP2 (newly introduced in system)*. Which means that, both arterial peristaltic pump 1 and arterial peristaltic pump 2 have to fail simultaneously to lead to the system level failure.

---

[3] The codes and associated properties are available at: http://save.seecs.nust.edu.pk/ projects/fvsahm/.

The effect of adding redundancy on the system reliability is further illustrated in Figs. 4a and b. In these figures, the horizontal axis represents the failure probability of individual failure events, while the vertical axis depicts the failure probability of subcomponents and the overall system. As discussed in Sect. 4, the SMV model of hemodialysis machine consists of multiple instances of 8 basic components. The failure probability of an individual event is assigned to every instance of the respective component and the collective failure behavior is computed using the corresponding fault tree. For example, there are five instances of the *pump* module, in the machine, namely, *EBC.APP1*, *EBC.VPP*, *EBC.HSP*, *BC.UFP* and *BC.BP*. Each instance can fail independently of the other and their collective failing behavior is presented in the graph. Likewise, there are 1, 3, 4, 1, 4, 1, 2 instances of *Disposable_system*, *Valve*, *Chamber*, *Meter*, *Sensor*, *Heater* and *Transducer*, respectively. The failure probability of the individual components is swept from 0 to 1 and the complete behavior of the failure of the hemodialysis system and its constituent components is captured in both figures. It is evident from the figures that the failure probability of the system with redundant components reaches 1 when failure probability of constituent basic events is below 0.1. Whereas, in the case of redundant components, the same probability is around 0.8 when the basic events failure probabilities are between 0.3 and 0.4. The decrease in slope with redundancy implies that for any given basic event failure probability, the likelihood of failure of a system with redundancy is less than the likelihood of failure of a system without redundancy. The relationship between cut-sets of FT and FMEA, as generated by xSAP, is elaborated in Fig. 3e, in the context of self test TLE. The graph is shown on a semilogarithmic scale to suppress the huge difference between FTA and FMEA cut-set values. These statistics were generated from the model having 21 basic failure events. According to the statistics displayed, there are obviously zero cut-sets with cardinality 0. While, the cut-sets with cardinality 1 for both FTA and FMEA are reported by xSAP to be 21 (note that FTA of the system without redundancy had 22 cut-sets with cardinality 1 and no cut-sets for higher cardinalities). This change (from 22 to 21) in cut sets by adding redundancy effects the system reliability as depicted in Fig. 4b. When the cardinality is increased to 2, the number of FT generated cut-sets decreases to 1, but the number of cut-sets reported by FMEA increases to 274. Upon further increasing the cardinality, we reach a stage where no cut-sets for FT were found. Whereas, for FMEA, the number of cut-sets further increases to 2045 and 10900 for cardinalities 3 and 4, respectively. During the formal safety analysis of the hemodialysis machine, it is observed that the number of cut-sets for FMEA reported by xSAP are generally greater than those of FT for the same property and cardinality. This is because the FMEA tables do not present minimal cut-sets leading to TLE, like fault trees. On the contrary, they consider all possible faults even if the faults are not contributing directly to TLE [9].

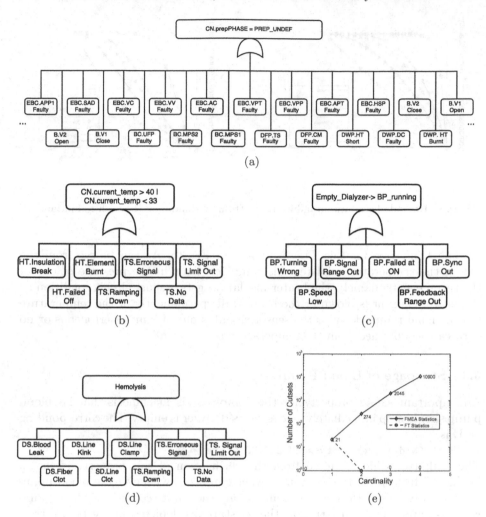

Fig. 3. Fault trees (a) self test of the hemodialysis machine (b) temperature control (c) blood pump stoppage (d) hemolysis (e) FMEA and FTA statistics

5.2   Temperature Control

We verify that *if the system is in the preparation phase and performs priming or rinsing or if the system is in the initiation phase, then the dialysate temperature shall remain between* 33 °C *and* 40 °C [20].

```
G ((CN.phase = PREPARATION & CN.tubingSystemPhase = PRIMING |
CN.prepPhase = RINSE_DIALYZER) | CN.phase = INITIATION ->
CN.current_temp > 33 & CN.current_temp < 40)
```

We transformed this property to an invariant TLE by asserting that the water temperature must always invariantly remain within 33° and 40 °C.

```
CN.current_temp > 40 | CN.current_temp < 33
```

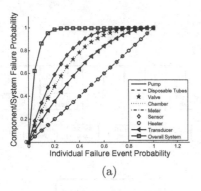 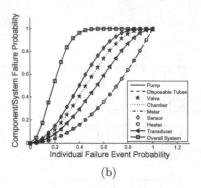

(a)   (b)

Fig. 4. Hemodialysis system failure (a) without redundancy (b) with redundancy

The Fault tree for this TLE is shown in Fig. 3b. As can be see from the figure, the temperature violates this condition limit in the presence of one of the seven events, namely, the heater insulation gets a short circuit condition or the heater element is blown or the heater fails permanently or the temperature sensor signal ramps down or the sensor signal is out of limit or erroneous or no data can be obtained from the temperature sensor at all.

5.3 Stoppage of Blood Pump

An important safety property for the hemodialysis machine is that its blood pump should stop immediately whenever its dialyzer is empty. The corresponding TLE is

`(TRUE -> CN.dialyzer_empty-> CN.EBC.BP.state = on)`

The fault tree which resulted from the verification of this property is shown in Fig. 3c. Intuitively, this undesired event can occur whenever the blood pump permanently fails at the on condition. Among the failure conditions where pump is not stopping and thus stuck at the on state, as depicted in the failure tree, are the pump turning in the wrong direction, its speed being too low but not halting, the signal of the pump being out of range, the pump explicitly failing at the on condition, the feedback signal of pump being out of range or the pump rotation being out of synchronization.

5.4 Hemolysis

The hemolysis is one of the most undesired conditions that must be averted during hemodialysis. In this condition, the red blood cells are damaged in the dialyzer. The conditions, which can cause the hemolysis are improper flow in the blood lines (due to clamping, kinking, etc.), the dialysate temperature exceeding 42 °C, low conductivity of dialysate, high arterial pressure, contaminated dialysate water (contaminations may include bleach, copper or nitrates), and a highly diluted dialysate [13]. As discussed in Sect. 4, many of these basic events leading to hemolysis are captured in the FEI semantics. We defined a property and named it hemolysis in our code and generated the corresponding fault tree, given in Fig. 3d. The failure events including kinking, clamping, fiber clotting, issues with conductivity meters, heaters, blood pressure are ORed together leading to hemolysis. In case of the emerging remote therapy scenarios, these failure events should be given extreme attention. Moreover, redundancy is strongly recommended here to prevent hemolysis.

6   Conclusion

This paper presents a formal safety assessment approach for a hemodialysis machine. The results obtained from this analysis are quite useful in assessing the safety levels of the hemodialysis machine and thus complement its previously verified functional correctness results. This work can be extended in many directions and one of the possible directions is to further refine the model of the system by adding more architectural details and more detailed failure modes for each device. Another direction is to come up with more interesting safety and security scenarios and check whether the model and thus the system design satisfies those properties or not.

References

1. Ahmed, W., Hasan, O.: Towards formal fault tree analysis using theorem proving. In: Kerber, M., Carette, J., Kaliszyk, C., Rabe, F., Sorge, V. (eds.) CICM 2015. LNCS (LNAI), vol. 9150, pp. 39–54. Springer, Cham (2015). https://doi.org/10.1007/978-3-319-20615-8_3
2. Arcaini, P., Bonfanti, S., Gargantini, A., Mashkoor, A., Riccobene, E.: Integrating formal methods into medical software development: the ASM approach. Sci. Comput. Program. (2017, in press)
3. Baier, C., Katoen, J.P., Larsen, K.G.: Principles of Model Checking. MIT Press, Cambridge (2008)
4. Banach, R.: Hemodialysis machine in hybrid Event-B. In: Butler, M., Schewe, K.-D., Mashkoor, A., Biro, M. (eds.) ABZ 2016. LNCS, vol. 9675, pp. 376–393. Springer, Cham (2016). https://doi.org/10.1007/978-3-319-33600-8_32
5. Barlow, R.E., Chatterjee, P.: Introduction to fault tree analysis. Technical report, DTIC Document (1973)
6. Barrett, C.W., Sebastiani, R., Seshia, S.A., Tinelli, C.: Satisfiability modulo theories. In: Handbook of Satisfiability, vol. 185, pp. 825–885 (2009)
7. Biere, A., Cimatti, A., Clarke, E.M., Fujita, M., Zhu, Y.: Symbolic model checking using SAT procedures instead of BDDs. In: Design Automation Conference, pp. 317–320. ACM (1999)
8. Biere, A., Cimatti, A., Clarke, E.M., Strichman, O., Zhu, Y.: Bounded model checking. Adv. Comput. 58, 117–148 (2003)
9. Bittner, B., et al.: The xSAP safety analysis platform. In: Chechik, M., Raskin, J.-F. (eds.) TACAS 2016. LNCS, vol. 9636, pp. 533–539. Springer, Heidelberg (2016). https://doi.org/10.1007/978-3-662-49674-9_31

10. Bozzano, M., Cimatti, A., Fernandes Pires, A., Jones, D., Kimberly, G., Petri, T., Robinson, R., Tonetta, S.: Formal design and safety analysis of AIR6110 wheel brake system. In: Kroening, D., Păsăreanu, C.S. (eds.) CAV 2015. LNCS, vol. 9206, pp. 518–535. Springer, Cham (2015). https://doi.org/10.1007/978-3-319-21690-4_36

11. Cavada, R., et al.: The NUXMV symbolic model checker. In: Biere, A., Bloem, R. (eds.) CAV 2014. LNCS, vol. 8559, pp. 334–342. Springer, Cham (2014). https://doi.org/10.1007/978-3-319-08867-9_22

12. Fayolle, T., Frappier, M., Gervais, F., Laleau, R.: Modelling a hemodialysis machine using algebraic state-transition diagrams and B-like methods. In: Butler, M., Schewe, K.-D., Mashkoor, A., Biro, M. (eds.) ABZ 2016. LNCS, vol. 9675, pp. 394–408. Springer, Cham (2016). https://doi.org/10.1007/978-3-319-33600-8_33

13. Fresenius Medical Care: 2008T Hemodialysis Machine, User Manual (2008)

14. Habermaier, A.: Design time and run time formal safety analysis using executable models. Ph.D. thesis, University of Augsburg (2016)

15. Hasan, O., Tahar, S.: Formal verification methods. In: Encyclopedia of Information Science and Technology, 3rd edn., pp. 7162–7170. IGI Global (2015)

16. Hoang, T.S., Snook, C., Ladenberger, L., Butler, M.: Validating the requirements and design of a hemodialysis machine using iUML-B, BMotion Studio, and co-simulation. In: Butler, M., Schewe, K.-D., Mashkoor, A., Biro, M. (eds.) ABZ 2016. LNCS, vol. 9675, pp. 360–375. Springer, Cham (2016). https://doi.org/10.1007/978-3-319-33600-8_31

17. Masci, P., Ayoub, A., Curzon, P., Lee, I., Sokolsky, O., Thimbleby, H.: Model-based development of the generic PCA infusion pump user interface prototype in PVS. In: Bitsch, F., Guiochet, J., Kaâniche, M. (eds.) SAFECOMP 2013. LNCS, vol. 8153, pp. 228–240. Springer, Heidelberg (2013). https://doi.org/10.1007/978-3-642-40793-2_21

18. Mashkoor, A.: Model-driven development of high-assurance active medical devices. Softw. Qual. J. **24**(3), 571–596 (2016)

19. Mashkoor, A.: The hemodialysis machine case study. In: Butler, M., Schewe, K.-D., Mashkoor, A., Biro, M. (eds.) ABZ 2016. LNCS, vol. 9675, pp. 329–343. Springer, Cham (2016). https://doi.org/10.1007/978-3-319-33600-8_29

20. Mashkoor, A., Sametinger, J.: Rigorous modeling and analysis of interoperable medical devices. In: Modeling and Simulation in Medicine Symposium. p. 5. Society for Computer Simulation International (2016)

21. Stamatis, D.H.: Failure Mode and Effect Analysis FMEA from Theory to Execution. ASQ Quality Press, Milwaukee (2003)

22. Zuckerman, D.M., Brown, P., Nissen, S.E.: Medical device recalls and the FDA approval process. Arch. Intern. Med. **171**(11), 1006–1011 (2011)

Automatic Decomposition of Java Open Source Pull Requests: A Replication Study

Victor da C. Luna Freire$^{(\boxtimes)}$, João Brunet, and Jorge C. A. de Figueiredo

Federal University of Campina Grande (UFCG), Campina Grande, PB, Brazil
victorfreire@copin.ufcg.edu.br

Abstract. The presence of large changesets containing several independent modifications (e.g. bug fixes, refactorings, features) can negatively affect the efficacy of code review. To cope with this problem, Barnett et al. developed ClusterChanges — a lightweight static analysis technique for decomposing changesets in different partitions that can be reviewed independently. They have found that ClusterChanges can indeed decompose such changesets and that developers agree with their decomposition. However, the authors' restricted their analysis to software that is: (i) closed source, (ii) written in C# and (iii) developed by a single organization. To address this threat to validity, we implemented JClusterChanges, a free and open source (FOSS) implementation of ClusterChanges for Java software, and replicated the original Barnett et al. study using changesets from Java open source projects hosted on GitHub. We found that open source changesets are similar to the changesets of the original study. Thus, our research confirms that the problem is relevant to other environments and provides a FOSS implementation of ClusterChanges that not only shows the feasibility of the technique in other contexts but can also be used to help future research.

Keywords: Modern code review · Changeset decomposition

1 Introduction

Developers have been increasingly applying lightweight code review processes known as "modern code review" (MCR) [1] because of the drawbacks of formal inspections [2–4]. MCR usually consists of reviewing changesets in a distributed and asynchronous manner with the assistance of specialized tools [5–7].

MCR is not trivial to perform though. In particular, understanding the code under review is one of the main challenges faced by developers [1]. The more independent modifications contained in a changeset, the harder it is to understand what has been changed and, consequently, review it [8]. This type of changeset has been called tangled changes [9] and composite changes [8] in previous research. In this paper, we refer to them as composite changesets.

Composite changesets are a significant problem. Researchers have estimated that as many as 17% of the changesets from open source software (OSS) are composite [9,10]. Furthermore, previous research indicates that developers would like

© Springer International Publishing AG 2018
A M. Tjoa et al. (Eds.): SOFSEM 2018, LNCS 10706, pp. 255–268, 2018.
https://doi.org/10.1007/978-3-319-73117-9_18

an automatic partitioning tool not only to help them understand the composite changesets under review [8,11,12] but also to improve the accuracy of software repository mining programs [9].

With this problem in mind, Barnett et al. [11] developed ClusterChanges – a lightweight static analysis technique for automatically partitioning changesets. Their evaluation of the technique had promising results. As a remarkable result, they found that, although ClusterChanges failed to detect some relationships between changes, it never marked two unrelated changes as being related, i.e. there were no false-positives. Furthermore, most of the software developers they interviewed agreed with the decomposition generated by ClusterChanges and all of them believe that the tool could be useful for understanding composite changesets [11].

Notwithstanding the excellent results, Barnett et al. [11] pointed out that their study suffers from the following threats to external validity: (1) the change-set sample only contains C# code and (2) the changesets are from a single organization. In addition, we also believe that a possible threat to external validity is that the analysis was restricted to closed source code, since OSS development practices tend to be significantly different [13,14].

Considering the aforementioned threats to validity, we replicated the quantitative substudy of the original study from Barnett et al. [11] using changesets from OSS projects written in Java by several organizations. More specifically, we (1) created JClusterChanges — a free and open source (FOSS) implementation of ClusterChanges for Java code changesets and (2) applied JClusterChanges to a sample of 1000 pull requests from the 10 most popular Java OSS projects hosted on GitHub. We had to create JClusterChanges to carry out the replication because the original implementation of ClusterChanges for C# software is not publicly available.

Our replication consisted of following the original study as close as possible except that we deliberately changed the context to better understand how widely applicable the results were, i.e., to address the threats to external validity. Replication is an important mechanism for assuring the reliability of scientific knowledge, due to the fact that designing and executing experiments is a complex and error-prone activity [15]. By means of this work, we increase the body of knowledge in Software Engineering and provide stronger evidence for previous work.

We obtained similar results to the original study. Although small and independent changesets are demanded in OSS projects [14], we observed that OSS changesets are often composite like the closed source changesets from Microsoft analyzed in the original study. Therefore, we found evidence that ClusterChanges is also valuable for OSS developers.

The main contributions of this work are:

- Evidence that the problem also exists in OSS projects, i.e. composite change-sets are common in OSS projects;
- Evidence that ClusterChanges is effective in other contexts;

- JClusterChanges: a FOSS implementation of ClusterChanges for changesets written in Java (publicly available with a live demo at: https://sites.google. com/site/jclusterchanges/)

2   Motivating Example

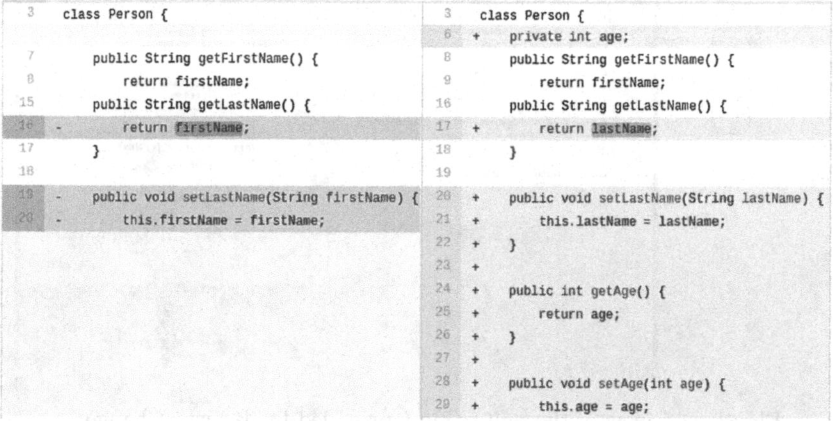

```
 3    class Person {                              3    class Person {
                                                  6  +     private int age;
 7        public String getFirstName() {          8        public String getFirstName() {
 8            return firstName;                    9            return firstName;
15        public String getLastName() {           16        public String getLastName() {
16  -         return firstName;                   17  +         return lastName;
17        }                                       18        }
18                                                19
19  -     public void setLastName(String firstName) {  20  +     public void setLastName(String lastName) {
20  -         this.firstName = firstName;         21  +         this.lastName = lastName;
                                                  22  +     }
                                                  23  +
                                                  24  +     public int getAge() {
                                                  25  +         return age;
                                                  26  +     }
                                                  27  +
                                                  28  +     public void setAge(int age) {
                                                  29  +         this.age = age;
```

Fig. 1. Shortened diff view of the pull request in GitHub [6].

Consider a pull request where a developer performed two independents tasks in a class called *Person* (Fig. 1). A pull request is equivalent to a changeset in the context of OSS development, i.e., it is a set of changes that should be reviewed by someone other than its author and merged into the main repository if it is deemed to be acceptable. One of the tasks in this pull request was to fix a bug where methods that should alter the *lastName* field were instead changing the *firstName* field (lines 17, 20–22). The other task was to store the age of a person (lines 6, 24–29).

Figure 1 shows how a developer assigned to review (the reviewer) such a pull request would typically view it. With typical code review tools, the reviewer has to understand on his own which changes are related to each other.

The ClusterChanges algorithm [11] identifies which diff-regions are related by analyzing the data dependencies between them. A diff-region is a contiguous set of source code lines that have been added or changed and it contains at most one class or method.

In our example, there are five diff-regions. Running JClusterChanges on this pull request yields two partitions, one containing diff-regions [6, 6], [24, 27], [28, 29] and the other containing diff-regions [17, 17] and [20, 23]. In particular, diff-regions [6, 6] and [24, 27] are marked as related by JClusterChanges because the former contains the definition of the variable *age* and the latter contains an use of that variable (def-use relationship).

Figure 2 shows how the JClusterChanges web application would display this pull request to the reviewer. When the reviewer selects a partition, the corresponding diff-regions are highlighted. Consequently, the user can review each partition independently without being confused by unrelated changes.

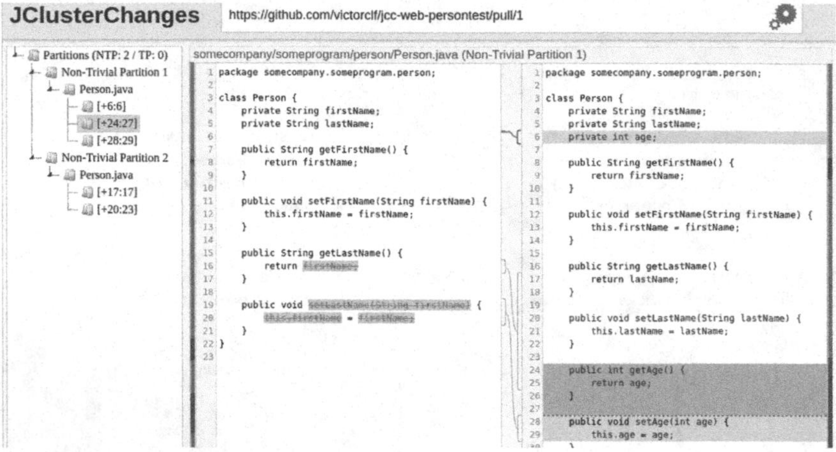

Fig. 2. Diff view of the pull request provided by JClusterChanges.

3   ClusterChanges

Given a changeset containing multiple diff-regions, ClusterChanges [11] aims to find a partitioning where each disjoint subset of the diff-regions can be reviewed independently from the others.

There are four basic definitions for understanding the technique:

Changeset. A changeset is a set of pair of files where each pair contains the original version of the file (before-file) and the modified version of the file (after-file). For the purposes of ClusterChanges, a pull request is equivalent to a changeset.

Diff-region. A diff-region is a contiguous set of source code lines that have been added or changed. Diff-regions are split at type and method boundaries.

Definition. A definition is a group of statements that introduces an entity into a program along with an identifier for referring to it. Such entities can be methods, fields and types for instance.

Use. A use is a reference to a definition by its identifier.

In order to determine which diff-regions are related, ClusterChanges searches for three possible relationships:

Def-use. If a diff-region f_1 has a definition d and a diff-region f_2 has a use u whose associated definition is d, then we say that there is a def-use relationship between diff-regions f_1 and f_2.

Use-use. Given a definition d that is present in the changeset but is not inside any diff-region, if a diff-region f_1 has a use u_1 whose associated definition is d and a diff-region f_2 has a use u_2 whose associated definition is also d, then we say that there is a use-use relationship between diff-regions f_1 and f_2.

Same enclosing method. ClusterChanges also considers diff-regions to be related if they are in the same method.

After identifying the relationships between the diff-regions, the changeset can be decomposed using graph theory and the resulting partitions are classified as either trivial or non-trivial. Trivial partitions are those that contain only diff-regions that belong to the same method or that contain a single diff-region. Non-trivial partitions are those which are not trivial partitions, i.e. they have multiple diff-regions that are not all enclosed by the same method.

3.1   Evaluation by Barnett et al.

First, the authors of the original study quantitatively evaluated ClusterChanges [11] by running their implementation on a random sample of 1000 changesets from the Microsoft Office project. Assuming that ClusterChanges correctly identifies non-trivial partitions (no false-positives), their results show that as much as 42% of the changesets can be decomposed.

Then, Barnett et al. divided the changesets into four groups based on their number of partitions and performed different analyses for each group:

- ≤ 1 **non-trivial partition:** Barnett et al. analyzed 50 of these changesets to determine if the partitioning was not obviously wrong by looking at the commit messages and the code changes. Although, 6 of those changesets had commit messages that suggested more than one task, they were all reasonably partitioned. Moreover, the authors found no false-positives.
- $[2, 5]$ **non-trivial partitions:** These were subjected to a qualitative evaluation described in the next paragraph.
- ≥ 6 **non-trivial partitions:** The authors of the original study did not analyze this group because only 1.4% of the changesets fall into it and it would take too much time to interview developers about these changesets.
- ≥ 10 **trivial partitions:** The authors analyzed 15 out of the 199 changesets that had at least 10 trivial partitions and concluded that missing relationships are what caused so many trivial partitions.

For their qualitative study, the authors conducted 20 semi-structured interviews with Microsoft developers who had recently submitted a changeset for code review that contained between 2 and 5 non-trivial partitions. 16 interviewees agreed that the non-trivial partitions were correct and complete, all of them agreed with the rationale behind ClusterChanges and 18 of them would like to use the tool in their next changesets.

4   JClusterChanges

In this section, we present JClusterChanges, our FOSS implementation of the ClusterChanges technique [11] for Java software projects.

We decided to implement ClusterChanges for Java instead of C# because (1) Java is a more popular programming language for OSS projects [16], (2) there are multiple OSS Java code parsers available, (3) in case Barnett et al. publicly release their implementation of ClusterChanges, our implementation is more valuable to the community if it targets a different language and (4) we had previous experience with the Java programming language.

A parser is needed in order to identify the relationships between diff-regions. We could not apply the Roslyn compiler as in the original study because it only works with C# code. Thus, we used the Eclipse Compiler for Java (ECJ) [17] for parsing Java code.

To verify and validate JClusterChanges, we applied automated test cases and analyzed the results it generated for changesets from real software projects.

JClusterChanges provides a command-line interface that takes as input a changeset represented by source code files and their corresponding diffs. After parsing the input files, JClusterChanges outputs a set of files in the comma-separated values (CSV) file format, which contain not only the partitioning of the changeset but also all definitions, uses, diff-regions, relationships between diff-regions that were identified.

We also developed a Web GUI for visualizing the results of JClusterChanges (Fig. 2). It improves the usability of JClusterChanges and allows users to try the tool without having to install it on their computers. Using the GUI, users can choose a pull request from GitHub and visualize the partitioning generated by JClusterChanges. Consequently, the user can review each partition independently.

5   Replication

The goal of this study was to address the threats to external validity from the original study. To accomplish this, we performed a replication of the original quantitative substudy by Barnett et al. [11] where we changed the population dimension as recommended by Gómez et al. classification of Software Engineering replications [18]. Hence, this is a changed-population/changed-experimenters replication.

This study can be divided into three phases. First, we randomly selected 1000 pull requests from the 10 most popular Java OSS projects hosted on GitHub. After that, we used JClusterChanges to automatically partition them. Finally, we analyzed the dataset similarly to the original study.

There are two main reasons for choosing OSS projects as context. First, it is a different context as desired, because researchers have shown OSS development practices to be significantly different from their closed source counterparts [13, 14]. Second, OSS projects have data easily accessible on the Internet, which facilitates data collection and replicability of empirical studies.

Our choice of GitHub [19] stems from the fact that not only it had over 100,000 OSS projects using pull-based software development in 2013 [20], but it also provides a REST API that makes it easy to mine data from it.

Out of all the Java OSS projects in GitHub, we mined the most popular ones because we hypothesized that these would have large numbers of diverse pull requests to analyze.

5.1 Data Collection

We chose 10 projects from GitHub by manually analyzing the OSS Java software projects with the most stars until we had selected 10 of them. We selected a project for the study if:

- it used GitHub's pull request system (most projects do not use pull requests [21]);
- it had at least 300 pull requests which contained Java source code (in 2014, 95% of GitHub projects had at most 25 pull requests [21]);
- it was targeted at the JVM (i.e. Android exclusive projects were not considered). We wanted to avoid compatibility issues.

In order to select 100 pull requests from each of those software projects, we:

1. Sampled 300 pull requests at random that had at least one Java source code after-file, since we are interested in analyzing Java code;
2. Executed JClusterChanges on these 300 pull requests;
3. Of these 300 pull requests, sampled 100 pull requests at random that were analyzed by JClusterChanges without errors or warnings (we discuss this further in Sect. 5.6).

5.2 Pull Request Sizes

Similarly to the original study, we use boxplots of three metrics to describe the sizes of the changesets in the dataset, namely files changed, methods changed and diff-regions (Fig. 3).

The boxplots of this study indicate that pull requests tend to be small. Nevertheless, the presence of numerous outliers show that big pull requests occur frequently. It is likely that these outliers contain independent modifications and, thus, it is likely that the problem is real, i.e. that composite changesets are not rare.

Since the original study data is not publicly available, we could only compare the results visually. The boxplots show that the changesets of this study are generally smaller than the ones from the original study.

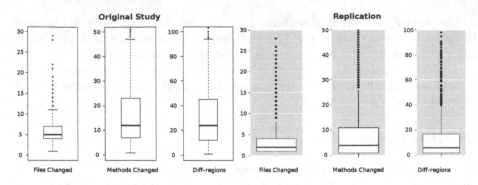

Fig. 3. Comparison between the boxplots of change sizes from the original study (left-hand side) and the ones from this study (right-hand side).

5.3 Partitions

According to the histogram of non-trivial partitions from this study (Fig. 4), the three most common cases in descending order are pull requests with: 1 (41.5%), 0 (36.9%) and 2 non-trivial partitions (12.2%). Moreover, 90.6% of the pull requests have at most 2 non-trivial partitions and 95.3% of the pull requests have at most 3 non-trivial partitions.

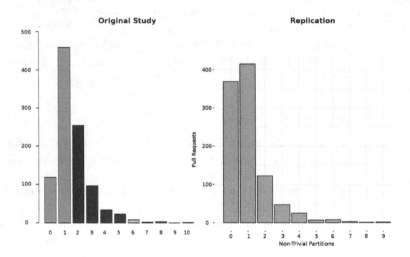

Fig. 4. Comparison between the histogram of non-trivial partitions of the original study (left-hand side) and the one from this study (right-hand side).

37% of the changesets did not have non-trivial partitions. This happens when the modifications are too small or consist of relationships not detected by JClusterChanges, thus the diff-regions are spread out in several trivial partitions. Since

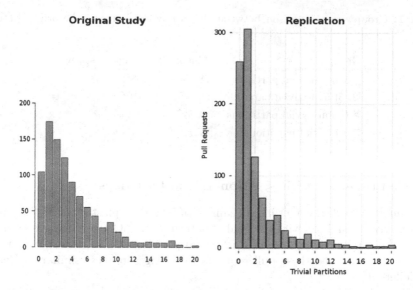

Fig. 5. Comparison between the histogram of trivial partitions of the original study (left-hand side) and the one from this study (right-hand side).

the median of diff-regions was small, the most frequent case was a changeset with few modifications.

Again, we could only compare the results visually because the original study data is not publicly available.

The histogram of non-trivial partitions obtained in this study is visually similar to the one from the original study (Fig. 4). More specifically, the tail of both distributions is similar and the most common cases are the same. But, the changesets from this study tend to have fewer non-trivial partitions.

As for the trivial partitions from this study (Fig. 5), the three most common cases in descending order are pull requests with: 1 (30.5%), 0 (25.9%) and 2 trivial partitions (12.6%). Unlike the distribution of non-trivial partitions, there is a long tail and 31% of the pull requests have more than 2 trivial partitions

A visual comparison between the histogram of trivial partitions from this study and the one from the original study (Fig. 5) shows a certain similarity between them. However, the changesets from this study tend to have fewer trivial partitions. Furthermore, while 4% of the changesets from the original study have more than 20 trivial partitions, 3% of the changesets from this study have more than 20 trivial partitions.

We followed the grouping strategy from the original study and performed a different analysis for each group. Table 1 summarizes the percentage of pull requests in each of the four groups. There is a marked difference between the proportions of pull requests with at most 1 non-trivial partition and the proportions of those with between 2 and 5 non-trivial partitions.

Table 1. Groupwise comparison between this study dataset and the original study one.

Group	This study	Original study
≤ 1 non-trivial partition	78.4%	58%
[2, 5] non-trivial partitions	20.1%	40%
≥ 6 non-trivial partitions	1.5%	1.4%
≥ 10 trivial partitions	7.7%	11.9%

5.4   Pull Requests with ≤ 1 Non-Trivial Partitions

We manually investigated a random sample of 50 pull requests that have at most one non-trivial partition with the goal of determining if ClusterChanges grouped unrelated diff-regions in the same non-trivial partition. As in the original study, we manually analyzed these pull requests following a process similar to Herzig and Zeller [10].

Only two pull requests clearly contained independent changes and JCluster-Changes separated those changes into different partitions as expected. Therefore, JClusterChanges never grouped unrelated diff-regions in the same partition in these 50 pull requests.

5.5   Pull Requests with > 10 Trivial Partitions

We manually investigated 15 of the 77 pull requests with more than 10 trivial partitions in order to determine what relationships ClusterChanges does not detect and, as a result, gain insight on how it can be improved.

We obtained results that are similar to the ones from the original study. The three most common relationships that JClusterChanges could not detect were:

– Refactoring patterns (e.g. code styling, formatting changes);
– Changes dependent on code not available in the pull request;
– Code called indirectly (e.g. methods meant to be called by a test framework).

5.6   Discussion

The similarity between the histograms of non-trivial partitions and trivial partitions of this study and the ones from the original study suggests that Cluster-Changes is as effective in the context of OSS projects as in the context of closed source software projects.

The boxplots of size metrics (Fig. 3) indicate that these dataset changesets are smaller than the ones analyzed in the original study. This suggests that pull requests tend to be more cohesive and less complex than the changes sent for review at companies such as Microsoft. We hypothesize that this is because pull requests are often created by outside developers who are not familiar with the code.

Given the smaller size of this dataset changes compared to the changes of the original study dataset, we expected to see fewer non-trivial partitions in this dataset and this prediction proved to be correct since there were about half as many changesets as the original study with more than 1 non-trivial partition. Nevertheless, the number of changesets with multiple partitions is significant and is evidence that large changesets with independent changes are also commonplace in OSS projects.

22% of the pull requests analyzed in this study have more than 1 non-trivial partition (Fig. 4). Considering that ClusterChanges never identified a false-positive, this means that at most 22% of the changesets are composite. Furthermore, this proportion is close to the estimates of 16% and 17% provided by past studies as to how many changesets in OSS projects are composite. This suggests that the partitioning is correct.

Our manual analysis of 50 pull requests provided further evidence that the def-use relationship is a fundamental one as claimed in the original study since we did not found any false positives. A false-positive would be an instance where JClusterChanges had put two unrelated diff-regions in the same partition and this did not happen in any of the pull requests analyzed. Such absence of false positives means that the tool provides an upper bound on the number of independent partitions within a changeset. Furthermore, we believe that this is of vital importance for user acceptance of the tool, because false positives have been a significant obstacle in the adoption of static analysis tools for finding bugs [22].

Although there were no false positives, we did observe several types of relationships between diff-regions that ClusterChanges did not detect. Diff-regions that were related by logical patterns but did not have code dependencies between them were a common type of false negative. A few real examples were: adding the prefix "Abstract" to the name of all abstract classes and adding final modifiers to fields. Tao et al. had some success using pattern matching techniques for detecting such relationships [10], so their approach could potentially be used to improve the efficacy of ClusterChanges with regards to these relationships.

We also frequently saw missed use-use relationships because these depended on definitions not present in the changeset, e.g. calls to a Logger API not present in the changeset and test cases for code that was not changed. One way to address this would be to modify ClusterChanges to consider the whole code base instead of just the files changed. But, future research is needed to determine whether this can be done efficiently since there would be a lot more source code for the tool to analyze.

One of the threats to validity of this study is that some changesets are not being fully analyzed by our tool. This seems to be caused by limitations in ECJ when parsing certain new features of Java. As this may result in missing relationships and seem to be an implementation issue unrelated to the technique itself, we have excluded such changesets from the dataset.

Another threat to validity is that we have not finished our replication of the qualitative study due to time constraints. Even though our results provide evidence that OSS developers face a similar situation to Microsoft developers and that ClusterChanges behave similarly in an OSS context, it is still possible that OSS developers do not agree with the partitionings or that they would not like to use the tool, since OSS development practices tend to be significantly different [13,14].

6   Related Work

We found two studies with goals similar to ClusterChanges. Dias et al. [23] created a technique for decomposing changes before developers commit them to avoid the creation of composite commits. Tao and Kim [10] also published a heuristic-based technique for automatically partitioning changesets but they used different heuristics.

The other studies focus on the impact of composite changes on mining software repositories (MSR). Herzig and Zeller [9] presented a technique that combines five heuristics to identify related changesets. Kirinuki et al. [24] devised a technique that is able to warn users if they are about to commit a potentially composite change by analyzing the history of the software repository. Nguyen et al. [25] used natural language processing algorithms to create a tool for decomposing changesets containing a mix of bug fixing code changes and unrelated non-fixing code changes.

7   Conclusion

To address the limitations of Barnett et al. evaluation of ClusterChanges [11], we created JClusterChanges, a FOSS implementation of ClusterChanges for Java software projects, and used it to evaluate the technique in the context of Java OSS projects from different organizations.

We obtained results similar to the ones in the original study. Hence, we have provided evidence that ClusterChanges is generalizable to other contexts and further evidence that the problem does exist. In addition, JClusterChanges shows that it is possible to implement the technique for other programming languages and it can be used to help future research on this subject, e.g. by using it as a baseline to evaluate other techniques and by extending its implementation to evaluate changes to the technique.

There are numerous possibilities for future work. Presently, we are working on a replication of the qualitative portion of the original ClusterChanges study. Another possibility would be to try to improve JClusterChanges according to the discussion on missing relationships from both this paper and the original study.

Finally, to aid future research and to encourage replication of this work, we provide the material and results of this research at: https://sites.google.com/site/jclusterchanges/.

References

1. Bacchelli, A., Bird, C.: Expectations, outcomes, and challenges of modern code review. In: Proceedings of the 2013 International Conference on Software Engineering, pp. 712–721. IEEE Press (2013)
2. Ciolkowski, M., Laitenberger, O., Biffl, S.: Software reviews: the state of the practice. IEEE Softw. 20(6), 46–51 (2003)
3. Harjumaa, L., Tervonen, I., Huttunen, A.: Peer reviews in real life - motivators and demotivators, pp. 29–36. IEEE (2005)
4. Shull, F., Seaman, C.: Inspecting the history of inspections: an example of evidence-based technology diffusion. IEEE Softw. 25(1), 88–90 (2008)
5. Gerrit team: Gerrit. https://www.gerritcodereview.com/. Accessed 21 July 2016
6. GitHub: Github's features. https://github.com/features. Accessed 21 July 2016
7. Phacility Inc: Phabricator. https://www.phacility.com/phabricator/. Accessed 21 July 2016
8. Tao, Y., Dang, Y., Xie, T., Zhang, D., Kim, S.: How do software engineers understand code changes? an exploratory study in industry. In: Proceedings of the ACM SIGSOFT 20th International Symposium on the Foundations of Software Engineering, Article no. 51. ACM (2012)
9. Herzig, K., Zeller, A.: The impact of tangled code changes. In: 2013 10th IEEE Working Conference on Mining Software Repositories (MSR), pp. 121–130. IEEE (2013)
10. Tao, Y., Kim, S.: Partitioning composite code changes to facilitate code review. In: Proceedings of the 2015 IEEE/ACM 12th Working Conference on Mining Software Repositories, pp. 180–190. IEEE, May 2015
11. Barnett, M., Bird, C., Brunet, J., Lahiri, S.K.: Helping developers help themselves: automatic decomposition of code review changesets. In: Proceedings of the 37th International Conference on Software Engineering. IEEE (2015)
12. Dias, M., Ducasse, S., Cassou, D., Uquillas-Gmez, V.: Do tools support code integration? a survey. J. Object Technol. 16(2), 1–20 (2016)
13. Mockus, A., Fielding, R.T., Herbsleb, J.D.: Two case studies of open source software development: Apache and Mozilla. ACM Trans. Softw. Eng. Methodol. (TOSEM) 11(3), 309–346 (2002)
14. Rigby, P.C., German, D.M., Cowen, L., Storey, M.A.: Peer review on open-source software projects: parameters, statistical models, and theory. ACM Trans. Softw. Eng. Methodol. 23(4), 1–33 (2014)
15. Basili, V.R., Shull, F., Lanubile, F.: Building knowledge through families of experiments. IEEE Trans. Softw. Eng. 25(4), 456–473 (1999)
16. Black Duck Software Inc: Open Hub - comparison between C# and Java with regard to monthly commits. https://www.openhub.net/languages/compare?language_name%5B%5D=csharp&language_name%5B%5D=java&language_name%5B%5D=-1&language_name%5B%5D=-1&measure=commits. Accessed 01 Aug 2016
17. The Eclipse Foundation: Eclipse Java development tools (JDT). https://www.eclipse.org/jdt/. Accessed 26 Nov 2015
18. Gómez, O.S., Juristo, N., Vegas, S.: Understanding replication of experiments in software engineering: a classification. Inf. Softw. Technol. 56(8), 1033–1048 (2014)
19. GitHub: About GitHub. https://github.com/about. Accessed 01 Aug 2016
20. Gousios, G., Pinzger, M., van Deursen, A.: An exploratory study of the pull-based software development model. In: Proceedings of the 36th International Conference on Software Engineering, pp. 345–355. ACM (2014)

21. Kalliamvakou, E., Gousios, G., Blincoe, K., Singer, L., German, D.M., Damian, D.: The promises and perils of mining GitHub. In: Proceedings of the 11th Working Conference on Mining Software Repositories, pp. 92–101. ACM (2014)
22. Bessey, A., Engler, D., Block, K., Chelf, B., Chou, A., Fulton, B., Hallem, S., Henri-Gros, C., Kamsky, A., McPeak, S.: A few billion lines of code later: using static analysis to find bugs in the real world. Commun. ACM **53**(2), 66–75 (2010)
23. Dias, M., Bacchelli, A., Gousios, G., Cassou, D., Ducasse, S.: Untangling fine-grained code changes. In: 2015 IEEE 22nd International Conference on Software Analysis, Evolution and Reengineering (SANER), pp. 341–350. IEEE (2015)
24. Kirinuki, H., Higo, Y., Hotta, K., Kusumoto, S.: Hey! Are you committing tangled changes? In: Proceedings of the 22nd International Conference on Program Comprehension, ICPC 2014, pp. 262–265. ACM, New York (2014)
25. Nguyen, H.A., Nguyen, A.T., Nguyen, T.N.: Filtering noise in mixed-purpose fixing commits to improve defect prediction and localization. In: 2013 IEEE 24th International Symposium on Software Reliability Engineering (ISSRE), pp. 138–147. IEEE (2013)

Transformation of OWL2 Property Axioms to Groovy

Bogumiła Hnatkowska$^{(\boxtimes)}$ and Paweł Woroniecki

Wrocław University of Science and Technology,
Wyb. Wyspiańskiego 27, 50-370 Wrocław, Poland
Bogumila.Hnatkowska@pwr.edu.pl,
192157@student.pwr.edu.pl

Abstract. Ontology is a formal representation of domain knowledge. It may be effectively used in software development – large parts of the object-oriented code can be automatically generated from existing domain ontologies. The paper is related to transformations from OWL2 to Groovy. It proposes transformations of OWL2 properties together with object property axioms. Many axioms, e.g. asymmetry, irreflexivity have not been considered in the existing literature up to now. Mapping of some others is incomplete. Proposed transformations preserve the OWL2 semantics of axioms, assuring model consistency with the original definition. The implemented rules either guarantee consistency of the source code by performing additional actions 'behind the scene' or prohibit inconsistency by throwing exceptions. As a result, their application can speed up the development process and produce the source code of high quality at the same time. All defined transformation rules were implemented and verified by several examples. A bigger case study confirmed the usability of the rules. Both the tool as well as the case study are publicly available.

Keywords: OWL2 · Groovy · Transformation rules · Property · Symmetry
Asymmetry · Transitivity · Reflexivity · Irreflexivity · Functional property
Inverse functional property

1 Introduction

Ontology can be defined as "a formal specification of a shared conceptualization" while "a conceptualization is a structured interpretation of a part of the world that people use to think and communicate about the world" [1]. In other words, ontology is a formal description of existing terms in the domain and relationships between them. This description can be reused for different purposes, e.g. for software development.

Object-oriented paradigm allows representing a complex reality with the use of classes. They are used to create instances communicating by exchange of messages. Typically, a subset of classes (called a model) serves as a representation of the specific domain. The model should be consistent with domain knowledge as much as possible, as it has a positive influence on source code quality.

The possible scenario of practical application of domain ontology in the development process can be as follows. Software developers are given a domain ontology or

© Springer International Publishing AG 2018
A M. Tjoa et al. (Eds.): SOFSEM 2018, LNCS 10706, pp. 269–282, 2018.
https://doi.org/10.1007/978-3-319-73117-9_19

part of it, which is correct, consistent, and complete (and handled by inference engine). Instead of spending hours on domain knowledge elicitation, e.g. by interviewing future users or domain experts, they automatically translate the ontology into a runnable source code, which doesn't need to be modified. The generated source code is delivered as a separate package. If the ontology is changed in any way, the transformation process can be repeated. The role of domain expert changes a little bit – it is a person responsible for finding or preparing the ontology or its part for the transformation purposes.

There exist many attempts to automatic translation from domain ontology to a selected programming language, e.g. Java [2–4]. Most of them focus on basic structural elements, for example define how to map ontology classes or class properties, neglecting important property features like symmetry, transitivity or functionality. Even if some property features are considered, e.g. in [4], the transformations are incomplete. So there is a need to extend transformation rules when it is possible. Properly defined transformation rules can be automatized, resulting in a source code of high quality and faster software development.

In this paper, we demonstrate a subset of transformation rules from OWL2 to Groovy. OWL2 is used as a specification language for many domain ontologies and is supported by dedicated tools, e.g. Protégé [5].

Groovy is a modern OO dynamic language with static compilation capabilities [6], and with some new features like traits, that can be effectively used for transformation purposes. These features allow to propose better transformations as well as to extend their scope (new transformation rules are defined for concepts typically not considered). Similarly to Java, Groovy is executed on the JVM machine. What is more, the Groovy code is shorter, and because of that more comprehensible, than equivalent code written in Java or C#.

The rest of the paper is structured as followed. Section 2 presents related works in deeper detail. Section 3 describes proposed basic transformations from OWL2 to Groovy. It brings necessary context to understand the way in which OWL2 properties are represented in Groovy – see Sect. 4 for details. Section 5 defines transformations for particular property axioms. Most of the transformation rules are illustrated with a simple example. A bigger case study was described in Sect. 6. Conclusions and further work are the content of Sect. 7.

2   Related Works

The best solutions for code generation of object-oriented (OO) languages based on OWL2 ontology were provided in [2–4]. However, they are not perfect.

OWL2 classes are typically transformed to OO classes (see [2, 4]) or interfaces (see [3]). The second approach is problematic as many parts of the source code must be implemented multiple times instead of reusing them. Java 8 default implementation of interfaces does not solve that problem as interfaces cannot implement a state.

OWL2 class axioms (e.g. *SubClassOf*, *EquivalentClasses*) and descriptions (e.g. *ObjectIntersectionOf*, *ObjectUnionOf*) are transformed to such implementation of setters/getters which prevents illegal operations performed by individuals. This logic is created dynamically (see [3]) or statically (see [4]). Dynamic implementation is hard to understand, debug and can decrease application performance. Static solutions, based on interfaces, usually lead to the repeated implementation of them in many places.

OWL2 property, regardless of its type (data property, object property), is represented as a class attribute (see [2, 4]) or as an interface with setters/getters and dynamically created implementation logic (see [3]). In the case of a data property, determination of property type may be difficult. There are many possible types in OWL2 (imported from XML Schema) that have no similar type in most OO languages. These are for example: *xsd:language* or *xsd:negativeInteger*. They may be mapped to the most similar types in the target language, e.g. *xsd:negativeInteger* is mapped to *BigInteger*, see [10, 11]. Such transformation is not exact. To overcome these problems an extra validation logic is needed to ensure correct attribute values. Such logic may be placed in setters. However, in such implementation there is no direct (static) information about attribute's type and the validation code is repeated in each setter for the same original type.

Transformation of property axioms (symmetry, reflexivity) is rarely considered in the literature. In [2] only selected axioms (functional and inverse properties) are addressed. Other axioms like symmetry, transitivity and inverse functionality are not covered. In [4], we can find the proposal of transformations for most of the axioms (except the properties: inverse functional, asymmetry, reflexive and irreflexive), but some of them seem to be too complicated. In particular, it concerns functional property which is transformed into a list of values, and then the uniqueness of the list is checked when any value is added to the list or removed from it. A simpler way to achieve such functionality is to set a simple type for the attribute (no collection type). In case of symmetry and transitive properties, only element addition was considered – there is no logic to ensure correct element removal.

To summarize, we expect the transformation:

– to be based on static mechanisms which are easier to understand and maintain,
– to be able to reuse implemented business logic rather than to repeat it many times,
– to cover as many class axioms and property axioms as possible.

3 OWL2 to Groovy Basic Class Transformations

In OWL2 "class can be understood as a set of individuals" [7]. An individual represents an object from the domain. It can be a member of many classes. Two classes can be related with *SubClassOf* axiom stating that each instance of the subclass is also an instance of its parent. In particular *Thing* class being the root of class hierarchy "represents the set of all individuals" [7].

In object-oriented languages like Groovy or Java, "class is a blueprint or prototype from which object is created" [8]. It is treated as a (reference) type serving as a descriptor representing the same structure of its instances [9]. One class (type) can be a subtype of another class. Class understood as a type is conformant to itself and all of its generalizations, so in consequence, an instance of type A can be used in the context in which its parent (B) is expected. However, in such a case widening reference conversion is applied meaning that the instances of *A* and *B* are not equivalent (in OWL2 in such a case we deal with the same instance) [6]. The fact that an instance is of specific class type cannot be interpreted as the synonym for "being a member of a set".

Above mentioned semantic differences are obstacles in defining OWL2 to OO mapping rules. However, they can be overcome by choosing proper OO language that provides necessary constructs. Groovy is an excellent destination language for OWL2 to OO language transformation. In contrast to Java, it enables effective mapping of many OWL2 elements including multiple class inheritance and relations between classes like equivalence, union, disjoint, intersection.

The most useful Groovy construct in the considered context is a trait. Traits in Groovy are placed between interfaces and classes. They allow to carry state and may contain the implementation of methods. Like interfaces, they cannot be instantiated but can be implemented by classes. Multiple inheritance of traits is also allowed. All these features make traits applicable in OWL2 to Groovy transformations.

3.1   Classes and Class (Multiple) Inheritance

OWL2 classes are typically transformed to OO classes or interfaces. We propose a mixture of both approaches where the OWL2 class is transformed to a trait, representing the class's state (such state can be reused by the subclasses), and a Groovy class with the name of the OWL2 class, which implements (directly or indirectly) the trait. So, OWL2 class *A* is transformed into two Groovy elements: *TraitA* and class *A* which implements *TraitA*. There is one root of all generated traits – *ThingTrait* (related to OWL2 supertype called *Thing*). *TraitA* contains properties of *A*, a list of *A* instances, a factory method (*create*) for creating new instances of *A* and a method (*removeInstance*) to remove a specific *A* instance. Both methods call appropriate methods from *TraitA* parent classes (to add or remove the instance from theirs instance lists). Class *A* contains only default private empty constructor – fields and methods are covered by *TraitA*.

OWL2 class inheritance is transformed to trait inheritance in Groovy. For example, mapping of class *A*, which extends *B* and *C*, results in the following Groovy structure: *TraitA* extending *TraitB* and *TraitC* – see Fig. 1.

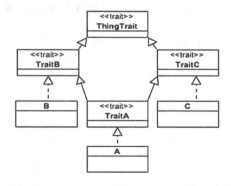

Fig. 1. Transformation rule for OWL2 (multiple) class inheritance

3.2 Equivalence of Classes

If OWL2 class *A* is equivalent to *B*, then it means that both names can be used interchangeably (they are synonyms). At the level of programming language, it means that instances of class *A* are also instances of class *B* and vice versa. That effect is achieved by the equivalence of traits (*TraitA* and *TraitB*) by defining one trait that extends both of them, and this common trait is implemented by classes *A* and *B* – see Fig. 2. *TraitAB* contains all elements that – in another case – would be implemented by *TraitA*, and *TraitB* appropriately. *TraitA* and *TraitB* are empty.

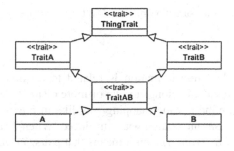

Fig. 2. Transformation rule for OWL2 equivalence class axiom

To create instances of *A* or *B* one can write:

```
TraitA a = A.create()
TraitB b = B.create()
```

After that it is possible to assign an instance of *A* to *B* (*B* to *A*) without casting:

```
a = b
```

3.3 Union of Classes

OWL2 class *A*, which is defined as the union of *B* and *C*, means that each instance of *B* or *C* is also an instance of *A*. Translation of such construct to Groovy results in the creation of three traits: *TraitA*, *TraitB*, and *TraitC*. Each object of *TraitA* may be cast to one of the types: *TraitB* or *TraitC* (depending on the class the object belongs to – object of *A* cannot be instantiated directly, but it must be *B* or *C*). See details in Fig. 3.

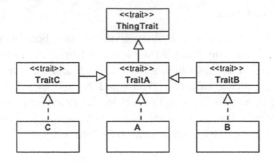

Fig. 3. Transformation rule for OWL2 union class axiom

3.4   Disjoint Classes

Another fundamental class transformation is related to disjoint classes. This axiom states that no OWL2 individual belongs to two or more disjoint classes simultaneously. It was not possible to define a static mapping rule like in previous cases using traits. Therefore *@DisjointClasses* annotation was introduced. When *TraitA* is annotated with *@DisjointClasses([TraitB, TraitC])* then it means that pairs: *TraitA* and *TraitB*, *TraitA* and *TraitC* are disjoint. The annotation is not enough alone – a validator that uses it is necessary. The validator scans all subtypes of *ThingTrait* (using reflection) to ensure that none of them extends two or more disjoint traits.

4   Transformation of Properties

OWL2 properties (both types: data property and object property) are mapped to Groovy attributes in generated traits. The domain of the property determines the trait in which the property is placed. It means that property can be applied only to objects of domain type. If the domain is defined as *D*, then the property must be placed in *DTrait* (implemented by class *D*). If no domain is specified, then the attribute is generated in *ThingTrait* (as *Thing* is the default domain in OWL2). The range of the property specifies the type of attribute. The default range is *ThingTrait*. The generated attributes have private visibility. Accessor methods are also generated to make them accessible.

By default, any attribute should be represented as a list because default cardinality of the OWL2 property is infinity. The only exception is when the upper bound of the cardinality is set to 1, or the attribute is marked as functional.

Let us consider the following fragment of OWL2 ontology (see Listing 1) containing object property called *madeFromGrape*.

```
Declaration( Class( :Wine ) )
Declaration( Class( :WineGrape ) )

Declaration( ObjectProperty( :madeFromGrape ) )
ObjectPropertyDomain( :madeFromGrape :Wine )
ObjectPropertyRange( :madeFromGrape :WineGrape )
```

Listing 1. Example of property defined in OWL2
(Source: https://www.w3.org/TR/owl-guide/wine.rdf [Accessed 01.03.2017])

The defined mapping rule translates it into the following Groovy code (see Listing 2).

```
class Wine implements WineTrait { }

trait WineTrait implements ThingTrait {
  private List<WineGrapeTrait> madeFromGrape
  // plus accessor methods: getter, setter
}
```

Listing 2. Property mapped from OWL2 to Groovy code

The domain of the *madeFromGrape* property is *Wine,* so it is placed in the *WineTrait* trait. Its range is *WineGrape* what is reflected in the attribute type: *List <WineGrapeTrait>*. According to the rule, the property is private, and there are accessor methods: getter and setter.

Some additional methods are added to increase property usability: *addMade-FromGrape* (to add a single grape), and *removeMadeFromGrape* (to remove a single grape).

Data property is also translated to an attribute placed in a proper trait. Its type is either a Groovy type – if it is an equivalent to original OWL2 datatype, e.g. String – or an immutable wrapper class otherwise. Such class accepts a value only in its constructor (no setters are defined) and validates it according to original type semantic. Then the value can be obtained using getter or type conversion (operator *as* in Groovy); for example, *NegativeInteger* wrapper class stores internally its value as an object of *BigInteger* type. Therefore, an instance of *NegativeInteger* may be converted to an instance of *BigInteger* (which is a convenient way to use it) or provide a getter that returns its value as *BigInteger*.

5 Transformation of Property Axioms

In further, selected axioms defining characteristics of object property are considered. They are symmetry, asymmetry, transitivity, functionality, inverse functionality, reflexivity and irreflexivity. For simplicity mapping rules presented in this section assume that attributes and accessors are defined directly in classes while in fact they are defined in traits implemented by classes.

Defined transformations try to preserve the original ontology semantics by:

– Automatic update of the model when it is possible
– Throwing exceptions when an operation can result in model inconsistency
– Use of built-in features of the Groovy language.

5.1 Symmetry

OWL2 symmetry axiom states that if an individual x is connected to an individual y, then y is also connected to x. As OWL2 properties are mapped to attributes in Groovy, then the mapping rule is expressed in terms of attributes.

Rule: if a symmetric attribute *attr* of object x contains value y, then the same attribute *attr* of object y must contain value x.

The rule is achieved by a proper construction of getter and setter for the symmetric attribute, as well as methods for attribute manipulation (*add*, *remove*). They must check (setter, add method) if parameters are connected with 'this' object and create the connection when necessary. If a new value is assigned, the old one symmetrically must be removed. *Remove* method does the opposite – called for one end automatically removes the other.

Let us consider the fragment of OWL2 ontology (see Listing 3) which declares that *adjacentRegion* is a symmetric property of class *Region* (property domain).

```
Declaration( Class( :Region ) )
Declaration( ObjectProperty( :adjacentRegion ) )
ObjectPropertyDomain( :adjacentRegion :Region )
ObjectPropertyRange( :adjacentRegion :Region )
SymmetricObjectProperty( :adjacentRegion )
```

Listing 3. Example of symmetric property defined in OWL2
(Source: https://www.w3.org/TR/owl-guide/wine.rdf [Accessed 01.03.2017])

Let us consider two regions: *r1* and *r2*. Assume also the existence of *addAdjacentRegion* method (in *Region*) that adds a single adjacent region. Invoking *addAdjacentRegion* on *r1* with *r2* passed as parameter means that *r2* must be added to *adjacetRegions* in *r1*, but also *r1* must be added to the same attribute's values list in *r2* to preserve symmetry.

Similarly, removing any value from *adjacentRegions* must also be done symmetrically, e.g. if *r2* is no longer an adjacent region of *r1* (it is removed from *adjacentRegions* values in *r1*), then *r1* must be deleted from the *adjacentRegions* list in *r2*.

An example of generated Groovy code that fulfills above requirements is presented in Listing 4 (setter, and *add* method).

```
private List<Region> adjacentRegions

void setAdjacentRegions(List<Region> adjacentRegions) {
  List<Region> oldValues = this.adjacentRegions ?: []
  List<Region> newValues = adjacentRegions ?: []
  List<Region> removedValues = oldValues - newValues
  List<Region> addedValues = newValues - oldValues
  removedValues.each {
    it.adjacentRegions?.remove(this)
    this.adjacentRegions?.remove(it)
  }
  addedValues.each { this.addAdjacentRegion(it) }
}

void addAdjacentRegion(Region adjacentRegion) {
  if (!this.adjacentRegions) {
    this.adjacentRegions = []
  }

  if (!this.adjacentRegions.contains(adjacentRegion)) {
    this.adjacentRegions.add(adjacentRegion)
    adjacentRegion.addAdjacentRegion(this)
  }
}
```

Listing 4. Symmetric property mapped from OWL2 to Groovy code

5.2 Asymmetry

OWL2 asymmetry axiom states that if an individual x is connected to an individual y, than y cannot be connected to x. Similarly to symmetry axiom, the mapping rule is expressed in terms of attributes.

Rule: if an asymmetric attribute *attr* of object x contains value y, then the same attribute *attr* of object y must not contain value x.

The rule is realized by a proper implementation of setter and *add* method. The methods check if any parameter is connected to 'this' object by the same property. If yes, an exception is thrown.

Let us consider *Person* class with *parents* property (with domain and range defined as *Person*), and two instances of *Person*: *p1* and *p2*. The property *parents* is declared asymmetric because if *p1* is a parent of *p2*, then *p2* must not be a parent of *p1*.

Parents setter checks the condition mentioned above. If any person passed to *setParents* contains 'this' object as its parent, then asymmetry rule is violated, and an exception is thrown. Otherwise, values are set correctly.

5.3   Transitivity

Transformation rule for transitivity axiom is also expressed regarding object's attributes.

Rule: if a transitive attribute *attr* of object *x* contains value *y* and the same attribute of object *y* contains value *z*, then the attribute of object *x* must contain value *z*.

Its transformation is quite similar to that defined for symmetric property with two small differences. The setter and *add* method do the connections transitively. *Remove* method throws an exception if transitivity rule is violated.

Let us consider the following fragment of OWL2 ontology (see Listing 5):

```
Declaration( Class( :Region ) )
Declaration( ObjectProperty( :placedIn ) )
ObjectPropertyDomain( :placedIn :Region )
ObjectPropertyRange( :placedIn :Region )
TransitiveObjectProperty( :placedIn )
```

Listing 5. Example of transitive property defined in OWL2
(Source: https://www.w3.org/TR/owl-guide/wine.r/df [Accessed 01.03.2017])

The example presents the *placedIn* property (of *Region* class) which is transitive. The *addPlacedIn* method adds a single value not symmetrically but transitively. Let us consider three regions: *r1*, *r2,* and *r3*. If *r3* is located in *r2* and one adds the fact that *r2* is located in *r1*, then the fact that *r3* is also located in *r1* must be added.

Because of transitivity, some attempts of values removal may be illegal. For example, if place *r1* is located in *r2*, and *r2* is located in *r3*, then *r1* must also be located in *r3*. In such a case *r1* cannot be deleted directly from the *placedIn* list of *r3* because it would change the state of the system to illegal. Such attempt of value removal results in throwing an exception. A programmer should delete instances gradually, first: remove *r1* from *r2*, and next – delete the others in any order: *r2* from *r3* and *r1* from *r3*.

5.4   Functionality

OWL2 functionality axiom states that for each individual *x* there can be at most one distinct literal *y* such that *x* is connected with *y* by functional property. In terms of attributes the same semantics can be expressed with the rule given below.

Rule: A functional attribute of object *x* can contain at most one unique value.

The semantics of functional attribute is ensured by the transformation which allows the attribute to contain only one value. It implies a proper type of the attribute which cannot be a collection or array; it could be *Person* but not *List <Person>*. Proposed transformation requires no additional validation logic.

An alternative approach would be to set attribute's type as *List* and validate that it does not contain more than one unique value. Such validation would have to be done in all methods that set or add new values to the attribute. It would be obviously more complicated than the first approach and bring no advantages over it.

5.5 Inverse Functionality

OWL2 inverse functionality axiom states that for each individual x there can be at most one individual y such that y is connected with x. The rule expressed regarding attributes is given below.

Rule: if an inverse functional attribute *attr* of object x contains value y, then value y must not be present in values of *attr* in any other object.

The rule is realized at Groovy side by storing the list of all objects of a given class in a static class attribute. Then, before setting a value of this attribute (setter, *add* method), it is checked if the value has not been already set in another object. When the rule is violated, the *InverseFunctionalPropertyException* is raised.

Let us consider the following fragment of OWL2 ontology (see Listing 6) where *children* property is introduced. It means that a specific child can be related to one woman only.

```
Declaration( Class( :Child ) )
Declaration( Class( :Woman ) )
Declaration( ObjectProperty( :children ) )
ObjectPropertyDomain( :children :Woman )
ObjectPropertyRange( :children :Child )
InverseFunctionalObjectProperty( :children )
```

Listing 6. Example of inverse functional property defined in OWL2

Implementation of the rule is demonstrated in the following Groovy code (see Listing 7). The static attribute used here is called *allWomen*.

```
class Woman implements WomanTrait {
  private static List<Woman> allWomen = [] // static attribute
  private List<Child> children

  Woman() { Woman.allWomen += this }

  void setChildren(List<Child> children)
     throws InverseFunctionalPropertyException {
    if (!children) { this.children = children; return }
    List<Child> childrenOfOtherWomen =
      (allWomen - this)*.children.flatten()
    List<Child> commonChildren =
      children.intersect(childrenOfOtherWomen)
    if (!commonChildren.isEmpty()) {
      throw new InverseFunctionalPropertyException()
    }
    this.children = children
  }
  List<Child> getChildren() { return this.children }
}
```

Listing 7. Inverse functional property mapped from OWL2 to Groovy code

Implementation of *addChild* and *removeChild* methods is not provided here due to limited space, but it is straightforward. The first method is a simplified version of the *setChildren* method. It checks if the new child exists in the list of children of any other woman. Implementation of *removeChild* removes the parameter (child) from the current woman's children list – no assertions are necessary in this case.

5.6   Reflexivity

OWL2 reflexivity axiom states that each individual is connected to itself.

Rule: a reflexive attribute of object *x* must contain value *x*.

This rule is assured by such implementation of the setter which throws an exception if the input parameter does not contain 'this' instance. It is combined with setting an initial attribute's value – its list of values contains 'this' value. A method removing attribute's values must not remove 'this' instance, so if this happens, it throws an exception. In consequence, the reflexive attribute always contains 'this' among its values.

Let us consider an example of reflexive property – *knows* (everybody knows self) of *Person* class. The methods *setKnows* and *addKnows* will check if among the parameters is 'this' instance. Otherwise, it will throw an exception. On the contrary, the *removeKnows* method will check if the parameter list does not contain 'this' instance and throw an exception when it does.

If the attribute is functional as well as reflexive, then it must be set to 'this', and its value cannot be changed, so there is no setter generated for such attribute – only getter. Additionally, it can be marked as a *final* field.

5.7   Irreflexivity

OWL2 irreflexivity axiom means that no individual is connected to itself, which is expressed in terms of attributes by the rule given below.

Rule: an irreflexive attribute of object *x* must not contain value *x*.

Mapping of the irreflexive attribute is similar to the mapping of reflexive one. However, there are two main differences: 'this' is not set as an initial value of the attribute, and values passed to the setter must not contain 'this' instance (in contrast to reflexive attribute where it must be present). The second condition must also be checked in the *add* method to prevent the addition of 'this' to attribute's values.

Let us consider the *marriedTo* property of *Person* class marked as irreflexive. The *setMarriedTo* method will check if a parameter list does not contain 'this' instance. Similarly, the *addMarriedTo* method will check if the parameter is different from 'this'.

6   Case Study

The correctness of implemented transformations was verified by several examples, including a bigger case study. In the case study, an ontology describing a shop selling products from different categories was used. This ontology was created by paper's authors. Both, the ontology and generated code are publicly available (see [12]). The ontology includes all axioms described here and contains two extra related to cardinality – not presented in the paper but supported by converter implementation.

The ontology (326 lines, 84 axioms at the first level) was transformed by the implemented engine to a set of 65 files organized in 5 packages. The package called *model* is the core one, including 13 Groovy classes with 14 accompanying traits written in 2011 code lines. No single class from application model had to be changed in this case to create a simple shop implementation where basic CRUD functionalities were provided, e.g. displaying products, orders, customers as well as their modifications. Only presentation and control layers were implemented – in total 180 lines of code (command-line user interface).

The case study could be easily extended, e.g. by introducing Object-Relational Mapping (to save data in a database), providing a graphical user interface or adding new useful functionalities. However, it was enough to confirm the usability of proposed transformation rule set.

The proposed approach should scale well for larger OWL2 models. Bigger ontology means bigger output package with model classes. Other source code packages will not be influenced by the ontology size as they contain auxiliary elements: declarations of thrown exceptions (exception package), definitions of data types (owlSimpleType package) or definitions of necessary validators (validator package).

7 Summary

In the paper, a set of transformation rules from OWL2 to Groovy was presented. The rules take into account transformation of OWL2 properties together with their features like symmetry, transitivity or functionality. Proposed rules fill the gap in similar transformations to Java language and address vulnerabilities in existing ones.

The rules were implemented in Groovy and are available as a jar file under the link [12]. The tool depends on OWLAPI [13]. The ontology may be provided in: OWL/XML [14], RDF/XML [15] or OWL Functional (used in this paper) [7].

The fact that Groovy is a target transformation language does not limit the usage of the approach to applications written only in Groovy. There exist integration mechanisms, e.g. API called JSR-223, which allows calling Groovy code from Java.

Domain experts can share their knowledge directly in ontology which is then automatically mapped to a source code, what speeds up the development process significantly. Generated code can be up to 80% of entire application source code. It is easy to understand by developers. The code can also be instrumented by annotations required by ORM frameworks or logs instructions. Moreover, the automatically generated code is less error-prone comparing to manually written one. Assuming correctness of transformation rules, it is always correct. Furthermore, domain ontologies may be effectively reused across many products. Reusability is also possible with manually written code, but as already mentioned, it is less readable to many domain experts. Besides, OWL2 ontologies may be obtained from external sources like the Internet. Automatic transformation rules allow to adopt them into own product immediately.

Known limitations of the proposed approach are as follows. The main assumption is that domain ontology which is translated to a source code is correct (syntactically and semantically), consistent and complete. Otherwise, the resulting source code will need to be modified or may not succeed at all. If the ontology is too wide, it is a task of a domain expert to select proper parts for transformations. Transformation rules cover many but not all OWL2 syntax constructs (not supported elements: axioms referring to anonymous classes, assertions, own datatype definitions, keys). Subsequently, we are going to propose transformation rules also for these elements. Provided solution is complete in the scope of considered OWL2 axioms, but the same validation logic must be repeated for many properties, e.g. if two or more properties are transitive. The problem can be addressed by the use of annotations and Aspect Oriented Programming (AOP).

References

1. Borst, W.N.: Construction of engineering ontologies for knowledge sharing and reuse. CTIT Ph.D-series No. 97–14, Enschede, The Netherlands (1997)
2. Athanasiadis, I.N., Villa, F., Rizzoli, A.E.: Ontologies, JavaBeans and relational databases for enabling semantic programming. In: 31th IEEE Annual International Computer Software and Applications Conference (COMPSAC), Beijing (2007)
3. Stevenson, G., Dobson, S.: Sapphire: generating java runtime artefacts from OWL ontologies. In: Salinesi, C., Pastor, O. (eds.) CAiSE 2011. LNBIP, vol. 83, pp. 425–436. Springer, Heidelberg (2011). https://doi.org/10.1007/978-3-642-22056-2_46
4. Kalyanpur, A., Pastor, D.J., Battle, S., Padget, J.: Automatic mapping of OWL ontologies into Java. In: Proceedings of Sixteenth International Conference on Software Engineering and Knowledge Engineering (SEKE), Banff (2004)
5. Protégé. http://protege.stanford.edu/. Accessed 27 June 2017
6. Groovy Language Documentation. http://groovy-lang.org/single-page-documentation.html. Accessed 27 June 2017
7. OWL2 Web Ontology Language. Structural Specification and Functional-Style Syntax, 2nd edn. https://www.w3.org/TR/owl2-syntax. Accessed 03 June 2017
8. Object-Oriented Programming Concepts. https://docs.oracle.com/javase/tutorial/java/concepts/index.html. Accessed 27 June 2017
9. OMG Unified Modeling Language, Version 2.5. http://www.omg.org/spec/UML/2.5. Accessed 27 June 2017
10. Ohlbach, H.J..: Java2OWL a system for synchronising Java and OWL. In: 4th International Conference on Knowledge Engineering and Ontology Development, pp. 15–24. SciTePress, Barcelona (2012)
11. Data Types and Data Binding in WebLogic Web Services. https://docs.oracle.com/cd/E13222_01/wls/docs100/webserv/data_types.html#wp209610. Accessed 22 May 2017
12. OWL2 to Groovy Converter. https://bitbucket.org/pworoniecki/owl-to-groovy/. Accessed 03 June 2017
13. The OWL API. http://owlapi.sourceforge.net/. Accessed 03 June 2017
14. OWL2 Web Ontology Language XML Serialization, 2nd edn. https://www.w3.org/TR/owl2-xml-serialization/. Accessed 03 June 2017
15. OWL2 Web Ontology Language Mapping to RDF Graphs, 2nd edn. https://www.w3.org/TR/2012/REC-owl2-mapping-to-rdf-20121211/. Accessed 03 June 2017

Graph Structure and Computation

Simple Paths and Cycles Avoiding Forbidden Paths

Benjamin Momège$^{(\boxtimes)}$

Inria Lille - Nord Europe, Villeneuve-d'Ascq, France
benjamin.momege@inria.fr

Abstract. A graph with forbidden paths is a pair (G, F) where G is a graph and F is a subset of the set of paths in G. A simple path avoiding forbidden paths in (G, F) is a simple path in G such that each subpath is not in F. It is shown in [S. Szeider, Finding paths in graphs avoiding forbidden transitions, DAM 126] that the problem of deciding the existence of a simple path avoiding forbidden paths in a graph with forbidden paths is NP-complete even when the forbidden paths are restricted to be transitions, i.e., of length two. We give an exact exponential time algorithm that decides in $O(2^n n^{2k+O(1)})$ time and $O(n^{k+O(1)})$ space whether there exists a simple path between two vertices of a given n-vertex graph where k is the length of the longest forbidden path. We also obtain an exact $O(2^n n^{2k+O(1)})$ time and $O(n^{k+O(1)})$ space algorithm to check the existence of a Hamiltonian path avoiding forbidden paths and for the graphs with forbidden transitions an exact $O^*(2^n)$ time and polynomial space algorithm to check the existence of a Hamiltonian cycle avoiding forbidden transitions. In the last section, we present a new sufficient condition for graphs to have a Hamiltonian cycle, which gives us some interesting corollaries for graphs with forbidden paths.

Keywords: Exponential time algorithms · Exact algorithms
Graph algorithms · Forbidden paths · Hamiltonian cycles

1   Introduction

Algorithms manipulating graphs are often used to solve concrete situations in many applied fields. Finding a path between two given points/vertices is a fundamental tool that often serves as a subroutine in many more complex algorithms and software, for example in flows: improving paths between a source and a sink, in scheduling: notion of constraint and critical path, in networks for routing operations, etc. Several well-known polynomial time algorithms are able to do this task: depth-first search (DFS) or breadth-first search (BFS) to find a shortest paths in unweighted graphs, Dijkstra for weighted graphs. They are widely available in software packages (like Maple and Mathematica) and are taught in most of the first level computer science or engineering courses all around the world (see a reference book on algorithms like [10]).

© Springer International Publishing AG 2018
A M. Tjoa et al. (Eds.): SOFSEM 2018, LNCS 10706, pp. 285–294, 2018.
https://doi.org/10.1007/978-3-319-73117-9_20

One of the most fundamental combinatorial problems is that of checking the existence of paths in graphs. In this paper we study a variant of this problem: consider a graph G with vertices s and t and a set F of paths in G called *forbidden paths*. The task is to find a simple (s,t)-path P such that no forbidden path appears as a subpath of P. We call the desired path a *path avoiding forbidden paths*. When the solution is restricted to a simple path, Szeider [19] uses a reduction from 3-SAT to show that the problem of checking the existence of a simple path avoiding forbidden paths is NP-Complete even when forbidden paths are transitions (paths of length two). When the solution is not restricted to a simple path, the problem has already been solved by Villeneuve and Desaulniers [20] and by Ahmed and Lubiw [2]. They found polynomial time algorithms to obtain a shortest (s,t)-path avoiding forbidden paths. The problem had not been studied before them.

More precisely, Villeneuve and Desaulniers [20] give an algorithm for a shortest (possibly non-simple) path avoiding forbidden paths. They preprocess the graph $G = (V_G, E_G)$ in $O((n+L)\log(n+L) + m + dL)$ time and $O(n+m+dL)$ space so that a shortest path from s to a query vertex can be found in $O(n+L)$ time, where $n = |V_G|$, $m = |E_G|$, d is the largest degree of a vertex, and L is the total size of all forbidden paths. They first build a deterministic finite automaton (DFA) from the set of forbidden paths using the idea of Aho and Corasick [3], which can detect in linear time whether a given path contains any of the forbidden paths. They then "insert" the DFA into G by replicating certain vertices of G in the manner introduced by Martins [11], and then they build a shortest path tree in this modified graph.

Ahmed and Lubiw [2] give two algorithms to compute shortest (possibly non-simple) path avoiding forbidden paths for the case when all the forbidden paths are not known a priori (more precisely, they can identify a forbidden path only after failing in their attempt to follow that path). Their algorithms are strictly more general than the one of Villeneuve and Desaulniers because these algorithms solve their problem in roughly the same time but in $O(n+m+L)$ space, and the algorithm has no a priori knowledge of the forbidden path. The algorithms take $O(fn\log n + fm)$ and $O((n+L)\log(n+L) + m + dL)$ time to find shortest path avoiding forbidden paths from s to all other vertices, where f is the number of forbidden paths. Their algorithms use a vertex replication technique similar to the one used to handle non-simple paths in other shortest path problems [11,20]. Their idea is to handle a forbidden path by replicating its vertices and deleting edges. The result is that one copy of the forbidden path is missing its last edge and the other copy its first edge. With that technique, they want to exclude the forbidden path but to allow all its subpaths. During their work, they identified the same problem as Villeneuve and Desaulniers: vertex replication can result in an exponential number of copies of any forbidden path that overlaps the current one. Villeneuve and Desaulniers solve this problem by identifying and compressing the overlaps of forbidden paths; such an approach was impossible for Ahmed and Lubiw since they didn't have access to the set of forbidden paths. Their idea is to couple vertex replication with the "growth" of a shortest path tree. Indeed, they proved that these extra copies are immaterial.

In their article, Ahmed and Lubiw [1] were motivated for the research on path avoiding forbidden paths by a problem in optical network routing from Nortel Network. Indeed, in an optical network, a ray of light may fail to reach the endpoint of a path P. This failure can occur because of various transmission impairments such as attenuation, crosstalk, dispersion and non-linearities [13, 18]. Moreover, it has been noticed that the ray of light doesn't reach the endpoint of P even if it is able to follow any subpath of P. Forbidden paths provide a straight-forward model of this situation. The path avoiding forbidden paths problem may also have applications in vehicle routing. Indeed, in some networks, it is not possible, while going from a point a towards a point b to continue towards point c. For example in several large streets of cities, it is forbidden to turn left at point b (on the way towards point c) and to cross a road (if one comes from point a preceding b). Many such transits are forbidden in all the countries; several other restrictions exist (no "U" turn for example). In other applications, a path can represent a list of incident tasks having precedence constraints that can be done to go from a certain state s of the system to another one t. However, due to some incompatibility features, a task c can be done after task b, except if the preceding task is a. For example state/task a can change the temperature of an object (for example a can be an industrial oven for workpieces) and going through b is not sufficient to lower this temperature (b can be a quick quality control of the piece). If task c does not bear such a temperature (for example if c puts pieces in a plastic envelope), it is then impossible to reach c, coming from b if b is directly reached by a. Several other studies have been done on graphs with forbidden transitions (paths of length two). For example, in [7] the authors want to find an Eulerian path in a graph representing biological data (from DNA sequencing) where not all transitions between these biological elements are allowed. Later, in [8], this practical problem serves as a motivation for a graph theoretic study. The authors prove, among other results, that finding an Eulerian path is NP-Complete when the graph contains forbidden transitions. All these concrete limitations are due to the system modeled by graphs (optical network, routes, systems of production, biological data etc.) in which not all the paths are possible because they have subpaths that are not allowed.

In [15], we addressed the problem of checking the existence of a simple path avoiding forbidden transitions. After the work of Szeider [19], we conjectured that the problem could be solved in $O^*(2^n)$ time and polynomial space. It is possible to find an $O^*(2^n)$ time algorithm using dynamic programming adapting the algorithms of Bellman [5,6] or Held and Karp [14] for the travelling salesman problem. However, their algorithms have the serious disadvantage of exponential space complexity which prohibits their use in many circumstances. Another algorithm using the principle of inclusion-exclusion with the same running time and polynomial space amenable to detecting if a graph (without forbidden paths) is Hamiltonian has been (re)discovered at least three times (see [4,16,17]). But when this method is adapted to our problem we only get an $O^*(3^n)$ time algorithm. Our idea was to find new sums where we can make a change of variables which reduces the number of operations to obtain an $O^*(2^n)$ time and polynomial space algorithm.

In this paper, we study the problem of checking the existence of a simple path avoiding forbidden paths. To be as general as possible we study the problem in directed graphs. We give a new exact exponential time algorithm that decides in $O(2^n n^{2k+O(1)})$ time and $O(n^{k+O(1)})$ space whether there exists a simple path between two vertices of a given n-vertex graph where k is the length of the longest forbidden path. This algorithm generalizes (for all k) and uses a faster and simpler techniques than the algorithm of [15]. We also obtain an exact $O(2^n n^{2k+O(1)})$ time and $O(n^{k+O(1)})$ space algorithm to check the existence of a Hamiltonian path avoiding forbidden paths and for the graphs with forbidden transitions an exact $O^*(2^n)$ time and polynomial space algorithm to check the existence of a Hamiltonian cycle avoiding forbidden transitions.

2   Preliminary Definitions

We refer to [9,12,21] for undefined notations. Except for the last section, we only consider simple directed graphs. We recall that a *path* of length ℓ in a graph is a sequence of $\ell + 1$ vertices (not necessarily distinct) such that from each of its vertices there is an arc to the next vertex in the sequence. A path is *simple* if all its vertices are distinct.

Definition 1. *A graph with forbidden paths is a pair (G, F) where $G = (V_G, E_G)$ is a graph and F is a subset of the set of paths in G. A path (resp. simple path, Hamiltonian path, Hamiltonian cycle) avoiding forbidden paths in (G, F) is a path (resp. simple path, Hamiltonian path, Hamiltonian cycle) in G such that no subsequence of consecutive elements of the path is in F. For a fixed positive integer k a graph with forbidden k-paths is a graph with forbidden paths (G, F) such that the length of the elements of F is less than or equal to k. A transition is a path of length two.*

We consider the following decision problems:

Simple Path Avoiding Forbidden Paths (SPAFP)

Input: An n-vertex graph with forbidden k-paths and two vertices s and t.
Output: Does there exist a simple (s, t)-path avoiding forbidden paths $((s, t)$-SPAFP) in the graph?

Theorem 1 (Szeider - [19]). *The problem SPAFP is NP-complete even for $k = 2$.*

The Hamiltonian path problem and the Hamiltonian cycle problem are problems of determining whether a Hamiltonian path or a Hamiltonian cycle exists in a given graph (whether directed or undirected). Recall that both problems are NP-complete even in graphs without forbidden paths (See [9]).

Hamiltonian Path Avoiding Forbidden Paths (HPAFP)

Input: An n-vertex graph with forbidden k-paths and two vertices s and t.
Output: Does there exist a Hamiltonian (s,t)-path avoiding forbidden paths $((s,t)$-HPAFP) in the graph?

Hamiltonian Cycle Avoiding Forbidden Transitions (HCAFT)

Input: An n-vertex graph with forbidden transitions.
Output: Does there exist a Hamiltonian cycle avoiding forbidden transitions in the graph?

In the Sects. 3 and 4 we present three algorithms:

- An exact $O(2^n n^{2k+O(1)})$ time and $O(n^{k+O(1)})$ space algorithm to solve the SPAFP problem. If a SPAFT exists, it also returns the length of the shortest,
- An exact $O(2^n n^{2k+O(1)})$ time and $O(n^{k+O(1)})$ space algorithm to solve the HPAFP problem,
- An exact $O^*(2^n)$ time and polynomial space algorithm to solve the HCAFT problem.

3   The Algorithms for the SPAFP and HPAFP Problems

Let (G, F) be a n-vertex graph graph with forbidden k-paths, A and T be subsets of V_G, ℓ a positive integer and s and t two vertices of G. We denote by P the set of paths (not necessarily simple) avoiding forbidden paths in (G, F). The proof of the following result is straightforward.

Lemma 1. *For $j \geq k$ we have $(x_0, \ldots, x_j) \in P$ if and only if $(x_i, \ldots, x_{i+k}) \in P$ for all $i \in \{0, \ldots j - k\}$.*

Definition 2. *Define $\mathcal{P}(A, \ell)$ as the number of (s, t)-paths (not necessarily simple) of length $\ell - 1$ that only visit vertices in A and that avoid the forbidden paths.*
Define $\mathcal{P}(A, \ell; v_1, v_2, \ldots, v_i)$ as the number of (s, v_i)-paths (not necessarily simple) of length $\ell - 1$ that only visit vertices in A, that avoid the forbidden paths, and whose last i visited vertices are $v_1, v_2, \ldots, v_i$ (in this order).

Lemma 2. *For fixed A, the values $\mathcal{P}(A, \ell)$ for $1 \leq \ell \leq n$ can be computed in $O(n^{2k+O(1)})$ time and $O(n^{k+O(1)})$ space.*

Proof. If $\ell < k$, we will still need to check against the paths in F, requiring $O(n^k)$ time for each (s, t)-path of length $\ell - 1$ that only visit vertices in A being checked.

If $\ell = k$, $\mathcal{P}(A, \ell; v_1, \ldots, v_k) = \begin{cases} 1 \text{ if } (v_1, \ldots, v_k) \in P \text{ and } v_1, \ldots, v_k \in A, \\ 0 \text{ else.} \end{cases}$

If $\ell > k$ and $v_k \notin A$, we have $\mathcal{P}(A, \ell; v_1, \ldots, v_k) = 0$.
If $\ell > k$ and $v_k \in A$, with the help of Lemma 1 we obtain:

$$\mathcal{P}(A, \ell; v_1, \ldots, v_k) = \sum_{v_0 \in A: (v_0, \ldots, v_k) \in P} \mathcal{P}(A, \ell - 1; v_0, \ldots, v_{k-1})$$

$$= \sum_{v_0 \in A: (v_0, \ldots, v_k) \text{ is good}} \mathcal{P}(A, \ell - 1; v_0, \ldots, v_{k-1}),$$

where $(v_0, \ldots, v_k) \in P$ is good if and only if $(v_j, \ldots, v_k) \notin F$ for $0 \le j \le k$.
We have $\{\mathcal{P}(A, \ell; v_1, \ldots, v_k) \mid (v_1, \ldots, v_k) \in A^k\}$

$$= \left\{ \sum_{v_0 \in A: (v_0, \ldots, v_k) \text{ is good}} \mathcal{P}(A, \ell - 1; v_0, \ldots, v_{k-1}) \mid (v_1, \ldots, v_k) \in A^k \right\}$$

and so we can compute this set from $\{\mathcal{P}(A, \ell - 1; v_0, \ldots, v_{k-1}) \mid (v_0, \ldots, v_{k-1}) \in A^k\}$ in $O(n^{2k+2})$ time (the cost of checking each path against paths in F could be $O(n^{k+1})$ time for each path in P in the worst case) and $O(n^{k+O(1)})$ space, and by induction from $\{\mathcal{P}(A, k; v_1, \ldots, v_k) \mid (v_1, \ldots, v_k) \in A^k\}$ in $O(n^{2k+3})$ time and $O(n^{k+O(1)})$ space. Finally, with the formula

$$\mathcal{P}(A, \ell) = \sum_{(v_1, \ldots, v_{k-1}) \in A^{k-1}} \mathcal{P}(A, \ell; v_1, \ldots, v_{k-1}, t)$$

valid for $\ell \ge k$ we compute $\mathcal{P}(A, \ell)$ in $O(n^{2k+O(1)})$ time and $O(n^{k+O(1)})$ space. This concludes the proof. $\square$

Definition 3. *Define $\mathcal{H}(T)$ as the number of Hamiltonian (s, t)-paths that avoid the forbidden paths in the subgraph induced by T.*

Lemma 3. $\mathcal{H}(T) = \sum_{A \subseteq T} (-1)^{|T \smallsetminus A|} \cdot \mathcal{P}(A, |T|)$.

Proof. Let P be a fixed path of length $|T| - 1$ that is counted in at least one of the terms $\mathcal{P}(A, |T|)$ of the sum

$$\sum_{A \subseteq T} (-1)^{|T \smallsetminus A|} \cdot \mathcal{P}(A, |T|). \tag{1}$$

Then we show that when P is simple, it contributes 1 to the sum, and when not simple, contributes 0. Indeed, the path P contributes

$$\sum_{U \subseteq A \subseteq T} (-1)^{|T \smallsetminus A|} \tag{2}$$

to the sum (1), where U is the set of vertices of P. Substituting $|T \smallsetminus A|$ by i the sum (2) is

$$\sum_{i=0}^{|T \smallsetminus U|} \binom{|T \smallsetminus U|}{i} (-1)^i,$$

and is equal to 0 if U is not equal to T, and to 1 otherwise. Thus, the sum (1) counts the number of (s,t)-paths of length $|T|-1$ avoiding forbidden paths and visiting each vertex of T, that is to say $\mathcal{H}(T)$. This concludes the proof. □

Now the number of simple (s,t)-paths of length $\ell-1$ that avoid the forbidden paths is obviously obtained by taking the sum

$$\sum_{T \subseteq V_G : |T|=\ell} \mathcal{H}(T)$$

of $\mathcal{H}(T)$ over all vertex subsets T of the graph such that $|T| = \ell$. It remains to derive a nicer-to-compute expression with the help of Lemma 3, e.g., as follows:

$$\sum_{T \subseteq V_G : |T|=\ell} \mathcal{H}(T) = \sum_{T \subseteq V_G : |T|=\ell} \sum_{A \subseteq T} (-1)^{|T \smallsetminus A|} \cdot \mathcal{P}(A, |T|)$$

$$= \sum_{A \subseteq V_G} \sum_{A \subseteq T \subseteq V_G : |T|=\ell} (-1)^{\ell - |A|} \cdot \mathcal{P}(A, \ell)$$

$$= \sum_{A \subseteq V_G} (-1)^{\ell - |A|} \cdot \mathcal{P}(A, \ell) \cdot \binom{n - |A|}{n - \ell}.$$

We deduce that the number of Hamiltonian (s,t)-paths that avoid the forbidden paths is

$$\sum_{A \subseteq V_G} (-1)^{n - |A|} \cdot \mathcal{P}(A, n),$$

and the number of simple (s,t)-paths that avoid the forbidden paths is

$$\sum_{\ell=1}^{n} \sum_{A \subseteq V_G} (-1)^{\ell - |A|} \cdot \mathcal{P}(A, \ell) \binom{n - |A|}{n - \ell}.$$

So the following algorithms are correct:

Algorithm 2. *Input: A graph with forbidden k-paths (G, F) and two vertices s and t.*
Output: Does there exist a (s,t)-HPAFP in (G, F)?

1. *Let $n := |V_G|$ and $R := 0$*
2. *For Each $A \subseteq V_G$ do $R := R + (-1)^{n-|A|} \cdot \mathcal{P}(A, n)$ end*
   If $R \geq 1$ then Return YES
3. *Return NO*

Algorithm 3. *Input: A graph with forbidden k-paths (G, F) and two vertices s and t.*
Output: Does there exist a (s,t)-SPAFP? If yes, what is the length of the shortest one?

1. *Let* $n := |V_G|$
2. *For* $\ell \leftarrow 1$ *To* n *do:*
   $R := 0$
   For Each $A \subseteq V_G$ *do* $R := R + (-1)^{\ell - |A|} \cdot \mathcal{P}(A, l) \cdot \binom{n - |A|}{n - \ell}$ *end*
   If $R \geq 1$ *then Return (YES,* ℓ) *end*
3. *Return NO*

Theorem 4. *Algorithms 2 and 3 are correct and run in* $O(2^n n^{2k + O(1)})$ *time and* $O(n^{k + O(1)})$ *space for every* n-*vertex graph with forbidden* k-*paths.*

Proof. In light of the above, algorithms are correct and the space complexity is bounded by $O(n^{k + O(1)})$. The time complexity of Algorithm 2 is bounded by

$$\sum_{i=1}^{n} \binom{n}{i} \cdot O(n^{2k + O(1)}) = O(2^n n^{2k + O(1)}).$$

The time complexity of Algorithm 3 is bounded by

$$\sum_{\ell=1}^{n} \sum_{i=1}^{n} \binom{n}{i} \cdot O(n^{2k + O(1)}) = O(2^n n^{2k + O(1)}).$$

This concludes the proof.   □

Remark 1. By repeating the Algorithm 2 for all ordered pairs of vertices (s, t) we check the existence of a HPAFP in (G, F) in $O(2^n n^{2k + O(1)})$ time.

4   The Algorithm for the HCAFT Problem

In this section (G, F) is a n-vertex directed graph with forbidden transitions (paths of length two). We use the abbreviation (s, t)-HPAFT for Hamiltonian (s, t)-path avoiding forbidden transitions.

Lemma 4. *A HCAFT cannot contain both arcs of a transition of* F.

Proof. Indeed, if a cycle contains two arcs ab and bc (with possibly $a = c$) of a transition of F, bc cannot be the successor of ab (otherwise the cycle would contain a transition of F). Thus, the vertex b appears twice in the cycle. This is a contradiction. This concludes the proof.   □

For each given arc $ts \in E_G$, we construct from (G, F) a graph with forbidden transition $(G_{s,t}, F_{s,t})$ as follows:

1. Delete the arc distinct from ts of each transition of F containing ts,
2. Remove all transitions containing the arc ts from F.

i.e. $V_{G_{s,t}} := V_G,$
         $E_{G_{s,t}} := E_G \smallsetminus (\{vt \mid (v, t, s) \in F\} \cup \{sv \mid (t, s, v) \in F\}),$
         $F_{s,t} := F \smallsetminus \{(v, t, s), (t, s, v) \mid v \in V_G\}.$

Theorem 5. *There is a HCAFT containing the arc ts in (G, F) if and only if there is a (s, t)-HPAFT in $(G_{s,t}, F_{s,t})$.*

Proof. If there is a HCAFT containing the arc ts in (G, F), then by Lemma 4, it does not contain the arc different from ts of each transition of F containing the arc ts. So the graph $(G_{s,t}, F_{s,t})$ contains the cycle and therefore a Hamiltonian (s, t)-path.

Conversely, suppose that there is a (s, t)-HPAFT in $(G_{s,t}, F_{s,t})$. By construction, this graph contains the arc ts and does not contain a transition of F containing this arc. So we can add this arc to the previous HPAFT to form a HCAFT in $(G_{s,t}, F_{s,t})$. This cycle does not contain any transition of F. It is therefore a HCAFT containing the arc ts in (G, F). This concludes the proof. $\square$

Corollary 1. *There is a HCAFT in (G, F) if and only if there exist an $st \in E_G$ such that there is a (s, t)-HPAFT in $(G_{s,t}, F_{s,t})$.*

Algorithm 6. *Input: A graph with forbidden transitions (G, F). Output: Does there exist a HCAFT in (G, F)?*

1. For Each arc $st \in E_G$:
Apply the Algorithm 2 to $G_{s,t}$
If Algorithm 2 returns YES then Return YES
2. Return NO

Corollary 2. *Algorithm 6 is correct and runs in $O^*(2^n)$ time and polynomial space for every n-vertex graph with forbidden transitions.*

Proof. By Corollary 1, Algorithm 6 is correct and has a polynomial space complexity. By Theorem 4 and Corollary 1 the time complexity is bounded by

$$n(n-1) \cdot O(2^n n^{4+O(1)}) = O^*(2^n).$$

This concludes the proof. $\square$

References

1. Ahmed, M., Lubiw, A.: Shortest paths avoiding forbidden subpaths. In: STACS, pp. 63–74 (2009)
2. Ahmed, M., Lubiw, A.: Shortest paths avoiding forbidden subpaths. Networks **61**(4), 322–334 (2013)
3. Aho, A.V., Corasick, M.J.: Efficient string matching: an aid to bibliographic search. Commun. ACM **18**(6), 333–340 (1975)
4. Bax, E.T.: Inclusion and exclusion algorithm for the Hamiltonian path problem. Inf. Process. Lett. **47**(4), 203–207 (1993)
5. Bellman, R.: Dynamic programming treatment of the travelling salesman problem. J. ACM **9**(1), 61–63 (1962)
6. Bellman, R.E.: Combinatorial processes and dynamic programming. In: Proceedings of 10th Symposium in Applied Mathematics, pp. 217–249 (1960)

7. Błażewicz, J., Kasprzak, M.: Computational complexity of isothermic DNA sequencing by hybridization. Discrete Appl. Math. **154**(5), 718–729 (2006)
8. Błażewicz, J., Kasprzak, M., Leroy-Beaulieu, B., de Werra, D.: Finding Hamiltonian circuits in quasi-adjoint graphs. Discrete Appl. Math. **156**(13), 2573–2580 (2008)
9. Bondy, J.A., Murty, U.S.R.: Graph Theory. Springer, London (2010)
10. Cormen, T.H., Leiserson, C.E., Rivest, R.L., Stein, C.: Introduction to Algorithms, 3rd edn. MIT Press, Cambridge (2009)
11. de Queiros, E., Martins, V.: An algorithm for ranking paths that may contain cycles. Eur. J. Oper. Res. **18**(1), 123–130 (1984)
12. Diestel, R.: Graph Theory. Graduate Texts in Mathematics, 173rd edn. Springer, Heidelberg (2012)
13. Gouveia, L., Patrício, P., de Sousa, A.F., Valadas, R.: MPLS over WDM network design with packet level QOS constraints based on ILP models. In: Proceedings of IEEE INFOCOM (2003)
14. Held, M., Karp, R.M.: A dynamic programming approach to sequencing problems. J. Soc. Ind. Appl. Math. **10**(1), 196–210 (1962)
15. Kanté, M.M., Laforest, C., Momège, B.: An exact algorithm to check the existence of (elementary) paths and a generalisation of the cut problem in graphs with forbidden transitions. In: van Emde Boas, P., Groen, F.C.A., Italiano, G.F., Nawrocki, J., Sack, H. (eds.) SOFSEM 2013. LNCS, vol. 7741, pp. 257–267. Springer, Heidelberg (2013). https://doi.org/10.1007/978-3-642-35843-2_23
16. Karp, R.M.: Dynamic programming meets the principle of inclusion and exclusion. Oper. Res. Lett. **1**(2), 49–51 (1982)
17. Kohn, S., Gottlieb, A., Kohn, M.: A generating function approach to the traveling salesman problem. In: Proceedings of the 1977 Annual Conference, ACM 1977, pp. 294–300. ACM, New York (1977)
18. Lee, K., Shayman, M.A.: Optical network design with optical constraints in IP/WDM networks. IEICE Trans. **88-B**(5), 1898–1905 (2005)
19. Szeider, S.: Finding paths in graphs avoiding forbidden transitions. Discrete Appl. Math. **126**(2–3), 261–273 (2003)
20. Villeneuve, D., Desaulniers, G.: The shortest path problem with forbidden paths. Eur. J. Oper. Res. **165**(1), 97–107 (2005)
21. West, D.B.: Introduction to Graph Theory, 2nd edn. Prentice Hall, Upper Saddle River (2000)

External Memory Algorithms for Finding Disjoint Paths in Undirected Graphs

Maxim Babenko[1,3] and Ignat Kolesnichenko[2,3(✉)]

[1] National Research University Higher School of Economics, Moscow, Russia
[2] Moscow Institute of Physics and Technology, Moscow, Russia
ignat1990@gmail.com
[3] Yandex LLC, Moscow, Russia

Abstract. Consider the following well-known combinatorial problem: given an undirected graph $G = (V, E)$, terminals $s, t \in V$, and an integer $k \geq 1$, find k edge-disjoint s–t paths in G or report that such paths do not exist.

We study this problem in the *external memory* (EM) model of Agrawal and Vitter, i.e. assume that only M words of *random access memory* (RAM) are available while the graph resides in EM, which enables reading and writing contiguous blocks of B words per single I/O. The latter external memory is also used for storing the output and some intermediate data.

For $k = 1$, the problem consists in finding a single s–t path in an undirected graph and can be solved in $Conn(V, E) = O\left(\frac{V+E}{V} Sort(V) \log\log \frac{VB}{E}\right)$ I/Os, where $Sort(N) = O\left(\frac{N}{B} \log_{M/B} \frac{N}{B}\right)$ is the complexity of sorting N words in external memory.

Our contribution is two novel EM algorithms that solve the problem for $k \leq \frac{M}{B}$. The first takes $O(k \cdot Conn(V, E))$ I/Os. The second one applies the ideas of Ibaraki–Nagamochi sparse connectivity certificates and takes $O\left((Sort(V + E) + k \cdot Conn(V, kV)) \cdot \log \frac{V}{M}\right)$ I/Os, which improves upon the first bound for sufficiently dense graphs.

Both algorithms outperform the naive approach based on successive BFS- or DFS-augmentations for a wide range of parameters $|V|$, $|E|$, M, B.

1 Introduction

Consider the following well-known combinatorial problem: given a undirected graph $G = (V, E)$ terminals $s, t \in V$, and integer $k \geq 1$, find k edge-disjoint s–t paths in G (or report that such paths do not exist). This problem, having intimate connections with network flow theory, dates back to the beginning of the 20th century. A multitude of efficient combinatorial algorithms are known to solve this problem but most are formulated in terms of the RAM model, where the cost of accessing each memory cell is $O(1)$.

Now suppose that graph G is huge; it cannot fit into RAM and is instead kept in a storage (say, HDD or SSD), which enables reading and writing contiguous

© Springer International Publishing AG 2018
A M. Tjoa et al. (Eds.): SOFSEM 2018, LNCS 10706, pp. 295–304, 2018.
https://doi.org/10.1007/978-3-319-73117-9_21

blocks of size B words (typically $B \ll M$) within a single I/O, while only $M \ll |V|, |E|$ words of the usual (*internal*, random access) memory are available. The external memory is also used for storing the output and any intermediate data the algorithm finds necessary. The complexity is measured as the number of I/Os (reads and writes) the algorithm performs in the worst case for inputs of a given size. This framework (introduced by Agrawal and Vitter [AV88]) proved to be a useful tool for analysing real-world algorithms dealing with huge volumes of data.

For example, consider the standard SORTING problem: given a sequence of N integers (each fitting into a machine word), the goal is to reorder its elements in non-decreasing order. The external memory version of MERGE-SORT algorithm solves this problem in $O(Sort(N))$ I/Os. Here $Sort(N) := O\left(\frac{N}{B} \log_{M/B} \frac{N}{B}\right)$; the latter can often be found as a part of various complexity estimates.

Assuming the EM model, the problem of finding disjoint paths becomes more intricate. Indeed, most RAM algorithms start with the empty collection of paths and then gradually improve it by running certain digraph traversals (e.g. BFS or DFS). Traversing a directed graph in external memory is known to be hard and takes $\Omega(V + E/B)$ I/Os for modern algorithms [MSS03]. (Hereinafter, in complexity bounds we identify sets with their cardinalities.)

Note that for $k = 1$ the problem is simpler: finding a spanning forest in an undirected graph can be done in $Conn(V, E) = O\left(\frac{V+E}{V} Sort(V) \log \log \frac{VB}{E}\right)$ I/Os [MR99]; note that $Conn(V, E) = o(V + E/B)$ for reasonable parameter values. Now it remains to check if s and t are in the same tree and, if so, compute a (unique) s–t path in that tree. The latter is known to be doable in $O(Sort(V + E))$ I/Os.

Our contribution is two novel EM algorithms that solve the problem for undirected graphs for moderate values of k; namely we assume that $k \leq \frac{M}{B}$. Our first algorithm takes $O(k \cdot Conn(V, E))$ I/Os and works best for sparse graphs. The second applies ideas of Ibaraki–Nagamochi sparse connectivity certificates and takes $O\left((Sort(V + E) + k \cdot Conn(V, kV)) \cdot \log \frac{V}{M}\right)$ I/Os, which gives a better bound for, e.g. $E > kV \cdot \log \frac{V}{M}$.

The rest of the paper is organized as follows. In Sect. 2 we introduce some basic definitions and notation that is used throughout the paper. Section 3 presents the first algorithm that employs the special structure of residual graphs to speed up finding augmenting paths. Section 4 discusses *sparse connectivity certificates* and presents the second algorithm, which improves upon the first one for sufficiently dense graphs. Finally in Sect. 5 we conclude with a number of observations and open questions.

2   Preliminaries

2.1   Flows and Packings

As it is widely known, there is an intimate connection between collections of vertex-simple edge-disjoint s-t paths (*packings*) and s–t integral *flows* in unit-capacitated networks. The latter can be equivalently described as follows. Suppose that some edges of G are made *directed* in such a way that: (i) all directed edges incident to s leave s; (ii) all directed edges incident to t enter t; (iii) for each $v \in V - \{s, t\}$ the number of directed edges entering v is equal to the number of directed edges leaving v. Then this (partial) orientation gives an s–t flow. The number of directed edges leaving s is always equal to the number of directed edges entering t; this common number is called the flow *value* and is denoted by $|f|$.

A packing can be trivially converted into a flow (by orienting all edges traversed by paths in the packing in the direction along the path from s to t). The reverse transformation is also possible: given a flow, one can decompose it into a collection of edge-disjoint s–t paths and circuits (by listing these components explicitly).

The latter transformation, while being trivially doable in linear time in the RAM model, is more challenging if the EM model is assumed. Fortunately, these exists an efficient algorithm that solves the problem in $O(Sort(V + E))$ I/Os. It reduces the decomposition to a variant of LIST-RANKING problem. Consider a linked list with N items (given by a collection of *links* (x, y) indicating that y is the immediate successor of x). The goal is to compute the *ranks* of its items, i.e. distances from the beginning of the list. While the task can be easily solved in $O(N)$ time in RAM, this straightforward approach involves $\Theta(N)$ random reads, which implies $O(N)$ I/Os bound in the EM model. A substantially better solution, which takes $O(Sort(N))$ I/Os, is known [AV88, MSS03].

Moreover, a similar algorithm can deal with linked lists consisting of multiple connected components, some of which could be cyclic. Instead of computing ranks the algorithm can list the items in these components explicitly (in the natural order induced by links).

With these techniques at hand, one can turn a flow into a packing as follows: consider the set of all directed edges and regard them as items. Sort these edges by their head vertices. Make a copy of the edge list and sort it by tail vertices. Now for each $v \in V - \{s, t\}$ one has the lists of all incoming and outcoming edges $\delta^{in}(v)$ and $\delta^{out}(v)$, resp. These lists are of equal size, so we may arbitrarily (and bijectively) match edges in $\delta^{in}(v)$ and $\delta^{out}(v)$ to form links between items. It remains to run a variant of LIST-RANKING algorithm [CGG+95] to decompose items (directed edges) into components (s–t paths and circuits). Among these components, we are only interested in s–t paths and may ignore circuits. The total complexity of this procedure is $O(Sort(V + E))$. The reader may refer to [Bab13] for more details.

2.2 Flow Augmentation

Our algorithms primarily work with flows rather than packings. Given a flow f, the standard augmenting path search may either reveal a way to increase the value of f or detect that it is already maximum, as follows. Consider the (partially directed) graph G_f (usually called *residual*) obtained from G by taking all undirected (w.r.t. f) edges and reversing the directions of all directed (w.r.t. f) edges. Now if G_f admits no s–t path (where directed edges must be traversed in the given direction and undirected can be traversed arbitrarily) then f is maximum. Otherwise, for such a path P (called *augmenting*) we alter f into f' as follows: all edges not traversed by P remain unchanged, all undirected edges traversed by P become directed in f' (and P induces a direction for them), and finally all directed edges traversed by P are reversed. This is the standard *flow augmentation procedure*; one can easily check that the resulting (partial) orientation f' is a flow obeying $|f'| = |f| + 1$.

These observations immediately imply the naive algorithm for finding k edge-disjoint s–t paths (typically referred to as the *Fulkerson–Ford algorithm*): start with the empty flow, run k augmentations; finally convert the flow into a packing. In the RAM model, this algorithm takes $O(k(V + E))$ time.

Unfortunately there exists a fundamental obstacle preventing this approach from yielding an efficient EM algorithm: while checking for s–t connectivity in undirected graphs is easy (takes $O(Conn(V, E)) = O(\frac{V+E}{V} \cdot Sort(V) \log \log \frac{VB}{E})$ I/Os [MR99]), residual graphs arising at intermediate steps are (partially) directed and no efficient EM digraph traversal is known; in particular both BFS and DFS take $\Omega(V + E/B)$ I/Os, which may easily be prohibitive.

3   Efficient External Memory Augmentation

We solve the above issue by exploiting the structure of residual graphs. Our approach takes $O(Conn(V, E))$ I/Os per augmentation step and thus enables to compute k edge-disjoint s–t paths in $O(k \cdot Conn(V, E))$ I/Os.

3.1   Ladder Graph

The idea is to replace the residual graph with another one, called the *ladder* graph H, which is constructed as follows. Let f be the current flow of value l, and $\mathcal{P} = \{P_1, \ldots, P_l\}$ be the current packing of s–t paths. We split vertices of G_f that appear in P_i to make paths P_i vertex-disjoint. Namely, let U be the set of vertices that belong to any P_i; for each $v \in U$ count the number $p(v)$ of paths P_i that contain v and make $p(v)$ copies $v^1, \ldots, v^{p(v)}$ of v. In particular, we have exactly l copies $s^1, \ldots, s^l$ of s and exactly l copies $t^1, \ldots, t^l$ of t. Directed edges of G_f are turned into directed edges of H.

In other words, H consists of l vertex-disjoint paths from t^i to s^i (for $i = 1, \ldots, l$). We call these paths $\mathcal{Q} = \{Q_1, \ldots, Q_l\}$ (where Q_i in H corresponds to P_i in G_f).

Now we add undirected edges to H to capture the reachability properties of the original G_f. First, we need to account for vertex splitting: for each $v \in U$ we add $p(v) - 1$ undirected edges of the form $\{v^i, v^{i+1}\}$ for $i = 1, \ldots, p(v) - 1$; we call them *glue* edges.

Second, we need to account for the undirected edges present in G_f. To this aim, we compute a spanning forest of the undirected part G_f^{undir} of G_f. For each such component Γ, let $u_1, \ldots, u_s$ be its vertices belonging to U. Recall that each

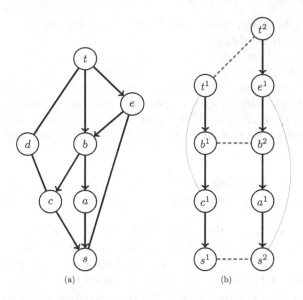

Fig. 1. Ladder graph construction. (a) Initial residual graph G_f; (b) Ladder graph H. Blue dashed indicates glue edges. Red thin indicates connectivity edges. (Color figure online)

of these vertices u is split into $p(u)$ copies in H. To capture the connectivity, we add $s - 1$ undirected edges between arbitrary copies of u_i and u_{i+1}, for $i = 1, \ldots, s - 1$; we call them *connectivity* edges. This completes the description of H.

One can easily see that each s–t path in G_f gives rise to an s^i–t^j path in H (for some i, j) and vice versa. Indeed, each s–t path in G_f can be split into maximal directed and undirected segments. Each directed segment induces a sequence of directed edges in H; since the endpoints of each consequent pair could be different copies v^α, v^β of the same $v \in U$, we may need to insert glue edges between.

Next, each undirected segment consists of edges from the same connected component Γ; we replace it with the appropriate sequence of connectivity edges.

An example of the original graph G_f and its corresponding ladder graph H is given in Fig. 1. Also this construction of H can be carried out in the EM settings; due to the lack of space we omit the relevant details.

Lemma 1. *Ladder graph H can be constructed in $O(Conn(V, E))$ I/Os.*

3.2 Finding Augmenting Paths

We now consider the problem of finding an augmenting path in H, i.e. a path connecting some s^i with some t^j. Like in most EM algorithms, all our graphs are given by files consisting of tuples describing edges. Vertices and edges are identified with numbers (or short tuples of numbers) and each edge is described by the ids of its endpoints. For graph H, its vertex ids explicitly encode ids of the originating vertices of G.

Recall that each path P_i in the current packing $\mathcal{P}$ in G is turned into a path Q_i in H and the latter paths are vertex-disjoint. We run LIST-RANKING for the directed part DIR of H to assign *ranks* to all vertices of H: copies s^i will have rank 0, the rank of each t^i coincides with the edge-length of the corresponding path Q_j ending in t^i; this assignment is given by file RANKS with tuples $(v\_id, rank, path\_id)$. *rank* is the above-mentioned rank, and *path_id* is an integer ranging from 1 to l and designating paths Q_i.

We take glue and connectivity edges and make them "symmetric" by adding edges (x, y) and (y, x) for each undirected edge $\{x, y\}$. The resulting file UNDIR consists of tuples with endpoints $(edge\_id, head\_id, tail\_id)$. We join (by sorting and merging) RANKS with UNDIR on condition $v\_id = tail\_id$ and split the result into files EDGES$_1, \ldots,$ EDGES$_l$ by *path_id* where EDGES$_i$ consists of tuples $(tail\_rank, tail\_id, head\_id, edge\_id)$ describing undirected edges of H that leave the vertices of Q_i, $i = 1, \ldots, l$; here *tail_rank* indicates the rank of vertex with id *tail_id*. These files EDGES$_i$ are furthermore sorted by *tail_rank*.

We execute a certain variant of graph traversal: maintain the set of reachable vertices R, which is initialized to be $\{s^1, \ldots, s^l\}$, then gradually examine edges leaving R and extend R until no more suitable edges remain or some t^j is added into R. The cornerstone of the efficient implementation is the following observation, which follows from the structure of H: if some $v \in V(Q_i)$ is added into R then all vertices of smaller rank (preceding v) in Q_i can also be immediately added to R. This enables to maintain an array of *border ranks* $b[1], \ldots, b[l]$ and assume that

$$R = \{v \in H \mid rank(v) \le b[path\_id(v)]\},$$

where $rank(v)$ and $path\_id(v)$ is the rank and the path id assigned to v, resp., by LIST-RANKING.

We start with $b[i] := 0$ for all $i = 1, \ldots, l$, and scan all EDGES$_i$ in parallel. From each EDGES$_i$, we read edges $e = (x, y)$ originating from vertices $x \in V(Q_i)$ with $rank(x) \le b[i]$. For each such e, let $j := path\_id(y)$; we update $b[j] := \max(b[j], rank(y))$ and proceed. These updates enable reads to progress. We stop either when some $b[i]$ becomes equal to the edge-length of Q_i (in which case some copy of t is reached and we have a breakthrough) or when for each EDGES$_i$ all edges with $tail\_rank \le b[i]$ are processed (in which case no augmenting path exists and the algorithm halts).

Note that border ranks are maintained in RAM. Also to enable reading from all EDGES$_i$ in parallel, we need Bl words of RAM to facilitate prefetch. This is feasible since $k \le \frac{M}{B}$.

The total I/O complexity of checking for the existence of an augmenting path is $O(Sort(V + E))$. In case of positive answer, however, we need to construct such a path explicitly and apply it to the current flow. The detailed proof of the following fact is rather technical and is omitted.

Lemma 2. *If the above algorithm reveals the existence of an augmenting path in H, then it is possible to construct one and augment f along it in $O(Sort(V+E))$ I/Os.*

Summing over all stages, we get

Theorem 1. *Given an undirected graph $G = (V, E)$, vertices $s, t \in V$, integer $k \geq 1$, and assuming the EM model, one can find k edge-disjoint s–t paths (or figure out that such paths do not exist) in $O(k \cdot Conn(V, E))$ I/Os.*

4 External Memory Sparsification

4.1 Sparse Connectivity Certificates

The complexity of the algorithm from Sect. 3 can be improved by applying the following idea: when graph G is sufficiently dense most of its edges are redundant and can be ignored. This intuition is formalized by the following

Theorem 2 [NI92]. *Given an undirected graph $G = (V, E)$, vertices $s, t \in V$, and integer $k \geq 1$, consider the sequence of undirected forests (regarded as edge sets) $F_1, \ldots, F_k$ constructed as follows: F_1 is a spanning forest in G; F_i is a spanning forest in $(V, E - F_1 - \ldots - F_{i-1})$ for $i = 2, \ldots, k$. Then, if G has k edge-disjoint s–t paths then $G' = (V, E')$, for $E' := F_1 \cup \ldots \cup F_k$ also has k edge-disjoint s–t paths.*

We call G' a *k-sparse certificate* for G. Note that G' has at most $k(|V| - 1)$ edges. In [NI92] it was shown how G' can be constructed from G in linear time. However, the latter algorithm only applies to the RAM model and requires $\Omega(V + E)$ I/Os in the EM model, which makes it impractical.

In this section we establish the following

Theorem 3. *Assuming the EM model, a k-sparse certificate for $G = (V, E)$ can be constructed in $O\left((Sort(V + E) + k \cdot Conn(V, kV)) \log \frac{V}{M}\right)$ I/Os.*

Together with Theorem 1 from Sect. 3 this implies

Theorem 4. *Given an undirected graph $G = (V, E)$, vertices $s, t \in V$, integer $k \geq 1$, and assuming the EM model, one can find k edge-disjoint s–t paths in G (or figure out that such paths do not exist) in $O\left((Sort(V + E) + k \cdot Conn(V, kV)) \log \frac{V}{M}\right)$ I/Os.*

4.2 Incremental Construction of Sparse Certificates

To prove Theorem 3, we need some better understanding of how spanning forests are constructed. A spanning forest F in G can be found as follows: initialize $F := \emptyset$, then scan all edges of G and *offer* each edge $e = \{x, y\}$ to F. If x and y are in distinct connected components of F then *accept* e into F (merging two components); otherwise *reject* (skip) e.

This implies some important observations:

- One may process edges in an arbitrary order and interrupt the process at any moment to get a spanning forest for the initial prefix of the edge set.
- One need not maintain F; instead it suffices to maintain the connected components of F.
- At any point, G can be replaced by another graph with all connected components of the current F contracted, loops and isolated vertices eliminated.

Now for the problem of constructing a sequence of spanning forests $F_1, \ldots, F_k$, we can state the following generic scheme: maintain a sequence of equivalence relations $\sim_1, \ldots, \sim_k$ on V such that $\sim_{i+1}$ is a refinement of $\sim_i$ for all $i = 1, \ldots, k - 1$. Initially all $\sim_i$ are *diagonal* ($x \sim_i y$ iff $x = y$ for all i).

Enumerate (in some order) pairs (e, i), where $e = \{x, y\} \in E$ and $i = 1, \ldots, k$ and offer e to $\sim_i$. If $x \not\sim_i y$ then $\sim_i$ accepts e and we merge the equivalence classes of x and y in $\sim_i$. If $x \sim_i y$ then $\sim_i$ rejects e, and we proceed to other pairs (e, i). The order in which (e, i) are tried is arbitrary as long as the following property holds: (e, i) is tried after all $(e, 1), \ldots, (e, i - 1)$.

Lemma 3. *The above generic scheme is correct, i.e. computes some spanning forests $F_1, \ldots, F_k$ as required by Theorem 2 (where F_i consists of edges accepted by $\sim_i$).*

Proof. Indeed, $\sim_1$ sees all edges of G in some order, and hence accepts a subset of edges forming a certain spanning forest F_1. Similarly $\sim_2$ sees all edges of G except for those accepted by $\sim_1$ and accepts a certain spanning forest F_2 of $(V, E - F_1)$, etc.

Like for the case of a single spanning forest, at any point G can be replaced by another graph with all equivalence classes of $\sim_k$ contracted, loops and isolated vertices eliminated. Since $\sim_{i+1}$ is a refinement of $\sim_i$ for $i = 1, \ldots, k - 1$, these contractions are well-defined for all $\sim_i$.

4.3   Sparse Certificates in External Memory

We now present an efficient algorithm for constructing k-sparse certificates in EM. The algorithm combines the above observations and the standard EM algorithms for computing spanning forests [MR99].

The algorithm works in *phases*, maintains the current graph $G = (V, E)$ and a sequence of equivalence relations $\sim_1, \ldots, \sim_k$, where $\sim_{i+1}$ is a refinement of $\sim_i$ for $i = 1, \ldots, k - 1$. Initially all $\sim_i$ are diagonal, i.e. $x \sim_i y$ iff $x = y$ for all $i = 1, \ldots, k$. At the beginning of a phase we *pick* some subset of edges of the current graph G. Then we offer all picked edges to $\sim_1$; those rejected by $\sim_1$ are offered to $\sim_2$, etc. All picked edges are removed from E as they cannot be of use anymore. Also at the end of the phase the algorithm contracts the equivalence classes of $\sim_k$, adjusts $\sim_i$ for $i = 1, \ldots, k - 1$ (recall that $\sim_k$ is the finest of these relations), rebuilds E (replacing each remaining edge with its image in the contracted graph), drops loops and isolated vertices. In particular, $\sim_k$ is always diagonal upon entering a phase. The goal of a phase is to decrease $|V|$ by a factor of $\frac{3}{4}$.

Partition V into V^- and V^+ as follows: vertices v with $\deg v < 4k$ go into V^-, the others go to V^+. Now for each vertex v, pick $\min(4k, \deg v)$ arbitrary incident edges. (An edge can be picked by just one of its endpoints or by both of them.) Totally we picked at most $4k|V|$ edges; this costs $O(Sort(V + E))$ I/Os. Process picked edges by running the connected components algorithm k times: first for all picked edges and $\sim_1$, then for the remaining picked edges (rejected by $\sim_1$) and $\sim_2$, and so on.

Let us bound the number of phases. Consider the equivalence classes of $\sim_k$ after all picked edges are handled (but before contractions). Three types of classes are possible: those fully contained in V^- (denote their number by N_1), those containing vertices from both V^- and V^+ (denote their number by N_2), and those fully contained in V^+ (denote their number by N_3). The latter are further divided into trivial components (with just one vertex; let there be N_3^1 such components) and nontrivial components (with at least two vertices; let there be N_3^2 such components). Note that N_1-components become isolated vertices (as we have picked all the edges incident to vertices in V^-) and thus vanish. Hence the next phase deals with a graph with at most $N_2 + N_3$ vertices. We have $|V|$ vertices in G in total, N_2 components of size at least 2, N_3^2 components of size at least 2, and N_3^1 components of size at least 1. Since these components are vertex-disjoint, one has $2N_2 + 2N_3^2 + N_3^1 \leq |V|$ and therefore $N_2 + N_3 \leq \frac{1}{2}(|V| + N_3^1)$.

It remains to bound N_3^1. A vertex v counts in N_3^1 iff $v \in V^+$ and no picked edges incident to v remained at the time the algorithm was handling $\sim_k$. Recall that at least $4k$ incident edges were picked for each $v \in V^+$. Therefore at least $4k \cdot N_3^1/2 = 2kN_3^1$ edges were accepted by $\sim_1, \ldots, \sim_{k-1}$. Each of the latter $k - 1$ forests contains up to $|V| - 1$ edges; hence $2kN_3^1 \leq (k-1)(|V|-1)$, which implies $N_3^1 \leq \frac{1}{2}|V|$.

Now we see that the next phase deals with at most $\frac{1}{2}(|V| + \frac{1}{2}|V|) = \frac{3}{4}|V|$ vertices. Hence after $O(\log \frac{V}{M})$ phases the number of vertices of the current graph becomes $O(M)$, i.e. the problem becomes *semi-external*. Clearly one needs just $O(V)$ RAM words to describe all the relations $\sim_1, \ldots, \sim_k$ (as their equivalence classes form a laminar family). At the last phase, the algorithm maintains all these relations in RAM, scans the edges in an arbitrary order and updates $\sim_i$ (by offering each edge e to $\sim_1, \ldots, \sim_k$, in this order).

Clearly all the above takes $O\left((Sort(V + E) + k \cdot Conn(V, kV)) \log \frac{V}{M}\right)$ in total, as claimed.

5   Conclusions

We have presented some improved EM algorithms for solving the edge-disjoint paths problem. These should be considered as just first steps since they raise more questions than answer. Clearly our approach is highly dependent on the structure of residual graphs and only works for undirected networks. For the latter, some improved flow algorithms are known [KL98, GR99] but they involve, e.g., flow decycling, shortest path augmentations, and dynamic connectivity data structures that are unlikely to be efficiently implementable in the EM settings.

Sparse certificates present another interesting challenge. While our algorithm benefits from graph sparsification, the complexity of constructing a k-sparse certificate seems unsatisfactory (and only improves upon the trivial $O(k \cdot Conn(V, E))$ algorithm for small values of k). In a sense, our sparsification algorithm is not fast, it is just not too slow compared with the subsequent augmentation procedure. Since the algorithm of Ibaraki and Nagamochi solves the problem in linear time in the RAM model, one should probably aim for an EM algorithm with complexity closer to $Sort(V + E)$.

References

[AV88]   Aggarwal, A., Vitter, J.S.: The input/output complexity of sorting and related problems. Commun. ACM **31**(9), 1116–1127 (1988)

[Bab13] Babenko, M.: Flow decompositions in external memory. In: van Emde Boas, P., Groen, F.C.A., Italiano, G.F., Nawrocki, J., Sack, H. (eds.) SOFSEM 2013. LNCS, vol. 7741, pp. 146–156. Springer, Heidelberg (2013). https://doi.org/10.1007/978-3-642-35843-2_14

[CGG+95] Chiang, Y.-J., Goodrich, M.T., Grove, E.F., Tamassia, R., Vengroff, D.E., Vitter, J.S.: External-memory graph algorithms. In: Proceedings of the Sixth Annual ACM-SIAM Symposium on Discrete Algorithms, SODA 1995, pp. 139–149 (1995)

[GR99]   Goldberg, A.V., Rao, S.: Flows in undirected unit capacity networks. SIAM J. Discret. Math. **12**(1), 1–5 (1999)

[KL98]   Karger, D.R., Levine, M.S.: Finding maximum flows in undirected graphs seems easier than bipartite matching. In: Proceedings of the Thirtieth Annual ACM Symposium on Theory of Computing, STOC 1998, pp. 69–78, ACM, New York (1998)

[MR99]   Munagala, K., Ranade, A.: I/O-complexity of graph algorithms. In: Proceedings of the Tenth Annual ACM-SIAM Symposium on Discrete Algorithms, SODA 1999, pp. 687–694. Society for Industrial and Applied Mathematics, Philadelphia (1999)

[MSS03] Meyer, U., Sanders, P., Sibeyn, J.F. (eds.): Algorithms for Memory Hierarchies: Advanced Lectures. LNCS, vol. 2625. Springer, Heidelberg (2003). https://doi.org/10.1007/3-540-36574-5

[NI92]   Nagamochi, H., Ibaraki, T.: A linear-time algorithm for finding a sparse k-connected spanning subgraph of a k-connected graph. Algorithmica **7**(5&6), 583–596 (1992)

On Range and Edge Capacity
in the Congested Clique

Tomasz Jurdziński$^{(\boxtimes)}$ and Krzysztof Nowicki

Institute of Computer Science, University of Wroclaw, Wroclaw, Poland
`tju@cs.uni.wroc.pl`

Abstract. The congested clique is a synchronous, message-passing model of distributed computing in which each computational unit (node) in each round can send message of $O(\log n)$ bits to each other node of the network, where n is the number of nodes.

Following recent progress in design of algorithms for graph connectivity and minimum spanning tree (MST) in the congested clique, we study these problems in limited variants of the congested clique. We show that MST can be computed deterministically and connected components can be computed by a randomized algorithm with optimal edge capacity $\Theta(\log n)$, while preserving the best known round complexity [6,13]. Moreover, our algorithms work in the rcast model with range $r = 2$, the weakest model of the congested clique above the broadcast variant ($r = 1$) in the hierarchy with respect to the range [2].

1 Introduction

Recently, the (unicast) congested clique model of distributed computation attracted much attention in algorithmic community. In this model, each pair of n nodes of a network is connected by a separate communication link. That is, the network forms an n-node clique. Communication is synchronous, each node in each round can send message of $O(\log n)$ bits to each other node of the network. Significantly, a node can send (possibly) different message to each other node of the network in a round. The main purpose of such a model is to understand the role of congestion in distributed computation.

The possibility of sending different messages to all neighbors makes the model very strong. Therefore, it is natural to consider quantitative measures of usage of the possibility of sending different messages through each outgoing link. Such approach was introduced recently in [2], parametrized by the range r, the maximum number of different messages a node can send in a round. We call the model with such a restriction the *rcast* congested clique.

The model. We consider the congested clique model with the following parameters: r – the maximum number of different messages a node can send over its

---

This work was supported by the Polish National Science Centre grant DEC-2012/07/B/ST6/01534.

© Springer International Publishing AG 2018
A. M. Tjoa et al. (Eds.): SOFSEM 2018, LNCS 10706, pp. 305–318, 2018.
https://doi.org/10.1007/978-3-319-73117-9_22

outgoing links in a round; b – the maximum size of a message (*bandwidth*); n – the number of nodes in the network/graph. The model with the above parameters will be denoted $\text{rcast}(n, r, b)$. Usually, we consider the model with $b = \log n$ and therefore the model $\text{rcast}(n, r, \log n)$ is also denoted $\text{rcast}(n, r)$.

We consider randomized algorithms in which a computational unit in each node of the input network can use private random bits in its computation. We say that some event holds with high probability (whp) for an algorithm A running on an input of size n if this event holds with probability $1 - 1/n^c$ for a given constant c.

Graph problems in the congested clique model. Graph problems in the congested clique model are considered in the following framework. The joint input to the n nodes of the network is an undirected n-node weighted graph $G(V, E, w)$, where each node corresponds to a node of the communication network and weights of edges are integers of polynomial size (i.e., each weight is a bit sequence of lenght $O(\log n)$). Each node u initially knows the network size n, its unique ID in $[n]$, the list of IDs of its neighbors in the input graph and the weights of its incident edges.

In the paper, we consider connected components problem (CC) and minimum spanning forest problem (MSF). Our goal is to compute CC or MSF of input graph, i.e., each node should know the set of edges inducing CC/MSF at the end of an execution of an algorithm. (Note that unlike a common definition of the connectivity problem, where the result should only specify the connected components, we require that the set of edges connecting the components has to be a part of the final solution.)

Complexity measures. The key complexity measure considered in context of the congested clique models is *round complexity* (or *time*) equal to the number of rounds in which an algorithm works for a given input size.

In order to provide accurate measure of the amount of information transmitted over communication links of a network, we consider the *edge capacity* measure. The *edge capacity* $\beta_A(i, n)$ is the (maximal) length (in bits) of messages which can be transmitted in the ith round of executions of the algorithm A on graphs of size n. The (total) edge capacity $B(A, n)$ is the sum of edge capacities of all rounds, $B_A(n) = \sum_i \beta_A(i)$. As n is usually known from the context, we use shorthands $\beta_A(i)$ and B_A for $\beta_A(i, n)$ and $B_A(n)$, respectively.

For further references we make the following observation concerning edge capacity of algorithms solving CC and MSF.

Fact 1. *Total edge capacity of any algorithm solving the connected components problem or the minimum spanning forest problem is $\Omega(\log n)$.*

For the rcast model, the *range* r is also a parameter determining complexity of an algorithm. That is, the range r means that a node u is allowed to transmit only r different messages in a round (i.e., each other node receives one of those r different messages from u).

Related work. The congested clique was studied in several papers, e.g. in [4–7,12–14]. The recent Lenzen's [12] constant time routing and sorting algorithm shows the power of the model. Lotker et al. [13] designed a $O(\log \log n)$ round deterministic algorithm for MSF (minimum spanning forest) (See also [11].) The best randomized solution for MSF in the unicast model works in $O(\log^* n)$ rounds [6], improving [7]. Reduction of the number of overall transmitted messages in the MST algorithms was studied in [15][1]. If messages can have $\sqrt{n} \log n$ bits, one can compute MSF in $O(1)$ of rounds, even if each node sends the same message to every other in a round [14]. Drucker et al. [5] explain the difficulty in obtaining lower bounds for cong. clique. In an extreme scenario of one-round protocols in which each node can send only one message has also been considered connectivity can be solved with public random bits, provided nodes can send messages of size $\Theta(\log^3 n)$ [1]. The rcast model of the congested clique was introduced in [2,3]. The authors showed the substantial difference between $r = 1$ and $r = 2$. Moreover, it was shown that an exponential increase of the range r may cause $\omega(1)$ drop in round complexity. The impact of a single message size b is also studied in [2,3]. One can observe that each step of the congested clique algorithm might be simulated in the rcast model with $r > 1$ in $\log_r n = O(\log n)$ rounds. This seems to diminish importance of the rcast hierarchy. However, the $\log_r n$ multiplicative factor becomes important in the case of problems of sublogarithmic round complexity, as it is in this paper.

Apart from purely theoretical and algorithmic interest, the model is closely related to other models of processing of large-scale graphs [8,10].

Our results. We show that MST can be computed deterministically and connected components can be computed by randomized algorithms with *optimal* edge capacity and in the rcast(2) model, the weakest model above a very weak broadcast congested clique (i.e., for $r = 1$) in the hierarchy of rcast(r) models. Significantly, our algorithms work also in the smallest known round complexity. Our results rely on new efficient distributed implementations of round efficient algorithms from [6,13] (these algorithms rely on basic primitives with large range and edge capacity).

Due to limited space, some proofs are omitted in the paper. The full exposition of the results is available in [9].

2 Graph Terminology and Tools for Capacity/Range Reduction

Given a natural number p, $[p]$ denotes the set $\{1, 2, \ldots, p\}$. For a graph $G(V, E)$ and $E' \subseteq E$, $C_1, C_2, \ldots, C_k \subset V$ is a partition of G into *components* with respect to $E' \subseteq E$ if C_is are pairwise disjoint, $\bigcup_{i \in [k]} C_i = V$, each C_i is connected with respect to the edges from E' and there are no edges $(u, v) \in E'$ such that $u \in C_i$ and $v \in C_j$ for $i \neq j$. That is, $C_1, \ldots, C_k$ are connected components of $G(V, E')$.

---

[1] The authors of [15] allow for different capacities of various edges in a round; this assumption makes their measure and results incomparable to ours.

A *fragment* of a graph $G(V, E, w)$ is a tree F which is a subgraph of a minimum spanning forest of G. A family $\mathbb{F}$ of fragments of $G(V, E, w)$ is a *partition* of G into fragments with respect to $E' \subseteq E$ if F_1 and F_2 have disjoint sets of nodes for each $F_1 \neq F_2$ from $\mathbb{F}$, each $v \in V$ belongs to some $F \in \mathbb{F}$ and each edge of each tree $F \in \mathbb{F}$ belongs to E'. Given a partition $\mathcal{C}$ ($\mathcal{F}$, resp.) of a graph $G(V, E)$ into components (fragments, resp.) and $v \in V$, C^v (F^v) denotes the component (the fragment, resp.) containing v. We will usually consider components with respect to a set of edges which are known to all nodes in the congested clique.

We say that a fragment (component, resp.) is *growable* if there is an edge connecting it with some other fragment/component in the considered graph. An edge (u, v) is *incident* to a fragment F (component C, resp.) wrt to some partition of a graph in fragments/components if it connects F with another fragment (component, resp.), i.e., $F^u \neq F^v = F$ or $F^v \neq F^u = F$ ($C^u \neq C^v = C$ or $C^v \neq C^u = C$, resp.).

Tools for capacity and range reduction. As tools to reduce edge capacity and range of congested clique algorithms, we introduce the *local broadcast* problem and the *global broadcast* problem. In the local broadcast problem, the following parameters are known to each node of a network: a set $T \subset V$, a set $R \subset V$, and a natural number b. Moreover, each node $v \in T$ has its own message M^u of length b. As a result of local broadcast, each node $v \in R$ receives the message M^u from each $u \in T$. As we show in Proposition 1, Algorithm 1 (LocalBroadcast) efficiently solves the local broadcast problem.

Algorithm 1. LocalBroadcast(T, R, b)

1: assign a segment S_i of nodes of size b to each $v \in T$
2: Round 1: each node v sends the jth bit of M^v to the jth node of its segment
3: Round 2: each node u (from the segment assigned to v) sends the bit received in Round 1 to all nodes from R

Proposition 1. *Algorithm 1 solves the local broadcast problem in $O(1)$ rounds with range $r = 2$ and capacity 1, provided $|T|b = O(n)$. It is possible to execute Algorithm 1 simultaneously for k triplets $(T_i, R_i, b_i)_{i \in [k]}$, as long as T_i's are pairwise disjoint, R_i's are pairwise disjoint and $|T_i|b_i \in O(n)$ for each $i \in [k]$.*

Assume that each node from a set $S \subseteq V$ of nodes knows (the same) message M of length b. The *global broadcast problem* is to deliver M to each node $v \in V$ of the network.

Proposition 2. *The global broadcast problem can be solved in one round with range $r = 1$ and edge capacity $\lceil \frac{b}{|S|} \rceil$.*

3 Deterministic Rcast Algorithm for MSF

In this section we provide a deterministic algorithm for minimum spanning forest (MSF) in the rcast model. First, we describe a generic algorithm for minimum spanning tree from [13]. Then we provide a new efficient rcast$(n, 2)$ version of this general algorithm. Finally, an algorithm optimizing the range r and achieving asymptotically optimal edge capacity is presented.

3.1 Generic MSF Algorithm

For a graph $G(V, E, w)$ and its partition into fragments, we say that an edge $e = (v, u)$ is *relevant* for a set $A \subseteq V$ if $F^v \neq F^u$ and e is the lightest edge connecting a node from A and a node from fragment F^u. Let $E_{A,\mu}$ denote the set of μ lightest relevant edges incident to the set $A \subset V$. Moreover, $\mathcal{N}_{F,\mu}$ for a fragment F denotes the set of fragments connected with F by edges from $E_{F,\mu}$.

The following lemma is applied in a round efficient algorithm for MSF [13].

Lemma 1. [13] *Let $\mathcal{F}$ be a partition of a graph $G(V, E)$ into fragments, let $E_{\mathcal{F}}$ be the set of edges in the trees of the partition $\mathcal{F}$. Then, given $E_{\mathcal{F}} \cup \bigcup_{F \in \mathcal{F}} E_{F,\mu}$ for $\mu > 0$, it is possible to determine a new partition $\mathcal{F}'$ of $G(V, E)$ such that the size of each growable tree of $\mathcal{F}'$ is at least $(\mu + 1) \min_{F \in \mathbb{F}} |F|$.*

Using Lemma 1, one can build MSF in *phases* using Algorithm 2 [13] in $O(\log \log n)$ rounds. Let $\mu_1 = 1$ and $\mu_i = \mu_{i-1}(\mu_{i-1} + 1)$ for $i > 1$. Phase i starts from a partition of the input graph into fragments of size $\geq \mu_i$ and ends with a new partition into fragments of size $\geq \mu_{i+1}$. Before the first phase, each node is considered as a separate fragment. At the beginning of the ith phase, the set E_{F,μ_i} of μ_i lightest relevant edges (or all relevant edges, if there are at most μ_i) is determined for each fragment F of the current partition. Then, this information is broadcasted to all nodes of the network. Using Lemma 1, each node can compute a new partition into fragments such that the size of the smalles growable fragment is increased at least $\mu_i + 1$ times.

Algorithm 2. Minimum Spanning Forest

1: $i \leftarrow 1$
2: $\mathbb{F} = \{\{v_1\}, \{v_2\}, \dots, \{v_n\}\}$
3: **while** $E \neq \emptyset$ **do**
4:     SelectEdges$(\mu_i, \mathbb{F})$
5:     announce edges from E_{F,μ_i}
6:     locally merge fragments, modify $\mathbb{F}$ appropriately
7:     $E \leftarrow E \setminus \{(u, v) | F^v = F^u\}$
8:     $i \leftarrow i + 1$

Lotker et al. algorithm essentially relies on the power of the unicast model, using linear range and super-logarithmic edge capacity.

Corollary 1. *The deterministic congested clique MSF algorithm from [13] works in $O(\log\log n)$ rounds with range $r = O(n)$ and edge capacity $O(\log n \cdot \log\log n)$.*

3.2 Minimum Spanning Forest Algorithm in rcast$(n, 2)$

In this section we will show an implementation of Algorithm 2 in $O(\log\log n)$ rounds, which is also efficient with respect to the range and edge capacity. As we discussed above, the only part of the Lotker et al. [13] implementation of Algorithm 2 with large range is the selection of the set of the lightest relevant edges for the current fragments. Therefore, in order to reduce the range without increasing round complexity, it is sufficient to design a new version of this part of Algorithm 2 for the sequence $\mu_1 = 1$ and $\mu_i = \mu_{i-1}(\mu_{i-1} + 1)$ for $i > 1$. We give such a solution in this section.

First, observe that the set of μ lightest relevant edges incident to a fragment F (i.e., $E_{F,\mu}$) is included in the union of μ lightest relevant edges incident to each node from F, i.e., $E_{F,\mu} \subseteq \bigcup_{v \in F} E_{v,\mu}$. Thus, in order to determine $E_{F,\mu}$, it is sufficient to distribute/broadcast information about $E_{v,\mu}$ for each $v \in F$ among nodes of F. This task corresponds to the local broadcast problem (see Sect. 2). More precisely, given a partition $\mathbb{F} = \{F_1, \ldots, F_k\}$ in phase i, each $v \in F_j$ is supposed to broadcast the message M^v of size $b_i = O(\mu_i \log n)$ (i.e., description of μ lightest relevant edges incident to v) to all nodes of F_j. Using Proposition 1, we can solve this task in $O(1)$ rounds with range $r = 2$ and edge capacity 1, provided

$$|F_i|\mu_i \log n \leq n. \tag{1}$$

However, for large fragments and/or large μ_i, this inequality is not satisfied. Therefore, we need a more general observation saying that μ lightest relevant edges incident to a set A (not necessarily a fragment) might be chosen from the sets of μ lightest edges incident to subsets A_j forming a partition of A.

Fact 2. *Let $\mathbb{F}$ be a partition of a graph in fragments and let $A_1, \ldots, A_k$ be a partition of the set of nodes of a fragment $F \in \mathbb{F}$. Then, for each $\mu \in \mathbb{N}$, $E_{F,\mu} \subseteq \bigcup_{j \in [k]} E_{A_j,\mu}$.*

Using Fact 2 we compute $E_{F,\mu}$ for a large fragment in the following way. The set F is split into small groups and μ lightest relevant edges are selected for each group and knowledge about them is distributed among nodes of the group. Then, the leader of each group is chosen and the task is reduced to choosing μ lightest relevant edges among the sets of μ edges known to the leaders. This reduces our problem to its another instance with smaller size of nodes. Another issue to deal with is to set the value of μ_i not too large for each i, in order to satisfy (1). The choice of parameters in Algorithm 3 guarantees that the task of selecting $\min\{\mu_i, n^{1/3}\}$ lightest relevant edges incident to each fragment is possible in $O(1)$ rounds with edge capacity 1.

Proposition 3. *Algorithm 3 determines the set $E_{F,\mu'}$ of μ' lightest relevant edges incident to each fragment $F \in \mathbb{F}$ in $O(1)$ rounds with edge capacity 1 and range $r = 2$, where $\mu' = \min\{n^{1/3}, \mu\}$. Moreover, $E_{F,\mu'}$ is known to each $v \in F$ for each $F \in \mathbb{F}$ at the end of an execution.*

Proof. Assume that n is large enough to satisfy $n^{1/3} > \log n$. First observe that the inequality $|A|\mu' \log n \leq n$ is satisfied when the last step of the algorithm is executed. If $|F|\mu' \log n \leq n$ then the claimed inequality holds, since $|A| = |F|$ in this case. Otherwise, the size of A is reduced to

$$k = \frac{|A|}{|A|/(\mu' \log n)} = \mu' \log n \leq n^{1/3} \log n < \frac{n^{2/3}}{\log n}.$$

Algorithm 3. SelectEdges($\mu, \mathbb{F}$)   ▷ the algorithm for node v

1: $\mu' \leftarrow \min\{n^{1/3}, \mu\}$
2: $n_{\max} \leftarrow n^{1/3}$
3: **for** each $F \in \mathbb{F}$ and each $v \in F$ simultaneously **do**
4:     $A \leftarrow$ the nodes of F
5:     $M^v \leftarrow \mu'$ lightest relevant edges incident to v
6:     **if** $|A|\mu' \log n > n$ **then**
7:         $n' \leftarrow \frac{|A|}{\mu' \log n}, k \leftarrow \lceil |A|/n' \rceil$
8:         split A into $A_1, \ldots, A_k$ such that $|A_i| = n'$ for $i < k$ and $|A_k| \leq n'$
9:         **for** each A_i simultaneously **do**
10:             LocalBroadcast($A_i, A_i, \mu' \log n$)
11:         let A_j denote the set which contains v
12:         $M^v \leftarrow \mu'$ lightest edges incident to A_j
13:         **if** ID(v) = $\min\{$ID(u) $| u \in A_j\}$ **then**
14:             $M^v \leftarrow \mu'$ lightest edges incident to A_j
15:         **else**
16:             v is removed from A
17:     LocalBroadcast($A, F, \mu' \log n$)
18:     v determines $E_{F,\mu'}$ on the basis of received messages   ▷ see Fact 2

The choice of n' guarentees also that $|A_j|\mu' \log n \leq |F| \leq n$ for each $j \in [k]$. Also, all fagments are pairwise disjoint, and all sets A_j are pairwise disjoint (as a disjoint subsets of fragments). Thus, all execution of LocalBroadcast last $O(1)$ rounds with edge capacity 1, by Proposition 1.

By Fact 2, the algorithm determines μ' lightest relevant edges for elements of partitions of F and eventually determines μ' lightest relevant edges for each $F \in \mathbb{F}$, i.e., $E_{F,\mu'}$. For each $F \in \mathbb{F}$, the set $E_{F,\mu'}$ is known to all element of F at the end of the execution of the algorithm, thanks to LocalBroadcast executed in the last step of the algorithm.

Lemma 2. *Assume that $\mu_1 = 1$ and $\mu_i = \min\{n^{1/3}, \mu_{i-1}(\mu_{i-1}+1)\}$ for $i > 1$. Then, an implementation of Algorithm 2 using the procedure SelectEdges from Algorithm 3 solves the MSF problem in $O(\log \log n)$ rounds with range $r = 2$.*

Proof. After an execution of SelectEdges, a designated node $v \in F$ for each fragment F knows μ_i edges which should be broadcasted to all nodes in step 5.

The definition of the sequence μ'_i and Lemma 1 guarantee that the smallest size of a fragment at the beginning of phase i is at least μ'_i. Using these facts, one can implement step 5 of Algorithm 2 in two rounds. In round 1, that the node $v \in F$ which knows $E_{F,\mu'}$ sends the jth edge from $E_{F,\mu'}$ to the jth element of F. In round 2, each node broadcasts an edge received in round 1 to the whole network. Thus, each iteration of the while-loop works (i.e., each phase) works in $O(1)$ rounds with range $r = 2$.

It remains to determine the number of iterations of the while-loop (i.e., the number of phases). For some $i = O(\log \log n)$ we get $\mu_i \geq n^{1/3}$. The smallest size of a (growable) component is larger than $n^{1/3}$ after $i = O(\log \log n)$ phases. For $j > i$, the smallest size of a growable component is increased (at least) $n^{1/3}$ times in the jth round. As a result, the size of the smallest component is n after the phase $i + 2$ which shows that the algorithm works in $O(\log \log n)$ rounds.

Reduction of total edge capacity

Our solution for the MSF from Lemma 2 reduces the range r to 2, but each phase requires sending $\Theta(\log n)$ bits by some nodes, because weights of some edges are transmitted by nodes in step 5 of Algorithm 2. In order to reduce (total) edge capacity, we modify the sequence $\{\mu_i\}$ again to make it possible that step 5 of Algorithm 2 requires $O(1)$ edge capacity for large fragments and edge capacities sum up to $O(\log n)$ for small fragments. More precisely, let

$$\mu_i = \begin{cases} 1 & \text{for } i \leq 2\log\log n \text{ (Stage 1)} \\ \min\{\mu_{i-1}^2/\log n, n^{1/3}\} & \text{for } i > 2\log\log n \text{ (Stage 2)} \end{cases}$$

Then, we implement Algorithm 2 as described in Lemma 2 for the new sequence $\{\mu_i\}_i$. One can verify that executions of SelectEdges can still be implemented in $O(1)$ rounds with capacity 1. However, to reduce also total edge capacity of the whole algorithm we change implementation of the part, where the edges from $E_{F,\mu}$ are announced for each F to the whole network (step 5 of Algorithm 2). Using Lemma 1, one can observe that the size of the smallest growable fragment is

- at least 2^{i-1} at the beginning of phase $i \leq 2\log\log n$;
- at least μ_i at the beginning of phase $i > 2\log\log n$.

In a phase of $i \leq 2\log\log n$ phases each fragment F has to broadcast a message M^F of $\Theta(\log n)$ bits describing the lightest relevant edge incident to F. We split this message into $|F|$ fragments, each of length $O(\frac{\log n}{|F|})$.

For $i > 2\log\log n$ and a fragment F we want to broadcast a description of $\frac{|F|}{\log n}$ edges, which consists of $O(\frac{|F|}{\log n} \log n) = O(|F|)$ bits. In order to do that it is enough that each node announces $O(1)$ bits to the whole network, cf. Proposition 2.

By analyzing this algorithm, we will prove the following result.

Theorem 1. *It is possible to calculate the minimum spanning forest in $O(\log \log n)$ rounds and with total capacity of communication edges $O(\log n)$ and range $r = 2$.*

Proof. **Number of rounds.** The first stage consists of $2 \log \log n$ rounds by definition. The second stage also consists of $O(\log \log n)$ rounds, however, we need a slightly more detailed analysis to show this fact.

At the beginning of the second stage, the size of all growable fragments is at least $\log^2 n$. Assume that the size of each growable fragment at the beginning of phase i is at least μ_i. Then, $\frac{\mu_i}{\log n}$ lightest relevant edges announced by each fragment satisfies $\frac{\mu_i}{\log n} \geq \mu_i^{1/2}$. Therefore, by Lemma 1, the size of the smallest growable fragment increases $\mu_i^{1/2} + 1$ times in a phase. Thus, the size of the smallest growable fragment in the ith phase during the second stage is limited from below by f_i defined as follows: $f_{1+2\log\log n} = \log^2 n$, $f_i = f_{i-1}^{3/2}$ for $i > 1 + 2 \log \log n$. For some $i \in \Theta(\log \log n)$, the size of the smallest fragment will be at least $n^{1/3}$. Then, as shown in the previous section (Lemma 2), we obtain MSF after $O(1)$ additional phases.

Total capacity of communication edges. In the first stage we have $O(\log \log n)$ phases, the size of the smallest growable fragment in the ith phase is at least 2^{i-1}. Thus total capacity of communication edges of the first stage is $O(\sum_i \frac{\log n}{2^i}) = O(\log n)$. In the second stage we have $O(\log \log n)$ phases, each is implemented in $O(1)$ rounds with edge capacity 1, thus total capacity of communication edges of those stages is $O(\log \log n)$. Therefore total capacity of communication edges of presented algorithm is $O(\log n + \log \log n) = O(\log n)$.

4 Randomized Rcast Algorithm for Connected Components

The fastest known randomized algorithm calculating Connected Components works in $O(\log^* n)$ communication rounds [6]. The algorithm works in phases. At the beginning of each phase, a partition of an input graph into components is known to all nodes. In a phase of the algorithm, the number of growable components drops from $\frac{n}{\log^2 x}$ to $\frac{n}{x}$. The key tool to make it possible is a special kind of *linear sketches*.

We first describe the linear sketches from Then, we briefly describe the $O(\log^* n)$ algorithm for connected components [6]. In the next part, we give an algorithm implementing the idea from [6] in the rcast$(n, 2)$ model. Finally, we provide a version of the algorithm with optimal total edge capacity and range 2.

4.1 Linear Sketches

In order to build sketches [6] for a graph with n nodes, a preprocessing is necessary. During the preprocessing, each (prospective) edge (u, v) is assigned an ID of size $O(\log n)$, based on a random seed of size $O(\log n)$. In order to build sketches for a given graph $G(V, E)$ with n nodes and a parameter $x \leq n$, the sets $E_1, E_2, \ldots, E_{10 \log x}$ included in E are chosen such that each edge $e \in E$ belongs E_j with probability $1/2^j$ and all random choices are independent. For $v \in V$ and $A \subset V$, let $E_j(v)$ be the set of elements of E_j incident to v and let $E_j(A)$ be the set of elements of E_j incident to A, i.e., $E_j(A) = \{\{u, v\} \in E_j \mid u \in A, v \notin A\}$. Then, sketch($\mathbb{X}$) for $\mathbb{X} \subseteq V$ is a table consisting of $10 \log x$ rows, each row contains a bit string of length $O(\log n)$. The jth row of sketch($\mathbb{X}$) is the xor of IDs of all elements of $E_j(\mathbb{X})$. The sequence of $\log x$ sketches for a set or a node will be called its *multi-sketch*. Thus, a multi-sketch is a table of $10 \log^2 x$ rows. By sketch$_r(A)$ and multi-sketch$_r(A)$ we denote the rth row of a sketch and a mutli-sketch of A, resp.

Proposition 4. [6] *1. It is possible to determine an edge $\{u, v\}$ such that $u \in A$ and $v \notin A$ from a sketch of $A \subset V$ with probability $\Omega(1)$, provided the number of edges $\{u, v\}$ such that $u \in A$, $v \notin A$ is at most x^5.*
2. The sketch of a set $A = A_1 \cup A_2 \subset V$ for disjoint sets A_1, A_2 is equal to sketch(A_1) xor sketch(A_2). That is, the ith row of sketch(A) is equal to the xor of the ith row of sketch(A_1) and the ith row of sketch(A_2).

4.2   Ghaffari-Parter $O(\log^* n)$ Connected Components Algorithm

Ghaffari-Parter algorithm for connected components in the unicast congested clique works in $O(\log^* n)$ phases, each phase consists of $O(1)$ rounds [6]. At the beginning of a phase, a partition $\mathbb{C}$ of an input graph into $O(n/\log^2 x)$ (growable) components is known to each node. As a result of the phase, the number of components is reduced to $O(n/x)$, whp. During the phase (see Algorithm 4):

 (i) multi-sketches are computed for each component and sent to the leader u^*;
 (ii) the leader u^* locally simulates $\log x$ steps of the Boruvka's algorithm, using obtained multi-sketches of components;
 (iii) the leader distributes information about new partition into components;
 (iv) each node v broadcast a random edge $\{u, v\}$ such that $C^u \neq C^v$ and a partition is updated using the broadcasted edges.[2]
 (v) non-growable components are deactivated.

Algorithm 4. CCLogstar   ▷ the algorithm for a node $v \in C_k$

1: $\mathbb{C} = \{\{v_1\}, \ldots, \{v_n\}\}$
2: **while** $\mathbb{C} \neq \emptyset$ **do**   ▷ i.e., while there are active components
3:     $x \leftarrow \min\{y \mid |\mathbb{C}| < \frac{n}{10 \log^2 x}\}$ ▷ $\mathbb{C}$ is the number of growable components
4:     Compute multi-sketches of all components from $\mathbb{C}$
5:     Distribute the multi-sketches in the network
6:     Update $\mathbb{C}$ by simulating $\Theta(\log x)$ rounds of Boruvka's alg., using sketches,
7:     Determine real edges which connect old components in the new ones
8:     Broadcast a random edge incident to each component, update $\mathbb{C}$ accordingly
9:     Deactivate (remove from $\mathbb{C}$) non-growable components.

The following result from [6] implies that Algorithm 4 determines connected components in $O(\log^* n)$ iterations of the while-loop, whp.

---
[2] Random edges are necessary in order to deal with components with degree $> x^5$, because sketches do not help much to find their neighbors.

Lemma 3. *An iteration of the while-loop Algorithm 4 reduces the number of non-growable components from $n/\log^2 x$ to at most n/x, whp.*

As the Ghaffari-Parter [6] distributed implementation of Algorithm 4 uses Lenzen's routing algorithm in each phase, and it also requires that nodes send independently chosen random messages of size $\Theta(\log n)$ on each edge (in a round), the edge capacity of this algorithm is $\Omega(\log n)$ in each phase and its range is $r = n$.

4.3 Range Efficient Algorithm for Connected Components

In order to implement a phase of Algorithm 4 in the rcast model with the range $r = 2$ and in $O(1)$ rounds, we need a new method of computing and distributing sketches. Assume that a partition $\mathcal{C}$ into components is known to all nodes at the beginning of a phase. Consider a *meta-graph*, whose nodes correspond to the current components, where C_i, C_j are connected by a *meta-edge* iff there is an edge $\{u, v\}$ such that $u \in C_i$ and $v \in C_j$. From the "point of view" of nodes it means that u and v are connected by an edge iff C^u and C^v are neighbors in the current meta-graph.

In our algorithm, the sketches are computed for the meta-graph and delivered to *all* nodes. On the basis of the sketches, each node can simulate $\log x$ steps of the Boruvka's algorithm on the meta-graph, merging components into larger ones. After determining new larger components, information about the real edges connecting merged input components (into new larger ones) are determined and broadcasted to all nodes. Below, we describe this strategy in more detail.

Computing sketches in a meta-graph. For computing (and broadcasting) multi-sketches in a meta-graph, each component C_i is associated with a *representative set* V_i of size $\log^2 x$. In the first round, each node v sends the bit 1 to each element of V_i for $i \in [\log^2 x]$ iff $(v, u) \in E$ for some $u \in C_i$. Otherwise, v sends 0 to each node of V_i. After such a round each node of V_i knows all neighbors of C_i in the meta-graph. In order to compute and distribute a multi-sketch of C_i in $O(1)$ rounds, we make the jth element of V_i (say, $v_{i,j}$) responsible for the jth row of the multi-sketch of C_i. For each edge $(C_i, C_{i'})$ such that $i > i'$, $v_{i,j}$ chooses with appropriate probability (i.e., $1/2^{1 + (j-1) \mod 10 \log x}$) whether this edge is included in the jth row of the multi-sketch. In the second communication round $v_{i,j}$ sends 1 to $v_{i',j}$ when the edge is included and 0 otherwise. Using own random choices and messages received in both rounds, $v_{i,j}$ computes the jth row of the multi-sketch of C_i and broadcasts it to the whole network. More precise description of the above strategy is presented in Algorithm 5.

Proposition 5. *Assume that Algorithm 5 is executed for a partition of an input graph in at most $n/\log^2 x$ components. Then, the algorithm determines multi-sketches of all nodes in the meta-graph and broadcasts them to the whole network in $O(1)$ rounds, with range $r = 2$ and edge capacity $O(\log n)$.*

Determining real edges connecting merged components. An offline simulation of the Boruvka's algorithm based on meta-edges derived from sketches

---

Algorithm 5. LinearSketches   ▷ the algorithm for a node $v \in C_k$

1:   $y \leftarrow 10 \log^2 x$
2:   Let C_k be the component containing v
3:   $V_i \leftarrow \{v_{i,1}, \ldots, v_{i,y}\}$ for $i \in [n/y]$, where $v_{i,j} = v_{(i-1)y+j}$
4:   Let $v = v_{p,r}$
5:   **for each** $j \in [n/y]$ **do**
6:      **if** $\{\{v, u\} \mid u \in C_j\} \neq \emptyset$ **then** $b_j \leftarrow 1$ **else** $b_j \leftarrow 0$
7:   **Round 1:** v sends b_j to each node of V_j for each $j \in [n/y]$
8:   $E(C_p) \leftarrow \{(C_p, C_l) \mid 1 \text{ received from some } u \in C_l\}$
9:   **for each** $e = (C_p, C_l) \in E(C_p)$ such that $l > p$:
       $b_l \leftarrow 1$ with probability $1/2^{1+(r-1) \bmod y}$, $b_l \leftarrow 0$ otherwise
10:   **Round 2:** $v = v_{p,r}$ sends b_l to $v_{l,r}$ for each $l \in [n/y]$
11:   **for each** $l < p$: set b_l to the bit received in Round 2 from $v_{l,r}$
12:   multi-sketch$_r(C_p) \leftarrow \text{xor}_{k \in [n/y]} b_k \cdot \text{ID}((C_p, C_k))$
13:   **Round 3:** $v_{p,r}$ sends multi-sketch$_r(C_p)$ to all nodes

---

gives a new partition into components $\mathcal{C}'$. Each component C' of this new partition is a connected subgraph of the meta-graph, with meta-edges connecting elements of C' known to all nodes (determined by sketches). In order to determine real edges connecting elements of C', a rooted spanning tree for C' is chosen arbitrarily but in the same way by each node $v \in C'$. For each node v, if v is adjacent to (u, v) such that C^u is the parent of C^v then v chooses such edge arbitrarily. Then, v broadcasts such chosen edge to the whole network.

Let CCLogstarR be a variant of Algorithm 4 where the steps 4 and 5 are implemented through Algorithm 5. In order to decode the real edges between joined components, we use the above described method. It requires 1 round with capacity $O(\log n)$ and range 1 for step 7 of our implementation of Algorithm 4.

Lemma 4. *Algorithm CCLogstarR identifies the connected components of the input graph in $O(\log^* n)$ communication rounds in the $rcast(n, 2)$ model, whp.*

4.4   Reduction of Total Edge Capacity

In this section we show that it is possible to achieve the optimal edge capacity $O(\log n)$ without increasing the range or round complexity of CCLogstarR.

Theorem 2. *There is a randomized algorithm in the $rcast(n, 2)$ congested clique that identifies the connected components of the input graph with total edge capacity $O(\log n)$ in $O(\log^* n)$ communication rounds, with high probability.*

The key idea of the proof of Theorem 2 is to distribute capacity load of nodes with help of the local broadcast and the global broadcast. Moreover, in order to distribute sketches in capacity-efficient way, we slow down an algorithm a bit. That is, the reduction of the number of components in a phase is not as efficient as originally; however, this weaker variant does not harm asymptotic complexity.

Conclusions

We have provided new efficient algorithms for MSF and connected components in the congested clique. An interesting research direction is to determine a relationship between adaptiveness (the number of rounds) and total capacity of communication edges.

References

1. Ahn, K.J., Guha, S., McGregor, A.: Analyzing graph structure via linear measurements. In: Proceedings of the Twenty-Third Annual ACM-SIAM Symposium on Discrete Algorithms, SODA 2012, Kyoto, Japan, 17–19 January 2012, pp. 459–467 (2012)
2. Becker, F., Anta, A.F., Rapaport, I., Rémila, E.: Brief announcement: a hierarchy of congested clique models, from broadcast to unicast. In: Proceedings of the 2015 ACM Symposium on Principles of Distributed Computing, PODC 2015, Donostia-San Sebastián, Spain, 21–23 July 2015, pp. 167–169 (2015)
3. Becker, F., Anta, A.F., Rapaport, I., Rémila, E.: The effect of range and bandwidth on the round complexity in the congested clique model. In: Proceedings of 22nd International Conference on Computing and Combinatorics, COCOON 2016, Ho Chi Minh City, Vietnam, 2–4 August 2016, pp. 182–193 (2016)
4. Becker, F., Montealegre, P., Rapaport, I., Todinca, I.: The simultaneous number-in-hand communication model for networks: private coins, public coins and determinism. In: Halldórsson, M.M. (ed.) SIROCCO 2014. LNCS, vol. 8576, pp. 83–95. Springer, Cham (2014). https://doi.org/10.1007/978-3-319-09620-9_8
5. Drucker, A., Kuhn, F., Oshman, R.: On the power of the congested clique model. In: ACM Symposium on Principles of Distributed Computing, PODC 2014, Paris, France, 15–18 July 2014, pp. 367–376 (2014)
6. Ghaffari, M., Parter, M.: MST in log-star rounds of congested clique. In: Proceedings of PODC 2016 (2016)
7. Hegeman, J.W., Pandurangan, G., Pemmaraju, S.V., Sardeshmukh, V.B., Scquizzato, M.: Toward optimal bounds in the congested clique: graph connectivity and MST. In: Proceedings of the 2015 ACM Symposium on Principles of Distributed Computing, PODC 2015, Donostia-San Sebastián, Spain, 21–23 July 2015, pp. 91–100 (2015)
8. Hegeman, J.W., Pemmaraju, S.V.: Lessons from the congested clique applied to mapreduce. Theor. Comput. Sci. 608, 268–281 (2015)
9. Jurdzinski, T., Nowicki, K.: MSF and connectivity in limited variants of the congested clique. CoRR, abs/1703.02743 (2017)
10. Klauck, H., Nanongkai, D., Pandurangan, G., Robinson, P.: Distributed computation of large-scale graph problems. In: Proceedings of the Twenty-Sixth Annual ACM-SIAM Symposium on Discrete Algorithms, SODA 2015, San Diego, CA, USA, 4–6 January 2015, pp. 391–410 (2015)
11. Korhonen, J.H.: Deterministic MST sparsification in the congested clique. CoRR, abs/1605.02022 (2016)
12. Lenzen, C.: Optimal deterministic routing and sorting on the congested clique. In: Fatourou, P., Taubenfeld, G. (eds.) ACM Symposium on Principles of Distributed Computing, PODC 2013, Montreal, QC, Canada, 22–24 July 2013, pp. 42–50. ACM (2013)

13. Lotker, Z., Pavlov, E., Patt-Shamir, B., Peleg, D.: MST construction in o(log log n) communication rounds. In: Proceedings of the Fifteenth Annual ACM Symposium on Parallel Algorithms and Architectures, SPAA 2003, pp. 94–100. ACM, New York (2003)
14. Montealegre, P., Todinca, I.: Brief announcement: deterministic graph connectivity in the broadcast congested clique. In: Proceedings of PODC 2016 (2016)
15. Pemmaraju, S.V., Sardeshmukh, V.B.: Super-fast MST algorithms in the congested clique using o(m) messages. In: 36th IARCS Annual Conference on Foundations of Software Technology and Theoretical Computer Science, FSTTCS 2016, 13–15 December 2016, Chennai, India, pp. 47:1–47:15 (2016)

Business Processes, Protocols, and Mobile Networks

Global vs. Local Semantics of BPMN 2.0 OR-Join

Flavio Corradini, Chiara Muzi$^{(\boxtimes)}$, Barbara Re, Lorenzo Rossi,
and Francesco Tiezzi

School of Science and Technology, University of Camerino, Camerino, Italy
{flavio.corradini,chiara.muzi,barbara.re,lorenzo.rossi,
francesco.tiezzi}@unicam.it

Abstract. Nowadays, BPMN 2.0 has acquired a clear predominance for modelling business processes. However, one of its drawback is the lack of a formal semantics, that leads to different interpretations, and hence implementations, of some of its features. This, as a matter of fact, results on process implementations using such features that do not fit with designers expectations, and that are not portable from one BPMN enactment tools to another. Among the BPMN elements particular ambiguous is the semantics of the OR-Join. Several formalisations of this element have been proposed in the literature, but none of them is derived from a direct and faithful translation of the current version of BPMN standard. In this work we instead provide direct, global and local, formalisations compliant with the OR-Join semantics reported in the BPMN 2.0 standard. In particular, the local semantics is devised to more efficiently determine the OR-Join enablement. The soundness of the approach is given by demonstrating the correspondence of the local semantics with respect to the global one.

1 Introduction

Nowadays, modelling is recognised as an important practice also in supporting software development. In particular, modelling business processes in complex organisations permits to better understand how organisations work and, at the same time, to support the development and continuous improvement of related IT systems [1]. In doing this, a challenge is to provide a precise semantics of the modelling languages used to guarantee that model behaviours do what they are supposed to do. We refer here to BPMN 2.0, the standard language for business process modelling [2]. Even if widely accepted, BPMN major drawbacks are related to the complexity of the BPMN meta-model semi-formal definition and to the possible misunderstanding of its execution semantics defined by means of natural text descriptions, sometimes containing misleading information [3]. These issues worsen when considering BPMN elements that have a particularly tricky behaviour, such as the OR-Join [4]. Roughly, this is used to synchronise two or more parallel flows according to specific (and non trivial) states on their execution status.

© Springer International Publishing AG 2018
A M. Tjoa et al. (Eds.): SOFSEM 2018, LNCS 10706, pp. 321–336, 2018.
https://doi.org/10.1007/978-3-319-73117-9_23

This paper aims at formally specifying the OR-Join semantics of BPMN process models. This paves the way not only to formal reasoning, but also to driven implementations of process-aware IT systems ensuring an execution of the OR-Join compliant with BPMN 2.0. We focus on the OR-Join not only because of its semantic complexity, but also due to its practical impact, as that is a convenient way to relax the synchronisation of parallel control flows [5]. Its use is also confirmed by the number of models containing it (316 out of 7.541 BPMN 2.0 collaborations available in the BPM Academic Initiative public repository [6]).

In providing a novel formal semantics of the OR-Join specification we are firstly motivated by the results of our literature review on the topic (see Sect. 3). In fact, already available formalisation attempts mainly refer to previous versions of BPMN and do not fit with the current 2.0 standard (see [7–10]). Instead, those that rely on BPMN 2.0, such as [11], only consider the restricted class of sound processes. In addition, we have also practical motivations concerning the implementation of process-aware IT systems. We have experimented with some popular BPMN modelling and enactment tools and we have observed that most of them relax, simplify or even avoid the implementation of the OR-Join (see Sect. 3). In other words, almost all considered tools are not fully compliant with the OMG standard, thus resulting incompatible each other and not faithful with the designer expectations based on the BPMN specification.

Tackling the above issues, the contribution of this paper is twofold. Firstly, we provide a direct formalisation compliant with the OR-Join semantics reported in the current BPMN 2.0 standard specification. The semantics informally described in the specification is based on global information about the state of the whole process model. Thus, a direct, one-to-one, formalisation of this description has to be given with a *global* style, i.e., it is based on a notion of state storing information about tokens distribution over the whole model. From the practical point of view, however, this global perspective does not fit with the distributed nature of many process aware IT systems, where a single synchronisation point may not be aware of the execution state of the other process elements. Moreover, the naive implementation of the global conditions enabling the OR-Join would turn out to be quite inefficient. Thus, we also provide a *local* variant of the semantics, devised to more efficiently determine the OR-Join enablement, as it depends only on information local to the considered OR-Join. This semantics fosters a compositional, hence more scalable, approach for enacting processes with OR-Joins.

To sum up, the global semantics has been introduced as the formal reference, while the local one to be used for implementations. The soundness of our approach is given by the formal proof of their correspondence.

2   BPMN 2.0 Overview

Here we concentrate on those BPMN elements related to the process behaviour we use in the following. We also introduce a running example used throughout the paper.

BPMN Standard. BPMN process diagrams consist of combinations of different elements that can be organised in four classes (Fig. 1). **Events** are used to represent something that can happen; they can be used to start or end the process. **Gateways** are used to join (merging incoming sequence edges) or split (forking into outgoing sequence edges) the flow of a process. Three types of gateways are available XOR, AND and OR. An *XOR gateway* gives the possibility to describe choices; it is activated each time the gateway is reached and, when executed, it activates exactly one outgoing edge. An *AND gateway* has to wait to be reached by all its incoming edges to start, and then all the outgoing edges are started in parallel. A *OR gateway* has to wait to be reached by an arbitrary number of its incoming edges to start, and then at least one of the outgoing edges is started (see Sect. 3 for more details). **Tasks** are used to represent specific works to perform. Finally, **Sequence Edges** are used to specify the internal flow of the process, thus ordering elements.

$\underset{\text{Start Event}}{\bigcirc}\ \underset{\text{End Event}}{\bigcirc}\ \underset{\text{XOR}}{\diamondsuit}\ \underset{\text{AND}}{\diamondsuit}\ \underset{\text{OR}}{\diamondsuit}\ \underset{\text{Task}}{\fbox{ }}\ \longrightarrow\ \text{Sequence Edge}$

Fig. 1. Considered BPMN 2.0 elements.

A key concept related to the BPMN process execution is the notion of *token* [2, Sect. 7.1.1]. Commonly, a token traverses, from a start event, the sequence edges of the process and passes through its elements enabling their execution, and it is consumed by an end event when terminates. The distribution of tokens in the process elements is called *marking*, therefore the *process execution* is defined in terms of marking evolution.

Running Example. The elements illustrated above can be combined in order to design models like the one in Fig. 2 modelling an order fulfilment process. This is the case of a customer-oriented manufacturing caring about the quality of the order and accepting the payment only when the customer is fully satisfied. The process shown starts, due to the presence of a *start event*, whenever a purchase order has been received from a costumer. In order to manufacture a product, material availability is checked and then raw materials have to be ordered. Two preferred suppliers provide different types of raw materials. Depending on the product to be manufactured, raw materials may be ordered from either Supplier 1 or Supplier 2, or from both. This is rendered by including related *tasks* in a

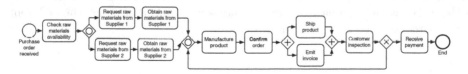

Fig. 2. An order fulfilment process diagram (revised version of model in [5]).

block composed of two OR *gateways*: an OR-Split, used to fork the flow into two branches after a decision; and an OR-Join that acts as a synchronisation point. Once raw materials are available, the product can be manufactured and the order confirmed. Then, tasks 'Ship product' and 'Emit invoice' can be performed independently from each other, so that they are put in a block between an AND-Split and an AND-Join enabling a parallel activation and a strict synchronisation before proceeding. The product is then inspected by the Customer: if he/she is unsatisfied, the product is manufactured again until he/she is pleased. Finally, when the Customer is satisfied the product is paid, and the process terminates by means of an *end event*.

In the rest of the paper and for the purpose of our study we intentionally left out tasks, since they do not affect the OR-Join execution [10]. Considering our running example, we get the process structure in Fig. 3.

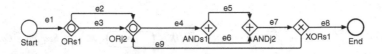

Fig. 3. The order fulfilment process structure.

3   Towards the OR-Join Formal Definition

Here we present in detail the semantics of BPMN 2.0 OR-Join as provided in the OMG specification. We also discuss related works, and give some preliminary notions we use throughout the paper to formalise the OR-Join behaviour.

From BPMN 2.0 Specification to Process Execution. The OR-Join semantics is quite complex, both from the definition point of view, in terms of formally expressing it, and from the computational point of view, in terms of determining whether an OR-Join is enabled. In our work we distil the characteristics of the OR-Join, from a detailed reading of the BPMN specification we report in Fig. 4 (where, as a matter of terminology, Inclusive Gateway stands for OR-Join, while Sequence Flow for sequence edge).

From the standard it is clear that the OR-Join has a *non-local semantics* and its activation may depend on the marking evolution considering the whole diagram. More in detail, given an OR-Join with a token in at least one of its incoming edges, it has to wait for a token that is in a path ending in a empty incoming edge of such OR-Join that does not visit the OR-Join itself. However, if this token is also in a path ending in a non-empty incoming edge, the OR-Join is activated and the execution can proceed.

The Inclusive Gateway is activated if:
- At least one incoming Sequence Flow has at least one token and
- For every directed path formed by sequence flow that:
  - (i) starts with a Sequence Flow f of the diagram that has a token,
  - (ii) ends with an incoming Sequence Flow of the inclusive gateway that has no token,
  - (iii) does not visit the Inclusive Gateway.
- There is also a directed path formed by Sequence Flow that:
  - (iv) starts with f,
  - (v) ends with an incoming Sequence Flow of the inclusive gateway that has a token,
  - (vi) does not visit the Inclusive Gateway.

Fig. 4. OR-Join semantics according to the OMG standard BPMN 2.0.

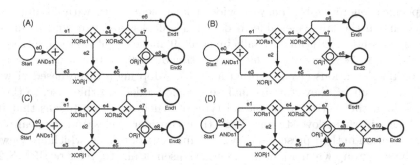

Fig. 5. OR-Join activation.

Let us consider the example in Fig. 5(A). In this case ORj1 has an incoming token in e_5, but it is not activated because it has to wait for the token in e_4 (corresponding to f in the definition in Fig. 4). Indeed, there is not another path from e_4 to e_5. However, if the token in e_4 moves to e_6, as in Fig. 5(B), the execution of ORj1 resumes, because now there is no marked path ending in e_7. Moreover, if we move the token in e_4 back to e_1, as in Fig. 5(C), quite surprisingly ORj1 is activated, since this token can follow the path leading to e_5. In this case, the OR-Join behaviour is quite anomalous; this is due to the fact that we are in presence of an unsafe model. Finally, to illustrate the effects of the condition "does not visit the *Inclusive Gateway*" in Fig. 4, let us consider a variant of the process where ORj1 is enclosed in a cycle (Fig. 5(D)). Also in this case ORj1 is activated; indeed, although the token in e_8 is in a path ending in an empty edge incoming in ORj1 (i.e., e_9), since it visits ORj1 this path is ignored.

OR-Join in the Literature. Most of the previous attempts to formalise the semantics of the OR-Join [7–10] are based on earlier versions of the BPMN standard, which provide different semantics for the OR-Join. Moreover, also when the same version of the standard is considered, different interpretations of the OR-Join behaviour, not always faithful to the specification, have been given. In particular, these differences regard the treatment of mutually dependent

OR-Joins (the so-called 'vicious circles') and of deadlock upstream an OR-Join. In fact, from a faithful translation of the standard, it results that mutually dependent OR-Joins are blocked, and that an OR-Join is not able to recognise that there is a deadlock on a path leading to it, thus it will wait forever. Below, we discuss the most significant related works.

Völzer [7] proposes a non-local semantics for the OR-Join in the BPMN 1.0 specification (2006) using workflow graphs. In case of vicious circles he argues that the intended meaning is not clear and hence they should be sort out by static analysis. This approach is then improved in [12], which quotes the 2010 version of the specification and gives an informal description of this one by means of inhibiting and anti-inhibiting paths. Dumas et al. [8] base their work on BPMN 1.0 and on the definition of the Synchronisation Merge pattern to which the specification refers to. They provide a local semantics, without imposing restrictions on the language, able to detect deadlocks upstream and to unlock mutually dependent OR-Joins. Thalheim et al. [9] make use of ASMs to introduce the OR-Join, by referring to the the specification of 2006, and make a comparison between the definitions given by other authors. Adopting a token-based view of workflow semantics, they start to analyse acyclic models. In this case, to threat the OR-Join, they introduce a special type of synchronisation tokens that fire flow objects in their downstream. They then consider cycles and, to deal with synchronisation in their presence, they introduce sets of tokens, which are viewed as a coherent group when a join fires. Christiansen et al. [10] refer to BPMN 2.0 - Beta 1, providing a global semantics directly in terms of a subset of BPMN. As for the vicious circle, they argue that, since informally BPMN specification does not include the resolution strategy and their work is a faithful translation, they do not consider it.

Differently from our work, the above approaches rely on past versions of the BPMN standard, which provide different semantics for the OR-Join with respect to the current 2.0 version. Thus, they cannot be applied as they are to the standard BPMN 2.0. Moreover, concerning the issues about vicious circles and deadlock upstream considered by some of those works, we have checked how they are dealt with by the current specification and, to be completely faithful with it, we have simply applied the same solution. Indeed, in the current description of the OR-Join semantics (Fig. 4), it does not seem to be any ambiguity about these two issues. The OR-Join is able to detect neither a vicious circle nor a deadlock upstream, thus in both cases its execution is blocked forever.

Recently, Prinz and Amme [11] propose a formalisation of the OR-Join semantics referred to the current version of the standard. However, they limit the work on *sound* workflow graphs, which identify a quite restricted class of BPMN processes [13]. In fact *soundness* is defined as the combination of properties concerning the dynamic behaviour of a process: option-to-complete, proper-completion, and no-dead-activities. Moreover, the proposed semantics does not fit with the standard as, for instance, it avoids vicious circles by determining which OR-Join in a circle has to wait and which one must proceed.

OR-Join Implementations. We have seen that in formalising the OR-Join semantics different interpretations have been given. The same has happened also for what concerns its implementation. Indeed, unfaithful implementations can be found in the most popular BPMN modelling and enactment tools. In particular, we have checked: Activiti [14], Camunda [15], Flowable [16], jBPM [17], ProcessMaker [18], Signavio [19], Stadust [20] and Sydle [21]. These BPMN tools provide their own interpretation of the BPMN standard, typically relaxing the OR-Join semantics. More specifically, Camunda and Flowable take advantage from the Activiti OR-Join implementation that in some cases keeps blocked a waiting token differently from what prescribed in the specification (see discussions above). A similar behaviour arises in Stadust. Instead, jBPM, Process Maker and Sydle relax the process structure handling only OR-Joins preceded by OR-Splits, and then enforce a simplified semantics. Last but not least, Signavio, and in particular its simulation feature, does not support the OR-Join at all.

Preliminaries. To define the formal semantics of a BPMN model we rely on information extracted from the model by means of a pre-processing step. This information consists of: *i.* paths from each OR-Join backward to the start event (and their suffix sub-paths) that do not visit the inclusive gateway; *ii.* sequence edges involved in a cycle; and *iii.* dependences between OR-Joins. We only consider models with one start event; this is not a limitation as in this setting each model can be rendered in this form.

For the purpose of our pre-processing, we consider a process model as a direct graph $G = (V, A)$ where: V is a set of *vertices*, ranged over by v and consisting of start events, end events, and gateways; and A is a set of *arrows*, consisting of triples (v_1, e, v_2) with $v_1 \neq v_2$ and $\mathsf{e} \in \mathbb{E}$, where $\mathbb{E}$ is the set of all (sequence) edges. Since edges are uniquely identified in a BPMN model, we have that for each (v_1, e, v_2) in A there exists no triple $(v_1', \mathsf{e}', v_2')$ in A with $\mathsf{e}' = \mathsf{e}$. This allows us to write, when convenient, (v_1, e, v_2) as e. Moreover, an OR-Join vertex is uniquely identified by the name of its outgoing edge.

A *path* in G, denoted by p, is a non-empty sequence of edges in A, where the third element of a triple is equal to the first of the next triple in the sequence, if any. A path that ends in its starting vertex is called *cycle*. For example, in the model in Fig. 3 we can observe the following cycle: $(\mathsf{e}_4, \mathsf{e}_6, \mathsf{e}_7, \mathsf{e}_9)$. Given a path p of the form $(v_0, \mathsf{e}_0, v_1), \ldots, (v_{k-1}, \mathsf{e}_{k-1}, v_k)$, notations $\mathsf{first}(p)$ and $\mathsf{last}(p)$ indicate the starting edge e_0 and the ending edge e_{k-1} of p, respectively.

We also refer with $\mathbb{P}$ the set of all the paths in G and we define $\mathcal{P} : \mathbb{E} \to 2^{\mathbb{P}}$ such a function that, given as input an edge $\mathsf{e} \in \mathbb{E}$ returns the set of all paths ending in the OR-Join uniquely identified by e and starting from all vertices between the start event and the OR-Join, which do not visit the considered OR-Join. Notably, this function returns a finite set of paths, because cycles within paths are not repeated. While computing $\mathcal{P}$, we can also compute the set $\mathbb{C} \subseteq \mathbb{E}$ of edges included in a cycle. Concerning the example in Fig. 3, we have $\mathcal{P}(\mathsf{e}_4) = \{(\mathsf{e}_2), (\mathsf{e}_3), (\mathsf{e}_1, \mathsf{e}_2), (\mathsf{e}_1, \mathsf{e}_3)\}$, and $\mathbb{C} = \{\mathsf{e}_4, \mathsf{e}_6, \mathsf{e}_7, \mathsf{e}_9\}$.

Finally, to properly formalise the OR-Join semantics in presence of vicious circles (i.e., to keep blocked the execution, see discussion above), we have to detect for each OR-Join the presence of OR-Joins from which it depends. This is expressed as a boolean predicate $noDep : \mathbb{E} \rightarrow \{true, false\}$, which taken as input an edge e identifying an OR-Join, it holds if no other OR-Join mutually depends with e.

To compute the pre-processing data mentioned above, we rely on existing graph theory procedures (the code is available at https://goo.gl/wv5Afu).

In particular, we use the *jGraphT* (www.jgrapht.org) Java library that is able to manage graphs. In this way, we capture cycles with the implementation of the Szwarcfiter and Lauer algorithm [22] and paths by using a Dijkstra-like algorithm [23].

4   Formalisation of the OR-Join Global Semantics

According to the OMG standard the semantics of the OR-Join requires global information about the state of the whole model. Here, we formalise this global perspective of the BPMN semantics. In particular, to enable a formal treatment of BPMN models including the OR-Join, we defined in Fig. 6 a BNF syntax of the model structure.

In the proposed grammar, the non-terminal symbol S represents *Process Structures*, while the terminal symbols, denoted by the sans serif font, are the considered elements of a BPMN model, i.e. events and gateways. The correspondence between the textual notation used here and the graphical notation of BPMN presented in Sect. 2 is as follows:

- e $\in \mathbb{E}$ denotes a sequence edge, while $E \in 2^{\mathbb{E}}$ a set of edges; we require $|E| > 1$ when E is used in joining and splitting gateways;
- start(e) represents a start event with outgoing edge e;
- end(e) represents an end event with incoming edge e;
- andSplit(e, E)   (resp. xorSplit(e, E), resp. orSplit(e, E)) represents an AND (resp. XOR, resp. OR) split gateway with incoming edge e and outgoing edges E;
- andJoin(e, E)   (resp. xorJoin(e, E), resp. orJoin(e, E)) represents an AND (resp. XOR, resp. OR) join gateway with incoming edges E and outgoing edge e;
- $S_1 \mid S_2$ represents a composition of structure elements in order to render a process structure in terms of a collection of elements.

To achieve a compositional definition, each sequence edge of the BPMN model is split in two parts: the part outgoing from the source element and the part incoming into the target element. The two parts are correlated by means of unique sequence edge names in the BPMN model. To avoid malformed structure models, we only consider structures in which for each edge labelled by e outgoing from an element, there exists only one corresponding edge labelled by e incoming into another node, and vice versa.

$S ::= \mathsf{start}(e) \mid \mathsf{end}(e) \mid \mathsf{andSplit}(e, E) \mid \mathsf{andJoin}(e, E) \mid \mathsf{xorSplit}(e, E)$
$\mid \mathsf{xorJoin}(e, E) \mid \mathsf{orSplit}(e, E) \mid \mathsf{orJoin}(e, E) \mid S_1 \mid S_2$

Fig. 6. Syntax of BPMN process structures.

The operational semantics we propose is given in terms of configurations of the form $\langle S, \sigma, \mathcal{P} \rangle$, where: S is a process structure; σ is the execution state, storing for each edge the current number of tokens marking it; and $\mathcal{P}$ is the function that associates to each OR-Join gateway all paths that are incoming to it, not visiting it, and starting from marked edges (it results from pre-processing, see Sect. 3). Specifically, a state $\sigma : \mathbb{E} \to \mathbb{N}$ is a function mapping edges to numbers of tokens. The state obtained by updating in the state σ the number of tokens of the edge e to n, written as $\sigma \cdot \{e \mapsto n\}$, is defined by $(\sigma \cdot \{e' \mapsto n\})(e) = n$ if $e' = e$ and $\sigma(e)$ otherwise. The *inital state*, where all edges are unmarked, is denoted by σ_0; formally, $\sigma_0(e) = 0 \ \forall e \in \mathbb{E}$.

The reduction relation over configurations, written $\to_G$ and defined by the rules in Fig. 7, formalises the execution of a process in terms of edge marking evolution. Since such execution only affects the process state, for the sake of presentation, we omit the structure and $\mathcal{P}$ from the target configuration of the transition. Moreover, since $\mathcal{P}$ is exploited only by the OR-Join rule, it will also be omitted from the source configuration. Thus, $\langle S, \sigma, \mathcal{P} \rangle \to_G \langle S, \sigma', \mathcal{P} \rangle$ shall be usually written as $\langle S, \sigma \rangle \to_G \sigma'$. Before commenting on the rules, we introduce the auxiliary functions they exploit. Function $inc : \mathbb{S} \times \mathbb{E} \to \mathbb{S}$ (resp. $dec : \mathbb{S} \times \mathbb{E} \to \mathbb{S}$), where $\mathbb{S}$ is the set of states, allows updating a state by incrementing (resp. decrementing) by one the value of an edge in the state. Formally, they are defined as follows: $inc(\sigma, e) = \sigma \cdot \{e \mapsto \sigma(e) + 1\}$ and $dec(\sigma, e) = (\sigma \cdot \{e \mapsto \sigma(e) - 1\}$. These functions extend to sets of edges as follows: $inc(\sigma, \varnothing) = \sigma$ and $inc(\sigma, \{e\} \cup E)) = inc(inc(\sigma, e), E)$ (the cases for dec are similar).

We now briefly comment on the operational rules. Rule *G-Start* starts the execution of a process when it is in its initial state (i.e., all edges are unmarked). The effect of the rule is to increment the number of tokens in the edge outgoing from the start event. For the sake of simplicity, the rule is defined in a way that, when the process execution terminates it can restart. Rule *G-End* instead is enabled when there is at least a token in the incoming edge of the end event, which is then removed. Rule *G-AndSplit* is applied when there is at least one token in the incoming edge of an AND-Split gateway; as result of its application the rule decrements the number of tokens in the incoming edge and increments that in each outgoing edge. Similarly, rule *G-AndJoin* decrements the tokens in each incoming edge and increments the number of tokens of the outgoing edge, when each incoming edge has at least one token. Rule *G-XorSplit* is applied when a token is available in the incoming edge of a XOR-Split gateway, the rule decrements the token in the incoming edge and increment the token in one of the outgoing edges. Rule *G-XorJoin* is activated every time there is a token in one of the incoming edges, which is then moved to the outgoing edge. Rule *G-OrSplit*

$$\langle \mathsf{start}(\mathsf{e}), \sigma_0 \rangle \rightarrow_G inc(\sigma_0, \mathsf{e}) \qquad\qquad (G\text{-}Start)$$

$$\langle \mathsf{end}(\mathsf{e}), \sigma \rangle \rightarrow_G dec(\sigma, \mathsf{e}) \qquad \sigma(\mathsf{e}) > 0 \qquad (G\text{-}End)$$

$$\langle \mathsf{andSplit}(\mathsf{e}, E), \sigma \rangle \rightarrow_G inc(dec(\sigma, \mathsf{e}), E) \qquad \sigma(\mathsf{e}) > 0 \qquad (G\text{-}AndSplit)$$

$$\langle \mathsf{andJoin}(\mathsf{e}, E), \sigma \rangle \rightarrow_G inc(dec(\sigma, E), \mathsf{e}) \qquad \forall \mathsf{e}' \in E . \sigma(\mathsf{e}') > 0 \qquad (G\text{-}AndJoin)$$

$$\langle \mathsf{xorSplit}(\mathsf{e}, \{\mathsf{e}'\} \sqcup E), \sigma \rangle \rightarrow_G inc(dec(\sigma, \mathsf{e}), \mathsf{e}') \qquad \sigma(\mathsf{e}) > 0 \qquad (G\text{-}XorSplit)$$

$$\langle \mathsf{xorJoin}(\mathsf{e}, \{\mathsf{e}'\} \sqcup E), \sigma \rangle \rightarrow_G inc(dec(\sigma, \mathsf{e}'), \mathsf{e}) \qquad \sigma(\mathsf{e}') > 0 \qquad (G\text{-}XorJoin)$$

$$\langle \mathsf{orSplit}(\mathsf{e}, E_1 \sqcup E_2), \sigma \rangle \rightarrow_G inc(dec(\sigma, \mathsf{e}), E_1) \qquad \sigma(\mathsf{e}) > 0 \quad E_1 \neq \varnothing \qquad (G\text{-}OrSplit)$$

$$\langle \mathsf{orJoin}(\mathsf{e}, E_1 \sqcup E_2), \sigma \rangle \rightarrow_G inc(dec(\sigma, E_1), \mathsf{e}) \qquad \begin{array}{l} \forall \mathsf{e}' \in E_1 . \sigma(\mathsf{e}') > 0 \qquad (G\text{-}OrJoin) \\ \forall \mathsf{e}' \in E_2 . \sigma(\mathsf{e}') = 0 \\ E_1 \neq \varnothing \qquad \forall p_1 \in \Pi . \exists p_2 \in \Pi_{p_1} \end{array}$$

$$\frac{\langle S_1, \sigma \rangle \rightarrow_G \sigma'}{\langle S_1 \mid S_2, \sigma \rangle \rightarrow_G \sigma'} \; (G\text{-}Int_1) \qquad\qquad \frac{\langle S_2, \sigma \rangle \rightarrow_G \sigma'}{\langle S_1 \mid S_2, \sigma \rangle \rightarrow_G \sigma'} \; (G\text{-}Int_2)$$

Fig. 7. BPMN global semantics.

is activated when there is a token in the incoming edge of an OR-Split gateway, which is then removed while a token is added in some outgoing edges (at least one). Notably, in the rule we make use of operator $\sqcup$, denoting the disjoint union of sets, i.e. $E_1 \sqcup E_2$ stands for $E_1 \cup E_2$ if $E_1 \cap E_2 = \varnothing$, it is undefined otherwise. Rules $G\text{-}Int_1$ and $G\text{-}Int_2$ deal with interleaving in a standard way.

We conclude by describing in detail the rule $G\text{-}OrJoin$ defining the semantics of the OR-Join gateway. The operator $\sqcup$ is used to split the set of edges incoming in the OR-Join into two disjoint sets, E_1 and E_2, such that one contains marked edges ($\forall \mathsf{e}' \in E_1 . \sigma(\mathsf{e}') > 0$) and the other one contains unmarked edges ($\forall \mathsf{e}' \in E_2 . \sigma(\mathsf{e}') = 0$). In describing the rule we quote the BPMN 2.0 specification to make clear the correspondence. *"The Inclusive Gateway is activated if"* the conditions for the rule applications are satisfied. Thus, the requirement *"At least one incoming Sequence Flow has at least one token"* is represented by condition $E_1 \neq \varnothing$. The second requirement *"For every directed path formed by Sequence Flow that (i)... (ii)... (iii)... There is also a directed path formed by Sequence Flow that (iv)... (v)... (vi)"* is represented by the condition $\forall p_1 \in \Pi . \exists p_2 \in \Pi_{p_1}$, where Π is the set of paths satisfying (i), (ii) and (iii), while the sets Π_p, one for each path p in Π, contain paths satisfying (iv), (v) and (vi). Formally, they are defined as $\Pi = \{p \in \mathcal{P}(\mathsf{e}) \mid \sigma(\mathsf{first}(p)) > 0 \wedge \mathsf{last}(p) \in E_2\}$ and $\Pi_p = \{p' \in \mathcal{P}(\mathsf{e}) \mid \mathsf{first}(p') = \mathsf{first}(p) \wedge \mathsf{last}(p') \in E_1\}$. In particular, a path p in Π is such that: *"(i) starts with a Sequence Flow f of the diagram that has a token"* ($\sigma(\mathsf{first}(p)) > 0$), *"(ii) ends with an incoming Sequence Flow of the inclusive gateway that has no token"* ($\mathsf{last}(p) \in E_2$), and *"(iii) does not visit the Inclusive Gateway"* (ensured by definition of $\mathcal{P}$). Instead, given a path p in Π, a path p' in Π_p is such that: *"(iv) starts with f"* ($\mathsf{first}(p') = \mathsf{first}(p)$, as f is the first edge of p), "*(v) ends with an incoming Sequence Flow of the inclusive gateway that has a token*" ($\mathsf{last}(p') \in E_1$), and "*(vi) does not visit the Inclusive Gateway*" (ensured again by definition of $\mathcal{P}$).

Example 1. The initial configuration of the process in Fig. 3 is $\langle S, \sigma_0 \rangle$ where:

$$S = \mathsf{start}(e_1) \mid \mathsf{orSplit}(e_1, \{e_2, e_3\}) \mid \mathsf{orJoin}(e_4, \{e_2, e_3, e_9\}) \mid \mathsf{andSplit}(e_4, \{e_5, e_6\})$$
$$\mid \mathsf{andJoin}(e_7, \{e_5, e_6\}) \mid \mathsf{xorSplit}(e_7, \{e_8, e_9\}) \mid \mathsf{end}(e_8)$$

By applying rule $G\text{-}Start$ the execution of the process starts by marking with a token the edge e_1. Rule $G\text{-}OrSplit$ can be then applied; it moves the token from e_1 to one (or more) outgoing edges of the OR-Split, say e_3. Now, all premises of rule $G\text{-}OrJoin$ are satisfied: $E_1 = \{e_3\} \neq \varnothing$, and the condition based in the universal quantification trivially holds as $\Pi = \varnothing$, since all paths with a token at the beginning and no token at the end, e.g. $(e_3, e_4, e_5, e_7, e_9)$, do visit the OR-Join, thus violating the requirement *(iii)*. Therefore, the rule can be applied and the token in e_3 moves to e_4. From there, the execution simply proceeds according to the semantics of AND and XOR gateways.

5 Formalisation of the OR-Join Local Semantics

The OR-Join semantics presented in the previous section perfectly fits with the informal definition given in the BPMN 2.0 standard specification. However, the evaluation of the OR-Join gateway activation (formalised by the premises of rule $G\text{-}OrJoin$) requires a global view of the process marking. From a practical perspective, this may complicate the implementation of the process control flow, also considering that the semantics of all other BPMN constructs is *local*, i.e. it relies only on the information about the marking of incoming and outgoing edges. Therefore, we propose in this section an alternative, yet equivalent, semantics of BPMN, including the OR-Join construct, that is local.

For the local semantics, we consider only *safe* models [24]. Safeness requires a model to not activate an edge more than once at the same time. This assumption is not too restrictive, since safeness is recognized as one of the most important correctness criteria for business process models [25]. The lack of this property, in fact, may cause issues concerning process execution, related e.g. to the proper termination of processes or to erroneous synchronizations among concurrent control flows [26].

To enable local treatment of the BPMN semantics, roughly the global state information of a process is spread over the edges of its structure, resulting on a *Marked Process*. Formally, the syntax of marked processes, denoted by M, is defined in Fig. 8. The only difference between the syntax of a marked process and a process structure is that in the former an edge is also characterised by a *type* T, indicating if it is part of a cycle (c) or not (nc), and by a *status* Σ, denoting whether a token is marking the edge (*live* status denoted by l), or may still arrive (*wait* status denoted by w), or will not arrive (*dead* status denoted by d). As

$M ::=$ start$(e.T.\Sigma)$ | andSplit$(e.T.\Sigma, E)$ | andJoin$(e.T.\Sigma, E)$ | xorSplit$(e.T.\Sigma, E)$
     | xorJoin$(e.T.\Sigma, E)$ | orSplit$(e.T.\Sigma, E)$ | orJoin$(e.T.\Sigma, E)$ | end$(e.T.\Sigma)$ | $M_1 | M_2$

$T ::=$ c | nc $\Sigma ::=$ l | w | d

Fig. 8. BPMN syntax of marked processes.

explained in Sect. 3, edge types are statically determined in the pre-processing. With abuse of notation, edge set notation E extends to marked edges.

Now, the operational semantics does not need to consider any more configurations with a state, but it is directly given in terms of marked processes. Formally, the operational semantics is defined by means of a labelled transition relation $M \xrightarrow{\alpha}_L M'$, meaning that "the marked process M performs a transition labelled by α and becomes M' in doing so". Labels α are used to propagate the effect of marking updates, resulting from the evolution of a subterm of the process, to the other subterms. They are triples of the form (w : E_1, d : E_2, l : E_3), indicating the edges whose status must be set to w, d and l, respectively. For the sake of simplicity, within labels, sets E_i contain just edge names (without type and status). Moreover, to improve readability, we omit a field of the triple when the associated edge set is empty, and we remove brackets {and} in case of singleton; for example, the label (w : $\varnothing$, d : $\varnothing$, l : {e}) is written l : e. Finally, to identify the initial status of a marked process M we rely on the boolean predicate $isInit(M)$, which holds when all edges of M have status w. Due to lack of space, we present below an excerpt of the operational semantics; we refer the interested reader to the companion technical report [27] for a complete account of definitions, operational rules, proofs of the correspondence results, and application to the running examples.

To define the labelled transition relation, we need a few auxiliary functions. First, we exploit $setDead(E)$ and $setWait(E)$ to change the status of gateway edges to d and w, respectively. Similarly, to check if the edges in E have live (resp. dead) status, we make use of the boolean function $isLive(E)$ (resp. $isDead(E)$). Finally, to distinguish the type T of edges in E we make use of boolean functions $isC(E)$ (resp. $isNC(E)$). All these functions are inductively defined on the structure of E.

In Fig. 9 we report some significant operational rules defining the evolution of live tokens in the BPMN local semantics. A start event has edges with non-cyclic type, as according to the BPMN standard it cannot have an incoming edge. Rule L-$Start$-NC annotates the edge e outgoing from the start event with l when the process is in the initial status (in fact, the edge has a w status before the transition), the corresponding label l : e is produced. Let us consider the OR-Join rules. L-$OrJoin$-NC is applied when the outgoing edge is of non-cyclic type, while L_1-$OrJoin$-C and L_2-$OrJoin$-C when it is of type c. In these latter cases, we also make use of the boolean predicate $noDep(e)$, defined in Sect. 3, to ensure that in case of vicious circles ($noDep(e) = false$) the rules cannot be applied, thus enforcing a deadlocked behaviour as prescribed by BPMN 2.0.

$$\mathsf{start}(e.nc.w) \xrightarrow{l:e}_L \mathsf{start}(e.nc.l) \hspace{4cm} (L\text{-}Start\text{-}NC)$$

$$\begin{array}{ll} \mathsf{orJoin}(e.nc.\varSigma, E_1 \sqcup E_2) \xrightarrow{(d:E_1 \sqcup E_2, l:e)}_L & E_1 \neq \varnothing \ \ isLive(E_1) \\ \hspace{0.5cm} \mathsf{orJoin}(e.nc.l, setDead(E_1 \sqcup E_2)) & isDead(E_2) \end{array} \hspace{1cm} (L\text{-}OrJoin\text{-}NC)$$

$$\begin{array}{ll} \mathsf{orJoin}(e.c.\varSigma, E_1 \sqcup E_2) \xrightarrow{(w:E_1, d:E_2, l:e)}_L & E_1 \neq \varnothing \ \ isLive(E_1) \\ \hspace{0.5cm} \mathsf{orJoin}(e.c.l, setWait(E_1) \sqcup setDead(E_2)) & isDead(E_2) \ \ isC(E_1) \\ & isNC(E_2) \ \ noDep(e) \end{array} \hspace{0.5cm} (L_1\text{-}OrJoin\text{-}C)$$

$$\begin{array}{ll} \mathsf{orJoin}(e.c.\varSigma, E_1 \sqcup E_2) \xrightarrow{(w:E_2, d:E_1, l:e)}_L & E_1 \neq \varnothing \ \ isLive(E_1) \\ \hspace{0.5cm} \mathsf{orJoin}(e.c.l, setDead(E_1) \sqcup setWait(E_2)) & isDead(E_2) \ \ isNC(E_1) \\ & isC(E_2) \ \ noDep(e) \end{array} \hspace{0.5cm} (L_2\text{-}OrJoin\text{-}C)$$

$$\mathsf{orJoin}(e.T.\varSigma, E) \xrightarrow{d:e}_L \mathsf{orJoin}(e.T.d, E) \hspace{1.5cm} isDead(E) \hspace{1cm} (D\text{-}OrJoin)$$

$$\frac{M_1 \xrightarrow{\alpha}_L M_1'}{M_1 \mid M_2 \xrightarrow{\alpha}_L M_1' \mid M_2 \star \alpha} \ (M\text{-}StatusUpd_l)$$

Fig. 9. BPMN local semantics (an excerpt).

The rules described so far are not enough for properly expressing the OR-Join behaviour only using local information. Other rules are indeed needed to propagate the dead status. They are applied when all incoming edges of a gateway are annotated with d, and propagate this information to the outgoing edges. As an example, we report here rule $D\text{-}OrJoin$. Finally, $M\text{-}StatusUpd$ allows the interleaving of the process element. It relies on the status updating function $M \star \alpha$, which returns a process obtained from M by updating the status of its edges according to the labelled sets they belong to in α.

We conclude the section with our main result, ensuring the soundness of our approach. In particular, we show the correspondence between the global and local semantics we provided. In order to do that we first need to illustrate the correspondence between the syntax used in the global formalisation and that used in the local version. The local notation is achieved by applying σ to the structure S, that is by distributing the token information included in σ on the edges of S. We recall, we consider only safe processes, thus $0 \leqslant \sigma(e) \leqslant 1$. Formally, we have the following definition; we rely here on auxiliary notations t and nl to denote an *undefined type*, which can be either c or nc, and a *not live* status, which can be either w or d.

Definition 1 (Syntax correspondence). *Let $\langle S, \sigma \rangle$ be a process configuration, then $S \cdot \sigma$ is inductively defined on the structure of S as follows (we show here only few cases of the definition, since the other are similar):*

$\mathsf{start}(e) \cdot \sigma = \mathsf{start}(e.t.(e \cdot \sigma)) \hspace{2cm} \mathsf{end}(e) \cdot \sigma = \mathsf{end}(e.t.(e \cdot \sigma))$

$\mathsf{orJoin}(e, E) \cdot \sigma = \mathsf{orJoin}(e.t.(e \cdot \sigma), (E \cdot \sigma)) \hspace{1cm} (S_1 \mid S_2) \cdot \sigma = S_1 \cdot \sigma \mid S_2 \cdot \sigma$

$where \ e \cdot \sigma = \begin{cases} l \ \text{if } \sigma(e) = 1; \\ nl \ \text{otherwise.} \end{cases} \hspace{1cm} \varnothing \cdot \sigma = \varnothing \hspace{1cm} (\{e\} \cup E) \cdot \sigma = \{e \cdot \sigma\} \cup (E \cdot \sigma).$

According to the above definition, a term $S \cdot \sigma$ represents a class of marked processes, i.e. all those processes with the same marking for what concerns the live status, but possibly different markings for the other two status and possibly different edge types (information that indeed are not considered at all in the global semantics). Therefore, to state that marked processes belong to a given class we use the relation $\equiv$, whose meaning is as follows: $M \equiv S \cdot \sigma$ means that M is syntactical equivalent to $S \cdot \sigma$, up to an instantiation of t and nl occurrences in $S \cdot \sigma$.

Finally, our results rely on the notion of *reachable* configuration/processes. In fact, the considered syntaxes are too liberal, as they allow terms that cannot be obtained (by means of transitions) from a process in its initial state.

Definition 2 (Reachable configuration/marked process). *A process configuration $\langle S, \sigma \rangle$ (resp. marked process M) is reachable if there exists $\langle S, \sigma' \rangle$ (resp. process M') such that $\sigma' = \sigma_0$ (resp. isInit(M')) and $\langle S, \sigma' \rangle \to_G^* \sigma$ (resp. $M' \xrightarrow{\alpha}{}_L^* M$).*

Now, we can formally define our results, stating that each step of the global semantics corresponds to one or more steps of the local semantics (Theorem 1) and vice versa (Theorem 2). Their proofs are given by induction on the derivation of the transitions.

Theorem 1. *Let $\langle S, \sigma \rangle$ be a reachable process configuration, if $\langle S, \sigma \rangle \to_G \sigma'$ then there exists M such that $M \equiv S \cdot \sigma$, $M \xrightarrow{\alpha}{}_L^+ M'$ and $M' \equiv S \cdot \sigma'$.*

Theorem 2. *Let M be a reachable marked process, with $M \equiv S \cdot \sigma$, if $M \xrightarrow{\alpha}{}_L M'$, then there exists M'' such that $M' \xrightarrow{\alpha}{}_L^* M''$, $\langle S, \sigma \rangle \to_G \sigma'$ and $M'' \equiv S \cdot \sigma'$.*

6   Concluding Remarks

In this paper we presented global and local direct formalisations of BPMN process models compliant with the OR-Join semantics reported in the BPMN 2.0 standard. In particular, the local semantics fosters a compositional, and hence more scalable, approach to enact business processes involving OR-Joins. The soundness of the proposed approach is given by the formal correspondence between the local and global semantics.

As a future work, we plan to validate the performance of the proposed global and local semantics over models coming from real scenarios. Moreover, we intend to use the OR-Join semantics to enable process verification and ensure process models correctness by design. Last but not least, we plan to extend enactment tools, such as Camunda [15], to implement process aware IT systems fitting with the proposed semantics.

References

1. Pastor, O.: Model-driven development in practice: from requirements to code. In: Steffen, B., Baier, C., van den Brand, M., Eder, J., Hinchey, M., Margaria, T. (eds.) SOFSEM 2017. LNCS, vol. 10139, pp. 405–410. Springer, Cham (2017). https://doi.org/10.1007/978-3-319-51963-0_31
2. OMG: Business Process Model and Notation (BPMN V 2.0) (2011)
3. Suchenia, A., Potempa, T., Ligęza, A., Jobczyk, K., Kluza, K.: Selected approaches towards taxonomy of business process anomalies. In: Pełech-Pilichowski, T., Mach-Król, M., Olszak, C.M. (eds.) Advances in Business ICT: New Ideas from Ongoing Research. SCI, vol. 658, pp. 65–85. Springer, Cham (2017). https://doi.org/10.1007/978-3-319-47208-9_5
4. van der Aalst, W.M., Desel, J., Kindler, E.: On the semantics of EPCs: a vicious circle. In: EPK, pp. 71–79 (2002)
5. Dumas, M., La Rosa, M., Mendling, J., Reijers, H.A.: Fundamentals of Business Process Management. Springer, Heidelberg (2013). https://doi.org/10.1007/978-3-642-33143-5
6. Kunze, M., Berger, P., Weske, M.: BPM academic initiative - fostering empirical research. In: BPM Demonstration Track, CEUR Workshop Proceedings, vol. 940, pp. 1–5 (2012)
7. Völzer, H.: A new semantics for the inclusive converging gateway in safe processes. In: Hull, R., Mendling, J., Tai, S. (eds.) BPM 2010. LNCS, vol. 6336, pp. 294–309. Springer, Heidelberg (2010). https://doi.org/10.1007/978-3-642-15618-2_21
8. Dumas, M., Grosskopf, A., Hettel, T., Wynn, M.: Semantics of standard process models with OR-Joins. In: Meersman, R., Tari, Z. (eds.) OTM 2007. LNCS, vol. 4803, pp. 41–58. Springer, Heidelberg (2007). https://doi.org/10.1007/978-3-540-76848-7_5
9. Thalheim, B., Sorensen, O., Borger, E.: On defining the behavior of OR-Joins in business process models. J. Univ. Comput. Sci. 15(1), 3–32 (2009)
10. Christiansen, D.R., Carbone, M., Hildebrandt, T.: Formal semantics and implementation of BPMN 2.0 inclusive gateways. In: Bravetti, M., Bultan, T. (eds.) WS-FM 2010. LNCS, vol. 6551, pp. 146–160. Springer, Heidelberg (2011). https://doi.org/10.1007/978-3-642-19589-1_10
11. Prinz, T.M., Amme, W.: A complete and the most liberal semantics for converging OR gateways in sound processes. Complex Syst. Inf. Model. Q. 4, 32–49 (2015). http://dblp.org/db/journals/csimq/csimq4
12. Gfeller, B., Völzer, H., Wilmsmann, G.: Faster Or-Join enactment for BPMN 2.0. In: Dijkman, R., Hofstetter, J., Koehler, J. (eds.) BPMN 2011. LNBIP, vol. 95, pp. 31–43. Springer, Heidelberg (2011). https://doi.org/10.1007/978-3-642-25160-3_3
13. Wynn, M.T., et al.: Business process verification-finally a reality!. Bus. Process Manag. J. 15(1), 74–92 (2009)
14. Alfresco Software Inc: Activiti v. 6.0. www.activiti.org (2017)
15. Camunda services GmbH: Camunda v. 7.7.0. www.camunda.com (2017)
16. Flowable: Flowable v. 6.1.0. www.flowable.org (2017)
17. Red Hat: jBPM v. 7.0.0. www.jBPM.org (2017)
18. ProcessMaker Inc.: Process maker v. 3.2. www.processmaker.com (2017)
19. Signavio Inc: Signavio v. 11.2.0. www.signavio.com (2017)
20. Stadust: Stadust v. 4.1.0. www.eclipse.org/stardust (2017)
21. Sydle: Sydle. www.sydle.com (2017)

22. Szwarcfiter, J.L., Lauer, P.E.: A search strategy for the elementary cycles of a directed graph. BIT Numer. Math. **16**(2), 192–204 (1976)
23. Dijkstra, E.W.: A note on two problems in connexion with graphs. Numer. Math. **1**(1), 269–271 (1959)
24. van der Aalst, W.M.P.: Workflow verification: finding control-flow errors using petri-net-based techniques. In: van der Aalst, W., Desel, J., Oberweis, A. (eds.) Business Process Management. LNCS, vol. 1806, pp. 161–183. Springer, Heidelberg (2000). https://doi.org/10.1007/3-540-45594-9_11
25. Dijkman, R.M., Dumas, M., Ouyang, C.: Semantics and analysis of business process models in BPMN. Inf. Softw. Technol. **50**(12), 1281–1294 (2008)
26. Corradini, F., Fornari, F., Muzi, C., Polini, A., Re, B., Tiezzi, F.: On avoiding erroneous synchronization in BPMN processes. In: Abramowicz, W. (ed.) BIS 2017. LNBIP, vol. 288, pp. 106–119. Springer, Cham (2017). https://doi.org/10.1007/978-3-319-59336-4_8
27. Corradini, F., Muzi, C., Re, B., Rossi, L., Tiezzi, F.: Global vs. Local Semantics of BPMN 2.0 OR-Join. Technical report, Univ. Camerino (2017). http://pros.unicam.it/documents.html

AODVv2: Performance vs. Loop Freedom

Mojgan Kamali[1]([envelope]), Massimo Merro[2]([envelope]), and Alice Dal Corso[2]

[1] Faculty of Science and Engineering, Åbo Akademi University, Turku, Finland
mojgan.kamali@abo.fi
[2] Dipartimento di Informatica, Università degli Studi di Verona, Verona, Italy
massimo.merro@univr.it

Abstract. We compare two evolutions of the Ad-hoc On-demand Distance Vector (AODV) routing protocol, i.e. DYMO and AODVv2-16. In particular, we apply *statistical model checking* to investigate the performance of these two protocols in terms of routes established and looping routes. Our modelling and analysis are carried out by the Uppaal Statistical Model Checker on 3×3 grids, with possibly lossy communication.

1 Introduction

Ad hoc networking has gained popularity and is applied in a wide range of applications, such as public safety and emergency response networks. Mobile Ad-hoc Networks (MANETs) are self-configuring networks that support broadband communication without relying on wired infrastructure. *Routing protocols* of ad-hoc networks are among the main factors determining performance and reliability of these networks. They specify the way of communication among different nodes by finding appropriate paths on which data packets must be sent.

In this work, we focus on two evolutions of the Ad-hoc On-demand Distance Vector (AODV) [21] protocol to investigate their performance and to analyse if they may yield routing loops. The protocol finds alternative routes *on demand* whenever needed, meaning that it is intended to first establish a route between a source node and a destination (*route discovery*), and then maintain a route between the two nodes during topology changes (*route maintenance*).

Most studies of wireless network protocols, especially for large scale networks, are mostly done by *simulation techniques* and test-bed experiments. These are valuable techniques for performance analysis, however they do not allow us to simulate all possible scenarios. As a consequence, unexpected behaviours and flaws appear many years after the development of protocols. Formal analysis techniques allow to screen protocols for flaws and to exhibit counterexamples to diagnose them. For instance, *model checking* [6] provides both an exhaustive search of all possible behaviours of the system, and exact quantitative results.

Statistical Model checking (SMC) [25] is a technique combining model checking and simulation, aiming at providing support for quantitative analysis as well as addressing the size barrier to allow analysis of large models. It relies on choosing sampling traces of the system and verifying if they satisfy the given property

© Springer International Publishing AG 2018
A. M. Tjoa et al. (Eds.): SOFSEM 2018, LNCS 10706, pp. 337–350, 2018.
https://doi.org/10.1007/978-3-319-73117-9_24

with a certain probability. In contrast to exhaustive approach, statistical model checking does not assure a 100% correct result, but it is possible to restrict the probability of an error occurring. In this work, we apply Uppaal SMC [8], the statistical extension of the Uppaal model checker [2] to support the composition of timed and/or probabilistic automata. In Uppaal SMC, two main statistical parameters α and ϵ, in the interval $[0, 1]$, must be specified by the user; the number of necessary runs is then computed by the tool using the Chernoff-Hoeffding bounds. The tool provides a value in the confidence interval $[p-\epsilon, p+\epsilon]$ indicating the probability p of the intended property. Parameters α and ϵ represent the probability of *false negatives* and probabilistic *uncertainty*, respectively.

Since its first definition, AODV has seen several versions and improvements. In particular, DYMO [22] is an evolution of AODV supporting *path accumulation*: whenever a control message travels via more than one node, information about all intermediate nodes is accumulated in the message and distributed to its recipients [7]. Several studies have shown that AODV, DYMO and AODVv2 suffer from *routing loops* [5,10,14,20], i.e. an established route stored in the routing tables at a specific point in time that visits the same node more than once before the intended destination is reached [11]. Caught packets in a routing loop can saturate the links and decrease the network performance. Thus, loop freedom is a critical and challenging property for any routing protocol.

Contributions. Our work has been motivated by a recent version of AODVv2, appearing in the AODVv2-16 Internet draft [24] and containing a number of modifications to overcome the looping problem of AODV and DYMO. As a first contribution, we have modelled in Uppaal SMC the core functionality of both AODVv2-16 and DYMO protocols for 3×3 grid topologies (9 nodes). While the model for AODVv2-16 is completely new, the model for DYMO is a refinement of those appearing in [7,15]. In both cases, we have adopted a *probabilistic model* for wireless communication to take into account both *message loss* and *link breakage* at different rates. As a second contribution, we have compared the performance of DYMO and AODVv2-16 with respect to four different workbenches: (i) route discovery, (ii) number of routes found, (iii) optimal route finding, (iv) and packet delivery. From our analysis, it emerges that DYMO performs significantly better than AODVv2-16 with respect to all workbenches, in particular in the presence of a significant message loss rate. Finally, as the third contribution, we investigate whether the models for the two protocols may yield routing loops under extreme conditions, such as message loss and link breakage. As expected, our model of DYMO faces a number of loops; however the corresponding Uppaal model for AODVv2-16 is loop free, with an accuracy of 99%, suggesting that the changes introduced in this version of the protocol help to reduce/remove loops.

Outline. In Sect. 2, we overview both DYMO and AODVv2-16. In Sect. 3, we discuss the Uppaal models of the two protocols based on their RFCs [22,24]. In Sects. 4 and 5, we present the results of our analysis with respect to performance and loop occurrences. In Sect. 6, we draw conclusions and review related work.

2   DYMO and AODVv2-16: Two Evolutions of AODV

This section provides a brief overview of DYMO and AODVv2-16 protocols. In both protocols, each node maintains a *routing table* (*RT*) containing information about the routes to be followed when sending messages to the other nodes of the network. The collective information in the nodes' routing table is at best a partial representation of network connectivity as it was at some times in the past; in the most general scenario, mobility together with node and communication failures continually modify that representation.

We report a scheme of the DYMO protocol [22] with an injected packet having the source node s and destination node d. When s receives the data packet, it first looks up an entry for d in its routing table. If there is no such entry, it broadcasts a `rreq` message through the network. Afterwards when an intermediate node receives the `rreq`, it first checks whether or not the information in the message is new. If this is not the case, the receiving intermediate node discards the `rreq` and the processing stops. If the information is new, the receiving node updates its routing table based on the information in the `rreq`. Then, it checks if it has a route to the destination d. If this information is provided, intermediate node sends a `rrep` back to the source s as well as to the destination d. By this, DYMO establishes *bidirectional* routes between originator and destination. On the other hand, if the intermediate node does not have any route to d, it adds its own address to the `rreq` and rebroadcasts the message.

When next intermediate node receives the rebroadcast `rreq`, it updates (if the message is new) the routing table entry associated with s and the corresponding intermediate sender node and repeats the same steps executed by the former intermediate node. Finally when the destination d receives the `rreq`, it updates its routing table for the source node s and all the intermediate nodes that have rebroadcast the `rreq`, and then sends a unicast `rrep` that follows the reverse path towards s. Each node receiving the `rrep` will update the routing table entry associated with d and intermediate nodes.

Nodes also monitor the status of alternative *active* routes to different destinations. Upon detecting the breakage of a link in an active route, an `rerr` message is broadcast to notify the other nodes about the link failure. The `rerr` message contains the information about those destinations that are no longer reachable toward the broken link. When a node receives an `rerr` from its neighbours, it invalidates the corresponding route entry for the unreachable destinations.

The architecture of the AODVv2-16 protocol [24] is quite similar to that of DYMO considering some differences. One of the main differences of AODVv2-16 is to avoid sending `rrep` by intermediate nodes. When AODVv2-16 broadcasts a `rreq`, it waits to get the `rrep` back only from the destination of the `rreq`. It means that intermediate nodes do not send the `rreps` to the source of the `rreq` even if they have active routes through the destination node. This behaviour will increase the time needed for route discovery (routing tables in AODVv2-16 are not updated as often as in DYMO), decreasing the performance of the protocol[1].

---

[1] Due to lack of space, we highlight the design differences between two protocols in [16].

2.1   Degrading Performance to Avoid Routing Loops

Different studies have proved the presence of loops in AODV, DYMO and
AODVv2 protocols [5,10,14,20]. Here, we report a simple example to show how
a loop can occur in DYMO, and how this is avoided in AODVv2-16.

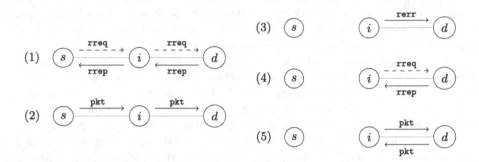

Fig. 1. Presence of a loop in DYMO.

The network in Fig. 1 consists of three nodes that are connected in a linear
topology. Let's assume that node s has a pkt to send to node d. It initiates
the route discovery and broadcasts a rreq. Node i gets the rreq, updates its
routing table for node s, adds itself as an intermediate node in the rreq of s, and
rebroadcasts the rreq, Fig. 1(1). Node s and d receive the rreq. Node s drops
the message since the received message is its own rreq and node d updates its
routing table for node s and i and since it is the rreq destination, it sends a
rrep back through the path to the originator of the rreq, i.e. node s. Node i gets
the rrep from d, updates its routing table for d, adds itself as an intermediate
node in rrep of d and sends the rrep to s. Finally, node s receives the rrep of
d, Fig. 1(1), updates its routing table for i and d and sends the pkt to node i
to be delivered to d, Fig. 1(2).

Afterwards, the link between s and i breaks and node i has a pkt to send
to s. Node i becomes aware of the link breakage and broadcasts an rerr to its
neighbours. Assume the rerr from i is lost in the reception of d, resulting in
node d not being notified about the link breakage, Fig. 1(3). Next when node i
has another pkt to send to s, and it knows already that there is no valid route to
s, it initiates a rreq to its neighbours. Node d receives the rreq and it has the
valid route to s. Node d, as the intermediate node, sends the rrep to i, Fig. 1(4).
Node i receives the rrep from d and updates its routing table for node s with
new information. In this situation, node i sends its pkt to d since node i's next
hop through s is d. Node d then sends the pkt to i as node d's next hop through
s is i. Finally, the pkt is circulated in a loop, Fig. 1(5).

Protocol designers have overcome the looping problem of DYMO by incorporating several changes in the new version (AODVv2-16). In this current version,
if route discovery is initiated the intermediate nodes which have active routes

through the destination do not send the `rrep` to the originator, meaning that the destination of the `rreq` has sole responsibility for sending the `rrep` back to the originator. By this, they have solved the problem of having loops in the network, but the performance level has decreased.

In AODVv2-16, the routing tables can be updated if:

> – "If AdvRte is more recent than all matching LocalRoutes. "
> – "If the sequence numbers are equal, Check that AdvRte is safe against routing loops compared to all matching LocalRoutes, If LoopFree(AdvRte, LocalRoute) returns TRUE, compare route costs:
> –If AdvRte is better than all matching LocalRoutes, it MUST be used to update the Local Route Set because it offers improvement.
> –If AdvRte is not better (i.e. it is worse or equal) but LocalRoute is Invalid, AdvRte SHOULD be used to update the Local Route Set because it can safely repair the existing Invalid LocalRoute." [[24], page 28]

Here, `LocalRoutes` stores previously received messages, `AdvRte` contains the information about newly received message, and `LoopFree(AdvRte, LocalRoute):= (Cost(AdvRte) <= Cost(LocalRoute))`.

There are more conditions in the specification of the AODVv2-16 indicating when to update routing tables, leading to less information being stored, hereby decreasing the performance. For instance, routing tables in AODVv2-16 are not updated in the scenario where sequence numbers are the same, the message is received via a longer path, and the link toward a destination is broken, although updating would have helped to fix broken paths. In addition, the sending of `rrep` by intermediate nodes is not specified in AODVv2-16. This leads to routes being established more slowly than in DYMO, since the `rreq` has to travel all the way to the destination node and `rrep` has to be sent back along the whole path, from the `rreq` destination to the `rreq` originator.

3   Uppaal Models of AODVv2-16 and DYMO

In this section, we briefly explain our AODVv2-16 automata and provide some modifications of the Uppaal SMC model of [15] for DYMO[2]. As in [15], both protocols are represented as parallel compositions of node processes, where each process is a parallel composition of two timed automata, the `Handler` and the `Queue`. This is because each node maintains a message queue to store incoming messages and a process for handling these messages; the workflow of the handler depends on the type of the message. Communication between nodes i and j is only feasible if they are neighbours, i.e. in the transmission range of each other. This is modelled by predicates of the form `isconnected[i][j]` which are true if and only if i and j can communicate. Communication between different nodes i and j are on channels with different names, according to the type of the control message being delivered (`rrep`, `rreq`, `rerr`).

Messages (arriving from other nodes) are stored in the queue, by using a function `addmsg()`. Only messages sent by nodes within the transmission range

---

[2] The reader can consult our models at http://users.abo.fi/mokamali/SOFSEM2018.

may be received. Unlike the model of [15] our Queue is essentially a probabilistic timed automata. Uppaal SMC features branching edges with associated weights for the probabilistic extension. Thus we define an integer constant loss, with $0 \leq$ loss ≤ 100, and a node can either lose a message with weight loss or receive it with weight $(100 -$ loss$)$.

The Handler automaton, modelling the message-handling protocol, is far more complicated and has around 22 locations. The implementation of the two protocols differs for this automaton. The Handler is busy while sending messages, and can only accept one message from the Queue once it has completely finished handling the previous message. Whenever it is not processing a message and there are messages stored in the Queue, the Queue and the Handler synchronise via channel imsg[ip], transferring the relevant message data from the Queue to the Handler. According to the specification of the protocols, the most time consuming activity is the communication between nodes, which takes 40 ms on average [22,24]. This is modelled in the Handler by means of a clock variable t, set to 0 before transmission, so that a delay between 35 and 45 ms is selected uniformly at random.

Based on DYMO and AODVv2-16 specifications, rreqs can be resent the maximum of 3 times in the presence of message loss. The major differences between AODVv2-16 and DYMO, are the absence of intermediate rreps and also conditions regarding updates of the routing tables. As we explained in Sect. 2, AODVv2-16 tries to find the whole path through the destination node and it does not rely on the rreps from intermediate nodes that have routes through the destination node (intermediate nodes do not generate any rrep message even if they have active routes through the destination node).

Finally, we report the main changes which have been introduced in our Uppaal SMC model of DYMO with respect to that proposed in [15]:

- In the DYMO model by [15], two connected nodes could get disconnected while a node is waiting to transmit a message (waiting time of 40 ms), which could cause a potential deadlock in the system. For our experiments, we modify this behaviour and assume that two connected nodes cannot get disconnected during this period of time which is the case in reality (the probability that two nodes disconnect upon communication is too low).
- We minimised the DYMO automaton of [15] by removing a number of redundant locations and transitions that were modelling the same procedure.
- We have also modelled the resending of rreq for the maximum number of 3 times, when control messages, i.e. rreq, rrep and rerr, can get lost. This was done by adding new locations and transitions.
- In the current version of DYMO Uppaal model, when a node receives a message from its neighbour it first checks the message sequence number. If it is recent then it updates its routing table for the message originator and for the stored intermediate nodes in the message. If the sequence number is not recent, the message is simply dropped without any routing table update.

For further details the reader is referred to our technical report [16].

4 Performance Analysis on Static Grids

We replay the experiments of [7,15] to compare DYMO and AODVv2-16 on
3×3 grid topologies with possibly lossy channels. Furthermore, we investigate
one more property, namely *packet delivery*. More precisely, we consider four
different workbenches to compare the two protocols: 1. A probabilistic analysis
to estimate the ability to successfully complete the protocol finding the requested
routes for a number of properly chosen scenarios; 2. A quantitative analysis to
determine the average number of routes found during the routing process in the
same scenarios; 3. A qualitative analysis to verify how good (i.e. short) are the
routes found by the routing protocol. 4. A probabilistic analysis to investigate
the number of delivered packets to their corresponding destinations. We conduct
our experiments using the following set-up: (i) 2.3 GHz Intel Quad-Core i7, with
16 GB memory, running the Mac OS X 10.11.6 "El Capitan"; (ii) Uppaal SMC
model-checker 64-bit version 4.1.19. The statistical parameters of false negatives
(α) and probabilistic uncertainty (ϵ) are both set to 0.01, leading to a confidence
level of 99%. For each experiment with these parameters, Uppaal SMC checks
several hundred runs of the model, up to 26492 runs (cf. Chernoff-Hoeffding
bound). We run our experiments for the message loss rates used in [7], namely
0%, 10% and 30%, and then also for 40% to obtain more precise results.

4.1 Successful Route Requests

In the first set of experiments we consider four specific nodes: A, B, C and D; each
with particular originator/destination roles. Our scenarios are a generalisation
of those of [15] (as we consider larger networks) and assign roles as follows:

(i)   A is the only originator sending a packet first to B and afterwards to C;
(ii) A is sending to B first and then B is also sending to C;
(iii) A is sending to B first and then C is sending to D.

Up to symmetry, varying the nodes A, B, C and D on a 3×3 grid, we have
5184 different configurations. From this number we deduct 4518 configurations
because they make little sense in our analysis, as the source and the destination
node coincide. This calculation yields 666 different configurations. As we will
repeat our simulations for four different loss rates, this makes in total 2664
experiments.

Initially, for each scenario no routes are known, i.e. the routing tables of each
node are empty. Then, with a time gap of 35–45 ms, two of the distinct nodes
receive a data packet and have to find routes to the packet's destinations. The
query in Uppaal SMC syntax has the following shape:

```
Pr[<=10000](<>(tester.final  &&  emptybuffers() &&
art[OIP1][DIP1].nhop!=0 && art[OIP2][DIP2].nhop!=0))
```

The first two conditions require the protocol to complete; here, `tester` refers
to a process which injects to the originators nodes (`tester.final` means

that all data packets have been injected), and the function `emptybuffers()` checks whether the nodes' message queue are empty and the `Handler` is idle (is not busy with processing messages). The third and the fourth conditions require that two different route requests are established. Here, `art[o][d].nhop` is the next hop in o's routing table entry for destination d. As soon as this value is set (is different to 0), a route to d has been established. Thus, the whole query asks for the probability estimate (Pr) satisfying the CTL-path expression `<>(tester.final && emptybuffers() && art[OIP1][DIP1].nhop!=0 && art[OIP2][DIP2].nhop!=0)` within 10000 time units (ms); as in [15] this bound is chosen as a conservative upper bound to ensure that the analyser explores paths to a depth where the protocol is guaranteed to have terminated.

In Table 1 we provide the results of our query for both models. More precisely, we report the average probability to satisfy the required property in all 666 configurations. This is done for four different loss rates. Note that in the case of perfect communication, our analysis shows that the probability to successfully establish a required route in our setting can be estimated to be at least 0.99. We should add here that increasing message loss rate leads an increase in the number of runs to complete the simulation. This is because unreliable communication channels make the routing process longer in order to resend control messages. In other words, the number of runs is affected by the lower success probability which requires a larger number of runs to provide confidence intervals.

Table 1. Route establishment on 3×3 grid networks ($\alpha = \epsilon = 0.01$).

	Loss = 0%	St. dev.	Loss = 10%	St. dev.	Loss = 30%	St. dev.	Loss = 40%	St. dev.
DYMO	0.99	0.00	0.99	0.00	0.89	0.06	0.65	0.14
AODVv2-16	0.99	0.00	0.98	0.00	0.72	0.14	0.45	0.20

We can see that on the 3×3 grid with perfect communication the reliability of the two protocols is quite similar. However, in the presence of message loss, DYMO performs better than AODVv2-16. In fact, the higher the loss rate, the bigger the gap between the two protocols. More precisely, with a 10% loss rate DYMO performs better than AODVv2-16, whereas with 30% and 40% loss rate the gap between two protocols becomes more obvious (DYMO performs much better than AODVv2-16). It should be also noticed that the results of the simulations on DYMO are more homogeneously distributed around the average probability, as it appears from the smaller standard deviation.

4.2   Number of Route Entries

The second analysis proposed in [15] takes into account the capability to build other routes while establishing a route between two specific nodes. Routing tables are updated whenever control messages are received. Both protocols update for the whole discovered paths by forcing *path accumulation* (storing the information about intermediate nodes in control messages).

We check the property:

```
E[<=10000,26492](max:total_knowledge())
```

where the function `total_knowledge()` counts the number of non-empty entries appearing in all routing tables built along a run of the protocol, and the function `max` returns for all runs of the simulation, the maximum number of non-empty entries. This calculation is done for all different configurations; the result of the analysis is the average over all configurations. The reader should notice that this kind of query is different from the previous one. It has the form `E[..](..)`, where the letter "E" stands for *expected value estimation*, as the result of the query is a value and not a probability. Since the number of runs is not determined by value estimation, we set 26492 runs for our simulations to guarantee a 99% confidence level. The time bound remains as 10000.

Table 2. Route quantity on 3×3 grid networks (26492 runs for each experiment).

	Loss 0%	St. dev.	Loss 10%	St. dev.	Loss 30%	St. dev.	Loss = 40%	St. dev.
DYMO	37.27	7.68	37.42	6.18	34.68	5.86	31.27	5.39
AODVv2-16	34.01	5.93	34.38	5.76	34.57	5.91	31.66	5.36

We repeat the same analysis of [15] on our 3×3 grid by considering four different loss rates. In total we did 2664 experiments, one for each configuration with a different loss rate. The results of our analysis are reported in Table 2. Table 2 shows that during the routing process DYMO establishes more routes than AODVv2-16 (37 versus 34 routes), in the absence of message loss. This gap remains the same when having 10% message loss rate. The analysis shows that increasing the rate of the message loss leads to have similar behaviour of DYMO and AODVv2-16 (having the same number of route entries).

4.3   Optimal Routes

The results of the previous section tell us that in our 3×3 grid, DYMO is more efficient than AODVv2-16 in populating routing tables while establishing routing requests. In this section, we provide a class of experiments to compare the ability of two protocols in establishing optimal routes, i.e. routes of minimal length, according to the network topology. As explained in [15,19], all ad-hoc routing protocols based on `rreq`-broadcast can establish non-optimal routes. This phenomenon is more evident in a scenario with unreliable communication.

We replay the same experiments of [15]. We checked the following property:

```
Pr[<=10000](<>(tester.final  &&  emptybuffers() &&
art[OIP1][DIP1].hops==min_path && art[OIP2][DIP2].hops==min_path1)).
```

Here, the third and the fourth conditions require that two different route requests are established. In fact, `art[o][d].hops` returns the number of hops necessary to reach the destination node d from the originator o, according to o's routing table. Furthermore, we require this number to be equal to the length of the corresponding optimal route (which has been previously computed).

In this experiment we are not interested in checking all non-empty routing entries but only those which are directly involved in the two routing requests. This property is checked on all 666 configurations with four different loss rates. Notice that this time we ask for a probability estimation, so the result is going to be a probability. The statistical parameters of our simulations are $\alpha = \epsilon = 0.01$.

Table 3. Optimal routing on 3×3 grid network. ($\alpha = \epsilon = 0.01$).

	Loss 0%	Stand. dev.	Loss 10%	Stand. dev.	Loss 30%	Stand. dev.	Loss = 40%	Stand. dev.
DYMO	0.94	0.20	0.84	0.18	0.67	0.17	0.48	0.17
AODVv2-16	0.95	0.19	0.86	0.18	0.58	0.19	0.37	0.19

Table 3 says that the probability to establish optimal routes in the two routing protocols is very close when having no message loss. Actually, in the presence of message loss, there is still a gap in favour of DYMO. This gap would become bigger if we would focus only on the optimality of the second route request, which is launched slightly after the first one. This is because DYMO works better than AODVv2-16 when routing tables are not completely empty.

4.4 Packet Delivery

The packet delivery property differs from the successful route request property, in that the route establishment property only checks if the source node has the information about the destination node, however the packet delivery property checks if the injected packets are delivered to the destination at the end. Indeed, there might be a situation where an originator node has the information about the destination node and sends its packet to the next node along the path to the destination node, but the next node itself does not have valid information about the destination node. As a consequence, all the packets stemming from the originator node will be lost, hence the packets cannot arrive at the destinations.

This property in Uppaal SMC syntax is as following:

```
Pr[<=10000](<>(tester.final  &&  emptybuffers()  &&  empty_queues()==0 &&
                packet_delivered()==2))
```

Here, the third and the fourth conditions require that the two packets are delivered at their destinations; `empty_queues()` is a function checking whether or not there is any packet in the queue of any nodes. When this function returns 0, it shows that there is no more packet in the queues of nodes. Function `packet_delivered()` returns the number of delivered packets which must be 2 at the end, given that we have injected two packets for our experiments. Thus, the whole query asks for the probability estimate (Pr) satisfying the CTL-path

expression <>(tester.final && emptybuffers() && empty_queues()==0 &&
packet_delivered()==2) within 10000 time units (ms); as in [15] this bound is
chosen as a conservative upper bound to ensure that the analyser explores to a
depth where the protocol is ensured to have terminated.

The results in Table 4 show that AODVv2-16 works worse than DYMO w.r.t.
the packet delivery property as it tries to find the whole path to the destination node, whereas DYMO relies on replying back from the intermediate nodes.
Moreover, routing tables in AODVv2-16 are not updated regularly due to the
more restricted routing table updates in AODVv2-16. Therefore, the probability
that all packets are delivered to the destination nodes is lower in AODVv2-16.

5 Loop Analysis on Grids with Link Breakage

We run our experiments, looking for loops on 3×3 grids during the routing
process, under the assumption that links between nodes can break with a *high
probability*. We model link breakage by modifying the Queue automaton so that
when a control message is received by the queue of a node (using a function
addmsg()) with probability of 100-loss, the link between one random node in
the network and the receiver can break with a fixed probability breaks. Since
link breakage is one of the main factors causing routing loops, we assign this
value to 80, so that with a very high probability the link between the sender and
the receiver fails. Furthermore, in order to increase the traffic in the network we
inject *three packets* in total. The slightly new scenario is explained below.

Table 4. Packet delivery on 3×3 grid networks ($\alpha = \epsilon = 0.01$).

	Loss 0%	Stand. dev.	Loss 10%	Stand. dev.	Loss 30%	Stand. dev.	Loss=40%	Stand. dev.
DYMO	0.99	0.00	0.98	0.00	0.78	0.09	0.50	0.16
AODVv2-16	0.99	0.00	0.97	0.01	0.60	0.16	0.35	0.18

We consider again four specific nodes: A, B, C and D; each with particular
originator/destination roles. We assign roles as follows: (i) A is the only originator sending the first packet to B, and afterwards sends the second and third
packets to C; (ii) A is sending to B first and then B is also sending the second
and third packets to C; (iii) A is sending to B first and then C is sending the
second and third packets to D.

For simplicity, in order to work with a reasonable number of experiments,
second and third packets have the same originators and destinations, so the
number of configurations up to symmetry will remain the same, i.e. 666. In our
experiments we check the number of loops in all 666 different configurations
(how many loops exist in the network) and we show how many configurations
have routing loops i.e. in how many configurations an injected packet can be
circulated between nodes. This gives 2664 experiments in total for each protocol.
Our experiments can be represented using the following Uppaal SMC syntax:

E[<=10000;26492](max:numberofloops())

Function `numberofloops()` counts the number of loops found along a run of the protocol, and the function `max` returns for all runs of the simulation, the maximum number of loops. We maintain the same number of runs as for performance analysis, i.e. 26492, to guarantee a 99% accuracy.

Table 5 depicts the maximum number of loops considering different message loss rate in different configurations for both protocols. The results of our analysis show that when message loss rate increases, the number of loops in the networks for DYMO also increases. For instance when having 0% message loss, the number of loops in the network is 1 and when message loss increases to 10% or more number of loops in the network increases to 2. Unlike DYMO, the rate of message loss does not have any effect on the number of loops in the network for AODVv2-16 as we cannot find routing loops while verifying AODVv2-16.

Table 5. Number of loops in different configurations.

	Loss 0%	Loss 10%	Loss 30%	Loss 40%
DYMO	1	2	2	2
AODVv2-16	0	0	0	0

Table 6. Number of configurations that have loops.

	Loss 0%	Loss 10%	Loss 30%	Loss 40%
DYMO	10	11	13	11
AODVv2-16	0	0	0	0

Table 6 shows the number of configurations having loops. Results for DYMO show with 0% message loss there are 10 configurations out of 666 that have loops in the network. This value is increased to 11 with 10% message loss, and when message loss is increased to 30%, the number of configurations that have loops goes up to 13. The table depicts when message loss increases to 40%, the number of configurations that have loops decreases to 11. In contrast to DYMO, there is no configuration in AODVv2-16 that has routing loops.

6 Conclusions and Related Work

Our work has been strongly inspired by recent version of AODVv2-16 [24] where several modifications were proposed to overcome looping problem of DYMO (and previous versions of AODVv2). We believe that the protocol designers accepted the performance hit in order to ensure that the protocol is loop free. To the best of our knowledge, our work is the first to investigate the looping property of AODVv2-16 and compare the performance of DYMO and AODVv2-16.

In this paper, we modelled the AODVv2-16 protocol and investigated the performance of the protocols DYMO and AODVv2-16 in 3×3 grids, with possibly lossy communication, as well as checking the loop freedom property for both protocols. Our analysis is performed using the Uppaal SMC (release 4.1.19). We were able to show how the performance of the more recent AODVv2-16 has been worsened compared to DYMO, especially in the case of lossy communication. DYMO can cause routing loops whereas our extensive analysis was not able to find loops in AODVv2-16. This result encourages us to pursue towards a formal proof of loop freedom for AODVv2-16.

Formal analysis of MANETs and their protocols is a challenging task, and their formal verification have attracted the attention from formal methods community [1, 3, 4, 7, 13, 15, 17, 18, 20]. There are number of papers which apply (statistical) model checking to AODV and its variants, to test the performances of the protocol(s). Fehnker et al. [9] used the Uppaal model checker [2] to analyse basic qualitative properties of the AODV routing protocol in all network topologies up to five nodes. Höfner and McIver [15] showed that AODV performs better than DYMO on the same topologies, relying on the Uppaal SMC model checker. On the contrary, Dal Corso et al. [7] showed that on larger networks (4×3 toroids) with lossy communication DYMO performs better than AODV.

There are also several studies on loop freedom of AODV and DYMO. van Glabbeek et al. [14] have studied the loop freedom of the AODV protocol and they have showed that AODV is not loop free and sequence numbers do not guarantee loop freedom. Namjoshi and Trefler [20] have investigated the looping property of AODVv2-04 and they have proved this protocol causes routing loops. There are several other studies that confirm existence of routing loops in AODV [5, 10, 12]. In a recent paper, Yousefi et al. [26] have applied their extension of actor-based modelling language bRebeca to model AODVv2-11 [23] (a previous version of AODVv2) where they have proved that the loop freedom property of AODVv2-11 does not hold. The authors had reported the existing loop scenario to protocol designers and the protocol has been modified in the newer version (AODVv2-13).

References

1. Battisti, L., Macedonio, D., Merro, M.: Statistical model checking of a clock synchronization protocol for sensor networks. In: Arbab, F., Sirjani, M. (eds.) FSEN 2013. LNCS, vol. 8161, pp. 168–182. Springer, Heidelberg (2013). https://doi.org/10.1007/978-3-642-40213-5_11
2. Behrmann, G., David, A., Larsen, K.G.: A tutorial on UPPAAL. In: Bernardo, M., Corradini, F. (eds.) SFM-RT 2004. LNCS, vol. 3185, pp. 200–236. Springer, Heidelberg (2004). https://doi.org/10.1007/978-3-540-30080-9_7
3. Benetti, D., Merro, M., Viganò, L.: Model checking ad hoc network routing protocols: ARAN vs. endairA. In: SEFM 2010, pp. 191–202. IEEE (2010)
4. Bhargavan, K., Obradovic, D., Gunter, C.A.: Formal verification of standards for distance vector routing protocols. J. ACM **49**(4), 538–576 (2002)
5. Bres, E., van Glabbeek, R., Höfner, P.: A timed process algebra for wireless networks with an application in routing. In: Thiemann, P. (ed.) ESOP 2016. LNCS, vol. 9632, pp. 95–122. Springer, Heidelberg (2016). https://doi.org/10.1007/978-3-662-49498-1_5
6. Clarke Jr., E.M., Grumberg, O., Peled, D.A.: Model Checking. MIT Press, Cambridge (1999)
7. Dal Corso, A., Macedonio, D., Merro, M.: Statistical model checking of Ad Hoc routing protocols in lossy grid networks. In: Havelund, K., Holzmann, G., Joshi, R. (eds.) NFM 2015. LNCS, vol. 9058, pp. 112–126. Springer, Cham (2015). https://doi.org/10.1007/978-3-319-17524-9_9

8. David, A., Larsen, K.G., Legay, A., Mikuăionis, M., Poulsen, D.B.: Uppaal SMC tutorial. STTT **17**(4), 397–415 (2015)
9. Fehnker, A., van Glabbeek, R., Höfner, P., McIver, A., Portmann, M., Tan, W.L.: Automated analysis of AODV using UPPAAL. In: Flanagan, C., König, B. (eds.) TACAS 2012. LNCS, vol. 7214, pp. 173–187. Springer, Heidelberg (2012). https:// doi.org/10.1007/978-3-642-28756-5_13
10. Fehnker, A., van Glabbeek, R.J., Höfner, P., McIver, A., Portmann, M., Tan, W.L.: A process algebra for wireless mesh networks used for modelling, verifying and analysing AODV. CoRR abs/1312.7645 (2013)
11. Garcia-Luna-Aceves, J.J.: A unified approach to loop-free routing using distance vectors or link states. SIGCOMM Comput. Commun. Rev. **19**(4), 212–223 (1989)
12. Garcia-Luna-Aceves, J.J., Rangarajan, H.: A new framework for loop-free on-demand routing using destination sequence numbers. In: MASS 2004, pp. 426–435. IEEE (2004)
13. van Glabbeek, R., Höfner, P., Portmann, M., Tan, W.L.: Modelling and verifying the AODV routing protocol. Distrib. Comput. **29**(4), 279–315 (2016)
14. van Glabbeek, R., Höfner, P., Tan, W.L., Portmann, M.: Sequence numbers do not guarantee loop freedom: AODV can yield routing loops. In: MSWiM 2013, pp. 91–100. ACM (2013)
15. Höfner, P., McIver, A.: Statistical model checking of wireless mesh routing protocols. In: Brat, G., Rungta, N., Venet, A. (eds.) NFM 2013. LNCS, vol. 7871, pp. 322–336. Springer, Heidelberg (2013). https://doi.org/10.1007/978-3-642-38088-4_22
16. Kamali, M., Merro, M., Dal Corso, A.: AODVv2: performance vs. loop freedom. Technical report. pp. 1177. TUCS - Turku Centre for Computer Science (2016)
17. Kamali, M., Höfner, P., Kamali, M., Petre, L.: Formal analysis of proactive, distributed routing. In: Calinescu, R., Rumpe, B. (eds.) SEFM 2015. LNCS, vol. 9276, pp. 175–189. Springer, Cham (2015). https://doi.org/10.1007/978-3-319-22969-0_13
18. Merro, M., Ballardin, F., Sibilio, E.: A timed calculus for wireless systems. TCS **412**(47), 6585–6611 (2011)
19. Miskovic, S., Knightly, E.W.: Routing primitives for wireless mesh networks: design, analysis and experiments. In: INFOCOM 2010, pp. 1–9. IEEE Press (2010)
20. Namjoshi, K.S., Trefler, R.J.: Loop freedom in AODVv2. In: Graf, S., Viswanathan, M. (eds.) FORTE 2015. LNCS, vol. 9039, pp. 98–112. Springer, Cham (2015). https://doi.org/10.1007/978-3-319-19195-9_7
21. Perkins, C., Belding-Royer, E., Das, S.: Ad hoc on-demand distance vector (AODV) Routing. RFC 3561 (Experimental) (2003)
22. Perkins, C., Stan, R., Dowdell, J.: Dynamic MANET on-demand (AODVv2) Routing draft-ietf-manet-dymo. Internet Draft 26 (2013)
23. Perkins, C., Stan, R., Dowdell, J., Steenbrink, L., Mercieca, V.: Ad Hoc On-demand Distance Vector (AODVv2) Routing draft-ietf-manet-aodvv2. Internet Draft 11 (2015)
24. Perkins, C., Stan, R., Dowdell, J., Steenbrink, L., Mercieca, V.: Dynamic MANET On-demand (AODVv2) Routing draft-ietf-manet-aodvv2. Internet Draft 16 (2016)
25. Sen, K., Viswanathan, M., Agha, G.A.: Vesta: a statistical model-checker and analyzer for probabilistic systems. In: QEST 2005, pp. 251–252. IEEE (2005)
26. Yousefi, B., Ghassemi, F., Khosravi, R.: Modeling and efficient verification of wireless ad hoc networks. CoRR abs/1604.07179 (2016)

Multivendor Deployment Integration for Future Mobile Networks

Manuel Perez Martinez[1], Tímea László[2], Norbert Pataki[3], Csaba Rotter[1(✉)], and Csaba Szalai[1]

[1] Nokia Bell Labs, Budapest, Hungary
{manuel.p.martinez,csaba.rotter,csaba.szalai}@nokia-bell-labs.com
[2] Nokia, Budapest, Hungary
timea.laszlo@nokia.com
[3] Department of Programming Languages and Compilers,
Eötvös Loránd University, Budapest, Hungary
patakino@elte.hu

Abstract. During the last few years, we have seen a tremendous explosion in the range of possibilities when speaking about software delivery. The web-scale IT capabilities have evolved drastically and complex web-based applications have adapted rapidly in an ever changing world where user experience is in the focus. Terms like *Agile*, *Cloudification*, *microservices* or *DevOps* are lately on the crest of the wave.

The focus of this paper, however, is not within the managed services providers, but with the network providers, or operators. These companies are experiencing similar challenges as described above especially with the imminent arrival of 5th generation mobile networks, but with a different set of constraints that make the adoption of the new paradigms or best practices a tough process. Along the paper we will cover the main bottlenecks that operators face in terms of adapting to the ever increasing network needs, paying especial attention to the multivendor nature and the extreme high availability expected in this kind of services. We present our tool for scheduling deployments in this special environment with the related workflows and leveraged DevOps best practices. Finally, we measure how a proof of concept tool helps to improve the delivery process in multivendor environments.

1 Introduction

Release management encompasses planning, coordinating, and verifying the deployment of software solutions into production. Release management requires collaboration by the development teams producing the solutions and the people responsible for your organizations operational IT infrastructure. In the case of organizations based on the agile development methodology, these people with the different responsibility areas may form several cross-functional teams, although

N. Pataki—Supported by the NKP-17-4 New National Excellence Program of the Ministry of Human Capacities.

© Springer International Publishing AG 2018
A M. Tjoa et al. (Eds.): SOFSEM 2018, LNCS 10706, pp. 351–364, 2018.
https://doi.org/10.1007/978-3-319-73117-9_25

even in these situations there could be a group of people responsible for governing the overall release management effort [11]. In the telecom industry the release procedure often spans over two or more organizations, as the development and operation are performed by distinct companies. On the other hand, the number of software releases per year has to be dramatically increased to cope with the ever-changing customer demands, affecting the release procedure as well [18].

New approaches have been appeared for software transition from development into production, such as continuous delivery (CD). The focus of continuous delivery is the release procedure automation [7]. Changes are committed to code repositories, builds and tests are run immediately as part of the continuous integration (CI) procedure. If all the changes are automatically deployed into production then we can speak about continuous deployment. This approach motivates the developers as well because they prefer faster deployment of the code they develop [23]. However, security of deployment pipelines also becomes important [6]. The DevOps approach is an extension of continuous delivery with feedback to the developers from production and intensive logging and monitoring that can be used for analysis to prevent problems and improve operational aspects [20].

Complex telecommunication systems typically consist of many components [1,22]. These components can be separated vendors or developed by different vendors and delivered to the operator who possesses the hardware and ensure several network functions – that can be selected from many different versions. It is the operator's responsibility that the subsystems are able to work together.

Continuous deployment in telecommunication industry requires coordination among the different vendors (or the delivery pipelines of the vendors). These vendors likely have different release procedure, schedule and might have whole different release frequency. Therefore, the introduction of DevOps is considered difficult in telecommunication services [15]. New technologies and approaches have been developed, adopted and fine-tuned for making this process easier. For instance, virtualization techniques (clouds and containerization) are widely-used in the telecom industry, as well.

However, there is no thoroughgoing toolchain to cover multivendor aspects of the deployment in complex telecommunication network nowadays [13]. This paper aims for providing a possible solution deployed to the operators premise to control and coordinate the releases of software components in a multivendor 5G telecommunication environment [4]. This architecture requires new approaches for deploying mobile networks and to be compliant with the DevOps paradigm [3]. The main cornerstones of 5G are automation and DevOps [27], thus we support existing CI/CD/DevOps pipelines with a new tool that finds the proper window for updating a network element, so it can increase the upgrade capacity at the operator side. We present different approaches for this tool, we compare them and propose a workflow how to use it.

This paper is organized as follows. We show the integration-related problems in Sect. 2. We present the existing techniques that motivate our work in Sect. 3. We particularize our solution in Sect. 4: the architecture details are described in the section. We measure how a specific application deployment can be gained speed in Sect. 5. Finally, this paper is concluded in Sect. 6.

2   Problems of Integration

The traditional software delivery process in telecommunication is milestone-based with upfront release planning, taking the form of project/release plans and spreadsheets. They rely on regular meetings between project office and the technical staff to keep them in sync.

The release handover process takes mostly manual planning for scheduling updates, requires additional and integration testing in staging. These processes are executed at the operator with the help of the vendor. Operator defines strait maintenance windows, in which slight service outages are tolerated. The software upgrade process is also executed most manually with incidental rollback method. Thus, these are slow, circumstantial, cumbersome processes which result in sub-optimal capacity of upgrading mobile network elements. In casual development continuous delivery can be used to increase delivery frequency and automate the delivery and deployment. Agile methodologies are able speed-up these processes, but it cannot solve all the problems in telecommunication software development because a telecommunication software significantly differs from a casual one in the following aspects [22]:

- *resilience*: usual IT application is much less complex as a telecommunication subsystem and thus detecting and fixing errors makes less time.
- *multivendor*: CD is typically applied in such IT product where the development and the operation is done by the very same company. So they usually have a single CI pipeline. We do not know any solution in IT that would synchronize among different CD pipelines belong to different vendors taking care of the security aspect as well. In contrast in telecommunication systems we need to synchronize different outputted artifacts and deployments from different vendors.
- *high availability*: In a telecommunication system five nines (99.999%) network availability is required while for a typical web-application 99% availability can be enough.

On the other hand, developing continuous deployment pipelines is hard, for instance, 15 companies have been analysed in 2015 and no company had an automatic pipeline all the way to deployment in a production environment [14]. However, tools, technologies and methodologies have been improved [10].

The delivery control systems in casual development supervise the delivery of a single component, so there is no need of synchronising the deployments of different DevOps pipelines. We are not aware of any tool in IT that would synchronize the output of distinct pipelines into production environment. Complex IT services and multivendor telecommunication systems require synchronization among the distinct pipelines providing quality and high availability.

As in the past it was usual to deliver just a few times a year, in the near future new releases should be deployed even every day [15]. This speed-up means problem regarding the increased amount of data, the compatibility and deployment scheduling of overlapping new release deployments.

Integration becomes more challenging when one deals with DevOps pipelines in multivendor environments [9]. The approaches of software architectures and the deployments processes have been changed, e.g. microservice-based architecture, which will be elaborated further, is gaining increasing popularity. This includes that the software is split into several components (services), which can and shall be deployed and operated separately, but it introduces additional operational and configuration complexity.

There are situations when the new release of a software component is no longer compatible to an other one because the public APIs and data schemas evolve time by time and the various software components should communicate with each other. Therefore the importance of spotting, tracking and resolving colliding software component versions is highly important. In some cases the software components are tightly coupled with each other, meaning that they cannot be updated independently. Software updates have to be carried out then in a predefined order.

Development team is likely to have separate CI pipeline set up for each software component. This pipeline guides the software components in its way from a software change to its release across several levels of test phases and quality assurance steps. This brings the need to create a common, automated way to deploy each software component to any test environment and to production as well.

The mentioned problems grow exponentially in a complex, multivendor-based telecommunication software system in which different subsystems are deployed and updated very frequently with DevOps approach. The existing approach cannot handle the complexity of the network, so new approaches are required to overcome this combinatorial explosion. In the 5G realm high availability (HA) is a very important aspect from the view of the operators [2]. Service outages are not acceptable from the view of end-users. Furthermore, so far only small maintenance windows (timeslots when updates and new releases can be deployed) have been allowed. This would not change in the 5G-based environment.

The traditional upgrade process causes suboptimal capacity of upgrading mobile network elements because of the long-term planning processes. Telecommunication operators are eager for frequent updates for the applied network elements, thus we define a new approach for making this processes faster and seamless. The solution guarantees proper timeslots for updating network element when a new release becomes available and performs the process. Thus, it increases the number of release updates at the operator side because correct timeframe for the separate, safe update of the different subsystems is ensured. This approach requires fine-grained network element architecture. However, there is a limit that should be approximated in the number of release updates.

3   Enablers

Continuous Delivery is a software development discipline which focuses on the deploymentability of developed software. Comprehensive testing is an important aspect because a deployable software always should be available [21]. It emphasizes the deployment automation for transparent deployment pipelines.

DevOps is an emerging methodology based on continuous delivery. The main missions of DevOps are: the development and operation affect each other, receiving feedback from operation to developers with comprehensive monitoring, logging that are continuously evaluated.

DevOps pipelines include many stages: starts with building, followed by different kinds of testing (e.g. component and integration testing) [24]. Comprehensive analysis requires static analyzers (e.g. [12]), vulnerability scanning, etc. After this phase, the automatic deployment of application starts [8]. Logging and monitoring supervise the working software and the problems in production are solved in a seamless way [16]. However, the development team is eager for feedback from the application which is in the production environment: e.g. what are the unused features or where are performance bottlenecks. The visibility of the whole process is guaranteed.

Microservice architecture is an approach to developing application as a set of small services, each running in its own process and communicating with lightweight mechanisms, often an HTTP resource API [19]. Services do not run on the same machine necessarily and they can be deployed independently, thus this architecture supports DevOps intensively [5]. Scaling of the application is much easier and fine-grained with microservices.

Using microservice architecture in telecommunication is not straightforward. For instance, well-defined boundaries and clean compositions are required in the case of this architecture because refactoring among services considered lumbering. Integration testing requires much more effort.

The Network Function Virtualization (NFV) Management and Orchestration (MANO) architecture aims at the flexible, transparent on-boarding and configuration of virtualized network functions (VNFs) and services composed of VNFs [17]. Networking, storage and virtual machines are included in the deployment. Virtualization breaks the coupling with specific equipment, thus NFV technology is able to virtualize a wide range of network function types, thus this is an ideal basis for multivendor environment.

The NFV MANO consists of three functional elements: the virtual infrastructure manager (VIM), the NFV orchestrator (NFVO) and the NFV manager (NFVM). The NFVO is responsible for on-boarding of new network services (NSs) and VNF packages. It handles the lifecycle management of the NS and global resource management. NFVO validates and authorizes network functions virtualization infrastructure (NFVI) resource requests. The VNF Manager handles lifecycle management of VNF instances. VIM controls and manages the NFVI compute, storage, and network resources.

NFV MANO architecture utilizes the virtualization techniques but virtualization has further benefits, as well. It is well-known that common staging environment should be similar to the production environment. The integration status can be tracked in the staging environment. However, different hardware elements may be available in staging and production because the production must be always available, so the hardware has high capacity. Fortunately, modern virtualization techniques are able to hide the details of hardware, thus the production and staging environment can be very similar, the only difference is the capacity of environments [25].

4 Our Technique

4.1 Approaches

A possible solution for the above mentioned challenges is a deployment control system (referred as *Deployment Manager*), deployed to the operators as part of the NFV orchestration and management solution.

The Deployment Manager provides the operators with a comprehensive view of software changes across a large collection of related software components, forming a single or multiple network service(s). It keeps track of available software artifacts delivered by different vendors and it gives aid for planning and scheduling system-level software upgrade.

Figure 1 shows a simple but descriptive setup and usage scenario involving the Deployment Manager. The operator has a network service consisting of three VNFs operated. Two of them are provided by a vendor, the other one is from another vendor. Deployment Manager runs in the operator's environment as part of the Service Orchestration Layer. It facilitates the Network Orchestration layer to deploy or update network services or the VNFs.

Each vendor has a fully automated development pipeline. The first part of each build pipeline follows the guideline of the continuous integration practice. The second part of the build pipeline is an internal deployment. During the internal deployment the solution is tested against functional and performance requirements with all the components provided by an other vendor emulated. The deployment procedure is also tested here.

If the software successfully passes all the phases, it can be deployed. We propose the *Deployment Scheduler* which is inside the Deployment Manager. The scheduler provides the appropriate date and time for the deployment to each pipeline. With its help the deployments will not overlap or hinder each other in any way. The main components of the Deployment Scheduler are the Decision Logic that uses the Component and the Compatibility Graphs and the Rule Engine that keeps track the already scheduled deployments in a database. This approach works in the following way: Deployment Scheduler receives schedule request containing compatibility info of the new component version. The Decision Logic stores the compatibility info of the new component version into the Compatibility Graph. The Decision Logic checks whether the new component version is compatible (based on Compatibility Graph, that was just updated) with all other component that the old version in the same component uses according to the Component Graph. The Decision Logic requests schedule from the

Rule Engine. The Rule Engine asks the Schedules database about the already scheduled deployments. Based on that and its rules the rule engine counts the next possible schedule for the given component version. The Rule Engine provides the schedule for the Decision Logic. The Decision Logic answers with the schedule response to the requester. Using a rule machine inside the Deployment Scheduler can implement any rules in terms of the schedule (dependencies, customer activities, etc.).

Another option is that the Deployment Scheduler is included in a more full-fledged *Delivery Manager* instead of the Deployment Manager. In this case during the software handover process to the operator the software with all its artifacts (release information, external configuration files and other metadata) gets uploaded to the Product and Service database inside the Delivery Manager. Based on the predefined rules and schedule, the Decision Logic performs the update of the corresponding VNF first in the staging environment. Deployment into the staging environment is part of the verification procedure: each software increment gets tested in an environment that is similar to the production. A software component passing this verification phase can now be deployed into production. It can be an immediate or a scheduled action (or may based on custom rules) and it might require formal approval as in the example of Fig. 1.

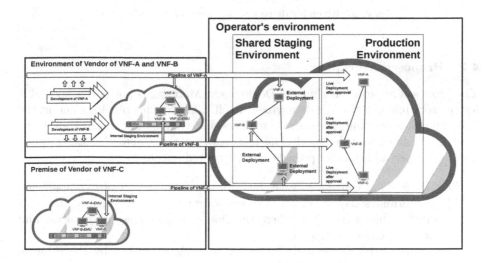

Fig. 1. Delivery control

An alternative would be to use only one common CD pipeline shared among the different vendors. Our opinion is this multivendor pipeline would rise security issues. Moreover, the development and test environment of the different vendors could not be separated because all of them need to have access to the administration of the pipeline, configuration of the test environments and the common version control systems. Building a common CD pipeline would also need intensive cooperation among the different vendors. So all in all, our solution provides better isolation and maintainability and proves to be easier to implement compared to the shared version.

The schematic picture of our solution can be seen in Fig. 2, the Deployment Scheduler that synchronizes the deployment of different products that are delivered by different pipelines controlled by the corresponding vendor. It shows an example when all the three pipelines are ready to deploy at the same time. They inform the Deployment Scheduler that decides the schedule of the deployments and responds to the pipelines to deploy accordingly.

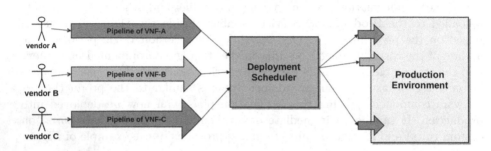

Fig. 2. Multivendor delivery with deployment scheduler

4.2   Proposed Workflow

The proposed approach is that the Deployment Manager is not only responsible for the schedule but also the deployment itself. The DevOps pipelines end at the delivery phase creating the software releases that they handle to our tool, to be stored, scheduled and deployed. The features that the *Comprehensive Deployment Manager* additionally provides are presented ahead:

- *Product/Service repository*: A database for the available software components. After a formal software release, the software artifacts are pushed into this repository. This is the place where the change logs, release information and operational guides are stored.
- *Deployment artifacts*: models for network services created by the solution architects that describe the VNFs and the required network setup, annotated with the corresponding software versions and lifecycle dependency graphs.
- *Deployment Scheduler*: The core part of the Comprehensive Deployment Manager. It helps to create release and deployment action plans according to the availability of the software components, assets and operational personnel. It aligns the different release trains of the vendors, ad-hoc releases and deployment windows. It supports several strategies from a fully automated, best-effort to a multiphased delivery process with fine-grained scheduling for every phase with manual approvals in between.

– *Asset Manager*: The release management team will work closely with the operations team to perform configuration management of the operational environment. To safely deploy into production they must know the current production and its dependencies comprehensively. The Asset Manager provides input for the release planner and scheduler to determine the status and availability of the necessary resources for software verification and operation.

– *Reporting*: The main role of the reporting subsystem is to provide all the contributors (solution architects, operation personnel, etc.) with release intelligence as an insight into the effectiveness of the release management effort. Predefined release metrics help the operator to gain insight and improve the release process. Such metrics can be:

  • number of pending software releases waiting in the "backlog"
  • number or rate of successful releases
  • number and duration of outages suffered during releases
  • percentage of releases by type (regular software update, security patch, emergency update, etc.)

The general software release management workflow (see Fig. 3) would look like as follows:

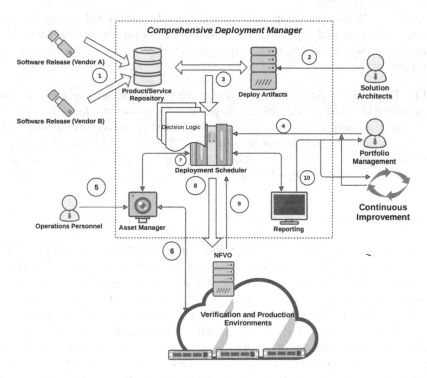

Fig. 3. Comprehensive deployment manager workflow

1. Software releases continuously provided by the various vendors are collected in the Product/Service Repository.
2. Solution Architects design the network services with all the necessary deployment artifacts.
3. With these two a network service becomes available for verification and for production use.
4. Portfolio and Release Management create a release plan with the corresponding ruleset and schedule, then upload them to the Release Planner and Scheduler.
5. Operations Personnel revises the current state of assets and resources according to the release plans.
6. Asset Manager keeps its state in sync with the verification and production environment.
7. Based on the release ruleset, the network service and asset availability the Decision Logic in the Release Planner and Scheduler triggers software deployment and release.
8. Release Planner and Scheduler delegates actions for deployment to the underlying network service orchestration and management layer.
9. Release Planner and Scheduler obtains feedback for the process state and the collected metrics.
10. With the Reporting component, the Comprehensive Deployment Manager provides views and reports of the release process for the management. This input is used for continuous improvement, i.e. further refinement of the release procedure.

The Deployment Scheduler uses a rule engine to determine schedule that can consider the deployment windows, priorities and not-yet-known dependencies among the components. The trivial rule engine just avoids overlapping of the deployment windows and provide schedule in a "first come, first served" basis, but there can be improved approaches. The operator has long-term information about the service usage and this can be used to detect the optimal update windows.

5   Measurements

We have developed a proof of concept tool for connecting existing CD/DevOps pipelines and scheduling the deployment of their output. Our tool defines a proper timeslot for execute deployment of a new release based on compatibility information, so this is the Deployment Scheduler in our approach. It implements a RESTful API for the communication. We have taken advantage of Neo4j graph databases [26] for components (products with version information). Components typically use each other, so in our database graph defines this relation. Another relation that is stored is the compatibility among the components.

We have prepared a distributed Hadoop cluster application to deploy according to the proposed approach. This application is deployed to cloud as a bunch of virtual machines with external volumes, connected via networks. We measure different (re)deployment times and analyse how we can speed up the deployment process. The deployment time includes three independent components: deployment of the resources (e.g. virtual machines, network ports, etc.), deployment of the software and the smoke test of the application.

The application consists of 6 virtual machines: 3 data nodes, an edge server, a distributed repository and a master node. All virtual machines have an attached volume and the nodes are connected with 7 networks. The different networks aim at different communication purposes (e.g. network for accessing the distributed repository). The virtual machines have different IP addresses on these networks. We distinguish the node releases based on compatibility information. There are node types which are compatible to the previously deployed virtual machines and there are node types which are incompatible to the previously deployed hosts. When a new incompatible node is deployed we have to redeploy all nodes with new compatible hosts. The edge and data nodes are compatible to every other nodes, but the master and repository releases are not.

We have configured the tool with different pipelines: first configuration of pipelines simulates the monolithic approach, the second one is the microservice-based. The first configuration redeploys all nodes when one of the pipelines has finished successfully because the published images are considered to be incompatible. The second one executed the incremental upgrade process if the compatibility is correct.

The entire deployment from scratch process takes 73 s for the cloud resources, 1525 s for the software configuration and 3 s for smoke test. This is the monolithic approach, but the deployment process should be more efficient, so we fine-grain the nodes of the cluster. The incremental update processes should speed up the progress because reconfiguration does not affect all nodes and sequential restarting can be avoided. The redeployment time of a single node is much better but we are not able to redeploy all nodes separately. We set the compatibility information into our proof of concept tool and receive update timeslots for upgrading the application.

Table 1. Application average deployment times

Scenario	Deployment of cloud resources	Software configuration	Smoke test
Application deployment	73 s	1525 s	3 s
Edge server redeployment	42 s	449 s	3 s
3 data nodes redeployment	43 s	383 s	3 s
3 data nodes and edge server redeployment	53 s	484 s	3 s

The average running times of different scenarios can be seen on Table 1. The table reflects that the fine-grained approach is worthwhile, the redeployment time is decreased regardless if it is related to the software configuration or the cloud resources. However, the software configuration time is improved better. On the other hand, in our case we cannot redeploy all the different node types. It is also seen that deployment times of different nodes vary but the number of nodes does not affect the runtime significantly. When the redeployment processes are faster we can effectively schedule the deployment of new releases and we can achieve better deployment capacity with less service outage compared to the former, monolithic approach. On the other hand, we cannot speed-up the smoke test with our approach, but operators also may take advantage of incremental, fast update processes and update the network service frequently.

6   Conclusion

DevOps is an emerging principle in the modern software development because it improves user experience from the view of end-users and it improves the operational tasks, as well. It is based on comprehensive testing, automatic deployment and release upgrade processes, feedback collection. However, the complex telecommunication systems in the 5G world also require DevOps-based frequent updates in the communication network. Operators work in a complex, multivendor environment with strong expectations of high availability. Using DevOps principles is not straightforward in this complex environment.

In this paper we argue for an approach that can be used in multivendor environment for synchronizing separate DevOps pipelines. Our work increases the update frequency and takes advantage of the deployment capacity at the operator side. This approach contains the Deployment Manager that is responsible for scheduling and deploying the scheduled VNFs. We have developed a proof of concept tool for this approach that makes proper schedule in multivendor environments based on compatibility information.

References

1. NGMN 5G white paper. White Paper, February 2015
2. Preliminary views and initial considerations on 5G RAN architecture and functional design. White Paper, March 2016. https://metis-ii.5g-ppp.eu/wp-content/uploads/white_papers/5G-RAN-Architecture-and-Functional-Design.pdf
3. 5G PPP Architecture Working Group: View on 5G Architecture. Technical report, 5G PPP Architecture Working Group (2016)
4. Agyapong, P.K., Iwamura, M., Staehle, D., Kiess, W., Benjebbour, A.: Design considerations for a 5G network architecture. IEEE Commun. Mag. **52**(11), 65–75 (2014)
5. Balalaie, A., Heydarnoori, A., Jamshidi, P.: Microservices architecture enables DevOps: migration to a cloud-native architecture. IEEE Softw. **33**(3), 42–52 (2016)
6. Bass, L., Holz, R., Rimba, P., Tran, A.B., Zhu, L.: Securing a deployment pipeline. In: 2015 IEEE/ACM 3rd International Workshop on Release Engineering, pp. 4–7, May 2015

7. Chen, L.: Continuous delivery: huge benefits, but challenges too. IEEE Softw. **32**(2), 50–54 (2015)
8. Cukier, D.: DevOps patterns to scale web applications using cloud services. In: Proceedings of the 2013 Companion Publication for Conference on Systems, Programming, & Applications: Software for Humanity. SPLASH 2013, pp. 143–152, ACM, New York (2013). http://doi.acm.org/10.1145/2508075.2508432
9. Fazal-Baqaie, M., Güldali, B., Oberthür, S.: Towards DevOps in multi-provider projects. In: Krusche, S., Lichter, H., Riehle, D., Steffens, A. (eds.) Proceedings of the 2nd Workshop on Continuous Software Engineering, pp. 18–21. CEUR-WS.org (2017). http://ceur-ws.org/Vol-1806/paper03.pdf
10. Fowley, F., Elango, D.M., Magar, H., Pahl, C.: Software system migration to cloud-native architectures for SME-sized software vendors. In: Steffen, B., Baier, C., van den Brand, M., Eder, J., Hinchey, M., Margaria, T. (eds.) SOFSEM 2017. LNCS, vol. 10139, pp. 498–509. Springer, Cham (2017). https://doi.org/10.1007/978-3-319-51963-0_39
11. Highsmith, J., Cockburn, A.: Agile software development: the business of innovation. Computer **34**(9), 120–127 (2001)
12. Horváth, G., Pataki, N.: Source language representation of function summaries in static analysis. In: Proceedings of the 11th Workshop on Implementation, Compilation, Optimization of Object-Oriented Languages, Programs and Systems, ICOOOLPS 2016, pp. 6:1–6:9, ACM, New York (2016). http://doi.acm.org/10.1145/3012408.3012414
13. Karl, H., Dräxler, S., Peuster, M., Galis, A., Bredel, M., Ramos, A., Martrat, J., Siddiqui, M.S., van Rossem, S., Tavernier, W., Xilouris, G.: DevOps for network function virtualisation: an architectural approach. Trans. Emerg. Telecommun. Technol. **27**(9), 1206–1215 (2016). https://doi.org/10.1002/ett.3084
14. Leppänen, M., Mäkinen, S., Pagels, M., Eloranta, V.P., Itkonen, J., Mäntylä, M.V., Männistö, T.: The highways and country roads to continuous deployment. IEEE Softw. **32**(2), 64–72 (2015)
15. Lwakatare, L.E., Karvonen, T., Sauvola, T., Kuvaja, P., Olsson, H.H., Bosch, J., Oivo, M.: Towards DevOps in the embedded systems domain: why is it so hard? In: 2016 49th Hawaii International Conference on System Sciences (HICSS), pp. 5437–5446, January 2016
16. Lwakatare, L.E., Kuvaja, P., Oivo, M.: Dimensions of DevOps. In: Lassenius, C., Dingsøyr, T., Paasivaara, M. (eds.) XP 2015. LNBIP, vol. 212, pp. 212–217. Springer, Cham (2015). https://doi.org/10.1007/978-3-319-18612-2_19
17. Mijumbi, R., Serrat, J., Gorricho, J.L., Latre, S., Charalambides, M., Lopez, D.: Management and orchestration challenges in network functions virtualization. IEEE Commun. Mag. **54**(1), 98–105 (2016)
18. Neely, S., Stolt, S.: Continuous Delivery? Easy! Just change everything (Well, maybe it is not that easy). In: 2013 Agile Conference, pp. 121–128, August 2013
19. Newman, S.: Building Microservices. O'Reilly, Sebastopol (2015)
20. Révész, Á., Pataki, N.: Containerized A/B testing. In: Budimac, Z. (ed.) Proceedings of the Sixth Workshop on Software Quality Analysis, Monitoring, Improvement, and Applications, pp. 14:1–14:8. CEUR-WS.org (2017). http://ceur-ws.org/Vol-1938/paper-rev.pdf
21. Roche, J.: Adopting DevOps practices in quality assurance. Commun. ACM **56**(11), 38–43 (2013). https://doi.org/10.1145/2524713.2524721
22. Rotter, C., Illés, J., Nyíri, G., Farkas, L., Csatári, G., Huszty, G.: Telecom strategies for service discovery in microservice environments. In: 2017 20th Conference on Innovations in Clouds, Internet and Networks (ICIN), pp. 214–218, March 2017

23. Savor, T., Douglas, M., Gentili, M., Williams, L., Beck, K., Stumm, M.: Continuous Deployment at Facebook and OANDA. In: Proceedings of the 38th International Conference on Software Engineering Companion. ICSE 2016, pp. 21–30, ACM, New York (2016). http://doi.acm.org/10.1145/2889160.2889223

24. Schaefer, A., Reichenbach, M., Fey, D.: Continuous integration and automation for DevOps. In: Kim, K.H., Ao, S.I., Rieger, B.B. (eds.) IAENG Transactions on Engineering Technologies: Special Edition of the World Congress on Engineering and Computer Science 2011, pp. 345–358. Springer, Netherlands (2013). https://doi.org/10.1007/978-94-007-4786-9_28

25. Sonkoly, B., Szabo, R., Jocha, D., Czentye, J., Kind, M., Westphal, F.J.: UNIFYing cloud and carrier network resources: an architectural view. In: 2015 IEEE Global Communications Conference (GLOBECOM), pp. 1–7, December 2015

26. Webber, J.: A programmatic introduction to Neo4j. In: Proceedings of the 3rd Annual Conference on Systems, Programming, and Applications: Software for Humanity. SPLASH 2012, pp. 217–218. ACM, New York (2012). http://doi.acm.org/10.1145/2384716.2384777

27. Ziegler, V., Theimer, T., Sartori, C., Prade, J., Sprecher, N., Albal, K., Bedekar, A.: Architecture vision for the 5G era. In: 2016 IEEE International Conference on Communications Workshops (ICC), pp. 51–56, May 2016

Mobile Robots and Server Systems

Patrolling a Path Connecting a Set of Points with Unbalanced Frequencies of Visits

Huda Chuangpishit[1], Jurek Czyzowicz[2], Leszek Gąsieniec[3],
Konstantinos Georgiou[1], Tomasz Jurdziński[4], and Evangelos Kranakis[5]([✉])

[1] Department of Mathematics, Ryerson University, Toronto, Canada
hoda.chuang@gmail.com, konstantinos@ryerson.ca
[2] Département d'informatique, Université du Québec en Outaouais,
Gatineau, Canada
Jurek.Czyzowicz@uqo.ca
[3] Department of Computer Science, University of Liverpool, Liverpool, UK
L.A.Gasieniec@liverpool.ac.uk
[4] Instytut Informatyki, Uniwersytet Wrocławski, Wrocław, Poland
Tomasz.Jurdzinski@ii.uni.wroc.pl
[5] School of Computer Science, Carleton University, Ottawa, Canada
evankranakis@gmail.com

Abstract. Patrolling consists of scheduling perpetual movements of a collection of mobile robots, so that each point of the environment is regularly revisited by any robot in the collection. In previous research, it was assumed that all points of the environment needed to be revisited with the same minimal frequency.

In this paper we study efficient patrolling protocols for points located on a path, where each point may have a different constraint on frequency of visits. The problem of visiting such divergent points was recently posed by Gąsieniec et al. in [14], where the authors study protocols using a single robot patrolling a set of n points located in nodes of a complete graph and in Euclidean spaces.

The focus in this paper is on patrolling with two robots. We adopt a scenario in which all points to be patrolled are located on a line. We provide several approximation algorithms concluding with the best currently known $\sqrt{3}$-approximation.

1 Introduction

In this paper we study efficient patrolling protocols by two robots for a collection of n points distributed arbitrarily on a path or a segment of length 1. Each point needs to be attended perpetually with *known* but often distinct minimal frequency, i.e., some points need to be visited more often than others.

J. Czyzowicz, K. Georgiou and E. Kranakis—Research supported in part by NSERC.
L. Gąsieniec—Research supported by Networks Sciences and Technologies (NeST).
T. Jurdziński—Research supported by the Polish National Science Centre grant DEC-2012/06/M/ST6/00459.

© Springer International Publishing AG 2018
A M. Tjoa et al. (Eds.): SOFSEM 2018, LNCS 10706, pp. 367–380, 2018.
https://doi.org/10.1007/978-3-319-73117-9_26

The problem was recently studied in [14] where a collection of n points was monitored with use of a single mobile robot. The points to be patrolled in [14] are located in nodes of a complete graph with edges of uniform (unit) length, as well as in Euclidean spaces, where the points are distributed arbitrarily. In their work the frequency constraints refer to *urgency factors* h_i, meaning that during a unit of time the urgency of point p_i grows by an additive term h_i, and the task is to design a schedule of perpetual visits to nodes which minimizes the maximum ever observed urgency on all points. In complete graphs and for any distribution of frequencies (urgency factors) the authors of [14] proposed a 2-approximation algorithm based on a reduction to the pinwheel scheduling problem, see, e.g., [6, 7, 15, 16, 19]. They also discuss more tight approximations for the cases with more balanced urgency factors. In Euclidean spaces [14] proposes several lower bounds and concludes with an $O(\log n)$-approximation for an arbitrary distribution of points and urgency factors.

In our formulation, we assume that both robots have unit speed, and we try to minimize the relative violation of visitation-frequency requirements, i.e. the worst case time between two visitations over the required largest waiting time of each point. Equivalently, one may think of the problem of finding the minimum possible speed s that both robots should patrol with that induces no violation for the visitation-frequency requirements. In such setting, our *patrolling* result refers naturally to a competitive ratio, which is defined by the ratio of the speed the robots attain in our algorithm divided by the speed in the optimal solution.

Specific to our model is the use of two robots, for which, as we show, one can achieve $\sqrt{3}$-approximation patrolling schedules. Notably, and maybe counter-intuitively, reducing the number of robots from two to one does not lead to constant approximation. An instructive example is when the central point has a very large visiting frequency (we can dedicate one robot to this point) comparing to the rest of the points on the line.

In the previous research on boundary and fence patrolling (cf. [11, 12, 17]) all points of the patrolled environment were supposed to be revisited with the same frequency. However, assigning different importance to distinct portions of the monitored boundary seems natural and observable in practice. A particular variation of this problem was studied in [10], where the authors focus on monitoring *vital* (possibly disconnected) parts of a linear environment, while the remaining *neutral* portions of the boundary need not be attended at all.

The problem of distinct attendance assigned to different portions of the environment, while of inherent combinatorial interest, is also observed in perpetual testing of virtual machines in cloud systems [1]. In such systems the frequency with which virtual machines are tested for undesirable symptoms may vary depending on the importance of dedicated cloud operational mechanisms.

The problem studied here is also a natural extension of several classical combinatorial and algorithmic problems referring to *monitoring* and *mobility*. This includes the *Art Gallery Problem* [20, 21] and its dynamic variant called the *k-Watchmen Problem* [24]. In a more recent work on *fence patrolling* [10, 11, 17] the efficiency of patrolling is measured by the *idleness* of the protocol, which is the time where a point remains unvisited (maximized over all time moments and all points of the environment). In [12] one can find a study on monitoring of linear environments by robots prone to faults. In [11,17] the authors assume robots have distinct maximum speeds which makes the design of patrolling protocols more complex, in which case the use of some robots becomes obsolete.

In a very recent work [18] Liang and Shen consider a line of points attributed with uniform urgency factors. For robots with uniform speeds, they give a polynomial-time optimal solution, and for robots with constant number of speeds they present a 2-approximation algorithm. For an arbitrary number of velocities they design a 4-approximation algorithm, which can be extended to a 2α-approximation algorithm family scheme, where integer $\alpha > 1$ is the tradeoff factor to balance the time complexity and approximation ratio.

2 Problem Statement and Definitions

An instance of the *Path Patrolling Problem of Points with Unbalanced Frequencies (PUF)* consists of points $S = \{y_i\}_{i=1,\ldots,n}$ in the unit interval, where $0 = y_1 < y_2 < \ldots < y_n = 1$. Each point y_i is associated with its *idleness time* $I(y_i) \in \mathbb{R}_+$, a positive real number which is also referred to as *visitation frequency requirement*.

A perpetual movement schedule of two robots r_1, r_2 of speed 1 will be referred to as a *patrolling schedule* (robots may change movement direction instantaneously, and at no cost). Given a patrolling schedule $\mathcal{A}$, we define the *waiting time* $w_\mathcal{A}(y_i)$ of each point y_i as the supremum of the time difference between any two subsequent visitations by any of r_1, r_2. When the patrolling schedule is clear from the context, we will drop the subscript in $w_\mathcal{A}$.

A patrolling schedule $\mathcal{A}$ is called *feasible* if for all i, $w_\mathcal{A}(y_i) \leq I(y_i)$. Schedule $\mathcal{A}$ is called c textit-feasible, or *c-approximation*, if $w_\mathcal{A}(y_i)/I(y_i) \leq c$, for each $i = 1, \ldots, n$. Thus a feasible patrolling schedule is also 1-approximation, or 1-feasible.

An instance of PUF that admits a feasible patrolling schedule will be called *feasible*. In this paper we are concerned with the combinatorial optimization problem of minimizing the worst (normalized) violation of the idleness times for feasible instances, i.e., we are concerned with finding good approximation patrolling schedules, in which robots' trajectories can be determined efficiently in the size of the given input. We will call such patrolling schedules *efficient*.

The problem considered here is a close relative of *Pinwheel scheduling* [15] modeled by points with non-uniform deadlines (visitation-frequencies) spanned by a complete network with edges of uniform length. The complexity of Pinwheel scheduling depends on its representation. In particular we know that in the standard multi-set representation the problem is in NP, however, we still don't known whether it is NP-hard. One can try to get closer to this answer either by studying particular instances of the problem which can be decided [16] or instead by seeking approximate solutions [14]. In this paper we adopted the latter.

We use the following concepts in the analysis of our patrolling schedules. We associate each point y_i with its *range* defined as the closed intervals $R(y_i) = \left[\max\left\{0, y_i - \frac{I(y_i)}{2}\right\}, \min\left\{1, y_i + \frac{I(y_i)}{2}\right\}\right]$. Intuitively, $R(y_i)$ is the ball around

y_i within which a robot can be moving introducing no violation to the visitation frequency requirement of y_i. We also group points y_i with respect to whether the extreme points fall within their range, i.e., we introduce:

$$S_{00} := \{y_i \in S : \ 0,1 \notin R(y_i)\}, S_{01} := \{y_i \in S : \ 0 \notin R(y_i) \ni 1\},$$
$$S_{10} := \{y_i \in S : \ 0 \in R(y_i) \not\ni 1\}, S_{11} := \{y_i \in S : \ 0,1 \in R(y_i)\}.$$

3   Summary of Results and Paper Organization

Our main contribution pertains to efficient patrolling schedules (algorithms) of feasible PUF instances. In particular, the patrolling schedules we propose are highly efficient and simple, meaning that robots' trajectories can be determined by a few critical turning points, which can be computed in linear time in the number of points of the PUF instance. In order to do so, we provide in Sect. 4 some useful properties that all feasible PUF instances exhibit, and in particular a characterization of instances with "no problematic points". For the latter instances, we also provide optimal feasible schedules (Theorem 1). Then we turn our attention to arbitrary feasible PUF instances. As a warm-up, we present in Sect. 5 a simple efficient 4-approximation patrolling schedule that does not require coordination between robots. Section 6 is devoted to the introduction of an elaborate and efficient $\sqrt{3}$-approximation patrolling schedule. The execution of the patrolling schedule requires robots to remember at most two special turning points (that can be found efficiently), and, in some cases, their coordination so that they never come closer than a predetermined critical distance. Its performance analysis is based on further properties of feasible PUF instances that are presented in Sect. 6.1. In particular, the $\sqrt{3}$-feasible patrolling schedule is the combination of Algorithms 1 and 2, presented in Sects. 6.2 and 6.3 respectively, each of them performing well for a different spectrum of a special structural parameter of the given instance that we call expansion. In the full paper [8] we also show that the analyses we provide for all our proposed algorithms are actually tight.

4   Characterization of (Some) Feasible PUF Instances

In this section we characterize feasible instances of PUF for which at least one of the extreme points falls within the range of each point.

Theorem 1. *An instance of* PUF *with* $S_{00} = \emptyset$ *is feasible if and only if the following conditions are satisfied:*

(1) $S_{10} \subset \bigcap_{x \in S_{10}} R(x) = X_{10}$, *and* $0 \in X_{10}$.
(2) $S_{01} \subset \bigcap_{x \in S_{01}} R(x) = X_{01}$, *and* $1 \in X_{01}$.
(3) $S \subset [\bigcap_{x \in S_{10}} R(x)] \cup \bigcap_{x \in S_{01}} R(x)] = X_{10} \cup X_{01}$

Moreover, if conditions (1)–(3) are satisfied, then there exists an efficient 1-approximation partition-based patrolling schedule, i.e. a schedule in which every y_i is visited only by one robot.

In order to prove Theorem 1 we need few observations.

Observation 1. *Assume $\mathcal{A}$ is a feasible patrolling schedule. Then, for each $x \in S$ and each time window of length at least $\frac{I(x)}{2}$ during an execution of $\mathcal{A}$, at least one robot is in $R(x)$.*

Proof. Reset time to $t_0 = 0$. Aiming at contradiction, assume there is no robot in $R(x)$ at $t \geq \frac{I(x)}{2}$. Since both robots have speed 1, no robot visited x in the period $[t - \frac{I(x)}{2}, t]$ and no robot is able to visit x in the period $[t, t + \frac{I(x)}{2}]$. Thus, $\mathcal{A}$ is not a feasible patrolling schedule. □

For simplicity, we may also assume that in any patrolling schedule (hence in feasible schedules as well), the position of robot r_1 in the unit interval is always to the left of the position of r_2, as otherwise we can exchange the roles of the robots whenever they swap while they meet. We summarize as follows.

Observation 2. *In any patrolling schedule of PUF, r_1 (r_2) is the only robot patrolling $y_1 = 0$ ($y_n = 1$), and r_1 stays always to the left of r_2.*

We are now ready to prove Theorem 1.

Proof (Theorem 1). First, we show implication ($\Rightarrow$) by contraposition. If Condition (1) is not satisfied, then there exists $x \in S_{10}$ such that $x \notin X_{10}$. Fix a feasible schedule $\mathcal{A}$. By Observation 2, we may assume that r_1 stays to the left of r_2, throughout the execution of the schedule. By Observation 1, there must be a robot in X_{10} at each time t. Thus, r_1 must be in X_{10} at each time t. Consequently, $x \in S_{10} \setminus X_{10}$ is visited only by r_2. But r_2 has to visit point $y_n = 1$, and by definition of S_{10} we know that $1 \notin R(x)$. Therefore, $\mathcal{A}$ is not a feasible schedule. By definition of S_{10}, for all $x \in S_{10}$, we have $0 \in R(x)$. Therefore $0 \in X_{10}$. A similar argument proves that Condition (2) is satisfied.

By (1) and (2), there exist $a, b \in (0, 1)$ such that $X_{10} = [0, a]$ and $X_{01} = [b, 1]$. Now suppose that Condition (3) is not satisfied. Then $a < b$, and there is a point $x \in S$ such that $a < x < b$, and therefore neither r_1 nor r_2 can visit x.

For implication ($\Leftarrow$), assume that (1)–(3) are satisfied. Consider a partition traversal A, where r_1 is searching $X_{10} \setminus X_{01}$ and r_2 is searching X_{01}. Then, by the definition of the ranges $R(x)$, X_{10} and X_{01}, the traversal A is feasible. □

The complication of instances when S_{00} is non empty is that in a feasible solution, points in S_{00} have to be interchangeably patrolled by both r_1, r_2, which further requires appropriate synchronization between them. Even though a characterization of feasibility for such instances is eluding us, we provide below a necessary condition. This condition will be useful also later on.

Lemma 1. *For every feasible instance of PUF, we have $S_{00} \subset \bigcap_{x \in S} R(x)$.*

Proof. Suppose to the contrary, that there are $x \in S_{00}$ and $y \in S$, such that $x \notin R(y)$. By Observation 1, a robot is always present inside $R(y)$. Therefore the other robot must visit x. Without loss of generality assume that $y < x$. The robot that visits y cannot pass the point $y + \frac{I(y)}{2} < x$. Also the robot that visits x cannot pass the point $x + \frac{I(x)}{2}$. Since $x \in S_{00}$ then $x + \frac{I(x)}{2} < 1$. This means that no robot can visit point $y_n = 1$. □

5 A Simple 4-Approximation Patrolling Schedule

In light of Theorem 1, it is interesting to study feasible instances of PUF that may have points that cannot be patrolled by one robot, i.e. for which $S_{00} \neq \emptyset$. As a warm-up, we provide a 4-feasible patrolling schedule for such instances. The advantage of this schedule is that robots' trajectories are simple and no coordination is required.

Theorem 2. *Feasible instances of* PUF *admit an 4-approximate patrolling schedule.*

Proof (Theorem 2). Let A be a feasible solution. Let $I = \min_{y \in S} I(y)$ and let $x \in S$ be such that $I(x) = I$. If $I \geq \frac{1}{2}$, then one robot patrolling the interval $[0, 1]$ gives a 4-approximation solution. Thus, we may assume that $I \leq \frac{1}{2}$.

According to Observation 1, at least one robot stays in $R(x)$ during A, at each time t. We claim that a nested traversal $\mathcal{A}$ in which one robot traverses $[0, 1]$ and the other robot traverses $R(x)$ is a 4-approximation.

We split the interval $[0, 1]$ into $A = [0, a]$, $R(x) = [a, a + I] = [a, 1 - b]$ and $B = [1 - b, 1]$, where $a + I + b = 1$. First, note that the waiting time of each $y \in R(x)$ during $\mathcal{A}$ is $w_{\mathcal{A}}(y) = 2I = 2I(x) \leq 2I(y)$. Thus, it remains to show that $w_{\mathcal{A}}(y) \leq 4I(y)$ for each point $y \in A \cup B$.

Without loss of generality assume that $|A| = a < b = |B|$. Using the assumption $I \leq \frac{1}{2}$ and $a + I + b = 1$, we have $a + b \geq \frac{1}{2}$, and therefore $b \geq \frac{1}{4}$. Using Observation 2, we consider a feasible schedule $\mathcal{B}$ in which r_1 is always to the left of r_2. By Observation 1, at least one robot stays in $R(x)$ at each time during $\mathcal{B}$. We consider the following cases:

(Case $y \in A$): As at each time moment there must exist a robot in $R(x)$, then in $\mathcal{B}$ robot r_1 has to stay in $R(x)$ while r_2 is traversing $B = [1 - b, 1]$ twice to visit $y_n = 1$ and return to $R(x)$. Therefore the waiting time $w_{\mathcal{B}}$ satisfies $I(y) \geq w_{\mathcal{B}} \geq 2b \geq 2\frac{1}{4} = \frac{1}{2}$. On the other hand $w_{\mathcal{A}}(y) = 2 = 4\frac{1}{2} \leq 4I(y)$.

(Case $y \in B$): Let $y' = y - (a + I)$, thus y' is the distance of y to $R(x)$. Consider a time t during the execution of $\mathcal{B}$ at which r_1 leaves $R(x)$ in order to visit the point 0. As r_2 must be in $R(x)$ at t, the last visit of y before t was at time $t' \leq t - y'$. Then, it has to stay in $R(x)$ for at least $2a + y'$. The time between two consecutive visits at y is at least $t + 2a + y' - (t - y') = 2a + 2y'$. On the other hand, in order to visit 1, r_2 has also time at least $2(1 - y')$ between two consecutive visits of y. Altogether $w_{\mathcal{B}}(y) \geq \max\{2(a + y'), 2(b - y')\}$. Thus $w_{\mathcal{B}}(y) \geq \frac{1}{2}[2(a + y') + 2(b - y')] = a + b \geq \frac{1}{2}$. On the other hand $w_{\mathcal{A}}(y) = 2$ and thus $w_{\mathcal{A}}(y) \leq 4w_{\mathcal{B}} \leq 4I(y)$.   □

6 A $\sqrt{3}$-Approximation Patrolling Schedule

The bottleneck toward patrolling instances of PUF is caused by points which require the coordination of both robots in order to be patrolled, i.e. instances in which $S_{00} \neq \emptyset$. In order to improve upon the 4-feasible schedule of Theorem

2, we need to understand better the visitation requirements of points in S_{00}, as well as their relative positioning in the path to be patrolled. The result of our analysis, and our main contribution, is an elaborate $\sqrt{3}$-feasible patrolling schedule.

Theorem 3. *Feasible instances of* PUF *admit an efficient* $\sqrt{3}$-*approximate patrolling schedule.*

In what follows, we explicitly assume that $S_{00} \neq \emptyset$, as otherwise, due to Theorem 1, we can easily find feasible schedules for instances of PUF that admit feasible solutions. Next, we introduce a key notion to our algorithms.

Definition 1. *Given an instance of* PUF *we identify critical points* $x_1, \ldots, x_4$ *that are defined as follows:* $\bigcap_{x \in S_{00}} R(x) = [x_1, x_4]$, *and* x_2, x_3 *are the left-most and rightmost points point in* S_{00}, *respectively. The instance is called* α-*expanding if* $x_1 = \frac{\alpha}{1+\alpha} x_4$.

Theorem 3 is an immediate corollary of the following Lemmata 2, 3 that we prove in subsequent Sects. 6.2 and 6.3, respectively. The lemmata are interesting in their own right, since they explicitly guarantee good approximate schedules as a function of the expansion of the given instance.

Lemma 2. *Feasible* α-*expanding instances of* PUF *admit an efficient* $(1+2\alpha)$-*approximate patrolling schedule.*

Lemma 3. *Feasible* α-*expanding instances of* PUF *admit an efficient* $\frac{2+\alpha}{1+\alpha}$-*approximate patrolling schedule.*

Lemmata 2, 3 above imply that any feasible α-expanding instance admits a $\min\left\{1 + 2\alpha, \frac{2+\alpha}{1+\alpha}\right\}$ feasible patrolling schedule. The achieved approximation is the worst when the instance is $\frac{\sqrt{3}-1}{2}$-expanding, in which case, the patrolling schedule is $\sqrt{3}$-feasible. This concludes the proof of Theorem 3.

Notably, our feasibility bounds above are tight. In the full paper [8] we show that for every α, there are feasible α-expanding PUF instances for which the performance of our patrolling schedules that prove Lemmas 2 and 3 (see Sects. 6.2, and 6.3) is equal to the proposed bound. Hence, the performance analysis of our patrolling schedule showing Theorem 3 cannot be improved.

6.1   Useful Observations for Feasible PUF Instances

In an α-expanding instance of PUF we have that $x_1 = \alpha(x_4 - x_1)$. If the instance is also feasible, then by Lemma 1 we have that $S_{00} \subset \bigcap_{x \in S} R(x)$. Since $S_{00} \subset S$, we obtain that $S_{00} \subset \bigcap_{x \in S_{00}} R(x) = [x_1, x_4]$. Also, it is easy to see that for the critical points $x_1, \ldots, x_4$ we have that $x_1 \leq x_2 < x_4$ and that $x_1 < x_3 \leq x_4$. In particular we may assume, without loss of generality, that $x_1 \leq 1 - x_4$, as otherwise we flip the order of all points. Also using Observation 2, we assume that the feasible schedule to the PUF instance has robot r_1 stay always to the left of r_2.

Lemma 4. *Consider a feasible patrolling schedule $\mathcal{A}$ for a PUF instance. Then*

(1) there is always a robot inside the interval $[x_1, x_4]$.
(2) the interval $[0, x_1)$ is only traversed by r_1 and the interval $(x_4, 1]$ is only traversed by r_2.
(3) $0 \in R(x)$ for all $x \in [0, x_1)$, and $1 \in R(x)$ for all $x \in (x_4, 1]$.
(4) $x_4 - x_3 \leq x_3 - x_1$ and $x_2 - x_1 \leq x_4 - x_1$.

Proof. The proof of (1) is a direct consequence of Observation 1 and the fact that $[x_1, x_4]$ is the intersection of the ranges of all of the points of S_{00}.

During the execution of $\mathcal{A}$ a robot needs to visit 0 and 1. Also, by (1) we know that there is always a robot inside $[x_1, x_4]$. Therefore while the robot r_2 is traversing $(x_4, 1]$ the robot r_1 has to stay inside $[x_1, x_4]$, and while robot r_1 is traversing $[0, x_1)$, the robot r_2 has to stay inside $[x_1, x_4]$. This implies that r_1 never passes x_4 and r_2 never passes x_1. This proves (2). Part (3) follows directly from (2).

We now prove the first inequality of (4). Suppose to the contrary that $x_4 - x_3 > x_3 - x_1$, and thus $x_3 < \frac{x_1 + x_4}{2}$. For all $x \in S_{00}$ we have that $x_4 \in R(x)$. Therefore for all $x \in S_{00}$, $x_4 \leq x + \frac{I(x)}{2}$. Moreover x_3 is the rightmost point of S_{00}, hence $x \leq x_3 < \frac{x_1 + x_4}{2}$. Consequently $x_4 \leq x + \frac{I(x)}{2} \leq x_3 + \frac{I(x)}{2} < \frac{x_1 + x_4}{2} + \frac{I(x)}{2}$. This implies that $I(x) > \frac{x_4 - x_1}{2}$. So for all $x \in S_{00}$ we have $x - \frac{I(x)}{2} \leq x - \frac{x_4 - x_1}{2} < \frac{x_1 + x_4}{2} - \frac{x_4 - x_1}{2} = x_1$. Therefore there is a point $y \in (0, 1)$ such that for all $x \in S_{00}$, $x - \frac{I(x)}{2} \leq y < x_1$. Hence $y \in \bigcap_{x \in S_{00}} R(x)$ and $y < x_1$. This contradicts the fact that x_1 is the leftmost point of the intersection of the ranges of all the points of S_{00}. The proof of the second inequality of (4) follows by an analogous argument. □

Lemma 5. *If there is a feasible solution for patrolling with two robots then the idle time of the points of S satisfy the following inequalities.*

$$I(x) \geq \begin{cases} \max\{2x, 2(1 - x - x_4 + x_1), x_4 - x_1\} & , x \in [0, x_1) \\ 2\max\{x_4 - x, x - x_1\} & , x \in [x_1, x_4] \\ \max\{2(1 - x), 2(x - x_4 + x_1), x_4 - x_1\} & , x \in (x_4, 1] \end{cases}$$

Proof. Let $\mathcal{A}$ be a feasible solution and $x \in S$.

First assume that $x \in [0, x_1)$. By (2) of Lemma 4, in $\mathcal{A}$ the points of $[0, x_1)$ are only visited by r_1 and $0 \in R(x)$. Thus, $I(x) \geq w_{\mathcal{A}}(x) \geq 2x$. Moreover robot r_1 has to stay inside the interval $[x_1, x_4]$ for at least $2(1 - x_4)$ while the robot r_2 is traversing the interval $(x_4, 1]$ to visit 1. The time length for r_1 to traverse from x to x_1, stay for at least $2(1 - x_4)$ inside $[x_1, x_4]$, and then traverse from x_1 to x is at least $2[(x_1 - x) + (1 - x_4)]$. Therefore, $I(x) \geq w_{\mathcal{A}(x)} \geq 2[(x_1 - x) + (1 - x_4)]$. On the other hand, by Lemma 1, we know that $x_3 \in R(x)$, and thus $\frac{I(x)}{2} \geq x_3 - x \geq x_3 - x_1$. By (3) of Lemma 4, $x_4 - x_3 \leq x_3 - x_1 \leq \frac{I(x)}{2}$. Therefore, $x_4 - x_1 = (x_4 - x_3) + (x_3 - x_1) \leq \frac{I(x)}{2} + \frac{I(x)}{2} = I(x)$. By the above discussion, and for all $x \in [0, x_1)$, we have $I(x) \geq \max\{2x, 2(1 - x - x_4 + x_1), x_4 - x_1\}$. A similar argument shows that for $x \in (x_4, 1]$ we have that $I(x) \geq \max\{2x, 2(1 - x - x_4 + x_1), x_4 - x_1\}$.

Now assume that $x \in [x_1, x_4]$. Then $x_1, x_4 \in R(x)$, and therefore $x - \frac{I(x)}{2} \leq x_1 \leq x_4 \leq x + \frac{I(x)}{2}$. This implies that $2(x - x_1) \leq I(x)$ and $2(x_4 - x) \leq I(x)$. So for all $x \in [x_1, x_4]$ we have $I(x) \geq \max\{x - x_1, x_4 - x\}$.

6.2 $(1 + 2\alpha)$-Approximate Patrolling Schedules (Proof of Lemma 2)

Given a feasible α-expanding instance of PUF and using its critical points as in Definition 1, we propose the following algorithm.

Algorithm 1

1: Robot r_1 starts anywhere in $[0, x_3]$, and robot r_2 starts anywhere in $[x_3, 1]$.
2: Repeat forever
3:     Robot r_1 zigzags inside $[0, x_3]$ and robot r_2 zigzags inside $[x_3, 1]$.

Next we show that Algorithm 1 is $(1 + 2\alpha)$-feasible, effectively proving Lemma 2. For this we analyze the waiting time $w(x)$ for all points $x \in S$.

Assume that $x \in [0, x_1)$. By Lemma 1, we know that $x_3 \in R(x)$. Moreover by (3) of Lemma 4, $0 \in R(x)$. Since r_1 zigzags inside $[0, x_3]$ then $w(x) \leq I(x)$.

Similarly, for $x \in (x_3, 1]$, by Lemmas 1 and 4 we have $\{x_3, 1\} \subset R(x)$. Since r_2 zigzags inside $[x_3, 1]$ then $w(x) \leq I(x)$.

Finally, let $x \in [x_1, x_3]$. First assume that $x < x_3$. Then in Algorithm 1 the point x is only visited by r_1. Since r_1 zigzags inside $[0, x_3]$ we have that $w(x) = 2\max\{x, x_3 - x\}$. We now compute the feasibility ratio. Clearly for the points $x \in [0, x_1) \cup (x_3, 1]$ we have that $\frac{w(x)}{I(x)} \leq 1$. So when $x \in [x_1, x_3]$, then by Lemma 5 $\frac{w(x)}{I(x)} \leq \frac{\max\{x, x_3 - x\}}{\max\{x - x_1, x_4 - x\}}$. First let $\max\{x - x_1, x_4 - x\} = x_4 - x$. Then $x \leq \frac{x_1 + x_4}{2}$. If $\max\{x, x_3 - x\} = x_3 - x$, as $x_3 \leq x_4$ we have that $\frac{w(x)}{I(x)} \leq 1$. If, on the other hand, $\max\{x, x_3 - x\} = x$, then we have

$$\frac{w(x)}{I(x)} \leq \frac{x}{x_4 - x} \leq \frac{\frac{x_1 + x_4}{2}}{x_4 - \frac{x_1 + x_4}{2}} \leq \frac{x_1 + x_4}{x_4 - x_1}$$

$$= \frac{(x_4 - x_1) + 2x_1}{x_4 - x_1} = 1 + \frac{2x_1}{x_4 - x_1}$$

$$= 1 + \frac{2x_1}{\frac{x_1}{\alpha}} \quad [\text{Using } x_1 = \alpha(x_4 - x_1)]$$

$$= 1 + 2\alpha.$$

Now let $\max\{x - x_1, x_4 - x\} = x - x_1$. Then $x \geq \frac{x_1 + x_4}{2}$. Moreover by (4) of Lemma 4, we have $x_3 \geq \frac{x_1 + x_4}{2}$. Therefore $x_3 - x \leq x - x_1$. If $\max\{x, x_3 - x\} = x_3 - x$ then $\frac{w(x)}{I(x)} \leq 1$. So assume that $\max\{x, x_3 - x\} = x$, in which case

$$\frac{w(x)}{I(x)} \leq \frac{x}{x - x_1} \leq \frac{x - x_1 + x_1}{x - x_1} = 1 + \frac{x_1}{x - x_1}$$

$$\leq 1 + \frac{x_1}{\frac{x_1 + x_4}{2} - x_1} = 1 + \frac{2x_1}{x_4 - x_1} = 1 + \frac{2x_1}{\frac{x_1}{\alpha}} = 1 + 2\alpha.$$

6.3 $\frac{2+\alpha}{1+\alpha}$-Approximate Patrolling Schedules (Proof of Lemma 3)

The distributed algorithm that achieves feasibility performance $\frac{2+\alpha}{1+\alpha}$ is quite elaborate. At a high level, the two robots maintain some distance that never drops below a certain carefully chosen threshold. During the execution of the patrolling schedule, there will always be some robot patrolling (zigzaging within) a certain subinterval defined by critical points of the given instance. When the robots move towards each other, and their distance reaches the certain threshold, then robots exchange roles; the previously zigzaging robot abandons the subinterval and goes to patrol its extreme point, while the other robot starts zigzaging within the subinterval. The formal description of our algorithm follows. The reader may also consult Fig. 1.

Fig. 1. The red arrow determines the patrolling area of r_1 and the blue arrow determines the patrolling area of r_2. (Color figure online)

Algorithm 2

1: Let $d = \frac{1}{1+\alpha}\min\{x_1, x_4 - x_1\}$.
2: Robot r_1 starts at $x_1 - d$ and robot r_2 at x_1.
3: Repeat forever
4:    *Patrolling Schedule of r_1:*
5:    **while** r_1 is inside the interval $[x_1, x_4]$ and the distance between the locations of r_1 and r_2 is at least d **do**
6:        Zigzag between points x_1 and x_4.
7:    Visit point 0, then visit point x_1, and then go to step 5.
8:    *Patrolling Schedule of r_2:*
9:    **while** r_2 is inside the interval $[x_1, x_4]$ and the distance between the locations of r_2 and r_1 is at least d **do**
10:        Zigzag between points x_1 and x_4.
11:    Visit point 1, then visit point x_4, and then go to step 9.

Note that each robot has an explicit segment in which the points are visited by only that robot, *i.e.* $[0, x_1)$ is the explicit segment of r_1 and $(x_4, 1]$ is the explicit segment of r_2. The trajectories of the robots overlap at $[x_1, x_4]$ where the points are visited by both r_1 and r_2. The movements of the robots have two states: zigzagging inside $[x_1, x_4]$ and traversing their explicit segments twice. More precisely, once a robot enters $[x_1, x_4]$ it zigzags inside $[x_1, x_4]$ until the other robot is at distance d. Then it leaves $[x_1, x_4]$, traverses its explicit segment twice, and the same process repeats perpetually.

Note that by the definition of d, we know that $\min\{x_1, x_4 - x_1, 1 - x_4\} \geq d$. Therefore, the original placement of r_1 at $x_1 - d$ is compatible with Algorithm 2.

The remaining of the section is devoted to proving that Algorithm 2 is $\frac{2+\alpha}{1+\alpha}$-approximate, effectively proving Lemma 3. As a first step, we calculate the worst case waiting times $w(x)$ of all points in S.

Lemma 6. *The waiting times of points in S for Algorithm 2 are as follows.*

$$w(x) \begin{cases} = 2\max\{x, 1 - x - d\} & , x \in [0, x_1) \\ \leq 2\max\{x - x_1, x_4 - x\} + d & , x \in [x_1, x_4] \\ = 2\max\{1 - x, x - d\} & , x \in (x_4, 1] \end{cases}$$

Proof. Recall that $x_1 \leq 1 - x_4$, and in particular $\min\{x_1, x_4 - x_1, 1 - x_4\} \geq d$.

Case $0 \leq x < x_1$: Point x is only visited by robot r_1. We now calculate the time interval between two consecutive visitations of x by r_1. We distinguish two subcases.

First consider the subcase where r_1 is moving to the left when it visits x. Before r_1 visits x again, it has to visit 0 and then return to x. Therefore, the time between the two visitations of x is $2x$.

Second consider the subcase in which r_1 is moving to the right when it visits x. Before r_1 visits x again, it has to visit x_1 (i.e. enter interval $[x_1, x_4]$), zigzag between points x_1 and x_4 until its distance to the other robots becomes d, and then r_1 exits the interval $[x_1, x_4]$ and return to x. Below we compute the total time between these two visitations of x by r_1.

(1a): r_1 traverses from x to x_1: it takes $x_1 - x$.

(1b): r_1 zigzags inside $[x_1, x_4]$: at the time that r_1 arrives at x_1 and starts zigzaging inside $[x_1, x_4]$, robot r_2 is at distance d from r_1 and it is moving to the right to visit 1 and return. Also, at the time that r_1 arrives at x_1 to exit the interval $[x_1, x_4]$, the distance between r_1 and r_2 is d and robot r_2 is moving to the left to zigzag inside the interval $[x_1, x_4]$. Therefore, the time r_1 spends inside the interval $[x_1, x_4]$ is equal to the time that r_2 spends to traverse from $x_1 + d$ to 1 and return to $x_1 + d$, which is $2(1 - x_1 - d)$.

(1c): r_1 traverses from x_1 to x: it takes $x_1 - x$.

Using (1a,1b,1c) above, we conclude that the total time between two consecutive visitations of x by r_1 is $2(1 - x - d)$.

Taking into consideration both subcases, the overall (worst case) waiting time of x is $2\max\{x, 1 - x - d\}$.

Case $x_4 < x \leq 1$: The analysis is analogous to the previous case.

Case $x_1 \leq x \leq x_4$: Point x is visited by both r_1 and r_2. We consider two subcases

(1) The two consecutive visits of x are by the same robot r_1 or r_2: this case occurs when either of r_1 or r_2 zigzags inside the interval $[x_1, x_4]$. Therefore $w(x) = 2\max\{x_4 - x, x - x_1\}$.

(2) The two consecutive visits of x are by different robots r_1 and r_2: this case occurs when one robot is exiting the interval $[x_1, x_4]$ and the other one is entering it.

First suppose that r_1 visits x and the next visit of x is performed by r_2. The worst waiting time in this case occurs when r_1 is about to visit x but the distance between r_1 and r_2 reduces to d and so r_1 turns away from x. Then r_2 visits x after at most d time steps. Note that since $x_1 \geq d$ the visit of x by r_2 is guaranteed. Therefore $w(x) \leq 2(x - x_1) + d$. Now assume that r_2 visits x and the next visit of x is performed by r_1. By a similar discussion we have that $w(x) \leq 2(x_4 - x) + d$. This implies that $w(x) \leq 2\max\{x - x_1, x_4 - x\} + d$.

By Subcases 1, 2 above we conclude that $w(x) \leq 2\max\{x - x_1, x_4 - x\} + d$, for all $x \in [x_1, x_4]$. ☐

The proof of Lemma 3 follows by upper bounding $\max_{x \in S}\left\{\frac{w(x)}{I(x)}\right\}$. Using Lemmas 5 and 6, we see that the approximation ratio of Algorithm 2 is no more than

$$\frac{w(x)}{I(x)} \leq \begin{cases} \frac{2\max\{x, 1-x-d\}}{\max\{2x, 2(1-x-x_4+x_1), x_4-x_1\}} & , x \in [0, x_1) \\ \frac{2\max\{x-x_1, x_4-x\}+d}{2\max\{x_4-x, x-x_1\}} & , x \in [x_1, x_4] \\ \frac{2\max\{1-x, x-d\}}{\max\{2(1-x), 2(x-x_4+x_1), x_4-x_1\}} & , x \in (x_4, 1] \end{cases} \quad (1)$$

Using that $d = \frac{\min\{x_1, x_4-x_1\}}{1+a}$, and the fact that the given instance is α-expanding, i.e. that $x_1 = \alpha(x_4 - x_1)$, and after some tedious and purely algebraic calculations, we see that $\frac{w(x)}{I(x)} \leq \frac{2+\alpha}{1+\alpha}$ for all $x \in S$, as wanted. Details can be found in the full paper [8].

7 Conclusion

The paper investigated the problem of patrolling a line segment by two robots when time-patrolling constraints are placed on the frequency of visitation of all the points of the line. As shown in this study, finding "efficient" trajectories that satisfy the requirements or even deciding on their existence for two robots turns out to be a highly intricate problem. Nothing better is known aside from the $\sqrt{3}$-approximation algorithm for two robots on a line presented in this work. The patrolling problem with constraints is also open for more general graph topologies (e.g., cycles, trees, etc.). Further, the case of patrolling with constraints for multiple robots is completely unexplored in all topologies, including for the line segment.

References

1. Alshamrani, S., Kowalski, D.R., Gąsieniec, L.: How reduce max algorithm behaves with symptoms appearance on virtual machines in clouds. In: Proceedings of IEEE International Conference CIT/IUCC/DASC/PICOM, pp. 1703–1710 (2015)
2. Baruah, S.K., Cohen, N.K., Plaxton, C.G., Varvel, D.A.: Proportionate progress: a notion of fairness in resource allocation. Algorithmica 15(6), 600–625 (1996)
3. Baruah, S.K., Lin, S.-S.: Pfair scheduling of generalized pinwheel task systems. IEEE Trans. Comput. 47(7), 812–816 (1998)

4. Bender, M.A., Fekete, S.P., Kröller, A., Mitchell, J.S.B., Liberatore, V., Polishchuk, V., Suomela, J.: The minimum backlog problem. Theoret. Comput. Sci. **605**, 51–61 (2015)
5. Bodlaender, M.H.L., Hurkens, C.A.J., Kusters, V.J.J., Staals, F., Woeginger, G.J., Zantema, H.: Cinderella versus the wicked stepmother. In: Baeten, J.C.M., Ball, T., de Boer, F.S. (eds.) TCS 2012. LNCS, vol. 7604, pp. 57–71. Springer, Heidelberg (2012). https://doi.org/10.1007/978-3-642-33475-7_5
6. Chan, M.Y., Chin, F.Y.L.: General schedulers for the pinwheel problem based on double-integer reduction. IEEE Trans. Comput. **41**(6), 755–768 (1992)
7. Chan, M.Y., Chin, F.: Schedulers for larger classes of pinwheel instances. Algorithmica **9**(5), 425–462 (1993)
8. Chuangpishit, H., Czyzowicz, J., Gasieniec, L., Georgiou, K., Jurdzinski, T., Kranakis, E.: Patrolling a path connecting set of points with unbalanced frequencies of visits (2012). http://arxiv.org/abs/1710.00466
9. Chrobak, M., Csirik, J., Imreh, C., Noga, J., Sgall, J., Woeginger, G.J.: The buffer minimization problem for multiprocessor scheduling with conflicts. In: Orejas, F., Spirakis, P.G., van Leeuwen, J. (eds.) ICALP 2001. LNCS, vol. 2076, pp. 862–874. Springer, Heidelberg (2001). https://doi.org/10.1007/3-540-48224-5_70
10. Collins, A., Czyzowicz, J., Gąsieniec, L., Kosowski, A., Kranakis, E., Krizanc, D., Martin, R., Morales Ponce, O.: Optimal patrolling of fragmented boundaries. In: Proceedings of the Twenty-fifth Annual ACM Symposium on Parallelism in Algorithms and Architectures, SPAA 2013, New York, USA, pp. 241–250 (2013)
11. Czyzowicz, J., Gąsieniec, L., Kosowski, A., Kranakis, E.: Boundary patrolling by mobile agents with distinct maximal speeds. In: Demetrescu, C., Halldórsson, M.M. (eds.) ESA 2011. LNCS, vol. 6942, pp. 701–712. Springer, Heidelberg (2011). https://doi.org/10.1007/978-3-642-23719-5_59
12. Czyzowicz, J., Gasieniec, L., Kosowski, A., Kranakis, E., Krizanc, D., Taleb, N.: When patrolmen become corrupted: monitoring a graph using faulty mobile robots. In: Elbassioni, K., Makino, K. (eds.) ISAAC 2015. LNCS, vol. 9472, pp. 343–354. Springer, Heidelberg (2015). https://doi.org/10.1007/978-3-662-48971-0_30
13. Fishburn, P.C., Lagarias, J.C.: Pinwheel scheduling: achievable densities. Algorithmica **34**(1), 14–38 (2002)
14. Gąsieniec, L., Klasing, R., Levcopoulos, C., Lingas, A., Min, J., Radzik, T.: Bamboo garden trimming problem (perpetual maintenance of machines with different attendance urgency factors). In: Steffen, B., Baier, C., van den Brand, M., Eder, J., Hinchey, M., Margaria, T. (eds.) SOFSEM 2017. LNCS, vol. 10139, pp. 229–240. Springer, Cham (2017). https://doi.org/10.1007/978-3-319-51963-0_18
15. Holte, R., Mok, A., Rosier, L., Tulchinsky, I., Varvel, D.: The pinwheel: a real-time scheduling problem. In: II: Software Track, Proceedings of the Twenty-Second Annual Hawaii International Conference on System Sciences, vol. 2, pp. 693–702, January 1989
16. Holte, R., Rosier, L., Tulchinsky, I., Varvel, D.: Pinwheel scheduling with two distinct numbers. Theoret. Comput. Sci. **100**(1), 105–135 (1992)
17. Kawamura, A., Kobayashi, Y.: Fence patrolling by mobile agents with distinct speeds. Distrib. Comput. **28**(2), 147–154 (2015)
18. Liang, D., Shen, H.: Point sweep coverage on path. Unpublished work https://arxiv.org/abs/1704.04332
19. Lin, S.-S., Lin, K.-J.: A pinwheel scheduler for three distinct numbers with a tight schedulability bound. Algorithmica **19**(4), 411–426 (1997)
20. Ntafos, S.: On gallery watchmen in grids. Inf. Process. Lett. **23**(2), 99–102 (1986)

21. O'Rourke, J.: Art Gallery Theorems and Algorithms, vol. 57. Oxford University Press, Oxford (1987)
22. Romer, T.H., Rosier, L.E.: An algorithm reminiscent of Euclidean-gcd for computing a function related to pinwheel scheduling. Algorithmica **17**(1), 1–10 (1997)
23. Serafini, P., Ukovich, W.: A mathematical model for periodic scheduling problems. SIAM J. Discret. Math. **2**(4), 550–581 (1989)
24. Urrutia, J.: Art gallery and illumination problems. Handbook Comput. Geom. **1**(1), 973–1027 (2000)

Exploring Graphs with Time Constraints by Unreliable Collections of Mobile Robots

Jurek Czyzowicz[1], Maxime Godon[1], Evangelos Kranakis[2], Arnaud Labourel[3], and Euripides Markou[4(✉)]

[1] Université du Québec en Outaouais, Gatineau, Canada
[2] School of Computer Science, Carleton University, Ottawa, Canada
[3] LIF, Aix-Marseille University & CNRS, Marseille, France
[4] University of Thessaly, Lamia, Greece
emarkou@dib.uth.gr

Abstract. A graph environment must be explored by a collection of mobile robots. Some of the robots, a priori unknown, may turn out to be unreliable. The graph is weighted and each node is assigned a deadline. The exploration is successful if each node of the graph is visited before its deadline by a reliable robot. The edge weight corresponds to the time needed by a robot to traverse the edge. Given the number of robots which may crash, is it possible to design an algorithm, which will always guarantee the exploration, independently of the choice of the subset of unreliable robots by the adversary? We find the optimal time, during which the graph may be explored. Our approach permits to find the maximal number of robots, which may turn out to be unreliable, and the graph is still guaranteed to be explored.

We concentrate on line graphs and rings, for which we give positive results. We start with the case of the collections involving only reliable robots. We give algorithms finding optimal times needed for exploration when the robots are assigned to fixed initial positions as well as when such starting positions may be determined by the algorithm. We extend our consideration to the case when some number of robots may be unreliable. Our most surprising result is that solving the line exploration problem with robots at given positions, which may involve crash-faulty ones, is NP-hard. The same problem has polynomial solutions for a ring and for the case when the initial robots' positions on the line are arbitrary. The exploration problem is shown to be NP-hard for star graphs, even when the team consists of only two reliable robots.

Keywords: Fault · Deadline · Exploration · Graph · Line · NP-hard
Ring · Robot · Star graph

J. Czyzowicz—Research supported in part by NSERC Discovery grant.
E. Kranakis—Research supported in part by NSERC Discovery grant.
A. Labourel—Research partially supported by the ANR project MACARON (anr-13-js02-0002).

A M. Tjoa et al. (Eds.): SOFSEM 2018, LNCS 10706, pp. 381–395, 2018.
https://doi.org/10.1007/978-3-319-73117-9_27

1   Introduction

Alice and Bob is a busy Ottawa couple with three kids Chris, Donald and Elsa. One day they need to pick up Elsa from the kindergarten, drive Donald to the wrestling practice and get Chris to the train station. They also need to get groceries, pick up wine and flowers before each store closes for a dinner party in their house. How should Alice and Bob share these tasks to minimize the effort and complete each one before its deadline?

An Ottawa School Bus Company needs to transport pupils to local schools before the start of their classes. Given the harsh Canadian climate, it is the norm rather than exception that a number of buses fail to function on any given day and an adequate replacement must be planned in advance. How should the buses allocate the tasks so as to successfully conclude the distribution of students while respecting the time deadlines?

Throughout this paper, the environment is modelled by a graph that must be serviced by a collection of mobile robots. The graph edges are weighted by numbers, representing the time it takes to traverse them. Each graph node is assigned a deadline, representing the maximal time moment to deliver a service to this node by some mobile robot. A number of robots may crash during their work. What is the minimal time needed to service a given graph by a collection of k robots? What is such a time if we assume that up to f unknown robots may crash during their work?

1.1   Preliminaries and Notation

We are given a weighted n-node graph $G = (V, E)$ with V its set of vertices, E its set of edges, and a set of k mobile robots initially placed at a subset of its nodes. The weight of an edge $\{v_i, v_j\}$ corresponds to the time it takes to be traversed by a robot. Each node v_i of the graph is assigned a deadline Δ_i, which is a positive real number. Robots walk along the edges of the graph with unit speed. The robots collaborate attempting to explore the entire graph. However, a subset of up to f robots may turn out to be unreliable and fail to collaborate. Unreliability refers to the robots which may be crash faulty in that they suffer from an (unspecified) passive, omission failure and then stop responding but are otherwise harmless. This subset of unreliable robots may be chosen by the adversary, which is assumed to know our algorithm beforehand. The exploration is successful if each graph node is visited before its deadline by at least one of the reliable robots.

We assume that nodes already explored "do not block passage" and can still be visited, even after their deadlines have expired, by robots on their way to reaching unexplored parts of the graph.

We denote by $t \to r_i(t)$ the trajectory of the i-th robot as a function of the time t, where $r_i(t)$ denotes the position of the i-th robot in the graph at time t, for $i = 1, 2, \ldots, k$. Note that at a given time t, a robot may be located in the interior of an edge.

By a schedule we mean a set of functions $r_i(t), i = 1, 2, \ldots, k$ which define the motion of the robots respecting their maximum unit speed. We say that the schedule *explores* the graph if for each node v_i there exists a robot r_j such that $r_j(t^*) = v_i$, for some time $t^* \leq \Delta_i$.

Given a time Δ, we study the *decision problem* whether the graph may be successfully explored before time Δ. We also look at the *optimization problem*, that is, the problem of ensuring that the reliable robots visit every node before expiration of its deadline, and the last explored node is visited as fast as possible. If for any schedule, the adversary can find a subset of f unreliable robots, so that any of the remaining $k - f$ robots fails to visit some node before its deadline, then the instance of the problem is deemed unsolvable.

1.2   Related Work

Searching a graph with one or more searchers has been widely studied in the mathematics literature (see, e.g. [14] for a survey). There is extensive literature on linear search (referring to searching a line in the continuous or discrete model), e.g., see [1] for optimal deterministic linear search and [11] for algorithms incorporating a *turn cost* when a robot changes direction during the search. Variants of search using collections of *collaborating* robots has also been investigated. The robots can employ either *wireless* communication (at any distance) or *face-to-face* communication, where communication is only possible among co-located robots. For example, the problem of *evacuation* [9] is essentially a search problem where search is completed only when the target is reached by the last robot. Linear group search in the face-to-face communication model has also been studied with robots that either operate at the same speed or with a pair of robots having distinct maximal speeds [2,6]. Linear search with multiple robots where some fraction of the robots may exhibit either *crash faults* or *Byzantine faults* is studied in [8,10], respectively.

The (Directed) Rural Postman Problem (DRPP) is a general case of the Chinese Postman Problem where a subset of the set of arcs of a given (directed) graph is 'required' to be traversed at minimum cost. [5] presents a branch and bound algorithm for the exact solution of the DRPP based on bounds computed from Lagrangian Relaxation. [7] studies the polyhedron associated with the Rural Postman Problem and characterizes its facial structure. [12] gives a survey of the directed and undirected rural postman problem and also discusses applications.

A scheduling problem considered by the research community concerns n jobs, each to be processed by a single machine, subject to arbitrary given precedence constraints; associated with each job j is a known processing time a_j and a monotone nondecreasing cost function $c_j(t)$, giving the cost that is incurred by the completion of that job at time t. [20] gives an efficient computational procedure for the problem of finding a sequence which will minimize the maximum of the incurred costs. Further, [20] also studies a class of time-constrained vehicle routing and scheduling problems that may be encountered in several transportation/distribution environments. In the single-vehicle scheduling problem with time window constraints, a vehicle has to visit a set of sites on a graph, and each site must be visited after its ready time but no later than its deadline. [23] studies the problem of minimizing the total time taken to visit all sites. [15] considers the problem of determining whether there exists a schedule on two identical processors that executes each task in the time interval between its start-time and deadline and presents an $O(n^3)$ algorithm that constructs such a schedule whenever one exists.

The author of [3] resolves the complexity status of the well-known Traveling Repairman Problem on a line (Line-TRP) with general processing times at the request locations and deadline restrictions by showing that it is strongly NP-complete. [21] considers the problem of finding a lower and an upper bound for the minimum number of vehicles needed to serve all locations of the multiple traveling salesman problem with time windows in two types of precedence graphs: the start-time precedence graph and the end-time precedence graph. [17] considers "the pinwheel", a formalization of a scheduling problem arising in satellite transmissions whereby a piece of information is transmitted for a set duration, then the satellite proceeds with another piece of information while a ground station receiving from several such satellites and wishing to avoid data loss faces a real-time scheduling problem on whether a "useful" representation of the corresponding schedule exists.

The work of [22] is very related to our work in that jobs are located on a line. Each job has an associated processing time, and whose execution has to start within a prespecified time window. The paper considers the problems of minimizing (a) the time by which all jobs are executed (traveling salesman problem), and (b) the sum of the waiting times of the jobs (traveling repairman problem). Also related is the research on Graphs with dynamically evolving links (also known as time varying graphs) which has been explored extensively in theoretical computer science (e.g., see [4,13,19]).

1.3 Outline and Results of the Paper

We consider first the collections of robots which are all reliable. We start in Sect. 2 with the case of a single robot on a line graph and we give an algorithm finding the shortest exploration time when the robot's starting position is given, is arbitrary, or it is arbitrary but restrained to some subset of line nodes. In Sect. 3 we study line exploration by a collection of robots at fixed or arbitrary positions on the line. We observe, that these algorithms may be extended to the ring case, although their complexity is slightly compromised.

In Sect. 4 we consider the case of unreliable robots. In one case, we show an unexpected result. If k robots are at given fixed initial positions on the line and up to f out of k robots may turn out to be crash-faulty, the problem of finding the optimal exploration time is NP-hard. This result holds even if the nodes' deadlines may be ignored (e.g. they are infinite for all nodes). For all other settings we give algorithms finding optimal exploration times. In Sect. 5 we extend our approach to the ring environment. However, the setting which was proven to be NP-hard for lines is polynomial-time decidable for the ring. Finally, we show that outside the line and ring environment the problem becomes hard. For a graph as simple as a star, already for the case of two robots, the exploration problem turns out to be NP-complete.

Because of the space constraints, all proofs and some illustrations are moved to an Appendix which can be found online in http://arxiv.org/abs/1710.00775.

2   Single Robot on the Line

In this section, we present algorithms that allow a single robot to solve the optimization problem on the line for two cases: when the robots' initial positions are given by an adversary, and when we have the possibility of choosing them ourselves.

We have a sequence of nodes $v_0 < v_1 < \cdots < v_{n-1}$ on the real line, and a robot r initially placed at initial position $r(0)$. We denote by v_s the starting node of the robot, i.e. $r(0) = v_s$.

Observation 1. *Without loss of generality we may assume that $\Delta_{s+1} < \Delta_{s+2} < \cdots < \Delta_{n-1}$. Indeed, if $\Delta_k \geq \Delta_{k+1}$ for some $k > s$ we can drop node v_k from consideration, since visiting v_{k+1} before its deadline implies that v_k is also visited before its deadline. For the same reason, we can also assume that $\Delta_0 > \Delta_1 > \cdots > \Delta_{s-1}$.*

Observation 2. *Without loss of generality we may consider only the solutions which consist of sequences that are increasing and decreasing at alternate nodes, respectively, i.e., sequences $r(0), r(t_1), r(t_2), \ldots, r(t_p)$ such that $0 \leq r(t_{2i}) < r(t_{2i+2})$, and $0 \geq r(t_{2i+1}) > r(t_{2i+3})$, for all i in the appropriate range. Moreover, each turning node $r(t_i)$ is located at some node $v_j, j = 0, 1, \ldots, n-1$.*

2.1   The Snapshot Graph

With these observations in mind, we define the fundamental concept of a directed, layered *snapshot graph* S which will form the basis of all subsequent algorithms.

Every node of the snapshot graph S represents a situation when a new node of the line is visited by the robot for the first time. Consequently, each node of S is denoted by a pair $(i, \bar{j})$ or $(\bar{i}, j)$, where $i \leq j$, $[i, j]$ is the interval of nodes already explored by the robot and the node of the line marked with the bar (either $\bar{i}$ or $\bar{j}$) denotes the current position of the robot.

Observe that the robot can advance its exploration in one of two ways: either by visiting the next unexplored node to the left of the interval already explored, or by visiting the next unexplored node to its right. These two possibilities generate the directed edges between the nodes of the snapshot graph. The weight of such an edge equals the time needed by the robot to traverse the path between robot positions in both nodes. Consequently, the nodes $(i, \bar{j})$ and $(\bar{i}, j)$ are placed at layer $j - i$ and the adjacencies in S are only between nodes of consecutive layers. Notice the following properties of the snapshot graph (see also Fig. 1 in the Appendix):

- The graph S has n layers numbered from 0 to $n-1$.
- There are n *source* nodes at the zeroth layer and $2(n-j)$ nodes at the j-th layer for each $j = 1, 2, \cdots, n-1$. Consequently, there are 2 *target* nodes (on the $(n-1)$-th target layer).
- The in-degree and the out-degree of each node is bounded by 2. Hence the complexity of the snapshot graph is $O(n^2)$.

Observe that, the solution to the optimization problem for the line corresponds to the shortest path from the source node representing the initial position of the robot to one of its target nodes, which respects the time constraints of all the nodes of L.

2.2   Given Initial Position of the Robot

We first present an algorithm which produces the optimal exploration path, assuming a given starting position v_s of the robot on the line. Consider the snapshot graph S described above. In order to obtain the optimal exploration path in the snapshot graph respecting the time constraints of L, we generate an all-targets shortest-time tree T whose root coincides with the node $(v_s, \bar{v}_s)$ of the snapshot graph corresponding to the initial position v_s of the robot. This is done in the following way.

We add a time counter *time* to every node of S. We set to zero the time counter of the initial node $(v_s, \bar{v}_s)$ and to ∞ the initial time counters of all other nodes of S. We then visit all nodes of S layer by layer. Consider a visit of any such node v, which corresponds to the first visit to node v_j of L. For each predecessor of v in S we consider the time equaling its time counter augmented by the weight of the edge joining it with v. Let Min denote the smaller of these values (we take an arbitrary one in the case of equality). If Min does not exceed the time constraint of v_j (i.e. $Min \leq \Delta_j$) we set the time constraint of v to Min and we add to T the edge from the corresponding predecessor of v. Otherwise, the time counter of v is set to ∞ and we leave v parentless.

Observe that, T is a tree, as each node has at most one parent. One of the two target nodes of the smaller time counter defines the optimal exploration time and the path to it in T corresponds to an optimal exploration path of L. Otherwise, there exists no exploration path respecting the node deadlines of the line graph.

For any node v of S we denote by $new(v)$ the index of the node of the line G which is newly explored when arriving at v. More exactly, $new(v) = j$, such that either $v = (i, \bar{j})$ or $v = (\bar{j}, k)$, for some $i \leq j \leq k \leq n-1$.

The following procedure InitStart indicates how to initialize the time counters of the nodes of S before running the main body of the algorithm. For each node i of the line L, which may be a starting position of a robot, we put a node $(i, \bar{i})$ of S to the set A. All nodes of A have their time counters initialized to 0.

Procedure InitStart(A, S) with A a subset of nodes of S at zeroth layer;

1 **for** *every node v of $V(S) \setminus A$* **do**
2    $time(v) = \infty$;
3 **for** *every node v of A* **do**
4    $time(v) = 0$;

Algorithm 1 describes pseudo-code that formalizes the previously outlined construction of a shortest-time tree.

Algorithm 1. Single Robot exploration on the line with given initial position v_s;

Input: A snapshot graph S and the starting position v_s of the robot
Output: An exploration tree with optimal exploration times

1 InitStart($\{v_s\}, S$);
2 **for** *layer $i = 0$ to $n - 1$* **do**
3   **for** *each arc $v \rightarrow w$ starting at layer i* **do**
4      $t = time(v) + weight(v, w)$;
5   **if** $t < time(w)$ *and* $t \leq \Delta_{new(w)}$ **then**
6        $time(w) = t$; $v = parent(w)$;

Please see the Appendix for an execution of Algorithm 1.

Theorem 1. *Consider a line graph G and a robot placed at its starting position v_s. Algorithm 1 correctly computes an optimal exploration path which satisfies the node deadlines in $O(n^2)$ time.*

2.3   Arbitrary Starting Position

We now consider a variation of the problem when the choice of the starting position of the robot is left to the user or it is restricted to be chosen from a subset of nodes of the line graph. We will show that Algorithm 1 also works in such a setting. We need, however, to modify the call to procedure InitStart in line 1 of Algorithm 1, so that its first parameter equals the set of all nodes of the line at which the robot may start. An example of its execution is presented in the Appendix.

Observe that, for any node w of the snapshot graph, the value of $time(w)$, computed by the algorithm, represents now the shortest exploration time ending at w starting from any node of the line graph. T is now a forest with the nodes of T, whose time counter remains at ∞ isolated in T (having no children or parent in T).

Corollary 1. *Let A be the subset of nodes of the line graph which we can choose for the starting position of the robot. Suppose that the first parameter of the call to procedure InitStart in line 1 of Algorithm 1 (A) equals the set of all nodes from zeroth level of S which correspond to the nodes of A. Such version of Algorithm 1 correctly computes in $O(n^2)$ time an optimal exploration path of the line graph, which satisfies the node deadlines. Moreover, for any sub-interval $[i, j]$ of the line, the algorithm computes an optimal robot starting position to explore $[i, j]$, the cost (time) of such exploration and the trajectory of the robot.*

3   Multiple Robots on the Line

In this section we consider line exploration by a collection of $k < n$ mobile robots. As before we study two variants of the time optimization problem. In the first setting, the distinct initial robot positions are given in advance. In the second setting, the initial positions of the robots are arbitrary, i.e. the algorithm identifies the initial placement of the robots, which results in the shortest exploration time respecting the node deadlines. Both variants are solved using versions of dynamic programming. We start with the following observation concerning the movement of the robots[1].

Observation 3. *There exists an optimal exploration solution in which the robots never change their initial order along the line. Moreover, the sub-intervals of the line explored by different robots are mutually disjoint.*

We use the following notation. Suppose that we need to explore an interval $[i, j]$ of the line respecting the deadlines of the nodes of $[i, j]$. For the setting when the robots are placed at given initial positions, for any pair of indices i, j, such that $0 \leq i \leq j \leq n-1$, we denote by $T_{i,j}$ the optimal time of exploration of the interval $[i, j]$ using the robots placed within $[i, j]$. When the initial placement of the robots is left to the algorithm, for any $1 \leq r \leq k$, we denote by $T_{i,j}^{(r)}$ the optimal time of exploration of the interval $[i, j]$ using r robots which may be placed at arbitrary initial positions within $[i, j]$.

3.1   Given Initial Positions

We start with the following observation

Observation 4. *Consider a line and a robot initially placed in its sub-interval $[i, j]$. Using Algorithm 1 the values $T_{i,j}$ for all $0 \leq i \leq j \leq n-1$, may be computed by the formula*

$$T_{i,j} = \min(time((i, \overline{j})), time((\overline{i}, j))) \tag{1}$$

---

[1] We remind the reader that all robots move with identical unit speed.

Let p_i denote the initial position of robot i. We assume that we have $0 \leq p_1 < p_2 < \cdots < p_k \leq n - 1$. By Observation 3 we need to partition the line into sub-intervals $[l_i, r_i]$ for $i = 1, 2, \ldots, k$ (with $l_1 = 1$ and $r_k = n$), each one explored by a different robot. The interval $[l_i, r_i]$, explored by robot i, contains its initial position p_i, but not an initial position of any other robot. Hence edges (r_i, l_{i+1}) for $i = 1, \ldots, k-1$, that we call *idle edges*, are never traversed by any robot. The following formula, is an obvious consequence of Observation 3,

$$T_{i,j} = \min_{p_q < m \leq p_{q+1}} \max(T_{i,m-1}, T_{m,j}), \tag{2}$$

for any $i \leq p_q, p_{q+1} < j$. Indeed, the idle edge $(m - 1, m)$, separating the sub-segments of operation of robots q and $q + 1$, is chosen so as to minimize the exploration time of interval $[i, j]$.

We give first an idea of our algorithm. We generate the snapshot graph, as described in Subsect. 2.2. Let's use the notation $p_0 = -1$ and $p_{k+1} = n$. For $m = 1, \ldots, k$ let S_m be the subgraph of S obtained by keeping the nodes $(\bar{i}, j)$ and $(i, \bar{j})$ such that $p_{m-1} < i, j < p_{m+1}$. In the first part of our algorithm, for each robot m, we run Algorithm 1 with inputs p_m and S_m, obtaining the optimal exploration time $T_{i,j}$ of each line sub-interval $[i, j]$, which contains exactly one starting position p_i, for $i = 1, 2, \ldots, k$.

In the second part of the algorithm, we combine exploration times of individual robots, in order to obtain the optimal exploration time $T_{0,j}$ using robots initially placed within $[0, j]$, subsequently for each j. Let r_j denote the number of robots initially placed in interval $[0, j]$ and suppose, that we computed the optimal exploration times of all intervals, which initially contain robots $1, 2, \ldots, r_j - 1$. When j exceeds p_{r_j} we use robot r_j and we determine the idle edges preceding the intervals of operation of r_j, resulting in the optimal exploration times of intervals, which initially contain robots $1, 2, \ldots, r_j$. The formal algorithm (Algorithm 2) can be found in the Appendix.

Theorem 2. *Algorithm 2 in $O(n^2)$ time computes the optimal exploration of the line by k robots initially placed at given initial positions $0 \leq p_1 < p_2 < \cdots < p_k \leq n - 1$.*

3.2 Arbitrary Initial Positions

This algorithm is also based on the dynamic programming approach for computing the table $T_{i,j}^{(r)}$, for all $1 \leq r \leq k$ and $0 \leq i < j \leq n - 1$. The values of $T_{0,n-1}^{(k)}$ represent the optimal exploration time of the line using k robots. We use the following formula, which works for any r, r_1, r_2, where $r_1, r_2 \geq 1$, $r = r_1 + r_2$ and any $0 \leq i < j \leq n - 1$.

$$T_{i,j}^{(r)} = \min_{i \leq k \leq j} \max\left(T_{i,k}^{(r_1)}, T_{k+1}^{(r_2)}\right). \tag{3}$$

Using Formula (3), the values of $T_{i,j}^{(r)}$ may be computed in a greedy manner for the increasing values of r. As Formula (3) may be naturally computed in $O(n)$ time, the total complexity of such a greedy approach is in $O(kn^3)$.

We give now a more efficient algorithm computing $T_{0,n-1}^{(k)}$. Observe first, that when $[i_1, j_1] \subseteq [i_2, j_2]$, then $T_{i_1,j_1}^{(r)} \leq T_{i_2,j_2}^{(r)}$. Consequently, when computing $T_{i,j}^{(r)}$, the value of index k which minimizes $\max(T_{i,k}^{(r-1)}, T_{i,k+1}^{(1)})$ may be found by a binary search (cf. function OptTime in the Appendix).

The following observation is easy.

Observation 5. *Consider two fixed numbers r_1, r_2 of robots. If for any interval $[i, j]$ of the line, $T_{i,j}^{(r_1)}$ and $T_{i,j}^{(r_2)}$ represent the optimal time of exploration of the interval by r_1 and r_2 robots, respectively, then function OptTime correctly computes in $O(\log n)$ time the optimal exploration time $T_{i,j}^{(r)}$ of the interval $[i, j]$ by $r = r_1 + r_2$ robots.*

The greedy approach would compute the values of table $T_{i,j}^{(r)}$ for any given r. Our algorithm below computes the values of $T_{i,j}^{(r)}$ when r is a power of 2 not exceeding k. Then, using formula 3, they are combined in $\lceil \log k \rceil$ steps, to compute the values of $T_{i,j}^{(k)}$. The formal algorithm (Algorithm 3) can be found in the Appendix.

The following theorem proves the correctness and the complexity of Algorithm 3.

Theorem 3. *Algorithm 3 computes in $O(n^2 \log n \log k)$ time the optimal time needed by k robots to explore the line.*

4   Line Exploration with Unreliable Collections of Robots

In this section we study the exploration problem when some of the robots may be faulty, i.e., when they fail to realize their exploration tasks. In this case, other robots need to help, so that eventually every node of the line is visited by some reliable robot before its deadline. Let there be given a weighted line L, containing n nodes with given deadlines and a collection of k robots at most f of which may turn out to be faulty. Consider a schedule for k robots on the line L. We say that the schedule is f-reliable in time Δ, if for any choice of f faulty robots by an adversary, each node of the line is visited by at least one non-faulty robot before its deadline and before time Δ.

Note that in the case of the presence of unreliable robots, it might be useful to initially place more than one robot at the same position. Consequently, we will assume that it is admissible for more than one robot to start from the same node of the line.

Observation 6. *If there can be f faulty robots, then to successfully explore a node v with deadline $\Delta(v)$, node v must be visited by at least $f + 1$ robots before time $\Delta(v)$.*

It is interesting to look at the *decision problem* as well as the *optimization problem* related to faulty agents. In the decision problem we look for an algorithm, which, given f and Δ, verifies whether there exists an f-reliable schedule in time Δ. In the optimization problem, we need an algorithm, which, for any given f, finds the minimal time interval Δ, which admits some f-reliable schedule in time Δ. Clearly, solving the optimization problem implies a solution to the decision problem and hardness of the decision problem implies hardness of the optimization problem. We are interested in both settings – for fixed and for arbitrary initial positions of the robots. As the case of the arbitrary starting positions is easier we discuss this variant first.

We prove the following theorem.

Theorem 4. *Let there be given a weighted line L, containing n nodes with given deadlines and a collection of k robots, which may be put at arbitrary starting positions on L. For any $0 < f < k$ the optimization problem involving up to f faulty robots may be solved in $O\left(n^2 \log n \log \left\lfloor \frac{k}{f+1} \right\rfloor \right)$ time.*

We now consider the more difficult case of given starting positions. Contrary to the case studied in the previous section, when the robots are assigned to fixed positions on the line, the existence of faulty robots leads to a problem which turns out to be NP-hard. In fact, the decision problem is hard, even in the case when all individual deadlines may be ignored (they are all larger than Δ), i.e. when the line does not have any node time constraints.

Exploration of the Line with Crash Faults (ELCF) problem
Instance: A line L, a multiset P of k starting positions of robots, a number of faults f and a time interval Δ.
Question: Is there an exploration strategy for the collection of k robots, which may include up to f faulty ones, such that each node of L is visited by at least one non-faulty robot before time Δ?

We construct a polynomial-time many to one reduction from the Numerical 3-Dimensional Matching problem (N3DM) which is a strongly NP-hard problem (referenced as [SP16] in [18]).

Theorem 5. *The ELCF decision problem is strongly NP-complete.*

5   The Ring Environment

In this section we show that most of the results for the line environment may be adapted to work on the ring. However, the $ELCF$ decision problem turns out to have a polynomial-time solution for the ring.

Suppose that the ring R contains nodes $0, 1, 2, \ldots, n-1$ in that counterclockwise order around R. Then every node i of the ring has a counterclockwise neighbour $(i + 1) \mod n$ and a clockwise neighbour $(i - 1) \mod n$. Consequently, in this section, all the ring node indices are implicitly taken modulo n. The approach used for the ring also starts by creating the snapshot graph, however slightly different from the one introduced in Sect. 2.1. The nodes of the snapshot graph are of the form $(i, \bar{j})$ and $(\bar{i}, j)$, where the node of the ring marked with the bar denotes the current position of the robot and $[i, j]$ is the segment of the ring already explored by the robot taken in the counterclockwise direction from i to j. Observe that, the terminal nodes of the snapshot graph, i.e. those which correspond to the exploration of every node of the ring, are now all nodes $(i, \bar{j})$ and $(\bar{i}, j)$, such that $(j - i) \mod n = 1$, i.e. i is the counterclockwise neighbour of j. Such snapshot graph also has $O(n^2)$ nodes of constant degree (see Fig. 5 in the Appendix). Consequently, by using the argument from Theorem 2 we have the following Observation.

Observation 7. *All values of $T_{i,j}$ for pairs (i, j), such that each pair denotes a counterclockwise segment around the ring containing an initial position of at most one robot, may be computed in amortized $O(n^2)$ time.*

Observe that, there exists an optimal solution for the ring with idle edges between initial positions of consecutive robots. By removing one such edge the ring becomes a line-segment. Consequently, most of our observations for lines may be applied for rings. In particular, for the case of robots which may be placed at arbitrary initial positions on the ring, the following Corollary is obvious.

Corollary 2. *In $O(n^2 \log n \log k)$ time it is possible to compute the optimal time of exploration of the ring of size n by a set of k robots, which may be placed at arbitrary initial positions.*

Indeed, it is sufficient to apply Algorithm 3, in which in lines 5 and 12 we consider all pairs (i, j) (rather than pairs for which $i < j$).

In the case of robots at given initial positions, the adaptation of the line algorithm to the ring case is also relatively easy, with some compromise on its time complexity. We have the following Proposition.

Proposition 1. *There exists an $O\left(n^2 + \frac{n^2}{k} \log n\right)$ algorithm for computing an optimal exploration of the ring R of size n using k mobile robots, initially placed at fixed positions on R.*

We now consider unreliable robots. Similarly to the line exploration case, every node of the environment must be explored $f + 1$ times by different robots before its deadline.

Consider first the case of robots which may be placed at arbitrary initial positions on the ring R. Suppose that we denote by $R^{(f+1)}$ a ring obtained in the following way. We cut R at any node v, obtaining a line segment starting and ending by a copy of v. We merge $f + 1$ copies of such segment, identifying the starting and the ending nodes of consecutive copies, obtaining a segment of $n(f + 1)$ nodes. Finally, we identify both endpoints of such segment obtaining a ring $R^{(f+1)}$. Observe that, covering R by k robots' exploration trajectories, so that each node of R is visited $f + 1$ times, is equivalent to exploring $R^{(f+1)}$ using k robots, so that each of its nodes is visited (once) before its deadline. As the size of $R^{(f+1)}$ is in $O(nf)$, from Corollary 2 we get.

Corollary 3. *Suppose that in an n-node ring we can place at arbitrary initial positions k robots, which may include up to f faulty ones. In $O(n^2 f^2 \log k(\log n + \log f))$ time it is possible to compute the optimal time of exploration of the ring.*

If the initial positions of the robots on the ring are given in advance, contrary to the case of the line segment, it is possible to decide in polynomial time whether there exists an f-reliable schedule in any given time Δ.

Proposition 2. *Consider a ring R of size n and k robots placed at given initial positions at the nodes of S. For any given time Δ it is possible to decide in polynomial time whether ring R may be explored by its robots within time Δ.*

6   NP-Hardness for Star Graphs

We gave exploration algorithms for lines and rings with time constraints on the nodes. It is easy to see that the exploration problem is hard for graphs, even for the case of a single robot and a graph with edges of unit length. Indeed, for a graph on n nodes, by setting all its node deadlines to $n - 1$, an instance of exploration problem is equivalent to finding a Hamiltonian path. However, we show below that the exploration problem is hard for graphs as simple as stars and already for two mobile robots. We construct a polynomial-time reduction from the Partition Problem [16].

Proposition 3. *The exploration problem respecting node deadlines for given starting positions of the robots is NP-hard. This problem is also NP-hard if the starting positions are arbitrary.*

7   Conclusion and Open Problems

We studied the question of exploring graphs with time constraints by collections of unreliable robots. When all robots are reliable we used dynamic programming to give efficient exploration algorithms for line graphs and rings. We showed, however, that the problem is NP-hard for graphs as simple as stars. We showed how to extend, in most cases, our solutions to unreliable collections of robots. One of our results is quite unexpected and important. Suppose that a collection of robots, placed on a line, may contain an unknown subset of robots (of bounded size), which turn out to be crash faulty. Verifying whether it is possible to explore the line within a given time bound is an NP-hard problem. The same problem on the ring has a polynomial-time solution.

An interested reader may observe that our positive results imply the possibility to compute the *resilience* of the configuration, i.e. given a time Δ, to find the largest value f, such that there exists a schedule assuring exploration when any set of f robots turns out to be unreliable.

In our paper, we did not actually produce schedules for our robots, but we only computed the optimal times when such schedules may be completed. However, from our work it is implicitly clear how to generate such schedules. We proved the optimality of the schedules but we did not prove the optimality of our algorithms. One of the possible open problems is to attempt to design algorithms of better time complexity.

References

1. Baeza Yates, R., Culberson, J., Rawlins, G.: Searching in the plane. Inf. Comput. **106**(2), 234–252 (1993)
2. Bampas, E., Czyzowicz, J., Gąsieniec, L., Ilcinkas, D., Klasing, R., Kociumaka, T., Pająk, D.: Linear search by a pair of distinct-speed robots. In: Suomela, J. (ed.) SIROCCO 2016. LNCS, vol. 9988, pp. 195–211. Springer, Cham (2016). https://doi.org/10.1007/978-3-319-48314-6_13
3. Bock, S.: Solving the traveling repairman problem on a line with general processing times and deadlines. Eur. J. Oper. Res. **244**(3), 690–703 (2015)
4. Casteigts, A., Flocchini, P., Quattrociocchi, W., Santoro, N.: Time-varying graphs and dynamic networks. In: Frey, H., Li, X., Ruehrup, S. (eds.) ADHOC-NOW 2011. LNCS, vol. 6811, pp. 346–359. Springer, Heidelberg (2011). https://doi.org/10.1007/978-3-642-22450-8_27
5. Christofides, N., Campos, V., Corberán, A., Mota, E.: An algorithm for the rural postman problem on a directed graph. Math. Program. Study **26**, 155–166 (1986)
6. Chrobak, M., Gąsieniec, L., Gorry, T., Martin, R.: Group search on the line. In: Italiano, G.F., Margaria-Steffen, T., Pokorný, J., Quisquater, J.-J., Wattenhofer, R. (eds.) SOFSEM 2015. LNCS, vol. 8939, pp. 164–176. Springer, Heidelberg (2015). https://doi.org/10.1007/978-3-662-46078-8_14
7. Corberán, A., Sanchis, J.M.: A polyhedral approach to the rural postman problem. Eur. J. Oper. Res. **79**(1), 95–114 (1994)
8. Czyzowicz, J., Georgiou, K., Kranakis, E., Krizanc, D., Narayanan, L., Opatrny, J., Shende, S.: Search on a line with Byzantine robots. In: ISAAC, LIPCS (2016)
9. Czyzowicz, J., Georgiou, K., Kranakis, E., Narayanan, L., Opatrny, J., Vogtenhuber, B.: Evacuating robots from a disk using face-to-face communication (extended abstract). In: Paschos, V.T., Widmayer, P. (eds.) CIAC 2015. LNCS, vol. 9079, pp. 140–152. Springer, Cham (2015). https://doi.org/10.1007/978-3-319-18173-8_10
10. Czyzowicz, J., Kranakis, E., Krizanc, D., Narayanan, L., Opatrny, J.: Search on a line with faulty robots. In: PODC, pp. 405–414 (2016)
11. Demaine, E.D., Fekete, S.P., Gal, S.: Online searching with turn cost. Theoret. Comput. Sci. **361**(2), 342–355 (2006)
12. Eiselt, H.A., Gendreau, M., Laporte, G.: Arc routing problems, part II: the rural postman problem. Oper. Res. **43**(3), 399–414 (1995)
13. Flocchini, P.: Time-varying graphs and dynamic networks. In: 2015 Summer Solstice: 7th International Conference on Discrete Models of Complex Systems (2015)
14. Fomin, F.V., Thilikos, D.M.: An annotated bibliography on guaranteed graph searching. Theoret. Comput. Sci. **399**(3), 236–245 (2008)
15. Garey, M.R., Johnson, D.S.: Two-processor scheduling with start-times and deadlines. SIAM J. Comput. **6**(3), 416–426 (1977)
16. Garey, M.R., Johnson, D.S.: Computers and Intractability, vol. 29. W. H. Freeman, New York (2002)
17. Holte, R., Mok, A., Rosier, L., Tulchinsky, I., Varvel, D.: The pinwheel: a real-time scheduling problem. In: Proceedings of the Twenty-Second Annual Hawaii International Conference on System Sciences. Software Track, vol. 2, pp. 693–702. IEEE (1989). Also, in Handbook of Scheduling Algorithms, Models, and Performance Analysis. CRC Press (2004)
18. Johnson, D.S.: The NP-completeness column: an ongoing guide. J. Algorithms **6**(3), 434–451 (1985)

19. Kuhn, F., Lynch, N., Oshman, R.: Distributed computation in dynamic networks. In: Proceedings of the Forty-Second ACM Symposium on Theory of Computing, pp. 513–522. ACM (2010)
20. Lawler, E.L.: Optimal sequencing of a single machine subject to precedence constraints. Manag. Sci. **19**(5), 544–546 (1973)
21. Mitrovic-Minic, S., Krishnamurti, R.: The multiple traveling salesman problem with time windows: bounds for the minimum number of vehicles. Simon Fraser University TR-2002-11 (2002)
22. Tsitsiklis, J.N.: Special cases of traveling salesman and repairman problems with time windows. Networks **22**(3), 263–282 (1992)
23. Young, G.H., Chan, C.-L.: Single-vehicle scheduling with time window constraints. J. Sched. **2**(4), 175–187 (1999)

The k-Server Problem with Advice in d Dimensions and on the Sphere

Elisabet Burjons[1][(✉)], Dennis Komm[1], and Marcel Schöngens[2]

[1] Department of Computer Science, ETH Zurich, Zürich, Switzerland
{elisabet.burjons,dennis.komm}@inf.ethz.ch
[2] CSCS, ETH Zurich, Lugano, Switzerland
schoengens@cscs.ch

Abstract. We study the impact of additional information on the hardness of the k-server problem on different metric spaces. To this end, we consider the well-known model of computing with advice. In particular, we design an algorithm for the d-dimensional Euclidean space, which generalizes a known result for the Euclidean plane. As another relevant setting, we investigate a metric space with positive curvature; in particular, the sphere. Both algorithms have constant strict competitive ratios while reading a constant number of advice bits with every request, independent of the number k of servers, and solely depending on parameters of the underlying metric structure.

Keywords: Online algorithms · Advice complexity
k-server problem · d-dimensional Euclidean space · Sphere
Positive curvature

1 Introduction

Online computation plays an important role for both theoretical and practical aspects of computer science. When studying online problems, we usually neglect the algorithm's time and space complexities, but face another challenge that is met in many real-world situations. The input is not known in advance to an *online algorithm*, but it arrives gradually in consecutive time steps; these chunks of input are called *requests*. Every request needs an immediate and usually definite *answer*. For instance, when considering paging or caching problems, the requests are given by page indices that need to be accessed by the CPU. If such a page is not in the cache at this point, an online algorithm answers by discarding a page currently in the cache to make space for the requested one. Of course, an optimal choice depends on future requests and the knowledge available is usually insufficient to guarantee creating an output of very high quality.

Being a powerful tool to measure the performance of online algorithms, *competitive analysis* was introduced in 1985 by Sleator and Tarjan [36], who applied it to the paging and list accessing problems. Here, the solution computed by the online algorithm at hand is compared to an optimal one. However, computing

© Springer International Publishing AG 2018
A M. Tjoa et al. (Eds.): SOFSEM 2018, LNCS 10706, pp. 396–409, 2018.
https://doi.org/10.1007/978-3-319-73117-9_28

such an optimal solution requires knowledge about the whole instance in general and can therefore never be achieved from a worst-case point of view. For an overview on competitive analysis and online algorithms, we refer to the literature [8, 22, 25, 27]. Throughout this paper, we consider the objective to minimize a given cost function; an online algorithm ALG is called *strictly c-competitive* if, for every instance of the given problem, its cost is at most c times as large as the optimal cost. The infimum of all c for which this holds is called the *(strict) competitive ratio* of ALG.

A complementing measurement is the *advice complexity* of an online problem that tries to answer a question along the lines of "how much information does one need to achieve a certain competitive ratio?" Other than allowing some lookahead or having some particular information (e.g., the size of an optimal solution, a specific knowledge about some requests etc.) about the input, this model allows *any* kind of such information; our interest only lies in its amount. To give a formal framework, we introduce an *oracle* that sees the whole input in advance, and that encodes binary information about this input onto an additional tape the algorithm may use during its computation. Online algorithms that have access to such an *advice tape* are called *online algorithms with advice*; we formalize this notion in the following definition.

Definition 1 (Online Algorithm with Advice). *Let $I = (x_1, \ldots, x_n)$ be an instance of some online minimization problem. An* online algorithm ALG *with advice computes the output sequence* $\text{ALG}^\phi(I) = (y_1, \ldots, y_n)$ *such that, for every i with $1 \leq i \leq n, y_i$ is computed from $\phi, x_1, \ldots, x_i$, where ϕ is the content of the advice tape, i.e., an infinite binary sequence.* ALG *is strictly c-competitive with advice complexity $b(n)$ if, for every n and for every input sequence I of length at most n, there is some ϕ such that $\text{cost}(\text{ALG}^\phi(I)) \leq c \cdot \text{cost}(\text{OPT}(I))$, and at most the first $b(n)$ bits of ϕ have been accessed during the computation of $\text{ALG}^\phi(I)$.*

Dobrev et al. [15, 16] were the first to investigate this setup using a slightly different setting. Here, the oracle was implicitly allowed to use an "end marker" as part of the advice, which led to effects that allowed to reduce the advice. As a consequence, this model was revised by both Hromkovič et al. [26] (see also Böckenhauer et al. [3, 4]) and Emek et al. [19, 20]; in this paper, we use the former model. For an overview on online algorithms with advice, we again refer to the literature [9, 17, 27]. The large number of problems analyzed within this model includes the paging problem [4], the knapsack problem [7], the set cover problem [14], and various scheduling problems [18, 28, 35]. Furthermore, there are some nontrivial connections between advice and randomization [2, 4, 23, 28].

In this paper, we study the *k-server problem*, where a number of entities (called *servers*) are moved through a metric space to certain points that are requested in an online fashion; the objective is to minimize the total distance traveled by the servers while covering all requests.

Definition 2 (k-Server Problem). *Let $\mathcal{M} = (P, \text{dist})$ be a metric space, where P is a (not necessarily finite) set of points and* $\text{dist} \colon P \times P \to \mathbb{R}$ *is a metric* *cost function, i.e., it satisfies* identity of indiscernibles, non-negativity, symmetry, *and the* triangle inequality *(which means that* $\operatorname{dist}(p_1, p_2) \leq \operatorname{dist}(p_1, p_3) + \operatorname{dist}(p_3, p_2)$ *for all* $p_1, p_2, p_3 \in P$ *). Furthermore, we are given a set of k servers, residing in some points from P. Let $C_i \subseteq P$ be the multiset of points occupied by servers at time step i with $0 \leq i \leq n$; a point occupied by j servers occurs j times in C_i. We also call C_i the* configuration *at time step T_i. The initial configuration C_0 is the configuration of the servers before any point is requested. Then, a point $x_i = p$ is requested and some servers may be moved yielding a new configuration C_{i+1}. The request x_i is satisfied if, after this movement of servers, some server resides at p, i.e., if $p \in C_{i+1}$. The* distance between two configurations C *and C' is given by the unique cost of a minimum-cost matching between C and C'. The k-server problem is the problem to satisfy all requests while minimizing the sum of the distances between all pairs of consecutive configurations.*

The k-server problem was introduced by Manasse et al. in 1988 [31], and it is beyond question one of the most famous and well-studied online problems. One of the reasons is that it generalizes a number of online problems, e.g., the aforementioned paging problem [8]. Another reason is that, in contrast to the paging problem, the k-server problem is still not fully understood despite a lot of effort.

The best known deterministic online algorithm is the *work function algorithm*, which was formally defined for the k-server problem by Chrobak and Larmore [11]. In 1995, Koutsoupias and Papadimitriou [30] showed that it achieves a competitive ratio of $2k - 1$; later, Emek et al. [21] proved that, as a consequence, the algorithm is also strictly $(4k - 2)$-competitive. However, it remains open whether there is a k-competitive online algorithm for general metric spaces; this is known as the *k-server conjecture*. For the randomized setting, there is an even larger gap. More specifically, the best known lower bound is $\Omega(\log k)$, which carries over from the paging problem, while the best known upper bound that only depends on k is intriguingly that implied by the deterministic one from Koutsoupias and Papadimitriou [30]. It is widely believed that there actually is a $\Theta(\log k)$-competitive randomized online algorithm, which is known as the *randomized k-server conjecture*.

In 2011, Bansal et al. [1] showed the existence of a randomized online algorithm that achieves an expected competitive ratio of $O(\log^2 k \log^3 m \log \log m)$, where m denotes the number of points in the underlying metric space. For more information about the k-server problem in deterministic or randomized settings, we refer to the literature [8,29].

Related Work

The advice complexity of the k-server problem was first studied by Emek et al. [19,20]. The authors considered a model where a fixed number of advice bits is supplied with every request, and designed an online algorithm that uses b bits of advice in every time step and that achieves a competitive ratio of $k^{O(1/b)}$, where $\Theta(1) \leq b \leq \log_2 k$.

Further investigations in the model we are using in this paper were made by Böckenhauer et al. [5,6]. There, it was shown that $\Omega(n \log k)$ advice bits are necessary to obtain an optimal output for all instances of length n. In essence, the idea of the proof is to give a reduction to guessing a permutation. If and only if an online algorithm with advice knows a permutation of the numbers $1, \ldots, k$, it can be optimal. It is easy to see that this bound is asymptotically tight [20]; indeed, in every time step, $\lceil \log_2 k \rceil$ advice bits suffice to encode the index of the server a fixed optimal algorithm uses. Moreover, the authors improved the previous results from Emek et al. Specifically, Böckenhauer et al. showed that there is an online algorithm with advice that is roughly $(2 \log_2 k / (b - 1))$-competitive while again using b advice bits in every time step. Renault and Rosén [34] further improved this bound by a factor of 2 by giving a roughly $(\log_2 k / (b - 2))$-competitive online algorithm with advice that also uses b advice bits per time step.

Furthermore, Renault and Rosén [34] investigated the k-server problem on the line, combining the "double coverage" strategy [12] with advice, and on graphs with a bounded caterpillar dimension. Gupta et al. [24] studied the k-server problem on special metric spaces, e.g., with bounded treewidth. For this large subclass of k-server instances, the authors gave both well-performing online algorithms with advice and hardness results.

Böckenhauer et al. [6] also observed an interesting connection between the randomized setting and online algorithms with advice, namely that a strong lower bound on the advice complexity could be used to disprove the randomized k-server conjecture.

It should be remarked that, to date, for neither deterministic, randomized, or advice algorithms, we have a complete picture of the k-server problem.

Finally, Böckenhauer et al. [6] also considered the k-server problem on the Euclidean plane, and designed an online algorithm with advice that reads a constant number b of advice bits in every time step, and that achieves a constant strict competitive ratio; here (other than for the general case), "constant" means independent of k. In order to put the results presented in this paper into context, and since our techniques are to some extent based on them, we now revisit this result in more detail. The proofs of the results presented in this section can also be found in the textbook by Komm [27]. Consider the subproblem of the k-server problem where the underlying metric space is the Euclidean plane; i.e., every point p from P has two coordinates, and the distance between any two points p_1 and p_2 is given by $\text{dist}(p_1, p_2) := \|p_1 - p_2\|_2$. For this setting, we revisit the online algorithm SEG2D for the k-server problem in the Euclidean plane that was introduced and analyzed by Böckenhauer et al. [6].

If, in any time step, the requested point is p, SEG2D divides the plane into 2^b disjoint *segments* $S_1, \ldots, S_{2^b}$ with their origin in p and with an angle of

$$\frac{2\pi}{2^b} =: \gamma \tag{1}$$

each, where $b \geq 3$ and thus $\gamma \leq \pi/4$; without loss of generality, we choose the x-axis as a boundary for one of the segments. Then, SEG2D reads b bits of advice

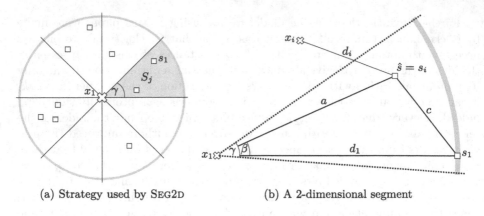

(a) Strategy used by SEG2D   (b) A 2-dimensional segment

Fig. 1. The construction used in the proofs of Lemma 1 and Theorem 1

that identify some segment S_j with $1 \le j \le 2^b$, and moves the closest server in S_j to p. The segment is chosen by the oracle such that a certain solution (which we describe later) uses a server from this segment. The idea is shown in Fig. 1a and explained in more detail in the proof of Theorem 1. In the following, let $r_{\text{plane}} := 1/(1 - 2\sin(\gamma/2))$.

Figure 1b shows the situation for the first time step T_1, where a point $x_1 = p$ is requested. SEG2D uses a server $\hat{s}$ (located at some point $\hat{p}$ in S_j), incurring a cost of a whereas the given solution uses a server s_1 (located at some point p_1) that causes cost d_1, where $d_1 \ge a$. The initial distance between the locations of s_1 and $\hat{s}$, i.e., p_1 and $\hat{p}$, is denoted by c. To show that SEG2D achieves a constant competitive ratio, the following technical lemma was proven.

Lemma 1 (Böckenhauer et al. [6]). *Let $a, d_1, c, r_{\text{plane}}$, and γ be as above. If d_1 is fixed, we have $a/(d_1 - c) \le r_{\text{plane}}$.* □

Now we are ready to analyze the competitive ratio of SEG2D. To this end, we need to take special care of the positions on which the servers are located at the beginning. As in Definition 2, a configuration C is a multiset of k points from P that are occupied by the servers. A configuration $C_{p \mapsto p'}$ is obtained from C by moving a server from $p \in C$ to p'. Recall that the *initial configuration* is the configuration before any request is served. In the following, we will simply speak of the initial configuration of a given instance.

Theorem 1 (Böckenhauer et al. [6]). SEG2D *has a strict competitive ratio of* $g := 1/(1 - 2\sin(\pi/2^b))$ *for the k-server problem in 2-dimensional Euclidean space, using $b \ge 3$ bits of advice per request.*

Proof Sketch. The proof is done by induction on the input length. We show that, for any input I with some initial configuration C, the first move of SEG2D can be made as described above, i.e., using the server $\hat{s}$ indicated by the advice. Moving $\hat{s}$ to x_1 leads to a new configuration C'. Then, we look at the suffix of I of length

$n - 1$ with initial configuration C' and argue that, by induction, there is some solution to this instance I' with some certain cost (note that this solution is not necessarily optimal). By induction, SEG2D's cost is at most g times larger on I'. An easy calculation shows that the first move of SEG2D in I is also not too expensive. It is crucial to note that the induction explicitly shows that SEG2D is at most g times worse than any given solution of I and C, which then also holds for an optimal one.   □

Our Contribution

In this paper, we present online algorithms with advice that achieve constant strict competitive ratios using a number of advice bits that is independent of the number k of servers for different metric spaces.

After having revisited the original proof in this section, we first give a generalization to three dimensions in Sect. 2. In Sect. 3, we consider d-dimensional Euclidean space. We can make use of Lemma 1 due to the fact that three points in d-dimensional space define a plane. The main issue we are facing is that we need to partition the space in a particular way; to this end, we use results from Rakhmanov et al. [33] and Damelin and Maymeskul [13] on the well-known problem of minimizing the discrete energy and point distribution on d-dimensional spheres [10]. Then we partition the space around these points using Voronoi diagrams [32]. One reason to treat the 3-dimensional case separately is that our bound is more constructive with respect to the values of advice bits b per time step for which it holds.

Our main result, presented in Sect. 4, deals with k-server on the sphere. Here, we design an algorithm that treats the sphere like a plane when only dealing with a small part of its surface, or that cleverly partitions the surface while again employing results from Rakhmanov et al. [33].

Due to space constraints, some of the proofs are omitted.

2   From Two Dimensions to Three Dimensions

We first discuss how to generalize the ideas presented in the preceding section. Suppose we are dealing with the k-server problem in 3-dimensional Euclidean space. Consider the online algorithm SEG3D with advice that acts analogously to SEG2D. For every request x_i with $1 \leq i \leq n$, it partitions the 3-dimensional space around x_i using a sphere. Consider a unit sphere $\mathbb{S}^2$ centered at x_i; b bits of advice allow us to divide its surface into 2^b areas and then give one of them as advice, i.e., the server used by the solution computed by the algorithm ALG (we compare against) lies within the "cone" defined by the corresponding area and the center x_i. In order to define these areas, we use a partitioning of $\mathbb{S}^2$ in surfaces of the same area and a small diameter, as stated by Rakhmanov et al. [33].

Theorem 2 (Rakhmanov et al. [33]). *For any $N \geq 2$, there is an area-regular partition of $\mathbb{S}^2$ into N parts with the diameter of each part being at most $7/\sqrt{N}$.*
    □

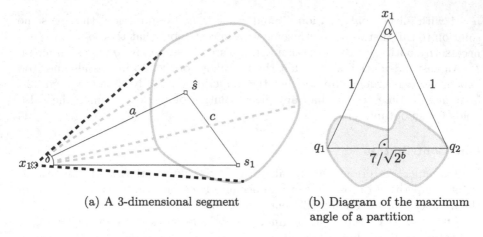

(a) A 3-dimensional segment

(b) Diagram of the maximum angle of a partition

Fig. 2. The construction used in the proof of Theorem 3

Let $S_1, \ldots, S_{2^b}$ denote the cones into which the space is partitioned. The advice encodes a cone S_j in which the server used by ALG is located. SEG3D uses the closest server from S_j to satisfy the current request. This way, with every request, SEG3D reads b bits of advice.

As in the 2-dimensional case, consider the first time step and the three points x_1, p_1, and $\hat{p}$. Recall that x_1 is requested, SEG3D serves x_1 with a server $\hat{s}$ located at $\hat{p}$ while the given solution serves x_1 with a server s_1 located at p_1. The idea of the following proof is that, since x_1, p_1, and $\hat{p}$ are located in some plane $\mathbb{P}$, we can use Theorem 1 to get an upper bound also for three dimensions. However, we need to bound the angle β of the triangle induced by x_1, p_1, and $\hat{p}$ on $\mathbb{P}$ in a different way. Here, we must consider the angle δ that results from the intersection of $\mathbb{P}$ and the current cone. In this case, we define the angle α as the maximum angle within one of the cones and observe that $\delta \leq \alpha$ for any plane $\mathbb{P}$, and α can be computed using Theorem 2.

Theorem 3. SEG3D *has a strict competitive ratio of* $1/(1 - 7/2^{b/2})$ *for the k-server problem in 3-dimensional Euclidean space, using* $b \geq 6$ *bits of advice per request.*

Proof. Theorem 2 ensures that each cone S_j has a diameter of at most $7/\sqrt{2^b}$ over the unit sphere $\mathbb{S}^2$. This means that, when taking the cone S_j, the maximum angle will be at most that determined by the isosceles triangle of base $7/\sqrt{2^b}$ and equal sides of length 1 as shown in Fig. 2b. Then the angle can be simply computed by the trigonometric equality $\sin(\alpha/2) = 7/2\sqrt{2^b}$, which gives $\alpha = 2\arcsin(7/(2\sqrt{2^b}))$.

Let S_j denote the cone indicated by the advice in time step T_1, i.e., the pyramid with apex x_1 that covers the points p_1 and $\hat{p}$, at which the servers s_1 and $\hat{s}$ are located. Since x_1, p_1, and $\hat{p}$ are in a plane $\mathbb{P}$, we can proceed analogously to the proof of Lemma 1. The only difference is that we need to bound the angle δ around x_1 that we obtain when intersecting S_j and $\mathbb{P}$. Clearly, $\beta \leq \delta \leq \alpha$; see Fig. 2. Consequently, α is an upper bound for the angle β.

Plugging $\gamma = \alpha$ into Lemma 1, we can give a proof analogously to that of Theorem 1, and it follows that the strict competitive ratio of SEG3D is at most $1/(1 - 7/2^{b/2})$, which finishes the proof. $\square$

3   From Three Dimensions to d Dimensions

Now we consider the d-dimensional Euclidean space. Suppose we are dealing with the k-server problem in this setting and consider the online algorithm SEGdD with advice that acts analogously to SEG2D and SEG3D.

First, we observe that, similarly as in the previous section, here, the first request x_1 together with the position of the server p_1 (that is used by the solution computed by the algorithm ALG we compare against) and the position $\hat{p}$ of the server $\hat{s}$ that serves the request for SEGdD are located in some plane $\mathbb{P}$. Hence, with the appropriate partition of the $(d-1)$-dimensional unit sphere into parts of small diameter, we can consider the d-dimensional cones projected from x_1 and use the same technique as in the previous section to generalize the result.

Consider a unit sphere $\mathbb{S}^{d-1}$ centered at the request x_i; again, the b bits of advice allow us to partition its $(d-1)$-dimensional hyperspace into 2^b parts and then give one of them as advice, i.e., the server used by ALG lies within the "cone" defined by the corresponding part of the hypersphere and the center x_i. In order to define these parts, we use a partition of $\mathbb{S}^{d-1}$ in parts of small diameter. First of all, given a distribution of N points in a sphere $\omega_N = \{u_1, \ldots, u_N\}$, its associated *Riesz s-energy* is given by

$$E_s(\mathbb{S}^{d-1}, \omega_N) := \sum_{1 \leq i < j \leq N} |u_i - u_j|^{-s}.$$

Observe that pairs of points that are far from each other make small contributions to the sum, whereas close points make larger contributions. Thus, distributions with small Riesz energy have all points far from one another.

A distribution is *s-extremal* if it attains minimal s-energy and can be written as $\omega_s^*(\mathbb{S}^{d-1}, N)$. We define the *mesh norm* $\rho(\mathbb{S}^{d-1}, \omega_N)$ of a distribution of N points by $\rho(\mathbb{S}^{d-1}, \omega_N) := \max_{y \in \mathbb{S}^{d-1}} \min_{x \in \omega_N} |y - x|$.

Damelin and Maymeskul [13] gave an upper bound for the mesh norm of s-extremal distributions for the class of compact sets $\mathcal{A}^{d-1}$ with some restrictions. A compact set A belongs to $\mathcal{A}^{d-1}$ if it fulfills the following conditions.

- $A \subseteq \mathbb{R}^{d'}$ for some $d' \geq d - 1$;
- A has a non-zero Hausdorff measure;
- A is a finite union of bi-Lipschitz images of compact sets in $\mathbb{R}^{d-1}$.

In particular, $(d-1)$-dimensional spheres (and ellipsoids in general) in $\mathbb{R}^d$ belong to $\mathcal{A}^{d-1}$ [13]. When this upper bound is applied to $\mathbb{S}^{d-1}$, we get the following corollary.

Corollary 1. *For any $N \geq 2$, any s-extremal distribution of N points on $\mathbb{S}^{d-1}, \omega_s^*(\mathbb{S}^{d-1}, N)$, has a mesh norm $\rho_s^*(\mathbb{S}^{d-1}, N)$ bounded by $\rho_s^*(\mathbb{S}^{d-1}, N) \leq CN^{-1/(d-1)}$, where C is a constant that only depends on d.*

Now, if we take the *Voronoi diagram* of such an s-extremal distribution with $N = 2^b$ points $\omega_s^* = \{u_1, \ldots, u_N\}$, it partitions $\mathbb{S}^{d-1}$ into convex $(d-1)$-dimensional parts $S_1^*, \ldots, S_N^*$ such that $u_i \in S_i^*$ for all i, and $y \in S_i^*$ if and only if $|y - x_i| \leq |y - x_j|$ for all $j \neq i$.

By the definition of S_i^* and using Corollary 1, we can conclude that the maximum diameter of S_i^* is $2\rho_s^*(\mathbb{S}^{d-1}, N) \leq C'N^{-1/(d-1)}$, where we set $C' := 2C$.

Recall that $S_1, \ldots, S_{2^b}$ denote the cones into which the space is partitioned, i.e., S_j is the cone projected from the center of the sphere to S_j^*. As above, the advice encodes a cone S_j in which the server used by ALG is located, and SEGdD uses the closest server from S_j to satisfy the current request.

As in the 2- and 3-dimensional cases, consider the first time step and the three points x_1, p_1, and $\hat{p}$. Again, we need to bound the angle β of the triangle induced by x_1, p_1, and $\hat{p}$ on $\mathbb{P}$ in a different way. Here, we must consider the angle δ that results from the intersection of $\mathbb{P}$ and the current cone. As in the case of three dimensions, we define α as the maximum angle within one of the cones. We observe that, for any plane with $\delta \leq \alpha$, this angle can be computed using Corollary 1 in exactly the same way as we did for SEG3D.

Theorem 4. *There is a constant C' solely depending on d such that SEGdD has a strict competitive ratio of $1/(1 - C'/2^{b/(d-1)})$ for the k-server problem in d-dimensional Euclidean space, using $b \geq (d-1)\log_2(C')$ bits of advice per request.*

Proof. Recall that Corollary 1 ensures each partition S_j^* has a diameter of at most $C'N^{-1/(d-1)} = C'2^{-b/(d-1)}$ if $N = 2^b$. This means that, when taking the cone S_j, the maximum angle will be that determined by the isosceles triangle of base $C'2^{-b/(d-1)}$ and equal sides of length 1 as in the 3-dimensional case. Then the angle can be simply computed by the trigonometric equality $\sin(\alpha/2) = C/2^{b/(d-1)}$, yielding $\alpha = 2\arcsin(C/(2^{b/(d-1)}))$.

Let S_j denote the cone indicated by the advice in time step T_1, i.e., the cone with apex x_1 that covers the points p_1 and $\hat{p}$, at which s_1 and $\hat{s}$ are located. Since x_1, p_1, and $\hat{p}$ are on a plane $\mathbb{P}$, we can again proceed analogously to the proof of Lemma 1. To this end, we again need to bound the angle δ around x_1 that we obtain when intersecting S_j and $\mathbb{P}$. Clearly, $\beta \leq \delta \leq \alpha$, and thus we ask when δ is maximized; see Fig. 2. Consequently, α is an upper bound for the angle β.

Again plugging $\gamma = \alpha$ into Lemma 1, we can give a proof analogously to that of Theorem 1, and it finally follows that the strict competitive ratio of SEGdD is at most $1/(1 - C'/2^{b/(d-1)})$, finishing the proof.   □

4   From None to Some Curvature

Now consider the k-server problem on the surface of a sphere $\mathbb{S}^2$. Without loss of generality, we assume that the radius of $\mathbb{S}^2$ is $R = 1$; this will help simplifying some computational steps, because, in this case, the shortest distance in radians between two points on $\mathbb{S}^2$ is their angle at the center of $\mathbb{S}^2$ [37].

Let us consider the following algorithm SEGSPH. For every request x_i with $1 \leq i \leq n$, SEGSPH gets $b + 1$ bits of advice with $b \geq 10$. The first such bit indicates whether the server used by the solution computed by the algorithm ALG (we compare against) is close to x_i or far from it. The threshold is at a distance of $1/p$ from x_i (where p depends only on b and will be fixed later). Then the other b bits indicate where the server used by ALG is located. $\mathbb{S}^2$ is divided in the following way. In the case that the server used by ALG is far away, SEGSPH divides the whole sphere into 2^b disjoint parts by selecting 2^b points on the surface distributed according to Theorem 2. We name the *parts* $P_1, \ldots, P_{2^b}$. SEGSPH serves the request x_i with the closest server to x_i within the part indicated by the advice (ignoring the servers at a distance less than $1/p$). Conversely, in the case that the server used by ALG is close, we want to assimilate the behavior to that of SEG2D in the Euclidean plane. To this end, SEGSPH divides the points closer than $1/p$ to x_i into 2^b disjoint *segments* $S_1, \ldots, S_{2^b}$ with their origin in x_i and with an angle of $2\pi/2^b =: \gamma$ (as already defined in (1)).

In the following, we analyze both cases separately.

4.1 The Far Case

Let ALG be an algorithm for the k-server problem on $\mathbb{S}^2$ that again serves the first request x_1 with a server located at p_1 that lies in a part P_j of the far partition. The request is served with cost $d_1 = \text{dist}(p_1, x_1)$, where dist is the distance function on the sphere. Now, SEGSPH serves x_1 with a server located at $\hat{p}$ in P_j with cost $a = \text{dist}(\hat{p}, x_1)$. Let the distance between p_1 and $\hat{p}$ be $c = \text{dist}(p_1, \hat{p})$. Recall that, as we are in the far case with $1/p \leq a \leq d_1$ and since the diameter of P_j, $\text{diam}(P_j)$, is at most $7/\sqrt{N}$ (as seen in Theorem 2), we have $c \leq 7/\sqrt{N}$.

As we want the close partition to be small and similar to the Euclidean plane, we will need $1/p < 1$. Moreover, since we want c to be small compared to d_1 and a, it is reasonable to make the size of $1/p$ larger than the size of one far part; so we define $1 < p < 2^{b/2}/7$. In the following, let $r_{\text{far}} := 1/(1 - (7p)/2^{b/2})$.

Lemma 2. *Let a, d_1, c, p, and P_j be as above. Then $a/(d_1 - c) \leq r_{\text{far}}$.*

Proof. Substituting r_{far} in $a + r_{\text{far}}c$, we obtain $a + r_{\text{far}}c = a + c/(1 - (7p)/2^{b/2})$, and since $c \leq \text{diam}(P_j) \leq 7/2^{b/2}$, it follows that $a + r_{\text{far}}c \leq a + 7/(2^{b/2} - 7p)$. It thus remains to prove that $a + 7/(2^{b/2} - 7p) \leq d_1/(1 - (7p)/2^{b/2})$, which is equivalent to

$$a + \frac{7}{2^{b/2} - 7p} \leq \frac{d_1 \cdot 2^{b/2}}{2^{b/2} - 7p}.$$

As $2^{b/2} - 7p > 0$, it suffices to show that $a \cdot (2^{b/2} - 7p) + 7 \leq d_1 \cdot 2^{b/2}$ or, equivalently, $7 - 7pa \leq 2^{b/2}(d_1 - a)$. Due to $d_1 \geq a$ and $a \geq 1/p$, the inequality follows and so does the lemma. $\qquad \square$

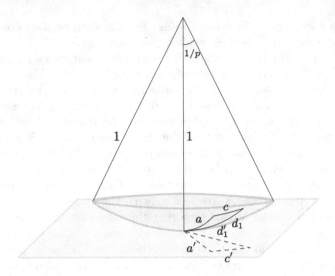

Fig. 3. Projection of a close server request to a surface

To be able to generalize the original theorem for both close and far partitions, we need a result similar to Lemma 2 for the close case, and then take the maximum of both "close competitive ratio" and "far competitive ratio" in order to have a bound on the general competitive ratio of SEGSPH.

4.2 The Close Case

The intuition is that the bound for the close partition should not be very different from that we already know for Euclidean plane, as in the limit for small distances, the surface of a sphere is homeomorphic to a plane.

Again, let ALG be an algorithm that serves x_1 with a server located at p_1, which lies in a segment S_j of the close partition. The request is served with cost $d_1 = \text{dist}(p_1, x_1)$. Now, SEGSPH serves x_1 with a server located at $\hat{p}$ in S_j with cost $a = \text{dist}(\hat{p}, x_1)$. As before, let the distance between p_1 and $\hat{p}$ be $c = \text{dist}(p_1, \hat{p})$. Recall that, as we are in the close case, $a \le d_1 < 1/p$ and that the maximum angle between a and d_1 is $\gamma = 2\pi/2^b$.

Now if we project the triangle $a d_1 c$ to the plane tangent to the sphere in x_1, we get a flat triangle as shown in Fig. 3. We label the sides of this triangle $a', d_1',$ and c'. Observe that $a' = \tan a, d_1' = \tan d_1, c' > c$, and the angle between a' and d_1' is at most γ. The specific values of c and c' can be computed using the cosine law in the sphere and in the plane, respectively. Now Lemma 1 in the plane holds for $a', d_1', c',$ and γ. Taking this into account, we can prove an analogous lemma for the spherical values $a, d_1, c,$ and γ.

First, the original lemma yields $a' + r_{\text{plane}} c' \le r_{\text{plane}} d_1'$ for the plane projection. Second, if we bound

$$k_0 a' \ge a \ge \frac{1}{k_0} a' \text{ and } k_1 (d_1' - c') \ge d_1 - c \ge \frac{1}{k_1}(d_1' - c'), \tag{2}$$

where k_0 and k_1 are two constants we determine in what follows, we can state $a/k_0 \leq a' \leq r_{\text{plane}}(d_1' - c') \leq r_{\text{plane}} k_1 (d_1 - c) \iff a \leq r_{\text{plane}} k_0 k_1 (d_1 - c)$, which is formalized by the following lemma. Let $r_{\text{close}} := (k_0 k_1)/(1 - 2\sin(\gamma/2))$.

Lemma 3. *Let $a, d_1, c, p,$ and S_k be as above. Then $a/(d_1 - c) \leq r_{\text{close}}$.* □

It remains to find k_0 and k_1 that satisfy (2). To find k_0, recall that $a' = \tan(a)$, so $k_0 \tan(a) \geq a$ if and only if $k_0 \geq 1$. On the other side, we have $a \geq \tan(a)/k_0$ if and only if $k_0 \geq \tan(a)/a$. Since $\tan(x)/x$ grows for $0 \leq x \leq \pi/2$, we just need to consider the maximum value for a. As we will require $p \geq 2.5$ for the next part of the proof, and $a \leq d_1 \leq 1/p \leq 0.4$, we get

$$\frac{\tan(a)}{a} \leq \frac{\tan(1/p)}{1/p} \leq \frac{\tan(0.4)}{0.4} < 1.06 = k_0$$

and a can be even smaller if we restrict the value of p further. However, restricting p has an effect on the number of advice bits needed per request as $2.5 \leq p \leq 2^{b/2}/7$ implies that $b \geq 10$.

We can prove that $d_1 - c \leq d_1' - c'$, which implies $k_1 \geq 1$. However, to find k_1, we need to find a bound for $k_1 \geq (d_1' - c')/(d_1 - c)$. First, we can show that $d_1' - c' \leq \tan a$, which implies $(d_1' - c')/(d_1 - c) \leq \tan a/(d_1 - c)$. Note that c grows with β and $\beta \leq \gamma = 2\pi/2^b$, yielding

$$\frac{d_1' - c'}{d_1 - c} \leq \frac{\tan(a)}{d_1 - c(\beta = 2\pi/2^b)}.$$

As a next step, we can show that $\tan(a)/(d_1 - c(\beta = 2\pi/2^b))$ grows with a, i.e., that the fraction is maximized if $a = d_1$. Then, we can prove that $\tan(d_1)/(d_1 - c)$ grows with d_1, and taking into account that $b \geq 10$, we can state

$$\frac{d_1' - c'}{d_1 - c} \leq \frac{\tan(0.4)}{0.4 - \arccos(\cos^2(0.4) + \sin^2(0.4)\cos(\pi/2^9))} \leq 1.17 = k_1.$$

We can finally multiply the values for k_0 and k_1, yielding $r_{\text{close}} = 1.25/(1 - 2\sin(\gamma/2))$ and plug this into Lemma 3.

4.3 Putting It Together

Finally, combining Lemmata 2 and 3 (i.e., using r_{far} and r_{close} in the corresponding cases) with the concrete values for k_0 and k_1, we can easily state the following theorem, which can be proven exactly as Theorem 1.

Theorem 5. *For $2.5 < p < 2^{b/2}/7$, SegSph has a strict competitive ratio of*

$$\max\left\{\frac{1.25}{1 - 2\sin(\pi/2^b)}, \frac{1}{1 - (7p)/2^{b/2}}\right\}$$

for the k-server problem on $\mathbb{S}^2$, using $b \geq 10$ bits of advice per request.

References

1. Bansal, N., Buchbinder, N., Mądry, A., Naor, J.: A polylogarithmic-competitive algorithm for the k-server problem. In: Proceedings of the FOCS 2011, pp. 267–276 (2011)
2. Böckenhauer, H.-J., Hromkovič, J., Komm, D., Královič, R., Rossmanith, P.: On the power of randomness versus advice in online computation. In: Bordihn, H., Kutrib, M., Truthe, B. (eds.) Languages Alive. LNCS, vol. 7300, pp. 30–43. Springer, Heidelberg (2012). https://doi.org/10.1007/978-3-642-31644-9_2
3. Böckenhauer, H.-J., Komm, D., Královič, R., Královič, R., Mömke, T.: On the advice complexity of online problems. In: Dong, Y., Du, D.-Z., Ibarra, O. (eds.) ISAAC 2009. LNCS, vol. 5878, pp. 331–340. Springer, Heidelberg (2009). https://doi.org/10.1007/978-3-642-10631-6_35
4. Böckenhauer, H.-J., Komm, D., Královič, R., Královič, R., Mömke, T.: Online algorithms with advice: the tape model. Inf. Comput. **254**, 59–83 (2017)
5. Böckenhauer, H.-J., Komm, D., Královič, R., Královič, R.: On the advice complexity of the k-server problem. In: Aceto, L., Henzinger, M., Sgall, J. (eds.) ICALP 2011. LNCS, vol. 6755, pp. 207–218. Springer, Heidelberg (2011). https://doi.org/10.1007/978-3-642-22006-7_18
6. Böckenhauer, H.-J., Komm, D., Královič, R., Královič, R.: On the advice complexity of the k-server problem. J. Comput. Syst. Sci. **86**, 159–170 (2017)
7. Böckenhauer, H.-J., Komm, D., Královič, R., Rossmanith, P.: The online knapsack problem: advice and randomization. Theoret. Comput. Sci. **527**, 61–72 (2014)
8. Borodin, A., El-Yaniv, R.: Online Computation and Competitive Analysis. Cambridge University Press, Cambridge (1998)
9. Boyar, J., Favrholdt, L.M., Kudahl, C., Larsen, K.S., Mikkelsen, J.W.: Online algorithms with advice: a survey. SIGACT News **47**(3), 93–129 (2016)
10. Brauchart, J.S., Grabner, P.J.: Distributing many points on spheres: minimal energy and designs. J. Complex. **31**(3), 293–326 (2015)
11. Chrobak, M., Larmore, L.: The server problem and online games. In: On-line Algorithms, Proceedings of a DIMACS Workshop. DIMACS Series in Discrete Mathematics and Computer Science. vol. 7, pp. 11–64. American Mathematical Society (1991)
12. Chrobak, M., Karloff, H.J., Payne, T.H., Vishwanathan, S.: New results on server problems. SIAM J. Discret. Math. **4**(2), 172–181 (1991)
13. Damelin, S.B., Maymeskul, V.: On point energies, separation radius and mesh norm for s-extremal configurations on compact sets in $\mathbb{R}^n$. J. Complex. **21**(6), 845–863 (2005)
14. Dobrev, S., Edmonds, J., Komm, D., Královič, R., Královič, R., Krug, S., Mömke, T.: Improved analysis of the online set cover problem with advice. Theoret. Comput. Sci. **689**, 96–107 (2017)
15. Dobrev, S., Královič, R., Pardubská, D.: How much information about the future is needed? In: Geffert, V., Karhumäki, J., Bertoni, A., Preneel, B., Návrat, P., Bieliková, M. (eds.) SOFSEM 2008. LNCS, vol. 4910, pp. 247–258. Springer, Heidelberg (2008). https://doi.org/10.1007/978-3-540-77566-9_21
16. Dobrev, S., Královič, R., Pardubská, D.: Measuring the problem-relevant information in input. Theor. Inf. Appl. (RAIRO) **43**(3), 585–613 (2009)
17. Dobrev, S., Královič, R., Královič, R.: Computing with advice: when knowledge helps. Bull. EATCS **110**, 35–51 (2013)

18. Dohrau, J.: Online makespan scheduling with sublinear advice. In: Italiano, G.F., Margaria-Steffen, T., Pokorný, J., Quisquater, J.-J., Wattenhofer, R. (eds.) SOFSEM 2015. LNCS, vol. 8939, pp. 177–188. Springer, Heidelberg (2015). https://doi.org/10.1007/978-3-662-46078-8_15

19. Emek, Y., Fraigniaud, P., Korman, A., Rosén, A.: Online computation with advice. In: Albers, S., Marchetti-Spaccamela, A., Matias, Y., Nikoletseas, S., Thomas, W. (eds.) ICALP 2009. LNCS, vol. 5555, pp. 427–438. Springer, Heidelberg (2009). https://doi.org/10.1007/978-3-642-02927-1_36

20. Emek, Y., Fraigniaud, P., Korman, A., Rosén, A.: Online computation with advice. Theoret. Comput. Sci. 412(24), 2642–2656 (2011)

21. Emek, Y., Fraigniaud, P., Korman, A., Rosén, A.: On the additive constant of the k-server work function algorithm. In: Bampis, E., Jansen, K. (eds.) WAOA 2009. LNCS, vol. 5893, pp. 128–134. Springer, Heidelberg (2010). https://doi.org/10.1007/978-3-642-12450-1_12

22. Fiat, A., Woeginger, G.J. (eds.): Online Algorithms: The State of the Art. LNCS, vol. 1442. Springer, Heidelberg (1998). https://doi.org/10.1007/BFb0029561

23. Gebauer, H., Komm, D., Královič, R., Královič, R., Smula, J.: Disjoint path allocation with sublinear advice. In: Xu, D., Du, D., Du, D. (eds.) COCOON 2015. LNCS, vol. 9198, pp. 417–429. Springer, Cham (2015). https://doi.org/10.1007/978-3-319-21398-9_33

24. Gupta, S., Kamali, S., López-Ortiz, A.: On advice complexity of the k-server problem under sparse metrics. Theory Comput. Syst. 59, 476–499 (2016)

25. Irani, S., Karlin, A.R.: On online computation. In: Hochbaum, D. (ed.) Approximation Algorithms for NP-Hard Problems, pp. 521–564 (1997). Chap. 13

26. Hromkovič, J., Královič, R., Královič, R.: Information complexity of online problems. In: Hliněný, P., Kučera, A. (eds.) MFCS 2010. LNCS, vol. 6281, pp. 24–36. Springer, Heidelberg (2010). https://doi.org/10.1007/978-3-642-15155-2_3

27. Komm, D.: An Introduction to Online Computation: Determinism, Randomization, Advice. Springer, Cham (2016). https://doi.org/10.1007/978-3-319-42749-2

28. Komm, D., Královič, R.: Advice complexity and barely random algorithms. Theor. Inf. Appl. (RAIRO) 45(2), 249–267 (2011)

29. Koutsoupias, E.: The k-server problem. Comput. Sci. Rev. 3(2), 105–118 (2009)

30. Koutsoupias, E., Papadimitriou, C.H.: On the k-server conjecture. J. ACM 42(5), 971–983 (1995). Association for Computing Machinery

31. Manasse, M.S., McGeoch, L.A., Sleator, D.D.: Competitive algorithms for on-line problems. In: Proceedings of the STOC 1988, pp. 322–333. Association for Computing Machinery (1988)

32. Preparata, F.P., Shamos, M.: Computational Geometry: An Introduction. Springer, New York (1985). https://doi.org/10.1007/978-1-4612-1098-6

33. Rakhmanov, E.A., Saff, E.B., Zhou, Y.M.: Minimal discrete energy on the sphere. Math. Res. Lett. 1, 647–662 (1994)

34. Renault, M., Rosén, A.: On online algorithms with advice for the k-server problem. Theory Comput. Syst. 56(1), 3–21 (2015)

35. Renault, M.P., Rosén, A., van Stee, R.: Online algorithms with advice for bin packing and scheduling problems. Theoret. Comput. Sci. 600, 155–170 (2015)

36. Sleator, D.D., Tarjan, R.E.: Amortized efficiency of list update and paging rules. Commun. ACM 28(2), 202–208 (1985)

37. Zwillinger, D.: Standard Mathematical Tables and Formulae, 32nd edn. CRC, Boca Raton (2011)

Automata, Complexity, Completeness

Deciding Universality of ptNFAs
is PSPACE-Complete

Tomáš Masopust[1(✉)] and Markus Krötzsch[2]

[1] Institute of Mathematics, Czech Academy of Sciences, Brno, Czech Republic
`masopust@math.cas.cz`
[2] cfaed, TU Dresden, Dresden, Germany
`markus.kroetzsch@tu-dresden.de`

Abstract. An automaton is partially ordered if the only cycles in its transition diagram are self-loops. We study the universality problem for ptNFAs, a class of partially ordered NFAs recognizing piecewise testable languages. The universality problem asks if an automaton accepts all words over its alphabet. Deciding universality for both NFAs and partially ordered NFAs is PSPACE-complete. For ptNFAs, the complexity drops to coNP-complete if the alphabet is fixed but is open if the alphabet may grow. We show, using a novel and nontrivial construction, that the problem is PSPACE-complete if the alphabet may grow polynomially.

1 Introduction

Piecewise testable languages form a strict subclass of *star-free languages* or, in other words, of the languages definable by the linear temporal logic. They are investigated and find applications in semigroup theory [2,25], in logic on words [9], in formal languages and automata theory [17], recently mainly in applications of separability [26], in natural language processing [10,28], in cognitive and sub-regular complexity [29], in learning theory [11,18], or in database theory in the context of schema languages for XML data [8,14,15,20]. They have been extended from words to trees [4,12].

Simon [31] showed that piecewise testable languages are exactly those regular languages whose syntactic monoid is $\mathcal{J}$-trivial and that they are characterized by *confluent, partially ordered DFAs*. An automaton is *partially ordered* if the only cycles are self-loops, and it is *confluent* if for any state q and any two of its successors s and t accessible from q by transitions labeled by a and b, respectively, there is a word $w \in \{a, b\}^*$ such that a common state is reachable from both s and t under w; cf. Fig. 1 (left) for an illustration.

Omitting confluence results in *partially ordered DFAs* (poDFAs) characterizing $\mathcal{R}$-*trivial languages* [6]. Lifting the notion of partial order from DFAs to NFAs, partially ordered NFAs (poNFAs) characterize the languages of level $\frac{3}{2}$ of the Straubing-Thérien hierarchy [30]; hence poNFAs are strictly more powerful than poDFAs. These languages are better known as *Alphabetical Pattern*

Supported by DFG grants KR 4381/1-1 & CRC 912 (HAEC), and by RVO 67985840.

A. M. Tjoa et al. (Eds.): SOFSEM 2018, LNCS 10706, pp. 413–427, 2018.
https://doi.org/10.1007/978-3-319-73117-9_29

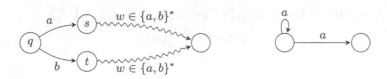

Fig. 1. Confluence (left) and the forbidden pattern of self-loop det. poNFAs (right)

Constraints, which are regular languages effectively closed under permutation rewriting used in algorithmic verification [5].

In our recent work, we showed that the increased expressivity of poNFAs is caused by self-loop transitions involved in nondeterminism. Consequently, $\mathcal{R}$-*trivial languages* are characterized by self-loop deterministic poNFAs (denoted by rpoNFAs from *restricted* poNFAs) [19]. A poNFA is *self-loop deterministic* if it does not contain the pattern of Fig. 1 (right). Our study further revealed that complete, confluent and self-loop deterministic poNFAs (denoted by ptNFAs from *piecewise testable*) characterize piecewise testable languages [21,23]. An NFA is *complete* if a transition under every letter is defined in every state.

In this paper, we study the *universality* problem of ptNFAs. The problem asks if an automaton accepts all words over its alphabet. The study of universality (and its dual, emptiness) has a long tradition in formal languages with many applications across computer science, e.g., in knowledge representation and database theory [3,7,32]. The problem is PSPACE-complete for NFAs [24]. Recent studies investigate the problem for specific types of regular languages, such as prefixes or factors [27].

Despite a rather low expressivity of poNFAs, the universality problem for poNFAs has the same worst-case complexity as for general NFAs, even if restricted to binary alphabets [19]. This is because poNFAs have a powerful nondeterminism. The pattern of Fig. 1 (right) admits an unbounded number of nondeterministic steps—the poNFA either stays in the same state or moves to another. Forbidding the pattern results in rpoNFAs where the number of nondeterministic steps is bounded by the number of states. This restriction affects the complexity of universality. Deciding universality for rpoNFAs is coNP-complete if the alphabet is fixed but remains PSPACE-complete if the alphabet may grow polynomially [19]. The growth of the alphabet thus compensates for the restriction on the number of nondeterministic steps. The reduced complexity is also preserved by ptNFAs if the alphabet is fixed [21] but is open if the alphabet may grow.

We solve this problem by showing that deciding universality for ptNFAs is PSPACE-complete if the alphabet may grow polynomially. To this aim, we use a novel and nontrivial extension of the construction for rpoNFAs [19]. Consequently, our result provides lower-bound complexities for the problems of inclusion, equivalence, and k-piecewise testability [21]. The results are summarized in Table 1.

Table 1. Complexity of deciding universality

	$|\Sigma| = 1$		$|\Sigma| = k \geq 2$		Σ is growing	
DFA	L-comp.	[16]	NL-comp.	[16]	NL-comp.	[16]
ptNFA	NL-comp.	(Theorem 1)	CONP-comp.	[21]	PSPACE-comp.	(Theorem 2)
rpoNFA	NL-comp.	[19]	CONP-comp.	[19]	PSPACE-comp.	[19]
poNFA	NL-comp.	[19]	PSPACE-comp.	[19]	PSPACE-comp.	[1]
NFA	CONP-comp.	[33]	PSPACE-comp.	[1]	PSPACE-comp.	[1]

2   Preliminaries

We assume that the reader is familiar with automata theory [1]. The cardinality of a set A is denoted by $|A|$ and the power set of A by 2^A. The empty word is denoted by ε. For a word $w = xyz$, x is a *prefix*, y a *factor*, and z a *suffix* of w. A prefix (factor, suffix) of w is *proper* if it is different from w.

Let $\mathcal{A} = (Q, \Sigma, \cdot, I, F)$ be a *nondeterministic finite automaton* (NFA). The language *accepted* by $\mathcal{A}$ is the set $L(\mathcal{A}) = \{w \in \Sigma^* \mid I \cdot w \cap F \neq \emptyset\}$. We often omit $\cdot$ and write Iw instead of $I \cdot w$. A *path* π from a state q_0 to a state q_n under a word $a_1 a_2 \cdots a_n$, for some $n \geq 0$, is a sequence of states and input symbols $q_0 a_1 q_1 a_2 \cdots q_{n-1} a_n q_n$ such that $q_{i+1} \in q_i \cdot a_{i+1}$, for $i = 0, \ldots, n-1$. Path π is *accepting* if $q_0 \in I$ and $q_n \in F$. We write $q_0 \xrightarrow{a_1 a_2 \cdots a_n} q_n$ to denote that there is a path from q_0 to q_n under the word $a_1 a_2 \cdots a_n$. Automaton $\mathcal{A}$ is *complete* if for every state q of $\mathcal{A}$ and every letter $a \in \Sigma$, the set $q \cdot a$ is nonempty. An NFA $\mathcal{A}$ is *deterministic* (DFA) if $|I| = 1$ and $|q \cdot a| = 1$ for every $q \in Q$ and every $a \in \Sigma$.

The reachability relation $\leq$ on states is defined by $p \leq q$ if there is a $w \in \Sigma^*$ such that $q \in p \cdot w$. An NFA $\mathcal{A}$ is *partially ordered (poNFA)* if the reachability relation $\leq$ is a partial order. For two states p and q of $\mathcal{A}$, we write $p < q$ if $p \leq q$ and $p \neq q$. A state p is *maximal* if there is no state q such that $p < q$.

A *restricted partially ordered NFA (rpoNFA)* is a poNFA such that for every state q and every letter a, if $q \in q \cdot a$ then $q \cdot a = \{q\}$.

A poNFA $\mathcal{A}$ over Σ with the state set Q can be turned into a directed graph $G(\mathcal{A})$ with the set of vertices Q where a pair $(p, q) \in Q \times Q$ is an edge in $G(\mathcal{A})$ if there is a transition from p to q in $\mathcal{A}$. For an alphabet $\Gamma \subseteq \Sigma$, we define the directed graph $G(\mathcal{A}, \Gamma)$ with the set of vertices Q by considering only those transitions corresponding to letters in Γ. For a state p, let $\Sigma(p) = \{a \in \Sigma \mid p \xrightarrow{a} p\}$ denote all letters labeling self-loops in p. We say that $\mathcal{A}$ satisfies the *unique maximal state* (UMS) property if, for every state q of $\mathcal{A}$, state q is the unique maximal state of the connected component of $G(\mathcal{A}, \Sigma(q))$ containing q.

Definition 1. *An NFA $\mathcal{A}$ is a ptNFA if it is partially ordered, complete and satisfies the UMS property.*

An equivalent notion to the UMS property for DFAs is confluence [17]. A DFA $\mathcal{D}$ over Σ is *(locally) confluent* if, for every state q of $\mathcal{D}$ and every pair of letters $a, b \in \Sigma$, there is a word $w \in \{a, b\}^*$ such that $(qa)w = (qb)w$. We generalize this notion to NFAs as follows. An NFA $\mathcal{A}$ over Σ is *confluent* if, for every state q of $\mathcal{A}$ and every pair of (not necessarily distinct) letters $a, b \in \Sigma$, if $s \in qa$ and $t \in qb$, then there is a word $w \in \{a, b\}^*$ such that $sw \cap tw \neq \emptyset$.

Lemma 1 [21]. *Complete and confluent rpoNFAs are exactly ptNFAs.*

3 Complexity of Universality for ptNFAs

We now study the universality problem for ptNFAs. If the alphabet is fixed, deciding universality for ptNFAs is coNP-complete and the hardness holds even if restricted to binary alphabets [21]. For unary alphabets, universality for ptN-FAs is decidable in polynomial time [19]. The following theorem improves this result.

Theorem 1. *Deciding universality of ptNFAs over a unary alphabet is an* NL-*complete problem.*

If the alphabet may grow polynomially, the universality problem for ptNFAs is open. In the rest of this paper we solve this problem by showing that the universality problem for ptNFAs is PSPACE-complete.

A typical proof showing PSPACE-hardness of universality for NFAs is to take a p-space bounded deterministic Turing machine $\mathcal{M}$, for a polynomial p, together with an input x, and to encode the computations of $\mathcal{M}$ on x as words over some alphabet Σ that depends on the alphabet and the state set of $\mathcal{M}$. One then constructs a regular expression (or an NFA) R_x representing all computations that do not encode an accepting run of $\mathcal{M}$ on x. That is, $L(R_x) = \Sigma^*$ if and only if $\mathcal{M}$ does not accept x [1].

The form of R_x is relatively simple, consisting of a union of expressions of the form

$$\Sigma^* K \Sigma^* \tag{1}$$

where K is a finite language with words of length bounded by $O(p(|x|))$.

Intuitively, K encodes possible violations of a correct computation of $\mathcal{M}$ on x, such as the initial configuration does not contain the input x, or the step from a configuration to the next one does not correspond to any rule of $\mathcal{M}$. These checks are local, involving at most two consecutive configurations of $\mathcal{M}$, each of polynomial size. They can therefore be encoded as a finite language with words of polynomial length.

The initial Σ^* of (1) then nondeterministically guesses a position in the word where a violation encoded by K occurs, and the last Σ^* reads the rest of the word if the violation check was successful.

This idea cannot be directly used to prove Theorem 2 for two reasons:

(i) Although expression (1) can easily be translated to a poNFA, it is not true for ptNFAs. The translation of the leading part $\Sigma^* K$ may result in the forbidden pattern of Fig. 1;

(ii) The constructed poNFA may be incomplete and its "standard" completion by adding the missing transitions to a new sink state may violate the UMS property.

A first observation to overcome these problems is that the length of the encoding of a computation of $\mathcal{M}$ on x is at most exponential with respect to the size of $\mathcal{M}$ and x. It would therefore be sufficient to replace the initial Σ^* in (1) by prefixes of an exponentially long word. However, such a word cannot be constructed by a polynomial-time reduction. Instead, we replace Σ^* with a ptNFA encoding such a word, which exists and is of polynomial size as shown in Lemma 2. There we construct, in polynomial time, a ptNFA $\mathcal{A}_{n,n}$ that accepts all words but a single one, $W_{n,n}$, of exponential length.

Since the language K of (1) is finite, and hence piecewise testable, there is a ptNFA for K. For every state of $\mathcal{A}_{n,n}$, we make a copy of the ptNFA for K and identify its initial state with the state of $\mathcal{A}_{n,n}$ if it does not violate the forbidden pattern of Fig. 1; see Fig. 2 for an illustration. We keep track of the words read by both $\mathcal{A}_{n,n}$ and the ptNFA for K by taking the Cartesian product of their alphabets. A letter is then a pair of symbols, where the first symbol is the input for $\mathcal{A}_{n,n}$ and the second is the input for the ptNFA for K. A word over this alphabet is accepted if the first components do not form $W_{n,n}$ or the second components form a word that is not a correct encoding of a run of $\mathcal{M}$ on x. This results in an rpoNFA that overcomes problem **(i)**.

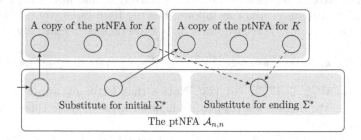

Fig. 2. Const. of an rpoNFA (solid edges) solving prob. (i), illustrated for two copies of the ptNFA for K, and its completion to a ptNFA (dashed edges) solving prob. (ii)

However, this technique is not sufficient to resolve problem **(ii)**. Although the construction yields an rpoNFA that is universal if and only if the regular expression R_x is [19], the rpoNFA is incomplete and its "standard" completion by adding the missing transitions to an additional sink state violates the UMS property. According to Lemma 1, to construct a ptNFA from the rpoNFA, we need to complete the latter so that it is confluent. This is not possible for every rpoNFA, but it is possible for our case because the length of the input that is of interest is bounded by the length of $W_{n,n}$. The maximal state of $\mathcal{A}_{n,n}$ is accepting, and therefore all the missing transitions can be added so that the paths required by confluence meet in the maximal state of $\mathcal{A}_{n,n}$. Since all words longer than $|W_{n,n}|$ are accepted by $\mathcal{A}_{n,n}$, we could complete the rpoNFA by adding paths to the maximal state of $\mathcal{A}_{n,n}$ that are longer than $|W_{n,n}|$. However, this cannot be done by a polynomial-time reduction, since the length of $W_{n,n}$ is exponential. Instead, we add a ptNFA to encode such paths in the formal definition of $\mathcal{A}_{n,n}$ as given in Lemma 2 below. We then ensure confluence by adding the missing transitions to states of the ptNFA $\mathcal{A}_{n,n}$ from which the unread part of $W_{n,n}$ is not accepted and from which the maximal state of $\mathcal{A}_{n,n}$ is reachable under the symbol of the added transition (cf. Corollary 1). The second condition ensures confluence, since all the transitions meet in the maximal state of $\mathcal{A}_{n,n}$. The idea is illustrated in Fig. 2. The details follow.

By this construction, we do not get the same language as defined by the regular expression R_x, but the language of the constructed ptNFA is universal if and only if R_x is, which suffices for universality.

Thus, the first step of the construction is to construct the ptNFA $\mathcal{A}_{n,n}$ that accepts all words but $W_{n,n}$ of exponential length. This automaton is the core of the proof of Theorem 2. The language considered there is the same as in our previous work [19, Lemma 17], where the constructed automaton is not a ptNFA.

Lemma 2. *For all integers $k, n \geq 1$, there exists a ptNFA $\mathcal{A}_{k,n}$ over an n-letter alphabet with $n(2k + 1) + 1$ states, such that the unique non-accepted word of $\mathcal{A}_{k,n}$ is of length $\binom{k+n}{k} - 1$.*

Proof. For positive integers k and n, we recursively define words $W_{k,n}$ over the alphabet $\Sigma_n = \{a_1, a_2, \ldots, a_n\}$ as follows. For the base cases, we set $W_{k,1} = a_1^k$ and $W_{1,n} = a_1 a_2 \ldots a_n$. The cases for $k, n > 1$ are defined recursively by setting

$$W_{k,n} = W_{k,n-1}\, a_n\, W_{k-1,n} = W_{k,n-1}\, a_n\, W_{k-1,n-1}\, a_n\, \cdots\, a_n\, W_{1,n-1}\, a_n.$$

The length of $W_{k,n}$ is $\binom{k+n}{n} - 1$ [23]. Notice that letter a_n appears exactly k times in $W_{k,n}$. We further set $W_{k,n} = \varepsilon$ whenever $kn = 0$, since this is useful for defining $\mathcal{A}_{k,n}$ below.

We construct a ptNFA $\mathcal{A}_{k,n}$ over Σ_n that accepts the language $\Sigma_n^* \setminus \{W_{k,n}\}$. For $n = 1$ and $k \geq 0$, let $\mathcal{A}_{k,1}$ be a DFA for $\{a_1\}^* \setminus \{a_1^k\}$ with k additional unreachable states used to address problem **(ii)** and included here for uniformity (see Corollary 1). $\mathcal{A}_{k,1}$ consists of $2k + 1$ states of the form $(i; 1)$ and a state max, as shown in the top-most row of states in Fig. 3, together with the given a_1-transitions. All states but $(i; 1)$, for $i = k, \ldots, 2k$, are accepting, and $(0; 1)$ is initial. All undefined transitions in Fig. 3 go to state max.

Given a ptNFA $\mathcal{A}_{k,n-1}$, we recursively construct $\mathcal{A}_{k,n}$ as defined next. The construction for $n = 3$ is illustrated in Fig. 3. We obtain $\mathcal{A}_{k,n}$ from $\mathcal{A}_{k,n-1}$ by adding $2k + 1$ states $(0; n), (1; n), \ldots, (2k; n)$, where $(0; n)$ is added to the initial states, and all states $(i; n)$ with $i < k$ are added to the accepting states. The automaton $\mathcal{A}_{k,n}$ therefore has $n(2k + 1) + 1$ states. The additional transitions of $\mathcal{A}_{k,n}$ consist of the following groups:

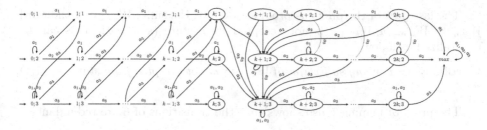

Fig. 3. The ptNFA $\mathcal{A}_{k,3}$ with $3(2k+1)+1$ states; all undefined transitions go to state max; dotted lines depict arrows from $(k+i,1)$ to $(k+1,3)$ under a_3, for $i = 2,3,\ldots,k$

1. Self-loops $(i;n) \xrightarrow{a_j} (i;n)$ for $i \in \{0,1,\ldots,2k\}$ and $a_j = a_1, a_2, \ldots, a_{n-1}$;
2. Transitions $(i;n) \xrightarrow{a_n} (i+1;n)$ for $i \in \{0,1,\ldots,2k-1\} \setminus \{k\}$;
3. Transitions $(k,n) \xrightarrow{a_n} max$, $(2k,n) \xrightarrow{a_n} max$, and the self-loop $max \xrightarrow{a_n} max$;
4. Transitions $(i;n) \xrightarrow{a_n} (i+1;m)$ for $i = 0,1,\ldots,k-1$ and $m = 1,\ldots,n-1$;
5. Transitions $(i;m) \xrightarrow{a_n} max$ for every accepting state $(i;m)$ of $\mathcal{A}_{k,n-1}$;
6. Transitions $(i;m) \xrightarrow{a_n} (k+1,n)$ for every non-accepting state $(i;m)$ of $\mathcal{A}_{k,n-1}$.

By construction, $\mathcal{A}_{k,n}$ is complete and partially ordered. It satisfies the UMS property because if there is a self-loop in a state $q \neq max$ under a letter a, then there is no other incoming or outgoing transition of q under a. This means that the component of the graph $G(\mathcal{A}_{k,n}, \Sigma(q))$ containing q is only state q, which is indeed the unique maximal state. Hence, it is a ptNFA. Equivalently, to see that the automaton is confluent, the reader may notice that the automaton has a single sink state.

We show that $\mathcal{A}_{k,n}$ accepts $\Sigma_n^* \setminus \{W_{k,n}\}$. The additional states of $\mathcal{A}_{k,n}$ and transitions 1, 2, and 3 ensure acceptance of every word that does not contain exactly k occurrences of a_n. The transitions 4 and 5 ensure acceptance of all words in $(\Sigma_{n-1}^* a_n)^i L(\mathcal{A}_{k-i,n-1}) a_n \Sigma_n^*$, for which the longest factor before the $(i+1)$th occurrence of a_n is not of the form $W_{k-i,n-1}$, and hence not a correct factor of $W_{k,n} = W_{k,n-1} a_n \cdots a_n W_{k-i,n-1} a_n \cdots a_n W_{1,n-1} a_n$. Together, these conditions ensure that $\mathcal{A}_{k,n}$ accepts every input other than $W_{k,n}$.

It remains to show that $\mathcal{A}_{k,n}$ does not accept $W_{k,n}$, which we do by induction on (k,n). We start with the base cases. For $(0,n)$ and any $n \geq 1$, the word $W_{0,n} = \varepsilon$ is not accepted by $\mathcal{A}_{0,n}$, since the initial states $(0;m) = (k;m)$ of $\mathcal{A}_{0,n}$ are not accepting. Likewise, for $(k,1)$ and any $k \geq 0$, we find that $W_{k,1} = a_1^k$ is not accepted by $\mathcal{A}_{k,1}$ (cf. Fig. 3).

For the inductive case $(k,n) \geq (1,2)$, assume that $\mathcal{A}_{k',n'}$ does not accept $W_{k',n'}$ for any $(k',n') < (k,n)$. We have $W_{k,n} = W_{k,n-1} a_n W_{k-1,n}$, and $W_{k,n-1}$ is not accepted by $\mathcal{A}_{k,n-1}$ by induction. Therefore, after reading $W_{k,n-1} a_n$, automaton $\mathcal{A}_{k,n}$ must be in one of the states $(1;m), 1 \leq m \leq n$, or $(k+1;n)$. However, states $(1;m), 1 \leq m \leq n$, are the initial states of $\mathcal{A}_{k-1,n}$, which does not accept $W_{k-1,n}$ by induction. Assume that $\mathcal{A}_{k,n}$ is in state $(k+1;n)$ after reading $W_{k,n-1} a_n$. Since $W_{k-1,n}$ has exactly $k-1$ occurrences of letter a_n, $\mathcal{A}_{k,n}$ is in state $(2k;n)$ after reading $W_{k-1,n}$. Hence $W_{k,n}$ is not accepted by $\mathcal{A}_{k,n}$. □

The last part of the previous proof shows that the suffix $W_{k-1,n}$ of the word $W_{k,n} = W_{k,n-1}a_nW_{k-1,n}$ is not accepted from state $(k+1;n)$. This can be generalized as follows.

Corollary 1. *For any suffix a_iw of $W_{k,n}$, w is not accepted from state $(k+1;i)$ of $\mathcal{A}_{k,n}$.*

The proof of Lemma 2 also shows that the transitions of 6 are redundant.

Corollary 2. *Removing from $\mathcal{A}_{k,n}$ the non-accepting states $(k+1,i),\ldots,(2k,i)$, for $1 \le i \le n$, and the corresponding transitions results in an rpoNFA that accepts the same language.*

A *deterministic Turing machine* (DTM) is a tuple $M = (Q,T,I,\delta,\sqcup,q_o,q_f)$, where Q is the finite state set, T is the tape alphabet, $I \subseteq T$ is the input alphabet, $\sqcup \in T \setminus I$ is the blank symbol, q_o is the initial state, q_f is the accepting state, and δ is the transition function mapping $Q \times T$ to $Q \times T \times \{L,R,S\}$; see Aho et al. [1] for details.

We now prove the main result, whose proof is a nontrivial generalization of our previous construction showing PSPACE-hardness of universality for rpoN-FAs [19].

Theorem 2. *The universality problem for ptNFAs is PSPACE-complete.*

Proof. Membership follows since universality is in PSPACE for NFAs [13].

To prove PSPACE-hardness, we consider a polynomial p and a p-space-bounded DTM $\mathcal{M} = (Q,T,I,\delta,\sqcup,q_o,q_f)$. Without loss of generality, we assume that $q_o \ne q_f$. A configuration of $\mathcal{M}$ on x consists of a current state $q \in Q$, the position $1 \le \ell \le p(|x|)$ of the read/write head, and the tape contents $\theta_1,\ldots,\theta_{p(|x|)}$ with $\theta_i \in T$. We represent it by a sequence

$$\langle\theta_1,\varepsilon\rangle \cdots \langle\theta_{\ell-1},\varepsilon\rangle\langle\theta_\ell,q\rangle\langle\theta_{\ell+1},\varepsilon\rangle \cdots \langle\theta_{p(|x|)},\varepsilon\rangle$$

of symbols from $\Delta = T \times (Q \cup \{\varepsilon\})$. A run of $\mathcal{M}$ on x is represented as a word $\#w_1\#w_2\# \cdots \#w_m\#$, where $w_i \in \Delta^{p(|x|)}$ and $\# \notin \Delta$ is a fresh separator symbol. One can construct a regular expression recognizing all words over $\Delta\cup\{\#\}$ that do not correctly encode a run of $\mathcal{M}$ (in particular are not of the form $\#w_1\#w_2\# \cdots \#w_m\#$) or that encode a run that is not accepting [1]. Such a regular expression can be constructed in the following three steps: we detect all words that

(A) do not start with the initial configuration;
(B) do not encode a valid run since they violate a transition rule;
(C) encode non-accepting runs or runs that end prematurely.

If $\mathcal{M}$ has an accepting run, it has one without repeated configurations. For an input x, there are $C(x) = (|T \times (Q \cup \{\varepsilon\})|)^{p(|x|)}$ distinct configuration words in our encoding. Considering a separator symbol $\#$, the length of the encoding of a run without repeated configurations is at most $1 + C(x)(p(|x|)+1)$, since every configuration word ends with $\#$ and is thus of length $p(|x|)+1$. Let n be the least number such that $|W_{n,n}| \geq 1 + C(x)(p(|x|) + 1)$, where $W_{n,n}$ is the word constructed in Lemma 2. Since $|W_{n,n}| + 1 = \binom{2n}{n} \geq 2^n$, it follows that n is smaller than $\lceil \log(1 + C(x)(p(|x|) + 1)) \rceil$, and hence polynomial in the size of $\mathcal{M}$ and x.

Consider the ptNFA $\mathcal{A}_{n,n}$ over the alphabet $\Sigma_n = \{a_1, \dots, a_n\}$ of Lemma 2, and define the alphabet $\Delta_{\#\$} = T \times (Q \cup \{\varepsilon\}) \cup \{\#, \$\}$. We consider the alphabet $\Pi = \Sigma_n \times \Delta_{\#\$}$ where the first letter is an input for $\mathcal{A}_{n,n}$ and the second letter is used for encoding a run as described above. Recall that $\mathcal{A}_{n,n}$ accepts all words different from $W_{n,n}$. Therefore, only those words over Π are of our interest, where the first components form the word $W_{n,n}$. Since the length of $W_{n,n}$ may not be a multiple of $p(|x|) + 1$, we add $\$$ to fill up any remaining space after the last configuration.

For a word $w = \langle a_{i_1}, \delta_1 \rangle \cdots \langle a_{i_\ell}, \delta_\ell \rangle \in \Pi^\ell$, we define $w[1] = a_{i_1} \cdots a_{i_\ell} \in \Sigma_n^\ell$ as the projection of w to the first component and $w[2] = \delta_1 \dots \delta_\ell \in \Delta_{\#\$}^\ell$ as the projection to the second component. Conversely, for a word $v \in \Delta_{\#\$}^*$, we write $\mathrm{enc}(v)$ to denote the set of all words $w \in \Pi^{|v|}$ with $w[2] = v$. Similarly, for $v \in \Sigma_n^*$, $\mathrm{enc}(v)$ denotes the words $w \in \Pi^{|v|}$ with $w[1] = v$. We extend this notation to sets of words.

Let $\mathrm{enc}(\mathcal{A}_{n,n})$ denote the automaton $\mathcal{A}_{n,n}$ with each transition $q \xrightarrow{a_i} q'$ replaced by all transitions $q \xrightarrow{\pi} q'$ with $\pi \in \mathrm{enc}(a_i)$. Then $\mathrm{enc}(\mathcal{A}_{n,n})$ accepts the language $\Pi^* \setminus \{\mathrm{enc}(W_{n,n})\}$. We say that a word w encodes an accepting run of $\mathcal{M}$ on x if $w[1] = W_{n,n}$ and $w[2]$ is of the form $\#w_1 \# \cdots \#w_m \#\$^j$ such that there is an $i \in \{1, 2, \dots, m\}$ for which $\#w_1 \# \cdots \#w_i \#$ encodes an accepting run of $\mathcal{M}$ on x, $w_k = w_i$ for all $k \in \{i+1, \dots, m\}$, and $j \leq p(|x|)$. That is, we extend the encoding by repeating the accepting configuration until we have less than $p(|x|) + 1$ symbols before the end of $|W_{n,n}|$ and fill up the remaining places with symbol $\$$.

For (A), we want to detect all words that do not start with the word

$$w[2] = \#\langle x_1, q_0 \rangle \langle x_2, \varepsilon \rangle \cdots \langle x_{|x|}, \varepsilon \rangle \langle \sqcup, \varepsilon \rangle \cdots \langle \sqcup, \varepsilon \rangle \#$$

of length $p(|x|) + 2$. This happens if (A.1) the word is shorter than $p(|x|) + 2$, or (A.2) at position j, for $0 \leq j \leq p(|x|) + 1$, there is a letter from the alphabet $\Delta_{\#\$} \setminus \{x_j\}$. Let $\bar{E}_j = \Sigma_n \times (\Delta_{\#\$} \setminus \{x_j\})$ where x_j is the jth symbol on the initial tape of $\mathcal{M}$. We can capture (A.1) and (A.2) in the regular expression

$$\left(\varepsilon + \Pi + \Pi^2 + \dots + \Pi^{p(|x|)+1} \right) + \sum_{0 \leq j \leq p(|x|)+1} (\Pi^j \cdot \bar{E}_j \cdot \Pi^*) \qquad (2)$$

Expression (2) is polynomial in size. It can be captured by a ptNFA as follows. Each of the first $p(|x|) + 2$ expressions defines a finite language and can easily be captured by a ptNFA (by a confluent DFA) of size of the expression. The disjoint union of these ptNFAs then form a single ptNFA recognizing the language $\varepsilon + \Pi + \Pi^2 + \dots + \Pi^{p(|x|)+1}$.

To express the language $\Pi^j \cdot \bar{E}_j \cdot \Pi^*$ as a ptNFA, we first construct the minimal incomplete DFA recognizing this language (states $0, 1, \dots, j, j+1, max$ in Fig. 4).

However, we cannot complete it by simply adding the missing transitions to a new sink state because it results in a DFA with two maximal states, max and the sink state, violating the UMS property. Instead, we use a copy of the ptNFA $enc(\mathcal{A}_{n,n})$ and add the missing transitions from state j under $enc(x_j)$ to state $(n+1;i)$ if $enc(x_j)[1] = a_i$; see Fig. 4. Notice that states $(n+1;i)$ are the states $(k+1;i)$ in Fig. 3. The resulting automaton is a ptNFA, since it is complete, partially ordered, and satisfies the UMS property—for every state q different from max, the component co-reachable and reachable under the letters of self-loops in q is only state q itself. The automaton accepts all words of $\Pi^j \cdot \bar{E}_j \cdot \Pi^*$.

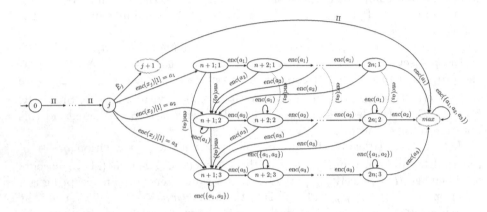

Fig. 4. A ptNFA accepting the language $\Pi^j \cdot \bar{E}_j \cdot \Pi^* + (\Pi^* \setminus \{enc(W_{n,n})\})$ illustrated for $\Sigma_n = \{a_1, a_2, a_3\}$; only the relevant part of $\mathcal{A}_{n,n}$ is depicted

We now show that any word w that is accepted by this automaton and that does not belong to $\Pi^j \cdot \bar{E}_j \cdot \Pi^*$ is such that $w[1] \neq W_{n,n}$, that is, it belongs to $\Pi^* \setminus \{enc(W_{n,n})\}$. Assume that $w[1] = W_{n,n} = ua_iv$, where a_i is the position and the letter under which the state $(n+1;i)$ of $\mathcal{A}_{n,n}$ is reached. Then v is not accepted from $(n+1;i)$ by Corollary 1. Thus, the ptNFA accepts the language $\Pi^j \cdot \bar{E}_j \cdot \Pi^* + (\Pi^* \setminus \{enc(W_{n,n})\})$. Constructing such a ptNFA for polynomially many expressions $\Pi^j \cdot \bar{E}_j \cdot \Pi^*$ and taking their union results in a polynomially large ptNFA accepting the language $\sum_{j=0}^{p(|x|)+1} (\Pi^j \cdot \bar{E}_j \cdot \Pi^*) + (\Pi^* \setminus \{enc(W_{n,n})\})$.

Notice that we ensure that the surrounding $\#$ in the initial configuration are present.

For **(B)**, we check for incorrect transitions. Consider again the encoding $\#w_1\# \ldots \#w_m\#$ of a sequence of configurations with a word over $\Delta \cup \{\#\}$. We can assume that w_1 encodes the initial configuration according to **(A)**. In an encoding of a valid run, the symbol at any position $j \geq p(|x|) + 2$ is uniquely determined by the symbols at positions $j - p(|x|) - 2, j - p(|x|) - 1$, and $j - p(|x|)$, corresponding to the cell and its left and right neighbor in the previous configuration. Given symbols $\delta_\ell, \delta, \delta_r \in \Delta \cup \{\#\}$, we can therefore define $f(\delta_\ell, \delta, \delta_r) \in \Delta \cup \{\#\}$ to be the symbol required in the next configuration. The case where $\delta_\ell = \#$ or $\delta_r = \#$ corresponds to transitions applied at the left and right edge of the tape, respectively; for the case that $\delta = \#$, we define $f(\delta_\ell, \delta, \delta_r) = \#$, ensuring that the separator $\#$ is always present in successor configurations as well. We extend f to $f \colon \Delta^3_{\#\$} \to \Delta_{\#\$}$. For allowing the last configuration to be repeated, we define f as if the accepting state q_f of $\mathcal{M}$ had a self loop (a transition that does not modify the tape, state, or head position). Moreover, we generally permit $\$$ to occur instead of the expected next configuration symbol. We can then check for invalid transitions using the regular expression

$$\Pi^* \sum_{\delta_\ell, \delta, \delta_r \in \Delta_{\#\$}} \mathrm{enc}(\delta_\ell \delta \delta_r) \cdot \Pi^{p(|x|)-1} \cdot \hat{f}(\delta_\ell, \delta, \delta_r) \cdot \Pi^* \tag{3}$$

where $\hat{f}(\delta_\ell, \delta, \delta_r)$ is $\Pi \setminus \mathrm{enc}(\{f(\delta_\ell, \delta, \delta_r), \$\})$. Note that (3) only detects wrong transitions if a long enough next configuration exists. The case that the run stops prematurely is covered in (C).

Expression (3) is not readily encoded in a ptNFA because of the leading Π^*. To address this, we replace Π^* by the expression $\Pi^{\leq |W_{n,n}|-1}$, which matches every word $w \in \Pi^*$ with $|w| \leq |W_{n,n}| - 1$. Clearly, this suffices for our case because the computations of interest are of length $|W_{n,n}|$ and a violation of a correct computation must occur. As $|W_{n,n}| - 1$ is exponential, we cannot encode it directly and we use $\mathrm{enc}(\mathcal{A}_{n,n})$ instead.

In detail, let E be the expression obtained from (3) by omitting the initial Π^*, and let $\mathcal{B}_1$ be an incomplete DFA that accepts the language of E constructed as follows. From the initial state, we construct a tree-shaped DFA corresponding to all words of length three of the finite language $\sum_{\delta_\ell, \delta, \delta_r \in \Delta_{\#\$}} \mathrm{enc}(\delta_\ell \delta \delta_r)$. To every leaf state, we add a path under Π of length $p(|x|) - 1$. The result corresponds to the language $\sum_{\delta_\ell, \delta, \delta_r \in \Delta_{\#\$}} \mathrm{enc}(\delta_\ell \delta \delta_r) \cdot \Pi^{p(|x|)-1}$. Let $q_{\delta_\ell \delta \delta_r}$ denote the states uniquely determined by the words in $\mathrm{enc}(\delta_\ell \delta \delta_r) \cdot \Pi^{p(|x|)-1}$. We add the transitions $q_{\delta_\ell \delta \delta_r} \xrightarrow{\mathrm{enc}(\hat{f}(\delta_\ell, \delta, \delta_r))} max'$, where max' is a new accepting state. The automaton is illustrated in the upper part of Fig. 5, denoted $\mathcal{B}_1$. It is an incomplete DFA for language E of polynomial size. It is incomplete only in states $q_{\delta_r \delta \delta_\ell}$ due to the missing transitions under $\mathrm{enc}(f(\delta_\ell, \delta, \delta_r))$ and $\mathrm{enc}(\$)$. We complete it by adding the missing transitions to the states of the ptNFA $\mathcal{A}_{n,n}$. Namely, for $z \in \{\mathrm{enc}(f(\delta_\ell, \delta, \delta_r)), \mathrm{enc}(\$)\}$, we add $q_{\delta_\ell \delta \delta_r} \xrightarrow{z} (n+1; i)$ if $z[1] = a_i$.

We construct a ptNFA $\mathcal{B}$ accepting the language $(\Pi^* \setminus \{\mathrm{enc}(W_{n,n})\}) + (\Pi^{\leq |W_{n,n}|-1} \cdot E)$ by merging $\mathrm{enc}(\mathcal{A}_{n,n})$ with at most $n(n+1)$ copies of $\mathcal{B}_1$, where we identify the initial state of each such copy with a unique accepting state of $\mathrm{enc}(\mathcal{A}_{n,n})$, if it does not violate the property of ptNFAs (Fig. 1). This is justified by Corollary 2, since we do not need to consider connecting $\mathcal{B}_1$ to non-accepting states of $\mathcal{A}_{n,n}$ and it is not possible to connect it to state max. We further identify state max' of every copy of $\mathcal{B}_1$ with state max of $\mathcal{A}_{n,n}$. The fact that $\mathrm{enc}(\mathcal{A}_{n,n})$ alone accepts $(\Pi^* \setminus \{\mathrm{enc}(W_{n,n})\})$ was shown in Lemma 2. This also implies that it accepts all words of length $\leq |W_{n,n}| - 1$ as needed to show that $(\Pi^{\leq |W_{n,n}|-1} \cdot E)$ is accepted. Entering states of (a copy of) $\mathcal{B}_1$ after

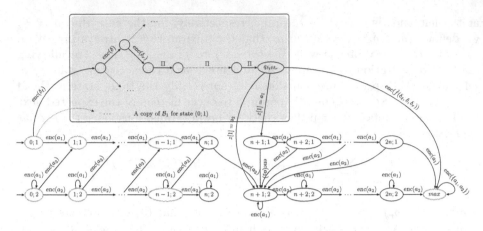

Fig. 5. ptNFA $\mathcal{B}$ consisting of $enc(\mathcal{A}_{n,n}), n = 2$, with, for illustration, only one copy of ptNFA $\mathcal{B}_1$ for the case the initial state of $\mathcal{B}_1$ is identified with state $(0;1)$ and state max' with state max

accepting a word of length $\geq |W_{n,n}|$ is possible but all such words are longer than $W_{n,n}$ and hence in $(\Pi^* \setminus \{enc(W_{n,n})\})$.

Let w be a word that is not accepted by (a copy of) $\mathcal{B}_1$. Then, there are words u and v such that u leads $enc(\mathcal{A}_{n,n})$ to a state from which w is read in a copy of $\mathcal{B}_1$. Since w is not accepted, there is a letter z and a word v such that uwz goes to state $(n + 1; i)$ of $\mathcal{A}_{n,n}$ (for $z[1] = a_i$) and v leads $enc(\mathcal{A}_{n,n})$ from state $(n + 1; i)$ to state max. If $u[1]w[1]a_iv[1] = W_{n,n,}$, then v is not accepted from $(n + 1; i)$ by Corollary 1, and hence $uwzv[1] \neq W_{n,n}$.

It remains to show that for every proper prefix $w_{n,n}$ of $W_{n,n}$, there is a state in $\mathcal{A}_{n,n}$ reached by $w_{n,n}$ that is the initial state of a copy of $\mathcal{B}_1$, and hence the check represented by E in $\Pi^{\leq|W_{n,n}|-1} \cdot E$ can be performed. In other words, if $a_{n,n}$ denotes the letter following $w_{n,n}$ in $W_{n,n}$, then there must be a state reachable by $w_{n,n}$ in $\mathcal{A}_{n,n}$ that does not have a self-loop under $a_{n,n}$. However, this follows from the fact that $\mathcal{A}_{n,n}$ accepts everything but $W_{n,n}$, since then the DFA obtained from $\mathcal{A}_{n,n}$ by the standard subset construction has a path of length $\binom{2n}{n} - 1$ labeled with $W_{n,n}$ without any loop. Moreover, any state of this path in the DFA is a subset of states of $\mathcal{A}_{n,n}$, therefore at least one of the states reachable under $w_{n,n}$ in $\mathcal{A}_{n,n}$ does not have a self-loop under $a_{n,n}$.

The ptNFA $\mathcal{B}$ thus accepts the language $\Pi^{\leq|W_{n,n}|-1} \cdot E + (\Pi^* \setminus \{enc(W_{n,n})\})$.

Finally, for **(C)**, we detect all words that (C.1) end in a configuration that is incomplete (too short), (C.2) end in a configuration that is not in the accepting state q_f, (C.3) end with more than $p(|x|)$ trailing \$, or (C.4) contain \$ not only at the last positions, that is, we detect all words where \$ is followed by a different symbol. For a word v, we use $v^{\leq i}$ to abbreviate $\varepsilon + v + \ldots + v^i$, and we define $\bar{E}_f = (T \times (Q \setminus \{q_f\}))$.

(C.1) $\Pi^* \text{enc}(\#)(\Pi + \ldots + \Pi^{p(|x|)}) \text{enc}(\$)^{\leq p(|x|)} +$
(C.2) $\Pi^* \text{enc}(\bar{E}_f)(\varepsilon + \Pi + \ldots + \Pi^{p(|x|)-1}) \text{enc}(\#) \text{enc}(\$)^{\leq p(|x|)} +$
(C.3) $\Pi^* \text{enc}(\$)^{p(|x|)+1} +$
(C.4) $(\Pi \setminus \text{enc}(\$))^* \text{enc}(\$) \text{enc}(\$)^*(\Pi \setminus \text{enc}(\$))\Pi^*$

$$(4)$$

As before, we cannot encode the expression directly as a ptNFA, but we can perform a similar construction as the one used for encoding (3).

The expressions (2)–(4) together then detect all non-accepting or wrongly encoded runs of $\mathcal{M}$. In particular, if we start from the correct initial configuration ((2) does not match), then for (3) not to match, all complete future configurations must have exactly one state and be delimited by encodings of $\#$. Expressing the regular expressions as a single ptNFA of polynomial size, we have thus reduced the word problem of polynomially space-bounded Turing machines to the universality problem for ptNFAs. $\square$

All missing proofs can be found in the full version of this paper [22].

References

1. Aho, A.V., Hopcroft, J.E., Ullman, J.D.: The Design and Analysis of Computer Algorithms. Addison-Wesley, Boston (1974)
2. Almeida, J., Costa, J.C., Zeitoun, M.: Pointlike sets with respect to R and J. J. Pure Appl. Algebra **212**(3), 486–499 (2008)
3. Barceló, P., Libkin, L., Reutter, J.L.: Querying regular graph patterns. J. ACM **61**(1), 8:1–8:54 (2014)
4. Bojanczyk, M., Segoufin, L., Straubing, H.: Piecewise testable tree languages. Logical Methods Comput. Sci. **8**(3) (2012)
5. Bouajjani, A., Muscholl, A., Touili, T.: Permutation rewriting and algorithmic verification. Inf. Comput. **205**(2), 199–224 (2007)
6. Brzozowski, J.A., Fich, F.E.: Languages of R-trivial monoids. J. Comput. Syst. Sci. **20**(1), 32–49 (1980)
7. Calvanese, D., De Giacomo, G., Lenzerini, M., Vardi, M.Y.: Reasoning on regular path queries. ACM SIGMOD Rec. **32**(4), 83–92 (2003)
8. Czerwiński, W., Martens, W., Masopust, T.: Efficient separability of regular languages by subsequences and suffixes. In: Fomin, F.V., Freivalds, R., Kwiatkowska, M., Peleg, D. (eds.) ICALP 2013. LNCS, vol. 7966, pp. 150–161. Springer, Heidelberg (2013). https://doi.org/10.1007/978-3-642-39212-2_16
9. Diekert, V., Gastin, P., Kufleitner, M.: A survey on small fragments of first-order logic over finite words. Int. J. Found. Comput. Science **19**(3), 513–548 (2008)
10. Fu, J., Heinz, J., Tanner, H.G.: An algebraic characterization of strictly piecewise languages. In: Ogihara, M., Tarui, J. (eds.) TAMC 2011. LNCS, vol. 6648, pp. 252–263. Springer, Heidelberg (2011). https://doi.org/10.1007/978-3-642-20877-5_26
11. García, P., Ruiz, J.: Learning k-testable and k-piecewise testable languages from positive data. Grammars **7**, 125–140 (2004)
12. García, P., Vidal, E.: Inference of k-testable languages in the strict sense and application to syntactic pattern recognition. IEEE Trans. Pattern Anal. Mach. Intell. **12**(9), 920–925 (1990)

13. Garey, M.R., Johnson, D.S.: Computers and Intractability: A Guide to the Theory of NP-Completeness. W. H. Freeman, New York (1979)
14. Hofman, P., Martens, W.: Separability by short subsequences and subwords. In: Arenas, M., Ugarte, M. (eds.) ICDT 2015. LIPIcs, vol. 31, pp. 230–246. Schloss Dagstuhl - Leibniz-Zentrum fuer Informatik (2015). https://doi.org/10.4230/LIPIcs.ICDT.2015.230
15. Holub, Š., Jirásková, G., Masopust, T.: On upper and lower bounds on the length of alternating towers. In: Csuhaj-Varjú, E., Dietzfelbinger, M., Ésik, Z. (eds.) MFCS 2014. LNCS, vol. 8634, pp. 315–326. Springer, Heidelberg (2014). https://doi.org/10.1007/978-3-662-44522-8_27
16. Jones, N.D.: Space-bounded reducibility among combinatorial problems. J. Comput. Syst. Sci. **11**(1), 68–85 (1975)
17. Klíma, O., Polák, L.: Alternative automata characterization of piecewise testable languages. In: Béal, M.-P., Carton, O. (eds.) DLT 2013. LNCS, vol. 7907, pp. 289–300. Springer, Heidelberg (2013). https://doi.org/10.1007/978-3-642-38771-5_26
18. Kontorovich, L., Cortes, C., Mohri, M.: Kernel methods for learning languages. Theor. Comput. Sci. **405**(3), 223–236 (2008)
19. Krötzsch, M., Masopust, T., Thomazo, M.: Complexity of universality and related problems for partially ordered NFAs. Inf. Comput. Part 1 **255**, 177–192 (2017). https://doi.org/10.1016/j.ic.2017.06.004
20. Martens, W., Neven, F., Niewerth, M., Schwentick, T.: BonXai: combining the simplicity of DTD with the expressiveness of XML schema. In: Milo, T., Calvanese, D. (eds.) PODS 2015, pp. 145–156. ACM (2015). https://doi.org/10.1145/2745754.2745774
21. Masopust, T.: Piecewise testable languages and nondeterministic automata. In: Faliszewski, P., Muscholl, A., Niedermeier, R. (eds.) MFCS 2016. LIPIcs, vol. 58, pp. 67:1–67:14. Schloss Dagstuhl - Leibniz-Zentrum fuer Informatik (2016). https://doi.org/10.4230/LIPIcs.MFCS.2016.67
22. Masopust, T., Krötzsch, M.: Universality of confluent, self-loop deterministic partially ordered NFAs is hard (2017). http://arxiv.org/abs/1704.07860
23. Masopust, T., Thomazo, M.: On Boolean combinations forming piecewise testable languages. Theor. Comput. Sci. **682**, 165–179 (2017)
24. Meyer, A.R., Stockmeyer, L.J.: The equivalence problem for regular expressions with squaring requires exponential space. In: Symposium on Switching and Automata Theory, pp. 125–129. IEEE Computer Society (1972). https://doi.org/10.1109/SWAT.1972.29
25. Perrin, D., Pin, J.E.: Infinite Words: Automata, Semigroups, Logic and Games, Pure and Applied Mathematics, vol. 141. Academic Press, Cambridge (2004)
26. Place, T., van Rooijen, L., Zeitoun, M.: Separating regular languages by piecewise testable and unambiguous languages. In: Chatterjee, K., Sgall, J. (eds.) MFCS 2013. LNCS, vol. 8087, pp. 729–740. Springer, Heidelberg (2013). https://doi.org/10.1007/978-3-642-40313-2_64
27. Rampersad, N., Shallit, J., Xu, Z.: The computational complexity of universality problems for prefixes, suffixes, factors, and subwords of regular languages. Fundamenta Informatica **116**(1–4), 223–236 (2012)
28. Rogers, J., Heinz, J., Bailey, G., Edlefsen, M., Visscher, M., Wellcome, D., Wibel, S.: On languages piecewise testable in the strict sense. In: Ebert, C., Jäger, G., Michaelis, J. (eds.) MOL 2007/2009. LNCS (LNAI), vol. 6149, pp. 255–265. Springer, Heidelberg (2010). https://doi.org/10.1007/978-3-642-14322-9_19

29. Rogers, J., Heinz, J., Fero, M., Hurst, J., Lambert, D., Wibel, S.: Cognitive and sub-regular complexity. In: Morrill, G., Nederhof, M.-J. (eds.) FG 2012-2013. LNCS, vol. 8036, pp. 90–108. Springer, Heidelberg (2013). https://doi.org/10.1007/978-3-642-39998-5_6

30. Schwentick, T., Thérien, D., Vollmer, H.: Partially-ordered two-way automata: a new characterization of DA. In: Kuich, W., Rozenberg, G., Salomaa, A. (eds.) DLT 2001. LNCS, vol. 2295, pp. 239–250. Springer, Heidelberg (2002). https://doi.org/10.1007/3-540-46011-X_20

31. Simon, I.: Hierarchies of events with dot-depth one. Ph.D. thesis, University of Waterloo, Canada (1972)

32. Stefanoni, G., Motik, B., Krötzsch, M., Rudolph, S.: The complexity of answering conjunctive and navigational queries over OWL 2 EL knowledge bases. J. Artif. Intell. Res. **51**, 645–705 (2014)

33. Stockmeyer, L.J., Meyer, A.R.: Word problems requiring exponential time: preliminary report. In: Aho, A.V., Borodin, A., Constable, R.L., Floyd, R.W., Harrison, M.A., Karp, R.M., Strong, R. (eds.) ACM Symposium on the Theory of Computing, pp. 1–9. ACM (1973). https://doi.org/10.1145/800125.804029

Theoretical Aspects of Symbolic Automata

Hellis Tamm[1]([⊠]) and Margus Veanes[2]

[1] Tallinn University of Technology, Tallinn, Estonia
hellis@cs.ioc.ee
[2] Microsoft Research, Redmond, USA
margus@microsoft.com

Abstract. Symbolic finite automata extend classical automata by allowing infinite alphabets given by Boolean algebras and having transitions labeled by predicates over such algebras. Symbolic automata have been intensively studied recently and they have proven useful in several applications. We study some theoretical aspects of symbolic automata. Especially, we study minterms of symbolic automata, that is, the set of maximal satisfiable Boolean combinations of predicates of automata. We define canonical minterms of a language accepted by a symbolic automaton and show that these minterms can be used to define symbolic versions of some known classical automata. Also we show that canonical minterms have an important role in finding minimal nondeterministic symbolic automata. We show that Brzozowski's double-reversal method for minimizing classical deterministic automata as well as its generalization is applicable for symbolic automata.

1 Introduction

Symbolic finite automata are finite state automata with an alphabet given by a Boolean algebra which can possibly have an infinite domain, and with transitions labeled by predicates over such algebra. Symbolic finite automata are a generalization of nondeterministic finite automata (NFAs), with a motivation for their introduction coming from practical applications which require handling of large or infinite alphabets.

Automata with predicates was first mentioned in [18]. We consider symbolic finite automata as defined in [4], where predicates are drawn from a decidable Boolean algebra. These automata have been intensively studied recently, for example, in the context of minimization of deterministic symbolic automata [5], computing forward bisimulations for nondeterministic symbolic automata [6], learning symbolic automata [9], and others.

We study some theoretical aspects of symbolic automata. We call the languages accepted by symbolic automata *symbolic regular languages*. These languages can be expressed with *symbolic regular expressions*. A similar symbolic

This work was supported by the Estonian Ministry of Education and Research institutional research grant IUT33-13.

A. M. Tjoa et al. (Eds.): SOFSEM 2018, LNCS 10706, pp. 428–441, 2018.
https://doi.org/10.1007/978-3-319-73117-9_30

generalization of regular expressions, called *extended regular expressions*, was used in [11] where also intersection and negation operators were supported.

We study *minterms* of symbolic automata, that is, the set of maximal satisfiable Boolean combinations of predicates of automata. It was pointed out in [4,5] that minterms can be used as a finite alphabet when adapting classical automata algorithms to the symbolic setting. This is because a symbolic automaton has a finite number of transition predicates, implying that the set of minterms is finite as well. We show that any symbolic regular language has a minimal set of minterms, the minterms of its minimal deterministic automaton. This set of minterms is unique up to predicate equivalence. We show that this set of canonical minterms can be used in place of a finite alphabet to define symbolic versions of some known NFAs, such as the *symbolic átomaton* and *canonical symbolic residual finite state automaton* of the language. Also we show that the minterms of a language have an important role in finding minimal nondeterministic symbolic automata.

We show that Brzozowski's double-reversal method for minimizing classical deterministic automata as well as its generalization is applicable for symbolic automata.

2 Symbolic Regular Languages and Symbolic Finite Automata

An *effective Boolean algebra* B has components $(\Sigma, \Psi, [\![\_]\!], \bot, \top, \vee, \wedge, \neg)$, where Σ is a set of *domain elements*, Ψ is a set of *predicates* closed under the Boolean connectives, and $\bot, \top \in \Psi$. The *denotation function* $[\![\_]\!] : \Psi \to 2^{\Sigma}$ is such that $[\![\bot]\!] = \emptyset$, $[\![\top]\!] = \Sigma$, and for all $\varphi, \psi \in \Psi$, $[\![\varphi \vee \psi]\!] = [\![\varphi]\!] \cup [\![\psi]\!]$, $[\![\varphi \wedge \psi]\!] = [\![\varphi]\!] \cap [\![\psi]\!]$, and $[\![\neg\varphi]\!] = \Sigma \setminus [\![\varphi]\!]$. If $[\![\varphi]\!] \neq \emptyset$, then φ is *satisfiable*. We require that checking satisfiability is decidable.

A predicate φ is a *subpredicate* of ψ, if $[\![\varphi]\!] \subseteq [\![\psi]\!]$.

Elements of Σ are *characters*. A *word* over Σ is a sequence $a_{i_1} \cdots a_{i_m}$, where $a_{i_j} \in \Sigma$, $j = 1, \ldots, m$. If $m = 0$, then we get the *empty* word, denoted by ε. The set of all words over Σ is denoted by Σ^*. We require that $\Sigma^n \cap \Sigma = \emptyset$ for $n \geq 2$.

We define a *symbolic regular expression* as follows:

- The constants ε and $\emptyset$ are symbolic regular expressions, denoting the languages $\{\varepsilon\}$ and $\emptyset$, respectively.
- For any predicate $\varphi \in \Psi$, φ is a symbolic regular expression, denoting the language $L(\varphi) = [\![\varphi]\!]$.
- For any symbolic regular expressions X and Y, the expressions $X + Y$, XY, and X^* are symbolic regular expressions, denoting respectively the languages $L(X) \cup L(Y)$, $L(X)L(Y)$, and $(L(X))^*$.

Any language defined by a symbolic regular expression is a *symbolic regular language*.

A *symbolic nondeterministic finite automaton (s-NFA)* is a quintuple $\mathcal{N} = (B, Q, \Delta, I, F)$, where $B = (\Sigma, \Psi, [\![\_]\!], \bot, \top, \vee, \wedge, \neg)$ is an effective Boolean algebra, called the *alphabet*, Q is a finite set of *states*, $\Delta \subseteq Q \times \Psi \times Q$ is a finite set of *transitions*, $I \subseteq Q$ is the set of *initial states*, and $F \subseteq Q$ is the set of *final states*. The *left language* of a state q of $\mathcal{N}$, denoted by $L_{I,q}(\mathcal{N})$, is the set of words $w \in \Sigma^*$ such that, either $w = \varepsilon$ and $q \in I$, or $w = a_1 \ldots a_k$ and there exist states $q_1, \ldots, q_k \in Q$ such that $(q_{i-1}, \varphi_i, q_i) \in \Delta$ and $a_i \in \llbracket \varphi_i \rrbracket$, with $q_0 \in I$ and $q_k = q$. The *right language*, or simply, the *language* of a state q of $\mathcal{N}$, denoted by $L_{q,F}(\mathcal{N})$, or simply, $L_q(\mathcal{N})$, is the set of words $w \in \Sigma^*$ such that, either $w = \varepsilon$ and $q \in F$, or $w = a_1 \ldots a_k$ and there exist states $q_1, \ldots, q_k \in Q$ such that $(q_{i-1}, \varphi_i, q_i) \in \Delta$ and $a_i \in \llbracket \varphi_i \rrbracket$, with $q_0 = q$ and $q_k \in F$. A state is *unreachable* if its left language is empty. A state is *empty* if its right language is empty. An s-NFA is *trim* if it does not have any unreachable or empty states. The *language accepted* by $\mathcal{N}$ is $L(\mathcal{N}) = \bigcup_{q \in I} L_q(\mathcal{N})$. Two s-NFAs are *equivalent* if they accept the same language. The *reverse* of an s-NFA $\mathcal{N} = (B, Q, \Delta, I, F)$ is the s-NFA $\mathcal{N}^R = (B, Q, \Delta^R, F, I)$, where $(q, \varphi, p) \in \Delta^R$ if and only if $(p, \varphi, q) \in \Delta$ for $p, q \in Q$ and $\varphi \in \Psi$. An s-NFA $\mathcal{N}$ is *normalized for predicates* if for all $p, q \in Q$ there is at most one predicate φ such that $(p, \varphi, q) \in \Delta$. Any s-NFA $\mathcal{N}$ can be normalized, resulting in the s-NFA $\mathcal{N}^N$, where all distinct transitions (p, φ_1, q) and (p, φ_2, q) from any state p to any state q have been replaced by a single transition $(p, \varphi_1 \vee \varphi_2, q)$. An s-NFA $\mathcal{N}$ is *complete* if for every $p \in Q$ and $a \in \Sigma$, there is a transition $(p, \varphi, q) \in \Delta$ with $a \in \llbracket \varphi \rrbracket$, $q \in Q$. If $\mathcal{N}_1 = (B, Q_1, \Delta_1, I_1, F_1)$ and $\mathcal{N}_2 = (B, Q_2, \Delta_2, I_2, F_2)$ are s-NFAs, then a map π from Q_1 into Q_2 is a *morphism* from $\mathcal{N}_1$ into $\mathcal{N}_2$ if and only if $\pi(I_1) \subseteq I_2$, $\pi(F_1) \subseteq F_2$, and for all states $p, q \in Q_1$ and $a \in \Sigma$ it holds that if $(p, \varphi_1, q) \in \Delta_1$ for some φ_1 such that $a \in \llbracket \varphi_1 \rrbracket$, then there is some φ_2 such that $(\pi(p), \varphi_2, \pi(q)) \in \Delta_2$ and $a \in \llbracket \varphi_2 \rrbracket$.

Sometimes it is useful to allow transitions on the empty word ε in a symbolic automaton. A *symbolic nondeterministic finite automaton with epsilon transitions (s-εNFA)* is $\mathcal{N} = (B, Q, \Delta, I, F)$, where B, Q, I, and F are as in an s-NFA, and $\Delta \subseteq Q \times (\Psi \cup \{\varepsilon\}) \times Q$.

Similarly to regular languages, one can show that symbolic regular languages are accepted by s-NFAs and *vice versa*.

We can apply the well-known Thompson's construction [15,17] to a symbolic regular expression, to obtain an s-εNFA. We present a slightly modified version of this construction in the following proposition:

Proposition 1. *Every symbolic regular language is accepted by an s-εNFA.*

Proof. An s-εNFA can be constructed from any symbolic regular expression, using structural induction which involves parts described as follows: First, the s-εNFAs for the constants ε and $\emptyset$ are respectively $\mathcal{N}_\varepsilon = (B, \{q\}, \emptyset, \{q\}, \{q\})$ and $\mathcal{N}_\emptyset = (B, \emptyset, \emptyset, \emptyset, \emptyset)$, and the s-$\varepsilon$NFA for any predicate $\varphi \in \Psi$ is $\mathcal{N}_\varphi = (B, \{q_1, q_2\}, \{(q_1, \varphi, q_2)\}, \{q_1\}, \{q_2\})$.

Now, let $\mathcal{N}_X = (B, Q_X, \Delta_X, I_X, F_X)$ be the s-εNFA for the expression X, and let $\mathcal{N}_Y = (B, Q_Y, \Delta_Y, I_Y, F_Y)$ be the s-εNFA for the expression Y, where the sets Q_X and Q_Y are disjoint. The s-εNFAs for the expressions XY, $X + Y$, and X^* are respectively $\mathcal{N}_{XY} = (B, Q_X \cup Q_Y, \Delta_X \cup \Delta_Y \cup (F_X \times \{\varepsilon\} \times I_Y), I_X, F_Y)$, $\mathcal{N}_{X+Y} = (B, Q_X \cup Q_Y \cup \{q_1, q_2\}, \Delta_X \cup \Delta_Y \cup (\{q_1\} \times \{\varepsilon\} \times (I_X \cup I_Y)) \cup ((F_X \cup F_Y) \times \{\varepsilon\} \times \{q_2\}), \{q_1\}, \{q_2\})$, and $\mathcal{N}_{X^*} = (B, Q_X \cup \{q_1, q_2\}, \Delta_X \cup (\{q_1\} \times \{\varepsilon\} \times (I_X \cup \{q_2\})) \cup (F_X \times \{\varepsilon\} \times (I_X \cup \{q_2\})), \{q_1\}, \{q_2\})$, where $q_1, q_2 \notin Q_X \cup Q_Y$. $\square$

Similarly to finite automata accepting regular languages, an s-εNFA can be converted to an equivalent s-NFA by eliminating epsilon transitions by standard methods.

An s-NFA $\mathcal{N} = (B, Q, \Delta, I, F)$ is a *symbolic deterministic finite automaton (s-DFA)* if $|I| = 1$ and if for all transitions $(p, \varphi, q), (p', \varphi', q') \in \Delta$ it holds that if $p = p'$ and $\varphi \wedge \varphi'$ is satisfiable, then $q = q'$. An s-NFA $\mathcal{N}$ can be *determinized* to obtain an equivalent s-DFA $\mathcal{N}^D = (B, Q^D, \Delta^D, \{s_0\}, F^D)$, using a symbolic version [16] of the well-known subset construction procedure. We present here a slightly modified variant of it which produces a complete and normalized s-DFA. Similarly to the classical subset construction, this procedure gradually forms the set Q^D of states, along with the set Δ^D of transitions of $\mathcal{N}^D$, including only reachable states, starting with $Q^D = \{I\}$ and $\Delta^D = \emptyset$. For every $s \in Q^D$, we do the following steps: first, we form the set S_s of states q of $\mathcal{N}$ such that there is a transition $(p, \varphi, q) \in \Delta$ from a state $p \in s$ to q with some $\varphi \in \Psi$; then, for all $q \in S_s$, let $\varphi_{s,q} = \bigvee_{(p,\varphi,q) \in \Delta, p \in s} \varphi$; for every $s' \subseteq S_s$, let $\varphi_{s,s'} = (\bigwedge_{q \in s'} \varphi_{s,q}) \wedge (\bigwedge_{q \in S_s \setminus s'} \neg \varphi_{s,q})$; if $\varphi_{s,s'}$ is satisfiable, then we add s' to Q^D (if $s' \notin Q^D$) and add the transition $(s, \varphi_{s,s'}, s')$ to Δ^D. Finally, we let $s_0 = I$ and $F^D = \{s \in Q^D \mid s \cap F \neq \emptyset\}$.

We assume for the rest of the paper that s-DFAs are complete. An s-DFA is *minimal* if it has the minimal number of states among all equivalent s-DFAs. We also require that a minimal s-DFA is normalized for predicates. A minimal s-DFA is unique up to renaming of states and equivalence of predicates [5]. In the minimal s-DFA, the languages of any two distinct states are different from each other. It is easy to see that every predicate occurring in any s-DFA with reachable states only, is a subpredicate of some predicate of the minimal s-DFA of the same language. This is because the minimal s-DFA can be obtained from any such s-DFA by merging some states and transitions.

3   Brzozowski's Theorem for Symbolic Automata

In this section we consider non-empty symbolic regular languages. We show the symbolic version of a (slightly modified) classical result by Brzozowski [2]:

Theorem 1. *If an s-NFA $\mathcal{N}$ has no empty states and $\mathcal{N}^R$ is an s-DFA, then $\mathcal{N}^D$ is minimal.*

Proof. Let $\mathcal{N} = (B, Q, \Delta, I, F)$ be an s-NFA with no empty states such that its reverse s-NFA $\mathcal{N}^R = (B, Q, \Delta^R, F, I)$ is an s-DFA. We note that F is a singleton set. If $|Q| = 1$, then $\mathcal{N}$ and $\mathcal{N}^R$ are the same automata. The determinized version $\mathcal{N}^D$ of $\mathcal{N}$ is complete and normalized, and has one or two states. In the former case $\mathcal{N}^D$ is clearly minimal. In the latter case, one of the states of $\mathcal{N}^D$ is the initial state with a non-empty language, and the other is an empty state, so the languages of these two states are different, implying that $\mathcal{N}^D$ is minimal.

We now consider the case where $|Q| \geq 2$. Let $q, q' \in Q$, with $q \neq q'$. We show that $L_q(\mathcal{N}) \cap L_{q'}(\mathcal{N}) = \emptyset$. Indeed, suppose that there is a word $w \in \Sigma^*$ such that $w \in L_q(\mathcal{N})$ and $w \in L_{q'}(\mathcal{N})$. If $w = \varepsilon$, then both q and q' must be final, but since $\mathcal{N}$ has only one final state, we have a contradiction. If $w = a_1 \ldots a_k$, where $k \geq 1$, then there are some states $q_{i-1}, q'_{i-1}, q_i \in Q$ such that $q_{i-1} \neq q'_{i-1}$, and transitions $(q_{i-1}, \varphi, q_i), (q'_{i-1}, \varphi', q_i) \in \Delta$ with $a_i \in [\![\varphi]\!]$ and $a_i \in [\![\varphi']\!]$. Therefore, $\varphi \wedge \varphi'$ is satisfiable, implying that $\mathcal{N}^R$ is not deterministic, a contradiction.

Now, let s_1 and s_2 be any two states of $\mathcal{N}^D$, where $s_1 \neq s_2$. We show that $L_{s_1}(\mathcal{N}^D) \neq L_{s_2}(\mathcal{N}^D)$. Indeed, because both s_1 and s_2 are subsets of Q, there is a state $q \in Q$ such that either $q \in s_1$ and $q \notin s_2$, or $q \in s_2$ and $q \notin s_1$. Since $L_{s_1}(\mathcal{N}^D) = \bigcup_{q \in s_1} L_q(\mathcal{N})$ and $L_{s_2}(\mathcal{N}^D) = \bigcup_{q \in s_2} L_q(\mathcal{N})$, and because we assumed that $L_q(\mathcal{N}) \neq \emptyset$ for any $q \in Q$, and showed above that $L_q(\mathcal{N}) \cap L_{q'}(\mathcal{N}) = \emptyset$ for every $q, q' \in Q$ with $q \neq q'$, it holds that $L_{s_1}(\mathcal{N}^D) \neq L_{s_2}(\mathcal{N}^D)$. Therefore, $\mathcal{N}^D$ is minimal. □

Based on Theorem 1, similarly to its classical version, it is possible to get a minimization algorithm for s-DFAs which we call *Brzozowski's minimization* or *double-reversal minimization* algorithm. By this algorithm, the minimal s-DFA of a language can be obtained from any s-NFA $\mathcal{N}$ by first applying the determinization procedure to the reverse $\mathcal{N}^R$ of $\mathcal{N}$ to obtain an s-DFA $\mathcal{N}^{RD}$ of the reverse language, and then applying determinization to its reverse $\mathcal{N}^{RDR}$ to obtain the s-DFA $\mathcal{N}^{RDRD}$. By Theorem 1, $\mathcal{N}^{RDRD}$ is a minimal s-DFA.

4   Minterms of Symbolic Automata

Let L be a symbolic regular language. Let $\mathcal{N}$ be an s-NFA of L and let $\mathcal{N}^N$ be the s-NFA obtained from $\mathcal{N}$ by predicate normalization. Let $\varphi_1, \ldots, \varphi_k$ be the predicates occurring in $\mathcal{N}^N$. Any satisfiable predicate $(\bigwedge_{i \in S} \varphi_i) \wedge (\bigwedge_{i \in \overline{S}} \neg\varphi_i)$ with $S \subseteq \{1, \ldots, k\}$ and $\overline{S} = \{1, \ldots, k\} \setminus S$ is a *minterm* of $\mathcal{N}$. Obviously, $\mathcal{N}$ and $\mathcal{N}^N$ have the same set of minterms. Also, it is easy to see that every predicate of $\mathcal{N}^N$ is a disjunction of minterms of $\mathcal{N}$. The minterms of $\mathcal{N}$ provide a partition of Σ.

We show that the minterms of any s-NFA of L are a refinement of the minterms of the minimal s-DFA of L.

Proposition 2. *Any minterm of an s-NFA of L is a subpredicate of some minterm of the minimal s-DFA of L.*

Proof. Let us first consider an s-NFA $\mathcal{N}$ that has only reachable states, and its normalized variant $\mathcal{N}^N$. We notice that the determinized versions $\mathcal{N}^D$ and $\mathcal{N}^{ND}$ of these two automata are the same s-DFAs (up to predicate equivalence). Let $s \subseteq Q$ be a state of $\mathcal{N}^{ND}$. Let $\varphi_1, \ldots, \varphi_k$ be the predicates occurring in $\mathcal{N}^N$ as the labels of out-transitions of the states $p \in s$, and let $\psi_1, \ldots, \psi_\ell$ be the predicates in $\mathcal{N}^{ND}$ which occur as the labels of out-transitions of s. According to how $\mathcal{N}^{ND}$ is constructed from $\mathcal{N}^N$, we notice that every ψ_j is a disjunction of predicates of the form $(\bigwedge_{i \in S} \varphi_i) \wedge (\bigwedge_{i \in \overline{S}} \neg\varphi_i)$, where $S \subseteq \{1, \ldots, k\}$ and $\overline{S} = \{1, \ldots, k\} \setminus S$, therefore any predicate $(\bigwedge_{i \in S} \varphi_i) \wedge (\bigwedge_{i \in \overline{S}} \neg\varphi_i)$ is a subpredicate of some ψ_j. Since $\mathcal{N}^{ND}$ is deterministic, $\psi_h \wedge \psi_j$ is not satisfiable if $h \neq j$, and thus

$(\bigwedge_{i \in S} \varphi_i) \wedge (\bigwedge_{i \in \overline{S}} \neg \varphi_i)$ is a subpredicate of $\psi_j \wedge (\bigwedge_{h \in \{1,...,\ell\}, h \neq j} \neg \psi_h)$. Because every minterm of $\mathcal{N}^N$ is a conjunction of predicates of the form $(\bigwedge_{i \in S} \varphi_i) \wedge (\bigwedge_{i \in \overline{S}} \neg \varphi_i)$, and every minterm of $\mathcal{N}^{ND}$ is a conjunction of predicates of the form $\psi_j \wedge (\bigwedge_{h \in \{1,...,\ell\}, h \neq j} \neg \psi_h)$, it is easy to see that every minterm of $\mathcal{N}^N$ is a subpredicate of some minterm of $\mathcal{N}^{ND}$. Because the minterms of $\mathcal{N}$ and $\mathcal{N}^N$ are equal, and the same holds for the minterms of $\mathcal{N}^D$ and $\mathcal{N}^{ND}$, we get that every minterm of $\mathcal{N}$ is a subpredicate of some minterm of $\mathcal{N}^D$.

Furthermore, because every predicate occurring in any s-DFA that has only reachable states, is a subpredicate of some predicate of the minimal s-DFA (see the end of Sect. 2), it is implied that any minterm of $\mathcal{N}^D$ is a subpredicate of some minterm of the minimal s-DFA of L. Thus, any minterm of $\mathcal{N}$ is a subpredicate of some minterm of the minimal s-DFA of L.

Now, let us consider the case where an s-NFA $\mathcal{N}$ has some unreachable states. It was shown above that any minterm of the reachable part of $\mathcal{N}$ is a subpredicate of a minterm of the minimal s-DFA. It is clear that every minterm of $\mathcal{N}$ is a subpredicate of some minterm of the reachable part of $\mathcal{N}$. We conclude that any minterm of $\mathcal{N}$ is a subpredicate of some minterm of the minimal s-DFA of L. □

Proposition 3. *Let $\mathcal{N}$ be an s-NFA and let $\mathcal{D}$ be the minimal s-DFA of L. Any minterm of $\mathcal{D}$ is a disjunction of minterms of $\mathcal{N}$.*

Proof. The minterms of $\mathcal{N}$ partition Σ, and so do the minterms of $\mathcal{D}$. Since by Proposition 2, any minterm of $\mathcal{N}$ is a subpredicate of some minterm of $\mathcal{D}$, we conclude that any minterm of $\mathcal{D}$ is a disjunction of minterms of $\mathcal{N}$. □

Considering that the minterms of any s-NFA of L are a refinement of the minterms of the minimal s-DFA of L, we call the latter the (canonical) minterms of L. Denoting the reverse language of L by L^R, we can show the following:

Proposition 4. *The minterms of L and L^R are the same.*

Proof. Let $\mathcal{D}$ be the minimal s-DFA of L. By Theorem 1, the minimal s-DFA of L^R can be obtained by reversing $\mathcal{D}$ and determinizing the resulting s-NFA $\mathcal{D}^R$ to get $\mathcal{D}^{RD}$. The set of transition predicates of $\mathcal{D}^R$ is the same as the set of transition predicates of $\mathcal{D}$, because reversing an automaton does not change predicates. Similarly, we get that the minterms of $\mathcal{D}^R$ are the minterms of $\mathcal{D}$. The predicates of $\mathcal{D}^{RD}$ are formed by using Boolean operations on predicates of $\mathcal{D}^R$, and the resulting predicates are disjunctions of minterms of $\mathcal{D}^R$. Thus, the minterms of $\mathcal{D}^{RD}$ are disjunctions of the minterms of $\mathcal{D}$.

By a similar reasoning as above we can obtain that the minterms of $\mathcal{D}$ are disjunctions of the minterms of $\mathcal{D}^{RD}$. We conclude that the minterms of $\mathcal{D}$ and $\mathcal{D}^{RD}$ are the same, that is, the minterms of L and L^R are the same. □

We note that although a symbolic regular language L can be defined over an infinite alphabet, the set of minterms of any s-NFA of L is finite, because an s-NFA has a finite number of transitions. It is pointed out in [4,5] that minterms can be used as an alphabet when adapting classical automata algorithms to the

symbolic setting. Based on the results above, every symbolic regular language
has a minimal set of minterms which is unique (up to predicate equivalence), with
the reverse language having the same set of minterms. This set of minterms can
be used in place of a finite alphabet to define several kind of symbolic automata
for a given language as will be shown in Sect. 6.

5   Quotients and Atoms of Symbolic Languages

Similarly to the case of regular languages, the *left quotient*, or simply *quotient*,
of a symbolic regular language L by a word $w \in \Sigma^*$ is the language $w^{-1}L =
\{x \in \Sigma^* \mid wx \in L\}$. There is one *initial* quotient, $\varepsilon^{-1}L = L$. A quotient is *final*
if it contains ε. Left quotients of L are the languages of the states of the minimal
s-DFA of L.

   Atoms of regular languages were introduced in [1] as non-empty intersections
of complemented or uncomplemented quotients of the language. In [10] it was
shown that atoms are the left congruence classes of the language. In the same
way, we can define atoms of symbolic regular languages. For a symbolic regular
language L, the *left congruence* $_L\equiv$ of L is defined as follows: for $x, y \in \Sigma^*$,
$x_L\equiv y$ if for every $u \in \Sigma^*$, $ux \in L$ if and only if $uy \in L$. An *atom* of L is a left
congruence class of L. Thus, an atom is a set of words which belong exactly to
the same quotients. That is, an atom of a language L with quotients $K_1, \ldots, K_n$
is any non-empty language of the form $\widetilde{K_1} \cap \cdots \cap \widetilde{K_n}$, where $\widetilde{K_i}$ is either K_i or
$\overline{K_i}$, and $\overline{K_i}$ is the complement of K_i with respect to Σ^*. It is easy to see that
every quotient K_i is a union of atoms. An atom is *initial* if it has L (rather than
$\overline{L}$) as a term; it is *final* if it contains ε. There is exactly one final atom, the atom
$\widehat{K_1} \cap \cdots \cap \widehat{K_n}$, where $\widehat{K_i} = K_i$ if $\varepsilon \in K_i$, and $\widehat{K_i} = \overline{K_i}$ otherwise.

   For any s-NFA $\mathcal{N} = (B, Q, \Delta, I, F)$ with a state set $Q = \{q_1, \ldots, q_n\}$ we can
define a language equation for each state q_i as

$$L_i = \bigcup_{(q_i, \varphi, q_j) \in \Delta} \llbracket \varphi \rrbracket L_j \cup L_i^\varepsilon, \quad i = 1, \ldots, n, \tag{1}$$

where $L_i^\varepsilon = \{\varepsilon\}$ if $q_i \in F$, and $L_i^\varepsilon = \emptyset$ otherwise. This is similar to the way the
language equations were defined for NFAs in [1]. Also similarly to what was done
in [1], we can obtain equations for atoms of L, using the language equations of
the minimal s-DFA of L. Namely, because quotients are the languages of the
states of the minimal s-DFA, and atoms are intersections of complemented or
uncomplemented quotients, we can express atoms by taking intersections of the
right sides of the equations of the minimal s-DFA, or their negations.

   We consider the minimal s-DFA $\mathcal{D} = (B, Q, \Delta, I, F)$ of L, with a state set
$Q = \{q_1, \ldots, q_n\}$. Since the language of any state q_i of $\mathcal{D}$ is some quotient K_i,
the equations

$$K_i = \bigcup_{(q_i, \varphi_{i_j}, q_j) \in \Delta} \llbracket \varphi_{i_j} \rrbracket K_j \cup K_i^\varepsilon, \quad i = 1, \ldots, n, \tag{2}$$

hold, where $K_i^\varepsilon = \{\varepsilon\}$ if $\varepsilon \in K_i$, and $K_i^\varepsilon = \emptyset$ otherwise. Because any atom A_h can be presented as an intersection $A_h = \bigcap_{i \in S_h} K_i \cap \bigcap_{i \in \overline{S_h}} \overline{K_i}$, where $S_h \subseteq \{1, \dots, n\}$ and $\overline{S_h} = \{1, \dots, n\} \setminus S_h$, we can compute the language equation for A_h from the following expression:

$$A_h = \bigcap_{i \in S_h} \left(\bigcup_{(q_i, \varphi_{i_j}, q_j) \in \Delta} [\![\varphi_{i_j}]\!] K_j \cup K_i^\varepsilon \right) \cap \bigcap_{i \in \overline{S_h}} \overline{\left(\bigcup_{(q_i, \varphi_{i_j}, q_j) \in \Delta} [\![\varphi_{i_j}]\!] K_j \cup K_i^\varepsilon \right)}. \qquad (3)$$

Since atoms are intersections of complemented or uncomplemented quotients, we can convert formula (3), similarly to how a logical formula is converted into its full disjunctive normal form, into the expression

$$A_h = [\![\varphi_{h_1}]\!] A_{h_1} \cup \cdots \cup [\![\varphi_{h_k}]\!] A_{h_k} \cup A_h^\varepsilon, \qquad (4)$$

where $\varphi_{h_1}, \dots, \varphi_{h_k}$ are obtained by applying Boolean operations on the predicates appearing in (3), $A_{h_1}, \dots, A_{h_k}$ are some atoms of L, and $A_h^\varepsilon = \{\varepsilon\}$ if $\varepsilon \in A_h$, and $A_h^\varepsilon = \emptyset$ otherwise. Clearly, $\varphi_{h_1}, \dots, \varphi_{h_k}$ are disjunctions of minterms of L. Based on this observation, we can state the following proposition:

Proposition 5. *Let φ be a minterm of L. If $aA_j \subseteq A_i$ holds for some $a \in [\![\varphi]\!]$ and atoms A_i, A_j of L, then $[\![\varphi]\!] A_j \subseteq A_i$ holds.*

More generally, we show the following:

Proposition 6. *Let φ be a minterm of L. If $aL_j \subseteq L_i$ holds for some $a \in [\![\varphi]\!]$ and unions of atoms L_i, L_j of L, then $[\![\varphi]\!] L_j \subseteq L_i$ holds.*

Proof. Let $aL_j \subseteq L_i$ hold for some $a \in [\![\varphi]\!]$ and languages L_i, L_j consisting of unions of atoms of L. Then for every $A_h \subseteq L_j$ there is an atom $A_g \subseteq L_i$ such that $aA_h \subseteq A_g$. By Proposition 5, for every $A_h \subseteq L_j$ there is an atom $A_g \subseteq L_i$ such that $[\![\varphi]\!] A_h \subseteq A_g$ holds. Therefore, $[\![\varphi]\!] L_j \subseteq L_i$ holds. $\qquad \square$

We will make use of Proposition 6 in the next section, where we define several s-NFAs for a given language.

6 Generating Symbolic Automata

In this section we consider the symbolic version of a method presented in [14] for generating NFAs from a set of languages. Similarly as in [14], we show that with this method we can define symbolic versions of some known NFAs. For the method to be able to work in the symbolic setting, minterms of a symbolic language prove to be very useful.

Let L be a symbolic regular language. We define a set $\{L_1, \dots, L_k\}$ of languages to be a *cover* of L, if every quotient K_j of L is a union of some L_i's. We say that a cover is *atomic* if every L_i is a union of atoms of L. We note that since L is the quotient of itself by the empty word ε, L is a union of some L_i's. We define the s-NFA based on an atomic cover $\{L_1, \dots, L_k\}$ as follows:

Definition 1. *The s-NFA generated by an atomic cover* $\{L_1, \ldots, L_k\}$ *of* L *is defined by* $\mathcal{G} = (B, Q, \Delta, I, F)$, *where* $Q = \{q_1, \ldots, q_k\}$, $I = \{q_i \mid L_i \subseteq L\}$, $F = \{q_i \mid \varepsilon \in L_i\}$, *and* $(q_i, \varphi, q_j) \in \Delta$ *if and only if* $[\![\varphi]\!]L_j \subseteq L_i$ *for* $q_i, q_j \in Q$ *and a minterm* φ *of* L.

Next, we present some properties of an s-NFA $\mathcal{G} = (B, Q, \Delta, I, F)$ generated by an atomic cover $\{L_1, \ldots, L_k\}$ of L. These results, originally presented for NFAs and general covers in [14], also fit into the symbolic setting. Proofs can be found in [14]; in the symbolic version, only minor adjustments are needed.

Proposition 7. *The following properties hold for s-NFA* $\mathcal{G}$:

1. $L_{q_i}(\mathcal{G}) \subseteq L_i$ *for every* $q_i \in Q$.
2. $L(\mathcal{G}) \subseteq L$.

We note that because of Proposition 6, it holds for every pair L_i, L_j of Definition 1 that whenever the inclusion $L_j \subseteq a^{-1}L_i$ holds for some $a \in \Sigma$, there is a transition (q_i, φ, q_j) of $\mathcal{G}$ such that $a \in [\![\varphi]\!]$. This property ensures that the following proposition holds:

Proposition 8. *The equality* $L_{q_i}(\mathcal{G}) = L_i$ *holds for every* $q_i \in Q$ *if and only if* $a^{-1}L_i$ *is a union of* L_j's *for every* L_i *and* $a \in \Sigma$.

Next property easily follows from Proposition 8:

Proposition 9. *If* $a^{-1}L_i$ *is a union of* L_j's *for every* L_i *and* $a \in \Sigma$, *then* $\mathcal{G}$ *accepts* L.

A simple example of an atomic cover is the set $A = \{A_1, \ldots, A_m\}$ of atoms of L, where A_m is the final atom. We can define a symbolic version of the NFA called the *átomaton* [1], as follows:

Definition 2. *The* symbolic átomaton *of* L *is the s-NFA* $\mathcal{A} = (B, Q, \Delta, I, \{q_m\})$, *where* $Q = \{q_1, \ldots, q_m\}$, $I = \{q_i \mid A_i \subseteq L\}$, *and* $(q_i, \varphi, q_j) \in \Delta$ *if and only if* $[\![\varphi]\!]A_j \subseteq A_i$ *for* $A_i, A_j \in A$ *and a minterm* φ *of* L.

It is known that for every atom A_i and $a \in \Sigma$, $a^{-1}A_i$ is a union of atoms [1]. Thus, by Proposition 8 it holds that $L_{q_i}(\mathcal{A}) = A_i$ for every $q_i \in Q$, and it follows from Proposition 9 that $L(\mathcal{A}) = L$. Also similarly to the classical case in [1], one can see that the predicate-normalized version of $\mathcal{A}^R$ is a minimal s-DFA of the reverse language L^R.

As another example of an atomic cover, consider the set $K' = \{K'_1, \ldots, K'_k\}$ of *prime* quotients of L, that is, those non-empty quotients of L which are not unions of other quotients. Based on this cover, we define an s-NFA as follows:

Definition 3. *The* canonical symbolic residual finite state automaton (canonical s-RFSA) *of* L *is the s-NFA* $\mathcal{R} = (B, Q, \Delta, I, F)$, *where* $Q = \{q_1, \ldots, q_k\}$, $I = \{q_i \mid K'_i \subseteq L\}$, *and* $(q_i, \varphi, q_j) \in \Delta$ *if and only if* $[\![\varphi]\!]K'_j \subseteq K'_i$ *for* $K'_i, K'_j \in K'$ *and a minterm* φ *of* L.

Since every quotient of L is a union of some prime quotients of L, for every prime quotient K_i' and $a \in \Sigma$, $a^{-1}K_i'$ is a union of prime quotients. In the same way as in the example above, one can see that the right language of a state $q_i \in Q$ is some prime quotient K_i', and that $L(\mathcal{R}) = L$. The classical NFA version of $\mathcal{R}$ is known as the *canonical residual finite state automaton* [7] of a language. *Residual finite state automata (RFSAs)* are NFAs where the languages of its states are some *residuals*, that is, quotients of the language. Some properties of RFSAs in the learning context have been studied in [8]. It would be interesting to study symbolic versions of these automata as well.

6.1 Generating Minimal s-NFAs

We show that atomic covers and minterms of the language can be used to find minimal s-NFAs. Our approach here is similar to the way of finding minimal NFAs in [14].

Let $\mathcal{N} = (B, Q, \Delta, I, F)$ be a trim s-NFA accepting a symbolic regular language L, with $Q = \{q_1, \ldots, q_k\}$. For every state q_i of $\mathcal{N}$, we define a language $C_i = \bigcap_{L_{q_i}(\mathcal{N}) \subseteq K_h} K_h$ as the intersection of all quotients of L which contain the right language of q_i as a subset. Clearly, the inclusion $L_{q_i}(\mathcal{N}) \subseteq C_i$ holds. Since every quotient is a union of atoms, C_i is also a union of atoms. Because the set of right languages of the states of $\mathcal{N}$ obviously forms a cover for L, the set of C_i's has the same property. We note that there may be some states q_i and q_j of $\mathcal{N}$, such that $q_i \neq q_j$, but $C_i = C_j$. Let the set of distinct C_i's be C.

Let $\mathcal{G}_C = (B, Q_C, \Delta_C, I_C, F_C)$ be the s-NFA generated by the cover C for the language L. We note that $|Q_C| \leq |Q|$. Let $\pi : Q \to Q_C$ be the mapping assigning to state q_i of $\mathcal{N}$, the state q_{C_i} of $\mathcal{G}_C$, corresponding to C_i.

Proposition 10. *The mapping π is a morphism from $\mathcal{N}$ into $\mathcal{G}_C$.*

Proof. First, if $q_i \in I$, then $L_{q_i}(\mathcal{N}) \subseteq K_1$, where $K_1 = L$. Since the inclusion $C_i \subseteq K_1$ holds, q_{C_i} is initial, that is, $\pi(q_i) \in I_C$.

Similarly, if $q_i \in F$, then $\varepsilon \in L_{q_i}(\mathcal{N})$, implying that $\varepsilon \in C_i$, and thus $q_{C_i} \in F_C$, that is, $\pi(q_i) \in F_C$.

We also show that for all states $q_i, q_j \in Q$ and $a \in \Sigma$, if $(q_i, \varphi, q_j) \in \Delta$ for some φ such that $a \in [\![\varphi]\!]$, then there is some φ' such that $(\pi(q_i), \varphi', \pi(q_j)) \in \Delta_C$ and $a \in [\![\varphi']\!]$. Let $(q_i, \varphi, q_j) \in \Delta$ such that $a \in [\![\varphi]\!]$ for some $q_i, q_j \in Q$ and $a \in \Sigma$. Then it holds that $L_{q_j}(\mathcal{N}) \subseteq a^{-1}L_{q_i}(\mathcal{N}) \subseteq a^{-1}C_i = a^{-1}\bigcap_{L_{q_i}(\mathcal{N}) \subseteq K_h} K_h = \bigcap_{L_{q_i}(\mathcal{N}) \subseteq K_h} a^{-1}K_h$. Therefore, $L_{q_j}(\mathcal{N})$ is a subset of some quotients $a^{-1}K_h$ such that $L_{q_i}(\mathcal{N}) \subseteq K_h$, implying that $C_j \subseteq \bigcap_{L_{q_i}(\mathcal{N}) \subseteq K_h} a^{-1}K_h$, that is, $C_j \subseteq a^{-1}C_i$. Thus, $aC_j \subseteq C_i$, and by Proposition 6, $[\![\varphi']\!]C_j \subseteq C_i$, where φ' is a minterm of L such that $a \in [\![\varphi']\!]$. It is implied that $(q_{C_i}, \varphi', q_{C_j}) \in \Delta_C$, that is, $(\pi(q_i), \varphi', \pi(q_j)) \in \Delta_C$.

We conclude that π is a morphism from $\mathcal{N}$ into $\mathcal{G}_C$. $\qquad\square$

Corollary 1. *For every state q_i of $\mathcal{N}$, the inclusion $L_{q_i}(\mathcal{N}) \subseteq L_{q_{C_i}}(\mathcal{G}_C)$ holds. Also, $L(\mathcal{G}_C) = L$.*

Proof. The morphism $\pi : Q \to Q_C$ implies that for every $q_i \in Q$, the inclusion $L_{q_i}(\mathcal{N}) \subseteq L_{q_{C_i}}(\mathcal{G}_C)$ holds, and also that $L(\mathcal{N}) \subseteq L(\mathcal{G}_C)$ holds.

Since $L(\mathcal{N}) = L$, and by Proposition 7, $L(\mathcal{G}_C) \subseteq L$, we conclude that $L(\mathcal{G}_C) = L$. $\square$

Now, let L_i be a union of some atoms of L. We define the *maximized* version of L_i to be the language $max(L_i) = \bigcap_{L_i \subseteq K_h} K_h$, that is, the intersection of all quotients which contain L_i as a subset. Since any quotient is a disjoint union of atoms, $max(L_i)$ is a union of atoms.

Based on the results above, we can obtain a minimal s-NFA of L as follows: we find an atomic cover $\{L_1, \ldots, L_k\}$ of L, consisting of the minimal number of languages L_i, then maximize L_i's to get the atomic cover $\{max(L_1), \ldots, max(L_k)\}$, and generate an s-NFA $\mathcal{G}$ using this maximized cover. If $\mathcal{G}$ accepts L, then $\mathcal{G}$ is a minimal s-NFA of L, otherwise it is not, and we try other covers in the order of increasing size until we generate an s-NFA which accepts L. The first such generated s-NFA is a minimal s-NFA for L. We note that a minimal cover and a minimal s-NFA are not necessarily unique.

7   Generalization of Brzozowski's Theorem

In this section we present a generalization of Theorem 1, which is similar to its classical version in [1]. Namely, we characterize the class of s-NFAs for which determinization produces a minimal s-DFA. The approach we take here is similar to what was used in [13] to prove an analogous result about obtaining a canonical RFSA.

First, we show the following proposition:

Proposition 11. *Given an s-NFA $\mathcal{N} = (B, Q, \Delta, I, F)$, the left language of a state s of $\mathcal{N}^D$ is $L_{\{I\},s}(\mathcal{N}^D) = \bigcap_{q \in s} L_{I,q}(\mathcal{N}) \cap \bigcap_{q \notin s} \overline{L_{I,q}(\mathcal{N})}$.*

Proof. Let $\mathcal{N} = (B, Q, \Delta, I, F)$ be an s-NFA. Let s be a state of $\mathcal{N}^D$ and let $w \in L_{\{I\},s}(\mathcal{N}^D)$ be a word in the left language of s. We prove the proposition by induction on the length of w. If $w = \varepsilon$, then $s = I$ is the initial state of $\mathcal{N}^D$. Also, since $\varepsilon \in L_{I,q}(\mathcal{N})$ for every $q \in I$, and $\varepsilon \notin L_{I,q}(\mathcal{N})$ for every $q \notin I$, it is clear that $\varepsilon \in L_{\{I\},s}(\mathcal{N}^D)$ if and only if $\varepsilon \in \bigcap_{q \in s} L_{I,q}(\mathcal{N}) \cap \bigcap_{q \notin s} \overline{L_{I,q}(\mathcal{N})}$.

Now, let $w = ua$ with $u \in \Sigma^*$ and $a \in \Sigma$. Let us assume that $u \in L_{\{I\},s'}(\mathcal{N}^D)$ holds for a state s' of $\mathcal{N}^D$ if and only if $u \in \bigcap_{q \in s'} L_{I,q}(\mathcal{N}) \cap \bigcap_{q \notin s'} \overline{L_{I,q}(\mathcal{N})}$. If $w \in L_{\{I\},s}(\mathcal{N}^D)$, then there is a state s' of $\mathcal{N}^D$, such that $u \in L_{\{I\},s'}(\mathcal{N}^D)$ and there is a transition $(s', \varphi_{s',s}, s)$ in $\mathcal{N}^D$ with $a \in \llbracket \varphi_{s',s} \rrbracket$. According to how $\mathcal{N}^D$ is constructed, $\varphi_{s',s} = (\bigwedge_{q \in s} \varphi_{s',q}) \wedge (\bigwedge_{q \in S_{s'} \setminus s} \neg \varphi_{s',q})$, where $\varphi_{s',q} = \bigvee_{(p,\varphi,q) \in \Delta, p \in s'} \varphi$ and $S_{s'}$ is the set of states q of $\mathcal{N}$ such that there is a transition from some state $p \in s'$ to q. Since by the induction assumption $u \in L_{I,q}(\mathcal{N})$ holds for $q \in s'$ and $u \notin L_{I,q}(\mathcal{N})$ holds for $q \notin s'$, it is clear that $ua \in L_{I,q}(\mathcal{N})$ holds for $q \in s$ and $ua \notin L_{I,q}(\mathcal{N})$ holds for $q \notin s$. This is equivalent to that $ua \in \bigcap_{q \in s} L_{I,q}(\mathcal{N}) \cap \bigcap_{q \notin s} \overline{L_{I,q}(\mathcal{N})}$. $\square$

Now, let us consider the minimal s-DFA $\mathcal{D} = (B, S, \Gamma, \{s_1\}, S_f)$ of a symbolic regular language L, with a state set $S = \{s_1, \ldots, s_n\}$. Let $L_i = L_{\{s_1\}, s_i}(\mathcal{D})$ be the left language of a state s_i, for $i = 1, \ldots, n$. It is easy to see that $L_i \cap L_j = \emptyset$ if $s_i \neq s_j$. Also, it is clear that for any s-DFA $\mathcal{D}'$ of L, there is a one-to-many correspondence between the L_i's and the states of $\mathcal{D}'$, such that every L_i is the union of the left languages of the corresponding states of $\mathcal{D}'$. We note that only if $\mathcal{D}'$ is minimal, this correspondence is one-to-one.

The following proposition holds:

Proposition 12. *For an s-NFA $\mathcal{N}$, $\mathcal{N}^D$ is minimal if and only if every left language of $\mathcal{N}$ is a union of L_i's.*

Proof. Let $\mathcal{N} = (B, Q, \Delta, I, F)$ be an s-NFA such that its determinized version $\mathcal{N}^D$ is a minimal s-DFA. Then for any state s_i of $\mathcal{N}^D$, the left language of s_i is L_i. Suppose that there is a state q_j of $\mathcal{N}$ such that its left language is not a union of L_i's. That is, for some word $u \in L_h$, $u \in L_{I, q_j}(\mathcal{N})$, but $L_h \not\subseteq L_{I, q_j}(\mathcal{N})$. Let s_u be a state of $\mathcal{N}^D$ such that $u \in L_{\{I\}, s_u}(\mathcal{N}^D)$. Since $\mathcal{N}^D$ is minimal, we know that $L_{\{I\}, s_u}(\mathcal{N}^D) = L_h$. By Proposition 11, we also know that $q_j \in s_u$ and $L_{\{I\}, s_u}(\mathcal{N}^D) \subseteq L_{I, q_j}(\mathcal{N})$. Therefore the inclusion $L_h \subseteq L_{I, q_j}(\mathcal{N})$ holds, a contradiction.

Conversely, let all the left languages of $\mathcal{N}$ be unions of L_i's. Since by Proposition 11 any left language of $\mathcal{N}^D$ is a Boolean combination of some left languages of $\mathcal{N}$, and because it is obvious that any left language of $\mathcal{N}^D$ is a subset of some L_i, we conclude that the left languages of $\mathcal{N}^D$ are exactly L_i's. Thus, $\mathcal{N}^D$ is minimal. $\square$

Similarly as in [1], we say that an s-NFA $\mathcal{N} = (B, Q, \Delta, I, F)$ is *atomic* if for every $q \in Q$, $L_q(\mathcal{N})$ is a union of atoms of $L(\mathcal{N})$.

Now we can state the following theorem:

Theorem 2. *For any s-NFA $\mathcal{N}$, $\mathcal{N}^D$ is minimal if and only if $\mathcal{N}^R$ is atomic.*

Proof. By properties of the symbolic átomaton (see Sect. 6), atoms of a language are equal to the reversed left languages of the states of a minimal s-DFA of the reverse language. Therefore, $\mathcal{N}^R$ is atomic if and only if every left language of $\mathcal{N}$ is a union of L_i's. We conclude by Proposition 12 that $\mathcal{N}^D$ is minimal if and only if $\mathcal{N}^R$ is atomic. $\square$

8   Related and Future Work

The work in [12] discusses the use of symbolic regular expressions over large but finite alphabets in the context of using regular expression derivatives [3] for matching. The paper does not use minterms to create predicates but a regular expression derivative induced equivalence relation over characters to create predicates. The paper states that in general it is not possible to compute such predicates without doing work that depends linearly on the size of the alphabet. This is clearly not possible if the alphabet is infinite. An interesting future work would be to extend the derivative based approach to symbolic regular expressions over arbitrary symbolic alphabets.

References

1. Brzozowski, J.A., Tamm, H.: Theory of átomata. Theor. Comput. Sci. **539**, 13–27 (2014)
2. Brzozowski, J.A.: Canonical regular expressions and minimal state graphs for definite events. In: Proceedings of the Symposium on Mathematical Theory of Automata, MRI Symposia Series, vol. 12, pp. 529–561. Polytechnic Press, Polytechnic Institute of Brooklyn, NY (1963)
3. Brzozowski, J.A.: Derivatives of regular expressions. J. ACM **11**(4), 481–494 (1964)
4. D'Antoni, L., Veanes, M.: The power of symbolic automata and transducers. In: Majumdar, R., Kunčak, V. (eds.) CAV 2017. LNCS, vol. 10426, pp. 47–67. Springer, Cham (2017). https://doi.org/10.1007/978-3-319-63387-9_3
5. D'Antoni, L., Veanes, M.: Minimization of symbolic automata. In: The 41st Annual ACM SIGPLAN-SIGACT Symposium on Principles of Programming Languages, POPL 2014, San Diego, CA, USA, 20–21 January 2014, pp. 541–554 (2014)
6. D'Antoni, L., Veanes, M.: Forward bisimulations for nondeterministic symbolic finite automata. In: Tools and Algorithms for the Construction and Analysis of Systems - 23rd International Conference, TACAS 2017, ETAPS 2017, Proceedings, Part I, Uppsala, Sweden, 22–29 April 2017, pp. 518–534 (2017)
7. Denis, F., Lemay, A., Terlutte, A.: Residual finite state automata. Fund. Informaticae **51**, 339–368 (2002)
8. Denis, F., Lemay, A., Terlutte, A.: Learning regular languages using RFSAs. Theor. Comput. Sci. **313**(2), 267–294 (2004)
9. Drews, S., D'Antoni, L.: Learning symbolic automata. In: Legay, A., Margaria, T. (eds.) TACAS 2017. LNCS, vol. 10205, pp. 173–189. Springer, Heidelberg (2017). https://doi.org/10.1007/978-3-662-54577-5_10
10. Iván, S.: Complexity of atoms, combinatorially. Inf. Process. Lett. **116**, 356–360 (2016)
11. Keil, M., Thiemann, P.: Symbolic solving of extended regular expression inequalities. In: 34th International Conference on Foundation of Software Technology and Theoretical Computer Science, FSTTCS 2014, 15–17 December 2014, New Delhi, India, pp. 175–186 (2014)
12. Owens, S., Reppy, J., Turon, A.: Regular-expression derivatives re-examined. J. Funct. Programm. **19**(2), 173–190 (2009)
13. Tamm, H.: Generalization of the double-reversal method of finding a canonical residual finite state automaton. In: Shallit, J., Okhotin, A. (eds.) DCFS 2015. LNCS, vol. 9118, pp. 268–279. Springer, Cham (2015). https://doi.org/10.1007/978-3-319-19225-3_23
14. Tamm, H.: New interpretation and generalization of the Kameda-Weiner method. In: 43rd International Colloquium on Automata, Languages, and Programming (ICALP 2016). Leibniz International Proceedings in Informatics (LIPIcs), vol. 55, Dagstuhl, Germany, Schloss Dagstuhl-Leibniz-Zentrum für Informatik, pp. 116:1–116:12 (2016)
15. Thompson, K.: Regular expression search algorithm. Commun. ACM **11**(6), 419–422 (1968)

16. Veanes, M., de Halleux, P., Tillmann, N.: Rex: symbolic regular expression explorer. In: Third International Conference on Software Testing, Verification and Validation, ICST 2010, pp. 498–507. IEEE Computer Society (2010)
17. Watson, B.W.: A taxonomy of finite automata construction algorithms. Computing science report 93/43. Eindhoven University of Technology (1995)
18. Watson, B.W.: Implementing and using finite automata toolkits. In: Extended finite state models of language, pp. 19–36. Cambridge University Press (1999)

Complete Algorithms for Algebraic Strongest Postconditions and Weakest Preconditions in Polynomial ODE'S

Michele Boreale$^{(\boxtimes)}$

Dipartimento di Statistica, Informatica, Applicazioni (DiSIA) "G. Parenti",
Università di Firenze, Viale Morgagni 65, I-50134 Firenze, Italy
michele.boreale@unifi.it

Abstract. A system of polynomial ordinary differential equations (ODE's) is specified via a vector of multivariate polynomials, or vector field, F. A safety assertion $\psi \longrightarrow [F]\phi$ means that the system's trajectory will lie in a subset ϕ (the postcondition) of the state-space, whenever the initial state belongs to a subset ψ (the precondition). We consider the case when ϕ and ψ are *algebraic varieties*, that is, zero sets of polynomials. In particular, polynomials specifying the postcondition can be seen as conservation laws implied by ψ. Checking the validity of algebraic safety assertions is a fundamental problem in, for instance, hybrid systems. We consider generalized versions of this problem, and offer algorithms to: (1) given a user specified polynomial set P and a precondition ψ, find the smallest algebraic postcondition ϕ including the variety determined by the valid conservation laws in P (relativized strongest postcondition); (2) given a user specified postcondition ϕ, find the largest algebraic precondition ψ (weakest precondition). The first algorithm can also be used to find the weakest algebraic *invariant* of the system implying all conservation laws in P valid under ψ. The effectiveness of these algorithms is demonstrated on a challenging case study from the literature.

Keywords: Ordinary differential equations · Postconditions
Preconditions · Invariants · Gröbner bases

1 Introduction

In recent years, there has been a renewed interest in computational models based on ordinary differential equations (ODE's), in such diverse fields as System Biology [2] and stochastic systems [23]. In particular, starting from [17], the field of hybrid systems has witnessed the emergence of a novel class of formal methods based on concepts from Algebraic Geometry – see e.g. [9,18,22] and references therein.

A system of ODE's can be seen as specifying the evolution over time, or *trajectory*, of certain variables of interest $x_1, ..., x_N$, describing for instance physical quantities (see Sect. 2). A fundamental problem in many fields is being able to

A M. Tjoa et al. (Eds.): SOFSEM 2018, LNCS 10706, pp. 442–455, 2018.
https://doi.org/10.1007/978-3-319-73117-9_31

prove or to disprove assertions of the following type. For each initial state in a given $\psi \subseteq \mathbb{R}^N$ (the precondition), the resulting system's trajectory will lie in a given set $\phi \subseteq \mathbb{R}^N$ (the postcondition). This is a *safety assertion* that, using a notation akin to Platzer's Dynamic Logic, we can write as $\psi \longrightarrow [F]\phi$, where F is the vector field specifying the system. Evidently, safety assertions can be considered as a continuous counterpart of Hoare's triples in imperative programs – see [14].

Here we are interested in the case where both ψ and ϕ are algebraic varieties, that is they are specified as zeros of (multivariate) polynomial sets, and the drifts f_i in $F = (f_1, ..., f_N)$ are polynomials themselves (Sect. 3). Although (sets of) trajectories can rarely be represented *exactly* as algebraic varieties, these provide overapproximations that may be useful in practice. In a valid safety assertion, the polynomials specifying the postcondition ϕ can be seen as system's *conservation laws* (e.g. energy or mass conservation) that are valid under the precondition ψ. Driven by the analogy with Hoare's triples, we find it natural to generalize the problem of checking the assertion $\psi \longrightarrow [F]\phi$ in two distinct ways. (1) Strongest postcondition: given a precondition ψ, find the smallest ϕ such that the assertion is valid; (2) weakest precondition: given a postcondition ϕ, find the largest ψ such that the assertion is valid. Problem (1) amounts to characterizing I_ψ, the set of *all* polynomials invariants (conservation laws) valid under ψ. This turns out to be awkward and motivates the introduction of a *relativized* version of this problem: for a user specified polynomial set P, compute $P \cap I_\psi$. Depending on P, this can be a lot easier than computing the whole I_ψ.

We offer complete algorithms that solve the relativized strongest postcondition (Sect. 4) and the weakest precondition (Sect. 5) problems. More precisely, the former problem is considered in the case where the set P is specified via a polynomial template. This way, for example, one can find at once all polynomial conservation laws of the system up to a given degree. As a byproduct of the first algorithm, we also get the weakest algebraic invariant that implies all laws in $P \cap I_\psi$. Both algorithms are based on building ascending chains of polynomial ideals: these represent, basically, more and more refined overapproximations of the (relativized) strongest postcondition and weakest precondition, respectively. Correctness and termination rely on a few concepts from Algebraic Geometry, notably Gröbner bases [8] (Sect. 2). We demonstrate the effectiveness of these algorithms reporting the outcomes we have obtained on a nontrivial system taken from the literature, using a preliminary implementation of our algorithms (Sect. 6). We compare our results with those obtained by other authors.

The present paper builds on and generalizes our previous work on initial value problems [6]. Recent contributions dealing with invariant generation for polynomial ODE's, in the context of hybrid systems, are reviewed and discussed in the concluding section (Sect. 7). Due to space limitations, all proofs and most examples have been omitted in the present version; they can be found in the full version [7].

2   Preliminaries

We review a few preliminary notions about ODE's, polynomials and Algebraic Geometry.

Polynomial ODE's. Let us fix an integer $N \geq 1$ and a set of N distinct variables $x_1, ..., x_N$. We will denote by $\mathbf{x}$ the vector $(x_1, ..., x_N)$. We let $\mathbb{R}[\mathbf{x}]$ denote the set of multivariate polynomials in the variables $x_1, ..., x_N$ with coefficients in $\mathbb{R}$, and let p, q range over it. Here we regard polynomials as syntactic objects. Given an integer $d \geq 0$, by $\mathbb{R}_d[\mathbf{x}]$ we denote the set of polynomials of degree $\leq d$. As an example, $p = 2xy^2 + (1/5)wz + yz + 1$ is a polynomial of degree $\deg(p) = 3$, that is $p \in \mathbb{R}_3[x, y, z, w]$, with monomials xy^2, wz, yz and 1. Depending on the context, with a slight abuse of notation it may be convenient to let a polynomial denote the induced function $\mathbb{R}^N \to \mathbb{R}$, defined as expected. In particular, x_i can be seen as denoting the projection on the i-th coordinate.

A (polynomial) *vector field* is a vector of N polynomials, $F = (f_1, ..., f_N)$, seen as a function $F : \mathbb{R}^N \to \mathbb{R}^N$. Throughout the paper, all definitions and statements refer to an arbitrarily fixed polynomial vector field F over a N-vector $\mathbf{x}$. The vector field F and an initial condition $\mathbf{x}_0 \in \mathbb{R}^N$ together define an *initial value problem* $\Phi = (F, \mathbf{x}_0)$, often written in the following form

$$\Phi : \begin{cases} \dot{\mathbf{x}}(t) = F(\mathbf{x}(t)) \\ \mathbf{x}(0) = \mathbf{x}_0. \end{cases} \tag{1}$$

The functions f_i in F are called *drifts* in this context. A *solution* to this problem is a differentiable function $\mathbf{x}(t) : D \to \mathbb{R}^N$, for some nonempty open interval $D \subseteq \mathbb{R}$ containing 0, which fulfills the above two equations, that is: $\frac{d}{dt}\mathbf{x}(t) = F(\mathbf{x}(t))$ for each $t \in D$ and $\mathbf{x}(0) = \mathbf{x}_0$. By the Picard-Lindelöf theorem [1], there exists a nonempty open interval D containing 0, over which there is a *unique* solution, say $\mathbf{x}(t) = (x_1(t), ..., x_N(t))$, to the problem. In our case, as F is infinitely often differentiable, the solution is seen to be *analytic* in D: each $x_i(t)$ admits a Taylor series expansion in a neighborhood of 0. For definiteness, we will take the domain of definition D of $\mathbf{x}(t)$ to be the largest symmetric open interval where the Taylor expansion from 0 of each of the $x_i(t)$ converges (possibly $D = \mathbb{R}$). The resulting vector function of t, denoted $\mathbf{x}(t)$, is called the *time trajectory* of the system. Note that both the time trajectory and its domain of definition do depend in general on the initial $\mathbf{x}_0$. We shall write them as $\mathbf{x}(t; \mathbf{x}_0)$ and $D_{\mathbf{x}_0}$, respectively, whenever we want to make this dependence explicit in the notation.

For any polynomial $p \in \mathbb{R}[\mathbf{x}]$, the function $p(\mathbf{x}(t)) : D \to \mathbb{R}$, obtained by composing p as a function with the time trajectory $\mathbf{x}(t)$, is analytic: we let $p(t)$ denote the extension of this function over the largest symmetric open interval of convergence (possibly coinciding with $\mathbb{R}$) of its Taylor expansion from 0. We will call $p(t)$ the *polynomial behaviour induced by p and by* the initial value problem (1). Again, fixing $N, \mathbf{x}$ and F once and for all, we shall write $p(t; \mathbf{x}_0)$ when we want to emphasize the dependence of this function from the initial value $\mathbf{x}_0$.

Lie derivatives. Given a differentiable function $g : E \to \mathbb{R}$, for some open set $E \subseteq \mathbb{R}^N$, the *Lie derivative of g along F* is the function $E \to \mathbb{R}$ defined as: $\mathcal{L}_F(g) \overset{\triangle}{=} \langle \nabla g, F \rangle = \sum_{i=1}^{N} (\frac{\partial g}{\partial x_i} \cdot f_i)$. The Lie derivative of the sum $h + g$ and product $h \cdot g$ functions obey the familiar rules

$$\mathcal{L}_F(h + g) = \mathcal{L}_F(h) + \mathcal{L}_F(g) \tag{2}$$
$$\mathcal{L}_F(h \cdot g) = h \cdot \mathcal{L}_F(g) + \mathcal{L}_F(h) \cdot g. \tag{3}$$

Note that $\mathcal{L}_F(x_i) = f_i$. Moreover if $p \in \mathbb{R}_d[\mathbf{x}]$ then $\mathcal{L}_F(p) \in \mathbb{R}_{d+d'}[\mathbf{x}]$, for some integer $d' \geq 0$ that depends on d and on F. This allows us to view the Lie derivative of polynomials along a polynomial field F as a purely syntactic mechanism, that is as a function $\mathcal{L}_F : \mathbb{R}[\mathbf{x}] \to \mathbb{R}[\mathbf{x}]$ that does not assume anything about the solution of (1). Informally, we can view p as a program, and taking Lie derivative of p can be interpreted as unfolding the definitions of the variables x_i's, according to the equations in (1) and to the formal rules for product and sum derivation, (2) and (3). More generally, we can define inductively $\mathcal{L}_F^{(0)}(p) \overset{\triangle}{=} p$ and $\mathcal{L}_F^{(j+1)}(p) \overset{\triangle}{=} \mathcal{L}_F(\mathcal{L}_F^j(p))$.

Example 1. The following system, borrowed from [10], will be used as a running example. Consider $N = 2$, $\mathbf{x} = (x, y)$ and the vector field $F = (y^2, xy)$. Let $p = x - y$. Examples of Lie derivatives are $\mathcal{L}_F(p) = y^2 - xy$ and $\mathcal{L}_F^{(2)}(p) = 2xy^2 - x^2y - y^3$.

The connection between Lie derivatives of p along F and the initial value problem (1) is given by the following equations, which can be readily checked. Here and in the sequel, we let $p(\mathbf{x}_0)$ denote the real number obtained by evaluating p at $\mathbf{x}_0$: $p(t; \mathbf{x}_0)_{|t=0} = p(\mathbf{x}_0)$ and and $\frac{d}{dt}p(t; \mathbf{x}_0) = (\mathcal{L}_F(p))(t; \mathbf{x}_0)$. More generally, we have the following equation for the j-th derivative of $p(t)$ $(j = 0, 1, ...)$: $\frac{d^j}{dt^j}p(t; \mathbf{x}_0) = (\mathcal{L}_F^{(j)}(p))(t; \mathbf{x}_0)$. In the sequel, we shall often abbreviate the syntactic Lie derivative $\mathcal{L}_F^{(j)}(p)$ as $p^{(j)}$, and shall omit the subscript $_F$ from $\mathcal{L}_F$ when clear from the context.

Algebraic Geometry preliminaries. We quickly review a few notions from Algebraic Geometry that will be used throughout the paper. A comprehensive treatment of these concepts can be found for instance in Cox et al.'s excellent textbook [8]. A set of polynomials $I \subseteq \mathbb{R}[\mathbf{x}]$ is an *ideal* if: (1) $0 \in I$ and (2) $p_1, ..., p_m \in I$ and $h_1, ..., h_m \in \mathbb{R}[\mathbf{x}]$ implies $\sum_{i=1}^{m} h_i p_i \in I$. The ideal generated by a set $P \subseteq \mathbb{R}[\mathbf{x}]$ is $\langle P \rangle \overset{\triangle}{=} \{\sum_{i=1}^{m} h_i p_i : m \geq 0 \text{ and } h_i \in \mathbb{R}[\mathbf{x}], p_i \in P \text{ for } i = 1, ..., m\}$. This is the smallest ideal containing P and as a consequence $\langle\langle P \rangle\rangle = \langle P \rangle$. Given an ideal I, a set P such that $I = \langle P \rangle$ is said to be *basis* for I. Hilbert's basis theorem implies that: (a) any ideal $I \subseteq \mathbb{R}[\mathbf{x}]$ has a finite basis; (b) any infinite ascending chain of ideals $I_0 \subseteq I_1 \subseteq \cdots$ stabilizes in a finite number of steps (*ascending chain condition*). Once a *monomial order* (e.g. lexicographic) is fixed, a multivariate version of polynomial division naturally arises – see [8] for the precise definition. A *Gröbner basis* of I (w.r.t. a fixed monomial order) is a finite basis G of I such that for any polynomial $p \in \mathbb{R}[\mathbf{x}]$ the *remainder* of the division of p by G, $r = p \bmod G$, enjoys following property: $p \in I$ iff $r = 0$. As a consequence, given a Gröbner basis G of I, the *ideal membership* problem $p \in I$ can be decided[1]. Ideal inclusion $I \subseteq J$ can be decided similarly. There are algorithms (e.g. Buchberger's) that, given a finite P and a monomial order, compute a Gröbner basis G such that $\langle G \rangle = \langle P \rangle$. This computation is potentially expensive.

The geometric counterpart of polynomial sets are algebraic varieties. Given a set of polynomials $P \subseteq \mathbb{R}[\mathbf{x}]$, the set of points in $\mathbb{R}^N$ annihilating all of them, $\mathbf{V}(P) \triangleq \{\mathbf{x} \in \mathbb{R}^N : p(\mathbf{x}) = 0 \text{ for each } p \in P\}$, is the *algebraic variety* represented by P. Ideals and algebraic varieties are connected as follows. For any set $A \subseteq \mathbb{R}^N$, the set of polynomials that vanish on A, $\mathbf{I}(A) \triangleq \{p : p(\mathbf{x}) = 0 \text{ for each } \mathbf{x} \in A\}$, is the ideal induced by A. Note that both $\mathbf{V}$ and $\mathbf{I}$ are inclusion reversing: $P \subseteq Q$ implies $\mathbf{V}(P) \supseteq \mathbf{V}(Q)$, and $A \subseteq B$ implies $\mathbf{I}(A) \supseteq \mathbf{I}(B)$. For A an algebraic variety and J an ideal, it is easy to see that $\mathbf{V}(\mathbf{I}(A)) = A$ and that $\mathbf{I}(\mathbf{V}(J)) \supseteq J$. We will have in general more than one ideal representing A.

3   Algebraic Safety Assertions and Invariants

We will be interested in *safety assertions* of the following type, where $\psi, \phi \subseteq \mathbb{R}^N$ are user specified algebraic varieties, which we call the *pre* and *postcondition*, respectively. Each of them is specified by a set of polynomials.

$$\text{Whenever } \mathbf{x}_0 \in \psi \text{ then for each } t \in D_{\mathbf{x}_0}, \mathbf{x}(t; \mathbf{x}_0) \in \phi. \tag{4}$$

The above assertion means that every trajectory starting in the precondition ψ will stay in the postcondition ϕ; hence necessarily $\psi \subseteq \phi$ for the assertion to hold. Using a notation akin to Platzer's Dynamic Logic's [14], the safety assertion (4) will be abbreviated as

$$\psi \longrightarrow [F] \, \phi. \tag{5}$$

A common technique for proving (5) is finding an algebraic variety χ such that $\psi \subseteq \chi \subseteq \phi$ and χ is an *algebraic invariant* for the vector field F, that is it satisfies $\chi \longrightarrow [F] \, \chi$. The invariance condition means that all trajectories starting in χ must remain in χ.

Let us now introduce two distinct generalizations of the problem of checking the safety assertion (5). These are the problems we will actually try to solve. In what follows, "finding" an algebraic variety means building a finite set of polynomials representing it. Also note that, in the present context, "smallest" means "strongest", and "largest" means "weakest".

Problem 1 (strongest postcondition). Given an algebraic variety ψ, find ϕ_ψ, the smallest algebraic variety ϕ such that (5) is true.

---

[1] Provided the involved coefficients can be finitely represented, e.g. are rational.

Note that ϕ_ψ always exists and is the intersection of all the varieties ϕ such that $\psi \longrightarrow [F]\,\phi$. Finding ϕ_ψ amounts to building (a basis of) an appropriate ideal I such that $\mathbf{V}(I) = \phi_\psi$. One such ideal is $I_\psi \triangleq \mathbf{I}(\phi_\psi)$. Unfortunately, computing I_ψ, or any other polynomial representation of ψ, appears to be computationally awkward. This motivates the introduction of a relativized version of the previous problem. In this version, a user specified set of polynomials P is used to tune the strength, hence precision, of the postcondition.

Problem 2 (strongest postcondition, relativized). Given a polynomial set $P \subseteq \mathbb{R}[\mathbf{x}]$ and an algebraic variety ψ, find a finite representation of $P \cap I_\psi$.

Of course, we have that $\mathbf{V}(P \cap I_\psi) \supseteq \mathbf{V}(I_\psi) = \phi_\psi$, which implies that $\psi \longrightarrow [F]\,\mathbf{V}(P \cap I_\psi)$. In other words, $P \cap I_\psi$ represents an overapproximation of the strongest postcondition. There is another meaningful way of generalizing the problem of checking (5).

Problem 3 (weakest precondition). Given an algebraic variety ϕ, find ψ_ϕ, the largest algebraic variety ψ such that (5) is true.

Let us now comment briefly on the relationships between the above introduced problems. It is not difficult to see that Problems 1 and 3 are both more general than the problem of checking (5) for given ψ *and* ϕ, based on the fact that one knows how to check inclusion between two varieties (see Sect. 2). The relativized Problem 2 too is more general than checking (5). Indeed, wanting to check the assertion $\psi \longrightarrow [F]\,\phi$, for *given* ψ and *given* $\phi = \mathbf{V}(Q)$, it is sufficient to let $P = Q$ in Problem 2 and then check if P is included in the computed $P \cap I_\psi$, that is if $P \subseteq I_\psi$.

Example 2. Let us reconsider the vector field F of Example 1. The variety $\psi = \mathbf{V}(\{p\}) = \mathbf{V}(\{x - y\})$ is the line $x = y$. Consider $\phi = \mathbf{V}(\{q\})$ where $q = x^2 - xy$. Let P the set of all polynomials of degree ≤ 2. We can consider the following problems. (a) Decide whether $\psi \longrightarrow [F]\,\phi$; (b) find a finite representation of $P \cap I_\psi$, that is all the conservation laws of degree at ≤ 2 that are satisfied, for each initial state in the line $x = y$ (relativized strongest postcondition); (c) find a finite representation of the largest algebraic variety ψ_ϕ such that $\psi_\phi \longrightarrow [F]\,\phi$ (weakest precondition). Note that solving (b) also yields a solution of (a).

In the following sections, we will provide complete algorithms for solving Problems 2 and 3. Concerning Problem 2, we shall give a method that works reasonably well for the case when the polynomial set P is specified by a polynomial template. Moreover, as a byproduct of this method, we will also get the weakest algebraic invariant included in $\mathbf{V}(P \cap I_\psi)$. The solution will also give us a handle on the more general and difficult Problem 1.

4   Strongest Postconditions

Our goal is to give a method to effectively compute $P \cap I_\psi$, for user specified variety ψ and polynomials set P. Following a well-established tradition in the field of hybrid systems, we shall consider the case when the user specifies P via a polynomial *template*, which we review in the next paragraph. Throughout the section, whenever we consider a Gröbner basis over the polynomial ring $\mathbb{R}[\mathbf{a}, \mathbf{x}]$, we shall assume a lexicographic monomial ordering[2] such that $a_i > x_j$ for each i, j. This way, whenever G is a Gröbner basis of an ideal $I \subseteq \mathbb{R}[\mathbf{a}, \mathbf{x}]$, then $G \cap \mathbb{R}[\mathbf{x}]$ is a Gröbner basis of the ideal $I \cap \mathbb{R}[\mathbf{x}]$ (see [8, Chap. 3, Sect. 1, Theorem 2]). In particular, for any finite set $G \subseteq \mathbb{R}[\mathbf{x}]$, we have that G is a Gröbner basis in $\mathbb{R}[\mathbf{a}, \mathbf{x}]$ if and only if it is in $\mathbb{R}[\mathbf{x}]$.

Templates. Fix a tuple of $n \geq 1$ of distinct *parameters*, say $\mathbf{a} = (a_1, ..., a_n)$, disjoint from $\mathbf{x}$. Let $Lin(\mathbf{a})$, ranged over by ℓ, be the set of *linear expressions* with coefficients in $\mathbb{R}$ and variables in $\mathbf{a}$; e.g. $\ell = 5a_1 + 42a_2 - 3a_3$ is one such expression[3]. A *template* [17] is a polynomial π in $Lin(\mathbf{a})[\mathbf{x}]$, that is, a polynomial with linear expressions as coefficients. For example, the following is a template: $\pi = (5a_1 + (3/4)a_3)xy^2 + (7a_1 + (1/5)a_2)xz + (a_2 + 42a_3)$. Note that $Lin(\mathbf{a})[\mathbf{x}] \subseteq \mathbb{R}[\mathbf{a}, \mathbf{x}]$, so, whenever convenient, we can consider a template as a polynomial in this larger ring. A *parameters valuation* is a vector $v = (r_1, ..., r_n) \in \mathbb{R}^n$. Given v, we will let $\ell[v] \in \mathbb{R}$ denote the result of replacing each parameter a_i with r_i, and evaluating the resulting expression; we will let $\pi[v] \in \mathbb{R}[\mathbf{x}]$ denote the polynomial obtained by replacing each ℓ with $\ell[v]$ in π. Given a set $S \subseteq \mathbb{R}^n$, we let $\pi[S]$ denote the set $\{\pi[v] : v \in S\} \subseteq \mathbb{R}[\mathbf{x}]$. The (formal) Lie derivative of π is defined as expected, once linear expressions are treated as constants; note that $\mathcal{L}(\pi)$ is still a template. It is easy to see that the following property is true: for each π and v, one has $\mathcal{L}(\pi[v]) = \mathcal{L}(\pi)[v]$. This property extends as expected to the j-th Lie derivative $(j \geq 0)$: $\mathcal{L}^{(j)}(\pi[v]) = \mathcal{L}^{(j)}(\pi)[v]$.

The POST algorithm. Given user specified algebraic variety ψ (the precondition) and polynomial template π specifying $P = \pi[\mathbb{R}^n]$, our objective is to compute $P \cap I_\psi$. Let us call $p \in \mathbb{R}[\mathbf{x}]$ a *polynomial invariant* for F and $\mathbf{x}_0$ if the function $p(t; \mathbf{x}_0)$ is identically 0. A polynomial invariant expresses a law which is satisfied by the solution of the initial value problem $(F, \mathbf{x}_0)$, that is, a conservation law. We will rely on the following two lemmas. The first one is just a reformulation of the definition of $I_\psi = \mathbf{I}(\phi_\psi)$. For the (easy) proof of the second, see e.g. [6].

Lemma 1. $I_\psi = \{p : p \text{ is a polynomial invariant for each } \mathbf{x}_0 \in \psi\}$.

Lemma 2. *Let* $p \in \mathbb{R}[\mathbf{x}]$. *Then* p *is a polynomial invariant for the initial value* $\mathbf{x}_0$ *if and only if for each* $j \geq 0$, $p^{(j)}(\mathbf{x}_0) = 0$.

The above two lemmas suggest the following strategy to compute the set $\pi[\mathbb{R}^n] \cap I_\psi$. We should identify those parameters valuations $v \in \mathbb{R}^n$, such that $\pi[v]$ is a polynomial invariant for each $\mathbf{x}_0 \in \psi$ (Lemma 1). That is, those v's such that for each $j \geq 0$ and for each $\mathbf{x}_0 \in \psi$, $\pi^{(j)}[v](\mathbf{x}_0) = 0$ (Lemma 2). Or,

---

[2] Any *elimination* ordering [8] for the parameters a_i could as well be considered.

[3] Note that linear expressions with a constant term, such as $2 + 5a_1 + 42a_2 - 3a_3$ are not allowed.

equivalently, $\pi^{(j)}[v] \in \mathbf{I}(\psi)$ for each $j \geq 0$. For each $j \geq 0$, the last condition imposes certain constraints on v, that is on the parameters of the template $\pi^{(j)}$. In order to make these constraints explicit, we shall rely on the following key lemma.

Lemma 3. *Let $G \subseteq \mathbb{R}[\mathbf{x}]$ be a Gröbner basis. Let π be a polynomial template and $r = \pi \bmod G$. Then r is linear in $\mathbf{a}$. Moreover, for each $v \in \mathbb{R}^n$, $\pi[v] \bmod G = r[v]$.*

Fix a Gröbner basis G of $\mathbf{I}(\psi)$. By the above lemma, for a fixed j, $\pi^{(j)}[v] \in \mathbf{I}(\psi)$ exactly when $r_j[v] = 0$, where $r_j = \pi^{(j)} \bmod G$. By seeing r_j as a polynomial in $Lin(\mathbf{a})[\mathbf{x}]$, the condition on v

$$r_j[v] = 0 \tag{6}$$

can be represented as a set of *linear* constraints on the parameters $\mathbf{a}$: indeed, a polynomial is zero exactly when all of its coefficients - in the present case, linear expressions in $\mathbf{a}$ - are zero[4]. This discussion leads to the method described below. We give below a mostly mathematical description of the algorithm. Additional computational aspects, including the determination of the basis G as well as a relaxation that guarantees soundness, are discussed in the full version [7].

The method can be seen as a generalization of the double chain algorithm of [6] to algebraic safety assertions. The basic idea is gradually refining the space of parameters valuations, starting from $\mathbb{R}^n$. More precisely, the algorithm builds two chains of sets: a descending chain of vector spaces, representing spaces of possible parameters valuations; and an (eventually) ascending chain of ideals, induced by those valuations. The ideal chain is used in the algorithm to detect the stabilization of the sequence. Fix a Gröbner basis G of $\mathbf{I}(\psi)$. For each $j \geq 0$, let $r_j \triangleq \pi^{(j)} \bmod G$. For each $i \geq 0$, consider the sets

$$V_i \triangleq \{v \in \mathbb{R}^n : r_j[v] \text{ is the 0 polynomial, for } j = 0, ..., i\} \tag{7}$$

$$J_i \triangleq \langle \bigcup_{j=0}^{i} \pi^{(j)}[V_i] \rangle. \tag{8}$$

It is easy to check that each $V_i \subseteq \mathbb{R}^n$ is a vector space over $\mathbb{R}$ of dimension $\leq n$: this stems from the linearity in $\mathbf{a}$ of the r_j's. Now let $m \geq 0$ be the least integer such that the following conditions are *both* true:

$$V_{m+1} = V_m \tag{9}$$

$$J_{m+1} = J_m. \tag{10}$$

The algorithm returns (V_m, J_m), written $\text{POST}(\psi, \pi) = (V_m, J_m)$. Note that the integer m is well defined: indeed, $V_0 \supseteq V_1 \supseteq \cdots$ forms an infinite descending

---

[4] For instance, if $\pi = (a_1 + a_2)x_1 + a_3 x_2$ then $\pi[v] = 0$ corresponds to the constraints $a_1 = -a_2$ and $a_3 = 0$.

chain of finite-dimensional vector spaces, which must stabilize in finitely many steps. In other words, we can consider the least m' such that $V_{m'} = V_{m'+k}$ for each $k \geq 1$. Then $J_{m'} \subseteq J_{m'+1} \subseteq \cdots$ forms an infinite ascending chain of ideals, which must stabilize at some $m \geq m'$. Therefore there must be some index m such that (9) and (10) are both satisfied, and we choose the least such m.

Let us say that a set of polynomials J is an *invariant ideal* for the vector field F if it is an ideal and $\mathcal{L}_F(J) \triangleq \{\mathcal{L}_F(p) : p \in J\} \subseteq J$. The next theorem states the correctness and relative completeness of POST. Informally, the algorithm outputs the largest space V such that $\pi[V] \subseteq I_\psi$ and the smallest invariant ideal J witnessing this inclusion.

Theorem 1 (correctness and relative completeness of Post). *For an algebraic variety ψ and a polynomial template π, let $\text{POST}(\psi, \pi) = (V, J)$. Then*

(a) $\pi[V] = \pi[\mathbb{R}^n] \cap I_\psi$;
(b) J is the smallest invariant ideal such that $J \supseteq \pi[V]$. Moreover, $J \subseteq I_\psi$.

Example 3. We reconsider the vector field F of Example 1. Let us consider $\psi = \mathbf{V}(\{x - y\})$. A Gröbner basis of $\mathbf{I}(\psi)$ is just $G = \{x - y\}$. We let π be the complete template of degree 2 (described below). We build the chain of sets V_i, J_i, for $i = 0, 1, \ldots$, with the help of a computer algebra system. Below, $v = (v_1, \ldots, v_6) \in \mathbb{R}^6$ denotes a generic parameters valuation.

- $\pi = a_6 xy + a_5 y^2 + a_4 x^2 + a_3 y + a_2 x + a_1$ and $r_0 = \pi \bmod G = a_4 y^2 + a_5 y^2 + a_6 y^2 + a_2 y + a_3 y + a_1$. Thus $V_0 = \{v : v_4 = -v_5 - v_6, v_2 = -v_3, v_1 = 0\}$ and $J_0 = \langle \pi[V_0] \rangle$;
- $\pi^{(1)} = a_6 x^2 y - 2 a_6 xy^2 + a_6 y^3 + a_3 xy - a_3 y^2$ and $r_1 = \pi^{(1)} \bmod G = 0$. Thus $V_1 = V_0$. Moreover $\pi^{(1)}[V_0] \subseteq J_0$, which implies $J_1 = \langle \pi[V_0] \cup \pi^{(1)}[V_0] \rangle = J_0$.

Thus $\text{POST}(\psi, \pi) = (V_0, J_0)$. A Gröbner basis of J_0 is $G_0 = G$.

Remark 1 (result template). Given a template π and $v \in \mathbb{R}^n$, checking if $\pi[v] \in \pi[V]$ is equivalent to checking if $v \in V$: this can be effectively done knowing a basis B of the vector space V (see [7]). In practice, it is sometimes more convenient to represent the whole set $\pi[V]$ returned by POST compactly in terms of a *new* m-parameters result template π' such that $\pi'[\mathbb{R}^m] = \pi[V]$. For instance, in the previous example, the result template $\pi' = a_1(y^2 - x^2) + a_2(xy - x^2) + a_3(y - x)$ represents $\pi[V_0]$, in the precise sense that $\pi[V_0] = \pi'[\mathbb{R}^3]$. The result template π' can in fact be built directly from π, by propagating the linear constraints on $\mathbf{a}$ (6) as they are generated.

Note that, while typically the user will be interested in $\pi[V]$, the ideal J as well may contain useful information, such as higher order, nonlinear conservation laws.

Corollary 1 (weakest algebraic invariant). *For an algebraic variety ψ and a polynomial template π, let $\text{POST}(\psi, \pi) = (V, J)$ and $\phi = \mathbf{V}(\pi[V])$. Then $\mathbf{V}(J)$ is the largest algebraic invariant included in ϕ.*

Finally, we show that the whole ideal I_ψ as well can be characterized in terms of the POST algorithm. For any $k \geq 0$, the *complete polynomial template* of degree k over a set of variables X is $\pi \overset{\triangle}{=} \sum_\alpha a_\alpha \alpha$, where α ranges over all monomials of degree $\leq k$ on the variables in X, and a_α ranges over distinct parameters.

Corollary 2 (characterization of I_ψ). *Let ψ be an algebraic variety. Let $k \geq 0$, π_k be the complete template of degree k over the variables in $\mathbf{x}$ and $(V, J) =$ POST(ψ, π_k). For k large enough, $J = I_\psi$.*

We leave open the problem of computing a lower bound on the degree k that is needed to recover I_ψ.

5   Weakest Preconditions

We first present a very simple algorithm solving Problem 3 in principle. Let $\phi = \mathbf{V}(P)$ be a user specified postcondition, with $P \subseteq \mathbb{R}[\mathbf{x}]$ a finite set of polynomials. We define inductively the sets P_j, $j \geq 0$, as follows: $P_0 \overset{\triangle}{=} P$ and $P_{j+1} = \mathcal{L}(P_j)$. For $j \geq 0$, we let

$$I_j \overset{\triangle}{=} \langle \cup_{i=0}^j P_i \rangle. \tag{11}$$

Let m the least integer such that $I_m = I_{m+1}$, which must exist as $I_0 \subseteq I_1 \subseteq \cdots$ forms an infinite ascending chains of ideals that must eventually stabilize. We let PRE$(\phi) \overset{\triangle}{=} I_m$. Note that the termination condition reduces to checking equality between two ideals, which can be effectively done (Sect. 2).

Theorem 2 (correctness and completeness of Pre). *Let ϕ be an algebraic variety and $I =$ PRE(ϕ). Then $\mathbf{V}(I) = \psi_\phi$.*

Example 4. We reconsider the vector field F of Example 1. Let us consider $\phi = \mathbf{V}(\{q\})$, where $q = x^2 - xy$. Let us compute the weakest precondition ψ_ϕ via PRE. With the help of a computer algebra system, it is easily checked that $q^{(2)} \in I_1 = \langle \{q, q^{(1)}\} \rangle$, where $q^{(1)} = -x^2y + 2xy^2 - y^3$ and $q^{(2)} = -x^3y + 4x^2y^2 - 5xy^3 + 2y^4$. This implies $I_2 = I_1$. Hence PRE$(\phi) = I_1$ and $\psi_\phi = \mathbf{V}(I_1)$.

Experimentally, we have found that PRE tends to scale badly with the degree of ϕ's defining polynomials (see Sect. 6). Under certain conditions, the following theorem may provide a more effective alternative for solving Problem 3, via the POST algorithm. In order to apply the result, it suffices to find *any* precondition ψ_0 and template π such that POST$(\psi_0, \pi) = (V, J)$ and $\mathbf{V}(\pi[V]) = \phi$. In particular, ψ_0 may consists of a singleton, a case for which it is trivial to obtain a basis of $\mathbf{I}(\psi_0)$ (see [7]).

Theorem 3 (weakest precondition via Post). *For an algebraic variety ψ_0 and template π, let POST$(\psi_0, \pi) = (V, J)$ and $\phi = \mathbf{V}(\pi[V])$. Then $\mathbf{V}(J) = \psi_\phi$.*

6 Experiments

We report below the outcomes we have obtained applying our algorithms to a challenging system taken from the literature. Two more extended examples (concerning collision avoidance and automatic discovery of Kepler laws from Newton's) are described in the full version [7]. The execution times reported below are for an implementation in Python under Sage, running on a Core i5 machine[5].

We consider the 6-th order longitudinal equations that capture the vertical motion (climbing, descending) of an airplane [20, Chap. 5]. The system is given by the equations below, where the variables have the following meaning: $u =$ axial velocity, $w =$ vertical velocity, $x =$ range, $z =$ altitude, $q =$ pitch rate, $\theta =$ pitch angle; we also have two equations encoding $\cos\theta$ and $\sin\theta$; we also introduce the following auxiliary variables (parameters, hence 0 derivative): $g =$ gravity acceleration, X/m, Z/m and M/I_{yy} whose meaning is described in [20] (see also [9,10]); and u_0, w_0, x_0, z_0, q_0, standing for the generic initial values of the corresponding variables. Overall, the system's vector field F consists of 17 polynomials over as many variables.

$$\dot{u} = X/m - g\sin\theta - qw \quad \dot{z} = -u\sin\theta + w\cos\theta \quad \dot{w} = Z/m + g\cos\theta + qu \quad \dot{q} = M/I_{yy}$$
$$\dot{x} = u\cos\theta + w\sin\theta \quad \dot{\theta} = q \quad \dot{\cos}\theta = -q\sin\theta \quad \dot{\sin}\theta = q\cos\theta.$$

In order to discover interesting polynomial invariants, we consider a complete template π of degree 2 over all the original system's plus two auxiliary variables[6], the latter representing the monomials qu and qw. So π is a linear combination of $n = 207$ monomials that uses as many parameters. We apply the approach underpinned by Theorem 3: we first pick up a precondition that requires $\theta = 0$ and assigns (generic) initial values to the remaining variables, $\psi_0 \stackrel{\triangle}{=} \mathbf{V}(\{\theta, \sin\theta, \cos\theta - 1, u - u_0, w - w_0, x - x_0, z - z_0, q - q_0\})$. We then run $\mathrm{POST}(\psi_0, \pi)$, which returns, after $m = 8$ iterations and about 26s, a pair (V, J). The vector space V corresponds to the following result template π'.

$$a_1 \cdot (\cos^2\theta + \sin^2\theta - 1) \quad + \quad a_2 \cdot (-(1/2)q^2 + \theta(M/I_{yy}) + (1/2)q_0^2) +$$
$$a_3 \cdot (uq\cos\theta + wq\sin\theta - (X/m)\sin\theta + (Z/m)\cos\theta - x(M/I_{yy}) - (M/I_{yy})x_0 + u_0q_0 + Z/m) +$$
$$a_4 \cdot (wq\cos\theta - uq\sin\theta - \theta g - (X/m)\cos\theta - (Z/m)\sin\theta - zM/I_{yy} - (M/I_{yy})z_0 + w_0q_0 + X/m).$$

Let $\phi \stackrel{\triangle}{=} \mathbf{V}(\pi'[\mathbb{R}^n])$ be the variety defined by the result template π'. The invariant ideal J returned by the algorithm represents the *weakest algebraic precondition* $\chi \stackrel{\triangle}{=} \mathbf{V}(J)$ such that $\chi \longrightarrow [F]\phi$: in other words, the largest algebraic precondition for which all instances of π' are polynomial invariants (Theorem 3).

---

[5] Code and examples available at http://local.disia.unifi.it/boreale/papers/Pre Post.py.

[6] We could dispense with them by considering a complete template of degree 3.

Moreover, χ is also the *weakest algebraic invariant* included in ϕ (Corollary 1). These findings generalize those in [9,10]. In particular, one obtains the polynomial invariants of [9,10] by letting $x_0 = z_0 = q_0 = 0$. By comparison, [9] reports that their method spent 1 hour to find a subset of all instances of π'. The method in [10] reportedly takes <1s on this system, but again only finds a subset[7] of instances of π'. Moreover, it cannot infer the largest invariant implying the discovered laws, as we do.

7   Further and Related Work

In the future, we plan to extend the present approach to systems where ψ and ϕ are specified as *semi*algebraic sets, in the vein of Liu et al.'s [11]; see also [19]. Our previous work [6] deals with initial values problems, where the precondition ψ always consists of a fixed singleton. The method introduced there has its roots in a line of research concerning weighted automata, bisimulation and Markov chains [3–5].

The study of the safety of hybrid systems can be shown to reduce constructively to the problem of generating invariants for their differential equations [14]. Many authors have therefore focused on the effective generation of invariants of a special type. For example, Tiwari and Khanna consider invariants generation based on *syzygies* and Gröbner basis [22]. Sankaranarayanan [18] characterizes greatest invariants in terms of a descending chains of ideals. This iteration does not always converge, thus a relaxation in terms of bounded-degree *pseudoideals* is considered: the resulting algorithm always converges and returns an invariant ideal, although with no guarantee of maximality [18, Theorem 4.1]. Ghorbal and Platzer [9] offer sufficient conditions under which all instances of a polynomial template are polynomial invariants [9, Prop.3]. Matringe et al. encode invariants constraints using symbolic matrices [16]. None of the above mentioned works offers (relative) completeness results for post-, preconditions or invariants, in the sense of our Theorems 1 and 3. Practically, this may reflect on the number and quality of the discovered invariants, as illustrated by our experimentin Sect. 6. Moreover, the computational prerequisites of some of these approaches, such as minimization of the rank of a symbolic matrix [9,16], appear to be quite more demanding than ours.

The recent work of Kong et al. [10] considers generation of invariant clusters, again based on templates. Nonlinear constraints on a template parameters are resolved via sum-of-squares (SOS) programming. The resulting approach also works for semialgebraic systems. Again, completeness guarantees in our sense are not offered, though – cf. the vertical airplane motion example in Sect. 6. Compared to theirs, our approach appears to be slower: but a few more tens seconds of execution time seem to be a fair price for completeness.

---

[7] For instance, one should compare the polynomial $\psi_3 = q^2 - 2\theta(M/I_{yy})$, which is part of the invariant cluster in [10], with our polynomial $-(1/2)q^2 + \theta(M/I_{yy}) + (1/2)q_0^2$ in the second summand of π' above.

Ideas from Algebraic Geometry have been fruitfully applied also in Program Analysis, see e.g. Müller-Olm and Seidl's [12], and [7] for a comparison with our work.

References

1. Arnold, V.I.: Ordinary Differential Equations. The MIT Press, Cambridge (1978). ISBN 0-262-51018-9
2. Blinov, M.L., Faeder, J.R., Goldstein, B., Hlavacek, W.S.: BioNet-Gen: software for rule-based modeling of signal transduction based on the interactions of molecular domains. Bioinformatics **20**(17), 3289–3291 (2004)
3. Bonchi, F., Bonsangue, M.M., Boreale, M., Rutten, J.J.M.M., Silva, A.: A coalgebraic perspective on linear weighted automata. Inf. Comput. **211**, 77–105 (2012)
4. Boreale, M.: Weighted bisimulation in linear algebraic form. In: Bravetti, M., Zavattaro, G. (eds.) CONCUR 2009. LNCS, vol. 5710, pp. 163–177. Springer, Heidelberg (2009). https://doi.org/10.1007/978-3-642-04081-8_12
5. Boreale, M.: Analysis of probabilistic systems via generating functions and Padé approximation. In: Halldórsson, M.M., Iwama, K., Kobayashi, N., Speckmann, B. (eds.) ICALP 2015. LNCS, vol. 9135, pp. 82–94. Springer, Heidelberg (2015). https://doi.org/10.1007/978-3-662-47666-6_7. Full version available as DiSIA working paper 2016/10. http://local.disia.unifi.it/wp_disia/2016/wp_disia_2016_10.pdf
6. Boreale, M.: Algebra, coalgebra, and minimization in polynomial differential equations. In: Esparza, J., Murawski, A.S. (eds.) FoSSaCS 2017. LNCS, vol. 10203, pp. 71–87. Springer, Heidelberg (2017). https://doi.org/10.1007/978-3-662-54458-7_5. Full version available as DiSIA working paper 2017/01. http://local.disia.unifi.it/wp_disia/2017/wp_disia_2017_01.pdf
7. Boreale, M.: Complete algorithms for algebraic strongest postconditions and weakest preconditions in polynomial ODE's. In: CoRR, abs/1708.05377. Full version of the present paper http://arxiv.org/abs/1708.05377 (2017)
8. Cox, D.A., Little, J., O'Shea, D.: Ideals, Varieties, and Algorithms. UTM. Springer, Cham (2015). https://doi.org/10.1007/978-3-319-16721-3
9. Ghorbal, K., Platzer, A.: Characterizing algebraic invariants by differential radical invariants. In: Ábrahám, E., Havelund, K. (eds.) TACAS 2014. LNCS, vol. 8413, pp. 279–294. Springer, Heidelberg (2014). https://doi.org/10.1007/978-3-642-54862-8_19. Extended version available from http://reports-archive.adm.cs.cmu.edu/anon/2013/CMU-CS-13-129.pdf
10. Kong, H., Bogomolov, S., Schilling, C., Jiang, Y., Henzinger, T.A.: Safety verification of nonlinear hybrid systems based on invariant clusters. In: HSCC 2017, pp. 163–172. ACM (2017)
11. Liu, J., Zhan, N., Zhao, H.: Computing Semi-algebraic Invariants for Polynomial Dynamical Systems. In: EMSOFT, pp. 97–106. ACM (2011)
12. Müller-Olm, M., Seidl, H.: Computing polynomial program invariants. Inf. Process. Lett. **91**(5), 233–244 (2004)
13. Platzer, A.: Differential dynamic logic for hybrid systems. J. Autom. Reasoning **41**(2), 143–189 (2008)
14. Platzer, A.: Logics of dynamical systems. In: LICS 2012, pp. 13–24. IEEE (2012)
15. Platzer, A.: The structure of differential invariants and differential cut elimination. Log. Methods Comput. Sci. **8**(4), 1–38 (2012)

16. Rebiha, R., Moura, A.V., Matringe, N.: Generating invariants for non-linear hybrid systems. Theor. Comput. Sci. **594**, 180–200 (2015)
17. Sankaranarayanan, S., Sipma, H., Manna, Z.: Non-linear loop invariant generation using Gröbner bases. In: POPL 2004, pp. 318–329. ACM (2004)
18. Sankaranarayanan, S.: Automatic invariant generation for hybrid systems using ideal fixed points. In: HSCC 2010, pp. 221–230 (2010)
19. Sogokon, A., Ghorbal, K., Jackson, P.B., Platzer, A.: A method for invariant generation for polynomial continuous systems. In: Jobstmann, B., Leino, K.R.M. (eds.) VMCAI 2016. LNCS, vol. 9583, pp. 268–288. Springer, Heidelberg (2016). https://doi.org/10.1007/978-3-662-49122-5_13
20. Stengel, R.F.: Flight Dynamics. Princeton University Press, Princeton (2004)
21. Tiwari, A.: Approximate reachability for linear systems. In: HSCC 2003, pp. 514–525. ACM (2003)
22. Tiwari, A., Khanna, G.: Nonlinear systems: approximating reach sets. In: HSCC 2004, pp. 600-614. ACM (2004)
23. Tribastone, M., Gilmore, S., Hillston, J.: Scalable differential analysis of process algebra models. IEEE Trans. Softw. Eng. **38**(1), 205–219 (2012)

Recognition and Generation

Influence of Body Postures on Touch-Based Biometric User Authentication

Kamil Burda[✉] and Daniela Chuda

Faculty of Informatics and Information Technologies,
Slovak University of Technology in Bratislava,
Ilkovičova 2, 842 16 Bratislava, Slovakia
{kamil.burda,daniela.chuda}@stuba.sk

Abstract. Due to user mobility, many factors may influence a user's touch screen behavior and consequently affect the accuracy of user authentication based on touch-screen behavioral biometrics. Existing studies have shown significant differences in typing behavior for different hand postures. In this paper we examine touch-based biometric user authentication when performing simple swipes under different body postures. Our proposed authentication method generates numerous features from the swipes and selects the most distinctive features using mutual information. Using an experimental dataset with 43 participants, we have concluded that performing swipes in different body postures has a negative impact on authentication accuracy and that several features based on finger touch size are not significantly affected by different body postures.

Keywords: User authentication · Behavioral biometrics
Touch screen · Body postures · Influencing factors

1 Introduction

Existing popular approaches to securing access to mobile devices may not be satisfactory due to their vulnerabilities such as observing a typed password or gesture over the shoulder or guessing the gesture according to the smudges left on the touch screen. User authentication may be enhanced by extracting biometric traits of a user. While physiological traits (such as fingerprints) require specialized and not commonly available hardware, behavioral traits can be observed from readily available sensors on mobile devices such as a touch screen.

Authenticating users based on behavioral biometrics requires building a user model, which involves logging raw data from one or more input devices or sensors, pre-processing the data (such as normalization), transforming the data to samples (often represented as vectors of features) and training the model on a subset of samples using methods ranging from simple distance metrics to machine learning algorithms. The resulting user model is then used to classify new samples and perform appropriate actions (such as accepting or rejecting a user). Common metrics for evaluating the accuracy of a biometric user model

© Springer International Publishing AG 2018
A M. Tjoa et al. (Eds.): SOFSEM 2018, LNCS 10706, pp. 459–468, 2018.
https://doi.org/10.1007/978-3-319-73117-9_32

include the false acceptance rate (FAR), false rejection rate (FRR) and equal error rate (EER).

Each biometric trait (such as keystroke dynamics or touch screen interaction) should possess a high degree of uniqueness (the ability to distinguish individuals) and permanence (invariance of the trait over time) [1]. In the context of mobile devices, many external factors can affect the user behavior due to user mobility, such as body postures (sitting, standing, walking), hand postures (fingers used to interact with the touch screen) or a user's physical condition. The factors can thus have a negative impact on the accuracy of biometric user modeling.

This paper revisits the feasibility of user authentication based on simple swipes performed on the touch screen of a mobile device when considering different body postures. The results provide the first step toward building a more accurate biometric user model based on the interaction with mobile devices under the influence of external factors.

We first describe existing approaches to behavioral biometrics on mobile devices, and discuss open problems in this field of study. The second part of this paper describes our proposed user authentication method when considering different body postures. Finally, we evaluate our method on an experimental dataset, discuss the results and possible ways of building upon the results.

2   Related Work

Touch screen biometrics have been predominantly studied for implicit user authentication. Several studies showed that typing passwords or PINs [2,3] or tapping objects [4] can be successfully exploited as a user authentication method, where the lowest EER achieved was 1%, 3.65% and 6.9%, respectively. Typical features extracted from the keystroke data include dwell time, flight time and features related to touch size, which were proven to significantly reduce the EER.

Comparable performance was found in performing simple touch screen swipes. A comprehensive study by Frank et al. [5] showed that such an approach results in EER below 4%. Other related studies, which also considered gestures such as zoom and pinch, achieved comparable performance [6,7]. Enhancing the lock pattern mechanism with touch screen biometrics resulted in approx. 10% EER in one study [8] and 90% classification accuracy in another [9]. Common features extracted from gestures include the swipe duration, velocity, start and end position, and touch size. Features extracted from different stages of each gesture may also prove useful as each user is assumed to exhibit different touch behavior at the start, middle and end of a gesture [5,10].

With each tap or gesture performed on the touch screen, the mobile device is slightly tilted or rotated, which can be tracked by data from accelerometer, gyroscope and geomagnetic sensors. Lin et al. [11] achieved 6.85% EER for authentication based on features from the accelerometer and geomagnetic sensor when performing touch screen swipes.

Several studies considered the influence of time on the accuracy of touch screen biometrics. The error rate has been shown to increase over sessions further apart in time [5, 12]. To the best of our knowledge, in most studies involving touch screen user authentication, other influencing factors were either not considered or minimized by performing experiments in a controlled environment.

The influence of hand postures on touch-screen behavior was studied by Buschek et al. [12, 13]. Based on an experiment involving typing a password on the touch screen in three different hand postures – thumb, two thumbs and index finger – the results suggest that typing behavior is strongly specific to hand postures. The best results were achieved for separate models for each posture combined in a probabilistic framework rather than a single model for all postures. In terms of the EER, binary classification methods outperformed anomaly detection methods [12].

The influence of body postures on touch screen biometrics was examined by Zheng et al. [2] for typing PINs in an experiment with 10 participants in four different postures – sitting, standing, lying and walking. Differences in individual postures for a single user were found, but not as significant as differences between a user and other users in a sitting posture.

Our previous study [14] showed that different body postures affect several touch screen features, especially touch size. Based on our observation, we perform user authentication under different body postures to determine their influence on user authentication error rate.

3   Method for User Authentication Under Different Body Postures

This section contains a detailed description of the proposed method of touch screen biometric user authentication. Overview of the method is depicted in Fig. 1.

Biometric user authentication can be represented as a binary classification problem, where the positive class is assigned to the mobile device owner and the negative class to the impostors attempting to gain unauthorized access to the device.

The method assumes a dataset containing raw data from the touch screen while performing simple swipes with arbitrary length and direction. In an experimental setup, we also assume that the raw data are logged from multiple users, each performing swipes in multiple postures.

On consumer smartphones, each touch screen interaction usually contains the following fields: timestamp, touch x, touch y and touch size. Additionally, touch screen gestures (strokes) can be easily distinguished by logging events such as touch-up and touch-down.

3.1   Data Pre-processing and Transformation

Once the raw data are available, we split the raw data to segments according to touch events. Each segment begins by a touch-down event and ends with a touch-up event and contains all data rows between these events. Segments whose

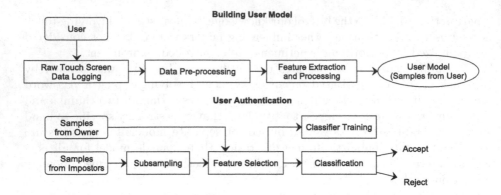

Fig. 1. Overview of the proposed method of touch screen-based user authentication

displacement (distance between end points) is lower than a given threshold are removed as they are not considered swipes, but rather button or key presses. Also, such segments would introduce noise in the samples that would confuse classifiers. The displacement threshold was determined manually based on the experimental dataset described in Sect. 4. An example of a touch swipe as a valid segment is shown in Fig. 2. Each point represents an xy touch coordinate logged at a given timestamp.

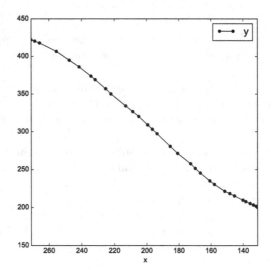

Fig. 2. An example of a touch screen swipe

From each segment we compute numerous features based on the combination of the following criteria:

1. statistic – mean, standard deviation, median, minimum, maximum, range (difference of maximum and minimum)
2. segment subset – entire segment, first n points, last m points, subset between the first n and last m points,
3. feature type – touch size, x-velocity, y-velocity, velocity magnitude, distance between trajectory and end-to-end line.

Examples of such computed features include the mean velocity magnitude, maximum touch size in the first 5 points, and so on. We also consider the following additional features:

1. ratio of swipe trajectory length and displacement,
2. timestamp (relative to the beginning of the segment) with the maximum distance of the swipe trajectory from the end-to-end line.

3.2   Feature Processing

Each feature set, hereinafter *sample*, is a vector comprising a user, posture and features computed from a single segment. Before being fed into a classifier, each sample needs to be further processed.

While raw data are dense and usually contain no missing values, some segments may not comprise enough data points, resulting in the fact that some features considering only a subset of points in such segments (e.g. between the first n and last m points) cannot be computed. In such a case, we impute (fill) missing values for these features based on the existing values of the same feature from other samples.

We scale each feature using the Z-score normalization as many classifiers are sensitive to feature values (treating them as weights). The high number of features considered during the classification may not be desirable in terms of classification speed and potentially performance. We therefore employ mutual information to select k features with the highest score.

3.3   Estimator Selection and Method Evaluation

We set samples extracted from one user for all postures as the device owner and the remaining samples as the impostors. We then perform estimator selection to determine the best parameters for feature processing methods and for the chosen classifier. We use the term *estimator* here to refer to both the chosen feature processing steps and the classifier because we also search for the best parameters for the feature processing steps.

Finally, we perform classification (user authentication) and determine the FAR and FRR of our method. We use the k-nearest neighbors (k-NN) and the random forest classifier (using the CART tree building algorithm) and compare the performance of these classifiers for user authentication. The rest of this section describes the details of estimator selection and user authentication.

Given that the impostor class contains samples from all other users, the number of samples in the impostor and owner class are highly imbalanced, which may result in the chosen classifier having good predictability of the impostor class, but not the owner class. We therefore balance the classes by subsampling the impostor class. The impostor samples are chosen randomly without replacement from any user and any posture.

We split the samples to train and test sets in the ratio of 3:1. The training set is used for estimator selection while the test set is held out for classification. Both sets are stratified to ensure a balanced number of samples for owner and impostor classes in each set.

To select the best estimator, we employ 10-fold stratified cross-validation (meaning that the class balance is maintained in each fold) and perform exhaustive search (i.e. training an estimator for every combination of parameters and selecting the best combination) to find parameters that yield the best cross-validation score. The parameters considered in estimator selection are specified in Table 1. We chose classification accuracy as the cross-validation score to compare the performance of individual estimators. The accuracy is a good indicator as the classes are assumed to be balanced (otherwise a different metric would have to be used).

Feature processing steps – imputation, scaling and selection – are performed on the train samples only and the imputed values, scaling parameters and selected features are then applied to the test samples.

Table 1. Parameters for determining the best estimator

Step	Parameter values
Imputation – strategy	Mean, median
Feature selection – mutual information – best k	10, 13, 16, 19
Classification – k-NN – k	1, 3
Classification – k-NN – distance metric	Manhattan, Euclidean
Classification – random forest – number of trees	5, 10
Classification – random forest – split criterion	Gini impurity, information gain

The entire process of estimator selection and method evaluation is repeated for each user. This implies that each user has a unique user model – different selected features and estimator parameters. We thus obtain u results for FAR, FRR and the list of selected features, where u is the number of users. From these individual results, we compute average FAR and FRR as a performance indicator of our user authentication method and the percentage of times a feature was selected among all users. Features selected the most often may indicate their low dependence on postures and high distinctiveness.

4   Evaluation

To evaluate our proposed method, we use a dataset from an experiment conducted in our previous study [14]. 43 participants (with one participant removed due to erroneous data) performed simple swipes on the touch screen of a smartphone. Each user was asked to drag a blue circle toward a black circle. The task was repeated 10 times for six postures: standing, sitting straight, sitting and leaning backward, sitting and leaning forward, sitting and leaning forwards with hands on a table and lying on a sitting bag. In each task the circles appeared in different random places on the touch screen, with a guaranteed minimum distance apart.

For each posture, each user managed to successfully perform at least 10 swipes. There may be more segments extracted in case the participant missed the target circle and so had to perform another swipe.

During segment extraction, we filtered segments not belonging to any task. The threshold for removing too short segments was set to 150 (which was determined manually based on the observation of the raw touch data). The number of remaining segments was 9–20 (11–12 on average) per user for each posture individually, and 61–99 (70 on average) per user for all postures.

Based on the number of touch-x and touch-y points for raw data per segment (7–102, 32 on average), we set the n and m parameters for segment subsets to 5 so that the method generates features such as the mean velocity from the first 5 points.

Swipe direction, trajectory length or swipe duration, which may exhibit good distinctiveness when used as features, are not considered due to random positions of the circles for each swipe. Moreover, while static authentication mechanisms may assume a swipe performed in a fixed starting position and direction, continuous authentication mechanisms cannot rely on this property due to the variety of gestures performed on the touch screen. To make our proposed method applicable for either scenario, we discard these features.

4.1 Results

Figures 3 and 4 show FAR and FRR for user authentication for each user and for each classifier separately. Average FAR and FRR from all users per each classifier are shown in Table 2.

The error rates vary widely across users and so do the individual error rates for each user. This may stem from the fact that the impostor samples were chosen randomly from any other user and posture and thus impostor samples for one posture may contain feature values similar to owner samples for one or more postures. Neither of the two examined classifiers can be overall considered more accurate for the experimental scenario, as k-NN exhibits higher FAR and random forest higher FRR on average.

The error rates, relatively high compared to similar studies, suggest that we cannot rely the touch-screen behavioral biometrics as a sole method for user authentication as they do not provide sufficient information to distinguish individuals, and that the chosen body postures have a strong impact on user authentication.

We can further examine the influence of postures by assessing which features were discarded most often (for all users). The features that were selected most

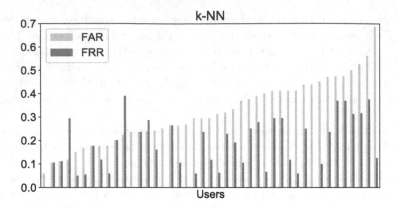

Fig. 3. User authentication FAR and FRR for each user (sorted by FAR) for the k-NN classifier

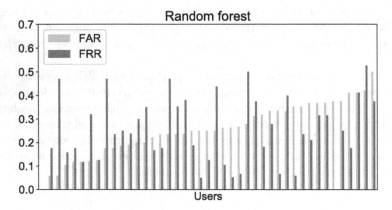

Fig. 4. User authentication FAR and FRR for each user (sorted by FAR) for the Random Forest classifier

often indicate their relative independence of postures and also their distinctiveness. Such features are specified in Table 3.

Features based on finger size thus still prove their usefulness for user authentication even if the user switches postures. Other features, such as touch velocity, proved to be not as distinctive under different postures, having been selected by less than in 18% of all users.

Table 2. Average FAR and FRR for user authentication for all users

Classifier	Average FAR	Average FRR
k-NN	32%	17%
Random forest	26%	25%

Table 3. Percentage of times a feature was selected per user (acting as the device owner) based on mutual information

Feature	% times selected
Size – mean between first 5 and last 5 points	81%
Size – mean	81%
Size – median between first 5 and last 5 points	74%
Size – mean from first 5 points	69%
Size – median	69%
Size – maximum between first 5 and last 5 points	65%
Size – maximum from first 5 points	62%
Size – minimum from first 5 points	60%
Size – maximum	58%
Size – median from last 5 points	55%
Size – minimum between first 5 and last 5 points	55%
Size – maximum from last 5 points	51%
Size – median from first 5 points	44%
Size – mean from last 5 points	34%

5   Conclusions and Future Work

In this paper we proposed a method for biometric user authentication based on performing a single swipe on the touch screen of a mobile device when considering various body postures as influencing factors. We have shown that finger touch size-based features can be usable for user authentication scenarios even under the influence of body postures.

The experimental results prompt us to rethink in what real-world scenarios the touch screen biometrics can be used reliably under various influencing factors so as to minimize their impact. In case of user authentication, imposing too many restrictions on the environment only to be successfully authenticated may significantly impact its usability.

In an endeavor of developing a seamless biometric user authentication method, an alternative approach to minimizing the influence of factors is to examine different approaches to processing raw data and classifying samples and considering additional sensors built-in mobile devices (such as accelerometer). Different sets of features from the touch screen could be extracted such as curvature or acceleration. User authentication accuracy could further be improved by considering a sequence of swipes, rather than a single swipe, to gain access to the mobile device.

Acknowledgments. This work was partially supported by the Scientific Grant Agency of the Slovak Republic, grant No. VG 1/0646/15 Adaptation of access to information and knowledge artifacts based on interaction and collaboration within web environment and the Slovak Research and Development Agency under the contract No. APVV-15-0508 Human Information Behavior in the Digital Space.

References

1. Jain, A.K., Ross, A.A., Nandakumar, K.: Introduction to Biometrics. Springer, Boston (2011). https://doi.org/10.1007/978-0-387-77326-1
2. Zheng, N., Bai, K., Huang, H., Wang, H.: You are how you touch: user verification on smartphones via tapping behaviors. In: 2014 IEEE 22nd International Conference on Network Protocols (ICNP), pp. 221–232, October 2014
3. Saevanee, H., Bhattarakosol, P.: Authenticating user using keystroke dynamics and finger pressure. In: 6th IEEE Consumer Communications and Networking Conference, CCNC 2009, pp. 1–2, January 2009
4. Chang, T.Y., Tsai, C.J., Lin, J.H.: A graphical-based password keystroke dynamic authentication system for touch screen handheld mobile devices. J. Syst. Softw. **85**(5), 1157–1165 (2012)
5. Frank, M., Biedert, R., Ma, E., Martinovic, I., Song, D.: Touchalytics: on the applicability of touchscreen input as a behavioral biometric for continuous authentication. IEEE Trans. Inf. Forensics Secur. **8**(1), 136–148 (2013)
6. Shahzad, M., Liu, A.X., Samuel, A.: Secure unlocking of mobile touch screen devices by simple gestures: you can see it but you can not do it. In: Proceedings of the 19th Annual International Conference on Mobile Computing and Networking, MobiCom 2013, pp. 39–50. ACM, New York (2013)
7. Bo, C., Zhang, L., Li, X.Y., Huang, Q., Wang, Y.: SilentSense: silent user identification via touch and movement behavioral biometrics. In: Proceedings of the 19th Annual International Conference on Mobile Computing and Networking, MobiCom 2013, pp. 187–190. ACM, New York (2013)
8. Angulo, J., Wästlund, E.: Exploring touch-screen biometrics for user identification on smart phones. In: Camenisch, J., Crispo, B., Fischer-Hübner, S., Leenes, R., Russello, G. (eds.) Privacy and Identity 2011. IAICT, vol. 375, pp. 130–143. Springer, Heidelberg (2012). https://doi.org/10.1007/978-3-642-31668-5_10
9. De Luca, A., Hang, A., Brudy, F., Lindner, C., Hussmann, H.: Touch me once and i know it's you!: implicit authentication based on touch screen patterns. In: Proceedings of the SIGCHI Conference on Human Factors in Computing Systems, CHI 2012, pp. 987–996. ACM, New York (2012)
10. Feng, T., Liu, Z., Kwon, K.A., Shi, W., Carbunar, B., Jiang, Y., Nguyen, N.: Continuous mobile authentication using touchscreen gestures. In: 2012 IEEE Conference on Technologies for Homeland Security (HST), pp. 451–456, November 2012
11. Lin, C.C., Liang, D., Chang, C.C., Yang, C.H.: A new non-intrusive authentication method based on the orientation sensor for smartphone users. In: 2012 IEEE 6th International Conference on Software Security and Reliability (SERE), pp. 245–252, June 2012
12. Buschek, D., De Luca, A., Alt, F.: Improving accuracy, applicability and usability of keystroke biometrics on mobile touchscreen devices. In: Proceedings of the 33rd Annual ACM Conference on Human Factors in Computing Systems, CHI 2015, pp. 1393–1402. ACM, New York (2015)
13. Buschek, D., De Luca, A., Alt, F.: Evaluating the influence of targets and hand postures on touch-based behavioural biometrics. In: Proceedings of the 2016 CHI Conference on Human Factors in Computing Systems, CHI 2016, pp. 1349–1361. ACM, New York (2016)
14. Chuda, D., Burda, K.: Toward posture recognition with touch screen biometrics. In: Proceedings of the 17th International Conference on Computer Systems and Technologies, CompSysTech 2016, pp. 293–299. ACM, New York (2016)

Michiko: Poem Models used in Automated Haiku Poetry Generation

Miroslava Hrešková[(✉)] and Kristína Machová

Technical University of Košice, Letná 9, 042 00 Košice, Slovak Republic
Miroslava.hreskova@student.tuke.sk,
kristina.machova@tuke.sk

Abstract. Computational creativity is a part of artificial intelligence that sets its goal to determine what is creativity and what does it mean to be creative - not only in humans, but in general. It also aims to mimic creativity by computer programs. There are multiple approaches and systems that are imitating creativity in different artistic forms. The approach proposed in this article suggests a method for automated generation of written text, specifically haiku poetry. Experiments with system that implements the proposed approach are presented.

Keywords: Computational creativity · Haiku · Poetry generation

1 Introduction

Definition of computational creativity from [1] states: "Computational creativity is the study and simulation, by computer means, of behavior, natural and artificial, which would, if observed in humans, be deemed creative." One of the main objectives of author's research is to generate haiku poetry that would be perceived by readers as artistically pleasing.

Certain areas of current research in computational creativity are focusing on developing approaches for autonomous creative tasks, e.g. creating pictures, composing music or writing prose and poetry. Some of such approaches are mentioned in Sect. 3.

According to [2], one of the main goals of computational creativity is to create a program that would exhibit human creativity. Also, the proposed approach aims to fulfill this goal by creating a system for automated haiku poetry generation using poem models.

Large poem corpus represents the basis for the knowledge discovery. Poem models and dictionary that are used for automated creation of the poems are extracted from the corpus. Section 4 is dedicated to the description of the approach and Michiko system, its implementation. Outputs of the generation were presented to real users for evaluation and results of the evaluation are also presented in this section.

2 Poetry

Poetry belongs to cultural heritage. It is used for expressing personal emotion or sharing ideas. It differs from prose mainly in strict formal rules defined by rhythm, metre, rhyme or word-stress pattern. That makes it more challenging to algorithmically generate poetry.

© Springer International Publishing AG 2018
A M. Tjoa et al. (Eds.): SOFSEM 2018, LNCS 10706, pp. 469–476, 2018.
https://doi.org/10.1007/978-3-319-73117-9_33

2.1   Haiku Poetry [3, 4]

Haiku is a famous genre of Japanese poetry. The founder of traditional haiku, Kyoshi, said that haiku should be "sketch from nature". As the quote suggests, a traditional haiku poem usually describes a person's feeling for nature.

Association with nature in haiku poetry is expressed by seasonal reference. There are two ways how to express it: directly naming the season (kigo) or by specific element of a season (kidai), e.g. falling leaves as a reference to autumn.

One haiku poem is a stanza consisting of 3 lines. Each line has fixed count of sound units (morae, similar to syllables in English). A traditional haiku poem consists of two parts. Each part creates a different image or aims to express a certain idea. These two parts are separated by cutting word (kireji) that is a word separating the images or ideas depicted in the poem.

First line of traditional haiku poem usually expresses an image using seasonal reference and ends with cutting word. The remaining 2 lines are used to create another image as a comparison, contrast or complement to the first one.

In the beginning of the 20th century, haiku was adapted to English and later also into other languages. Foreign adaptation consists of 3 lines of 5-7-5 syllables, since morae does not have an equivalent in other languages. Foreign haiku does not always follow strict rules of traditional haiku poem. Therefore, topics are not limited to nature and often haiku in other language does not conform to the formal haiku rules.

The proposed approach creates English haiku poems about nature. Poems are generated in 3 lines and conform to traditional 5-7-5 syllable pattern.

2.2   Basic Properties of Poetry

According to [5], poetic text must hold all the following three properties:

- Meaningfulness: the poem is human-understandable – it expresses certain idea or message under some interpretation
- Grammaticality: poem has to follow grammar and lexical rules
- Poeticness: poem has poetic features specific for the poetry genre (rhythm, meter, rhyme, etc.)

Approach to generation of poetry, described in this article, aims to follow mostly the rule of grammaticality and poeticness. Grammaticality is ensured by extraction of poem models from corpus of existing poems from human authors. Poeticness is provided by following the formal rules of haiku poem – creating 3 lines of 5-7-5 syllables and by using haiku-specific dictionary of words to fill the model with. Next step is to implement methods of artificial intelligence in order to achieve certain level of meaningfulness.

3   Related Works

Language provides a space for creativity - in generation of novel sentences, rhymes, metaphors, analogies, ideas, etc. This section mentions some approaches to computational creativity in language, specifically poetry.

3.1   Chinese Poetry Generation with Recurrent Neural Networks

Approach in [6] aims to generate classical Chinese poetry with formal and rhythmic constraints. It leverages neural networks and uses them to probabilistically generate the poem verse by verse. The poem topic is user-selected based on number of keywords provided as an input.

Poem corpus is used as training set for learning individual Chinese characters, their combinations and relations (how they form poem verses).

3.2   Constraint Satisfaction-Based Generator of Topical Indonesian Poetry

An input to the system, described in [7], is an Indonesian news article and corpus containing poems written by famous Indonesian authors. Article is user-selected input and it is used for keyword extraction. Poetry corpus is used for creating sentence templates and obtaining of poetic words, fifty most frequently used words in poetry corpus.

The system creates poetry from the collection of templates combined with a particular set of words. All possible combinations of templates, filled by keywords and poetic words, are created. These combinations are candidates for a line in the output poem. Candidates are filtered by applying poetic constraints, e.g. number of syllables, rhyme, rhythm or number of lines.

Thorough evaluation of the system was performed. Experiment was conducted with 180 participants that were asked to determine whether a poem is written by a human or generated by computes. The results showed that 57% of the respondents thought that the generated poems were authored by humans.

3.3   Automatic Analysis of Rhythmic Poetry with Applications
   to Generation and Translation

In [8], statistical analysis of poetry corpus is described. It is further used for generation of poems and their translation from Italian to English. Large set of sonnets is the subject for analysis. Unsupervised learning is used to reveal word-stress patterns. 3 different corpuses were used.

The results from word-stress analysis together with trigram model built from love poems is used to create poems with lines in a certain meter to generate poetry.

3.4   Computational Creativity for Automatic Generation of Poetry
   in Bengali

System described in [9] automatically generates a line of poetry as a response to user's one-line poetry input. The goal is to create appropriate verse that has the same rhythmic structure and rhymes with the input verse.

At first, rhyme structure understanding of the given user input has to be performed. For this purpose, corpus of Bengali poems is used as a training set for a classifier that predicts rhyme syllables and syllable sequence patterns. Bigrams are used to prune the list of candidate words and weighted sentence aggregation used to generate the actual system output.

3.5   Automated Haiku Generation Using Vector Space Model

Approach presented in [10] aims to create haiku poems. To achieve this, set of 500 most common words used in haiku writing (available online) is used as keyword set. These keywords are then searched in different blogs.

Articles are parsed into sentences and parts of the sentences, containing searched keyword, are gathered. Vector Space Model (VSM) and Term Frequency–Inverse Document Frequency (TF-IDF) are used to select sentence fragments and combine them into poems.

4   Poem Models in Michiko Poetry Generation System

Poem model defines basic structure of haiku poem to be generated. It contains knowledge on how to create the output poem by filling these models with words from dictionary based on their part of speech and syllable count.

Example model

Numeral – noun
Preposition – adjective – noun – noun
Noun – noun – noun

1 – 4
1 – 2 – 2 – 2
2 – 1 – 2

Example of generated poem from the above stated model:

each January
in frozen sunshine brightness
cutting pine branches

The corpus is a large set that consists of haiku poems written by human authors [12, 13]. It is used for two main goals:

- creating dictionary of words - splitting poems into words, gathering metadata for each word
- extracting poem models - list of parts of speech, each with certain syllable count

It is important to note, that the algorithm implementing the proposed approach is not using nor quoting whole haiku poems nor the verses from the corpus. It only uses the poems to extract information that is further used to create new poems in haiku generation process. Haiku corpus is not saved in database, only models and dictionary, extracted from the poems, are saved.

Michiko system (available online at [11]) implements an approach to generate haiku poems based on the usage of poem models. Several experiments were carried out to improve the performance of Michiko system that is implementing the proposed approach. Conducted experiments, together with results, are presented in this section.

4.1   Words in Dictionary

Haiku poem has a characteristic topic – the topic of nature. To achieve that generated poem is thematically consistent with haiku genre, dictionary is created by using words from the corpus. The corpus is a large set of haiku poems written by human authors from online haiku portals available at [12, 13]. This dictionary provides the word set for selection into the output poem.

The approach relies on the fact that human-authored haiku from the corpus are conforming to the haiku rules in terms of content. Testing with potential users showed that output poems contained some haikus with words not related to the typical haiku topics (which are expressing feeling, nature and its beauty), probably used by authors in some figurative speech. However, the approach does not consider meaning of the word. To solve this issue, only haiku-specific words are kept in dictionary and another experiment was carried out.

One word can be used in multiple haikus. The more often the word is used, the higher is its specificity for haiku poem and its probability to occur in haiku (except of words from general vocabulary).

For each unique word in dictionary, number of occurrences in haiku corpus was counted. Based on this, different occurrence thresholds were used for dictionary creation. Original dictionary and 4 of its subsets (with words that have their occurrence count higher than a selected threshold of 3, 5, 10 and 15 occurrences) were used in poetry generation in order to determine the right threshold that would create haiku-specific dictionary.

With each dictionary, 30 poems were created and evaluated by 3 participants. Their evaluation of poem generation showed that the most thematically balanced poems were produced by dictionary created with threshold of 5 occurrences. When too low occurrence threshold is set, dictionary contains too many words that are not thematically consistent for haiku genre, e.g. microwave. When too high threshold is used, all haiku-specific words are removed and only general vocabulary remains.

Table 1 shows dictionary size (total number of words in dictionary) for each threshold and its percentage share of dictionary size when all words extracted from corpus are used (when occurrence threshold equals 1).

Table 1. Experiment 1 – words in dictionary.

Threshold	Number of remaining words in dictionary	Percentage of remaining words in dictionary
1	7035	100%
3	3192	45.4%
5	1728	26.4%
10	1074	15.3%
15	625	8.9%

4.2   Gathering Metadata

Proposed approach creates poems by filling poem models with words based on their syllable count and part of speech. These properties of words are considered as metadata, providing basic information on when and where can be the word used in the resulting poem. Thus, dictionary of words with these metadata available is a precondition to successfully generate haikus. Corpus contains 8 107 haikus and 73 309 words in total, from which 9 117 were unique.

Originally, online tools [14, 15] for word metadata extraction were used. A separate application was created and used to carry out the metadata extraction, containing separate tools for syllable count and another for part of speech determination. Each word in dictionary was searched. HTML of the page was parsed in order to find the required metadata which was saved to a database. This process was long and demanding on computational power. It also proved to be unreliable, since it was able to acquire metadata for only approximately 60% of the dictionary.

Thus, metadata determination was implemented using Words API [16]. With the usage of Words API, 17% increase in dictionary coverage was observed. The results of this experiment are indicated in Table 2.

Table 2. Experiment 2 – metadata gathering.

Dictionary used	Words found	Percentage of words found
Online dictionary with online tool for syllable counting	5471	60%
Words API	7035	77%

Database of Words API contains 150,000 words and, besides part of speech and syllable count, it also provides more features, such as list of synonyms, antonyms or rhymes. Another advantage of Words API is that it provides complex information about searched word at one place (no need for separate tools) and using it is much quicker.

4.3   Haiku Generation Testing

Proposed approach was implemented as web application and made available for testing by real users at [11]. Based on main properties that poetic text has to conform to (according to [5]), users were asked to take into account following criteria for poem evaluation:

- Form – haiku poem consists of 3 lines and each line conforms to 5-7-5 syllable pattern
- Content – generated poem contains words related to nature and/or expressing emotions
- Meaning – the poem can be considered as meaningful, there is idea recognizable behind the verses

In sum, 254 poems were evaluated. Users evaluate each poem as neutral and as positive or negative with a degree of strength ranging from 1 to 3. Table 3. presents count of user evaluations belonging to each class and its percentage share of the total number of evaluations. Table 4. shows average values of positive and negative evaluation.

Table 3. Experiment 3 – evaluation count.

Evaluation class	Number of evaluations	Percentage of evaluations
Positive evaluation (points ranging from 1 to 3)	127	50%
Neutral evaluation (0 points)	35	13.7%
Negative evaluations (points ranging from −3 to −1)	92	36.3%

Table 4. Experiment 3 – evaluation statistics.

Statistics	Average evaluation value
Average positive evaluation value (points ranging from 1 to 3)	1.3
Average negative evaluation value (points ranging from 3 to −1)	−2.1

5 Conclusion

The proposed approach and application are work in progress. Its goal is to create haiku poems that would be considered by users as aesthetically pleasing.

Haiku poems originally capture a picture of nature, the changes of the season. Thus, the next goal is to implement generating haiku thematically – based on user-selected season.

Computational creativity, especially creating prose and poetry, is a suitable way to make the interaction between human and robot more natural - by improving robots' natural language generation.

Another goal of the research is to enrich the poems with recitation performed by a robot to create human-like recitation – speech with appropriate speed and voice pitch supported by non-verbal expression such as posture, hand and head movements to make robots' appearance more natural and human-like.

The biggest advantage of creative software (compared to human creativity) is its ability of "thinking outside the box" - since computers are not limited by conventions, customs, attitudes, etc. and can explore areas in art that people would not. Another pro is the ability of computers to analyze large text sets for knowledge, greater memory capacity to store extracted knowledge and more computational power for knowledge discovery. Correct poem structure is always kept – conforming to strict poetic formal or rhythmical rules.

Disadvantage of computational poetry generation (and computational text generation in general), often viewed as a challenge, is abiding grammar rules, creating meaningful text representing certain idea or using figures of speech.

Acknowledgment. The work presented in this paper was partially supported by the Slovak Grant Agency of the Ministry of Education and Academy of Science of the Slovak Republic under grant no. 1/0493/16 and by the Slovak Research and Development Agency under the contract No. APVV-16-0213.

References

1. Cardoso, A., Veale, T., Wiggins, G.A.: Converging on the divergent: the history (and future) of the international joint workshops in computational creativity. AI Mag. **30**(3) (2009)
2. Computational Creativity. Accessed 1 Mar 2017. http://computationalcreativity.net/home/about/computational-creativity/
3. Díaz-Agudo, B., Gervás, P., González-Calero, P.A.: Poetry generation in COLIBRI. In: Craw, S., Preece, A. (eds.) ECCBR 2002. LNCS (LNAI), vol. 2416, pp. 73–87. Springer, Heidelberg (2002). https://doi.org/10.1007/3-540-46119-1_7
4. Haiku Poetry. Accessed 10 Oct 2016. https://www.poets.org/poetsorg/text/haiku-poetic-form
5. Rahman, F., Manurung, R.: Multiobjective optimization for meaningful metrical poetry. In: Proceedings of the 2nd International Conference on Computational Creativity (2011)
6. Zhang, X., Lapata, M.: Chinese poetry generation with recurrent neural networks. In: EMNLP (2014)
7. Rashel, F., Manurung, R.: Pemuisi: a constraint satisfaction-based generator of topical Indonesian poetry. In: 5th International Conference on Computational Creativity, ICCC (2014)
8. Greene, Erica, Bodrumlu, T., Knight, K.: Automatic analysis of rhythmic poetry with applications to generation and translation. In: Proceedings of the 2010 Conference on Empirical Methods in Natural Language Processing. Association for Computational Linguistics (2010)
9. Das, A., Gambäck, B.: Poetic machine: Computational creativity for automatic poetry generation in Bengali. In: 5th International Conference on Computational Creativity, ICCC (2014)
10. Wong, M., Chun, A.H.W.: Automatic haiku generation using VSM. In: Li, Q., Chen, S.Y., Xu, A. (eds.) WSEAS International Conference on Proceedings of Mathematics and Computers in Science and Engineering, no. 7. World Scientific and Engineering Academy and Society (2008)
11. Michiko. Accessed 01 Mar 2017. http://michiko.azurewebsites.net/
12. Haiku Dictionary. Accessed 10 Mar 2017. http://www.ahapoetry.com/aadoh/h_dictionary.htm
13. Daily Haiku. Accessed 10 Mar 2017. http://www.dailyhaiku.org/
14. Syllable count. Accessed 10 Mar 2017. http://www.syllablecount.com/
15. YourDictionary. Accessed 10 Mar 2017. http://www.yourdictionary.com/
16. Words API. Accessed 10 Mar 2017. https://www.wordsapi.com

Optimization, Probabilistic Analysis, and Sorting

House Allocation Problems with Existing Tenants and Priorities for Teacher Recruitment

Ana Paula Tomás[(✉)]

DCC & CMUP, Faculdade de Ciências, Universidade do Porto, Porto, Portugal
`apt@dcc.fc.up.pt`

Abstract. We study a variant of house allocation problems with application to a real-world job assignment problem where some applicants cannot result unmatched. Such applicants hold posts initially, which enter the market if they can get strictly better posts. All applicants are strictly ordered by priority in a single master list. Their preference lists may be incomplete and may contain ties. We seek a matching that assigns the best possible post to each applicant, taking into account their preferences, priorities and initial posts. We give algorithms for solving the problem in polynomial time for three different cases.

1 Introduction

Many real-world problems can be modelled as matching problems with preferences, under some specific constraints and optimality criteria [18]. For many applications, these problems arise in the context of *centralised matching schemes* (a.k.a. clearinghouses) that assign applicants to posts. Algorithmic aspects of matching problems with ordinal preferences have been extensively studied after Gale and Shapley seminal work on the Stable Marriage Problem (SM) and variants [5]. For a recent comprehensive survey, we refer to [15]. Every agent reports his/her preferences, as a *preference list*, which can be strictly or partially ordered and complete or incomplete, modelling situations where it is allowed or disallowed to express indifference and unacceptable pairs. These problems are often modelled by two-sided markets, where each agent on one side has preferences over agents of the other side [5,19]. Nevertheless, the situations where the markets are one-sided, in the sense that only one side plays an active role, expressing preferences, are ubiquitous in practice. These include Housing Markets (HM) and House Allocation (HA) problems [1,3,20,23], where most frequently the goal is to find a Pareto optimal matching. In a Pareto optimal matching no agent can improve his allocation without making any other agent worse off. In housing markets, each active agent owns an indivisible item, that is called *a house*, whereas

---

A. P. Tomás—This work was partially supported by CMUP (UID/MAT/00144/2013), which is funded by FCT (Portugal) with national (MEC) and European structural funds through the programs FEDER, under the partnership agreement PT2020. The author gratefully acknowledges the support of COST Action IC1205 on Computational Social Choice (ECOST-STSM-IC1205-210914-046248).

A. M. Tjoa et al. (Eds.): SOFSEM 2018, LNCS 10706, pp. 479–492, 2018.
https://doi.org/10.1007/978-3-319-73117-9_34

in house allocation no agent owns a specific house. In [1], Abdulkadiroglu and Sönmez introduce an hybrid model, *"house allocation with existing tenants"*, where some agents own a house and some are newcomers. Agents have *strict* preferences over houses and each existing tenant is allowed to keep his current house. The allocation must be *individually rational*, which means that no agent may receive a house inferior to his own one. They propose two algorithms: the Top Trading Cycles mechanism and YRMH-IGYT "you request my house, I get your turn". A strict ordering of the agents is required, which can be a random ordering or an hierarchical ordering defined by seniorities, for example. In addition, these algorithms work for strict preferences only and, consequently, if there are ties, a tie-breaking rule is used to eliminate indifference.

We study variants of the house allocation problem with existing tenants and priorities, *without a tie-breaking rule*. An instance involves a set of agents A and a set of houses H. The agents are ranked according to some criteria and define a single strictly ordered *master list*. Every agent provides a *preference list*, which may contain ties and be incomplete. Each house has a capacity that can be any integer. We look for a matching that assigns the best possible house to each agent, in view of their preferences and the priorities given by the master list. Here, a matching can be a one-to-one matching, for unit capacities (HA), or a many-to-one matching, in the capacitated case (CHA). Some agents own a house initially (which, in CHA, corresponds to a vacancy in a house) and their houses enter the market but cannot be assigned to other agents unless they can move to a strictly better house.

In the sequel, we call the problem *TRP* and define the matchings we look for as *applicant-optimal weakly stable matchings*. TRP because the initial motivation for this work was a real-world problem, involving teacher recruitment in Portugal [24,25]. Amendments to the teacher recruitment legislation are made almost every year and, sometimes, they are troublesome. In the Fall 2004 and 2014, there was a deep concern due to some failures in the allocation of teachers to schools. The main recruitment program has a national scope and is centralised. There are thousands of applicants but very few posts. Applicants are strictly ranked and when they hold permanent posts, they cannot result unmatched. In the worst case, they keep their current post. Their preference lists can contain ties. Since in-service-time is one of the parameters used for ranking the candidates, we need matching mechanisms that can produce optimal solutions, under the constraints imposed by the law. That raised the question of whether TRP could be solved in polynomial time, which led us to address the problem, without being aware of some complementary regulation that established a tie-breaking rule. This rule resolves ties using an ordering defined by school codes. Although it has a drastic impact on the matching, it was not clearly stated in the main decree, in 2004. It was introduced in 2006 as a result of [24]. The problem that arose in 2014 resulted from another amendment. For the sake of transparency, an hiring scheme that was running in a completely decentralised way in the previous years was centralised. It involved fixed-term contracts in public schools with some autonomy. Each institution (school or school cluster) had its own master list. First, there was a bug in the formula used to produce the master lists. But, more importantly, there was really a problem since, for these offers, the preference lists of the candidates are not sorted. The candidates apply for schools, and just state whether they are willing to accept only full-time posts in that school or also a part-time position (there are at least two types of workload intervals). No candidate has a post initially. That renders the allocation problem NP-hard if, for instance, we seek a stable matching of maximum size. The Stable Marriage Problem with Ties and Incomplete lists (SMTI) can be reduced to this problem and it is known that SMTI is NP-hard, even under quite severe restrictions on the number and lengths of ties [16]. But, as for the main competition, for each institution, no candidate can overpass a "better" candidate who is still unmatched. So, the centralised matching mechanism mimicked the decentralised scheme and some applicants got many offers simultaneously for a final choice (about a hundred offers in some cases reported in the news). That raised controversy and caused significant delays. After some rounds, the control was given back to the school directors, for the remaining vacancies. In a subsequent amendment, the procedure was decentralised again. These two situations motivate our paper, which revises and extends [25]. It is worthwhile mentioning that TRP was inspired by the teachers recruitment problem, but should not be regarded as a model for the overall problem.

TRP has no relation to the problem of assigning teachers to schools studied in [4]. It is related, but not equivalent, to HA with existing tenants and to profile-based optimal problems (e.g., rank-optimal matchings [9,11], greedy maximum matching [14], fair matchings [8], lexicographic maximum stable matchings [10]), and the weighted popular matching problem [17,21]. All of them can be seen as HA problems, with very distinct goals and properties, that are exploited by the proposed matching mechanisms despite being grounded and employing standard matching theory tools and techniques. The notion of applicant-optimal stable matchings is close to that of *strong priority matchings*, recently defined in [13]. The Serial Dictatorship Mechanism with Ties (SDMT-1) introduced in that work can be seen as a particular case of the algorithm we gave for TRP.

The rest of paper is structured as follows. In Sect. 2, we introduce some notation and describe the problem formally. In Sect. 3 we show that TRP is polynomially solvable. In Sects. 4–6, we give algorithms for solving specific variants: TRP with strictly ordered preference lists and unit capacities, with ties and unit capacities, and the capacitated version (also with ties).

2   Problem Definition and Notation

An instance of TRP involves a set of agents $A = \{a_1, a_2, \ldots, a_{n_1}\}$ and a set of houses $H = \{h_1, h_2, \ldots, h_{n_2}\}$, with $A = A_E \cup A_N$ and $H = H_0 \cup H_V$, being A_E the set of existing tenants, A_N the set of new agents, H_0 the set of occupied houses and H_V the set of vacant houses. Each house h has a capacity $c(h)$, that can be any integer. If $c(h) < 0$ then no new agent can be assigned to h unless $1 - c(h)$ tenants who initially own h are assigned a new house in the matching.

For each agent a_i, let $\Gamma_{i,1}, \Gamma_{i,2}, \ldots, \Gamma_{i,\gamma_i}$ be his preference list, in strictly increasing order. Each $\Gamma_{i,l}$ is a set of houses for which a_i has the same preference, which is defined by $rank_{a_i}(h) = l$, for all $h \in \Gamma_{i,l}$, for $1 \le l \le \gamma_i$. In real-life applications, such as [24], γ_i is limited by a constant, which we denote by U, that can be much smaller than the total number of vacancies.

Each agent a_i has *a last resort house*, which is the house a_i holds, if a_i is a tenant. Otherwise, we define it as a dummy house h_0 (for a one-to-one matching, we could clone it, and define a dummy house for each applicant). We assume that A is strictly ordered by decreasing priority, through a master list, and that $rank_h(a_i) = i$, if a_i does not hold h and, otherwise, $rank_h(a_i) = 0$, for all $h \ne h_0$. For convenience, we introduced the dummy house h_0 with an unbounded number of vacancies. In this way, TRP can be seen as an instance of SMTI, for unit capacities (or of the Hospital/Residents problem, with ties, for generic capacities). We look for a matching M that is *weakly stable*, which means that there is no pair (a, h) such that agent a strictly prefers house h to $M(a)$ (i.e., $rank_a(h) < rank_a(M(a))$) and h is unassigned or strictly prefers a to $M(h)$ (i.e., $rank_h(a) < rank_h(M(h))$, if h is not free). For the capacitated version, the second part is rephrased to h is under-subscribed or strictly "prefers" a to the lowest ranked agent assigned to it in M.

A solution to TRP is an *applicant-optimal weakly stable matching* $M^\star$ of the applicants (agents) to posts (houses). *Optimal* means that $\zeta(M^\star) \le_{lex} \zeta(M)$, for every weakly stable matching M, where $\le_{lex}$ stands for the lexicographic order in $(\mathbb{N} \cup \{\infty\})^{n_1}$. The *rankings profile* $\zeta(M)$ of a matching M is the tuple $(z_1, \ldots, z_{n_1})$, where z_i is the rank of $M(a_i)$ in the preference list of a_i. We define $rank_{a_i}(h_0) = \infty$, since h_0 essentially means that a_i gets "no house" ("no post"). This notion of profile is distinct from the one addressed in other works (e.g. [8,9,11,14]), but it is essentially the one studied in [13] for *strong priority matchings*. In a rank-maximal (or greedy) matching the profile is given by the number of applicants that are matched to their first choice, to their second choice, and so forth [9,11].

Example 1. Let us consider the following two scenarios. In Case A, no agent owns a house, whereas, in Case B, all of them own houses initially.

Case A	Case B
$a_1 : \{h_1, h_2, h_3, h_4\}$	$a_1 : \{h_3\}, \{h_2\}, (\text{holds } h_1)$
$a_2 : \{h_1, h_2, h_3, h_4\}$	$a_2 : \{h_1\}, (\text{holds } h_2)$
$a_3 : \{h_1\}$	$a_3 : \{h_1\}, (\text{holds } h_3)$
$a_4 : \{h_2\}$	

In case B, the matching $\{(a_1, h_2), (a_2, h_1), (a_3, h_3)\}$ is the solution of TRP. The matching $\{(a_1, h_1), (a_2, h_2), (a_3, h_3)\}$ is weakly stable, because every agent gets the house he owns initially (for which he is top rank), but is not a solution of TRP. The matching $\{(a_1, h_3), (a_2, h_2), (a_3, h_1)\}$ is not weakly stable but its rankings profile is $\le_{lex}$-minimum. In case A, $\{(a_1, h_1), (a_2, h_2), (a_3, h_0), (a_4, h_0)\}$ is weakly stable but not a TRP-solution, because its profile is not $\le_{lex}$-minimum. The matching $\{(a_1, h_3), (a_2, h_4), (a_3, h_1), (a_4, h_2)\}$ is a solution to TRP.

Before we proceed, we note that the existence of tenants and the requirement that the matching must be weakly-stable and optimal in the above sense make TRP distinct from the weighted popular matching problem, studied in [17,21]. In that variant of popular matchings [2], applicants have weights (used to define priorities) and a matching M is weighted popular if there is no matching M' such that the applicants preferring M' to M overweight the applicants preferring M to M'. Example 2 shows that an optimal weighted popular matching is not a TRP-matching.

Example 2. Consider three agents a_1, a_2 and a_3, given in decreasing priority (weight) order, and three houses h_1, h_2 and h_3, being h_1 and h_3 the houses that a_2 and a_3 hold initially. Suppose that a_1 strictly prefers h_1 to h_2 and is not interested in h_3, a_2 only wants h_3 and a_3 only wants h_1, that is:

$$a_1 : \{h_1\}, \{h_2\} \qquad a_2 : \{h_3\}, \text{ (holds } h_1) \qquad a_3 : \{h_1\}, \text{ (holds } h_3)$$

The matching $M_1 = \{(a_1, h_2), (a_2, h_1), (a_3, h_3)\}$ is the unique solution to TRP but $M_2 = \{(a_1, h_2), (a_2, h_3), (a_3, h_1)\}$ is more popular than M_1. Even if it seems nonsense to adopt M_1 instead of the unstable matching M_2, stability is crucial for some real-life applications to avoid controversy.

Hence, TRP seeks a matching where every agent a_i gets a house among the best he can get in all weakly stable matchings that guarantee the same for $a_1, \ldots, a_{i-1}$, which seems fair. We will see that TRP is polynomially solvable, in contrast to some variants of the Stable Marriage Problem with master preference lists studied in [10] and of SMTI [12,16].

3   Polynomial Time Complexity

In this section we present a reduction of TRP with unit capacities to a sequence of at most t maximum-weight matching problems in bipartite weighted graphs, where $t = |A_E|$ is the number of existing tenants. To reduce the problem we introduced *edge weights* that guarantee weak stability but are exponential. This kind of reduction to weighted matching was previously independently introduced in [9,11], for solving greedy (rank-maximal) matching problems. We consider a relaxation of TRP where we no longer require that the existing tenants get a real house. Thus, we extend the preference list of a_i:

$$\tilde{\Gamma}_{a_i} : \begin{cases} \Gamma_{i,1}, \Gamma_{i,2}, \ldots, \Gamma_{i,\gamma_i}, \{h_j\}, \{h'_i\} & \text{if } a_i \text{ holds } h_j \\ \Gamma_{i,1}, \Gamma_{i,2}, \ldots, \Gamma_{i,\gamma_i}, \{h'_i\}, & \text{if } a_i \notin A_E \end{cases}$$

where h'_i is the last resort house (a dummy house), which is different for every applicant. We denote by Ω_i the rank of the last resort house, in each case, i.e., $\gamma_i + 2$ and $\gamma_i + 1$, respectively, and define the weight $w(a_i, \tilde{\Gamma}_{i,z})$ of every house that belongs to $\tilde{\Gamma}_{i,z}$, by $w(a_i, \tilde{\Gamma}_{i,z}) = \tilde{r}_i(\Omega_i - z + 1)$, for $1 \leq z \leq \Omega_i$, with $\tilde{r}_{n_1} = 1$ and $\tilde{r}_{i-1} = (U + 3)\tilde{r}_i$, for $1 < i \leq n_1$. Let $G' = (A \cup H', E')$ be the resulting weighted graph, where A is the set of agents, $H' = H \cup \{h'_i \mid i \in A\}$ is the set of houses and the set of edges is given by $E' = \{\langle a_i, h\rangle \mid h \in \tilde{\Gamma}_{a_i, z}, \text{for } 1 \leq z \leq \Omega_i\}$, with weights defined by w. The weight function w has been chosen in such a way that no group of agents of a lower rank (i.e., lower priority) may violate weak stability to globally increase the sum of the weights of their assignments. This is the key result for the proof of Proposition 1, since it implies that any maximum weight matching in G' is weakly stable and applicant-optimal in G'.

Proposition 1. *If $A_E = \emptyset$, a maximum weight matching in G' is a solution to TRP (with unit capacities) for the weight function w, with G' defined above.*

Proof. Since every agent can be assigned his last resort house h'_i and all weights are positive integers, every maximum weight matching in G' is a maximum cardinality matching in G'. Let $(\beta_1, \ldots, \beta_{n_1})$ and $(\beta'_1, \ldots, \beta'_{n_1})$ be the weights of the houses assigned to $a_1, \ldots, a_{n_1}$ in two maximum cardinality matchings. We will see that the weight function ensures that, for all i_0, if $\sum_{i=i_0}^{n_1} \beta_i \geq \sum_{i=i_0}^{n_1} \beta'_i$ then $\beta_{i_0} \geq \beta'_{i_0}$. Considering the upper and lower bounds of the weights of the edges incident to a_i in G', we have $\beta_i \leq \tilde{r}_i(\Omega_i - 1 + 1) = \tilde{r}_i \Omega_i < \tilde{r}_i(U + 3) = \tilde{r}_{i-1}$ and $\beta'_i \geq \tilde{r}_i(\Omega_i - \Omega_i + 1) = \tilde{r}_i$. Therefore

$$\sum_{i=i_0}^{n_1} \beta_i - \sum_{i=i_0}^{n_1} \beta'_i < (\beta_{i_0} - \beta'_{i_0}) + \sum_{i=i_0+1}^{n_1} (\tilde{r}_{i-1} - \tilde{r}_i) = (\beta_{i_0} - \beta'_{i_0}) + \tilde{r}_{i_0} - 1$$

and $\beta_{i_0} - \beta'_{i_0} = \tilde{r}_{i_0}(-z_{i_0} + z'_{i_0})$, for some z_{i_0} and z'_{i_0}, which define the ranks of the houses assigned to a_{i_0} in each case. If we assume, by contradiction, that $\beta_{i_0} < \beta'_{i_0}$, then $z'_{i_0} < z_{i_0}$ and $\sum_{i=i_0}^{n_1} \beta_i - \sum_{i=i_0}^{n_1} \beta'_i < \tilde{r}_{i_0}(z'_{i_0} - z_{i_0} + 1) - 1 < 0$. Hence, for all i_0, if $\sum_{i=i_0}^{n_1} \beta_i \geq \sum_{i=i_0}^{n_1} \beta'_i$ then $\beta_{i_0} \geq \beta'_{i_0}$. This property implies that if $M^\star$ is a maximum weight matching in G' then $M^\star$ is a weakly stable matching in G' and $\zeta(M^\star)$ is lexicographically minimum among the weakly stable matchings in G'. If $A_E = \emptyset$, this means that $M^\star$ is a solution to TRP.   □

If $A_E \neq \emptyset$, any maximum weight matching $M^\star$ in G' that violates the constraints imposed by tenure is not a TRP-solution, but provides relevant information. Indeed, all agents matched in $M^\star$ to their last resort (as well, as any $a_i \in A_E$ that gets the house h_j he owns) cannot get a better house other than their (real) last resort. Hence, we can assign them their last resort house, remove them and their houses from the graph, and repeat the procedure until all tenants are matched to real houses (which requires no more than t iterations).

Corollary 1. *TRP can be solved in $O(\sqrt{\min(n_1, n_2)}\, m\, n_1 \max(1, t))$ for unit capacities, where $t = |A_E|$ and $m = \sum_i \sum_j |\Gamma_{i,j}|$ is the total length of the preference lists, assuming that $\max_i \gamma_i \leq U$, for a constant U.*

Proof. In [6], Goldberg *et al.* show that a matching of maximum weight in a weighted bipartite graph can be found in $O(\sqrt{r}m \log C)$ time, where r is the size of the smaller side of the graph, m is the number of edges, and C is the largest absolute value of an arc-cost. In our model, the largest weight $C \leq \tilde{\Gamma}_{1,1} = r_1 \Omega_1 < (U + 3)^{n_1}$ and, in the worst case, we repeat the procedure t times.   □

Although we considered the case of unit capacities, we can conclude that the capacitated version is solvable in pseudo-polynomial time, since we can clone each house to reduce the problem to the unit capacity case. The case where $c(h)$ is negative, for some h, can be handled in the same way, as that means that the vacancies created by tenants that moved from h to other houses cannot be assigned to newcomers unless more than $|c(h)|$ tenants move and create some real vacancies. Otherwise, their vacancies are extinguished.

In the remaining sections we develop specific algorithms for TRP that improve these complexity bounds.

4   TRP for Strict Preferences and Unit Capacities

We start by considering the case where the preference lists of the agents are strictly ordered and $c(h) = 1$, for all $h \in H$. Algorithm 1 adapts the applicant-oriented version of Gale-Shapley Algorithm to solve TRP in $O(m + n)$ time. It assumes that the preference lists of the existing tenants contain the houses they own, whereas, for newcomers, they contain the dummy house h_0, as last resort.

Algorithm 1. TRP for strictly ordered preference lists (last resort in $Prefs$)

1: $M := \emptyset;\ I := i := 1;$
2: **while** $i \leq n_1$ **do**
3:     $h_j := Prefs[a_i].\text{pop}();$
4:     **if** h_j is free or h_j is the dummy house h_0 **then**
5:         $M := M \oplus \{\langle a_i, h_j \rangle\};$ $\triangleright$ assigns a_i to h_j
6:         $i := I + 1;\ I := I + 1;$ $\triangleright$ all agents from 1 to I were matched
7:     **else**
8:         $a_k := M(h_j);$
9:         **if** $(k > i$ and $a_k \neq \text{HOLDS}(h_j))$ or $(k < i$ and $a_i = \text{HOLDS}(h_j))$ **then**
10:             $M := M \oplus \{\langle a_k, h_j \rangle, \langle a_i, h_j \rangle\};\ i := k;$ $\triangleright$ a_k becomes free
11:         **end if**
12:     **end if**
13: **end while**

Proposition 2. *When the preference lists of the agents contain no ties (i.e., $\Gamma_{i,l}$ is a singleton for all i and l), TRP with unit capacities admits a unique solution. This matching can be found by Algorithm 1 in $O(n + m)$, where m is the total length of the preference lists, and $n = n_1 + n_2$.*

Proof. TRP with unit capacities and strictly ordered preference lists can be encoded as an instance of the Stable Marriage Problem with Incomplete Lists, as we discussed above. It is known that the applicant-oriented version of the Gale-Shapley algorithm [5,7] computes the stable matching that is optimal from the point of view of the applicants in $O(m + n)$ time. For strict preferences, this matching is the unique solution of TRP. $\square$

5   TRP with Ties and Unit Capacities

We will see now that, when the preference lists may contain ties, TRP can be solved as a sequence of maximum cardinality bipartite matching problems on reduced sub-graphs, combined with an effective propagation of the stability constraints. This structural property is important for an efficient time and space complexity. Our algorithm (Algorithm 2) is given below in pseudocode. It assumes that the last resort houses are not in the preference lists.

Algorithm 2. TRP for preference lists with ties (last resort not in $Prefs$)

1: Define all agents and houses to be free and define $Reject[h_j] := \infty$, for all j;
2: $M := \emptyset$; $G := (A \cup H, \emptyset)$; $I := i := 1$; $ok := \texttt{false}$;
3: **while** $i \leq n_1$ **do**
4:     **while** $ok = \texttt{false}$ and not $Prefs[a_i]$.ISEMPTY() **do**
5:         $ok :=$ INSERTNEWLEVEL(i);
6:     **end while**
7:     **if** $ok = \texttt{false}$ **then**
8:         $h_j :=$ HOLDS(a_i);
9:         delete a_i from A;   ▷ set a_i as "definitely assigned"
10:        **if** $h_j \neq h_0$ **then**
11:            $Reject[h_j] := 0$;   ▷ can delete h_j from G also
12:        **end if**
13:        **if** h_j is free **then**   ▷ h_0 is assumed to be free always
14:            $M := M \oplus \{\langle a_i, h_j \rangle\}$;
               $i := I + 1$; $I := I + 1$;
15:        **else**   ▷ a_i holds h_j and h_j is no longer free
16:            $a_k := M(h_j)$;   ▷ a_k was matched to h_j in M
17:            $M := M \oplus \{\langle a_k, h_j \rangle, \langle a_i, h_j \rangle\}$;   ▷ a_k looses h_j to assign a_i
18:            $i := k$; $ok := \texttt{true}$;   ▷ try to match a_k at the same level
19:        **end if**
20:    **else**
21:        **if** there is an augmenting path P starting at a_i **then**   ▷ found by BFS
22:            $M := M \oplus P$; $i := I + 1$; $I := I + 1$;   ▷ agents from 1 to I matched
23:        **else**
24:            $k :=$ index of the lowest ranked agent in the Hungarian tree (root a_i);
25:            **if** $k > i$ **then**
26:                $P :=$ an alternating path from a_i to a_k (i.e., a switching path);
27:                $M := M \oplus P$;   ▷ a_k becomes free and a_i matched
28:                $i := k$;
29:                DELETEEDGESANDUPDATEREJECTIONLEVEL(k);
30:            **end if**
31:        **end if**
32:        $ok = \texttt{false}$;   ▷ the current graph must be updated to insert a new tie
33:    **end if**
34: **end while**

For a matching M, an *alternating path* is a simple path that alternates between matched and free edges. An *augmenting path* is an alternating path that starts and ends with a free vertex. The function INSERTNEWLEVEL(i) looks for the next preference level Γ_{i,z_i} that contains some feasible house (one whose rejection level is greater than or equal to i). Returns `true` if it succeeds in finding such a house and adds the corresponding edges to the current graph. Otherwise returns `false`. The function DELETEEDGESANDUPDATEREJECTIONLEVEL(k) deletes all edges incident to a_k in the current graph and updates the rejection level of the corresponding houses (this is not important to prevent some agent with lower priority to be matched to them, but can improve the runtime of the algorithm). The operator $\oplus$ denotes the symmetric difference, as usual.

Our algorithm works iteratively and uses a sequence of reduced graphs. The existence of tenants and ties requires a specialized treatment, although other algorithms follow a similar approach (e.g., the algorithm given in [17] for finding weighted popular matchings and their extension to the weighted capacitated house allocation problem [21]). At each stage, the idea is to try to augment a partial matching to provisionally (or even definitely) match one more agent, using the master list to define the order in which the agents are considered. For each agent a_i, only one preference tie Γ_{i,z_i} is active in each iteration. The algorithm adds Γ_{i,z_i} to the graph and looks for an augmenting path starting at a_i using the provisonal matching M.

When we try to assign a house to a tenant a_i, and there remain no choices for a_i (the preference list is empty), then a_i must be assigned the house he owns. If this house was (provisionally) assigned to another agent, say a_k, then a_k becomes free and, in the next iteration, the algorithm looks for a house to a_k. In doing that, it can reach a situation that forces some agent with lowest priority to become free. Therefore, when no augmenting path remains, we look for alternating paths that start at the exposed (unmatched) agent a_i and end at an agent a_k such that $k > i$. We will refer to them as *switching paths*. If a_i cannot be matched to any house in Γ_{i,z_i}, we record it, by decreasing the *rejection level* of the houses in Γ_{i,z_i} to $i - 1$. Then, we remove the edges defined by Γ_{i,z_i} and introduce the edges defined by the next tie $\Gamma_{i,1+z_i}$. The rejection level is set to zero when the house is assigned to the agent that owns it initially (another way to understand this is to consider that they both leave the matching scheme).

In each iteration, the algorithm looks for a house for a_i. It searches for augmenting paths, starting at a_i, using breadth-first search (BFS). This can be done in $O(|E_G|)$ for the current graph G (e.g., [22]). If no augmenting path is found then, without increasing the time complexity, we can look for the agent a_k with the lowest rank that was visited by the *Hungarian tree* rooted at a_i. This agent can be a_i itself. If it is an agent a_k with lower priority then the algorithm uses the switching path from a_i to a_k to update the matching.

Example 3. Suppose $A = \{a_1, a_2, a_3, a_4\}$, a_4 owns h_1, each house has unit capacity and $\Gamma_{1,1} = \{h_1, h_2, h_3, h_4\}$, $\Gamma_{2,1} = \{h_1\}$, $\Gamma_{2,2} = \{h_2\}$, $\Gamma_{3,1} = \{h_1\}$, $\Gamma_{3,2} = \{h_2\}$, $\Gamma_{4,1} = \{h_2\}$. Figure 1 sketches the idea of our algorithm. Thick solid edges indicate the current matching. In the end, $M = \{(a_1, h_3), (a_2, h_2), (a_4, h_1), (a_3, h_0)\}$, meaning that a_3 results unmatched.

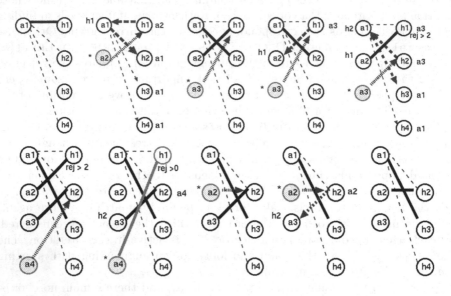

Fig. 1. Looking for a TRP matching.

Theorem 1. *Algorithm 2 outputs a solution to TRP with unit capacities in $O(n_1^2 K \max(1, t))$ time, where K is the maximum number of houses equally ranked by some agent and t is the number of existing tenants.*

Proof. The main **while** loop keeps the invariant that the agents $a_i, a_{I+1}, \ldots, a_{n_1}$ are free in M and M is a weakly stable matching whose profile is lexicographically minimum for $\{a_1, \ldots, a_I\} \setminus \{a_i\}$; $z^M(a_p) \leq z^{M'}(a_p)$, for all p, for every lexicographically minimum weakly stable matching M' that matches $\{a_1, \ldots, a_I\}$.

Now, we proceed by induction.

– When we check $i \leq n_1$ for the first time, the loop invariant holds trivially.
– Let us assume that the condition holds at the beginning of a given iteration.
– Suppose that $ok = $ false in line 4. Then we move from one preference level to the next one because there remain no feasible houses in the previous level. All such houses had a rejection level smaller than i, which implies that we have to move to the next tie of $Prefs[a_i]$.
– If $ok = $ false in line 7, there remain no options in the preference list of a_i. Therefore a_i must be assigned to his last resort. We assume that $\textsc{Holds}(a_i)$ returns h_0 when a_i is not an existing tenant. If $h_j \neq h_0$, then the algorithm checks whether h_j is free (line 13) or not (line 16). If it is free, all agents from 1 to I are matched and no blocking pair can arise in a subsequent step

involving h_j. If h_j is not free (line 16), $a_k := M(h_j)$ becomes free and h_j will be definitely assigned to a_i (who owns it initially [lines 9–12]). In this case, we have to check whether a_k can get a house in the current tie Γ_{k,z_k}. For that reason ok is set to true in line 18.

- (line 21) Suppose that ok = true and an augmenting path P w.r.t. M is found. Then $M \oplus P$ is weakly stable matching and lexicographically minimum for $\{a_1, \ldots, a_I\}$, because every agent that was matched in M is matched at the same tie, and $(a_i, (M \oplus P)(a_i))$ is no longer a *blocking pair* for the matching (i.e., a pair that raises a stability conflict). Since $z(\cdot)$ has not changed, we conclude that the stated condition holds at the beginning of the next iteration for $[a_{I+1}, \ldots, a_{n_1}]$ and $M := M \oplus P$.
- (lines 24–29) We check whether there is a switching path from a_i to a_k, for some $k > i$. The agent a_k with the lowest priority (line 24) cannot be assigned to any house in his current preference level. Here we assume that G contains no edge that was ruled out by an update of the rejection level of some house (this can be implemented in a lazy fashion during the search for augmenting paths).

The main while-loop terminates because the tuple $(I, D, i, z(a_i))$ increases lexicographically in each iteration: $n_1 - I + 1$ agents remain unmatched, D is number of agents assigned to their *last resort* (the house they own or h_0), and $z(a_i)$ identifies the current tie $\Gamma_{i,z(a_i)}$ for the current agent a_i.

The time bound $O(n_1^2 K \max(1, t))$ follows from the fact that there are at most $O(n_1 K)$ edges in the graph and we can expand the Hungarian tree to continue the search for augmenting paths for a_i, when a_i is the same as in the previous iteration, so that the whole procedure takes $O(n_1 K)$. The time bound is smaller than the one given in Corollary 1, since $n_1 K \leq \min(n_1 K, m)$. $\square$

6   Extensions to the Capacitated TRP with Ties

In the teacher recruitment setting, it is important to consider also the assignment of applicants to schools rather than to posts. Each school may have a number of vacancies, all corresponding to identical posts. Due to demographic reductions, some schools in Portugal have *negative vacancies* nowadays. The law says that whenever a teacher that holds such a vacancy applies for another permanent position and gets it, his vacancy cannot be assigned to another candidate. That is, a school that has $|c(h)|$ negative vacancies may admit new teachers only if more than $|c(h)|$ tenured applicants move from it. The algorithm given previously may be adapted to solve TRP (with non-unitary capacities) in polynomial time. As for the previous model, we initially define the capacity of each house as the number of the published vacancies plus the number of agents that are trying to move from it. An *augmenting path* with origin at a_i terminates at a house that has a positive capacity currently or at a provisionally assigned agent of lower priority. When an agent a_i has to be assigned to the house h_j he holds initially and the current capacity of h_j is zero, the agent with the lowest priority provisionally assigned to that house becomes unmatched, if there is any. Otherwise, a_i is definitely assigned to his house, which necessarily ends up with negative capacity. The algorithm, stated as Algorithm 3, is based on the model of TRP as a flow network and adapts the algorithm for computing a maximum s-t flow. Since TRP is defined by a bipartite graph, and the directed edges from A to H have unit capacity, we do not have to introduce a source s and a sink t explicitly.

Algorithm 3. TRP for generic capacities and ties (last resort not in $Prefs$)

1: Define all agents and houses to be free and define $Reject[h_j] := \infty$, for all j;
2: $M := \emptyset$; $G := (A \cup H, \emptyset)$; $I := i := 1$; $ok := \texttt{false}$;
3: **while** $i \leq n_1$ **do**
4:     **while** $ok = \texttt{false}$ and not $Prefs[a_i].\textsc{isEmpty}()$ **do**
5:         $ok := \textsc{InsertNewLevel}(i)$;
6:     **end while**
7:     **if** $ok = \texttt{false}$ **then**
8:         set a_i as "definitely assigned"; $h_j := \textsc{holds}(a_i)$;
9:         **if** h_j is under-subscribed or all agents assigned to h_j hold h_j **then**
10:             $M := M \oplus \{(a_i, h_j)\}$; update residual graph; $i := I + 1$; $I := I + 1$;
11:         **else**   ▷ a_i holds h_j and h_j is full
12:             $a_k :=$ the lowest ranked agent provisionally assigned to h_j;
13:             $M := M \oplus \{(a_k, h_j), (a_i, h_j)\}$; and update residual graph (delete a_i)
14:             $Reject[h_j] := k - 1$;
15:             $i := k$; $ok := \texttt{true}$;   ▷ try to match a_k at the same level
16:         **end if**
17:     **else**
18:         **if** there is an augmenting path starting at a_i ($s \to a_i \rightsquigarrow t$) **then**
19:             $P :=$ an augmenting path starting at a_i (breadth-first search);
20:             $M := M \oplus P$; and update residual graph
21:             $i := I + 1$; $I := I + 1$;   ▷ all agents from 1 to I were matched
22:         **else**
23:             $k :=$ the lowest ranked agent reached from a_i in the residual graph;
24:             **if** $k > i$ **then**
25:                 $P :=$ a path from a_i to a_k in the residual graph (switching path);
26:                 $M := M \oplus P$; and update residual graph ▷ a_k is free and a_i matched
27:                 $i := k$; $\textsc{DeleteEdgesAndUpdateRejectionLevel}(k)$;
28:             **end if**
29:         **end if**
30:         $ok = \texttt{false}$;   ▷ the current graph must be updated
31:     **end if**
32: **end while**

---

7 Conclusion

Several variants of the Stable Marriage Problem with ties where individual preference lists may be derived from master lists are NP-hard, for weak stability [10]. These results carry over to the corresponding Hospital/Resident problems with ties. Although TRP is related to these problems, the kind of matching we seek renders TRP polynomially solvable. Hence, for the teacher recruitment problem we could discard tie breaking rules that usually lead to unfair allocations [24].

Acknowledgments. The author would like to thank Katarína Cechlárová and anonymous reviewers for insightful comments.

References

1. Abdulkadiroğlu, A., Sönmez, T.: House allocation with existing tenants. J. Econ. Theory **88**, 233–260 (1999)
2. Abraham, D.J., Irving, R.W., Kavitha, R., Mehlhorn, K.: Popular matchings. In: Proceedings of the 16th Annual ACM-SIAM Symposium on Discrete Algorithms (SODA 2005), pp. 424–432. SIAM (2005)
3. Cechlárová, K., Manlove, D.F.: The exchange-stable marriage problem. Discret. Appl. Math. **125**(1–3), 109–122 (2005)
4. Cechlárová, K., Fleiner, T., Manlove, D.F., McBride, I.: Stable matchings of teachers to schools. Theoret. Comput. Sci. **653**, 15–25 (2016)
5. Gale, D., Shapley, L.S.: College admissions and the stability of marriage. Am. Math. Monthly **69**, 9–15 (1962)
6. Goldberg, A.V., Kaplan, H., Hed, S., Tarjan, R.E.: Minimum cost flows in graphs with unit capacities. In: Mayr, E.W., Ollinger, N. (eds.) STACS 2015, pp. 406–419 (2015)
7. Gusfield, D., Irving, R.W.: The Stable Marriage Problem - Structure and Algorithms. MIT Press, Cambridge (1989)
8. Huang, C.C., Kavitha, R., Mehlhorn, K., Michail, D.: Fair matchings and related problems. Algorithmica **74**, 1184–1203 (2016). https://doi.org/10.1007/s00453-015-9994-9
9. Irving, R.W.: Greedy matchings. University of Glasgow, Computing Science Department Research report, TR-2003-136, April 2003
10. Irving, R.W., Manlove, D.F., Scott, S.: The stable marriage problem with master preference lists. Discret. Appl. Math. **156**(15), 2959–2977 (2008)
11. Irving, R.W., Kavitha, T., Mehlhorn, K., Michail, D., Paluch, K.: Rank-maximal matchings. In: Proceedings of the 15th Annual ACM-SIAM Symposium on Discrete Algorithms (SODA 2004), pp. 68–75. SIAM (2004)
12. Iwama, K., Miyazaki, S., Morita, Y., Manlove, D.: Stable marriage with incomplete lists and ties. In: Wiedermann, J., van Emde Boas, P., Nielsen, M. (eds.) ICALP 1999. LNCS, vol. 1644, pp. 443–452. Springer, Heidelberg (1999). https://doi.org/10.1007/3-540-48523-6_41
13. Krysta, P., Manlove, D., Rastegari, B., Zhang, J.: Size versus truthfulness in the House Allocation problem. In: Proceedings of the EC 2014 15th ACM Conference on Economics and Computation, pp. 453–470. ACM (2014)
14. Kwanashie, A., Irving, R.W., Manlove, D.F., Sng, C.T.S.: Profile-based optimal matchings in the student/project allocation problem. In: Kratochvíl, J., Miller, M., Froncek, D. (eds.) IWOCA 2014. LNCS, vol. 8986, pp. 213–225. Springer, Cham (2015). https://doi.org/10.1007/978-3-319-19315-1_19
15. Manlove, D.F.: Algorithmics of Matching Under Preferences. World Scientific, Singapore (2013)

16. Manlove, D.F., Irving, R., Iwama, K., Miyazaki, S., Morita, Y.: Hard variants of stable marriage. Theoret. Comput. Sci. **276**, 261–279 (2002)
17. Mestre, J.: Weighted popular matchings. ACM Trans. Algorithms **10**(1), 2 (2014)
18. Niederle, M., Roth, A.E., Sönmez, T.: Matching. In: The New Palgrave Dictionary of Economics, 2nd edn. Palgrave Macmillan (2007)
19. Roth, A.E.: The evolution of the labor market for interns and residents: a case study in game theory. J. Polit. Econ. **92**, 991–1016 (1984)
20. Shapley, L., Scarf, H.: On cores and indivisibility. J. Math. Econ. **1**, 23–37 (1974)
21. Sng, C.T.S., Manlove, D.F.: Popular matchings in the weighted capacitated house allocation problem. J. Discret. Algorithms **8**, 102–116 (2010)
22. Wolsey, L.A.: Integer Programming. Wiley-Interscience, Hoboken (1998)
23. Yuan, R.: Residence exchange wanted: a stable residence exchange problem. Eur. J. Oper. Res. **90**, 536–546 (1996)
24. Tomás, A.P.: Emparelhamentos, casamentos estáveis e algoritmos de colocação de professores. Technical report DCC-2005-02, DCC - FC & LIACC, University of Porto (2005). (in Portuguese). www.dcc.fc.up.pt/Pubs/TR05/dcc-2005-02.pdf
25. Tomás, A.P.: Weak stable matchings with tenants and ties. Presented at CSCLP 2006: Annual ERCIM Workshop on Constraint Solving and Constraint Logic Programming, Lisbon, Portugal, June 2006

Runtime Distributions and Criteria for Restarts

Jan-Hendrik Lorenz[(✉)]

Institut für Theoretische Informatik, Universität Ulm, 89069 Ulm, Germany
jan-hendrik.lorenz@uni-ulm.de

Abstract. Randomized algorithms sometimes employ a restart strategy. After a certain number of steps, the current computation is aborted and restarted with a new, independent random seed. In some cases, this results in an improved overall expected runtime. This work introduces properties of the underlying runtime distribution which determine whether restarts are advantageous. The most commonly used probability distributions admit the use of a scale and a location parameter. Location parameters shift the density function to the right, while scale parameters affect the spread of the distribution. It is shown that for all distributions scale parameters do not influence the usefulness of restarts and that location parameters only have a limited influence. This result simplifies the analysis of the usefulness of restarts. The most important runtime probability distributions are the log-normal, the Weibull, and the Pareto distribution. In this work, these distributions are analyzed for the usefulness of restarts. Secondly, a condition for the optimal restart time (if it exists) is provided. The log-normal, the Weibull, and the generalized Pareto distribution are analyzed in this respect. Moreover, it is shown that the optimal restart time is also not influenced by scale parameters and that the influence of location parameters is only linear.

1 Introduction

Restart mechanisms are commonly used in day-to-day life. For example, when waiting for an email response, it is common to send the original email again after some time. Therefore it is not surprising that restart strategies are used in subjects as diverse as biology (e.g. [20]), physics (e.g. [7]) and computer science (e.g. [9,21]). There are at least two large fields in computer science which utilize restarts. On the one hand network protocols often have a retransmission timer (e.g. TCP, see [19]), after a timeout the loss of the package is assumed and therefore the message is resent. On the other hand, probabilistic algorithms often restart after a certain number of steps without finding a solution, those algorithms are especially common for constraint satisfaction problems (CSP) and the well-known satisfiability problem (SAT). Although in practical use, our impression is that the power of this algorithm paradigm is still underestimated. Restarts can be used to improve the performance of an algorithm in regards to various measures. For example, restarting the algorithm can help to improve the completion probability when a deadline is present. This model was studied by

© Springer International Publishing AG 2018
A M. Tjoa et al. (Eds.): SOFSEM 2018, LNCS 10706, pp. 493–507, 2018.
https://doi.org/10.1007/978-3-319-73117-9_35

Wu [23] while Lorenz [12] examined completion probabilities for parallel algorithms using restarts. Another measure which can benefit from restarts is the expected runtime.

An important class of distributions for which restarts often improve the expected runtime is the so-called class of heavy-tailed distributions. Heavy-tailed distributions have a tail which decays slower than an exponential. Crovella et al. [6] showed that transmission times in the world wide web follow a power-law tail which is a subclass of heavy-tailed distributions. Gomes et al. [9] observed that some instances in CSP also show a power-law tail, while Caniou and Codognet [5] examined that the log-normal distribution is a good fit for some problems in constraint satisfaction. The log-normal distribution also belongs to the class of heavy-tailed distributions.

Luby et al. [14] introduced two of the most important restart strategies. The fixed cut-off strategy always restarts after the same (fixed) number of steps. They showed that this strategy is optimal for a certain (possibly infinite) number of steps. However, in general finding the right number of steps before restarting requires extensive knowledge of the distribution. The second strategy which Luby et al. introduced is called Luby's (universal) strategy which slowly increases the restart times. This strategy does not require any knowledge of the underlying distribution and compared to the optimal strategy the expected runtime of a process utilizing Luby's strategy is only higher by a logarithmic factor.

Since Luby's strategy does not require any a-priori knowledge of the distribution, it is nowadays more commonly used than the fixed cut-off strategy. One could, however, argue that better strategies are possible since, in a few cases, some information is available prior to the experiment. For instance, for many algorithms, the distribution for a certain class of problems has been observed empirically. Arbelaez et al. [2] use a machine learning approach to predict the runtime distributions of several randomized algorithms. This knowledge can be used to obtain a better restart strategy for this class of problems. Then, a speedup of, at least, a logarithmic factor can be expected (compared to Luby's strategy). Such a factor cannot be ignored in practice.

Choosing the wrong restart strategy can result in expected runtimes which are much worse than not restarting at all. On the other hand, a good choice regarding the restart strategy can result in a super-exponential speedup. We believe that not enough attention has been paid to this field of research.

Our contribution: A condition for the usefulness of restart (Theorem 1) and a condition for optimal restart times (Theorem 2) is obtained. It is shown that scale parameters neither influence the usefulness nor the optimal restart times (Theorems 3 and 4). The log-normal and the generalized Pareto distribution are analyzed for the usefulness of restarts and their optimal restart times. The Weibull distribution is also studied for its optimal restart times. Parameter settings for all these distributions for which restarts are useful are obtained. Finally, it is shown that the influence of location parameters on the usefulness of restarts is limited. This is, for all distributions discussed here, restarts are still useful when a location parameter is present. The influence of a location Parameter on the optimal restart time is just linear.

2   Preliminaries

In this section, the notation used throughout this work is introduced. Let X be a real-valued random variable. Then $F_X(t) = \Pr(X \le t)$ is the cumulative distribution function (cdf) of X and its derivative $f_X(t) = \frac{d}{dt}F(t)$ is the density function of X. In many cases the quantile function of the random variable X is helpful, it is defined as follows:

Definition 1 [18]. *Let X be a real-valued random variable with cumulative distribution function $F_X : \mathbb{R} \to [0,1]$. Then the Quantile function $Q_X : [0,1] \to \mathbb{R}$ is given by*

$$Q_X(p) = \inf\{x \mid F(x) \ge p\}. \tag{1}$$

For continuous, strictly monotonically increasing cumulative distribution functions F_X the quantile function Q_X is the inverse function of F_X.

Luby et al. defined the fixed cut-off strategy.

Definition 2 [14]. *Let X be a random variable describing the runtime of a probabilistic algorithm $\mathcal{A}$ on some specific input. Given any value $t \in \mathbb{R}_+$ a new algorithm $\mathcal{A}_t$ is obtained by restarting $\mathcal{A}$ after time t has passed without finding a solution. Then X_t is a random variable describing the runtime of $\mathcal{A}_t$.*

When talking about restarts, restarts using the fixed cut-off strategy are meant. The notion of usefulness is often used in this work. Restarts are called useful if there is a $t > 0$ with $E[X_t] < E[X]$. Throughout this work, only real-valued random variables such that F_X, f_X and Q_X exist are considered. If it is clear from the context, the subscript X is omitted for the functions defined here. For the results presented here, we assume that the number of restarts is not limited.

3   Main Results

Before employing a restart strategy, it should first be considered under which conditions restarts are useful at all. Moorsel and Wolter [16] obtained a condition for the usefulness of restarts: Let T be a random variable describing the runtime of the process if there is a $t > 0$ with $E[T] < E[T - t \mid T > t]$, then restarts are useful. They showed that this condition is sufficient and necessary if the mean $E[T]$ exists. This is a property which is often shown by heavy-tailed distributions. However, there are heavy-tailed distributions which do not fulfill their conditions, and there are also light-tailed distributions which do fulfill this condition. In this section, another condition for the usefulness of restarts is provided and it is applied to several distributions.

3.1   Effective Restarts

There are several ways to describe a dataset. Two of the most commonly used values are the median and the mean, both of which describe a 'typical' value for this dataset. If the mean lies to the right of the median one can speak of (positively) skewed data. While outliers contribute linearly to the mean, the median is very resistant to outliers. Therefore a big difference between the median and the mean can be explained by either many outliers or a few, but extreme outliers. In both of these cases, restarts can be an efficient way to reduce outliers. Thus comparing the mean to the median yields a simple condition for the usefulness of restarts: If $Q(0.5)/E[X] < 0.5$, then restarts are beneficial. This holds because the expected runtime $E[X_{Q(p)}]$ is bounded from above by $\frac{Q(p)}{p}$. This idea can be easily generalized. If the mean is large because of a small number of disproportionately long runs, but there are also many short runs, then restarts are useful. Measuring this inequality is a well-known field in economics which is known as income inequality metrics. One of those metrics, the Lorenz curve, turns out to be helpful in the following.

Definition 3 [13]. *Let X be a real-valued random variable. Then the Lorenz curve $L : [0,1] \to [0,1]$ is given by:*

$$L(p) = \frac{\int_0^p Q(x)\mathrm{d}x}{E[X]}. \tag{2}$$

The derivative L' of L is given by $L'(p) = \frac{Q(p)}{E[X]}$. If the mean is infinite, then it is clear that restarts are always useful as long as some quantile exists. This is a property which can, for example, be observed for some power-laws. The next theorem provides a necessary and sufficient condition.

Theorem 1. *Let X be a real-valued random variable, then restart are useful if and only if there is a $p \in [0,1)$ such that*

$$(1-p)L'(p) + L(p) < p. \tag{3}$$

Proof. The expected runtime with an unbounded number of restarts after $Q(p)$ steps is given by (see [22]):

$$E[X_{Q(p)}] = \frac{1-p}{p}Q(p) + E[X \mid X < Q(p)] \tag{4}$$

The conditional expectation $E[X \mid X < Q(p)]$ is defined by $\frac{\int_0^{Q(p)} x f(x)\mathrm{d}x}{p}$ which is equivalent to $\frac{\int_0^p Q(u)\mathrm{d}u}{p}$. This can be obtained by substitution $u = F(x)$. Inserting these identities into $E[X] > E[X_{Q(p)}]$ and dividing by $E[X]$ yields:

$$p > (1-p)L'(p) + L(p). \tag{5}$$

This completes the proof. □

The difference with the condition in [16] is that the existence of $E[X]$ is not required. Also, since p is limited to $[0,1)$ it is algorithmically easy to find intervals for which restarts are useful, while in the condition in [16] the variable is often unbounded. If the condition in Eq. 3 would be an equality instead of an inequality, then the condition would describe quantiles where restarts are neither harmful nor helpful. Wolter [22] showed that for the exponential distribution restarts are neither helpful nor harmful.

3.2 Optimal Restarts

In the previous section, a condition for the usefulness of restarts was introduced. This section focuses on optimal restart times. Wolter [22] provided a relationship between the optimal restart times and the inverse hazard rate. Here a condition for the optimal restart time is shown by using quantile functions. This classification is used to analyze the optimal restart times of several distributions. It is shown that a condition for the optimal restart time can be expressed solely in terms of the quantile function.

Theorem 2. *Let X be a real-valued random variable with the quantile function Q and its antiderivative $\mathfrak{Q}$. Then all optimal restart times $Q(p)$ have to fulfill:*

$$(p-1)Q(p) + p(1-p)Q'(p) - \mathfrak{Q}(p) + \mathfrak{Q}(0) = 0, \tag{6}$$

where Q' is the derivative of the quantile function Q.

Proof. The expected runtime under restart after $Q(p)$ steps is given by:

$$E[X_{Q(p)}] = \frac{1-p}{p}Q(p) + \frac{\mathfrak{Q}(p) - \mathfrak{Q}(0)}{p}. \tag{7}$$

By equating the derivative with zero the function can be minimized. After multiplying the derivative with p^2 the obtained condition is:

$$(p-1)Q(p) + p(1-p)Q'(p) - \mathfrak{Q}(p) + \mathfrak{Q}(0) = 0, \tag{8}$$

where Q' is the derivative of Q. This completes the proof.   □

Next, the influence of scale parameters on the condition from Theorem 2 is investigated.

3.3 Scale Parameter

In this section, it is shown that for every continuous family of distributions there is one parameter which does not have an effect: the scale parameter.

Definition 4 [15]. *Let X be a real-valued, continuous random variable with cdf F_X. A new random variable Y with cdf F_Y is obtained by the identity $F_X(x) = F_Y(\frac{x}{\beta})$ for $\beta > 0$. The parameter β is called a scale-parameter. This is denoted as $Y \overset{d}{=} \beta X$.*

With this definition, the main results of the section can be derived.

Theorem 3. *Let X be a real-valued, continuous random variable such that restarts are useful. Then for $Y \overset{d}{=} \beta X$ restarts are also useful for every $\beta > 0$.*

Proof. Let X and $Y = \beta X$ be random variables with $\beta > 0$. Then the quantile function Q_Y, its antiderivative $\mathfrak{Q}_Y$ and the mean $E[Y]$ are given by:

$$Q_Y(p) = \beta Q_X(p), \tag{9}$$
$$\mathfrak{Q}_Y(p) = \beta \mathfrak{Q}_X(p), \tag{10}$$
$$E[Y] = \beta E[X] \tag{11}$$

Thus, Y fulfills the condition from Theorem 1 iff X fulfills it.   □

Since the derivative Q'_Y is given by $Q'_Y = \beta Q'_X$, the result can be extended to show that scale parameters do not change the optimal restart time. The proof is similar in its nature and is therefore omitted.

Theorem 4. *Let X be a real-valued, continuous random variable and let $q \in (0,1)$ be such that $Q_X(q)$ is the optimal restart time. Let $\beta > 0$ be a positive, real number, then $Q_{\beta X}(q)$ is the optimal restart time for the random variable βX.*

These findings show that scale parameters can be ignored in the analysis for restart times. For several commonly used distributions the properties from Theorems 1 and 2 can be applied.

3.4 Log-Normal

Due to the central limit theorem, the log-normal distribution arises by the product of n i.id random variables. Barrero et al. [4] observed log-normally distributed times of several evolutionary algorithms, including genetic programming, particle swarm optimization, and genetic algorithms. Muñoz et al. [17] empirically showed that the runtime of several path planning algorithms such as A^* and $Theta^*$ follow log-normal distributions. Frost et al. [8] argued that the runtime of several backtracking algorithms follow log-normal distributions in the case of unsolvable binary CSP instances. Arbelaez [1] studied the runtime distributions of two SAT solvers and found that for randomly generated instances the log-normal distribution is a good fit. Thus, the log-normal distribution is commonly used to describe the runtime of local search algorithms. The log-normal distribution is defined as follows:

Definition 5 [18]. *Let X be a real-valued random variable. If there are parameters $\mu > 0, \sigma > 0$, such that the random variable U with*

$$U = \frac{\log(X) - \mu}{\sigma} \tag{12}$$

is standard normal distributed, then X is said to be log-normally distributed. In this case the mean $E[X]$ and the quantile function Q_X are given by

$$E[X] = e^{\mu + \sigma^2/2}, \tag{13}$$
$$Q_X(p) = e^{\mu + \sigma\sqrt{2}\,\mathrm{erf}^{-1}(2p-1)}, \tag{14}$$

where erf^{-1} is the inverse error function.

The erf^{-1} function is not analytically solvable, but there are numerical approaches. An antiderivative $\mathfrak{Q}$ of Q_X and the derivative Q' can be obtained by calculations:

$$\mathfrak{Q}(p) = -\frac{1}{2}e^{\mu+\sigma^2/2}\mathrm{erf}\left(\frac{\sigma}{\sqrt{2}} - \mathrm{erf}^{-1}(2p-1)\right), \tag{15}$$

$$Q'(p) = e^{\mu+\sqrt{2}\cdot\sigma\cdot\mathrm{erf}^{-1}(2p-1)+\left(\mathrm{erf}^{-1}(2p-1)\right)^2}\sigma\sqrt{2\pi}. \tag{16}$$

where erf is the error function which only can be computed numerically. With these definitions the usefulness of restarts for the log-normal distribution can be estimated.

Theorem 5. *Let X be a log-normal distributed random variable. Then there is a $p \in (0,1)$ such that*

$$E[X_{Q(p)}] < E[X]. \tag{17}$$

Proof. Due to Theorem 3, the scale parameter e^μ can be ignored for the analysis of the usefulness of restarts. Therefore, let $\mu = 0$. Note that $E[X_{Q(p)}]$ converges to $E[X]$ as p approaches one. The derivative with respect to p of the expected runtime $E'[X_{Q(p)}]$ is obtained similarly to Theorem 2 and is given by:

$$E'[X_{Q(p)}] = \frac{(p-1)}{p^2}Q(p) + \frac{(1-p)}{p}Q'(p) - \frac{1}{p^2}(\mathfrak{Q}(p) + \mathfrak{Q}(0)). \tag{18}$$

The limit of $E'[X_{Q(p)}]$ as p approaches one is analyzed. In this case, it can be seen that $\frac{(p-1)}{p^2}Q(p)$ converges to zero and $\frac{1}{p^2}(\mathfrak{Q}(p) + \mathfrak{Q}(0))$ converges to $E[X]$. Therefore the analysis focuses on the limit of $(1-p)Q'(p)$.

$$\lim_{p\to 1}(1-p)Q'(p) = \lim_{p\to 1}\frac{(1-p)}{e^{-\sqrt{2}\cdot\sigma\cdot\mathrm{erf}^{-1}(2p-1)-\left(\mathrm{erf}^{-1}(2p-1)\right)^2}}\sigma\sqrt{2\pi} \tag{19}$$

$$= \lim_{p\to 1}\frac{\sigma\sqrt{2}e^{\sqrt{2}\cdot\sigma\cdot\mathrm{erf}^{-1}(2p-1)}}{\sqrt{2}\sigma + \mathrm{erf}^{-1}(2p-1)} = \lim_{p\to 1}\sigma^2 e^{\sigma\sqrt{2}\mathrm{erf}^{-1}(2p-1)} \to \infty \tag{20}$$

This limit is obtained by applying L'Hospital's rule twice. Thus, since $E[X_{Q(p)}]$ converges to $E[X]$ and $E'[X_{Q(p)}]$ approaches positive infinity, there is a $p \in (0,1)$ with $E[X_{Q(p)}] < E[X]$. □

Figure 1 shows parameter combinations for p and σ for which restarts are useful. Since neither the error function nor the inverse error function can be solved analytically, numerical methods have been used to obtain those results.

The optimal restart times, as presented in Theorem 2, are shown in Fig. 2a. It can be seen that for high σ values the optimal restart time quickly approaches $Q(0)$, while for small σ values the optimal restart time converges to $Q(1)$.

Figure 2b shows the comparison of a log-normal distribution without restarts to a log-normal distribution with restart at the optimal time. The plot has the same shape for all values of μ, and only the values on the y-axis differ. It can be

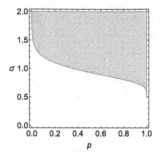

Fig. 1. A regionplot for the log-normal distribution. The blue area denotes parameter settings which fulfill the condition from Theorem 1. For $\sigma < 0.48$ the numerical approach could not find values of p such that restarts are useful. For high values of σ even low values of p yield an improved expected runtime under restart, while for low values of σ only very high values of p improve the expected runtime. (Color figure online)

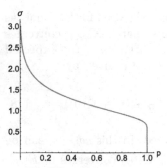

(a) The brown line denotes parameter settings of σ and p which minimize the expected runtime under restart.

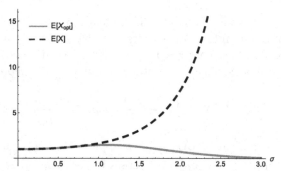

(b) This plot shows the expected runtime for a log-normal distribution without restart as a dashed line. The blue line represents the expected runtime with restarts at the optimal restart time.

Fig. 2. The figures show the optimal restart quantiles for a log-normal distribution with $\mu = 1$ on the left, and the expected runtime and the optimal mean with restarts on the right. (Color figure online)

observed for values up to approximately $\sigma \approx 0.8$ the difference in the expected runtime is marginal. On the other hand, while the expected value $e^{\mu+\frac{\sigma^2}{2}}$ behaves super-exponentially for increasing values of σ, the expected runtime with restarts after an optimal number of steps starts to decrease at about $\sigma \approx 1.1$. Therefore, in real applications restarts should only be employed for high values of σ.

3.5   Generalized Pareto

The Pickands–Balkema–de Haan theorem (see [3]) states that the excess probability $\Pr(X - u \leq y \mid X > u) = \frac{F(u+y)-F(u)}{1-F(u)}$ converges in distribution towards the generalized Pareto distribution for a large number of distributions as $u \to \infty$. Due to this, it can be used to model the tail of distributions. The generalized Pareto distribution (GP) includes the exponential, the Pareto, and the uniform distribution. Since the Pareto distribution is a subclass of the GP, the GP is also well suited to describe power-law decays in the tail. Corvella et al. [6] observed that network transmission times follow a power-law in the tail. Gomes and Selman [9] found that the runtime of the quasi-group completion problem is also well described by a power-law. At this point, the generalized Pareto distribution is formally defined:

Definition 6 [18]. *Let X be a real-valued random variable. If the cdf F_X is given by*

$$F_X(x) = 1 - \left(1 + \frac{kx}{\sigma}\right)^{-1/k} \qquad (21)$$

for $\sigma > 0, k \in \mathbb{R}$, then X has a generalized Pareto (GP) distribution.

For $k < 1$ the mean of the GP is given by $E[X] = \frac{\sigma}{1-k}$, otherwise the mean is infinite. For $k = 0$ the GP is equivalent to the exponential distribution, and for all $k > 0$ it takes the form of a Pareto distribution. For $k \le -0.5$ the GP has finite support, and for $k = -1$ it becomes a uniform distribution. Compare [18] for these results. The Quantile function Q, an antiderivative $\mathfrak{Q}$ and the derivative Q' are given by:

$$Q(p) = \frac{\sigma}{k}\left((1-p)^{-k} - 1\right), \qquad (22)$$

$$\mathfrak{Q}(p) = -\frac{\sigma}{k}\left(p + \frac{(1-p)^{1-k}}{1-k}\right), \qquad (23)$$

$$Q'(p) = \sigma(1-p)^{-1-k}. \qquad (24)$$

These definitions can be used to analyze the usefulness of restarts.

Theorem 6. *Let X be a generalized Pareto distribution, there is a $p \in [0,1)$ with*

$$E[X_{Q(p)}] < E[X] \qquad (25)$$

if and only if $k > 0$.

Proof. Due to Theorem 3, the scale parameter σ does not influence the usefulness of restarts. Therefore, define $\sigma = 1$ for the rest of this proof. For the case $k \ge 1$ the mean is infinite. Thus, restarts are useful for all $p \in (0,1)$. Thus, only the case where $k < 1$ is considered. Then the Lorenz curve L and its derivative L' are given by:

$$L(p) = \frac{\mathfrak{Q}(p) - \mathfrak{Q}(0)}{E[X]} = \frac{1}{k}\left(1 - (1-p)^{1-k} - (1-k)p\right), \qquad (26)$$

$$L'(p) = \frac{Q(p)}{E[X]} = \frac{1-k}{k}\left((1-p)^{-k} - 1\right). \qquad (27)$$

By inserting the Lorenz function and its derivative in inequality 3, the following can be obtained by some calculations:

$$p > -(1-p)^{1-k} + 1 \tag{28}$$
$$\Leftrightarrow k \log (1-p) < 0 \tag{29}$$

For $p \in (0,1)$ the left side of the equation $k \log (1-p)$ is negative if and only if k is positive. Therefore restarts are useful for all $p \in [0,1)$ iff $k > 0$. $\qquad\square$

This is consistent with other results in this field. Wolter [22] showed that Restarts are useful for the Pareto distribution, they are not useful for the uniform distribution and are neither helpful nor harmful for the exponential distribution. The result presented here is stronger since all of those three distributions are subclasses of the generalized Pareto distribution while other distributions can be obtained by using different parameters. The next theorem analyzes the optimal restart time.

Theorem 7. *Let X be a generalized Pareto distributed random variable with $k > 0$, then the optimal restart time is zero and the optimal expected runtime under restart $E[X_{Q(0)}]$ is $E[X_{Q(0)}] = \sigma$.*

Proof. Due to Theorem 4, the scale parameter σ does not have any influence on the optimal restart time. Hence, it can be set to $\sigma = 1$ for the analysis. Then the condition as in Theorem 2 is:

$$\frac{1}{k}\left(\frac{1}{1-k} - p - \frac{(1-p)^{1-k}}{1-k} + (1-p)\left((1-p)^{-k} - 1\right)\right) - p(1-p)^{-k} = 0. \tag{30}$$

By transforming the equation, this condition can be simplified to $(1-p)^{-k}(1 - kp) = 1$. This is obviously true for $p = 0$. Actually, it can also be shown that $p = 0$ is the only value which fulfills the condition. Differentiating $(1-p)^{-k}(1-kp)$ with respect to p yields $\frac{(k-1)kp}{(1-p)^k(p-1)}$. For $k \in (0,1)$ this is strictly positive, and for $k \in (1,\infty)$ this is strictly negative for $p \neq 0$. For this reason, the condition is either strictly monotonically increasing or strictly monotonically decreasing. Therefore, every other value of p does not fulfill Eq. 30. The expected runtime is given by $E[X_{Q(p)}] = \frac{1-p}{p}Q(p) + \frac{Q(p)-Q(0)}{p}$. In case of GP the limit exists for $p \to 0$, it can be obtained by applying L'Hospital's rule and is given by $E[X_{Q(0)}] \to Q'(0) = \sigma$. $\qquad\square$

It is noteworthy that the expected runtime does not depend on the shape parameter k anymore. When comparing expected runtimes under restart with the expected runtimes without restarts $E[X] = \frac{\sigma}{1-k}$ for $k \in (0,1)$, it is easy to see that for $k \to 0$ both runtimes converge against σ. This is consistent with the fact that the generalized Pareto distribution becomes the exponential distribution for $k = 0$.

3.6   Weibull

The Weibull distribution was extensively analyzed by Wolter [22]. The Weibull distribution is one of the three limiting distributions of the Fisher-Tippett-Gnedenko Theorem in case of the minimum value (see for example [11]). Therefore it is a likely candidate when observing the minimum of n i.id random variables $X_1, \ldots, X_n$. Frost et al. [8] observed that the runtime distributions of several backtracking algorithms can be reasonably well described by Weibull distributions for solvable binary CSP instances at the 50% satisfiability point. Hoos and Stützle [10] examined the runtime of a SAT-solver (GSAT). They found that for non-optimal parameter settings the runtime can be described as a Weibull distribution. Barrero et al. [4] studied generation based models without selective pressure, they argue that the generations-to-success can be modeled by a Weibull distribution. The Weibull distribution is defined as follows:

Definition 7 [18]. *Let X be a real-valued random variable. The random variable X has a Weibull distribution if and only if*

$$F_X(x) = 1 - e^{-(\frac{x}{a})^k} \tag{31}$$

for some fixed $k > 0$. Then the quantile function Q_X is given by:

$$Q_X(p) = a(-\log(1-p))^{1/k}. \tag{32}$$

Wolter [22] showed that restarts are always useful for $k < 1$. In case $k > 1$ restarts are always harmful and in case $k = 1$ the Weibull distribution becomes the exponential distribution, therefore restarts are neither useful nor harmful. The same results can be obtained by the technique from Theorem 1. The derivative Q' and an antiderivative $\mathfrak{Q}$ of Q are given as follows:

$$Q'(p) = a\frac{(-\log(1-p))^{\frac{1}{k}-1}}{k(1-p)}, \tag{33}$$

$$\mathfrak{Q}(p) = a\gamma\left(1 + \frac{1}{k}, -\log(1-p)\right), \tag{34}$$

where $\gamma(z, x) = \int_0^x t^{z-1}e^{-t}dt$ is the incomplete gamma function. The optimal restart time is analyzed in the next theorem.

Theorem 8. *Let X be a Weibull distributed random variable with $k < 1$. Then the optimal restart time is zero and the optimal expected runtime under restart is $E[X_{Q(0)}] = 0$.*

The proof is similar to the case of the GP. It is presented in the full version of this article[1]. It is remarkable that the optimal expected runtime in the case of $k < 1$ is not dependent on any parameter of the distribution.

---

[1]   https://arxiv.org/abs/1709.10405

3.7 Location Parameter

Up to now, several multiplicative variants of random variables X were discussed. Nonetheless, many commonly used distributions require an additive location parameter $b \in \mathbb{R}$ which shifts the support of the cdf. In this section, the results are augmented with this extension and it is shown that the influence of the location parameter b is limited.

In the following, let X be a random variable without location parameter and let $Y = X + b$ be a random variable with some location parameter b. The expected value is known to be a linear function, therefore $E[Y] = E[X] + b$. Similar results follow easily for the quantile function. Since $F_Y(x) = F_X(x - b)$ holds $Q_Y(p) = Q_X(p) + b$ directly follows. Then an antiderivative of Q_Y is given by $\mathfrak{Q}_X(p) + pb$ where $\mathfrak{Q}_X$ is an antiderivative of Q_X. Define $c \in \mathbb{R}$ such that $b = cE[X]$. With these identities the usefulness of restarts can be reestimated:

$$E[X] + b > \frac{1-p}{p}(Q_X(p) + b) + b + \frac{1}{p}(\mathfrak{Q}_X(p) - \mathfrak{Q}_X(0)) \tag{35}$$

$$\Leftrightarrow p + (p-1)c > (1-p)L'_X(p) + L_X(p) \tag{36}$$

is the new condition for the usefulness of restarts. This inequality assumes $E[X] > 0$, for $E[X] < 0$ the 'greater than' sign becomes a 'less than' sign. However, this only makes sense if the location parameter shifts the support of the distribution to strictly positive values. It can be shown that the condition for the optimal restart time only changes by the location parameter itself. This can be shown by similar transformations; the proof is therefore omitted.

Theorem 9. *Let X be a random variable and let $Y = X + b$ be a random variable with location parameter $b \in \mathbb{R}$. Then the condition for the optimal restart time for Y is:*

$$(p-1)Q_X(p) + p(1-p)Q'_X(p) - \mathfrak{Q}_X(p) + \mathfrak{Q}_X(0) = b. \tag{37}$$

If Q'_X dominates $(1-p)$ in the neighborhood of $p = 1$, then the left side of Eq. 37 approaches infinity. This implies that restarts are useful for an arbitrarily large b since $E[X_{Q(1)}] = E[X]$. This is the case for all distributions considered in this article.

Corollary 1. *Let X be log-normal, GP, or Weibull distributed, with parameters such that restarts are useful. Let $b \in \mathbb{R}_+$, then there is a $p \in (0, 1)$ with*

$$E[(X + b)_{Q(p)}] < E[X + b]. \tag{38}$$

Note, that this is not a general property which is true for all distributions which admit useful restarts. Counterexamples are distributions with a finite support. With this relationship, it is reasonable to analyze distributions without location parameters and scale parameters. This simplifies the analysis whether a restart strategy should be employed and if so, which strategy should be chosen.

4   Discussion

This work discussed the relationship between the quantile function and restarts using the fixed cut-off strategy. Theorem 1 uses the quantile function and its antiderivative to provide a condition for the usefulness of restarts, while Theorem 2 established a condition for the optimal restart times. It was proven in Theorems 3 and 4 that scale parameters can be ignored in the context of restarts. In Sect. 3.7 it was shown that the influence of location parameters on the usefulness of restarts is limited. For a large group of distributions the usefulness of restarts is not affected at all by the presence of a location parameter. Secondly, the optimal restart times are just linearly influenced by a location parameter. Therefore, it often suffices to analyze the remaining parameters.

Several commonly used distributions were observed for their usefulness under restart. In the following, the log-normal distribution (compare Sect. 3.4) and the generalized Pareto distribution (compare Sect. 3.5) were discussed. It was shown that in the case of the log-normal distribution restarts are always useful. In case of the generalized Pareto distribution, restarts are useful iff the shape parameter k is greater than zero. The optimal restart times and optimal expected runtimes under restart of the log-normal, the generalized Pareto and the Weibull distribution were discussed. The expected runtime without restart for the log-normal distribution increases super-exponentially in σ. For the log-normal distribution, it was numerically observed that for increasing parameter σ the optimal restart time is decreasing. And while the expected value without restarts increases super-exponentially, the expected value with restart at the optimal time starts to decrease at about $\sigma \approx 1.1$. It is also interesting to see that for low values of σ the speedup with restarts is marginal. This is especially important if the parameters of the distribution are not completely known. Figure 3 represents an example of this behavior. This shows that choosing a suboptimal restart time can easily result in expected runtimes under restart which are worse than not employing a restart strategy. Therefore, in practice it can be better to not employ a restart strategy if the parameters are estimates and σ is estimated to be low.

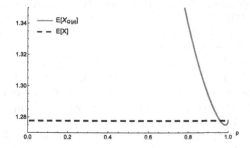

Fig. 3. This figure depicts the expected runtime of a log-normally distributed random variable X with $\mu = 0$ and $\sigma = 0.7$ as a dashed line. The blue line is the expected runtime with restart after $Q_X(p)$ steps. (Color figure online)

For the Weibull distribution, it was shown that the optimal restart time and the expected runtime is zero. A similar behavior was observed for the GP distribution. The optimal restart time is also zero, its optimal expected runtime under restart, however, approaches σ. It is noteworthy that in these two cases the expected runtime is no longer dependent on the shape parameter and in the case of the Weibull distribution also not dependent on the scale parameter. For algorithms, an intuitive description of the restart quantile zero in, e.g., runtime distributions with location b and scale a emerges from the optimum restart condition $(p-1)Q_X(p) + p(1-p)Q'_X(p) - \mathfrak{Q}_X(p) + \mathfrak{Q}_X(0) = b/a$. If $a \gg b$, the optimal restart time approaches $Q(0) = b$, i.e., the algorithm's behavior before b dominates all subsequent steps. It is also remarkable that some distributions which show suboptimal behavior without restarts yield low runtimes when an optimal restart strategy is applied.

References

1. Arbelaez, A., Truchet, C., Codognet, P.: Using sequential runtime distributions for the parallel speedup prediction of SAT local search. Theory Pract. Logic Program. **13**(4–5), 625–639 (2013)
2. Arbelaez, A., Truchet, C., O'Sullivan, B.: Learning sequential and parallel runtime distributions for randomized algorithms. In: ICTAI 2016: 28th International Conference on Tools with Artificial Intelligence, San Jose, California, USA, pp. 655–662. IEEE (2016)
3. Balkema, A.A., De Haan, L.: Residual life time at great age. Ann. Probab. 792–804 (1974)
4. Barrero, D.F., Muñoz, P., Camacho, D., R-Moreno, M.D.: On the statistical distribution of the expected run-time in population-based search algorithms. Soft. Comput. **19**(10), 2717–2734 (2015)
5. Caniou, Y., Codognet, P.: Sequential and parallel restart policies for constraint-based local search. In: Proceedings of the 2013 IEEE 27th International Symposium on Parallel and Distributed Processing Workshops and Ph.D. Forum, pp. 1754–1763. IEEE Computer Society (2013)
6. Crovella, M.E., Taqqu, M.S., Bestavros, A.: Heavy-tailed probability distributions in the World Wide Web. Pract. Guide Heavy Tails **1**, 3–26 (1998)
7. Evans, M.R., Majumdar, S.N.: Diffusion with stochastic resetting. Phys. Rev. Lett. **106**(16), 160601 (2011)
8. Frost, D., Rish, I., Vila, L.: Summarizing CSP hardness with continuous probability distributions. In: Proceedings of the Fourteenth National Conference on Artificial Intelligence and Ninth Conference on Innovative Applications of Artificial Intelligence, AAAI 1997/IAAI 1997, pp. 327–333. AAAI Press (1997)
9. Gomes, C.P., Selman, B., Crato, N.: Heavy-tailed distributions in combinatorial search. In: Smolka, G. (ed.) CP 1997. LNCS, vol. 1330, pp. 121–135. Springer, Heidelberg (1997). https://doi.org/10.1007/BFb0017434
10. Hoos, H.H., Stützle, T.: Evaluating las vegas algorithms: pitfalls and remedies. In: Proceedings of the Fourteenth Conference on Uncertainty in Artificial Intelligence, pp. 238–245. Morgan Kaufmann Publishers Inc. (1998)
11. Kotz, S., Nadarajah, S.: Extreme Value Distributions: Theory and Applications. World Scientific, Singapore (2000)

12. Lorenz, J.H.: Completion probabilities and parallel restart strategies under an imposed deadline. PloS one **11**(10), e0164605 (2016)
13. Lorenz, M.O.: Methods of measuring the concentration of wealth. Publ. Am. Stat. Assoc. **9**(70), 209–219 (1905)
14. Luby, M., Sinclair, A., Zuckerman, D.: Optimal speedup of Las Vegas algorithms. Inf. Process. Lett. **47**(4), 173–180 (1993)
15. Meyer, J.: Two-moment decision models and expected utility maximization. Am. Econ. Rev. 421–430 (1987)
16. Van Moorsel, A.P., Wolter, K.: Analysis and algorithms for restart. In: Proceedings of the First International Conference on the Quantitative Evaluation of Systems, pp. 195–204 (2004)
17. Muñoz, P., Barrero, D.F., R-Moreno, M.D.: Run-time analysis of classical path-planning algorithms. In: Bramer, M., Petridis, M. (eds.) Research and Development in Intelligent Systems XXIX, pp. 137–148. Springer, London (2012). https://doi.org/10.1007/978-1-4471-4739-8_10
18. Norman, L., Kotz, S., Balakrishnan, N.: Continuous Univariate Distributions, vol. 1. Wiley Series in Probability and Mathematical Statistics: Applied Probability and Statistics (1994)
19. Paxson, V., Allman, M., Chu, J., Sargent, M.: Computing TCP's retransmission timer. Technical report (2011)
20. Reuveni, S., Urbakh, M., Klafter, J.: Role of substrate unbinding in Michaelis-Menten enzymatic reactions. Proc. Natl. Acad. Sci. U.S.A. **111**(12), 4391–4396 (2014)
21. Schöning, U.: A probabilistic algorithm for k-SAT and constraint satisfaction problems. In: Proceedings of the 40th Annual Symposium on Foundations of Computer Science, FOCS 1999, p. 410. IEEE Computer Society, Washington, DC (1999)
22. Wolter, K.: Stochastic Models for Fault Tolerance: Restart, Rejuvenation and Checkpointing. Springer Science & Business Media, Heidelberg (2010). https://doi.org/10.1007/978-3-642-11257-7
23. Wu, H.: Randomization and restart strategies. Master's thesis, University of Waterloo (2006)

Inversions from Sorting with Distance-Based Errors

Barbara Geissmann[✉] and Paolo Penna

Department of Computer Science, ETH Zurich, Zurich, Switzerland
barbara.geissmann@inf.ethz.ch

Abstract. We study the number of inversions after running the INSERTION SORT or QUICKSORT algorithm, when errors in the comparisons occur with some probability. We investigate the case in which probabilities depend on the difference between the two numbers to be compared and only differences up to some threshold τ are prone to errors. We give upper bounds for this model and show that for constant τ, the expected number of inversions is *linear* in the number of elements to be sorted. For INSERTION SORT, we also yield an upper bound on the expected number of runs, i.e., the number of consecutive increasing subsequences.

1 Introduction

We study the problem of sorting a sequence of distinct elements when the algorithm performs pairwise comparisons, but *errors* in the comparisons occur with some probability. A basic question here is to understand the structure of the output sequence for a given algorithm and given error comparabilities. In particular, here we focus on the *number of inversions* of the output sequence.[1]

Our study is in part motivated by the problem of designing *energy-efficient* algorithms for sorting, where errors are deliberately introduced in order to spend less energy on a single comparison (see e.g. the survey [17] and references therein for studies on the trade-off between energy saving and errors probability at a hardware level).

Indeed, it is well known that the *number of comparisons* made by INSERTION SORT is $n - 1 + I$ where I is the number of inversions of the input sequence. This suggests a natural approach to save energy spent in the computation:

1. First run some sorting algorithm using *low energy* comparisons. This will save energy, but introduces errors in the computation, meaning that the output is not guaranteed to be a sorted sequence in general.
2. Second run INSERTION SORT at *full energy* so that comparisons are always correct. If the sequence produced by the previous step has "few" inversions, then this step will cost significantly less than running INSERTION SORT directly at full energy, or even an $O(n \log n)$-time algorithm at full energy.

---

[1] The number of inversions of a sequence $\sigma = (\sigma_1, \ldots, \sigma_n)$ is the number of pairs (i, j) with $i < j$ such that $\sigma_i > \sigma_j$.

© Springer International Publishing AG 2018
A M. Tjoa et al. (Eds.): SOFSEM 2018, LNCS 10706, pp. 508–522, 2018.
https://doi.org/10.1007/978-3-319-73117-9_36

We ask the following question: *Under which conditions is the above approach effective?*

Since the expected number of inversions in a random sequence is $\Theta(n^2)$ we aim to *presort* an input sequence such that the expected number of inversions is low. The most natural approach is to run the same algorithm, INSERTION SORT, twice (first at low energy and then at full energy). However, it might also be beneficial to *mix* different algorithms and use another sorting algorithm at low energy. Motivated by these questions, we study the number of inversions that INSERTION SORT and QUICKSORT produce for a certain family of error probabilities (next section).

A similar idea has been introduced by Funke et al. [7], who distinguish between *cheap* (floating-point arithmetic) and *expensive* (exact geometric computation) comparisons in computational geometry. Their primary goal is not to save energy, but instead to save time and speedup their computations.

1.1   Our Contributions

We are interested in the number of inversions that single runs of two classical sorting algorithms, namely, INSERTION SORT and QUICKSORT, produce when the input sequence is a permutation of the integers 1 to n. We introduce a simple model in which the probability that a comparison between two elements (integers) is correct depends on the *difference* (we will call it *distance*) between the two elements we are comparing.

To get a feeling of our model, consider the following special case: All comparisons are correct, except those where the two elements are at distance 1, in which case $0 < q < 1$ is the probability of error. The two algorithms guarantee the following:

1. INSERTION SORT. The *expected* number of inversions is less than $n \cdot \frac{q}{1-q}$.
2. QUICKSORT. The number of inversions is *guaranteed* to be at most n.

In fact, we consider a more general type of errors that depend on the distance of the compared elements:

- *Distance-based errors.* The probability of error in a comparison between two elements x and y depends only on their distance $d = |x - y|$ and it is fully specified by a vector $p = (p_1, p_2, \ldots)$, where p_d is the probability of an error in a distance-d comparison. Note that this is a very general model as, for instance, it is possible that errors between distance-1 elements are less likely than errors at distance 2.

A natural restriction to the model above is to assume a maximum distance in which comparison errors can occur:

- *Threshold error probabilities* [1,7]. This is the case in which all distances up to some constant threshold τ are prone to errors, and higher distance comparisons are always correct. We additionally assume errors occur with probability at most $q < 1$.

For INSERTION SORT, we show that the *expected* number of inversions is $O(n)$ for threshold error probabilities (Theorem 1). The analysis of QUICKSORT on the same model provides an interesting comparison. We indeed show that QUICKSORT *always* returns a sequence with no more than $\tau \cdot n$ inversions, for any threshold τ as above, and that this analysis is tight (Theorem 2). Note for example that, if $\tau < \frac{n-1}{2}$, then QUICKSORT will never output the reversed sequence, while this is possible with INSERTION SORT (though very unlikely). Note that this holds even if comparisons below the threshold τ fail in adversarial fashion.

Our analysis on the number of inversions of INSERTION SORT can be extended to the *weighted number of inversions*, a natural variant in which inversions are weighted according to the distance of the inverted elements [9]. We provide this in the full version.

Finally, we study the number of *runs*, that is, the number of consecutive increasing (sorted) subsequences. This is what one should try to minimize if, in the above combination of two algorithms in cascade, the second algorithm would be MERGE SORT, instead of INSERTION SORT. Indeed, it is well-known that MERGE SORT can be implemented to run in time $O(n \cdot \log R)$, where R is the number of runs in the input. We show that INSERTION SORT has a rather *high* expected number of runs, namely $R = \Theta(n)$ for threshold error probabilities (Theorem 3). This means that the combination INSERTION SORT $\rightarrow$ MERGE SORT is not effective (the second algorithms makes $\Theta(n \log n)$ comparisons at full energy in expectation). In contrast, the combinations INSERTION SORT $\rightarrow$ INSERTION SORT and QUICKSORT $\rightarrow$ INSERTION SORT result in $O(n)$ comparisons at full energy (in expectation or guaranteed, respectively).

1.2   Related Work

Our distance-based error model with threshold error probabilities includes some of the other models studied previously in the literature. The closest model is perhaps the one studied by Funke et al. [7] and Ajtai et al. [1], where comparisons are *always correct* if the difference between the elements is above a *certain threshold* τ (the same as our threshold errors, but with no assumptions on the probabilities below the threshold). In Ajtai et al. [1], the threshold τ represents the *just noticeable difference unit* or *difference threshold* in the psychophysics literature [19]. Funke et al. [7] distinguish between *cheap* and *expensive* comparisons. In their terminology, only cheap comparisons between numbers whose difference is at most τ are prone to errors. They proved that MERGE SORT and HEAP SORT with cheap comparisons return a sequence with $O(\tau n \log n)$ inversions, while QUICKSORT outputs at most $2\tau n$ inversions.

Distance-based error probabilities that decrease exponentially with the distance d of the elements, e.g., $p_d = 1/(1 + \lambda^{2d})$ with $\lambda > 1$, have been studied for certain random processes by Geissmann and Penna [9].

Alonso et al. [2] studied the expected number of inversions of QUICKSORT when the probability of error is q for each comparison. They showed that the number of inversions is $\Theta(n^2 q)$ in expectation for nearly the whole range of q, including cases where q depends on n. Note that, for our threshold error model, we obtain stronger guarantees (not just in expectation). Hadjicostas and Lakshmanan [10–12] consider well-known sorting algorithms under the assumption that at most e comparisons fail during the execution. They showed lower and upper bounds on the number of inversions for BUBBLE SORT, (straight) INSERTION SORT and recursive MERGE SORT. In particular, for INSERTION SORT, these bounds are 0 and $\frac{n^2 e}{2(e+1)} + O(n)$. Lakshmanan et al. [14] adapted the (binary) INSERTION SORT algorithm to return the correctly sorted sequence using $O(n \log n + ne)$ comparisons, where e is again the number of errors.

For recurring errors, Braverman and Mossel [3] showed how to find a so-called maximum likelihood order of the elements, such that the maximum dislocation of an element is $O(\log n)$ and the total dislocation of all elements is $O(n)$ with high probability. By the inequality of Diaconis and Graham [5], this implies also $O(n)$ inversions. However, the time to compute such an order is exponential in γ, with $p = \frac{1}{2} - \gamma$. Klein et al. [13] provided a polynomial-time algorithm for the same upper bound on the maximum dislocation. The results of Geissmann et al. [8] imply that the number of inversions in the output of any algorithm cannot be guaranteed to be smaller than $2e$ if the number of recurring errors is bounded by some parameter e.

For independent errors, Feige et al. [6] gave an algorithm that sorts n numbers with probability $1 - Q$ in a decision-tree of depth $\Theta(n \log(n/Q))$, where $Q \in (0, 1/2)$ is a so-called tolerance parameter that can be chosen freely in this interval.

Finally, among others, Yao and Yao [20] and Leighton et al. [15,16] studied error tolerant sorting networks. For a more detailed review of the literature in the field of sorting and searching while coping with errors in comparisons, or even in memory, we refer to the surveys of Cicalese [4] and Pelc [18].

1.3   Preliminaries

Error Model. We consider the problem of sorting a sequence of n integer elements consisting of a permutation of the set $\{1, 2, \dots, n\}$. We call the sequence $(1, 2, 3, \dots, n)$ the *sorted order*, and the sequence $(n, n - 1, n - 2, \dots, 1)$ the *reverse order* of these elements. The *number of inversions* in any sequence $\sigma = (\sigma_1, \dots, \sigma_n)$ is the number of pairs i, j with $i < j$ and $\sigma_i > \sigma_j$. For instance, there are two inversions in $\sigma = (1, 3, 4, 2)$, namely $(3, 2)$ and $(4, 2)$.

We assume that a comparison takes an unordered pair of elements as input and returns an order of these two elements, e.g., for an input $\{x, y\}$ the output is either (x, y) or (y, x). If the comparison operates correctly, the first element in the output is smaller than the second one. The probability that a comparison is correct depends on the difference between the two numbers that are compared. Specifically, we are given a vector of probabilities

$$p = (p_1, p_2, \dots),$$

where $p_d \in [0, 1)$ for all d, and a comparison between two elements x and y with absolute difference $d = |x - y|$ *fails* with probability p_d. Hereafter, we will always address this absolute difference of two elements as their *distance*.

In this paper, we consider the case in which errors occur only if the two elements are at distance smaller than a fixed constant threshold τ.

Definition 1 (Critical Comparisons). *Let* $\tau := \max\{d \mid p_d > 0\}$ *be the maximum distance for which a comparison error might happen. We say that a comparison between two elements is critical if their distance is at most* τ.

The following quantity will play a key role in the analysis:

$$\Pi_p := \prod_{d=1}^{\tau} (1 - p_d)^d. \tag{1}$$

Insertion Sort. We consider the non-optimized[2] INSERTION SORT algorithm: on an arbitrary input sequence, the algorithm iterates and grows a sorted output sequence by processing one element in every iteration. The algorithm finds for the element in process its correct position in the already sorted subsequence by repeated comparisons and swaps with its left neighboring element until this neighbor is smaller (or none is left). Hence, the algorithm moves the element to the left until it is correctly placed.

If some comparisons can fail, it might happen that an element is not placed in its correct position. This in turn implies that the subsequence which we assume to be already sorted in fact might contains some inversions.

Example 1. Suppose we run INSERTION SORT on the reverse sequence $(5, 4, 3, 2, 1)$. Erroneous comparisons are shown in boldface. The symbol '•' in the sequence determines the progress of the algorithm, i.e., the elements on the left are already processed and the first element on the right is the next element that will be inserted.

	5 • 4 3 2 1
$(4, 5)$	4 5 • 3 2 1
$(3, 5), (\mathbf{3}, \mathbf{4})$	4 3 5 • 2 1
$(2, 5), (\mathbf{2}, \mathbf{3})$	4 3 2 5 • 1
$(1, 5), (1, 2), (1, 3), (1, 4)$	1 4 3 2 5 •

While two comparisons failed, the output contains three inversions: $(4, 3)$, $(4, 2)$, and $(3, 2)$. There would be seven inversions, had the comparison between 1 and 5 also failed.

---

[2] We find the correct position of an element by linear search not by binary search.

Quicksort. We consider the QUICKSORT algorithm: Starting with an arbitrary input sequence, the algorithm choses an arbitrary[3] element, compares every other element with this pivot and places it either left or right of the pivot, according to the outcome of their comparison. Then, the algorithm continues recursively with the elements placed left of the pivot and with those placed right of the pivot.

If a comparison fails, this partition into left and right also fails and the wrongly placed element causes inversions (with the pivot and possibly also with elements on the other side of the pivot), that will remain during the further execution of QUICKSORT.

Example 2. We simulate QUICKSORT on the numbers 1 to 5. We assume that our first pivot element is 3. We show erroneous comparisons in boldface. In a first step, we compare all elements to the pivot and put them either left or right of it:

$$\boxed{3}\ 5\ \ 4\ \ 2\ \ 1$$

$$(5,3),(\mathbf{4},\mathbf{3}),(2,3),(\mathbf{1},\mathbf{3})\qquad 4\ \ 2\ \boxed{3}\ 5\ \ 1$$

Then, we recurse on the two subsequences left and right of the pivot:

$$\boxed{4}\ 2\ \ 3\ \ 5\ \ 1\qquad\qquad 4\ \ 2\ \ 3\ \boxed{5}\ 1$$

$$(2,4)\qquad 2\ \boxed{4}\ 3\ \ 5\ \ 1\qquad (1,5)\qquad 4\ \ 2\ \ 3\ \ 1\ \boxed{5}$$

The output sequence of the algorithm is $(2,4,3,1,5)$ which contains the four inversions $(2,1)$, $(4,3)$, $(4,1)$, and $(3,1)$.

2   Inversions of Insertion Sort

In this section we prove the following result.

Theorem 1. *For error probabilities p with threshold τ and an arbitrary input sequence of size n, the expected number of inversions after one run of* INSERTION SORT *is at most*

$$n \cdot \frac{(1 - \Pi_p)^{1/\tau}}{(1 - (1 - \Pi_p)^{1/\tau})^2},$$

where Π_p is defined as in (1).

Note that Theorem 1 implies that the expected number of inversions is linear for threshold error probabilities (constant τ and $p_i < 1$ for $i \leq \tau$), because in this case Π_p is a strictly positive constant. In Sect. 2.3 we provide a tight bound for $\tau = 1$.

---

[3] The analysis on the number of inversions appearing after one run of QUICKSORT holds for arbitrarily chosen pivots. In particular, it also holds for random pivots.

2.1   Useful Definitions

In order to compute the expected number of inversions in the output sequence, we partition the sequence into blocks such that all inversions occur inside the blocks:

Definition 2 (Block). *In a sequence σ, a block is a minimal subsequence of elements in σ such that each of these elements has only inversions with elements in the same block.*

We distinguish two types of blocks: *trivial* blocks of size one and *non-trivial* blocks of size larger than one. Observe that elements in adjacent trivial blocks are sorted and an element in a non-trivial block is inverse to at least one other element in this block. Such a partition into blocks is possible in every sequence and, as it will turn out, we can upper bound the number of inversions if we know the expected block size after one execution of INSERTION SORT. Consider Fig. 1 for an example of blocks.

output sequence σ	3	2	1	4	5	7	6	8	10	9
sorted order	1	2	3	4	5	6	7	8	9	10
BS_{σ_j}	0	0	3	1	1	0	2	1	0	2
Y_{σ_j}	0	1	2	0	0	0	1	1	0	1
X_{σ_j}	0	0	1	1	1	0	1	1	0	1

Fig. 1. An output sequence σ along with the resulting blocks (gray boxes). For each block, we identify its smallest element (variable X_i) and associate to it the size of the block (variable BS_i). Variables Y_i indicate the number of elements larger than i in its block and are used to upper bound the number of inversions. Note that the variables X_i, BS_i, Y_i belong to element i, and X_{σ_j}, BS_{σ_j}, Y_{σ_j} to the element at position j in σ.

2.2   Bound the Number of Inversions (Proof of Theorem 1)

The maximum number of inversions in a (non-trivial) block of size S is equal to $\binom{S}{2}$, which is the number of pairs of elements in S. Consider an output sequence σ and let the random variable BS_i for $i \in [n]$ be equal to the size of the block in σ that contains i as its smallest element, and zero otherwise (if i is not the smallest element in its block). Furthermore, let Y_i be the random variable that denotes the number of elements larger than i in the same block (see Fig. 1). Observe now that the sum of all binomial coefficients $\binom{BS_i}{2}$ is equal to the sum of all Y_i, that is

$$\sum_{i=1}^{n} \binom{BS_i}{2} = \sum_{i=1}^{n} Y_i.$$

Let I denote the number of inversions in the output sequence of INSERTION SORT. By linearity of expectation, the expected number of inversions in the output sequence is

$$\mathrm{E}[I] \leq \mathrm{E}\left[\sum_{i=1}^{n} \binom{BS_i}{2}\right] = \mathrm{E}\left[\sum_{i=1}^{n} Y_i\right] = \sum_{i=1}^{n} \mathrm{E}[Y_i]. \tag{2}$$

The following lemmas will be used to bound the expected values of the Y_is. To this aim, let X_i be the random variable indicating whether i is the smallest element in its block, i.e., $X_i = 1$ if this is the case and $X_i = 0$ otherwise.

Lemma 1. *Let σ be an output sequence of* INSERTION SORT. *Then, $i \in [n]$ is the smallest element in its block, i.e. $X_i = 1$, if and only if all critical comparisons between elements in $[i - \tau, i - 1]$ and in $[i, i + \tau - 1]$ made by the algorithm did not fail.*

Proof. First, observe that $X_i = 1$ is equivalent to saying that σ does not contain any inversion between an element in $[1, i - 1]$ and an element in $[i, n]$: Whenever i is the smallest element in a block, all elements smaller than i lie on the left of this block in σ and all elements larger than i lie either in the same block as i or on the right of this block. Thus, no element smaller than i is inverse to i or an element larger than i.

This implies that if $X_i = 1$, all comparisons that were made during the algorithm between one element in $[1, i - 1]$ and one in $[i, n]$ turned out correct, where the only critical comparisons are those of elements in $[i - \tau, i - 1]$ with elements in $[i, i + \tau - 1]$.

For the other direction, we show that if no critical comparison between $[i - \tau, i - 1]$ and $[i, i + \tau - 1]$ fails, then σ contains no inversions between $[1, i - 1]$ and $[i, n]$. Consider INSERTION SORT in execution: in its iteration, an element from $[1, i - 1]$ passes all elements from $[i, n]$. Similarly, an element from $[i, n]$ never passes any one from $[1, i - 1]$. Thus, the algorithm maintains the following invariant after every iteration: in the sorted subsequence, the elements from $[1, i - 1]$ are on the left of those from $[i, n]$. $\square$

Lemma 2. *For any integer k and any $i \in [n]$ such that $i + k\tau \leq n$,*

$$\Pr[X_i = X_{i+\tau} = \cdots = X_{i+k\tau} = 0] \leq (1 - \Pi_p)^{k+1}.$$

Proof. Let $relevant_j$ be the set of pairs (a, b) such that $a \in [j - \tau, j - 1]$ and $b \in [j, j + \tau - 1]$. By Lemma 1, $X_j = 0$ for $j \in [n]$ if and only if at least one critical comparison $(a, b) \in relevant_j$ failed. Let $n_d^j \geq 0$ be the number of comparisons $(a, b) \in relevant_j$ made by the algorithm such that $|a - b| = d$. Then, the probability that at least one critical comparison $(a, b) \in relevant_j$ failed is

$$F^j := \left(1 - \prod_{d=1}^{\tau} (1 - p_d)^{n_d^j}\right). \tag{3}$$

Since the set of relevant comparisons, $relevant_j$ and $relevant_{j'}$, of any two distinct elements j and j' in $\{i, i + \tau, \ldots, i + k\tau\}$ are disjoint, and different comparisons fail independently with probability p_d, we have

$$\Pr[X_i = X_{i+\tau} = \cdots = X_{i+k\tau} = 0] \leq F^i \cdot F^{i+\tau} \cdots F^{i+k\tau}. \tag{4}$$

We next show that $F^j \leq 1 - \Pi_p$ for any j. Observe that, for every $d = 1, 2, \ldots, \tau$, there are exactly d possible pairs (a, b) with $a \in [i - \tau, i - 1]$ and $b \in [i, i - \tau]$ and such that $|a - b| = d$. This implies $n_d^j \leq d$, and thus

$$\prod_{d=1}^{\tau} (1 - p_d)^{n_d^j} \geq \prod_{d=1}^{\tau} (1 - p_d)^d = \Pi_p, \tag{5}$$

where the equality is the definition of Π_p in Eq. (1). By combining (3), (4), and (5) we obtain the desired bound.   □

Observe that Y_i is equal to the number of consecutive elements $j > i$ such that $X_j = 0$. The expected value of Y_i is thus

$$E[Y_i] = \sum_{k=1}^{n-i-1} k \cdot \Pr[X_{i+1} = X_{i+2} = \cdots = X_{i+k} = 0, X_{i+k+1} = 1], \tag{6}$$

$$\leq \sum_{k=1}^{n-i-1} k \cdot \Pr[X_{i+1} = 0, X_{i+1+\tau} = 0, \ldots, X_{i+1+\lfloor k/\tau \rfloor} = 0]$$

$$\leq \sum_{k=0}^{\infty} k \cdot (1 - \Pi_p)^{\lceil k/\tau \rceil} \leq \frac{(1 - \Pi_p)^{1/\tau}}{(1 - (1 - \Pi_p)^{1/\tau})^2}, \tag{7}$$

where the second inequality is by Lemma 2. Equations (2) and (7) give now the following upper bound on the expected number of inversions, which concludes the proof of Theorem 1:

$$E[I] \leq \sum_{i=1}^{n} E[Y_i] \leq n \cdot \frac{(1 - \Pi_p)^{1/\tau}}{(1 - (1 - \Pi_p)^{1/\tau})^2}.$$

2.3   The Case $\tau = 1$

In this section, we study the special case, where $\tau = 1$, and show a tight upper bound on the expected number of inversions after running INSERTION SORT. To get a feeling for the specialty of this case, we start with an observation for general τ, which strengthens the intuition that a bad input sequence is one for which INSERTION SORT has to succeed in many critical comparisons to output the sorted order. In other words, the more inversions an input sequence contains, the more unlikely it is that INSERTION SORT removes all of them.

For any $2 \leq \tau \leq n - 1$, if the input sequence is the reverse order, then (by Lemma 1) in order to get the sorted order, INSERTION SORT has to perform all critical comparisons and each one has to be correct. In contrast, if the input is an arbitrary sequence where many pairs are already in their correct order, the number of (correct) critical comparisons made during INSERTION SORT is smaller. However, even for $\tau = 1$, INSERTION SORT has to succeed in *every* distance-1 comparison for *any* input sequence, since every adjacent pair of elements in the output gets compared during INSERTION SORT and is placed according to the result of this comparison.

Lemma 3. *If we assume $\tau = 1$ and start with the reverse order $(n, \ldots, 1)$, then every distance-1 comparison is made during the execution of* INSERTION SORT.

Proof. Initially all elements larger than an element i are on its left, and all elements smaller than i are on its right. When i is processed, i is compared only to elements that are larger, and all comparisons are certainly correct until i is compared to $i+1$. If this comparison fails, i stops moving to the left. Otherwise, i moves to the first position. □

From Lemma 3 we learn that the reverse order is the worst input for $\tau = 1$, because the algorithm makes all critical comparisons in every possible execution. Moreover, an element i is either placed to the right of $i+1$ or to the (temporally) first position. We now show that in the former case, no further element will be placed between i and $i+1$.

Lemma 4. *For $\tau = 1$, after the execution of* INSERTION SORT, *the elements within a block are in reverse order.*

Proof. By contradiction, assume that a block contains two adjacent elements i and j (in this order), with $i > j$, and their absolute difference is larger than one. During INSERTION SORT, every element gets compared to its left and its right neighbor of the final sequence. Furthermore, the relative order of the already inserted elements is never again changed during the execution of the algorithm. This implies that there has been a comparison between i and j that failed (since $i > j$ is on the left of j), which is a contradiction to $\tau = 1$. Therefore, all elements in a block lie in reverse order. □

Lemma 4 implies that for $\tau = 1$, the number of inversions in the output sequence is indeed equal to the sum of all variables Y_i, and that $\Pr[X_i = 1] = \Pi_p = 1 - p_1$. Using Eq. (6), we can thus obtain a better upper bound on the expected number of inversions for $\tau = 1$:

$$E[Y_i] \leq \sum_{k=0}^{\infty} k \cdot p_1^k \cdot (1 - p_1) = \frac{p_1}{1 - p_1}, \qquad \text{and} \qquad E[I] \leq n \cdot \frac{p_1}{1 - p_1}.$$

3   Inversions of Quicksort

In this section we study the number of inversions of QUICKSORT, as opposed to INSERTION SORT considered before. In favour of QUICKSORT is the fact that it

usually requires $O(n \log n)$ comparisons[4], which is, for many inputs, better than
INSERTION SORT. Moreover, [7] proved that the number of inversions is at most
$2\tau \cdot n$ in the threshold error model. We next provide a *tight* bound:

Theorem 2. *For threshold τ and an arbitrary input sequence of size n, a tight
upper bound on the number of inversions after one execution of* QUICKSORT *is*
$\tau \cdot n$.

3.1   Proof of Theorem 2

To prove an upper bound on the number of inversions in output sequences of
QUICKSORT, we imagine a slight modification of the algorithm, such that the
output consists of *marked* and *non-marked* elements[5]:

- Whenever an element i is compared to a pivot and this comparison fails, we
  mark i for this failure.

Example 3. Assume during our QUICKSORT algorithm, we consider the numbers
1 to 5 with 2 being the first pivot. Suppose that all comparisons are correct,
except for the one between 2 and 4. The output is $(1, \bar{4}, 2, 3, 5)$, with 4 being the
only marked element.

Observe that whenever two elements are inverse in the output sequence, there
has been a common pivot (possibly one of those two) during the execution of
QUICKSORT that placed them to opposite sides, and at least one of them to the
wrong side. In order to bound the number of inversions in the output sequence
we conclude the following:

1. All non-marked elements in the output sequence of QUICKSORT are sorted.
   Thus, every inversion in this sequence includes at least one marked element.
2. The difference between two inverse elements, one marked and the other one
   non-marked, is at most τ. The difference between two inverse elements, both
   marked, is at most 2τ.

Consider now any element i in an output sequence of QUICKSORT and let L_i
denote the set of larger elements on its left and R_i the set of smaller elements
on its right, such that $|L_i| + |R_i|$ equals the number of inversions that include i.
Note that every element in L_i is inverse to every element in R_i, and recall that,
by Item 2, two inverse elements differ by at most 2τ. Therefore, $|L_i| + |R_i| \le 2\tau$.
Observe that for every inversion between two elements $i < j$, we have $j \in L_i$
and $i \in R_j$, which implies that every inversion is counted twice in the sum
$\sum_i |L_i| + |R_i| \le 2\tau \cdot n$. Hence, there cannot be more than $\tau \cdot n$ inversions in
the output sequence. A tight example is the output sequence that consists of
blocks of size $2\tau + 1$ with elements inside a block in reverse order. There are
$\binom{2\tau+1}{2}$ inversions per block and $\frac{n}{2\tau+1}$ such blocks, which results in exactly $n \cdot \tau$
inversions in total.

---

[4] See [7] for a analysis of the time complexity of QUICKSORT with errors.
[5] This modification of marking the elements is purely imaginary; the QUICKSORT algo-
    rithm does not know the correctness of a comparison.

4   Runs in Insertion Sort

In this section, we study the expected number of *runs* in the output of INSERTION SORT, that is, the number of increasing (sorted) subsequences. We prove the following result:

Theorem 3. *For error probabilities p with constant threshold τ and an arbitrary input sequence of size n, the expected number of runs after one execution of* INSERTION SORT *on an arbitrary input sequence of size n is $\Theta(n)$.*

4.1   Relation Between the Number of Blocks and Runs

An output sequence of INSERTION SORT consists of *trivial* and *non-trivial* blocks. All elements in consecutive trivial blocks are in the same run, since this subsequence is strictly increasing. Elements in non-trivial blocks, however, cannot all be in the same run, since every non-trivial block contains at least one inversion. Therefore, in every non-trivial block, there ends and starts at least one run (see Fig. 2 for an example).

Lemma 5. *In any sequence, the number of runs is larger than the number of non-trivial blocks.*

Proof. Let R denote the number of runs and B the number of non-trivial blocks. Then, $R \geq B + 1$, since the first run starts with the first element of the sequence and ends somewhere in the first non-trivial block and each non-trivial block contains at least one inversion, thus at least one start of a new run.   □

Fig. 2. The relation between number of runs and number of non-trivial blocks.

4.2   Consecutive Trivial Blocks (Proof of Theorem 3)

Observe that if we remove all trivial blocks from a sequence, the number of runs is still the same[6]. Between any two consecutive non-trivial blocks there is a number (possibly zero) of consecutive trivial blocks. We show that, in expectation, both the number of consecutive trivial blocks and the size of non-trivial blocks is "small", which then implies that the number of non-trivial blocks must be "large".

Lemma 6. *For error probabilities p and an arbitrary input sequence of size n, the expected number of elements in a subsequence of consecutive trivial (size one) blocks is at most $1/p_1^2$ in the output sequence of* INSERTION SORT.

---

[6] This is true if and only if the sequence contains at least one non-trivial block.

Proof. Note that elements in consecutive trivial blocks differ by one. In INSERTION SORT, every two *neighbors* in the output sequence have been compared with each other, and sorted accordingly. Therefore, for k consecutive trivial blocks in the output, at least $k-1$ distance-1 comparisons have been performed correctly. Let T_i denote the number of elements in the i-th subsequence of consecutive trivial blocks. Then it holds for all i,

$$\Pr[T_i = k] \leq (1 - p_1)^{k-1}, \qquad \text{and} \qquad \mathrm{E}[T_i] \leq \frac{1}{1 - p_1} \sum_k k(1 - p_1)^k \leq \frac{1}{p_1^2}.$$

□

Lemma 7. *For error probabilities p with threshold τ and an arbitrary input sequence of size n, the expected size of a non-trivial block in the output sequence of* INSERTION SORT *is at most* $2 + \frac{(1-\Pi_p)^{1/\tau}}{(1-(1-\Pi_p)^{1/\tau})^2}$.

Proof. We proceed similar to the proof of Theorem 1 and Lemma 2. Since the size of a non-trivial block is at least two, we need to bound the expected number of additional elements. Without loss of generality, assume that $i - 1$ and i are the two smallest elements in a non-trivial block. Then, the expected size of this block is at most

$$2 + \sum_{k=1}^{n-i} k \cdot Pr[X_{i+1} = \cdots = X_{i+k} = 0, X_{i+1+k} = 1] \leq 2 + \frac{(1 - \Pi_p)^{1/\tau}}{(1 - (1 - \Pi_p)^{1/\tau})^2}.$$

□

The output sequence of INSERTION SORT consists of repetitions of a possibly empty subsequence of consecutive trivial blocks and one non-trivial block. We call one of such repetitions a *unit* and shall argue that the expected number of units in the output is in $\Omega(n)$. (Note that only the very last unit might not contain a non-trivial block.) By Lemmas 6 and 7, the expected length l of a unit is at most

$$l \leq 2 + \frac{(1 - \Pi_p)^{1/\tau}}{(1 - (1 - \Pi_p)^{1/\tau})^2} + \frac{1}{p_1^2},$$

which is constant for constant values of τ. Thus, the expected number of units is at least $n/l \in \Omega(n)$, which implies that the expected number of non-trivial blocks is also linear. Finally, by Lemma 5, the expected number of runs is linear.

5   Conclusion and Open Questions

It would be interesting to investigate whether other restrictions on the error probabilities still guarantee a linear number of inversions. In particular, whether a constant value of Π_p is in general sufficient to guarantee a linear number of inversions. One such an example is the model in [9] where the error probability decreases exponentially with the distance, and for which Π_p is indeed constant.

Our upper bound on the number of inversions for INSERTION SORT (Theorem 1) grows exponentially in τ. The analysis of the case $\tau = 1$ suggests that our analysis can be improved. The exact growth as a function in τ is an interesting research direction. It would be also interesting to prove lower bounds, that is, show that any sorting algorithm must produce $f(\tau) \cdot n$ inversions in expectation, for a suitable function f.

One of the motivations for studying the number of inversions of the output (or other measures of "unsortedness") is the combination of two or more algorithms, some of them running at low energy. Our analysis on the number of inversions and runs, for example, suggests that certain combinations are better than others: one should prefer the combination 'INSERTION SORT $\rightarrow$ INSERTION SORT' to the combination 'INSERTION SORT $\rightarrow$ MERGE SORT'. There are other combinations of low-energy and full-energy algorithms that could be considered, as well as whether a three-stage combination could bring any improvement.

Acknowledgements. This research has been supported by the Swiss National Science Foundation (SNFS project 200021_165524).

References

1. Ajtai, M., Feldman, V., Hassidim, A., Nelson, J.: Sorting and selection with imprecise comparisons. ACM Trans. Algorithms **12**(2), 19 (2016)
2. Alonso, L., Chassaing, P., Gillet, F., Janson, S., Reingold, E.M., Schott, R.: Quicksort with unreliable comparisons: a probabilistic analysis. Comb. Probab. Comput. **13**(4–5), 419–449 (2004)
3. Braverman, M., Mossel, E.: Noisy sorting without resampling. In: Proceedings of the 19th Annual ACM-SIAM Symposium on Discrete Algorithms (SODA), pp. 268–276 (2008)
4. Cicalese, F.: Fault-Tolerant Search Algorithms - Reliable Computation with Unreliable Information. MTCSAES. Springer, Heidelberg (2013). https://doi.org/10.1007/978-3-642-17327-1
5. Diaconis, P., Graham, R.L.: Spearman's footrule as a measure of disarray. J. Roy. Stat. Soc.: Ser. B (Methodol.) **39**(2), 262–268 (1977)
6. Feige, U., Raghavan, P., Peleg, D., Upfal, E.: Computing with noisy information. SIAM J. Comput. **23**(5), 1001–1018 (1994)
7. Funke, S., Mehlhorn, K., Näher, S.: Structural filtering: a paradigm for efficient and exact geometric programs. Comput. Geom. **31**(3), 179–194 (2005)
8. Geissmann, B., Mihalák, M., Widmayer, P.: Recurring comparison faults: sorting and finding the minimum. In: Kosowski, A., Walukiewicz, I. (eds.) FCT 2015. LNCS, vol. 9210, pp. 227–239. Springer, Cham (2015). https://doi.org/10.1007/978-3-319-22177-9_18
9. Geissmann, B., Penna, P.: Sort well with energy-constrained comparisons. arXiv e-prints, arXiv:1610.09223, October 2016
10. Hadjicostas, P., Lakshmanan, K.B.: Bubble sort with erroneous comparisons. Australas. J. Comb. **31**, 85–106 (2005)
11. Hadjicostas, P., Lakshmanan, K.B.: Measures of disorder and straight insertion sort with erroneous comparisons. ARS Combinatoria **98**, 259–288 (2011)

12. Hadjicostas, P., Lakshmanan, K.B.: Recursive merge sort with erroneous comparisons. Discret. Appl. Math. **159**(14), 1398–1417 (2011)
13. Klein, R., Penninger, R., Sohler, C., Woodruff, D.P.: Tolerant algorithms. In: Demetrescu, C., Halldórsson, M.M. (eds.) ESA 2011. LNCS, vol. 6942, pp. 736–747. Springer, Heidelberg (2011). https://doi.org/10.1007/978-3-642-23719-5_62
14. Lakshmanan, K.B., Ravikumar, B., Ganesan, K.: Coping with erroneous information while sorting. IEEE Trans. Comput. **40**(9), 1081–1084 (1991)
15. Leighton, F.T., Ma, Y.: Tight bounds on the size of fault-tolerant merging and sorting networks with destructive faults. SIAM J. Comput. **29**(1), 258–273 (1999)
16. Leighton, F.T., Ma, Y., Plaxton, C.G.: Breaking the theta (n log^2 n) barrier for sorting with faults. J. Comput. Syst. Sci. **54**(2), 265–304 (1997)
17. Palem, K.V., Lingamneni, A.: Ten years of building broken chips: the physics and engineering of inexact computing. ACM Trans. Embed. Comput. Syst. **12**(2s), 87 (2013)
18. Pelc, A.: Searching games with errors - fifty years of coping with liars. Theoret. Comput. Sci. **270**(1–2), 71–109 (2002)
19. Thurstone, L.L.: A law of comparative judgment. Psychol. Rev. **34**(4), 273 (1927)
20. Yao, A.C.-C., Yao, F.F.: On fault-tolerant networks for sorting. SIAM J. Comput. **14**(1), 120–128 (1985)

Filters, Configurations, and Picture Encoding

An Optimization Problem Related to Bloom Filters with Bit Patterns

Peter Damaschke[1]([⊠]) and Alexander Schliep[2]

[1] Department of Computer Science and Engineering,
Chalmers University, 41296 Gothenburg, Sweden
`ptr@chalmers.se`
[2] Department of Computer Science and Engineering,
University of Gothenburg, Gothenburg, Sweden
`schliep@cse.gu.se`

Abstract. Bloom filters are hash-based data structures for membership queries without false negatives widely used across many application domains. They also have become a central data structure in bioinformatics. In genomics applications and DNA sequencing the number of items and number of queries are frequently measured in the hundreds of billions. Consequently, issues of cache behavior and hash function overhead become a pressing issue. Blocked Bloom filters with bit patterns offer a variant that can better cope with cache misses and reduce the amount of hashing. In this work we state an optimization problem concerning the minimum false positive rate for given numbers of memory bits, stored elements, and patterns. The aim is to initiate the study of pattern designs best suited for the use in Bloom filters. We provide partial results about the structure of optimal solutions and a link to two-stage group testing.

Keywords: Bloom filter · Genomics · Antichain · Group testing
Disjunct matrix

1 Introduction

The following scenario appears in various applications of computing: A large set S of data is maintained. Further elements may be added to S, but usually elements are never removed. Many queries of the form "$s \in S$?" must be answered, where s is any element from the domain of discourse. To facilitate quick answers, a certain rate of false positives is permitted: The system may sometimes claim $s \in S$ although actually $s \notin S$. However, false negatives are not allowed: The system must recognize that $s \in S$ whenever this is the case. A popular example of a data structure providing this functionality is the Bloom filter [2].

The word filter in the name indicates their use in avoiding accesses to the set S, in particular if slow accesses over networks or to disks become necessary. If these costly operations only happen for items passing the filter, the computational cost of many operations can be reduced, if the filter data structure allows inserts and queries in a time- and space-efficient manner. A number of database products (Google BigTable, Apache Cassandra, and Postgresql)

© Springer International Publishing AG 2018
A M. Tjoa et al. (Eds.): SOFSEM 2018, LNCS 10706, pp. 525–538, 2018.
https://doi.org/10.1007/978-3-319-73117-9_37

and web proxies (Squid) use Bloom filters; they have also been used to accelerate network router performance [23].

A specific application area in which Bloom filters have become a central data structure is the bioinformatics analysis of high-throughput DNA sequencing data from clinical or genomics experiments. In its analysis the k-mer, a consecutive substring of k characters in a *DNA read*, or string obtained from a sequencing instrument, is a fundamental unit for two reasons: First, the nodes of the *de Bruijn*-graph [7] are k-mers. The *de Bruijn*-graph is the most frequently used data structure in *de novo* genome assembly [25], the process of assembling complete genomes from the many fragments obtained from a sequencing instrument. Second, due to the way the errors are distributed in DNA sequencing reads, frequent k-mers seen a number of times represent the error-free sequence of the genome, whereas k-mers seen only once are erroneous. This explains the importance of identifying frequent k-mers [21] and their use in error correction, gene expression analysis and metagenomics, to list just a few applications.

The size of the problem instances are huge. A DNA sequencing data set of a human genome might contain 240 billion k-mers in its 2.4 billion reads. One expects about 3 billion k-mers to be frequent, and there could be up to 270 billion distinct erroneous k-mers for $k = 31$ [21]. Consequently, the filters have to be large too, in the tens of Gigabyte range, which amplifies the effect of cache misses. As the cost of the Bloom filter operations makes up a large proportion of the total running time, constants, complexity and details of cache behavior matter and a better understanding of these aspects of the filters will have impact on many practical applications. In the following, we first introduce the particular type of Bloom Filter we will study and motivate the hypothesis pursued in this study.

1.1   Blocked Bloom Filters with Bit Patterns

Bloom filters [2] are a classic implementation of the filtering idea introduced in the previous section. Although they have some issues (deletions are not supported, and the space is 1.44 times larger than optimal) and alternatives came up more recently in theory [11,19] and practice [13], Bloom filters remain an important and widely used data structure due to their conceptual simplicity.

Some basic notation is needed for the subsequent descriptions. A *vector* always means a bit vector, if not said otherwise. For vectors x, y of equal length, let $x \cap y$ and $x \cup y$ denote the bit-wise AND and OR, respectively. We write $y \leq x$ if y is contained in x, that is, for every entry 1 in y, the entry at the same position in x is 1 as well. We write $y < x$ if $y \leq x$ and $y \neq x$. For a set or multiset X of vectors, $\bigcup X$ is the vector obtained by joining all vectors in X by $\cup$. The *complement* of a vector x is obtained by flipping all bits. To *set a bit* means to assign value 1 to it. We wish to store a subset S of a universal set U.

Bloom filters with bit patterns have been proposed in [20], and standard Bloom filters appear as a special case of them. Their work can be described as follows. (A formal definition would be lengthy.) The filter consists of a vector of m bits, whose length m is chosen depending on parameters of the application. The filter uses a hash function $h : U \longrightarrow \{0, 1\}^m$, assigning a vector to every element $s \in U$. We call this vector the *pattern* of s. Let d be the number of elements in $S \subset U$, and let $x_1, \ldots, x_d$ be their patterns. Only the vector $x := x_1 \cup \ldots \cup x_d$ is stored. In order to test whether $s \in S$, one takes the pattern y of s and checks whether $y \leq x$. If not, then clearly $s \notin S$. If $y \leq x$, then $s \in S$ is assumed. Hence $s \notin S$ is a false positive if and only if $y \leq x_1 \cup \ldots \cup x_d$. In particular, any collision of patterns, $y = x_i$, causes a false positive.

Specifically, the *standard Bloom filter* uses a fixed k and builds the pattern by setting up to k bits, chosen by k independent hash functions with values in $\{1, \ldots, m\}$; note that the k bits are not necessarily distinct. For variations of this original idea and theoretical analysis of their properties, in particular, the false positive rate versus space, see, e.g., [3,8,15,18].

A *blocked Bloom filter* consists of many small blocks. A hash function first chooses a block (or blocks are partly predetermined, as the elements may be already grouped in some way), and then the blocks work like usual Bloom filters. Blocked Bloom filters with bit patterns have been proposed in [20]. It is one way to reduce both cache misses and hashing, which make up for the major part of the running time in some applications. Different applications can have very different demands on the false positive rate, memory space, time complexity, cache- and hash-efficiency, etc., therefore it is worthwhile to have a variety of filters with different strengths regarding these parameters.

Getting back to the description of blocked Bloom filters with bit patterns, the n patterns to be used are precomputed, by random sampling of k bits per pattern, and stored. While the space needed for the patterns is negligible compared to the entire filter, too large an n, say larger than the Level-1 or Level-2 cache will lead to deteriorating performance. Too small an n will lead to more collisions and increase the errors rate, which can be remediated by increasing filter size. Collision resolution mechanisms may be used to get roughly the same number d of elements per block. Hashing can be drastically reduced even without deteriorating the asymptotic false positive rate [15], but these results are shown for $d \to \infty$ whereas we are interested in blocks with small d and prescribed n.

1.2   Specific Problems and Our Contributions

Our hypothesis, prompted by observations with random k-set designs in combinatorial group testing [16], is that the exact choice of random k-bit patterns does have an effect in particular in light of small n. Also, it is not obvious that random k-bit patterns indeed attain optimal performance.

To our best knowledge, a study is missing that asks which set of bit patterns (i.e., which image of the hash function) is optimal to use in this approach to blocked Bloom filters, depending on the mentioned parameters m, d, n. The present paper is mainly devoted to this question.

We consider arbitrary probability distributions on the m-bit vectors (resulting from the part of the hash function that assigns patterns to elements in a block), and we ask which ones minimize the *false positive rate (FPR)*:

Definition 1. *Let m and d be fixed positive integers. Consider any probability distribution on the set of m-bit vectors. Draw $d + 1$ vectors $x_1, \ldots, x_d$ and y*

randomly and independently from the given distribution. We define the false positive rate (FPR) of the distribution, for the given d, as the probability of the event $y \leq x_1 \cup \ldots \cup x_d$. The true negative rate (TNR) is the probability of the complementary event. We abbreviate the FPR and TNR for a fixed d by $FPR(d)$ and $TNR(d)$, respectively. (Thus $TNR(d) + FPR(d) = 1$.) We refer to the probability of the event $y \leq x_1 \cup \ldots \cup x_d$, where the x_i are fixed and only y is random, as a conditional FPR.

Problem. *Given m, d, n, devise a probability distribution on the m-bit vectors that assigns positive probabilities to at most n vectors and minimizes $FPR(d)$.*

First we look at $d = 1$. This is not yet the realistic case, because a block would barely hold just one element. We start with this case rather for theoretical reasons, as it already provides some structural insights. We show that the best $FPR(1)$ is achieved by a random vector with a fixed number of 1s, which is $m/2$ (rounded if m is odd). Note that these vectors form the largest antichain (with respect to $\leq$) due to Sperner's theorem [24]. While the result is not surprising, its proof is not that straightforward: Clearly, the more vectors we use, the smaller can we make the probability of collisions ($y = x_1$), and this is the only type of false positives caused by an antichain. But it must also be shown that using even more vectors, partly being in $\leq$ relation, is not beneficial. Our argument is based on edge colorings in bipartite graphs and resembles the "sizes of shadows" in one of the proofs of Sperner's theorem, yet our objective is different. (The proof also closes a gap in a proof step of a side result, Theorem 4, in [5].) This start result raises further interesting points addressed in the sequel.

First, notice that a random vector with some *fixed* number of *distinct* bits has the optimal FPR, and its specification needs less than $\log_2 2^m = m$ random bits, whereas, e.g., setting a fixed number of independent random bits has a worse FPR and needs $\Theta(m \log m)$ random bits (more than $m/2$ specifications of one out of m position, requiring $\Theta(\log m)$ bits each).

Getting to the real case with general d (and also with limited n), one may wonder if random vectors with some fixed number k of 1s (depending on m and d) yield optimal $FPR(d)$ as well. This conjecture will be disproved already by a counterexample being as small as $m = 2$ and $d = 2$, but then we also obtain the following general result (that will point to a modified conjecture; see below): Some distribution with minimum $FPR(d)$ has a support of a form that we call a weak antichain. While an antichain forbids any vectors in $\leq$ relation, in a weak antichain we do allow such pairs of vectors provided that they differ in only one bit. (In [4] we proved that another combinatorial optimization problem shares the same property, also the basic proof idea of "quartet changes" is the same, however the proof details are problem-specific.) The relevance of this general theorem is that families of bit patterns in Bloom filters can be restricted to weak antichains, since other designs have only worse FPR values.

Note that setting k independent random bits with replacement violates the weak antichain property, which naturally leads to the idea of patterns, too. On the other hand, the proposal in [20] was just to use a "table of random k-bit patterns". The small example of non-optimality and the weak antichain property suggest that it might be good to use some mixture of patterns with two consecutive numbers, k and $k + 1$, of 1 entries. This seems also plausible because for any given d and m one would hardly expect one optimal k that jumps when m grows.

We do not manage to solve the general optimization problem considered here, however its difficulty is explained by our last contribution that might be the main result: We show that FPR minimization is, essentially, equivalent to the (notoriously difficult) construction of optimal almost disjunct matrices, which are designs being known from the group testing problem. The connection between Bloom filters and group testing has been noticed earlier here and then, but we are not aware of an explicit result on their relationship, as provided here.

2 Preliminaries

In this section we collect some special notation and known facts, in the order of appearance in the paper, except disjunct matrices and group testing which fit more naturally in the technical sections.

We call the number of 1s in a vector u its *level*. (This number is also known as the Hamming weight, but later we want to avoid confusion with another weight.) We also use the phrase "level k" to denote the *set* of all vectors with the same number k of bits 1.

We consider probability distributions Φ on finite sets only. The *support* of Φ, denoted $supp(\Phi)$, is the set of elements u (in our case: vectors) with nonzero probability $p(u) > 0$. The distribution Φ is *uniform* on $supp(\Phi)$ if all these $p(u) > 0$ are equal.

As said before, $p(u)$ denotes the probability of vector u in a given distribution. Sometimes it is more convenient to write p_U instead, where U is the set of positions of bits 1 in u. We also omit commas and brackets. For instance, $p(1, 0, 1)$ is written as p_{13}. If $U = \emptyset$, we write p_0.

We presume that standard graph- and order-theoretic concepts not explained here are widely known. A classic theorem by König (1916) states that every bipartite graph with maximum degree Δ allows an *edge coloring* with Δ colors. That is, we can color the edges in such a way that edges with the same color always form a *matching*, i.e., they are pairwise disjoint. Different proofs and many algorithmic versions have been given later, see, e.g., [14].

An *antichain* in a partial order (e.g., in the partial order of m-bit vectors under the $\leq$ relation), is a subset without any pairs $y < x$. Sperner's theorem [24] states (rephrased) that the largest antichain in the set of m-bit vectors is simply the set of all vectors on level k, where $k = \lfloor m/2 \rfloor$ or $k = \lceil m/2 \rceil$. Slightly relaxing the notion of antichain, we call a set A of m-bit vectors a *weak antichain* if for all vectors $u, v \in A$ with $u \leq v$, vector v has at most one 1 entry more than vector u.

Let y be a vector and X a tuple of d vectors (which are in general not distinct). We define $f(y, X) = 1$ if $y \leq \bigcup X$, and $f(y, X) = 0$ otherwise. Note that $FPR(d)$ in Definition 1 is the weighted sum of all $f(y, X)$, where the weight of (y, X)

is the probability that $d + 1$ vectors independently drawn from the distribution happen to be y and the vectors of X in the given order.

We say that a probability distribution Φ on the m-bit vectors is *dominated* by another distribution Ψ if, for every d, the FPR of Ψ is no larger than that of Φ. We call Φ *undominated* if Φ is not dominated by any $\Psi \neq \Phi$. Clearly, from the point of view of getting optimal FPR, only undominated distributions need to be considered.

Every probability distribution on finitely many elements and with rational numbers as probability values can be equivalently viewed as a uniform distribution on copies of the elements: Let q be a common denominator of all probabilities. Then we may represent every element of probability p/q as p distinct copies labeled by the element. We refer to these copies as *units*, and every unit is chosen with probability $1/q$. Notationally we may not always distinguish between a unit and its label, if this causes no confusion.

Let e denote Euler's number. Logarithms are meant with base 2 if not said otherwise.

3   False Positive Rate for One Element

Theorem 1. *For every $m > 1$, the uniform distribution on a median level, i.e., on the level $\lfloor m/2 \rfloor$ or $\lceil m/2 \rceil$, attains the smallest $FPR(1)$.*

Proof. For any probability distribution Φ on the m-bit vectors, observe that $FPR(1) = \sum_u p(u)^2 + \sum_{u<v} p(u) \cdot p(v)$, where the sums are taken over all vectors. Let k be the lowest level containing any vectors in $supp(\Phi)$, and assume that $k \leq (m-1)/2$. We construct a weighted bipartite graph as follows. The vertices are all vectors $u \in supp(\Phi)$ on level k, and all vectors v on level $k+1$ (including those with zero probability). We use the terms vector and vertex interchangeably. The edges are all pairs (u, v) with $u < v$. The weight of a vertex is its probability, and the weight of an edge (u, v) is $p(u) \cdot p(v)$.

Note that every vertex on level $k + 1$ has a degree at most $k + 1$, and every vertex on level k has exactly the degree $m - k \geq k + 1$. By König's theorem there exists an edge coloring with $m - k$ colors. Clearly, every vertex on level k is incident to exactly one edge of each color. Since $m > 1$, we have $m - k \geq 2$. The total edge weight of the bipartite graph is $b := \sum_{u<v} p(u) \cdot p(v)$, where u and v are restricted to vertices on level k and $k+1$, respectively. The color class of a color c is the set of all edges of this color c. Let M be a color class with minimum total edge weight, among all colors c. This weight can be at most $b/2$, since $m - k \geq 2$.

Now we modify the probabilities. For every vertex u on level k and its partner v in M, we set $p(u) := 0$ and $p(v) := p(v) + p(u)$. Notice that v exists, and different vertices u have different partners v. The contribution of levels k and $k+1$ to $FPR(1)$ decreases by b as we destroy all edges, and at the same time it increases by at most $2b/2 = b$ because every new $p(v)^2$ becomes $(p(v)+p(u))^2 = p(v)^2 + 2p(u) \cdot p(v) + p(u)^2$. In words: For every $(u, v) \in M$, the squared vertex weight $p(u)^2$ just "moves into" $p(v)^2$, and the doubled edge weight is added. The sum of all doubled edge weights in M is bounded by $2b/2$. Finally, no further positive terms in $FPR(1)$ are created by moving probability mass to level $k+1$: There are no further vertices w with $p(w) > 0$ on lower levels, and for any $w > v$ on higher levels we have already $w > u$ by transitivity. Altogether it follows that we can empty the level k without increasing $FPR(1)$.

By symmetry, $FPR(1)$ is not affected if we take the complements of all vectors. Thus the same reasoning applies also to the highest level k that intersects $supp(\Phi)$, assuming that $k \geq (m+1)/2$. By iterating the procedure we can move all probability mass into the level $m/2$ if m is even, or into one of $\lfloor m/2 \rfloor$ or $\lceil m/2 \rceil$ if m is odd. As the last step, the sum of squares of a fixed number of values with a fixed sum is minimized if these values are equal. $\qquad\square$

In Theorem 1 we did not limit the size of the support, i.e., the number n. of patterns. Now let n be prescribed. Due to Theorem 1, if $n > \binom{m}{\lfloor m/2 \rfloor}$, we would still take only a median level and no further vectors, and if $n \leq \binom{m}{\lfloor m/2 \rfloor}$, we can take the uniform distribution on any antichain of n vectors to achieve the best $FPR(1)$ which is then $1/n$.

4 Weak Antichains

Theorem 2. *For every m, every probability distribution on the m-bit vectors is dominated by some probability distribution whose support is a weak antichain.*

Proof. Let u and v be vectors such that $u \leq v$, and v has at least two 1 entries more than u. Clearly, we can get two vectors w and w' such that $w \cap w' = u$, $w \cup w' = v$, and u, v, w, w' are four distinct vwctors. Now let Φ be any probability distribution on the vectors with $u, v \in supp(\Phi)$, that is, Φ contains two such units u and v, and is therefore not a weak antichain. We replace one unit u with one unit w, and we replace one unit v with one unit w'. We call such a replacement a *quartet change*. We study how a quartet change affects the FPR.

In certain subsets (of sequences of vectors) with even cardinality we will pair up all members, i.e., divide them completely into disjoint pairs, and we refer to the members of every such pair as *partners*. In the following, observe that distinct units carrying the same label are still considered distinct (as units), and that to "appear" in a sequence means "at least once".

Every argument (y, X) of f, where y is a unit and X is a sequence of d units, belongs to exactly one of the following cases:

(a1) Both u and v are not y, nor do they appear in X.
(a2) Both u and v are not y, and exactly one of them appears in X.
(a3) Both u and v are not y, and both appear in X.
(b1) Unit y is one of u and v, and both u and v do not appear in X.
(b2) Unit y is one of u and v, and y appears in X.
(b3) Unit y is one of u and v, and only the unit other than y appears in X.

Note that, in general, y itself may appear in X.

Since we are working with units, all (y, X) have the same probability, hence $FPR(d)$ is simply the unweighted sum of all $f(y, X)$. In each of the cases we prove that $FPR(d)$ cannot increase by the quartet change.

Case (a1). Trivially, $f(y, X)$ is not affected by the quartet change.

Case (a2). We pair up the arguments of f that belong to this case: The partner of every (y, X) is defined by replacing all occurrences of our unit u with v, or vice versa. Let X_u and X_v be any such partners containing u and v, respectively, with unions $x_u := \bigcup X_u$ and $x_v := \bigcup X_v$. We define X_w as the sequence obtained from X_u by replacing all occurrences of the unit u with w, and $x_w := \bigcup X_w$. Finally, $X_{w'}$ and $x_{w'}$ are defined similarly. In the distribution after the quartet change, X_w and $X_{w'}$ are partners.

We claim that $f(y, X_u) + f(y, X_v) \geq f(y, X_w) + f(y, X_{w'})$. This claim follows from two observations: If both $y \leq x_w$ and $y \leq x_{w'}$, then $y \leq x_w \cap x_{w'} = x_u \leq x_v$, where the inner equality is true by the distributive law for $\cap$ and $\cup$. If only one of the former inequalities holds, say $y \leq x_w$, then we still have $y \leq x_v$.

Case (a3). Consider any such argument (y, X) as specified in this case, and let X' be the sequence obtained from X by the quartet change. Let $x := \bigcup X$ and $x' := \bigcup X'$. We claim that $f(y, X) \geq f(y, X')$. To show this claim, we use that $w \cup w' = v$: If $y \leq w \cup w'$ then trivially $y \leq v$. Together with the distributive law this shows: If $y \leq x'$ then $y \leq x$.

Case (b1). Again we pair up the arguments of f that belong to the case: This time, (u, X) and (v, X) are partners, and the claim is that $f(u, X) + f(v, X) \geq f(w, X) + f(w', X)$. With $x := \bigcup X$ observe the following: If both $w \leq x$ and $w' \leq x$, then $u \leq v = w \cup w' \leq x$. If only one of the former inequalities holds, say $w \leq x$, then we still have $u \leq x$.

Case (b2). The same unit appears in the role of y and also in X, and it is replaced with the same unit at all occurrences. Thus we have $f(y, X) = 1$ before and after the quartet change.

Case (b3). We pair up the arguments (u, X_v) and (v, X_u), where X_u is obtained from X_v by replacing all occurrences of our unit u with v. Note that we also obtain X_v from X_u in the opposite direction. We define X_w and $X_{w'}$ as in case (1). We also adopt the earlier notations for the unions.

We claim that $f(u, X_v) + f(v, X_u) \geq f(w, X_{w'}) + f(w', X_w)$. To show the claim, first note that trivially $w \leq x_w$ and $w' \leq x_{w'}$. Now, if also both $w \leq x_{w'}$ and $w' \leq x_w$, then $u \leq v = w \cup w' \leq x_w \cap x_{w'} = x_u \leq x_v$, where the first equality holds by definition, and the second equality was already used in case (1). If only one of the former inequalities holds, say $w \leq x_{w'}$, then it suffices to observe that $u \leq v$.

Finally, it is not hard to see that a sequence of quartet changes cannot cycle. Hence we always arrive at a weak antichain dominating the original distribution.   □

5 Some Special Cases

The following propositions are proved by using extremal value calculations and Theorem 2; a full version is available at www.cse.chalmers.se/~ptr.

Proposition 1. *Among all distributions whose support is contained in the levels 0 and 1, the distribution minimizing $FPR(d)$ is the following:*

For $d \geq m$, assign probability $1 - m/(d+1)$ to the zero vector, and $1/(d+1)$ to every vector on level 1.
For $d < m$, assign probability $1/m$ to every vector on level 1.
Moreover, for $d < m$, the (unrestricted) distribution minimizing $FPR(d)$ does not have the zero vector in the support.

Proposition 2. *For $m \geq 2$ and $d \geq 2$, the support of any distribution minimizing $FPR(d)$ does not include the vector on level m.*

Although these propositions treat only special aspects of our FPR minimization problem, they lead to some interesting conclusions:

Consider $m = 2$ and $d = 2$. Proposition 2 yields $p_{12} = 0$. Thus we can apply Proposition 1, and therefore the best distribution is $p_0 = p_1 = p_2 = 1/3$. Already this small example shows that Theorem 1 does not generalize to $d > 1$ in the way that the optimal $FPR(d)$ is always attained by the uniform distribution on some single level. But together with Theorem 2 it suggests that the minimum $FPR(d)$ might be attained by some distribution whose support is in at most two consecutive levels, and where all vectors on the same level have equal probabilities.

Whatever the conjecture is, it is not easy to see how the arguments in Theorem 1 can be generalized to $d > 1$. Informally, movements of probability mass from the lowest level upwards create larger unions $x_1 \cup \ldots \cup x_d$. This makes it tricky to control the FPR, since probabilities can no longer be assigned to the edges of some graph.

So far we have usually assumed an unlimited number n of vectors in the support. The problem earns an extra dimension when a maximum n is prescribed as well, as in the following section.

6 Using Almost Disjunct Matrices

Disjunct matrices (see definitions below) are test designs for non-adaptive group testing [9], and relaxed versions are applied to two-stage group testing. In *non-adaptive group testing*, d unknown elements in a set of n elements have a specific property called *defective*, and these defective elements must be identified by m simultaneous group tests: A *group test* indicates whether a certain subset contains some defective or not. In *two-stage group testing* the aim is the same, but the job of the first stage is only to limit the possible defectives to a subset of candidates, which are then tested individually in the second stage. (There is also a version where the second stage can apply yet another non-adaptive group testing scheme, but this problem version is not relevant in our current context.) Remarkably, two-stage group testing can accomplish a query number exceeding the information-theoretic lower bound only by a constant factor [6,12], which is not possible in one stage.

We call a binary matrix (d, ε)- *disjunct* if $y \le x_1 \cup \ldots \cup x_d$ happens with probability at most ε, when $x_1, \ldots, x_d$ are columns chosen independently and uniformly at random, and y is uniformly chosen among the remaining vectors, distinct from all x_i. (The definition in [1,17] is slightly different, as it requires the x_i to be distinct as well, but the difference is marginal for $d \ll n$.) A $(d, 0)$-disjunct matrix is simply called d- *disjunct*. Informally we also refer to (d, ε)-disjunct matrices as *almost disjunct*. For the use of (almost) disjunct matrices in group testing we refer to the cited literature. In our context, the n columns are the patterns in a Bloom filter with m bits.

The event $y \le x_1 \cup \ldots \cup x_d$ can occur for two reasons: either (1) a collision $y = x_i$ happens for some i, or (2) y is in the union of d vectors other than y. We name the probabilities of (1) and (2) the *collision* and *containment probability*, respectively.

Proposition 3. *Among all distributions with a fixed support of size $n \ge d + 1$, the uniform distribution on the support has the smallest collision probability, which equals $1 - (1 - 1/n)^d$.*

Proof. We denote the n probabilities by $q_1, \ldots, q_n$. The probability of no collision equals $\sum_{i=1}^{n} q_i (1 - q_i)^d$. We want to maximize this expression under the constraint $\sum_{i=1}^{n} q_i = 1$. From the first and second derivative one can see that the function $q(1 - q)^d$ is increasing if and only if $q < 1/(d + 1)$, and concave if and only if $q < 2/(d+1)$. It follows that, in an optimal solution, all $q_i < 2/(d+1)$ are equal, and $q_i \ge 2/(d+1)$ holds for at most one index. Denote the small and large value s and r, respectively. The assumption $n \ge d+1$ implies $s < 1/n \le 1/(d+1)$. Hence we can decrease r and increase s so as to preserve the sum constraint and improve the objective. It follows that, in an optimal solution, an index i with $q_i = r$ cannot exist. Finally we get $q_i = 1/n$ for all i. $\square$

By virtue of Proposition 3 we focus now on filters that use a distribution being uniform on its support. We remark that, by simple calculation, $1 - (1 - 1/n)^d = d/n - O((d/n)^2)$, which is essentially d/n.

Proposition 4. *Any (d, ε)-disjunct $m \times n$ matrix enables a Bloom filter with m bits, n patterns, and $FPR(d) \le 1 - (1 - 1/n)^d + (1 - 1/n)^d \varepsilon$, where the patterns are assigned uniformly to the elements. The converse holds also true.*

Proof. Given a matrix as indicated, we take the uniform distribution on its columns. The collision probability is $1 - (1 - 1/n)^d$. The containment probability, in the event of no collision, is bounded by ε, by the definition of (d, ε)-disjunctness. Conversely, suppose that we have a Bloom filter as indicated. Again, the collision probability is equal to $1 - (1 - 1/n)^d$ because of the uniform distribution. Since $FPR(d) \le 1 - (1 - 1/n)^d + (1 - 1/n)^d \varepsilon$ is assumed, the containment probability in the case of no collision cannot exceed ε. Hence we can view the patterns as the columns of some (d, ε)-disjunct $m \times n$ matrix. $\square$

Proposition 4 states that, at least for uniform distributions, constructing Bloom filters with bit patterns that are optimal (in terms of FPR, space, and amount of patterns and hash bits) is essentially equivalent to constructing optimal almost-disjunct matrices. The next natural question concerns the possible trade-offs between the parameters. The smallest possible row number of d-disjunct matrices behaves as $m = \Theta(d^2/\log d)\log n$ [10]. Unfortunately, with $\varepsilon := d/n$ this leads to $m/d = \Theta(d/\log d)(\log d + \log(1/\varepsilon))$, i.e., the space per element ratio is by a $\Theta(d/\log d)$ factor worse than in standard Bloom filters where $m/d = 1.44\log(1/\varepsilon)$. For $d = 1$ we remark that the optimal 1-disjunct matrices are the Sperner families, and according to Theorem 2 they have optimal $FPR(1)$. But for $d > 1$, using d-disjunct matrices quickly becomes unsuitable.

The picture becomes better with (d, ε)-disjunct matrices. As mentioned in [1, 17], it is possible to achieve $m = \Theta(d\log n)$ due to [26] (and hence the additional $\Theta(d/\log d)$ factor disappears), although the cited result was not constructive. But it was not noticed in [1,17] that a special type of (d, ε)-disjunct matrices with $m = \Theta(d\log n)$ rows and even better properties is known as well [6,12]. We will utilize them now.

A binary matrix is called (d, f)-resolvable if, for any d distinct columns $x_1, \ldots, x_d$, the inclusion $y \leq x_1 \cup \ldots \cup x_d$ holds for fewer than f columns y other than the x_i [12]. Note that any (d, f)-resolvable matrix is also $(d, f/(n - d))$-disjunct, and the resulting false positive probability bound holds even conditional on every tuple $x_1, \ldots, x_d$, not only averaged over all tuples. A counterpart of Proposition 4 holds for resolvable matrices and conditional FPR.

Specifically, Theorem 2 in [12] provides, for every integer $f > 0$, a (d, f)-resolvable matrix with $m = 2(d^2/f)\log(en/d) + 2d\log(en/f) + 2(d/f)\log n$ rows. This yields, in a few steps: $m/d = 2(d/f)\log(en/d) + 2\log(en/f) + (2/f)\log n = (2(d + f + 1)/f)\log(n/d) + 2(d/f)\log e + 2\log(d/f) + 2\log e + (2/f)\log d$. For notational convenience we define $r = d/n$, $s = f/n$, and $t = (d+f)/n$. We assume bounded ratios r/s and s/r and (for studying the asymptotics for growing n) we neglect the terms that do not depend on n. Then the above equation simplifies to $m/d = 2(1 + r/s)\log(1/r)$. Further rewriting gives $m/d = 2t/(t-r)\cdot\log(1/r)$, which we use below.

It is not totally obvious that the most efficient resolvable matrices, that maximize n for given m and d, also yield the smallest $FPR(d)$ of Bloom filters of this type. While the collision probability improves (i.e., decreases) for growing n, the containment probability increases, as the relation between n and the fixed m becomes worse. But, in fact, we can establish monotonicity.

Proposition 5. *When the columns of the (d, f)-resolvable matrices from [12] are used as patterns in a Bloom filter, then $FPR(d)$ decreases for growing n.*

Proof. Let C denote the factor for which $m = Cd\log n$. Note that $C \geq 2$. Solving $m/d = 2t/(t-r)\cdot\log(1/r)$ for t yields $t = r/(1 - (2/\ln 2)(d/m)\ln(1/r))$. Taking the derivative with repect to r by using the quotient rule yields the denominator $1 - (2/\ln 2)(d/m)(\ln(1/r) + 1)$. We have the following chain of equivalent inequalities: $1 - (2/\ln 2)(d/m)(\ln(1/r) + 1) > 0 \iff \ln(1/r) < \ln 2 \cdot$

$(m/2d) - 1 \iff 1/r < (1/e) \cdot 2^{m/(2d)} \iff n/d < (1/e) \cdot 2^{Cd \log n/(2d)} \iff n < (d/e) \cdot 2^{(C/2) \log n} \iff n < (d/e) \cdot n^{C/2}$, and the latter one is true for $C \geq 2$. Hence the derivative is positive in the relevant range of r, therefore t decreases with growing $1/r$, and the assertion follows.   □

On the other hand, a larger n requires more space to store the patterns and more hashing. Still, the use of patterns is advantageous in this respect: In a design with n patterns, only $\log n$ hash bits per element are needed. A standard Bloom filter needs $\Theta((m/d) \log m) = \Theta(\log n \cdot \log m)$ hash bits per element. The constants depend on the desired FPR, but the extra $\Theta(\log m)$ factor remains.

Another remark is that the resolvable matrices in [12] consist again of randomly chosen vectors where a fixed number of bits is set, and Bloom filters are explicitly mentioned as the inspiration. The opposite direction, namely, using randomly chosen vectors with a fixed number of 1s as bit patterns in blocked Bloom filters, was proposed in [20]. However, the known resolvable matrices are not necessarily optimal. (In general, constructions of improved test designs are a major theme in group testing research.) An intriguing question is whether there are better designs with a given number n of patterns, and this is our optimization problem.

7   Concluding Remarks

The actual construction of improved almost-disjunct matrices, and hence of better bit patterns for Bloom filters, is beyond the scope of this paper. Our partial results suggest that certain designs with vectors from *two* neighbored levels might be optimal. We notice that the construction of combinatorial designs with certain "almost-properties" gained new momentum recently [22].

We intend to design large-scale simulation experiments, to gain insights for real and simulated workloads of using Bloom filters with bit patterns. We expect to see differences between various pattern choices when viewing the FPR, as the number of items in the filter increases. There may not necessarily be differences in the FPR for the nominal design parameter representing the number of items, but in how the FPR behaves up to this point and beyond.

Yet another aspect could not be addressed here: Cache considerations prevent making the number n of patterns arbitrarily large, as the pattern storage needs to fit within primary or at least secondary caches. One possible approach to increase n (and thus reduce the FPR) in the same pattern storage would be the computation of the actually needed patterns on-the-fly from hash values, using only a small amount of auxiliary memory. Naturally, the design of the patterns must allow fast calculation. We are wondering if such designs exist, that do not compromise the other parameters too much.

Acknowledgment. We are grateful to the reviewers for encouragement and for careful comments that helped improve the notation and fix a calculation mistake.

References

1. Barg, A., Mazumdar, A.: Almost Disjunct Matrices from Codes and Designs. CoRR abs/1510.02873 (2015)
2. Bloom, B.H.: Space/time trade-offs in hash coding with allowable errors. Comm. ACM **13**, 422–426 (1970)
3. Broder, A., Mitzenmacher, M.: Network applications of Bloom filters: a survey. Internet Math. **1**, 485–509 (2004)
4. Damaschke, P.: Calculating approximation guarantees for partial set cover of pairs. Optim. Lett. **11**, 1293–1302 (2017)
5. Damaschke, P., Muhammad, A.S.: Randomized group testing both query-optimal and minimal adaptive. In: Bieliková, M., Friedrich, G., Gottlob, G., Katzenbeisser, S., Turán, G. (eds.) SOFSEM 2012. LNCS, vol. 7147, pp. 214–225. Springer, Heidelberg (2012). https://doi.org/10.1007/978-3-642-27660-6_18
6. De Bonis, A., Gasieniec, L., Vaccaro, U.: Optimal two-stage algorithms for group testing problems. SIAM J. Comput. **34**, 1253–1270 (2005)
7. de Bruijn, N.G.: A combinatorial problem. Koninklijke Nederlandse Akademie v. Wetenschappen **49**, 758–764 (1946)
8. Dillinger, P.C., Manolios, P.: Bloom filters in probabilistic verification. In: Hu, A.J., Martin, A.K. (eds.) FMCAD 2004. LNCS, vol. 3312, pp. 367–381. Springer, Heidelberg (2004). https://doi.org/10.1007/978-3-540-30494-4_26
9. Du, D.Z., Hwang, F.K.: Pooling Designs and Nonadaptive Group Testing. World Scientific, New Jersey (2006)
10. Dyachkov, A.G., Vorobev, I.V., Polyansky, N.A., Shchukin, V.Y.: Bounds on the rate of disjunctive codes. Probl. Inf. Transm. **50**, 27–56 (2014)
11. Eppstein, D.: Cuckoo filter: simplification and analysis. In: Pagh, R. (ed.) SWAT 2016. LIPIcs, vol. 53, paper 8, Dagstuhl (2016)
12. Eppstein, D., Goodrich, M.T., Hirschberg, D.S.: Improved combinatorial group testing algorithms for real-world problem sizes. SIAM J. Comput. **36**, 1360–1375 (2007)
13. Fan, B., Andersen, D.G., Kaminsky, M., Mitzenmacher, M.: Cuckoo filter: practically better than Bloom. In: Seneviratne, A., et al. (eds.) CoNEXT 2014, pp. 75–88. ACM (2014)
14. Kapoor, A., Rizzi, R.: Edge-coloring bipartite graphs. J. Algorithms **34**, 390–396 (2000)
15. Kirsch, A., Mitzenmacher, M.: Less hashing, same performance: building a better Bloom filter. Random Struct. Algorithms **33**, 187–218 (2008)
16. Knill, E., Schliep, A., Torney, D.C.: Interpretation of pooling experiments using the Markov Chain Monte Carlo method. J. Comput. Biol. **3**, 395–406 (1996)
17. Mazumdar, A.: Nonadaptive Group Testing with Random Set of Defectives. CoRR abs/1503.03597 (2016)
18. Mitzenmacher, M., Upfal, E.: Probability and Computing: Randomized Algorithms and Probabilistic Analysis. Cambridge University Press, Cambridge (2005)
19. Pagh, A., Pagh, R., Srinivasa Rao, S.: An optimal Bloom filter replacement. In: SODA 2005, pp. 823–829 (2005)
20. Putze, F., Sanders, P., Singler, J.: Cache-, hash-, and space-efficient Bloom filters. ACM J. Exp. Algorithms **14**, Article 4.4 (2009)
21. Roy, R.S., Bhattacharya, D., Schliep, A.: Turtle: identifying frequent k-mers with cache-efficient algorithms. Bioinformatics **14**, 1950–1957 (2014)

22. Sarkar, K., Colbourn, C.J., de Bonis, A., Vaccaro, U.: Partial covering arrays: algorithms and asymptotics. In: Mäkinen, V., Puglisi, S.J., Salmela, L. (eds.) IWOCA 2016. LNCS, vol. 9843, pp. 437–448. Springer, Cham (2016). https://doi.org/10.1007/978-3-319-44543-4_34
23. Song, H., Dharmapurikar S., Turner J., Lockwood, J.: Fast hash table lookup using extended Bloom filter: an aid to network processing. In: Guérin, R., Govindan, R., Minshall, G.: SIGCOMM 2005, pp. 181–192. ACM (2005)
24. Sperner, E.: Ein Satz über Untermengen einer endlichen Menge. Math. Zeitschrift **27**, 544–548 (1928)
25. Zerbino, D.R., Birney, E.: Velvet: algorithms for de novo short read assembly using de Bruijn graphs. Genome Res. **18**, 821–829 (2008)
26. Zhigljavsky, A.: Probabilistic existence theorems in group testing. J. Stat. Plann. Infer. **115**, 1–43 (2003)

Nivat's Conjecture Holds for Sums of Two Periodic Configurations

Michal Szabados[(✉)]

Department of Mathematics and Statistics,
University of Turku, 20014 Turku, Finland
micsza@utu.fi

Abstract. Nivat's conjecture is a long-standing open combinatorial problem. It concerns two-dimensional configurations, that is, maps $\mathbb{Z}^2 \to \mathcal{A}$ where $\mathcal{A}$ is a finite set of symbols. Such configurations are often understood as colorings of a two-dimensional square grid. Let $P_c(m,n)$ denote the number of distinct $m \times n$ block patterns occurring in a configuration c. Configurations satisfying $P_c(m,n) \leq mn$ for some $m,n \in \mathbb{N}$ are said to have low rectangular complexity. Nivat conjectured that such configurations are necessarily periodic.

Recently, Kari and the author showed that low complexity configurations can be decomposed into a sum of periodic configurations. In this paper we show that if there are at most two components, Nivat's conjecture holds. As a corollary we obtain an alternative proof of a result of Cyr and Kra: If there exist $m,n \in \mathbb{N}$ such that $P_c(m,n) \leq mn/2$, then c is periodic. The technique used in this paper combines the algebraic approach of Kari and the author with balanced sets of Cyr and Kra.

1 Introduction

Let $\mathcal{A}$ be a finite set of symbols and d a positive integer, the dimension. A *d-dimensional symbolic configuration* c is an element of $\mathcal{A}^{\mathbb{Z}^d}$, that is, a map assigning a symbol to every vertex of the lattice $\mathbb{Z}^d$. The symbol at position $v \in \mathbb{Z}^d$ is denoted c_v.

For a non-empty finite domain $D \subset \mathbb{Z}^d$, the elements of $\mathcal{A}^D$ are *D-patterns*. We can observe patterns in a given configuration, the D-pattern occurring in c at position $v \in \mathbb{Z}^d$ is the map

$$p \colon D \to \mathcal{A}$$

$$u \mapsto c_{v+u}.$$

The number of distinct D-patterns occurring in c, denoted $P_c(D)$, is the *D-pattern complexity* of c. We say that c has *low complexity* if $P_c(D) \leq |D|$ holds for some D.

M. Szabados—Research supported by the Academy of Finland Grant 296018.

A M. Tjoa et al. (Eds.): SOFSEM 2018, LNCS 10706, pp. 539–551, 2018.
https://doi.org/10.1007/978-3-319-73117-9_38

We study what conditions on complexity imply that a configuration is periodic, that is, when there exists a non-zero vector u such that $c_v = c_{v+u}$ for all $v \in \mathbb{Z}^d$. The situation in one dimension was described by Morse and Hedlund [MH38], let us denote $[\![n]\!] = \{0, \ldots, n-1\}$:

Theorem (Morse–Hedlund). *Let c be a one-dimensional symbolic configuration. Then c is periodic if and only if there exists $n \in \mathbb{N}$ such that $P_c([\![n]\!]) \leq n$.*

As a corollary, non-periodic one-dimensional configurations satisfy $P_c([\![n]\!]) \geq n + 1$. Those for which equality holds for every n are *Sturmian words*, they are a central topic of combinatorics on words and have connections to discrete geometry, finite automata and mathematical physics [Lot02, AS03, DL99]. Note that Sander and Tijdeman [ST00] extended the Morse–Hedlund theorem for patterns of other shapes than $[\![n]\!]$, they showed that in fact any low complexity one-dimensional symbolic configuration is periodic.

Nivat's conjecture [Niv97] is a natural extension of the theorem to two-dimensions. To simplify notation we write $P_c(m, n) = P_c([\![m]\!] \times [\![n]\!])$.

Conjecture (Nivat). If a two-dimensional symbolic configuration c satisfies $P_c(m, n) \leq mn$ for some $m, n \in \mathbb{N}$, then it is periodic.

Nivat's conjecture is tight in the sense that there exist non-periodic configurations satisfying $P_c(m, n) = mn+1$ for all $m, n \in \mathbb{N}$, all such configurations were classified by Cassaigne [Cas99]. Note that the conjecture is not an equivalence, the opposite implication is easily seen to be false.

There have been a number of partial results towards the conjecture. Cyr and Kra [CK16] proved that having $P_c(3, n) \leq 3n$ for some $n \in \mathbb{N}$ implies periodicity, which was an improvement on a previous result with constant 2 [ST02]. In another direction, there are results showing that having $P_c(m, n) \leq \alpha mn$ for some $m, n \in \mathbb{N}$ implies periodicity for a suitable real α. The best result to date is also by Cyr and Kra [CK15] with $\alpha = 1/2$, which improved on previous constants $\alpha = 1/16$ [QZ04] and $\alpha = 1/144$ [EKM03]. Recently, Kari and the author [KS15] proved an asymptotic version of the conjecture: If $P_c(m, n) \leq mn$ for infinitely many pairs $(m, n) \in \mathbb{N}^2$, the configuration is periodic.

The Morse–Hedlund theorem does not analogously generalize to higher dimensions. There exists a three-dimensional configuration with low block complexity which is not periodic [ST00].

Our contributions

In [KS15], Kari and the author introduced an algebraic view on symbolic configurations. Following their definition, let a *configuration* be any formal power series in d variables $x_1, \ldots, x_d$ with complex coefficients, that is, an element of

$$\mathbb{C}[[X^{\pm 1}]] = \left\{ \sum_{v \in \mathbb{Z}^d} c_v X^v \mid c_v \in \mathbb{C} \right\}$$

where X^v is a shorthand for $x_1^{v_1} \cdots x_d^{v_d}$.[1] If the configuration has only integer coefficients it is called *integral*, if they come from a finite set the configuration is *finitary*. A symbolic configuration can be identified with a finitary integral configuration if the symbols from $\mathcal{A}$ are chosen to be integers. Kari and the author in [KS15] proved:

Theorem (Decomposition theorem). *Let c be a low complexity d-dimensional finitary integral configuration. Then there exists $k \in \mathbb{N}$ and periodic d-dimensional configurations $c_1, \ldots, c_k$ such that $c = c_1 + \cdots + c_k$.*

Note that the summands do not have to be finitary configurations. The minimal possible number of components k in the decomposition plays an important role. In this paper we prove:

Theorem 1. *Let c be a two-dimensional configuration satisfying $P_c(m, n) \leq mn$ for some $m, n \in \mathbb{N}$. If c is a sum of two periodic configurations then it is periodic.*

In the proof of the asymptotic version of Nivat's conjecture given in [KS16], configurations which are a sum of horizontally and vertically periodic configuration had to be handled separately using a rather technical combinatorial approach. Theorem 1 is of particular interest since it covers this case.

In this paper we revisit the method of Cyr and Kra [CK15, CK16]. They approach Nivat's conjecture from the point of view of symbolic dynamics. They use a refined version of the classical notion of expansiveness of a subshift, a so called *one-sided non-expansiveness*. A key definition of theirs is that of a *balanced set* – it is a shape $D \subset \mathbb{Z}^2$ which satisfies a particular condition on the complexity $P_c(D)$. (Note that this notion is different from balancedness usual in combinatorics on words.) The crucial tool they developed is a combinatorial lemma which links one-sided non-expansiveness and balanced sets to periodicity of a configuration. However, in order to obtain the main result of the paper from the lemma it still takes a rather lengthy technical analysis.

We combine the algebraic method with ideas of Cyr and Kra. We start the exposition with a very basic introduction to the topic of symbolic dynamics. In Sect. 2 we define a subshift, in Sect. 3 we fix some geometric terminology, and in Sect. 4 we give definitions of non-expansiveness and one-sided non-expansiveness of a subshift.

In Sect. 5 we introduce a simplified version of a balanced set and prove Lemma 4 which connects balanced sets with periodicity using the ideas of Cyr and Kra. We use the lemma together with decomposition theorem to prove Theorem 1 in Sect. 6. As a corollary, we obtain an alternative proof of Theorem 1.2 of [CK15], the main result of their paper:

Theorem (Cyr, Kra). *Let c be a configuration satisfying $P_c(m, n) \leq mn/2$ for some $m, n \in \mathbb{N}$. Then c is periodic.*

---

[1] For the most of this paper, however, it is enough to consider configurations to be elements of $\mathbb{C}^{\mathbb{Z}^d}$.

2   Symbolic Dynamics and Subshifts

Let us recall basic facts from symbolic dynamics, for a comprehensive reference and proofs see [Kůr03].

Symbolic dynamics studies $\mathcal{A}^{\mathbb{Z}^d}$ as a topological space. Let us first make $\mathcal{A}$ a topological space by endowing it with the discrete topology. Then $\mathcal{A}^{\mathbb{Z}^d}$ is considered to be a topological space with the product topology.

Open sets in this topology are for example sets of the following form. Let $D \subset \mathbb{Z}^d$ be finite and $p \colon D \to \mathcal{A}$ arbitrary. Then

$$Cyl(p) := \left\{\, c \in \mathcal{A}^{\mathbb{Z}^d} \mid \forall v \in D \colon c_v = p_v \,\right\}$$

is an open set, also called a *cylinder*. In fact, the collection of cylinders $Cyl(p)$ for all possible p forms a subbase of the topology on $\mathcal{A}^{\mathbb{Z}^d}$.

For a vector $u \in \mathbb{Z}^d$, the *shift* operator $\tau_u \colon \mathcal{A}^{\mathbb{Z}^d} \to \mathcal{A}^{\mathbb{Z}^d}$ is defined by $(\tau_u(c))_v = c_{v-u}$. Informally, τ_u shifts a configuration in the direction of vector u.

The set $\mathcal{A}^{\mathbb{Z}^d}$ is called the *full shift*. A subset $X \subset \mathcal{A}^{\mathbb{Z}^d}$ is called a *subshift* if it is a topologically closed set which is invariant under all shifts τ_u:

$$\forall u \in \mathbb{Z}^d \colon c \in X \Rightarrow \tau_u(c) \in X.$$

Subshifts are the central objects of study in symbolic dynamics.

Let c be a symbolic configuration. We denote by X_c the *orbit closure* of c, that is, the smallest subshift which contains c. It can be shown that c contains exactly those configurations c' whose finite patterns are among the finite patterns of c. In particular, for any $c' \in X_c$ and a finite domain D we have $P_{c'}(D) \le P_c(D)$.

Example 1. Let us give an example of taking orbit closure. Let $c \in \{0,1\}^{\mathbb{Z}^2}$ be such that $c_{ij} = 1$ if $i = 0$ or $j = 0$, and $c_{ij} = 0$ otherwise. When pictured, the configuration c consists of a large cross with its center at $(0,0)$. The orbit closure X_c then consist of four types of configurations: a cross, a horizontal line, a vertical line and all zero configurations, with all possible translations, see Fig. 1. It is easy to see that any pattern which occurs in them also occurs in c, and not difficult to prove that those are all such configurations.   □

Fig. 1. Four types of configurations in the orbit closure X_c from Example 1. The gray color corresponds to value 1, white is 0.

3 Geometric Notation and Terminology

In the sequel we will be concerned with the geometry of $\mathbb{Z}^2$. Let us establish some notation and terminology.

We view $\mathbb{Z}^2$ as a subset of the vector space $\mathbb{Q}^2$. A *direction* is an equivalence class of $\mathbb{Q}^2\backslash\{(0,0)\}$ modulo the equivalence relation $u \sim v$ iff $u = \lambda v$ for some $\lambda > 0$. By a slight abuse of notation, we identify a non-zero vector $\boldsymbol{u} \in \mathbb{Z}^2$ with the direction $\boldsymbol{u}\mathbb{Q}^+$.

Let $\boldsymbol{u} \in \mathbb{Z}^2$ be non-zero. An (undirected) *line* in $\mathbb{Z}^2$ is a set of the form

$$\{v + q\boldsymbol{u} \mid q \in \mathbb{Q}\} \cap \mathbb{Z}^2$$

for some $v \in \mathbb{Z}^2$. We call both $\boldsymbol{u}$ and $-\boldsymbol{u}$ a *direction* of the line. We define a *directed line* to be a line augmented with one of the two possible directions.

Let ℓ be a directed line in direction $\boldsymbol{u}$ going through $v \in \mathbb{Z}^2$. The *half-plane* determined by ℓ is defined by

$$H_\ell = \{v + \boldsymbol{w} \mid \boldsymbol{w} \in \mathbb{Z}^2, w_1 u_2 - u_1 w_2 \geq 0\}.$$

With the usual choice of coordinates it is the half-plane "on the right" from the line. Let $H_{\boldsymbol{u}}$ denote the half-plane determined by the directed line in direction $\boldsymbol{u}$ going through the origin.

We say that a non-empty $D \subset \mathbb{Z}^2$ is *convex* if D can be written as an intersection of half-planes. *Convex hull* of D, denoted $Conv(D)$, is the smallest convex set containing D. Assume ℓ is a directed line in direction $\boldsymbol{u}$ such that $D \subset H_\ell$ and $\ell \cap D$ is non-empty. If $|\ell \cap D| > 1$ we call it the *edge* of D in direction $\boldsymbol{u}$, otherwise we call it the *vertex* of D in direction $\boldsymbol{u}$. Note that a vertex is a vertex for many directions, but an edge has a unique direction (as long as D is not contained in a line). See Fig. 2 for an example.

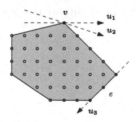

Fig. 2. A convex set. The point v is a vertex of the set for both directions $\boldsymbol{u_1}$ and $\boldsymbol{u_2}$. The set of three marked points e is the edge in direction $\boldsymbol{u_3}$.

Let $\boldsymbol{u}$ be a direction and ℓ, ℓ' two directed lines in direction $\boldsymbol{u}$. If

$$S = H_\ell \backslash H_{\ell'}$$

is non-empty, then S is called a *stripe* in direction $\boldsymbol{u}$. We call ℓ, ℓ' the *inner* and *outer* boundary of S respectively. Let $S^\circ = S\backslash \ell$ be the *interior* of S.

For $A, B \subset \mathbb{Z}^2$, we say that A *fits in* B if there exists a translation of A which is a subset of B.

4   Non-expansiveness and One-Sided Non-expansiveness

It can be verified that the topology on $\mathcal{A}^{\mathbb{Z}^d}$ is compact and also metrizable. Note that shift operators τ_u are continuous maps on $\mathcal{A}^{\mathbb{Z}^d}$. Expansiveness can be defined in general for a continuous action on a compact metric space, the definition is however too general for our purposes. We give a definition specific to the case of $\mathcal{A}^{\mathbb{Z}^2}$.

Let $X \subset \mathcal{A}^{\mathbb{Z}^2}$ be a subshift and u a direction. Then u is an *expansive direction* for X if there exists a stripe S in direction u such that

$$\forall c, e \in X: \quad c{\restriction}_S = e{\restriction}_S \;\Rightarrow\; c = e.$$

Informally speaking, u is an expansive direction for X if a configuration in X is uniquely determined by its coefficients in a wide enough stripe in direction u.

A two-dimensional configuration is *doubly periodic* if it has two linearly independent period vectors. The following classical theorem links double periodicity of a configuration with expansiveness. It is a corollary of a theorem by Boyle and Lind [BL97].

Theorem 2. *Let c be a symbolic configuration. Then c is doubly periodic iff all directions are expansive for X_c.* □

Let $X \subset \mathcal{A}^{\mathbb{Z}^2}$ be a subshift and u a direction. Then u is a *one-sided expansive direction* for X if

$$\forall c, e \in X: \quad c{\restriction}_{H_u} = e{\restriction}_{H_u} \;\Rightarrow\; c = e.$$

Equivalently, u is a one-sided expansive direction for X if there exists a wide enough stripe S in direction u such that $\forall c, e \in X: c{\restriction}_S = e{\restriction}_S \Rightarrow c{\restriction}_{H_{-u}} = e{\restriction}_{H_{-u}}$. See Fig. 3 for a comparison of the notion of expansiveness and one-sided expansiveness.

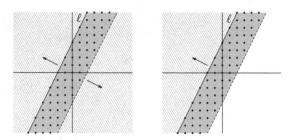

Fig. 3. The figure on the left illustrates expansiveness – values of the configuration inside the stripe determine the whole configuration. On the right we see one-sided expansiveness in direction $(1, 2)$ – values in the half-plane H_ℓ, or equivalently in a wide enough stripe, determine the values in the half-plane $\mathbb{Z}^2 \backslash H_\ell$.

Example 2 (Ledrappier's subshift). It is possible for a subshift to be one-sided expansive but non-expansive in the same direction. Consider a subshift $X \subset \{0,1\}^{\mathbb{Z}^2}$ consisting of configurations c which satisfy $c_{ij} \equiv c_{i,j+1} + c_{i+1,j+1}$ (mod 2). Upper half-plane of a configuration determines the whole, since any single row determines the one below it. Therefore $(-1,0)$ is a one-sided expansive direction for X. However, no stripe in direction $(-1,0)$ determines a configuration from the subshift; for any row, there are always two possibilities for the row above it (they are complements of each other). Any horizontal stripe can be extended to the upper half-plane in infinitely many ways.   □

We are primarily interested in non-expansive directions. In our setup, it is known that there are only finitely many of them, we omit the proof for space reasons.

Lemma 1. *Let c be a low complexity two-dimensional configuration. Then there are at most finitely many one-sided non-expansive directions for X_c.*   □

For later use it will be practical to define non-expansiveness explicitly. Let $X \subset \mathcal{A}^{\mathbb{Z}^2}$ be a subshift and S a stripe in direction $\boldsymbol{u}$. We say that S is an *ambiguous stripe in direction $\boldsymbol{u}$* if there exist $c, e \in X$ such that

$$c{\upharpoonright}_{S^\circ} = e{\upharpoonright}_{S^\circ}, \quad \text{but} \quad c{\upharpoonright}_S \neq e{\upharpoonright}_S . \tag{1}$$

We say that $c \in X$ *contains* an ambiguous stripe S if there exists $e \in X$ satisfying (1). Informally, a stripe is ambiguous if its interior does not determine the inner boundary.

Definition. Let $\boldsymbol{u}$ be a direction and $X \subset \mathcal{A}^{\mathbb{Z}^2}$ a subshift. Then $\boldsymbol{u}$ is *one-sided non-expansive direction* if there exists an ambiguous stripe in direction $\boldsymbol{u}$ of arbitrary width.

We leave the proof that this is the converse of the earlier definition of one-sided expansiveness to the reader.

5   Balanced Sets

Let c be a fixed symbolic configuration.

Definition 1. Let $B \subset \mathbb{Z}^2$ be a finite and convex set, $\boldsymbol{u}$ a direction and E an edge or a vertex of B in direction $\boldsymbol{u}$. Then B is $\boldsymbol{u}$-balanced if:

(i) $P_c(B) \leq |B|$
(ii) $P_c(B) < P_c(B \backslash E) + |E|$
(iii) Intersection of B with all lines in direction $\boldsymbol{u}$ is either empty or of size at least $|E| - 1$.

The three conditions of the definition can be interpreted as follows. The first one simply states that B is a low complexity shape. The second condition limits the number of $(B \backslash E)$-patterns which do not extend uniquely to a B-pattern, there is strictly less than $|E|$ of them. The third condition is implied if the length of the edge in direction u is smaller or equal to the length of the edge in the opposite direction, as can be seen in the next proof.

Lemma 2. *Let c be such that $P_c(m, n) \leq mn$ holds for some $m, n \in \mathbb{N}$ and u be a direction. Then there exists a u-balanced or $(-u)$-balanced set. Moreover, if u is horizontal or vertical, then there exists a u-balanced set.*

Proof. Let D be an $m \times n$ rectangle, we have $P_c(D) \leq |D|$. Let us define a sequence of convex shapes $D = D_0 \supset D_1 \supset \cdots \supset D_k = \emptyset$ such that $D_i \backslash D_{i+1}$ is the edge of D_i in direction $(-1)^i u$. Informally, the sequence represents shaving off an edge (or a vertex) of the shape alternately in directions u and $-u$. See Fig. 4 for an illustration.

Consider the expression $P_c(D_i) - |D_i|$ as a function of i. For $i = 0$ its value is non-positive and for $i = k$ its value is 1. Let $i \in [0, k - 1]$ be smallest such that $0 < P_c(D_{i+1}) - |D_{i+1}|$, then we have

$$P_c(D_i) - |D_i| \leq 0 < P_c(D_{i+1}) - |D_{i+1}|.$$

Denote $E = D_i \backslash D_{i+1}$, it is an edge or a vertex of D_i in direction u or $-u$. Adding $|D_i|$ to the inequality and rewriting gives $P(D_i) \leq |D_i| < P(D_i \backslash E) + |E|$.

We show that $B = D_i$ is a balanced set by showing that (iii) of Definition 1 holds. Without loss of generality let the direction of E be u. Then, by construction, the length of E is smaller or equal to the edge in direction $-u$. In fact, if we consider the convex hull of B in $\mathbb{Q}^2$, any line in direction u intersects it in a line segment longer or equal to d, the length of the edge. Any line segment of length at least d in direction u intersects either none or at least $|E| - 1$ integer points, and we are done.

If u is either horizontal or vertical, instead of alternating the direction of shaved off edges, we can always shave off the edge in direction u. It will be always the shortest edge in direction u, therefore verification of part (iii) goes through. $\square$

Next we present Lemma 4 which connects non-expansiveness and balanced sets with periodicity, based on the method of Cyr and Kra. Periodicity in the proof first arises in a stripe from the use of Morse–Hedlund theorem. This part of the proof follows Lemma 2.24 from [CK15]. The periodicity is then extended to the whole configuration by the following lemma, which is a corollary of Lemma 39 from [KS16]. We omit the proof for space reasons.

Lemma 3. *Let c be a two-dimensional configuration and D a non-empty finite subset of $\mathbb{Z}^2$ such that $P_c(D) \leq |D|$. Let S be a stripe in direction u such that D fits in S. If S° is periodic with a period in direction u then also c is periodic with a period in direction u.* $\square$

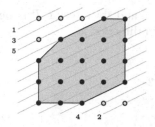

Fig. 4. Shaving off edges or vertices of a 5×5 rectangle alternately in directions $(2,1)$ and $(-2,-1)$. Small numbers indicate the order in which the edges or vertices were removed.

Lemma 4. *Let c be a configuration and B a $\boldsymbol{u}$-balanced set. Assume that c contains an ambiguous stripe for X_c in direction $\boldsymbol{u}$ such that B fits in the stripe. Then c is periodic in direction $\boldsymbol{u}$.*

Proof. Let E be the edge or vertex of B in direction $\boldsymbol{u}$, denote S the stripe and let ℓ be the inner boundary of S in direction $\boldsymbol{u}$. Without loss of generality assume $B \subset S$, $E \subset \ell$, and that $\boldsymbol{u}$ is not an integer multiple of a smaller vector. Let $e \in X_c$ be such that Eq. 1 holds.

Denote points in E consecutively by $e_1, \ldots, e_n$ (see Fig. 5). Define a sequence $B = D_n \supset \cdots \supset D_1 \supset D_0 = B \backslash E$ by setting $D_{i-1} = D_i \backslash \{e_i\}$. Consider the values $P(D_i) - |D_i|$. Since B is a balanced set, by (ii) we have $P_c(D_n) - |D_n| < P_c(D_0) - |D_0|$, let $k \in [0, n-1]$ be such that

$$P_c(D_{k+1}) - |D_{k+1}| < P_c(D_k) - |D_k|.$$

Adding $|D_{k+1}|$ to both sides yields $P_c(D_{k+1}) < P_c(D_k) + 1$. On the other hand, $P_c(D_k) \leq P_c(D_{k+1})$ since $D_k \subset D_{k+1}$, and therefore we have $P_c(D_k) = P(D_{k+1})$. In other words, a D_k-pattern uniquely determines the value at position e_{k+1}.

We will show that $\forall i : c\!\upharpoonright_{D_k + iu} \neq e\!\upharpoonright_{D_k + iu}$. For the contrary, assume that there is j such that $c\!\upharpoonright_{D_k + ju} = e\!\upharpoonright_{D_k + ju}$. Using the property of D_k, we have $c\!\upharpoonright_{e_{k+1} + ju} = e\!\upharpoonright_{e_{k+1} + ju}$. Therefore $c\!\upharpoonright_{D_k + (j+1)u} = e\!\upharpoonright_{D_k + (j+1)u}$ and we can proceed by induction to show $c\!\upharpoonright_{D_k + j'u} = e\!\upharpoonright_{D_k + j'u}$ for all $j' > j$. Analogously, by constructing sets D_i by removing edge points from the other end, it can be shown that also $c\!\upharpoonright_{D_k + j'u} = e\!\upharpoonright_{D_k + j'u}$ for all $j' < j$. We proved $c\!\upharpoonright_S = e\!\upharpoonright_S$, which is a contradiction with ambiguity of S.

We have that all $(B \backslash E)$-patterns $c\!\upharpoonright_{(B \backslash E) + iu}$ have at least two possible extensions into a B-pattern. Part (ii) of Definition 1 implies that there are at most $|E| - 1$ such patterns. Let T be a thinner stripe in direction $\boldsymbol{u}$ defined by $T = \bigcup_{i \in \mathbb{Z}} (B \backslash E) + i\boldsymbol{u}$. Using part (iii) of Definition 1, values of c on every line $\lambda \subset T$ in direction $\boldsymbol{u}$ contain at most $|E| - 1$ distinct subsegments of length at least $|E| - 1$. By Morse–Hedlund theorem, the values on the line repeat periodically. Therefore $c\!\upharpoonright_T$ is periodic in direction $\boldsymbol{u}$.

B fits in the stripe $T \cup \ell$ and its interior T is periodic in direction $\boldsymbol{u}$. By Lemma 3 also c is periodic in direction $\boldsymbol{u}$.   □

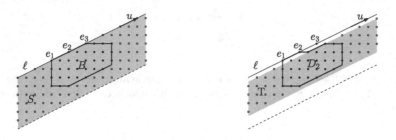

Fig. 5. Illustration of the proof of Lemma 4.

6   Main Result

Theorem (Theorem 1). *Let c be a two-dimensional configuration satisfying $P_c(m,n) \leq mn$ for some $m, n \in \mathbb{N}$. If c is a sum of two periodic configurations then it is periodic.*

Proof. For contradiction assume c is non-periodic and denote c_1, c_2 periodic configurations such that $c = c_1 + c_2$. Let $\boldsymbol{u_1}, \boldsymbol{u_2}$ be their respective vectors of periodicity. If they are linearly dependent, c is periodic and we are done. Otherwise, define a parallelogram

$$D = \{\, a\boldsymbol{u_1} + b\boldsymbol{u_2} \mid a, b \in [0, 1) \,\} \cap \mathbb{Z}^2.$$

We can choose $\boldsymbol{u_1}, \boldsymbol{u_2}$ large enough so that an $m \times n$ rectangle fits in. We can also assume that $\boldsymbol{u_2} \in H_{\boldsymbol{u_1}}$. Denote $D_j = D + j\boldsymbol{u_2}$ and define a sequence of stripes $S_j = \bigcup_{i \in \mathbb{Z}} D_j + i\boldsymbol{u_1}$. The setup is illustrated in Fig. 6.

Assume that there are $j \neq j'$ such that $c\!\restriction_{D_j} = c\!\restriction_{D_{j'}}$. We claim that then $c\!\restriction_{S_j} = c\!\restriction_{S_{j'}}$. Note that since $c = c_1 + c_2$, for $\boldsymbol{v} \in \mathbb{Z}^2$ we have

$$(c_{(\boldsymbol{v}+\boldsymbol{u_1})+j\boldsymbol{u_2}} - c_{(\boldsymbol{v}+\boldsymbol{u_1})+j'\boldsymbol{u_2}}) - (c_{\boldsymbol{v}+j\boldsymbol{u_2}} - c_{\boldsymbol{v}+j'\boldsymbol{u_2}}) = 0.$$

In particular, if $c_{\boldsymbol{v}+j\boldsymbol{u_2}} = c_{\boldsymbol{v}+j'\boldsymbol{u_2}}$, then also $c_{(\boldsymbol{v}+\boldsymbol{u_1})+j\boldsymbol{u_2}} = c_{(\boldsymbol{v}+\boldsymbol{u_1})+j'\boldsymbol{u_2}}$. Since $c_{\boldsymbol{v}+j\boldsymbol{u_2}} = c_{\boldsymbol{v}+j'\boldsymbol{u_2}}$ holds for $\boldsymbol{v} \in D$, it also holds for $\boldsymbol{v} \in D + \boldsymbol{u_1}$, and by induction $c\!\restriction_{S_j} = c\!\restriction_{S_{j'}}$.

Since c is finitary there are only finitely many possible D-patterns, let N be an upper bound on their number. There are also finitely many stripe patterns $c\!\restriction_{S_j}$ since the pattern in S_j is determined by the pattern in D_j. Because c is not periodic, there exists $k \in \mathbb{Z}$ such that $c\!\restriction_{S_k} \neq c\!\restriction_{S_{k-N!}}$.

By Lemma 2, there is either a $\boldsymbol{u_1}$-balanced or $(-\boldsymbol{u_1})$-balanced set B, without loss of generality assume the former. Since c is non-periodic, by Lemma 4 there is no ambiguous stripe in c in direction $\boldsymbol{u_1}$ in which B fits. B fits in any stripe

S_j, therefore values in any stripe S_j determine the values in the whole half-plane on the side of the inner boundary of S_j.

By pigeonhole principle, there are $j < j' \in [0, N]$ such that $c\lceil_{S_{k+j}} = c\lceil_{S_{k+j'}}$. The two stripes extend uniquely to the half-planes on the side of their inner boundary. Therefore the half-plane $H = \bigcup_{i \leq j'} S_i$ has period $(j' - j)\mathbf{u_2}$. Since $j' - j$ divides $N!$ and $S_k, S_{k-N!} \subset H$, we have a contradiction with $c\lceil_{S_k} \neq c\lceil_{S_{k-N!}}$. $\qquad\square$

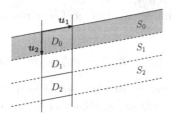

Fig. 6. Proof of Theorem 1.

Corollary 1. *If a non-periodic configuration c is a sum of two periodic ones, then $P_c(m, n) \geq mn + 1$ for all $m, n \in \mathbb{N}$.* $\qquad\square$

We finish the exposition by reproving the result of Cyr and Kra from [CK15]. To do that, we need additional theory from [KS16]. Multiplication of a two-dimensional configuration c by a polynomial $f \in \mathbb{C}[x_1, x_2]$ is well defined. If $fc = 0$, we call f an *annihilator* of c. The following two lemmas we state without a proof, they are direct corollaries of Corollary 24 and Lemma 32 of [KS16], respectively.

Lemma 5. *Let c be a low complexity two-dimensional integral configuration. Then there exists $k \in \mathbb{N}$ and polynomials $\phi_1, \ldots, \phi_k \in \mathbb{C}[x_1, x_2]$ with the following properties:*

Every annihilator of c is divisible by $\phi_1 \cdots \phi_k$. Furthermore, c can be written as a sum of k, but no fewer periodic configurations. If g is a product of $0 \leq \ell < k$ of the polynomials ϕ_i, then gc can be written as a sum of $k - \ell$, but no fewer periodic configurations. $\qquad\square$

Any polynomial in $\mathbb{C}[x_1, x_2]$ can be written as $f = \sum_{v \in \mathbb{Z}^2} a_v X^v$. The *support* of f, denoted $supp(f)$, is defined as the finite set of vectors $v \in \mathbb{Z}^2$ such that $a_v \neq 0$. We say that f *fits* in a subset $D \subset \mathbb{Z}^2$ if its support fits in D.

Lemma 6. *Let c be a finitary configuration. Then the symbols of $\mathcal{A}$ can be changed to suitable integers such that if $P_c(D) \leq |D|$ for some $D \subset \mathbb{Z}^d$, then there exists an annihilator f which fits in $-D$.* $\qquad\square$

Theorem 3. *Let c be a configuration such that $P_c(m, n) \leq mn/2$ for some $m, n \in \mathbb{N}$. Then c is periodic.*

Proof. Assume that the symbols of $\mathcal{A}$ have been renamed as in Lemma 6, then there exists f an annihilator of c which fits in an $m \times n$ rectangle. By Lemma 5, we can write $f = \phi_1 \cdots \phi_k h$. If $k \leq 2$ then c is periodic by Theorem 1. Assume $k \geq 3$, we will show that it leads to a contradiction.

Let $g = \phi_3 \cdots \phi_k$, $c' = gc$ and let $m_g, n_g \in \mathbb{N}$ be smallest such that g fits in an $(m_g + 1) \times (n_g + 1)$ rectangle, see Fig. 7. Note that an $(m - m_g) \times (n - n_g)$ block in c' is determined by multiplication by g from an $m \times n$ block in c. Therefore $P_c(m, n) \geq P_{c'}(m - m_g, n - n_g)$.

By Lemma 5, c' is a sum of two but no fewer periodic configurations. Thus it is not periodic, and by Theorem 1,

$$P_c(m, n) \geq P_{c'}(m - m_g, n - n_g) > (m - m_g)(n - n_g).$$

Let v be an arbitrary vertex of the convex hull of $-supp(g)$. Consider all translations of $-supp(g)$ which are a subset of the rectangle $[\![m]\!] \times [\![n]\!]$, denote R the locus of v under these translations. There are $(m - m_g)(n - n_g)$ such translations, therefore the size of R is the same number.

Now let us define a shape $U = [\![m]\!] \times [\![n]\!] \backslash R$. It is a shape such that no polynomial multiple of g fits in $-U$. In particular no annihilator of c fits in $-U$, and thus by Lemma 6,

$$P_c(m, n) \geq P_c(U) > |U|.$$

Since either $(m - m_g)(n - n_g) = |R| \geq mn/2$ or $|U| \geq mn/2$, we have $P_c(m, n) > mn/2$, a contradiction. $\square$

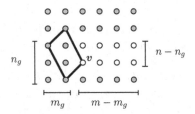

Fig. 7. Proof of Theorem 3. The quadrilateral depicts the convex hull of $-\text{supp}(g)$ for a polynomial g, positioned in the bottom left corner of an $m \times n$ block. The white points form the set R and the shaded points form the set U. We have $|U| \geq mn/2$ or $|R| \geq mn/2$.

References

[AS03] Allouche, J., Shallit, J.: Automatic Sequences: Theory, Applications, Generalizations. Cambridge University Press, Cambridge (2003)

[BL97] Boyle, M., Lind, D.: Expansive subdynamics. Trans. Am. Math. Soc. **349**(1), 55–102 (1997)

[Cas99] Cassaigne, J.: Double sequences with complexity mn+1. J. Autom. Lang. Comb. **4**(3), 153–170 (1999)

[CK16] Cyr, V., Kra, B.: Complexity of short rectangles and periodicity. Eur. J. Comb. Part A **52**, 146–173 (2016)

[CK15] Cyr, V., Kra, B.: Nonexpansive $\mathbb{Z}^2$-subdynamics and Nivat's conjecture. Trans. Am. Math. Soc. **367**(9), 6487–6537 (2015)

[DL99] Damanik, D., Lenz, D.: Uniform spectral properties of one-dimensional quasicrystals, I. Absence of eigenvalues. Commun. Math. Phys. **207**(3), 687–696 (1999)

[EKM03] Epifanio, C., Koskas, M., Mignosi, F.: On a conjecture on bidimensional words. Theoret. Comput. Sci. **299**(1–3), 123–150 (2003)

[KS15] Kari, J., Szabados, M.: An algebraic geometric approach to Nivat's conjecture. In: Halldórsson, M.M., Iwama, K., Kobayashi, N., Speckmann, B. (eds.) ICALP 2015. LNCS, vol. 9135, pp. 273–285. Springer, Heidelberg (2015). https://doi.org/10.1007/978-3-662-47666-6_22

[KS16] Kari, J., Szabados, M.: An algebraic geometric approach to Nivat's conjecture. arXiv:1605.05929 (2016)

[Kůr03] Kůrka, P.: Topological and Symbolic Dynamics. Collection SMF, Société mathématique de France (2003)

[Lot02] Lothaire, M.: Algebraic Combinatorics on Words. Encyclopedia of Mathematics and Its Applications. Cambridge University Press, Cambridge (2002)

[MH38] Morse, M., Hedlund, G.A.: Symbolic dynamics. Am. J. Math. **60**(4), 815–866 (1938)

[Niv97] Nivat, M.: Invited talk at ICALP, Bologna (1997)

[QZ04] Quas, A., Zamboni, L.Q.: Periodicity and local complexity. Theoret. Comput. Sci. **319**(1–3), 229–240 (2004)

[ST00] Sander, J.W., Tijdeman, R.: The complexity of functions on lattices. Theoret. Comput. Sci. **246**(1–2), 195–225 (2000)

[ST02] Sander, J.W., Tijdeman, R.: The rectangle complexity of functions on two-dimensional lattices. Theoret. Comput. Sci. **270**(1–2), 857–863 (2002)

Encoding Pictures with Maximal Codes of Pictures

Marcella Anselmo[1], Dora Giammarresi[2], and Maria Madonia[3(✉)]

[1] Dipartimento di Informatica, Università di Salerno,
Via Giovanni Paolo II, 132, 84084 Fisciano, SA, Italy
manselmo@unisa.it
[2] Dipartimento di Matematica, Università di Roma "Tor Vergata",
Via della Ricerca Scientifica, 00133 Roma, Italy
giammarr@mat.uniroma2.it
[3] Dipartimento di Matematica e Informatica, Università di Catania,
Viale Andrea Doria 6/a, 95125 Catania, Italy
madonia@dmi.unict.it

Abstract. A picture is a two-dimensional counterpart of a string and it is represented by a rectangular array of symbols over a finite alphabet Σ. A set X of pictures over Σ is a code if every picture over Σ is tilable in at most one way with pictures in X. Recently, the definition of *strong prefix code* was introduced as a decidable family of picture codes, and a construction procedure for *maximal strong prefix (MSP)* codes was proposed. Unfortunately, the notion of completeness cannot be directly transposed from strings to pictures without loosing important properties. We generalize to pictures a special property satisfied by complete set of strings that allow to prove interesting characterization results for MSP codes. Moreover, we show an encoding algorithm for pictures using pictures from a MSP code. The algorithm is based on a new data structure for the representation of MSP codes.

1 Introduction

A picture is represented by a rectangular array of symbols over a finite alphabet Σ and it is taken as the two-dimensional counterpart of a string. The set of all pictures over Σ is usually denoted by Σ^{**} and a picture language is then a subset of Σ^{**}. The general and ambitious intent of the researchers is to generalize the well established theory of string languages to picture languages in a way to exploit all the richness of having two dimensions. Unfortunately, many definitions and properties cannot be directly transposed to two dimensions and many problems become very difficult, sometimes even undecidable.

In the last two decades, two dimensional codes were studied in different contexts. In particular a *picture code* is a subset X of Σ^{**} such that every picture over Σ is tilable in at most one way with pictures in X. Most of the results show

Partially supported by INdAM-GNCS Project 2017, FARB Project ORSA138754 of University of Salerno and FIR Project 375E90 of University of Catania.

ⓒ Springer International Publishing AG 2018
A M. Tjoa et al. (Eds.): SOFSEM 2018, LNCS 10706, pp. 552–565, 2018.
https://doi.org/10.1007/978-3-319-73117-9_39

that in the 2D context we loose important properties. A major result due to D. Beauquier and M. Nivat states that the problem whether a finite set of pictures is a code is undecidable, and the same result holds also for dominoes [10]. Other related results on two-dimensional codes can be found in [1,12,15,17,18].

Among the first attempts to define a decidable subclass of picture codes we mention the definition of *prefix code* [5,6]. Pictures are considered with the preferred scanning direction from the top-left corner to the bottom-right one. Moreover, the notion of a picture p *prefix* of a picture q is used when p coincides with the "top-left portion" of q. Prefix picture codes inherit some properties from the original family of prefix string codes and several non trivial examples can be exhibited. Nevertheless, it is worth to say that the definition is sometimes difficult to manage, since the presence of a specific picture in the code depends on a tiling combination of (possibly) many other pictures in the same set and it involves a special kind of polyominoes.

An interesting class of pictures codes are the *strong prefix codes* introduced in [4,9]. They have a more practicable and usable definition based on the notion of *prefix-overlaps* between pictures. Two pictures p and q prefix-overlap if they coincide in the common part when p is layed on q by superposing their top-left corners. Then, a set of picture X is said *strong prefix* if no pairs of pictures in X prefix-overlap.

Finite strong prefix sets are again a decidable family of picture codes with a simple polynomial decoding algorithm. *Maximal strong prefix (MSP)* sets are also studied and it is proved that it is decidable whether a given finite strong prefix set is maximal. Some interesting results concerning the measure of strong prefix codes are given in [7,8] together with an effective procedure to construct *all* (maximal) strong prefix codes of pictures, starting from the "singleton" pictures containing only one alphabet symbol.

All those results naturally promote the class of strong prefix codes of pictures to be the right generalization in two dimensions of the important class of prefix string codes that plays an important role in several applications, as for example the Huffman coding algorithm (see [11,13] for a complete reference). The strength of maximal prefix codes of strings lies in the fact that they are right-complete that is any string w can be encoded as $w = x_1 x_2 \ldots x_k y$ where all the factors x_i are strings from the code and y itself is a prefix (possibly empty) of a string in the code. The notion of right-completeness can be naturally transposed to two dimensions and called *br-completeness* (cf. [4,9]). Unfortunately maximal strong prefix codes of pictures are not in general br-complete and this implies that they cannot be effectively used in general to encode pictures (as one would expect from a code!). The main reason is due to the different shapes of the pictures; it is not always possible to concatenate pictures avoiding holes or overlaps.

In this paper, we identify a property characterizing the complete sets of strings and generalize it to sets of pictures. We say that a set of pictures X is *br-full* if for any picture p over Σ and for any position (i, j) in p there is a picture x in X that can be placed on p by putting the top-left corner of x on position

(i, j) and all the symbols in the superposed positions coincide. We prove that a strong prefix code of pictures X is maximal if and only if it is br-full. Moreover, using this property, we show a unique way to tile a generic picture p over Σ with pictures in X, by using some prefixes of pictures in X chosen in an appropriate way. This is called *decomposition with cuts*. In the last part of the paper we introduce a data structure, called *extension-tree*, to represent a maximal strong prefix code. In the finite case, it allows to design an efficient algorithm to find the unique encoding for any picture p that is related to its decomposition with cuts in X.

2   Preliminaries

We recall some definitions about two-dimensional languages (see [14]). In the following, we will consider only finite languages, even if some definitions and results, given throughout the paper, apply to both finite and infinite languages.

A *picture* over a finite alphabet Σ is a two-dimensional rectangular array of elements of Σ. Given a picture p, $|p|_{row}$ and $|p|_{col}$ denote the number of rows and columns, respectively, while $size(p) = (|p|_{row}, |p|_{col})$ and $area(p) = |p|_{row} \times |p|_{col}$ denote the picture *size* and *area*, respectively. We also consider all the empty pictures, referred to as $\lambda_{m,0}$ and $\lambda_{0,n}$, for all $m, n \geq 0$; they correspond to all pictures of size $(m, 0)$ or $(0, n)$. The set of all pictures over Σ of fixed size (m, n) is denoted by $\Sigma^{m,n}$, while Σ^{m*} and Σ^{*n} denote the set of all pictures over Σ with fixed number of rows m and columns n, respectively. The set of all pictures over Σ is denoted by Σ^{**}, while Σ^{++} refers to the set Σ^{**} without the empty pictures. A *two-dimensional language* (or *picture language*) over Σ is a subset of Σ^{**}. Any string on Σ can be viewed as a one-row picture in Σ^{**}.

In order to locate a position in a picture, it is necessary to put the picture in a reference system. The set of coordinates $dom(p) = \{1, 2, \ldots, |p|_{row}\} \times \{1, 2, \ldots, |p|_{col}\}$ is referred to as the *domain* of a picture p. We let $p(i, j)$ denote the symbol in p at coordinates (i, j). We assume the top-left corner of the picture to be at position $(1, 1)$, and fix the scanning direction for a picture from the top-left corner (tl-corner, for short) toward the bottom-right corner (br-corner, for short).

A *subdomain* of $dom(p)$ is a set d of the form $\{i, i + 1, \ldots, i'\} \times \{j, j + 1, \ldots, j'\}$, where $1 \leq i \leq i' \leq |p|_{row}$, $1 \leq j \leq j' \leq |p|_{col}$, also specified by the pair $[(i, j), (i', j')]$. The portion of p corresponding to positions in subdomain $[(i, j), (i', j')]$ is denoted by $p[(i, j), (i', j')]$. Then, a picture x is a *subpicture of* p if $x = p[(i, j), (i', j')]$, for some $1 \leq i \leq i' \leq |p|_{row}$, $1 \leq j \leq j' \leq |p|_{col}$.

Prefixes of pictures are special subpictures. Given pictures x, p, with $|x|_{row} \leq |p|_{row}$ and $|x|_{col} \leq |p|_{col}$, picture x is a *prefix* of p, denoted $x \trianglelefteq p$, if x is a subpicture of p corresponding to its top-left portion, i.e. if $x = p[(1, 1), (|x|_{row}, |x|_{col})]$; x is a *proper prefix* of p if, moreover, $x \neq p$.

Dealing with pictures, two concatenation products are classically defined. Let $p, q \in \Sigma^{**}$ be pictures of size (m, n) and (m', n'), respectively. The *row* and the *column concatenation* of p and q, denoted by $p \ominus q$ and $p \oslash q$, are defined by juxtaposing p and q vertically and horizontally, respectively. They are partial operations, defined only if $n = n'$ and if $m = m'$, respectively, as:

$$p \ominus q = \boxed{\begin{array}{c} p \\ \hline q \end{array}} \qquad\qquad p \odot q = \boxed{\;p\;|\;q\;}\,.$$

These operations can be extended to define row and column concatenations, and *row* and *column stars* on languages. We consider another interesting star operation for picture languages, as introduced by Simplot in [19], *the tiling star*. The idea is to compose pictures in some way to cover a rectangular area as, for example, in the following figures.

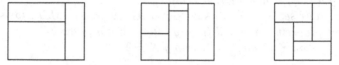

The tiling star of X, denoted by X^{**}, is the set that contains all the empty pictures together with all the non-empty pictures p whose domain can be partitioned in disjoint subdomains $\{d_1, d_2, \ldots, d_k\}$ such that any subpicture p_h of p associated with the subdomain d_h belongs to X, for all $h = 1, \ldots, k$. Then X^{++} denotes the set X^{**} without the empty pictures. In the sequel, if $p \in X^{++}$, the partition $t = \{d_1, d_2, \ldots, d_k\}$ of $dom(p)$, together with the corresponding pictures $\{p_1, p_2, \ldots, p_k\}$, is called a *tiling decomposition* of p in X.

2.1   Two-Dimensional Codes

Let us recall the definitions of codes and strong prefix codes of pictures given in [4–6,9], together with some examples. Let Σ be a finite alphabet. $X \subseteq \Sigma^{++}$ is a *code* iff any $p \in \Sigma^{++}$ has at most one tiling decomposition in X.

Example 1. Let $\Sigma = \{a, b\}$ be the alphabet and let $X = \left\{ \boxed{a\ b},\ \boxed{\begin{array}{c} a \\ b \end{array}},\ \boxed{\begin{array}{cc} a & a \\ a & a \end{array}} \right\}$. It is easy to see that X is a code. Any picture $p \in X^{++}$ can be decomposed starting at the top-left-corner and checking the subpicture $p[(1,1),(2,2)]$; it can be univocally decomposed in X. Then, proceed similarly for the next contiguous subpictures of size $(2, 2)$.

Example 2. Let $X = \left\{ \boxed{a\ b},\ \boxed{b\ a},\ \boxed{\begin{array}{c} a \\ a \end{array}} \right\}$. Notice that no picture in X is prefix of another picture in X. Nevertheless, X is not a code. Indeed, picture $\boxed{\begin{array}{c} a\ b\ a \\ a\ b\ a \end{array}}$ has the two following different tiling decompositions in X: $t_1 = \boxed{\begin{array}{c|c} a\ b & a \\ \hline a\ b & a \end{array}}$ and $t_2 = \boxed{\begin{array}{c|c} a & b\ a \\ \hline a & b\ a \end{array}}$.

Taking inspiration from the family of prefix codes of strings, the *strong prefix* sets of pictures have been defined in [4,9]. Note that the strong prefix sets are codes.

The definition of strong prefix set is based on the notion of prefix-overlap; two pictures p and q *prefix-overlap* if for any $(i,j) \in \text{dom}(p) \cap \text{dom}(q)$, $p(i,j) = q(i,j)$. Moreover, p and q *strictly prefix-overlap* if they prefix-overlap, but neither $p \trianglelefteq q$, nor $q \trianglelefteq p$ (cf. [9]). For example, in the following figure, picture p and q strictly prefix-overlap:

$$\begin{array}{|cc|} \hline a & b \\ a & a \\ \hline \end{array} \qquad\qquad \begin{array}{|cccc|} \hline a & b & a & a \\ \hline \end{array} \qquad\qquad \begin{array}{|cc|cc|} \hline a & b & a & a \\ a & a & & \\ \hline \end{array}$$

$$p \qquad\qquad\qquad\qquad q \qquad\qquad\qquad p \text{ and } q \text{ prefix-overlap}$$

Definition 1. *Let $X \subseteq \Sigma^{++}$. X is strong prefix if for any pictures p, q in X with $p \neq q$, p and q do not prefix-overlap.*

A strong prefix set $X \subseteq \Sigma^{++}$ is maximal strong prefix (MSP, for short) over Σ if it is not properly contained in any other strong prefix set over Σ; that is, $X \subseteq Y \subseteq \Sigma^{++}$ and Y strong prefix imply $X = Y$.

Example 3. The following language X is strong prefix; no two pictures in X prefix-overlap. Moreover, in [9] it is proved that X is a maximal strong prefix code.

$$X = \left\{ \begin{array}{|ccc|} \hline a & b & a \\ \hline \end{array}, \begin{array}{|ccc|} \hline a & b & b \\ \hline \end{array}, \begin{array}{|c|} \hline b \\ b \\ \hline \end{array}, \begin{array}{|cc|} \hline a & a \\ a & a \\ \hline \end{array}, \begin{array}{|cc|} \hline a & a \\ a & b \\ \hline \end{array}, \begin{array}{|cc|} \hline a & a \\ b & a \\ \hline \end{array}, \begin{array}{|cc|} \hline a & a \\ b & b \\ \hline \end{array}, \begin{array}{|cc|} \hline b & a \\ a & a \\ \hline \end{array}, \begin{array}{|cc|} \hline b & a \\ a & b \\ \hline \end{array}, \begin{array}{|cc|} \hline b & b \\ a & a \\ \hline \end{array}, \begin{array}{|cc|} \hline b & b \\ a & b \\ \hline \end{array} \right\}.$$

The results in [7–9] describe an effective procedure to construct *all* (maximal) strong prefix codes of pictures, starting from the "singleton" pictures containing only one alphabet symbol. The construction in some sense extends the literal representation of prefix codes of strings in terms of trees. It is based on the notion of *extension* of a picture. The set of extensions of a picture p to some bigger size (m, n), is the set of all pictures of fixed size (m, n), obtained by adding some columns to the right and some rows to the bottom of p filled with all possible combinations of alphabet symbols. Formally, the *set of extensions* of p to a bigger size (m, n) is $E_{(m,n)}(p) = \{q \in \Sigma^{m,n} \mid p \text{ is a proper prefix of } q\}$. The next characterization result will be used in Sect. 5 to define a data structure to handle the MSP codes.

Proposition 1 [9]. *$X \subseteq \Sigma^{++}$ is a finite maximal strong prefix code if and only if there exists a finite sequence of picture languages over Σ, $X_1, X_2, \ldots, X_k$, such that $X_1 = \Sigma^{1,1}$, $X = X_k$, and for $i = 1, \ldots, k-1$, $X_{i+1} = (X_i \setminus \{p_i\}) \cup E_{(m_i,n_i)}(p_i)$, for some $p_i \in X_i$, $m_i, n_i \geq 0$.*

3   Completeness for Sets of Strings

Completeness for a set of strings is a property which guarantees that any string on the alphabet can be decomposed using the strings in the set. When the set of strings is a code we have some further uniqueness result (as discussed later).

Usually, in the literature (see for example [11]) a set of strings S over an alphabet Σ is defined right-complete if any string $w \in \Sigma^*$ is a prefix of some string $s \in S^*$. We will adopt an equivalent definition, more suitable for our purposes, since it can be then extended in two dimensions.

Definition 2. *A set of strings S over an alphabet Σ is right-complete if any string $w \in \Sigma^*$ can be written as $w = xy$ where $x \in S^*$ and y is a prefix of some string in S.*

It is well-known that all maximal *prefix codes* are right-complete. More precisely, a prefix code is right-complete if and only if it is maximal prefix. Hence, the maximal prefix codes can be used to uniquely encode all the strings on the alphabet, as follows.

Let S be a maximal prefix code on Σ and w be any string over Σ. The string w can be decomposed as a concatenation of factors in S, and, possibly, at the end, a prefix of a string in S; more precisely, $w = x_1 x_2 \ldots x_k y$ with $x_1, x_2, \ldots, x_k \in S$ and y a prefix of some string in S. Note that y could be the prefix of more than one string in S. If one wants to uniquely determine one string in S whose prefix is y, one could decide, for example, to consider the smallest string x_{k+1} in S in the lexicographic order. With this assumption, the *encoding* of w is the sequence of the strings $x_1, x_2, \ldots, x_k, x_{k+1} \in S$ together with their position inside w.

If S is a maximal prefix code over Σ then any string over Σ has a unique encoding in S. We are going to generalize this result to the pictures. Our point of view will be that the last string x_{k+1} in S in the decomposition of w has been "cut", since we have found the obstacle of the right border of the string.

The notion of completeness is not able to capture the maximality of (strong) prefix codes in the two dimensions. Let us introduce the definition of a new property on languages of strings, the right-fullness. This property is equivalent to the right-completeness for strings. On the contrary, in two dimensions, it results in a different property which will be able to capture the notion of maximality.

Definition 3. *A set of strings S over an alphabet Σ is right-full if for any string $w \in \Sigma^*$, $w = a_1 a_2 \cdots a_n$, with $a_1, a_2, \cdots, a_n \in \Sigma$, and any position i, $1 \le i \le n$, either there exists a non-empty $x \in S$, such that $x = a_i \cdots a_{i+|x|-1}$ or $a_i \cdots a_n$ is a prefix of a string in S.*

Proposition 2. *A set of strings S over an alphabet Σ is right-complete iff it is right-full.*

The proof of Proposition 2 is mainly based on the observation that the definition of right-fullness is equivalent to the following one. A set $S \subseteq \Sigma^*$ is right-full if, for any string $w \in \Sigma^*$, either there exists a string in S which is a prefix of w, or w is a prefix of a string in S. We have preferred to state it as above, because it describes more explicitly the point of view that we will adopt for the encoding problem in two dimensions.

4   Completeness for Sets of Pictures

The theory of codes of strings is well established. Any string on a given alphabet Σ can be encoded on a (prefix) code on Σ, provided that the code is right- complete, or, equivalently, right-full, as described in the previous section. For picture languages, the notion that generalizes the right-completeness of string languages is the br-completeness, where "br" indicates that the picture is read starting from the position $(1,1)$ and going towards the bottom-right corner. It was introduced in [9] and it refers to the notion of covering. Informally, a picture p is *covered* by pictures in a set X, if p can be tiled (without holes and overlapping) with pictures that possibly exceed p throughout the bottom or the right border (cf. [5,9]).

Definition 4. *A set $X \subseteq \Sigma^{**}$ is br-complete if every picture $p \in \Sigma^{**}$ can be covered by pictures in X.*

Unfortunately, in two dimensions the equivalence between br-completeness and maximality holds only in a very weak form, i.e. only when the code X is a set of strings or "thick" strings.

Proposition 3 [9]. *Let $X \subseteq \Sigma^{**}$ be a finite maximal strong prefix code. X is br-complete if and only if $X \subseteq \Sigma^{m*}$ or $X \subseteq \Sigma^{*n}$, $n, m \geq 1$.*

As a result of the previous proposition, if X is a MSP code that is not br-complete, then, when one tries to cover a picture p with pictures in X, one possibly gets holes where no picture code fits. We illustrate such situation in the following example.

Example 4. Consider the set X of Example 3. X is a MSP code, but X is not

br-complete. Indeed, consider the picture $p = \begin{array}{|cccc|} \hline b & b & a & b \\ b & b & b & b \\ a & b & a & b \\ \hline \end{array}$. It can be easily

verified that p cannot be covered with pictures in X. Two different attempts of coverings are given below. Always, some positions (printed in bold) remain uncovered leaving holes in the covering.

b	b	a	b	a
b	b	b	b	
a	**b**	a	b	

b	b	a	b	b
b	b	**b**	**b**	
a	b	a	**b**	

Note that, in the previous example, a picture of X that matches the uncovered positions does exist; the problem is that it does not fit exactly in the hole. In the following, with this example in mind, we will introduce the definition of *br-full* set of pictures which extends Definition 3 for strings. First, let us state an auxiliary definition.

Definition 5. *Given $x, p \in \Sigma^{**}$ and $(i, j) \in \text{dom}(p)$, we say that x matches p in position (i, j) if the subpicture $p[(i, j)(|p|_{row}, |p|_{col})]$ and x prefix-overlap.*

Definition 6. *A set of pictures X over an alphabet Σ is br-full if for any picture $p \in \Sigma^{**}$, and any position $(i, j) \in \text{dom}(p)$, there exists $x \in X$ such that x matches p in position (i, j).*

As already recalled, differently from the string case, the class of MSP codes does not coincide with the class of br-complete codes. On the contrary, the property which captures the maximality, in the case of the pictures, is the br-fullness.

Proposition 4. *Let $X \subseteq \Sigma^{**}$ be a strong prefix code of pictures. X is a maximal strong prefix code of pictures if and only if X is br-full.*

Proof. Suppose that X is a maximal strong prefix code of pictures and that X is not br-full. Then, there exist a picture $p \in \Sigma^*$ and a position $(i, j) \in \text{dom}(p)$ such that, for any $x \in X$, x does not match p in position (i, j). Therefore, the subpicture $q = p[(i, j)(|p|_{row}, |p|_{col})]$ of p is such that, for any $x \in X$, q and x do not prefix-overlap. This implies, in particular, that $q \notin X$. Hence, $X \cup \{q\}$ is a strong prefix code that properly contains X, contradicting the maximality of X.

Suppose now that X is br-full. Let $p \in \Sigma^{**} \setminus X$ and consider position $(1, 1)$ of p. Since X is br-full then there exists $x \in X$ such that x matches p in position $(1, 1)$, i.e. p and x prefix-overlap. Therefore $X \cup \{p\}$ is not strong prefix and, hence, X is a maximal strong prefix code. $\qquad\square$

Proposition 5. *Let $X \subseteq \Sigma^{**}$. If X is br-complete then it is br-full. The converse does not hold.*

Proof. Suppose that X is br-complete. To prove that X is br-full, consider a picture $p \in \Sigma^*$ and a position $(i, j) \in \text{dom}(p)$. We have to show that there exists $x \in X$ that matches p in position (i, j). Since X is br-complete, the subpicture $q = p[(i, j)(|p|_{row}, |p|_{col})]$ of p can be covered by (pictures in) X. In the covering of q, let $x \in X$ be the picture that covers position $(1, 1)$. Then, trivially, we have that q and x prefix-overlap and, therefore, x matches p in position (i, j).

Now we show that not any br-full set is a br-complete set. Indeed, consider the set X of Example 3. In the same example, it is stated that X is a maximal strong prefix code and therefore, from Proposition 4, X is br-full. But, as noted in the Example 4, X is not br-complete. $\qquad\square$

In general, a MSP code is not br-complete and, therefore, it is not possible to cover any picture in X, since some holes could remain in its covering. On the other hand, any MSP code is br-full. The problem is that, in some cases, the picture of X that matches the positions of the holes cannot be placed, due to some kinds of obstacles. We will solve this problem, as in the string case, by introducing the possibility of cutting the pictures, and, then, introducing some prefixes. Hence, we propose a relaxed definition of the decomposition of pictures, called *decomposition with cuts*.

Note that, in the covering of a string w, an element of the set S may be cut only at the right border of w, since this is the only possible obstacle. In the covering of a picture p, three different kinds of obstacles can be found; the right border of p, the bottom border of p and the border of some picture "already" placed in the covering. Which pictures are "already" placed depends on the scanning strategy used to examine the picture p.

In the string case, only one possible scanning strategy exists once one starts from the leftmost position (the one that goes to the right). In the case of pictures, starting from the top-left corner, we can follow many different scanning strategies to reach the bottom-right one (cf. [2, 3, 16]). In this paper, we choose to consider a scanning strategy that starts from position $(1, 1)$ and then proceeds always choosing the next position higher and leftmost, i.e. by following the lexicographic order of the positions.

Let $X \subseteq \Sigma^{**}$, $M_X = max\{|x|_{row}, |x|_{col}$ for $x \in X\}$, and $a \in \Sigma$ be a fixed symbol. In the next definition, for any picture $p \in \Sigma^{**}$, we will consider the picture $\overline{p}$ obtained from p by adding M_X columns filled by a to its right and M_X rows filled by a to its bottom. The reason is to obtain the uniqueness result stated in Proposition 6.

Definition 7. *Let* $X \subseteq \Sigma^{**}$ *and* $p \in \Sigma^{**}$ *be a picture of size* (m, n). *A decomposition with cuts of* p *in* X *is a partition of* $dom(p)$ *in disjoint subdomains* $\{d_1, d_2, \dots, d_k\}$ *such that, supposing that the domains are ordered by their tl-corners, for any* $\ell = 1, \dots, k$, *the subpicture* p_ℓ *of* p *associated with the subdomain* $d_\ell = [(i_\ell, j_\ell), (i'_\ell, j'_\ell)]$ *satisfies one of the following conditions*

(1) $p_\ell \in X$
(2) p_ℓ *is a proper prefix of* x_ℓ, *for some* $x_\ell \in X$ *that matches* $\overline{p}$ *in position* (i_ℓ, j_ℓ), *and if* $|p_\ell|_{row} < |x_\ell|_{row}$ *then* $i'_\ell = m$; *if* $|p_\ell|_{col} < |x_\ell|_{col}$ *then either* $j'_\ell = n$ *or* $j'_\ell + 1$ *is the minimum index* j, $j > j_\ell$, *such that* (i_ℓ, j) *belongs to* $d_1 \cup d_2 \cup \dots \cup d_{\ell-1}$.

Condition (2) in the previous definition represents the situation when a cut is done on the picture x_ℓ matching p in the considered position (i_ℓ, j_ℓ). This cut may be done either because x_ℓ, when put in position (i_ℓ, j_ℓ), falls out p, or because it occupies some positions already occupied by some of the previously determined pictures $p_1, p_2, \dots, p_{\ell-1}$. Notice that following a prescribed scanning strategy guarantees that we use cut pictures as in Condition (2) only if we are forced and this assures the uniqueness of this kind of decomposition.

Example 5. Continuing Example 4, we give below a decomposition with cuts for the picture p. The bold printed subpictures correspond to the pictures in X that were cut (they are prefixes of $\boxed{a \quad b \quad a}$).

b	b	**a**	**b**
b	b	b	b
a	**b**	a	b

Proposition 6. *Let* $X \subseteq \Sigma^{**}$ *be a maximal strong prefix code. Then, any picture* $p \in \Sigma^{**}$ *has a unique decomposition with cuts in* X.

Proof. Let $p \in \Sigma^{**}$. The crucial observation is that, since X is a maximal strong prefix code, then for any position $(i, j) \in dom(p)$, there exists one and only one $x \in X$ which matches $\overline{p}$ in position (i, j). Subsequently, some attention has to be paid in order to guarantee that also the cuts of such pictures are done in a uniquely determined way. In order to find a decomposition with cuts in X of p, consider the positions of $dom(p)$ in lexicographic order, starting from position $(1, 1)$. Therefore, the subdomains $d_1, d_2, \dots, d_k$ will be obtained in the order of their tl-corners.

Let $x_{(1,1)} \in X$ be the unique picture of X that matches $\bar{p}$ in position $(1,1)$. Then, set $d_1 = \mathrm{dom}(p) \cap \mathrm{dom}(x_{(1,1)})$. Note that the subpicture p_1 of p associated with d_1 is such that either $p_1 = x_{(1,1)} \in X$ (in the case that $x_{(1,1)}$ is a prefix of p) and hence it satisfies condition (1) in Definition 7, or p_1 is a proper prefix of $x_{(1,1)} \in X$ that satisfies condition (2) in Definition 7. In both cases, d_1 is uniquely defined.

Suppose, now, that the subdomains $d_1, d_2, \ldots, d_{\ell-1}$ have been uniquely determined. In order to determine d_ℓ, consider the smallest position (i_ℓ, j_ℓ) in lexicographic order such that $(i_\ell, j_\ell) \in \mathrm{dom}(p) \setminus (d_1 \cup d_2 \cup \cdots \cup d_{\ell-1})$. Let $x_\ell \in X$ be the unique picture of X that matches $\bar{p}$ in position (i_ℓ, j_ℓ) and set $d_\ell = [(i_\ell, j_\ell), (i'_\ell, j'_\ell)]$ where i'_ℓ and j'_ℓ are determined in the following way. If $i_\ell + |x_\ell|_{row} - 1 \leq |p|_{row}$, then $i'_\ell = i_\ell + |x_\ell|_{row} - 1$; otherwise, $i'_\ell = |p|_{row}$. Two different cases can occur for j'_ℓ, following that x_ℓ, when put in position (i_ℓ, j_ℓ), does not cover any position occupied by the already determined pictures $p_1, p_2, \ldots, p_{\ell-1}$, or not. More precisely, in the first case, position $(i_\ell, j) \notin (d_1 \cup d_2 \cup \cdots \cup d_{\ell-1})$ for any $j \in \{j_\ell + 1, \ldots, j_\ell + |x_\ell|_{col} - 1\}$, in the second case $(i_\ell, j) \in (d_1 \cup d_2 \cup \cdots \cup d_{\ell-1})$ for some $j \in \{j_\ell + 1, \ldots, j_\ell + |x_\ell|_{col} - 1\}$. In the first case, if $j_\ell + |x_\ell|_{col} - 1 \leq |p|_{col}$, then $j'_\ell = j_\ell + |x_\ell|_{col} - 1$; if, instead, $j_\ell + |x_\ell|_{col} - 1 > |p|_{col}$ then $j'_\ell = |p|_{col}$. In the second case, let $\bar{j}$ be the minimum index $j \in \{j_\ell + 1, \ldots, j_\ell + |x_\ell|_{col} - 1\}$, such that the position (i_ℓ, j) belongs to $(d_1 \cup d_2 \cup \cdots \cup d_{\ell-1})$, and set $j'_\ell = \bar{j} - 1$.

Note that the subpicture p_ℓ of p associated with d_ℓ is such that either $p_\ell = x_\ell \in X$ (in the first case when furthermore $i_\ell + |x_\ell|_{row} - 1 \leq |p|_{row}$, $j_\ell + |x_\ell|_{col} - 1 \leq |p|_{col}$), and hence p_ℓ satisfies condition (1) in Definition 7, or p_ℓ is a proper prefix of $x_\ell \in X$ that satisfies condition (2) in Definition 7. In both cases, d_ℓ is uniquely defined. □

5   The Extension Tree and the Encoding Algorithm

In this section we present a data structure to represent a maximal strong prefix code of pictures X, called *extension tree*. The extension tree will be then used in an algorithm that, given any picture p, finds its unique encoding in X. The efficiency of the algorithm relies mainly on the data structure to represent X that we are going to describe.

Let us introduce the extension trees.

An extension tree is a rooted tree where each node v corresponds to a picture $pict(v)$ and the edges are labeled by a single row or column over the alphabet. Moreover, an operation $op(v)$ is associated to every node v; the operation is either a row or a column concatenation. The picture associated to the root is an empty picture, while the pictures associated to the root's children are all possible pictures of size $(1,1)$. Subsequently, the pictures associated to the children of a node v are all the extensions of the picture $pict(v)$, which are obtained by concatenating pict(v) with all possible single rows or all possible single columns over the alphabet. The type of operation (either row or column concatenation) is dictated by the field op. More precisely, let v be any node in T and (m, n) be the size of $pict(v)$. The pictures associated to the children of v are all the extensions of $pict(v)$ to size $(m+1, n)$ if $op(v) = \ominus$, to size $(m, n+1)$ if $op(v) = \oplus$.

Definition 8. *An extension tree on Σ is a rooted labeled tree T where*

- *every node v has two auxiliary fields: $op(v) \in \{\ominus, \oplus\}$ and $pict(v) \in \Sigma^{**}$*
- *$op(roo(T)) = \oplus$, $pict(root(T)) = \lambda_{1,0}$*
- *the children of a node v are given in an ordered list, denoted $Children(v)$*
- *every edge (v, w), with $w \in Children(v)$, is labeled by a row or a column of symbols in Σ, denoted* label(v, w), *such that*
  - *if $op(v) = \ominus$ then $\{label(v,w) \mid w \in Children(v)\} = \Sigma^{1,|pict(v)|_{col}}$, and $pict(v) \ominus label(v, w) = pict(w)$,*
  - *if $op(v) = \ominus$ then $\{label(v,w) \mid w \in Children(v)\} = \Sigma^{|pict(v)|_{row},1}$, and $pict(v) \oplus label(v, w) = pict(w)$.*

The language represented by T is the set $L(T) = \{pict(v) \mid v$ is a leaf of $T\}$.

We will assume that, for any node v, the list of outgoing edges is ordered following the lexicographic order of the labels, where the labels are viewed as strings. The same order is inherited by the related list $Children(v)$.

Note that any extension of a picture p to a bigger size can be obtained as a sequence of simple extensions by one row or column. This observation, together with Proposition 1, allows to prove the following result. Proposition 7 highlights the analogy existing between the extension trees for the MSP picture codes in two dimensions, and the literal representation of maximal prefix string codes, in one dimension.

Proposition 7. *The language represented by an extension tree is a maximal strong prefix code. Vice versa, any maximal strong prefix code can be represented by an extension tree.*

Example 6. Consider again the language X in Example 3. Here below is an extension tree that represents X. The pictures corresponding to the nodes $v_1, v_2, \ldots, v_{16}$ are, respectively

$$\boxed{a}, \boxed{b}, \boxed{a\ a}, \boxed{a\ b}, \boxed{\begin{smallmatrix}b\\a\end{smallmatrix}}, \boxed{\begin{smallmatrix}b\\b\end{smallmatrix}}, \boxed{\begin{smallmatrix}a\ a\\a\ a\end{smallmatrix}}, \boxed{\begin{smallmatrix}a\ a\\a\ b\end{smallmatrix}}, \boxed{\begin{smallmatrix}a\ a\\b\ a\end{smallmatrix}}, \boxed{\begin{smallmatrix}a\ a\\b\ b\end{smallmatrix}}, \boxed{a\ b\ a}, \boxed{a\ b\ b}, \boxed{\begin{smallmatrix}b\ a\\a\ a\end{smallmatrix}}, \boxed{\begin{smallmatrix}b\ a\\a\ b\end{smallmatrix}}, \boxed{\begin{smallmatrix}b\ b\\a\ a\end{smallmatrix}}, \boxed{\begin{smallmatrix}b\ b\\a\ b\end{smallmatrix}}.$$

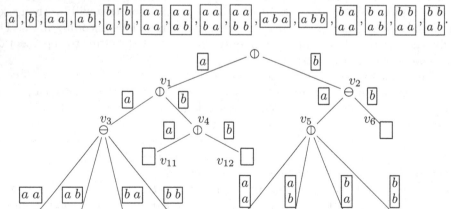

Let us first draw some considerations on the size of an extension tree in relation to the size of the represented language, where the size of a language X is defined as $size(X) = \sum_{x \in X} area(x)$.

Let T be an extension tree and $X = L(T)$. For any leaf v of T, the depth of v is given by $|pict(v)|_{row} + |pict(v)|_{col} - 1$. Therefore, the height of the extension tree for X is given by the maximum of $|x|_{row} + |x|_{col} - 1$, for all $x \in X$. Then, the number of nodes of T is less than $\sum_{x \in X}(|x|_{row} + |x|_{col} - 1)$, that is strictly less than the size of X. The number of children of a node v is equal to $|\Sigma|^\ell$, where $\ell = |pict(v)|_{col}$ if op(v) $= \ominus$, $\ell = |pict(v)|_{row}$, otherwise. Finally, the size of the set of the labels of all the edges in T is strictly less than the size of X.

Let us sketch how to use the extension tree T of X to find a picture $x \in X$ that matches a given position (i, j) of a picture p, in time proportional to $area(x)$. The idea is similar to the one used to find a factor of a string in a prefix set represented by its literal representation. Start from the root of T and follow a path toward a leaf, scanning the positions around (i, j), as dictated by the information in the nodes of the tree. If the operation in the reached node is $\ominus$ then read the symbols of p that are in the row to the bottom of the visited portion; otherwise, read the column to the right. Then, follow the edge out of v with the read label. When a leaf w is reached then $pict(w)$ matches p in position (i, j).

Recall that the length of the list of edges outgoing from v is equal to $|\Sigma|^\ell$, where $\ell = |pict(v)|_{col}$ if op(v) $= \ominus$, $\ell = |pict(v)|_{row}$, otherwise. Then, since the list is ordered, the time to access the right edge is proportional to $\log_2 |\Sigma|^\ell = \ell \log_2 |\Sigma|$ (by executing a binary search). Therefore, the overall time to possibly find the picture in X that matches (i, j) is proportional to the area of x, on a fixed alphabet Σ.

Let us now focus on the encoding problem. First, we fix the definition.

Definition 9. *Let $X \subseteq \Sigma^{**}$ and $p \in \Sigma^{**}$ be a picture of size (m, n). An encoding of p in X is a sequence $((d_1, x_1), (d_2, x_2), \ldots, (d_k, x_k))$ where $\{d_1, d_2, \ldots, d_k\}$ is a partition of $\mathrm{dom}(p)$ in disjoint subdomains ordered by their tl-corners, and for any $\ell = 1, \ldots, k$, $x_\ell \in X$ is a picture that matches $\bar{p}$ in the tl-corner of d_ℓ, while the subpicture p_ℓ of p associated with the subdomain $d_\ell = [(i_\ell, j_\ell), (i'_\ell, j'_\ell)]$ satisfies one of the following conditions*

(1) $p_\ell \in X$ and then $x_\ell = p_\ell$

(2) p_ℓ is a proper prefix of x_ℓ, and if $|p_\ell|_{row} < |x_\ell|_{row}$ then $i'_\ell = m$; if $|p_\ell|_{col} < |x_\ell|_{col}$ then either $j'_\ell = n$ or $j'_\ell + 1$ is the minimum index j, $j > j_\ell$, such that (i_ℓ, j) belongs to $d_1 \cup d_2 \cup \cdots \cup d_{\ell-1}$.

Example 7. Continuing Example 5, an encoding of p in X is

$((d_1, \begin{array}{c}\boxed{b}\\\boxed{b}\end{array}), (d_2, \begin{array}{c}\boxed{b}\\\boxed{b}\end{array}), (d_3, \boxed{a\ b\ a},), (d_4, \begin{array}{c}\boxed{b\ b}\\\boxed{a\ b}\end{array}), (d_5, \boxed{a\ b\ a},)))$, where $d_1 = [(1, 1), (2, 1)]$,

$d_2 = [(1, 2), (2, 2)]$, $d_3 = [(1, 3), (1, 4)]$, $d_4 = [(2, 3), (3, 4)]$, $d_5 = [(3, 1), (3, 2)]$.

There is a one-to-one correspondence between the encodings of a picture p in a MSP code X and the decompositions with cuts of p in X. Therefore, we can obtain the following result as a corollary of Proposition 6.

Corollary 1. *Let $X \subseteq \Sigma^{**}$ be a maximal strong prefix code. Then, any picture $p \in \Sigma^{**}$ has a unique encoding in X.*

For the rest of the section, we will sketch an algorithm that takes a MSP code X and a picture p and finds the unique encoding of p in X as described in Definition 9.

The algorithm follows the steps described in the proof of Proposition 6. It adds the pairs (d_i, x_i) to an initially empty list, in the lexicographic order of the tl-corners of d_i's. In order to keep track of the positions occupied by the domains already determined, it uses an auxiliary array $COMB$ of length $|p|_{col}$. Indeed, since the algorithm processes the positions of $dom(p)$ in lexicographic order, at any step, the occupied positions altogether look like a "comb"; if a position $(\bar{i}, \bar{j})$ is occupied then all the positions above it (i.e. positions $(i, \bar{j})$ with $i \leq \bar{i}$) are already occupied. Then, for any $i = 1, 2, \ldots, |p|_{col}$, $COMB(i) = j$ if j is the maximum index such that (i, j) is occupied.

The algorithm starts in position $(1, 1)$ of p and looks for the picture $x_1 \in X$ that matches $\bar{p}$ at position $(1, 1)$, as discussed above. Then, it sets $d_1 = dom(p) \cap dom(x_1)$, adds (d_1, x_1) to the list to return and updates $COMB$ array. Suppose, now, that the algorithm has constructed the list $((d_1, x_1), (d_2, x_2), \ldots, (d_{\ell-1}, x_{\ell-1}))$. In order to determine (d_ℓ, x_ℓ), it uses the $COMB$ array to find the smallest position (i_ℓ, j_ℓ) that is not yet occupied. Then, it finds the unique picture x_ℓ in X that matches $\bar{p}$ in position (i_ℓ, j_ℓ), sets $d_\ell = [(i_\ell, j_\ell), (i'_\ell, j'_\ell)]$ where i'_ℓ and j'_ℓ are set as in the proof of Proposition 6, and updates the $COMB$ array. The overall running time of the algorithm is $O(\sum_{\ell=1}^{k} area(x_\ell))$, on a fixed alphabet.

Let $Enc(p) = \{x_1, \ldots, x_k\}$. Note that the pictures $x_1, \ldots, x_k$ do not in general form a tiling decomposition of p, since they may overlap each other. Hence, in general, $\sum_{\ell=1}^{k} area(x_\ell) \geq area(p)$. On the other hand, one can observe that each position (i, j) of p, can be covered by at most $j - 1$ pictures in $Enc(p)$, because no two pictures in $Enc(p)$ may cover (i, j) and have their tl-corners in the same column. Finally, the algorithm runs in $O(mn^2)$ time, where (m, n) is the size of p.

References

1. Aigrain, P., Beauquier, D.: Polyomino tilings, cellular automata and codicity. Theor. Comput. Sci. **147**, 165–180 (1995)
2. Anselmo, M., Giammarresi, D., Madonia, M.: Tiling automaton: a computational model for recognizable two-dimensional languages. In: Holub, J., Žd'árek, J. (eds.) CIAA 2007. LNCS, vol. 4783, pp. 290–302. Springer, Heidelberg (2007). https://doi.org/10.1007/978-3-540-76336-9_27

3. Anselmo, M., Giammarresi, D., Madonia, M.: A computational model for tiling recognizable two-dimensional languages. Theor. Comput. Sci. **410**(37), 3520–3529 (2009)
4. Anselmo, M., Giammarresi, D., Madonia, M.: Strong prefix codes of pictures. In: Muntean, T., Poulakis, D., Rolland, R. (eds.) CAI 2013. LNCS, vol. 8080, pp. 47–59. Springer, Heidelberg (2013). https://doi.org/10.1007/978-3-642-40663-8_6
5. Anselmo, M., Giammarresi, D., Madonia, M.: Two dimensional prefix codes of pictures. In: Béal, M.-P., Carton, O. (eds.) DLT 2013. LNCS, vol. 7907, pp. 46–57. Springer, Heidelberg (2013). https://doi.org/10.1007/978-3-642-38771-5_6
6. Anselmo, M., Giammarresi, D., Madonia, M.: Prefix picture codes: a decidable class of two-dimensional codes. Int. J. Found. Comput. Sci. **25**(8), 1017–1032 (2014)
7. Anselmo, M., Giammarresi, D., Madonia, M.: Structure and measure of a decidable class of two-dimensional codes. In: Dediu, A.-H., Formenti, E., Martín-Vide, C., Truthe, B. (eds.) LATA 2015. LNCS, vol. 8977, pp. 315–327. Springer, Cham (2015). https://doi.org/10.1007/978-3-319-15579-1_24
8. Anselmo, M., Giammarresi, D., Madonia, M.: Infinite two-dimensional strong prefix codes: characterization and properties. In: Dennunzio, A., Formenti, E., Manzoni, L., Porreca, A.E. (eds.) AUTOMATA 2017. LNCS, vol. 10248, pp. 19–31. Springer, Cham (2017). https://doi.org/10.1007/978-3-319-58631-1_2
9. Anselmo, M., Giammarresi, D., Madonia, M.: Structure and properties of strong prefix codes of pictures. Math. Struct. Comput. Sci. **27**(2), 123–142 (2017)
10. Beauquier, D., Nivat, M.: A codicity undecidable problem in the plane. Theor. Comp. Sci **303**, 417–430 (2003)
11. Berstel, J., Perrin, D., Reutenauer, C.: Codes and Automata. Cambridge University Press, Cambridge (2009)
12. Bozapalidis, S., Grammatikopoulou, A.: Picture codes. ITA **40**(4), 537–550 (2006)
13. Crochemore, M., Rytter, W.: Text Algorithms. Oxford University Press, Oxford (1994)
14. Giammarresi, D., Restivo, A.: Two-dimensional languages. In: Rozenberg, G., Salomaa, A. (eds.) Handbook of Formal Languages, vol. III, pp. 215–267. Springer, Heidelberg (1997). https://doi.org/10.1007/978-3-642-59126-6_4
15. Grammatikopoulou, A.: Prefix picture sets and picture codes. In Proceedings of the CAI 2005, pp. 255–268. Aristotle University of Thessaloniki (2005)
16. Lonati, V., Pradella, M.: Strategies to scan pictures with automata based on Wang tiles. RAIRO - Theor. Inf. Appl. **45**(1), 163–180 (2011)
17. Moczurad, M., Moczurad, W.: Some open problems in decidability of brick (labelled polyomino) codes. In: Chwa, K.-Y., Munro, J.I.J. (eds.) COCOON 2004. LNCS, vol. 3106, pp. 72–81. Springer, Heidelberg (2004). https://doi.org/10.1007/978-3-540-27798-9_10
18. Moczurad, W.: Decidability of multiset, set and numerically decipherable directed figure codes. Discret. Math. Theor. Comput. Sci. **19**(1) (2017)
19. Simplot, D.: A characterization of recognizable picture languages by tilings by finite sets. Theor. Comput. Sci. **218**(2), 297–323 (1991)

Machine Learning

ARCID: A New Approach to Deal with Imbalanced Datasets Classification

Safa Abdellatif[1]([✉]), Mohamed Ali Ben Hassine[1], Sadok Ben Yahia[1], and Amel Bouzeghoub[2]

[1] University of Tunis El Manar, Faculty of Sciences of Tunis,
LIPAH-LR11ES14, El Manar, 2092 Tunis, Tunisia
{Safa.abdellatif,mohamedali.benhassine}@fst.utm.tn,
sadok.benyahia@fst.rnu.tn
[2] Institut Mines-TELECOM, TELECOM SudParis,
UMR CNRS Samovar, 91011 Evry Cedex, France
amel.bouzeghoub@it-sudparis.eu

Abstract. Classification is one of the most fundamental and well-known tasks in data mining. Class imbalance is the most challenging issue encountered when performing classification, i.e. when the number of instances belonging to the class of interest (minor class) is much lower than that of other classes (major classes). The class imbalance problem has become more and more marked while applying machine learning algorithms to real-world applications such as medical diagnosis, text classification, fraud detection, etc. Standard classifiers may yield very good results regarding the majority classes. However, this kind of classifiers yields bad results regarding the minority classes since they assume a relatively balanced class distribution and equal misclassification costs. To overcome this problem, we propose, in this paper, a novel associative classification algorithm called Association Rule-based Classification for Imbalanced Datasets (ARCID). This algorithm aims to extract significant knowledge from imbalanced datasets by emphasizing on information extracted from minor classes without drastically impacting the predictive accuracy of the classifier. Experimentations, against five datasets obtained from the UCI repository, have been conducted with reference to four assessment measures. Results show that ARCID outperforms standard algorithms. Furthermore, it is very competitive to Fitcare which is a class imbalance insensitive algorithm.

Keywords: Associative classification · Imbalanced datasets
Machine learning · Data mining

1 Introduction

With the huge advance of technology, enterprises are daily collecting massive information from multiple sources. Collecting, preprocessing and then taking advantages of these large amounts of data was really challenging at the time. In

A. M. Tjoa et al. (Eds.): SOFSEM 2018, LNCS 10706, pp. 569–580, 2018.
https://doi.org/10.1007/978-3-319-73117-9_40

this respect, data mining techniques have been shown to be of benefit to handle such overwhelming data. Indeed, through a computational processus, useful knowledge is unveiled. A range of data mining techniques namely association rule mining, classification and clustering have been well developed and applied in several domains.

Associative classification is the integration of association rule mining and classification in order to build classifiers that can predict class labels for unseen data [1]. Techniques based on this approach have yield good accuracy comparing to other classification techniques. However, mining imbalanced datasets was considered as one of the top ten data mining challenges since most of the machine learning (ML) algorithms assume that datasets have balanced class distribution [29]. A dataset is called imbalanced when the number of instances belonging to the class of interest (minor class) is much lower than the ones of other classes (major classes). Association rules belonging to minor classes are rare as compared with ones that predict major classes. Consequently, this yields to a misclassification of the testing samples belonging to minor classes. Generally, classifiers aim to minimize the error rate and maximize the accuracy. They assume that the misclassification errors cost equally which is not the case of many real-world domains. For example, in a medical diagnostic problem where the disease cases are usually quite rare as compared with normal populations, the recognition goal is to detect people with these diseases. Hence, a good classifier is the one that provides a high accuracy on the disease class. Also worth of cite, in fraud detection domain, fraudulent transactions are rare as compared with legitimate transactions. However, missing a fraudulent example is much more expensive than classifying a non-fraudulent as fraudulent. The problem of imbalanced datasets classification is encountered in many other domains ranging from sentiment analysis and text classification, network intrusion detection and many others.

To overcome this problem, we introduce in this paper a novel associative classification algorithm called Association Rule-based Classification for Imbalanced Datasets (ARCID). ARCID is based on three phases which are generating, filtering and selecting rules. The first phase consists in generating frequent rules from each class of the training set using a local support. The second phase consists in filtering rules generated during the first phase. To do so, a new ranking and pruning technique is proposed based on multiple criteria aggregation in order to keep simultaneously rules with a high predictive accuracy and those which are rare but of primary interest. The last phase consists in predicting the class label of the new data. Experimentations, against five real-world datasets obtained from the UCI repository [21] and using different rule-based and non-rule-based approaches, have been conducted with reference to four assessment measures in order to evaluate the performance of the proposed approach.

The remainder of this paper is organized as follows. Section 2 recalls the basic concepts related to associative and imbalanced datasets classification. The proposed approach is described in Sect. 3. Experimental results are shown in Sect. 4. Conclusion and perspectives are sketched in Sect. 5.

2   Background and Related Work

We provide, in the following, the basic concepts related to this work.

2.1   Classification Based on Association Rules

Let D be a training dataset containing $|D|$ instances and $I = \{I1, I2, \ldots, Im+1\}$ a set of m + 1 distinct items. Each instance of D is a set of items of I. The pattern of the form X $\rightarrow$ Y is called association rule (AR) where X and Y are disjoint subsets of I. Using an ARs mining technique on the training set D, frequent itemsets are mined and ARs are generated. Class Association Rule (CAR) is an AR where X is a subset of items and Y is a class label.

Associative Classification (AC) is a rule-based approach which first discovers from the training set a complete set of CARs and then uses it to predict class labels of new data objects [2]. Several studies [2,3] have shown that AC approaches are able to achieve more accurate classifiers than traditional approaches namely decision trees, rule induction and probabilistic approaches.

AC typically consists of three phases. The first phase consists in generating a set of CARs using a given training set. The second phase consists in ranking and pruning the complete set generated in the first phase in order to discard useless rules and select the important ones. The final phase consists in predicting the class label of the testing set instances based on the collection of CARs retained.

Several AC algorithms have been proposed namely CBA, CPAR, MMAC, MCAR, CMAR and many others [26]. These algorithms use several methodologies to generate, rank, prune and select rules for data prediction. To generate rules, several AR mining techniques have been proposed such as Apriori [1] (as used in CBA), FP-Growth [12] (as used in CMAR), FOIL [24] (as used in CPAR), etc. To eliminate redundant and inefficient rules, several pruning techniques have been proposed such as database coverage (as used in CBA, CMAR, MMAC and MCAR), redundant rules pruning (as used in CMAR) and interesting measures based pruning (as used in CMAR and CBA). The last phase of an AC algorithm is to assign the appropriate class label to the new data. Several methods use the single rule class assignment approach [20] such as CBA, MCAR and MMAC while other methods like CMAR and CPAR use the class assignment based on group of rules approach [27].

2.2   Imbalanced Data Sets Classification

Dealing with class imbalance has become a common problem faced in data mining. A dataset is imbalanced when it contains a small number of training instances which belong to the class of interest (also called the minority or positive class), while other instances make the other class (called the majority or negative class) [16]. The class imbalance problem has become more marked while applying ML algorithms to real-world problems. Researchers around the world have treated actively this problem for years [14]. In fact, major studies were dedicated especially to evaluation metrics and classification techniques.

Evaluation metrics. In ML, several assessment measures have been proposed in order to evaluate the performance of a classifier. The common measures are:

- *Accuracy and error rate:* These measures are the most commonly used metrics for classifier's performance evaluation. They evaluate the overall effectiveness of the algorithm by estimating the proportion of instances that are correctly (accuracy)/incorrectly (error rate) classified. However, they are not appropriate in the case of imbalanced datasets since they place more interest on the majority class.
- *Precision, Recall and F-measure:* Precision calculates the number of errors made in predicting instances as being of some label l. However, Recall assesses the goodness of a classifier in not leaving out instances that should have been predicted with the label l. F-measure combines Precision and Recall into a single measure that reflects the goodness of a classifier in the presence of rare classes [25]. F-measure provides more information about the efficiency of a classifier than the accuracy metric. Hence, it has been used for the evaluation of classifiers with imbalanced data in several fields such as text classification, fraud detection and churn prediction.
- *Geometric mean (Gmean):* Gmean is one of standard evaluation measures used in an imbalanced dataset classifier. It was suggested by [18] as the product of the prediction accuracies of minor and major classes. Gmean measures the performance balance of a classifier between the minority and majority classes. A high Gmean value can only be achieved with high prediction accuracies on both classes.

Classification techniques. To resolve the problem of imbalanced data sets, several solutions have been proposed both at the data as well as the algorithmic level.

At the data level, proposed works aim to modify the data itself by rebalancing classes before applying any algorithm. The most common techniques related to this approach are oversampling and undersampling. The oversampling approach tends to increase the population of minority class by replicating its instances. Several oversampling techniques have been proposed recently namely random oversampling, SMOTE [5] and Borderline SMOTE [11]. The main advantage of these techniques is that there is no loss of data. However, it may lead to an overfitting and a computational overhead. The undersampling approach tends to decrease the population of the majority class by ignoring a large number of its instances. Many undersampling techniques have been proposed such as random undersampling, Tomek links [28], Condensed Nearest Neighbor Rule [13] and One-sided selection [19]. The main drawback of these techniques is that potentially useful information may be lost during the sampling process.

At the algorithmic level, proposed solutions deal with modifying the classifier itself. It is about trying to adapt existing algorithms to the problem of imbalanced datasets in order to reveal the minority class. Several works have adopted this strategy mainly Fitcare [7] which is one of the well-known competitors of our proposed approach. Other works, based on Cost-Sensitive Learning

[15], also adopt the same strategy. They tend to modify the classifier by applying a misclassification cost to the incorrectly classified instance. Learn only the rare class approach is also classified in this category. It consists in only learning from the minor class by treating major class' instances as outliers. HIPPO [17] and RIPPER [8] are examples of this approach.

3 Proposed Approach: ARCID

Generally, in a context of a data mining classification problem, classical classifiers aim to minimize the error rate and maximize the accuracy. They assume also a balanced class distribution and an equal cost of misclassification errors. Nevertheless, in many real-world applications, data extracted from the web is imbalanced and the difference between misclassification errors is considerable. Consider, for example, a case of fraud detection where the fraudulent cases only represent 1% and the non-fraudulent ones represent 99%. In this case, traditional classifiers offer an excellent accuracy (99%) since they predict correctly all non-fraudulent examples, however, they omit fraudulent ones which are very important in our case. To overcome this issue and to avoid problems caused by data-based classification strategy described in the last section, we choose to adopt the algorithmic based strategy.

ARCID (Association Rule-based Classification for Imbalanced Datasets), our proposed approach, is an associative rule-based classification technique which aims to extract significant knowledge from imbalanced datasets by emphasizing on information extracted from minor classes without drastically impacting the predictive accuracy of the classifier. ARCID is based on three main phases: (1) generating, (2) filtering, and (3) selecting rules for class prediction.

3.1 Rule Generation

In this phase, two main problems are faced: (1) Managing the overwhelming number of CARs generated from real-life datasets and (2) Removing redundant rules conveying the same information. To overcome these problems, ARCID uses the IGB algorithm [9]. This algorithm provides a reduced set of rules which are information lossless, generic, non-redundant, and informative. To adapt IGB to our context, ARCID starts by scanning the training set to create instances' groups based on their class labels. Each resulting group contains instances belonging to the same class. Then, for each group, the support measure is applied to reduce the search space and generate frequent rules. Since we work on a homogeny group, i.e. containing instances belonging to the same class, a local support is used regarding the whole data set. Hence, rules with low support in the whole dataset and frequent in their own class have the chance to be generated.

3.2 Ranking, Pruning and Selecting Relevant CAR Rules

To deal with the huge set of rules generated in the previous phase and to guarantee a high accuracy in classification without neglecting rules belonging to rare classes, we propose a new technique for ranking and pruning rules based on the combination of two different criteria (measures). Our main idea consists in:

1. Ranking then selecting top k rules using two interestingness measures that highlight respectively two kinds of rules:
   - Rules that have a very high predictive accuracy (because of their high support value) and generally belong to major classes.
   - Rules that are rare (because of their low support value), interesting in many applications and generally belong to minor classes.

In order to select the best two measures that verify conditions mentioned above, we carried out several experiments using five binary datasets chosen from the UCI repository [21]. These experiments are carried as follows: (i) Rules are generated using the IGB algorithm with a local support for each class (ii) These rules are then sorted using eight different measures each individually. (iii) The sorted rules are used for the prediction of class labels for the testing dataset. A Rule is selected for prediction of a test instance if it has the highest rank according to a specific measure which minimizes the classification error rate. Figures 1 and 2 show the result of classification (considering minor class in Fig. 1 and major class in Fig. 2) applied on different datasets using different measures separately.

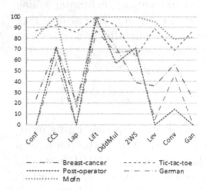

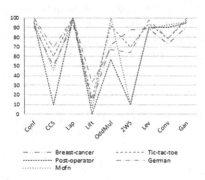

Fig. 1. Correct prediction for minor class

Fig. 2. Correct prediction for major class

The x−axis shows the different measures while the y−axis shows the percentage of instances correctly classified. For example, in Fig. 1, the LaPlace measure only correctly classifies 20% (resp. 0% and 16%) of instances belonging to the minor class of the Breast-cancer dataset (resp. German and Mofn) while the lift measure correctly classifies the majority of these instances (96% for Breast−cancer, 87% for German and 100% for Mofn). In Fig. 2, the results are inverted. In fact, we notice that the LaPlace measure classifies correctly the majority of instances belonging to the major class while the use of the lift measure yields poor results (i.e. low percentage of instances correctly classified). We may conclude that lift (resp. Laplace) is the best–suited measure for minor (resp. major) classes prediction since it increases the number of instances correctly classified. If we had used other measures, these instances would have been misclassified. At the end of this stage, we obtain two lists of CARs having the same content but sorted according to Lift (*Lift_list*) and LaPlace (*LaPlace_list*) measures.

2. Selecting top K rules from both obtained lists. The parameter k is chosen as follows: From the list of rules ranked by the lift measure, we discard those having a Lift value less than or equal to one (i.e. rule's antecedent and rule's conclusion are negatively correlated or independent). The k parameter is the number of rules maintained and will be used to prune Laplace_list.

3. Selecting common rules that are the result of the intersection operator applied on the pruned lists. The resulting set Common_list contains relevant rules that are suitable for instances classification in minor and major classes.

3.3 Class Prediction

In this phase, two methods can be used for class prediction [20,27]. The first method selects the class label of the highest ranked rule (based on a defined measure) which matches the test instance. The second method selects the class label using an aggregate value (the highest). This value corresponds to the average of a defined measure for each group of rules predicting the same class and matching the test instance. If no rule matches the test instance, the minor class is assigned to it.

4 Experimental Evaluation

4.1 Data Collection and Experimental Setup

In this study, five real-world datasets obtained from the UCI repository [21] are selected to evaluate ARCID. Datasets are summarized in Table 1. Each dataset includes the number of instances, the number of attributes and the imbalance ratio (IR) which is defined as the ratio of major class' instances divided by the minor class' instances. All the datasets are binary class. The next version handling the multi-class imbalance classification problem stands as the hottest forthcoming issue that we plan to tackle.

Experiments were carried out on a Windows 8 PC equipped with an Intel Core i7-4720, 2.6 GHz processor and 8 GB of RAM. Our approach is compared to several well-known classification approaches including the non-rule-based ones like Naive Bayes (NB) [22] and Random Forest (RF) [6], the rule-based ones like C4.5 [23] and CBA [20], and those handling the class imbalance problem such as Fitcare [7] and RIPPER [8]. Fitcare is kindly provided by its author [7] while the others are available in WEKA software System [10]. The four assessment metrics [4] used in this comparison are Global accuracy, Gmean, F-measure and per-class accuracy of minor class.

Table 1. Datasets used for the evaluation

Datasets	# Instances (#Maj/#Min)	# Attributes	Imbalance ratio
Breast Cancer	286 (201/**85**)	10	2.36
Tic-tac-toe	425 (276/**149**)	10	1.68
Mofn	1323 (1031/**292**)	11	3.53
Post-operator	88 (64/**24**)	9	2.66
German	1001 (701/**300**)	25	2.33

4.2 Results of the Experiments

Before evaluating and comparing ARCID to the other state-of-art approaches, experiments were conducted in order to choose the best-suited method for the class prediction phase. Table 2 presents the results obtained from the application of the two methods (highest ranked rule and the average of measures) using four assessment measures over five datasets. It is clearly observed that the proposed classifier using the highest ranked rule based method yields better results than the one using the average of measures for all the assessment measures. For this reason, it will be used in the remainder.

Table 2. Comparaison of ARCID's performance using the highest ranked rule based method and the average of measures based method

Datasets	Global accuracy		Gmean		Accuracy (Min. class)		FM (Min. class)	
	HRR	AVG	HRR	AVG	HRR	AVG	HRR	AVG
Breast cancer	72.34	69.14	0.67	0.67	64	64	0.55	0.52
Tic-tac-toe	72.71	58.49	0.77	0.63	92.3	84.6	0.67	0.55
Mofn	68.81	67.15	0.77	0.75	100	97.6	0.59	0.57
Post-operator	59.25	59.25	0.34	0.32	14.3	14.3	0.15	0.15
German	67.27	51.65	0.66	0.57	64.8	73.6	0.54	0.45
Avg	68.07	61.13	0.64	0.58	67.08	66.82	0.5	0.448
Avg rank	1	1.8	1	1.8	1.2	1.4	1	1.8

In the following, we perform a thorough experimental comparison between ARCID and the state-of-art approaches using the four assessment measures mentioned above.

Global accuracy. Global accuracy is the proportion of instances which are correctly classified. The results of the experiments are presented in Table 3. It shows that the state-of-art algorithms are better ranked than ARCID. This could be explained by the fact that they pursue on maximizing the global accuracy and minimizing the error rate to which minor class rarely contributes. However, if we take a look at the average of global accuracies of all classifiers, we may notice that even if ARCID emphasis on efficiently predicting the instances of minor classes, it gives pretty good results whenever compared to other approaches.

Table 3. Global accuracies (%) for all classification techniques

Datasets	ARCID	Specific rule-based		Standard rule-based		Non-rule-based	
		Fitcare	Ripper	CBA	C4.5	NB	RF
Breast cancer	72.34	63.82	74.73	78.68	74.73	75.78	66.31
Tic-tac-toe	72.71	100	98.59	69.01	80.75	72.71	89.2
Mofn	68.81	87.68	90.23	82.03	85.54	86.71	94.23
Post-operator	59.25	48.14	71.4	71.42	71.42	71.42	71.42
German	67.27	61.7	71.55	_	75.44	76.04	77.24
Avg	68.07	72.26	81.3	75.28	77.57	77.57	77.57
Avg rank	5.6	4.6	**2.6**	4.4	3.2	2.8	2.6

Gmean. As we mentioned above, the state-of-art classifiers yield better results than the ARCID in terms of accuracy. In the case of imbalanced datasets, accuracy puts more focus on major classes than minor classes which makes it a misleading indicator. For this reason, we have proposed to use an additional metric which is Gmean in order to measure the balance between classification performances on the minority and majority classes. According to the results presented in Table 4, ARCID gets the best rank compared to other approaches. In fact, it can be observed that ARCID performs slightly better than Fitcare and RIPPER. However, it outperforms all standard rule-based and non-rule-based approaches by several ranks.

Performance in minority classes. In the case of imbalanced datasets classification problem, minority classes are generally grasping interest. To evaluate the performances of the different methods in classifying instances of minor classes, two measures are used: the per-class accuracy and the F-measure.

Per-class accuracy results. Results obtained from the experiments are depicted in Table 5. As may be seen, ARCID provides statistically better results. We may conclude that ARCID is an efficient algorithm when it comes to correctly predicting the class label on the minor class instances since it tends to focus on the accuracy of the minor class while trading off the accuracy of major class.

Table 4. GMean results for all classification techniques

Datasets	ARCID	Specific rule-based		Standard rule-based		Non-rule-based	
		Fitcare	Ripper	CBA	C4.5	NB	RF
Breast cancer	0.67	0.62	0.59	0	0.47	0.66	0.41
Tic-tac-toe	0.77	1	0.97	0	0.68	0.61	0.83
Mofn	0.77	0.83	0.85	0.61	0.65	0.64	0.26
Post-operator	0.34	0.46	0	0	0	0	0.34
German	0.66	0.58	0.58	0	0.66	0.66	0.64
Avg rank	**2.2**	2.4	3	5.8	3.6	3.4	4.4

Table 5. Per-class accuracy of minor classes

Datasets	ARCID	Specific rule-based		Standard rule-based		Non-rule-based	
		Fitcare	Ripper	CBA	C4.5	NB	RF
Breast cancer	64	60	40	0	24	52	20
Tic-tac-toe	92.3	100	95.5	0	50	43.9	71.2
Mofn	100	75.9	78.4	37.9	44	41.4	75
Post-operator	14.3	42.8	0	0	0	0	12.5
German	64.8	52.7	40.7	48.4	47.3	52.7	47.3
Avg rank	**1.6**	1.8	3.6	5.8	4.8	4.6	4.4

F-measure results. To ensure that the results are not biased towards minor classes, the per-class accuracy is dropped in favor of the F-measure. The F-measure results are reported in Table 6. ARCID is ranked the first which owe to the fact that it asserts an absence of a bias towards minor classes.

Table 6. F-measure results of minor classes

Datasets	ARCID	Specific rule-based		Standard rule-based		Non-rule-based	
		Fitcare	Ripper	CBA	C4.5	NB	RF
Breast cancer	0.55	0.46	0.45	0	0.33	0.53	0.23
Tic-tac-toe	0.67	1	0.97	0	0.61	0.5	0.8
Mofn	0.59	0.74	0.78	0.48	0.58	0.58	0.85
Post-operator	0.15	0.3	0	0	0	0	0.2
German	0.54	0.43	0.43	0	0.54	0.52	0.52
Avg rank	**2.4**	2.6	3.4	6.4	4	4	3.2

5   Conclusion

This paper dealt with imbalanced datasets problems. In fact, in these datasets, important information related to minor classes are omitted by classical classifiers which tend generally to focus on prevalent classes and ignore minor ones. This process, called imbalanced datasets classification, could produce high realistic value in many real-world applications (security, medicine, counter-terrorism, etc.). This paper proposed a novel associative classification algorithm called ARCID in order to handle problems mentioned above. ARCID aims to emphasize on rare but important information from minor classes without drastically impacting the predictive accuracy. The performance of ARCID is assessed on five datasets with reference to four evaluation measures. Experimentations show that ARCID outperforms standard algorithms. However, it is very competitive to Fitcare. In our future work, we intend to extend our approach to handle the multi-class imbalanced learning problem. Moreover, we plan to use dataset meta features in order to find the best measures for filtering and selecting rules phases. Furthermore, we plan to apply our proposed approach in text mining and sentiment analysis domains.

References

1. Agrawal, R., Srikant, R.: Fast algorithms for mining association rules in large databases. In: Proceedings of 20th International Conference on Very Large Data Bases, VLDB 1994, Santiago de Chile, Chile, 12–15 September 1994, pp. 487–499 (1994)
2. Ali, K., Manganaris, S., Srikant, R.: Partial classification using association rules. In: Proceedings of the Third International Conference on Knowledge Discovery and Data Mining (KDD-1997), Newport Beach, California, USA, 14–17 August 1997, pp. 115–118 (1997)
3. Antonie, M., Zaïane, O.R.: An associative classifier based on positive and negative rules. In: Proceedings of the 9th ACM SIGMOD Workshop on Research Issues in Data Mining and Knowledge Discovery, DMKD 2004, Paris, France, 13 June 2004, pp. 64–69 (2004)
4. Bekkar, M., Djemaa, H.K., Alitouche, T.A.: Evaluation measures for models assessment over imbalanced data sets. J. Inf. Eng. Appl. 3(10), 2–4 (2013)
5. Bowyer, K.W., Chawla, N.V., Hall, L.O., Kegelmeyer, W.P.: SMOTE: synthetic minority over-sampling technique. CoRR abs/1106.1813 (2011). http://arxiv.org/abs/1106.1813
6. Breiman, L.: Random forests. Mach. Learn. 45(1), 5–32 (2001)
7. Cerf, L., Gay, D., Selmaoui-Folcher, N., Crémilleux, B., Boulicaut, J.: Parameter-free classification in multi-class imbalanced data sets. Data Knowl. Eng. 87, 109–129 (2013)
8. Cohen, W.W.: Fast effective rule induction. In: Proceedings of the Twelfth International Conference on Machine Learning, pp. 115–123 (1995)
9. Gasmi, G., Yahia, S.B., Nguifo, E.M., Slimani, Y.: $\mathcal{IGB}$: a new informative generic base of association rules. In: Ho, T.B., Cheung, D., Liu, H. (eds.) PAKDD 2005. LNCS, vol. 3518, pp. 81–90. Springer, Heidelberg (2005). https://doi.org/10.1007/11430919_11

10. Hall, M., Frank, E., Holmes, G., Pfahringer, B., Reutemann, P., Witten, I.H.: The WEKA data mining software: an update. ACM SIGKDD Explor. Newsl. **11**(1), 10–18 (2009)

11. Han, H., Wang, W.-Y., Mao, B.-H.: Borderline-SMOTE: a new over-sampling method in imbalanced data sets learning. In: Huang, D.-S., Zhang, X.-P., Huang, G.-B. (eds.) ICIC 2005. LNCS, vol. 3644, pp. 878–887. Springer, Heidelberg (2005). https://doi.org/10.1007/11538059_91

12. Han, J., Pei, J., Yin, Y., Mao, R.: Mining frequent patterns without candidate generation: a frequent-pattern tree approach. Data Min. Knowl. Discov. **8**(1), 53–87 (2004)

13. Hart, P.E., Nilsson, N.J., Raphael, B.: A formal basis for the heuristic determination of minimum cost paths. IEEE Trans. Syst. Sci. Cybern. **4**(2), 100–107 (1968)

14. Hido, S., Kashima, H., Takahashi, Y.: Roughly balanced bagging for imbalanced data. Stat. Anal. Data Min.: ASA Data Sci. J. **2**(5–6), 412–426 (2009)

15. Holmes, J.H.: Differential negative reinforcement improves classifier system learning rate in two-class problems with unequal base rates. In: Genetic Programming, pp. 635–642 (1998)

16. Hu, B., Dong, W.: A study on cost behaviors of binary classification measures in class-imbalanced problems. CoRR abs/1403.7100 (2014)

17. Japkowicz, N., Myers, C., Gluck, M., et al.: A novelty detection approach to classification. In: IJCAI, vol. 1, pp. 518–523 (1995)

18. Kubat, M., Holte, R.C., Matwin, S.: Machine learning for the detection of oil spills in satellite radar images. Mach. Learn. **30**(2–3), 195–215 (1998)

19. Kubat, M., Matwin, S.: Addressing the curse of imbalanced training sets: one-sided selection. In: Proceedings of the Fourteenth International Conference on Machine Learning (ICML 1997), Nashville, Tennessee, USA, 8–12 July 1997, pp. 179–186 (1997)

20. Liu, B., Hsu, W., Ma, Y.: Integrating classification and association rule mining. In: Proceedings of the Fourth International Conference on Knowledge Discovery and Data Mining (KDD-1998), New York City, New York, USA, 27–31 August 1998, pp. 80–86 (1998)

21. Merz, C.: UCI repository of machine learning databases (1996). http://www.ics.uci.edu/~mlearn/MLRepository.html

22. Mitchell, T.M.: Machine Learning. McGraw Hill Series in Computer Science. McGraw-Hill (1997)

23. Quinlan, J.R.: C4.5: Programs for Machine Learning. Morgan Kaufmann, Burlington (1993)

24. Quinlan, J.R., Cameron-Jones, R.M.: FOIL: a midterm report. In: Brazdil, P.B. (ed.) ECML 1993. LNCS, vol. 667, pp. 1–20. Springer, Heidelberg (1993). https://doi.org/10.1007/3-540-56602-3_124

25. Rijsbergen, C.J.V.: Information Retrieval. Butterworth, London (1979)

26. Sasirekha, D., Punitha, A.: A comprehensive analysis on associative classification in medical datasets. Indian J. Sci. Technol. **8**(33), 3–5 (2015)

27. Thabtah, F., Cowling, P., Peng, Y.: Multiple label classification rules approach. J. Knowl. Inf. Syst. **9**, 109–129 (2006)

28. Tomek, I.: An experiment with the edited nearest-neighbor rule. IEEE Trans. Syst. Man Cybern. **6**, 448–452 (1976)

29. Yang, Q., Wu, X.: 10 challenging problems in data mining research. Int. J. Inf. Technol. Decis. Mak. **5**(04), 597–604 (2006)

Fake Review Detection via Exploitation of Spam Indicators and Reviewer Behavior Characteristics

Ioannis Dematis[1(✉)], Eirini Karapistoli[2], and Athena Vakali[1]

[1] Informatics Department, Aristotle University of Thessaloniki,
Thessaloniki, Greece
{icdematis,avakali}@csd.auth.gr
[2] CapriTech Limited, 10-12 Mulberry Green,
Old Harlow, Essex CM17 0ET, UK
irene@capritech.co.uk

Abstract. The rapid spread of Internet technologies has redefined E-commerce, since opinion sharing by product reviews is an inseparable part of online purchasing. However, e-commerce openness has attracted malicious behaviors often expressed by fake reviews targeting public opinion manipulation. To address this phenomenon, several approaches have been introduced to detect spam reviews and spammer activity. In this paper, we propose an approach which integrates content and usage information to detect fake product reviews. The proposed model exploits both product reviews and reviewers' behavioral traits interlinked by specific spam indicators. In our proposed method, a fine-grained burst pattern detection is employed to better examine reviews generated over "suspicious" time intervals. Reviewer's past reviewing history is also exploited to determine the reviewer's overall "authorship" reputation as an indicator of their recent reviews' authenticity level. The proposed approach is validated with a real-world Amazon review dataset. Experimentation results show that our method successfully detects spam reviews thanks to the complementary nature of the employed techniques and indicators.

Keywords: Fake review · Reviewer behavior · Spam indicators

1 Introduction

E-commerce has been radically affected by the rapid spread of Web and Internet technologies which enabled tremendous user-generated content (UGC) production and sharing. Consumers publicly and continuously declare and share opinions for purchased products or services and assess quality and value-for-money. A recent study [1] demonstrated that online reviews are quite important to prospective buyers as around 90% of consumers read and incorporate online reviews in their decision-making. Moreover, it has been reported that 88% of consumers trust online reviews as much as personal recommendations.

Such online reviewing impact has opened the floor to "non-honest" activities which aim to either capitalize on or manipulate user reviews for particular products or services.

© Springer International Publishing AG 2018
A M. Tjoa et al. (Eds.): SOFSEM 2018, LNCS 10706, pp. 581–595, 2018.
https://doi.org/10.1007/978-3-319-73117-9_41

It is now evident that professional "spammers" are repeatedly hired to populate the online reviewing space with fake reviews [2, 3] due to competition and/or profit reasons. This large scale of deceptive reviews has emerged as a significant problem attracting the scientific community's interest. Research efforts mostly aim to improve fake review detection towards re-establishing online opinions validity and credibility.

Fake review detection is a mostly recent research field [4], which initially focused on duplicated review content and review context. Such text analysis was mostly based on machine learning (classifiers) at word or sentence level which targeted the detection of spam reviews by performing supervised learning classification of review content [5–7]. However, the absence of a globally reliable training set of annotated review instances necessary to empower supervised learning approaches led to a shift in research focus [8]. Reviewer behavior was found to hold an abundance of spam indicators including excessive reviewing [9], rating manipulation [10–13], bursty behavior [14–16], etc.

While recent approaches have displayed promising and highly accurate results by featuring a variety of spam indicators, there is a lack of lightweight methods that successfully combine review features and extensive reviewer activity analysis, and work on a fine-grained (product) level, i.e., processing a product's string of reviews to detect fakes. Additionally, in-depth models are usually hard to adapt and be integrated into functional reviewing sites, while most streamlined and focused approaches result in loss of information.

In this paper, we examine the most important spam indicators relative to review spam and leverage on a reviewer's behavior characteristics, which are exploited for review labeling in two classes of "honest" or "spam". Our main goal is to maintain a core part of information associated with online reviewing to feed a generalized methodology, which will be adaptive and computationally effective. The dataset of the proposed work includes commonly available review metadata, which are used to identify bursty review arrival patterns and track reviewer activity. Moreover, past reviewing history is exploited to gain additional indications for a reviewer's overall reputation, which aids in determining the genuine or deceptive nature of the reviewer's more recent reviews.

Thus, our main contributions are as follows:

- Proposition of an adaptive fake review detection model which integrates a wide and heterogeneous number of review and reviewer traits.
- Determination of a reviewer's reputation profile based on reviewer history analysis.
- Inclusion of burst pattern detection not as sole focus but as an additional technique.
- Computational efficiency by implementing a lightweight and non-complex review scoring approach.

The remainder of this paper is organized as follows. Section 2 offers an overview of existing work in the field of review spam detection. In Sect. 3 the problem definition is laid down. Sections 4 and 5 describe the proposed methodology and experimentation results of our study, respectively. Finally, Sect. 6 concludes this paper summarizing our findings.

2   Related Work

Over the last decade, considerable research has been conducted in the field of opinion spam detection of online reviews. The most relevant literature is summarized with emphasis on detecting spam reviewing activity.

Review text analysis. Identification of fake reviews was initially studied as a task of detecting duplicated review text, since content duplication has been recognized as a common spammer practice, in which the same review is reproduced numerous times (semantically or textually). Indeed, the cosine similarity between review contents is often proposed as an effective detection feature [5, 17]. These duplicate and near-duplicate reviews originally served as the positive class for review content classification approaches [4, 5, 17]. The release of the gold-standard dataset [6, 7] of annotated review instances though, procured by employing the Amazon Mechanical Turk (AMT) service, sparked a new interest in supervised learning. Classifiers, built on the aforementioned gold-standard dataset and based on word n-gram [6, 7, 18] or character n-gram features [19], displayed high detection accuracy across both positive and negative sentiment. However, the reliability of the training set of review instances remains a debatable factor in regards to its applicability on real world review cases, as the knowledge and psychology of AMT workers is allegedly not accurately representative of real professional spammers [20].

Graph-based approaches. Certain studies [21, 22] proposed an heterogenous graph representation to model the interconnections between reviewers, reviews and online stores in order to detect irregularities. Using these interconnections, it is possible to iteratively determine the trustworthiness of reviewers, the reliability of stores and the honesty of reviews. FraudEagle [23], an unsupervised network-based framework, consists of a bipartite network of reviewers and products, with edges representing a positive or negative review rating. It initializes the vertices and then iteratively propagates the respective values across the network via the edges until convergence is achieved, which implies consistent scores between neighboring nodes.

Burst pattern discovery. There has been increasing focus on the aspect of time in regards to studying spam reviewing activity. Given that most reviewers create only a single review for a given product, i.e., singleton review, the authors of [14] observed the bursty arrival pattern of singletons, as well as their temporal correlation to rating, and built a multidimensional time series for each product based on average rating, total number of reviews and the ratio of singleton reviews. A joint anomaly detection on these temporally correlated abnormal sections revealed suspicious singleton review activity. Another study [15] asserted that reviews and reviewers, appearing in the same burst of a product's reviewing activity, are often related and thus, using a graph representation to model author interconnections, successfully identified review spammers. The computational costs of analyzing the entire string of a product's reviews led [9] to only analyze and consider those reviews fallen in bursty time intervals on the grounds that they are most likely to contain suspicious activity.

Rating manipulation analysis. Spammers attempt to promote or demote a product by manipulating its overall ranking. As a result, the identification of the proportion of ratings disagreeing with the majority opinion has already been studied as a standalone detection technique or as part of a wider combination of spam indicators and features [11, 12]. A considerable number of early ratings, as well as extreme ratings, have also been linked to suspicious behavior [8, 11]. Furthermore, spammers have been found to distort their distribution of review scores leaving behind a trail of distributional foot-prints, which can be used to assist in the discovery of spam reviewers [13].

Group spammers detection. Deceptive reviewers often work in collaboration with each other in order to promote or demote a particular product or service. Using frequent pattern mining, [24] found candidate spammer groups and ranked them with SVM RANK based on a number of group related features. The authors of [25] applied a frequent itemset mining method on Amazon review data to extract candidate groups and rank them according to the probability of spamming. A more recent approach [26] used the co-bursting spammer relations to model a co-bursting network, which suc-cessfully detected spammer groups.

In short, most methods utilizing a graph-based model [15, 21, 23] and examining various behavior footprints [8, 11, 12] perform an in-depth analysis of reviewing activity, however their (computational) complexity and/or focus on spammer detection does not enable a dedicated product-level approach akin to already established spam review filtering systems. A few approaches [9, 14] did focus on a product-based analysis by taking as input a product's reviews and identifying burst patterns and suspicious reviews, though they suffer from loss of information by ignoring reviews created outside of bursty time intervals. Moreover, they lack an in-depth analysis of reviewer activity and behavior.

In contrast, the proposed method bridges the existing gaps by introducing an effective fake review detection model that operates on a fine-grained (product) level, utilizes burst pattern discovery (detecting suspicious time intervals) as an additional analysis technique and integrates reviewer past and present activity.

3   Problem Definition

Before detailing our approach towards detecting fake reviews, we describe the main concepts of this study and present the issues our method addresses.

To start with, for a given product p we consider a set of n reviews $R = \{r_1, \ldots, r_n\}$ and a set of m reviewers or authors $A = \{a_1, \ldots, a_m\}$ where $m \leq n$, and n, m vary depending on the product. It is apparent that review and reviewer constitute the core entities in our study:

Definition 1 (User Review). *A user review r_i refers to a review written by a user or consumer for a product or a service p based on their experience as a user of the reviewed product. A review usually includes the following information:*

$r_{i,c}$: *A relatively short passage of text or comment expressing the user's experience and judgement of the reviewed product.*

$r_{i,rt}$: *The rating given to the reviewed product with its range typically at the [1, 10] or [1, 5] scales.*

$r_{i,t}$: *The creation date and time of the review.*

$r_{i,a}$: *The author ID of the review.*

Definition 2 (Reviewer). *A reviewer $a(r_i)$ is a person who formally assesses a used product or service p by authoring a review r_i. A reviewer is associated with a set $R_{a,j}$, where $|R_{a,j}| > 0$, defined as the set of all reviews that $a(r_i)$ has written for p.*

Most fake review detection methods focus only on a product's reviews, lacking the deep level (across multiple products) analysis of spammer detection methods. Our goal is to propose a spam review detection approach satisfying the following criterion:

Problem Definition 1 (Fake Review Detection). *Detect spam in online reviews with a model that (1) operates on a product level, (2) exploits all available data relative to reviews and (3) analyzes past and present reviewer activity.*

As we will show in the subsequent section, a hybrid approach combining indicators of spam for review and reviewer, can successfully determine whether the former is fake or honest.

4   Proposed Model

Our approach attempts to create a robust fake review detection system by considering a variety of well-established and accepted by the scientific community spam features linked to both review and reviewer behavior. With regard to the product-level processing, our model receives as input a set of n reviews $R = \{r_1, \ldots, r_n\}$ associated with a product. Then, for each review r_i we extract the necessary information and metadata including review text, review rating, timestamp and reviewer ID, which we first study across some basic spam indicators. We also use burst pattern discovery as a complementary analysis tool to identify bursty time intervals and pinpoint "suspicious" reviews, which we then examine across two additional spam indicators. Thus, our method considers all reviews of a product (no loss of information), while probing further into the most high-risk ones. Lastly, the history of an author's past reviewing activity is taken into account as it can affect their overall reputation as a user and subsequently, as a spam or honest reviewer. During analysis of a review, its author's associated set of past reviews $Hist_{a,j}$ is investigated and studied across a number of features and behavior characteristics as an additional measure of reviewer trustworthiness and ultimately, review spam level. We determine the review spam level by applying a linear weighted scoring function [11] to the review and define a spam score

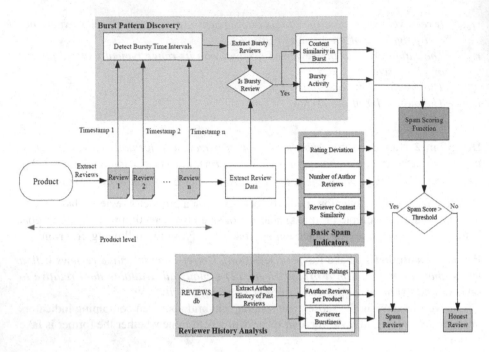

Fig. 1. Overview of the proposed method's workflow.

threshold to which we compare each review's accumulated score. Thus, our method outputs as fake those reviews whose score exceeds the threshold and as honest those reviews whose score does not exceed the threshold. On overview of the proposed method can be seen in Fig. 1.

4.1 Basic Spam Indicators

This section presents and describes the 3 basic spam indicators used in our model to detect spam in online reviews.

- **Rating Deviation (RD)**

A spam review will typically aim at increasing or decreasing a product's overall rank by manipulating its mean score towards a particular direction and, consequently, deviates from the mean.

Considering $S_{mean}(p)$ as the mean rating of a product p and normalizing according to a 5-star rating scale, the rating deviation score [0, 1] of a review r_i is found to be:

$$RD(r_i) = \frac{\left| r_{i,rt} - S_{mean}(p) \right|}{4} \tag{1}$$

- **Number of Reviews (NR)**

It is a common spammer practice to create multiple reviews for the same product in order to exert greater influence on public opinion and manipulate the mean rating.

Naturally, the spam score of a review r_i created by reviewer $a(r_i)$ should also be affected by the number of reviews $|R_{a,j}|$ the author has contributed for the same product:

$$NR(a(r_i)) = |R_{a,j}| \tag{2}$$

- **Content Similarity (CS)**

Spammers often reproduce the same review text as authoring original content would prove time consuming. Therefore, we can detect spammers by considering the overall content similarity of their reviews. In accordance with the existing literature [5, 17], we use the cosine similarity for this purpose.

The content similarity score [0, 1] of a reviewer $a(r_i)$, attributed to review r_i, is the average of the similarities of each review $r_j \in R_{a,j}$:

$$CS(a(r_i)) = Avg \left(\frac{\sum_{z=1}^{|R_{a,j}|} cosine(r_j, r_z)}{|R_{a,j}|} \right), j \neq z \tag{3}$$

4.2 Burst Pattern Detection

Spammers typically create a large quantity of reviews in a reasonably short time period in order to quickly negate the effects of and dominate honest opinions. Such excessive posting can lead to the appearance of sudden increases in a product's reviewing activity, creating "bursts" or peaks in certain time intervals. Our model incorporates a burst pattern detection technique, which has already been used successfully in the past [9], as a means of narrowing down the most suspicious time intervals and, subsequently, the most potentially harmful reviews. While the authors of [9] only considered these reviews, missing the rest of a product's reviews, we believe that they should not be the sole focus of a detection model as spam could also exist outside of bursts as well. So, we merely subject these reviews, as well as their respective reviewers, to further analysis with 2 additional spam indicators. Thus, our method investigates all reviews of a product for the existence of spam, analyzing more thoroughly those created in bursty time intervals.

The algorithm for burst pattern discovery is presented below.

Algorithm 1 Algorithm to detect bursty time intervals for a product associated with n reviews $R = \{r_1, ..., r_n\}$. Inputs are the corresponding review creation dates $T = \{d_1, ..., d_n\}$ and the time window dt, which divides the product's timeline into intervals $\{I_1, ..., I_k\}$ of duration dt, where I_j is the number of reviews posted during the j-th interval. dt is set to 7 days [9]. Output is whether I_j is bursty.

1: **Input:** $T = \{d_1, ..., d_n\}$, dt

2: **Output:** whether interval I_j is bursty

3: $len = d_n - d_1$ // Measured in days

4: $k = \#Intervals = \frac{len}{dt}$

5: $I = \{I_1, ..., I_k\}$

6: $Avg(I_j) = \frac{n}{k}, \ 1 \leq j \leq k$ // Average number of reviews per interval

7: **for** $j = 1 : k$ **do**

8:     **if** $I_j > Avg(I_j)$ **then**

9:         **if** $j = 1$ & $I_j > I_{j+1}$ **then** $I_j \leftarrow$ Bursty

10:        **else if** $1 < j < k$ & $I_{j-1} < I_j > I_{j+1}$ **then** $I_j \leftarrow$ Bursty

11:        **else if** $j = k$ & $I_j > I_{j-1}$ **then** $I_j \leftarrow$ Bursty

12: **end for**

We then extract the reviews fallen in bursty intervals and apply the 2 following spam indicators to them.

- **Content Similarity in Burst (CSBu)**

A high enough similarity score between a review and other reviews of the same "burst" could indicate that a review is suspiciously resembling other reviews.

We thus calculate the cosine similarity between r_i and all other $I_j - 1$ reviews of the same burst:

$$CSBu(r_i) = \begin{cases} \frac{\sum_{z=1}^{I_j} cosine(r_i, r_z)}{I_j - 1} - 0.5, & \frac{\sum_{z=1}^{I_j} cosine(r_i, r_z)}{I_j - 1} > 0.5 \\ 0, \ otherwise \end{cases} \tag{4}$$

Assuming that a similarity score of 0.5 is considered normal, we have modified the CSBu metric so as to only affect those reviews that display higher similarity than normal to not penalize reviews simply for being posted in a bursty time interval.

- **Bursty Activity (BuA)**

A spammer is expected to create large numbers of reviews in small bursts of activity to quickly manipulate the general opinion. We assume that an honest reviewer would create at most 2 bursty reviews, so the bursty activity score for a reviewer $a(r_i)$, and subsequently for his/her reviews, is measured as:

$$BuA(a(r_i)) = \begin{cases} 1, & bursty\ reviews\ > 2 \\ 0, & otherwise \end{cases} \qquad (5)$$

4.3 Reviewer Reputation

There is ample available information in regards to author past reviewing activity, which could empower our model to better evaluate a reviewer's overall reputation and, ultimately, the trustworthiness of his/her review(s), via a reviewer-level analysis. This leads us to the following definition:

Definition 3 (Author Reputation). *Author reputation refers to a reviewer's general trustworthiness based on their behavior and activity across their past reviews.*

A reviewer $a(r_i)$ is associated with a set of reviews $Hist_{a,j}$, his/her past reviewing history, across a number of distinct products, which our model exploits by considering 3 addition reviewer history-based spam indicators.

- **Extreme Rating (EXR)**

Most spammers resort to extreme ratings (e.g. 1 or 5 in a 5-star scale) in order to rapidly increase or decrease the mean score of a product.

To this end, the amount of extreme ratings on a 5-star scale among all past ratings $RS_{a,j}$ of an author $a(r_i)$ is collected, and divided by the total number of given ratings $|RS_{a,j}|$ leading to the reviewer's ratio [0, 1] of extreme ratings, which ultimately adds to his/her overall reputation score:

$$EXR(a(r_i)) = \frac{|RS_{a,j} \in \{1,5\}|}{|RS_{a,j}|} \qquad (6)$$

- **Number of Reviews per Product (NRP)**

Due to the impact of excessive reviewing, we also consider a reviewer's relevant behavior on past reviewed products. To this end, we measure the average number of reviews a reviewer $a(r_i)$ writes per product by dividing the size of his reviewing history $Hist_{a,j}$ with the number of reviewed products $n_{a,p}$:

$$NRP(a(r_i)) = \frac{|Hist_{a,j}|}{n_{a,p}} \qquad (7)$$

- **Reviewer Burstiness (RBu)**

Spammers tend to create all their reviews in great volume and in a short time window (burst) in order to quickly dominate honest reviews. Examining a time window of $\delta = 30$ days [8], the burstiness score of a reviewer $a(r_i)$ is measured like so:

$$RBu(a(r_i)) = \begin{cases} 0, LR(a(r_i)) - FR(a(r_i)) > \delta \\ 1 - \frac{LR(a(r_i)) - FR(a(r_i))}{\delta}, \text{ otherwise} \end{cases} \quad (8)$$

where $LR(a(r_i))$ indicates creation date of the reviewer's last and more recent review, while $FR(a(r_i))$ represents the creation date of the first written review by this reviewer account.

Taking into consideration the above 3 history-based spam indicators, we propose measuring a reviewer's reputation by adding the accumulated indicator scores. Thus, we introduce the following combined method that models trustworthiness or reputation for a reviewer $a(r_i)$. Each generated score is multiplied by a respective weight according to the desired impact of the indicator on the final score:

$$Rep(a(r_i)) = \frac{1}{2} EXR(a(r_i)) + \frac{1}{2} NRP(a(r_i)) + RBu(a(r_i)) \quad (9)$$

A low score is indicative of good reputation, while a high score is implying suspicious behavior.

4.4 Spam Scoring Function

We now introduce our linear weighted scoring function, which combines the individual scores generated by each previously mentioned indicator and outputs an overall spam score for each review. Thus, the spam score of a review r_i, written by a reviewer $a(r_i)$, is measured by the following method:

$$S(r_i) = RD(r_i) + \frac{1}{3} NR(a(r_i)) + 1.5 CS(a(r_i)) + 2 CSBu(r_i) + BuA(a(r_i)) + Rep(a(r_i)) \quad (10)$$

The weights of our model's indicator scores are empirically selected based on feature significance as well as value range. Content Similarity in Burst (CSBu) has a value of $[0, 0.5]$ so we give it a weight of 2 to increase its impact, while Extreme Rating (EXR) is considered the weakest indicator, since an honest reviewer could also resort to extreme ratings, and is given a smaller weight. The two spam features (NR, NRP) linked to excessive reviewing are given relatively low weights to counterbalance their potentially high values. Finally, we believe that reviewer Content Similarity (CS) provides strong evidence of spam so we increase its weight accordingly.

Finally, a defined threshold separates the fake reviews from the genuine reviews. After examining the expected score values for honest reviews, as well as for spam reviews, we set the threshold to 3. Thus, reviews with spam scores exceeding the threshold are marked as fake, while reviews with spam scores lower than the threshold are considered genuine.

5 Experimental Analysis

We will now evaluate the effectiveness of the proposed methodology. We conduct experiments on a dataset of real-world reviews and report our findings.

5.1 Dataset

We procured the Amazon review dataset, crawled by [4], to conduct our experiments. The initial dataset is comprised of 5.838.041 reviews of 1.230.915 products created by 2.146.057 reviewers. To facilitate experiments, we sample this dataset to acquire a smaller and easier to evaluate dataset. We exclude from the sampling process those products with less than 5 reviews as lacking attention from users. Our final dataset is comprised of 244.882 reviews, 175.146 reviewers and 13.768 Amazon products.

5.2 Evaluation by Supervised Text Classification

Evaluation has always been a significant barrier in developing highly reliable review spam detection systems. The difficulty stems from the absence of real-world ground truth data of spam reviews necessary for evaluation and model building. A common solution is employing human evaluators and experts to annotate review instances. However, this method includes human subjectivity in the evaluation process.

In this paper, we utilize a different evaluation approach already used successfully in the past [8, 15]. It relies on supervised text classification of the reviews labeled by our method, which are used to represent the positive and negative class, respectively. We iterate over all products in our dataset and score their reviews. Then, all reviews are ranked in descending order, with the top-2000 representing the positive (spam) class and the bottom-2000 representing the negative (honest) class. We choose the top-2000 reviews, as they are heavy spam cases and feature more spam-like text. A Naïve Bayes classifier is then built on these reviews based on UNIGRAM features and the Bag-of-Words model. We perform 10-fold cross validation and report the results. Given the limitation that it is sometimes hard to determine review authenticity by content alone, classification accuracy won't be completely representative of our actual accuracy nor will it allow for a safe comparison to other methods. It will however indicate whether our model is effective and has accurately labeled the evaluation reviews. Accuracy is measured with the established metrics of precision, recall and F-score to ensure consistency with other works in the field.

5.3 Experimentation Results

In order to display the impact of all employed techniques of our model, we first evaluate the effectiveness of the 3 basic review spam indicators. Then, we perform fake review detection with the addition of burst pattern detection. Finally, we include reviewer reputation in the detection process and observe its impact.

For the reviewer reputation scoring phase, we use the entire non-sampled Amazon dataset, which contains ample information regarding reviewer history across a range of distinct products, as our sample dataset may not feature enough information.

Table 1 reports the results of our model's effectiveness after performing 10-fold cross-validation of the classification of our dataset reviews. Surprisingly, the inclusion of burst pattern discovery seems to be lowering accuracy by 1% compared to the results of the basic spam indicators. The difference, however, is small enough to be attributed to the limitations of review text classification so no real conclusion can be made. The addition of reviewer reputation though displayed a considerable improvement in detection accuracy, reporting nearly 75%. Considering again the limitations of our evaluation method, this is a very positive result, which attests to the importance of reviewer reputation in discovering spam reviews. This makes us confident that complementing basic spam indicators and burst pattern discovery with analysis of reviewer past activity allows our model to successfully detect harmful fake reviews.

Table 1. Results of 10-fold cross validation for different combinations of indicators.

Method	Precision	Recall	F-score
Basic	67.6	66.2	65.4
Basic + burst pattern	66.9	65.2	64.3
Basic + burst pattern + reviewer reputation	75.2	75	**74.9**

On top of supervised text classification as an evaluation method, we present a thorough examination of 5 unique review scoring cases. Table 2 displays the respective scores of a sample of 5 reviews of our dataset for all 8 employed spam indicators. The first review has accumulated a very high spam score due to its author's extensive reviewing (NR = 37) on the same product. We also observe that the CS score is quite low, which means that the reviewer created reviews of distinct content to obfuscate their activity. The second, fourth and fifth reviews on the table feature scores close to the defined threshold and are mostly the result of duplicated or near-duplicated content (NR > 1 and CS $\approx$ 1). Three of the reported reviews are also unreasonably similar to other reviews of the same bursty time interval (CSBu > 0), which we discover thanks to our burst pattern technique. Finally, the inclusion of reviewer past history analysis truly shines with the detection of the second sample review, which is a singleton review. Owing mostly to the extremely high NRP score, our method revealed the reviewer's past spamming activity, which in turn weighs down on their recent review.

Table 2. Review scoring examples for 5 spam reviews of the Amazon dataset.

RD	CS	NR	CSBu	BuA	EXR	NRP	RBU	Spam score
0.03	0.3	37	0.0	1	1.0	1.0	0.26	20.69
0.05	1.0	2	0.0	0	0.68	1.01	0.0	3.06
0.15	0.0	1	0.0	0	1.0	57	0.0	29.48
0.07	0.98	3	0.29	1	1.0	1.0	0.0	5.13
0.06	0.99	2	0.49	0	1.0	1.0	0.0	4.22

Overall, our proposed model has displayed positive detection accuracy on the Amazon review dataset. We detected 6.168 fake reviews (2.5% of reviews), that constitute both serious and minor cases of review spamming. In reality, spam percentage is even higher, due to singleton reviews. While we have detected singletons, there are more that can only be captured by specialized techniques [14], which are not our focus. Moreover, we have found that most spam is owed to reviewers reproducing the same (or marginally altered) review twice or thrice, leading to a spam score close to the defined threshold. The most extreme cases of spamming, featuring high spam scores, are those of a reviewer creating multiple reviews for a single product and putting the effort to author dissimilar content in order to avoid detection.

6   Conclusion

In this paper, we propose a new approach for detecting spam reviews. We exploit a variety of different spam indicators on a product level relative to both review and reviewer behavior in order gather and utilize every bit of available information. Moreover, our model features additional analysis features based on burst pattern discovery, which enables the identification of suspicious time intervals and reviews. Finally, we measure reviewer reputation, by examining their history of past reviews and activity, to better determine the authenticity of their more recent reviews. The evaluation of our proposed method was performed on a dataset of Amazon product reviews and the experimentation results showed that our combined method is effective in detecting harmful fake reviews.

As future work, we plan to modify the introduced methodology to better account for singleton spam reviews. While these reviews as individual pieces of content lack the influence on a product's overall rating and popularity, however, in unison they could pose a real threat to unsuspecting review readers and consumers.

Acknowledgments. The authors acknowledge research funding from the European Union's Horizon 2020 research and innovation programme under the Marie Skłodowska-Curie grant agreement No. 691025.

References

1. The Impact of Online Reviews on Customers' Buying Decisions [Infographic]. http://www.business2community.com/infographics/impact-online-reviews-customers-buying-decisions-infographic-01280945#k4Q7iGGLamrml8iA.97
2. Ott, M., Cardie, C., Hancock, J.: Estimating the prevalence of deception in online review communities. In: Proceedings of the 21st International Conference on World Wide Web, pp. 201–210. ACM (2012)
3. Wang, Z.: Anonymity, social image, and the competition for volunteers: a case study of the online market for reviews. B.E. J. Econ. Anal. Policy 10(1), 1–33 (2010)
4. Jindal, N., Liu, B.: Opinion spam and analysis. In: Proceedings of the 2008 International Conference on Web Search and Data Mining, pp. 219–230. ACM (2008)
5. Lin, Y., Zhu, T., Wang, X., Zhang, J., Zhou, A.: Towards online anti-opinion spam: spotting fake reviews from the review sequence. In: 2014 IEEE/ACM International Conference on Advances in Social Networks Analysis and Mining (ASONAM), pp. 261–264. IEEE (2014)

6. Ott, M., Choi, Y., Cardie, C., Hancock, J.T.: Finding deceptive opinion spam by any stretch of the imagination. In: Proceedings of the 49th Annual Meeting of the Association for Computational Linguistics: Human Language Technologies, Portland, Oregon, USA, pp. 309–319 (2011)

7. Ott, M., Cardie, C., Hancock, J.T.: Negative deceptive opinion spam. In: Proceedings of the 2013 Conference of the North American Chapter of the Association for Computational Linguistics: Human Language Technologies, Atlanta, Georgia, USA, pp. 309–319 (2013)

8. Mukherjee, A., Kumar, A., Liu, B., Wang, J., Hsu, M., Castellanos, M., Ghosh, R.: Spotting opinion spammers using behavioral footprints. In: Proceedings of the 19th ACM SIGKDD International Conference on Knowledge Discovery and Data Mining, pp. 632–640. ACM (2013)

9. Heydari, A., Tavakoli, M., Salim, N.: Detection of fake opinions using time series. Expert Syst. Appl. **58**, 83–92 (2016)

10. Jindal, N., Liu, B., Lim, E.-P.: Finding unusual review patterns using unexpected rules. In: Proceedings of the 19th ACM International Conference on Information and Knowledge Management, pp. 1549–1552. ACM (2010)

11. Lim, E.-P., Nguyen, V.-A., Jindal, N., Liu, B., Lauw, H.W.: Detecting product review spammers using rating behaviors. In: Proceedings of the 19th ACM International Conference on Information and Knowledge Management, pp. 939–948. ACM (2010)

12. Savage, D., Zhanga, X., Yua, X., Choua, P., Wang, Q.: Detection of opinion spam based on anomalous rating deviation. Expert Syst. Appl. **42**(22), 8650–8657 (2015)

13. Feng, S., Xing, L., Gogar, A., Choi, Y.: Distributional footprints of deceptive product reviews. ICWSM **12**, 98–105 (2012)

14. Xie, S., Wang, G., Lin, S., Yu, P.S.: Review spam detection via temporal pattern discovery. In: Proceedings of the 18th ACM International Conference on Knowledge Discovery and Data Mining, pp. 823–831. ACM (2012)

15. Fei, G., Mukherjee, A., Liu, B., Hsu, M., Castellanos, M., Ghosh, R.: Exploiting burstiness in reviews for review spammer detection. ICWSM **13**, 175–184 (2013)

16. Ye, J., Kumar, S., Akoglu, L.: Temporal opinion spam detection by multivariate indicative signals. In: ICWSM, pp. 743–746 (2016)

17. Lau, R.Y., Liao, S., Kwok, R.C.W., Xu, K., Xia, Y., Li, Y.: Text mining and probabilistic language modeling for online review spam detecting. ACM Trans. Manag. Inf. Syst. **2**(4), 1–30 (2011)

18. Feng, S., Banerjee, R., Choi, Y.: Syntactic stylometry for deception detection. In: Proceedings of the 50th Annual Meeting of the Association for Computational Linguistics: Short Papers-Volume 2, pp. 171–175. Association for Computational Linguistics (2012)

19. Fusilier, D.H., Montes-y-Gómez, M., Rosso, P., Cabrera, R.G.: Detection of opinion spam with character n-grams. In: Gelbukh, A. (ed.) CICLing 2015. LNCS, vol. 9042, pp. 285–294. Springer, Cham (2015). https://doi.org/10.1007/978-3-319-18117-2_21

20. Mukherjee, A., Venkataraman, V., Liu, B., Glance, N.: Fake review detection: classification and analysis of real and pseudo reviews. Technical report UIC-CS-2013–03, University of Illinois at Chicago (2013)

21. Wang, G., Xie, S., Liu, B., Yu, P.S.: Review graph based online store review spammer detection. In: 2011 IEEE 11th International Conference on Data Mining (ICDM), pp. 1242–1247. IEEE (2011)

22. Fayazbakhsh, S., Sinha, J.: Review spam detection: a network-based approach. Final Project Report: CSE 590 (2012)

23. Akoglu, L., Chandy, R., Faloutsos, C.: Opinion fraud detection in online reviews by network effects. ICWSM **13**, 2–11 (2013)

24. Mukherjee, A., Liu, B., Wang, J., Glance, N., Jindal, N.: Detecting group review spam. In: Proceedings of the 20th International Conference Companion on World Wide Web, pp. 93–94. ACM (2011)
25. Mukherjee, A., Liu, B., Glance, N.: Spotting fake reviewer groups in consumer reviews. In: Proceedings of the 21st International Conference on World Wide Web, pp. 191–200. ACM (2012)
26. Li, H., Fei, G., Wang, S., Liu, B., Shao, W., Mukherjee, A., Shao, J.: Bimodal distribution and co-bursting in review spam detection. In: Proceedings of the 26th International Conference on World Wide Web, pp. 1063–1072. International World Wide Web Conferences Steering Committee (2017)

Mining Spatial Gradual Patterns: Application to Measurement of Potentially Avoidable Hospitalizations

Tu Ngo[1,2], Vera Georgescu[2], Anne Laurent[3(✉)], Thérèse Libourel[4], and Grégoire Mercier[2]

[1] Department of Information and Communication Technology, University of Science and Technology of Hanoi, Hanoi, Vietnam
[2] Economic Evaluation Unit, University Hospital of Montpellier, Montpellier, France
[3] LIRMM, University of Montpellier, Montpellier, France
laurent@lirmm.fr
[4] Espace-Dev, University of Montpellier, Montpellier, France

Abstract. Gradual patterns aim at automatically extracting co-variations between variables of data sets in the form of *"the more/the less"* such as *"the more experience, the higher salary"*. This data mining method has been applied more and more in finding knowledge recently. However, gradual patterns are still not applicable on spatial data while such information have strong presence in many application domains. For instance, in our work we consider the issue of *potentially avoidable hospitalizations*. Their determinants have been studied to improve the quality, efficiency, and equity of health care delivery. Although the statistical methods such as regression method can find the associations between the increased potentially avoidable hospitalizations with its determinants such as lower density of ambulatory care nurses, there is still a challenge to identify how the geographical areas follow or not the tendencies. Therefore, in this paper, we propose to extend gradual patterns to the management of spatial data. Our work is twofold. First we propose a methodology for extracting gradual patterns at several hierarchical levels. In addition, we introduce a methodology for visualizing this knowledge. For this purpose, we rely on spatial maps for allowing decision makers to easily notice how the areas follow or not the gradual patterns. Our work is applied to the measure of the potentially avoidable hospitalizations to prove its interest.

Keywords: Data mining · Gradual patterns · Spatial maps
Cartography visualization · Potentially avoidable hospitalizations

1 Introduction

1.1 Problem Statement

It is often estimated that over 90% of the information integrate spatial information. In many cases, this important component has not yet been taken into

© Springer International Publishing AG 2018
A M. Tjoa et al. (Eds.): SOFSEM 2018, LNCS 10706, pp. 596–608, 2018.
https://doi.org/10.1007/978-3-319-73117-9_42

account for specific designs and implementations. However, such spatial information are currently taking more and more importance with the emergence of Internet of Things and popular applications integrating spatial information (e.g., Google maps).

In this context, it is important to analyze the information at several levels of granularity with upscaling and downscaling features. Public policies are especially targeted in such analyses as actions can be taken at different levels of administrative entities (cities, regions, states,...). In our context, we focus on potentially avoidable hospitalizations. We aim at extracting gradual patterns so as to analyze the co-variations of descriptors and highlight some actionable features. Gradual patterns are of the form *the more/less A_1,..., the more/less A_n*. Such co-variations can not easily be aggregated through spatial levels of granularity and some knowledge that could be relevant at some level could be called into question at some other level. Thus, we aim at helping decision makers to navigate through the most relevant features and levels of granularity.

In this paper, we introduce a generic method for extracting and analyzing gradual patterns from spatial data at several levels of granularity. Our method is based on the extraction of gradual patterns. One key point is then to deal with aggregation from one level to the upper level.

This method is applied to a real case for analyzing potentially avoidable hospitalization that are both societal and financial issues in public policies.

1.2   Use Case

The use case we are working on is meant at helping decision makers from the public health system. Typically, in France, the public health decision makers can have an impact on the determinants related to health care such as the density of physicians, nurses, or the density of hospital beds, but they have no influence on socio-economic determinants such as poverty and education. Potentially avoidable hospitalizations (PAH) are hospital episodes that could have been avoided if patients had received timely and effective primary care. Avoiding these admissions by improving access to primary care could result in a substantial decrease in costs and could enhance patients' quality of life [1]. The main objective for avoiding these hospitalizations is to enhance the health care services where and when it is feasible by working on actionable features.

In this work, we consider two levels of granularity: geographic code and department levels where the patients live. This geographic code level corresponds roughly to the postal code level (n = 5,590) while the department level is similar to the county level in the United States (n = 96). It should be noted that French overseas territories were excluded because most data is lacking.

In addition, this research is conducted on the datasets with the age- and sex-standardized rates of PAH. The standardization for the rates of PAH is necessary to allow for an unbiased comparison between spatial elements [5]. The datasets are provided by the Ministry of Health data that is the national hospital discharge database (fr. Programme de Médicalisation des Systèmes d'Information PMSI). It includes data from all French hospitals, whether public or private, and for all payers. Discharge data are obtained at the patients' residence geographic code level. The reliability and validity of the PMSI are high for various acute and chronic conditions, especially since 2007 [6]. This research has been approved by the National Committee on Information Technology and Civil Liberties (Reference number CNIL/DE-2014-134).

The PAH potential determinants including the rates of ambulatory care nurses (per 1,000 people), the rates of general practitioners, the rates of specialist physicians, the annual median patient incomes, percentage of education level beyond high school, the mortality ratios, and the rates of acute care hospital beds had been collected from French Ministry of Health and from the National Institute for Statistics and Economic Studies (INSEE).

This research is the next step of one of the previous finding [1] of a French national project on PAH funded by the French Ministry of Health. That previous research has found the associations between the standardized rates of PAH with higher mortality ratio, lower density of ambulatory care nurses, lower median income, and lower education levels and other effects [1].

Those findings are useful for policy makers. However, that research does not help answer which areas to increase the rate of the nurses, for instance, in order to reduce the numbers of PAH. Hence, another research should be conducted for the answers and it is the main aim of this research.

1.3 Approach Proposal

The approach proposed in this paper is an extension of [4]. It considers the extraction of gradual patterns at several spatial granularity levels that are then compared and plotted on spatial maps. The rest of this paper details this approach. We first detail the methodology proposed, described here as a workflow integrating the use of a spatial database and spatial maps. We also discuss how to deal with the extraction and study of gradual patterns at several granularity levels.

The approach we introduce here is generic. Although it has been tested and assessed on real data from French public health, it can be used on any data containing spatial information and which attribute domains are partially ordered so as to allow gradual patterns to be extracted, as recalled below with the basic concepts associated to gradual patterns.

2 Related Works

2.1 Around Gradual Patterns

Gradual patterns consider tendencies in terms of correlation of the attribute variations [2]. A gradual pattern is in the form of "the more/the less A_1, ..., the more/the less A_n" such as *"the more experience, the higher salary"* or *"the older a subject, the less his memory"*.

A **gradual item** is defined as a pair (i, v) in which i is an attribute of the given dataset and v is variation with $v \in \{\uparrow, \downarrow\}$ in which $\uparrow$ stands for increasing variation and ↓ stands for decreasing variation. A **gradual pattern** is a set of gradual items denoted by $\{(i_1, v_1), ..., (i_n, v_n)\}$.

For example, given that we have a dataset with three attributes: A, B, and C as shown in Table 1, (A, ↓) is a gradual item and {(A, ↓), (C, ↑)} is a gradual pattern.

Table 1. An example dataset

Objects	A	B	C
Obj 1	4	6	12
Obj 2	1	9	13
Obj 3	2	10	10
Obj 4	5	8	11
Obj 5	3	7	14

Support of Gradual Patterns. The support value of a gradual pattern indicates to which extent it is true in a given dataset. There are several ways to compute such a value [2,3]. In this paper, we consider the approach based on precedence graphs.

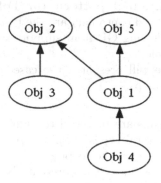

Fig. 1. Precedence graph for the gradual pattern {(A, ↓), (C, ↑)} with the example dataset.

A precedence graph is considered for one given gradual pattern and represents the partial order of the objects from the database through paths. For instance, when considering the data from Table 1 and the gradual pattern {(A,↓), (C,↑)}, then Obj 3 ≺ Obj 2 as 2 > 1 and 10 < 13.

The **support value of a gradual pattern** is given by the maximum length of all paths from the precedence graph over the total number of objects.

Returning back to the example precedence graph (Fig. 1), the value of *maxLength* is 3 and there are 5 objects. Hence, we have:

Support({(A, ↓), (C, ↑)})= $\frac{3}{5}$ = 0.6

A gradual pattern is said to be frequent if its support is higher than a given support threshold.

Gradual Patterns and Spatial Information. Gradual patterns have been applied in various application domains, as biology, psychology, etc. They have also been studied in the framework of spatial information [4] which proposes a method to visualize on spatial maps the information about to which extent a geographical object (e.g., a city) participates in each gradual pattern. On the other hand, each gradual pattern can be represented by a precedence graph that indicates which paths a spatial object belongs to. For example, on the precedence graph (Fig. 1), [Obj 2] are on two paths: The first one is [Obj 4] → [Obj 1] → [Obj 2] and the other one is [Obj 3] → [Obj 2]. The **lengths** of these paths are 3 and 2 respectively.

Definition. The **item support value of an object** is the **max length** of all the paths the object is on.

Back to the example above, the item support value of [Obj 2] is 3 because the lengths of all the paths [Obj 2] is on are {3, 2} as mentioned above.

On the other side, since our approach is applied on several hierarchical levels of the spatial objects, there are insider-level objects and container-level objects (in our case, they are geographic codes and department codes respectively).

Definition. The **follow-gradual pattern (or Follow-GP) insiders** of a container-level object (denoted container) are the insider-level objects (denoted insiders) in the container having GP item support values that are not smaller than a user-defined threshold.

Later in this paper, we will present a use case of this definition when we discuss about aggregation maps.

Spatial Maps. Spatial maps are powerful to highlight information related to locations [10]. There are several types of spatial maps such as choropleth and symbol maps [10,13]. However, in the scope of this paper, introduce choropleth maps. Choropleth maps use colors to represent the data associated with an area by filling the shape of that area with different colors. The data could be categorical or numerical. With categorical data, choropleth maps (categorized maps in QGIS) use a different color for each category. When there are only two categories, these maps can be called binary maps as the two categories could be converted into binary values (0 and 1). With numerical data, choropleth maps (graduated maps in QGIS) use color progression for the different ranges of data with the principle that the darker colors the higher values of data. In this study, we use these choropleth maps (with QGIS) for the knowledge visualization.

2.2 Multiple-Level Analysis of Spatial Information

Statistics. Statistical methods have been developed and applied widely in data analysis in many domains such as health sciences [11,12]. In our previous work

[1], a multilevel mixed model (regression model with two hierarchical levels) was used to assess disparities in PAH in France in 2012 and analyze their determinants. The result of the research has indicated that the increased PAH were associated with higher mortality, lower density of acute care beds and ambulatory care nurses, lower median income, and lower education levels. It also suggests that primary care organizations play a role in geographic disparities in PAH [1]. However, this statistical method did not take into account the spatial information.

SOLAP. While On-Line Analytical Processing (OLAP) technologies allow fast, easy, and interactive exploration and analysis of data without any expert assistance [7,8], they are not optimized to spatial data. On the other hand, Geographic Information Systems (GIS) are powerful tools for detailed spatial data analysis, but they are not meant to support analytical needs which mostly require summarized information, aggregated data, trends analysis, spatio-temporal comparisons, interactive exploration of data, geographic knowledge discovery in large amounts of data, etc. [9]. The solution of combining the strengths of GIS and the strengths of OLAP tools gives birth to Spatial OLAP (SOLAP) technologies [8]. Like OLAP, these decision making technologies allow easier and faster navigation of geo-spatial databases relying on several levels of information granularity, cross-tabulated data, explicit spacetime integration and more tightly integrated modes of visualization [7]. As SOLAP technologies are very promising, they have been applied in many domains such as surveillance of climate-related health vulnerabilities [9] or public debate [7]. Related to our work, SOLAP technologies could be an interesting extension to our project.

3 Extracting Spatial Gradual Patterns

As mentioned in the Introduction section, our goal is to extract associations between potential determinants and spatial objects and to visualize the results with spatial maps to help decision makers to navigate through hierarchical levels.

Considering our use case, we aim in particular at retrieving the potential determinants impacting the rates of PAH by extracting gradual patterns from different levels of spatial information (geographic codes and department codes). The patterns are then plotted on spatial maps as a reference for the decision makers. In this paper, we present our approach to achieve that goal.

3.1 Process Flow

Our implementation approach includes several steps that are described in the process flow detailed below.

Step 1: Find gradual patterns at several granularity levels. At this first step of the process the gradual patterns are extracted at all granularity levels (geographic code and department levels in our use case). Given a support threshold, the output of this step is a list of frequent gradual patterns for every level with their support values.

Step 2: Select gradual patterns for mining. At this step, experts help select some gradual patterns from the output of the first step. A gradual pattern is selected based on both its relevance and the inclusion of actionable variables and its high gradual pattern support value.

Step 3: For every selected gradual pattern, find item support values of spatial objects. At this third step, for every selected gradual pattern, the item support value is computed of every element from every granularity level (e.g., every geographic code and every department code).

Step 4: Find number of follow-GP insiders for every container-level element. This step is only processed at the insider-level. In this step, for every selected gradual pattern, a threshold is defined for the item support values. In addition, a join table contains an insider (e.g., geographic code) is in which container (e.g., department). The output of this step is a dataset with the number of follow-GP insiders for every container. This output is used to update the shape file[1] at the container-level.

Step 5: Update findings into the shape files at all levels. At this step, all the findings found on the previous step for all granularity levels will be updated into the corresponding shape files (geographic codes and departments for our use case). The findings include the item support values of the spatial objects and number of follow-GP insiders for container-level objects.

Step 6: Visualize the findings with the shape files by GIS software. In this step, any GIS software such as QGIS can be used to visualize the findings on spatial maps with the shape files.

3.2 Use Case

As mentioned in the Introduction section, we have applied this approach to our real datasets that have two hierarchical levels: geographic codes (n = 5,590) and department codes (n = 96). In this section, we present the obtained results. For this purpose, an R package has been developed.

At the geographic code level, the following PAH potential determinants are available:

– Rates of general practitioners per 1,000 people (denoted as *Generalists*)
– Annual median incomes (denoted as *Median income*)
– Percentage of education level beyond high school (denoted as *Education*)
– Rates of ambulatory care nurses per 1,000 people (denoted as *Nurses*)
– The rates of ambulatory care specialists per 1,000 people is also available, but there are many geographic codes in which there are no specialists, hence we did not include it when we search for the gradual patterns.

---

[1] Popular geo-spatial vector data format for geographic information system (GIS) software.

At department code level, besides the potential determinants we have at geographic code level, we also have the data of the followings:

- Standard mortality ratio (denoted as *Mortality ratio*)
- Number of acute care hospital beds per 1,000 people (denoted as *Beds*)
- Percentage of CMU-c recipients[2] (denoted as *CMUc recipients*)

Select Gradual Patterns for Mining. The **Find Gradual Patterns** step has generated the list of gradual patterns with their support values. From that list, the experts have selected the following gradual patterns for mining based on their high support values and their relevance to the purpose of the project.

At the geographic code level:

- {(Median income, ↓), (PAH, ↑)} (denoted as *INC* in Figs. 7 and 8)
- {(Education, ↓), (PAH,↑)} (denoted as *EDU* in Figs. 7 and 8)
- {(Nurses, ↓), (PAH, ↑)} (denoted as *NUR* in Figs. 7 and 8).

At the department level:

- {(Nurses, ↓), (PAH, ↑)}
- {(Mortality ratio, ↑), (PAH, ↑)}
- {(Generalists, ↓), (PAH, ↑)}
- {(Specialists, ↓), (PAH, ↑)}
- {(Education, ↓), (PAH, ↑)}.

Find Item Support Values. In this step, at each hierarchical level, for every selected gradual pattern, we need to find the item support value of every spatial element. For the purpose of demonstration, in this paper, we only present the item support values of the gradual pattern {(Nurses, ↓), (PAH, ↑)}. For the purpose of visualization, we divided these values into 5 groups for each level, at both the geographic code (Fig. 2) and department code (Fig. 3) levels.

4 Dealing with Spatial Maps and Hierarchies

4.1 Navigating Through Hierarchical Levels

In this section, we present how hierarchies can be dealt with in the context of spatial data and gradual patterns. In our approach, we take advantages of the current GIS software (QGIS in our case) to navigate through hierarchical levels. In particular, we use choropleth maps to plot the gradual patterns at each level as layers (as in QGIS). The navigation bar of the GIS software allows us to easily switch among the maps (rolling up or down between the hierarchical levels). In addition, We can pre-compute the aggregation values for the higher level

---

[2] In France, CMU-c recipients are people who are given special rights for a free complementary health care complementary insurance.

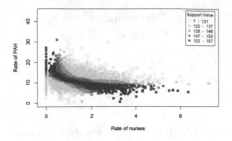

Fig. 2. Item support values of {(Nurses, ↓), (PAH, ↑)} at geographic code level

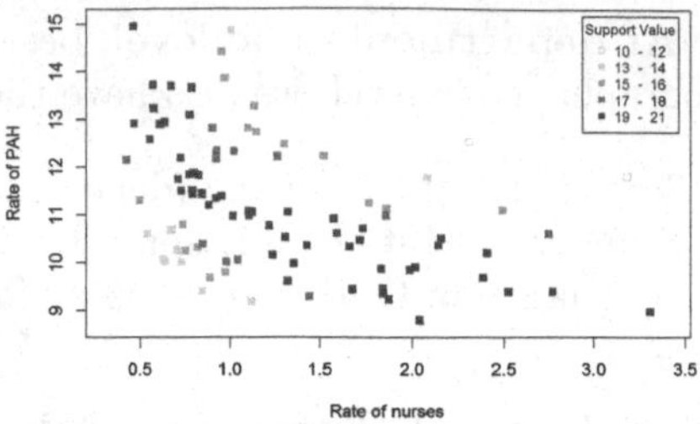

Fig. 3. Item support values of {(Nurses, ↓), (PAH, ↑)} at department code level

(department in our case) from the lower level one (geographic codes in our case). The aggregation values are computed based on the number of follow-GP insiders (step 4 in the process flow). The aggregation values show how insider-level elements of a container-level object participate in a selected gradual pattern. Because the gradual patterns are computed independently at each spatial level, the aggregation values work like the connecting values between the two hierarchical levels. Therefore, by visualizing these values, we would find the valuable information in analysis of hierarchical spatial data.

4.2 Use Case

In our work, we implemented two aggregation values. The first one is to show percentage of geographic codes inside a department following a selected gradual pattern. The second one is to display the best gradual patterns in each department. The best gradual pattern is simply defined is the gradual pattern whose number of follow-GP is the biggest compared with the other gradual patterns.

As we have mentioned, for every selected gradual pattern, we need to find the number of follow-GP geographic codes for every department. In order to do that, thresholds are needed. In our case, the experts have selected the following thresholds (Table 2).

Table 2. Thresholds for the numbers of follow-GP insiders

#	Gradual pattern	Threshold
1	{(Median income, ↓), (PAH, ↑)}	165
2	{(Education, ↓), (PAH, ↑)}	161
3	{(Nurses, ↓), (PAH, ↑)}	153

After setting the threshold for each gradual pattern, the number of follow-GP geographic codes of every department can be obtained as shown in the same template (Table 3).

Table 3. Number of follow-GP geographic codes of department with gradual pattern {(Nurses, ↓), (PAH, ↑)}

#	Department code	Number of follow-GP
1	01	6
2	13	25
3	02	10
...	...	...

4.3 Finding Visualization on Spatial Maps

As mentioned in the process flow, in order to visualize the findings above, we need to import them into the corresponding shape files at the hierarchical levels. This step can be conducted by SQL commands on database management system (DBMS) with spatial extension (postgresql and postgis in our case).

Graduated Maps for Item Support Values. These maps (Figs. 4 and 5) facilitate the decision makers to find out how an area (geographic code and department) follows a selected gradual pattern through its item support value, the higher item support value the better it follows the gradual pattern.

 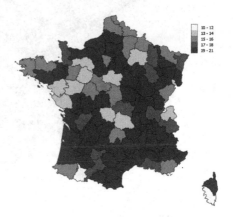

Fig. 4. Graduated map for item support values of {(Nurses, ↓), (PAH, ↑)} at geographic code level

Fig. 5. Graduated map for item support values of {(Nurses, ↓), (PAH, ↑)} at department code level

Aggregation Maps at Container-Level from the Insider-Level. In these maps, we visualize the aggregation values on spatial maps. In our case, we implemented two types of the aggregation maps:

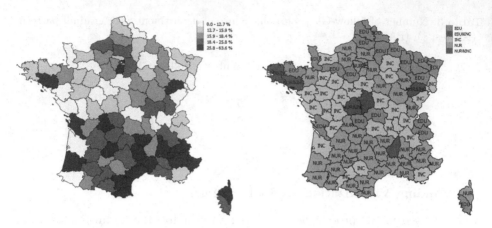

Fig. 6. Percentage of geographic codes inside department codes following $\{(\text{Nurses}, \downarrow), (\text{PAH}, \uparrow)\}$

Fig. 7. Best gradual patterns at each department code

Fig. 8. Multiple-gradual-pattern map at geographic code level

The first type is to display the *percentage of geographic codes inside department codes following a selected gradual patterns* (Fig. 6).

The second aggregation map is the *best gradual pattern map* (Fig. 7). For example, on the map above (Fig. 7), EDU & INC indicates that the departments have the have the same numbers of follow-GP geographic codes for $\{(\text{Education}, \downarrow), (\text{PAH}, \uparrow)\}$ and $\{(\text{Median income}, \downarrow), (\text{PAH}, \uparrow)\}$.

Multiple-Gradual-Pattern Maps. This type of spatial maps (Fig. 8) is to display multiple gradual patterns on a same map. This type of maps could be useful for the decision makers as they can analyze the association between many different determinants on the spatial objects. In particular, in our case, the decision makers want to see which gradual patterns the geographic codes follow.

5   Conclusions

In this paper, we have presented an approach of using gradual pattern method to not only find the correlation of the attribute variations as the regression method does but also to mine geographical data and to identify how an object participates in the associations between attribute variations through the gradual pattern item support values of spatial elements. The visualization of the spatial areas is crucial.

In our work, we have applied our method to study which areas participate in the association between primary care and PAH. This work is of high interest to national- and regional-level health authorities. Indeed, the latter might focus their efforts and investments on these areas in order to maximize the efficiency at the health system level.

This paper describes the method of using spatial maps with shape files and GIS software as tools for the decision making people. In particular, this paper gives some ideas of visualizing the gradual pattern support values of the geographic codes and the departments the on the spatial maps. These maps might be the useful references for decision makers at the French Ministry of Health when they want to reduce the numbers of PAH in France.

Further work includes the integration of these proposals in the context of Spatial OLAP systems in order to provide end-users with integrated fluid solutions for navigating through the spatial data and hierarchies with such complex measures (gradual patterns).

Acknowledgements. We would like to thank University of Science and Technology of Hanoi (USTH) and the DIM department from the CHU of Montpellier for funding this work.

References

1. Mercier, G., Georgescu, V., Bousquet, J.: Geographic variation in potentially avoidable hospitalizations in France. Health Aff. **34**, 836–843 (2015)
2. Laurent, A., Lesot, M.-J., Rifqi, M.: GRAANK: exploiting rank correlations for extracting gradual itemsets. In: Andreasen, T., Yager, R.R., Bulskov, H., Christiansen, H., Larsen, H.L. (eds.) FQAS 2009. LNCS (LNAI), vol. 5822, pp. 382–393. Springer, Heidelberg (2009). https://doi.org/10.1007/978-3-642-04957-6_33
3. Di-Jorio, L., Laurent, A., Teisseire, M.: Mining frequent gradual itemsets from large databases. In: Adams, N.M., Robardet, C., Siebes, A., Boulicaut, J.-F. (eds.) IDA 2009. LNCS, vol. 5772, pp. 297–308. Springer, Heidelberg (2009). https://doi.org/10.1007/978-3-642-03915-7_26

4. Aryadinata, Y.S., Lin, Y., Barcellos, C., Laurent, A., Libourel, T.: Mining epidemiological dengue fever data from Brazil: a gradual pattern based geographical information system. In: Laurent, A., Strauss, O., Bouchon-Meunier, B., Yager, R.R. (eds.) IPMU 2014. CCIS, vol. 443, pp. 414–423. Springer, Cham (2014). https://doi.org/10.1007/978-3-319-08855-6_42

5. Nelson, G.S.: Reporting healthcare data: understanding rates and adjustments. In: PharmaSUG 2014 Conference Proceedings, San Diego, United States (2014)

6. Goldberg, M., Coeuret-Pellicer, M., Ribet, C., Zins, M.: Epidemiological studies based on medical and administrative databases : a potential strength in France. Med. Sci. **28**(4), 430–434 (2012)

7. McHugh, R., Roche, S., Bédard, Y.: Towards a SOLAP-based public participation GIS. J. Environ. Manage. **90**(6), 2041–2054 (2008)

8. Rivest, S., Bédard, Y., Proulx, M.-J., Nadeau, M., Hubert, F., Pastor, J.: SOLAP technology: merging business intelligence with geospatial technology for interactive spatio-temporal exploration and analysis of data. J. Int. Soc. Photogrammetry Remote Sens. (ISPRS) **60**(1), 17–33 (2005)

9. Bernier, E., Gosselin, P., Badard, T., Bédard, Y.: Easier surveillance of climate-related health vulnerabilities through a Web-based spatial OLAP application. Int. J. Health Geographics. **8**(18) (2009)

10. Magnuson, L.: Data Visualization: A Guide to Visual Storytelling for Libraries. Rowman and Littlefield publishers, Maryland (2016)

11. Auget, J.-L., Balakrishnan, N., Mesbah, M., Molenberghs, G.: Advances in statistical methods for the health sciences: applications to cancer and AIDS studies, genome sequence analysis, and survival analysis. Statistics for Industry and Technology. Birkhuser, Basel (2007). https://doi.org/10.1007/978-0-8176-4542-7

12. Ott, L.R., Longnecker, M.: An Introduction to Statistical Methods and Data Analysis. Duxbury, Australia (2001)

13. Zhang, L., Guo, Q., Jiao, L.: Design and implementation of decision-making support system for thematic map cartography. Int. Arch. Photogrammetry, Remote Sens. Spat. Inf. Sci. **37** (2008)

Text Searching Algorithms

New Variants of Pattern Matching
with Constants and Variables

Yuki Igarashi$^{(\boxtimes)}$, Diptarama, Ryo Yoshinaka, and Ayumi Shinohara

Graduate School of Information Sciences, Tohoku University,
6-6-05 Aramaki Aza Aoba, Aoba-ku, Sendai, Japan
{yuki_igarashi,diptarama}@shino.ecei.tohoku.ac.jp
{ry,ayumi}@ecei.tohoku.ac.jp

Abstract. Given a text and a pattern over two types of symbols called constants and variables, the *parameterized pattern matching problem* is to find all occurrences of substrings of the text that the pattern matches by substituting a variable in the text for each variable in the pattern, where the substitution should be injective. The *function matching problem* is a variant of it that lifts the injection constraint. In this paper, we discuss variants of those problems, where one can substitute a constant or a variable for each variable of the pattern. We give two kinds of algorithms for both problems, a convolution-based method and an extended KMP-based method, and analyze their complexity.

Keywords: Pattern matching · Parameterized pattern matching
Function matching · Parameterized pattern queries

1 Introduction

The *parameterized pattern matching* problem was proposed by Baker [4] about a quarter of a century ago. Problem instances are two strings called a pattern and a text, which are sequences of two types of symbols called constants and variables. The problem is to find all occurrences of substrings of a given text that a given pattern matches by substituting a variable in the text for each variable in the pattern, where the important constraint is that the substitution should be an injective map. She presented an algorithm for this problem that runs in $O(n \log n)$ time using *parameterized suffix trees*, where n is the length of text.

By removing the injective constraint from the parameterized pattern matching problem, Amir *et al.* [1] proposed the *function matching* problem, where the same variable may be substituted for different variables. Yet another but an inessential difference between parameterized pattern matching and function matching is in the alphabets. The function matching problem is defined to be constant-free in the sense that patterns and texts are strings over variables. However, this simplification is inessential, since it is known that the problem with variables and constants is linear-time reducible to the constant-free case [2]. This reduction technique works for the parameterized pattern matching as well. Their

© Springer International Publishing AG 2018
A M. Tjoa et al. (Eds.): SOFSEM 2018, LNCS 10706, pp. 611–623, 2018.
https://doi.org/10.1007/978-3-319-73117-9_43

Table 1. The time complexity of our proposed algorithms

Problem	Convolution-based method	Extended KMP-based method	
		Preprocessing	Query
PVC-matching	$O(|\Sigma_P|n\log m)$	$O(|\Pi_P||\Sigma_P|m^2)$	$O(|\Pi_P|\lceil\frac{m}{w}\rceil n)$
FVC-matching		$O(|\Pi_P|(|\Sigma_P|+|\Pi_P|)m^2)$	$O(|\Pi_P|^2\lceil\frac{m}{w}\rceil n)$

deterministic algorithm solves this problem in $O(|\Pi|n\log m)$ time, where n and m are the lengths of the text and pattern, respectively, and $|\Pi|$ is the number of different symbols in the pattern. After that, Amir and Nor [3] introduced the *generalized function matching* problem, where one can substitute a string of arbitrary length for a variable. In addition, both a pattern and a text may contain "don't care" symbols, which are supposed to match arbitrary strings.

The parameterized pattern matching problem and its extensions have been of great interest not only to the pattern matching community [13] but also to the database community. Du Mouza *et al.* [7] proposed a variant of the function matching problem, where texts should consist solely of constants and a substitution maps variables to constants, which is not necessarily injective. Let us call their problem *function matching with variables-to-constants, FVC-matching* in short.[1] The function matching problem is linear-time reducible to this problem by simply assuming the variables in a text as constants. Therefore, this problem can be seen as a generalization of the function matching problem. Unfortunately, as we will discuss in this paper, their algorithm is in error.

In this paper, we introduce a new variant of the problem by du Mouza *et al.* with the injective constraint, which we call *parameterized pattern matching with variables-to-constants mapping (PVC-matching)*. For each of the FVC-matching and PVC-matching problems, we propose two kinds of algorithms: a *convolution-based method* and an *extended KMP-based method*. The convolution-based methods and extended KMP-based methods are inspired by the algorithm of Amir *et al.* [1] for the function matching problem and the one by du Mouza *et al.* [7] for the FVC-matching problem, respectively. As a result, we fix the flaw of the algorithm by du Mouza *et al.* The convolution-based methods for both problems run in $O(|\Sigma_P|n\log m)$ time, where Σ_P is the set of constant symbols that occur in the pattern P. Our KMP-based methods solve the PVC-matching and FVC-matching problems with $O(|\Sigma_P||\Pi_P|m^2)$ and $O(|\Pi_P|(|\Sigma_P|+|\Pi_P|)m^2)$ preprocessing time and $O(|\Pi_P|\lceil\frac{m}{w}\rceil n)$ and $O(|\Pi_P|^2\lceil\frac{m}{w}\rceil n)$ query time, respectively, where Π is the set of variables and w is the word size of a machine (Table 1). The convolution-based methods and KMP-based methods work more efficiently than the trivial $O(mn)$ algorithm if the pattern contains few different constants and few different variables, respectively.

---

[1] They called the problem *parameterized pattern queries*. However, to avoid misunderstanding the problem to have the injective constraint, we refrain from using the original name in this paper.

A full version of this paper [10] includes pseudo codes and experimental results for these algorithms.[2]

2   Preliminaries

For any set Z, the cardinality of Z is denoted by $|Z|$. Let Σ be an alphabet. We denote by Σ^* the set of strings over Σ. The empty string is denoted by ϵ. The concatenation of two strings $X, Y \in \Sigma^*$ is denoted by XY. For a string X, the length of $X = X[1]X[2] \cdots X[n]$ is denoted by $|X| = n$. The substring of X beginning at i and ending at j is denoted by $X[i : j] = X[i]X[i + 1] \cdots X[j - 1]X[j]$. Any substrings of the form $X[1 : j]$ and $X[i : n]$ are called a *prefix* and a *suffix* of X. For any number k, we define $X[k : k-1] = \epsilon$. The set of symbols from a subset Δ of Σ occurring in X is denoted by $\Delta_X = \{ X[i] \in \Delta \mid 1 \leq i \leq n \}$.

This paper is concerned with matching problems, where strings consist of two kinds of symbols, called *constants* and *variables*. Throughout this paper, the sets of constants and variables are denoted by Σ and Π, respectively. Variables are supposed to be replaced by another symbol, while constants are not.

Definition 1. *For a function* $\pi : \Pi \to (\Sigma \cup \Pi)$, *we extend it to* $\hat{\pi} : (\Pi \cup \Sigma)^* \to (\Pi \cup \Sigma)^*$ *by*

$$\hat{\pi}(X) = \hat{\pi}(X[1])\hat{\pi}(X[2]) \cdots \hat{\pi}(X[n]), \text{ where } \hat{\pi}(X[i]) = \begin{cases} \pi(X[i]) & (X[i] \in \Pi) \\ X[i] & (\text{otherwise}) \end{cases}$$

Parameterized match [4] and function match [1][3] are defined as follows.

Definition 2. *Let* P *and* Q *be strings over* $\Sigma \cup \Pi$ *of the same length. String* P *is said to* parameterized match *(resp.* function match*) string* Q *if there exists an injection (resp. function)* $\pi : \Pi \to \Pi$, *such that* $\hat{\pi}(P) = Q$.

The parameterized pattern matching problem (resp. function matching problem) is to find all occurrences of substrings of a given text that a given pattern parameterized matches (resp. function matches).

The problems we discuss in this paper allow variables to be mapped to constants and variables.

Definition 3. *Let* P *and* Q *be strings over* $\Sigma \cup \Pi$ *of the same length. String* P *is said to* parameterized match with variables-to-constants mapping *(resp.* function match with variables-to-constants mapping*), shortly* PVC-match *(resp.* FVC-match*), string* Q *if there exists an injection (resp. function)* $\pi : \Pi \to (\Sigma \cup \Pi)$, *such that* $\hat{\pi}(P) = Q$.

---

[2] Source codes are available at https://github.com/igarashi/matchingwithvcmap.
[3] Amir *et al.* [1] defined the problem so that strings are over a single type of symbols, which can be seen as variables. This restriction is inessential [2].

Problem 1. Let P and T be strings over $\Sigma \cup \Pi$ of length m and n, respectively. The *parameterized pattern matching problem with variables-to-constants mapping* (resp. *function matching problem with variables-to-constants mapping*), shortly *PVC-matching* (resp. *FVC-matching*) asks for all the indices i where pattern P *PVC-matches* (resp. *FVC-matches*) substring $T[i : i + m - 1]$ of text T.

Table 2 summarizes those four problems.

Table 2. Definition of problems

Problems	Admissible mappings	
	Type	Injection constraint
PVC-matching	$\Pi \to (\Pi \cup \Sigma)$	Yes
FVC-matching[7]		No
Parameterized matching [4]	$\Pi \to \Pi$	Yes
Function matching [1]		No

We can assume without loss of generality that the text T solely consists of constants. This restriction is inessential since one can regard variables occurring in T as constants. Under this assumption, the FVC-matching problem is exactly *parameterized pattern queries* [7].

Example 1. Let $\Sigma = \{a, b\}$ and $\Pi = \{A, B\}$. Consider pattern $P = \text{ABAb}$ and text $T = \text{ababbbb}$. Then, the answer of PVC-matching problem is $\{1, 2\}$, since P PVC-matches $T[1 : 4] = \text{abab}$, $T[2 : 5] = \text{babb}$. On the other hand, the answer of FVC-matching problem is $\{1, 2, 4\}$ since P FVC-matches $T[1 : 4] = \text{abab}$, $T[2 : 5] = \text{babb}$, $T[4 : 7] = \text{bbbb}$. Note that we have $\hat{\pi}(P) = T[4 : 7]$ for π with $\pi(A) = \pi(B) = b$, which is not injective.

Throughout this paper, we arbitrarily fix a pattern $P \in (\Sigma \cup \Pi)^*$ of length m and a text $T \in \Sigma^*$ of length n.

3   Convolution-Based Methods

In this section, we show that the FVC-matching problem can be solved in $O(|\Sigma_P| n \log m)$ time by reducing the problem to the function matching problem and the wildcard matching problem, for which several efficient algorithms are known. The PVC-matching problem can also be solved using the same reduction technique with a slight modification.

For strings P of length m over $\Sigma \cup \Pi$ and T of length n over Σ, we define $\Pi' = \Pi_P \cup \Sigma_T$. Let $P_* \in (\Sigma \cup \{*\})^*$ be a string obtained from P by replacing all variable symbols in Π with *don't care symbol* $*$. Let $P_\Pi \in \Pi'^*$ be a string obtained from P by removing all constant symbols in Σ. Moreover, for $1 \leq i < n - m$, let T_i' be a string defined by $T_i' = v(1)v(2) \cdots v(m)$, where $v(j) = T[i + j - 1]$ if $P[j] \in \Pi$ and $v(j) = \epsilon$ otherwise. Note that both the lengths of T_i' and P_Π are equal to the total number of variable occurrences in P.

Example 2. For $T = \mathsf{aabcbc}$ and $P = \mathsf{AaBBb}$ over $\Pi = \{\mathsf{A}, \mathsf{B}\}$ and $\Sigma = \{\mathsf{a}, \mathsf{b}, \mathsf{c}\}$, we have $P_* = *\mathsf{a}**\mathsf{b}$, $P_\Pi = \mathsf{ABB}$, $T_1' = \mathsf{abc}$, and $T_2' = \mathsf{acb}$.

For both FVC-matching and PVC-matching problems, the following lemma is useful to develop algorithms to solve them.

Lemma 1. *P FVC-matches (resp. PVC-matches) $T[i : i+m-1]$ if and only if*

1. *P_* wildcard matches $T[i : i + m - 1]$, and*
2. *P_Π function matches (resp. parameterized matches) T_i'.*

Lemma 1 suggests that the FVC-problem would be reducible to the combination of wildcard matching problem and function matching problem.

The wildcard matching problem (a.k.a. Pattern matching with don't care symbol) [8] is one of the fundamental problems in pattern matching. There are many algorithms for solving the wildcard matching problem [5,8,11]. For example, Cole and Hariharan [5] gave an algorithm which runs $O(n \log m)$ time by using convolution.

However, Lemma 1 does *not* imply the existence of a *single* string T' such that P FVC-matches $T[i : i+m-1]$ if and only if P_* wildcard matches $T[i : i+m-1]$ and P_Π function matches $T'[i : i + m - 1]$. A Naive application of Lemma 1 to compute T_i' explicitly for each i requires $O(mn)$ time in total.

We will present an algorithm to check whether P_Π function matches (parameterized matches) T_i' for all $1 \le i < n - m$ in $O(\log |\Sigma| n \log m)$ time in total. Without loss of generality, we assume that Σ and Π are disjoint finite sets of positive integers in this section, and for integers a and b, the notation $a \cdot b$ represents the multiplication of a and b but not the concatenation.

Definition 4. *For integer arrays A of length n and B of length m, we define an integer array R by $R[j] = \sum_{i=1}^{m} A[i + j - 1] \cdot B[i]$ for $1 \le j \le n - m + 1$. We denote R as $A \otimes B$.*

In a computational model with word size $O(\log m)$, the discrete convolution can be computed in time $O(n \log n)$ by using the Fast Fourier Transform (FFT) [6]. The array R defined in Definition 4 can also be computed in the same time complexity by just reversing array B.

Amir *et al.* [1] proved the next lemma for function matching.

Lemma 2 [1]. *For any natural numbers $a_1, \cdots, a_k$, the equation $k \cdot \sum_{i=1}^{k} (a_i)^2 = (\sum_{i=1}^{k} a_i)^2$ holds if and only if $a_i = a_j$ for any $1 \le i, j \le k$.*

Let $\boldsymbol{T}$ be the string of length n such that $\boldsymbol{T}[i] = (T[i])^2$ for every $1 \le i \le n$. For a variable $x \in \Pi_P$, let c_x denote the number of occurrences of x in P, and let P_x be the string of length m such that $P_x[j] = 1$ if $P[j] = x$ and $P_x[j] = 0$ otherwise, for every $1 \le j \le m$. By Lemma 2, we can prove the following lemma.

Lemma 3. *All the symbols (values) in T_i' at every position j satisfying $P_\Pi[j] = x$ are the same, if and only if the equation $c_x \cdot ((\boldsymbol{T} \otimes P_x)[i]) = ((T \otimes P_x)[i])^2$ holds.*

Thus, P_Π function matches T_i' if and only if the equation in Lemma 3 holds for all $x \in \Pi_P$. Both the convolutions $\boldsymbol{T} \otimes P_x$ and $T \otimes P_x$ can be calculated in $O(n \log m)$ time by simply dividing T into $2 \times \frac{n}{2m}$ overlapping substrings of length $2m$. For parameterized pattern matching problem, we have only to check additionally whether the value $(T \otimes P_x)[i]/c_x$ is unique among all $x \in \Pi_P$.

Theorem 1. *The FVC-matching problem and PVC-matching problem can be solved in $O(|\Sigma_P| \, n \log m)$ time.*

4   KMP-Based Methods

Du Mouza *et al.* [7] proposed a KMP-based algorithm for the FVC-matching problem, which, however, is in error. In Sect. 4.1, we propose a correction of their algorithm, which runs in $O(|\Pi|^2 \lceil \frac{m}{w} \rceil n)$ query time with $O(|\Pi|(|\Sigma_P| + |\Pi|)m^2)$ preprocessing time, where w denotes the word size of a machine. This algorithm will be modified in Sect. 4.2 so that it solves the PVC-matching problem in $O(|\Pi| \lceil \frac{m}{w} \rceil n)$ query time with $O(|\Pi||\Sigma_P|m^2)$ preprocessing time.

The KMP algorithm [12] solves the standard pattern matching problem in $O(n)$ time with $O(m)$ preprocessing time. We say that a string Y is a *border* of X if Y is simultaneously a prefix and a suffix of X. A border Y is *nontrivial* if Y is not X itself. For the preprocessing of the KMP algorithm, we calculate the longest nontrivial border b_k for each prefix $P[1 : k]$ of pattern P, and store them as *border array* $B[k] = |b_k|$ for each $0 \leq k \leq m$. Note that $b_0 = b_1 = \epsilon$. In the matching phase, the KMP algorithm compares symbols $T[i]$ and $P[k]$ from $i = k = 1$. We increment i and k if $T[i] = P[k]$. Otherwise we reset the index for P to be $k' = B[k - 1] + 1$ and resume comparison from $T[i]$ and $P[k']$.

4.1   Extended KMP Algorithm

This subsection discusses an algorithm for the FVC-matching problem. In the matching phase, our extended KMP algorithm compares the pattern and a substring of the text in the same manner as the classical KMP algorithm except that we must maintain a function by which prefixes of the pattern match some substrings of the text. That is, our extended KMP algorithm compares symbols $T[i]$ and $P[k]$ from $i = k = 1$ with the empty function π. If $P[k]$ is not in the domain $\operatorname{dom}(\hat{\pi})$ of $\hat{\pi}$, we expand π by letting $\pi(P[k]) = T[i]$ and increment i and k. If $\hat{\pi}(P[k])$ is defined to be $T[i]$, we increment i and k. Otherwise, we say that *a mismatch occurs at position k with a function π*. Note that the mismatch position refers to that of P rather than T. When we find a mismatch, we must calculate the appropriate position j of P and function π' with which we resume comparison. If instances are variable-free, the position is solely determined by the longest border size of $P[1 : k]$ and we have no function. In the case of FVC-matching, the resuming position depends on the function π in addition to k.

Example 3. Let us consider the pattern $P = \texttt{AABaaCbC}$ where $\varPi = \{\texttt{A}, \texttt{B}, \texttt{C}\}$ and $\varSigma = \{\texttt{a}, \texttt{b}\}$ in Fig. 1. If the concerned substring of the text is $T' = \texttt{bbbaaabb}$, a mismatch occurs at $k = 8$ with a function π such that $\pi(\texttt{A}) = \pi(\texttt{B}) = \texttt{b}$ and $\pi(\texttt{C}) = \texttt{a}$. In this case, we can resume comparison with $P[7]$ and $T'[8]$, since we have $\hat{\pi}'(P[1 : 6]) = T'[2 : 7]$ for π' such that $\pi'(\texttt{A}) = \pi'(\texttt{C}) = \texttt{b}$ and $\pi'(\texttt{B}) = \texttt{a}$. On the other hand, for $T'' = \texttt{bbaaaabb}$, the first mismatch occurs again at $k = 8$ with a function ρ such that $\rho(\texttt{A}) = \texttt{b}$ and $\rho(\texttt{B}) = \rho(\texttt{C}) = \texttt{a}$. In this case, one cannot resume comparison with $P[7]$ and $T''[8]$, since there is no ρ' such that $\hat{\rho}'(P[1 : 6]) = T''[2 : 7]$, since $P[1] = P[2]$ but $T''[2] \neq T''[3]$. We should resume comparison between $P[4]$ and $T''[8]$ with ρ' such that $\rho'(\texttt{A}) = \texttt{a}$ and $\rho'(\texttt{B}) = \texttt{b}$, for which we have $\hat{\rho}'(P[1 : 3]) = T''[5 : 7]$. Note that $\rho'(\texttt{C})$ is undefined.

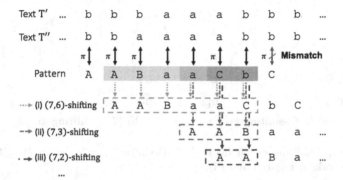

Fig. 1. Examples of possible shifts in the extended KMP algorithm

The goal of the preprocessing phase is to prepare a data structure by which one can efficiently compute the *failure function* in the matching phase:

Input: the position $k + 1$ (where a mismatch occurs) and a function π whose domain is $\varPi_{P[1:k]}$,

Output: the largest position $j + 1 < k + 1$ (at which we will resume comparison) and the function π' with domain $\varPi_{P[1:j]}$ such that $\hat{\pi}'(P[1 : j]) = \hat{\pi}(P[k - j + 1 : k])$.

We call such π a *preceding function*, π' a *succeeding function* and the pair (π, π') a (k, j)-*shifting function pair*. The substrings $P[1 : j]$ and $P[k-j+1 : k]$ may not be a border of $P[1 : k]$ but under preceding and succeeding functions they play the same role as a border plays in the classical KMP algorithm. The succeeding function π' is uniquely determined by a preceding function π and positions k, j. The condition for functions π and π' form a (k, j)-shifting function pair can be expressed using the (k, j)-*shifting graph* (on P), defined as follows.

Definition 5. *Let $\varPi'$ be a copy of $\varPi$ and P' be obtained from P by replacing every variable in $\varPi$ with its copy in $\varPi'$. For two numbers k, j such that $0 \leq j < k \leq m$, the (k, j)-shifting graph $G_{k,j} = (V_{k,j}, E_{k,j})$ is defined by*

$$V_{k,j} = \Sigma_P \cup \Pi_{P[k-j+1:k]} \cup \Pi'_{P'[1:j]},$$

$$E_{k,j} = \{\, (P[k-j+i], P'[i]) \mid 1 \le i \le j < k \text{ and } P[k-j+i] \ne P'[i] \,\}.$$

We say that $G_{k,j}$ is invalid if there are distinct $p, q \in \Sigma_P$ that belong to the same connected component. Otherwise, it is valid.

Note that $G_{k,0} = (\Sigma_P, \emptyset)$ is valid for any k. Figure 2 shows the $(7,6)$-shifting and $(7,3)$-shifting graphs for $P = \mathtt{AABaaCbC}$ in Example 3. Using functions π and π'

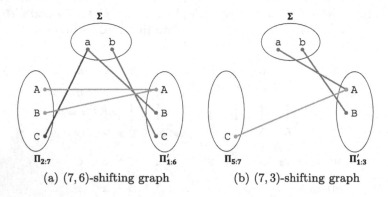

(a) $(7,6)$-shifting graph   (b) $(7,3)$-shifting graph

Fig. 2. The $(7,6)$-shifting graph (a) and $(7,3)$-shifting graph (b) on $P = \mathtt{AABaaCbC}$, which corresponds to Fig. 1(i) and (ii).

whose domains are $\mathrm{dom}(\pi) = \Pi_{P[k-j+1:k]}$ and $\mathrm{dom}(\pi') = \Pi_{P[1:j]}$, respectively, let us label each node $p \in \Sigma$, $x \in \Pi$, $x' \in \Pi'$ of $G_{k,j}$ with $p, \pi(x), \pi'(x)$, respectively. Then (π, π') is a (k,j)-shifting pair if and only if every node in each connected component has the same label. Obviously $G_{k,j}$ is valid if and only if it admits a (k,j)-shifting function pair.

Thus, the resuming position should be $j + 1$ for a mismatch at $k + 1$ with a preceding function π if and only if j is the largest such that $G_{k,j}$ is valid and

(a) if $x \in \Pi$ and $p \in \Sigma$ are connected in $G_{k,j}$, then $\pi(x) = p$,
(b) if $x \in \Pi$ and $y \in \Pi$ are connected in $G_{k,j}$, then $\pi(x) = \pi(y)$.
    In that case, we have $\hat{\pi}'(P[1:j]) = \hat{\pi}(P[k-j+1:k])$ for π' determined by
(c) $\pi'(x) = \hat{\pi}(y)$ if $x' \in \Pi'_{P[1:j]}$ and $y \in \Pi \cup \Sigma$ are connected.

We call the conditions (a) and (b) the (k,j)-preconditions and (c) the (k,j)-postcondition. Note that every element in $\Pi'_{P'[1:j]}$ is connected to some element in $\Pi_{P[k-j+1:k]} \cup \Sigma_P$ in $G_{k,j}$ and thus π' is well-defined.

Remark 1. The algorithms EDGESCONSTRUCTION (preprocessing) and MATCH (matching) by du Mouza *et al.* [7] do not treat the condition induced by two nodes of distance more than 1 correctly. For example, let us consider the pattern $P = \mathtt{AABaaCbC}$ in Example 3. For a text $T = \mathtt{bbaaaabbb}$, the first mismatch occurs at $k = 8$, where $\hat{\rho}(P[1:7]) = \mathtt{bbaaaab}$ for $\rho(\mathtt{A}) = \mathtt{b}$ and $\rho(\mathtt{B}) = \rho(\mathtt{C}) = \mathtt{a}$. To have (ρ, ρ') a $(7,6)$-shifting pair for some ρ', it must hold $\rho(\mathtt{A}) = \rho(\mathtt{B})$. That is, one can resume the comparison at position 7 only when the preceding function assigns the same constant to A and B. The preceding function ρ in this case does not satisfy this constraint. However, their algorithm performs this shift and reports that P matches T at position 2.

To efficiently compute the failure function, our algorithm constructs another data structure instead of shifting graphs. The *shifting condition table* is a collection of functions $A_{k,j} : \Pi_{P[k-j+1:k]} \rightarrow \Pi_{P[k-j+1:k]} \cup \Sigma_P$ and $A'_{k,j} : \Pi'_{P'[1:j]} \rightarrow \Pi_{P[k-j+1:k]} \cup \Sigma_P$ for $1 \leq j < k \leq m$ such that $G_{k,j}$ is valid. The functions $A_{k,j}$ can be used to quickly check the (k,j)-preconditions (a) and (b) and $A'_{k,j}$ is for the (k,j)-postcondition (c). Those functions satisfy the following property: for each connected component $\alpha \subseteq V_{k,j}$, there is a representative $u_\alpha \in \alpha$ such that

- if $\alpha \cap \Sigma \neq \emptyset$, then $u_\alpha \in \Sigma$,
- if $\alpha \cap \Sigma = \emptyset$, then $u_\alpha \in \Pi$,
- for all $x \in \alpha \cap \Pi$, $A_{k,j}(x) = u_\alpha$,
- for all $x' \in \alpha \cap \Pi'$, $A'_{k,j}(x') \in \alpha \cap (\Pi \cup \Sigma)$.

Note that $G_{k-1,j-1}$ is a subgraph of $G_{k,j}$, where the difference is at most two nodes and one edge. Hence, we can compute $A_{k,j}$ and $A'_{k,j}$ from $A_{k-1,j-1}$ and $A'_{k-1,j-1}$ in $O(\log|\Pi|)$ worst-case time and $O(\mathcal{A}(|\Pi|))$ amortized time, where $\mathcal{A}(n)$ is the inverse-Ackermann function, by using Union-Find data structure [14]. Moreover, when computing $A_{k,j}$ and $A'_{k,j}$, we can verify the validity of $G_{k,j}$.

Lemma 4. *The shifting condition table can be calculated in $O(\log|\Pi|m^2)$ time.*

Suppose that we have a mismatch at position $k+1$ with a preceding function π. By using the shifting condition table, a naive algorithm may compute the failure function in $O(k|\Pi|^2)$ time by finding the largest j such that π satisfies the (k,j)-precondition and then compute a function π' satisfying the (k,j)-postcondition with which we resume comparison at $j+1$. The calculation of π' can be done in $O(|\Pi|)$ time just by referring to the array $A'_{k,j}$. We next discuss how to reduce the computational cost for finding j by preparing an elaborate data structure in the preprocessing phase.

Du Mouza et al. [7] introduced a bitmap data structure concerning the precondition (a), which can be constructed using $A_{k,j}$ in the shifting condition table as follows. Here we extend the domain of $A_{k,j}$ to Π by defining $A_{k,j}(x) = x$ for each $x \in \Pi \setminus \Pi_{P[k-j+1:k]}$.

Definition 6 [7]. *For every $0 \leq j < k \leq m$, $x \in \Pi$ and $p \in \Sigma_P$, define*

$$r^k_{x,p}[j] = \begin{cases} 0 & (G_{k,j} \text{ is invalid or } A_{k,j}(x) \in \Sigma \setminus \{p\}) \\ 1 & (otherwise) \end{cases}$$

Lemma 5 [7]. *A preceding function π satisfies the (k,j)-precondition (a) if and only if $\bigwedge_{x \in \Pi} r^k_{x,\pi(x)}[j] = 1$.*

We define a data structure corresponding to the (k,j)-precondition (b) as follows.

Definition 7. *For every $0 \leq j < k \leq m$ and $x, y \in \Pi$, define*

$$s_{x,y}^{k}[j] = \begin{cases} 0 & (G_{k,j} \text{ is invalid or } A_{k,j}(x) = y) \\ 1 & (\text{otherwise}) \end{cases}$$

Lemma 6. *A preceding function π satisfies the (k,j)-precondition (b) if and only if $\bigwedge_{\substack{x,y \in \Pi \\ \pi(x) \neq \pi(y)}} s_{x,y}^{k}[j] = 1$.*

Therefore, we should resume comparison at $j + 1$ for the largest j that satisfies the conditions of Lemmas 5 and 6. To calculate such j quickly, the preprocessing phase computes the following bit sequences. For every $x \in \Pi$, $p \in \Sigma_P$ and $1 \leq k \leq m$, let $r_{x,p}^{k}$ be the concatenation of $r_{x,p}^{k}[j]$ in ascending order of j:

$$r_{x,p}^{k} = r_{x,p}^{k}[0] r_{x,p}^{k}[1] \cdots r_{x,p}^{k}[k-1],$$

and for every $x, y \in \Pi$ and $1 \leq k \leq m$, let

$$s_{x,y}^{k} = s_{x,y}^{k}[0] s_{x,y}^{k}[1] \cdots s_{x,y}^{k}[k-1].$$

Calculating $r_{x,p}^{k}$ and $s_{x,y}^{k}$ for all $x, y \in \Pi$, $p \in \Sigma_P$ and $1 \leq k \leq m$ in the preprocessing phase requires $O(|\Pi|(|\Sigma_P| + |\Pi|)m^2)$ time in total. When a mismatch occurs at $k + 1$ with a preceding function π, we compute

$$J = \bigwedge_{x \in \Pi} r_{x,\pi(x)}^{k} \wedge \bigwedge_{\substack{x,y \in \Pi \\ \pi(x) \neq \pi(y)}} s_{x,y}^{k}.$$

Then the desired j is the right-most position of 1 in J. This operation can be done in $O(\lceil \frac{m}{w} \rceil |\Pi|^2)$ time, where w denotes the word size of a machine. That is, with $O(|\Pi|(|\Sigma_P| + |\Pi|)m^2)$ preprocessing time, the failure function can be computed in $O(|\Pi|^2 \lceil \frac{m}{w} \rceil)$ time. For most applications, we can assume that m is smaller than the word size w, i.e. $\lceil \frac{m}{w} \rceil = 1$.

Theorem 2. *The FVC-matching problem can be solved in $O(|\Pi|^2 \lceil \frac{m}{w} \rceil n)$ time with $O(|\Pi|(|\Sigma_P| + |\Pi|)m^2)$ preprocessing time.*

4.2   Extended KMP Algorithm for PVC-Match

In this subsection, we consider the PVC-matching problem. We redefine the *(mis)match* and *failure function* in the same manner as described in the previous section except that all the functions are restricted to be injective. We define $G_{k,j}$ exactly in the same manner as in the previous subsection. However, the condition represented by that graph should be strengthened in accordance with the injection constraint on matching functions. We say that $G_{k,j}$ is *injectively valid* if for each $\Delta \in \{\Sigma, \Pi, \Pi'\}$, any distinct nodes from Δ are disconnected. Otherwise, it is *injectively invalid*. There is a (k,j)-shifting injection pair if and only if $G_{k,j}$ is injectively valid.

For $P = \texttt{AABaaCbC}$ in Example 3 (see Fig. 2), the $(7,6)$-shifting graph $G_{7,6}$ for $P = \texttt{AABaaCbC}$ is valid but injectively invalid, since $\texttt{A}$ and $\texttt{B}$ are connected. On the other hand, $G_{7,3}$ is injectively valid.

In the PVC-matching, the condition for an injection pair (π, π') to be (k,j)-shifting is described using the graph labeling by (π, π') as follows:

– two nodes are assigned the same label if and only if they are connected.

Under the assumption that $G_{k,j}$ is injectively valid, the (k,j)-precondition on a preceding function π is given as

(a) if $x \in \Pi$ and $p \in \Sigma$ are connected, then $\pi(x) = p$,
(b') if $x \in \Pi$ and $x' \in \Pi'$ are connected and $y' \in \Pi' \setminus \{x'\}$ and $p \in \Sigma$ are connected, then $\pi(x) \neq p$.

Since each connected component of an injectively valid shifting graph $G_{k,j}$ has at most 3 nodes, it is cheap to compute the function $F_{k,j} : V_{k,j} \to 2^{V_{k,j}}$ such that $F_{k,j}(u) = \{v \in V_{k,j} \mid u \text{ and } v \text{ are connected in } G_{k,j}\}$. For technical convenience, we assume $F_{k,j}(u) = \emptyset$ for $u \in \Pi \setminus V_{k,j}$. Using $P[k], P[j]$, and $F_{k-1,j-1}$, one can decide whether $G_{k,j}$ is injectively valid and can compute $F_{k,j}$ (if $G_{k,j}$ is injectively valid) in constant time.

Suppose that we have a preceding function π at position k. By using the function $F_{k,j}$, a naive algorithm can compute the failure function in $O(k|\Pi|)$ time. We define a bitmap $t^k_{x,p}[j]$ to check if π satisfies preconditions (a) and (b').

Definition 8. *For every* $0 \leq j < k \leq m$, $x \in \Pi$ *and* $p \in \Sigma_P$, *define*

$$t^k_{x,p}[j] = \begin{cases} 0 & (G_{k,j} \text{ is injectively invalid or } F_{k,j}(x) \cap \Sigma \not\subseteq \{p\} \\ & \text{or } |(F_{k,j}(x) \cup F_{k,j}(p)) \cap \Pi'| = 2) \\ 1 & (\text{otherwise}) \end{cases}$$

The conditions $F_{k,j}(x) \cap \Sigma \not\subseteq \{p\}$ and $|F_{k,j}(x) \cap F_{k,j}(p) \cap \Pi'| = 2$ in Definition 8 for $p = \pi(x)$ correspond to the (k,j)-preconditions (a) and (b'), respectively.

Lemma 7. *Suppose that* $G_{k,j}$ *is injectively valid. The preceding function* π *satisfies the* (k,j)-*preconditions (a) and (b') if and only if* $\bigwedge_{x \in \Pi} t^k_{x,\pi(x)}[j] = 1$.

Proof. Suppose that π violates the (k,j)-precondition (a). There are $x \in \Pi$ and $q \in \Sigma$ which are connected in $G_{k,j}$ such that $\pi(x) \neq q$. Then $q \in F_{k,j}(x) \cap \Sigma \not\subseteq \{\pi(x)\}$ and $t^k_{x,\pi(x)}[j] = 0$. Thus $\bigwedge_{y \in \Pi} t^k_{y,\pi(y)}[j] = 0$. Suppose that π violates the (k,j)-precondition (b'). There are $x \in \Pi$, $x' \in \Pi'$, and $y' \in \Pi' \setminus \{x'\}$ such that $x' \in F_{k,j}(x)$ and $y' \in F_{k,j}(\pi(x))$. Then $(F_{k,j}(x) \cup F_{k,j}(\pi(x))) \cap \Pi' = \{x', y'\}$ and thus $\bigwedge_{y \in \Pi} t^k_{y,\pi(y)}[j] = t^k_{x,\pi(x)}[j] = 0$.

Suppose that $\bigwedge_{y \in \Pi} t^k_{y,\pi(y)}[j] = 0$. Then there is $x \in \Pi$ for which $t^k_{x,\pi(x)}[j] = 0$, and either $F_{k,j}(x) \cap \Sigma \not\subseteq \{\pi(x)\}$ or $|(F_{k,j}(x) \cup F_{k,j}(\pi(x))) \cap \Pi'| = 2$. In the former case, there is $p \in (F_{k,j}(x) \cap \Sigma) \setminus \{\pi(x)\}$, which means that x and p are connected but $\pi(x) \neq p$. This violates the (k,j)-precondition (a). In the latter case, there are distinct $x', y' \in \Pi'$ such that $x' \in F_{k,j}(x)$ and $y' \in F_{k,j}(\pi(x))$. That is, x and x' are connected and y' and $\pi(x)$ are connected, which violates the (k,j)-precondition (b'). $\qquad\square$

In the preprocessing phase, we calculate

$$t_{x,p}^k = t_{x,p}^k[0] t_{x,p}^k[1] \cdots t_{x,p}^k[k-1]$$

for all $x \in \Pi$, $p \in \Sigma_P$ and $1 \leq k \leq m$, which requires $O(|\Pi||\Sigma_P|m^2)$ time. When a mismatch occurs at $k+1$ with a function π, we compute

$$J = \bigwedge_{x \in \Pi} t_{x, \pi(x)}^k$$

where the desired j is the right-most position of 1 in J. We resume comparison at $j+1$. The calculation of the failure function can be done in $O(|\Pi|\lceil \frac{m}{w} \rceil)$ time, where w denotes the word size of a machine.

Theorem 3. *The PVC-matching problem can be solved in $O(|\Pi|\lceil \frac{m}{w} \rceil n)$ time with $O(|\Pi||\Sigma_P|m^2)$ preprocessing time.*

5   Concluding Remarks

In this paper, we proposed efficient algorithms for the FVC-matching and PVC-matching problems. The FVC-matching problem has been discussed by du Mouza *et al.* [7] as a generalization of the function matching problem, while the PVC-matching problem is newly introduced in this paper, which can be seen as a generalization of the parameterized pattern matching problem. We have fixed a flaw of the algorithm by du Mouza *et al.* for the FVC-matching problem. Moreover, the experimental results [10] show that our algorithms run more effecient than the trivial $O(mn)$ algorithm.

There can be further variants of matching problems. For example, one may think of a pattern with don't care symbols in addition to variables and constants. This is not interesting when don't care symbols appear only in a pattern in function matching, since don't care symbols can be assumed to be distinct variables. However, when imposing the injection condition on a matching function, don't care symbols play a different role from variables. This generalization was tackled in [9]. We can consider an even more general problem by allowing texts to have variables, where two strings P and S are said to match if there is a function π such that $\hat{\pi}(P) = \hat{\pi}(S)$. This is a special case of the *word equation problem*, where a string instead of a symbol can be substituted, and word equations are very difficult to solve in general. Another interesting restriction of word equations may allow to use different substitutions on compared strings, i.e., P and S match if there are functions π and ρ such that $\hat{\pi}(P) = \hat{\rho}(S)$. Those are interesting future work.

Acknowledgements. This work is supported by Tohoku University Division for Interdisciplinary Advance Research and Education, ImPACT Program of Council for Science, Technology and Innovation (Cabinet Office, Government of Japan), and JSPS KAKENHI Grant Number JP15H05706.

References

1. Amir, A., Aumann, Y., Lewenstein, M., Porat, E.: Function matching. SIAM J. Comput. **35**(5), 1007–1022 (2006)
2. Amir, A., Farach, M., Muthukrishnan, S.: Alphabet dependence in parameterized matching. Inf. Process. Lett. **49**(3), 111–115 (1994)
3. Amir, A., Nor, I.: Generalized function matching. J. Discrete Algorithms **5**(3), 514–523 (2007)
4. Baker, B.S.: Parameterized pattern matching: algorithms and applications. J. Comput. Syst. Sci. **52**(1), 28–42 (1996)
5. Cole, R., Hariharan, R.: Verifying candidate matches in sparse and wildcard matching. In: Proceedings of the Thirty-Fourth Annual ACM Symposium on Theory of Computing, pp. 592–601. ACM (2002)
6. Cormen, T.H., Leiserson, C.E., Rivest, R.L., Stein, C., et al.: Introduction to algorithms, vol. 44, pp. 97–138. MIT Press, Cambridge (1990)
7. Du Mouza, C., Rigaux, P., Scholl, M.: Parameterized pattern queries. Data Knowl. Eng. **63**(2), 433–456 (2007)
8. Fischer, M.J., Paterson, M.S.: String-matching and other products. Technical report, DTIC Document (1974)
9. Igarashi, Y.: A study on the parameterized pattern matching problems for real data (in Japanese). Bachelor thesis, Tohoku University (2017)
10. Igarashi, Y., Diptarama, Yoshinaka, R., Shinohara, A.: New variants of pattern matching with constants and variables. CoRR abs/1705.09504 (2017)
11. Iliopoulos, C.S., Rahman, M.S.: Pattern matching algorithms with don't cares. In: Proceedings of the 33rd SOFSEM, pp. 116–126. Citeseer (2007)
12. Knuth, D.E., Morris Jr., J.H., Pratt, V.R.: Fast pattern matching in strings. SIAM J. Comput. **6**(2), 323–350 (1977)
13. Mendivelso, J., Pinzón, Y.J.: Parameterized matching: solutions and extensions. In: Stringology, pp. 118–131. Citeseer (2015)
14. Tarjan, R.E.: Efficiency of a good but not linear set union algorithm. J. ACM (JACM) **22**(2), 215–225 (1975)

Duel and Sweep Algorithm for Order-Preserving Pattern Matching

Davaajav Jargalsaikhan[(✉)], Diptarama, Yohei Ueki, Ryo Yoshinaka,
and Ayumi Shinohara

Graduate School of Information Sciences, Tohoku University,
6-6-05 Aramaki Aza Aoba, Aoba-ku, Sendai, Japan
{davaajav,ry,ayumi}@ecei.tohoku.ac.jp,
{diptarama,yohei_ueki}@shino.ecei.tohoku.ac.jp

Abstract. Given a text and a pattern over an alphabet, the classic exact matching problem searches for all occurrences of the pattern in the text. Unlike exact matching, *order-preserving pattern matching* (OPPM) considers the relative order of elements, rather t han their real values. In this paper, we propose an efficient algorithm for the OPPM problem using the "duel-and-sweep" paradigm. For a pattern of length m and a text of length n, our algorithm runs in $O(n + m \log m)$ time in general, and in $O(n + m)$ time under an assumption that the characters in a string can be sorted in linear time with respect to the string size. We also perform experiments and show that our algorithm is faster than the KMP-based algorithm.

Keywords: Order-preserving pattern matching · Duel-and-sweep

1 Introduction

The exact string matching problem is one of the most widely studied problems. Given a text and a pattern, the exact matching problem searches for all occurrence positions of the pattern in the text. Many pattern matching algorithms have been proposed such as the well-known Knuth-Morris-Pratt algorithm [15], Boyer-Moore algorithm [2], and Horspool algorithm [13]. These algorithms preprocess the pattern first and then match the pattern from its prefix or suffix when comparing it with the text. Vishkin proposed two algorithms for pattern matching, pattern matching by duel-and-sweep [18] and pattern matching by sampling [19]. Both algorithms match the pattern to a substring of the text from some positions which are determined by the property of the pattern, instead of its prefix or suffix. These algorithms are developed also for parallel processing.

Furthermore, variants of Vishkin's duel-and-sweep algorithm have been developed for other types of pattern matching. Amir et al. [1] proposed a duel-and-sweep algorithm for the two-dimensional pattern matching problem. Cole et al. [7] generalized it for two-dimensional parameterized pattern matching. The aim of this paper is to show that the duel-and-sweep paradigm is also useful for

© Springer International Publishing AG 2018
A M. Tjoa et al. (Eds.): SOFSEM 2018, LNCS 10706, pp. 624–635, 2018.
https://doi.org/10.1007/978-3-319-73117-9_44

another variant of pattern matching, namely, *order-preserving pattern matching* (OPPM).

Unlike the exact matching problem, OPPM considers the relative order of elements, rather than their real values. Order-preserving matching has gained much interest in recent years, due to its applicability in problems where the relative order matters, such as share prices in stock markets, weather data or musical notes. The difficulty of OPPM mainly comes from the fact that we cannot determine the isomorphism by comparing the symbols in the text and the pattern on each position independently; instead, we have to consider their respective relative orders in the pattern and in the text.

Kubica et al. [16] and Kim et al. [14] independently proposed the same solution for OPPM based on the KMP algorithm. Their KMP-based algorithm runs in $O(n + m \log m)$ time. Cho et al. [6] brought forward another algorithm based on the Horspool algorithm that uses q-grams, which was proven to be experimentally fast. Crochemore et al. [8] proposed useful data structures for OPPM. On the other hand, Chhabra and Tarhio [5], Faro and Külekci [10] proposed filtration methods which are practically fast. Moreover, faster filtration algorithms using SIMD (Single Instruction Multiple Data) instructions were proposed by Cantone et al. [3], Chhabra et al. [4] and Ueki et al. [17]. They showed that SIMD instructions are effective in speeding up their algorithms.

In this paper, we propose a new algorithm for OPPM based on the duel-and-sweep technique. Our algorithm runs in $O(n + m \log m)$ time which is as fast as the KMP based algorithm. Moreover, we perform experiments to compare those algorithms, which show that our algorithm is faster than the KMP-based algorithm.

The rest of the paper is organized as follows. In Sect. 2, we give preliminaries on the problem. We describe our algorithm for the OPPM problem in Sect. 3. Section 4 shows some experimental results that compare the performance of our algorithm with the KMP-based algorithm. In Sect. 5, we conclude our work and discuss future directions.

2 Preliminaries

We use Σ to denote an alphabet of integer symbols such that the comparison of any two symbols can be done in constant time. Σ^* denotes the set of strings over the alphabet Σ. For a string $S \in \Sigma^*$, we will denote the i-th element of S by $S[i]$ and the substring of S that starts at the location i and ends at j as $S[i:j]$. We say that two strings S and T of equal length n are *order-isomorphic*, written $S \approx T$, if

$$S[i] \leq S[j] \iff T[i] \leq T[j] \text{ for all } 1 \leq i, j \leq n.$$

For instance, $(12, 35, 5) \approx (25, 30, 21) \not\approx (11, 13, 20)$.

In order to check the order-isomorphism of two strings, Kubica et al. [16] defined useful arrays[1] $Lmax_S$ and $Lmin_S$ by

$$Lmax_S[i] = j \ (j < i) \ \text{ if } \ S[j] = \max_{k<i}\{S[k] \mid S[k] \leq S[i]\}, \tag{1}$$

$$Lmin_S[i] = j \ (j < i) \ \text{ if } \ S[j] = \min_{k<i}\{S[k] \mid S[k] \geq S[i]\}. \tag{2}$$

We use the rightmost (largest) j if there exist more than one such j. If there is no such j then we define $Lmin_S[i] = 0$ and $Lmax_S[i] = 0$. From the definition, we can easily observe the following properties. Unless $Lmax_S[i] = 0$ or $Lmin_S[i] = 0$,

$$S[Lmax_S[i]] = S[i] \quad \Longleftrightarrow \quad S[i] = S[Lmin_S[i]], \tag{3}$$

$$S[Lmax_S[i]] < S[i] \quad \Longleftrightarrow \quad S[i] < S[Lmin_S[i]]. \tag{4}$$

Lemma 1 [16]. *For a string S, let $sort(S)$ be the time required to sort the elements of S. $Lmax_S$ and $Lmin_S$ can be computed in $O(sort(S) + |S|)$ time.*

Thus, $Lmax_S$ and $Lmin_S$ can be computed in $O(|S| \log |S|)$ time in general. Moreover, the computation can be done in $O(|S|)$ time under a natural assumption [16] that the characters of S are elements of the set $\{1, \ldots, |S|^{O(1)}\}$. By using $Lmax_S$ and $Lmin_S$, the order-isomorphism of two strings can be decided as follows.

Lemma 2 [6]. *For two strings S and T of length n, assume that $S[1:j] \approx T[1:j]$ for some $j < n$. Moreover assume that $Lmax_S[j+1] \neq 0$ and $Lmin_S[j+1] \neq 0$. Let $i_{max} = Lmax_S[j+1]$ and $i_{min} = Lmin_S[j+1]$. Then $S[1:j+1] \approx T[1:j+1]$ if and only if either of the following two conditions holds.*

$$S[i_{max}] = S[j+1] = S[i_{min}] \ \wedge \ T[i_{max}] = T[j+1] = T[i_{min}], \tag{5}$$

$$S[i_{max}] < S[j+1] < S[i_{min}] \ \wedge \ T[i_{max}] < T[j+1] < T[i_{min}]. \tag{6}$$

Corollary 1. *Suppose that $P[1:j-1] \approx Q[1:j-1]$ and $P[1:j] \not\approx Q[1:j]$ for two strings P and Q of length at least j. For $i_{max} = Lmax_P[j]$ and $i_{min} = Lmin_P[j]$, if $i_{max}, i_{min} \neq 0$, we have*

$$P[j] = P[i_{max}] \ \wedge \ Q[j] \neq Q[i_{max}]$$
$$\vee \ P[j] = P[i_{min}] \ \wedge \ Q[j] \neq Q[i_{min}]$$
$$\vee \ P[j] > P[i_{max}] \ \wedge \ Q[j] \leq Q[i_{max}]$$
$$\vee \ P[j] < P[i_{min}] \ \wedge \ Q[j] \geq Q[i_{min}].$$

The order preserving-pattern matching problem is defined as follows.

---

[1] Similar arrays $Prev_S$ and $Next_S$ are introduced in [12].

Definition 1 (OPPM problem).

Input: A text $T \in \Sigma^*$ of length n and a pattern $P \in \Sigma^*$ of length $m \leq n$.
Output: All occurrence positions of substrings of T that are order-isomorphic to P.

Hasan et al. [12] proposed a modification to Z-function, which Gusfield [11] defined for ordinary pattern matching, to make it useful from the order-preserving point of view. For a string S, the *(modified) Z-array* of S is defined by

$$Z_S[i] = \max_{1 \leq j \leq |S|-i+1} \{j \mid S[1:j] \approx S[i:i+j-1]\} \quad \text{for each } 1 \leq i \leq |S|.$$

In other words, $Z_S[i]$ is the length of the longest substring of S that starts at position i and is order-isomorphic to some prefix of S. An example of Z-array is illustrated in Table 1.

Table 1. Z-array of a string $S = (18, 22, 12, 50, 10, 17)$. For instance, $Z_S[3] = 3$ because $S[1:3] = (18, 22, 12) \approx (12, 50, 10) = S[3:5]$ and $S[1:4] = (18, 22, 12, 50) \not\approx (12, 50, 10, 17) = S[3:6]$. $Lmax_S$ and $Lmin_S$ are also shown.

	1	2	3	4	5	6
S	18	22	12	50	10	17
Z_S	6	1	3	1	2	1
$Lmax_S$	0	1	0	2	0	3
$Lmin_S$	0	0	1	0	3	1

Lemma 3 [12]. *For a string S, the Z-array Z_S can be computed in $O(|S|)$ time, assuming that $Lmax_S$ and $Lmin_S$ are already computed.*

Note that in their original work, Hasan et al. [12] assumed that each character in S is distinct. However, we can extend their algorithm by using Lemma 2 to verify order-isomorphism even when S contains duplicate characters.

In the remainder of this paper, we fix a text T of length n and a pattern P of length m.

3   Duel-and-sweep Algorithm for Order-Preserving Matching

In this section, we will propose an algorithm for OPPM based on the "duel-and-sweep" paradigm [1,18]. The duel-and-sweep paradigm screens all substrings of length m of the text, called *candidates*, in two stages, called the *dueling* and *sweeping* stages. Suppose when P is superimposed on itself with the offset

$a < m$, the two overlapped substrings of P are not order-isomorphic. Then it is impossible that two candidates with offset a are both order-isomorphic to P. The dueling stage lets each pair of candidates with such an offset a "duel" and eliminates one based on this observation. This test is quick but not perfect. This stage can remove many candidates, although there would still remain candidates which are actually not order-isomorphic to the pattern. On the other hand, it is guaranteed that if distinct candidates that survive the dueling stage overlap, their prefixes of certain length are order-isomorphic. The sweeping stage takes the advantage of this property when checking the order-isomorphism between surviving candidates and the pattern so that this stage can be done also quickly.

Prior to the dueling stage, the pattern is preprocessed to construct a *witness table* based on which the dueling stage decides which pair of overlapping candidates should duel and how they should duel.

3.1   Pattern Preprocessing

For each offset $0 < a < m$, the original duel-and-sweep algorithm [18] saves a position i such that $P[i] \neq P[i + a]$. However, in order-preserving pattern matching, the order-isomorphism of two strings cannot be determined by comparing a symbol in one position. We need two positions as a *witness* to say that the two strings are not order-isomorphic. Therefore, for each offset $0 < a < m$, when the overlapped regions obtained by superimposing P on itself with offset a are not order-isomorphic, we use a pair $\langle i, j \rangle$ of locations called *a witness pair for the offset a* if either of the following holds:

- $P[i] = P[j]$ and $P[i + a] \neq P[j + a]$,
- $P[i] > P[j]$ and $P[i + a] \leq P[j + a]$,
- $P[i] < P[j]$ and $P[i + a] \geq P[j + a]$.

Next, we describe how to construct a *witness table* for P, that stores witness pairs for all possible offsets a ($0 < a < m$). The witness table WIT_P is an array of length $m - 1$, such that $WIT_P[a]$ is a witness pair for offset a. In the case when there are multiple witness pairs for offset a, we take the pair $\langle i, j \rangle$ with the smallest value of j and some $i < j$. When the overlap regions are order-isomorphic for offset a, which implies that no witness pair exists for a, we express it as $WIT_P[a] = \langle 0, 0 \rangle$. Table 2 shows an example of a witness table.

Table 2. Witness table WIT_P for a string $P = (18, 22, 12, 50, 10, 17)$. For instance, the witness pair $WIT_P[2]$ for offset 2 is $\langle 2, 4 \rangle$, due to $P[2] = 22 < 50 = P[4]$ and $P[2 + 2] = 50 > 17 = P[4 + 2]$. On the other hand, $WIT_P[4] = \langle 0, 0 \rangle$, since $P[1:2] \approx P[5:6]$.

	1	2	3	4	5	6
P	18	22	12	50	10	17
WIT_P	$\langle 1, 2 \rangle$	$\langle 2, 4 \rangle$	$\langle 1, 2 \rangle$	$\langle 0, 0 \rangle$	$\langle 0, 0 \rangle$	–

Algorithm 1. Algorithm for constructing the witness table WIT_P

```
1  Function Witness(P) /* Construct the witness table WIT_P                    */
2      compute the Z-array Z_P for the pattern P;
3      for a = 1 to m − 1 do
4          j = Z_P[a + 1] + 1, i_min = Lmin_P[j] and i_max = Lmax_P[j];
5          if j = m − a + 1 then WIT_P[a] = ⟨0, 0⟩;
6          else if i_max = 0 then WIT_P[a] = ⟨i_min, j⟩;
7          else if i_min = 0 then WIT_P[a] = ⟨i_max, j⟩;
8          else if P[i_min] = P[j] ∧ P[i_min + a] ≠ P[j + a]
9                  ∨ P[i_min] > P[j] ∧ P[i_min + a] ≤ P[j + a] then
10             └  WIT_P[a] = ⟨i_min, j⟩

11         else
12             └  WIT_P[a] = ⟨i_max, j⟩
```

Lemma 4. *For a pattern P of length m, Algorithm 1 constructs WIT_P in $O(m)$ time assuming that Z_P is already computed.*

Proof. Clearly the algorithm runs in $O(m)$ time.

We show that for each $1 \le a < m$, Algorithm 1 computes $WIT_P[a]$ correctly. Recall that $Z_P[a + 1]$ is the length of the longest prefix of $P[a + 1 : m]$ that is order-isomorphic to a prefix of P. Let $j = Z_P[a + 1] + 1$, for which we have $P[1 : j − 1] \approx P[1 + a : j − 1 + a]$. Suppose that $j = m − a + 1$. This means that $P[1 : j − 1] \approx P[1 + a : j − 1 + a] = P[1 + a : m]$, i.e., there is no witness pair for the offset a. Indeed Algorithm 1 gets $WIT_P[a] = \langle 0, 0 \rangle$ for this case.

Otherwise, we have $P[1 : j] \not\approx P[1 + a : j + a]$. Let $i_{max} = Lmax_P[j]$ and $i_{min} = Lmin_P[j]$. If $i_{max} = 0$, $P[j] < P[k]$ for all $k < j$. Note that $i_{min} \ne 0$ by $j \ge 2$. Since $P[1 : j − 1] \approx P[1 + a : j − 1 + a]$ and $P[1 : j] \not\approx P[1 + a : j + a]$, there exists $1 \le k < j$ such that $P[j + a] \ge P[k + a]$. By $P[i_{min}] \le P[k]$ and $(P[i_{min}], P[k]) \approx (P[i_{min} + a], P[k + a])$, we have $P[i_{min} + a] \le P[k + a] \le P[j + a]$. Therefore, $\langle i_{min}, j \rangle$ is a witness pair for the offset a. The case where $i_{min} = 0$ can be discussed in the exactly symmetric way.

Let us assume $i_{min} \ne 0$ and $i_{max} \ne 0$. If $P[i_{min}] = P[j] \land P[i_{min} + a] \ne P[j + a]$ or $P[i_{min}] > P[j] \land P[i_{min} + a] \le P[j + a]$, clearly $\langle i_{min}, j \rangle$ is a witness pair for a. Otherwise, by Corollary 1, either $P[i_{max}] = P[j] \land P[i_{max} + a] \ne P[j + a]$ or $P[i_{max}] < P[j] \land P[i_{max} + a] \ge P[j + a]$ holds, in which case $\langle i_{max}, j \rangle$ is a witness pair for a. □

3.2   Dueling Stage

Let us denote the candidate that starts at the location x as $T_x = T[x : x + m − 1]$. In the dueling stage, we "duel" all pairs of overlapping candidates T_x and T_{x+a} such that $WIT_P[a] \ne \langle 0, 0 \rangle$. Witness pairs are used in the following manner. Suppose that $WIT_P[a] = \langle i, j \rangle$, where $P[i] < P[j]$ and $P[i + a] \ge P[j + a]$, for example. Then, it holds that

---

Algorithm 2. Dueling

---

1 **Function** Dueling(x, a) /* Duel between candidates T_x and T_{x+a} */
2     $\langle i, j \rangle = WIT_P[a]$;
3   **if** $P[i] = P[j]$ **then**
4   **if** $T[x + a + i - 1] \neq T[x + a + j - 1]$ **then** **return** x;
5   **else** **return** $x + a$;
6   **if** $P[i] < P[j]$ **then**
7   **if** $T[x + a + i - 1] \geq T[x + a + j - 1]$ **then** **return** x;
8   **else** **return** $x + a$;
9   **if** $P[i] > P[j]$ **then**
10   **if** $T[x + a + i - 1] \leq T[x + a + j - 1]$ **then** **return** x;
11   **else** **return** $x + a$;

- if $T[x + a + i - 1] \geq T[x + a + j - 1]$, then $T_{x+a} \not\approx P$,
- if $T[x + a + i - 1] < T[x + a + j - 1]$, then $T_x \not\approx P$.

Based on this observation, we can safely eliminate either candidate T_x or T_{x+a} without looking into other locations. We can perform this process similarly for other equality/inequality cases. This process is called *dueling*. The procedure for all cases of the dueling is described in Algorithm 2.

On the other hand, if T_x and T_{x+a} do not overlap or the offset a has no witness pair, i.e. $P[1:m-a] \approx P[a+1:m]$, no dueling is performed on them. We say that a position x *is consistent with* $x + a$ if either $0 < a < m$ and $WIT_P[a] = \langle 0, 0 \rangle$ or $a \geq m$. Note that the consistency property is determined by a and P only, and x and T are irrelevant. The consistency property is transitive.

Lemma 5. *For any a, b and x such that $1 \leq a < a + b < m$ and $1 \leq x < m - a - b$, if x is consistent with $x + a$ and $x + a$ is consistent with $x + a + b$, then x is consistent with $x + a + b$.*

Proof. Since x is consistent with $x + a$, it follows that $P[1:m-a] \approx P[a+1:m]$, so that $P[b+1:m-a] \approx P[(a+b)+1:m]$. Moreover, since $x + a$ is consistent with $x + a + b$, it follows that $P[1:m-b] \approx P[b+1:m]$, so that $P[1:m-b-a] \approx P[b+1:m-a]$. Thus, $P[1:m-(a+b)] \approx P[(a+b)+1:m]$, which implies that x is consistent with $x + a + b$. □

The whole process of the dueling stage is shown in Algorithm 3, which follows Amir et al. [1] for ordinary pattern matching. This stage eliminates candidates until all surviving candidates are pairwise consistent. The algorithm uses a stack to maintain candidates which are consistent with each other. A new candidate y will be pushed to the stack if the stack is empty. Otherwise y is checked by comparing it to the topmost element x of the stack. By Lemma 5, if x is consistent with y, all the other elements in the stack are consistent with y, too. Thus we can push y to the stack. On the other hand, if x is not consistent with y, we should exclude one of the candidates by dueling them. If x wins the duel,

---

Algorithm 3. The dueling stage algorithm

```
 1  Function DuelingStage(P, T)
 2      create stack;
 3      for y = 1 to n − m + 1 do
 4          while stack is not empty do
 5              pop x from stack;
 6              if y − x ≥ m or WIT_P[y − x] = ⟨0, 0⟩ then
 7                  push x and y to stack;
 8                  break;
 9              else
10                  z = Dueling(x, y − x);
11                  if z = x then
12                      push x to stack;
13                      break;
14          if stack is empty then
15              push y to stack;
```

---

we put x back to the stack, discard y, and get a new candidate. If y wins the duel, we exclude x and continue comparison of y with the top element of the stack unless the stack is empty. If the stack is empty, y will be pushed to the stack. Figure 1 gives an example run of the dueling stage.

Lemma 6 [1]. *The dueling stage can be done in $O(n)$ time by using WIT_P.*

3.3 Sweeping Stage

The goal of the sweeping stage is to prune inconsistent candidates until all remaining candidates are order-isomorphic to the pattern P. Suppose that we need to check whether some surviving candidate T_x is order-isomorphic to P. It suffices to successively check the conditions (5) and (6) in Lemma 2, starting from the leftmost location in T_x. If the conditions are satisfied for all locations in T_x, then $T_x \approx P$. Otherwise, $T_x \not\approx P$, and obtain a mismatch position j.

A Naive implementation of sweeping requires $O(n^2)$ time. Algorithm 4 takes advantage of the fact that all the remaining candidates are pairwise consistent, we can reduce the time complexity to $O(n)$ time. Suppose there is a mismatch at position j when comparing P with T_x, that is, $T_x[1 : j − 1] \approx P[1 : j − 1]$ and $T_x[1 : j] \not\approx P[1 : j]$. If the next candidate is T_{x+a} with $a < j$, since $P[1 : j − a − 1] \approx P[a + 1 : j − 1] \approx T_x[a + 1 : j − 1] = T_{x+a}[1 : j − a − 1]$, we can start comparison of P and T_{x+a} from the position where the mismatch with T_x occurred. If $P \approx T_x$, the above discussion holds for $j = m + 1$. Therefore, the total number of comparison is bounded by $O(n)$, by applying the same argument on the complexity of the KMP algorithm for exact matching.

Lemma 7. *The sweeping stage can be completed in $O(n)$ time.*

		1	2	3	4	5	6	7	8	9	10	stack
$y = 1$	add T_1	8	13	5	21	14	18	20	25	15	22	1
$y = 2$	exclude T_2	8	13	5	21	14	18	20	25	15	22	1
		12	50	10	17							
			12	50	10	17						
$y = 3$	add T_3	8	13	5	21	14	18	20	25	15	22	1,3
$y = 4$	exclude T_4	8	13	5	21	14	18	20	25	15	22	1,3
				12	50	10	17					
					12	50	10	17				
$y = 5$	add T_5	8	13	5	21	14	18	20	25	15	22	1,3,5
$y = 6$	exclude T_5	8	13	5	21	14	18	20	25	15	22	1,3,6
	add T_6					12	50	10	17			
							12	50	10	17		
$y = 7$	exclude T_6	8	13	5	21	14	18	20	25	15	22	1,3,7
	add T_7						12	50	10	17		
								12	50	10	17	

Fig. 1. An example run of the dueling stage for $T = (8, 13, 5, 21, 14, 18, 20, 25, 15, 22)$, $P = (12, 50, 10, 17)$, and $WIT_P = (\langle 1, 2 \rangle, \langle 0, 0 \rangle, \langle 0, 0 \rangle)$. First, the position 1 is pushed to the stack. Next, T_2 duels with T_1 and then T_2 loses because $P[1] < P[2]$ and $T_2[1] > T_2[2]$. The next position 3 is pushed to the stack by $WIT_P[3 - 1] = \langle 0, 0 \rangle$. Similarly, T_4 loses against T_3, and 5 is accepted to the stack. For $y = 6$, T_5 is removed and T_6 is added because $P[1] < P[2]$, $T_6[1] < T_6[2]$, and 3 is consistent with 6. Finally T_7 defeats T_6 and the contents of the stack become 1, 3, and 7.

By Lemmas 4, 6, and 7, we summarize this section as follows.

Theorem 1. *Given a text T of length n and a pattern P of length m, the duel-and-sweep algorithm solves the OPPM Problem in $O(n + m \log m)$ time. Moreover, the running time is $O(n + m)$ under the natural assumption that the characters of P can be sorted in $O(m)$ time.*

4 Experiments

In order to compare the performance of proposed algorithm with the KMP-based algorithm [14, 16] on solving the OPPM problem, we performed two sets of experiments. In the first experiment set, the pattern size m is fixed to 10, while the text size n is changed from 100000 to 1000000. In the second experiment set, the text size n is fixed to 1000000 while the pattern size m is changed from 5 to 100. We measured the average of running time and the number of comparisons for 50 repetitions on each experiment. We used randomly generated texts and patterns with alphabet size $|\Sigma| = 1000$. Experiments are executed on a machine with Intel Xeon CPU E5-2609 8 cores 2.40 GHz, 256 GB memory, and Debian Wheezy operating system.

Algorithm 4. The sweeping stage algorithm

---

1 **Function** SweepingStage()
2   **while** *there are unchecked candidates to the right of* T_x **do**
3   let T_x be the leftmost unchecked candidate;
4   **if** *there are no candidates overlapping with* T_x **then**
5   **if** $T_x \not\approx P$ **then** eliminate T_x;
6   **else**
7   let T_{x+a} be the leftmost candidate that overlaps with T_x;
8   **if** $T_x \approx P$ **then** start checking T_{x+a} from the location $m - a + 1$;
9   **else**
10   let j be the mismatch position;
11   eliminate T_x;
12   start checking T_{x+a} from the location $j - a$;

The results of our experiments are shown in Figs. 2 and 3. We can see that our algorithm is better than the KMP-based algorithm in running time and the number of comparisons when the pattern size and text size are large. However, our algorithm was slower when the pattern is very short, namely $m = 5$. The reason why the proposed algorithm makes fewer comparisons than the KMP-based algorithm may be explained as follows. The KMP-based algorithm relies on Lemma 2, which compares symbols at three positions[2] to check the order-isomorphism between a prefix of the pattern and a substring of the text when the prefix is extended by one. On the other hand, the dueling stage of our algorithm compares only two positions determined by the witness table. By pruning candidates in the dueling phase, the number of precise tests of order-isomorphism in the sweeping stage is reduced.

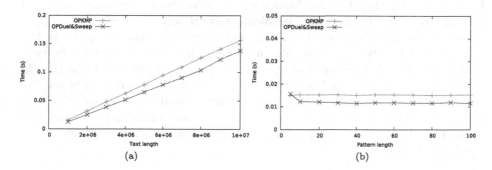

Fig. 2. Running time of the algorithms with respect to (a) text length, and (b) pattern length.

---

[2] Each of (5) and (6) of Lemma 2 involves four (in)equalities but checking three is enough thanks to the properties (3) and (4).

634   D. Jargalsaikhan et al.

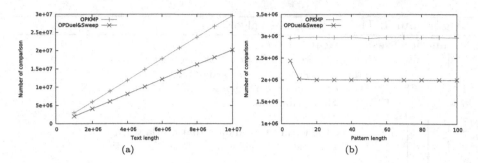

Fig. 3. Number of comparisons in the algorithms with respect to (a) text length, and (b) pattern length.

5   Discussion

We proposed a new algorithm for the OPPM problem by extending Vishkin's duel-and-sweep algorithm [18] for the exact matching problem. Our algorithm runs in linear time, that is theoretically fast. The experimental results showed that our algorithm is practically faster than the KMP-based algorithm [14,16], which has the same theoretical running time. Actually, our algorithm makes fewer comparisons than the KMP-based algorithm.

Since Vishkin's algorithm has been designed for parallel computing [18], we expect that our duel-and-sweep algorithm for order preserving pattern matching could also be extended for parallel computing. This extension is not trivial because the periodicity property of a string in order preserving pattern matching is different from the one in ordinary pattern matching.

Another potential of the duel-and-sweep paradigm is in solving *two-dimensional* pattern matching problems. Amir et al. [1] and Cole et al. [7] have designed duel-and-sweep algorithms for solving two-dimensional exact and parameterized pattern matching problems, respectively. Currently no fast algorithm for the two-dimensional order-preserving pattern matching problem has been proposed. Actually we have already developed a dueling algorithm for two-dimensional OPPM that runs in linear time with respect to the input text size [9]. However, we do not have a linear time algorithm for the sweeping stage yet. We hope the two-dimensional OPPM problem can be solved more efficiently by finding a more sophisticated method based on some combinatorial properties, like Cole et al. did for the two-dimensional parameterized matching problem. This is left for future work.

Acknowledgements. This work is supported by Tohoku University Division for Interdisciplinary Advance Research and Education, ImPACT Program of Council for Science, Technology and Innovation (Cabinet Office, Government of Japan), and JSPS KAKENHI Grant Number JP15H05706.

References

1. Amir, A., Benson, G., Farach, M.: An alphabet independent approach to two-dimensional pattern matching. SIAM J. Comput. **23**(2), 313–323 (1994)
2. Boyer, R.S., Moore, J.S.: A fast string searching algorithm. Commun. ACM **20**(10), 762–772 (1977)
3. Cantone, D., Faro, S., Külekci, M.O.: An efficient skip-search approach to the order-preserving pattern matching problem. In: PSC, pp. 22–35 (2015)
4. Chhabra, T., Külekci, M.O., Tarhio, J.: Alternative algorithms for order-preserving matching. In: PSC, pp. 36–46 (2015)
5. Chhabra, T., Tarhio, J.: A filtration method for order-preserving matching. Inf. Process. Lett. **116**(2), 71–74 (2016)
6. Cho, S., Na, J.C., Park, K., Sim, J.S.: A fast algorithm for order-preserving pattern matching. Inf. Process. Lett. **115**(2), 397–402 (2015)
7. Cole, R., Hazay, C., Lewenstein, M., Tsur, D.: Two-dimensional parameterized matching. ACM Trans. Algorithms **11**(2), 12:1–12:30 (2014)
8. Crochemore, M., Iliopoulos, C.S., Kociumaka, T., Kubica, M., Langiu, A., Pissis, S.P., Radoszewski, J., Rytter, W., Waleń, T.: Order-preserving indexing. Theor. Comput. Sci. Pattern Matching **638**, 122–135 (2016). Text Data Structures and Compression
9. Davaajav, J.: A study on the two-dimensional order-preserving matching problem. Bachelor thesis, Tohoku University (2017)
10. Faro, S., Külekci, M.O.: Efficient algorithms for the order preserving pattern matching problem. In: Dondi, R., Fertin, G., Mauri, G. (eds.) AAIM 2016. LNCS, vol. 9778, pp. 185–196. Springer, Cham (2016). https://doi.org/10.1007/978-3-319-41168-2_16
11. Gusfield, D.: Algorithms on Strings, Trees and Sequences: Computer Science and Computational Biology. Cambridge University Press, Cambridge (1997)
12. Hasan, M.M., Islam, A.S., Rahman, M.S., Rahman, M.S.: Order preserving pattern matching revisited. Pattern Recogn. Lett. **55**, 15–21 (2015)
13. Horspool, R.N.: Practical fast searching in strings. Softw. Pract. Experience **10**(6), 501–506 (1980)
14. Kim, J., Eades, P., Fleischer, R., Hong, S.H., Iliopoulos, C.S., Park, K., Puglisi, S.J., Tokuyama, T.: Order-preserving matching. Theor. Comput. Sci. **525**, 68–79 (2014)
15. Knuth, D.E., Morris Jr., J.H., Pratt, V.R.: Fast pattern matching in strings. SIAM J. Comput. **6**(2), 323–350 (1977)
16. Kubica, M., Kulczyński, T., Radoszewski, J., Rytter, W., Waleń, T.: A linear time algorithm for consecutive permutation pattern matching. Inf. Process. Lett. **113**(12), 430–433 (2013)
17. Ueki, Y., Narisawa, K., Shinohara, A.: A fast order-preserving matching with q-neighborhood filtration using SIMD instructions. In: SOFSEM (Student Research Forum Papers/Posters), pp. 108–115 (2016)
18. Vishkin, U.: Optimal parallel pattern matching in strings. In: Brauer, W. (ed.) ICALP 1985. LNCS, vol. 194, pp. 497–508. Springer, Heidelberg (1985). https://doi.org/10.1007/BFb0015775
19. Vishkin, U.: Deterministic sampling - a new technique for fast pattern matching. SIAM J. Comput. **20**(1), 22–40 (1991)

Longest Common Prefixes with k-Mismatches and Applications

Hayam Alamro, Lorraine A. K. Ayad, Panagiotis Charalampopoulos$^{(\boxtimes)}$, Costas S. Iliopoulos, and Solon P. Pissis

Department of Informatics, King's College London, London, UK
{hayam.alamro,lorraine.ayad,panagiotis.charalampopoulos, costas.iliopoulos,solon.pissis}@kcl.ac.uk

Abstract. We propose a new algorithm for computing the longest prefix of each suffix of a given string of length n over a constant-sized alphabet of size σ that occurs elsewhere in the string with Hamming distance at most k. Specifically, we show that the proposed algorithm requires time $\mathcal{O}(n(\sigma R)^k \log \log n (\log k + \log \log n))$ on average, where $R = \lceil (k + 2)(\log_\sigma n + 1) \rceil$, and space $\mathcal{O}(n)$. This improves upon the state-of-the-art average-case time complexity for the case when $k = 1$ [23] by a factor of $\log n / \log^3 \log n$. In addition, we show how the proposed technique can be adapted and applied in order to compute the longest previous factors under the Hamming distance model within the same complexities. In terms of real-world applications, we show that our technique can be directly applied to the problem of genome mappability.

1 Introduction

The longest common prefix (LCP) array is a commonly used data structure alongside the suffix array (SA). The LCP array stores the length of the longest common prefix between two adjacent suffixes of a given string as they are stored (in lexicographical order) in the SA [22]. A typical use of the combination of the SA and the LCP array is to simulate the suffix tree [30] functionality using less space [1]. This use has inspired many researchers to focus on engineering the construction of the LCP array [17].

However, there are many practical scenarios where the LCP array may be applied without making use of the SA. The LCP array provides us with essential information regarding repetitiveness in a given string and is therefore a useful data structure for analysing textual data in areas such as molecular biology, musicology, or natural language processing.

It is also quite common to account for potential alterations within sequences. For example, they can be the result of DNA replication or sequencing errors in DNA sequences. Alterations may also be introduced in the scope of plagiarism

P. Charalampopoulos—Supported by the Graduate Teaching Scholarship scheme of the Department of Informatics at King's College London and by the A.G. Leventis Foundation.

© Springer International Publishing AG 2018
A M. Tjoa et al. (Eds.): SOFSEM 2018, LNCS 10706, pp. 636–649, 2018.
https://doi.org/10.1007/978-3-319-73117-9_45

attempts in natural languages. In this context, it is natural to define the longest common prefix with k-mismatches. Given a string $x[0..n-1]$, the longest common prefix with k-mismatches for every suffix $x[i..n-1]$ is the length of the longest common prefix of $x[i..n-1]$ and any $x[j..n-1]$, where $j \neq i$, with up to k mismatches. Note that for the mismatches we make use of the Hamming distance model throughout.

Molecular Biology. Repeated sequences are a common characteristic of genomes. One type in particular, namely *interspersed repeats*, are known to occur in all eukaryotic genomes. These repeats have no repetitive pattern and appear irregularly within DNA sequences [20]. Occurrences of single nucleotide polymorphism exist within genomes, where a mutation of a single nucleotide takes place during cell division. This results in the existence of interspersed repeats that are not identical [21]. Identifying the positions of where these repeats occur has been linked to genome folding locations and phylogenetic analysis [27].

Computational Musicology. Sequential patterns of varying length are a key feature of musical compositions. Chords are made up of three or more simultaneously played notes and a chord progression is made up of two or more chords, where the order plays a significant role in determining the tone of a musical piece. Minor changes can exist in the transitions between chords. The analysis of these harmonic progressions contributes to the analysis and categorisation of musical genres [6]. Another example is *ostinato*, a motif that persistently repeats in the same musical voice; it is used to define the tone of a piece of music [8]. It commonly refers to exact repetition, but also covers repetition with variations.

Natural Language Processing. Natural language text collections are increasing rapidly and massively, thus becoming a source of several analysis tasks such as text classification. For instance, an important task is to identify similar or duplicate documents in large text collections for detecting plagiarism or for obtaining more realistic text statistics. To this end, many repetition-based strategies have been suggested. One of these approaches is based on computing the common repeated lengths of a document's text in other documents of the collection to derive whether the document is repeated in the text collection or not [19].

State of the Art. The problem of computing the longest common prefixes with k-mismatches was introduced by Manzini in [23]; an algorithm was presented to solve the problem only for $k = 1$ in time $\mathcal{O}(nL_{\mathrm{ave}} \log n / \log \log n)$ using $\mathcal{O}(n)$ extra space for a string of length n over a constant-sized alphabet, where L_{ave} is the average value in the LCP array. We show that this value is $\Omega(\log n)$ (see Lemma 3). This value is known to be $\mathcal{O}(\log n)$ [18] on average, and so the algorithm of [23] works in time $\mathcal{O}(n \log^2 n / \log \log n)$ on average for $k = 1$.

Our Contribution. Due to our motivational applications we focus on linear-space solutions. Given a string x of length n over a constant-sized alphabet of size σ and an integer $0 < k < n$, and setting $R = \lceil (k+2)(\log_\sigma n + 1) \rceil$, we make the following threefold contribution:

1. We improve upon the result of [23] by presenting an algorithm for computing the longest common prefixes with 1-mismatch requiring time $\mathcal{O}(n \log n \log^2 \log n)$ on average using $\mathcal{O}(n)$ extra space. In fact we show how our technique can be generalised to work for arbitrary k; the average-case time complexity then becomes $\mathcal{O}(n(\sigma R)^k \log \log n(\log k + \log \log n))$ using $\mathcal{O}(n)$ extra space.

2. We apply our technique to compute the related longest previous factor (LPF) with k-mismatches for every suffix of x within the same complexities. The LPF with k-mismatches of the suffix $x[i..n-1]$ is the length of the longest prefix of $x[i..n-1]$ that occurs before i in x with at most k mismatches.

3. We also apply our technique to construct a data structure of size $\mathcal{O}(n)$ in average-case time $\mathcal{O}(n(\sigma R)^k \log \log n(\log k + \log \log n))$ using $\mathcal{O}(n)$ extra space that answers queries of the following type in $\mathcal{O}(1)$ time per query: return the smallest m such that at least α of the substrings of x of length m do not occur more than once in x with at most k mismatches. This data structure is a more general solution to the genome mappability problem [12].

2   Preliminaries

2.1   Strings

We begin with some basic definitions and notation. Let $x = x[0]x[1]\ldots x[n-1]$ be a *string* of length $|x| = n$ over a finite ordered alphabet Σ of size $|\Sigma| = \sigma = \mathcal{O}(1)$. For two positions i and j on x, we denote by $x[i..j] = x[i]\ldots x[j]$ the *substring* (sometimes called *factor*) of x that starts at position i and ends at position j. By ε we denote the *empty string* of length 0. We recall that a *prefix* of x is a substring that starts at position 0 ($x[0..j]$) and a *suffix* of x is a substring that ends at position $n-1$ ($x[i..n-1]$).

Let y be a string of length m with $0 < m \leq n$. We say that there exists an *occurrence* of y in x, or, more simply, that y *occurs in* x, when y is a substring of x. Every occurrence of y can be characterised by a starting position in x. We thus say that y occurs at the *starting position* i in x when $y = x[i..i+m-1]$.

The *Hamming distance* between two strings x and y, with $|x| = |y|$, is defined as $d_H(x, y) = |\{i : x[i] \neq y[i], i = 0, 1, \ldots, |x|-1\}|$. If $|x| \neq |y|$, we set $d_H(x, y) = \infty$. If two strings x and y are at Hamming distance at most k, we write $x \approx_k y$, and we say that x and y have k-*mismatches* or have *at most* k *mismatches*.

Let x be a string of length $n > 0$. The *suffix tree* $\mathcal{T}(x)$ of x is a compact trie representing all suffixes of x. The nodes of the trie which become nodes of the suffix tree are called *explicit* nodes, while the other nodes are called *implicit*. Each edge of the suffix tree can be viewed as an upward maximal path of implicit nodes starting with an explicit node. Moreover, each node belongs to a unique path of that kind. Thus, each node of the trie can be represented in the suffix tree by the edge it belongs to and an index within the corresponding path. We let $\mathcal{L}(v)$ denote the *path-label* of a node v, i.e., the concatenation of the edge labels along the path from the root to v. We say that v is path-labelled $\mathcal{L}(v)$. Additionally, $\mathcal{D}(v) = |\mathcal{L}(v)|$ is used to denote the *string-depth* of node v. Node v

is a *terminal* node if its path-label is a suffix of x, that is, $\mathcal{L}(v) = x[i .. n-1]$ for some $0 \leq i < n$; here v is also labelled with index i. It should be clear that each substring of x is uniquely represented by either an explicit or an implicit node of $\mathcal{T}(x)$, called its *locus*. In standard suffix tree implementations, we assume that each node of the suffix tree is able to access its parent. Once $\mathcal{T}(x)$ is constructed, it can be traversed in a depth-first manner to compute $\mathcal{D}(v)$ for each node v. The suffix tree of a string of length n can be computed in time and space $\mathcal{O}(n)$ [30].

We denote by SA the *suffix array* of x. SA is an integer array of size n storing the starting positions of all (lexicographically) sorted non-empty suffixes of x, i.e. for all $1 \leq r < n$ we have $x[\mathsf{SA}[r-1] .. n-1] < x[\mathsf{SA}[r] .. n-1]$ [22]. Let $\mathsf{lcp}(r, s)$ denote the length of the longest common prefix between $x[\mathsf{SA}[r] .. n-1]$ and $x[\mathsf{SA}[s] .. n-1]$ for positions r, s on x. We denote by LCP the *longest common prefix* array of x defined by $\mathsf{LCP}[r] = \mathsf{lcp}(r-1, r)$ for all $1 \leq r < n$, and $\mathsf{LCP}[0] = 0$. The inverse iSA of the array SA is defined by $\mathsf{iSA}[\mathsf{SA}[r]] = r$, for all $0 \leq r < n$. It is known that SA, iSA, and LCP of a string of length n, over a constant-sized alphabet, can be computed in time and space $\mathcal{O}(n)$ [13, 26].

The *permuted* LCP *array*, denoted by PLCP, has the same contents as the LCP array but in different order. Let i^- denote the starting position of the lexicographic predecessor of $x[i .. n-1]$. For $i = 0, \ldots, n-1$, we define $\mathsf{PLCP}[i] = \mathsf{LCP}[\mathsf{iSA}[i]] = \mathsf{lcp}(\mathsf{iSA}[i^-], \mathsf{iSA}[i])$, that is, $\mathsf{PLCP}[i]$ is the length of the longest common prefix between $x[i .. n-1]$ and its lexicographic predecessor. For the starting position j of the lexicographically smallest suffix we set $\mathsf{PLCP}[j] = 0$. For any $k \geq 0$, we define $\mathsf{lcp}_k(y, z)$ as the largest $\ell \geq 0$ such that $y[0 .. \ell-1]$ and $z[0 .. \ell-1]$ exist and are at Hamming distance at most k, that is, have at most k mismatches; note that lcp_k is defined for a pair of strings. We analogously define the *permuted* LCP *array with k-mismatches*, denoted by PLCP_k. For $i = 0, \ldots, n-1$, we have that

$$\mathsf{PLCP}_k[i] = \max_{j=0,\ldots,n-1,\ j \neq i} \mathsf{lcp}_k(x[i .. n-1], x[j .. n-1]).$$

The computational problem in scope can be formally stated as follows.

PLCP WITH k-MISMATCHES
Input: A string x of length n and an integer $0 < k < n$
Output: PLCP_k and P_k; $\mathsf{P}_k[i] \neq i$, for $i = 0, \ldots, n-1$, is such that $x[i .. i + \ell - 1] \approx_k x[\mathsf{P}_k[i] .. \mathsf{P}_k[i] + \ell - 1]$, where $\ell = \mathsf{PLCP}_k[i]$

Example 1. Consider the string `acababbac` and $k = 1$. The following table gives arrays PLCP_1 and P_1.

i	0	1	2	3	4	5	6	7	8
$\mathsf{PLCP}_1[i]$	4	3	4	3	3	3	3	2	1
$\mathsf{P}_1[i]$	2	3	0	1	2	2	3	0	1

Our Analysis Model. When we state average-case time complexities for our algorithms, we assume that the input is a string x of length n over a constant-sized alphabet Σ of size $\sigma > 1$ with the letters of x being independent and identically distributed random variables, uniformly distributed over Σ.

2.2   Advanced Data Structure Tools

Let $\mathcal{T}$ be a rooted tree of size n with integer weights on nodes each of magnitude at most n. We require that the root weight is zero and the weight of any other node is strictly larger than its parent's weight. A node v is a *weighted ancestor* of a node u at depth ℓ if v is the highest ancestor of u with weight at least ℓ.

Lemma 1 [4]. *After $\mathcal{O}(n)$-time preprocessing, weighted ancestor queries of nodes of a tree $\mathcal{T}$ can be answered in $\mathcal{O}(\log \log n)$ time per query.*

The following corollary applies Lemma 1 to the suffix tree of a string x of length n.

Corollary 1. *After $\mathcal{O}(n)$-time preprocessing, the locus of any substring $x[i \mathinner{.\,.} j]$ in $\mathcal{T}(x)$ can be found in $\mathcal{O}(\log \log n)$ time.*

Definition 1. *Given a string x and a substring y of x, we denote by $range(x, y)$ the range in the SA of x that represents the suffixes of x that have y as a prefix.*

Every node u in $\mathcal{T}(x)$ corresponds to an SA range $range(x, \mathcal{L}(u))$. We can precompute $range(x, \mathcal{L}(u))$ for all explicit nodes u in $\mathcal{T}(x)$ in $\mathcal{O}(n)$ time while performing a depth-first traversal of the tree. We also make use of the following lemma for a string x of length n.

Lemma 2 [14]. *Let y and z be two substrings of x. Given the SA and the iSA of x, as well as $range(x, y)$ and $range(x, z)$, $range(x, yz)$ can be computed in time $\mathcal{O}(\log \log n)$ after $\mathcal{O}(n \log \log n)$-time and $\mathcal{O}(n)$-space preprocessing.*

3   Longest Common Prefixes with k-Mismatches

We first show the following lower bound which is related to the time complexity of the algorithm in [23].

Lemma 3. *The average value in the LCP array of any string x of length n over an alphabet Σ of size σ is $\Omega(\log_\sigma n)$.*

Proof. First note that $\sum_i \mathsf{LCP}[i] \leq \sum_i \max\{\mathsf{LCP}[i], \mathsf{LCP}[i+1]\} \leq 2 \sum_i \mathsf{LCP}[i]$. We thus consider $\max\{\mathsf{LCP}[i], \mathsf{LCP}[i+1]\}$ (i.e. the length of the longest common prefix of $x[i \mathinner{.\,.} n-1]$ with any other suffix of x) instead of $\mathsf{LCP}[i]$ to simplify the proof. We know that $\max\{\mathsf{LCP}[i], \mathsf{LCP}[i+1]\}$ is equal to the string-depth of the parent of the leaf with path-label $x[i \mathinner{.\,.} n-1]\$$, $\$ \notin \Sigma$, in the suffix tree of $x\$$.

Consider the suffix tree of $x\$$. Each node can have at most $\sigma + 1$ leaves attached to it. We have at most σ^r non-leaf nodes at depth r. Hence we can obtain a brute force lower bound by assuming that we have a complete tree—of the required depth so that it has $n + 1$ leaves in total—with $\sigma + 1$ leaves in all of its nodes (note that this is impossible). This required depth is the smallest t such that $(\sigma + 1)(1 + \sigma + \ldots + \sigma^t) \geq n$; $t = \Omega(\log_\sigma n)$. It is then clear that nodes in the two deepest levels have attached to them at least half of the $n + 1$ leaves; this concludes the proof.   □

We next present an algorithm for the problem PLCP WITH 1-MISMATCH and then explain how it can be extended to solve problem PLCP WITH k-MISMATCHES. The proposed algorithm essentially consists of two different parts:

1. Computing *long* PLCPs in average-case time $\mathcal{O}(n)$;
2. Computing *short* PLCPs in worst-case time $\mathcal{O}(n \log n \log^2 \log n)$.

Notably, both parts use $\mathcal{O}(n)$ extra space for arbitrary k.

We initialize PLCP_1 and P_1 for each i based on the longest common prefix of $x[i .. n - 1]$ (i.e. not allowing any mismatches) that occurs elsewhere using the SA and the LCP array; this can be done in $\mathcal{O}(n)$ time.

Computing Long PLCPs. The first part is a slight modification of the algorithm presented in Sect. 3 of [3] for the problem of 1-mappability. In this problem, we are asked to compute for each substring of length m of a given string of length n the number of other occurrences of this substring in the string with at most 1 mismatch. The algorithm of [3] was shown to solve this problem in average-case time $\mathcal{O}(n)$ for values of m greater than or equal to $3 \log_\sigma n + 3$ using space $\mathcal{O}(n)$.

The algorithm presented in [3] computes all pairs of suffixes that share a prefix of length at least m with at most 1 mismatch. When such a pair is considered, the algorithm has already precomputed enough information (using longest common extension queries) that allows us to retrieve the longest common prefix with 1-mismatch of these two suffixes in $\mathcal{O}(1)$ time. This is merely because a longest common extension query may extend beyond length m: it is interrupted only by the second mismatch (or the ends of the string).

Hence, if we set $m = R = \lceil 3 \log_\sigma n \rceil + 3$, it is trivial to store, within the same complexities, $\mathsf{PLCP}_1[i]$ and $\mathsf{P}_1[i]$ for every i for which $x[i .. i + R - 1]$ has 1-mappability greater than 0 (i.e. $x[i .. i + R - 1]$ occurs elsewhere in x with at most 1 mismatch). Note that these are the positions i for which we have that $\mathsf{PLCP}_1[i] \geq R$. We thus arrive at the following lemma.

Lemma 4. *We can compute $\mathsf{PLCP}_1[i]$ and $\mathsf{P}_1[i]$ for each i for which $\mathsf{PLCP}_1[i] \geq R$ in average-case time $\mathcal{O}(n)$ using $\mathcal{O}(n)$ extra space.*

Computing Short PLCPs. Let S be the set of starting positions of m-length substrings that have 1-mappability 0 for $m = R$. For each $i \in S$, we have that $\mathsf{PLCP}_1[i] < R = \mathcal{O}(\log n)$. We proceed to compute $\mathsf{PLCP}_1[i]$ and $\mathsf{P}_1[i]$ for each $i \in S$ as follows; see also Fig. 1 for an illustration.

We first locate the node v in $\mathcal{T}(x)$ with path-label $x[i .. n - 1]$—this is a terminal node. We then consider each explicit ancestor u of v in $\mathcal{T}(x)$; note that

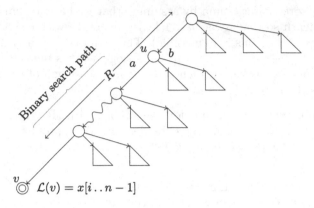

Fig. 1. Illustration; binary search along the shown path for the longest common prefix with 1 mismatch of $\mathcal{L}(v)$ and $\mathcal{L}(u)bx[i + \mathcal{D}(u) + 1 .. i + \lfloor(R + \mathcal{D}(u) - 1)/2\rfloor]$.

for each such u we have that $\mathcal{D}(u) < R - 1$ since $\mathsf{PLCP}_1[i] < R$. For each such u we perform the following. Suppose that the first edge label of the outgoing edge from u that lies on the path from the root to v is $a \in \Sigma$. For each other outgoing edge from u, say with first edge label $b \in \Sigma$, $b \neq a$, we wish to find the longest prefix of $\mathcal{L}(u)bx[i + \mathcal{D}(u) + 1 .. i + s]$, where $s = \min\{R - 2, n - 1 - i\}$, that is a substring of x and the starting position of one of its occurrences. The longest of these strings is precisely the longest prefix of $x[i .. n - 1]$ that occurs elsewhere in x with at most 1 mismatch.

We will find this by performing binary search on the subpath of the path from the root to v that corresponds to $x[i + \mathcal{D}(u) + 1 .. i + s]$ as follows. We first compute $range(x, y)$ for $y = \mathcal{L}(u)bx[i + \mathcal{D}(u) + 1 .. i + \lfloor(s + \mathcal{D}(u) + 1)/2\rfloor]$. If $range(x, y) = [p, q] \neq \emptyset$ we set $\mathsf{PLCP}_1[i] = \max\{\mathsf{PLCP}_1[i], |y|\}$ (and $\mathsf{P}_1[i] = \mathsf{SA}[p]$ if PLCP_1 has changed) and go down the path; else, the range is empty and we thus go up the path. We proceed with binary search in the same manner.

We can move along the path and find auxiliary ranges (e.g. $range(x, x[i + \mathcal{D}(u)+1 .. i+\lfloor(s+\mathcal{D}(u)+1)/2\rfloor])$) stored in explicit nodes of $\mathcal{T}(x)$ using weighted ancestor queries in time $\mathcal{O}(\log\log n)$ per query due to Corollary 1. Note that the range of an implicit node z along an edge (f, g) is equal to that of the explicit node g. We can then merge these ranges in time $\mathcal{O}(\log\log n)$ due to Lemma 2. Hence, each step of the binary search requires time $\mathcal{O}(\log\log n)$. The path-label of the considered path has length $\mathcal{O}(\log n)$ because $R = \lceil 3\log_\sigma n\rceil + 3$, and hence we do $\mathcal{O}(\log\log n)$ iterations for the binary search. Thus, each binary search takes time $\mathcal{O}(\log^2\log n)$ in total. We formalise the described algorithm in the pseudocode presented below.

Lemma 5. *Given the set of positions $S = \{i|\mathsf{PLCP}_1[i] < R\}$, we can compute $\mathsf{PLCP}_1[i]$ and $\mathsf{P}_1[i]$, for all $i \in S$, in worst-case time $\mathcal{O}(n\log n\log^2\log n)$ using $\mathcal{O}(n)$ extra space.*

Proof. The outer loop of PLCP₁SHORT iterates through positions of x that have 1-mappability 0 for $m = R$; these are at most n. For each of these, the algorithm considers its explicit ancestors; there are $\mathcal{O}(\log n)$ of them. For each such ancestor u it performs $\deg(u) = \mathcal{O}(\sigma) = \mathcal{O}(1)$ binary searches, each of which takes time $\mathcal{O}(\log^2 \log n)$ as described above. Thus, algorithm PLCP₁SHORT takes worst-case time $\mathcal{O}(n \log n \log^2 \log n)$. The extra space used is clearly $\mathcal{O}(n)$.   □

PLCP₁SHORT(x, n, S, R)

1    $\mathcal{T}(x) \leftarrow$ SUFFIXTREE(x)
2   **for** each explicit node $u \in \mathcal{T}(x)$ **do**
3        $\mathcal{D}(u) \leftarrow$ string-depth of u
4        $\mathcal{I}(u) \leftarrow range(x, \mathcal{L}(u))$
5   Preprocess $\mathcal{T}(x)$ for weighted ancestor queries
6   **for** $i \in S$ **do**
7        $v \leftarrow$ node with path-label $x[i \,.. \, n - 1]$
8   **for** each explicit node u ancestor of v in $\mathcal{T}(x)$ **do**
9           $a \leftarrow x[i + \mathcal{D}(u)]$
10   **for** each outgoing edge from u with first edge label $b \neq a$ **do**
11   PATHBINARYSEARCH$(i, u, b, \mathcal{D}(u) + 1, \min\{R - 2, n - 1 - i\})$

PATHBINARYSEARCH(i, u, b, j_1, j_2)

1    $w \leftarrow$ NODE$(i + \mathcal{D}(u) + 1, i + \lfloor (j_1 + j_2)/2 \rfloor)$
2    $[p, q] \leftarrow range(x, \mathcal{L}(u)b\mathcal{L}(w))$
3   **if** $[p, q] \neq \emptyset$ **then**
4        $\ell \leftarrow |\mathcal{L}(u)b\mathcal{L}(w)|$
5   **if** PLCP₁$[i] < \ell$ **then**
6   PLCP₁$[i] \leftarrow \ell$
7   P₁$[i] \leftarrow$ SA$[p]$
8   **if** $j_1 \neq j_2$ **then**
9   PATHBINARYSEARCH$(i, u, b, \lfloor (j_1 + j_2)/2 \rfloor, j_2)$
10   **else if** $j_1 \neq j_2$ **then**
11   PATHBINARYSEARCH$(i, u, b, j_1, \lfloor (j_1 + j_2)/2 \rfloor)$

By combining Lemmas 4 and 5 we arrive at the following result.

Theorem 6. *Problem* PLCP WITH 1-MISMATCH *can be solved in average-case time* $\mathcal{O}(n \log n \log^2 \log n)$ *using* $\mathcal{O}(n)$ *extra space.*

Theorem 6 improves upon the state-of-the-art average-case time complexity for the case where only 1 mismatch is allowed by a factor of $\log n / \log^3 \log n$ (see Lemma 3 and [23]). Notably, our technique can be extended to work for arbitrary k as follows. We first set $R = \lceil (k+2)(\log_\sigma n + 1) \rceil$ so that the adapted algorithm from [3] requires time $\mathcal{O}(kn)$ on average. Then for each position i with PLCP$_k[i] < R$ we have $\mathcal{O}(k \log n)$ branching nodes for the first mismatch—similar to the above. Suppose that for some explicit node u, ancestor of v, where $\mathcal{L}(v) = x[i \,.. \, n - 1]$ and u has an outgoing edge with first edge label $b \neq x[i + \mathcal{D}(u)]$, the longest prefix of $\mathcal{L}(u)bx[i + \mathcal{D}(u) + 1 \,.. \, i + s]$, where $s = \min\{R - 2, n - 1 - i\}$, that occurs in x is $x[p \,.. \, q]$. In order to allow for a second mismatch, we consider every ancestor of node u_b, where $\mathcal{L}(u_b) = x[p \,.. \, q]$, with string-depth larger than $\mathcal{D}(u) + 1$, and proceed in a similar fashion.

Each branching step allows for an extra mismatch. We only consider $\mathcal{T}(x)$ up to string-depth R and hence the possible branching options are $\mathcal{O}((\sigma R)^k)$. Each binary search is now performed on a path with path-label of length $\mathcal{O}(k \log n)$. Each iteration of the binary search takes time $\mathcal{O}(\log \log n)$ for the level ancestor query and for merging the ranges. We thus arrive at the following result.

Theorem 7. *Problem* PLCP WITH k-MISMATCHES *can be solved in average-case time* $\mathcal{O}(n(\sigma R)^k \log \log n(\log k + \log \log n))$, *where* $R = \lceil (k+2)(\log_\sigma n+1) \rceil$, *using* $\mathcal{O}(n)$ *extra space.*

Remark 1. Alternatively, in the second part of our algorithm (Computing Short PLCPs), we can perform the binary search with the aid of the data structure presented by Cole et al. in [9]. This data structure is of size $\mathcal{O}(n \frac{(c_1 \log n)^k}{k!})$ and can be built in time $\mathcal{O}(n \frac{(c_1 \log n)^k}{k!})$, where $c_1 > 1$ is a constant. We can then answer whether a given substring of x occurs elsewhere in x with at most k mismatches (as well as the starting position of one of its occurrences) in time $\mathcal{O}(\frac{(c_2 \log n)^k \log \log n}{k!})$, where $c_2 > 1$ is another constant. With this modification, the average-case time required by our algorithm becomes $\mathcal{O}(n \frac{(\log n)^k}{k!}(c_1^k + c_2^k(\log \log n(\log k + \log \log n))))$. The $\omega(n)$ space required for this data structure is however impractical for real-world datasets. Note that the efficient solutions of Thankachan et al. for the related *longest common factor with k-mismatches* problem also require space $\omega(n)$ when $k = \omega(1)$ [28,29].

4   Longest Previous Factors with k-Mismatches

The longest previous factor (LPF) array gives, for each position i in a string x, the length of the longest factor of x that occurs both at i and to the left of i in x. The LPF array is central in many text compression techniques as well as in the most efficient algorithms for detecting motifs and repetitions occurring in a text [11]. A time-space optimal (linear) algorithm that computes the LPF array is known for some time [10].

In this section, we present how the algorithm presented in Sect. 3 can be adapted to compute the LPF array with k-mismatches within the same complexities. We naturally define the *LPF array with k-mismatches*, denoted by LPF_k, as follows. We set $\mathsf{LPF}_k[0] = -1$ and for $i = 1, \ldots, n-1$, we have that

$$\mathsf{LPF}_k[i] = \max_{j=0,\ldots,i-1} \mathsf{lcp}_k(x[i \mathinner{.\,.} n-1], x[j \mathinner{.\,.} n-1]).$$

The problem in scope can be formally defined as follows.

LPF WITH k-MISMATCHES

Input: A string x of length n and an integer $0 < k < n$

Output: LPF_k and P_k; $\mathsf{P}_k[0] = -1$ and $\mathsf{P}_k[i] < i$, for $i = 1, \ldots, n-1$, is such that $x[i \mathinner{.\,.} i + \ell - 1] \approx_k x[\mathsf{P}_k[i] \mathinner{.\,.} \mathsf{P}_k[i] + \ell - 1]$, where $\ell = \mathsf{LPF}_k[i]$

Example 2. Consider the string `acababbac`. The following table gives arrays LPF_1 and P_1.

i	0	1	2	3	4	5	6	7	8
$\mathsf{LPF}_1[i]$	-1	1	4	3	3	3	3	2	1
$\mathsf{P}_1[i]$	-1	0	0	1	2	2	3	0	1

First, let us recall that a range minimum query (RMQ) data structure over an array of size n can be constructed in time and space $\mathcal{O}(n)$, and can then answer range minimum queries in $\mathcal{O}(1)$ time per query (see [7] for the details).

The following two modifications to the algorithm presented in Sect. 3 suffice to transform it to an algorithm that solves problem LPF WITH k-MISMATCHES:

1. When running the average-case k-mappability algorithm and considering a pair of suffixes starting at positions r, q, $r < q$, $\mathsf{LPF}_k[r]$ remains unchanged, while we only update $\mathsf{LPF}_k[q]$ (along with $\mathsf{P}_k[q]$) if $\mathsf{LPF}_k[q] < \mathsf{lcp}_k(x[r\mathinner{..}n - 1], x[q\mathinner{..}n - 1])$.
2. In the second part of the algorithm described above, while processing the suffix starting at position i, if at any step of the algorithm the obtained SA range $[p, q]$ (corresponding to node z in $\mathcal{T}(x)$) is not empty, we also have to check whether it contains a position smaller than i. We do this by employing the RMQ data structure over the suffix array. If $\mathsf{SA}[\mathsf{RMQ}_{\mathsf{SA}}(p, q)] > i$, we treat the range as if it were empty and go up the path. If $\mathsf{SA}[\mathsf{RMQ}_{\mathsf{SA}}(p, q)] < i$, we go down the path after checking whether $\mathsf{LPF}_k[i] < \mathcal{D}(z)$; if yes, we set $\mathsf{LPF}_k[i] = \mathcal{D}(z)$ and $\mathsf{P}_k[i] = \mathsf{SA}[\mathsf{RMQ}_{\mathsf{SA}}(p, q)]$.

Theorem 8. *Problem LPF WITH k-mismatches can be solved in average-case time $\mathcal{O}(n(\sigma R)^k \log \log n (\log k + \log \log n))$, where $R = \lceil (k + 2)(\log_\sigma n + 1) \rceil$, using $\mathcal{O}(n)$ extra space.*

5 Application of LCP with k-Mismatches to Genome Mappability

The focus of this section is directly motivated by the well-known and challenging application of *genome re-sequencing*—the assembly of a genome directed by a reference sequence. New developments in sequencing technologies [25] allow whole-genome sequencing to be turned into a routine procedure, creating sequencing data in massive amounts. Short sequences, known as *reads*, are produced in huge amounts (tens of gigabytes); and in order to determine the part of the genome from which a read was derived, it must be mapped (aligned) back to some reference sequence that consists of a few gigabases. A wide variety of short-read alignment techniques and tools have been published in the past years to address the challenge of efficiently mapping tens of millions of reads to a genome, focusing on different aspects of the procedure: speed, sensitivity, and accuracy [15]. These tools allow for a small number of errors in the alignment.

The re-sequencing method starts with matching a *seed* of each read to the genome. This, for example, could be a short prefix of the read (the accuracy is usually higher in the prefix of the read). We then *extend* this match until the total number of errors exceeds a predefined threshold or until a match is found [2]. Considering errors is necessary due to genetic variation as well as sequencing errors; most of these errors are single-base substitutions [24]. It is suitable to allow for a small number k of errors in the seed part.

The k-*mappability* problem was first introduced in the context of genome analysis in [12] (and in some sense earlier in [5]), where a heuristic algorithm was proposed to approximate the solution. The aim from a biological perspective is to compute the mappability of each region of a genome sequence; i.e. for every substring of a given length of the sequence, we are asked to count how many other times it occurs in the genome with up to a given number of errors. This is particularly useful in the application of genome re-sequencing. By computing the mappability of the reference genome, we can then assemble the genome of an individual with greater confidence by first mapping the segments of the DNA that correspond to regions with low mappability. Interestingly, it has been shown that genome mappability varies greatly between species and gene classes [12].

Formally, we are given a string x of length n and integers $m < n$ and $k < m$, and we are asked to count, for each length-m substring y of x, the number occ of other length-m substrings of x that are at Hamming distance at most k from y. We then say that this substring has k-mappability equal to occ. Hence, a more general question to ask is the following: *What is the minimal value of m that forces at least α of the starting positions in the reference genome to have k-mappability equal to 0?* We formalise this question as a data structure problem.

GENOME MAppability
Input: A string x of length n and an integer $0 < k < n$
Query: $\text{LEN}_{x,k}(\alpha)$ that represents the smallest m such that at least $\alpha > 0$ of the substrings of x of length m do not occur more than once in x with at most k mismatches

---

We can solve this problem by first making the following crucial observation.

Observation 9. *A substring $x[i\mathinner{.\,.}i+m-1]$ of a string x does not occur more than once in x with at most k mismatches if and only if $m > PLCP_k[i]$.*

Our construction works as follows. We first compute the PLCP_k array for x. We then sort its elements in ascending order using bucket sort in time $\mathcal{O}(n)$ and store them in a new array $\mathcal{A}_k$. Based on Observation 9, $\text{LEN}_{x,k}(\alpha)$ is given by the smallest m for which $\mathcal{A}_k[\alpha+m-2]+1 \leq m$. We show the following property on the values of $\mathcal{A}_k$.

Property 1. $\mathcal{A}_k[i+1] \leq \mathcal{A}_k[i]+1$.

Proof. Note that either $\text{PLCP}_k[i+1] \geq \text{PLCP}_k[i]$ or $\text{PLCP}_k[i+1] = \text{PLCP}_k[i]-1$. Thus considering the values in the PLCP_k array from the left to the right they start from $\mathsf{PLCP}_k[0]$ and then as we move one position to the right, this value either increases or stays the same or drops by 1. $\mathsf{PLCP}_k[n-1]$ is equal to either 0 or 1. Hence, for every integer $d \in [\min_i\{\mathsf{PLCP}_k[i]\}, \max_i\{\mathsf{PLCP}_k[i]\}]$ there exists a j, $0 \le j \le n-1$, such that $\mathsf{PLCP}_k[j] = d$ and thus the lemma follows. (Note that $\mathcal{A}_k$ is just the sorted PLCP_k array.) $\qquad\square$

For each α, $0 < \alpha \le n-1$, we denote by $m_\alpha \in [k+1, n-\alpha+1]$ the smallest integer—if it exists—for which $\mathcal{A}_k[\alpha+m_\alpha-2]+1 \le m_\alpha$ holds. In fact, we know by Property 1 that if such an m_α exists, then

$$\mathcal{A}_k[\alpha + r - 2] + 1 \le r, \text{ for all } m_\alpha \le r \le n - \alpha + 1.$$

Moreover, we have that $m_\alpha \le m_{\alpha+1}$, since

$$\mathcal{A}_k[\alpha + m_{\alpha+1} - 2] + 1 \le \mathcal{A}_k[\alpha + 1 + m_{\alpha+1} - 2] + 1 \le m_{\alpha+1}.$$

We can thus precompute m_α, for all $0 < \alpha \le n-1$, and store them in an array $\mathcal{B}_k[\alpha] = m_\alpha$ in time $\mathcal{O}(n)$ while scanning array $\mathcal{A}_k$ from left to right: we start by computing m_1 and apply the inequality $m_\alpha \le m_{\alpha+1}$ to obtain $m_2, \ldots, m_{n-1}$. If such an integer m_α does not exist, we set $\mathcal{B}_k[\alpha] = 0$. We can then answer query $\mathsf{LEN}_{x,k}(\alpha)$ in time $\mathcal{O}(1)$: the answer is $\mathcal{B}_k[\alpha]$.

Example 3. Consider the string $x = \texttt{acababbac}$ and $k = 1$. The following table gives arrays PLCP_1, $\mathcal{A}_1$, and $\mathcal{B}_1$. For $\alpha = 3$, we have that $\mathsf{LEN}_{x,k}(3) = \mathcal{B}_1[3] = 4$.

i	0	1	2	3	4	5	6	7	8
$\mathsf{PLCP}_1[i]$	4	3	4	3	3	3	3	2	1
$\mathcal{A}_1[i]$	1	2	3	3	3	3	3	4	4
$\mathcal{B}_1[i]$	-	4	4	4	4	5	0	0	0

We thus obtain the following result.

Theorem 10. *Array $\mathcal{B}_k$ can be computed in time $\mathcal{O}(n)$ from array PLCP_k.*

Corollary 2. *We can construct an $\mathcal{O}(n)$-sized data structure in average-case time $\mathcal{O}(n(\sigma R)^k \log \log n(\log k + \log \log n))$, where $R = \lceil (k+2)(\log_\sigma n + 1) \rceil$, using $\mathcal{O}(n)$ extra space that answers GENOME MAPPABILITY queries in $\mathcal{O}(1)$ time per query.*

6 Final Remarks

We have presented a new algorithm for computing the longest prefix of each suffix of a given string of length n over a constant-sized alphabet of size σ that occurs elsewhere in the string with Hamming distance at most k. The proposed algorithm requires time $\mathcal{O}(n(\sigma R)^k \log \log n(\log k + \log \log n))$ on average, where $R = \lceil (k+2)(\log_\sigma n + 1) \rceil$, and $\mathcal{O}(n)$ extra space.

We have then shown that the proposed technique can be adapted and applied for computing the longest previous factors under the Hamming distance model within the same complexities. Finally, we have shown that our technique can be applied to construct an $\mathcal{O}(n)$-sized data structure that can answer queries related to genome mappability [12] in $\mathcal{O}(1)$ time per query.

We anticipate that this new technique would be applicable in several contexts where we have to compute longest repeating factors under the Hamming distance model subject to some additional requirements. For instance, one such problem is computing the longest factor of a string occurring in another string with k-mismatches, also known as the LCF with k-mismatches problem [16,28].

References

1. Abouelhoda, M.I., Kurtz, S., Ohlebusch, E.: Replacing suffix trees with enhanced suffix arrays. J. Discret. Algorithms **2**(1), 53–86 (2004)
2. Altschul, S.F., Gish, W., Miller, W., Myers, E.W., Lipman, D.J.: Basic local alignment search tool. J. Mol. Biol. **215**(3), 403–410 (1990)
3. Alzamel, M., Charalampopoulos, P., Iliopoulos, C.S., Pissis, S.P., Radoszewski, J., Sung, W.-K.: Faster algorithms for 1-mappability of a sequence. In: COCOA. LNCS, vol. 10628, pp. 109–121. Springer International Publishing (2017). https://doi.org/10.1007/978-3-319-71147-8_8
4. Amir, A., Landau, G.M., Lewenstein, M., Sokol, D.: Dynamic text and static pattern matching. ACM Trans. Algorrithms **3**(2), 19 (2007)
5. Antoniou, P., Daykin, J.W., Iliopoulos, C.S., Kourie, D., Mouchard, L., Pissis, S.P.: Mapping uniquely occurring short sequences derived from high throughput technologies to a reference genome. In: ITAB, pp. 1–4. IEEE Computer Society (2009)
6. Barthet, M., Plumbley, M.D., Kachkaev, A., Dykes, J., Wolff, D., Weyde, T.: Big chord data extraction and mining. In: CIM (2014)
7. Bender, M.A., Farach-Colton, M.: The LCA problem revisited. In: Gonnet, G.H., Viola, A. (eds.) LATIN 2000. LNCS, vol. 1776, pp. 88–94. Springer, Heidelberg (2000). https://doi.org/10.1007/10719839_9
8. Bufe, C.: Understandable Guide to Music Theory: The Most Useful Aspects of Theory for Rock, Jazz, and Blues Musicians. See Sharp Press, Tucson (1994)
9. Cole, R., Gottlieb, L.-A., Lewenstein, M.: Dictionary matching and indexing with errors and don't cares. In: STOC 2004, pp. 91–100. ACM (2004)
10. Crochemore, M., Ilie, L., Iliopoulos, C.S., Kubica, M., Rytter, W., Waleń, T.: Computing the longest previous factor. Eur. J. Comb. **34**(1), 15–26 (2013)
11. Crochemore, M., Ilie, L., Smyth, W.F.: A simple algorithm for computing the Lempel Ziv factorization. In: DCC, pp. 482–488. IEEE Computer Society (2008)
12. Derrien, T., Estellé, J., Sola, S.M., Knowles, D., Raineri, E., Guigó, R., Ribeca, P.: Fast computation and applications of genome mappability. PLoS ONE **7**(1), e30377 (2012)
13. Fischer, J.: Inducing the LCP-array. In: Dehne, F., Iacono, J., Sack, J.-R. (eds.) WADS 2011. LNCS, vol. 6844, pp. 374–385. Springer, Heidelberg (2011). https://doi.org/10.1007/978-3-642-22300-6_32
14. Fischer, J., Köppl, D., Kurpicz, F.: On the benefit of merging suffix array intervals for parallel pattern matching. In: CPM 2016. LIPIcs, vol. 54, pp. 26:1–26:11. Schloss Dagstuhl - Leibniz-Zentrum fuer Informatik (2016)

15. Fonseca, N.A., Rung, J., Brazma, A., Marioni, J.C.: Tools for mapping high-throughput sequencing data. Bioinformatics **28**(24), 3169–3177 (2012)
16. Grabowski, S.: A note on the longest common substring with k-mismatches problem. Inf. Process. Lett. **115**(6–8), 640–642 (2015)
17. Kärkkäinen, J., Kempa, D.: Faster external memory LCP array construction. In: ESA. LIPIcs, vol. 57, pp. 61:1–61:16. Schloss Dagstuhl - Leibniz-Zentrum fuer Informatik (2016)
18. Karlin, S., Ghandour, G., Ost, F., Tavare, S., Korn, L.J.: New approaches for computer analysis of nucleic acid sequences. Proc. Natl. Acad. Sci. U.S.A. **80**(18), 5660–5664 (1983)
19. Khmelev, D.V., Teahan, W.J.: A repetition based measure for verification of text collections and for text categorization. In: ACM SIGIR 2003, pp. 104–110. ACM (2003)
20. Kolpakov, R., Bana, G., Kucherov, G.: MREPS: efficient and flexible detection of tandem repeats in DNA. Nucleic Acids Res. **31**(13), 3672–3678 (2003)
21. Liang, K.-H.: Bioinformatics for Biomedical Science and Clinical Applications. Woodhead Publishing Series in Biomedicine. Woodhead Publishing, Cambridge (2013)
22. Manber, U., Myers, E.W.: Suffix arrays: a new method for on-line string searches. SIAM J. Comput. **22**(5), 935–948 (1993)
23. Manzini, G.: Longest common prefix with mismatches. In: Iliopoulos, C., Puglisi, S., Yilmaz, E. (eds.) SPIRE 2015. LNCS, vol. 9309, pp. 299–310. Springer, Cham (2015). https://doi.org/10.1007/978-3-319-23826-5_29
24. Médigue, C., Rose, M., Viari, A., Danchin, A.: Detecting and analyzing DNA sequencing errors: toward a higher quality of the bacillus subtilis genome sequence. Genome Res. **9**(11), 1116–1127 (1999)
25. Metzker, M.L.: Sequencing technologies - the next generation. Nat. Rev. Genet. **11**(1), 31–46 (2010)
26. Nong, G., Zhang, S., Chan, W.H.: Linear suffix array construction by almost pure induced-sorting. In: DCC, pp. 193–202. IEEE (2009)
27. Smit, A.F.A.: Interspersed repeats and other mementos of transposable elements in mammalian genomes. Curr. Opin. Genet. Dev. **9**(6), 657–663 (1999)
28. Thankachan, S.V., Apostolico, A., Aluru, S.: A provably efficient algorithm for the k-mismatch average common substring problem. J. Comput. Biol. **23**(6), 472–482 (2016)
29. Thankachan, S.V., Chockalingam, S.P., Liu, Y., Apostolico, A., Aluru, S.: ALFRED: a practical method for alignment-free distance computation. J. Comput. Biol. **23**(6), 452–460 (2016)
30. Weiner, P.: Linear pattern matching algorithms. In: SWAT 1973, pp. 1–11. IEEE Computer Society (1973)

Data and Model Engineering

Managing Reduction in Multidimensional Databases

Franck Ravat[1], Jiefu Song[1(✉)], and Olivier Teste[2]

[1] IRIT – Université Toulouse I Capitole, 2 Rue du Doyen Gabriel Marty,
31042 Toulouse Cedex 09, France
{ravat,song}@irit.fr
[2] IRIT – Université Toulouse II Jean Jaurès, 1 Place Georges Brassens,
31703 Blagnac Cedex, France
teste@irit.fr

Abstract. Dealing with large amount of data has always been a key focus of the Multidimensional Database (MDB) community, especially in the current era when data volume increases more and more rapidly. In this paper, we outline a conceptual modeling solution allowing reducing data in MDBs. A MDB after reduction is modeled with multiple states. Each state is valid during a period of time and aggregates data from a more recent state. We propose three alternatives of reduced MDB modeling at the logical level: (i) the *flat* modeling integrates all states into one single table, (ii) the *horizontal* modeling converts each state into a fact table and some dimension tables associated with a temporal interval and (iii) the *vertical* modeling breaks down a reduced MDB into separate tables, each table includes data from one or several states. We evaluate query execution efficiency in MDBs with and without data reduction. The result shows data reduction is an interesting solution, since it significantly decreases execution costs by 98.96% during our experimental assessments.

Keywords: Data reduction · Relational multidimensional design
Experimental assessments

1 Introduction

Multidimensional Databases (MDBs) are widely used in decision-support systems. A MDB organizes data according to analysis subjects (i.e. facts) and analysis axes (i.e. dimensions). A fact includes a set of numeric indicators (i.e. measures), while a dimension contains one or several granularities (i.e. levels). In today's highly competitive business context, data coming from both inside and outside a company are periodically added and then permanently stored in a MDB [1, 6]. The huge amount of data in a MDB slows down query execution, not to mention that decision-makers may easily get lost while facing all detailed data during analyses. Meanwhile, all data do not keep the same informative value over time. While detailed information is important for recent data, it may be of less interest for older data [11].

Reducing data can avoid an overly large MDB. It allows decreasing the amount of useless data and thus increasing query execution efficiency [13]. As detailed data lose

© Springer International Publishing AG 2018
A M. Tjoa et al. (Eds.): SOFSEM 2018, LNCS 10706, pp. 653–666, 2018.
https://doi.org/10.1007/978-3-319-73117-9_46

their informative value over time, a data reduction solution should allow selectively deleting useless data in a MDB. Moreover, it is necessary to aggregate data progressively, so that information is not lost after reduction but represented in a summarized form for comparative or trend analyses. This is achieved by eliminating a MDB's content deprecated for business analyses.

Our aim is to support effective and efficient decision-making by storing only data of high informative value over time in a MDB. In our previous work [9], we proposed a conceptual modeling solution for *MDBs with data reduction* (i.e. reduced MDBs). As modeling solutions at the logical level are seldom studied for MDBs whose schema changes over time, this paper focuses on the relational modeling of reduced MDBs. Some algorithms are proposed to automatically transform a conceptual reduced MDB into different relational forms. We carry out some experimental assessments to compare query execution efficiency in reduced and unreduced MDBs.

The paper is organized as follows: Sect. 2 discusses the representative work related to data reduction; Sect. 3 describes three relational modeling solutions and a schema design process for reduced MDBs; Sect. 4 illustrates the benefits of reduced MDBs through some experimental assessments.

2 Related Work

Data reduction is a technique originally used in the data mining field [7]. In this context, data reduction aims at improving the accuracy of mining results by extracting significant and relevant features of sources. In the database field, data reduction is adapted to automatically delete expired data which are no longer of interest. We can cite the work [3] which enables data reduction by deleting content in materialized views. In the MDB field, related work focuses on reducing data in a fact. The authors of [12] describe a solution for the progressive aggregation and deletion of data in a fact. A set of criteria is proposed to summarize data according to higher granularities. The authors of [5] present a complete data reduction process. They study the conception, implementation, and influence of data reduction in a MDB's fact.

The above-mentioned work only allows reducing a fact. Our previous work [9] generalizes the reduction to a complete MDW. Consequently, both facts and dimensions can be reduced. Moreover, unlike some automatic reduction solutions, our proposed approach involves decision-makers in a reduction process. A designer determines with a decision-maker within which temporal interval a MDB schema is valid. As detailed information is often irrelevant to analyses over an old period, a MDB schema includes different contents over time. The further we look back in time, the fewer detailed data a MDB schema contains.

Specifically, a reduced MDB is composed of a set of *states* $E = \{E_1; \ldots; E_n\}$. The state E_n is the latest state including the most complete schema, while the other states consist of a succession of reduced schemas over time. Each *state* $E_i (E_i \in E)$ corresponds to a star schema including a *fact* F_i and a set of *dimensions* D_i with necessarily a temporal dimension. The *state* E_i is stamped with a validation period $T_i = [t^i_{start}; t^i_{end}]$ defined on the temporal dimension. The *fact* F_i contains a set of *measures*, $M^{Fi} = \{m_1; \ldots; m_p\}$ while a *dimension* $D_k(D_k \in D_i)$ includes a set of *attributes* $A^{Dk} = \{a_1; \ldots; a_q\}$ organized in different *levels*. We distinguish two types of attributes: a *parameter* $p_x(p_x \in A^{Dk})$ is an attribute allowing identifying an unique *level* on the dimension D_k, while a *weak attribute* is a non-identifier attribute providing descriptive information to a *parameter*.

Based on this conceptual reduced MDB modeling, our previous work [9] extends the work [10] by proposing some operators for multidimensional analyses on reduced data. These operators allow (i) choosing analysis subjects and axes (i.e. *Display*), (ii) aggregating data (i.e. *Drilldown* and *Rollup*), (iii) changing analysis axes (i.e. *Rotate*), and (iv) filtering analysis results (i.e. *Select*).

In this paper, we complete our work [9] by studying modeling alternatives at the logical level. The efficiency of each alternative will be studied through some experimental assessments.

3   Relational Modeling of MDBs with Data Reduction

In this section, we describe the logical modeling of reduced MDBs. This modeling is based on three relational modeling alternatives. An algorithm is proposed for each alternative to automate the transformation from a conceptual reduced MDB into a relational reduced MDB.

3.1   Case Study

A MDB contains a fact, named *Sales*, which includes one measure named *Amount*. The measure can be calculated along three dimensions, namely *Products*, *Customers* and *Times*. The current MDB contains all sale data from 1990 to 2017. However, since most today's products and customers did not exist before, the MDB is reduced by creating three states as follows: (i) the latest state E_3 contains all detailed data within all dimensions from 2010 to 2017; (ii) the second state E_2 includes aggregated data starting from products' *Range*, customers' *Town* and sale date ID_{Time} between 2000 to 2010; (iii) the oldest state E_1 supports historical sales analyses by products' *Sector* and *Year* from 1900 to 2000. Figure 1 shows the reduced MDB's states according to the graphical notation proposed in [4].

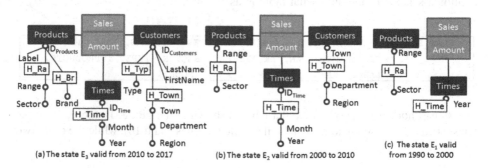

(a) The state E_3 valid from 2010 to 2017   (b) The state E_2 valid from 2000 to 2010   (c) The state E_1 valid from 1990 to 2000

Fig. 1. Reduced MDB schema evolutions over time

3.2   *Flat* Modeling of a Reduced MDB

The first alternative is called *flat* modeling. It integrates all states into one single flat table. All attributes and all measures before data reduction constitute the columns of a flat table. We propose the following algorithm for the *flat* modeling.

Algorithm 1. *Flat Modeling*

Input: a reduced MDB composed of a set of states $\mathcal{E} = \{E_1; ...; E_n\}$.

Output: a flat table T_{Flat} = (<u>SynKey</u>, $\mathcal{A}_{Flat}$, $\mathcal{M}_{Flat}$), where SynKey is a synthetic key; $\mathcal{A}_{Flat}=\{a_1; ...; a_m\}$ is a set of attributes; $\mathcal{M}_{Flat}=\{m_1; ...; m_p\}$ is a set of measures.

Begin

1. *Find the latest state E_n of the reduced MDB, $E_n \in \mathcal{E}$, $E_n=\{F_n; \mathcal{D}_n; T_n\}$;*
2. *Create the schema of the flat table T_{Flat}, set $\mathcal{A}_{Flat} \leftarrow \bigcup_{D_i \in \mathcal{D}_n} A^{D_i}$, set $\mathcal{M}_{Flat} \leftarrow \mathcal{M}^{F_n}$;*
3. For each $E_i \in \mathcal{E}$
4. | For each $a_k \in \mathcal{A}_{Flat}$ do,
5. | | If $a_k \notin \bigcup_{D_j \in \mathcal{D}_i} A^{D_j}$ then *assign the NULL value to the instances of a_k;*
6. | End for
7. | For each $m_s \in \mathcal{M}_{Flat}$ do,
8. | | If $m_s \notin \mathcal{M}^{F_i}$ then *assign the NULL value to the instances of m_s;*
9. | End for
10. | *Insert into T_{Flat} with tuples $(i_{a_1}, ..., i_{a_m}, i_{m_1}, ..., i_{m_p})$, such as $\forall i_{a_k} \in \{i_{a_1}; ...;$*
    | *$i_{a_m}\}$, $i_{a_k} \in dom(a_k)$ and $\forall i_{m_s} \in \{i_{m_1}; ...; i_{m_p}\}$, $i_{m_s} \in val(m_s)$;*
11. End for

End

After creating the structure of a flat table (*cf.* lines 1 and 2), the algorithm extracts data from each state and loads the flat table. Specifically, if the attribute a_k (or the measure m_s) from the flat table does not exist in the state E_i, the algorithm assigns the *NULL* value to its instances (*cf.* lines 3–9). Then, measure instances and related attribute instances from each state are loaded in the flat table (*cf.* line 10). The time span of a flat table corresponds to the union of all states' temporal intervals.

Example. We apply the algorithm 1 to the reduced MDB of our case study. The relational schema of the output flat table is as follows.

```
FLAT_SALES (SYNKEY, IDTIME, MONTH, YEAR, IDCUSTOMERS, LASTNAME,
            FIRSTNAME, TOWN, DEPARTMENT, REGION, TYPE, IDPRODUCTS,
            LABEL, RANGE, SECTOR, BRAND, AMOUNT)
```

A snapshot[1] of instances in the flat table is shown in the Fig. 2. Instances from the latest state E_3 are directly loaded in the flat table (*cf.* lines 3 and 10), while the other two

---

[1] For the sake of simplicity, all snapshots in this section include only the dimension *Products*.

time span [1990, 2017]

	SYNKEY		...		IDPRODUCTS		LABEL		RANGE		SECTOR		BRAND		AMOUNT
E_3	1 ...				1		P1		R1		S1		B1		100
	2 ...				2		P2		R1		S1		B2		150
	3 ...				3		P3		R2		S1		B2		300
E_2	4 ...				null		null		R1		S1		null		240
	5 ...				null		null		R2		S1		null		320
E_1	6 ...				null		null		null		S1		null		540

Fig. 2. A snapshot of instances organized according to the *flat* modeling

states E_2 and E_1 are loaded with *NULL* value as placeholder for the deleted attributes' instances (cf. lines 3–6 and 10).

3.3   *Horizontal* Modeling of a Reduced MDB

The second relational modeling alternative is named *horizontal*. Each state is implemented through a *fact table* and a set of *dimension tables*. The algorithm of the *horizontal* modeling is as follows.

Algorithm 2. *Horizontal Modeling*

Input: a reduced MDB composed of a set of states $\mathcal{E} = \{E_1; ...; E_n\}$.

Outputs:

— a set of fact tables $\mathcal{T}_{Fact} = \{T_{F_1}; ...; T_{F_n}\}$, such as $\forall T_{F_i} \in \mathcal{T}_{Fact}$, $T_{F_i} = (\underline{SynKey_i}, \mathcal{FKey_i}, \mathcal{M}_i)$ implements the fact F_i of the state E_i, where $SynKey_i$ is a synthetic primary key; $\mathcal{FKey_i}$ is a set of foreign keys; $\mathcal{M}_i$ is a set of measures in T_{F_i}.

— a set of dimension tables $\mathcal{T}_{Dim} = \{T_{D_1^{E_1}}; ...; T_{D_w^{E_n}}\}$, such as $\forall T_{D_j^{E_i}} \in \mathcal{T}_{Dim}$, $T_{D_j^{E_i}} = (\underline{Key_{T_{ji}}}, \mathcal{A}_{T_{ji}})$ implements the dimension D_j of the state E_i, where $Key_{T_{ji}}$ is a primary key of the dimension table; $\mathcal{A}_{T_{ji}}$ is a set of attributes.

Begin

1.   For each state $E_i \in \mathcal{E}$, $E_i = \{F_i; \mathcal{D}_i; T_i\}$

2. | *Create a fact table* $T_{F_i} = (\underline{SynKey_i}, \mathcal{FKey_i}, \mathcal{M}_i)$, *where* $\mathcal{FKey_i} \leftarrow \emptyset$, $\mathcal{M}_i \leftarrow \mathcal{M}^{F_i}$;

3. | For each dimension $D_j \in \mathcal{D}_i$

4. | *Find the parameter* p_1 *on the lowest granularity of* D_j;

5. | $\mathcal{FKey_i} \leftarrow \mathcal{FKey_i} \cup \{p_1\}$;

6. | *Create a dimension table* $T_{D_j^{E_i}} = (\underline{Key_{T_{ji}}}, \mathcal{A}_{T_{ji}})$, *set* $Key_{T_{ji}} \leftarrow p_1$, $\mathcal{A}_{T_{ji}} \leftarrow \mathcal{A}^{D_i} \backslash \{p_1\}$;

7. | *Insert attribute instances within* D_j *into* $T_{D_j^{E_i}}$;

8. | End for

9. | *Insert measure instances within* F_i *with related parameter instances into* T_{F_i}

10. End for

End

The *horizontal* modeling creates a fact table T_{F_i} for each state E_i. Each fact table includes all measures from the fact F_i and a set of foreign keys (*cf.* lines 1 and 2). Each foreign key consists of the parameter on the lowest granularity of a dimension from the state E_i (*cf.* line 5). Each dimension D_j is converted into a dimension table as follows: the parameter p_1 of the lowest granularity on D_j is used as a primary key, while other attributes on the dimension (i.e. $\mathcal{A}^{Di} \backslash \{p_1\}$) are directly added in the dimension table (*cf.* lines 3–6). Consequently, the time span of a fact table and a dimension table corresponds to the temporal interval of the involved state.

Example. According to the algorithm 2, the reduced MDB of the case study is implemented through 3 fact tables and 8 dimension tables.

E3_TIMES	(IDTIME, MONTH, YEAR)
E3_CUSTOMERS	(IDCUSTOMERS, LASTNAME, FIRSTNAME, TOWN, DEPARTMENT, REGION, TYPE)
E3_PRODUCTS	(IDPRODUCTS, LABEL, RANGE, SECTOR, BRAND)
E3_SALES	(SYNKEY, IDTIME#, IDCUSTOMERS#, IDPRODUCTS#, AMOUNT)
E2_TIMES	(IDTIME, MONTH, YEAR)
E2_CUSTOMERS	(TOWN, DEPARTMENT, REGION)
E2_PRODUCTS	(RANGE, SECTOR)
E2_SALES	(SYNKEY, IDTIME#, TOWN#, RANGE#, AMOUNT)
E1_TIMES	(YEAR)
E1_PRODUCTS	(SECTOR)
E1_SALES	(SYNKEY, YEAR#, SECTOR#, AMOUNT)

Figure 3 displays a snapshot of instances in the reduced MDB implemented according to the *horizontal* modeling.

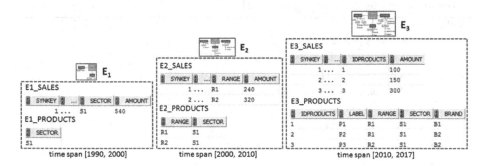

Fig. 3. A snapshot of instances organized according to the *horizontal* modeling

3.4   *Vertical* Modeling of a Reduced MDB

The third alternative is named *vertical* modeling. It gathers common components among states into separate tables called vertical tables. Each vertical table includes measures and attributes shared by some states. We propose the following algorithm for the *vertical* modeling.

Algorithm 3. *Vertical Modeling*

Input: a reduced MDB composed of a set of states $\mathcal{E} = \{E_1, ..., E_n\}$.

Output: a set of vertical tables $\mathcal{T}_V = \{T_{V_1}, ..., T_{V_n}\}$, such as $\forall T_{V_i} \in \mathcal{T}_V$, $T_{V_i} = \{\underline{\text{SynKey}_i}, \mathcal{A}_i, \mathcal{M}_i\}$ is a vertical table for a subset of states, where SynKey_i is a synthetic key; $\mathcal{A}_i$ is a set of attributes; $\mathcal{M}_i$ is a set of measures.

Begin

1. For each i from 1 to n (n=|$\mathcal{E}$|)

2. | Create a vertical table $T_{V_i} = \{\underline{\text{SynKey}_i}, \mathcal{A}_i, \mathcal{M}_i\}$, where

    — $\mathcal{A}_i \leftarrow \cup_{D_k \in \mathcal{D}_i} \mathcal{A}^{D_k}$ such as $\mathcal{D}_i$ is the set of dimensions from the state E_i;

    — $\mathcal{M}_i \leftarrow \mathcal{M}^{F_i}$ such as F_i is the fact from the state E_i;

3. | For each $E_x \in \mathcal{E}$

4. | | *Insert into* T_{V_i} *instances of attributes* $\mathcal{A}_i$;

5. | | *Insert into* T_{V_i} *aggregated values of measures* $\mathcal{M}_i$ *from* E_x *according to* $\mathcal{A}_i$;

6. | End For

7. | $\mathcal{E} \leftarrow \mathcal{E} \setminus \{E_i\}$;

8. End for

End

According to the definition of the data reduction, attributes and measures from an old state E_i must exist in a more recent state E_j (i < j). Therefore, to gathers common components in a subset of states $\{E_i, ..., E_n\}$ ($1 \leq i \leq n$), the ith vertical table T_{V_i} groups together attributes and measures from the ith state (*cf.* lines 1 and 2). Then, for each state E_x in $\{E_i, ..., E_n\}$, instances of each attribute in $\mathcal{A}_i$ are retrieved from the state E_x and then loaded in T_{V_i}. Based on the attribute instances, values of each measure in $\mathcal{M}_i$ from E_x are aggregated and then inserted into T_{V_i} (*cf.* lines 3–6). Consequently, each vertical table T_{V_i} covers a time span from the state E_i to the latest state E_n.

Example. After applying the algorithm 3 to our case study, we obtain the following three vertical tables.

```
VTABLE1  (SYNKEY, YEAR, SECTOR, AMOUNT)
VTABLE2  (SYNKEY, IDTIME, MONTH, YEAR, TOWN, DEPARTMENT, REGION,
         RANGE, SECTOR, AMOUNT)
VTABLE3  (SYNKEY, IDTIME, MONTH, YEAR, IDCUSTOMERS, LASTNAME,
         FIRSTNAME, TOWN, DEPARTMENT, REGION, TYPE, IDPRODUCTS,
         LABEL, RANGE, SECTOR, BRAND, AMOUNT)
```

The snapshot presented in Fig. 4 indicates a state of reduced MDB is implemented through one or several vertical tables. For instance, data from the latest state E_3 are found within all vertical tables: (i) *VTABLE3* includes the sale *amount* from 2010 to 2017 by *IDProducts*; (ii) *VTABLE2* aggregates the *amount* from the state E_3 according to products' *range*; (iii) *VTABLE3* further aggregates the *amount* from the state E_3 according to product's *sector*.

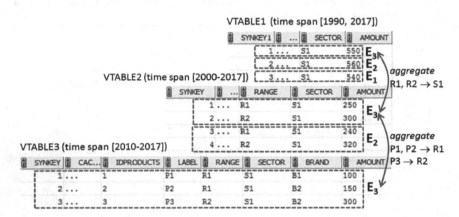

Fig. 4. A snapshot of instances organized according to the *vertical* modeling

3.5 Comparison Among Relational Modeling Alternatives

A conceptual reduced MDB can be transformed into various relational schemas. Extracting the same data requires applying different queries to different relational schemas with different data redundancy ratios.

The *flat* modeling consists of a simplistic way which converts the whole reduced MDB into one relation. It frees queries from joins, regardless of the number of involved dimensions. However, the *flat* modeling causes high data redundancy: attribute instances are repetitively stored in the relation with related measure instances.

The *horizontal* modeling is a more complex method which converts measures and attributes from one state into independent relations. It minimizes data redundancy by associating attribute instances with related measure instances through *primary key - foreign key* relationships. However, the *horizontal* modeling requires joins in queries involving dimension tables.

The *vertical* modeling converts measures and attributes shared by several states into separate relations. This modeling has multiple advantages. On one hand, queries involving several dimensions do not have to include joins. On the other hand, data redundancy is reduced to attribute instances within some high levels on dimensions.

To accurately and quantitatively study the influences of different relational modeling alternatives on query execution efficiency, the remainder of this paper focuses on some experimental assessments.

4   Experimental Assessments

In this section, we carry out some experimental assessments by executing queries in reduced and unreduced MDBs populated with data according to different volumes.

4.1   Protocol

The objective of our experimental assessments is twofold: (i) studying if all relational modeling alternatives for reduced MDBs help improving query execution efficiency and (ii) identifying the most efficient relational modeling of reduced MDBs. Existing multidimensional data benchmarks (e.g. TPC-DS[2] and SSB [8]) are designed to measure a system's performance [2]. They do not allow testing the effect of different reduced modeling solutions, since the included MDB is composed of only one state.

Facing this issue, we have to generate our own data during the experimental assessments. The MDB of our case study is used and populated with synthetic data. Three reduced MDB implementations, namely *flat*, *horizontal* and *vertical*, are built according to the relational modeling alternatives (*cf.* Sect. 3). Two unreduced MDBs are used as baseline to assess the impact of data reduction: (i) the *unreduced flat* MDB integrates all attributes and measures before reduction into one table and (ii) the *unreduced horizontal* MDB includes one fact table and three dimension tables without reduction. The number of tuples as well as redundancy ratio of attribute instances according to MDB implementation and scale factor is shown in Table 1.

Table 1. Scale factors and number of tuples with attribute instance redundancy ratio.

Relational modeling	Number of tuples and redundancy ratio of attribute instances			
	$SF1$	$SF2$	$SF3$	$SF4$
Unreduced flat	10^6 (99.0%)	2.5×10^7 (99.6%)	10^8 (99.9%)	4×10^8 (99.9%)
Unreduced horizontal	10^6 ($\approx$0%)	2.5×10^7 ($\approx$0%)	10^8 ($\approx$0%)	4×10^8 ($\approx$0%)
Flat	3.2×10^5 (97.8%)	8×10^6 (99.9%)	3.2×10^7 (99.9%)	1.27×10^8 (99.9%)
Horizontal	3.2×10^5 ($\approx$0%)	8×10^6 ($\approx$0%)	3.2×10^7 ($\approx$0%)	1.27×10^8 ($\approx$0%)
Vertical	3.4×10^5 (91.6%)	8.4×10^6 (92.4%)	3.4×10^7 (92.5%)	1.34×10^8 (92.5%)

During the experimental assessment, we consider only queries producing full answers in MDBs before and after data reduction. Meanwhile, different queries should involve different dimensions in different states during querying. Table 2 shows our proposed 12 queries. Specifically, queries Q_1–Q_3 involve one dimension in one state; queries Q_4–Q_7 involve multiple dimensions in one state; queries Q_8 and Q_9 involve different dimensions in two states; Q_{10}–Q_{12} involve different dimensions in all states.

---

[2] http://www.tpc.org/tpcds/.

Table 2. 12 queries involving different dimensions and time spans.

Query	No. of dimensions	Time span and state
Q_1: Annual sale amount for the last three years	1	[2014, 2017] E_3
Q_2: Annual sale amount in 2008	1	[2008, 2008] E_2
Q_3: Annual sale amount before 2000	1	[1990, 2000] E_1
Q_4: Sale amount by customer from 2010 to 2012	2	[2010, 2012] E_3
Q_5: Monthly sale amount by town from 2000 to 2005	2	[2000, 2005] E_2
Q_6: Monthly sale amount by town and sector in 2012	3	[2012, 2012] E_3
Q_7: Annual sale amount by town and sector from 2000 to 2005	3	[2000, 2005] E_2
Q_8: Monthly sale amount since 2000	1	[2000, 2017] E_2, E_3
Q_9: Annual sale amount per town from 2002 to 2012	2	[2002, 2012] E_2, E_3
Q_{10}: Annual sale amount	1	[1990, 2017] E_1, E_2, E_3
Q_{11}: Annual sale amount per sector	2	[1990, 2017] E_1, E_2, E_3
Q_{12}: Total sale amount	n/a	[1990, 2017] E_1, E_2, E_3

For each query, we record the *execution costs* provided by the *Explain Plan* command of the Oracle 12c DBMS without any optimization techniques (e.g. index and table partitioning). The hardware configuration is as follows: $2 \times$ CPU@2.33 GHz with 2 cores, 128 GB RAM and 1 TB SSD Disk in RAID6.

4.2 Observations and Discussions

In this section, we study the query execution costs in reduced and unreduced MDBs of different scale factors.

Observation. From Fig. 5, we can see the same trend is found in MDBs of different scale factors. The lowest execution costs of the twelve queries come from different implementations of reduced MDB. Specifically, for queries covering a time span within the temporal interval of one state, regardless of the scale factor and the number of dimensions included, (i) the lowest execution costs of Q_1, Q_4 and Q_6 (within the temporal interval of E_3) are found within the *vertical* MDB; (ii) the lowest execution costs of Q_2, Q_5 and Q_7 (within the temporal interval of E_2) are produced by the *horizontal* MDB; (iii) both the *vertical* and the *horizontal* MDBs are cost-efficient for Q3 (within the temporal interval of E_1). All queries involving multiple states are more efficiently computed within the *vertical* MDB (from Q8 to Q12), regardless of the MDB volume and the number of states as well as dimensions involved.

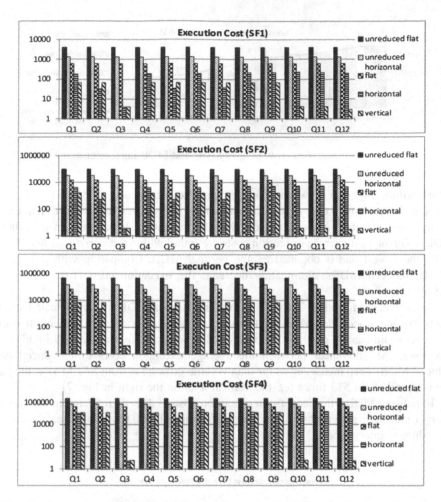

Fig. 5. Query execution costs in reduced and unreduced MDBs of different scale factors

Discussion. Based on the above observations, we can conclude that regardless of the scale factor, reduced MDBs always produce lower execution costs than unreduced MDBs. The execution costs in reduced MDBs (i) are not significantly influenced by the number of dimensions involved in a query but (ii) highly depend on the time span involved in a query. The more a query and a reduced MDB implementation share in terms of time span, the lower the execution costs become. When a query only involves old states, the influence of time span is weakened by the small volume of data within the *horizontal* and the *vertical* MDBs.

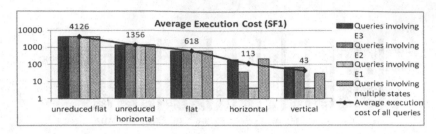

Fig. 6. Average execution costs by query type and MDB implementation of *SF1*

Observation. Figure 6 shows the average query execution costs in MDBs of the scale factor *SF1* according to query type. No matter how many states are involved in queries, the average execution costs in reduced MDBs are always lower than in unreduced MDBs. The highest average execution costs are found within the *unreduced flat* MDB, while the lowest one is obtained by the *vertical* MDB. Comparing with unreduced MDBs, reduced MDBs significantly decrease the execution costs: from 54.4% to 98.96%.

As we can see from Fig. 7, the same trend is found in MDBs of larger scale factors. From the *unreduced flat* MDB to the *vertical* MDB, the average execution costs decrease significantly: over 100 times (*cf.* the vertical axis on the left in Fig. 7). Moreover, the differences between the average execution costs in unreduced and reduced MDBs keep increasing as the data volume grows; i.e. from *SF1* to *SF4*, the gap has widened about 513 times (*cf.* the vertical axis on the right in Fig. 7).

In reduced MDBs, the decrease in execution costs is directly reflected in the gain in query runtime. Figure 8 shows the average runtime in MDBs of the scale factor 4 according to query type.

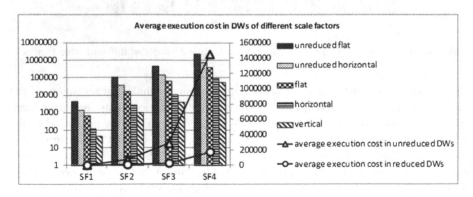

Fig. 7. Average execution costs of all queries in MDBs of different scale factors

Discussion. All reduced MDBs allow significantly saving the query execution costs, regardless of the scale factor and the query type. More importantly, the results of our experimental assessments show the scalability of our proposal: the larger the MDB is, the more significant the decrease in execution costs becomes after data reduction. The most efficient relational modeling is the *vertical* MDB. It groups measure instances and related attribute instances from one state together and implements them in one table. Consequently, data redundancy is reduced, while queries involving multiple dimensions are freed from joins in a *vertical* reduced MDB.

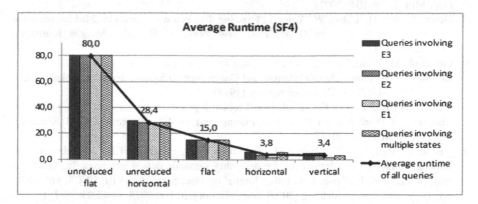

Fig. 8. Average runtime of queries involving different states in the largest MDBs

5 Conclusion

Our aim is to support effective and efficient decision-making by storing only data of high informative value over time in a MDB. In this paper, we outline a conceptual modeling solution allowing reducing both facts and dimensions in MDBs. A reduced MDB is modeled with multiple states. Each state is valid for a period of time.

Three relational modeling alternatives are proposed for reduced MDBs. The *flat* modeling integrates all measures and attributes from all states into one single flat table. The *horizontal* modeling converts each state into a fact table and a set of dimension tables. The *vertical* modeling gathers common measures and attributes shared by states into vertical tables. Different relational modeling alternatives (i) require different numbers of joins in analysis queries and (ii) bring in different degrees of data redundancy.

We carry out some experimental assessments to evaluate query execution efficiency in reduced and unreduced MDBs. The result shows the data reduction is a scalable solution: the larger the MDB is, the more significant the improvement in query execution efficiency becomes after the data reduction. During our experimental assessments, the improvement in terms of query execution costs ranges from 54.4% to 98.96%. The most significant decrease in query execution costs is found in the *vertical* MDB, which makes it the most efficient relational modeling of reduced MDBs.

In the future, we intend to study the performance of our proposed relational modeling alternatives in other types of DBMS. As more and more NoSQL systems nowadays are adopted to deal with large amount of data, it would be necessary to study new data reduction strategies in the context of NoSQL. One of our ongoing work focuses on reducing data in *graph* databases and *triple store* (RDF) databases.

References

1. Berkani, N., Bellatreche, L., Benatallah, B.: A value-added approach to design bi applications. In: Madria, S., Hara, T. (eds.) DaWaK 2016. LNCS, vol. 9829, pp. 361–375. Springer, Cham (2016). https://doi.org/10.1007/978-3-319-43946-4_24
2. Darmont, J., Bentayeb, F., Boussaid, O.: Benchmarking data warehouses. Int. J. Bus. Intell. Data Min. **2**, 79–104 (2007)
3. Garcia-Molina, H., Labio, W., Yang, J.: Expiring data in a warehouse. In: 24rd International Conference on Very Large Data Bases, New York, pp 500–511. Morgan Kaufmann Publishers Inc. (1998)
4. Golfarelli, M., Maio, D., Rizzi, S.: Conceptual design of data warehouses from E/R schemes. In: Thirty-First Annual Hawaii International Conference on System Sciences, Kohala Coast, HI, pp. 334–343. IEEE Computer Society (1998)
5. Iftikhar, N., Pedersen, T.B.: A rule-based tool for gradual granular data aggregation. In: International Workshop on Data Warehousing and OLAP, Glasgow, United Kingdom, pp. 1–8. ACM Press (2011)
6. Nebot, V., Berlanga, R., Pérez, J.M., Aramburu, M.J., Pedersen, T.B.: Multidimensional integrated ontologies: a framework for designing semantic data warehouses. In: Spaccapietra, S., Zimányi, E., Song, I.-Y. (eds.) Journal on Data Semantics XIII. LNCS, vol. 5530, pp. 1–36. Springer, Heidelberg (2009). https://doi.org/10.1007/978-3-642-03098-7_1
7. Okun, O., Priisalu, H.: Unsupervised data reduction. Signal Process. **87**, 2260–2267 (2007). https://doi.org/10.1016/j.sigpro.2007.02.006
8. O'Neil, P., O'Neil, E., Chen, X., Revilak, S.: The star schema benchmark and augmented fact table indexing. In: Nambiar, R., Poess, M. (eds.) TPCTC 2009. LNCS, vol. 5895, pp. 237–252. Springer, Heidelberg (2009). https://doi.org/10.1007/978-3-642-10424-4_17
9. Ravat, F., Song, J., Teste, O.: OLAP analysis operators for multi-state data warehouses. Int. J. Data Warehous. Min. **12**, 20–53 (2016)
10. Ravat, F., Teste, O., Tournier, R., Zurfluh, G.: Algebraic and graphic languages for OLAP manipulations. Int. J. Data. Warehous. Min. **4**, 17–46 (2008)
11. Skyt, J., Jensen, C.S., Pederson, T.B.: Specification-based data reduction in dimensional data warehouses. In: 18th International Conference on Data Engineering, p. 278. IEEE Computer Society (2002)
12. Udo, I.J., Afolabi, B.: Hybrid data reduction technique for classification of transaction data. J. Comput. Sci. Eng. **6**, 12–16 (2011)

UML2PROV: Automating Provenance Capture in Software Engineering

Carlos Sáenz-Adán[1](✉), Beatriz Pérez[1], Trung Dong Huynh[2], and Luc Moreau[3]

[1] Department of Mathematics and Computer Science, University of La Rioja,
Logroño, La Rioja, Spain
{carlos.saenz,beatriz.perez}@unirioja.es

[2] Department of Electronics and Computer Science, University of Southampton,
Southampton, UK
tdh@ecs.soton.ac.uk

[3] Department of Informatics, King's College London, London, UK
luc.moreau@kcl.ac.uk

Abstract. In this paper we present UML2PROV, an approach addressing the gap between application design, through UML diagrams, and provenance design, using PROV-Template. PROV-Template is a declarative approach that enables software engineers to develop programs that generate provenance following the PROV standard. The main contributions of this paper are: (i) a mapping strategy from UML diagrams (UML State Machine and Sequence diagrams) to templates, (ii) a code generation technique that creates libraries, which can be deployed in an application by creating suitable artefacts for provenance generation, and (iii) a demonstration of the feasibility of UML2PROV implemented with Java, and a preliminary quantitative evaluation that shows benefits regarding aspects such as design, development and provenance capture.

Keywords: Provenance data modeling and capture
PROV-Template · UML

1 Introduction

Over the last few years, there has been a growing interest in the origin of data, in order to enable its rating, validation, and reproducibility. In this context, the term *provenance* has emerged to refer to "the information about entities, activities, and people involved in producing a piece of data or thing, which can be used to form assessments about its quality, reliability or trustworthiness" [1].

This interest in provenance has led to various point solutions developed to capture provenance (such as PASS [2], PERM [3], Taverna [4], Vistrails [5] or Kepler [6]). The need for interoperability between systems has been a driver for the creation of the PROV standard [1,7,8], a conceptual data model for provenance, and its serialization to various Web technologies. Since PROV's aim is the interoperable exchange of provenance information, toolkits supporting PROV [9,10] have been facilitating the software engineer's task of creating, storing, reading and exchanging provenance; however, such toolkits do not help

© Springer International Publishing AG 2018
A M. Tjoa et al. (Eds.): SOFSEM 2018, LNCS 10706, pp. 667–681, 2018.
https://doi.org/10.1007/978-3-319-73117-9_47

decide what information should be included in provenance, and how software should be designed to allow for its capture. Therefore, the ability to consider the use of provenance, specially during the software engineering design phase, has become critically important to support the software designer in making provenance-enabled systems. PrIMe [11], the *Provenance Incorporation Methodology*, is the first provenance-focused methodology for adapting applications to make them provenance-aware. Although the application of this methodology has demonstrated promising results, PrIMe is standalone, and does not integrate with existing software engineering methodologies, which makes it challenging to use in practice.

In contrast, design techniques have been proposed to shorten the development time of software products, as well as to increase their quality, avoiding developers from expending extra time and efforts during subsequent phases. Among such techniques, the Unified Modelling Language (*UML*) [12] is widely accepted as the de-facto method for designing object-oriented software systems. However, the *UML* design methodology offers no specific support for provenance. Specifically, *UML* does not provide the means to express elements of response to provenance questions, such as the activity that lead to a specific result, or the elements involved in its creation. In fact, our experience in developing software applications augmented with support for provenance is that the inclusion of provenance within the design phase can entail significant changes to an application design [11]. This is a cumbersome task for the designers and programmers alike, since they have to be knowledgeable about provenance, to deal with complex diagrams, and to maintain an application's provenance-specific code base. In short, the gap between software engineering design methodologies and provenance engineering can result in applications generating provenance that is not aligned with what the application actually does, or that is not fit for purpose. Against this background, PROV-Template [13] is a recent development allowing the structure of provenance to be described declaratively: a provenance *template* is a document containing placeholders (referred as *variables*). An *expansion algorithm* instantiates a *template* with values, which are contained in *bindings* associating *variables* with concrete values. Although this approach reduces the development and maintenance effort, separating responsibilities between software and provenance designers, it still requires designers with provenance knowledge.

The aim of this paper is to propose UML2PROV, an approach that addresses the gap between application design, through *UML* diagrams, and provenance design, by means of PROV-Template. The contributions of this paper are as follows: (i) a mapping of *UML* diagrams (*UML* State Machine and Sequence diagrams) to templates according to a set of transformation rules, (ii) a code generation technique that creates libraries, that need to be linked with the application to generate provenance, and (iii) a demonstration of the feasibility of UML2PROV by implementing it with Java, whose preliminary quantitative evaluation shows significant benefits of the approach. These benefits, which will appeal to designers in early stages of the development process, are mainly: (1) *design/development*, since we provide a way to include provenance capabilities

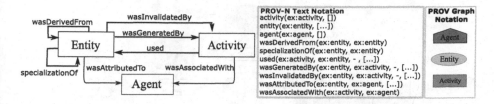

Fig. 1. PROV UML Class Diagram with graphical and textual PROV notation [7,8]

during the design phase *without* changing the way in which software designers use *UML* (provenance generation is handled automatically from such *UML*), and (2) *capturing provenance*, since the provenance capture is performed automatically thanks to UML2PROV's code generation technique, which provides clear benefits over the more traditional approach of provenance capture.

This paper is organized as follows. We outline the background of this research in Sect. 2. In Sect. 3, we give an overview of UML2PROV. Sections 4 and 5 describe our approach, while Sect. 6 presents a complete implementation of it. A quantitative evaluation is provided in Sect. 7, while Sect. 8 discusses related work. Finally, conclusions and further work are set out in Sect. 9.

2 Background

In this section, we first introduce the PROV standard for provenance and provide an overview of the main insights concerning the use of PROV-Template. Second, we highlight key aspects of the *UML* diagrams used in this work.

2.1 The PROV Standard and PROV-Template

PROV [1] is a World Wide Web Consortium (W3C) standard that aims to facilitate the publication and interchange of provenance among applications. PROV is fully specified in a family of documents, which cover various of its aspects such as modeling, serialization, access, interchange, translation and ways to reason over it. For the purpose of our paper, we illustrate PROV focusing on the PROV Data Model (PROV-DM) [7], which is a conceptual model that forms the basis for the remainder PROV family of specifications, and the PROV Notation (PROV-N) [8], a textual representation suitable for human consumption.

PROV is based around three concepts, together with their relationships which are depicted in the left part of Fig. 1. In the right part, we also show the PROV-N representation of these concepts, together with their graphical notation. More specifically, an *Entity* is a physical, digital, conceptual or other kind of thing. An *Activity* is a set of actions that act upon or with *entities* during a specific time frame. Finally, an *Agent* refers to something which takes responsibilities of *entities* or *activities* through attribution or association, respectively.

As shown in Fig. 1, these concepts are associated through relationships such as usage (*used*), which represents an activity beginning to utilize an entity, generation (*wasGeneratedBy*) used when an activity produces a new entity, derivation

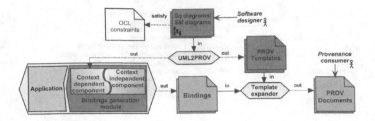

Fig. 2. The UML2PROV approach. The red and blue colours are used to refer to *design time* and *runtime* aspects of the approach, respectively. (Color figure online)

(*wasDerivedFrom*) which denotes an entity update, invalidation (*wasInvalidatedBy*) used when an activity starts the destruction or invalidation of an entity, association (*wasAssociatedWith*) which indicates that an agent had a role in an activity, attribution (*wasAttributedTo*) which shows an agent bearing the responsibility for an entity, and specialization (*specializationOf*) used when an entity shares the aspects of another entity, but also has more specific aspects.

PROV-Template [13] is a declarative approach to creating PROV compliant provenance-enabled applications. It consists of three main key elements: *provenance templates*, *bindings*, and a *provenance template expansion algorithm*. The overall process supported by PROV-Template is as follows. The *provenance templates* are firstly designed and embedded in the application's code, which logs the values in the form of *bindings* during its execution. Finally, provenance is automatically generated by *template expansion*. For further details regarding PROV and PROV-Templates, the reader is referred to [1,7,8] and [13], respectively.

2.2 UML Diagrams

UML [12] distinguishes two major categories of diagrams: *structural* diagrams are concerned with the static structure of a system, whereas *behavioural* diagrams capture the behavioural features of a system, including aspects concerning its runtime execution. This latter type of diagrams describes the dynamics between objects of a system in terms of states, interactions, collaborations, etc. Since provenance bears a strong relation with all the data taken part in producing a final item (that is, information related to involved *entities* together with the different *states* they go through over time, conducted *activities*, *interactions* among such entities, etc.), we considered *UML Sequence Diagrams* (*Sq Diagrams*) and *UML State Machine Diagrams* (*SM Diagrams*), to be the most suitable ones for our purpose. Briefly speaking, *Sq Diagrams* are used to model the *interactions* among collaborating objects in terms of *messages* exchanged from a *sender* to a *receiver's lifeline*. *SM Diagrams* specify the various states that an object goes through during its lifecycle. They mainly consist of *states*, *transitions* and other types of *vertexes* called *pseudostates*. For the sake of brevity, we do not delve into more detail regarding *Sq* and *SM Diagrams*; we refer the reader to [12].

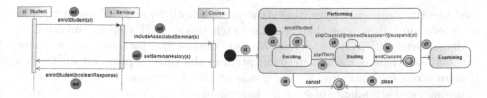

Fig. 3. On the left side, a *Sq diagram* showing the interaction between **Student**, **Seminar** and **Course**. On the right side, the *SM diagram* of the **Seminar** class.

3 Overview: Generating PROV Templates from UML

In this section, we provide an overview of the UML2PROV approach identifying its key facets, and distinguishing its different stakeholders: *software designers* and *provenance consumers*. We illustrate our explanations by means of Fig. 2, where *design time* elements (red) are distinguished from *runtime* elements (blue). *Design time* facets are the *Sq/SM diagrams*, the associated *PROV templates* generated from those, and the *bindings generation module*. In particular, this module is composed by two main components: a *context-independent component*, which contains the bindings's generation code that is common to all applications, and a *context-dependent component*, which is generated from the system's *UML* diagrams and includes the bindings's generation code specific to the concrete application. The *runtime execution* facets consist of the values logged by the application, in the form of *bindings*, and the *PROV documents*.

Software designers are responsible for creating the *Sq* and *SM diagrams* based on the concrete domain's requirements (see upper part of Fig. 2). Since *UML Sq* and *SM diagrams* show interconnected behavioural views of an overall system, before applying our approach, those diagrams must satisfy a set of Object Constraint Language (OCL) [14] rules we have defined to ensure that those diagrams are consistent with each other (for details about these rules, we refer to [15]). UML2PROV takes as input the *UML* diagrams satisfying such rules, and automatically generates: PROV *templates*, as defined by the *UML* to templates mapping (Sect. 4), and the *context-dependent component* in the *bindings generation module* (Sect. 5). UML2PROV determines (1) what provenance information is considered from the *Sq/SM diagrams* to be captured, and (2) how the application is wrapped with the functionality needed to allow such a capture (i.e. the functionality implemented by the *bindings generation module*).

Finally, the *provenance consumer* uses the provenance *template expander* to generate *PROV documents* from both the *templates* and the *bindings*. By distinguishing among the different stakeholders, we allow them having clearly defined roles and focusing on their specific responsibilities, avoiding task collision.

4 From UML Diagrams to Provenance Templates

In this section, we present the mapping from *Sq* and *SM diagrams* satisfying our OCL constraints, to provenance templates. We have defined a set of patterns that identify commonly appearing structures on both *Sq* and *SM diagrams* and a set of translation rules that translate each single *UML* element involved in such patterns to PROV elements. We only outline the patterns due to space constraints, whereas a complete description of the rules is provided in [15]. To illustrate our explanations, we use a case study of a system that manages the enrolment and attendance of students to seminars of a University course. Figure 3 shows two *Sq* and *SM diagrams* defined for such a case study.

4.1   From Sequence Diagrams to Templates

We illustrate our translation approach by means of the *SeqP1-SeqP4* patterns presented in Fig. 4, together with the template of Fig. 5 which shows the translation of the *message* m1 from the case study's *Sq diagram* in Fig. 3.

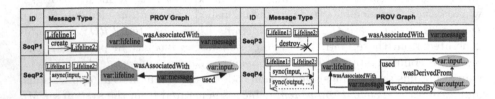

Fig. 4. Sq diagrams' patterns and their provenance templates

```
1 agent(var:lifeline,[prov:type='exe:Student'])          6  wasAssociatedWith(var:message, var:lifeline,-,[])
2 activity(var:message,[prov:type='exe:enrolStudent',     7  used(var:message,var:input0,-,[prov:role='exe:st'])
3       tmpl:startTime = '...', tmpl:endTime='...'])       8  wasGeneratedBy(var:output0,var:message,-,
4 entity(var:input0, [prov:value='var:input0value'])      9       [prov:role='exe:booleanResponse'])
5 entity(var:output0, [prov:value='var:output0value'])  10  wasDerivedFrom(var:output0,var:input0)
```

Fig. 5. An extract of a template generated from the case study's Sq diagram.

For each pattern identified, the sender *object lifeline* is mapped to a prov:Agent (identified by `var:lifeline`) that assumes the responsibility of such an *object* (e.g. in line 1 of Fig. 5 we show how the *object* `Student` is translated into a prov:Agent). The *message* sent is modelled as a prov:Activity (identified by `var:message`) that represents the invocation of the message's *operation* (e.g. the *message* `enrolStudent` is mapped to the prov:Activity showed in lines 2–3 of Fig. 5). Additionally, when an *object lifeline* sends a *message* to another *lifeline*, a new prov:wasAssociatedWith relationship is generated between the *message* identified by `var:message`, and the sender *lifeline* identified by `var:lifeline` (e.g. the statement in line 6 of Fig. 5 shows this relationship).

Patterns *SeqP2* and *SeqP4* depict the communication between two *lifelines* through a reply *asynchronous/synchronous message* with *arguments*. Each *message's argument* is modelled as a prov:Entity, identified by `var:input`... Additionally, to assert that the *argument* is a parameter of the request *message*, the relationship prov:used links the *message* `var:message` and the *argument*

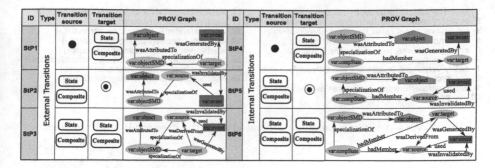

Fig. 6. Patterns identified in *SM diagrams*

`var:input`... Focusing on the *message* `m1` in Fig. 3, the *argument* `st` is translated into the prov:Entity showed in line 4 of Fig. 5, together with the link between the identifiers of both the *argument* and the *message*, shown in line 7.

SeqP4 additionally encompasses a *reply message* with an *output argument*. Additionally, the *output argument* is modelled as a prov:Entity (identified by `var:output`...) that was "generated" as part of the *reply*. Thus, the relationship prov:wasGeneratedBy is created between the *message* identified by `var:message` and the *argument* `var:output`... Regarding the reply *message* `m4` in Fig. 3, the *output argument* is translated into the prov:Entity showed in line 5 of Fig. 5, while its relation with the *message* prov:Activity is shown in lines 8–9.

We note that in PROV two relationships of the form (`B`, prov:used, `A`) and (`C`, prov:wasGeneratedBy, `B`) are usually enriched with (`C`, prov:wasDerivedFrom, `A`) to express the dependency of `C` on `A`. This structure refers to a provenance construction called *Use-generate-derive triangle* [16] which includes the three elements involved. *SeqP4* in Fig. 4 depicts such a situation between the request's and the response's *arguments*: when both request and reply *messages* have *arguments*, we use the prov:wasDerivedFrom relationship. In line 10 of Fig. 5 we reflect such a situation between the *input* and *output arguments* of `enrolStudent`.

4.2   From State Machine Diagrams to Templates

We now present the mapping from *SM diagrams* to provenance templates. Our explanation is illustrated by using the *StP1-StP6* patterns presented in Fig. 6 and the *provenance template* showed in Fig. 7, which depicts an extract of the translation resulted from the case study's *SM diagram* in Fig. 3.

SM Diagrams represent the evolution of an *object* using *transitions* between *states*. In fact, among the patterns depicted in Fig. 6, we can identify four common UML elements shared by all of them. (1) The *object* whose behaviour is modelled by the *SM diagram* is translated into a prov:Agent identified by `var:object` (e.g. in line 1 of Fig. 7 the object `Seminar` whose behaviour is modelled by the *SM diagram* in Fig. 3 is translated into a prov:Agent). (2) The *object*'s *state machine* is represented as a prov:Entity (identified by `var:objectSMD`).

```
1  agent(var:object,[prov:type='exe:Seminar'])              11  wasAttributedTo(var:objectSMD, var:object,[])
2  entity(var:objectSMD,[prov:type='exe:StateMachine'])     12  used(var:event,var:source,-)
3  activity(var:event,[prov:type='exe:enrolStudent',        13  wasInvalidatedBy(var:source, var:event,-)
4      tmpl:startTime = '...', tmpl:endTime='...'])          14  wasGeneratedBy(var:target,var:event,-)
5  entity(var:source, [exe:state='exe:Enroling',            15  wasDerivedFrom(var:target,var:source)
6      prov:type='exe:Seminar'])                             16  specializationOf(var:performing, var:objectSMD)
7  entity(var:target, [exe:state='exe:Enroling',            17  hadMember(var:performing,var:source)
8      prov:type='exe:Seminar'])                             18  hadMember(var:performing,var:target)
9  entity(var:performing, [exe:state='exe:Performing',
10     prov:type='exe:Seminar'])
```

Fig. 7. An extract of a template generated from the case study's *SM diagram*.

Additionally, `var:objectSMD` is related to the *object*, identified by `var:object`, using prov:wasAttributedTo relationship (e.g. the *object*'s *state machine* of Fig. 3 is translated into the prov:Entity in line 2, which is associated with the corresponding *object* by means of line 11). (3) The *event* that triggers a *state* change is translated into a prov:Activity identified by `var:event` (e.g. the *event* `enrolStudent` is represented by the prov:Activity in lines 3–4 of Fig. 7). Finally, (4) the *state*, *simple* or *composite*, which denotes the *object*'s situation is mapped to a prov:Entity identified by `var:source`, `var:target` or `var:compState`. For example, the *source state*, the *target state*, and the *composite state* involved in the transition `t3` of Fig. 3 are translated into the prov:Entity showed in lines 5–6, 7–8, 9–10 of Fig. 7, respectively. To represent that the source *state* influences the outcome of a *transition*, we adopt the prov:used relationship between the source *state* identified by `var:source` and the *event* identified by `var:event`. Additionally, to represent that the *object* is no longer in the source *state*, the relationship prov:wasInvalidatedBy links the source *state* `var:source` and the *event* `var:event`. Finally, to represent that the target *state* results from the triggering of the *transition*, a prov:wasGeneratedBy relationship links the target *state* `var:target` and the *event* `var:event`. For instance, focusing on the *transition* `t3` in Fig. 3, the source *state* `Enroling` represented by a prov:Entity and the *event* `enrolStudent` represented by a prov:Activity are linked by the relationships prov:used and prov:wasInvalidtedBy depicted in lines 12 and 13 of Fig. 7. In addition, the target *state* `Enroling` represented by a prov:Entity is related to the *event* `enrolStudent` represented by a prov:Agent by means of the relationship prov:wasGenereatedBy shown in line 14.

Although these patterns share the previous cited aspects, the complete translation of all the elements within a *SM diagram* depends on the particular nuances such as the target/composite elements and the type of *transition* (internal or external). Whenever the *transition* is not enclosed within a *composite state* (*StP1-StP3*), its *source* and *target states* are related to the *state machine*, identified by `var:objectSMD`, through prov:specializationOf. In contrast, if the *transition* is enclosed within a *composite state* (*StP4-StP6*), its *source* and *target states* (identified by `var:source` and `var:target`, respectively) are related to the *composite state* (identified by `var:compState`) through prov:hadMember. Additionally, the *composite state* is related to the *state machine* using prov:specializationOf. For instance, since the *transition* `t3` in Fig. 3 is enclosed in a *composite state*, it follows the pattern *StP6*. Thus, its source and target *states* are related to the *composite state* by the statements in lines 17 and 18 of Fig. 7, while the *composite state* is linked to the *state machine* by line 16.

Finally, similarly to Sect. 4.1, *StP3* and *StP6* exploit the *Use-generate-derive triangle* [16] among the source *state* var:source, the *event* var:event and the target *state* var:target. Thus, we define a direct relationship between both the var:source and the var:target by means of the prov:wasDerivedFrom relationship, representing the fact that the *target* state is a consequence of the triggering of the *transition* from the *source state*. In line 15 of Fig. 6 we reflect such a situation between the *source* and *target states* of transition t3.

5   Bindings Generation Strategy

As explained in Sect. 2, the PROV-Template approach takes a *provenance template* together with a set of *bindings* as input of the *template expansion* process. Such a process replaces variables in the *provenance templates* by real values in the *bindings*, producing *PROV documents*. Obtaining the *bindings* becomes a key focus of the runtime execution, requiring adaptation of existing application code. Although a manual adaptation of the source code is a valid option to extract *bindings*, software engineers would need to expend a great deal of effort on traversing the overall application's source code, and adding suitable instructions to generate the *bindings* structures. Thus, it would constitute a tedious, time-consuming and error prone process. To avoid that, PROV2UML creates *bindings* automatically by applying the *Proxy Pattern* [17], thus requiring minor modifications, without obfuscating the existing code with new statements.

Briefly speaking, the *Proxy Pattern* provides a surrogate for another object to control its behaviour. It is mainly intended to manage the access to objects' methods, allowing us to modify their behaviour. This benefit has led to a wide use of this pattern in, for example, Aspect-Oriented Programming (AOP)-based frameworks. The *Proxy Pattern* is composed of the following four elements. (1) The *Subject Interface* includes all the methods implemented by the *Real Subject*. (2) The *Real Subject* is the object whose behaviour we want to modify, must implement the *Subject Interface*. (3) The *Proxy* element also implements the *Subject Interface* so that it can be used in any location where the *Real Subject* can be used. The *Proxy* element maintains a reference to the *Real Subject* and executes its own code before and after the *Real Subject*'s usual execution. (4) The *Client* element is in charge of invoking the *Subject*, which allows the *Client* to interact with the *Proxy* as though it were the *Real Subject*. Thus, the *Proxy* constitutes the intermediary between the *Client* and the *Real Subject*. This pattern helps us collect suitable information to construct the *bindings* before and after the usual execution of the objects' methods. Harnessing the potential of this pattern to generate the *bindings* has two main advantages: (1) we deal with the concept of proxy independently of any programming language, and (2) this solution is suitable for both already developed applications, and applications yet to be developed. In particular, the *Proxy* element wraps the *Real Subject* allowing us to extract *provenance* information for each method defined in the *Subject Interface*.

{"var":{
  "source":[{"@id":"exe:Seminar@57fa26b7_1"}],
  "event":[{"@id":"exe:enrolStudent_1"}],
  "lifeline":[{"@id":"exe:Student@28180122"}],
  "performing":[{"@id":"exe:Performing_1"}],
  "objectSMD":[{"@id":"exe:Seminar@57fa26b7_0"}],
  "object":[{"@id":"exe:Seminar@57fa26b7"}],

  "eventStartTime":[{"@type":"xsd:dateTime",
    "@value":"2017-02-09T11:54:24"}],
  "target":[{"@id":"exe:enrolStudent_1"}],
  "eventEndTime":[{"@type":"xsd:dateTime",
    "@value":"2017-02-09T11:54:24"}]},
  "vargen":{},
  "context":{"exe":"http://uml2prov.../execution#"}}

Fig. 8. Example of bindings collected from the method `enrolStudent` in Fig. 3

When a method is called, the *Proxy* intercepts the method invocation and gathers concrete information about the system execution (e.g. time) and specific information about the method (such as the parameters). We note that each captured value is directly related to a variable included in a provenance template (e.g. `var:message` value is given by the name of the method).

In Fig. 8, we show an example of bindings in JSON format representing the bindings captured when the *transition* `t3` in Fig. 3 is triggered. More specifically, it shows the *bindings* between several variables appearing in the provenance templates of Fig. 7 and their corresponding values; for example, the variable `event` is associated with the concrete value `exe:enrolStudent_1`.

6   Implementation

In this section, we discuss a reference implementation of UML2PROV in Java. Regarding the translation of *UML* to provenance templates, we have chosen Extensible Stylesheet Language Transformations (XSLT) [18] to implement the patterns. More specifically, we have defined two XSLT transformation files, each one tackling a type of diagram (*Sq* and *SM diagrams*). The diagrams are expected to be encoded in XMI format, a standardized XML representation for UML diagrams supported by mainstream UML designers such as UML 2 Eclipse plug-in, Modelio [19] or Papyrus [20]. We use Papyrus which not only is able to represent *UML* diagrams graphically, serialising them into XMI, but it is also able to check OCL constraints on UML diagrams, that is, it allows us to verify our OCL constraints on the source diagrams before applying UML2PROV. The XMI files are taken as input by each XSLT transformation, which automatically generates the corresponding provenance templates in PROV-N.

Aiming at generating bindings for Java applications, we provide a Java class named as `ProxyProvGenerator` which relies on the `java.lang.reflect` package. Basically, this class has a method which receives a *subject object* implementing its corresponding *subject interface* and then, the method returns the *subject object*'s *proxy*. Such a *proxy* is created with all the bindings generation instructions within. The `ProxyProvGenerator` is application independent since it is agnostic about the *subject object* given. Providing the `ProxyProvGenerator` to the software developer is enough to automatically generate a proxy for each *subject object* with provenance capturing capabilities. Thus, this class constitutes the *context-independent component* in the *bindings generation module*.

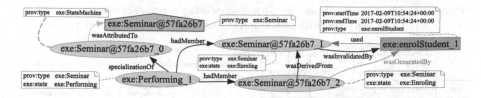

Fig. 9. Expanded PROV document

We have applied the UML2PROV implementation to the case study in Fig. 3 obtaining 3 and 6 templates from the *Sq diagram* and the *SM diagram*, respectively (Figs. 5 and 7 show actual extracts of such provenance templates). Figure 9 depicts the PROV document generated from the set of bindings shown in Fig. 8 and the template from Fig. 7, by applying the *template expander*.

7 Quantitative Evaluation and Discussion

This section evaluates the strengths and weaknesses of UML2PROV. More specifically, we have applied it to five case studies and analysed the results in the light of several criteria pertaining to *design time*: (1) the number of generated provenance template elements, (2) the time that took to generate the templates, and (3) the amount of automatically generated code. As for *runtime execution*, we discuss (4) how much provenance is being generated after expansion.

Table 1 depicts the results given by applying UML2PROV to the five case studies, organized depending on the type of diagram. The first case study (CS1) corresponds to the complete seminars' system. The remainder case studies, which have been selected from Internet because their diagrams are varied in size, are associated to a water system (CS2), a system representing the Model-View-Controller pattern (CS3), a phone call system (CS4), and an elevator system (CS5). The relevant documents related to the case studies can be found on [15].

Regarding the analysis of (1) the number of provenance template elements that are generated, and (2) the time that took to generate such templates, we study the relation between the number of UML elements and the number of PROV elements, as well as, the relation between the number of UML elements and the translation time taken. With this study we check the capability of UML2PROV to handle the growing amount of UML elements and its potential to accommodate such a growth. In particular, we observe that the average time (in *Sq* and *SM diagrams*) is significantly larger for the CS5 case study, but likewise, the average size of generated PROV elements for this application is larger. This confirms that the cost per UML element remains constant. To validate this, we applied Pearson's correlation test and obtained a ρ-value of 0.9978 (relating to *Sq diagrams'* elements) and a ρ-value of 0.9713 (relating to *SM diagrams'* elements) showing a strong correlation. Similarly, we have computed the Pearson's correlation coefficient to measure the strength of the linear association between the number of source *UML* elements and the generated PROV elements,

Table 1. Results obtained from the cases studies using a personal computer, Intel (R) CoreR^{TM} i7 CPU, 3.6 GHz, with 16 GB RAM, running Windows 10 Enterprise.

Id	UML Elements			PROV elements			Interf. code lines	Avera. time (ms)
	Diagr. Type	Num. Diagr.	Num. Diagr. Elemen.	Templ. Num.	Num. PROV Elemen.	Var. Num.		
CS1	SqD	1	10	3	18	83	11	45.4
	SMD	3	19	9	146			25
CS2	SqD	4	18	8	40	88	12	53
	SMD	2	22	8	163			22
CS3	SqD	1	17	5	34	56	13	50.2
	SMD	4	20	6	148			23.6
CS4	SqD	1	12	5	25	84	11	47.2
	SMD	3	16	8	117			22.2
CS5	SqD	2	50	9	67	131	47	90.4
	SMD	5	52	13	369			37.4

Legend:

Num. Diagr. Number of SqD and SMD diagrams modelling the system.

Num. Diagr. Elemen. The total number of elements within each diagram (lifelines, messages, arguments, transitions, and simple and composite states).

Templ. Num. The number of generated PROV templates.

Num. PROV Elemen. The number of PROV template elements.

Var. Num. The number of variables in these templates.

Inferf. code lines. The lines of code in the generated subject interfaces.

Avera. Time (ms). The average time taken by 12 executions of the translation process.

obtaining a ρ-value of 0.9660 (for *Sq diagrams'* elements) and a ρ-value of 0.9996 (for *SM diagrams'* elements), which demonstrates good performance results.

As for the code required to be created for bindings generation, as explained in Sect. 5, UML2PROV only requires the *Subject Interfaces* to be created, which are used together with the `ProxyProvGenerator` class. Since such interfaces are automatically generated by UML2PROV from the source *UML* diagrams, software developers do not have to develop them manually, and thus, they do not need to write the number of lines of code presented in Table 1 (see column "Interf. code lines"). Without using UML2PROV, software developers would have to write additional code within the application to create bindings. Typically, for each variable in a template, a method call is needed to assign a value to it, thus, a developer would need to write one line of code for each variable in a template. In our five case studies, although being relatively small, these number of lines of code are presented in column "Var. Num." in Table 1. With UML2PROV, writing such code is not required, since the proxy constructs that automatically.

Finally, regarding the provenance obtained after expansion, we would like to note that, in case of a repetitive cycle or sequence of actions in the *Sq diagrams*, the number of PROV documents obtained after the expansion process grows proportionally to the length of these cycles or sequences.

8   Related Work

Although provenance has been widely addressed from different perspectives [21–24], to the best of our knowledge, it has been scarcely investigated from the point of view of determining the provenance to be generated as software is being designed. In contrast to our proposal, other works undertake the development of provenance-aware systems by means of weaving provenance generation instructions into programs, which makes code maintenance a cumbersome task. Examples of these include PASS [25], which is a storage system which supports the automatic collection and maintenance of provenance; PERM [3], which is a provenance database middleware that enables provenance computation; and finally, workflow systems such as Taverna [4], Vistrails [5] and Kepler [6] which incorporate provenance capabilities into the workflow system.

Alternatively, there are different approaches that include provenance generation instructions into source code. For instance, Ghosal et al. [26] extract provenance from log files, Cheney et al. [27,28] use statistic analysis to create executables that produce provenance information, and Brauer et al. [29] use an Aspect-Oriented Architecture to interweave aspects generating provenance. This approach bears relationship with our work since, as discussed previously, the *Proxy Pattern* used in our approach is widely applied in AOP. However, UML2PROV not only gives a general solution to include provenance with minimum interferences with the original system, but it also addresses the design of the provenance to be generated using PROV-Template [11].

Finally, it is worth mentioning the standalone methodology PrIMe [11]. It could be said that UML2PROV complements PrIMe, since UML2PROV integrates the design of provenance by means of PROV-Templates with the design of applications using the well-known de-facto standard notation *UML*.

9 Conclusions and Future Work

Bridging the gap between application design and provenance design remains an adoption hurdle for provenance technology. In this paper, we present UML2PROV that addresses such a challenge for the particular case of *Sq* and *SM Diagrams*, taken as design methodology, and PROV-Template, used as provenance design. Our contributions are as follows: (i) a mapping of *UML* diagrams to provenance templates, (ii) a code generation technique that creates libraries to be linked with the application to generate provenance, and (iii) a demonstration of the feasibility of UML2PROV by providing an implementation, and a preliminary quantitative evaluation that shows significant benefits of the approach. Our evaluation shows that our approach significantly reduces efforts in design time, resulting in an increased productivity. The automated provenance capture also provides clear benefits over the traditional approach of provenance capture, showing the amount of code that software developers will need to write without UML2PROV. The experiments also confirm that the approach is tractable, requiring milliseconds for generating PROV templates.

Although our proposal takes into account two of the most used *UML* behavioural diagrams, considering a wider number of *UML* elements, including other kind of *UML Diagrams* (such as *UML* Activity Diagrams), and other elements (such as *SM Diagram*'s *pseudostates*, not considered in our patterns) to constitute a more complete provenance-aware methodology, is a line of further work. Additionally, using a strategy based on, for example, *UML* stereotypes, to monitoring only concrete messages, constitutes an interesting direction of further work. We use XSLT as a first attempt to implement our patterns; other approach of future work is to consider using a Model Driven Development (MDD) tool chain based on MDD-based tools such as ATL [30] and XPand [31]. Finally, performing a systematic quantitative evaluation of the approach and a study of the quality of provenance being generated from a real situation (involving users, designers or developers) constitute another line of future work.

Acknowledgements. This work was partially supported by the spanish MINECO project EDU2016-79838-P, and by the University of La Rioja (grant FPI-UR-2015).

References

1. Groth, P., Moreau, L. (eds.): PROV-Overview. An Overview of the PROV Family of Documents. W3C Working Group Note NOTE-prov-overview-20130430, World Wide Web Consortium, April 2013. http://www.w3.org/TR/2013/NOTE-prov-overview-20130430/
2. Holland, D., Braun, U., Maclean, D., Muniswamy-Reddy, K.K., Seltzer, M.I.: Choosing a data model and query language for provenance. In: Proceedings of the International Provenance and Annotation Workshop, IPAW 2008, pp. 98–115 (2008)
3. Glavic, B., Alonso, G.: Perm: processing provenance and data on the same data model through query rewriting. In: Proceedings of the 25th IEEE International Conference on Data Engineering, ICDE 2009, pp. 174–185 (2009)
4. Wolstencroft, K., Haines, R., Fellows, D., Williams, A., Withers, D., Owen, S., Soiland-Reyes, S., Dunlop, I., Nenadic, A., Fisher, P., et al.: The Taverna workflow suite: designing and executing workflows of Web Services on the desktop, web or in the cloud. Nucleic Acids Res. **41**, 557–561 (2013). Oxford University Press
5. Silva, C.T., Anderson, E., Santos, E., Freire, J.: Using vistrails and provenance for teaching scientific visualization. Comput. Graph. Forum **30**(1), 75–84 (2011)
6. Altintas, I., Barney, O., Jaeger-Frank, E.: Provenance collection support in the kepler scientific workflow system. In: Moreau, L., Foster, I. (eds.) IPAW 2006. LNCS, vol. 4145, pp. 118–132. Springer, Heidelberg (2006). https://doi.org/10.1007/11890850_14
7. Moreau, L., Missier, P., Belhajjame, K., B'Far, R., Cheney, J., Coppens,S., Cresswell, S., Gil, Y., Groth, P., Klyne, G., Lebo, T., McCusker, J., Miles, S., Myers, J., Sahoo, S., Tilmes, C. (eds.): PROV-DM: The PROV Data Model. W3CRecommendation REC-prov-dm-20130430, World Wide Web Consortium (2013). http://www.w3.org/TR/2013/REC-prov-dm-20130430/
8. Moreau, L., Missier, P., Cheney, J., Soiland-Reyes, S. (eds.): PROV-N: The Provenance Notation. W3C Recommendation REC-prov-n-20130430, World Wide Web Consortium, April 2013. http://www.w3.org/TR/2013/REC-prov-n-20130430/
9. A library for W3C Provenance Data Model supporting PROV-JSON, PROV-XML and PROV-O (RDF), October 2017. https://pypi.python.org/pypi/prov. Accessed Oct 2017
10. ProvToolbox: Java library to create and convert W3C PROV data model representations. http://lucmoreau.github.io/ProvToolbox/. Accessed Oct 2017
11. Miles, S., Groth, P.T., Munroe, S., Moreau, L.: Prime: a methodology for developing provenance-aware applications. ACM Trans. Softw. Eng. Methodol. **20**(3), 8:1–8:42 (2011)
12. OMG.: Unified Modeling Language (UML). Version 2.5 (2015). http://www.omg.org/spec/UML/2.5/. Accessed 1 Mar 2015
13. Moreau, L., Batlajery, B.V., Huynh, T.D., Michaelides, D., Packer, H.: A templating system to generate provenance. IEEE Trans. Softw. Eng. (2017, in Press). http://eprints.soton.ac.uk/405025/
14. OMG: Object Constraint Language, Version 2.4 (2014). http://www.omg.org/spec/OCL/2.4/PDF. Accessed 3 Feb 2014

15. Supplementary material of UML2PROV (October 2017). https://uml2prov.github.io/. Accessed Oct 2017
16. Kwasnikowska, N., Moreau, L., Bussche, J.V.D.: A formal account of the open provenance model. ACM Trans. Web 9(2), 10:1–10:44 (2015)
17. Gamma, E., Helm, R., Johnson, R., Vlissides, J.: Design patterns: elements of reusable object-oriented software. Addison Wesley, Boston (1995)
18. XSL Transformations (XSLT) Version 3.0: W3C Recommendation 8 June 2017, February 2017. https://www.w3.org/TR/xslt-30/
19. Modelio, UML modeling tool: Version 3.6, February 2017. http://www.modeliosoft.com/. Accessed Oct 2017
20. Papyrus, Modeling environment: Version 2.0.2 (Neon release), January 2017. https://eclipse.org/papyrus/. Accessed Oct 2017
21. Tan, W.C.: Provenance in databases: past, current, and future. IEEE Data Eng. Bull. 30(4), 3–12 (2007)
22. Davidson, S.B., Freire, J.: Provenance and scientific workflows: challenges and opportunities. In: Proceedings of the 2008 ACM SIGMOD International Conference on Management of Data, MOD 2008, pp. 1345–1350. ACM, New York (2008)
23. Moreau, L.: The foundations for provenance on the Web. Found. Trends Web Sci. 2(2–3), 99–241 (2010)
24. Simmhan, Y.L., Plale, B., Gannon, D.: A Survey of Data Provenance Techniques. Technical report 612 Extended version of SIGMOD Record (2005). http://www.cs.indiana.edu/pub/techreports/TR618.pdf
25. Glavic, B., Dittrich, K.R.: Data Provenance: A Categorization of Existing Approaches. In: Proceedings of Datenbanksysteme in Büro, Technik und Wissenschaft, BTW 2007, pp. 227–241 (2007)
26. Ghoshal, D., Plale, B.: Provenance from log files: a bigdata problem. In: Proceedings of the Joint EDBT/ICDT 2013 Workshops, pp. 290–297. ACM (2013)
27. Cheney, J., Ahmed, A., Acar, U.A.: Provenance as dependency analysis. Math. Struct. Comput. Sci. 21(6), 1301–1337 (2011). Cambridge University Press, Cambridge
28. Cheney, J.: Program slicing and data provenance. IEEE Data Eng. Bull. 30(4), 22–28 (2007)
29. Brauer, P.C., Fittkau, F., Hasselbring, W.: The aspect-oriented architecture of the CAPS framework for capturing, analyzing and archiving provenance data. In: Ludäscher, B., Plale, B. (eds.) IPAW 2014. LNCS, vol. 8628, pp. 223–225. Springer, Cham (2015). https://doi.org/10.1007/978-3-319-16462-5_19
30. Jouault, F., Kurtev, I.: Transforming models with ATL. In: Bruel, J.-M. (ed.) MODELS 2005. LNCS, vol. 3844, pp. 128–138. Springer, Heidelberg (2006). https://doi.org/10.1007/11663430_14
31. XPand: Eclipse platform (2017). https://wiki.eclipse.org/Xpand. Accessed Oct 2017

Validating Data from Semantic Web Providers

Jacques Chabin[1], Mirian Halfeld-Ferrari[1], Béatrice Markhoff[2],
and Thanh Binh Nguyen[1(⊠)]

[1] Université d'Orléans, INSA CVL, LIFO, Orléans, France
binh@univ-orleans.fr
[2] Université Francois Rabelais de Tours, LI, Tours, France

Abstract. As the Linked Open Data and the number of semantic web
data providers hugely increase, so does the critical importance of the
following question: how to get usable results, in particular for data mining
and data analysis tasks? We propose a query framework equiped with
integrity constraints that the user wants to be verified on the results
coming from semantic web data providers. We precise the syntax and
semantics of those user quality constraints. We give algorithms for their
dynamic verification during the query computation, we evaluate their
performance with experimental results, and discuss related works.

Keywords: Semantic web data · User quality constraint
Query rewriting

1 Introduction

There exist now very large knowledge bases on the web of Linked Open Data,
as DBpedia, Yago or BabelNet. The largest ones contain millions of entities and
billions of facts about them (attribute values and relationships with other entities) [20]. Applications are needed to help humans exploring this huge knowledge
network, performing data analysis and data mining tasks. Promising recent proposals are currently experimented on only one semantic web data source [7,10],
and these processes can be expected to be even more helpful when they will
deal with several linked open data sets. One crucial point for such applications,
and in particular for data mining algorithms, is that the data collection and
pre-processing steps have to be *safe and sound.*

In order to help semantic web data mining tool designers for performing
the data collection and pre-processing steps, we propose a semantic web data
validator [4]. The idea is to extend a query environment over semantic graph
databases with a mechanism for filtering answers according to a user customized
context. In this paper, we use the term "user" for the query-writer. The *user
context* is composed of *(i)* the *view* she/he has defined on the needed semantic
web data and *(ii)* a set of *personalization tools*, such as integrity constraints,
confidence degrees, etc. In this paper, we only deal with integrity constraints,

This work is supported by Girafon Project, funded by Region Centre Val de Loire.

that we call *user quality constraints,* leaving the other kinds of personalization tools for other discussions (see [4, 6]).

User quality constraints are restrictions imposed on query results. Both the constraints and the queries are expressed in terms of the user's view of data. The constraint verification is triggered by a query and consists in filtering its answers. In this way, there may be some inconsistencies within sources, but the answers given to the user are filtered to ensure their consistency w.r.t. her/his constraints. The following example illustrates the kind of constraints a user can define and what are their effects on query answers.

Example 1. Let us consider a query $q_1(X) \leftarrow teacherOf(X, Y)$ in a context with two constraints:

$$c_p : teacherOf(X, Y) \rightarrow professor(X).$$
$$c_n : teacherOf(X, Y), takesCourse(X, Y) \rightarrow \bot.$$

The first constraint is to verify that each teacher of a course is a professor. The second constraint disallows to accept, in the query answers, a person who teaches a course while she/he is enrolled in the same course. Suppose the database is as in Fig. 1. Although $\{Bob, Tom, Alice, Ann\}$ are answers to query q_1, $\{Alice, Ann\}$ are invalid w.r.t. c_p, while $\{Tom\}$ causes a violation of constraint c_n. Only $\{Bob\}$ satisfies all constraints. Thus, the answer to q_1 in the user context consisting of $\{c_p, c_n\}$ is $\{Bob\}$.

From Example 1, it can be noticed that when a constraint is triggered by instantiated atoms in the query's body, it requires auxiliary appropriate queries to verify its side effect. For instance, the fact $teacherOf(Bob, DB)$ triggers both c_p and c_n, thus queries like $q_{11}() \leftarrow professor(Bob)$ and $q_{12}() \leftarrow takesCourse(Bob, DB)$ are produced

teacherOf(Bob, DB)	professor(Bob)
teacherOf(Bob, Java)	professor(Tom)
teacherOf(Tom, Java)	takesCourse(Tom, Java)
teacherOf(Alice, DB)	takesCourse(Bob, Java)
teacherOf(Ann, DB)	reasearchesIn(Ann, DB)
	reasearchesIn(Bob, DB)

Fig. 1. Database instance

to verify whether Bob is a professor and whether Bob is registered in the Database course. It is easy to see that, when dealing with a big amount of data, the impact of such auxiliary queries may be important. Even though most of them are simple queries, they can lead to a system overloading. A solution to avoid such issue is *to integrate as much as possible the constraints into the query,* in such a way that the answers will not only satisfy the initial query, but they will also respect all integrated constraints.

This paper is organized as follows: in Sect. 2, we present the overall query framework with user context, and precise the syntax and semantics of user quality constraints. In Sect. 3 we give algorithms for their dynamic verification during the query computation. In Sect. 4 we evaluate their performance with experimental results, and discuss related works.

2   A Querying Framework with Constraints

2.1   Querying Environment

Our query processing framework is depicted in Fig. 2. It comprises two distinct parts which communicate: *Data validation*, responsible for checking constraints satisfaction, and *Data providers* for computing answers to the queries issued from the data validation part. The later may actually integrate several end-data-providers, or it may connect only one provider. For ensuring that the final answers to the user's queries satisfy all user constraints, a dialogue between the two parts is established, for getting intermediate results and sending subsidiary queries.

The user defines her/his *context* by setting her/his view on the queried sources, a set of datalog

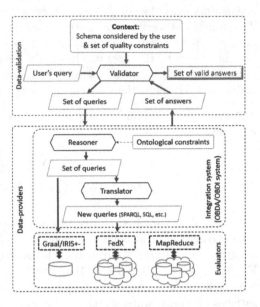

Fig. 2. Query system overview

predicates as explained in next section, and a set of quality constraints involving these predicates. The user's *query* involves these predicates, so quality constraints can be used as rewriting-rules to reformulate each query q, resulting in a union of conjunctive queries whose answers, contained in q's answers, are valid w.r.t. the user quality constraints.

Afterwards, these conjunctive queries are sent to the *Data providers* part, which evaluates them against data stored on sources. The query evaluation process is transparent to the validation step, in particular, answers that are entailed are treated in the same way as those that actually exist in sources. We respect the potential ontological dimension of semantic web sources, while interpreting the *user constraints* using the closed-world assumption. Indeed, as it deals with semantic data, the evaluating process performed by the *Data providers* part relies on the open-world assumption, where ontological constraints are used to deduce new information. Ontological constraints are used as rewriting-rules to reformulate a query into a set of new conjunctive queries, for taking into account integration information (OBDA/OBDI Systems [3,18]), or for dealing with incomplete information issues [3,11,12,15]. But such rewritings are performed by the *Data providers* part, independently from the *Data validation* part.

Our system may be deployed with various data management systems by using a module that translates datalog+− queries [5] (used by Graal[1]) into SPARQL for FedX [19], and HIVE-SQL for MapReduce (as proposed in [4]).

---

[1] https://graphik-team.github.io/graal/.

2.2   Constraints

Our constraints are expressed in a first-order logic formalism. We consider an alphabet made up of three disjoint sets const, var and pred, of constants, variables and predicate names, respectively. A term t is either a variable or a constant and an *atom* is a formula $p(x_1, x_2, \ldots, x_n)$ where p is a predicate name and each x_i is a term. A *substitution* is a total mapping $\sigma : \text{var} \to T$ from variables to terms. A *homomorphism* from a set of atoms A_1 to a set of atoms A_2, all over the same schema R, is a substitution h from the set of terms of A_1 to the set of terms of A_2 such that: (i) if t is a constant, then $h(t) = t$, and (ii) if $r(t_1, \ldots, t_n)$ is in A_1, then $h(r(t_1, \ldots, t_n)) = r(h(t_1), \ldots, h(t_n))$ is in A_2. The notion of homomorphism naturally extends to conjunctions of atoms. Two atoms A_1 and A_2 are *unifiable* if and only if there exists a substitution σ s.t. $\sigma(A_1) = \sigma(A_2)$. Furthermore, if two atoms A_1 and A_2 are unifiable then there exists a *most general unifier* (mgu) θ s.t. $\theta(A_1) = \theta(A_2)$.

A *conjunctive query* (CQ) q of arity n over a given schema is a logical rule of the form $q(\mathbf{X}) \leftarrow \phi(\mathbf{X}, \mathbf{Y})$, where $\phi(\mathbf{X}, \mathbf{Y})$ is a conjunction of atoms over the schema, q is a n-ary predicate and $\mathbf{X}, \mathbf{Y}$ are sequences of terms. Given a logical rule r, we denote by $body(r)$ the rule's antecedent by $head(r)$ its consequent.

Our *user quality constraints* [4] are also logical rules. We define a user *context* as a set $\mathcal{C}$ of constraints, composed of three subsets, as follows:

Positive constraints $(\mathcal{C}_P)$: Each positive constraint has the form

$$\forall \mathbf{X}, \mathbf{Y}\ L_1(\mathbf{X}, \mathbf{Y}) \to \exists \mathbf{Z}\ L_2(\mathbf{X}, \mathbf{Z})$$

$L_1(\mathbf{X}, \mathbf{Y})$ and $L_2(\mathbf{X}, \mathbf{Z})$ are atoms and $\mathbf{Z}$ are existential variables.

Negative constraints $(\mathcal{C}_N)$: Each negative constraint is a rule having the form

$$\forall \mathbf{X}\ \phi(\mathbf{X}) \to \bot$$

where $\phi(\mathbf{X})$ is an atom $L_1(\mathbf{X})$ or a conjunction of two atoms $L_1(\mathbf{X}_1), L_2(\mathbf{X}_2)$, which have a non-empty intersection between the terms in $\mathbf{X}_1$ and $\mathbf{X}_2$. We refer to $\mathcal{C}_{N1}$ and $\mathcal{C}_{N2}$ as sets of negative constraints having only one atom and two atoms, respectively. Negative constraint is a special case of denial constraint with at most two occurrences of database literals.

Equality-generating dependency constraints without nulls $(\mathcal{C}_K)$: each EGD is a rule having the general form

$$\forall X_1, X_2, \mathbf{Y}, \mathbf{Z}_1, \mathbf{Z}_2\ L_1(\mathbf{Y}, X_1, \mathbf{Z}_1), L_2(\mathbf{Y}, X_2, \mathbf{Z}_2) \to X_1 = X_2.$$

where $\mathbf{Y}$ is a sequence of common terms of L_1 and L_2 that has at least one element. Notice that EGD include functional dependency (and thus, key constraints) having the form $L_1(\mathbf{Y}, X_1, \mathbf{Z}_1), L_1(\mathbf{Y}, X_2, \mathbf{Z}_2) \to X_1 = X_2$.

In the rest of this paper, for simplicity, we will omit the quantifiers. We say that a constraint c is triggered by an atom A when there is a homomorphism h from $body(c)$ to A. Positive constraints are a special case of linear tuple generating dependency (TGD [2]) which contain only one atom in the head. When $\mathbf{Z}$ is not empty, the homomorphism h is extended to h' such that, for each existential variable $z \in \mathbf{Z}$, $h'(z)$ is a new fresh variable. It is well-known that facts from a database instance may trigger such constraints, and the *chase* procedure [17] is the standard process for the generation of new facts from a database instance and a set of dependencies (TGD or EGD) [2]. It can also be used to decide containment of conjunctive queries in the presence of constraints [14]. In this paper, we consider that the set of positive constraints is weakly acyclic, which guarantees the decidability of query containment [9]. In Example 1, c_p and c_n are illustrations for the definitions of positive and negative constraints above. An example of EGD constraints can be as follows:

$$c_k : worksFor(X, Y, Z), headOf(X, W) \rightarrow Z = W.$$

It states that if a person X is the head of W and if she is working for organization Y in department Z then W must be the department Z.

3   Validating Semantic Web Query Outputs

Given a user's query q, the validation of its result on the basis of user's quality constraints in $\mathcal{C}$ can be performed in two ways: by rewriting q to take into account the constraints in $\mathcal{C}$, or by the evaluation of auxiliary queries, composed on the basis of initial results obtained for q. Even if the choice between these two processes depends on the query evaluation power of data providers, it is important to study their *costs and benefits* in a common framework. To do so, in this paper, we use Graal [1] as conjunctive query evaluator for both techniques. More precisely, we focus on testing and comparing the performance of our validation approach in the following two scenarios: (1) the rewriting of q on the basis of constraints in $\mathcal{C}$, followed by the rewritten-query evaluation, and (2) what we call the naive solution, *i.e.* evaluate q, then build and evaluate multiple auxiliary queries on the basis of q's answers. This section summarizes these two scenarios, and in Sect. 4 we analyse in details their respective validation performance.

3.1   Query Rewriting with Constraints

Given a CQ q and a set of constraints $\mathcal{C}$, let us consider examples to illustrate the situations our query rewriting algorithm tackles with.

Example 2. Query q_1 below looks for professors who were born in a foreign country. Constraints establish a user's context imposing a professor to be associated with a course (c_{p_a}) offered by a department (c_{p_b}). Moreover, the user is interested only in professors working in the public sector (c_{p_c}).

$$q_1(X_1) \leftarrow professor(X_1), placeOfBirth(X_1, Z_1), foreignCountry(Z_1).$$

$$c_{p_a} : professor(X) \rightarrow teacherOf(X, Y).$$

$$c_{p_b} : teacherOf(X, Y) \rightarrow offeredCourseIn(Y, Z).$$

$$c_{p_c} : professor(X) \rightarrow employeeGov(X).$$

In this context, we see $body(q_1)$ as a set of atoms capable of triggering constraints and producing new atoms that should be added to the query's body. This operation corresponds to a chase computation [17], which starts with the atoms in $body(q_1)$. Special attention is required in the use of variable renaming. The new rewritten query, that the system should send to data providers, is:

$q'_1(X_1) \leftarrow professor(X_1), teacherOf(X_1, Y_1), offeredCourseIn(Y_1, Y_2),$
        $employeeGov(X_1), placeOfBirth(X_1, Z_1), foreignCountry(Z_1).$ □

When the query, or the constraints, contain *constants*, the above rewriting technique should be revised, as illustrated by the following example.

Example 3. Consider query q_2, and constraint c_{p2} imposing restrictions on database teachers - they should do research in the database domain:

$$q_2(X) \leftarrow teacherOf(X, Y).$$

$$c_{p2} : teacherOf(Z, DB) \rightarrow researchesIn(Z, DB).$$

Notice that no restriction is imposed on teachers in other domains. Here we cannot apply the chase as in Example 2, because a query $q'_2(X) \leftarrow teacherOf(X, DB), researchesIn(Z, DB)$ would ignore the teachers of all other domains. In this case, our proposal is to replace q_2 by the union of the two following queries:

$$q_{2.1}(X) \leftarrow teacherOf(X, Y), \neg teacherOf(X, DB).$$

$$q_{2.2}(X) \leftarrow teacherOf(X, Y), teacherOf(X, DB), researchesIn(X, DB).$$ □

Algorithm 1 summarizes our rewriting solution. In this algorithm the input is composed of a conjunctive query, and positive and negative constraints. However, negative constraints in $\mathcal{C}_{N2}$, *i.e.*, those having the form $L_1(\mathbf{X_1}), L_2(\mathbf{X_2}) \rightarrow \bot$ are transformed into two equivalent formulas: $L_1(\mathbf{X_1}) \rightarrow \neg L_2(\mathbf{X_2})$ and $L_2(\mathbf{X_2}) \rightarrow \neg L_1(\mathbf{X_1})$. In this way, negative constraints receive a similar treatment as positive constraints. For instance, from Example 1, the constraint c_n can be written as $c_{n_1} : teacherOf(X, Y) \rightarrow \neg takesCourse(X, Y)$ and $c_{n_2} : takesCourse(X, Y) \rightarrow \neg teacherOf(X, Y)$. Query q_1 is then rewritten as $q_1(X) \leftarrow teacherOf(X, Y), \neg takesCourse(X, Y)$.

In Algorithm 1, Function RewriteWithConstraints is the main program, which ensures that each query is rewritten by taking into account all positive and negative constraints in $\mathcal{C}$. It calls Function Integrate, the kernel of our rewriting method, which computes the new queries that replace the given query q, by integrating in q the restrictions imposed by the given constraint c.

The instantiation of constraints *w.r.t.* the atoms L in q's body is done on line 15 by using a *mgu* θ, and c' is the resulting constraint, instantiated with constants in q. Then, on line 18, we consider the cases where c' can be triggered by L. This happens when θ is a variable renaming, or, when it replaces variable in c by constants in L (afterwards, there may still exists a homomorphism ν from $body(c')$ to L). For instance, consider query q_3 and constraint c_3 as follows:

$$q_3(X) \leftarrow professor(Bob), teacherOf(Bob, X)$$
$$c_3 : professor(X) \rightarrow inDept(X, Y)$$

With $L = professor(Bob)$ and $\theta = \{X/Bob\}$, we obtain $c'_3 : professor(Bob) \rightarrow inDept(Bob, Y_1)$, where Y_1 is a new variable resulting from variable renaming performed by *createRule* (line 19). Similarly, in Example 2, for $L = professor(X_1)$ and $\theta = \{X/X_1\}$ we obtain $c'_{p_a} : professor(X_1) \rightarrow teacherOf(X_1, Y_1)$.

When the homomorphism ν exists, the query's body is completed with the head of c' (line 19). The loop on line 5 ensures that the query's body will be completed with all the atoms obtained by triggered constraints. Notice that the idea here is to use a chase procedure applied to rules that respect some syntactic restrictions. Indeed, our current implementation deals with a set of weakly acyclic TGD [9]. Roughly, a set of TGD is acyclic if it does not allow for cascading of labelled null creation during the chase. Example 2 illustrates a rewritten query obtained by following the above steps.

Algorithm 1. *RewriteWithConstraint*

Input:　A conjunctive query q and a set of constraints $\mathcal{C} = \mathcal{C}_P \cup \mathcal{C}_N$

Output:　A set of queries Q s.t. each $q' \in Q$ does not contain explicit contradictions and the answers of q' respect $\mathcal{C}_P \cup \mathcal{C}_N$. Notice that we can get $Q = \emptyset$ as output.

1　**Function** RewriteWithConstraint(q, $\mathcal{C}$):
2　　$Q = \{q\}$;
3　　**repeat**
4　　　$hasChanged$ = false;
5　　　**foreach** $c \in \mathcal{C}$ **do**
6　　　　**foreach** $q \in Q$ **do**
7　　　　　Q' = Integrate(q, c);
8　　　　　**if** $(|Q'| = 1$ *and* $q' \in Q'$ *is more restricted than* q) *or* $(|Q'| > 1)$ **then**
9　　　　　　$Q = Q \backslash \{q\} \cup Q'$;
10　　　　　　$hasChanged$ = true;

11　　**until** *not hasChanged*;
12　　**return** Q;

13　**Function** Integrate(q, c):
14　　$Q' = \{q\}$;
15　　**foreach** $L \in body(q)$ *s.t.* $\exists mgu$ $\theta : \theta(L) = \theta(body(c))$ *and not* $tested(L, c)$ **do**
16　　　$c' = createRule(\theta(head(c)), \theta(body(c)))$;
17　　　**foreach** $q' \in Q'$ **do**
18　　　　**if** $\exists$ *homomorphism* ν *from* $body(c')$ *to* L **then**
19　　　　　$q_1 = createRule(head(q'), body(q') \wedge \nu(head(c')))$;
20　　　　　$Q'' = \{q_1\}$;

21　　　　**else**
22　　　　　$q_1 = createRule(head(q'), body(q') \wedge \neg\theta(body(c')))$;
23　　　　　$q_2 = createRule(head(q'), body(q') \wedge \theta(body(c')) \wedge \theta(head(c')))$;
24　　　　　$Q'' = \{q_1, q_2\}$;

25　　　　$Q'' = Simplify\_Verify(Q'')$;
26　　　**if** $(|Q''| = 1$ *and* $q'' \in Q''$ *is more restricted than* q') *or* $(|Q''| > 1)$ **then**
27　　　　$Q' = Q' \backslash \{q'\} \cup Q''$;

28　　　markTested(L,c);
29　　　//Mark L as already tested *w.r.t. c, i.e.* $tested(L, c)$ = true

30　　**return** Q';

When the homomorphism ν does not exist, we are dealing with constants that cannot map to variables or with different constants. Let us consider Example 3, after executing line 15 of Algorithm 1 with $L = teacherOf(X, Y)$. We have $c'_{p2} : teacherOf(Z, DB) \rightarrow researchesIn(Z, DB)$ (no changes w.r.t. c_{p2}). No homomorphism from $body(c')$ to L is possible. Line 22 deals with results that are *not* concerned by the constraint. In this case, the query body is completed with the negation of the constraint's body. Thus, in our Example 3, $q_{2.1}$ selects people who do not teach DB. With the database instance of Fig. 1, the answer for $q_{2.1}$ is Tom. Then, on line 23, we deal with results *concerned* by the constraint. In Example 3, $q_{2.2}$ selects two kinds of people: (*i*) those who are database researchers and *only* teach DB and (*ii*) those who teach and do research in the database domain but also teach other subjects. Continuing with our example, the desired answers for q_2 are Bob, Ann and Tom. With our algorithm, Bob and Ann are not answers for $q_{2.1}$, but they are answers to $q_{2.2}$. The result of q_2 is the union of the answers for $q_{2.1}$ and $q_{2.2}$.

Rewritten queries, put in the set Q'', are sent to function *Simplify_Verify* (line 25) that, for each query, removes redundant atoms. This function also ensures that Q'' does not contain queries with explicit contradiction. In other words, the function checks whether: (*i*) there is no two atoms having the form $L(\mathbf{X})$ and $\neg L(\mathbf{X})$ in the query body and (*ii*) atoms in the query body cannot trigger a negative constraint.

We use query containment (see, for instance [2] for a revision on the subject) to decide whether a rewritten query replaces a given one. On line 27, notice that at each iteration step, the set Q' contains the most restricted rewritten queries obtained so far. Each iteration step considers an atom in the query body and one single constraint. The output of the Integrate function is the set Q', which contains the most restricted rewritten queries obtained for one query w.r.t. one constraint c. Then, on line 9, the replacement of the original query q is considered. If only one query q' results from Integrate, q is replaced by q' only when q' is more restricted than q. Otherwise, when more than one rewritten queries result from Integrate, q is replaced by them.

The query obtained after only chasing the original query w.r.t. positive constraints corresponds to the universal plan of [8]. However, when dealing with negative constraints, even when Integrate performs only lines 17–20 to rewrite a given query, the rewritten query may contain negative atoms.

3.2 Building Auxiliary Queries

Given a query q, to ensure its answer consistency w.r.t. user's quality constraints, instead of dealing with query rewriting, one can consider the generation of subqueries from the initial answers obtained from q. Let h_t be the homomorphism used to produce tuple t as an answer to the query q. We want to check whether t is valid w.r.t. constraints. Tuple t is considered valid only when *all* constraints triggered during the validation process are satisfied.

Let $L(\mathbf{X})$ be an atom of $body(q)$. The instantiated atom $h_t(L(\mathbf{X}))$ may trigger a constraint c. According to the type of c, an auxiliary query q' is created:

- For $c \in \mathcal{C}_P$ the auxiliary boolean query is $q'() \leftarrow h_t(L_0(\mathbf{X}_0))$ where $L_0(\mathbf{X}_0) = head(c)$. The resulting tuple t is valid $w.r.t.$ c if the answer of q' is positive. Notice however that each fact f resulting from the instantiation of $h_t(L_0(\mathbf{X}_0))$ on the database may trigger another constraint. The validation process continues until no constraint is triggered and corresponds to a chase procedure, establishing a dialogue between the validator and the providers.
- For $c \in \mathcal{C}_N$ and assuming that c has the form $L(\mathbf{X}), L_0(\mathbf{X}_0) \rightarrow \bot$ the auxiliary boolean query is $q'() \leftarrow h_t(L_0(\mathbf{X}_0))$. Tuple t is valid $w.r.t.$ c if the answer of q' is negative. Clearly, if c has the form $L(\mathbf{X}) \rightarrow \bot$, the verification is straightforward.
- For $c \in \mathcal{C}_K$, assuming that c has form $L(\mathbf{Y}, X_1, \mathbf{Z}_1), L_0(\mathbf{Y}, X_2, \mathbf{Z}_2) \rightarrow X_1 = X_2$ and $\mathbf{X} = \mathbf{Y} \cup X_1 \cup \mathbf{Z}_1$, the auxiliary query is $q'(X_2) \leftarrow h_t(L_0(\mathbf{Y}, X_2, \mathbf{Z}_2))$. Tuple t is valid $w.r.t.$ c if the answer set is a singleton containing the tuple value $h_t(X_1)$.

3.3   Complete Validation

Finally, Algorithm 2 is responsible for validating the result of a query q $w.r.t.$ a set of constraints $\mathcal{C}$. Algorithm 1 rewrites the query only $w.r.t.$ positive and negative constraints. Then it must be completed by the generation of auxiliary queries, from the answers of the rewritten queries, at least for dealing with EGD constraints in $\mathcal{C}$. On line 2 of Algorithm 2, Function $RewriteWithConstraint$ returns a set Q of rewritten queries. Afterwards, Function $Eval$ evaluates all queries in Q (line 3), and answers are stored in the set Solutions. On line 5, $\mathcal{C}_{check}$ is the set of the constraints which are not addressed by Algorithm 1. Function $Valid$ verifies whether an answer sol is valid $w.r.t.$ $\mathcal{C}_{check}$ by generating corresponding auxiliary queries, as sketched in Sect. 3.2.

Algorithm 2.

    Input: A conjunctive query q and a set of constraints $\mathcal{C}$.
    Output: Answers of q respecting $\mathcal{C}$.

1   AnsSet $= \emptyset$;
2   $Q = RewriteWithConstraint(q, \mathcal{C})$;
3   Solutions $= Eval(Q)$;
4   $Cache = CreateCache()$;
5   $\mathcal{C}_{check} = remainingConstraints(\mathcal{C})$;
6   **foreach** $sol \in$ Solutions *where* $sol = (t, h_t)$ **do**
7   **if** $Valid(sol, \mathcal{C}_{check}, Cache)$ **then**
8   AnsSet $:= $ AnsSet $\cup \{t\}$;

9   **return** $AnsSet$;

---

4   Experimental Results and Related Works

Our main goal is to compare the overall performance between (i) our first scenario, $i.e.$ the query rewriting approach performed by Algorithm 2 when only the

EGD constraints are not considered by Function *RewriteWithConstraint*, and (*ii*) our second scenario, the naive approach, performed by Algorithm 2 when Function *RewriteWithConstraint* is simply not applied. Both approaches compute the same *valid* answers (whose number is given in column 5 and 6 in Table 1(a) for the given conjunctive query, *i.e.* answers that satisfy the given set of quality constraints. Another important goal of experiments is to analyze features that affect the computation efficiency, such as the size of datasets, the size of queries, the number and type of constraints, etc.

Table 1. Rewriting approach

	Trig.	Num.Rew.Que.		Max num.	Valid answers	
	cons.	w.opt.	wo.opt.	atoms	1 univ.	5 univ.
Q1	4	1	4	7	523	3331
Q2	1	1	1	2	7861	36682
Q3	2	2	2	5	3599	23749
Q4	0	1	1	2	10735	67702
Q5	6	6	8	14	50	59
Q6	8	2	8	13	6631	36538
Q7	6	2	8	13	21	220

		1 university		5 universities	
	RewTime	EvalTime	Total	EvalTime	Total
Q1	0.043	0.372	0.415	0.492	0.535
Q2	0.001	0.429	0.430	6.388	6.389
Q3	0.007	0.124	0.131	0.804	0.811
Q4	0	0.111	0.111	0.692	0.692
Q5	0.048	0.702	0.75	0.773	0.821
Q6	0.011	20.522	20.533	122.285	122.296
Q7	0.01	3.193	3.203	162.105	162.115

(a) Queries and Rewritten Queries   (b) Rewriting, Evaluation-Verification (s)

Table 2. Evaluation and verification in the Naive approach (s)

	1 university					5 universities				
	Eval.	Verif.	Total	Init.ans.	Num.Que.	Eval.	Verif.	Total	Init.ans.	Num.Que.
Q1	0.965	1.172	2.137	1548	2072	1.191	7.14	8.331	10095	13426
Q2	0.153	49.952	50.105	7861	7861	1.038	t/o	t/o	36682	-
Q3	0.041	1.515	1.556	3599	3599	2.59	10.709	13.299	23749	23749
Q4	0.026	0.072	0.098	10735	0	0.166	0.43	0.596	67702	0
Q5	0.227	1.704	1.931	50	200	0.735	1.363	2.098	59	236
Q6	9.205	57.948	67.153	6631	39786	16.108	t/o	t/o	36538	-
Q7	4.772	0.535	5.307	96	159	292.216	0.712	292.928	645	1305

We performed experiments using a HP ZBook laptop equipped with a quad-core Intel i7-4800MQ processors at 2.7 GHz and 16 Gb of RAM. We developed Java programs using Graal, a Java toolkit dedicated to knowledge-base querying within the framework of existential rules (*e.g.* Datalog+−). We used the LUBM[2] benchmark, which describes the organizational structure of universities with 43 classes and 32 properties, and provides a generator of synthetic data with varying size. For analyzing the impact of the size of databases on the tested solutions, we created two versions of datasets containing data of 1 and 5 universities, containing 86, 165 and 515, 064 triples, respectively. These datasets are loaded and managed directly by Graal, which converts them from RDF/XML to Dlgp, its supported data format. Inspired by the 14 test queries of LUBM, we devised 7 queries and 12 constraints written in Dlgp (4 positive,

---

[2] Lehigh University: http://swat.cse.lehigh.edu/projects/lubm/.

5 negative, and 3 keys)[3]. The queries spread from simple queries with few atoms ($Q1$, $Q2$) to more complex queries ($Q6$, $Q7$), and may contain constants ($Q5$). Some constraints also involve constants ($Cp2$, $Cp3$, $Cp4$). Column 1 in Table 1(a) contains the number of constraints triggered by each query. The second and third columns present the number of rewritten queries either applying the simplification query-containment test (Function $Simplify\_Verify$), or not. Theoretically, a query that involves n constraints can be rewritten into 2^n reformulations in the worst case. Experimental results show that in some cases ($Q1$, $Q6$, $Q7$), Function $Simplify\_Verify$ significantly reduces the number of rewritings. Column 4 shows the maximum number of atoms in rewritten queries, which demonstrates that the more constraints are used in the rewriting procedure, the more complex are the rewritings (number atoms or joins).

We now turn our attention to the time of rewriting and complete evaluation-verification, reported in Table 1(b), which contains the following information: (i) the time needed for rewriting, indicated in Column $RewTime$; (ii) the time needed for evaluating all queries obtained from the rewriting step, shown in column $EvalTime$, for the two tested datasets; (iii) the total time for performing these two steps (Column $Total$). Rewritings are very fast and the evaluation time is clearly the major part in the total time, in all cases. Furthermore, the evaluation time is directly proportional to the size of the tested dataset. Moreover, the rewritten-query complexity affects the evaluation time, for instance, $Q6$ and $Q7$ have 13 atoms in their body and their evaluation times on 5 universities are the biggest ones. Interestingly, $Q5$ has 14 atoms and does not need so much time for the evaluation. The reason is that $Q5$ contains a constant, which highly reduces its querying space. In summary, these first experiments demonstrate how the dataset size, the query complexity, the number of involved constraints and the presence of constants in initial and rewritten queries, impact the overall time of the rewriting-and-evaluating approach for processing a query with user-constraints.

Concerning now the experimental results for the naive approach, shown in Table 2, we have, for each dataset: (i) the time needed for evaluating the initial query in Column $Eval.$; (ii) the time necessary for generating and executing auxiliary queries to verify all answers obtained from the previous evaluation step, in Column $Verif.$; (iii) the overall processing time in Column $Total.$ (iv) the number of answers before constraint verification in Column $Init.Ans.$; and (v) the number of auxiliary queries generated, in Column $Num.$ $Queries$. Naturally, the dataset size has a similar effect as in the rewriting approach. However, the number of generated auxiliary queries plays an even more significant role in the total processing time. Intuitively, this number depends (i) on the size of the initial answer set and (ii) on the number of involved constraints. We can notice that, contrary to the rewriting approach, the complexity of the query has little effects on the total execution time in the naive approach. See, for instance, $Q6$ and $Q7$ which have similar complexity. However, $Q6$ has many answers, provoking the

---

[3] Details in the technical report: http://www.univ-orleans.fr/lifo/rapports.php?annee=2017.

generation of many sub-queries. Indeed, the verification step is carried out by generating simple sub-queries for each answer *w.r.t.* each constraint.

Perhaps one of the most meaningful observation provided by our experiments is that, when the dataset size increases, the rewriting approach is clearly far more efficient than the naive approach. This is specially the case when the initial query gives a large number of answers, no matter if it is a simple or a complex query, and these answers trigger a lot of constraints: $Q2$ and $Q6$ are typical examples of such cases, which induce a time-out for 5 universities. For $Q4$, which triggers no constraint, the naive approach is better or similar to the rewriting one.

Related Works. We already mentioned the main works related to our proposal in Sect. 2.1. Firstly, ontological-constraints-based query-rewritings in Ontology-Based Data Access (OBDA) systems [3,18] and rewritings in incomplete information querying systems [11,12,15] inspired our solution. In [16] we also find different semantics for query answering over inconsistent Datalog$^\pm$ ontologies. Their goal is to propose corrections to the database, while ours is to avoid answering on the basis of inconsistent data. Indeed, we designed our solution with traditional database constraints that must be verified, while in those works ontological constraints are seen as inference rules. Our user constraints allows us to verify answer sets and eliminate those answers that do not comply with the user needs. For instance, coming back to c_p given in Introduction, which enforces that all person who teaches is a professor, the answer $teacherOf(Bob, DB)$ is valid only if $professor(Bob)$ is true in the provided answers, *i.e.* the fact $professor(Bob)$ is not inferred from the user constraints.

For this reason, our rewriting algorithm is based on traditional results in the database domain already cited in Sect. 2.2 [2,14,17]. We are currently studying to what extent our proposed user-context is covered by the traditional framework of answering queries using views, for which a general rewriting algorithm is presented in [8], and further improved in [13]. We already mentioned this algorithm, called C & B for its two phases (Chase and BackChase), at the end of Sect. 3.1. It first constructs a canonical rewriting called *UniversalPlan* by using TGDs rules, which play the same role as our positive constraints, and then it searches minimal reformulations among the candidates in the *UniversalPlan*, using EGDs rules. But how it could apply to our context is not obvious, because we already mentioned that, in general, the Chase can not be directly used with constraints containing constants, excepted when there exists a homomorphism from the constraint's atoms to the query's atom (see Lines 17–20 in Algorithm 1).

5   Conclusion

We presented a solution for validating a set of user quality constraints when performing query evaluation, in the semantic web context. A naive way to verify them is to generate auxiliary queries after having got the result set from the evaluation of the user query. Our experiments have put in evidence that these auxiliary queries, generally simple but performed on huge data sets, sometimes lead to overload the system. Integrating as much as possible the constraints into the original user query can help to overcome this drawback. We presented an algorithm for such a constraint-query integration, and provided experimental results that demonstrate its benefits regarding total query-with-constraints processing time. Both techniques are correct and complete. In other words, given the query Q and the constraints C, (i) there is no answer to Q that satisfies C, but is not in the answer set of both methods (completeness); (ii) all the answers produced by both algorithms are answers to Q that respect C (correction). Our immediate future works will concern extending our experiments to take into account the data provider features and capabilities (*e.g.* not all of them can evaluate complex queries).

References

1. Graal. https://graphik-team.github.io/graal/
2. Abiteboul, S., Hull, R., Vianu, V.: Foundations of Databases, vol. 8. Addison-Wesley, Reading (1995)
3. Abiteboul, S., Manolescu, I., Rigaux, P., Rousset, M.-C., Senellart, P.: Web Data Management. Cambridge University Press, New York (2011)
4. Bamha, M., Chabin, J., Halfeld-Ferrari, M., Markhoff, B., Nguyen, T.B.: Personalized environment for querying semantic knowledge graphs: a mapreduce solution. Technical report, LIFO- Université d'Orléans, RR-2017-06 (2017)
5. Calì, A., Gottlob, G., Lukasiewicz, T.: A general datalog-based framework for tractable query answering over ontologies. J. Web Semant. **14**, 57–83 (2012)
6. Chabin, J., Halfeld-Ferrari, M., Nguyen, T.B.: Querying semantic graph databases in view of constraints and provenance. Technical report, LIFO- Université d'Orléans, RR-2016-02 (2016)
7. d'Amato, C., Tettamanzi, A.G.B., Minh, T.D.: Evolutionary discovery of multi-relational association rules from ontological knowledge bases. In: Blomqvist, E., Ciancarini, P., Poggi, F., Vitali, F. (eds.) EKAW 2016. LNCS (LNAI), vol. 10024, pp. 113–128. Springer, Cham (2016). https://doi.org/10.1007/978-3-319-49004-5_8
8. Deutsch, A., Popa, L., Tannen, V.: Query reformulation with constraints. SIGMOD Rec. **35**(1), 65–73 (2006)
9. Fagin, R., Kolaitis, P.G., Miller, R.J., Popa, L.: Data exchange: semantics and query answering. Theor. Comput. Sci. **336**(1), 89–124 (2005). Database Theory
10. Galárraga, L., Razniewski, S., Amarilli, A., Suchanek, F.M.: Predicting completeness in knowledge bases. In: WSDM, pp. 375–383 (2017)
11. Gottlob, G., Orsi, G., Pieris, A.: Ontological queries: rewriting and optimization. In: ICDE, pp. 2–13 (2011)
12. Gottlob, G., Orsi, G., Pieris, A.: Query rewriting and optimization for ontological databases. CoRR, abs/1405.2848 (2014)
13. Ileana, I., Cautis, B., Deutsch, A., Katsis, Y.: Complete yet practical search for minimal query reformulations under constraints. In: Proceedings of the 2014 ACM SIGMOD International Conference on Management of Data, SIGMOD 2014. ACM, New York, pp. 1015–1026 (2014)
14. Johnson, D.S., Klug, A.C.: Testing containment of conjunctive queries under functional and inclusion dependencies. J. Comput. Syst. Sci. **28**(1), 167–189 (1984)
15. Lembo, D., Lenzerini, M., Rosati, R., Ruzzi, M., Savo, D.F.: Inconsistency-tolerant query answering in ontology-based data access. Web Semant. Sci. Serv. Agents World Wide Web **33**, 3–29 (2015)

16. Lukasiewicz, T., Martinez, M.V., Simari, G.I.: Inconsistency handling in datalog+/− ontologies. In: ECAI 2012–20th European Conference on Artificial Intelligence. Including Prestigious Applications of Artificial Intelligence (PAIS-2012) System Demonstrations Track, Montpellier, France, 27–31 August, 2012, pp. 558–563 (2012)
17. Maier, D., Mendelzon, A.O., Sagiv, Y.: Testing implications of data dependencies. ACM Trans. Database Syst. 4(4), 455–469 (1979)
18. Poggi, A., Lembo, D., Calvanese, D., De Giacomo, G., Lenzerini, M., Rosati, R.: Linking data to ontologies. In: Spaccapietra, S. (ed.) Journal on Data Semantics X. LNCS, vol. 4900, pp. 133–173. Springer, Heidelberg (2008). https://doi.org/10.1007/978-3-540-77688-8_5
19. Schwarte, A., Haase, P., Hose, K., Schenkel, R., Schmidt, M.: FedX: optimization techniques for federated query processing on linked data. In: Aroyo, L., Welty, C., Alani, H., Taylor, J., Bernstein, A., Kagal, L., Noy, N., Blomqvist, E. (eds.) ISWC 2011. LNCS, vol. 7031, pp. 601–616. Springer, Heidelberg (2011). https://doi.org/10.1007/978-3-642-25073-6_38
20. Weikum, G., Hoffart, J., Suchanek, F.M.: Ten years of knowledge harvesting: lessons and challenges. IEEE Data Eng. Bull. 39(3), 41–50 (2016)

Author Index

Abdellatif, Safa   569
Ablayev, Farid   197
Alamro, Hayam   636
Ambainis, Andris   197
Anselmo, Marcella   552
Ayad, Lorraine A. K.   636

Babenko, Maxim   295
Beck, Harald   87
Bellomarini, Luigi   3
Ben Hassine, Mohamed Ali   569
Ben Yahia, Sadok   569
Boreale, Michele   442
Bouzeghoub, Amel   569
Breu, Ruth   153
Broy, Manfred   19
Brunet, João   255
Burda, Kamil   459
Burjons, Elisabet   396

Chabin, Jacques   682
Charalampopoulos, Panagiotis   636
Chaudron, Michel R. V.   47
Chuangpishit, Huda   367
Chuda, Daniela   459
Corradini, Flavio   321
Czyzowicz, Jurek   367, 381

Dal Corso, Alice   337
Damaschke, Peter   525
Dao-Tran, Minh   87
de Figueiredo, Jorge C. A.   255
Dematis, Ioannis   581
Diptarama   611, 624
Dony, Christophe   180
Doty, David   212
Dreier, Jan   125

Eiter, Thomas   87

Farwick, Matthias   153
Fernandes-Saez, Ana   47

Gąsieniec, Leszek   367
Geissmann, Barbara   508
Georgescu, Vera   596
Georgiou, Konstantinos   367
Giammarresi, Dora   552
Godon, Maxime   381
Gogoglou, Antonia   94
Gottlob, Georg   3

Hadj Kacem, Ahmed   180
Haeusler, Martin   153
Halfeld-Ferrari, Mirian   682
Hartmann, Tim A.   137
Hasan, Osman   241
Hebig, Regina   47
Henzinger, Monika   40
Hnatkowska, Bogumiła   269
Hoffmann, Clemens   111
Ho-Quang, Truong   47
Hrešková, Miroslava   469
Huynh, Trung Dong   667

Igarashi, Yuki   611
Iliopoulos, Costas S.   636

Jalonen, Joonatan   227
Jargalsaikhan, Davaajav   624
Jolak, Rodi   47
Jurdziński, Tomasz   305, 367

Kallel, Sahar   180
Kamali, Mojgan   337
Karapistoli, Eirini   581
Kari, Jarkko   227
Kessler, Johannes   153
Khadiev, Kamil   197
Khadieva, Aliya   197
Khan, Shahid   241
Kolesnichenko, Ignat   295
Komm, Dennis   396
Kranakis, Evangelos   367, 381
Krötzsch, Markus   413
Kuinke, Philipp   125

Labourel, Arnaud 381
László, Tímea 351
Laurent, Anne 596
Libourel, Thérèse 596
Lorenz, Jan-Hendrik 493
Luna Freire, Victor da C. 255

Machová, Kristína 469
Madonia, Maria 552
Manolopoulos, Yannis 94
Markhoff, Béatrice 682
Markou, Euripides 381
Martinez, Manuel Perez 351
Mashkoor, Atif 241
Masopust, Tomáš 413
Mercier, Grégoire 596
Merro, Massimo 337
Mlynčár, Andrej 168
Molter, Hendrik 111
Momège, Benjamin 285
Moreau, Luc 667
Muzi, Chiara 321

Ngo, Tu 596
Nguyen, Thanh Binh 682
Nowakowski, Emmanuel 153
Nowicki, Krzysztof 305

Pataki, Norbert 351
Penna, Paolo 508
Pérez, Beatriz 667
Pieris, Andreas 3
Pissis, Solon P. 636

Ramachandran, Gowri Sankar 67
Rástočný, Karol 168
Ravat, Franck 653
Re, Barbara 321

Rossi, Lorenzo 321
Rossmanith, Peter 125
Rotter, Csaba 351

Sáenz-Adán, Carlos 667
Sallinger, Emanuel 3
Schliep, Alexander 525
Schöngens, Marcel 396
Shinohara, Ayumi 611, 624
Singh, Ritesh Kumar 67
Song, Jiefu 653
Sorge, Manuel 111
Szabados, Michal 539
Szalai, Csaba 351

Tamm, Hellis 428
Teste, Olivier 653
Tibermacine, Chouki 180
Tiezzi, Francesco 321
Tomás, Ana Paula 479
Trojer, Thomas 153
Tsikrika, Theodora 94

Ueki, Yohei 624

Vakali, Athena 581
Veanes, Margus 428

Weyns, Danny 67
Woroniecki, Paweł 269

Xuan, Ba Le 125

Yoshinaka, Ryo 611, 624

Zhu, Shaopeng 212

Printed in the United States
By Bookmasters